Reference
and
Information Services

Recent Titles in
Library and Information Science Text Series

Reference and Information Services

An Introduction

FOURTH EDITION

Richard E. Bopp and
Linda C. Smith, Editors

Library and Information Science Text Series

LIBRARIES UNLIMITED

AN IMPRINT OF ABC-CLIO, LLC
Santa Barbara, California • Denver, Colorado • Oxford, England

Library of Congress Cataloging-in-Publication Data

Reference and information services : an introduction / Richard E. Bopp and Linda C. Smith, editors. — 4th ed.
     p. cm. — (Library and information science text series)
   Includes bibliographical references and indexes.
   ISBN 978-1-59158-365-3 (hardcover : acid-free paper) — ISBN 978-1-59158-374-5 (pbk. : acid-free paper) — ISBN 978-1-59884-817-5 (ebk.)
   1. Reference services (Libraries)   2. Information services.   I. Bopp, Richard E.
   II. Smith, Linda C.
   Z711.R443   2011
   025.5'2—dc22   201100855

ISBN: 978-1-59158-365-3
         978-1-59158-374-5 (pbk.)
EISBN: 978-1-59884-817-5

15   14   13   12   4   5   6

This book is also available on the World Wide Web as an eBook.
Visit www.abc-clio.com for details.

Libraries Unlimited
An Imprint of ABC-CLIO, LLC

ABC-CLIO, LLC
130 Cremona Drive, P.O. Box 1911
Santa Barbara, California 93116-1911

This book is printed on acid-free paper ∞

Manufactured in the United States of America

Copyright Acknowledgments

Every reasonable effort has been made to trace the owners of copyright materials in this book, but in some instances this has proven impossible. The editors and publishers will be glad to receive information leading to more complete acknowledgments in subsequent printings of the book and in the meantime extend their apologies for any omissions.

FirstSearch screenshots are used by permission of OCLC. FirstSearch® is a registered trademark of OCLC Online Computer Library Center, Inc.

Contents

x Contents

Part II: Information Sources and Their Use

15—ALMANACS, YEARBOOKS, AND HANDBOOKS 439

Lori S. Mestre

16—BIOGRAPHICAL SOURCES 471

Jeanne Holba Puacz

Preface

This new fourth edition of *Reference and Information Services* reflects the dramatic changes shaped by rapidly developing technologies over the past 10 years. In the process, it takes the introduction to reference sources and services significantly beyond the content of the first three editions. In Part I, "Concepts and Processes," chapters have been revised and updated to reflect new ideas and methods in the provision of reference service in an era when many users have access to the Web. In Part II, "Information Sources and Their Use," discussion of each source type has been updated to encompass key resources in print and on the Web, where an increasing number of freely available sources join those purchased or licensed by libraries.

A number of new authors are contributors to this fourth edition, bringing to their chapters their experience as teachers of reference or as practitioners in various types of libraries.

Discussions of services in Part I integrate digital reference as appropriate to each topic, such as how to conduct a reference interview online using instant messaging. Boxes interspersed in the text are used to present scenarios for discussion, to highlight key concepts, or to present excerpts from important documents. Each chapter concludes with an updated list of additional readings to guide further study.

Discussions of sources in Part II place more emphasis on designing effective search strategies using both print and electronic resources. The chapter on selection and evaluation of sources addresses the changing nature of reference collections and how to evaluate new types of sources. As in Part I, boxes are used to generate thought and discussion. In these chapters, they highlight the content, structure, and advantages of various reference sources, both print and electronic. Each chapter concludes with a comprehensive list of all reference sources discussed in that chapter.

Despite these updates and changes, the fourth edition of this text has the same goal as its predecessors, to provide students and practitioners with an overview of current reference sources, issues, and services.

Richard E. Bopp
Associate Professor of Library Administration, Emeritus
University Library
University of Illinois at Urbana-Champaign

Linda C. Smith
Professor and Associate Dean for Academic Programs
Graduate School of Library and Information Science
University of Illinois at Urbana-Champaign

Acknowledgments

A number of individuals assisted the editors or authors in the creation of this fourth edition of *Reference and Information Services*. We would like here to express our gratitude to them for their valuable contributions.

First, we would like to thank the editorial and production staff at Libraries Unlimited, an imprint of ABC-CLIO, for their patience and support during a project that took much longer than we anticipated.

The authors of several chapters in the fourth edition built on the work of authors who contributed to the third edition. We would like to acknowledge our debt to Bryce Allen, Charles A. Bunge, Holly Crawford, Constance A. Fairchild, Laura R. Lucio, Susan Miller, and Ellen D. Sutton for helping shape earlier editions of this text.

Sandra L. Wolf of the University of Illinois at Urbana-Champaign Library provided support to authors in locating articles and verifying bibliographic information.

Susan M. Bopp assisted in photocopying and mailing chapters during the editing process.

Finally, we express our gratitude to all others who have helped in any way in the revision of this text. We hope all mentioned here will take pride in the finished product, to which they have been essential contributors.

Contributors

David A. Cobb
Retired from position as Curator,
  Harvard Map Collection
Harvard University
Chapter 19

Prudence W. Dalrymple
Research and Teaching Professor and
  Director, Institute for Healthcare
  Informatics
College of Information Science &
  Technology
Drexel University
Chapter 4

Stephanie R. Davis-Kahl
Public Services Librarian, The Ames
  Library
Illinois Wesleyan University
Chapter 17

Eric Forte
Member Services Consultant
OCLC
Chapter 22

Jim Hahn
Orientation Services Librarian,
  Undergraduate Library, and Assistant
  Professor of Library Administration
University of Illinois at Urbana-
  Champaign
Chapter 11

Frances Jacobson Harris
University Laboratory High School
  Librarian and Professor of Library
  Administration
University of Illinois at Urbana-
  Champaign
Chapter 12

Lisa Janicke Hinchliffe
Coordinator for Information Literacy
  Services and Associate Professor of
  Library Administration
University of Illinois at Urbana-
  Champaign
Chapter 8

M. Kathleen Kern
Associate Reference Librarian and
   Associate Professor of Library
   Administration
University of Illinois at Urbana-
   Champaign
Chapter 3

Josephine Z. Kibbee
Retired from position as Head of
   Reference and Professor of Library
   Administration
University of Illinois at Urbana-
   Champaign
Chapter 11

Kathleen M. Kluegel
Retired from position as English
   Librarian and Associate Professor of
   Library Administration
University of Illinois at Urbana-
   Champaign
Chapters 5, 6

Mary Mallory
Government Information Access
   and Collections Coordinator and
   Associate Professor of Library
   Administration
University of Illinois at Urbana-
   Champaign
Chapter 22

Lori S. Mestre
Head, Undergraduate Library and
   Associate Professor of Library
   Administration
University of Illinois at Urbana-
   Champaign
Chapter 15

Carol Bates Penka
Retired from position as Assistant
   Reference Librarian and Assistant
   Professor of Library Administration
University of Illinois at Urbana-
   Champaign
Chapter 20

Jeanne Holba Puacz
Adjunct Lecturer
Graduate School of Library and
   Information Science
University of Illinois at Urbana-
   Champaign
Chapter 16

Richard E. Rubin
Associate Provost for Extended
   Education and Professor, School of
   Library and Information Science
Kent State University
Chapter 2

Linda C. Smith
Professor and Associate Dean for
   Academic Programs
Graduate School of Library and
   Information Science
University of Illinois at Urbana-
   Champaign
Chapters 4, 13, 21

Joseph E. Straw
Reference and Instruction Librarian and
   Associate Professor
Marietta College
Chapter 14

David A. Tyckoson
Associate Dean, Madden Library
California State University, Fresno
Chapter 1

Jo Bell Whitlatch
Retired from position as Associate
   Dean
San José State University Library
Chapter 10

Lynn Wiley
Head of Acquisitions and Associate
   Professor of Library Administration
University of Illinois at Urbana-
   Champaign
Chapter 7

Melissa A. Wong
Adjunct Lecturer
Graduate School of Library and
   Information Science
University of Illinois at Urbana-
   Champaign
Chapter 18

Beth S. Woodard
Reference Librarian & Training
   Coordinator and Associate Professor
   of Library Administration
University of Illinois at Urbana-
   Champaign
Chapters 3, 9

Part I

Concepts and Processes

History and Functions of Reference Service

Chapter

1

David A. Tyckoson

INTRODUCTION

Think what a library would be without reference service. Try to imagine a library with a great collection, an excellent catalog, lots of subject guides, a rich assortment of electronic resources, clean restrooms, and good signage, but with no one to provide direct assistance to the user. Can such a library exist? Can the users of the library function effectively with no assistance? Are catalogs, indexes, databases, and finding tools so good that users are able to figure them out on their own?

From our perspective in the early 21st century, it is difficult to imagine a library without reference service. From the Library of Congress to the smallest one-room, one-person school library, reference service is ingrained as an expected part of what libraries provide. With the increasing complexity and quantity of information available in and through libraries, users need ever more assistance in identifying, retrieving, and evaluating the specific information that fits their needs. In other words, they need help. This is what reference librarians do. Whether it is called reference service, information service, customer service, research service, help desk, or some other new trendy name, the service is intended to help the users of the library find what they want. For the purposes of this book, the term used is "reference service."

Although reference service is common today in all libraries, such has not always been the case. Throughout most of the history of librarianship, libraries did *not* offer reference service. It is only in relatively recent times that such service has been offered to library users. To understand why reference service is so universal, the following sections look back at the factors behind its establishment, beginning with the fundamental roles and functions of the library in society.

THE LIBRARY AND THE COMMUNITY

Libraries do not exist in isolation. Every library serves a specific, defined community. The library exists as a resource for that specific community, not as an independent institution in and of itself. Public libraries serve the residents of a certain geographic area, most often a city or county. Academic libraries serve the faculty, staff, and students at the college or university. School libraries serve the teachers and students attending a specific school. Medical libraries serve the doctors, nurses, staff, and patients of the hospital. Law libraries serve the attorneys and staff of the firm. Corporate libraries serve the management and employees of a specific company. With very few exceptions, libraries are not independent agencies; they exist to serve the information needs of a very specific community.

In each case, the function of the library is to provide information to its parent community. When members of the community need information, the primary objective of the library is to fill those information needs. Whether those needs relate to research, business, or entertainment, the members of the community turn to the library for certain types of information. Most libraries, especially public and academic libraries, also allow people from outside the primary community to use their collections and facilities. However, the primary focus needs to be on the people who make up the parent community. If a library fails to serve its primary clientele, it will not remain in business. A library that is perceived as vital to its community will receive the support, staff, and funding to maintain its role as the information utility for the community. A library that does not fill the needs of its parent community will slowly wither, will become marginalized, and may even close. To serve the community effectively, librarians must learn who composes that community, what their information needs are, and how those needs are changing. Know the community, and one will know what the library should contain, which services to offer, and what level of support to expect in return.

WHAT LIBRARIES DO

Libraries perform three basic functions in order to fill the information needs of their communities. Each of these functions is extremely detailed and highly complex, yet all of the activities of the library can be reduced to one of these three factors. The functions of the library have evolved over time as libraries and their parent communities have coevolved. To fully understand reference service, one first needs to understand how it relates to the other functions of the library.

Collections

Historically, the first function of libraries was to select, collect, and preserve information. From ancient times, librarians have collected and retained documents of interest to their parent communities. From the scrolls in the Great Library of Alexandria to the books chained to the desks of the Bodleian Library, to the scientific journals of the National Library of Medicine, to the children's books of the local public library, each library has had and continues to have as its first role the accumulation of information of interest to its community. This information takes many forms, which today include books, journals, microforms, photographs, compact discs, videos, DVDs, Web sites, MP3s, computer files, and any other form of information storage from the past. In response to the needs of the community, librarians will also collect any new information formats that will be developed in the future. The popular image of the library as a warehouse for materials—whether via row after row of books on shelving, cabinets of microfilm or audio CDs, or a Web page full of links—comes directly from this collection function. This is the oldest historical function of libraries: to find, select, acquire, and preserve documents of interest to the community. It remains a vital role to this day. Part II of this book (chapters 13–22) discusses collections for reference service.

Organization

The second function of libraries is to organize the information that is collected. The fact that librarians organize information is intuitively obvious, but it is a much more recent function than collecting. Historically, this was the second function to arise in libraries, evolving as a corollary to the first function. As libraries grew in size, it became more and more difficult for users (and librarians) to find the information in which they were interested. When libraries were very small, the user could simply browse the entire collection to find what was needed. As the size of libraries grew, other methods of organization were required.

From alphabetical order to AACR II and from MARC to metadata, librarians have developed a wide variety of methods for organizing and finding materials in their collections. Most of these tools were developed by librarians primarily for self-assistance. As libraries grew larger, it became much more difficult for librarians to know where to find specific documents or pieces of information within the overall collection. As a result, librarians developed concepts such as subject headings, main entries, authority files, call numbers, and controlled vocabularies. Although libraries must have always had some kind of organization, the first true catalogs were developed as inventory control devices in the latter half of the 15th century.[1] Although no precise date can be given for when librarians began to organize information on a large scale, they have been doing so for approximately 500 years.

Over time, organizational tools became more and more sophisticated, with author, title, and later even subject entries included. By the early 19th century, librarians had developed a number of codes that described how such information would be organized, resulting in publication of the famous 91 rules of Panizzi in 1841 and Cutter's *Rules for a Dictionary Catalog* in 1876. Today we use AACR II, MARC records, HTML, XML, EAD, OpenURL, and metadata coding to describe our collections. Tomorrow, new schema will be developed that will be applied to as-yet-undeveloped forms of information or that will better organize materials in our collections. However, the central function remains the same: to tell the users what information is included in the library and to help them retrieve that information.

Librarians have become quite sophisticated in organizing and indexing the materials contained within their collections. Using the technology of the times, from scrolls to books to cards to databases, librarians have been and continue to be leaders in the theory and practice of indexing and cataloging information. Google (http://www.google.com)

and Yahoo! (http://www.yahoo.com) may tell their users what exists on the Web, but librarian-developed tools such as *INFOMINE* (http://infomine.ucr.edu) and the *ipl2* (http://www.ipl.org) tell users where the useful information is located. A big difference exists between these two types of Web indexes: the former rely on automatic linking and indexing of resources, whereas the latter include only sources that have been evaluated by librarians. For more on the organization function, see chapter 4.

Service

The third and historically most recent function of libraries is to provide direct assistance to users in their search and retrieval of information, what librarians now call reference service. This aspect of librarianship is by far the youngest of the three functions, having not been practiced until the mid- to late-1800s. Although everyone today has grown up with this function of the library and tends to take this service for granted, it was truly a revolutionary concept when first introduced. For understanding of how revolutionary the idea of reference service really was, a look back in time at what society was like in that era is required.

HISTORICAL DEVELOPMENT OF REFERENCE SERVICE

Universal Education and Public Libraries

That reference service was developed at all is linked to two different, yet related 19th-century ideals: universal education and public libraries. These two movements transformed the fabric of American society. Universal education was the concept that all children in the United States, no matter what class, race, or religion, would be able to receive free public education. Reasons for establishing universal education for all school-age children varied widely and were often at cross-purposes to one another.[2] Business leaders saw universal education as a way to create better workers. Labor leaders saw it as a way for people to move up in society. Religious leaders saw it as a way to make it possible for more people to read the Bible. Politicians saw it as a way to create a single national identity among a varied immigrant population. Regardless of the true motivations for establishing universal education, state and local governments throughout the nation established free public schools, which did in fact result in a more highly educated society. As a direct result of universal education, the literacy rate in the United States rose significantly.

Data on literacy prior to 1870 is difficult to obtain, and rates varied widely from region to region.[3] Estimates of literacy rates in the 1850s range from 90 percent in Massachusetts to 60 percent in the Southern states. However, these figures count only white males. Female literacy rates tended to be lower than that for males, ranging from 2–4 percent less in the Northeast to 10–15 percent less in the South. Literacy among the free black population was estimated at 50 percent, and the literacy rate of slaves was 5–10 percent. The literacy rate for Native Americans would have been even lower. By 1870, the literacy rate had risen to 88.5 percent in the white population and 20.5 percent in the non-white population.[4] As more and more people learned to read, they became more and more interested in doing so.

At the same time as universal education was becoming the norm, the concept of the free public library was being established. To convince the city fathers that such an institution would be a necessary and valuable component of the community, the trustees of the Boston Public Library made these arguments:

> The question is not what will be brought about by a few individuals of indomitable will and an ardent thirst for improvement, but what is most for the advantage of the mass of the community. In this point of view we consider that a large public library is of the utmost importance as the means of completing our system of public education.[5]

That the public library was viewed as a component of universal education is emphasized again later in that same report (emphases in the original document):

> And yet there can be no doubt that such reading ought to be furnished to all, as a matter of public policy and duty, on the same principle that we furnish free education, and in fact, as a part, and the most important part, of the education of all. For it has been rightly judged that,—under political, social and religious institutions like ours,—it is of paramount importance that the means of general information should be so diffused that the largest possible number of persons should be induced to read and understand questions going down to the very foundations of social order, which are constantly presenting themselves, and which we, as a people, are constantly required to decide, and do decide, either ignorantly or wisely. That this *can* be done,—that is, that such libraries *can* be collected, and that they will be used to a much wider extent than libraries have ever been used before, and with much more important results, there can be no doubt; and if it can be done *anywhere,* it can be done *here* in Boston; for no population of one hundred and fifty thousand souls, lying so compactly together as to be able, with tolerable convenience, to resort to one library, was ever before so well fitted to become a reading, self-cultivating population, as the population of our own city is at this moment.
>
>   To accomplish this object, however,—which has never yet been attempted,—we must use means which have never before been used; otherwise the library we propose to establish, will not be adjusted to its especial purposes. Above all, while the rightful claim of no class,—however highly educated already,—should be overlooked, the first regard should be shown, as in the case of our Free Schools, to the wants of those, who can, in no other way supply themselves with the interesting and healthy reading necessary for their farther education.[6]

The Boston Public Library did, in fact, become a reality and opened its doors to the public—all of the public—on March 20, 1854. It was an instant success. In less than six months of operation, more than 35,000 volumes were borrowed.[7] When given an opportunity to read, the public responded at an overwhelming rate, borrowing an average of one book for every two people living in the city, and this at a time when the concept of borrowing books was new to the majority of the population and not yet a common practice. The concept of the free public library was rapidly adopted by other municipalities, with 188 such libraries having been established in 11 different states by 1876.[8]

This is all an interesting aspect of library history, but what does the development of universal education and public libraries have to do with reference service? Reference service came about as a direct result of these two innovations. Universal education taught the public to read, and public libraries offered material to read. As Melvil Dewey put it,

> The school teaches them to read; the library must supply them with reading which will serve to educate, and so it is that we are forced to divide popular education into two parts of almost equal importance and deserving equal attention: the free school and the free library.[9]

The newly literate members of society knew how to read, but not how to use a library. They came into the library in ever-increasing numbers but did not know what they wanted to read. Naturally, they asked the librarians for advice. By 1876, the idea of reference service had been born.

Samuel Green and the Founding of Reference Service

The first discussion of any type of direct service by librarians to help library users was a paper presented by Samuel Swett Green at the first conference of the American Library Association in Philadelphia. His paper, "Personal Intercourse and Relations between Librarians and Readers in Popular Libraries," outlined the concept of the

---

BOX 1.1
WHY DO WE CALL IT "REFERENCE SERVICE"?[10]

When the idea of helping library users was first proposed, the terms "reference service" and "reference librarian" had yet to be coined. However, the term "reference book" was already widely in use. Reference books were originally known as the books, such as catalogs, indexes, and bibliographies, that one consulted to find references to other sources. By the 1870s, any library book that did not circulate was being called a reference book.

In the first paper discussing reference service, Samuel Green called it "personal intercourse between librarians and readers." Fortunately, that phrase was quickly shortened to "aid to readers." Later, the term "assistance to readers" came into more widespread use as the service end of reference began to be more widely recognized. Because the librarians who helped readers tended to use the books that were located in the reference collection, they gradually became known as reference librarians. In 1885, Melvil Dewey became the first to hire staff with the title of "reference librarian" when he organized the first multiple-librarian (i.e., two-person) reference department at Columbia College. "Reference work" was what "reference librarians" did. The name caught on, and the rest, as they say, is history.

---

librarian interacting with and assisting the reader; he did not use the phrase "reference service" because that term had not yet been developed. His paper was published with a shorter title in the first volume of *Library Journal*[11] and is universally recognized as the first professional discussion of what we now call reference service.

That reference service arose in the public library instead of academic institutions is directly related to the democratic ideals of the free public library. Rather than being developed within the walls of academe, where students were theoretically seeking to build upon the knowledge of the past, it was in the people's university, the free public library, that the concept took hold. Samuel Rothstein, who studied the development of reference services in academic libraries, accounts for the lack of interest among academics as follows:

> Actually, the student of that era was little inclined to make much use of the college librarian in any case. The idea of research had as yet scarcely reached American universities, and the teaching methods in undergraduate courses still emphasized the traditional reliance upon the textbook. The student had little occasion to borrow books from the library, and his demands for personal assistance must have been even more rare.[12]

However, some positive reaction to the concept of personal assistance was found in academic institutions. In the discussion that followed Green's presentation, Otis Robinson of the University of Rochester heartily endorsed the concept.[13] At the London Conference the following year, Reuben Guild of Brown University described the availability of librarians to the public (faculty and students) at his university.[14] Within a decade of Green's paper, Melvil Dewey had embraced the idea of reference service in the Columbia College (now Columbia University) Library. Dewey was the first to establish a team of librarians to provide personal assistance to users and was the first to use the phrase "reference department" when referring to that team. Rothstein indicates, "Under Dewey's dynamic and positive leadership, the Columbia College Library had already recognized that such assistance was more than just another aid or subsidiary activity, that the personal help given to individual readers was a necessary and integral part of the library's educational function."[15] As the teaching methods used in colleges and universities evolved into a more research-based model, the use of the library by students increased to the point where reference service became established in academic libraries. More traditional academic institutions took longer to adopt this idea, but eventually reference service was available in virtually any public or academic library in the United States.

Original Functions of the Reference Librarian

So what exactly does a reference librarian do? Green's original paper on the topic consists primarily of examples of the types of questions asked by users of public libraries. However, embedded in those examples are four distinct functions of the reference librarian. Briefly stated, they are as follows:

1. *Teach people how to use the library and its resources.* Although some scholars may have known their way around catalogs, indexes, and the stacks, most of the newly literate members of society were unfamiliar

with what libraries contained and how to find what they wanted. The first function of the librarian providing personal assistance to readers was to teach them how to find things in the library. Green states, "Give them as much assistance as they need, but try at the same time to teach them to rely upon themselves and become independent."[16]

2. *Answer readers' questions.* Green's paper provides myriad examples of the types of questions asked by users of the public library, ranging from simple factual queries to in-depth research projects. The librarian was expected to be able to answer—or more accurately, to provide sources that would answer—all of these types of questions. As Green states so succinctly, "persons who use a popular library for purposes of investigation generally need a great deal of assistance."[17] He then presents three pages of examples of the type of assistance that readers in his library have needed.

3. *Aid the reader in the selection of good books.* People wanted to read but did not know what was worth reading. One of the major roles of the librarian was to serve as a readers' advisor, recommending material that fit each reader's interests and ability. Green, in discussing his (female) reference librarian, comments, "I am confident that in some such way as this a great influence can be exerted in the direction of causing good books to be used.... Only let her aim at providing every person who applies for aid with the best book he is willing to read."[18]

4. *Promote the library within the community.* Underlying all of Green's examples is the concept that by being personally available to members of the community, the librarian would generate support from the community, which of course would lead to more use of the library and greater financial support. Green closes his paper by stating, "The more freely a librarian mingles with readers, and the greater the amount of assistance he renders them, the more intense does the conviction of citizens, also, become, that the library is a useful institution, and the more willing do they grow to grant money in larger and larger sums to be used in buying books and employing additional assistants."[19] In other words, if you help them, they will come—and provide funding!

Changes since 1876: Technology

Much has changed since 1876. The area that is most obviously different is the technology used in libraries. Whereas librarians in Green's time had essentially two formats, books and periodicals, librarians today use a wide range of resources. The reference librarian today is more likely to consult a computer than a book in response to a question. Various types of machines are found throughout the library. Technology has transformed the way that libraries operate and the way that readers use the library. Over the decades, the library has gone from a place that relied on paper and pencil to one that uses silicon chips and electrons. Roughly in chronological order by the decade of their adoption in libraries, some of the technologies that have affected libraries are listed in Figure 1.1.

Although this is a vast array of technologies, each of which has had a profound impact on libraries, all of these technologies can be broken down into three distinct categories: technology that stores information; technology that reproduces information; and technology that communicates. The technologies in Figure 1.1 can be divided into these three categories as illustrated in Figure 1.2.

1890s	Typewriter		Cassette tape
1920s	Telephone		Telefacsimile
	Radio	1980s	Personal computer
1930s	Phonodisc		Printer
1940s	Television		Floppy disk
	Microfilm		Audio compact disc
1950s	Tape recording		CD-ROM
	Slide		E-mail
	Punch card		Electronic mailing lists
	Thermofax copier	1990s	World Wide Web
1960s	Photocopier		Internet chat
	Filmstrip		E-commerce
	Microfiche		Laptop computer
	Microcard		Wireless
	Telex		telecommunication
1970s	Mainframe computer	2000s	iPod
	Modem		USB storage device
	Video recording		

Figure 1.1. Technology arranged chronologically.

Storage	Reproduction	Communication
Phonodisc	Typewriter	Telephone
Microfilm	Thermofax copier	Radio
Punch card	Photocopier	Television
Tape recording	Mainframe computer	Telex
Slide	Telefacsimile	Modem
Filmstrip	Personal computer	Telefacsimile
Microfiche	Printer	E-mail
Microcard	Laptop computer	Electronic mailing lists
Video recording		World Wide Web
Cassette tape		Internet chat
Mainframe computer		E-commerce
Personal computer		Wireless
Floppy disk		
Audio compact disc		
CD-ROM		
Laptop computer		
iPod		
USB storage device		

Figure 1.2. Technology arranged by function.

Some of these technologies are used to perform more than one of the three listed functions (such as the computer), but each technology enhances the ability of the library to function in one or more ways. Each of these technologies is a tool that enhances library service but does not fundamentally change the nature of that service. The next several years will undoubtedly bring about even more technological developments. The only certainty is that technological change will continue to occur, probably at an even more rapid pace. Chapters 5 and 6 provide more details on the impact of technology on reference service.

Changes since 1876: Diversity

The other major change in libraries over the past 130 years has been in the nature of the populations that libraries serve. Since the 19th century, the population of the United States has become much more diverse. Whereas the users of libraries in Green's time were primarily English-speakers of European descent, users of libraries in the United States today come from all over the world and speak dozens of languages. As our communities have changed to incorporate immigrants from Asia, Africa, and Latin America, our libraries also have changed to include more materials about other cultures in more and more languages.

Diversity is not only ethnic in nature. In the 1870s, libraries existed to serve adults. During the ensuing years, libraries have established a number of specialized services and departments for various segments of the population, including children, teens, senior citizens, veterans, persons with disabilities, students, teachers, the business community, unemployed persons, and virtually any other discrete population not served by basic library programs. Diversity has had an impact on reference service by creating the need to respond to these demographic changes. For more on diversity and reference service, see chapter 12.

FUNCTIONS OF THE REFERENCE LIBRARIAN TODAY

So what do reference librarians do today? With all of these changes in technology and the continuing diversity of our users, what is reference like now? Surprisingly (or perhaps not), the actual functions of the reference librarian have changed very little over the years. A century after Green first discussed reference service, Thomas Galvin listed the functions of the modern reference librarian as follows:

1. Assistance and instruction (formal or informal) in the use of the library.
2. Assistance in the identification and selection of books, journals, and other materials relevant to a particular information need.
3. Provision of brief, factual information of the "ready reference" variety.[20]

In the 1980s, a series of essays was commissioned in honor of Margaret Monroe, the esteemed library science educator at the University of Wisconsin. These essays were collected into a Festschrift. The main body of the work consists of four survey articles that present the state of reference and public service at that time. These chapters are titled simply "Information," "Instruction," "Guidance," and "Stimulation" (the latter referring to promotion of the use of the library's human and material resources).[21]

More recently, in her dictionary of librarianship, Joan Reitz has defined reference services as

> including but not limited to answering substantive questions, instructing users in the selection of appropriate tools and techniques for finding information, conducting searches on behalf of the patron, directing users to the location of library resources, assisting in the evaluation of information, referring patrons to resources outside the library when appropriate, keeping reference statistics, and participating in the development of the reference collection.[22]

The role of the reference librarian today is also reflected in the definitions of a reference transaction and reference work, adopted by the Reference and User Services Association (RUSA) of the American Library Association:

Reference Transactions are information consultations in which library staff recommend, interpret, evaluate, and/or use information resources to help others to meet particular information needs. Reference transactions do not include formal instruction or exchanges that provide assistance with locations, schedules, equipment, supplies, or policy statements.

Reference Work includes reference transactions and other activities that involve the creation, management, and assessment of information or research resources, tools, and services.[23]

Although these definitions do not mention the public relations role of the librarian, the functions described today are otherwise essentially the same as those mentioned by Green. In other words, the services offered by reference librarians today are the same as those Green proposed and practiced a century ago.

REFERENCE SERVICE: VARIETIES AND APPROACHES

Styles of Reference Service

Although what librarians do has remained fairly constant over the years, the relative importance of those functions has varied tremendously. From the inception of reference service, there has been a debate over to what degree librarians should instruct users as opposed to answering their questions. From the time that the first questions were asked by curious readers, the librarian has had to determine whether it is appropriate to *conduct* research for the patron or to *instruct* the patron in how to do that research. This debate has raged for at least a century and is one that is still appropriate today.

In one of the early textbooks on reference service, James Wyer described three different philosophies of reference service, which he labeled "conservative," "moderate," and "liberal."[24] In his landmark history of reference service, Samuel Rothstein calls these same philosophies "minimum," "middling," and "maximum."[25] No matter how we name them, these philosophies define the range of possible reference services. Simply stated, these alternatives are as follows:

1. *Conservative or minimum.* The primary role of the librarian is to teach patrons how to use the library. The librarian helps users find sources but does not read or interpret those sources for the user. The library is seen as an extension of instruction. Not surprisingly, this approach is most common in academic libraries.

2. *Moderate or middling.* The librarian teaches the user how to use sources but also provides answers to many questions. The librarians do not do homework assignments for students but will search exhaustively to find answers for research and factual questions. This model is most common in public libraries.

3. *Liberal or maximum.* The librarian takes the user's question, conducts the research, finds appropriate material, and presents it to the user. In some cases, the librarian even writes a summary or analysis of the information found. This type of reference service is most often found in special libraries, including hospital libraries, law libraries, and corporate libraries.

The conservative/minimum philosophy emphasizes instruction over answers, the liberal/maximum philosophy emphasizes answers over instruction, and the moderate/middling philosophy comprises equal parts of each. All reference services fall somewhere within this overall spectrum; exactly where depends on the needs and expectations of the parent community.

Types of Reference Service

Within these philosophies and functions of the reference librarian, several particular types of reference service have been developed. Some common forms of reference service include readers' advisory, ready reference, research consulting, subject specialists, bibliographic verification and citation, interlibrary loan and document delivery, instruction, literacy programs, and outreach and marketing.

Readers' Advisory

Readers' advisory is the process of recommending sources to library users. In her dictionary, Joan Reitz defines this service narrowly: "a readers' advisor recommends specific titles and/or authors, based on knowledge of the patron's past reading preferences, and may also compile lists of recommended titles"[26] Although this is the classic image of the readers' advisor, the application of that concept is much broader. Any reference librarian who recommends sources based on the user's needs is in fact doing readers' advisory service. Whether a book, database, or Web site, the librarian chooses the source for the user based on the librarian's skill level and the nature of the user's question. The public librarian who recommends one fiction writer over another, the academic librarian who recommends one subject database over another, and the special librarian who recommends one journal over another are all involved in readers' advisory work.

Ready Reference

Ready reference is the provision of short, factual answers to highly specific questions. Answers to these questions are verifiable as accurate or inaccurate. Following are examples of ready-reference questions: "What is the population of Chicago?" "How many apples were grown in Washington State in 2010?" "Who played the role of Stella in the film version of *A Streetcar Named Desire*?" "What is the address of the headquarters of Microsoft?"

Answering ready-reference questions is the popular image of the reference librarian. This image has been popularized by media, as in the portrayals by Katharine Hepburn and her staff in the film *Desk Set*.[27] However, ready reference has never been the primary function of reference service and is rapidly becoming an even smaller component of the reference librarian's duties. In the past, reference librarians did more ready reference simply because the sources required to answer such questions were in library collections and not in the hands of the users. With the development of the Web and search tools such as Yahoo! and Google, users have the tools to find this type of information on their own. As a result, there is less need to consult a librarian for ready reference. Ready reference is more common in public libraries than in academic or special libraries, but it is in decline in all types of libraries.

Research Consulting

A more common form of reference service is assisting users with research questions. In this case, the librarian may suggest sources, search terms, and pathways that will lead to material relevant to the research project. These questions do not have single, factual answers but have many possible results that vary depending on the researcher's interests and needs. Following are some examples of research questions: "Why did the various ethnic groups in Chicago settle in the neighborhoods that they now occupy?" "What is the effect of pesticides on apple production?" "What is Stella's psychological background in *A Streetcar Named Desire*?" "How did Microsoft grow into a company that dominates the information industry?"

Each of these examples corresponds to one of the ready-reference examples in the previous section but is much more complex. With research questions, there is not one single answer that can be verified as categorically correct or incorrect. Instead, a wide range of possible approaches, search strategies, and potential sources are available, each leading in a different direction. The role of the librarian as a research consultant is to find out what aspects of the problem the user is interested in and to suggest possible search strategies that will lead the user toward the best solution. As a research consultant, the librarian may get the user started in the research, but the user will do most of the searching. The user may return several times during the process. Research consulting is more common in academic and research libraries than in other types, but it is becoming the dominant form of reference service in all libraries.

Subject Specialists

Many large libraries hire librarians to be specialists in a specific subject field or discipline. These librarians immerse themselves in the subject area, usually selecting materials for the collection as well as assisting users with specialized research. Although subject specialists can be assigned to cover any discipline, they are most common in areas that society sees as requiring more specialized knowledge to succeed, such as law, medicine, the sciences, and business. Subject specialists often have advanced degrees within their field of specialization. They work closely with researchers in the community and handle very complex questions. Subject specialists are most often found in academic libraries, large public libraries, and special libraries.

Bibliographic Verification and Citation

Bibliographic verification is the process of reading, identifying, and interpreting citations to information sources. Those sources include books, journals, theses, Web pages, manuscripts, or any other form of publication. In the process of verification, the librarian usually finds other reference sources that cite the same publication, corrects errors, and determines where to find the desired information. As information becomes more and more complex, verification is a growing activity for reference librarians. This is the primary activity of interlibrary loan librarians, whose entire operation depends on citations.

A newer function related to bibliographic verification is helping users to correctly cite the information sources that they have used. Students, researchers, and the general public all need to be able to provide accurate citations to their sources so that others will be able to find those sources. With the wide range of available citation styles, such as APA (from the *Publication Manual of the American Psychological Association*), MLA (from the *MLA Handbook for Writers of Research Papers*), and Chicago (from *The Chicago Manual of Style*), and an ever-growing number of formats, users find it increasingly difficult to accurately cite the information sources that they use. Add to that the relatively new format of the Web, and users are very confused about citations. Aiding users with citations is a rapidly growing function of the reference librarian. This is extremely common in academic and school libraries where students are learning how to cite material, but citations are a common area of query in public and special libraries as well. Reference librarians are often responsible for maintaining good standards in citations and references.

Interlibrary Loan and Document Delivery

Interlibrary loan is the process of sharing material between libraries. One library may loan a physical item to another library for a specific period of time or may copy the original and deliver it to the requesting library. Interlibrary loan is a common service in most libraries of all types because it extends the range of material available to users beyond the home library's collection. Most libraries belong to consortia that determine which materials may be borrowed or photocopied. Using established codes[28] and copyright guidelines,[29] libraries regularly exchange material in all formats. When cooperative union catalogs such as OCLC were adapted for interlibrary loan, the process was made significantly easier, and the volume of traffic among lending libraries rose tremendously.

Interlibrary loan librarians spend a lot of time doing bibliographic verification. Their primary responsibility is to search for material requested by users, verify that the information is accurate, determine that the home library does not own it, and identify potential lending partners who can provide the material. Software packages such as ILLiad and Clio make the processing of requests much easier for the librarian, allowing the same staff to handle an increasing volume of requests. For more about interlibrary loan, see chapter 7.

Instruction

Green's first function of the reference librarian was to instruct readers about the library. That instruction role continues well into the 21st century. Instruction tends to take two forms: direct and indirect. Direct instruction is characterized by the librarian communicating directly to the user and is delivered through any of a number of channels. It may come in a one-on-one situation in which the librarian teaches the user as they work together on a query; it may be done in a voluntary group environment, through workshops or classes that teach general or specific skills to those who choose to attend; or it may be a required part of a specific course or assignment in which the instructor wants all students to use library resources. Required instruction is more common in academic libraries, whereas voluntary and one-on-one instruction are features of reference service in all libraries.

Reference librarians also provide indirect instruction. In indirect instruction, the librarian does not communicate directly with the user, but communicates through instructional tools. In order to assist users with common problems, librarians write guides or pathfinders that describe how and where to approach various research problems. Some guides cover specific issues, such as how to use the catalog, a database, or a specific reference source. Other guides may be directed at a specific discipline, such as bibliographies or Web pages of useful materials in music or education. Guides may be in print or electronic form and are updated as needed. Indirect instruction is provided in anticipation of user needs. For more about instruction, see chapter 8.

Literacy Programs

In addition to providing resources for the literate segment of society, libraries have continued to play a role in education itself. Many librarians conduct literacy programs that are designed to teach reading skills to those members of the community who have not acquired such skills through other channels. Frequently, these programs are aimed at adults who have not completed their schooling, for whom English is a second language, or who are new immigrants to the community. Literacy programs are most common in public libraries. These programs continue the historic role of the public library in educating members of the communities that they serve.

Outreach and Marketing

Public relations is as important in today's libraries as it was back in Samuel Green's time. Green realized the value of having the public interact directly with librarians, and this type of personal interaction has been a symbol of reference service ever since. However, librarians today have gone beyond this passive approach of waiting for users to come to the library and now work to generate interest in their communities. Academic and public libraries frequently have staff whose primary responsibility is to work with specific segments of the community to increase library awareness and use within those populations. In the academic environment, the library may target outreach efforts at specific disciplines or departments, or toward specific types of users, such as faculty or graduate students. In public libraries, outreach is often directed at segments of the community, such as teens, senior citizens, minorities, or members of clubs or interest groups. Outreach activities continue to grow in libraries and are often a part of the reference librarian's duties.

Models of Reference Service

Samuel Green saw great value in having the librarian interact directly with the users of the library. The method by which that interaction happens may take many different forms, including service at a reference desk, roving reference, tiered reference, reference by appointment, and service to remote users.

Reference Desk

In this traditional model of reference service, the librarian staffs a desk or counter at a fixed location within the library. That location is usually in a prominent position within the building so that users can easily find it. The materials consulted by the reference librarians—books, indexes, computers, and so on—are usually found adjacent to the librarian for easy access. Users approach the desk when they have a question. The librarian may work with the user at the desk or take the user to the appropriate sources or facilities elsewhere in the building. One distinguishing characteristic of the reference desk model is that the user initiates the transaction, not the librarian.

Roving Reference

In order to provide more proactive reference service, some reference librarians wander through the library looking for users who may have questions. This has the advantage of offering assistance to users where they are already working on their questions; of allowing more hesitant users to be helped; and of eliminating any physical barriers that the desk itself poses to users. The roving method is distinguished by the fact that the librarian is the one who initiates the reference transaction by approaching the potential user. The main problems with roving are that users sometimes are unsure whether the person who approaches them really is a librarian and that users who do have a question do not know where to go if they want to find the librarian. Roving is used in many libraries, often as an adjunct to the traditional reference desk.

Tiered Reference Service

Tiered service is a model in which staff members with varying levels of skills answer different levels of queries. The theory behind tiered reference is that staff will answer questions that best fit their training. Paraprofessionals or student assistants staff an information desk and answer directional questions and basic questions regarding library holdings, as well as ready-reference questions, freeing up reference librarians to answer all of the research-level questions. When a user comes to the desk with a complex question, that user is referred to the reference librarian on duty, who is often in a private office or another area of the building, away from the busy atmosphere of the information desk. A benefit of tiered reference is that high-level staff is not wasted on routine directional questions. The problem with this method is that many users simply accept the information provided at the first level of service and do not follow through with the referral. This method of reference service is also known as the Brandeis method because it was first popularized at Brandeis University.[30] Tiered reference service has not been widely adopted. However, those institutions that do use this approach are predominantly academic libraries.

Reference by Appointment

A more extreme version of tiered reference is reference service by appointment. In this method, users who wish to consult a reference librarian must make an appointment to meet with the librarian. The benefit of this method is that the individual has the full attention of the librarian for an extended period of time. The disadvantage of appointment-based service is that many users do not want to wait for an appointment and simply accept whatever information they can find on their own. Appointment-based reference service is most often used with subject specialists in research and special libraries.

Service to Remote Users

All of the service models mentioned here require that the user be physically in the library building in order to receive assistance. In Green's day, that was most likely the case. Unless a user wrote a letter to the librarian, the only way to make any use of the library was to go in person to the physical library building. In today's environment, advances in telecommunications have made it very easy for people to use just about any library from almost any physical location. Using technologies such as the telephone, e-mail, chat, instant messaging, or social networking tools, individuals can communicate instantly with librarians at a distance. As a result, libraries have developed special reference services based on those technologies.

Reference service has been available by telephone for many years. This is such a popular service in urban public libraries that such libraries often have separate telephone reference departments handling hundreds or thousands of calls each day. More recently, most libraries have established e-mail accounts or Web forms that allow users to submit questions. Some have initiated virtual reference services using chat, instant messaging, or other software that allows the librarian to communicate over the Web with users. Because of the technical requirements of some of these virtual reference services, they are often established in cooperative ventures with other libraries or with commercial companies. These services succeed when the community members served by the library are frequent users of those communication technologies. Virtual reference is now offered by a number of public and academic libraries. However, despite much hype, the level of use of virtual reference has never approached that of in-person and telephone reference.

The Personal Nature of Reference Service

Whether they are physically present or not, people who ask reference librarians for assistance are at a psychological disadvantage. They have a need, and library staff members are the ones who may be able to help them. Because users are not certain how to proceed, they rarely state exactly what they want. This is where the reference interview comes into play.

The reference interview is a set of questioning skills that enables the librarian to work with the user to figure out what the query really is. A good interview is a conversation between the librarian and user that identifies and clarifies what the user is looking for. In many cases, the user has not thought deeply about the topic, and the librarian helps the user determine the parameters of the information need. By using good interview skills, the librarian can help the user define the information need and come up with some search possibilities to satisfy that need.

In addition to discussing the research need of the user, the reference interview serves a psychological role in the reference process. People asking for help often feel at a disadvantage when they reach the point at which they ask, whether that help is from a doctor, lawyer, or librarian. Society encourages people to figure things out on their own. When they cannot and need to ask another person for assistance, they can feel as if they have failed.

It is very important that people feel comfortable in asking for our help and that each user is treated with dignity and respect. Most of the time, reference librarians are not helping users find specific, factual information but are helping the user to identify sources and suggesting search strategies. In this regard, reference service is more like counseling the user than providing answers. Reference service is about developing a relationship between the user and the librarian, not about a specific answer to a question. In order to help librarians work with users, RUSA has developed a set of guidelines to assist librarians with the behavioral nature of the reference process.[31] For more information on the reference interview, see chapter 3.

Even the most skilled reference librarians have limits to what they can offer. In some subject areas, especially law and medicine, the librarian needs to be very careful about giving advice to users. Even in his original paper, Green recognized that librarians cannot provide answers to all questions:

> There are obvious limits to the assistance which a librarian can undertake to render. Common-sense will dictate them. Thus no librarian would take the responsibility of recommending books to give directions for the treatment of diseases. Nor would he give legal advice nor undertake to instruct applicants in regard to the practical manipulations of the workshop or laboratory.[32]

In light of recent events and the current political climate (including the USA PATRIOT Act), formerly theoretical ethical issues for reference librarians have become practical realities. Ethical questions such as the provision of information that has the potential to harm society (e.g., how to build a bomb) are now concrete issues that reference librarians encounter in their daily lives. For more on the ethics of reference service, see chapter 2.

How Are Reference Librarians Doing?

Reference service has become a standard component of library services, but is it achieving its goals? Are reference librarians really effective in teaching people to use the library, answering their questions, recommending resources, and promoting the library in the community? Evaluation and assessment of reference service present a number of challenges.

On a superficial level, reference staff can easily measure the quantity of reference transactions. Most reference departments keep statistical tallies that indicate how many users ask questions. This data is used to fill annual reports and is an indication of the busyness of the reference department. Sometimes these statistical tallies are divided by type of question, by subject field, or by type of user. Many different methods of tracking statistics are used, from simple tick marks to data tracking software. No matter what method of statistics collection is being used, a disturbing trend has emerged: fewer and fewer reference transactions are occurring each year.

The decline in reference statistics first emerged as a trend in the 1990s and, in the beginning, was reported anecdotally. More detailed analysis of reference statistics indicates that the decline in questions is a reality. The 2006 statistical report from the Association of Research Libraries shows a steady and dramatic decline in reference transactions from the mid-1990s through 2005, with 48 percent fewer questions recorded in 2005 compared to 1991.[33] Other studies indicate a similar, although perhaps not as dramatic, decline. Collectively, reference librarians are answering many fewer questions than a decade ago.

Statistics such as this are measures of quantity, but how can one also measure quality? In the 1970s, the idea of unobtrusive testing of reference service was developed. This assessment method involves asking questions of librarians and comparing the answers received with the previously known correct answer. This method was popularized by Peter Hernon and Charles McClure in the 1980s.[34] The results of these studies were disturbing: reference librarians gave correct answers only slightly more than one half of the time. This gave rise to what Hernon and McClure called the "55 percent rule": whenever a user asks a question, there is a 55 percent chance of getting the correct answer. This is clearly not very good. The results of unobtrusive testing have pointed out areas in which improvement can be made through staff training, collection enhancement, and other techniques to improve the accuracy of responses to factual questions. For more on reference assessment, see chapter 10.

Because assessment techniques were producing such discouraging results, reference librarians went through a true crisis of conscience during the 1980s and 1990s. This era was bracketed by two classic articles on the state of reference service: William Miller's "What's Wrong with Reference?"[35] and the follow-up 15 years later by David Tyckoson, "What's Right with Reference?"[36] In between these two publications, reference librarians did a lot of collective soul searching. The most critical viewpoint about reference service was expressed by Jerry Campbell, who attempted to shake reference to its conceptual foundation by proposing that libraries essentially eliminate the reference component of library service.[37]

Some of the most prominent efforts to review reference services were the "Rethinking Reference" institutes organized by Anne Lipow.[38] These seminars reexamined each of the roles traditionally played by reference librarians, from the reference desk to instruction to management. Some librarians, including Steve Coffman, looked to the commercial sector for ideas about customer service.[39] Some very innovative new services came out of this period of reflection, most notably the concept of cooperative 24/7 virtual reference. Reference librarians may answer fewer questions now than in the past, but they handle more complex questions in more innovative ways.

THE FUTURE OF REFERENCE

What will happen next in reference service? Will this newest role of the library remain a standard feature for years to come, will it fade into history, or will something else take its place? In another century, will reference service be viewed as an aberration of the 20th century, or will it still be a common service offered by libraries to their future communities? Of course, no one can say for sure. Many have made an attempt to predict what reference service will be like in future years, including a panel of experts who were invited to write papers for ALA/RUSA on this topic.[40] The best indication of the value of reference service comes from the most important critics, the users. When asked, users consistently rate reference service as one of the most important features of the library. In survey after survey in every type of library, it is clear that users still place a very high value on Samuel Green's "personal intercourse between librarians and readers."

However, the fact that reference is popular now does not necessarily mean it will remain so in the future. Following are three possible scenarios in which the current model of reference service will cease to exist:

1. *Information tools become so easy to use that people no longer need assistance using them.* Although users currently have the ability to find and retrieve more information than at any previous time in human history, they still need help finding the information that they actually want amid the torrent of results. Although new tools do get better and make information easier to get, reference librarians still have a role in teaching people how to use them and in evaluating the results. In addition, the quantity and complexity of information are so vast that people will always need assistance in finding and using that information. Despite the advances in technology and tools, this scenario is extremely unlikely to occur.

2. *Information becomes entirely commercialized, requiring each user to pay for any and all information obtained.* This scenario is slightly more likely than the first, but still highly unlikely. Although information has become more of a commodity in the last few decades, libraries serve as information utilities, purchasing information collectively for the use of all members of their communities. In addition, in a democratic society, federal and state governments will have an obligation to make information produced by government agencies widely available. Some producers in the commercial sector will require users to pay directly for access to information, but the vast majority of human knowledge will still be available through libraries.

3. *Parent communities no longer value libraries and the services that they provide.* Sadly, this is the most likely scenario to occur. A few public libraries have closed or threatened to close in places ranging from Corning, New York, to Salinas, California. Many corporations have already closed their libraries in efforts to reduce costs. Some students (and a few professors) have the idea that everything that they need is on the Web. If reference service is to wither away, it will be due to the decline of the library as a useful institution in the community. For this reason, Green's concept of promoting the value of the library to the community will become ever more important.

Despite these scenarios, there can be little doubt that reference service will be as common in libraries one hundred years from now as it is today. However, the tools used will be vastly different, and the people served will be an even more inclusive community. Reference librarians in the future will continue to teach users about

BOX 1.2
THE IMPORTANCE OF PEOPLE

My earliest personal recollection of using the library was at the Glenview Public Library in suburban Chicago. Back in the 1960s, I would ride my bike to the library and be amazed at its contents. When everyone else was discovering rock and roll, I was listening to folk and blues. Because we lived outside of the town limits, my family did not have a library card. Nonetheless, the seemingly elderly librarians (who probably were all of 35 years old at the time) helped me find and explore a whole world of music by introducing me to the Folkways series of recordings. They never questioned my lack of library card and not only let me listen to whatever I wanted in their collection, but even made suggestions, telling me that if I liked one particular recording, I should try listening to other similar ones. I would sit in the library for hours with headphones firmly attached, listening to old LPs.

When I think back to those early library experiences, I cannot remember what I listened to, only that the recommendations of the librarians made that experience so much better. As in Joan Durrance's "willingness to return" studies,[41] it is the people whom I remember, not the building or the collections. The image of those helpful librarians 40 years ago has stayed with me all this time—and may have played a subconscious role in my becoming a reference librarian myself.

What are your earliest recollections of libraries? If you are like many of us, it is the people who stand out, not the books, the magazines, the recordings, or the computers. The reference librarian is the public face of the library. Remember that when you move on to the staff side of the desk, you may be influencing someone's image of libraries and librarians, just as the librarians at the Glenview Public Library influenced me.

information, answer questions, recommend sources, and promote the library within the community. Those studying to become reference librarians need to keep in mind the reasons that reference service was created, for they are the same reasons that it is needed today and will be needed in the future.

NOTES

1.   For the history of cataloging and catalogs, see Eugene R. Hanson and Jay E. Daily, "Catalogs and Cataloging," in *Encyclopedia of Library and Information Science*, ed. Allen Kent and Harold Lancour, vol. 4 (New York: Marcel Dekker, 1970), 242–98.

2.   Gerald Lee Gutek, "Arguments for Universal Education," in *An Historical Introduction to American Education* (New York: Crowell, 1970), 51–52.

3.   Lee Soltow and Edward Stevens, *The Rise of Literacy and the Common School in the United States: A Socioeconomic Analysis to 1870* (Chicago: University of Chicago Press, 1981), 247 pp.

4.   U.S. Bureau of the Census, "Percent Illiterate in the Population, by Race and Nativity: 1870–1969," Series H 664–668, *Historical Statistics of the United States: Colonial Times to 1970* (Washington, D.C.: Government Printing Office, 1975), 1:382.

5.   Trustees of the Public Library of the City of Boston, *Upon the Objects to Be Attained by the Establishment of a Public Library*, City Document no. 37 (Boston: J. H. Eastburn, Printer, July 1852), 9. Reprinted by G.K. Hall, 1975.

6.   Ibid., 15–16.

7.   Elizabeth W. Stone, *American Library Development, 1600–1899* (New York: H. W. Wilson, 1977), 158.

8.   William F. Poole, "Some Popular Objections to the Public Libraries," *American Library Journal* 1 (November 30, 1876): 45–51.

9.   Melvil Dewey, "The Profession," *American Library Journal* 1 (September 30, 1876): 6.

10.   Summarized from Samuel Rothstein, "The Genesis of Reference Service: 1875–1895," *The Development of Reference Services through Academic Traditions, Public Library Practice and Special Librarianship* (Boston: Gregg Press, 1972), 25–27. ACRL monographs no. 14.

11.   Samuel S. Green, "Personal Relations between Librarians and Readers," *American Library Journal* 1 (November 30, 1876): 74–81.

12.   Samuel Rothstein, "The Development of the Concept of Reference Service in American Libraries, 1850–1900," *Library Quarterly* 21 (January 1953): 4.

13.   O. H. Robinson, "Librarians and Readers," *American Library Journal* 1 (November 30, 1876): 123–24.

14.   Reuben A. Guild, "Access to Librarians," *Library Journal* 2 (January–February 1877): 278.

15.   Samuel Rothstein, "Melvil Dewey and Reference Work at Columbia," in *The Development of Reference*, 27–28.

16.   Green, "Personal Relations between Librarians and Readers," 80.

17.   Ibid., 74.

18.   Ibid., 79.

19. Ibid., 81.

20. Thomas J. Galvin, "Reference Services and Libraries," in *Encyclopedia of Library and Information Science*, ed. Allen Kent and Harold Lancour, vol. 25 (New York: Marcel Dekker, 1978), 220–21.

21. Gail A. Schlachter, ed., *The Service Imperative for Libraries: Essays in Honor of Margaret E. Monroe* (Littleton, CO: Libraries Unlimited, 1982), 21–154.

22. Joan M. Reitz, "Reference Services," *Dictionary for Library and Information Science* (Westport, CT: Libraries Unlimited, 2004), 602.

23. American Library Association, Reference and User Services Association, *Definitions of Reference*. http://www.ala.org/ala/mgrps/divs/rusa/resources/guidelines/definitionsreference.cfm.

24. James I. Wyer, *Reference Work: A Textbook for Students of Library Work and Librarians* (Chicago: American Library Association, 1930), 6–7.

25. Samuel Rothstein, "Reference Service: The New Dimension in Librarianship," *College & Research Libraries* 22 (January 1961): 11–18.

26. Joan M. Reitz, "Reader's Advisory," *Dictionary for Library and Information Science* (Westport, CT: Libraries Unlimited, 2004), 592.

27. Walter Lang, director, *Desk Set* (20th Century Fox, 1957), 103 min. Starring Spencer Tracy and Katharine Hepburn. Available on DVD and VHS. As relevant today as it was when it was filmed 50 years ago, this is still the best library-themed film ever made.

28. American Library Association, Reference and User Services Association, Interlibrary Loan Committee, *Interlibrary Loan Code for the United States* (Chicago: American Library Association, January 2008). http://www.ala.org/ala/mgrps/divs/rusa/resources/guidelines/interlibrary.cfm.

29. National Commission on New Technological Uses of Copyrighted Works (CONTU), "CONTU Guidelines on Photocopying under Interlibrary Loan Arrangements," in *Final Report of the Commission* (Washington, D.C.: CONTU, 1979), 54–55. http://www.cni.org/docs/info.policies/CONTU.html.

30. Virginia Massey-Burzio, "Reference Encounters of a Different Kind," *Journal of Academic Librarianship* 18 (November 1992): 276–86.

31. American Library Association, Reference and User Services Association, Management and Operation of User Services Section, Management of Reference Committee, "Guidelines for Behavioral Performance of Reference and Information Service Providers" (Chicago: American Library Association, June 2004). http://www.ala.org/ala/mgrps/divs/rusa/resources/guidelines/guidelinesbehavioral.cfm.

32. Green, "Personal Relations between Librarians and Readers," 78.

33. Martha Kyrillidou and Mark Young, *ARL Statistics 2004–2005* (Washington, D.C.: Association of Research Libraries, 2006), 8–9. http://www.arl.org/stats/annualsurveys/arlstats/stats0405.shtml.

34. Peter Hernon and Charles McClure, "Unobtrusive Reference Testing: The 55 Percent Rule," *Library Journal* 111 (April 15, 1986): 37–41.

35. William Miller, "What's Wrong with Reference?" *American Libraries* 15 (May 1984): 303–6, 321–22.

36. David A. Tyckoson, "What's Right with Reference?" *American Libraries* 30 (May 1999): 57–63.

37.   Jerry D. Campbell, "Shaking the Conceptual Foundations of Reference: A Perspective," *Reference Services Review* 20 (Winter 1992): 29–35.

38.   Anne G. Lipow, *Rethinking Reference in Academic Libraries* (Berkeley, CA: Library Solutions Institute, 1993), 242 pp.

39.   Steve Coffman, "Reference as Others Do It," *American Libraries* 30 (May 1999): 54–56.

40.   Ilene Rockman, ed., "Special Issue: The Future of Reference," *Reference Services Review* 31 (2003): 7–104.

41.   Joan C. Durrance, "Factors That Influence Reference Success: What Makes Questioners Willing to Return?" *The Reference Librarian* 49/50 (1995): 243–65.

ADDITIONAL READINGS

Cheng, Yungrang Laura, ed. "Special Section on Virtual Reference Services." *Bulletin of the American Society for Information Science and Technology* 34 (December–January 2008). http://www.asis.org/Bulletin/Dec-07/index.html

> This series of five papers discusses different aspects of virtual reference services: the history (and possible future) of virtual reference services, participatory librarianship, evaluation of virtual reference services, implementation of professional and ethical standards, and understanding non-users of virtual reference services.

Green, Samuel S. "Personal Relations between Librarians and Readers." *American Library Journal* 1 (November 30, 1876): 74–81.

> In the very first article ever published about reference service, Green discusses the need for providing service, gives examples of the types of service needed, and outlines the role of the librarian in providing service.

Katz, William A. *Introduction to Reference Work*, 8th ed., 2 vols. New York: McGraw-Hill, 2002.

> This two-volume reference textbook, first published in 1969, covers reference sources and services. The first volume introduces some basics of reference librarianship, followed by discussion of reference sources arranged by type of source. The second volume addresses reference services and reference processes, covering such topics as the reference interview, information literacy instruction, and evaluation of reference services.

Lipow, Anne G., ed. *Rethinking Reference in Academic Libraries*. Berkeley, CA: Library Solutions Press, 1993. 242 pp.

> The institutes on which this volume is based explored the need for changes in reference services to respond to changes in user needs, information delivery, and society in general. Topics discussed include new staffing patterns, new administrative structures, new physical arrangements, and serving users who are at a distance from the library. Among several useful appendices is an annotated bibliography on the topic of "rethinking reference."

Miller, William, and Rita M. Pellen, eds. "Reforming Reference." *The Reference Librarian* 48, no. 2 (2007): 1–60.

> This collection includes four papers presented by William Miller, Brian Mathews, James Rettig, and Jerry Campbell at a session at the 2007 national conference of the Association of College and Research Libraries on "The Reference Question—Where

Has Reference Been? Where Is Reference Going?" In addition, Anna Carlin's selective annotated bibliography of literature about reference services from 1984 to the present highlights factors that have contributed to challenge and change in reference services over the last 20 years.

Pomerantz, Jeffrey. "Collaboration as the Norm in Reference Work." *Reference & User Services Quarterly* 46 (Fall 2006): 45–55.

The progress of technology has allowed reference services to become more collaborative. Pomerantz discusses several possibilities for collaboration in reference work: between potential users (e.g., the imposed query); between the librarian and the user (e.g., the traditional reference transaction); between librarians, both within a library (e.g., colleagues collaborating on answering a question) and across libraries (e.g., through electronic mailing lists); and between services (e.g., question-swapping consortia).

Rettig, James. "Reference Service: From Certainty to Uncertainty." *Advances in Librarianship* 30 (2006): 105–43.

Drawing on his own experience in academic libraries as well as the published literature, Rettig traces changes in reference service over a period of 30 years, highlighting trends in the areas of technology, rethinking reference, development of new services, assessment, collaboration, reference collections, and instruction.

Rockman, Ilene, ed. "Special Issue: The Future of Reference." *Reference Services Review* 31, no. 1 (2003): 7–104.

Five prominent reference librarians present their personal views of what the future of reference may look like, and other authors respond to these forecasts.

Rothstein, Samuel. *The Development of Reference Services through Academic Traditions, Public Library Practice and Special Librarianship.* Chicago: Association of College and Research Libraries, 1955. ACRL Monographs Number 14. Reprinted by Gregg Press in 1972.

Rothstein's comprehensive history of the first few decades of reference service compares the development of reference work in academic, public, and special libraries.

Schlachter, Gail A., ed. *The Service Imperative for Libraries: Essays in Honor of Margaret E. Monroe.* Littleton, CO: Libraries Unlimited, 1982. 215 pp.

Compiled in honor of a prominent reference instructor, these essays present a thorough review of the four functions of reference service (instruction, answering questions, readers' advisory, and public relations), in addition to providing discussions of education for and assessment of reference services.

Thomsen, Elizabeth. *Rethinking Reference: The Reference Librarian's Practical Guide for Surviving Constant Change.* New York: Neal-Schuman, 1999. 290 pp.

Thomsen provides an overview of reference service in modern times, covering all aspects of reference service, including the history of reference, communication skills, answering questions, instruction, and the Internet.

Chapter

2

Ethical Aspects of Reference Service

Richard E. Rubin

INTRODUCTION AND HISTORICAL BACKGROUND

On a day-to-day basis, librarians seldom focus their attention on the ethical implications of their professional actions. Nonetheless, ethical principles form an important framework that guides professional conduct. The ethical foundation of reference service shares, to a large extent, the general principles of library and information service. Therefore, this discussion embodies an analysis of the broader obligations of the profession as a whole. Understanding the ethical issues and principles of the field is best achieved by first providing a historical context. The values of a profession are not absent one day, only to appear fully formed the next; they are part of evolutionary changes in the profession and the society. For this reason, it is important to examine briefly the values that form the foundation of contemporary ethics for reference service.

When public libraries were first established in the mid- to latter part of the 19th century, library service was limited. "Closed shelving" restricted access to all but library staff. There were no reference desks. Desks, when present, served primarily as places where books were checked out or returned. It was probably not a particularly hospitable environment for asking questions. One library historian described the public library of this period as "inflexible, coldly authoritarian, and elitist."[1] If library users had questions, the users likely left without asking any staff member to help them. These reluctant researchers were called "shy enquirers" by pioneering librarians, who recognized that the library was an important place to find information and that the librarian was obligated to provide it.[2] As Samuel Green, librarian of the Worcester Free Public Library and a former American Library Association president, put it,

> The ideal library is one which invites everybody who has a question to ask . . . to come to the library and put his question, with the assurance that he

will be kindly received, his question sympathetically considered, and every effort made to find the answer desired.[3]

Near the end of the 19th century, access to library collections was liberalized. Open shelves where library users could freely browse materials became increasingly common, and an information function separate from the circulation function emerged. A library worker was assigned to an "information desk."[4] This worker answered library users' questions, referred users to other departments, and prepared reference lists on various subjects.[5] In larger organizations, reference departments were headed by trained reference librarians aided by reference assistants. The importance of this new function in libraries led Samuel Green, in 1896, to refer to libraries as "Bureaus of Information."[6]

As reference work evolved, it was imbued with the moral cast of the latter half of the 19th century, an unabashedly moralistic period. It was not uncommon to read or hear public leaders, such as Andrew Carnegie, speak of the need for moral development among the citizenry and the obligation of those with wealth or power to direct this moral development. Public libraries were viewed as institutions through which this moral duty could be discharged. The nature of this duty has been described variously as helping Americans improve themselves and become educated citizens or as socializing and controlling immigrant populations unfamiliar with American ways.[7] In any event, libraries and library service of the late 19th century were intended to educate and inculcate values, and librarians interpreted this function as a social or moral duty. This could be seen most conspicuously in the careful control and selection of materials based on these beliefs. The modern concept of intellectual freedom played little or no role in library service.

According to Melvil Dewey, perhaps the leading spokesman of American librarianship in the 19th century, the civilizing power of librarians could hardly be exaggerated. If librarians performed their duty properly, they could guide library users from good to better. The moral power of librarians was so great that Dewey felt that they could shape the thinking of their entire community.[8] A young Winston Churchill echoed this view when he addressed the New Hampshire Library Association in 1903 on the unfortunate rising tide of mediocre books: "It is the duty of the library to separate this wheat from a mass of chaff. And to just such an extent—and it is a very great extent—is the librarian the custodian of public morals and the moulder of public men."[9] The predominantly female composition of the library workforce was consistent with these moralistic views. Women were considered civilizers and domesticators of the society in general and of library users in particular. Their congeniality and gentility were expected to serve as models of proper library behavior.[10]

Such a heavy responsibility required a librarian of considerable moral character. The pressures must have been great. Corinne Bacon, a Connecticut reference librarian, noted in her address to the Connecticut Library Association in 1902, "If anything is impressed upon us nowadays, it is the seriousness of our profession as librarians, the importance, nay, the necessity of attaining physical, mental and moral perfection."[11] She also suggested that the reference librarian have the characteristics of "approachableness, omniscience, tact, patience, persistence, accuracy, knowledge of one's tools, knowledge of one's town, and familiarity with current events."[12] She added a "sense of humor" as well.

In 1904, G. T. Clark, librarian at the San Francisco Public Library, gave these paragons of virtue a heavenly quality:

> Many of those coming to the library are unaccustomed to the use of its tools, unfamiliar with the literature of the topic in hand and indiscriminating in the value of authorities. The reference librarian must make up for all these deficiencies and furthermore should be possessed of an angelic disposition, and be filled with an unquenchable desire to assist fellow beings.[13]

Providing good reference service was clearly important to reference librarians early in the 20th century. These good intentions, however, were frustrated by the lack of professional training and resources. In 1926, Robert J. Usher reported a lack of in-depth reference books and a notable lack of articles on reference service. He lamented that poor training meant that

> the beginner in reference work must find his way, slowly, learning by doing, profiting by mistakes in which the innocent reader is, unfortunately, too often the loser. . . . I grant that not much more than an elementary knowledge of reference work can be expected from the new graduated library school student . . . without further training in research work the result must be an impaired service to the public.[14]

Other frustrations included the desire on the part of some library users to turn reference librarians into their "private secretaries or private tutors."[15] Some reference patrons were more exasperating than others. Corinne Bacon, for example, placed reference patrons into one of three classes:

1. The select few who know just what they want, state their want with clearness and expect you to meet it. It is a joy to work for them.
2. The people who expect nothing of you, apologize for disturbing you, and break out into a fever of gratitude over the slightest assistance. These are amusing.
3. The people who expect you to do all their work for them. These are irritating.[16]

Despite inadequate training and some difficult library users, librarians acknowledged and embraced the duty to provide good reference service. In 1904, Miss McLoney, librarian at the Des Moines Public Library, enumerated the primary elements of reference work:

1. A spirit of willingness on the part of the reference librarian which counts nothing too troublesome that will secure the desired result.
2. Having the resources of the library brought out to the fullest extent and made available.
3. Cultivation of the mental alertness which will quickly suggest possible sources of information upon obscure subjects concerning which catalog, index and bibliography may not offer what is needed.

4. Persistence. It very rarely is necessary to send inquirers away from the library without at least partial information upon the subject which they are looking up, and this never should be done until the fact is established beyond question that the library can not give the desired help.[17]

Although today's reference librarian is no longer considered an arbiter of moral conduct or poor thinking, many aspects of the elements just listed are reflected in modern reference service: (1) a service-oriented perspective, (2) the responsibility to select and organize collections to maximize effectiveness, (3) strong knowledge of subjects and the principles and practices of fields, and (4) a commitment to either answering the question or referring to a source that can. These values are a strong foundation for any ethical code for information providers and resonate in the "Guidelines for Behavioral Performance of Reference and Information Service Providers," adopted by the Reference and User Services Association (RUSA) in 2004.[18] (See chapter 3 for additional discussion.)

ETHICAL GUIDANCE IN THE CONTEMPORARY ETHICAL ENVIRONMENT

Although it might be possible to impose a singular moral perspective on reference conduct, the heterogeneity of contemporary society and the increasing importance of tolerance for differing ideas as a guiding principle of our profession make such an approach impractical and undesirable. Today's information environment and the reference librarian's role within it are increasingly complex and multifaceted. In addition, given the many types of libraries that exist today, there are many distinct ethical issues unique to each. Archivists, for example, confront issues regarding restricted access to records that might be in conflict with increased access in a public library. Information managers in private organizations might have greater restrictions on providing service than reference librarians working in a public setting. Given this variety, not all ethical standards can be applied or interpreted in the same way. Nonetheless, a general pattern regarding ethical obligations is evident in various professional codes.

Ethical or Professional Codes

Reference librarians, as well as librarians in general, are guided by a variety of professional codes or guidelines. These include the aforementioned RUSA "Guidelines for Behavioral Performance of Reference and Information Service Providers," the American Library Association's (ALA) "Code of Ethics" (see Box 2.1), the American Society for Information Science and Technology's (ASIS&T) "ASIS&T Professional Guidelines" (see Box 2.2), the Society of American Archivists' "Code of Ethics for Archivists" (see Box 2.3), the Medical Library Association's "Code of Ethics for Health Sciences Librarianship" (see Box 2.4), and the American Association of Law Libraries' "AALL Ethical Principles" (see Box 2.5).[19]

BOX 2.1
AMERICAN LIBRARY ASSOCIATION
CODE OF ETHICS

As members of the American Library Association, we recognize the importance of codifying and making known to the profession and to the general public the ethical principles that guide the work of librarians, other professionals providing information services, library trustees and library staffs.

Ethical dilemmas occur when values are in conflict. The American Library Association Code of Ethics states the values to which we are committed, and embodies the ethical responsibilities of the profession in this changing information environment.

We significantly influence or control the selection, organization, preservation, and dissemination of information. In a political system grounded in an informed citizenry, we are members of a profession explicitly committed to intellectual freedom and the freedom of access to information. We have a special obligation to ensure the free flow of information and ideas to present and future generations.

The principles of this Code are expressed in broad statements to guide ethical decision making. These statements provide a framework; they cannot and do not dictate conduct to cover particular situations.

I.   We provide the highest level of service to all library users through appropriate and usefully organized resources; equitable service policies; equitable access; and accurate, unbiased, and courteous responses to all requests.

II. We uphold the principles of intellectual freedom and resist all efforts to censor library resources.

III. We protect each library user's right to privacy and confidentiality with respect to information sought or received and resources consulted, borrowed, acquired or transmitted.

IV. We respect intellectual property rights and advocate balance between the interests of information users and rights holders.

V.   We treat co-workers and other colleagues with respect, fairness, and good faith, and advocate conditions of employment that safeguard the rights and welfare of all employees of our institutions.

VI. We do not advance private interests at the expense of library users, colleagues, or our employing institutions.

VII. We distinguish between our personal convictions and professional duties and do not allow our personal beliefs to interfere with fair representation of the aims of our institutions or the provision of access to their information resources.

VIII.   We strive for excellence in the profession by maintaining and enhancing our own knowledge and skills, by encouraging the professional development of co-workers, and by fostering the aspirations
of potential members of the profession.

Adopted by the ALA Council, June 28, 1997; amended January 22, 2008. Reprinted with the
permission of the American Library Association.

BOX 2.2
ASIS&T PROFESSIONAL GUIDELINES

Dedicated to the Memory of Diana Woodward

ASIS&T recognizes the plurality of uses and users of information technologies, services, systems and products as well as the diversity of goals or
objectives, sometimes conflicting, among producers, vendors, mediators, and
users of information systems.

ASIS&T urges its members to be ever aware of the social, economic, cultural, and political impacts of their actions or inaction.

ASIS&T members have obligations to employers, clients, and system users,
to the profession, and to society, to use judgement and discretion in making
choices, providing equitable service, and in defending the rights of open inquiry.

Responsibilities to Employers/Clients/System Users

* To act faithfully for their employers or clients in professional matters.
* To uphold each user's, provider's or employer's right to privacy and
confidentiality and to respect whatever proprietary rights belong to
them, by limiting access to, providing proper security for and ensuring proper disposal of data about clients, patrons or users.
* To treat all persons fairly.

Responsibility to the Profession

To truthfully represent themselves and the information systems which they
utilize or which they represent, by
* not knowingly making false statements or providing erroneous or
misleading information
* informing their employers, clients or sponsors of any circumstances
that create a conflict of interest
* not using their position beyond their authorized limits or by not using
their credentials to misrepresent themselves
* following and promoting standards of conduct in accord with the best
current practices

- undertaking their research conscientiously, in gathering, tabulating or interpreting data; in following proper approval procedures for subjects; and in producing or disseminating their research results
- pursuing ongoing professional development and encouraging and assisting colleagues and others to do the same
- adhering to principles of due process and equality of opportunity.

Responsibility to Society

To improve the information systems with which they work or which they represent, to the best of their means and abilities by

- providing the most reliable and accurate information and acknowledging the credibility of the sources as known or unknown
- resisting all forms of censorship, inappropriate selection and acquisitions policies, and biases in information selection, provision and dissemination
- making known any biases, errors and inaccuracies found to exist and striving to correct those which can be remedied.

To promote open and equal access to information, within the scope permitted by their organizations or work, and to resist procedures that promote unlawful discriminatory practices in access to and provision of information, by

- seeking to extend public awareness and appreciation of information availability and provision as well as the role of information professionals in providing such information
- freely reporting, publishing or disseminating information subject to legal and proprietary restraints of producers, vendors and employers, and the best interests of their employers or clients.

Information professionals shall engage in principled conduct whether on their own behalf or at the request of employers, colleagues, clients, agencies or the profession.

Adopted May 1992. Reprinted with the permission of the American Society for Information Science & Technology, Silver Springs, MD.

BOX 2.3
CODE OF ETHICS FOR ARCHIVISTS

Preamble

The Code of Ethics for Archivists establishes standards for the archival profession. It introduces new members of the profession to those standards, reminds experienced archivists of their professional responsibilities, and serves as a model for institutional policies. It also is intended to inspire public confidence in the profession.

This code provides an ethical framework to guide members of the profession. It does not provide the solution to specific problems.

The term "archivist" as used in this code encompasses all those concerned with the selection, control, care, preservation, and administration of historical and documentary records of enduring value.

I. Purpose

The Society of American Archivists recognizes the importance of educating the profession and general public about archival ethics by codifying ethical principles to guide the work of archivists. This code provides a set of principles to which archivists aspire.

II. Professional Relationships

Archivists select, preserve, and make available historical and documentary records of enduring value. Archivists cooperate, collaborate, and respect each institution and its mission and collecting policy. Respect and cooperation form the basis of all professional relationships with colleagues and users.

III. Judgment

Archivists should exercise professional judgment in acquiring, appraising, and processing historical materials. They should not allow personal beliefs or perspectives to affect their decisions.

IV. Trust

Archivists should not profit or otherwise benefit from their privileged access to and control of historical records and documentary materials.

V. Authenticity and Integrity

Archivists strive to preserve and protect the authenticity of records in their holdings by documenting their creation and use in hard copy and electronic formats. They have a fundamental obligation to preserve the intellectual and physical integrity of those records.

Archivists may not alter, manipulate, or destroy data or records to conceal facts or distort evidence.

VI. Access

Archivists strive to promote open and equitable access to their services and the records in their care without discrimination or preferential treatment, and in accordance with legal requirements, cultural sensitivities, and institutional policies. Archivists recognize their responsibility to promote the use of records as a fundamental purpose of the keeping of archives. Archivists may place restrictions on access for the protection of privacy or confidentiality of information in the records.

VII. Privacy

Archivists protect the privacy rights of donors and individuals or groups who are the subject of records. They respect all users' right to privacy by maintaining the confidentiality of their research and protecting any personal information collected about them in accordance with the institution's security procedures.

VIII. Security/Protection

Archivists protect all documentary materials for which they are responsible and guard them against defacement, physical damage, deterioration, and theft. Archivists should cooperate with colleagues and law enforcement agencies to apprehend and prosecute thieves and vandals.

IX. Law

Archivists must uphold all federal, state, and local laws.

Approved by the SAA Council, February 5, 2005. Reprinted with permission.

BOX 2.4
CODE OF ETHICS FOR HEALTH SCIENCES LIBRARIANSHIP

Goals and Principles for Ethical Conduct

The health sciences librarian believes that knowledge is the sine qua non of informed decisions in health care, education, and research and the health sciences librarian serves society, clients, and the institution by working to ensure that informed decisions can be made. The principles of this code are expressed in broad statements to guide ethical decision making. These statements provide a framework; they cannot and do not dictate conduct to cover particular situations.

Society

- The health sciences librarian promotes access to health information for all and creates and maintains conditions of freedom of inquiry, thought, and expression that facilitate informed health care decisions.

Clients

- The health sciences librarian works without prejudice to meet the client's information needs.
- The health sciences librarian respects the privacy of clients and protects the confidentiality of the client relationship.
- The health sciences librarian ensures that the best available information is provided to the client.

Institution

- The health sciences librarian provides leadership and expertise in the design, development, and ethical management of knowledge-based information systems that meet the needs and obligations of the institution.

Profession

- The health sciences librarian advances and upholds the philosophy and ideals of the profession.
- The health sciences librarian advocates and advances knowledge and standards of the profession.
- The health sciences librarian conducts all professional relationships with courtesy and respect.
- The health sciences librarian maintains high standards of professional integrity.

Self

- The health sciences librarian assumes personal responsibility for developing and maintaining professional excellence.
- The health sciences librarian shall be alert to his or her institution's code of ethics and its conflict of interest, disclosure, and gift policies.

Used with permission of the Medical Library Association, Chicago. Copyright (c) 1994 Medical Library Association.

BOX 2.5
AALL ETHICAL PRINCIPLES

Preamble

When individuals have ready access to legal information, they can participate fully in the affairs of their government. By collecting, organizing, preserving, and retrieving legal information, the members of the American Association of Law Libraries enable people to make this ideal of democracy a reality.

Legal information professionals have an obligation to satisfy the needs, to promote the interests and to respect the values of their clientele. Law firms, corporations, academic and governmental institutions and the general public have legal information needs that are best addressed by professionals committed to the belief that serving these information needs is a noble calling and that fostering the equal participation of diverse people in library services underscores one of our basic tenets, open access to information for all individuals.

Service

We promote open and effective access to legal and related information. Further we recognize the need to establish methods of preserving, maintaining and retrieving legal information in many different forms.

We uphold a duty to our clientele to develop service policies that respect confidentiality and privacy.

We provide zealous service using the most appropriate resources and implementing programs consistent with our institution's mission and goals.

We acknowledge the limits on service imposed by our institutions and by the duty to avoid the unauthorized practice of law.

Business Relationships

We promote fair and ethical trade practices.

We have a duty to avoid situations in which personal interests might be served or significant benefits gained at the expense of library users, colleagues, or our employing institutions.

We strive to obtain the maximum value for our institution's fiscal resources, while at the same time making judicious, analytical and rational use of our institution's information resources.

Professional Responsibilities

We relate to our colleagues with respect and in a spirit of cooperation.

We distinguish between our personal convictions and professional duties and do not allow our personal beliefs to interfere with the service we provide.

We recognize and respect the rights of the owner and the user of intellectual property.

We strive for excellence in the profession by maintaining and enhancing our own knowledge and skills, by encouraging the professional development of co-workers, and by fostering the aspirations of potential members of the profession.

Approved by the AALL membership, April 5, 1999. Reprinted by permission of the American Association of Law Libraries.

Taken as a whole, these codes suggest that ethical obligations occur on at least four levels: (1) *individual level*—librarians have an obligation to act ethically to each individual they serve; (2) *organizational level*—librarians have an ethical obligation to act in the best interest of their organization; (3) *professional level*—librarians have an ethical obligation to promote standards of professional conduct established by the accepted professional organizations; and (4) *societal level*—librarians, like all individuals, have an ethical obligation to serve the best interests of the society as a whole.

The obligations noted in the codes manifest themselves in the manner in which reference work is conducted. They include the obligations to (1) provide the highest level of services to all library users and information seekers, treating all individuals with respect and courtesy; (2) protect the confidentiality and privacy of library users and information seekers; (3) respect the intellectual freedom of library users through equal, open, and nondiscriminatory access to information; (4) respect intellectual property or other proprietary interests; (5) pursue continuing education to improve professional skills; (6) advance the interest of the library user and information seeker over the interest of the librarian; and (7) improve the system or processes of the organization.

Professional codes are not magic formulas. Although the guidelines or precepts may be helpful, they are usually relatively brief statements. The many subtleties raised while discussing the code and the reasoning behind the code are usually lost in the final version. Consequently, attempts to interpret the code in the myriad situations that might arise are often difficult. In addition, ethical codes in the information professions are not supported by sanctions in case of violation. For example, violating the Code of Medical Ethics might lead to a physician's license being suspended or revoked. The information professions have no such sanctions.

Nonetheless, professional codes are often a product of considerable thought and reflect professional consensus. They highlight many important ethical responsibilities of librarians in general, as well as reference librarians in particular. They provide important guidance in difficult situations, and despite the lack of sanctions, the general acceptance of such codes provides considerable normative support to regulate the conduct of information professionals.

Competencies and Ethical Behavior

Although ethical codes represent the core ethical guidance of the profession, in 2003 the Reference and User Services Association of the ALA adopted specific professional competencies. Because competencies imply specific types of behavior, it is reasonable that many of these behaviors would possess ethical dimensions. In fact, the behaviors listed in the RUSA "Professional Competencies for Reference and User Services Librarians"[20] provide an excellent example of a reference librarian performing ethically. To meet the goals identified by the RUSA competencies, a librarian

- "provides services that are responsive to user needs";
- "effectively designs and organizes reference and user services to meet the needs of the primary community";
- "provides high quality services by carefully analyzing both information sources and services";

- "monitors the most relevant information sources to routinely update knowledge of current developments in reference and user services";
- "effectively utilizes new knowledge to enhance reference and user services practices";
- "shares expertise with colleagues and mentors newer staff";
- "actively contributes to improving professional practice through engaging in projects with colleagues and enhancing individual skills through independent learning";
- "conducts research to determine what types of reference services to provide and to what types of users these services will be provided";
- "effectively communicates the nature of the reference and information services that are provided to users being served";
- "consistently and systematically evaluates the effectiveness of the marketing of reference and information services";
- "treats the user as a collaborator and partner in the information seeking process";
- "works closely with colleagues to provide quality service to users";
- "develops collaborative relationships within the profession to enhance service to users";
- "develops and maintains partnerships beyond the library and the profession to strengthen services to users";
- "effectively uses tools and techniques to survey users and their information needs";
- "assesses the effectiveness of information services provided to users";
- "assesses and evaluates resources in all formats in terms of objective standards and how well it meets the library's user needs";
- "evaluates new or existing services for a match between user capabilities and service technological requirements";
- "evaluates the format, access, and presentation aspects of resources as part of the overall assessment of the value of tools"; and
- "effectively identifies and employs evaluation techniques that measure staff performance."

The considerable burden placed on reference librarians in their day-to-day work environment to meet all their professional responsibilities is often grossly underestimated. In fact, the duties are great, and meeting one's professional obligations is a formidable challenge.

The First Amendment as an Ethical Guide

In addition to professional codes of conduct and competencies, librarianship as a profession is grounded in the ethical obligation to protect the First Amendment rights of library users and hence to protect the right of access to information. The First Amendment, among other things, protects the right of free speech and press. The right to speak or publish is hollow, however, unless citizens also have a right to gain access to the ideas that are spoken or otherwise produced. Public institutions whose primary purpose is to disseminate ideas play a critical role in protecting the First Amendment; attempts to restrict access to such ideas are violations of this right.

Libraries, especially public libraries, have consciously and concertedly associated themselves with protecting the First Amendment rights of American citizens, especially since the middle of the 20th century. Protecting the right of access to ideas and information is a commonly accepted ethical obligation in the library profession, usually subsumed under the broader obligation to protect the intellectual freedom of library users. The reference librarian shares these obligations and meets them by providing all users with the complete information they seek in a confidential manner.

SOME MAJOR ETHICAL ISSUES FACING REFERENCE LIBRARIANS AND OTHER INFORMATION PROFESSIONALS

Many ethical issues confront reference librarians. The brief discussions that follow are intended to identify some of the more common ethical concerns and to challenge readers to think carefully about how they might deal with them.

The Tension between Protecting the Right of Access and Protecting Individuals or Society from Harm

If an individual who is unfamiliar to you comes to the reference desk and requests material on how to build a bomb, do you provide it?
If an individual comes to the reference desk and asks if there is any material on how to freebase cocaine, do you provide it?
Should the library provide open access to the Internet for library users of all ages?

One of the most important ethical tensions in librarianship involves situations in which the rights of individuals come into conflict with their own welfare or that of others. As a rule, reference librarians are expected to withhold judgment regarding the nature of the inquiry. D. J. Foskett described this view in 1962 as the "Creed of the Librarian": in executing professional responsibilities, the librarian should have "no politics, no religion, no morals."[21] Such neutrality is considered essential to protect all information to which the citizenry has a constitutional right. There is little doubt that the ALA "Library Bill of Rights"[22] (see Box 2.6) and the ALA "Code of Ethics" support this perspective. When an individual asks for information, it is the professional duty of the reference librarian to provide that information. But what if that information may cause direct harm to the individual asking for it or to others? (See Box 2.7.)

BOX 2.6
LIBRARY BILL OF RIGHTS

The American Library Association affirms that all libraries are forums for information and ideas, and that the following basic policies should guide their services.

I. Books and other library resources should be provided for the interest, information, and enlightenment of all people of the community the library serves. Materials should not be excluded because of the origin, background, or views of those contributing to their creation.

II. Libraries should provide materials and information presenting all points of view on current and historical issues. Materials should not be proscribed or removed because of partisan or doctrinal disapproval.

III. Libraries should challenge censorship in the fulfillment of their responsibility to provide information and enlightenment.

IV. Libraries should cooperate with all persons and groups concerned with resisting abridgment of free expression and free access to ideas.

V. A person's right to use a library should not be denied or abridged because of origin, age, background, or views.

VI. Libraries that make exhibit spaces and meeting rooms available to the public they serve should make such facilities available on an equitable basis, regardless of the beliefs or affiliations of individuals or groups requesting their use.

Adopted June 19, 1939, by the ALA Council; amended October 14, 1944; June 18, 1948; February 2, 1961; June 27, 1967; January 23, 1980; inclusion of "age" reaffirmed January 23, 1996.

Reprinted with the permission of the American Library Association.

BOX 2.7
CASE STUDY: TO BE OR NOT TO BE

Melissa, a 15-year old, comes into the Jonestown Public Library from time to time. None of the reference librarians in the library know her well, but when Melissa passes the desk, she usually says "hi" as she goes by to any staff member who is stationed there. She is not a behavioral problem, although rarely, a staff member may have to tell her to keep her voice down. The reference staff is aware that Melissa has had "some problems," and there is a rumor that last year she tried to hurt herself.

Melissa approaches the reference librarian. She looks like she has been crying; her eyes are a little red, and her face is slightly puffy. In a slightly shaky voice, she asks, "I've been looking for a book, but it's not on the shelf. It's called *Final Exit*. Can you tell me where it is?" You know that *Final Exit* is a book on how to commit suicide. You also know that it has just been returned and is on a cart ready for reshelving.

Questions

Should the librarian retrieve the book from the cart and give it to Melissa?
Should any other actions be taken?
Exactly what would you say to Melissa?
Can you think of other reference questions that might present ethical problems
at the reference desk?

The issue of causing harm has recently been highlighted by debates over unrestricted access to the Internet. Because the Internet contains a variety of materials that may be considered violent, hateful, or sexually explicit, serious concern has been expressed about the common library policy that permits young people as well as adults to consult any part of a library collection. If such a policy is extended to the Internet, it is argued, detrimental effects could result to the young people exposed to such material. Consequently, a particularly active debate has ensued regarding the use of electronic filters that can block Web sites that contain offensive materials, especially those that are sexually explicit. On the face of it, such an argument seems sensible. Proponents of filters consider them appropriate in part because their use affirms and preserves the traditional character of library collections; that is, in general, libraries do not collect pornographic materials. Using filters that remove such sites makes Internet access consistent with other selection practices and protects young users from potentially harmful exposure.

Filters raise numerous ethical concerns. They violate fundamental tenets of reference work by denying access to information to some individuals but not others. Generally, the library profession has established the standard that all individuals have equal rights to information. Discriminating on the basis of age, for example, is expressly prohibited by the "Library Bill of Rights." This prohibition has been extended specifically to the electronic environment in the ALA policy "Access to Electronic Information, Services, and Networks." In addition, filters have not been shown to be entirely successful, and their inability to distinguish appropriate sexual information from pornographic sites threatens constitutionally protected speech. Complications have also arisen when certain types of federal assistance may be dependent on the library's use of filters. In cases where filtering is legally mandated, the issue of how much filtering should be employed becomes an additional ethical consideration.

Concern over the implementation of filters has led the American Library Association to issue a variety of official statements cautioning libraries against their use: "Resolution on the Use of Filtering Software in Libraries," the "ALA Intellectual Freedom Committee Statement on Library Use of Filtering Software," and "Guidelines and Considerations for Developing a Public Library Internet Use Policy."[23]

Underlying the library profession's concern about filtering and the temptation to restrict materials because of their potential harm is the concept of intellectual freedom. The principle of intellectual freedom supports the belief that people have a fundamental right to the ideas produced in a society and that society functions best when the flow of ideas is unimpeded. Given this view, it is inappropriate for librarians to make judgments regarding the appropriateness of particular information for a particular individual. The reference librarian is expected not to guess how a particular piece of information will be used, but to provide the information to the information seeker. Otherwise, the reference librarian is given license to decide which reasons for use are valid and which are pernicious. Such a view would allow for considerable mischief.

Despite the strength of this argument, some writers maintain that there are even deeper issues at stake. Robert Hauptman, for example, argues that reference librarians, just like everyone else, have an ethical duty to protect others. Hauptman contends that "censorship is never warranted, but it should not be confused with a refusal to aid and abet egregiously antisocial acts."[24] Hauptman fears that professional education emphasizing the "Library Bill of Rights" becomes dogma that replaces thoughtful reflection on the specific situation and the ethical dilemmas that may arise.[25] In 1975, Hauptman conducted an experiment in libraries directly related to this issue. Self-described as "young, bearded, deferential," Hauptman visited 13 public and academic libraries. After determining he was talking to a reference librarian, he indicated that he needed information on a "small explosive device" and wanted to know about the properties of cordite. He even indicated he was interested in whether a small amount would destroy a "normal suburban house." Hauptman reported that none of the librarians invoked ethical grounds for refusing to cooperate, and the vast majority tried to supply the information.[26] A similar finding occurred in a follow-up experiment conducted by Robert Dowd in 1989. Dowd asked reference librarians how to freebase cocaine.[27] The situations created by Hauptman and Dowd remind us that our ethical duty extends to the protection of others and the society at large, not just to the library user. These dilemmas are difficult because one must always weigh harm done to individuals and the society at large when the right to information is deprived based on the speculation of reference librarians.

Nonetheless, the issues Hauptman raises are provocative, and the implication that librarians as professionals have an obligation to be thoughtful and reflective is doubly important when dealing with ethical dilemmas. Whether they fear that information provided will be harmful to others or to the individual, there will remain a residue of uneasiness when reference librarians provide information they suspect might be used for untoward purposes. At present, the professional codes and guidelines and professional education offer the most solid framework for providing reference service.

Issues Related to Equality of Access to Information

Is it ever appropriate to violate the confidentiality or privacy of library patrons? Do children have the same rights to information as adults?

The central ethical principle guiding reference librarians is "equality of access." This notion is explicitly stated or inherent in the various codes and guidelines of the profession. For example, the ALA "Code of Ethics" calls for "equitable access," the ASIS&T "Professional Guidelines" exhort information scientists to "promote open and equal access to information," and the "Code of Ethics for Health Sciences Librarianship" "promotes access to health information for all." A variety of situations challenge this principle.

Privacy and Confidentiality

The concepts of privacy and confidentiality are explicit parts of many ethical codes in the information professions and are vital to the provision of information services. Although not specifically identified in the U.S. Constitution, a right to privacy has been recognized in a variety of court cases as an important right of citizens.

For individuals to feel comfortable seeking information, they must be confident that their queries and the answers given to their queries are confidential. Significant First Amendment issues arise if such confidences are broken. Making reference inquiries and responses public may create what is referred to as a "chilling effect" on the First Amendment rights of library users. If library users feel that they could be subjected to public exposure, embarrassment, or sanction, they are not likely to pursue the information they need. Reference librarians are therefore ethically obligated to conduct their reference interviews in a manner that is minimally intrusive, and their queries should be directed only toward those factors that would help satisfy information needs. Similarly, they must prevent, as far as possible, intrusions into the privacy of their users. This notion is linked to Fourth Amendment protections regarding unlawful search and seizure as well as to First Amendment rights. Generally speaking, the reference librarian is ethically obligated to keep the content of reference questions confidential, even when queried by government officials.

These rights were conspicuously challenged in the 1970s when the federal government made a concerted effort to investigate certain types of reference inquiries, especially in academic libraries. The FBI began the Library Awareness Program, the purpose of which was to try to identify foreign agents in the United States who were attempting to gather unclassified scientific and technical information that could give their countries a technological advantage. The FBI suspected that library collections were a perfect place for such agents to get this information. Consequently, they began making inquiries of librarians concerning individuals making such requests. The existence of this program was not revealed until 1987, when it was exposed by an incident at Columbia University. Following considerable protests by the American Library Association, the FBI decided to discontinue the program, although its revival is still a possibility.

More recently, there is considerable concern that the USA PATRIOT Act compromises the confidentiality of reference queries as well as other library activities, such as the circulation of library materials. Under this act, federal authorities can assert the power to investigate the nature and content of reference queries of individual patrons, and such investigations may be conducted with fewer safeguards for the subject of these investigations or the library institution.

Reference librarians have an ethical obligation to protect the privacy and confidentiality of library user inquiries, but is that obligation absolute? If a teenager who appears upset asks for information on committing suicide, is there any obligation to report the individual's apparent distress to a school counselor? If law enforcement investigators believe that the information requested and provided to a library user might reasonably cause harm to others, does the reference librarian have an obligation to reveal the content of the reference transaction?

As with most ethical dilemmas, no single answer produces perfect solutions. Under extraordinary circumstances, one might imagine grounds for transgressing the basic ethical tenets of privacy and confidentiality, but it is clear that such tenets are fundamental to professional practice, and their violation must generally be considered a serious breach of the professional duty of reference librarians (see Box 2.8).

BOX 2.8
CASE STUDY: A CASE OF HONOR OR PRIVACY

Mary Smith is a reference librarian at the Martinville College Library, a small liberal arts college. Recently, a college student came into the library and requested help on the Internet terminal. The student indicated she was looking for help on preparing a term paper on James Joyce because she had to do one in Dr. Jones's introductory literature class. Mary knows Dr. Jones very well and considers her a good friend.

The student brought with her the name of a particular Web site, and she wanted to know how to find it. Mary recognized the name of the site because it had become popular among some of the students. It was a site that provided access to copies of term papers prepared by students around the country.

Mary took the student to the terminal and briefly instructed her regarding how to use the search engines to locate the Web site. The student stayed at the terminal for about 20 minutes. The last 10 minutes were spent printing off a fairly lengthy document. Just before the student left, she approached the desk and thanked Mary for the help. Mary could see that she had a copy of a paper in her hand.

Not long after the student left, Mary went to the terminal and saw that the student had printed off a term paper on James Joyce titled "James Joyce: Portrait of an Artist as an Old Man." The paper was authored by Patricia Van Doren. Mary felt some pangs of guilt. There is a clear plagiarism policy at the college that says that students and staff must report evidence of plagiarism. Mary wondered if she should say anything, but she didn't.

Several weeks later, Dr. Jones was having lunch with Mary at a local restaurant. Dr. Jones was talking about her classes when she commented that recently she had received a couple of term papers that really worried her. The style and quality of writing far exceeded the students' regular performances, and she feared that someone had written their papers for them. She mentioned that one paper, prepared by a female student on James Joyce, was particularly troubling. The paper was finely written, and she simply didn't think that particular student could do that kind of work. Dr. Jones expressed frustration that she couldn't really do much about it.

Mary didn't know what to do about it either.[28]

Questions

What are Mary's ethical obligations?
What, if anything, should Mary say to Dr. Jones?

Should she mention the student specifically?

Should she mention the term paper database without mentioning the student?

If Dr. Jones mentioned that she had heard of term paper databases and asked Mary if she knew if they were being used by her students, what should Mary say?

Disparate Levels of Service

The reference librarian in most public libraries today encounters a wide variety of library users. Despite the differences in clientele, librarians are expected to provide equal library service. This was not always so. In 1911, for example, the highly respected librarian John Cotton Dana suggested that the amount of time devoted to a reference question depended on three things—(1) the significance of the query: whether the answers provided would add to the body of knowledge, be instructive to groups or individuals, or be merely of recreational interest or frivolous; (2) the claim or status of the inquirer: an individual such as a library trustee or government official would likely receive greater time; and (3) the probability of success or ease in finding the answer.[29]

Although modern professional codes remind us to treat all individuals equally, today's reality suggests that Dana's criteria still prevail. For example, it is becoming more common today, given the difficult financial circumstances of many libraries, that special information services or special reference collections for special groups can be offered only if additional financial support is provided by them. Hence, libraries may provide special services to business and industry but not fine arts. Although it is clear that providing services to an important part of the library community is ethically appropriate, this raises another important ethical dilemma: devoting one's resources and energies to one group often means providing service of less quality to other groups. Because both fiscal and human resources are limited, if the technology "haves" are the groups emphasized by information services, then the technology "have-nots" might be deprived of resources and energy.

Sometimes concern has been expressed regarding the equality of service provided to certain groups, most notably children. Do children receive treatment equal to that given to adults? Do some reference policies discriminate against service for children? For example, in a public library, are homework questions treated the same way as if an adult had asked a similar question? In an academic library, are students' information queries treated the same way as are faculty members'? Are exceptions regarding library rules in the reference department more likely to be made for a faculty member, administrator, or board member than for a student?

The Internet has also raised the specter of differential treatment in regard to service. As noted earlier, Internet terminals may be restricted or filtered for young people. In the academic setting, different types of Internet services are available for some groups and not others. For example, students might be allowed access to both search and e-mail functions, but the general public might be able to use only the search functions.

The fundamental tenets of the profession suggest that providing unequal service is an unethical act, yet an ethical tension remains, reflecting the ethical obligation to protect and promote the survival of the library. Is it wrong to provide special services to those who are likely to influence, for better or worse, the future of the library? As information technologies increase in number and sophistication, it behooves reference librarians to consider who is being served and why. Who is being included and who is being excluded or ignored?

Copyright Issues

Copyright is one of the most complex issues facing today's reference librarians (see chapter 7 for a discussion of copyright in the context of interlibrary loan and document delivery). Copying information has been a service available in libraries for decades. The central issue regarding copyright focuses on the idea of "fair use." Fair use is a concept under the copyright law that permits an individual, under specific conditions, to make a copy of something without the permission of the copyright owner. Four basic criteria are considered when determining whether a particular use is a fair use:

1. the purpose and character of the use, including whether such is of a commercial nature or is for nonprofit educational purposes;
2. the nature of the copyrighted work;
3. the amount and substantiality of the portion used in relation to the copyrighted work as a whole; and
4. the effect of the use upon the potential market for, or value of, the copyrighted work.[30]

Use is more likely to be considered "fair use" when the purpose is educational, when it is a print item rather than a video, when only a small portion of the item is copied, and when the copy has little demonstrative effect on the profits that could be gained if the item were purchased from the copyright owner.

Copying, however, has become more complicated with the introduction of electronic technologies, especially access to the Internet and the Web. The Web provides vast amounts of otherwise unavailable information that can be rapidly copied or downloaded with little effort. This situation is both good and bad. It is good in that people and librarians have access to a tremendous amount of information. It is bad if librarians and library users do not respect the intellectual property rights of those who produce the information. This tension can be seen in the ALA "Code of Ethics," which asserts the intellectual freedom rights of library users, exhorts librarians to provide the highest levels of service, and insists that librarians concomitantly respect the intellectual property rights of information producers.

Reference librarians tend to take very liberal positions regarding the copying of material; "educational" use is often assumed, as is the trivial effect on the market for the creator or producer of the product. This is not surprising; after all, reference librarians ensure the information rights of library users. This seems like a manifestly ethical act. By the same token, it is reasonable to assume that copyright owners have a legal and moral right to protection from copying of their work and the right to benefit from the creation of their intellectual products. Excessive copying of materials is likely to be a violation of law, and violating the law is usually considered to be an unethical act. What roles should librarians play in explaining copyright obligations and monitoring uncontrolled copying of copyrighted material? Do librarians do enough to caution library users concerning copying activity? As information becomes more and more fluid and easily transferred, the ethical tensions in this area are likely to increase, and there will be greater and greater reliance on reference librarians to consider the role and limits of their actions.

This problem is highlighted as librarians provide more and more bibliographic instruction, especially in the academic environment. It is common during such instruction to provide substantive information on accessing full-text databases or downloading images. Are librarians providing students with the means to easily misuse such material? If so, what specific additional obligations should the librarian meet to ensure that students are aware of the ramifications of copyright violations and plagiarism?

DIGITAL REFERENCE

In general, the rise of digital reference is an exciting prospect. In its most elementary form, digital reference is providing references services electronically. It might be a synchronous activity in which the user and librarian are interacting "live," or it might be asynchronous, in which the user asks a question electronically, and it is subsequently answered by a librarian. The advantages are obvious. Information seekers from remote and convenient locations can have 24/7 access to information professionals, who, in turn, have access to the world of digitally available information.

Of course, the basic ethical issues implicated in regular reference processes, such as confidentiality and privacy, apply in the digital environment. However, the vulnerability to ethical violations may increase because of the nature of the technology itself. For example, in the electronic environment, it is often possible to track an individual's identity, queries, and precise use of electronic databases because an electronic trail may be preserved. These records should be treated with the same respect for confidentiality and privacy as circulation records. There is also the ethical issue of availability of and access to digital reference services. It is clear from a variety of studies that there are groups of individuals who remain part of the digital divide. These groups do not have the same access to digital services for at least two reasons: they lack the computer equipment and network access, and they do not have the training to use the equipment even if it is available. If librarians devote more and more of their resources and time to digital reference, then service to those who do not have technological access will be negatively affected. Such disparities in library service imply not that digital reference service is unethical, but only that digital reference raises ethical implications that must be concomitantly addressed. As the digital environment grows, there is no doubt that the ethical concerns will grow as well.

CONCLUSION

Ethical considerations and obligations in reference work are many and are related in complex ways. Librarians bring to their workplace their own personal convictions and beliefs, and library users bring their own needs, purposes, and values as well. In this heterogeneous environment, the information professions provide some consistency regarding ethical conduct by identifying through their professional codes and education those behaviors that have been accepted as ethically responsible.

As a rule, the underlying ethical obligation of reference librarians, as of all library workers, is to provide the highest level of service to each library user. This not only entails providing accurate and complete information to every inquirer; it also requires that each library user be treated in an ethical and professional manner.

It is easy to think that ethical concerns arise only in particular circumstances or when dealing with particular library users or questions. Certainly, these situations must be pondered carefully. It is equally important to realize that ethical obligations are fulfilled during each reference transaction. Every day, every time a question is asked, reference librarians fulfill or abrogate their ethical obligations. RUSA, in its guidelines, has identified clearly how these daily obligations are fulfilled. A brief restatement of these obligations represents an apt summary of what is meant by ethical and professional reference service. Reference librarians must

1. be approachable;
2. demonstrate a genuine interest in each library user's query;
3. listen carefully to each question and make the needed inquiries to truly understand what is being asked;
4. conduct thorough and accurate searches, or provide library users with the needed information to conduct the searches themselves; and
5. follow up with each library user to determine whether the user's information needs have actually been met.[31]

In the broadest context, if reference librarians perform these functions, their ethical obligations will be satisfied, and library users and the society as a whole will be well served.

NOTES

1. Michael Harris, "The Purpose of the American Public Library: A Revisionist Interpretation of History," *Library Journal* 98 (September 15, 1973): 2511.

2. James Duff Brown, "The Shy Enquirer," *The Library World* 13 (1911): 365.

3. Samuel S. Green, "Libraries as Bureaus of Information," *The Library Journal* 21 (July 1896): 324.

4. W. E. Foster, "The Information Desk," *The Library Journal* 19 (November 1894): 368.

5. Ibid., 368–69.

6. Green, "Libraries as Bureaus of Information," 324.

7. Harris, "The Purpose of the American Public Library," 2510–11.

8. Melvil Dewey, "The Profession," *Library Journal* 114 (June 15, 1989): 5.

9. Winston Churchill, "The Mission of the Public Library," *Library Journal* 28 (March 1903): 116.

10.   Dee Garrison, "The Tender Technicians: The Feminization of Public Librarianship, 1876–1905," *Journal of Social History* 6 (Winter 1972–1973): 131–56.

11.   Corinne Bacon, "Reference Work from the Librarian's Point of View," *The Library Journal* 27 (November 1902): 927.

12.   Ibid., 929.

13.   G. T. Clark, Librarian, San Francisco Public Library, in "Reference Work with the General Public," *Public Libraries* 9 (February 1904): 58.

14.   Robert J. Usher, "Some Needs in Reference Work," *The Library Journal* 51 (September 15, 1926): 761, 762.

15.   W. W. Bishop, "The Amount of Help to Be Given to Readers," *Bulletin of the American Library Association* 2 (September 1908): 327.

16.   Bacon, "Reference Work from the Librarian's Point of View," 930.

17.   Miss McLoney, "Reference Work with the General Public," *Public Libraries* 9 (February 1904): 64.

18.   Reference and User Services Association, "Guidelines for Behavioral Performance of Reference and Information Service Providers." http://www.ala.org/ala/mgrps/divs/rusa/re sources/guidelines/guidelinesbehavioral.cfm.

19.   Ethics policies for the American Library Association can be found at http://www.ala.org/ ala/issuesadvocacy/proethics/codeofethics/codeethics.cfm; for the American Society for Information Science & Technology at http://www.asis.org/AboutASIS/professional-guidelines. html; for the Society of American Archivists at http://www.archivists.org/governance/hand book/app_ethics.asp; for the Medical Library Association at http://www.mlanet.org/about/eth ics.html; and for the American Association of Law Libraries at http://www.aallnet.org/about/ policy_ethics.asp.

20.   Reference and User Services Association, "Professional Competencies for Reference and User Services Librarians." http://www.ala.org/ala/mgrps/divs/rusa/resources/guidelines/ professional.cfm.

21.   D. J. Foskett, *The Creed of the Librarian—No Politics, No Religion, No Morals* (London: Library Association, 1962), 13 pp.

22.   *Library Bill of Rights.* http://www.ala.org/ala/issuesadvocacy/intfreedom/librarybill/ index.cfm.

23.   "Intellectual Freedom Statements and Policies: Internet." http://www.ala.org/ala/ aboutala/offices/oif/statementspols/statementspolicies.cfm#internet.

24.   Robert Hauptman, "Professional Responsibility Reconsidered," *RQ* 35 (Spring 1996): 329.

25.   Robert Hauptman, "Professionalism or Culpability? An Experiment in Ethics," *Wilson Library Bulletin* 50 (April 1976): 626–27.

26.   Ibid., 626.

27.   Robert C. Dowd, "I Want to Find out How to Freebase Cocaine or Yet Another Unobtrusive Test of Reference Performance," *The Reference Librarian* 25/26 (1989): 483–93.

28.   For a discussion of term paper Web sites, see Gregory L. Anderson, "Cyberplagiarism: A Look at the Web Term Paper Sites," *College & Research Libraries News* 60 (May 1999): 371–73, 394; for a discussion of strategies for detecting and deterring cyberplagiarism, see Jennifer R. Sharkey and F. Bartow Culp, "Cyberplagiarism and the Library: Issues and Solutions," *Reference Librarian* 91–92 (2005): 103–16.

29. John Cotton Dana, "Misdirection of Effort in Reference Work," *Public Libraries* 16 (March 1911): 108.

30. 17 U.S.C. Section 107.

31. Reference and User Services Association, "Guidelines." http://www.ala.org/ala/mgrps/divs/rusa/resources/guidelines/guidelinesbehavioral.cfm.

ADDITIONAL READINGS

American Library Association, Reference and User Services Association (RUSA). "Professional Competencies for Reference and User Services Librarians." http://www.ala.org/ala/mgrps/divs/rusa/resources/guidelines/professional.cfm.

These guidelines are designed to identify the critical competencies for effective performance of reference services. Covering such areas as access, organization and design of services, marketing, outreach, evaluation, and professional development, the competencies clarify the goals and responsibilities of reference librarians, many of which have ethical implications.

Barsh, Adele, and Amy Lisewski. "Library Managers and Ethical Leadership: A Survey of Current Practices from the Perspective of Business Ethics." *Journal of Library Administration* 47 (2008): 27–67.

The authors examine library managers' role in ethical leadership within their organizations. Concepts of business ethics and moral development are explored, as well as the research literature on ethics and values in the library profession. The article reports on a survey conducted by the authors identifying ethical issues confronted by practitioners and the role of ethical codes.

Buchanan, Elizabeth A., and Katherine A. Henderson. *Case Studies in Library and Information Science Ethics*. Jefferson, NC: McFarland, 2009. 165 pp.

This work contains more than 100 case studies divided into five categories: intellectual freedom, privacy, intellectual property, professional ethics, and intercultural information ethics. Theoretical as well as practical issues are raised and discussed. Discussion questions are also included.

Carbo, Toni, and Martha M. Smith. "Global Information Ethics: Intercultural Perspectives on Past and Future Research." *Journal of the American Society for Information Science and Technology* 59 (2008): 1111–23.

The authors review the widening application of the concept of information ethics (IE) to many disciplines and across national boundaries. The article discusses the application of IE in library and information science education, ethics courses, conferences, and professional journals and identifies a variety of articles that provide perspectives on global information ethics.

Danielson, Elena S. "Ethics and Reference Services." *The Reference Librarian* 56 (1997): 107–24.

This article explores the ethical ramifications of reference service in the archival environment. Reference codes are discussed, as well as issues related to the use of the Internet, responsibilities of ownership, equitable access, providing information about archives versus providing information from the archives, and privacy concerns.

Del Vecchio, Rosemary A. "Privacy and Accountability at the Reference Desk." *The Reference Librarian* 38 (1992): 133–40.

> Del Vecchio explores the extent to which reference librarians are obligated to protect the privacy of library users and the expectations of library users regarding their privacy. The legal responsibilities regarding maintaining privacy are discussed, as well as the obligations identified in professional codes.

Froehlich, Thomas J. "Ethical Considerations of Information Professionals." *Annual Review of Information Science and Technology* 27 (1992): 291–319.

> This substantial literature review covers a number of issues on ethics and information professionals. Froehlich surveys the major concerns and examines such areas as privacy, confidentiality, and legal liabilities. He also includes discussions of the principles proposed for ethical action, the concerns of theoreticians and researchers, and the ethical code established by the American Society for Information Science and Technology.

Gosseries, Alex. "A Case for Restricted Access." *Journal of Information Ethics* 12 (Spring 2003): 56–66.

> This article explores the possible reasons asserted for restricting access to information and the tests for determining access to information. Concepts such as "standing" and "merit" of request are reviewed. The "worst possible recipient" test is discussed and its implications identified for open access to information.

Hauptman, Robert, ed. "Ethics and the Dissemination of Information." *Library Trends* 40 (Fall 1991): 199–375.

> This collection of articles covers a wide range of topics on ethics in library and information science. Authors include Rosemary Ruhig Du Mont, Rhoda Garoogian, John Swan, Thomas Froehlich, Norman Stevens, and others. Among the topics discussed are ethical issues related to management, user confidentiality, law librarianship, ethics in health sciences libraries, and ethical issues in technology transfer.

Hauptman, Robert. "Professional Responsibility Reconsidered." *RQ* 35 (Spring 1996): 327–29.

> This article reviews earlier articles by Hauptman and Dowd on the propensity of reference librarians to ignore the possible social ramifications of their actions and suggests that librarians remain insensitive to the possible harmful impact of their actions. Hauptman expresses concern that librarians fail to take responsibility for their actions and rely too heavily on their educational indoctrination.

International Review of Information Ethics. Stuttgart, Germany: International Center for Information Ethics, 2004–. Semiannual.

> This journal, formerly the *International Journal of Information Ethics*, is the official journal of the International Center for Information Ethics. Central themes include the impact of the ethics of information technology on people and society.

Isaacson, David. "Is the Correct Answer the Right One?" *Journal of Information Ethics* 13 (Spring 2004): 14–18.

> This article explores the potential ethical dilemmas that arise when a library user is not happy with the answer provided by the reference librarian, even if that answer is correct.

Journal of Information Ethics. Edited by Robert Hauptman. Jefferson, NC: McFarland, 1992–. Semiannual.

> This journal explores a wide variety of topics in the area of information ethics, including ethical issues related to Internet use, secrecy, privacy, professional values, use of images, and the workplace.

Lindsey, Jonathan A., and Ann E. Prentice. *Professional Ethics and Librarians*. Phoenix, AZ: Oryx Press, 1985. 103 pp.

The authors review the historical and philosophical foundations of ethics codes in general. The text includes a detailed discussion of the development of the ALA "Code of Ethics," with verbatim reproductions of earlier versions of the code and commentary on the code by several notable librarians.

Mason, Richard O., Florence M. Mason, and Mary J. Culnan. *Ethics of Information Management*. Thousand Oaks, CA: Sage, 1995. 324 pp.

This text is a general treatise on the ethical and moral dimensions of handling information. Among the areas covered are the ethical challenges facing information professionals; understanding the nature of information; the relationship of information to decision making, power, and information policy; the foundations of ethical theory; and societal and organizational issues that relate to ethical decision-making for information professionals.

McMenemy, David, Alan Poulter, and Paul F. Burton. *A Handbook of Ethical Practice: A Practical Guide to Dealing with Ethical Issues in Information and Library Work*. Oxford, England: Chandos Publishing, 2007. 153 pp.

This book aims to discuss the ethical issues facing librarians in the modern era. It includes a review of the key contemporary and historical ethical challenges, an examination of some of the professional association codes of ethics, and a discussion of case studies focused on the key ethical themes identified.

Moore, Adam D., ed. *Information Ethics: Privacy, Property, and Power*. Seattle: University of Washington, 2005. 455 pp.

This book contains a variety of articles dealing with the ethical dimensions of information. Areas covered include understanding ethical frameworks (e.g., utilitarianism), moral and legal issues related to intellectual property, privacy, freedom of speech, and governmental control of information.

Preer, Jean. *Library Ethics*. Westport, CT: Libraries Unlimited, 2008. 255 pp.

This text promotes the need for ethical awareness and explores the field's professional identity and values, including service and access obligations, conflicts of interest, and confidentiality. Specific ethical examples from library history are examined. A variety of codes of ethics are also included.

Rockenbach, Barbara. "Image Ethics: Security and Manipulation of Digital Images." *Journal of Information Ethics* 9 (Fall 2000): 66–71.

This article explores the vulnerability of digital images to manipulation, processing, and change. The article reviews methods of image security and manipulation and the ethical implications for the role of information providers.

Rubin, Richard E., and Thomas J. Froehlich. "Ethical Aspects of Library and Information Science." In *Encyclopedia of Library and Information Science*, 3rd ed. Boca Raton, FL: CRC, 2010. 3: 1743–57.

The authors provide an overview of the ethical responsibilities of librarians and information scientists and the ethical issues that they confront. The discussion covers the major areas of ethical concern such as privacy, selection, and copyright; it also includes consideration of the values of information professionals and the factors that affect ethical deliberations.

Shachaf, Pnina. "A Global Perspective on Library Association Codes of Ethics." *Library and Information Science Research* 27 (Autumn 2005): 513–33.

> This study reports the analysis of the codes of ethics from library associations in 28 different countries in order to identify the set of shared values. The most frequently identified principles were professional development, integrity, confidentiality or privacy, and free and equal access to information.

Smith, Martha M., ed. "Information Ethics." Special issue. *North Carolina Libraries* 51 (Spring 1993): 2–37.

> This issue of *North Carolina Libraries* is devoted to information ethics. Articles were prepared by Martha Smith, Gene Lanier, Susan Rathbun, Jennifer McLean, Lee Finks, and others. Topics covered include the general area of professional ethics, as well as the unauthorized practice of law, archival management, and ethics in library and information science education. An ethics bibliography is also included.

Sturges, Paul. "Information Ethics in the Twenty First Century." *Australian Academic & Research Libraries* 40 (December 2009): 241–51.

> The authors explore information ethics from the perspective of published codes, the professional literature, conference proceedings, and education programs. Authors note that a specific subdiscipline of information ethics has now been well established.

Chapter

The Reference Interview

M. Kathleen Kern and Beth S. Woodard

INTRODUCTION

The reference interview is where library science becomes an art. It is about the skills of listening and communicating. Like painting, there is both process and talent involved in the reference interview; knowledge of technique is essential, but each librarian will develop his or her own style. A good searcher—a librarian skilled at information retrieval—may not necessarily be good at interactions with users. Fortunately, good communication skills can be developed, and many minds in library science have contributed to researching and documenting the communication skills that librarians need to complement their knowledge of information sources.

The concept of the reference interview has been around since early in the 20th century, but it was often called the librarian–user "conversation," and it focused more on the information needed to supply the user with resources and not on the interpersonal skills necessary to conduct the interview. It was not until 1954, when David Maxfield applied interviewing principles from the counseling field to the reference interview, that acceptance, understanding, communication, and collaboration were identified as important to a successful reference interview.[1]

Some writers describe the reference interview as a dialogue, with the reference librarian taking the responsibility for finding out the information need of the user and providing the information for him or her. Others[2] suggest that this interaction should be described as a "partnership" in which both partners are equals and have mutual goals. The reference interview is a dialogue between the user and librarian in which the librarian's objective is clarification and understanding of the user's question as a means to meet the user's information need, and the user's objective is to have the librarian understand and meet the information need.

Reference interviewing has been the subject of much research and analysis. This scrutiny has resulted in evidence that the quality of the interaction that the user has with the librarian is important. Some studies have even found that a positive interaction, one in which the user feels that the librarian has listened and been concerned, is more important to the user's willingness to return with another question than the accuracy of the answers that are received.[3]

Some reference questions are straightforward and do not require a high degree of interaction between the reference librarian and the user to be successful. Others require a great deal of negotiation. Experienced librarians can provide examples of instances in which users with seemingly simple questions often have more complex information needs that they have not yet acknowledged or realized. Robert Taylor called these needs that are felt but not yet consciously formulated *visceral need*.[4] The librarian's ability to help the user vocalize these needs and clarify their exact nature has been identified as an important aspect of user satisfaction with reference service.[5]

This chapter considers the reference interview as a dialogue between the librarian and the user, from the initial conversation to the stages of defining the user's question, finding the answer to the user's question, engaging in any negotiation required, and performing follow-up, with a focus on patterns and steps.

OVERVIEW OF THE REFERENCE INTERVIEW PROCESS

The Reference and User Services Association (RUSA) of the American Library Association has studied the reference interview process in great detail. The RUSA "Guidelines for Behavioral Performance of Reference and Information Service Providers," excerpted in Box 3.1, outlines in a linear way the elements of best practice in reference interviewing. However, because the reference interview is a process and, like most processes, is in fact an iterative process with steps repeated and returned to as necessary, the guidelines alone do not give an accurate picture of the process. The diagram in Box 3.2 is based on the RUSA behavioral guidelines and attempts to illustrate that communication techniques such as asking questions, paraphrasing, and providing information are appropriate throughout the reference interview, not merely at certain stages.

BOX 3.1
EXCERPTS FROM THE RUSA "GUIDELINES FOR BEHAVIORAL PERFORMANCE OF REFERENCE AND INFORMATION SERVICE PROVIDERS"

1.0 Approachability

Approachability behaviors, such as the initial verbal and non-verbal responses of the librarian, will set the tone for the entire communication process, and will influence the depth and level of interaction between the staff and the patrons.... To be approachable, the librarian:

1.1 Establishes a "reference presence" wherever patrons look for it.
1.2 Is poised and ready to engage approaching patrons. The librarian is aware of the need to stop all other activities when patrons approach and focus attention on the patrons' needs.
1.3 Acknowledges others waiting for service.
    1.3.1 Employs a system of question triage to identify what types of questions the patrons have when more than two patrons are waiting....

2.0 Interest

A successful librarian must demonstrate a high degree of interest in the reference transaction. While not every query will contain stimulating intellectual challenges, the librarian should be interested in each patron's informational need.... To demonstrate interest, the librarian:

2.1 Faces the patron when speaking and listening.
2.2 Focuses attention on the patrons.

3.0 Listening/Inquiring

The reference interview is the heart of the reference transaction and is crucial to the success of the process. The librarian must be effective in identifying the patron's information needs and must do so in a manner that keeps patrons at ease. Strong listening and questioning skills are necessary for a positive interaction. As a good communicator, the librarian:

3.1 Communicates in a receptive, cordial, and encouraging manner.
3.2 Uses a tone of voice and/or written language appropriate to the nature of the transaction.
3.3 Allows the patrons to state fully their information need in their own words before responding.
3.4 Identifies the goals or objectives of the user's research, when appropriate.
3.5 Rephrases the question or request and asks for confirmation to ensure that it is understood.
3.6 Seeks to clarify confusing terminology and avoids excessive jargon.
3.7 Uses open-ended questioning techniques to encourage patrons to expand on the request or present additional information....
3.8 Uses closed and/or clarifying questions to refine the search query....
3.9 Maintains objectivity and does not interject value judgments about subject matter or the nature of the question into the transaction.

4.0 Searching

As an effective searcher, the librarian:

4.1 Finds out what patrons have already tried, and encourages patrons to contribute ideas.

4.2 Constructs a competent and complete search strategy....

4.3 Explains the search strategy and sequence to the patrons, as well as the sources to be used.

4.4 Attempts to conduct the search within the patrons' allotted time frame.

4.5 Explains how to use sources when appropriate.

4.6 Works with the patrons to narrow or broaden the topic when too little or too much information is identified.

4.7 Asks the patrons if additional information is needed after an initial result is found.

4.8 Recognizes when to refer patrons to a more appropriate guide, database, library, librarian, or other resource.

4.9 Offers pointers, detailed search paths (including complete URLs), and names of resources used to find the answer, so that patrons can learn to answer similar questions on their own.

5.0 Follow-up

The reference transaction does not end when the librarian leaves the patrons....For successful follow-up, the librarian:

5.1 Asks patrons if their questions have been completely answered.

5.2 Encourages the patrons to return if they have further questions....

5.3 Roving...is an excellent technique for follow-up.

5.4 Consults other librarians or experts in the field when additional subject expertise is needed.

5.5 Makes patrons aware of other appropriate reference services (email, etc.)

5.6 Makes arrangements, when appropriate, with the patrons to research a question even after the reference transaction has been completed.

5.7 Refers the patrons to other sources or institutions when the query cannot be answered to the satisfaction of the patron.

5.8 Facilitates the process of referring patrons to another library or information agency....

5.9 Takes care not to end the reference interview prematurely.

RUSA, "Guidelines for Behavioral Performance of Reference and Information Services Providers," http://www.ala.org/ala/mgrps/divs/rusa/resources/guidelines/guidelinesbehavioral.cfm.

BOX 3.2
REFERENCE INTERACTION PROCESS

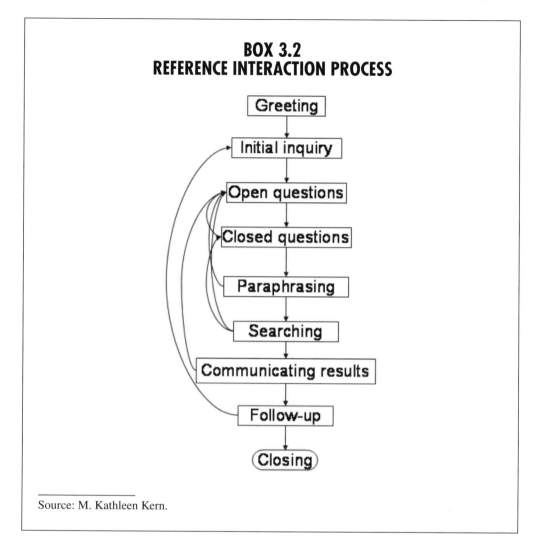

Source: M. Kathleen Kern.

To be complete, a "reference interview" extends beyond the stage of interviewing users about their information needs. The interaction does not end with the confirmation that the librarian understands the user's inquiry; it encompasses searching, presentation of results, and follow-up. In many ways, it is better to think of this as the "reference interaction," or perhaps the "reference dialogue," because it is a two-way communication between a user and a librarian in which both contribute to the process. The user brings the question and the understanding of what is needed. The librarian brings understanding of available resources and asks questions to encourage the user to explain any expectations and to help the librarian match available resources with the user's information needs. It is only the user who can determine the extent to which the information provided is relevant or accurate. Thus, the reference interaction starts and ends with the user, regardless of which person speaks the first or last word.

Opening the Interview

Approachability

First impressions are said to be lasting ones. How the librarian first appears to users will affect their attitude toward the librarian and may shape the phrasing of their questions; it may sway a user's decision to ask a question at all. The reference librarian should always appear welcoming. Some users may feel that their questions are stupid or that they are bothering the librarian by asking for assistance. A smile goes a long way and encourages reluctant or shy users to approach the reference desk and ask their question. Making eye contact with users as they come near the reference desk establishes a connection and expresses that the librarian is there to help.

It is important not to appear involved in other work because this will increase user perception that the librarian is too busy or important to answer questions. Users often open an interaction with "Sorry to bother you...." Users should never feel that their questions are bothersome or an interruption. It is, after all, exactly why the reference librarian is available. Libraries' policies differ on whether librarians are allowed to take other work (such as collection development or report writing) with them to the desk, but if other projects are worked on while at the reference desk, the librarian must be even more aware of approachability factors and look up frequently from other tasks and be conscious of users in the area.

Greeting

A simple greeting such as "Hi, how may I help you?" will establish that the librarian is available to help the user and allay any fears that he or she is in the wrong place or that the librarian is busy. Tone should, of course, be pleasant. Professionalism dictates that librarians sound enthusiastic about providing assistance even if the heat in the building has failed or they are covering a colleague's shift and have been working at the reference desk for several hours. Each user should be treated as a new and interesting interaction.

Library and clientele will dictate the formality of the greeting, and telephone greetings are often a little more formal than in-person. With experience, a reference service provider can learn to adapt his or her communication style to one more consistent with the user's preferences.

Online greetings for chat and instant messaging are often pre-scripted but should avoid sounding too automated and cold. It is frequently effective to follow up a pre-scripted greeting with a personalized one, incorporating the user's name or screen ID to establish rapport. The interaction might look like this:

RefLibrarian: Hi, welcome to the Library's Ask-A-Librarian Service. How may I help you?
SportsFan1:   Who won last night's baseball game?
RefLibrarian: Hi, SportsFan!
                 Which baseball game are you interested in?

Sometimes the reference desk is busy and a queue forms. Users may linger farther from the desk if they see that the librarian is involved in helping someone else.

Smiling at and greeting the waiting users is a way to let them know that they have been seen and that someone will be with them presently. Again, a simple statement such as "Hi, I'll be with you soon" reassures the users that they have been noticed.

Interest

The need for a friendly demeanor extends beyond the initial contact with the users. For the reference interaction to be successful, the users must feel that they have the reference librarian's attention and that the librarian is truly listening to what is said. Undoubtedly, there will be questions in which the librarian has no personal interest or that have been encountered 10 times already that day. The librarian should react the same way as when listening to a friend: nod, smile, encourage.

Show of interest during in-person encounters is primarily nonverbal. The user can see that someone is paying attention when that person is looking at him or her and appears focused and alert. When the user is remote, reaching the reference service by telephone or online communications, these visual cues are missing. Verbal expressions of interest are very important in telephone conversations; an "okay" or an "I see" can substitute for a nod. When the interaction occurs via online communications, typing must substitute for verbal and visual indicators of interest. The librarian should be sure not to leave the user hanging. Break apart long sentences with ellipses and send the fragments of thought, indicate to the user that a few minutes are needed to search or to think, and send some type of communication at least every two minutes—even if it is just to say that the search is still in process. The librarian does not want to give the impression that he or she has given up or gone away.

Body Language

The body language of the service provider can go a long way toward communicating an openness and willingness to listen to a user's query. Maintaining an open stance, facing the user squarely instead of at an angle, and leaning forward in the chair are all positive nonverbal messages that the service provider is ready to pay attention to the other person. Other considerations include being at the same eye level, which might mean standing if the person approaches the desk in a standing posture, or taking a seat if the individual is in a wheelchair. Reducing reference-desk clutter also allows the service provider to concentrate attention on the question at hand. Roving, or walking around the service area to where the users might have questions, is another way of inviting queries with positive body language. Simple things such as taking fingers off the computer keyboard or putting down a held pencil can also reduce the distractions perceived by the user.

Question Negotiation

The questioning process seeks to (1) elicit the user's question in his or her own words; (2) make information available that the librarian needs to understand the inquiry to an extent that enables effective searching and accurate provision of information; and (3) verify that the librarian and user share the same understanding of the information need. It is after this shared agreement is confirmed that the search process can begin. Several communications strategies are used during question nego-tiation: *open questions*, *closed questions*, *encouragers*, and *active listening*. The first two strategies encourage users to describe their information needs in their own terms and to provide the librarian with specifics required to match the vast array of available information with those needs. The strategies of active listening make users aware that the librarian is interested, concerned, and attentive to their question. As Mary Ellen Bates has observed, "The time you invest in the reference interview is time you don't spend later re-doing your work when you finally figure out what your client really wanted."[6]

Open Questions

After the greeting and the user's initial question, the reference interview almost always starts with the librarian asking an open question. An open question is one to which there is no fixed answer; it cannot be answered with a yes or no, nor does it draw its response from a set of predetermined choices, as in multiple choice responses. Open questions encourage users to talk about the information need using their own terms.[7] There are many possibilities for open questions, and some inquiries will naturally pres-ent obvious questions to ask. For example, the user who approaches the desk needing travel guides prompts the librarian to inquire, "What part of the world are you inter-ested in?" Open questions seek to elicit descriptive answers and typically begin with "what," "when," "where," and "how." Box 3.3 lists some possible open questions.

BOX 3.3
OPEN QUESTIONS

- That is a broad topic. Do you have something more specific in mind?
- Can you tell me more about [topic]?
- What materials have you already examined?
- What do you already know about this subject?
- What kind of information are you looking for?
- When you say [topic], what do you mean?
- We have a number of books/articles about [topic]. Was there some-thing in particular you were looking for?
- I'm not sure if I know what [topic] is/means. Could you tell me some more about it?
- How much information are you looking for?
- Is there a particular aspect of or type of information about [topic] that you are interested in finding information on?

Discussion questions:
Everyone has their own style of asking questions. Can you think of other open questions to ask? How would you phrase them?

At times, the user's question may be unfamiliar, and the open questions will seek to draw out more explanation as well as inform the librarian about the topic area. An example of this is the user who says, "I need to write a paper about top quarks." An open question to ask here might be "Could you tell me more about top quarks? What field of study does that relate to?" If the librarian is comfortable doing so, it is okay to let the user know if terms are unfamiliar; it is better to ask for clarification than to blunder ahead without direction.

Each librarian has his or her own style of speech, and each service provider develops his or her own approach to asking open questions. It is important to realize that the reference interview is a dialogue, not an interrogation. The user is not (likely) willfully withholding information but may not have provided everything that the librarian needs to know to meet the information need. The questions asked should display interest and maintain approachability. The librarian should avoid using any words that are judgmental and may cause the user to back away from communication, such as saying that a question is "too broad" or that the user needs "to focus" on an area. Keep the choice of words and tone positive.

Closed Questions

After the user's topic is known, often the librarian needs to know more before searching for an answer. How much information does the user need? Is he or she interested in articles or books, or does it matter? Is there a particular time period for the information: recent or historical? Closed questions ask for a yes or no response or present the user with options from which to choose. Closed questions tend to focus narrowly and distinctly on a particular subject or source and help further the librarian's understanding of the user's information need.

Closed questions are asked after the open questions to avoid leading the user in a particular direction or narrowing the options too soon. Even if the user's initial question is very broad or not yet well-formed, it is the user who needs to decide and define the information need. Users view librarians as the authorities on information and may think that the information they want is not available if the suggestions given are not what they have in mind.

Consider this scenario:

Patron: Do you have anything on athletes and drugs?
Librarian: Are you looking for legislation or statistics?
Patron: Well, I wanted to read athletes' stories. What they've written. I don't know if you have anything like that. So, statistics, I guess.

This user did reveal a preference, but not all users will. Users often do not know what is available from the library and will try to match their question with what they think they will be able to find. When presented with a list of options, users may be hesitant to say something that is not on the list, even if that is what they want. It is good practice when presenting a list to leave an "other" option. For example, "Are you interested in Canada, England, or somewhere else?" Box 3.4 gives sample closed questions and provides some questions for discussion.

BOX 3.4
CLOSED QUESTIONS

- Do you need books or magazine and journal articles?
- Are you looking for current or historical information?
- What time period does your information need to be about?
- Are you interested in information on [topic 1] or [topic 2]?
- Do you want advanced material or something basic?
- What material have you already looked at? *Or* Where have you already looked?

Discussion questions:

When might it be appropriate to use closed questions early in the negotiation process? Can you think of some examples?

Would it ever be appropriate to ask an open question at the end of a reference interview? Can you think of examples?

Neutral Questioning

When direct questions might offend the user, a technique called *neutral* or *sense-making questioning* can be used to elicit further information. By using questions such as "If you could tell me the kind of problem you are working on, I will get a better of idea of what would help you,"[8] the librarian can gain valuable background information. Questions about why the information is needed and to what use the information will be put help the librarian understand the context from which the information need arose.

Like open questions, neutral questions strive to get the user to talk more fully about the information need. Although neutral questions, according to Dervin and Dewdney,[9] are most effective early in the interview process to help the librarian see the question more in the way the user does, they can also be used later in the process when materials judged by the librarian to be useful are not seen as relevant by the user. In general, neutral questions help the librarian to avoid reaching premature and inaccurate conclusions about the user's need based on the librarian's experience, biases, or history with that user.

Asking Why

There is no consensus in the literature on whether or how the librarian should ask the user why the information being sought is needed. Because many questions—such as those regarding health, regarding legal issues, or even about kinds of services—have their roots in personal and private situations, asking this question can destroy the trust established throughout the interview process. Alfred Benjamin, in *The Helping Interview*, discusses his objections to the use of asking why because of the tension caused in the interview and the frequent withdrawal by the interviewee.[10] However, sometimes, in order to better serve the user, the librarian needs to determine "the level of treatment and amount of information needed"[11] and needs to ask "why."

If possible, dealing solely with the question and information volunteered by the user is the best strategy for the librarian to follow. In situations where the librarian needs to make a recommendation for a tool to use and does not have adequate information to make a decision, one possibility is to ask how the information is going to be used. Although this is not as abrupt as asking why, it is very close and could still give offense. Suggesting alternatives and allowing the user to choose the appropriate tool is another method and illustrates the cyclical nature of the reference interview process.

Encouragers

Noncommittal acknowledgements of what the user is saying indicate that one is listening and seem to encourage the user. These types of open question are sometimes called "encouragers."[12] These questions overtly encourage the users to more fully reveal their information needs. Questions such as "Can you tell me more about this topic?" and even short questions such as "Yes?" or "Okay, what else?" can be very effective ways of getting the user to further explain the question so that the librarian can begin thinking about where to start in the search for an answer. Nonverbal encouragers can include head-nodding, eye contact, and facial expressions that match what the speaker is saying. As with neutral questioning, encouragers help the librarian to see the question as much as possible from the viewpoint of the user and to gain more insight into the background that produced the question.

Language

Librarians have the responsibility to use clear language, free of jargon, so that users can understand. Dina Cramer notes that "the reference interview is supposed to elicit the real questions, but it can't if people mean different things by the words they use."[13] So when a questioner uses a word in the commonly understood sense, but the librarian uses the same word to mean something else, the librarian must be aware that misunderstandings can occur. Such words as "bibliography" and "biography" are commonly recognized as problematic. Dina Cramer further suggests that librarians not use the word "citation" because to the user it might refer to a traffic ticket.

Active Listening

Because good communication involves both getting the message across and understanding what the other person is saying, the use of active listening techniques helps ensure not only that the message is received accurately but also that it was understood. Research shows that people listen at about 25 percent efficiency,[14] meaning that of everything one hears, only 25 percent is likely to be interpreted correctly. In order to turn hearing into listening, one must focus on what a person is saying, pay attention to what is said, and concentrate on understanding. So a mere restate-ment of the perceived message is not enough. The message needs to be restated in one's own words, or paraphrased. Active listening involves not only paraphrasing but also asking clarifying questions and understanding the nature of the problem fully before attempting to assist with the user's information need. Feedback from the user, then, is also an essential element of active listening. With straightforward questions, the librarian may simply need to paraphrase the question before begin-ning the search. In more complex questions, however, the librarian may need to renegotiate the question several times during the interview and the search process.

BOX 3.5
BRINGING IT ALL TOGETHER: PRACTICE GETTING TO THE REAL QUESTION

Instructions:

Divide into pairs. Each person in the pair has a different question and scenario,[15] and they will take turns being the user and asking the reference question. The other person's role is to ask the user questions to determine his or her information need.

Guidelines:

Keep in mind the different types of questioning skills used in the reference interview.

Focus on the question-negotiation part of the reference interview. Do not focus on the searching aspect. Try *not* to think about sources that you would use to answer the question. What follow-up questions would you ask to clarify what the user wants? What information do you need to know?

Assessment (to be performed by the "user" and the "librarian"):

Was the user welcomed/greeted?

How was interest in the user's question shown?

What kinds of questions were asked? (open, closed, why, neutral, encouragers)

Were open-ended questions asked? Was more than one open-ended ques-tion asked?

Were neutral questions or encouragers used to keep the user talking?

Was sensitivity to "why" the user needed the information shown? How did the librarian get to this information?

Were closed questions used appropriately?

Was the user's question restated or paraphrased in the process?

User and librarian should compare and discuss assessments.

Searching

It is important not to start searching too early in the interview process. If the librarian jumps ahead to searching before establishing a shared understanding of what the user wants, then a lot of time can be wasted, and frustration may result for both the user and the librarian. Once the search process has been started, however, the librarian can continue to ask questions, refining what the user wants and adjusting the search strategy accordingly. This can be a helpful approach particularly when the user has been cryptic or uncertain, when the user has declined to narrow a broad topic, or when there is a lot of available information on a topic.

Sometimes searching is done without the user present, and this presents its own set of challenges in the reference interview. Ideally, more of the communication must be done up-front, and then communication should be continued when the results are presented to the user, to avoid constant back-and-forth by telephone or delays in the searching while waiting for the user to return.

Asking the user what the final answer might look like is a technique suggested by Tim Buckley Owen.[16] For example, if the user is asking about migration patterns, does the user want the information in the form of statistics, graphs, charts, or diagrammatic maps? Knowing the kind of answer the user is expecting can help guide the selection of the tools or resources that will provide that kind of answer.

Involving the User

Just like questioning, searching is a joint process with the user. What form and extent this collaboration takes is affected by the reference environment (discussed later in this chapter). A basic principle for most situations is that the search process should be transparent for the user, so that the user can see and understand what the librarian is doing. This keeps the dialogue open and allows the user to offer further information and the librarian to continue to ask questions.

In most environments, the librarian should explain the search process as it is happening, when possible and appropriate. Discretion should be used here to match the level of user involvement in the search process with the time the user is willing to spend. In some situations it may be appropriate to show a user how to find a call number for a book; in others it is more appropriate to provide the call number. In some libraries, particularly corporate libraries, where the librarian performs the research for the user with minimal involvement from the user, the search process is explained in a very brief summary when the requested information is delivered.

One of the most effective ways to involve the users is to work alongside them at a table with reference books or at a computer terminal with access to the library's databases. In this way, users can be instructed how to search (or can be shown search results) and can provide immediate feedback as to the relevance of what has been found. For example, when users see that there is a lot of information about their chosen topic, they may narrow the topic, and the search results can be used to spark ideas for a more refined search. Remember that it is difficult for users to frame their questions because they are often not aware of what information might be available on their topic. Catherine Ross, Kirsti Nilsen, and Patricia Dewdney call this "inclusion" and suggest that it involves these basic steps: restating the problem; describing briefly what steps are going to be taken and why these are the appropriate steps; and, if appropriate, indicating the amount of time these steps might take.[17] Box 3.6 gives two scenarios regarding involving the user and some possible discussion questions.

BOX 3.6
INVOLVING THE USER

Scenario 1

User:	I need to find *One Flew Over the Cuckoo's Nest*.
Librarian:	[Types title in online catalog.]
	That is at 813 K474O1973.
User:	Thanks! [Patron walks away to bookshelves.]

Scenario 2

User:	I need to find *One Flew Over the Cuckoo's Nest*.
Librarian:	Let's look this up in the library's catalog together. [Moves with user to nearby terminal.]
Librarian:	Now type the title in here. [Points to form on screen.]
User:	Okay. Are any of these videos?
Librarian:	Yes. This one, number four of your search results, is a video. It is located at our media desk; just ask for it by the title, and they will get it for you.
User:	Thanks! So these others are books? I think that I'll get that too.

In these scenarios, the second librarian instructed the user in using the catalog, also eliciting more information (availability of a video) in the process of the search. The librarian could have arrived at the user wanting a video through questioning rather than instruction. Consider these questions:

- How would the user's demeanor have affected the decision to give the user the call number or instruct in using the catalog?
- Would one scenario be preferable if you knew more about the user's demographics, such as age or status as a university student?
- How might different library settings affect the decision to instruct the user?
- What would have been the best course of action if there had been a line of users at the desk? Would that influence the course of the reference interview?
- Is it always better to instruct? How would you determine the teachable moment?

If a question may have been misinterpreted by the librarian, searching with the user provides a comfortable opportunity for realignment. Users may be hesitant to reapproach a librarian to point out that a mistake has been made because they may fear seeming rude, but while librarian and user are viewing and discussing the same search results or reference book, it is easier to continue the dialogue.

Presentation of Answers

When the question has a definite factual answer, the answer should be given to the user and a source for the information provided. If the user was not present during the searching part of the process, some communication regarding what was done to find the information (search terms, other sources consulted) may be presented as well.

In recent years, librarians have found that they are asked factual "ready-reference" questions less often and receive a higher proportion of questions that involve assisting users with finding information where there is not a single, brief answer. There seems to be a trend of moving away from asking for the number of a specific hotel in Virginia Beach to asking how they can research lodging and travel options for their next vacation. In these cases, the answer is really providing the user with a set of options about where to look and some strategies for doing research. Returning to the example of the user looking for information on athletes and drug use, the answer is the librarian's guidance with choosing and using one or two databases (an article index and the library's catalog perhaps) in which the user will be able to search, examine results, and determine appropriateness of content.

When providing information, it is important to cite the source. Authority is an important aspect of information. Because a source may have a particular bias or perspective, knowing the source is vital to users' evaluation of the information, whether or not they requested identification of the source. Speak clearly, particularly via telephone, spelling unusual or difficult terms, and check to see if the answer is understood.

Lastly, verify that the answer matches the scope of the user's question and that the level or amount of information given is what was desired. For example, a user looking for the definition of "heaven" may want a simple dictionary definition to quote or something more lengthy and explanatory regarding how a particular religion views heaven. Although the early stages of the reference interview ideally would have determined the scope of the information need, presentation of answers is always a good time to verify that the information presented is what was expected. The user continues to think about the question during the search process and may need supplementary information or may have changed from the original question slightly.

Closing

Librarian: Does this information answer your question?
User: Yes, I think that this is good for now.
Librarian: Great. If you think of anything else, just ask. We are here today until 10.
User: Okay. Thanks!

Closing the reference interview properly is important because it is the last communication with the user and can affect the way that the user remembers the entire interaction. The end of the reference interview should always leave open the opportunity for the user to say more. Asking, "Does this completely answer your question?" or "Is there anything else that I can help you with today?" gives the user the opportunity to ask for further information or to say that something different is required than what was found. Asking appropriate follow-up questions has been demonstrated to improve the accuracy of the answer provided by the librarian.[18] Similarly, an invitation to return reminds the user that there is always the opportunity to ask for more (or different) information. It is also a pleasant reminder that librarians are always available to help with the user's information needs.

Follow-Up

If the user remains in the library, it is a nice touch for the librarian to follow up with the user to confirm that the information was adequate and nothing else is required. In a corporate setting, or one where librarians have a close connection with their remote users, a follow-up telephone call may achieve the same end. In other settings, this type of follow-up would seem intrusive, so whether to do this is at the discretion of the librarian, based on how it fits with the library environment.

Referrals

Sometimes the librarian or library will not have the answer that the user needs. In these cases it is appropriate to refer the user to another person, library, or organization. It is kind to the user to first confirm that the referral destination can indeed help the user and that someone is available. Users resent being treated like footballs—passed from one person to another.

Confirming that a referral is appropriate not only helps the user; it helps the next person or organization that works with the user because that helper will be prepared, and the user will not be upset over being misdirected. Librarians, in their zeal to be helpful, may find it difficult to let go of a question and can have the tendency to hang on too long to questions that could be better or more quickly answered by other librarians or experts in the field. A call to verify that there is another expert willing and available to help the user can ease the librarian's anxiety over parting with a question. Christopher Nolan suggests that an unsuccessful interview should always end with a referral.[19]

Negative Closure

When a reference interview is ended abruptly without a real examination of the user's question or an adequate attempt to meet the user's information need, this is called *negative closure*.[20] Nolan suggests that there are three reasons interviews terminate prematurely: (1) the librarian was unsuccessful in answering the user's query and did not make an appropriate referral; (2) whether because of frustration or futility, lack of patience, or poor communication skills, some interviews end early because they are simply not going well; and (3) interviews can be closed for policy or institutional factors such as time of day, queues of other users waiting, and costs.[21]

Everyone has experienced negative closure in some service interaction, whether in a library, a retail store, or elsewhere. Some classic examples and their library manifestations include pointing ("the encyclopedias are over there") and vague, unhelpful responses ("try looking in the 700s"). Box 3.7 illustrates other ways in which negative closure can occur.

Negative closure also encompasses taking the user's question at face value, bypassing the reference interview, and beginning to work without asking questions or providing explanations. Research consistently finds that in about 50 percent of reference interactions, there is no reference interview.[22] Other types of negative closure are blind or unmonitored referrals without confirming that the other person can help and providing a call number without follow-up confirmation with the user that the information was actually helpful. Ross found that this error happens in about one-third of the accounts of negative closure.[23]

Too often the librarian's questions relate to the library system instead of the context of the user's information need. In these instances, the librarian asks questions that may be answered by the user but that may not be understood by the user or that have little bearing on the user's question. An example is asking the user whether an answer from an encyclopedia or a dictionary is needed, without providing context as to how information in one would differ from information in the other. Or the librarian may respond to the user's request for *Time* magazine by asking, "Are you looking for the unbound periodicals section?" rather than asking what date is needed. With these examples, closed questioning has become a type of negative closure.

BOX 3.7
EXAMPLES OF NEGATIVE CLOSURE

- Implying that the user should have done something else before asking for reference help
- Trying to get the user to accept more easily found information instead of the information actually asked for
- Warning the user to expect defeat because the topic is too hard, obscure, large, elusive, or otherwise unpromising
- Encouraging the user to abort the transaction voluntarily
- Signaling nonverbally that the transaction is over by turning away, by tone of voice, or by starting another activity
- Stating explicitly that the search has reached a dead end
- Claiming that the information is not in the library or else does not exist at all
- Telling the user that he or she will track down a document but then never returning[24]

In general, then, the closure of the reference interview is extremely important, and care should be taken to ensure that the answer provided is to the question intended by the user, both throughout the interview process and at the end of the interaction.

Librarian Self-Follow-Up

Another aspect of follow-up is the reference librarian's self-reflection concerning the interaction. Particularly in instances where the interaction did not go well, or the librarian was unsuccessful in finding an answer, an analysis of each aspect of the reference interview can point out areas for improvement. Box 3.8 provides an evaluation sheet that can be used for self-evaluation or in conjunction with a trusted peer.

BOX 3.8
REFERENCE INTERVIEW EVALUATION SHEET

1. Approachability + Interest
    - Was a greeting given beyond the standard welcome message? Y N
    - Was interest shown (via attentive comments, etc.) to the user's questions? Y N

2. Question Negotiation
    - Was there any question negotiation or a reference interview? Y N
    - Number of open ended questions asked: _____
    - Number of closed questions asked: _____
    - Was the user's question restated or paraphrased before searching began? Y N

3. Searching
    - Was the user kept updated on the status of the search? Y N
    - Were sources cited to the user (e.g., names of databases, books, etc.)? Y N
    - Appropriateness of sources:
    1 (not appropriate)—5 (extremely appropriate) _____
    - Amount of information given:
    1 (too little)—3 (just right)—5 (too much) _____
    - When appropriate, amount of library instruction given:
    N/A—1(none)—2 (basic instruction)—5 (sufficient instruction) _____
    - How completely was the question answered?
    1 (not answered)—3 (somewhat answered)—5 (fully answered)
    _____
    - If referrals were given, were they appropriate and monitored? Y N

4. Follow-Up
    - Did the librarian confirm that the answer was understood? Y N
    - Was a follow-up question asked that addressed the specific question? Y N
    - Was the user asked to check back, when appropriate? Y N N/A

Adapted from an evaluation sheet developed by David Ward, Reference Services Librarian, Undergraduate Library, University of Illinois at Urbana-Champaign.

PERSONALITY QUALITIES OF REFERENCE LIBRARIANS

The communication skills necessary to conduct good reference interviews can be learned with appropriate study and training, but not everyone can be an effective reference librarian. Although no two authors agree on the qualities needed in a good reference librarian, certain qualities and skills are commonly mentioned, and not all can be learned efficiently and effectively. In an attempt to summarize several authors, Charles Patterson listed good memory, thoroughness, orderliness, accuracy, imagination, an inquisitive mind, logicalness, an outgoing personality, the ability to interact, and a desire to help people.[25] This section provides just one possible list of qualities necessary for excellence in reference interviews.

Service Orientation

"Service orientation" is a phrase used in many advertisements for reference positions,[26] referring to an innate desire or commitment to helping others. This desire to help is expressed through approachability, friendliness, open-mindedness, and interest in each user as an individual. Individuals who like people are more likely to accept people as they are and resist making assumptions based on superficial observations. Enjoying the "give-and-take of human interaction"[27] is highlighted by Elaine and Edward Jennrich as extremely important, given that many reference librarians do not have private offices and must deal with people during most of their working day.

This interest in helping should be accompanied by flexibility in working with people of diverse personalities, appearances, and backgrounds. If the librarian is open and self-revealing, users will respond correspondingly and be more forthcoming and thus be more satisfied with the human relations aspect of the reference service provided.[28]

Patience and Persistence

Successful reference librarians exhibit a great deal of patience with individuals who have difficulty expressing themselves or with frustrated, angry, impatient, arrogant, insensitive, or shy individuals. In such situations, the librarian may need to spend more time eliciting information and listening to the user talk, and the user needs to feel that the librarian is not in a hurry to go do something else.

Reference librarians also need to have patience with their own inadequacies in the search process, realizing that no one person can possibly know everything and be everything to everyone. In dealing with difficult questions—difficult because of delicate negotiations or complex or puzzling queries—the librarian needs to remain calm and composed, so that the user does not lose trust in the librarian or regret asking the question. When faced with questions that seem insurmountable, librarians may need to tell users that they have to get back to them later in the day or week because of the complexity of the question. The librarian may wish to discuss the question with colleagues to broaden the range of options to pursue.

Sensitivity

Richard Bopp has suggested that "sensitivity is the surest way to transform the desire to help into effective results."[29] Librarians with sensitivity know how to set the tone of the communication—more formally and objectively or through casual conversation and more obvious personal interest in the question. A sensitive individual can adapt to the communication style preferred by the individual being interviewed. Problems of communication with those different from the librarian, such as groups including children, older adults, individuals with disabilities, nonnative language speakers, or individuals intimidated by the setting or the tools in libraries, are more readily addressed when the librarian is open to the uniqueness of the individual. An insensitive reference librarian can destroy the chance to negotiate the reference interview successfully by not perceiving the unique needs and concerns that must be addressed.

Self-Control

Negotiating a successful reference interview requires a certain amount of discipline, or self-control. Discipline helps counteract the impulse to skip the reference interview and take the question at face value. It can be very tempting to treat the sixth person who asks a seemingly simple question differently from the first one. Discipline is also needed to give each user the proper amount of concentration in the midst of a variety of distractions in the reference environment. Particularly in hectic atmospheres, it is important for users to feel that they have the librarian's full attention.

The exercise of self-control to encounter the next reference query without the baggage of the previous one—especially with time constraints, failed search strategies, or a difficult librarian–user interaction—is important. Every librarian has shifts when he or she hits the right tone in almost every encounter. Conversely, every reference librarian has times when nothing seems to go right. Martin Seligman, in *Learned Optimism*, talks about optimists' and pessimists' views of good and bad events as permanent, pervasive, and personal, and he stresses that individuals can change their viewpoints by monitoring their self-talk.[30] For example, after a difficult reference encounter, does one say, "Man that was a tough one! What was it about that interaction that was so difficult?" (temporal, isolated, external to self). Or does one say, "I really blew that one; I'll never be a good reference librarian!" (permanent, pervasive, personal). This self-control results in handling negative emotions and false leads in a way that does not compromise the user's trust in the librarian as a competent provider and also will help the librarian maintain a more positive frame of mind about the job.

Persistence, *dedication*, and *commitment* are terms that connote the ability to stick with something in the face of difficulties or obstacles. In a difficult situation, the librarian whose failures seem permanent, pervasive, and personal is more likely to give up on a reference question or send the user away out of frustration. The librarian who is sure that he or she can effect a satisfactory outcome is more likely to stay with the task and explore alternative solutions to help the user. At times, the librarian may have more interest and persistence regarding the question than the user does, and the librarian should be looking for clues that would indicate this.

Flexibility and Sense of Humor

The ability to jump quickly from one subject to another is another good trait for a reference librarian, whether in a specialized setting or a general one.[31] Handling in-person and virtual reference questions at the same time, a combination of telephone and virtual inquiries, or three virtual queries at once can be challenging and stressful and requires the flexibility to handle more than one query at the same time and the ability to move from one to the other smoothly.

Flexibility can be thought of as another aspect of imagination and creativity, the ability to change directions by looking at the question from another perspective or to borrow ideas from other contexts.

A sense of humor is often cited as a good quality for a reference librarian.[32] In general, the use of humor can help relieve stress, put people at ease, and establish rapport. Care should be taken, however, not to make individuals the focus of that humor.

Good Judgment

Librarians must continuously make decisions in their interactions with users. Deciding which sources to consult is actually among the easier decisions faced by reference librarians. The area of interpersonal communication requires application of professional judgment to determine appropriate questions and responses based on the interaction so far: the content and tone of the user's communication. This is not about jumping to conclusions or making snap judgments about a user, but about careful consideration of all that has been observed during the interaction and the ability to remain open to new cues from the user.

A few of the areas requiring professional judgment are matching the level of the answer to the user, determining the teachable moment, and knowing when to not ask too much. Examining each of these areas in turn, matching the level of the answer to the user requires being aware of the user's comfort with the library and amount of previous library experience. It also includes knowing how much information the user is seeking. Some of this can be ascertained through questioning during the reference interview, but attention to the user's level of facility with using the library resources and to the degree of sophistication in how the question is framed and presented is vital. Librarians can easily overwhelm users with resources about a topic or information about libraries and research. Impatience, boredom, or glassy eyes are extreme indicators that the user either has lost interest or is overwhelmed.

Teaching is a primary mission in some libraries and not employed at all in others. Library type is always a factor in determining whether it is appropriate to instruct the user. Of equal importance is the user's willingness to learn. If the user is impatient or uninterested, the librarian can teach, but it is unlikely that the user will retain any learning. It may be more suitable to provide the information needed and tell the user the search process being used: "I will look up that book in the catalog, using the 'title' search." Some searches are complex or convoluted because of the nature of the information being sought, and these are rarely good opportunities for learning unless the user is a dedicated researcher or openly expresses interest. Nonetheless, in many settings it is necessary to have users research for themselves and evaluate the results of the findings. In these cases the librarian should present the research process in steps, working with the user, and pay attention to nonverbal cues and signs of frustration or understanding. Leave the user to examine the results of the first part of the search (e.g., finding newspaper articles) and return later to explain the next step (e.g., finding books) or invite the user to return to the desk when ready to move to the next part of the research process.

Sometimes users have questions that may be of a sensitive or personal nature. This can be uncomfortable for both users and the librarians. It is imperative that librarians remain impartial and not let personal beliefs or experiences affect their responses. Avoid forming opinions about the user's needs or uses for the information. That is not to say that the librarian should be uncaring, but caring is best exemplified by avoiding intrusions into the user's privacy. Good judgment is needed to avoid asking questions of the user that may be seen as intrusive and to regulate one's tone of voice. Medical, legal, and social or personal welfare questions are the most frequent examples in this category. An example would be a user asking for information on local drug treatment centers. There are many reasons users might ask this question. The librarian's most immediate thought may be that the user wants to know for herself or for a family member or a friend who is seeking treatment. The user's appearance may be a factor in this conclusion. However, there are many other reasons the user may require this information: a student's research paper, a community member's desire to volunteer, a business person's interest in marketing a new product, a social worker's job search, and so on. Most importantly, it is not the concern of the librarians why the information is needed. Questions should be neutral; the librarian should ask about the type of information needed and avoid "why" questions. Open-ended questions allow the user the freedom to define the need, but a hesitant user may be prompted with a more closed query, such as "Are you looking for names and addresses, types of treatment provided, or something else?" Occasionally, a user may divulge more than the librarian wishes to know, in which case it is prudent to bring the user back to questions that the librarian can help with while still maintaining a caring disposition.

Knowledge and Confidence

A good reference librarian has the ability to match users' queries to available resources and knows how to use resources effectively. In order to achieve this, the librarian should develop a broad knowledge of resources by reading a daily newspaper and possibly a weekly newsmagazine or subscribing to a news blog to keep up with current events.[33] Richard Bopp has suggested that because many humanities graduates are drawn to reference work and work at general reference desks, a specialized source for non-specialists, such as *Scientific American*, might be included in the librarian's regular reading.[34]

Similarly, a thorough knowledge of reference sources is necessary for selecting the resource appropriate in a particular situation. Time and experience in dealing with these sources are necessary to gain mastery over them. The successful reference professional is familiar with a broad range of reference sources in different formats. There are, in reality, a relatively small number of multipurpose reference sources, but knowing the content of these materials will give the librarian confidence to know when to go beyond them to other resources. Knowledge of local collections, and the broader availability of resources in distant or remote collections, is also important. Good knowledge of information sources inspires the confidence of the user and contributes to the trust that is needed to enter into a successful reference transaction.

REFERENCE ENVIRONMENTS

The physical and social environment where the reference interaction occurs plays a substantial role in its success. Care should be taken to create an environment that allows for the librarian to engage the user in a careful, thorough discussion of the user's needs. Without the appropriate environment to do so, the reference librarian faces difficult obstacles before the question is even asked.

A friendly, attractive environment easily located and with good signage will attract users and more questions, both in person and virtually. Service points should be well marked and highly visible. A logical, highly visible arrangement should make it easy to find help and particular items within the collection.

Friendly, approachable staff should be seen from throughout the area. Reference staff should be walking the floor or scanning the floor if they are at the desk. When reference staff work at the desk and eye contact is minimal, users feel that the staff are "too busy" to be bothered.

Unlike many other professionals who have the option of conducting interviews in a private setting, reference librarians often conduct interviews in public spaces where the chances of being interrupted or having the conversation overheard by others are high. When others are standing by waiting for service, their presence gives questioners little privacy and places pressure on the librarian to finish the interview prematurely. Telephone interruptions may be an irritant to the user and a distraction to the librarian. Even if librarians tell callers that they are busy and will call back, the interview may be adversely affected by this interruption. Interacting with another user via the telephone is at least visibly obvious to users at the desk, whereas chat or instant messaging (IM) queries are not. All the user can see is that the librarian is typing on a computer, and it is not obvious that he or she is actually interacting with someone.

Using tiered services, such as a separate desk for screening telephone calls or staffing virtual reference services in a different location, such as an office, are options that can be explored to minimize interruptions to user–librarian interactions. Having an individual on call, or standby, during peak hours to handle waiting users or staff the desk, to enable another colleague to continue a more involved query away from the desk, is another option. Scheduling interactions that are likely to be longer and more involved away from the desk is yet another. Consultations, particularly if some screening has gone on beforehand, allow the reference librarian to spend uninterrupted time with the user.

One of the notable trends in library staffing in the past few decades has been the replacement of professionals by paraprofessionals. The proper mix of paraprofessionals and professionals can yield considerable success. For optimal success, orientation, on-the-job training, and continuing education opportunities should be reflected in appropriate policies. Measures of success should also be highly visible in mission, goals, and objectives and in the regular evaluation of reference staff.

At service desks with multiple functions, where a variety of staff members work, such as the more recent information commons settings in academic libraries where information technology (IT) staff and librarians work side-by-side, it is important that minimum-level competencies be established for shared responsibilities. Some libraries have combined reference and circulation desks, so that users have one place to go for all services. With combined desks, it may be advisable to minimize user confusion about whom to ask what questions through signs and nametags or through employing a triage model, in which one or two staff greet users and then direct the question to the appropriate person at the desk. The desks also may be arranged so that all staff will greet patrons, help those they can, and redirect questions to other staff as needed. These combined service operations generally involve basic cross-training so that all staff can field basic questions and make appropriate referrals. This is not expected to result in IT staff able to assist with research or with reference librarians adept at using all software. In any case, combined desks with multiple functions require flexibility and collegiality on the part of all staff.

INTERVIEWS FOR SPECIFIC SITUATIONS

Dealing with Multiple Users and Queues

Sometimes the reference desk is busy, and more than one user is waiting for an answer. It is of little consequence whether these users are all at the desk in person, or one is on the telephone, or another has contacted the library via instant messaging. The result is that the librarian will need to make a decision about which individual to help first and how to make all users contacting the library feel like their questions are important. Unlike banks and the post office, the reference desk does not have stanchions, numbers are not taken, and of course no one likes to wait in line even when there are such queuing devices. What is a librarian to do?

Acknowledging waiting users is vital. The librarian should smile and nod at users waiting in line, verbally greet them, and let them know that someone will assist them shortly. For telephone queries, the librarian should pick up the ringing phone, warmly greet the caller, and ask if he or she can hold. Electronically, the librarian should respond to the IM or chat and let the user know that staff members are assisting other users and will be with the user soon. These actions reassure users that they are not being ignored, and for remote users, the acknowledgment confirms that the library is open and staffed with helpful people.

Users may be helped on a "first come, first served" basis. This is easy but not always practical for the librarian or the user. A user waiting for directions may be frustrated by waiting behind a user who is working on research for a 10-page paper. Therefore, asking waiting users how they could be helped is effective. If all questions are of an in-depth nature, ask the later-arriving users to wait; if some questions are easy or quick to answer, handle those first, and then full attention can be devoted to the more complicated questions. It is possible to start with one user, get to the search stage, and then help another user while the first user looks over search results. Obviously, there are limits to how long users can be expected to wait. It might be more considerate to take a phone number and return the call of the telephone user—perhaps

---

BOX 3.9
EXERCISE: WHOM WOULD YOU HELP IN WHAT ORDER AND WHY?

Telephone call: User wants to know whether the library owns a particular book.

In-person: User is looking for articles on how media images affect anorexia in teenage girls.

Instant messaging: User is encountering difficulty in accessing one of the library's online journal subscriptions.

What would you do if all three of these users arrived within the space of three minutes? Does it matter to you if the instant messaging question is from a prominent community member or if the in-person user is a student or teacher? How might your approach be different if all of the users were in-person?

---

with an answer if the question was taken. Constant interruptions while the librarian is helping with that 10-page paper may be interpreted as lack of interest.

Some libraries have tiered reference services where short questions are handled at one desk and longer questions at another. This may alleviate some juggling of questions of various types, but any reference desk can get busy at any time with any type of question, necessitating judgment (there is that word again) about priorities. Most libraries do not set priorities by a set policy, but strive to be equitable in how they treat all users and place equal importance on all inquiries regardless of mode of communication, type of user, or content of question. It is then up to the librarian working the desk at a given moment to determine the appropriate way in which to serve a queue of users.

Some compromises suggested by Tim Buckley Owen to immediately providing answers to users include suggesting sources, suggesting alternative libraries or individual sources of information, asking for thinking time, and offering a "quick and dirty" answer.[35] Certainly, if any of these techniques are utilized, follow-up is more important than ever.

Angry or Upset Users

The complexity of information and the variety of ways in which libraries organize and provide access to their collections can cause confusion, frustration, and even anger on the part of library users. Whether it is restrictive library policies that cause irritation, incomplete collections, inadequate services by library staff, or a frustrating event prior to the library visit, library users can be quite angry and upset when dealing with reference staff. In such a situation, individuals in public services positions are vulnerable to angry reactions by library users for even minor irritations. For whatever reason, reference staff will need to be ready to deal effectively with a user who is difficult to handle. On occasion, reference librarians may have to deal with individuals

---

BOX 3.10
REFLECTIVE STATEMENTS

Practice acknowledging the user's feelings in the following situations. Use simple, reflective statements. Do not try, in the exercise, to solve the user's problem; just work on exhibiting an understanding of the user's frustration. Do this exercise with another person, if someone is available; this exercise will work for any mode of communication: online, in-person, or telephone.

- The books that I want are always checked out. The library never has anything that I need.
- Why does the library close so early? You used to be open later.
- I can't believe that you charge for printing. Where I used to live, they didn't charge for printing.
- This catalog is stupid. I can't find anything!
- You canceled the most important journal in my field. How can the library do that?
- These DVDs are inappropriate for the library. You shouldn't spend money on that.

---

who are mentally ill or under the influence of inappropriate medication, but only the more common situation involving angry or irritated users is discussed here.

Nowhere is professional judgment more in evidence then when a librarian is confronted with an angry or upset user. The library literature offers a variety of resources to help librarians prepare themselves to deal with such situations.[36] In general, these works suggest using not only general communication skills, including the active listening and questioning techniques discussed throughout this chapter, but also using *empathetic listening.*

Empathetic listening requires acknowledging the feelings of others. This acknowledgment is uncomfortable for most people,[37] but when strong emotions stand in the way of resolving an issue, these feelings need to be addressed. In general, the librarian should acknowledge the user's feelings and link them with the specific facts of the situation in a statement. The statement should include acknowledgment of responsibility, the reflection of emotion or feeling, and the description of the event and facts. "You [responsibility] feel [insert feeling word] when [event]." This statement acknowledges the credibility of the user and demonstrates that the librarian as a listener accepts the user as a person as well. These statements exhibit empathy, not sympathy. In contrast, "absorbing or agreeing with the sentiments of the patron"[38] has the potential to interfere with the librarian's helping role.[39]

Once the user's feelings have been acknowledged, then the librarian must take some action to address the user's problem, starting with asking what the user wants the librarian to do to solve the problem. Often, the librarian cannot take the action that the user wants and will have to identify alternative solutions or bring in a supervisor with greater authority to clarify library policies or to review whether an exception can be made to the current policy.

If an exception cannot be made or alternative solutions found to satisfy the user, the librarian can promise to review the policies and procedures in light of the user's frustrations. Willingness to rethink policies and procedures acknowledges that these need constant updating and that libraries are responsive to users' needs.

Written policies available to users and to staff members are essential[40] to minimize conflicts. Without written policies, users may attempt to intimidate librarians into deviating from established policy for their benefit. Other staff members may unwittingly cause problems by deviating from established policy without informing the users that they are making an exception, which thus allows the user to establish an unrealistic expectation of the services the next staff member can and should provide.

Reference staff should also explore opportunities to discuss conflict situations and look for ways to avoid similar problems in the future. After each difficult situation, staff should discuss mechanisms to respond. Sometimes the user simply wants more than the library can provide, but repeated complaints—such as inadequate access to computers and electronic databases or unhappiness over canceled reference sources—should be referred to administrators for further consideration or review. Whether or not expressions of frustration and anger are justified, a user-centered reference service will be willing to regularly reexamine its responses to expressed user needs.

Imposed Queries

Questions asked by a user on behalf of another person, called *imposed queries*[41] or secondhand interactions,[42] are seen in all types of libraries. Individuals ask questions to glean information for someone else—their children, spouses, parents, friends, or employers or other individuals—or for situations that do not arise out of their own curiosity, as is the case with school assignments or work projects. Gross's survey of public libraries found that about 25 percent of questions were imposed queries, or those asked at someone else's request;[43] the Transform Inc. survey in Maryland revealed that 90 percent of the children's reference questions were school-related.[44] Because such users often have incomplete or misunderstood information regarding the information requested, it is more important than ever for librarians to seek to understand the context from which the question arose. "When questions are imposed and not self-generated, they are very apt to be presented to reference staff as an 'ill-formed query'...because the person asking the question might not fully understand it."[45]

When librarians in school, public, or academic libraries encounter a number of questions from different students related to the same topic, it is easy to jump to the conclusion that the questions arise from some sort of homework assignment. It is important, even if it appears that the question is one heard before, to conduct a reference interview.

Children tend to have broad initial requests more frequently than adults, so when their initial queries are vague, it is important for the librarian to not jump to the immediate conclusion that the question is related to a homework assignment. However, when children's questions are generated from someone else rather than generated out of their own curiosity, they often do not have the additional information the reference librarian would like to have.

Not surprisingly, there are differences of opinion regarding whether a librarian should ask if the question arises from a homework assignment, just as there are about asking "why." The 1997 Maryland study suggests asking open questions of the child to elicit more information and asking about an assignment only if the child cannot provide enough information about the question. This same study found that reference interviews started with broad initial questions about 70 percent of the time, but that "librarians appear to have a problem using more than one open probe in questioning children,"[46] indicating the need to use more open questions in working with children in the reference interview.

When it is obvious that the questioner is working from a homework assignment, it is certainly appropriate to ask whether the student has a copy of the teacher's written instructions to look at. Sometimes talking to the teacher, the person who asked the original question, is appropriate, to avoid placing the student in the middle. Likewise, it is important when dealing with children to talk to the child rather than an accompanying parent in negotiating the question. Further explorations of reference interviews with children, as well as other special populations, are found in chapter 12.

Catherine Ross and colleagues point out that "when a user says that the material is needed 'for a friend,' this formulation is sometimes a defensive strategy to avoid self-disclosure about a sensitive topic." If so, then the individual is in a good position to answer questions about the information need because it is in reality their own. Also problematic are the situations in which the individual is acting as an "information gatekeeper," bringing information to others.[47] Again, asking for ways in which the other person will be using the information will be helpful.

When an employee asks a question on behalf of a boss or supervisor, the individual may not know the context of the information need. "One approach in handling the issue of getting past the intermediary to the ultimate client is to provide the go-between, often a secretary or administrative assistant, with a written list of questions you need answered before you can proceed with the research."[48] The librarian may need to teach the individual elements of the reference interview in order for that person to go back to the originator of the question for more information. Another alternative is to create a search form. Ross, Nilsen, and Dewdney's advice for creating an e-mail reference form works equally well in this situation—eliciting information on the user's eligibility for the service, history of the question, gaps in current information, how the information will be used, features of the perfect answer, and time constraints.[49]

Readers' Advisory

No question at the reference desk can be more challenging than "Can you recommend a good book?" Because the focus of the interview is on helping readers find books that they want to read, usually pleasure reading and most often fiction books, the readers' advisory interview is very different from other reference interviews.[50]

Joyce Saricks and Nancy Brown point out that most fiction readers "are not looking for a book on a particular subject. They want a book with a particular 'feel.'"[51] Sometimes additional books by the same author, or within a specific genre, will satisfy the reader, but sometimes the reader is looking for something else. So the first aim of the librarian in a readers' advisory interview is to get the user to talk about the books he or she has enjoyed in the past. A good open question that works for readers' advisors is "Can you tell me about a book you've read and really enjoyed?" followed by a further probe, "What particularly did you like about it?"[52] When the user talks about the kinds of books he or she has enjoyed, the librarian should listen for information regarding several characteristics. These can include pacing—fast-paced action and excitement, witty dialogue, or lengthy descriptions; characterization—focus on a single character or several with interconnected story lines; themes—love, war, survival, revenge, coping with illness, the conflict of good and evil, and so on; settings—past, present, or future and geographic setting; and the atmosphere or tone—soothing and comforting or challenging and quirky.

There is no single right answer to a readers' advisory question, but there are answers that are wrong, particularly if librarians offer recommendations based on their own personal tastes or attempt to change the users' reading tastes. "The role of the readers' adviser is to help narrow down choices to a manageable number of suggestions that match the reader's stated interest and tastes."[53]

It is beyond the scope of this chapter to discuss resources for assisting librarians in making readers' advisory selections, but a knowledge of genres and new titles for fiction and a thorough knowledge of the subject field and important titles in that field for nonfiction are vital. Guidance for the selection of fiction works can be found in *The Reader's Advisor Online*, discussed in chapter 20, and on the Reference and User Services Association Web site, in the Collection Development and Evaluation Section, Readers' Advisory Committee.[54]

In closing the readers' advisory interview, it is especially important to encourage the reader to return for more assistance, especially to return with feedback regarding the book or books suggested by the librarian. Further clarification can assist the librarian in understanding better the user's tastes as well as the particular work or genre.[55] Saricks and Brown note that ongoing relationships with individual users over a period of time can improve the readers' advisory interview as the librarian develops familiarity with the reader's tastes. Although these kinds of interactions generally occur in public libraries, similar relationships in academic libraries can occur with individuals pursuing long-term scholarly endeavors.

Remote Users

Telephone

Libraries have been receiving questions by telephone for more than 130 years.[56] Communication via telephone in the reference environment has its own challenges. As mentioned previously, the lack of nonverbal cues is an impediment in the telephone interview. Although some emotions are easily communicated via tone of voice (such as annoyance or anger), others (such as lack of interest or confusion) are not as easily communicated by vocal inflection. Further, in the absence of facial expressions and body language, it is easier to misinterpret another's tone of voice. This works both ways, with the potential for the librarian to misunderstand the user as well as for the user to misunderstand the librarian. Unhelpful awkwardness might arise if the user perceives the librarian as uninterested or the librarian thinks that the user sounds annoyed.

It is effective when answering the phone to smile because this affects the tone of voice and sounds more welcoming. A typical telephone greeting such as "Hello" or "Good morning" starts the conversation off in a friendly manner. Additionally, telephone greetings usually contain the name of the library or reference desk, to assure the user that the correct number has been reached. An open question such as "How may I help you?" invites the user to state their question.

The rest of the question negotiation is really the same via telephone as it is in person. Open and closed questions and paraphrasing are still good practice. It is even possible to instruct inquirers in the use of library resources while they are on the telephone. This is particularly true when the inquirer is using the online library catalog or electronic databases and is able to be working at a computer while talking on the telephone with a librarian. For other questions, the librarian and inquirer may not want to stay on the telephone that long. When the questions require instruction as part of the answer, and it will take the librarian more than a couple of minutes to find an answer, it is kindest to ask inquirers whether they would prefer a call back or would like to hold. No one enjoys waiting on hold for a long time, so inquirers who are on hold should be reassured every few minutes that the librarian is still working on their question and given the option for a call back.

Ambient noise and inaudible inquirers can be a problem with telephone calls. A reference desk may have too much in-person activity to allow the librarian to hear someone on the phone clearly, or the acoustics of the room may be bad. A particularly busy telephone also may make it difficult to work with in-person users. Libraries deal with staffing telephone reference in different ways. Some have a desk that is in a different location, staffed separately from the in-person reference desk. It is more common for libraries to staff the telephone from the same desk as in-person queries and to have a volume control to help them better hear callers on the telephone.

E-mail, Mail, and Fax

Reference queries received via e-mail, mail, and fax all have an asynchronous nature in that the librarian cannot interview the user in real time. All three interactions can result in substantial delays in responses to users. All three are appealing because users can submit the question whenever it occurs to them. Those who live at a distance, who have mobility constraints, or who are more comfortable using written rather than verbal communication because of language skills or shyness may prefer to use these types of written communications. For librarians, these transactions have some advantages. It has been suggested that the users formulate and present their questions more effectively when they formally write them out rather than speak them.[57]

Because the user is not present in person or in real time, there is more time for thought and reflection, and questions can be deferred to quieter times. It is easier to refer questions to the appropriate person or expert, and the workload is more easily distributed to others. E-mail software can capture and save the queries and responses for later analysis or evaluation. Some back-and-forth communication may be needed to clarify the question, but this can be difficult to achieve via e-mail because the user may view a request for clarification as being put off or may become frustrated with the amount of time that the interaction is taking. Ultimately, as Joseph Straw writes, "reference librarians must be able to write messages that are organized, concise, and logical. A well-written response not only answers a question eloquently, but it also tells the user about the importance that the library places on the question."[58]

Chat and Instant Messaging

Real-time chat and instant messaging services augment but do not replace e-mail services in libraries. One advantage that virtual reference services have over e-mail, fax, and mail is the ability to conduct the reference interview in real time and to eliminate the waiting time. Other advantages of virtual transactions are the ability to escort the user through complex searches, provide instruction in using resources, and assist users in evaluating the results. Possibilities of cooperative ventures could even allow answers to be given 24/7 by librarians not in the library where the user is a patron. The librarian may be at home, on another campus, or even on another continent. The disadvantages of this communication mode are that there are no visual or aural cues, and the communication is more labor-intensive because typing requires more time and concentrated effort than speaking. Electronic reference interviews require the same skills as traditional reference interviews, but some additional considerations should be taken into account.

Chat interactions utilize a more casual tone than that to which most librarians are accustomed. The exchanges of text utilize shorter phrases than in speech and often incorporate commonly accepted abbreviations. Buff Hirko and Mary Ross state that "economy of phrase is invaluable, along with the ability to break a longer answer into brief one- or two-line parts that can be quickly sent."[59] Although the abbreviations used in online communication initially may be unfamiliar, there are sources[60] that provide explanation, and these may be bookmarked or distributed to staff for their reference. Use of abbreviations may be less frequent than expected because there are varying levels of formality in online communication, just as in spoken discourse. As with any reference interview, the librarian should be aware of and responsive to the user's formality but should not feel obligated to use abbreviations or slang because this may come across as contrived.

Keeping the user informed is one of the most challenging aspects of the virtual environment, with the librarian needing to let the user know what he or she is doing, such as still looking, sending a Web page, or guiding to the online catalog. Appropriate responses to common questions and situations can be selected from pre-scripted messages, such as initial greetings, prompts for additional information, search instructions, technical messages, advising the user to please wait or that the librarian is still searching, and so on. In one study of chat communication, "lengthy, formal scripts were seen as impersonal, and overuse of them implied lack of either interest or interview skills on the part of the library operator."[61] Scripts should be used to facilitate the flow of conversation but should not become the conversation. Attention to the tone of the scripts is important to avoid a robotic or unwelcoming tone.

The question of the importance of the reference interview was addressed as the topic of the 2002 RUSA President's Program.[62] Catherine Ross and Jana Ronan, along with respondents David Tyckoson and Kathleen Kern, upheld the importance of the reference interview and provided best practices for librarians. The availability of chat transcripts for analysis led to a flurry of research on interpersonal communications in libraries. Marie Radford's examination of transcripts from Maryland AskUsNow! and the Samuel Swett Green Award competition investigated rapport-building techniques used by both librarians and inquirers in chat communication as well as barriers to effective communication.[63] The practitioner will find the examples of each type of communication strategy and failure to be a useful training and self-assessment tool. Jody Fagan and Christina Desai also provide examples from actual transcripts to support their recommendations for best practices in chat and instant messaging reference.[64]

Instant messaging has recently become a popular communication technology in libraries. As it relates to the reference interview, IM is similar to chat in the way that communication occurs and in best practices to be used by the librarian in interacting with the user. New communications technologies are continually explored by the general public and libraries. Voice-over IP (VoIP) and online videoconferencing technologies that deliver real-time voice and video over the Internet have yet to gain significant use by the general population and so have not been incorporated into reference services by many libraries. If these technologies are implemented by libraries, librarians will need to adapt reference interview techniques to these new environments.

CONCLUSION

The effectiveness of reference service depends on the ability of library staff to conduct a successful reference interview. This is a constant, regardless of the mode of communication. Catherine Ross, Kirsti Nilsen, and Patricia Dewdney state, "The process of finding out what the user really wants is the bedrock of successful reference, upon which everything else depends. The most comprehensive understanding of the sources is wasted if the information intermediary is looking for the wrong thing. The need to understand what the user really wants to know remains the same, whether the reference transaction is face-to-face, over the telephone, or computer-mediated through asynchronous e-mail or real-time chat."[65]

Successful reference interactions require a variety of interpersonal skills and traits in addition to questioning: genuine interest in users' information needs, ability to establish trust and confidence, flexibility, professional judgment, and knowledge of research tools and reference sources. User satisfaction not only with the answer provided but also with the interaction with the librarian is the ultimate goal. As research by Joan Durrance and others has shown, personal interaction is as significant a factor in user satisfaction and willingness to return as being given a correct answer.[66] Thus, just as approachability is the beginning of a reference interview, facility with the reference interview is the beginning of an excellent reference librarian.

NOTES

1.   David K. Maxfield, "Counselor–Librarianship: A New Departure," *Occasional Papers*, no. 38 (Urbana: University of Illinois Library School, March 1954), 39 pp.

2.   Celia Hales Mabry, "The Reference Interview as Partnership: An Examination of Librarian, Library User, and Social Interaction," *The Reference Librarian* 83/84 (2003): 41–56.

3.   Joan C. Durrance, "Factors That Influence Reference Success: What Makes Questioners Willing to Return?" *The Reference Librarian* 49/50 (1995): 243–65; Patrica Dewdney and Catherine Sheldrick Ross, "Flying a Light Aircraft: Reference Service Evaluation from a User's Viewpoint," *RQ* 34 (Winter 1994): 217–30; Marie L. Radford, *The Reference Encounter: Interpersonal Communication in the Academic Library* (Chicago: Association of College and Research Libraries, 1999), 242 pp.

4.   Robert S. Taylor, "Question-Negotiation and Information Seeking in Libraries," *College & Research Libraries* 29 (May 1968): 182.

5.   Dewdney and Ross, "Flying a Light Aircraft," provides examples.

6.   Mary Ellen Bates, "Finding the Question Behind the Question," *Information Outlook* 2 (July 1998): 19.

7.   Geraldine B. King, "The Reference Interview: Open & Closed Questions," *RQ* 12 (Winter 1972): 159.

8.   Brenda Dervin and Patricia Dewdney, "Neutral Questioning: A New Approach to the Reference Interview," *RQ* 25 (Summer 1986): 511.

9.   Ibid., 506–13.

10.   Alfred Benjamin, *The Helping Interview*, 3rd ed. (Boston: Houghton Mifflin, 1981), 85–96.

11.   Fred Oser, "Referens Simplex or the Mysteries of Reference Interviewing Revealed," *The Reference Librarian* 16 (1987): 72.

12.   Catherine Sheldrick Ross and Patricia Dewdney, *Communicating Professionally*, 2nd ed. (New York: Neal-Schuman, 1998), 22–23.

13.   Dina C. Cramer, "How to Speak Patron," *Public Libraries* 37 (November/December 1998): 349.

14.   Madelyn Burley-Allen, *Listening: The Forgotten Skill*, 2nd ed. (New York: Wiley, 1995), 3.

15.   Lists of questions can be acquired at https://netfiles.uiuc.edu/bswoodar/www/Reference%20Interview%20Questions%20and%20Scenarios.doc or obtained from other sources such as Buff Hirko and Mary Bucher Ross, *Virtual Reference Training: The Complete Guide to Providing Anytime Anywhere Answers* (Chicago: American Library Association, 2004), 111–16.

16.   Tim Buckley Owen, *Success at the Enquiry Desk: Successful Enquiry Answering Every Time*, 4th rev. ed. (London: Facet, 2003), 27.

17.   Catherine Ross, Kirsti Nilsen, and Patricia Dewdney, *Conducting the Reference Interview* (New York: Neal-Schuman, 2002), 113. Other resources on inclusion are Gillian Michell and Roma M. Harris, "Evaluating the Reference Interview: Some Factors Influencing Patrons and Professionals," *RQ* 27 (Fall 1987): 95–105; and Marilyn Domas White, "The Dimensions of the Reference Interview," *RQ* 20 (Summer 1981): 373–81.

18.   Ralph Gers and Lillie J. Seward, "Improving Reference Performance: Results of a Statewide Study," *Library Journal* 110 (November 1, 1985): 32–35; Lillie Seward Dyson, "Improving Reference Services: A Maryland Training Program Brings Positive Results," *Public Libraries* 31 (September/October 1992): 284–89; Laura Isenstein, "Get Your Reference Staff on the STAR Track," *Library Journal* 117 (April 15, 1992): 34–37.

19.   Christopher W. Nolan, "Closing the Reference Interview: Implications for Policy and Practice," *RQ* 31 (Summer 1992): 513–23.

20.   Catherine S. Ross and Patricia Dewdney, "Negative Closure: Strategies and Counter-Strategies in the Reference Transaction," *Reference & User Services Quarterly* 38 (1998): 151–63.

21.   Nolan, "Closing the Reference Interview."

22.   Mary Jo Lynch, "Reference Interviews in Public Libraries," *Library Quarterly* 48 (April 1978): 119–42, found that about 50 percent of the library staff chose to conduct a reference interview; Patricia Dewdney, "The Effects of Training Reference Librarians in Interview Skills: A Field Experiment" (Ph.D. diss., University of Western Ontario, 1986), found that of 629 nondirectional questions, 57 percent, or 332 cases, had interviews; Catherine Sheldrick Ross and Kirsti Nilsen, "So Has the Internet Changed Anything in Reference? The Library Visit Study, Phase 2," *Reference & User Services Quarterly* 40 (Winter 2000): 147–55, found that of 261 transactions, 129 reference interviews were conducted.

23.   Ross, Catherine Sheldrick, "The Reference Interview: Why It Needs to Be Used in Every (Well, Almost Every) Reference Transaction," *Reference & User Services Quarterly* 43, no. 1 (Fall 2003): 41.

24.   Ross and Dewdney, "Negative Closure," 151–63.

25.   Charles D. Patterson, "Personality, Knowledge, and the Reference Librarian," in *Reference Services and Technical Services*, ed. Gordon Stevenson and Sally Stevenson (New York: Haworth Press, 1984), 167.

26.   Gillian Allen and Bryce Allen, "Service Orientation as a Selection Criterion for Public Service Librarians," *Journal of Library Administration* 16, no. 4 (1992): 68.

27.   Elaine Z. Jennerich and Edward J. Jennerich, *The Reference Interview as a Creative Art*, 2nd ed. (Englewood, CO: Libraries Unlimited, 1997), 37.

28.   Marilyn J. Markham, Keith H. Stirling, and Nathan M. Smith, "Librarian Self-Disclosure and Patron Satisfaction in the Reference Interview," *RQ* 22 (Summer 1983): 372–73.

29.   Richard E. Bopp, "Reference Interview," in *Reference and Information Services: An Introduction*, ed. Richard E. Bopp and Linda C. Smith, 3rd ed. (Englewood, CO: Libraries Unlimited, 2001), 50.

30.   Martin E. P. Seligman, *Learned Optimism* (New York: Alfred A. Knopf, 1991), 319 pp.

31.   S. D. Neill, "Problem Solving and the Reference Process," *RQ* 14 (Summer 1975): 314.

32.   Jennerich and Jennerich, *Reference Interview as a Creative Art*, 36; Nancy S. Osborne, "Librarian Humor in Classroom and Reference," *ERIC* document ED349018, 1992.

33.   Juris Dilevko and Elizabeth Dolan, "Reference Work and the Value of Reading Newspapers," *Reference & User Services Quarterly* 39 (Fall 1999): 71–81.

34.   Bopp, "Reference Interview," 51.

35.   Owen, *Success at the Enquiry Desk*, 67.

36.   Rhea Joyce Rubin, "Anger in the Library: Defusing Angry Patrons at the Reference Desk (and Elsewhere)," *The Reference Librarian* 31 (1990): 39–51; Mark R. Willis, *Dealing with Difficult People in the Library* (Chicago: American Library Association, 1999), 195 pp.; and numerous articles in Kwasi Sarkodie-Mensah, ed., *Helping the Difficult Patron: New Approaches to Examining and Resolving a Long-Standing and Ongoing Problem* (New York: Haworth Press, 2002), 303 pp.

37.   Madelyn Burley-Allen, *Listening: The Forgotten Skill: A Self-Teaching Guide*, 2nd ed. (New York: Wiley, 1995), 128.

38.   Glenn S. McGuigan, "The Common Sense of Customer Service: Employing Advice from the Trade and Popular Literature of Business to Interactions with Irate Patrons in Libraries," *The Reference Librarian* 75/76 (2002): 201.

39. Brian Quinn, "How Psychotherapists Handle Difficult Clients: Lessons for Librarians," *The Reference Librarian* 75/76 (2002): 188.

40. Rhea Joyce Rubin, "Anger in the Library: Defusing Angry Patrons at the Reference Desk (and Elsewhere)," *The Reference Librarian* 31 (1990): 47; Willis, *Dealing with Difficult People,* 109–17.

41. Melissa Gross, "The Imposed Query," *RQ* 35 (Winter 1995): 236–43; and "Imposed versus Self-Generated Questions: Implications for Reference Practice," *Reference & User Services Quarterly* 39 (Fall 1999): 53–61.

42. Ross, Nilsen, and Dewdney, *Conducting the Reference Interview,* 136–42.

43. Gross, "The Imposed Query," 236–43; Gross, "Imposed versus Self-Generated Questions," 53–61.

44. Mary Lee Blatchford, Marjorie Ann Crammer, Susan Paznekas, and Stacey Aldrich, "Quality of Reference Service to Children: A Pilot Study from Maryland" (paper presented at the Public Library Association Conference, Kansas City, MO, 1998). Quoted in Melvin K. Burton, "Reference Interview: Strategies for Children," *North Carolina Libraries* 56 (Fall 1998): 110–13.

45. Ross, Nilsen, and Dewdney, *Conducting the Reference Interview*, 137.

46. Melvin K. Burton, "Reference Interview: Strategies for Children," quoting Blatchford et al., "Quality of Reference Service to Children," 5.

47. Ross, Nilsen, and Dewdney*, Conducting the Reference Interview*, 139.

48. Bates, "Finding the Question behind the Question," 20.

49. Ross, Nilsen, and Dewdney, *Conducting the Reference Interview*, 208, with acknowledgement to Carole Farber, University of Western Ontario.

50. Mary K. Chelton, "Read Any Good Books Lately? Helping Patrons Find What They Want," *Library Journal* 118 (May 1, 1993): 33–37.

51. Joyce G. Saricks and Nancy Brown, *Readers' Advisory Service in the Public Library*, 2nd ed. (Chicago: American Library Association, 1997), 35.

52. Ross, Nilsen, and Dewdney, *Conducting the Reference Interview*, 162.

53. Ibid., 163.

54. American Library Association, Reference and User Services Association, Collection Development Section, Readers' Advisory Committee. http://www.ala.org/ala/mgrps/divs/rusa/development/readersadvisory101/index.cfm

55. Saricks and Brown, *Readers' Advisory Service*, 77.

56. M. Kathleen Kern, "Have(n't) We Been Here Before? Lessons From Telephone Reference," *The Reference Librarian* 41, no. 85 (2003): 1–17.

57. Eileen G. Abels, "The E-mail Reference Interview," *RQ* 35 (Spring 1996): 348.

58. Joseph E. Straw, "A Virtual Understanding: The Reference Interview and Question Negotiation in the Digital Age," *Reference & User Services Quarterly* 39 (Summer 2000): 376–79.

59. Buff Hirko and Mary Bucher Ross, *Virtual Reference Training: The Complete Guide to Providing Anytime Anywhere Answers* (Chicago: American Library Association, 2004), 12.

60. For a comprehensive list, see NetLingo's list at http://www.netlingo.com/acronyms.php.

61.   Hirko and Ross, *Virtual Reference Training*, 13.

62.   Kathleen Kluegel, Catherine Sheldrick Ross, Jana Ronan, Kathleen Kern, and David Tyckoson, "The Reference Interview: Connecting in Person and in Cyberspace," *Reference & User Services Quarterly* 43 (Fall 2003): 37–51.

63.   Marie Radford, "Encountering Virtual Users: A Qualitative Investigation of Interpersonal Communication in Chat Reference," *Journal of the American Society for Information Science and Technology* 57 (2006): 1046–59.

64.   Jody C. Fagan and Christina M. Desai, "Communication Strategies for Instant Messaging and Chat Reference Services," *The Reference Librarian* 79/80 (2002/2003): 121–55.

65.   Ross, Nilsen, and Dewdney, *Conducting the Reference Interview*, ix.

66.   Durrance, "Factors That Influence Reference Success," 243–65.

ADDITIONAL READINGS

Benjamin, Alfred. *The Helping Interview*. 3rd ed. Boston: Houghton Mifflin, 1981. 177 pp.

> This book, by a practicing rehabilitation counselor, is full of honest self-examination and important insights regarding the techniques that make an interview effective. Written in the first person, it contains many examples to illustrate its points. It is a marvelous introduction to the psychological aspects of the type of interviewing in which a professional seeks to help a client in some way.

Durrance, Joan C. "Factors That Influence Reference Success: What Makes Questioners Willing to Return?" *The Reference Librarian* 49–50 (1995): 243–65.

> Durrance seeks to expand the evaluation of reference encounters beyond the provision of successful information service (accuracy of answers) to include other aspects such as the quality of the reference interview and the provision of instruction and guidance. In her "Willingness to Return" study, she uses the willingness of users to return to the same librarian at a later time with another question to study what factors users consider important in the reference interaction. She found that such interpersonal qualities as approachability, ability to listen, and interest in the user's question were among the behaviors most often associated with success as judged by users.

Fine, Sara. "Reference and Resources: The Human Side." *Journal of Academic Librarianship* 21 (January 1995): 17–20.

> In this short but thought-provoking essay, Fine discusses librarians' assumptions about themselves and their users and how these assumptions can affect the service provided. She argues that better awareness of their own assumptions about themselves and their users will help reference librarians improve their service to those users.

Gross, Melissa. "The Imposed Query." *RQ* 35 (Winter 1995): 236–43.

Gross, Melissa. "Imposed versus Self-Generated Questions: Implications for Reference Practice." *Reference & User Services Quarterly* 39 (Fall 1999): 53–61.

> In these two thought-provoking articles, Melissa Gross discusses reference interviewing when the question asked is posed not by the originator of the question but by an agent of that person, such as a secretary, student, family member, or other individual. In the first article, she reviews some of the relevant literature and develops a model for imposed queries. The second article delves more specifically into the problems associated with these questions and suggests solutions.

Howze, Philip C., and Felix E. Unaeze. "All in the Name of Service: Mediation, Client Self-Determination, and Reference Practice in Academic Libraries." *RQ* 36 (Spring 1997): 430–37.

Howze and Unaeze apply the concept of "client self-determination" (or self-empowerment), borrowed from social work, to the field of reference librarianship. They argue that the reference librarian's role as a mediator between users and information sources is best carried out when the librarian encourages users to "become full participants in their own outcomes."

Jennerich, Elaine Z., and Edward J. Jennerich. *The Reference Interview as a Creative Art.* 2nd ed. Englewood, CO: Libraries Unlimited, 1997. 128 pp.

This book provides an excellent overview of the reference interview, including sections on skills, training, evaluation, and special kinds of interviews. It is thoroughly grounded in the literature, and the bibliography is extensive.

Kluegel, Kathleen, Catherine Sheldrick Ross, Jana Ronan, Kathleen Kern, and David Tyckoson. "The Reference Interview: Connecting in Person and in Cyberspace" (presentations and responses from the RUSA President's Program, 2002 ALA Annual Conference, Atlanta, June 17, 2002). *Reference & User Services Quarterly* 43 (Fall 2003): 37–51.

This set of articles examines whether the reference interview is a necessary component of online reference interactions. These articles represent an early look at the reference interview process in the synchronous chat environment and how the reference interview is changed in the online environment. Issues of immediacy, lack of visual cues, and user expectations are addressed by library and information science faculty member Ross and practitioners Ronan, Tyckoson, and Kern.

Kovacs, Diane K. *The Virtual Reference Handbook: Interview and Information Delivery Techniques for the Chat and E-Mail Environments.* New York: Neal-Schuman, 2007. 132 pp.

In this handbook Kovacs offers guidance on how to adapt face-to-face reference interview skills to the virtual environment, using both chat and e-mail. Her discussion encompasses strategies for developing the needed technical, communication, and reference skills.

Luo, Lili. "Chat Reference Competencies: Identification from a Literature Review and Librarian Interviews." *Reference Services Review* 35 (2007): 195–209.

Based on a thorough review of the chat reference literature and interviews with experienced librarians, three types of chat reference competencies are identified: core competencies for general reference, competencies for general reference but highlighted in the chat environment, and competencies specific to chat reference service.

Murphy, Sarah Anne. "The Reference Narrative." *Reference & User Services Quarterly* 44 (Spring 2005): 247–52.

This article examines the reference interview using the rhetorical narrative or "text." Reference, like medicine, is a human endeavor requiring interpretation of objective, subjective, and ambiguous texts. There are three types of texts that come together in the reference interview: the user's text, the librarian's text, and the institution's text. These make up the narrative through which the librarian may interpret the user's information needs, empathize with the user's experience in using the library institution, and collaborate with the user to focus the information need to achieve the desired outcome.

Radford, Marie L. "Communication Theory Applied to the Reference Encounter: An Analysis of Critical Incidents." *Library Quarterly* 66 (April 1996): 123–37.

Radford, Marie L. *The Reference Encounter: Interpersonal Communication in the Academic Library.* ACRL Publications in Librarianship, no. 52. Chicago: American Library Association, 1999. 242 pp.

Both of these Radford titles report qualitative studies of reference interactions, using detailed interviews with both the librarian and the user to understand their perceptions of the encounter. Among other conclusions, Radford suggests that users value highly the "relational messages that are communicated along with the information" and that librarians and library educators should focus more on the development of communication skills in training for reference service. She includes extensive quotations from users and librarians. Radford found that librarians were likely to talk about issues of content, such as the amount or quality of information, whereas users looked at relational factors such as pleasantness, helpfulness, and similar qualities in determining the success or failure of a reference transaction.

Ross, Catherine Sheldrick, and Patricia Dewdney. *Communicating Professionally.* 2nd ed. How-to-Do-It Manuals for Librarians, no. 58. New York: Neal-Schuman, 1998. 322 pp.

Ross and Dewdney discuss the skills required for effective communication and apply them to various library activities, from group activities and formal presentations to the one-to-one communication found in the reference interview. Of most relevance here are the sections on listening and question negotiation and on the types and stages of reference interviews. The book is very readable, and the annotated readings appended to each section are very helpful.

Ross, Catherine Sheldrick, Kirsti Nilsen, and Marie L. Radford. *Conducting the Reference Interview.* 2nd ed. How-to-Do-It Manuals for Librarians, no. 166. New York: Neal-Schuman, 2009. 290 pp.

An outgrowth of years of research on reference interview effectiveness and countless workshops on conducting the reference interview, this work provides excellent summaries of the research as well as some practical suggestions for individual study or group interactions to improve the librarian's ability to understand what the user wants. The use of case studies, checklists, and exercises makes this a valuable tool for training on the reference interview, engaging the reader in active learning.

Taylor, Robert S. "The Process of Asking Questions." *American Documentation* 13 (October 1962): 391–96.

Taylor, Robert S. "Question-Negotiation and Information Seeking in Libraries." *College & Research Libraries* 29 (May 1968): 178–94.

These seminal articles are among the most frequently cited discussions of the application of communication principles to the reference interview. Taylor focuses on the ways questions are formulated by the user and how they are presented to the reference librarian. The second article, in particular, discusses principles of question negotiation that librarians should follow to accurately understand the user's information need.

Chapter

4

Organization of Information and Search Strategies

Prudence W. Dalrymple and
Linda C. Smith

INTRODUCTION

Students preparing for a career working to make information accessible to users face greater challenges today than they did even just a few years ago. The conceptual underpinnings and structure of the bibliographic universe as it has been organized by librarians and information specialists for decades are now being modified and adjusted to meet the tremendous demands of the information age. Procedures are being streamlined so that principles of bibliographic organization can be applied to ever-larger amounts of material. At the same time, material is being made available to the public through the Internet in unprecedented quantities, frequently without any regard to the principles that have been established by librarians. Today's library and information science students must deal with both universes, one that is carefully structured and organized and another that often seems chaotic or assembled according to what appears to be a different set of rules. During the transition from traditional library organization to that based on digital models, librarians need to understand both worlds and perhaps begin to devise ways in which the librarian's traditional store of knowledge can be brought to bear on the multitude of information available electronically.

The premise of this chapter is that reference librarians should understand the power and benefit of organizational schema, first by understanding the principles of traditional bibliographic organization of published materials. By gaining an understanding of these principles and how they can be exploited for information retrieval, librarians will be prepared to devise effective search strategies. They can also work to design organizational plans that can be applied to other emerging types of information sources. Information professionals who are committed to providing access to information and materials directly to users can contribute to the creation of a more orderly and satisfying digital universe. Searching any information system is easier when the librarian is familiar with how it is organized (if it is organized). Conceptualization of the various strategies that can be employed to make searching effective and efficient can also be demonstrated to users through information literacy instruction (see chapter 8) or point-of-access assistance, and these same strategies can be incorporated into the design of print and electronic materials to aid the user.

The process of organizing information to make it available to persons seeking to use it is known as *bibliographic control*, and it is an activity basic to librarianship. Indeed, the history of librarianship in the United States is closely associated with the development of bibliographic organization schemes, such as Melvil Dewey's classification scheme, and the extensive bibliographic activities of the nation's libraries, such as the Library of Congress, the National Library of Medicine, and the National Agricultural Library. Since the 19th century, considerable time, money, and effort have been expended to design, implement, and maintain local, regional, national, and international systems of bibliographic control to ensure that the universe of published information is made accessible. Today, the rapid growth of the Internet has led to a growing appreciation of the principles of organization that librarians have established and sustained. Although the Internet is far from organized in the traditional sense, several initiatives are underway that build on librarians' traditional bibliographic practice; an understanding of the principles of bibliographic organization will enable reference librarians to use these enhancements and even to contribute to their growth and development. The purpose of this chapter is to introduce and explain these concepts and to indicate possible future directions.

Bibliographic universe refers to the totality of published items, regardless of date, format, or location. *Bibliographic control* refers to the organizing of these items, or rather the organizing of the representations of these items, so that they may be identified and located. The most common methods of ordering and providing access in libraries traditionally have been by author, by title, and by subject. Other ways of organizing materials such as archives are interesting for comparative purposes but are outside the scope of this chapter. Availability of information resources in digital form has also made virtually every character string in the text accessible, but for reasons that will become apparent, such expanded access can sometimes be a mixed blessing.

Although the concept of bibliographic control is simple, the practice of organizing information is complex and can be confusing to beginning librarians and library users. The universe of published materials may be partitioned in several ways: by publishing mode (e.g., books versus articles), by format (e.g., print versus electronic), or by subject area (e.g., general versus specific subject). These traditional types have been augmented by new categories of materials in hybrid and evolving formats such as Web sites, electronic journals, and consolidated sites consisting of resources hyperlinked to other sites and sources. For simplicity's sake, this chapter emphasizes two main approaches to organizing these materials: catalogs and indexes. The bibliographic principles underlying their design and the ways they are evolving are discussed. The process of searching for information by applying the principles of bibliographic control is described, and general search strategies are explained.

BOX 4.1
DEFINING BIBLIOGRAPHIC CONTROL

The bibliographical universe is not under effective bibliographical control until anyone can discover those of its inhabitants that will suit his or her purposes.

—Patrick Wilson, "The Catalog as Access Mechanism"[1]

THE LIBRARY CATALOG

For many years, the library catalog was the primary means of locating and accessing items in a library's collection; indeed, the function of the catalog was to display the holdings of a particular library. Over the last several decades, however, the catalog's function has evolved so that it not only reflects the library's collection but also acts as an access mechanism to resources beyond the library. At the same time, as it has broadened its scope, it also has deepened to include sources that indicate the contents of items (e.g., journals) held by a library, such as indexes and citation databases. Although the records that make up a library's catalog may be drawn from a shared cataloging resource such as the Online Computer Library Center (OCLC), the catalog itself is specific to that particular library's collection. Bibliographic records are selected from the national database and may undergo modifications, such as the addition of a local call number or volume holdings statement. Consulting a national database answers the question "Does an item exist?" Consulting the catalog answers the questions "Does the library own or provide access to the item?" and "Where can the item be found?"

A library's catalog is cumulative, including all materials held in a collection, regardless of date of publication or date of acquisition. In large libraries or library systems, the contents of the catalog may be a combination of several libraries. In these instances, the catalog is known as a *union catalog*. (Local circumstances may preclude representation in the catalog of all holdings of all libraries within a system. When the catalog is not fully representative, this fact should be made clear to users and librarians.)

The catalog is composed of representations or surrogates of bibliographic objects, including books, journals, audio and video materials, maps, and other nonprint items. These representations are called *bibliographic records*. In a card catalog, the bibliographic record was printed on a set of cards; in an online catalog, the bibliographic record consists of machine-readable information encoded in digital format. The machine-readable version of a bibliographic record conforming to certain standards for content and structure of the data is called a MAchine-Readable Cataloging (MARC) record. When the whole universe of intellectual resources is taken into consideration, bibliographic records are seen to be only one component. To describe the resources available on the Internet, librarians (and others) are currently engaged in creating various *metadata* schemes for records, describing various types of materials. Examples of these schemes are the Dublin Core, the Encoded Archival Description (EAD), and the Text Encoding Initiative (TEI) *Guidelines for Electronic Text Encoding and Interchange*.[2] Many of these approaches are based on traditional principles and modified to take advantage of the electronic format, whereas others embody a whole new approach.

Historically, the catalog provided three major types of access points for a given item: author, title, and subject. In a card catalog, this meant that there was a card created for each author, title, and subject (usually two or three subjects as described by subject headings). The subject headings used in catalogs are selected from established subject heading lists—the *Library of Congress Subject Headings* (LCSH)[3]or the *Sears List of Subject Headings*,[4] for example—during the cataloging process. The use of standardized lists ensures that the terminology and format of the headings remain consistent. A *shelf list*, a file arranged by call number, provides control over the collection and access by classification number. It takes its name from the fact that it reflects the arrangement of items on the shelf; where no actual shelf exists, a shelf list offers the opportunity to browse by classification number. A single item, then, was represented by several cards in the catalog; to save labor and space, the number of cards was usually limited, and the list of the various cards in the set appeared only on the main entry card.

As online catalogs gradually replaced card catalogs, cataloging principles began to change as well. Underlying the online catalog's structure is the MARC record (see Figure 4.1) showing which fields can be retrieved. All the bibliographic information associated with a specific piece is displayed in the various fields of the MARC record, along with the tag that identifies it. In Figure 4.1, the 100 field in the MARC record for the book *The Medical Library Association Essential Guide to Becoming an Expert Searcher* shows that the main entry is the author, Terry Ann Jankowski. Catalogers consulted the cataloging rules to select one access point as the main entry—author or title, for example. Although the MARC record retains the concept of a main entry, which is reflected in the "100" field, some catalogers have now begun to question whether the concept of the main entry is outmoded.[5]

The shift from paper to electronic format has increased the number of possible subject access points. In Figure 4.1, the 650 fields are the subject headings; in this case, subject headings from two lists are displayed, the Library of Congress and the *Medical Subject Headings* (MeSH) lists. The source of the subject heading is indicated by the digit to the right of the 650. Six subject headings from *Library of Congress Subject Headings* and two subject headings from *Medical Subject Headings* are assigned to this book. When each subject entry necessitated the production and filing of a card, fewer subject headings were used, usually just two or three, but catalogers are no longer so limited in the number of subject headings they assign. More subject headings increase the possibility of retrieving that item using the authorized term from the subject heading list. This information, particularly the subject tracings, can be very useful because it shows how the cataloger chose to represent that particular item and can suggest terminology to use in searching. The ability to gain an overview of the full bibliographic record is often ignored by the catalog user (patron and reference librarian alike) when only the brief entry is displayed. Many systems allow the user to review brief listings but then to request a display of the full record to determine the subject terminology that has been used to create the record and provide access to the item.

000	01896cam a2200445 a 450
001	5698132
005	20081212105141.0
008	080926s2008 nyua b 001 0 eng
010	__ la 2008026988
035	__ la (OCoLC)ocn180755587
040	__ la DLC lc DLC ld BTCTA ld BAKER ld YDXCP ld UKM ld C#P ld CDX ld BWX ld WAU
015	__ la GBA889506 l2 bnb
016	7_ la 014669851 l2 Uk
020	__ la 9781555706227 (pbk. : alk. paper)
020	__ la 1555706223 (alk. paper)
029	1_ la AU@ lb 000043203610
050	00 la Z675.M4 lb J36 2008
082	00 la 026/.61 l2 22
049	__ la UIUU
100	1_ la Jankowski, Terry Ann, ld 1951-
245	14 la The Medical Library Association essential guide to becoming an expert searcher : lb proven techniques, strategies, and tips for finding health information / lc Terry Ann Jankowski.
260	__ la New York : lb Neal-Schuman Publishers, lc c2008.
300	__ la xiii, 137 p. : lb ill. ; lc 28 cm.
440	_0 la Medical Library Association guides
504	__ la Includes bibliographical references (p. 107-116) and index.
650	_0 la Medical libraries lx Reference services.
650	_0 la Searching, Bibliographical lx Study and teaching (Higher)
650	_0 la Searching, Bibliographical lv Problems, exercises, etc.
650	_0 la Online bibliographic searching lv Problems, exercises, etc.
650	_0 la Database searching lv Problems, exercises, etc.
650	_0 la Information literacy lx Study and teaching (Higher)
650	_2 la Databases, Bibliographic.
650	_2 la Information Storage and Retrieval lx methods.
710	2_ la Medical Library Association.

Figure 4.1. Example of a MARC record.

INDEXES

Just as it is essential to understand some basic principles of cataloging, it is important to understand some basic principles of indexing. This need is even more critical when converting print to electronic media and merging indexing and cataloging files. It may be helpful to recall that *index* means "to point to." Indexes "point to" information located somewhere else; here, *index* refers to a tool that is used to locate information within a document. The most familiar index is the one found at the back of a book, which is used to find where certain topics are discussed within the text.

The indexes discussed in this chapter are indexes to published periodical literature. This kind of index is produced on a regular schedule and provides access to the topical contents of a group of publications. The group indexed may be determined by a variety of criteria; topic, language, publication type, and country of origin are some of the most common criteria. For example, the *Readers' Guide to Periodical Literature*[6] indexes a group of popular magazines published in the United States, *Education Index*[7] includes only publications whose primary focus is education, and *Index Medicus*[8] (now available online as part of *MEDLINE*) indexed medical journals published throughout the world in a variety of languages. The criteria used in selecting materials to include for indexing are usually explained in the introductory pages of a print index and are essential reading for effective use of the index. Explanations of indexes in electronic form should be included in the systems presented to users. All too often, users are uninformed about what they are actually searching.

Indexes are published in book or electronic form and may be cumulative for a year or for longer time periods. Most print indexes are arranged in alphabetical order by subject, and some provide a separate listing by author. When indexes are published in electronic form, many more points of access are available. This is a definite advantage, but there are also costs, as is pointed out in the later section on search strategies.

Unlike a library's catalog, the domain of an index is unrelated to the library's collection. From the searcher's perspective, then, an index represents what has been published in a particular subject area during a specified time period; to determine whether a particular library holds an item, some additional searching must be undertaken. Although this may seem quite obvious, it becomes less clear when online indexes are presented to the user alongside or through the same terminal as an online catalog. Many libraries now subscribe to services that provide full-text articles online even when they do not own the periodical itself, so it is important for reference librarians to inform users of what resources are available to them. Unless these distinctions are made very clear, users may expect to obtain all the items listed in an index, just as they would expect to locate all the items listed in a library's catalog. These distinctions become even less clear when a single interface is used to provide access to all materials.

BEYOND CATALOGS AND INDEXES

Few reference librarians today would attempt to provide information to users without referring to the Internet. The wealth of materials available on the Internet

Each Dublin Core definition refers to the resource being described. For the purposes of Dublin Core metadata, a resource will typically be an information or service resource, but may be applied more broadly.

Element: Title
Definition: A name given to the resource.

Element: Creator
Definition: An entity primarily responsible for making the resource.

Element: Subject
Definition: The topic of the resource.

Element: Description
Definition: An account of the resource.

Element: Publisher
Definition: An entity responsible for making the resource available.

Element: Contributor
Definition: An entity responsible for making contributions to the resource.

Element: Date
Definition: A associated with an event in the life cycle of the resource.

Element: Type
Definition: The nature or genre of the resource.

Element: Format
Definition: The file format, physical medium, or dimensions of the resource.

Element: Identifier
Definition: An unambiguous reference to the resource within a given context.

Element: Source
Definition: A related resource from which the described resource is derived.

Element: Language
Definition: A language of the resource.

Element: Relation
Definition: A related resource.

Element: Coverage
Definition: The spatial or temporal topic of the resource, the spatial applicability of the resource, or the jurisdiction under which the resource is relevant.

Element: Rights
Definition: Information about rights held in and over the resource.

Adapted from *Dublin Core Metadata Element Set, Version 1.1: Reference Descriptions*, http://dublin core.org/documents/2010/10/11/dces/.

Figure 4.2. Dublin Core definitions.

makes it imperative to be comfortable searching in this environment. The way in which metadata schemes improve access to materials may not conform to traditional bibliographic principles, but there are similarities. The Dublin Core, for example, provides a set of descriptive elements not unlike those provided by the MARC record (see Figure 4.2). The Dublin Core, however, does not require use of particular standard vocabularies in subject indexing; a subject may be expressed in keywords or key phrases. The extent to which materials on the Web will be brought into the bibliographic universe associated with the catalog is a topic of continuing philosophical and practical discussion.

PRINCIPLES OF BIBLIOGRAPHIC CONTROL

Despite the differences in scope between catalogs and indexes, some underlying principles of bibliographic control are addressed by both: arrangement, collocation and authority control, and depth and comprehensiveness of indexing. Each of these principles is defined and discussed in the following sections. Although much of the work of libraries is carried out through electronic means, the principles and terminology are best understood in the traditional format; once understood, they can be adapted and applied to the digital environment. In fact, some principles that appear to be nearly irrelevant in the digital world are included here not only for historical reasons but also because they exemplify utilitarian benefits that may be achieved in new and different ways as the digital environment evolves and matures.

Arrangement

The physical arrangement of the catalog has been used to improve retrieval capability for the user. For purposes of this discussion, the catalog is regarded as a file, a group of objects arranged in an arbitrary or meaningful order. An example of a file arranged in arbitrary order is a dictionary catalog, in which the records are arranged in alphabetical order. An example of meaningful order can be found in a classified catalog, in which the records are arranged by classification number to reflect a subject arrangement.

In classified catalogs, materials on similar subjects are filed together as they would appear on the shelf according to the classification plan. Users of a classified catalog must consult a schedule or plan to determine the appropriate class numbers for a particular topic before beginning to search, in much the same way as the index of a book is consulted to locate discussions of a particular topic. Classified catalogs are seldom used in the United States; they are more common in Europe. In a dictionary catalog, the searcher may approach the file directly, as one might consult an encyclopedia or a dictionary. In large libraries especially, dictionary card catalogs were divided into two alphabets, one containing author/title entries and one containing subject entries only. In online catalogs and indexes, the same effect can be achieved by limiting the search key to a particular field.

Some of the characteristics of both dictionary and classified arrangements have produced interesting problems and attempts at new solutions in the online environment. For example, the ability to browse through a meaningful order (typical of a classified catalog) is supported in the BUBL Information Service's use of the Dewey Decimal Classification System (http://bubl.ac.uk/) to provide access to selected Internet resources. Searchers can browse the classification schedule in order to gain a sense of related topics. In many online catalogs, related subject headings can be displayed for browsing.[9]

Collocation and Name Authority Control

A basic tenet of cataloging is the principle of collocation, which means that similar materials are gathered together at a single location. In other words, one of the functions of cataloging is to ensure that all materials by Shakespeare are filed together and that all materials about aardvarks are located at the same point in the file. Although this may seem quite simple and obvious, the cumulative nature of the catalog, combined with the practice of using popular (and therefore changing) terminology for subject headings, makes total collocation difficult to achieve. At the same time, the experience of searching the Internet illustrates dramatically the potential benefit of "collocating" all materials in one place accessible to the searcher.

From their inception, catalogs were designed to be searched directly by the library user and are presumed to be self-explanatory. The use of popular words and terms as subject headings facilitates searching directly without first consulting a list of subject headings or requiring any specific training or subject expertise. Multiple-word phrases are sometimes combined and inverted for purposes of collocation; for example, "Insurance" and "Insurance, health" appear together in an alphabetical display. The maintenance of linkages between terms is referred to as the *syndetic structure* of the subject headings. Cross-references are used to make intellectual links between the new and old terms; in electronic files, hyperlinks can be established between terms, terms can be mapped automatically to one another, or global changes can accomplish what previously required the addition of cards to the catalog.

Collocation works in a catalog because terminology can be confined to a specific field. That is, books *by* Shakespeare and books *about* Shakespeare can be differentiated because Shakespeare as an author is tagged differently than Shakespeare as a subject. A biography of Shakespeare would appear in the subject catalog, but if the title of the biography were *Shakespeare*, it would also appear in the author/title sequence. In libraries where the card catalog was divided, one alphabetical sequence included entries for authors and titles, and another alphabetical sequence had entries for subjects (the "subject catalog"). Although this division was designed to assist the user by reducing the size of the file that needed to be searched, the benefit was sometimes not recognized by the user. In the online catalog, the same effect can be accomplished by limiting the search key to the subject field or the author field rather than simply using a keyword approach. By specifying the search key as "subject" or "author," the searcher can reduce the size of the retrieval set.

An essential requirement for achieving collocation is maintenance of *authority control*, whether of author's names, subjects, or titles. For example, author-name authority control ensures that all existing permutations of an author's name—P. S. Winnicott, Pamela Smith Winnicott, Pamela S. Winnicott, or Pamela Smith (if Winnicott were a name acquired or dropped by a change in marital status)—are linked so that all the works written by this individual are gathered together at a particular location in the catalog. The sheer size of the bibliographic universe and the complexity of modern knowledge (the "information explosion") have made authority control one of the biggest challenges in cataloging today, driven in part by the mounting cost of comprehensive authority work.[10]

Subject Authority Control

Subject authority control has as its objective the gathering together in one place of items on a particular topic. A few attempts at searching in a file that has no subject authority control should convince even the skeptic of the benefit that comes from assigning terms that represent the intellectual contents of an item. Although some titles may describe accurately the contents of some items, particularly in the scientific and technical world, titles of items are not necessarily indicative of intellectual content. To retrieve these items, some method of naming or pointing to the contents of the piece is required. In cataloging, this process is known as *subject cataloging* and is defined as the application of subject headings and the creation of subject entries. For periodicals, this process is known as indexing and consists of using terms called descriptors to "point to" the contents of the piece. Lists of *subject headings* such as the LCSH indicate those headings that are preferred and/or related (cross-references and "see also" references), and lists of *descriptors* are displayed in a *thesaurus* that indicates not only preferred terms through cross-references but also broader and narrower terms. These lists are referred to as *controlled vocabularies*, and the relationships among terms are known as the *syndetic structure* of the vocabulary.

Because of the richness of the English language, many similar terms can be used to represent a single idea; a system of controlled vocabulary links these many terms to a single term. All items that are about this topic are thus collocated together, improving retrieval for the user. This benefit obviously has economic implications both for indexing and for cataloging, but it is still a fundamental objective of bibliographic control. Correct, consistent use of authority control and controlled vocabulary provides quality control; that is, these techniques ensure that materials are represented reliably and consistently, so that the user may depend on consistent results when using proper search and retrieval techniques.

Classification, indexing, and subject cataloging have as their goal the grouping together of similar items for easy retrieval, but in electronic bibliographic systems, the way in which these various systems work together is beginning to shift. The distinctions between subject cataloging and indexing have blurred, although it is useful to recall the historical origins, as described in the next section on coordinate headings. The benefits of syndetic structure can be overlooked and underutilized when the relationships among terms and the context of these terms are not made apparent to the user. The meaning of a particular term may vary considerably depending on the context. For example, the term "stress" can refer to psychological stress, mechanical stress, or the physical stress of a cardiac stress test.

Retrieval from a file will be much more precise if the person assigning the subject terms is able to specify which meaning is intended. Similarly, searchers will be able to focus their retrieval if they are able to select the appropriate meaning of the term by specifying the context. Some librarians are questioning the basic premise that the best (or only) way to achieve reliable subject access is to use standardized vocabulary.[11]

Without standardized vocabulary, however, a greater burden is placed on the searcher, whether user or reference librarian, to construct a search that is both comprehensive and specific enough to meet the need.

Depth and Comprehensiveness of Indexing

For many years, one distinctive feature of an index compared with a catalog was the depth and comprehensiveness of indexing. Indexing is most often associated with articles, whereas cataloging is associated with separately published works such as books. The bibliographic record for cataloging is standardized on a national or even international level, whereas the indexing record, known as the *unit record*, may differ from index to index. Despite these differences, however, one of the most important elements of the unit record is the set of descriptors used to describe the intellectual contents of the document. Before electronic catalogs and indexes became so prevalent, articles generally had many more descriptors attached to them than books had subject headings.

Descriptors in a thesaurus are linked by references indicating relationships, such as "broader" term, "narrower" term, and "related" term. Although recent editions of the LCSH include narrower term/broader term designations, LCSH was not originally designed to function as a true thesaurus.[12] Although the difference between a subject heading list and a thesaurus is debated among librarians, one difference is that the syndetic structure of a thesaurus is more rigorous and hierarchical than that of a subject heading list. Another difference lies in the way a thesaurus is constructed. Many thesauri are created a priori as reflections of the nature of the subject field. They are representations of knowledge within a specific subject area. The topics and their interrelationships are represented through terms regardless of the existence of documents within those areas. Other thesauri are more like subject heading lists, in that terms are introduced by virtue of *literary warrant*; that is, they are derived from the published literature of the subject field. When a term has been used sufficiently to warrant its use in a subject heading or as a descriptor, it is considered for inclusion in the list.

Subject headings sometimes capture more than one concept per heading by *pre-coordinating* the terms. For example, a book titled *Children's Books and Magazines: A Market Study* is about the children's book publishing industry. The subject heading for this book is "Children's literature-Publishing-United States." The concept "children" is pre-coordinated with the concept "literature" to make the subject heading "children's literature." Other types of literature may also be represented by pre-coordinated headings. Further, the subject heading for this book is composed of another term, "publishing," and finally, the geographical location "United States." Although all of these terms further describe what the book is about, they do not serve as access points except in electronic formats, such as an online catalog, in which keyword searching is available.

The concept of a pre-coordinated heading makes greatest sense when thinking about the challenges faced in preparing a print index. Pre-coordination performs the same function as the AND operator in a Boolean search (see chapter 5). When Boolean searching (or its equivalent) was not available, pre-coordination saved the time of the searcher. When controlled vocabularies with pre-coordinated headings and syndetic structures are not available, a much greater burden rests on the ingenuity of the searcher. Terms may be pre-coordinated in various sequences to assist the searcher or indexer in selecting the appropriate term. By inverting the order of terms, similar terms can fall together; for example, "insurance, accident"; "insurance, health"; and "insurance, life" fall together when they are inverted. In another example, the order of terms is essential to the meaning: invert the terms in "venetian blind," and you get a "blind venetian"! The power that coordinate searching brought to the world of information retrieval is nicely presented in a history by Frederick Kilgour.[13]

In print indexes, unlike card catalogs, the descriptors attached to the item are not usually listed as part of the entry in the index. It is therefore impossible to see what other aspects of an article have been brought out by the indexer. In electronic systems, however, the searcher can request that the descriptors be displayed. Examining the descriptors can often provide insight into other aspects of a topic covered by an article or can suggest additional terminology to be incorporated in a subsequent search. Figures 4.3 and 4.4 show the descriptors from the online version of *ERIC* and the subject headings for the same item in an online catalog.

Accession Number	ED464640
Author	McClure, Charles R. Ryan, Joe. Bertot, John Carlo.
Institution	Florida State Univ., Tallahassee. Information Use Management and Policy Inst.
Sponsoring Agency	American Library Association, Washington, DC., National Foundation on the Arts and Humanities, Washington, DC. Inst. of Museum and Library Services.
Title	Public Library Internet Services and the Digital Divide: The Role and Impacts from Selected External Funding Sources.
Page Count	191
Peer Reviewed	N/A
Date of Publication	2002-01
ERIC Subject Headings	Access to Information *Federal Aid Federal Programs *Internet *Library Development *Library Services *Public Libraries Questionnaires Tables (Data)
Identifiers	Digital Divide, E Rate (Internet), Library Services and Technology Act 1996.

Figure 4.3. Report listed in *ERIC*.

Author:	McClure, Charles R.
Title:	Public library Internet services and the digital divide : the role and impacts from selected external funding sources / by Charles R. McClure, Joe Ryan, John Carlo Bertot.
Published:	Tallahassee, Fla. : Information Use Management and Policy Institute, School of Information Studies, [2002]
Physical Description:	xii, 163 p. ; 28 cm.
Includes:	Includes bibliographical references (p. 110-116)
Subject (LCSH):	Public libraries—Finance.
	Internet—Public libraries.
	Digital divide—United States.
	Internet access for library users—United States.
Other Name:	Ryan, Joe, 1951-
	Bertot, John Carlo.
	Florida State University. Information Use Management and Policy Institute.
	Chief Officers of State Library Agencies (U.S.)

Figure 4.4. Report listed in online catalog.

THE CONCEPT OF SEARCH STRATEGY

A *search strategy* may be broadly defined as a conscious approach to decision making to solve a problem or achieve an objective. The typical library user may employ an approach to searching that is more or less conscious and more or less informed, but the professional librarian is expected to apply knowledge and judgment in approaching information work. In this chapter, search strategies are discussed in the context of librarians seeking to assist users to find information by consulting resources that have been brought under some form of bibliographic control. The purpose is to familiarize beginning librarians with the ways they can exploit the power of bibliographic control to find answers to reference questions more effectively. Although some reference will be made to search strategies for items not under bibliographic control, fuller discussion of this topic is included in chapter 6.

These principles are described at a general level that differentiates them from heuristics or searching "tips" that apply to specific situations. For these, the reader is referred to the current library literature, wherein descriptions of such techniques appear regularly.[14] At the outset of any discussion of search strategy, it is useful to note that certain parameters will affect how any reference search is carried out:

- What is wanted
- What is known about what is wanted

- What resources are available
- How those resources are constructed
- What is known about the structure of those resources

Each of these questions is dealt with in different parts of this text. Because this chapter deals with the organization of information, the discussion of search strategy focuses particularly on how knowledge of bibliographic structures may be used to improve search results. Chapter 3 discusses ways for librarians to determine exactly what a user wants. It is worth noting, however, that this is not always clear at the time the search request is received or the reference question is posed. Rather, in the process of conducting an in-depth reference interview, the librarian and the user may come to understand more clearly what is wanted, and the focus of the search may change.

Examining the search patterns of both librarians and users to improve information access is an important research area in library and information science. Although early research focused primarily on patterns displayed by reference librarians answering questions from print sources, recent work has examined the search behavior of librarians conducting online searches. As users do more and more searching by themselves, a stream of research looking at how users access information on their own is continuing to grow. The study of both cognitive and affective aspects of the search process encourages librarians to become more aware of user needs at any given point and enables librarians to make appropriate interventions to facilitate the searches. By studying how students feel at various stages of preparing a term paper, librarians may become aware that the search for information is not solely an intellectual process; it may be accompanied by a wide variety of feelings, including uncertainty, anxiety, confusion, relief, disappointment, or confidence.[15]

One of the benefits of electronic bibliographic information systems has been the opportunity to observe how people actually search. Many long-standing assumptions about the ways in which people look for information using the tools provided by librarians have fallen by the wayside. Fortunately, librarians have worked with system designers to provide enhancements based on these observations, and information system design advanced dramatically in the 21st century's first decade. Many of the research studies that led to these advancements depended on users' ability to describe what they did while they were doing it; others used the electronic "paper trails" known as transaction logs that captured users' interactions with systems.

The insights that have emerged from this research can be useful to beginning reference librarians because they illustrate ways in which various features of information systems can be exploited in creative ways to produce better results. These patterns can also provide guidance to librarians who are responsible for creating search aids to be used while searching in environments that are not organized according to bibliographic principles. Models of how individuals search the Internet are not fully developed yet, but early research suggests that searchers use a highly interactive approach. This makes sense because there are few organizing principles used in putting items up on the Web, and the protocols used by search engines are usually not explicitly stated. Searchers must then interact with the system to deduce what works best for a given query and for a given search engine. Modeling search processes can be helpful in designing instruction or in helping searchers improve their results. The growing availability of direct user access to electronic information systems has stimulated interest in modeling the search processes of casual (untrained) users as well as those of librarians.[16]

A critical component in search strategy is the selection of terminology. As discussed earlier in this chapter, the use of thesauri and controlled vocabularies lends power to the searcher who understands and can exploit them. Because search term selection is so powerful, research has explored how searchers select terms and how they monitor and correct their strategy based on feedback. This process has its origins in manual searching, as described in an early exploration of search strategy by Marcia Bates, and has been further developed in electronic environments.[17] For example, Bates's tactic, called TRACE, refers to using the information already found to derive additional search terms and to examine the way in which the document has been represented. In a catalog search, the searcher uses the subject headings as potentially relevant search terms in refining the search. As electronic retrieval systems have evolved, more and more of them have begun to facilitate the searcher's use of the subject terms (subject headings or index terms) to assist the searcher in coming up with additional search terms or in understanding the cataloger or indexer's approach. Just as examining the subject tracings on catalog cards improved manual searches, this same technique can be used in an online catalog by displaying the subject headings.

In print indexes, the list of descriptors is not displayed, and TRACE cannot be used. In an electronic environment, however, TRACE may be used by displaying the fields in the unit records that list the descriptors used. Some system designers have incorporated the TRACE tactic as a feature of the interface. In some systems, the user is prompted to ask for a listing of the descriptors with the suggestion that they can be incorporated into the search; in others, the list is provided automatically. Such a feature is known as *automatic query expansion* and is an example of how a manual technique can inspire system enhancement.[18]

THE ELECTRONIC ENVIRONMENT

Structured files possess certain fields and attributes that can be used as retrieval tools. Knowledge of the file structure facilitates effective searching. In becoming familiar with any reference source (file), one of the first questions to ask is "What portions of the file are directly accessible for searching purposes?" Another way of putting this question is to ask, "What fields are searchable?" For example, in an electronic file, if one does not know the fields and which ones are searchable, one must resort to keyword searching throughout the file. Many false hits will likely occur. If the term "white," for example, is searched only in the names field, the retrieval will be much more accurate than if the whole file were searched for the term, where the search would pick up "white" in the title, the subject headings, and possibly the publisher and imprint fields.

In a print reference tool, the analog for the searchable fields is the type of indexes to a given work that are available. Knowing in advance whether a reference book has a names index or only a subject index will determine how easily and effectively it can be searched. Some reference texts have numerous indexes that enable the librarian to identify just the right piece of information very quickly. For example, the *Physicians' Desk Reference*[19] has numerous indexes that are particularly effective in drug searching. Although reference librarians are expected to be able to search and retrieve information from sources that are not organized, searching unstructured files requires an extra measure of ingenuity to compensate for the lack of bibliographic organization.

The principles of bibliographic control in catalogs and indexes may differ on a number of dimensions because of fundamental differences in how each is expected to function for the user. However, assumptions about the function of catalogs and indexes have been challenged with the nearly universal adoption of online catalogs and wide availability of electronic indexes. As reference tools become more widely available in electronic form, and the Web continues to grow in both size and sophistication, a discussion of search strategy based on the purpose of the tool becomes less relevant. What is of greatest concern to both user and librarian is how to exploit the power of the organizational principles in conjunction with the power of electronic retrieval. Because of the different functions of catalogs and indexes, the models used to describe a typical search have been assumed to differ as well. Generally speaking, the index search is conducted to identify items about a particular topic and is therefore inherently a subject or topical search. Both records loaded into a database and the format of a print index place primary emphasis on subject access. It has generally been assumed that catalog searches are known item searches, whereby users seek to locate particular items about which they possess some specific information: an author or a title, for example. The searcher enters the catalog, identifies the item, and goes to the shelf to locate it. The search may be broadened by browsing the shelves nearby, using the subject classification scheme to identify more items. This model may be described as moving from the specific to the general.

In an index, the searcher moves from the general topic to a specific aspect of the topic. In some indexes, the entries are arranged to reflect a hierarchical structure, with more general articles first, followed by more specific aspects listed underneath. The general-to-specific structure is readily apparent at first glance into the print index. The electronic version of such an index does not reveal this structure so easily. On the other hand, by using the power of coordinated searching, specificity in searching can be achieved.

Recently, some research has been done on the approach that most users take when searching the Web. Because there is no controlled vocabulary (descriptors or subject headings), search engines do not generally enable users to specify that the character string is to be searched only as a subject or only as a name. When a searcher is able to specify an exact name or phrase, this frequently helps reduce the retrieval, but there is little assistance in differentiating homographs or synonyms.

Another way of improving searching is through system design. Increasingly, librarians are taking an active role in creating or adapting systems to meet the needs of their users. Appropriate didactic interventions, such as Help screens, can be built into the system interface, or the machine can be programmed to modify strategies automatically to achieve better results. Software for *federated searching* supports simultaneous searching of multiple online databases or Web resources.

STRATEGIES FOR BIBLIOGRAPHIC SEARCHING

Two strategies, specific-to-general and general-to-specific, enable the searcher to exploit bibliographic structure to achieve an objective. These strategies may be applied to solving problems such as vocabulary selection and reference tool selection. Other strategies assist the searcher in capitalizing on specific system properties to improve the efficiency and quality of an information search. Two such properties are context and feedback.

The Specific-to-General Approach

The *specific-to-general approach* is defined as a search in which the searcher has a known relevant item or topic in mind and wishes to find others like it. For example, when a requester knows the author and title of a book and wishes to find similar books by different authors, the subject headings can be examined and then used to locate additional items. As pointed out earlier, this strategy works well in bibliographic systems that display descriptors, such as card catalogs and online databases and catalogs (see Box 4.2).

The first step is to locate the known item in the file. Assuming the information about the item is complete and correct, locating it in the file can usually be done through an author or title search. Although an author/title search is not always easy, especially when the file is large or the entry is complex (e.g., for corporate authors, such as U.S. government agencies), it is usually straightforward and unambiguous. Once the record is located, the searcher may examine the subject terms assigned to the work and immediately incorporate those terms in a subsequent search for more items. This direct entry into an information file eliminates the need to think of possible subject terms on one's own and also makes consulting a thesaurus or list of subject headings optional. Of course, the terms located initially may also be used as entry terms into a thesaurus or list of subject headings. One of the reasons the

---

BOX 4.2
FINDING RELATED ITEMS

Suppose the user has just finished reading the book *The Shallows: What the Internet Is Doing to Our Brains* by Nicholas Carr. She would like to continue reading in the same area, but she has no idea how to go about finding books on similar subjects. By looking up the book in the online catalog, she discovers that the subject headings applied to the book are "Neuropsychology," "Internet—Physiological effect," and "Internet—Psychological aspects." Because her interest is really in the psychological aspects, she decides to look further under "Internet—Psychological aspects." Using the library's online catalog, she finds that there are 12 books with that subject heading. By browsing through the list, she finds some titles of interest, including *Oxford Handbook of Internet Psychology* and *Cognition in a Digital World*. These will be a good start for further reading.

specific-to-general approach works well is that it provides a specific, unambiguous entry point of known accuracy into an information file.

When used in an online database search, this technique is usually called *citation pearl growing*. The initial citation is the point of entry, or seed of the pearl, and the search is expanded outward by selecting subject terms from the descriptor fields of the unit record. The successive expansions constitute the layers of the pearl. Another example of this strategy in online searching is the most-specific-facet-first approach. For example, a proper name or a highly specialized term or phrase is used as the entry point. Because most online systems allow searchers to enter free text or keywords, almost any specific term can be used as an entry point. If the retrieval is sufficient and of good quality, the search can be terminated; if larger retrieval is desired, both free-text terms obtained from titles or abstracts and controlled vocabulary terms obtained from lists of descriptors can be added to expand the retrieval.

Citation indexing, discussed in more detail in chapter 21, works on the same principle. A specific known item is used as an entry point to the index or database, and other items, assumed to be similar in subject matter because their authors cite the known item, can then be located. Citation searches may result in somewhat different retrieval because it is the judgment of the authors of the works, rather than that of the indexers, on which the links between items are established. Acknowledging the diversity of both indexing practices and citation habits, fully comprehensive results may be achieved by conducting multiple searches using both indexing and citation links.

Still another example of the specific-to-general approach is reflected in queries in reference interviews in which requesters are asked to supply a known citation as a starting point. Here, the requester makes the judgment as to the relevance of a particular item to the topic of the request (the information need). Such information may be invaluable to the reference librarian in fully understanding what is meant by the user's information request and in resolving any potential ambiguities.

General characteristics of the specific-to-general approach are its highly interactive quality and the need for continual review of results. With this degree of interactivity, however, there is always the danger that the searcher will become lost or distracted during the search; therefore, it is essential to know when to stop expanding the search and cycling through the process.

The General-to-Specific Approach

The key to effective searching when moving from the general to the specific is the syndetic structure that provides a logical overview or map of the concepts and vocabulary of a particular topic area. Because items are indexed to the most specific aspects of a topic, it is crucial to determine the correct level of specificity. This can be accomplished quickly and easily by scanning a thesaurus. For example, the thesaurus used in indexing medical literature, known as *Medical Subject Headings* (MeSH),[20] provides terms for the leg bones of the human body. The four bone terms listed are *femur, fibula, patella,* and *tibia.* Articles dealing with fractures of the fibula would therefore be indexed at the most specific level: fibula and fractures. The femur, however, has an additional level of specificity that describes two particular locations on the femur: femur head and femur neck. A fracture of the femur that is located at the head of the femur must therefore be indexed at the most specific level: femur head and fractures. The best (and sometimes only) way to determine the level of specificity is to consult the thesaurus. The importance of the thesaurus to constructing a successful search has led some database producers to provide the thesaurus online. In addition, some thesauri (of which MeSH is an example) provide a display of terms in a hierarchical structure. In MeSH, this display is known as the *tree structure*, as shown in Figure 4.5.

The alphabetical listing and the tree structure can be used together to determine the correct level of specificity. In the alphabetical listing, an interpretive note is made at "leg bones," and the appropriate place in the tree structure is indicated by means of an alphanumeric code: A02.835.232.043.650. As pointed out earlier, some indexes incorporate syndetic structure either through classification or by the arrangement of items under a heading, or with both.

A further enhancement to some online systems (e.g., *MEDLINE*) is an Explode feature that captures several terms at various levels within the hierarchy below the starting term with a single command. Once a term is located in the hierarchy, it may be exploded, and the search expanded very quickly; this can be done without sacrificing precision because it is possible to determine ahead of time which terms will be included. In the example used in the previous paragraphs, an online searcher could explode the term "femur," thereby capturing all articles dealing with the femur, the femur head, and the femur neck. The explosion also may occur higher up in the tree, capturing all the terms for leg bones.

Unfortunately, not all bibliographic systems have thesauri, nor are the thesauri always readily available in libraries. Fortunately, more and more publishers have recognized the value of making their subject headings and thesauri available, especially

Musculoskeletal System	A02
Skeleton	A02.835
Bone and Bones	A02.835.232
Bones of Lower Extremity	A02.835.232.043
Foot Bones	A02.835.232.043.300
Metatarsal Bones	A02.835.232.043.300.492
Tarsal Bones	A02.835.232.043.300.710
Calcaneus	A02.835.232..043.300.710.300
Talus	A02.835.232.043.300.710.780
Toe Phalanges	A02.835.232.043.300.800
Leg Bones	A02.835.232.043.650
Femur	A02.835.232.043.650.247
Femur Head	A02.835.232.043.650.247.343
Femur Neck	A02.835.232.043.650.247.510
Fibula	A02.835.232.043.650.321
Patella	A02.835.232.043.650.624
Tibia	A02.835.232.043.650.883

From http://www.nlm.nih.gov/mesh/trees2008/A02.html.

Figure 4.5. Tree structure from *Medical Subject Headings* (MeSH).

in electronic sources. Without them, it is difficult to grasp the scope of the subject matter or the syndetic structure of the index. Another problem is the number of subject heading schemes and controlled vocabularies that populate the bibliographic universe. These controlled vocabularies differ in degree of specificity, frequency of updating, availability, and structure. The librarian working in a general reference setting must cope with several different controlled vocabularies on a daily basis.

A single controlled vocabulary that encompasses many subject areas and is in widespread use (e.g., LCSH) provides consistency for librarians and users, but specialized thesauri developed by subject experts provide a greater degree of flexibility and specificity. In some specialized areas, there has been an attempt to rationalize controlled vocabulary to provide consistent access across a number of indexes. For example, the Unified Medical Language System (UMLS) provides a systematic linking of terms from both clinical and bibliographic vocabularies.[21]

In addition to moving up and down a hierarchical list of descriptors, syndetic structure supports moving horizontally through the use of cross-references and "see also" references. As pointed out earlier, one of the advantages of a controlled vocabulary is collocation: gathering similar works together despite individual variance in title words or abstracts. Once the searcher has arrived at the correct location in an information source, the list of descriptors may be scanned to select more specific items.

One of the difficulties, however, is selecting the correct terminology to arrive at the desired spot in the file. In a system without cross-references, the searcher must use the allowed term (in the correct spelling and grammatical form) to locate any materials. Cross-references permit the searcher to move from an entry term that is not used to a controlled vocabulary term that is used. Using an incorrect term results in no retrieval (manual or online), creating the usually false impression that nothing exists on the given topic. Maintaining a cross-reference structure assists the user because it can increase the number of entry points; knowledge of the topic, a good imagination, and a large vocabulary can also be assets to the searcher.

The ability to allow users to match their terminology to the systems' is so important that various schemes for enhancing the number of entry points have been proposed. Some of these involve providing expanded lists of words that can be used as entry points (sometimes called "super thesauri"), encouraging reference librarians to add cross-references to catalogs and allowing users to add their own terms to local databases through tagging.[22] These ideas serve to focus attention on an important problem in searching. A nearly universal problem when employing the general-to-specific approach in an electronic environment is the creation of large retrieval sets. The inexperienced searcher can risk losing important and valuable information if the size of the retrieval set is not reduced systematically and carefully. Karen Markey proposes a number of enhancements to online catalogs that could improve the precision of search results.[23] Whether these enhancements are accomplished through functions programmed into the system or whether they are invoked by the librarian while searching, the end result is the same: the retrieval is more manageable in size, of better quality, and ultimately of more use to the requester.

Context and Feedback

The preceding discussion suggests that the specific-to-general approach is particularly well suited to electronic environments, whereas the general-to-specific approach works best when the searcher wants a quick overview of a topic by scanning a print source or when a screen display facilitates a quick and effective grasp of the materials retrieved. This highlights the importance of context in developing a search strategy. In print sources, displays of syndetic structure inform the searcher of the context in which terminology is to be understood, as well as creating a visual map of the structure of a discipline. In online sources, however, these visual cues are often not available. As anyone familiar with the English language can attest, context plays a major part in resolving ambiguity when terms have several meanings. For example, stress can be understood in a psychological context ("stressed out" from exams), in a physical context (metals undergo stress), or in a medical context (stress as exertion).

The effect of ambiguity on searching can be substantial, particularly in large online systems (catalogs or databases that contain files covering many disciplines). Entering the term "stress" (meaning psychological stress) in an online catalog will retrieve a large number of items, but only a portion of them will deal with psychological stress. In some systems, the only way to determine which ones are relevant is to display all the items (no small task when 300 items are retrieved). Reviewing a few items and discovering that some of them deal with stress in metals will reveal semantic ambiguities, however, and indicate that another concept or term must be added to limit the search to the appropriate subject area. A very easy way to do this is to use Boolean AND with a psychological term such as "role conflict," which fixes the search in the appropriate context where further refinements can take place. This model for searching is often called the *building-block approach* and is widely used in online searching.

In online databases where the subject content is consistent throughout the file, a different strategy is necessary. For example, in *PsycINFO* (the online version of *Psychological Abstracts*),[24] the use of a general psychological term would be unnecessary because the psychological context is implicit. In fact, including general psychological terminology in a search in *PsycINFO* may be counterproductive because indexing of articles is done at a specific level. It is unlikely that such a general concept would be indexed, and therefore, the search would retrieve little or nothing. Ironically, this tactic is sometimes referred to as *overspecifying* a search. What this means is that the searcher has not taken into account the implicit context of the file and has constructed a redundant search strategy (see Box 4.3 for an example).

The importance of context is often overlooked because it is often taken for granted. The tremendous growth of online and Web searching, wherein contextual clues are all but lost, has served to reemphasize the potential value of context in resolving ambiguity and providing clues as to meaning and direction in searching. The context supplies a kind of feedback that is invaluable to the searcher. Feedback about the progress of a search, particularly in an online environment, has come to be a valued component of system design. Features such as menus that assist the searcher in formulating (and reformulating) a search strategy, Help screens that can be invoked by the user as needed, and display of retrieved items in order of their relevance to the query are becoming more common as online system design continues to evolve.

Although online feedback may be more explicit, subtle forms of feedback can be observed in print formats. Hierarchical displays in indexes; evidence of the scope of an area, such as the amount of catalog space or the number of pages in an index allocated to a particular topic; and even the age of the catalog cards themselves often exert a subtle influence on the direction of a search.[25] By recognizing the existence and

---

BOX 4.3
EFFECTS OF FAILING TO RECOGNIZE
THE CONTEXT OF A SEARCH

In looking for articles about the psychological effects of foster care, the searcher selects an appropriate database (*PsycINFO*) but fails to recognize that virtually all articles in this file deal with psychological aspects of phenomena. Looking for recent articles published in the past four years, the searcher correctly enters the publication year limits and uses the descriptor "foster care," which retrieves 762 articles, but also chooses to create a free-text phrase "psychological effects," which retrieves 377 articles. When the two search statements are combined, the result is one article. Although this article is relevant, it is likely that the number of relevant articles is much greater. The searcher's requirement that the words "psychological effects" appear in the bibliographic record has resulted in an unrealistically restricted retrieval. In this case a different approach is needed to narrow the retrieval set, such as combining "foster care" with another descriptor expressive of the searcher's interest in the topic, such as "resilience (psychological)."

---

value of feedback in refining or changing direction in a search, librarians can become aware of the role feedback plays in their own search strategies, and they can also incorporate feedback mechanisms in the programs and systems they provide to users.

Choice of Reference Tool

Little has been said so far in this chapter about the choice of reference tool. Selecting an appropriate reference tool or database affects the search strategy; together, tool selection and search strategy determine the effectiveness of the search. Strategies that are appropriate for the various types of tools discussed in Part 2 are presented along with the tools themselves. Guides to reference sources identified in chapter 13 assist the searcher in identifying appropriate sources. As explained in chapter 5, librarians are increasingly involved in developing gateways or portals to guide users in the selection of electronic resources.

SUMMARY AND CONCLUSION

An understanding of the way in which the bibliographic universe is organized is essential to effective, efficient searching. The two primary types of access mechanisms discussed in this chapter are library catalogs and indexes, each of which is presented as an ideal type—catalogs providing access to a particular library's collection and indexes providing access to journal articles in a particular subject area. In actuality, each of these types exists in less pure forms, and the distinctions between them are becoming less clear-cut, particularly when they coexist in the same electronic environment. Despite, and perhaps because of, the increasing complexity of the bibliographic world, it is important to keep in mind the fundamental principles of bibliographic control such as arrangement, collocation and authority control, and depth and comprehensiveness of indexing.

Exploiting the power of bibliographic organization to conduct effective, efficient searches takes practice and experience. Thinking critically about the process as one goes along, as well as observing the behavior of others (librarians and users alike), can yield valuable insight into how best to assist and instruct others to find information. Although the searching process will vary from individual to individual, two general strategies for searching, specific-to-general and general-to-specific, can be used effectively. The selection of appropriate reference tools, a critical component to the success of a search, can be made easier by consulting bibliographies of reference works or online gateways, and the selection of appropriate terminology can be facilitated by consulting sources that link various controlled vocabularies together. The application of online and computer technologies has affected the bibliographic world, both by making it more complex and by offering librarians the challenge and the means to improve access to information.

NOTES

1.   Patrick Wilson, "The Catalog as Access Mechanism: Background and Concepts," *Library Resources & Technical Services* 27 (January/March 1983): 5–6.

2.   Priscilla Caplan, *Metadata Fundamentals for All Librarians* (Chicago: American Library Association, 2003), 192 pp.

3.   U.S. Library of Congress, Cataloging Policy and Support Office, *Library of Congress Subject Headings*, 32nd ed., 6 vols. (Washington, D.C.: Library of Congress, 2010).

4.   Minnie Earle Sears, *Sears List of Subject Headings*, 20th ed., ed. Joseph Miller (New York: H. W. Wilson, 2010), 872 pp.

5.   Michael Gorman, "Yesterday's Heresy—Today's Orthodoxy: An Essay on the Changing Face of Descriptive Cataloging," *College & Research Libraries* 50 (November 1989): 626–34.

6.   *Readers' Guide to Periodical Literature*, 1900–. (New York: H. W. Wilson, 1905–).

7.   *Education Index*, 1929–. (New York: H. W. Wilson, 1932–).

8.   *Index Medicus* (Washington, D.C.: National Library of Medicine, 1960–2004).

9.   Thomas Mann, "Why LC Subject Headings Are More Important Than Ever," *American Libraries* 34 (October 2003): 52–54.

10.   Michael Gorman, "Authority Control in the Context of Bibliographic Control in the Electronic Environment," *Cataloging & Classification Quarterly* 38 (October 2004): 11–22.

11.   Alva T. Stone, "That Elusive Concept of Aboutness: The Year's Work in Subject Analysis, 1992," *Library Resources & Technical Services* 37 (July 1993): 277–97.

12.   Mary Dykstra, "LC Subject Headings Disguised as a Thesaurus," *Library Journal* 113 (March 1, 1988): 42–46; and "Can Subject Headings Be Saved?" *Library Journal* 113 (September 15, 1988): 55–58.

13.   Frederick G. Kilgour, "Origins of Coordinate Searching," *Journal of the American Society for Information Science* 48 (April 1997): 340–48.

14.   Examples of such articles appear regularly in the journals *Online* and *Searcher*.

15.   Carol Collier Kuhlthau, *Seeking Meaning: A Process Approach to Library and Information Services*, 2nd ed. (Westport, CT: Libraries Unlimited, 2004), 247 pp.

16.   Marcia J. Bates, "Indexing and Access for Digital Libraries and the Internet: Human, Database, and Domain Factors," *Journal of the American Society for Information Science* 49 (November 1998): 1185–205; Carol Collier Kuhlthau, "Learning in Digital Libraries: An Information Search Process Approach," *Library Trends* 45 (Spring 1997): 708–24.

17.   Marcia J. Bates, "Information Search Tactics," *Journal of the American Society for Information Science* 30 (July 1979): 205–14; Amanda Spink and Tefko Saracevic, "Interaction in Information Retrieval: Selection and Effectiveness of Search Terms," *Journal of the American Society for Information Science* 48 (August 1997): 741–61; Mirja Iivonen and Diane H. Sonnenwald, "From Translation to Navigation of Different Discourses: A Model of Search Term Selection during the Pre-Online Stage of the Search Process," *Journal of the American Society for Information Science* 49 (April 1998): 312–26.

18.   Micheline Hancock-Beaulieu and Stephen Walker, "An Evaluation of Automatic Query Expansion in an Online Library Catalogue," *Journal of Documentation* 48 (December 1992): 406–21.

19.   *Physicians' Desk Reference* (Montvale, NJ: Medical Economics, 1946–).

20.   U.S. National Library of Medicine, *Medical Subject Headings*. http://www.nlm.nih.gov/mesh/.

21.   Unified Medical Language System. http://www.nlm.nih.gov/research/umls/.

22.   Peter J. Rolla, "Can User-Supplied Data Improve Subject Access to Library Collections?" *Library Resources & Technical Services* 53 (July 2009): 174–84.

23.   Karen Markey, "The Online Library Catalog: Paradise Lost and Paradise Regained?" *D-Lib Magazine* 13 (January/February 2007). http://www.dlib.org/dlib/january07/markey/01markey.html.

24.   *Psychological Abstracts* (Washington, D.C.: American Psychological Association, 1927–2006). Included online in *PsycINFO*.

25.   Stanley Wilder, "Baker's Smudges," *Library Journal* 131 (September 1, 2006): 30–32.

ADDITIONAL READINGS

Beall, Jeffrey. "The Weaknesses of Full-Text Searching." *Journal of Academic Librarianship* 34 (2008): 438–44.

Noting that over the past 15 years, most information retrieval has gone from searching based on rich metadata to full-text searching, Beall provides a detailed analysis of the challenges posed by this shift.

Breeding, Marshall. "Automation Marketplace 2010: New Models, Core Systems." *Library Journal* 135 (April 1, 2010): 22–36.

In his latest annual update on library automation systems, Breeding describes trends in the modern interface to online catalogs. Such systems offer relevancy-ranked results, a single search box, faceted navigation, and enriched content beyond the basic MARC records.

Caplan, Priscilla. *Metadata Fundamentals for All Librarians*. Chicago: American Library Association, 2003. 192 pp.

Defining metadata as "structured information about an information resource of any media type or format," Caplan divides the contents of her book into two parts. Part 1 presents an informative tutorial on metadata principles and practice, and Part 2 has a series of chapters on different metadata schemes, including library cataloging, Dublin Core, and others.

Chowdhury, G. G., and Sudatta Chowdhury. *Organizing Information: From the Shelf to the Web*. London: Facet Publishing, 2007. 230 pp.

This text covers both library approaches (catalogs and bibliographies, classification, subject indexing) and non-library approaches (e.g., Internet-based) to organizing information, including the principles, tools, and techniques needed to do this effectively.

Library of Congress, Working Group on the Future of Bibliographic Control. *On the Record: Report of the Library of Congress Working Group on the Future of Bibliographic Control*. Washington, D.C.: Library of Congress, 2008. 44 pp. http://www.loc.gov/biblio graphic-future/news/lcwg-ontherecord-jan08-final.pdf.

Convened by the Library of Congress, the Working Group considered bibliographic control in general and investigated issues relating to management of library data and catalogs as well as the current technology context. The Working Group envisions a future for bibliographic control that will be collaborative, decentralized, international in scope, and Web-based.

Mann, Thomas. *Library Research Models: A Guide to Classification, Cataloging and Computers*. New York: Oxford University Press, 1993. 248 pp.

By presenting a variety of models for searching, Mann raises the reader's awareness of the extent to which expectations affect results. The author focuses on the analysis of extensive information searches rather than short reference queries. His years of experience as a librarian in large research libraries led him to propose a "methods of searching" model that provides a lively counterpoint to traditional assumptions that have guided library practice.

O'Dochartaigh, Niall. *Internet Research Skills: How to Do Your Literature Search and Find Research Information Online*. Los Angeles: Sage, 2007. 169 pp.

Cautioning that "the Internet is not an organized system," the author provides a clear and concise guide to search strategies for students in the humanities and social sciences. Chapters cover books; articles; subject guides; searching keyword search engines; interaction, news, and multimedia; governments, archives, and statistics; and evaluation and citation.

Taylor, Arlene G., and Daniel N. Joudrey. *The Organization of Information*. 3rd ed. Westport, CT: Libraries Unlimited, 2009. 512 pp.

This introductory text gives an excellent overview of the principles of organizing recorded information of various types. Within a broad context, the authors enable the reader to see how organization facilitates use regardless of the specific set of principles used or the type of materials organized.

Wakimoto, Jina Choi. "Scope of the Library Catalog in Times of Transition." *Cataloging & Classification Quarterly* 47 (2009): 409–26.

Writing in response to the question "What should the scope of the catalog be, particularly an academic library catalog?," Wakimoto argues that users will be best served if coverage is expanded to provide access to electronic resources, e-books and e-journals, digital collections, and selected Web resources. She also advocates enriching records to provide more complete descriptions through the inclusion of tables of contents and summaries.

White, Howard D., Marcia J. Bates, and Patrick Wilson. *For Information Specialists: Interpretations of Reference and Bibliographic Work*. Norwood, NJ: Ablex, 1992. 310 pp.

> This collection of essays by three seminal writers in the field of storage and retrieval of bibliographic materials provides insight into the tools and processes of information work. The authors move between highly conceptual themes that are often provocative and idiosyncratic and specific and practical suggestions for exploiting the principles and practice of bibliographic organization in strategic ways. The volume contains essays by Bates and Wilson that are expansions of the works cited in this chapter.

Younger, Jennifer A. "Resources Description in the Digital Age." *Library Trends* 45 (Winter 1997): 462–87.

> This article provides the reader with an overview of the ways in which the library community is addressing the need for a comprehensive, updated approach to describing items in a digital environment. The author links the traditional accomplishments of cataloging and indexing to new approaches such as metadata and does so in the context of the fundamental objectives of the library catalog.

Chapter

5

Electronic Resources for Reference

Kathleen M. Kluegel

This is a reference book. It is not a printout of the Internet.[1]

INTRODUCTION

Many of the chapters in this book identify specific electronic resources for reference service. Others refer to the role of electronic resources in the provision of reference service. This chapter puts these resources into the context of the history and development of electronic information resources. The focus here is on those resources that might be termed "professional grade" reference tools, that is, resources that were developed as reference works or as parts of the reference infrastructure. Another goal is to show the structure that changes bits and bytes into information resources and the relation between structure and function. With this perspective, one can analyze how a tool works and how to identify its structure and then can translate that structure into effective search strategies. These skills transcend any medium and any information delivery option.

The chapter also examines the revolution in the creation and distribution of digital information of all kinds in the context of information services. This revolution has transformed the role of the reference librarian in information delivery services. It is changing the fundamental definition of the reference collection as well. Professional reference tools are now used in a context of blogs, news feeds, and other formal and informal resources that everyone can access and use. This has further ramifications in the design and organization of information services in and through the library.

HISTORY OF ELECTRONIC RESOURCES

No discussion of electronic resources for reference would be complete without mentioning a few key early players. In the mid-1960s the National Library of Medicine in the United States created computer programs that enabled highly trained searchers to retrieve citations to relevant literature from its internal databases through a batch searching system called MEDLARS (Medical Literature Analysis and Retrieval System). When it went online in the early 1970s, it became *MEDLINE* (MEDLARS ONLINE). The *MEDLINE* system was critical to the diffusion of medical information to researchers across the country. Similarly, the National Technical Information Service system was developed to make reports of federally funded research projects accessible to the research and development work of the nation's universities and businesses. Another early player in the advancement of sophisticated information retrieval systems was Lockheed's Dialog system, which started out as a means to allow company-wide sharing of aerospace and engineering information. By the mid-1970s, the Dialog information system had been applied to proprietary abstracting and indexing databases from many disciplines and made available to reference librarians and information centers in the United States and abroad on a cost-per-use charging system. Parallel developments were made by the System Development Corporation (SDC) and the Bibliographic Retrieval Services (BRS) corporations as well. They all provided powerful searching capabilities on the abstracting and indexing databases across nearly all disciplines. The book *A History of Online Information Services: 1963–1976* by Charles P. Bourne and Trudi Bellardo Hahn provides a more detailed introduction to the early days of information systems.[2]

Because of the complexities of the search and retrieval systems and the associated costs of the databases, the early information retrieval systems were used by trained and experienced reference librarians at the computer keyboard. Individual researchers, for the most part, did not have the time or inclination to learn the necessary codes and formulas for successful searching.

In time, these early mediated systems developed end-user versions that were intended to be easily searched by individuals without specialized training. The typical end-user systems were distributed to libraries with the data and the search system written on CD-ROMs. These end-user systems provided much of the searching power of the mediated database search systems but without their associated time and cost pressures. Although the vast majority of these systems have migrated to the Web, there are still some legacy CD-ROM databases to be found in most large libraries.

Now there has been a vast expansion of the world of end-user searching far beyond the scope of the local CD-ROM workstation and far beyond the walls of the reference room. The primary audience for current electronic information resources is the end user. With the development of the Web, combined with the proliferation of low-cost computers, the mass audience needed to support these expanded services now exists. The Web provides a common platform for the delivery of electronic resources to users: it is format-independent. One of the Web's primary attractions is the ability to provide access to electronic resources to any location on the globe. Librarians are now able to provide resources to their users wherever they happen to be. To provide these services, each library subscribes to proprietary Web-based resources for the library's primary user community. Many libraries, of course, also provide links to

---

BOX 5.1
THE LAW OF THE INSTRUMENT

If a new tool has been acquired, everything must be processed with that tool. This law is best demonstrated by a two-year-old and a hammer. The next best demonstration is the Web: If a library has a Web site, everything must go up on the Web.

---

more scholarly and authoritative free Web sites and resources. The proprietary Web resources, such as indexes and abstracts, are the focus of the next section.

When electronic resources are redesigned for the Web, much of the structure of the command-based search services is built into the search screen. In place of highly structured search command languages, most of these services provide a point-and-click interface with a "fill in the box" search window designed for easy searching by the end user. These point-and-click interfaces resemble the Web search engines such as Google and Yahoo. The results are displayed on the screen for review. The user can select items to be printed or downloaded. In some cases, with a few more clicks, the user will be connected to a site with the full text of the source online, ready to be read, downloaded, imported into the user's own database, and/or printed. This system for providing electronic information services can be seen at thousands upon thousands of workstations in homes, offices, and libraries throughout the world.

One consequence of the change in the primary focus for electronic resources is the change in the way reference librarians use their expertise and understanding of databases. A few years ago, their role was to serve as an intermediary between the complex database search system and the person needing the information. Now it is to serve as coach and tutor for the end user conducting the search. Another critical role is to guide the user to the appropriate information resource. In any of these roles, an understanding of the concepts and mechanics of information retrieval is essential for reference librarians. It can be argued that it is more important to fully understand a search system when one is a coach because of the consequences of an error. If, as an experienced searcher, one mis-remembers a feature, the resulting search failure is readily apparent and can be corrected immediately. If one makes a similar error as a coach, the inexperienced user may never realize the error or the implications of the error, never understanding why the search failed. The next two sections enable the reference librarian to understand the deep structure of databases and explain the concepts and mechanics of information retrieval.

DATABASES

The term "database" needs to be explored more fully to gain an understanding of and appreciation for it. A *database* is a set of information items formatted into defined structures with additional elements designed to assist retrieval. In the current context, the information is likely to be text. The text can be a basic bibliographic citation including the authors' names and identifying the source; it can be an enhanced citation including subject headings and abstracts; or it can be the full text of the article or report. Text can also include numbers and charts. In a database, these elements have been assigned to fields, which are defined, organized, and labeled according to the rules of the database.

Frequently, each field has a particular format for the elements within it. For example, an author's name is likely to be structured with the surname first, followed by a comma and some elements of the forenames. This structure for names is ubiquitous, appearing in the telephone directory, personal address books, endnotes, and the like, so that it is nearly invisible to us. The more formal term for the kinds of structures and elements that we use to organize and index information is *metadata*.

The term metadata is defined as "data about data" or "data associated with data." We encounter, use, manipulate, and create metadata many times a day every day. One example is seen in the organization and arrangement of our daily newspaper. Each part of the newspaper is assigned to a section and, in the world of print, a page. Online, each article may have a particular URL. The section is a metadata element, as is the page number. These metadata elements are shown in the "What's inside" index that newspapers put on the front page or on the inside front page. In the case of a newspaper where the full text is online, the "What's inside" index is more likely displayed as a menu along the left side of the "front page" of that day's newspaper. Each article is composed of many elements, and each element has a role to play in the display, arrangement, and retrieval of the article. For example, pieces of metadata are attached to the headline. Some of it drives the display so that the headline appears in a larger, bolder font than the body of the article. Hidden elements of the headline metadata allow the newspaper's users to search for words in the headline and retrieve the needed article.

In the kinds of databases under discussion, such as an abstracting and indexing service, the kinds and roles of metadata grow in complexity. This database design with metadata elements is the result of very deliberate decisions by database producers and has consequences for searching. Box 5.2 shows a made-up example of how a typical entry from a telephone directory could be structured in the database.

In the telephone directory example in Box 5.2, the field labels allow the printing software to accomplish two essential tasks: sorting and formatting. The sorting can be imagined as a series of sets of slots. Each record will be sent through the appropriate slot at each level for further sorting. At each level, the sorting becomes finer. We are most familiar with telephone directories in which the following sorting and formatting rules are embedded: the initial sort would be at the record type, which determines the segment of the directory; the second level would be at the initial letter of the surname; and so forth. The sorting rules for the ordering of records in which the first several elements are identical would be complex. For example, with very common surnames, the differences between entries might occur at the street address level. With very unusual surnames, the sorting algorithm could stop at the surname level. Decisions about how to deal with compound surnames or hyphenated forenames would have to be built into the sorting software.

Once the records were sorted, the field labels would be used to determine formatting. The surname element would be in bold, at the furthest left place in the column.

BOX 5.2
SAMPLE DATABASE ENTRY

Record Number = qs122333
Record Type = Residential
Surname = Hunkle
First Forename = Welkins
First Middle Initial = Q
First Title = DDS
Street Address = 123 Maple Avenue
City = Hometown
Telephone Number = 555-6789
Second Forename = Pat
Second Middle Initial = Q
Second Title = MD
Street Address = 123 Maple Avenue
City = Hometown
Telephone Number = 555-1234

The forename and initials elements would then be set in lighter typeface, indented under the surname header. The street address would be abbreviated and put on the same line as the telephone number. From this simple example, one can see the kind of decision making that is required to build a database with enough structure for it to be functional. The developers have to anticipate all the forms of the information and take into account all the possible variations.

When applied to a database of bibliographic citations, this database-building process becomes very complex. Even a very basic bibliographic metadata structure has to deal with the huge variety of names, journal titles, languages, abbreviations, volume and issue numbering, and pagination. All of the relevant data elements must have a field that supports their form. For example, ISSN numbers need to be 8 characters long, ISBN numbers 10 (or 13, depending on the date of the item). To be of more use, the database structure must be explicitly built and labeled to support subject headings, descriptors, identifiers, and other elements that can also be added to the record. These elements are usually the results of human indexing.

SEARCHING CAPABILITIES

If a database remains a static set of information records, the structural elements identified in the previous section would determine how the information could be arranged and presented. For example, the telephone directory sorted, formatted, and printed for our hypothetical town can be viewed as a static database. As a static database, the telephone directory is useful but not very interesting. When the telephone directory or any other set of information becomes a dynamic and searchable database, it becomes more complex and interesting. The number of access points grows from one to many, and one gains the power to manipulate the entries. How does the searching process work in databases?

One of the more important capabilities of search engines is to create sets that meet user-defined criteria and manipulate them. Search engines use logic, algorithms, and character-string matching to accomplish this. "Searching" the telephone book with one's eyes involves similar processes. One looks for names that match the initial surname string in the query. Within that list, further searching looks for a match on the forename, even if it is there only as an initial. To choose among the possible matches, the searcher checks the address to see if it matches what is known about the person. With search systems and databases, the fields, data elements, and structure of a database interact with the search engine capabilities in highly specific ways to create the information retrieval possibilities. One of the more important tools used in search systems is Boolean logic.

Boolean Logic

Boolean logic is a form of symbolic logic named after George Boole, the 19th-century English mathematician who developed it. Boolean logic uses common words as logical operators in very specific ways to create and manipulate sets. Some of these Boolean operators are AND, OR, and NOT.

The Boolean operator OR is used to create a set by making an item eligible for inclusion if it meets at least one of the stated criteria: an item would be included in a set if it meets the condition A OR the condition B OR the condition C, and so on. In creating a set of citrus fruit, one might use the following Boolean string: oranges OR grapefruit OR lemons OR limes OR kumquats. This set is more inclusive than a set that has a single criterion for acceptance—for example, oranges. One way to visualize Boolean logic is with Venn diagrams. In these diagrams, shadings indicate the results of each of the operators. The Venn diagram for OR is shown in Figure 5.1.

The Boolean operator AND is used to make a more restrictive set by requiring that an item meet both the conditions stated to be included in the final set: an item

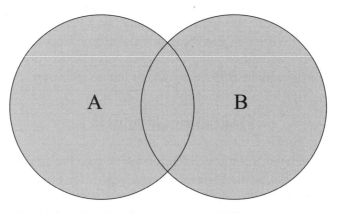

Figure 5.1. The Boolean operator OR in a Venn diagram.

would be included only if it meets condition A AND condition B. One could use the Boolean AND to create a set containing only those books written by Isaac Asimov which contained the word "robot." The Boolean string would be "Isaac Asimov AND robot." The Venn diagram for AND is shown in Figure 5.2.

The Boolean AND and the Boolean OR are concepts that the beginning searcher may have trouble keeping straight. The use of the terms is somewhat at odds with the ordinary usage of the English words "and" and "or." In ordinary English usage, "or" implies a choice—to select one item is to exclude the others—whereas the Boolean OR expands and includes all of the items. An example from a restaurant can highlight this difference. On a breakfast menu, one might be offered toast or a muffin or a bagel. From the customer's perspective, the English "or" means the customer must select an item from the "breakfast bread" set. Viewing this menu from the restaurant's perspective, it has used the Boolean OR ("toast" OR "muffin" OR "bagel") to create the set "breakfast breads."

The Boolean AND and the English "and" produce different outcomes as well. The English "and" works through addition: it adds all the items joined by the "and." The Boolean AND selects items that include all the named elements. To highlight this difference, one can look at another restaurant example. In a restaurant that allows one to choose one item from column A *and* one from column B *and* one from column C, the result of an order will be a plate that contains three items. The result of a Boolean search for A AND B AND C is one item that contains all three elements, an unlikely dish in any restaurant.

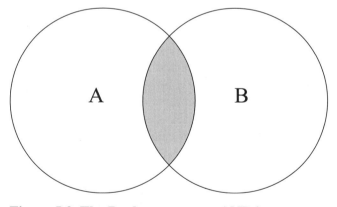

Figure 5.2. The Boolean operator AND in a Venn diagram.

BOX 5.3
RESULTS OF A BOOLEAN SEARCH

If you send a reference librarian to the store with a Boolean list of "sugar" AND "flour" AND "eggs," you will get a cookie.

The Boolean operator NOT (sometimes AND NOT) is also used to make a more restrictive set. It first creates a set of items that meet the condition A and then removes from the set those items that also meet condition B. To create a set of trees that were not deciduous, one would use the Boolean NOT to exclude deciduous from the set of trees. The Boolean string would be "trees NOT deciduous." The Venn diagram for NOT is shown in figure 5.3.

Boolean operators form the essential machinery for making computerized information retrieval precise and effective. With Boolean logic, one can manipulate databases containing a million records to produce the single item that contains all and only the information specified by the user. It is most effective on databases that have a higher proportion of structured text and relatively little unstructured or "free" text.

Truncation

Another capability for database manipulation occurs because of the computer's vast list-making potential. It can compile a set of materials that meet multiple criteria simultaneously. The term "truncation" refers to shortening a word or eliminating some characters from a longer term to pick up variants. It is a form of the Boolean operator OR. In truncation, the computer is told to put into a single set all those items that share a common sequence of characters, even if they do not share all the same characters. This process can also be called a "wildcard" search or *stemming*. For example, when a user searches for the truncated term "librar," the computer is asked to make a set of items that contain the term "library" or "libraries" or "librarians" or "librarian" or "librarianship." The symbols used to indicate truncation will vary from system to system. The asterisk (*) is one symbol that is commonly used, but others, including the question mark (?), the colon (:), and the plus sign (+), are also used in different systems.

Truncation can take place to the left, to the right, or in the middle of the core characters. Truncation can also involve the replacement of several characters or a single character. In the previous example, because the truncation occurred to the right of the core characters, it is called right-hand truncation. It can be further described as a multiple-character truncation. If the truncation occurs to the left of the core characters, it is left-hand truncation. For example, left-hand truncation with the core characters "ship" would retrieve, at least, all the records containing any of the terms

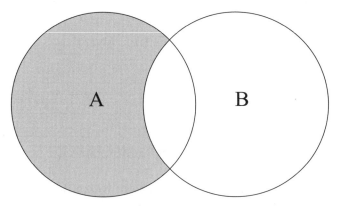

Figure 5.3. The Boolean operator NOT in a Venn diagram (A NOT B).

"librarianship," "guardianship," "statesmanship," "leadership," and "starship." When truncation occurs in the middle of the core characters, it is called *internal truncation*. An example of internal truncation would be "Labo#r" where the "#" is the internal truncation symbol. If this were a single-character substitution system, in which the symbol can stand for either nothing or a single character, this term would pick up items that contained the terms "labor" or "labour." If it is a multiple-character system, in which the symbol can stand for more than one alternate character, the set could include "labor," "labour," "laborer," or "labourer."

Frequently, systems allow one to select a single-character or multiple-character truncation method in order to tailor the search to one's needs. Truncation allows the user to acknowledge and compensate for some amount of uncertainty in the source information, as well as for other, more predictable variations in the database. When using truncation, the searcher must take care to avoid unwanted hits, such as "re-adjustment" from a search for a truncated term such as "read:" or "Warsaw" from truncating "war?"

In Web-based search engines, stemming or truncation is often applied without any express action on the part of the searcher. Each term input is matched to a set of terms that have the same stem. These multiple variants on the stem are then searched in the database or file.

Stemming and truncation are some of the ways to accomplish "fuzzy matches," that is, to count as a match those terms that are "close" to the ones input. "Close" can be defined in several ways. With stemming and truncation, the definition is tied to matching the first several characters of the term. With other forms, the terms can be determined to be matching based on other factors, such as common misspellings.

The searches that have been described here are usually termed "keyword" searches, to identify that the matches are conducted in areas of the document that have been coded for searching. Typically, in structured databases such as an abstracting database, keyword searches operate on meaning-carrying words or terms in the citation and abstract of the item. Parts of the record such as the author's name or the name of the journal are usually excluded from the list of keywords that are operated upon. Keyword searching, even when used with Boolean operators, is a somewhat hit-or-miss way to find material in the database. In the typical interface, the results are not broken down into matches per term, so that one cannot assess the effectiveness or retrieval power of each term in the end results. Typically, a search engine responds with the advice "you might try another strategy" only when the results are zero. In large databases with abstracts, it is unusual to find zero matches. A keyword search works only as well as the searcher is correct in assumptions about spelling, structure, and formatting of terms within the database, as well as about the content of the database. Most search systems also provide ways for the searcher to learn more about all these aspects of the database through specialized functions. Search systems usually provide a browseable display of terms that have a relationship with the term of interest.

Displaying the Index

An additional feature of some of the search engines used with electronic reference sources is the ability to display a range of terms in a context. This is a function of the computer's ability to build and display multiple indexes to a single database. A primary index, called the *inverted index* or inverted file, is built on an alphabetical basis, in which each retrievable word in the database is listed in a single sequence. This inverted index is part of the reason that a computer is able to manipulate the file at incredible speeds. It goes directly to the term requested, which is linked to the records containing that term. Without the inverted index, the computer would have to scan the entire database looking for the requested sequence of characters. The main inverted file is called the *basic index*. In an operation that may be called "browse" or "expand" or "neighbor," the computer displays the requested section of the basic index, as shown in Figure 5.4. This allows one to see a term while it is surrounded by the terms immediately preceding and succeeding it alphabetically. Often, there is an identification of the number of records in the database that contain that term. This feature allows one to identify the most productive terms to retrieve a concept. It brings to the eye some of the perhaps unanticipated terms that are in close proximity and allows one to preview the effects of truncation.

A variation of the basic index occurs in those databases that have a controlled indexing vocabulary. In these databases, the producers create and maintain a list of subject headings, called *descriptors*, that must be used by the indexers to identify the subject of the item. Descriptors are another metadata element. Frequently, these descriptors are linked with other related subject headings through the use of concepts such as "related term," "broader term," and "narrower term." When such relationships exist among the descriptors, the result is called a *thesaurus*. In some databases, an index of the descriptors is created. In others, the thesaurus itself is an index, with the related terms identified and directly retrievable. Figure 5.5 is 2 examples of an online

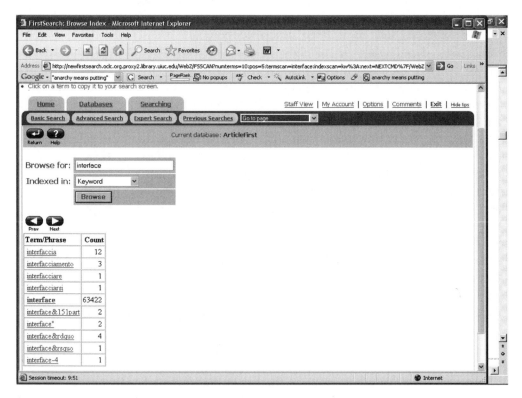

Figure 5.4. Basic index display from *Article1st* on FirstSearch.

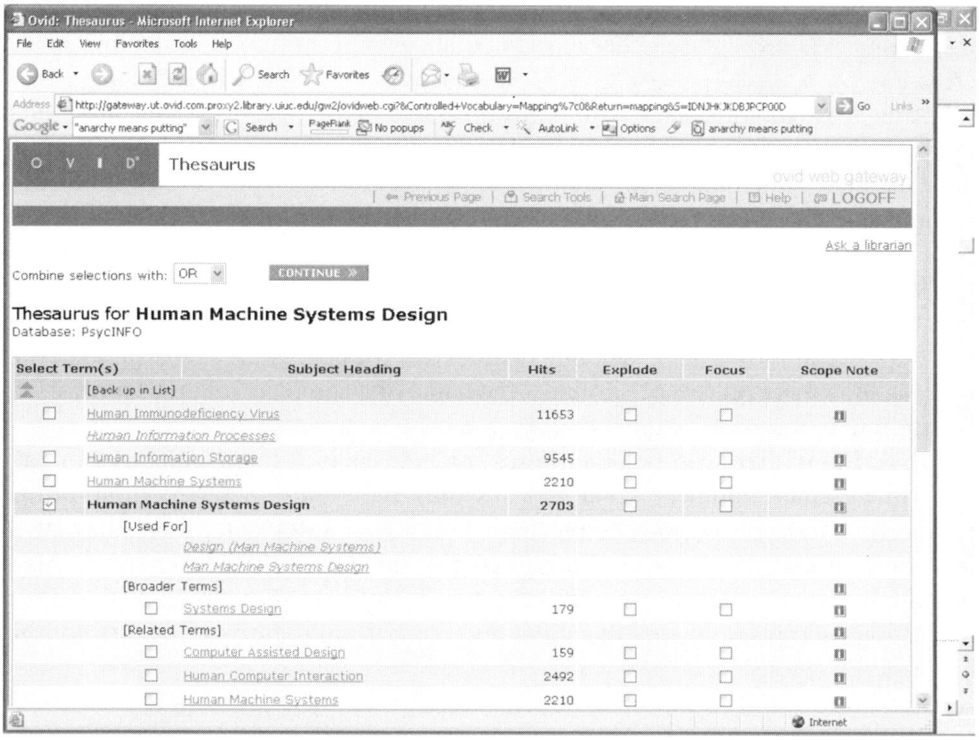

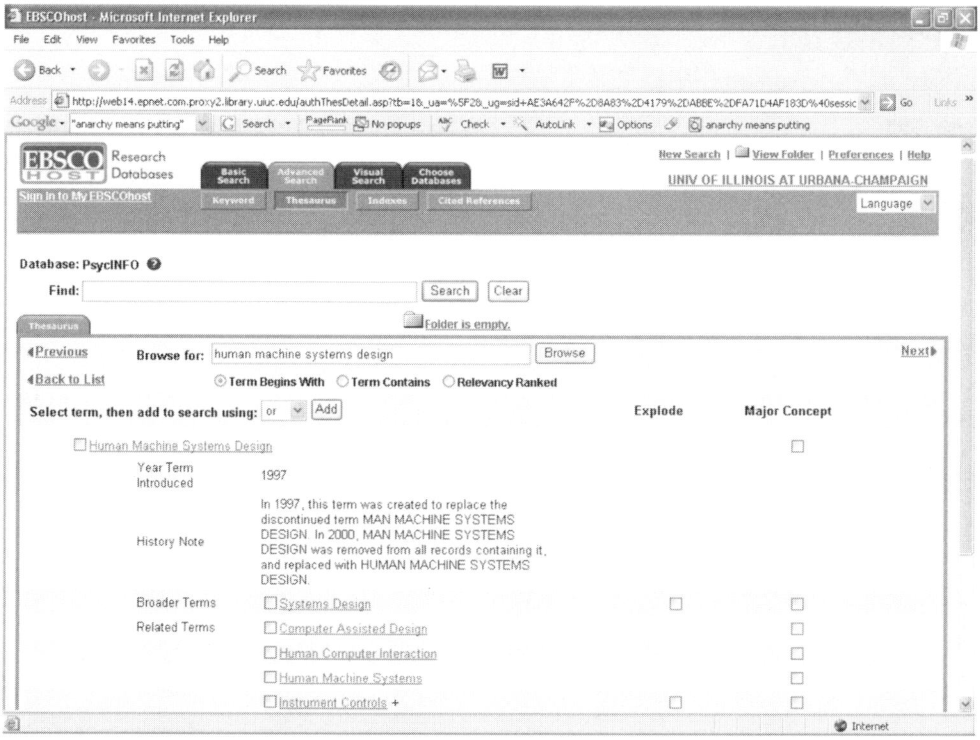

Figure 5.5. Online thesaurus display from *PsycInfo* on Ovid and EBSCO.

thesaurus display. The display identifies the subject heading and the synonyms it replaces, and it allows the searcher to manipulate each term further to explore related terms.

A database might also contain terms that have more meaning if they are used to build yet another kind of index of metadata, one in which the function of the term is made explicit. For example, an author's name has more meaning and is more easily manipulated if it can be seen in the context of other authors' names. This can be seen most readily when imagining how to search for authors whose names are also nouns, for example, Hill, Stone, and Case. These names are much more useful when pulled into a separate formatted index with the standard rules for name display. One can pick out variations of a single author's name if this list is organized on a surname-first basis, as shown in Figure 5.6. Similarly, the name of a company might be more useful if it appears in a context of other company names or variants.

In addition, there can be other bases for indexes in a single database. In databases that contain numbers, some indexes may show these numbers in an ordinal list. For example, in business directories containing sales data, there may be an index that shows sales in order from largest to smallest, or there may be scales of magnitude for sales figures, showing the ranges. In other directories, ZIP codes or population figures may be more salient and could form their own indexes within a database.

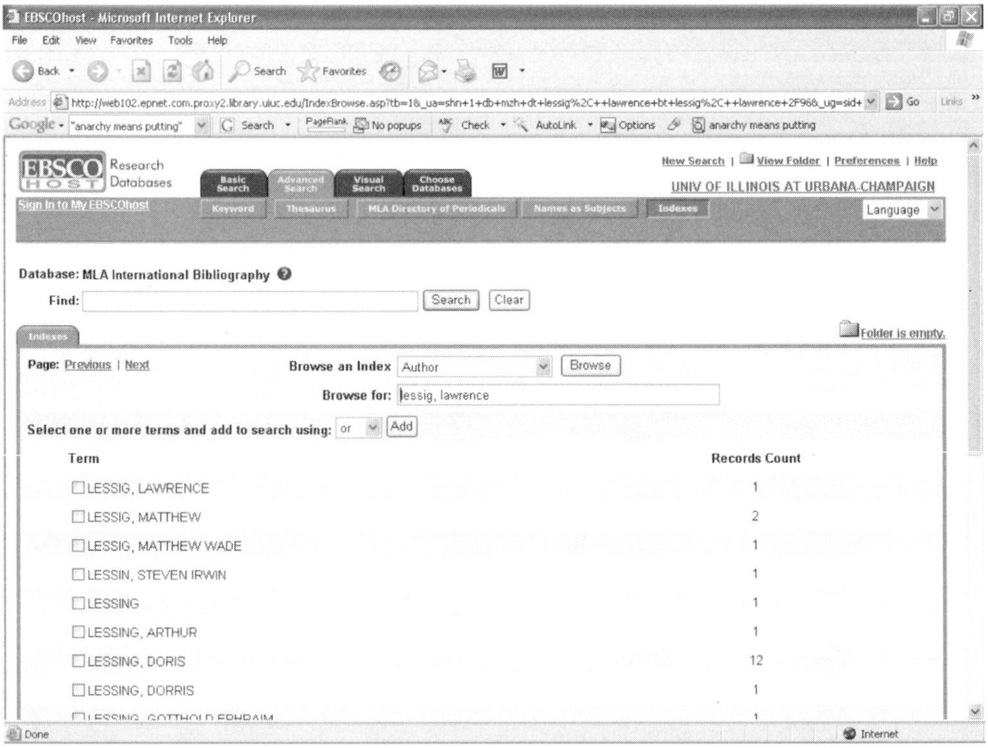

Figure 5.6. Author index display from *MLA International Bibliography* on EBSCO.

Positional Searching

An additional aspect of the basic index allows for great precision in identifying material. Each term in the basic index has markers that show its position in each of the records in which it appears. Most computer retrieval systems allow a searcher to specify a particular positional relationship between two terms, called *proximity*. A system will have a set of specialized proximity operators that name the positional relationship needed. For example, to specify that two terms must be right next to each other, one could use an "adjacency" operator. In some search interfaces, the proximity operator is expressed through the use of quotation marks, which restrict the search to retrieving only those records where the phrase is exactly as written. One could also specify that the terms be within a determined number of words or in the same sentence, field, or paragraph. Proximity operators are a refinement on the Boolean AND operator, further specifying the conditions in which an item is determined to "match" through the positional relationship with another term. In this way, a searcher can specify that the system retrieve only those items that contain a phrase, such as "quality circles," even if that phrase is not a descriptor in the database.

Proximity operators use coded data about the word position of each searchable term in a database to determine retrieval. As each term from each document in the database is added to the basic index, it is coded with details on its position within the document. This would include its location in a document, field, paragraph, and sentence. An example of this type of coding is shown in Figure 5.7. This system of proximity-coded searching is very fast, given that it depends on simple mathematical handling of the positional codes of the search terms.

In this hypothetical example, the coded numbers in the parentheses refer to the record number, the paragraph, the sentence, and the word within the sentence. To find the term "quality" in the same sentence as "design," the search system will look at the record number for each term. If the record number matches, it will compare paragraph numbers for each term with the same record number. If both paragraph numbers match, it will look for matching sentence numbers. If all three numbers for both terms match, the document will be retrieved by the search system. For the system to select the phrase "quality circles," the numbers for record, paragraph, and sentence must match, and the word numbers must differ by one. In most systems that offer proximity searching, the searcher can specify word order as well as degrees of closeness. This provides a great deal of precision in retrieval. It is critical to remember that each search system will have its own way to specify proximity. For many search systems, there is a special operator used to indicate proximity, such as *adj* or *near*. Other systems have two operators: one is used if word order is important, and the other if word order does

"Quality (RN1,P1,S1,W1) circles (RN1,P1,S1,W2) in (RN1,P1,S1,W3) database (RN1,P1,S1,W4) management (RN1,P1,S1,W5)   and   (RN1,P1,S1,W6)   design (RN1,P1,S1,W7)."

The (RN1,P2,S1,W1) study (RN1,P2,S1,W2)....

Figure 5.7. Positional coding for proximity retrieval.

not matter. Typically, one is able to specify the number of words that can separate the terms. The searcher can specify that the first term must be within one, two, three, or any other number of words of the second term. In such a system, the search statement could look like this: S *guide n/3 Internet*. This would retrieve documents containing such phrases as "a new guide to the Internet," "world wide Internet guide," and so on, because the two terms are within three words of one another.

In any search system, there are elements that are included in the record for display purposes but are not searchable. In an online catalog system, for example, the bibliographic record is likely to show the size and number of pages in a monograph. However, there are no online catalog systems that will allow one to search and retrieve items based on either the size of the pages or their numbers, even though this would be a feature that some librarians would use at least from time to time to restrict their searches to retrieve materials usable in the time available to the patron.

The power of the computer to create, manipulate, display, and retrieve these multiple indexes to a single file is very important to users. When this is combined with the power of Boolean logic, it multiplies the possibilities for creatively manipulating databases to retrieve the needed information. Multiple access points and the ability to combine them also allow retrieval of materials for which the information is incomplete. If one knows the author's surname, a word from the title, and a decade in which the book was published, combining these elements with a Boolean AND is very likely to produce a set that contains the needed item and very few others.

Creating Search Strategies

The various search operators described previously can be used in combination with one another to create the complete search strategy. In most cases, search strategies are built step-by-step, incorporating information from each stage into refining, expanding, or modifying the original search. For example, one can put in three keywords combined with Boolean ANDs to get a very rough and ready estimate of the quantity of materials that may be of interest in a database. Scanning a few records retrieved in this way can point the way to improve the search. One record may have a subject heading or descriptor that encapsulates one aspect of the search topic more effectively than the keywords with which one began. This can also confirm that the database is likely to be productive because it has records with appropriate and relevant subject headings.

Beyond Boolean

Although Boolean logic is quite effective in many databases, it may be less effective in databases made up of full-text documents. These full-text databases tend to be quite unstructured, with natural language dominating whatever structured indexing language is associated with the text. In the course of a 10-page article, for example, many terms occur at least once and could therefore be retrieved in a simple Boolean search. Phrase searching, though more precise, will miss many documents because of the natural variations in expression in full-text materials.

An alternative search design that is more effective in these full-text databases looks beyond mere occurrence and tries to measure the relative importance of the terms within a document, through *weighting*. In weighting, the frequency with which a term appears in the database and in a document forms a ratio that helps determine how important that term is in the search and how much weight to give its appearances. A term that occurs frequently in one document while occurring relatively infrequently in the database as a whole will be more heavily weighted than another term that occurs with comparable frequency in both. A term, for example, that occurs in only 2 documents out of 100 will be weighted much more highly than one that occurs in 90 of the 100 documents. In *relevancy rankings*, the higher the proportion of search terms in a document, the higher the ranking in predicted relevancy. This is based on the logical assumption that if one compares two documents of the same size, the document with a high number of occurrences of a term is likely to be more "about" that term than the one with a low number of occurrences of that same term. With these search parameters, documents will be retrieved and displayed based on the relative weights and relevancy of the search terms.

In Figure 5.8, the sample sentence shows an example of a highly skewed document. The relevancy ranking for this document for the term "bird" is very high and for the term "seed" quite low.

Search Strategy

Understanding the search concepts discussed in this chapter is important in achieving effective and efficient searches. It is equally important to understand that these searching functions are expressed in different ways and combinations in each search system. Each system has an underlying set of operating assumptions that will govern the search and display process. These assumptions are called *defaults*. For example, a search system may have the Boolean AND as its default operator. In any search with two terms, it will search each term separately and combine the sets with the Boolean AND. Another search system may have a proximity operator as its default and will look for each set of two terms as a phrase. Each of these default operators will produce substantially different results for the same two search terms. Similarly, each search system will have a default display option. In nearly every system, a searcher is able to override the default option on a search-by-search basis. Sometimes it is a matter of finding a search menu and changing the operator. In other cases, it is necessary to explicitly type in the search operator. In any case, it is essential to discover what the search system defaults are. The concept of search defaults is one that can be a challenge to articulate to the user because defaults are typically invisible. Few search systems put an explanation in the "Keyword" search box that they are using the Boolean AND or proximity operators, for example. Users typically do not approach a search screen with an understanding of the underlying assumptions and operations at work.

> "The word *bird* is used in a great many phrases in English, for example, bird bath, bird seed, bird feeder, bird song, song birds, bird brain, eat like a bird, bird's eye, birds of a feather, a little bird told me, bird of paradise, and bird nest."

Figure 5.8. A sample document that would rank high on a search for "bird."

The steps that a searcher takes to find a set of materials that meet an information need make up the *search strategy*. The search strategy operates within the framework of the search system's mechanisms and the database structure and content. The goal of the search strategy to retrieve "all and only" the ideal set of relevant materials remains largely unattainable. Most of the decisions a searcher makes in the search strategy are made to achieve the appropriate balance between the two aims of information retrieval: precision and recall. *Precision* refers to getting only relevant material. *Recall* refers to getting all the relevant material. In a world where language is unambiguous and indexing is perfect, precision and recall would be the same. But in this world, because language is ambiguous and indexing imperfect, precision and recall are largely incompatible goals. For example, the word "program" is used to represent at least three rather different concepts. This affects precision because a search on the term "program" for one of these concepts will retrieve unrelated material that refers to either of the other two meanings of the term, which thus reduces precision. On the other hand, because of synonyms and changes in terminology over time, there are often a multitude of terms to describe a single concept. Searching for every possible term to achieve perfect recall is a demanding task. As a result, search strategies are a compromise between precision and recall.

Information professionals learn these concepts as well as search-building techniques as part of their professional training and experience. A reference librarian develops the equivalent of a pre-flight checklist for databases, with features, structures, and logical elements forming a matrix to be checked against the new or revised database, interface, or delivery system. The experienced reference librarian approaches a new electronic resource with this set of expected functions and capabilities and investigates the ways in which they are supported, displayed, or invoked.

An examination of the opening screen reveals some of the possibilities. A sample search or two will identify further answers. For example, a reference librarian might try to search for a compound surname, a surname with a prefix, or a hyphenated surname. The search system will respond with the desired item or will reveal how it deals with improperly formatted names. If the search screen is uninformative about the default search operators, a multiword search, with and without the Boolean operator explicitly typed in, will be revealing. Help commands can be invoked to see if they illuminate effective search strategies. This is standard exploratory behavior for reference librarians and information specialists because they have these elements in their mental framework (see Box 5.4). Alas, it remains largely an attribute of information

---

BOX 5.4
DOCUMENTING SEARCH FEATURES

A new electronic resource has been acquired by the reference librarian. You have been asked to write preliminary documentation on its search interface for the other reference librarians to use. You might start with how to search simple and compound names. How to search for exact phrases in titles might be another element. Make a list of the other search functions and features that you would test in the development of this documentation.

professionals because very few users have enough experience in structured information sources and retrieval to have derived these conceptual elements.

Bibliographic Control

One of the important efforts of librarians over many decades has been to provide bibliographic control over the cumulative cultural record, much of which has been recorded in print in books, journals, conference proceedings, government documents, and pamphlets. *Bibliographic control* is the term for the organization of representations of published items regardless of format, date, or location. Bibliographic control of these enormous numbers of items requires a substantial investment in the information infrastructure.

One can imagine a relatively simple system to arrange a list containing a hundred items, with the author's name being the primary sorting element, the title the secondary, and so on. We have seen these lists of citations at the end of books or dissertations, for example. When we expand the universe of items to be uniquely identified, represented, described, and sorted into the millions, the structures to support the enterprise must be scaled up dramatically. Entire sets of rules of description are required. The current set of rules to consistently describe these items is called the *Anglo-American Cataloguing Rules*. The second edition of this book was revised in 2002 by the Joint Steering Committee for Revision of AACR of the American Library Association. Similarly, subject access to the materials in the bibliographic universe requires a comprehensive set of subject headings, provided in the form of the *Library of Congress Subject Headings* (LCSH) list. Necessarily, this title is updated frequently and in 2010 was in its 32nd edition. The third element of this bibliographic control triangle is the classification number or call number. The primary control for call numbers is the *LC Classification Outline*, created by the Library of Congress in 1903 (with the original title *Classification. Outline scheme of classes*); under its present title, this publication was in its 7th edition in 2003. For libraries using the Dewey Decimal system, there is a corresponding title, *Dewey Decimal Classification and Relative Index*. Originally devised by Melvil Dewey, it has been updated and revised since his original design and was in its 23rd edition as of 2011. Among these three titles are thousands of pages of rules and formulas and words and phrases for metadata construction to describe, collocate, and index millions upon millions of items, ranging from pamphlets to tomes to e-books and Web sites. These rules and formulas allow the reference librarian to say with assurance, "This book is this book and not another one."

The locus for an important part of bibliographic control for these millions of items is in the online union catalog or *bibliographic utility*. Its very name suggests heavy-duty work in the library. Utilities provide us with the essential resources we need: electricity, water, and heat. Bibliographic utilities at their center provide essential bibliographic control through their large databases of shared cataloging. The records in the database are created by the combined efforts of large libraries, such as the Library of Congress, other national libraries, and contributing member libraries in many countries. The major online union catalog in the United States is *WorldCat* (from OCLC), with more than 25,900 contributing member libraries and institutions. In 2006, as a result of a merger with OCLC, the Research Libraries Group's Research Libraries Information Network (RLIN) online catalog was integrated into the *WorldCat* database. *WorldCat*'s services are discussed further in chapter 20.

Bibliographic utilities have at the heart of their databases a set of bibliographic records in a specific machine-readable form, called MARC. MARC stands for MAchine-Readable Cataloging, and it is both a standard format and a set of records conforming to that standard. In 1968, the Library of Congress developed the first MARC format for monographs in English. MARC standards for other languages and other materials followed. The members of the bibliographic utilities contribute their acquisition and cataloging records in MARC format to the databases. In this instance, librarians are database producers as well as database users. After its integration of the RLIN bibliographic records, *WorldCat* contained (as of March 2011) around 219 million records for materials that date from 1000 B.C.E. These 219 million records had 1.7 billion individual holdings (see a sample record in Figure 5.9).

WorldCat began with cataloging and acquisitions librarians and staff as its primary creators and users, as did RLIN. Although reference librarians were not the central focus of these bibliographic utilities, they soon discovered how useful these utilities were in finding bibliographic records for materials that may have been cataloged anywhere in the country. These bibliographic utilities expanded their user base from cataloging and interlibrary loan departments to include reference and other public service staff. When the databases moved to the Web, they expanded their user base to include the public. Now merged, the integrated online union catalog provides an end-user interface to its rich bibliographic database. Only a few years ago, access to an online union catalog was as far from the experience of the typical library user as it could be; now it is a click away from anywhere. In addition, there are thousands

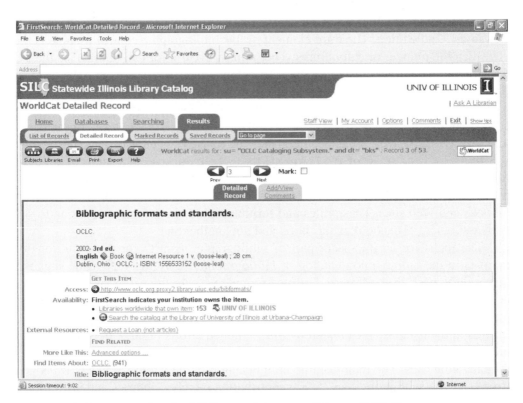

Figure 5.9. An example of a bibliographic record from OCLC.

of individual library online catalogs from around the world accessible over the Web. Cooperative efforts are underway to produce national and international union catalogs accessible from computers anywhere in the world. As just one example, in Figure 5.10, we see the KVK (Karlsruhe Virtueller Katalog), which allows the user to search many catalogs from around the world simultaneously. Of course, each catalog's interface and results may be in the original language, and that can present some linguistic challenges.

ELECTRONIC RESOURCES AND THE END USER

A walk around a typical reference room will reveal a number of computers with users working at them. This is not a big change. For more than two decades, library users have been using computer terminals to search the library's online catalog for materials of interest. What has changed is the size and shape of the information space available through the computer screen.

The transformation of bibliographic utilities and international union catalogs into end-user databases is emblematic of the changes in reference service. Where once a reference librarian had to walk back to the cataloging or interlibrary loan area to consult the database, now grade school students can link to *WorldCat* from their home computers and discover new books by their favorite authors. Researchers can

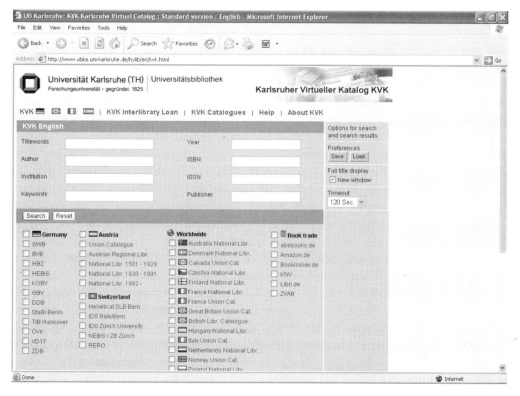

Figure 5.10. A sample listing of online union catalogs provided by Unversität Karlsruhe Library.

search *WorldCat* and solve many bibliographic puzzles on their own, without consulting reference librarians. This direct access empowers users and gives them control over meeting their own information needs.

Electronic resources that were once the province of bibliographers and reference librarians are now essential parts of the end-user repertoire. This development has escalated the level of questions brought to the reference desk. Now users are likely to say, "Can you help me find this? I couldn't find it in *WorldCat*." The bibliographic detective skill required to solve these problems is of a higher level. Instead of coming to the desk with a simple verification question about an English-language monograph, the researcher comes with a partial citation to a Hungarian-language conference proceeding. The ironic effect of having millions of bibliographic records available for all the library's users is the creation of more difficult challenges for reference librarians. Expectations about what is possible with electronic resources are very high. In addition, each reference librarian needs to develop a set of tactful explanations for how one was able to find something in *WorldCat* that the user had missed.

Structures Invisible to the Casual Observer

The expansion of the user base of electronic resources has ramifications for how search systems look and function. Many of the changes are positive ones, with some of the arcane requirements of command mode searching giving way to a simpler point-and-click system on the Web. For the most part, the search engine and its interface have taken on more of the work in the search process. Instead of typing in the code for the different fields, the searcher can slide down a menu for that field. The interface interprets the different clicks and formats the search statement into the necessary codes that the search engine can understand. However, as the search engine migrates from command mode to the Web version, the search capabilities are often reduced. There is an assumption on the part of database producers and vendors that end users either do not know or do not care about the kinds of distinctions that the highly structured database contains. Formerly distinct fields such as "descriptor," "identifier," and "title" are all merged into a single category and labeled as keyword searches. Although this tendency may increase the chances for retrieval of material from the database, it severely restricts the possibilities of refining a search. On one hand, retrieving something rather than nothing is probably useful for the end user; on the other hand, retrieving a great many items of only middling relevance can be highly frustrating.

Many of the codes and labels for internal structures of databases have become invisible. It is assumed that the user will recognize that this part is an author because it is a person's name, and that part is the author's affiliation because it is the name of an organization. Using explicit labels or even formatting the display to indicate different fields or structural elements is not very common in these database designs. The fact that the internal structure is invisible rather than nonexistent is more important than it might seem at first glance. These invisible structural elements tend to be focused on spaces and punctuation. In some cases, a trivial error in formatting a name can result in substantial differences in retrieval. For example, keeping or omitting a comma in a name search can be significant. The choice of hyphenating a compound word or separating the elements with a space can also yield substantial differences. If the user is fortunate, the search system will ignore the variation and retrieve the appropriate material. A less sophisticated search system may recognize the error and suggest alternative input choices. An alternative response from the search engine would be to display the list of names that are closest to the one input, as interpreted and understood by the search engine. If the names look a bit odd—for example, if they are all hyphenated or are at the end of the alphabet—the alert user may be able to use the clues to devise a different strategy to produce a list of names that look more like the one desired.

Not all search engines generate that kind of helpful feedback to assist the user in improving a search strategy. In the least sophisticated systems, one receives no matches or an artificially low (or high) result without realizing that an error has occurred. This is a consequence of the invisibility of the defaults that the search system employs. It is also the result of a lack of a built-in "Is this what you mean?" response that would at least alert the user to what the search system thinks the user is asking for. Many of the tools that are now available to end users make assumptions about the sophistication and experience of the user that perhaps do not match the actual attributes of the typical user.

Part of the reason users may misinterpret the results of a search lies with the user. Users have a significant amount of faith that the computer is providing help to them—that is, that the computer "understands" what they asked for and has provided "the answer." When a user receives a set with 1 item in it because of the inadvertent matching of misspellings or receives a set of 7 items out of a possible 50 that would match the user's needs, most of the time, the user believes that these are the correct results and goes away. Figure 5.11 the consequences of a very minor error in structuring a name search in a database. Few users come to any electronic resource with a well-developed sense of likely results, nor do they come with an effective yardstick with which to measure their success. Any results are the right results. That it was ever thus is a small comfort to reference librarians and interface designers alike.

Another potential area of miscommunication between the search system and the user is how the system handles words or phrases the user inputs. In some systems, there is automatic truncation of search terms or phrases. In others, the terms are searched exactly as input unless there is an explicit use of the system's truncation symbol. In some systems, the words are searched as a phrase, whereas in others there is an implicit Boolean AND between the terms. In still other systems, the terms are searched with relevancy ranking and weighting. Not all search systems make their searching choices apparent. The challenge for the user is to identify the search mechanism at work and to devise search strategies that are effective in this system. A problem for even the very alert user moving between two or more search systems is that these important search system features may be confounded or confused.

The internal organization of an electronic resource may not be evident to the user, nor might the user be aware that an electronic resource has internal organization. This is in contrast to a printed reference source, which has to make its organization and arrangement clear in order to be used at all. A print source provides one or more structures to make the contents accessible. If it is organized along alphabetical lines, perhaps there will be an index providing additional terms to supplement the cross-references provided within the tool. One can think of an encyclopedia providing alphabetical entries supported by cross-references and a subject index. If a print tool

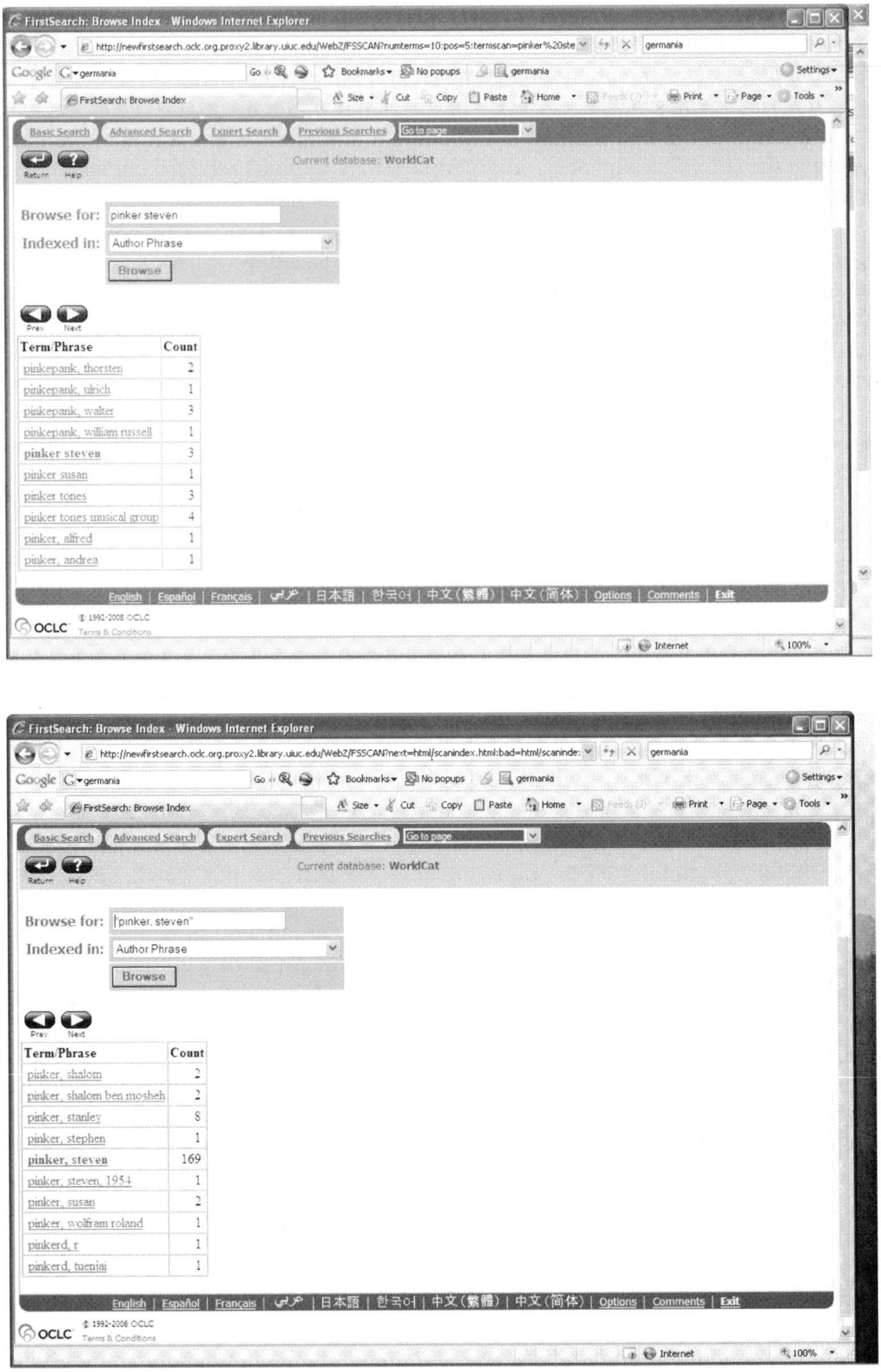

Figure 5.11. Incorrect and correct name search in *WorldCat*.

is organized in a subject hierarchy, a table of contents will be provided outlining the arrangement. The *Handbook of Latin American Studies* is an example of a tool with the entries arranged in a topical hierarchical outline. An alphabetical index is likely to be included in such a hierarchical tool.

These alternative access structures can be a big help if the information one has about a question does not match the organizational pattern. In *Bartlett's Familiar Quotations*, for example, the body is arranged broadly by date and within a date range alphabetically by the surname. However, because not everyone can correctly place a name in the appropriate era, an index by name is provided. As required by the nature of this tool, it also provides an extensive index by keyword in the quotation. In a reference tool on the Web, the context and the organization of the information are likely to be invisible. A piece of information will be brought to the screen in response to the search query. All that can be determined is whether the piece on the screen has the answer to the query. Internal structure can sometimes be discerned from the format of the query screen or the style of the displayed results. In any case, such structures may be irrelevant to the interaction because the searcher may not be able to use that knowledge as an alternative approach to the resource. Internal navigation within the tool is most likely to be limited to the query screen, rather than another access mechanism or browseable display.

The User and the Interface

Electronic resources differ from print materials in the way they are delivered to the user, whether the user is in the library, at home, in the office, or at an Internet café halfway around the world. Electronic resources exist as multiple potential realities rather than a single, fixed reality. Just as water has no fixed shape or size, electronic resources have similar fluid properties. They arrive through an electronic "pipe" with a computer for a faucet. The particular reality that exists for any user will differ in appearance and capabilities depending on the size of the pipe and the type of faucet being used to access the resource. The version one finds on the Web through a broadband connection may differ in substantive as well as graphical ways from the version reached through one's mobile phone. There may be an all-text option or a low-graphics version of a resource. The fluid nature of the resource is a challenge for reference librarians as they seek to describe a resource helpfully and unambiguously for users.

In addition, the resource itself is subject to change without notice. The interface can change markedly from one version to the next. New screens, new options, a new "look and feel" can leave a user unsure how to proceed with a formerly familiar resource. A database may be made available through another provider. An abstracting and indexing resource can add links to full-text sites. A resource can do all these things simultaneously and throw in a name change at the same time. Again, the reference librarian seeking to describe an electronic resource is at a significant disadvantage in this task. Indeed, a description of a single database can begin to resemble a rap sheet for a career criminal, with an extensive "also known as" list to describe the many possible names under which a user may recognize a particular resource. When corporate mergers or realignments are added to the mix, the task becomes truly daunting. Name changes are relatively uncommon in the world of print reference resources.

When they occur, catalogers deal with them with a simple addition to the cataloging record. Users looking for the item under old or new names are successful. Likewise, the guides to reference resources, such as Balay's *Guide to Reference Books* or *The New Walford Guide to Reference Resources*, provide access under previous names. With the slippery nature of the electronic resource, it is hard to pin down just what is to be named or described and how one might do this. To put it another way, one may not know a reference book by its cover, but at least it has one. What is the equivalent of an electronic resource's cover? How can the librarian make a label for a resource that is accurate, up-to-date, and durable in the face of all these changes?

When using electronic resources made available by the library, end users will very likely have to switch from one interface to another. Figure 5.12 is an example of how the same database, *ERIC*, looks on the first screen of two different systems: FirstSearch and Ovid.

Both Ovid and FirstSearch offer an advanced search screen in addition to the basic search screen shown. So in this case, for a single database, there are four different search screens offering different search capabilities and strategies, not to mention different citation handling and printing options. Most of the time, of course, each database will be available on a single system in a library. However, because many libraries subscribe to several systems to cover the full range of information sources, the complexity of searching choices and strategies for the user trying to find information through multiple interfaces remains.

All the end-user systems, whether on CD-ROMs or over the Web, are intended to be user-friendly, but some are more successful in their design than others. Many systems offer two or more levels of searching, designed for both novice searchers and users with more searching experience. For the novice, there might be a single search box, labeled "Quick Search" or some such inviting term, which leads the user to type in the term of choice. For the more experienced searcher, there might be a multi-box search screen with each box offering a menu of search/field options.

In some systems, there is an expert option, in which the search interface more greatly resembles the command-line searching of the days of yore. Whatever advanced options are offered, they all provide more searching power, greater efficiency in handling citations, or just faster searching than the "quick search" of the beginner's screen. Many studies assess users' success in retrieving information from the library's online catalog and abstracting and indexing services. One source of the overall lack of success for users is the mismatch between users' assumptions about "the computer" and the actual search mechanisms at work. One example is a study conducted by Eric Novotny at Pennsylvania State University involving novice and experienced online catalog users.[3] The users of the library's catalog revealed untested and unfounded assumptions about the results of their searches. Developing point-of-use instruction that can assist users in developing a better search strategy or expanding the search vocabulary is time-consuming and very hard to do well. It can be even harder to get the user to respond to these guides. In those systems that have different search levels, the levels frequently have little in common, so the searcher moving from the basic to the advanced is faced with learning new terminology and new techniques. Search systems in which there is a "skills ladder" in which to build on skills and concepts from one level to the next are rare. As a result, it is difficult for the user to develop the skills needed to use the higher levels successfully. This results in the user either remaining

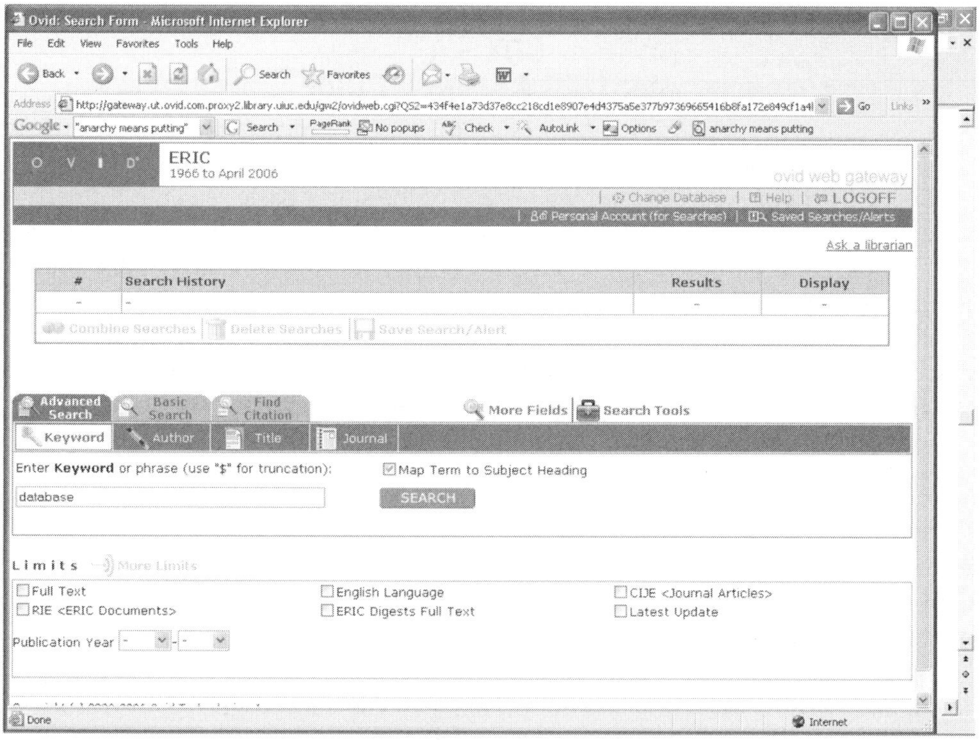

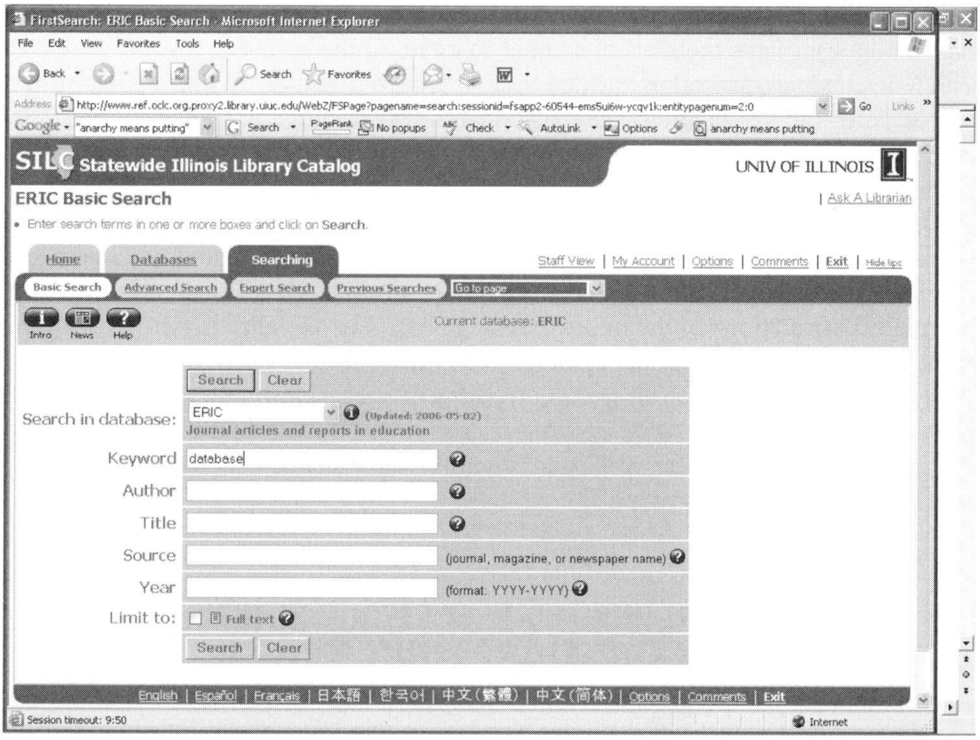

Figure 5.12. One database and multiple interfaces—*ERIC* on Ovid and FirstSearch.

BOX 5.5
WRITING A SEARCH GUIDE

A popular electronic resource has just come out in a new release. The new version has two levels of searching instead of the single basic search it formerly had. You are going to be writing a new user guide for the resource. Knowing that most users will use a guide only if it is very short, you need to make some early choices. Will you write a guide for the basic level and add a note that users should ask at the reference desk if they need help with the advanced search, or will you write a guide that will assist users in determining which kind of search they will need to use, with some examples of correct searches? Will your decisions be the same if you intend to mount the guide on the Web as well as have a print version available?

at an unsophisticated level or needing individualized training and instruction in the higher-level search techniques.

As the discussion on search capabilities indicated, the concepts that enable efficient and effective searching are not necessarily known, recognized, or understood by the end user. If a search window offers Boolean searching, how likely is it that the user will know whether this function is needed for an effective search? Nor does the average user have the kind of sample searches at the ready that would reveal the search mechanisms at work in the database. It is hard to imagine a user with a "Top 10 List of Things to Learn about Database Searching" resource in a shirt pocket, briefcase, or backpack. It is almost equally hard to imagine that the end user understands the need for such a list.

Not all electronic information resources make it clear to the casual user (or the reference librarian) what the database contains, in terms of degree of coverage of the listed journals, the dates of coverage, and the like. Users may start with very optimistic expectations of the online coverage based on the enthusiastic descriptions of the possibilities of electronic resources as portrayed by television and its commercials. Users also will be carrying their feelings of success from their searches on the Web. It is easy to imagine the frustrated user saying, "If I can find the stuff I need on _____ [insert favorite Web search engine name here], why can't I find what I need on the library's Web pages?"

INTEGRATING END-USER RESOURCES INTO
USER-CENTERED REFERENCE SERVICES

Paying for access to electronic resources is just one step in developing effective reference service. Systems and services must be created and implemented that allow the user to identify the resources available, select the appropriate resources, access them, search them to discover the needed information, handle the output, and ultimately use the information discovered. These systems and services need to be site-independent; that is, the remote user and the user in the library should be able to follow the same path with the same ease and the same chance of success.

Reference Service Environment

For the purposes of this discussion, the reference service environment consists of the physical surroundings of the reference service point, the reference presence in the library Web space, the equipment used in the provision of the service, the reference staff, the reference collection, and the reference service policies. This reference matrix is a dynamic, interlinked one, with changes in any area affecting and shaping each of the others. At the very center of this reference service matrix is the user. Each element of the environment must be designed with the user's needs in mind. It is essential that the different user groups that make up a reference library's community be considered in this design.

One set of users to be considered in the design are reference librarians themselves. They are the most intensive users of the resources. It would be much easier to design reference environments if reference librarians were the only user community. If this were the case, when physical reference environments were designed in libraries, the tools could be put wherever the reference librarians need them. They could be moved as often as needed. If a "professionals only" information space were designed for the Web, the same principles would apply. Librarians know their own strengths and weaknesses and can evaluate the success of the design in real time. If something did not work the way it was intended, this would make itself evident to the developer, often the same person as the user, right away. Modifications could be undertaken on the fly to remedy the situation. Communicating to those affected by the change would be straightforward; an e-mail to one's colleagues or a note left at the reference desk would suffice, or one could let the modified user environment speak for itself.

When the reference environment is opened to the many user communities served, this has consequences for the ability to design the information space. In the physical reference room, the needs of the independent user of the reference tools must be balanced against the needs of the reference staff. It might be very convenient for reference librarians to have all the almanacs at the reference desk, but it would not be a successful location for the users. Similarly, as the many elements of the physical reference collection migrate to the information space on the Web, reference librarians seek to arrange the electronic resources for ready access by virtual users. To direct those users who may not know the formal names of different kinds of reference tools, the reference space may use the language of questions to identify resources by function. For example, the reference space could pose these choices: "Looking for a quick fact or definition? Click here for almanacs and dictionaries." "Trying to find a longer explanation for a concept? Click here for general and specialized encyclopedias."

In this scenario, those users who know the type of tool they need can recognize it, and those who are less familiar can try to select the appropriate resource by the kind of question they have in mind. In any design, it is essential to provide a link to real help, such as a telephone number for the reference desk, with hours of service, for example, in addition to a link for "ask a reference question" e-mail service. With the provision of virtual reference services, with the user and the reference librarian work-ing together in shared Web spaces in real time through specialized software, the help can be tailored immediately to the user's needs. A technology that is even more ac-cessible is instant messaging, and some reference departments are finding their users in that space. It lacks the shared browsing of Web pages offered by virtual reference services, but the speed and ease of the technology counterbalances that lack. Guiding the user to appropriate resources, suggesting search strategies, and helping the user cope with the variety of information resources are all accomplished as a team, with the librarian serving as coach, guide, teacher, and navigator.

Another aspect of the reference environment changes with the translation of ref-erence resources to the Web. As opposed to traditional print reference tools, which are located within a physical environment and provide a context for the information they contain, Web-based tools exist without a frame of reference. Typically, a print source has a call number that simultaneously identifies its subject matter and locates it next to other reference tools on the same subject. Print tools are often clustered by func-tion within the reference room, with atlases collected together and perhaps indexes arranged on tables. This physical co-location can provide some benefits through ser-endipity, bringing to the user's attention an unknown or forgotten title. These features of location and context are largely or entirely absent from the Web.

Most Web-based tools exist in complete isolation from one another. Perhaps titles that are produced by a single publisher or that are made available through an aggrega-tor will be identified on a single selection screen. More often, the URL is a context-less anchor to a single tool. (Box 5.6 provides an elegant expression to the Web space experience.) Some reference tools may lend themselves to a post hoc consumer clus-tering through bookmarks and the like, but these are frail structures in contrast to the rugged and durable outlines of the LC or Dewey classification schemes. In addition, these post hoc groupings require constant updating.

Managing Access

Electronic resources can come to a library and its users through many different consortial arrangements. A library can be a member of a state-wide consortium, a regional consortium, or a consortium based on type of library or other bases. Each of these consortia may provide electronic resources to its member libraries for use by the libraries' user communities. These arrangements greatly expand the pool of resources available to the members of the consortium. Typically, there are substantial discounts for the resources acquired by consortia. This results in more effective expenditures of the scarce resource dollars. The benefits of these arrangements are clear, but some complications arise as well. The licensing arrangements for each consortium can di-vide a reference library's users into groups with differing access rights and different

---

BOX 5.6

"There are no fixed points in space." —Albert Einstein

service options. With overlapping domains of "citizenship" in different cooperative agreements, different users may find that some resources are available only under certain conditions, for example when they are in the library, and that other resources are not available at all.

Managing access for these multiple-user communities is a challenge. The library seeks to make as many resources available to as many of its users as possible while not violating the licensing terms. A library can develop alternative strategies to deal with these multiple and overlapping citizenship issues. Many libraries define their licensed primary-user community to include all those who use the resources in-person at the library. These users may be thought of as wearing a temporary identification badge. For the length of their visit, they are part of the organization.

The extension of temporary citizenship works for those who use licensed resources in-person. For remote users, the library must be able to ascertain their eligibility to use the resource. One way to do this is through Internet addresses associated with the library or licensing agency. The librarian or agency identifies the set of Internet addresses, called IP ranges, that belong to its primary user group. Anyone using a computer with an IP address in the correct range is allowed access to the resource. Others will be turned away. This is most effective for a campus or a company with a unique set of IP domains. The strategy can also be used for some broad-based electronic resources. For example, Indiana has made some electronic resources available to everyone in the state through its INSPIRE program. All of the public IP ranges that are in Indiana are allowed access to these resources.

The other way to determine membership in a group is through *authentication*. Authentication is a two-step process for assuring that the person is truly the person and is on the list of eligible users, typically through matching a name and password with an entry in the user database. For example, in the INSPIRE program, if Indiana residents want to use the service through a national Internet service provider, they need to register and be added to the INSPIRE user database. When they log on, their computer is checked against the database before they are allowed to use the service.

It is a challenge to make the authentication process reliable, efficient, and unobtrusive. It is nearly impossible to make the properly authenticated session also anonymous. Many of the library's users are aware that the library is committed to keeping the activities of its users confidential, but they are also aware that there is a difference between confidential and anonymous. Because of authentication, there is a chance that these sessions will not remain confidential. Users who wish to maintain anonymity may have to do their research in the library on computers that have direct access to the needed resources.

EXPANDING RESOURCES

The changes in technology can be summed up in one word: more. More speed, more images, more formats, more channels, and more resources. The future is likely to be more of the same. Is the result just more reference service, or are there some fundamental differences in how these resources are developed and used?

In the beginning of the end-user revolution, there were relatively few resources available. Many of them were known to the user in their print format. The move to electronic form meant faster, easier, more flexible searching within familiar boundaries. The users had some idea about the kind of material that they would receive from their searches. One of the roles of the reference librarian was to guide the user from the print to the electronic version. User instruction was largely one-to-one and took place in the reference room or at the information desk.

By 2010, the tidal wave of electronic resources had washed away virtually all knowledge of the existence of print resources and swept all signposts from the emerging reference resource landscape. The end user's information universe has expanded from a tidy solar system to an immense and expanding galaxy. Just as a galaxy is filled with neutron stars, supernovas, quasars, suns, and planets beyond counting, the end user's information space has become much more complex. It begins with indexes and abstracts and includes full-text electronic journals, dictionaries, encyclopedias, directories, and datasets, to name just a few resources. This has transformed the role of reference librarians in helping users navigate this space.

As the number and type of electronic resources grows, the challenge becomes one of assisting users in identifying and selecting the appropriate resource for their needs. In person, the reference librarian can guide the end user from source to source, pacing the information flow to suit the user's knowledge and experience. The reference librarian is also able to see whether the user is working successfully alone or some additional guidance is needed. Similarly, if the interaction with the user happens as part of the virtual reference service, the real-time user interactions guide the reference librarian in the selection and utilization of resources. To deliver the same guidance to those users who are far beyond the walls of the reference room, reference librarians have provided *gateways* or *portals*. These gateways on the Web can be thought of as maps to the library's information space and are designed to guide the user to the correct resources. They attempt to divide resources into familiar categories and keep similar kinds of resources together. In some ways, the gateways work to simulate the arrangement of a reference room on the screen. Creating a set of virtual index tables, encyclopedia cases, and dictionary stands on the library's gateway page may help the user identify where to begin.

Some gateways may be built as a series of branching menus with multiple layers of choices. Each choice brings a new set of choices to the screen until the user reaches the final layer. This strategy assists the user by breaking down an enormous amount of information into smaller, more manageable pieces. Instead of having to deal with 250 or 2,500 electronic resources of all types in one long list, one can choose among perhaps five categories. These could be arranged on a subject basis or on another functional basis. This approach has some distinct advantages over scrolling through screens of resources. It is important that the menus be very well designed, with clear, unambiguous, and comprehensive choices and very flexible detours back to previous levels for an alternate set of choices.

If gateways are based on a database of databases, they can provide a kind of flexibility and responsiveness that is unavailable in traditional guides to reference sources. A carefully designed database of databases can include inclusive and exhaustive lists of subjects and topics for each of the resources, based on the vocabulary of that discipline. The gateway can be built on the fly in response to a user's query. For example, a user may come to the gateway and be invited to type in some words from a topic of interest. The gateway software will search for resources that contain that topic and present to the user tools such as subject encyclopedias, abstracting and indexing sources, and even Web sites of possible interest.

This approach, though an interesting and valuable alternative to a more static style of gateway, has a problem that may be termed the "Salvador Dali" problem. That is, a user will type in a term such as "Salvador Dali" rather than "art history" or "modern art" or "twentieth-century art" or another more generalized description of the subject. If so, the user's search may not result in a match in the database of electronic resources because the resources are not indexed to that level of granularity or detail. The converse problem, the "History" problem, occurs when a user types in a topic that is so broad that it matches nearly every resource in the system. Devising appropriate guidance mechanisms for these searches will be a long-term challenge for reference librarians, as will be the development of the descriptors for each of the resources.

Some developments in software systems are designed to assist users in selecting and searching across multiple resources. The most common term for this development is *federated searching*. In federated search systems, a library selects a group of resources, typically including the online catalog, major abstracting and indexing tools, and some reference tools, and provides a simple interface to the user that will allow a search across all the tools simultaneously. The librarian may design the search interface to cluster broad-based resources together or offer choices among subject categories or a combination of the two approaches. The challenge in these systems is to select tools that can be made to work together and present the disparate results in a way that is intelligible to the user. Typically, the federated search system necessarily makes some compromises in the way the resources are searched and is not able to support the native system search capabilities in the cross-search environment. However, it can go some distance in reducing the user's frustration in conducting searches serially across a variety of resources. And it can bring to the experienced library user's eye resources that had not been discovered earlier. Success with federated searches is improving as librarians and vendors work together to match user behavior and expectations within the limitations of computing power and resource compatibility.

Of course, the users of the virtual reference room are similar to the users of the physical reference room. They may not know where to start or how to frame their question. They may not understand the relationship between and among different kinds of reference resources. So to supplement the electronic gateway to the virtual reference room, some libraries have created research guides on their Web pages to assist users. Some of these are virtual pathfinders with step-by-step guides to research in an area. Duke University (http://library.duke.edu/research/help/), Los Angeles Public Library (http://www.lapl.org/resources/guides/), Cornell University (http://olinuris.library. cornell.edu/ref/research/tutorial.html), and the New York Public Library (http://www. nypl.org/collections/nypl-recommendations/research-guides) are just a few libraries that have developed research guides on the Web.

Translating the intellectual and functional concepts of information resources into the visual and verbal structures of the computer screen takes good imagination and design skills. Providing enough information to support intelligent decision-making processes within the constraints of computer screens is a challenge. This challenge is addressed through a variety of mechanisms. One strategy is "layering" the screen so that additional information about a resource is accessible through a mouse-over or as a pop-up. Creating an "About this Database" icon that links to fuller descriptions of the resources is another strategy. Adding to the challenge is the constantly changing array of reference resources. Reference collections have always been dynamic. Reference librarians add resources as they become available, replace older editions with new ones, and deaccession materials as they lose their utility. However, the rate of change for electronic resources is substantially higher than for traditional print resources. In addition to the "changes by choice," in which a library changes its subscriptions to add or delete a title, there are the changes in the nature of the resources that remain in the collection. Given the very fluid state of electronic resources, how can the library's gateway service lead novice users to the "new" resource while helping experienced users recognize that it is a new incarnation of the one they used last week?

DEFINITION OF THE REFERENCE COLLECTION

The revolution in reference is causing some fundamental changes in the way reference librarians acquire, describe, think about, and use their collections (see chapter 13). In times of rapid transition, it can be helpful to see both the past and the present as preludes to discovering possible routes to the future. Following is a description of the "classic" reference collection.

The reference collection is a distinct set of print and electronic resources selected and acquired by reference librarians and made available within a recognizable space to local user communities. Reference librarians thrive on the challenge of identifying the right set of reference resources that they can consult to deal with the information needs of their users, within budgetary and space constraints.

Reference librarians have developed the criteria for assessing the quality of these tools, and they apply these criteria in choosing items for the reference collection. The crucial challenges for reference librarians are establishing intellectual control over the content of the collection and reflecting that control in ways that benefit users. These challenges are more readily met because of the rigorous selection and evaluation process for each resource as it is acquired. Because the reference collection has a structure and a shape built by the reference librarians who use it, integrating new tools and resources into the working collection is a nearly automatic process. The reference librarian's mental map of the intellectual content of the reference collection is well developed and well maintained. This mental map is reflected in the physical arrangement of the room, with materials organized for effective use.

As the reference collection migrates to electronic form, what elements of the earlier definition remain? Some of them remain virtually unchanged; others continue in modified form. One area that warrants extensive exploration is selection and acquisition. This is where the traditional, orderly processes of reference collection development have changed the most.

The first step of selection is the identification of forthcoming tools of possible interest. The reference librarian tries to keep aware of new tools that will be released in the near future. However, because electronic resources are so fluid in nature, this identification is an amorphous process. Between the time of announcement and the time of appearance in the marketplace, many resources undergo extensive revisions of concept and execution. Some resources are offered on a basis that is similar to a prospectus. If the proposed tool generates enough interest and orders, it will continue through the development cycle to a production version. If not, it may be withdrawn for redesign or be delayed until there are sufficient purchasers. A tool that was identified as being of some interest in April might be of much greater or lesser interest by September when it is released. The version that was available for evaluation might be very different from the version that is delivered. Much of the time, it is an improved version, but not always.

Another factor that is important in the selection of electronic resources, although it played a negligible role in the print collection, is the availability of a resource from multiple sources. Many resources are available in different configurations at a substantial difference in price. For example, the *MLA International Bibliography* is currently available through three vendors. The same original *MLA International Bibliography* database forms the core of these different products. However, in some very real sense, *MLA International Bibliography* is not the same database in all these cases. It may be too much to assert that the interface *is* the product. It is not too much to assert that it is impossible to evaluate a resource without evaluating the interface. For some tools, evaluation of a resource for selection and acquisition into the reference collection is based at least as much on the interface as on the content. This represents a change in emphasis from the selection for the print collection. In the print world, essentially all reference collections have at least one reference tool that is nearly impossible to use. Reference librarians put up with the difficulties of use because the content comes in only one print package. The economies of print publishing ensure that. In the reference room, the reference librarian is available to serve as the intermediary between the print tool and the user. There is no expectation that the user will learn the eccentricities of arrangement and access.

By contrast, in the electronic reference collection, the expectation is that the end user will be using the electronic resource independently, without a reference librarian to serve as an intermediary. If the resource content is offered with an interface that is difficult for end users or that is confusing or lacks important features, many librarians will pass. They will wait with some assurance that another company will offer the same content in a package that has better features. If it is a crucial resource, then perhaps it will be selected but kept on a "wait and see" basis until it improves or there is an alternative.

In weighing one version of a resource against another, some factors are difficult to balance. Perhaps one source offers a longer run of the database, but another may offer a smaller subset of the database at a significant discount. It is very hard to weigh the costs of not offering the older citations. A third source provides the users with more options for citation handling, which is a popular feature for the library's many remote users. Perhaps a fourth source is the least expensive to acquire but requires that the library mount the database on its own server. If the library already owns a server, the marginal costs for mounting and maintaining an additional database may be fairly low. Perhaps the library is in a consortium that is considering a multi-database package that includes the database but with an interface that is less user-friendly than one of the alternatives. Finding ways to evaluate the array of choices on all these factors is one of the continuing challenges faced by the reference librarian.

After the rigorous evaluation process, each electronic resource is considered for addition to the collection. The process of adding resources to the collection is called *acquisition.* However, in the realm of electronic resources, the concept of acquisition has been redefined into something more equivalent with leasing than with ownership. Although some titles in some electronic formats can be purchased on a permanent basis, most are acquired on much more temporary terms. Electronic resources are made available to a defined group of users for a defined period of time. It is this increasingly ephemeral nature of the reference collection that has created some cognitive dissonance among reference librarians. The concept of the reference collection used to carry with it a notion of permanence. For example, there is nothing temporary in the impression given by the hundreds of sage and gold volumes that make up the *National Union Catalog of Pre-1956 Imprints.* The *Oxford Dictionary of National Biography* will be of interest and value well into this century, at least. Any library that owns these reference tools will keep them available for decades.

By contrast, a reference librarian can look at a computer screen and realize that a tool that was there yesterday is gone today. That is an unsettling moment. These moments are occurring with great frequency at reference desks everywhere. Nearly equally unsettling is the realization that a tool has been added to the reference collection as a nearly invisible piece of a consortial package. Because this is the new reality, it pays to approach the reference desk with an open mind, ready to adjust one's strategies to the day's resources.

If a reference tool meets the selection criteria and has been added to the collection, its role in reference service needs to be settled. The reference librarians decide just how and where an item is to be "virtually shelved," that is, into which synthetic context the tool will be added. The electronic map of the virtual reference room will be updated. The new resource will be listed or linked from the cluster of electronic tools that it is most like, for example, with dictionaries or indexes or biographical sources. While the new item is being linked and listed, it is likely that the other tools of its kind will be reassessed in light of the new resource. Perhaps a realignment of resources is in order. A single category might be divided into two if the original list gets too long to be easily managed or navigated. It is understood that this intellectual integration of the electronic resource is a critical step in the continuing management of the reference collection.

The impermanence of electronic resources can lead to some caution in the intellectual integration process. It is hard to invest much scarce human capital into developing aids and guides for yet another resource whose time in the collection may be measured in months rather than years. On the other hand, it is essential to make each reference tool fully accessible and available for use while it is part of the collection. With the transformation of the reference room and the reference collection into an access node rather than a depository, developing a comprehensive access system is essential. One can claim a distinction between a tool that is not owned and one that is unavailable or invisible, but it is a distinction without a difference for the user.

In evaluating a reference tool, one factor to consider is cost. A more important factor is value. One can measure the price of a reference tool in terms of absolute cost. This is easy to do by just reading the invoice. It is harder to measure the value of a reference tool. One way to begin to measure value is to look at cost per use. In terms of cost per use, a $40 item that is not used in a year is more expensive than the $4,000 database that is used once a day. The costs of making the resource more usable through training sessions, user guides, publicity, or demonstrations may very well be recovered in the added value of the resource for its users: the cost per use will go down because of the increased number of users. It is nearly impossible to accurately measure the number of times a print tool is used, but most reference librarians have a general sense of use. Usage is likely to be expressed in general terms such as "very frequently," "occasionally," "rarely," or "never." This is in contrast with electronic tools that are typically set up to produce usage reports. Thus, comparing print and electronic tools on cost-per-use is a somewhat speculative process, but it can help clarify the evaluation of their utility for the users of the reference collection.

When evaluating an electronic reference tool, at least one other cost factor must be considered as well: "soft costs." Unlike "hard costs," soft costs cannot be measured in dollars and cents. Soft costs are paid in time, energy, and frustration. They are paid by the users who spend excessive time trying to figure out a search system. Users pay soft costs whenever they fail to find an item that is in the system. It can be helpful to think about a hypothetical interface in which the search button is just an unlabeled arrow. Some users will figure out that this means "search." Other users will try other buttons first and then try the arrow. Still other users will ask for help. Other users will quit. Every library that owns this resource will create a guide of some kind indicating that the arrow button means search. Each individual action that is needed to compensate for the unclear button adds a little bit to that system's soft costs. Perhaps for any one library, the cost is not that much, but when multiplied by the number of users of all the libraries, it adds up. At some point, the soft costs exceed the hard costs of the system. All systems come with soft costs, but it is useful to keep in mind that these will vary across systems. It is worthwhile to evaluate the interface for a resource in terms of likely soft costs as well as hard costs. Whether the soft costs outweigh the value of the resource is a question that may have a different answer in each library.

Another factor in evaluating an electronic reference tool is accessibility. For electronic resources, one form of accessibility is greatly improved: physical access. Consulting an electronic reference tool can be accomplished without a visit to the physical reference room. This eliminates a variety of architectural and meteorological barriers to access. It also removes time barriers. A tool may be consulted whenever electricity is available, rather than when a library is open and staffed. It requires a computer and a connection to the Internet or some other information appliance that includes communication with the Web. It is difficult, but not impossible, to imagine a search of library resources on one's cell phone. The challenge of the small keyboard and screen can be overcome with sufficient determination. The devices one can use to access electronic resources are not free but are rapidly becoming available for a minimal investment. The library and its resources are able to reach a much larger portion of the library's user communities than ever before.

However, electronic resources bring their own accessibility challenges. Some Web-based resources' primary interfaces are highly dependent on good vision and fine-motor skills. Maneuvering a mouse and clicking the buttons can be difficult for some users. Assistive computer programs are widely available, as well as other kinds of adaptive technology that address these issues. An example of these assistive programs is StickyKeys, which makes it possible to do the two- and three-key combinations that are often required for computer operations. The all-too-familiar "Control-Alt-Delete" key combination requires significant two-handed dexterity. StickyKeys makes it possible to do this one keystroke at a time.

Not all interface accessibility concerns are fully addressed by the technology, however. An all-text version, for example, works better with most screen-reading technology than an image-based interface. Some resources come with alternative interfaces that can meet the needs of a variety of users. In evaluating electronic resources, those that come with alternative interfaces are preferable to those that depend on assistive and adaptive technologies.

An essential element of the evaluation of reference resources is the involvement of the end user. Experienced reference librarians have a great deal of information about how end users interact with information resources. They have developed insights into how the user views the information universe. However, this knowledge is necessarily limited in a variety of ways. Librarians do not always know what questions to ask. More is known about the users with whom librarians have contact than about those who do not come in or call. More is known about those users who have overcome the barriers to access reference service than about those whom the barriers have turned away. Not all barriers may even be known.

In trying to evaluate a reference tool or interface from an end-user point of view, the librarian's experience is a two-edged sword. On the one hand, this experience has revealed how some users approach and use a reference tool. On the other hand, it has made some parts of the experience opaque. It is nearly impossible to recapture that original feeling of innocence in the face of an electronic reference tool. Librarians can see the information on the screen in a way that the novice cannot. Some parts of the screen may as well be empty for as much as a new user is able to glean from them. In any interface, no matter how a "fill in the blank" option is phrased or labeled, a reference librarian will have a clue as to what to do next. At a minimum, the librarian will know to check that the little cursor bar is inside the box before trying to type. This knowledge is far from universal. A librarian will most likely notice that some symbol or icon is a toggle switch and will be able to make a reasonable estimate of its function and impact.

Many of the users do not see the buttons or do not fully understand the ramifications of these choices. As librarians evaluate these tools, it is critical to be aware of how these differences in experience affect perceptions of usability. With those real limits on knowledge of user behavior, it would be a foolhardy reference librarian indeed who feels competent to fully assess and evaluate the usability of any reference resource for end users.

In view of these factors, it becomes critical to develop and use formal and informal pathways for user feedback on electronic reference tools. For those tools that are available from different sources, setting up a formal evaluation process where users can test and compare the interfaces as part of the initial selection process would be an excellent start. For a modest outlay of library resources to pay a set of willing subjects and to hire recorders and transcribers to capture the interactions, one can gain an enormous amount of information on which to base a decision.

If paying persons to help is not feasible, perhaps groups such as the Friends of the Library could be invited to participate in the evaluation as volunteers. Library staff members could take notes of their observations. The volunteers' reward would be information on topics of interest and a sense of contribution; the librarians' reward would be insight into how well the interfaces matched their users' needs. In either scenario, one could be assured that the evaluation and selection process had included the most important stakeholders, the users themselves. Providing feedback to the database producers is an effective way to close the development loop and encourage more usability in the next version of the interface.

For internally developed electronic resources such as Web pages and gateways, this user evaluation needs to be incorporated into the design and development phase. It also needs to be a periodic feature of the implementation phase. This is one area where the flexibility and impermanence of the electronic medium is an overlooked feature. Librarians would like to view their gateways, portals, and guides as finished products, whereas they need to be viewed as permanently under construction. Although no one likes a Web site that is in constant flux, one that evolves over time to a more usable version is welcomed.

If "user-centered information services" is to be anything but a slogan on annual reports, reference librarians and reference departments need to develop and maintain an active user perspective on their resources and services. This can involve user surveys and interviews, as well as surveys and interviews with people who do not use the library. Identifying barriers to use is an important step toward removing them.

CONCLUSION

Reference librarians find themselves trying to manage the fire-hose flow of information into drinking-fountain streams of information that the user can handle. The step-down mechanisms of gateways, searchable databases of databases, menus, guides, and links are demanding all the imagination, skill, research, energy, work, and luck that can be mustered. The rewards for this effort have been substantial and widespread. Millions of users who connect to the library's computer system can initiate a set of activities that go far beyond the answers reference librarians once provided to the question "May I help you?"

From the library's gateway, the system authenticates the user's status within the library's service communities; queries the user about information needs; provides access to specialized information resources; identifies electronic abstracting and indexing resources; links to the full text of the documents; allows desktop delivery of articles that are from collections a thousand miles away; connects with the local, expanded online catalog; identifies a variety of print and digital resources available; sends the print resources to the user's location; provides access to a very large portion of the monographic works of the world; and interacts with an interlibrary lending component to arrange delivery of those works not held by the local library. All these functions can happen in less time than it takes to drive to the library, find a parking spot, dig under the front seat for change for the parking meter, climb the marble stairs to the library, and approach the reference desk looking hopeful.

NOTES

1. *Unshelved,* November 3, 2005. http://www.unshelved.com/2005-11-3.

2. Charles P. Bourne and Trudi Bellardo Hahn, *A History of Online Information Services, 1963–1976* (Cambridge, MA: MIT Press, 2003), 493 pp.

3.   Eric Novotny, "I Don't Think, I Click: A Protocol Analysis Study of Use of a Library Online Catalog in the Internet Age," *College & Research Libraries* 65 (November 2004): 525–37.

ADDITIONAL READINGS

Bell, Suzanne S. *Librarian's Guide to Online Searching.* 2nd ed. Westport, CT: Libraries Unlimited, 2009. 287 pp.

This book combines tutorial material on database structure and basic search techniques with discussions of search strategy development for major databases in a variety of subject areas. Suzanne Bell also offers guidance on evaluating databases and choosing the right resource in response to a question.

Breeding, Marshall. "Next-Generation Library Catalogs." *Library Technology Reports* 43, no. 4 (July 2007). 44 pp.

This issue of *Library Technology Reports* is devoted to the developments in the area of "next-generation library catalogs." Marshall Breeding identifies and explores the concepts, goals, and current achievements in this area of library automation, including faceted navigation, relevancy ranking, and enriched content. He then provides a detailed look at the major next-generation catalogs.

Cervone, Frank. "What We've Learned from Doing Usability Testing on OpenURL Resolvers and Federated Search Engines." *Computers in Libraries* 25, no. 9 (October 2005): 10–14.

This article identifies some of the major challenges and opportunities in implementing federated search engines and OpenURL resolvers in a major academic research library. The findings are based on three years of usability tests.

Johnson, Peggy, ed. *Virtually Yours: Models for Managing Electronic Resources and Services.* Chicago: American Library Association, 1999. 165 pp.

This volume is an edited set of papers presented at the RUSA/ALCTS Joint Institute in 1997. Collection development librarians and reference librarians shared their visions for a future in which seamless, integrated, dynamic collections are acquired, processed, and made available to the user through the collaborative efforts of the entire library staff.

LIBLICENSE: Licensing Digital Information: A Resource for Librarians. http://www.library.yale.edu/~llicense/index.shtml.

This Web site focuses on the topic of licensed electronic resources in libraries. As the introduction states, "these materials will serve as a useful starting point towards providing librarians with a better understanding of the issues raised by licensing agreements in the digital age." Although the site makes clear that these resources are not a substitute for legal advice and opinion, they can be used as a starting point in examining any potential license. Examples of model licensing principles and preferred licensing language offer solid help to the reference librarian working with these increasingly important issues.

Lipinski, Tomas A., ed. *Libraries, Museums, and Archives: Legal Issues and Ethical Challenges in the New Information Era.* Lanham, MD: Scarecrow Press, 2002. 335 pp.

In this book, Lipinski brings together more than a dozen authors who address the topics at the intersection of information technology and legal issues, such as the Americans with Disabilities Act, information ethics, and privacy concerns, among others.

Lipow, Anne G. "'In Your Face' Reference Service." *Library Journal* 124 (August 1999): 50–52.

This article can be seen as a wake-up call to reference librarians to develop methods to deal with the information needs of the remote user wherever and whenever they arise. Lipow proposes some thought-provoking organizational and technological innovations as ways to make reference service more visible and available.

Mates, Barbara T. *Adaptive Technology for the Internet: Making Electronic Resources Accessible to All*. Chicago: American Library Association, 2000. 192 pp.

This volume provides a snapshot of available adaptive and assistive technology that can bring the promise of the Web and the Internet to the widest possible audience. Doug Wakefield and Judith Dixon are contributors who bring experienced voices to the discussion. This resource includes information on Web sites, vendors, manufacturers, and consultants that can help a library on its path to full accessibility.

Walker, Geraldene, and Joseph Janes. *Online Retrieval: A Dialogue of Theory and Practice*. 2nd ed. Englewood, CO: Libraries Unlimited, 1999. 312 pp.

Although it focuses on the traditional search services and systems, this comprehensive book includes searching techniques for the Web. Extensive examples and illustrations help illuminate the concepts and commands of efficient searching.

Understanding Electronic Information Systems for Reference

Kathleen M. Kluegel

INTRODUCTION

Chapter 5 presented the history and development of electronic resources for reference, exploring the expansion of these resources far beyond the reference room walls and the consequences for reference service. This chapter examines the structures that underlie the creation and distribution of these resources, beginning with a look at the history of the Internet. Next, the terms and concepts of the Internet needed to understand the current generation of electronic resources and services are introduced. An analysis of Internet and Web tools and how they work follows, creating a framework for understanding and developing the next generation of products and services. The final section focuses on some of the fascinating challenges facing reference librarians in the digital information age.

HISTORY OF THE INTERNET

The Internet has a brief but explosive history. What has become the Internet began as ARPAnet, an experimental high-speed network linking computers at Department of Defense research sites in the early 1970s. Its major goal was to develop a distributed computer network that could withstand disruptions. The only computers on ARPAnet belonged to the Department of Defense and its major contractors. In the mid-1980s, the National Science Foundation developed its own network, NSFnet, in order to link its five supercomputer sites around the country. Many universities wished to connect to one of these supercomputer sites to do research. Because of the enormous costs that would have accompanied running telephone lines crisscrossing the country, a series of regional networks was developed around each of the supercomputer sites. The design of these regional networks resembled that of ARPAnet, and they interconnected with one another. Any computer connected at any point on any of the regional networks could communicate with any other computer. These networks and similar networks developed and expanded around the world to form the Internet. The Internet has become a ubiquitous phenomenon that is growing at an unbelievable rate. People have devised various ways to assess the size of the Internet and the Web. One set of illustrative statistics can be found in the article "Lessons for the Future Internet: Learning from the Past" by Michael M. Roberts. He notes that as late as 1985, there were fewer than 100 hosts on the Internet; now there are more than 500 million.[1]

INTERNET TERMS AND CONCEPTS

In spite of the nearly universal presence of the Internet and the Web in daily life, there is often little awareness of the elements that make them possible. The following section focuses on the underlying concepts, structures, and services that make up the Internet. Understanding these fundamental Internet concepts prepares one to assimilate future developments and innovations. These concepts also are useful in interpreting the sometimes cryptic messages that computers display when accessing the Internet and the Web. Knowing the terminology of network structures facilitates communication with technical systems staff as well.

Protocols

It is helpful to think of the Internet as a many-layered information environment. Some concepts form the foundation on which the other layers depend. The most critical element in the understanding of the Internet and the Web is the concept of protocols. *Protocols* are formal agreements on the form and style of communication to assure reliable information transfers. In diplomatic circles, protocols are rules of speech and behavior that have been codified to assure clear communication across cultural or linguistic boundaries. These rules help diplomatic interactions and reduce areas of possible confusion. On a more familiar level, a protocol is an agreement—for example, "We will all use the 24-hour clock when we talk about time."

By establishing and using this and other protocols, one can assure clear and unambiguous communication. Computers connected to the Internet transfer information using protocols. It is almost impossible to overstate the importance of protocols in the area of electronic networks. Without protocols, there could be no computer network because information created in one computer environment could not be used, shared, transferred, or seen by someone using a different computer.

The essential protocol for national and international networks is TCP/IP (Transmission Control Protocol/Internet Protocol). TCP/IP governs the transport of information from one computer to another, independent of the kind of data. It ensures that information created in one computer will be received by another, unchanged by the process. TCP/IP forms the fundamental transport level for the Internet. It can be thought of as the foundation for the Internet. Specialized kinds of information may require that additional protocols be defined to enable successful exchanges. These protocols form layers that are carried on top of the TCP/IP layer. The railway system provides a useful analogy. TCP/IP forms the railroad tracks. The various kinds of additional protocols are the different kinds of engines and cars that can ride those rails. The content is carried in the appropriate rail cars.

One very important protocol supported by browsers on the Web is support for file transfers from one machine to another. The File Transfer Protocol (FTP) is the standard, high-level Internet protocol for transferring files. It is less well-known now than some of the other Web protocols because the common Web browsers provide transparent support for it, typically calling it a *download* or a *save*. FTP enables users at any Internet site to retrieve files, documents, data, or programs from many other Internet sites. It is the way that shareware and other programs are delivered from a server and downloaded to the user's computer. Nearly every user of the Web has used FTP to download the programs, plug-ins, or other files that update or enhance their Web browsers.

The TCP/IP protocol provides the rules that allow one computer to establish a connection to another computer on the Internet. The TCP/IP protocol is incorporated into TELNET, a program that is much less widely used today than in the past. However, a brief discussion of TELNET can put other protocols in perspective and can clarify concepts intrinsic to the Web. TELNET links a remote computer to the user's display and keyboard as if the user's computer were directly connected to the distant machine. To the users of the Internet, TELNET is rather like riding on a swan; that is, the user gets a very smooth ride, but the TELNET swan is paddling like crazy beneath the surface, making links, exchanging protocol parameters, and transferring information across the multiple boundaries.

TELNET provided an essential bridge to the development of the Web. It allowed the wider use of resources without the need to transfer the resource from one environment to another. Large databases were built on and resided on a single host computer with multiple remote users. Because TELNET provides remote access to the resource that is identical to the local access, no loss of functionality occurs. Typically, the TELNET host computer asks for users to log on. This logon allows the host computer to allocate a portion of its resources to each session.

TELNET is called a *stateful* protocol because the user's computer and the server computer maintain an active connection. Stateful search systems maintain each session in real time with information kept in an active mode. This allows a user to refer to previous elements of the interaction and reuse information without reentering it.

Client–Server Computing

The *client–server model* is another important element of networked computing systems. In client–server programs, the functions of the program are split into two components. The *client* is the "face" of the program. It is the part of the program the human user sees on the screen and interacts with. The client accepts the commands of the user and then interacts with the *server* portion of the system, using the protocols incorporated into its design to translate the commands into the language of the computer performing the task. After the server completes the task, it provides the results to the client to translate them into the response the user sees on the screen. Typically, the client program is first designed to work with one set of machines or on one operating system, called the *platform*.

The primary platforms for personal computers are Microsoft Windows, Macintosh OS, and Linux. Because each of these platforms is unique in its programming language and rules, client programs have to be modified to work on the other platforms. The process of modifying software to work on different platforms is called *porting*. (See Box 6.1 for another illustration of these concepts.)

The client–server model of computer systems allows different tasks to be allocated to the different modules. For example, in search systems, the user interface is typically a client-supported activity. The client provides a screen designed to assist the user with the desired task. It may further provide help screens. By shifting these functions to a local client, the server has more free resources to support the primary function. An online public access catalog (OPAC) is an example of a client–server system. In a typical OPAC, the interface is a client program that is loaded and runs on the computers used to access the catalog. It shows the user a screen with search options and help screens. The user interacts with the interface and enters information about the needed materials, such as a title, an author, or a topic. Acting as a silent, behind-the-screen "invisible butler," the interface translates the user information into the precise search commands used by the OPAC's search engine and sends the command to the server. The server responds with a stream of coded bibliographic and circulation information about the item. The client translates this stream of bits and bytes into a formatted display that the user can understand. Typically, the display will have additional options for locating a particular item, searching for related items, and the like. The client portion of the program supports all of these activities. The advantages for the user of this "invisible butler" acting as interpreter are substantial. The user does not have to spend time and energy learning the precisely formatted search commands. This frees the user to focus on accomplishing the task of finding the needed materials in the OPAC. The search interface screen can be designed to provide a helpful and supportive search environment with user-friendly features such as pop-up help screens or interpretive glosses.

The search system has some advantages as well. Because the client serves as the translator between the user and the server, the server can operate more efficiently on the actual search and retrieval functions. Thus, the workload is shared across the processors, resulting in faster search response time and the ability to support a larger number of users.

BOX 6.1
THE SCREWDRIVER AS A CLIENT–SERVER MODEL

The screwdriver handle takes the user input, the gripping and twisting, and translates that energy into an input the screw understands, the bit. The screw and screwdriver also demonstrate the importance of standards and protocols: the slot in the screw is machined to a standard shape, width, and depth to match the standard dimensions of the screwdriver. One could further stretch the model by positing the changeable-bit screwdriver as an example of porting.

The diversity of the computers that make up the Internet and the Web make the client–server model the only feasible one. The millions upon millions of personal computers from a myriad of manufacturers use a wide range of client programs to access the Internet. A wide variety of Web servers run a number of server software programs. Both the client programs and the server programs are designed around the Internet protocols.

The specialized client programs developed for the Web are called *browsers*. Browsers such as Firefox, Opera, and Internet Explorer are programs or a cluster of interrelated programs and applications that are developed to work with the different protocols and conventions that make up the Web. Browsers interact with the Web servers that hold the millions of files that make up the pages, images, sounds, and data of the Web.

Hypertext Transfer Protocol

The most important protocol in the Web is the Hypertext Transfer Protocol (HTTP). *Hypertext* is the term used to describe files of two main types. The original meaning refers to any document that can be read in a nonlinear way with different paths through the text. This results in a different experience for each reader, depending on the choices made at each juncture. The other, more common meaning of hypertext, and its extension *hypermedia*, is a file or document that contains links to other files. These linked files can contain text, data, sound, and/or images and can reside on one or many computers connected to the Web. HTTP provides the support for moving or viewing these files across the Web.

Files and documents on the Web are coded to protocols. In the case of text, the most widely used Web protocol at this time is HyperText Markup Language (HTML). HTML is an application of the Standard Generalized Markup Language (SGML) International Standards Organization (ISO) standard. Markup languages provide a consistent and unambiguous way to describe the structural parts of a document, independent of content. These descriptions, or tags, can be thought of as a particular kind of editing code, related to the codes that have been used by blue-pencil-wielding editors for years, with the double-underline to mean capitalize and the double-stroke P to indicate a new paragraph. HTML and SGML tags can be read and understood by humans as well as by machines. The HTML protocol includes a set of predetermined codes for the functional parts of a document. These codes have been incorporated into the standard Web browser and include header, paragraph, list, and so on. Web browsers interpret these codes in order to display the documents or files correctly. Typefaces, font size, placement on page, blank spaces, indentations, and other display elements are implemented according to the HTML protocol as interpreted by the particular Web browser of the user. Specialized programs can be used to create HTML-coded documents. HTML coding is supported by major word processing programs, such as Microsoft Word, as well. The value of adding HTML codes to a document goes beyond the aesthetics of the display. These codes turn a page of undifferentiated plain text into a structured document that is much easier to read and interpret.

URL

Other HTML codes also support the existence, formatting, and utilization of hypertext links to other documents. These interconnected, linked documents and files form the Web. Each document or file has a unique address, the Uniform Resource Locator (URL). The URL is built by following another protocol. Each element of the URL has a specific function and can be parsed. The part of the URL that is before the colon specifies the type of access protocol. For example, the URL can begin with "http:"—which indicates that the resource is a hypertext or hypermedia file and will be retrieved using the HTTP protocol. The part of the URL after the colon is interpreted in ways that are specific to the access method. In general, two slashes (//) after the colon indicate that the elements that follow identify the machine where the resource is located. The term *machine* as used here can be a single computer or a cluster of computers working together as if a single machine. The address part of the URL following the slashes is called the *domain name*.

Each address on the Web must be registered to assure its uniqueness. Naming conventions govern the appearance of the domain name. In the United States, the top-level domain names have one of several main endings: edu, biz, org, com, gov, net, and so on. Each ending lets the user anticipate the kind of organization or service that is available through that Web site. Although the categories are not absolute, in general, ".edu" is used for educational organizations, ".org" for nonprofit organizations, ".com" or ".biz" for commercial sites, ".gov" for units of government, and ".net" for organizations that support Internet access and Web services.

The number of domain name endings in the United States will likely expand to further refine the nature of the entities that make up the Web. The Internet Corporation for Assigned Names and Numbers (ICANN) is responsible for the coordination of names and addresses in the Web, and it also is responsible for the designation of top-level domain names. It maintains registries of domain names and addresses so that each one is assigned to only one entity, although each entity can have more than one domain name. One can register similar domain names such as www.mycompany.com and mycompany.com in order to assure that people wishing to reach the "my company" Web site can do so whether or not they include the "www" part of a typical URL. In other parts of the world, there are similar patterns governing domain name conventions. In countries outside of the United States, domain names generally include an abbreviation for the country of origin as well as an element designating the kind of service provider.

As an example of a URL that follows the current domain naming conventions, a URL such as http://www.ala.org tells the user that the resource is a hypertext one and that it is located on the machine registered to the American Library Association, a not-for-profit organization. The pattern for a URL from another country would produce, for example, the address http://auniversity.ac.uk, identifying a fictitious academic site in the United Kingdom. A URL for a commercial site in Australia might look like this: http://mycompany.com.au.

Browsers for the Web present the user with an interface that allows the direct input of a known URL or a search of the content of the Web to discover documents that meet the user's needs. Once a URL has been selected, the browser goes to the appropriate Web server, finds the requested file, delivers it to the user's desktop, and displays it according to the HTML coding included in the file.

HTTP and URLs combine to transform the product of publication from a static, linear document to a dynamic, hypertext one. For example, if an author is creating an international travel guide, it can be done as a printed book or as a document on the

BOX 6.2
THE POWER OF HYPERTEXT

In writing this chapter, for example, the author wished many times that it could be created as a hypertext document, with links from terms and concepts to pages of explanation and examples. Using hypertext would also provide an opportunity to link to relevant Web sites.

Web. In a book or other fixed text format, the author would have to include as much information as possible while providing readers with contact information such as telephone numbers and addresses of organizations that may have additional material. Constraints of size would determine some choices for the author.

In contrast, on the Web, the author would be able to incorporate much of the information through links to relevant Web sites anywhere in the world. For example, the author could provide a link to the U.S. Department of State International Travel Information Web site (http://travel.state.gov/travel). This link would bring the user directly to the most complete and up-to-date information about places the user wishes to visit, with tips about travel in general and current travel warnings. This hypertext travel publication would provide each user with a unique experience, in that some links will be explored by some readers but not others, or links may be explored in a different sequence. Many of the linked pages will be part of other hypertext documents on the Web, which can themselves be explored or not, as the reader chooses.

Stateful or Stateless?

The most commonly deployed version of HTTP is HTTP/1.0. HTTP/1.0 is called a stateless protocol because each HTTP request opens a new TCP connection, starts the session, interacts with the server, fills the request, and closes the TCP connection. Web pages that have embedded images, for example, fill each image request as a separate TCP connection to the server. Each HTTP request is executed as an independent interaction without any knowledge of the requests that came before it. Consequently, browsers are limited in their ability to incorporate previous information into their searches or other World Wide Web interactions. Statelessness has far-reaching implications for searching on the Web and for manipulating the results of that search.

Looking at the full URL in the browser window during successive steps of a Web interaction can be very revealing. At each stage of the process, the browser adds elements to the URL to produce a particular address string that will be translated into the needed next action. For example, if one clicks a button to see the next page of a Web site, the URL in the browser address bar will likely show additional codes added to the original in order to retrieve that page. This stateless search process is not particularly efficient when compared with a typical stateful search. In a stateful system, the material meeting the requirements would be available on the server and the pages displayed in any order with a simple display command.

BOX 6.3
URL EXAMPLES

The Web server in a stateless session adds elements to the URL in order to create a sequential experience for the user. For example, the *International Herald Tribune* Web site has multipage stories. The first page of the story might have a URL like this made-up example—www.iht.com/2006/10/5/news/pie.php—and the next page would have the URL www.iht.com/2006/10/5/news/pie.php?page=2.

The Web has "overhead costs" in the relatively inefficient TCP connections that must be reestablished with every interaction. Everyone using the Internet and the Web pays these costs through reduced speed of response and lost bandwidth. In ordinary Web usage, the implications of statelessness for most activities are relatively minor. One becomes accustomed to the sometimes lengthy waits for the next set of possible sites of interest. Or the converse occurs when one waits for a very large document to be transmitted in its entirety, although only a small segment is of actual interest.

Statelessness has much larger implications for database searching. The self-contained nature of a stateless interaction is at odds with the kinds of step-by-step searches that are typical of a command-line database search. Concept building, searching for synonyms, and combining concepts are all components of a traditional, stateful database search. Traditional online search systems provide the mechanisms that allow searchers to create very complex searches with several parameters in order to retrieve a very focused body of materials. It is more cumbersome and more difficult to achieve these same results in a stateless search environment. In order to support these complex search activities, nearly all of the commercial database sites have developed search programs that achieve pseudo-statefulness using technologies such as cookies and JavaScript. The servers use these mechanisms to keep track of search results and documents. This results in a search experience that is very similar to a stateful one. These pseudo-stateful systems have their own associated costs and inefficiencies for the server and for the user, but these costs are more than balanced by the effective retrieval of relevant materials.

The current statelessness of the Web is both a feature and a flaw. On the one hand, statelessness allows many more people to use a single resource than a stateful session would. The Web server can send out the little packets of information very quickly without having to expend any internal resources on keeping track of the transactions. One can think of the stateless Web server as a Pez dispenser, sending the little candies down a chute as quickly as it can flip its top. A stateful session would require the Web server to keep track of which user has seen which page and to keep the pages in order. The server would have to allocate internal resources such as memory and programming for these management tasks. In stateful sessions, each user is allocated an amount of memory or disk space on the server machine to store the intermediate results of searches. The sets have to be numbered and counted and ordered. In addition, stateful sessions require a one-to-one match between a user and a port or socket. When the server is out of ports, no more users can log on.

Stateless servers open and close sessions so quickly that a queue of browser requests can move along briskly. This statement is put to the test during busy times at very popular sites, but very large commercial Web sites can be designed to handle a million hits, whereas stateful servers reach their limits at much lower levels. In addition, once the Web resource has been transferred to the user's computer, it is a local resource, which can be quickly accessed without interacting with the Web server. It can be stored on a temporary basis in a cache or on a permanent basis on the user's computer.

Researchers who study traffic over the Web have determined that, on the whole, persistent TCP connections would be around 20 percent more efficient than temporary TCP connections and statelessness on the Web. Consequently, the HTTP Working Group of the Internet Engineering Task Force has created an HTTP protocol called HTTP/1.1, which supports persistent connections. This means that once a browser connects to a Web server, it can receive multiple files through the same connection. HTTP/1.1 also supports pipelining, which is the sending of multiple requests over a single persistent TCP connection. Balachander Krishnamurthy and colleagues discuss the development of HTTP/1.1 and the implications of the protocol in their article.[2]

Because of the demands placed on server resources by persistent TCP connections, HTTP/1.1 incorporates rules that allow servers or clients to terminate the connection as needed. One of the important factors in the development of the new hypertext protocol is the requirement that HTTP/1.1 maintain backward compatibility with HTTP/1.0. This means that the functions, commands, and codes that were used in HTTP/1.0 will still be correctly interpreted by browsers and servers using HTTP/1.1. This backward compatibility is essential because although most newer versions of Web browsers support HTTP/1.1, there is a large installed base of older clients that do not. In addition, not all Web servers support HTTP/1.1. The requirement of maintaining backward compatibility adds to the complexity and inconsistencies within HTTP/1.1 that would not be present if the developers had been free to develop the protocol in isolation.

Other Significant Protocols

A variant of the regular HTTP protocol is called Secure Hypertext Transfer Protocol (S-HTTP). This protocol assures that the information submitted is secure and protected. This protocol is usually represented to the Web browser as "https://." One will normally encounter the S-HTTP protocol when completing a form that requires important personal or financial information. One use for S-HTTP is *authentication*, certifying to the Web server that one is authorized to use a particular Web resource. If the user has to log on in order to use a Web resource, the process is likely to be conducted with the S-HTTP protocol.

Web browsers can be configured to alert a user when entering and leaving a secure Web space, so that the user does not inadvertently submit sensitive information over an insecure connection. The site or server that performs the authentication may have www-s as the first element of the URL to identify it as a secure server. Other kinds of security protocols are in use throughout the Web. Some of them involve encryption, which scrambles the information so thoroughly that even if the data are intercepted, they cannot be interpreted without the decryption key. Different encryption programs have different levels of protection. Commercial Web sites frequently identify the strength of their encryption protection as a way of clarifying the level of safety of the information transmitted.

As the preceding discussions have documented, each resource on the Internet and the Web is created with a set of rules based on common protocols. HTML, for example, is designed to format plain text. But plain text must itself be based on common standards in order to be understood and interpreted correctly. The most basic format for text is plain ASCII, which is an international standard for representing letters and numbers. ASCII includes upper- and lowercase letters, punctuation marks, and numbers from 0 to 9 (essentially all the characters represented by an English-language typewriter keyboard). Each character is a seven-bit combination with numeric values from 32 to 128. Plain ASCII text does not contain any formatting information beyond spaces and line breaks. Features such as underlining or boldface or different type fonts require encoding elements beyond the seven-bit limit, as does representing non-ASCII characters from other alphabets or characters from languages such as Japanese, Chinese, and Korean. Computer programs use characters beyond the basic ASCII set, namely the full binary character set, and these must be encoded as well, if they are to be transmitted across the Internet.

Beyond information that is communicated through plain text or numbers, there is information that relies on patterns or relationships among the elements. For example, spreadsheets and other databases contain information in the formatting, with cells, rows, and columns carrying vital elements that must be maintained in transferring data from one setting to another. Because several of the Internet protocols are built on the seven-bit limit for file transmission, various encoding systems have been developed to allow the transmission of complex text files and binary files within these constraints. In each of these systems, ASCII characters are used to represent non-ASCII information. The HTML markup language is an example of complex formatting codes being carried through regular seven-bit ASCII characters. The following is an example of HTML code that a Web browser will understand and use to turn the regular font ASCII text phrase "Web-Based Reference Sources" into a larger, bold font heading for a Web page: <font size = +2>Web-Based Reference Sources</font>
.

One of the mechanisms for supporting distribution of graphic, non-textual, or complex text files is the Multipurpose Internet Mail Extensions (MIME) specification. MIME allows for the use of an extended set of characters and the representation of contents other than plain text. This protocol makes it possible to represent arbitrarily complex data structures based on a standardized meta-language. MIME compliance has been built into the major e-mail packages and Web browsers, allowing users of those packages to receive these complex files with their formatting and images intact.

META Tags

There is a special category of HTML tags, called META tags, that deserves some explanation here. HTML META tags are the Web implementation of *metadata*, a term that can be translated as "data about data," as discussed in chapter 5. HTML META tags are a set of tags that can be used to describe the content of the Web page without affecting its appearance in any way. META tags frequently include information about the creator of the document, the primary subject matter, and the date of creation. One way to think about META tags in HTML documents is as catalog records that are included in the document, readable by programs but kept off-screen and out of sight. The user can, of course, use the "view source" or "page source" option in the Web browser to see all the tags, cascading style sheets, META tags, and formatting codes in plain ASCII. This can be a useful way to see how different effects are achieved and how the page is documented. The information contained in HTML META tags is understood and used by the servers and clients that make up the Web. Content-related META tags are used by Web search engines as part of the information gathered about Web pages by their crawlers.

Beyond HTML

As noted in the earlier discussion, HTML is a specialized form of SGML designed to operate over the Web. HTML uses a predefined set of markup tags that are incorporated into Web browsers. It is well suited to the handling and display of relatively simple documents over the Web. However, complex documents need more structure than is supported by the limited set of HTML tags. Knowing that the full-sized edition of SGML can handle even extremely complex, multilayered documents, one might propose that the full-sized SGML set would be the solution for handling these documents in the Web environment. However, SGML cannot be used to mark up or tag documents for transmission over the Web because the standard full-featured SGML parser (the program that reads and interprets the tags) is too large to be incorporated into Web browsers.

Given the need for encoding complex document structure and the limitations of even an expanded HTML set of tags, an alternative coding solution is needed. Another markup language designed to handle complex documents and other data sets over the Web is expanding its scope of content and applications. Like HTML, Extensible Markup Language (XML) is based on SGML. The "extensibility" of XML refers to the ability of users to define specialized tags as needed. However, it is important to realize that XML is not created by adding a larger set of HTML-like tags to those currently available. Instead, XML needs to be understood as a simplified form of SGML. The first XML is designed to function with a streamlined SGML parser that can be included in every Web browser. It may seem contradictory to say that XML is designed to handle extremely complex documents and yet is referred to as a simplified version of SGML. XML transcends the contradiction by creating a streamlined parser with few, if any, predefined tags. The definitions of the tags for each document will have to accompany it, either through scripts or through style sheets. This allows the parser to remain small while allowing it to deal with the potentially infinite variety of tags that a user can create in XML.

Although XML is not backward compatible with HTML, HTML documents can be readily converted to XML. XML is a platform-independent, vendor-independent, and media-independent language for publishing. XML also supports the interchange of data and information between dissimilar databases. Jon Bosak describes some of the ways that an XML system could enhance client-side manipulations of data.[3] Customized displays of documents and a phone book sorted by first name instead of by last name are just two of the examples. In an article in *EContent* titled "X Marks the Spot," Bob Doyle both provides a clear description of XML in content-creation contexts and compares a dozen XML authoring tools.[4] Because XML creates one standardized system of publishing that supports formats as dissimilar as books, printed newspapers, complex data structures, and Web documents, XML is likely to be of increasing importance in the years to come.

Future Developments

Protocols for the Web are constantly being created. The success of a protocol depends on the number of applications, such as Web browsers, that adopt it. For example, in 1999, MP3 was developed as a new protocol for compressing digital audio files for distribution over the Web. Because it is very effective at reducing the size of audio files without a significant loss of quality, it rapidly became a very popular Web format. Because of its popularity, small portable MP3 players for these files were developed and sold. The iPod from Apple Inc. is one example of the successful implementation of the MP3 protocol. Although MP3 is the current informal standard for compressed audio files, it is not clear at this time whether MP3 will be adopted as a formal international standard. At some point, a protocol can assume the de facto status of a standard if it effectively functions as one.

Another protocol that is gaining in importance for communication is the Voice over Internet Protocol (VoIP). This protocol allows for ordinary voice conversations to be carried over the Internet's broadband carriers rather than over traditional telephone lines or cell phone signals. VoIP is itself built on other Internet protocols and standards, including TCP/IP, while conforming to the ITU-T H.323 standard for sending voice and video using the Internet. Because of technical challenges relating to emergency services (e.g., 9-1-1) and security, it is not clear whether VoIP will evolve into a ubiquitous communication system or remain a niche solution.

As this discussion of file formats demonstrates, the Internet and the Web have to be learned simultaneously as medium and as message, as protocol and as content. A resource that can be imported through FTP has to be understood as resource and as format. Using TELNET to manipulate a distant resource can be understood both as local and as distant process. Digitized images or multimedia that are on the Internet can best be understood and manipulated as intrinsically part of the protocols and standards used to create and support them. The closest analogy might be a person encountering the printed word for the first time in the form of a book. Comprehending the book as simultaneously format, content, protocol, and standard would be necessary to assimilate and use it. Learning to "read" the structure of the Internet and the Web follows the same pattern.

BOX 6.4
IF YOU BUILD IT, THEY WILL COME

If you design a protocol that solves a problem more efficiently and more elegantly than previous solutions, the applications will follow.

PROLIFERATING RESOURCES

The Internet is so vast that knowing what is on it is literally impossible. It contains resources that did not exist even in the imagination 10 years ago. It is a self-determining entity that is growing and developing in many directions simultaneously. Many of the millions of users are also contributors to the Internet, formally through database projects such as *Wikipedia*[5] or more informally through personal Web pages, electronic mailing lists and discussion groups, and forums. One way to imagine this is as a gigantic supermarket bulletin board, with everyone free to contribute postings on any topic at any time. The Web proves the old axiom that there is freedom of the press for anyone who owns one. The Web has made it possible for nearly everyone to be a publisher.

INTERNET SOLUTIONS

People seeking to understand the Internet and use it effectively have a variety of options available. Several print guides aid in the discovery of Internet and Web resources. These include the column "Internet Resources," published in each issue of *College & Research Libraries News*.[6] Each of the columns focuses on a particular subject area and identifies authoritative resources that deal with the topic. Columns in newspapers and magazines identify sites that address consumer, health, travel, entertainment, and other information needs. However, the vast majority of such aids are contained within the Internet itself. It may seem paradoxical to turn to the Internet for help in solving Internet problems, but it can be a very effective strategy. In this section, some of the most widely available systems for navigating the Internet and Web are described.

Web search engines, such as Google, Bing, and Yahoo! Search, are some of the ways that people discover resources on the Web. Yet there is a nearly universal feeling of uncertainty in using them. Some of the questions that arise include the following: Which one works best for this request? Is the coverage complete? How can the search be made more effective? No hard and fast answers are available to any of these questions, but learning the principal mechanisms behind the search engines can help determine the proximate answers for any given question on any given day. It can also help formulate more effective search strategies.

What is commonly called a Web search engine is really a Web search system consisting of three major components: the crawler (or spider), the index, and the search engine itself. The *crawler* is a robot program that is sent out on the Web to discover new Web pages and explore the other Web pages at each site. The crawler

---

BOX 6.5
EVERYONE IS AN AUTHOR

It has been said that more people write poetry than read it. Is this true of the Web as well? If true, is it a problem?

brings this information back to the base. The information for each Web page (the URL, the title, words and phrases from the page, etc.) is added to the *index*. The *search engine* operates on the information contained in the index. When a search is conducted, the search engine looks through its index and identifies all the pages that "match" the search query.

If all search engines are based on these same three components, how does one explain their differences in action? This chapter discusses the differences in general. For a more thorough examination, one can go to the Web site *Search Engine Showdown: The Users' Guide to Web Searching*, created by Greg R. Notess, which provides very useful descriptions, comparisons, and reviews of search engines.[7] It is important to understand, however, that none of the search engines separately and not even all of them together index the Web in its entirety. There is a site, www.worldwidewebsize. com, that tries to measure the size of the indexed Web—that is, the part of the Web that the search crawlers have retrieved and put into their respective databases.

One difference in search engines lies in the number of pages at each Web site that are selected for indexing. Some Web crawlers identify only the top-level page or top- and second-level pages at each site; others follow all the URL extensions for each site. For example, although all Web crawlers would index a page with the hypothetical URL http://theuniversityofwonderful.edu, some would omit the third-level URL, http://theuniversityofwonderful.edu/library/information.html. This leads to some difficult choices for Web site developers. On the one hand, a single, main URL gives all the pages a unifying identity and clearly marks all the pages, regardless of level, as belonging to the overarching organization. On the other hand, it can make most of the pages invisible to at least some search engines. If each sub-unit of the main organization has its own top-level URL, this makes more Web pages retrievable, but also makes it more difficult for users of the page to recognize the internal relationships of the pages with one another and to explore the organizational hierarchy. This alternative approach would yield URLs that followed this pattern: http://home.universityof- wonderful.edu, http://library.universityofwonderful.edu, http://englishdepartment.uni versityofwonderful.edu, and so forth.

Another difference lies in how each search engine indexes a page that the crawler identifies. Some search engines select every word from the entire Web page for their indexes. Other search engines use formulas that determine what words from which parts of the page are included in the index. For example, a search engine might select all the words from the title and the first 20 lines of the text, supplemented by the hundred most frequently used words in the entire document.

The relative position of terms and phrases within the document is an important element in determining content. A document is likely to put its primary subject in the title and the first paragraph of the document rather than the last paragraph. Terms encountered for the first time in the last paragraph are not very likely to have received a comprehensive treatment.

Another difference among search engines is the way they determine what a Web page is about. As discussed in chapter 5, it is a reasonable operating assumption that a document that uses a term many times is more "about" that term than is one that uses it only once or twice. Some search engines count the words and phrases contained in the page and use ratio formulas to determine the most important terms. As an additional strategy to try to identify key concepts, a search engine might use statistical frequency to analyze clusters of terms in relation to one another to see if meaningful patterns emerge. Other search engines look at the titles and keywords of pages that are linked to the original page to further reinforce or refine the subject of the page. A page that has the keyword *spider*, for example, and also has links to pages containing the words *spider*, *silk*, and *arachnids* is more likely to be about the eight-legged creatures than about Web search crawlers.

Some search engines provide another layer of structure for their indexes by identifying the field for selected terms. Typical fields that some search engines include are title, named person, URL elements, and dates associated with the page. These search engines allow the search to specify the kind of information needed to satisfy the search request. These search engines function a bit like the database search systems discussed in chapter 5. Like those database search engines, the Web search engines require that field limits be constructed according to specific patterns to work correctly. As Randolph Hock notes, some search field elements are interpreted differently by different systems.[8] The date field, in particular, is one that can mean any one of several dates associated with a page: date updated, date created, date indexed, and so forth. Each search engine has a link to a help screen or a guide for advanced searching that will clarify how to format a field search and provide examples of its correct use. Each one also provides a menu that will assist with field searching among infrequent users of a particular search engine.

Search engines strive to achieve the goals of recall and precision while dealing with the millions of pages and hundreds of millions of indexing terms contained within the Web. In the context of searches, *recall* refers to the retrieval of *all* the pages that are relevant to the query, whereas precision refers to retrieving *only* the pages that are relevant to the query. The challenges faced by search engines in achieving these incompatible goals are substantial. One often hears the phrase "comparing apples and oranges" in reference to the difficulty of comparing the relative merits of disparate objects. On the Web, this challenge can be described as "comparing apples, oranges, eagles, mountains, elephants, and petunias." Pages differ in their size, audience, design, content, and structure. They are created by earnest third-graders and eminent professors. They vary in accuracy, reliability, availability, and readability. The language each uses in its content differs from another.

Like snowflakes, no two Web pages are alike. However, Web pages, unlike snowflakes, are made up of a variety of elements. A Web page may be all text or mostly images, full of sound or completely silent. A search engine combing the indexes of the Web has to develop strategies for dealing with this overwhelming diversity in ways that allow the users to take advantage of the rich resources available. All the decisions on depth of indexing, patterns, field labels, and other indexing algorithms have an impact on how each search engine achieves this goal.

To achieve recall, Web search engines use a variety of techniques. One of the principal methods is *truncation*, or *stemming*. The search words that are input are stripped of their endings, and all the words in the index that match the stem are added to the retrieval results. For example, if the search query includes the term "swimmers," the search engine would stem the word and search for those terms in the index that begin with the root "swim-." Thus, "swims," "swimming," "swim," and "swimmer" would all be counted as a match for the search term and retrieved. This is just one matching rule that each search engine defines for itself. Another rule concerns capitalization of search terms. Some search engines disregard the case of the search query, and both capitalized and lowercase terms are considered a match. Other search engines are case-sensitive and include the case of the search term as an element in determining a match. In concept-based search engines, terms from the search query are processed in a way similar to how one might look through a thesaurus, and a set of synonyms is searched in the index. In these systems, the list of terms to be searched is developed through statistical analysis of Web pages and thus is subject to a degree of imperfect assumptions about the exact relationship between any one term and a concept. All of these search rules and algorithms have as their aim retrieving a comprehensive set of Web pages for each search query.

To achieve precision, each Web search engine tries to assure that the documents retrieved are focused on the search query. Relevancy scores and ranking are the two primary ways to achieve this precision. Frequency of occurrence of a term is one way of calculating relevancy. Another factor that Web engines take into account in determining relevancy is the degree to which other Web pages with the same search terms link to one another. In addition, in general, Web pages with more links to them are likely to have been found valuable by their users.

Web search engines that provide searches limited to particular fields can be effective in improving precision on search terms that might otherwise be too generic to be useful. For example, a search for the radio show *This American Life* can be done several ways. If the three words are entered as plain text in a basic search on Google, the search produces over 84 million hits. When restricted to a particular field search, with the title in quotation marks—allintitle:"This American Life"—the search produced only 295,000 hits. In both cases the main homepage for the show is the first item retrieved. All the items on the first several screens refer specifically to the radio program, with links to podcasts and particular shows. However, even this strategy is not always effective. In spite of the simple-looking interface with its little search box, each Web search engine is supremely sensitive to the formatting of search queries. Seemingly minor differences in search string construction, such as the presence or absence of quotation marks, plus signs, and spaces, can produce disproportionate differences in results. Experimentation with these and many other formulations in several search engines produces results that are sometimes difficult to understand in the context of how the search engine is expected to handle these searches. Experience and review are recommended as strategies for maximizing the effectiveness of any search engine for particular kinds of questions.

The preceding example focused on what might be called the "known item search," in which the searcher is seeking one particular page. This type of search might also be called a closed-end search. It is a search for an item that will be recognized if retrieved. The hoped-for page may or may not exist on the Web, but the search statement is constructed to find it if it exists. This type of search is common when trying to find a corporation or an organization home page, for example. When one is searching for the Folger Shakespeare Library's home page, it will be clear whether one has found it or not. By contrast, the more open-ended search is one in which the user is looking for information about a topic. The searcher may have to retrieve and examine many pages and make comparisons among them to determine which best serves the information need at this time. The search engines' indexing and retrieval decisions can have a profound effect on these searches as well. Stemming or synonym searching is likely a more helpful feature when trying to find information on a topic than when searching for a single known page. The open-ended search needs a different formulation of its search query than a closed-end search. In contrast to the tightly focused query for the known-item search, the open-ended search is likely to be more broadly constructed. It might include fairly general terms describing the topic and perhaps some synonyms for the key concept. As an example, a search for resources that discuss privacy issues on the Web will look different from a search for the privacy watchdog group the Center for Democracy & Technology.

It is useful to realize that search engines are not working in isolation as they develop and refine their indexing and retrieval rules. With the increased importance of the Web for businesses and organizations, there is a dynamic interplay between search engines and the Web page designers. The search engines want to serve their users by providing the best, most relevant sites for each search. Web page designers want to assure their clients that their pages will be retrieved and displayed as many times as possible. Understanding that Web search engines look for frequency and density of keywords as part of their measures of relevancy, some Web page designers will repeat keywords and phrases many times throughout a document to assure their pages get indexed with these terms. To counteract this ploy, some Web search engines apply reduction formulas in their relevancy measures if search terms are repeated excessively. Although some search results may be affected somewhat by these competing strategies, the overall impact is relatively small.

It is important to remember that new Web search engines are introduced and new features are added to current search engines nearly every other week. In addition, there is a growing set of metasearch sites, which simultaneously search on several search engines.

In the face of all this simultaneous choice and change, reference librarians seeking to use search engines more proficiently may need to pursue their goal through the parallel strategies of intensive and extensive searches. The intensive part of the strategy is to learn one or two search engines very well, so that the underlying logic of the indexing and retrieval system becomes clear. This quest can be facilitated by using some of the search engine tutorials available over the Web. The extensive part of the strategy is to selectively explore a new search engine or metasearch site regularly. For example, one could conduct the same search on a familiar search engine and a completely new search engine. Comparing the results and the facility with which each one identified useful resources can expand and sharpen one's search skills. With this approach, one gains the ease and skills with searches that will produce efficient and effective search techniques.

BOX 6.6
FLAW OR FEATURE?

Discussions of the Web and its search engines usually end up revolving around a question: Is it a flaw or is it a feature? Frequently, an aspect of a search engine—automatic stemming, for example—will be a flaw for one search and a feature for another.

Whatever the search parameters of search engines, they are largely limited to searches on the "surface Web" or the "publicly indexable Web," that is, the Web of static URLs. Search engines cannot mine the riches of the "deep Web," which consists of structured databases that have query interfaces that generate dynamic links. In the deep or hidden or invisible Web, these databases respond with lists of information in response to a direct search query. The structured databases of the deep Web include such widely used sites as Amazon.com and the other subject- or content-specific databases that must be queried directly by users to create specific responses that meet the criteria.

Some parts of the deep Web are the proprietary databases that form the central resources of libraries, such as *LexisNexis* and *JSTOR*. Measuring the invisible Web presents difficulties that are discussed in a paper by Yanbo Ru and Ellis Horowitz, "Indexing the Invisible Web: A Survey."[9] Chris Sherman and Gary Price identify the multiple ways in which the invisible Web remains invisible to Web crawlers and name four kinds of invisibility: the Opaque Web, the Private Web, the Proprietary Web, and the Truly Invisible Web.[10]

Given the mix of proprietary and subscription materials that form the invisible Web, finding a single approach to making this material available to users is a challenge for reference librarians. Most users are not familiar with the multiple databases that libraries offer to provide this access. And the databases are frequently focused on a single discipline or a few interrelated disciplines. One strategy that can be considered is incorporating specialized Web search engines into the reference mix. One such program is Google Scholar.[11] Google Scholar is a program created by Google to index part of the deep Web and to make the results available to scholars and researchers everywhere. Google has arranged with publishers of scholarly material to enable the identification of their materials through Google Scholar. Automated processing of journal articles and book chapters creates an index to the material included in these arrangements. The number of publishers who have joined Google Scholar is growing as they realize the wider audiences their publications can reach through this service. Of course, Google Scholar cannot offer the full text of the material it indexes. Access to the full content of the books and journals depends on the individual library of each user. Google Scholar offers libraries an opportunity to make the links to the full text of the articles through their "Library Links Program."

BOX 6.7
THE DEEP WEB "BY THE NUMBERS"

The deep Web is a subject of a great deal of research. Some of that research is being conducted at the University of Illinois at Urbana-Champaign. An especially useful article is by Kevin Chen-Chuan Chang, Bin He, Chengkai Li, Mitesh Patel, and Zhen Zhang, titled "Structured Databases on the Web: Observations and Implications," *ACM SIGMOD Record* 33 (September 2004): 61–70. It provides statistical measurements of the deep and open Web.

INTERNET CHALLENGES

This section describes some of the challenges for reference librarians in using the Internet and its resources for reference. Many of the challenges of the Internet can be expressed as questions: Who created the resource? How can these resources be identified and cataloged? What is the authority of the resource? How can one be sure that the resource received or used is identical to the original? What are the intellectual property rights of the resource creator? How are these rights recognized and supported? Who is eligible to use these resources? The following section identifies some solutions being developed to help librarians answer these questions.

Internet Resource Description

One of the implementations of metadata is focused on a standard description of Internet and Web resources. The OCLC Online Computer Library Center and the National Center for Supercomputing Applications (NCSA) have worked together to help develop a standard set of metadata elements called the Dublin Core Metadata Element Set. It is named after OCLC's home city of Dublin, Ohio, where the initial conferences took place. The Dublin Core is a simple content description model for electronic resources.[12] This cooperative effort is designed to assist in the identification, description, and retrieval of Web resources. The Dublin Core defines a set of structured elements that are intended to be used by authors to describe their Web resources. The current set of metadata elements includes the Web resource title, creator, subject, description, publisher, contributor, date, type, format, identifier, source, language, relation, coverage, and rights. If the Dublin Core is adopted by a large number of Web resource developers, it will facilitate consistent identification and retrieval of these resources.

Metadata elements associated with Web resources form two classes of META tags: META HTTP-EQUIV tags are so called because, like regular HTTP tags, they guide the actions of the Web browser in the formatting and display of the Web resource. The other group, META NAME tags, are tags that are unrelated to the formatting and display functions. The Dublin Core is one set of META NAME tags. Search engine rules vary in their treatment of META NAME tags on Web pages. Some engines use them to index the page and its content, whereas others index the information contained in some META NAME tags, like a keyword tag, but ignore others. Still others ignore all META NAME tags. Because META NAME tags do not affect the display of Web resources, they can be used to provide meaningful content and description for a Web page that does not have extensive text. For example, many Web resources do not have meaningful titles. If a Web page is titled "My World," this title does not tell the search engines or directories anything about the content.[13] If the rest of the first page is equally lacking in semantic content, perhaps because it is covered with images of your world, or because it just has the first names of the members of a circle of friends, for example, there is nothing for a Web search engine to index or retrieve. A Web page developer can use META NAME tags to provide meaningful content and description while leaving the visual design elements uncluttered by text.

Standards

The Internet and the Web provide reference librarians with connectivity to a wide variety of electronic bibliographical resources. Many of these resources, such as online catalogs and indexing and abstracting services, are supported through proprietary systems developed by vendors and suppliers. These proprietary systems require that the resources be searched using the disparate search interfaces provided by each system developer. The multiplicity of search interfaces is a barrier to efficient use of the resources. The solution to the problem is a third-party system that can interoperate with disparate systems and provide a single user interface. This is an information retrieval standard, known in the United States as the ANSI/NISO Z39.50-2003, Information Retrieval: Application Service Definition and Protocol Specification; internationally as the ISO 23950; and informally as Z39.50.

Z39.50

The Z39.50 standard provides a client–server electronic information system design "blueprint." Information system and database developers are using this blueprint to design their systems in ways that make it possible for users of one system to access databases in another system using one set of commands, regardless of the hardware or software of the host system. Each system or database can be designed with its own unique features and search functions and search interface, but each of these is mapped to a corresponding Z39.50 element. Because Z39.50 includes the information needed to program an encoder/decoder for translating commands from one system to another, it provides a translating function that allows one system to correctly interoperate with another. When each system uses Z39.50, this allows users of each of these online catalogs to maximize the search options supported by the other and creates the largest possible common ground. It also provides for the translation of the incoming record(s) to a standard format that will be readily understood by the user. Although Z39.50 maximizes the common ground between dissimilar or different systems, it cannot supply the pieces missing from either. An option has to exist in both systems in order to be available through the Z39.50 interface. For example, if one online catalog supports adjacency searching, and another does not, the adjacency searching option will not be offered through the Z39.50 interface.

Z39.50 shows the promise and the limitations of interoperability. Z39.50 is a big advance in the move toward mutual intelligibility of different catalog systems. However, as with any translating device, Z39.50 cannot be truly idiomatic. Each system has variations in the search engine and in the specific search choices in system design and implementation. It is important that reference librarians understand that variations in indexing and retrieval decisions will have real impacts on the search results. This is a particularly subtle and important area of user education as well. Because Z39.50 can provide a familiar "look and feel" to resources, highlighting this distinction for the users will be a formidable challenge indeed.

Metasearch

As users face the bewildering and ever-expanding range of materials and sources in libraries, they often find the task of discovering the material they need overwhelming. The users contrast the complex, multilayered library search process with the simplicity of the typical one-line box of the Web's search engines and they wonder why the library is "so hard." The difficulty of meeting this challenge is one libraries have struggled with for some time. One approach created in the 2000s was federated searching, or metasearching. WebFeat (since December 2010 merged with and replaced by Serials Solutions 360 Search) and Ex Libris MetaLib are just two of the search systems that provide a single interface for multiple resources in an effort to reduce the information load on the user. Through the inclusion of the online catalog, abstracting and indexing services, and aggregator services in a federated search, the user receives results from across disparate electronic information sources simultaneously. Metasearch engines use a variety of protocols and standards in order to conduct their searches. They typically conduct the search in one of two major ways. One approach transfers the search terms into the different databases' search boxes to be operated on according to each database's native interface. The other approach interrogates the databases using Z39.50 or XML protocols.[14]

In order to be included in a federated search system, the database must have implemented the OpenURL standard (NISO/ANSI Z39.88-2004) and digital object identifier (DOI) technologies, which provide durable and consistent links to items in a database. While the federated search provides the user with lists of databases and catalogs that contain information on the topic, it does not provide evaluation or ranking of the resources. Depending on how the original search term was entered and interpreted by the search engine, results across databases may under-represent or over-represent the amount of useful information in each. The user must select from a list of database titles that are unlikely to be familiar in order to explore the results for each. Each search interface will be different in its approach to managing the list of results. But the federated search process does present to the user a broader array of information than he or she is likely to find on his or her own. Because the databases selected typically have links to full-text articles online, the user will be able to access them and determine their usefulness in rapid fashion. A fuller discussion of metasearching and the standards and protocols associated with it is in the two-part article "NISO Metasearch Initiative Targets Next Generation of Standards and Best Practices" in *Against the Grain*.[15]

Web-Scale Discovery Systems and Services

Beyond the library's catalog, journal subscriptions and aggregator resources are institutional repositories of digital resources, created and curated by the organization, and open archive sources such as HathiTrust and OAIster materials. Many of these resources are nearly invisible to their potential users because of the enormous number of sources any library is likely to have. Spotting them in an A–Z list and understanding their potential usefulness is beyond the skill set of the average or even above average user. In order to bring these disparate resources to the screens of users and researchers in a single search interface with a single merged and ranked list of results, federated searching services have recently been succeeded by the more comprehensive Web-scale discovery systems and services. This area of user discovery resources is very new and the several systems offering Web-scale discovery are in a state of nearly constant development and change. Among the Web-scale discovery services are EBSCO Discovery Service, Ex Libris Primo Central, Serials Solutions Summons, Innovative Interfaces Encore Synergy, and *WorldCat* Local. Both Ex Libris and Serials Solutions have incorporated their federated search engines into the new Web-scale discovery system either as an add-on or as an integral component.

In early 2011 some general outlines of the services are visible and are likely to be recognizable through the future versions of the products. In brief, these Web-scale discovery systems work with publishers, aggregators, integrated library systems, and institutional repositories to create a single index of the metadata of the millions of items in the service. These Web-scale discovery systems depend on additional protocols, including OAI-PMH (Open Archives Initiative Protocol for Metadata Harvesting) and API (Application Programming Interface). This comprehensive centralized index is made up of preharvested, preaggregated, and normalized metadata. The initial search interface is a single box but there are advanced search screens in each system. Results from a search inquiry are sorted and presented by complexly weighted relevancy factors. Each system also offers post-search manipulation of the results with menus of factors, for example, type of material, dates, language, author, and scope. A click on the link to the individual item in the library's collection, or a full-text article, or a link resolver will bring the user to the particular material needed. A comprehensive description of these systems is beyond the scope of this chapter. A full description of the Web-scale discovery systems is available in a January 2011 report by Jason Vaughan.[16] Vaughan includes an extremely valuable chapter on factors that differentiate the search systems as well as a chapter of questions each library will wish to consider as part of the evaluation process.

Future of Standardization

The Web has provided both the means and the necessity for this standardization. These standards and associated protocols will foster the development of compatible information resources and the integration of information from disparate sources. The reference librarian will be able to master these formats and retrieval mechanisms and be in a position to navigate the networks with expectations of success.

Technological Ripples

With each new shift and development in information technology, reference librarians face another challenge, the challenge of innovation. Each new technology provides solutions that previous technologies did not or could not provide. Each new technology also brings its own set of problems seeking resolution, although these may be hidden from view. No doubt, the typewriter instituted a substantial change in the way many tasks were accomplished at the time of its adoption throughout libraries. It was the first step in providing full catalog information at each access point.

In earlier times, due in part to the laborious nature of writing catalog cards with pen and ink, full information was provided only at the main entry card, with brief information at all other access points. Because of the higher transcription speeds possible with the typewriter, labor-saving policies of this kind became less necessary. The benefit of this technology for reference was substantial. Consistently formatted cards with more information at each access point saved the time and energy of reference librarians with every use of the catalog. These benefits had to be weighed against the costs of adopting the new technology. The costs of adoption included the expense of acquiring the typewriters, but also included training costs and maintenance costs. There were policy issues as well. Although each member of the library staff was likely to be able to write on catalog cards, it is likely that not all of them would be provided with a typewriter.

The problems the technology presented are somewhat less apparent. Each user of the typewriter had to be trained to be proficient with the machine. In the beginning, layouts of the keyboard were not standard. The QWERTY keyboard became standard neither because of its "user friendliness" nor because of its "human-factors design" but because it reduced the jamming of the mechanical keys. The QWERTY keyboard shows some of the long-term consequences of standard development.

The standard can long outlive its origins in necessity and can, in some cases, actively slow the pace of development. If the typewriter had been invented in an English-speaking country after the invention of the transistor, for example, its keyboard would likely be standardized according to the frequency of use of letters in the English language. Typographical errors would likely be much less frequent in this case, and the average speed of typing would likely be much higher.

Technical innovations create policy issues as well. Each library had to weigh the cost and benefit factors associated with typewriters and determine the best distribution. Typewriters were relatively expensive machines. How few could the library purchase while still gaining the advantage of the technology? As in any early innovation, not every manufacturer survived. Thus, some libraries had a variety of typewriters for which there were no longer parts or service available. These are some of the costs of adoption of new technologies.

In any environment, there will be early technology adapters who usually pay substantial premiums in terms of human resources to learn and manage new technologies. The expectation is that these costs will be recouped in the advantages offered by the change. Many times, this strategy pays off, but in other situations, the investment has to be written off as a learning experience.

Some costs are associated with late adoption of new technologies as well. Staff time and energy have to be expended to keep the old system functional. Technical support becomes more difficult to find as those with expertise in the old system move on. Being out-of-step with the rest of the library systems also has costs. Cooperative arrangements are more difficult, expensive, or just impossible because of the incompatibility of the old technology with the new. Effective management of technology requires a careful balance between the costs of adoption and the costs of non-adoption. It is likely that the organization's experience with previous generations of technology will shape the corporate culture in this regard. One position may be described by the old saying "once burned, twice shy," which suggests caution and delay as important elements in the technology adoption policy. On the other hand, as Mark Twain noted, "We should be careful to get out of an experience only the wisdom that is in it—and stop there; lest we be like the cat that sits down on a hot stove lid. She will never sit down on a hot stove lid again—and that is well; but also she will never sit down on a cold one any more."[17] This suggests that adoption assessment needs to focus on the particular strengths, weaknesses, costs, and benefits of each opportunity rather than the number of months since first deployment. There are lessons that can be learned too well.

Orphan Technologies

One of the continuing challenges of electronic resources is that technological innovation often leads to technological obsolescence. Most technological innovations have one of two relationships with the previous generation of hardware and software. The relationship can be one of backward compatibility in which the new technology accommodates the old. For example, newer CD-ROM drives usually play CD-ROMs compiled under older standards. This is largely a result of the size and importance of the installed base of the older technology. It would take a brave standard to render millions upon millions of CD audio and CD-ROM discs obsolete. It is likely to happen someday, but not yet. One complication of backward compatibility is the likelihood that the newer technology is unable to be as innovative, efficient, or radical as it could be. It represents a compromise between the possible and the achievable.

With many other technologies, the relationship is succession, in which the new technology supersedes the older technology and leaves it behind. This is the result when the projected improvements cannot be achieved within the framework of the old. In another historical (if more recent) example, the larger capacity of the 3.5" disks depended on a change in the way data is written and read that was incompatible with the old 5.25" floppy disks. Therefore, the newer disks superseded the old and produced a large number of old diskettes cannot be read on any current computer. At the time of the introduction of the smaller diskette size, most computers came with two disk drives, one for each size. Those users who had stored important data on the larger floppies had to migrate their data to the new format while the equipment supporting the old format was available.

Not everyone took advantage of this migration window. Consequently, there are offices and desk drawers throughout the land that have floppies that are for all practical purposes unusable. It may be that some large computer labs and specialized data recovery companies can transfer the content to a more modern format, but this is an undertaking that most users do not pursue. The floppy diskette is just one more step in a long line of orphan technologies, ranging from the original 80-column punch cards to computer tapes of various outmoded sizes, as well as a variety of other computer disk sizes. For data storage, the DVD and the flash drive are rapidly replacing CD-ROMs and other disks.

Electronic Archiving

A topic related to orphan technology is electronic archiving. At this time, electronic archiving is essentially an oxymoron. As the preceding examples show, that data continue to exist in a physical sense on an uncorrupted disk or a perfectly preserved CD-ROM does not mean that the data have been archived. If the data exist on only one medium, and if the last machine to read that particular format has broken beyond repair, the existence of the physical medium does not equal preservation. At this time, preservation of electronic content consists of a series of migrations from medium to medium. This requires a serious commitment of resources to set up a regular review and updating of all the electronic formats held in a collection. Decisions about what to keep will vary with the library's mission.

When it comes to content that is on the Web, archiving becomes even more problematic. To begin with, archiving has two different meanings within the context of the Web. One meaning refers to making the collected communications available as a searchable file. One such archive is the Liblicense-L archive at Yale at http://www.library.yale.edu/~llicense/ListArchives/. One can go to the archive and search on a topic related to the licensing of electronic resources by libraries. It will list the items that contain that term and provide a list of threaded discussions. This type of Web archive is straightforward. It requires an investment of time and equipment to maintain, but each message is a self-defined, self-contained unit. A message may refer to previous messages, often by incorporation, but is itself the unit of analysis.

As more and more of the world's cultural and intellectual content migrates to the Web, there is concern about the impermanence of the record. This issue is the focus of the other kind of archiving of Web content. Some of the issues associated with this broader aspect of archiving of the Web are discussed by Peter Lyman and Brewster Kahle, including what types of digital artifacts to archive, who will take responsibility for archiving, and what technologies are available for this purpose.[18]

Some organizations do a periodic preservation of their Web sites, as a "snapshot." A copy is made and saved of all the current pages of a site. One fundamental issue that confronts the library wishing to archive the content of its Web site is defining what is meant by a Web page. Most Web pages contain links to other pages. Some of these linked Web pages contain a substantial portion of the content of the linking page. However, retrieving these related pages and including them in any preservation process is beyond the scope of these Web site projects. If it were technically possible, intellectual property rights issues would greatly impede the inclusion of these linked pages. In any case, because of the tremendously dynamic nature of the Web, any decision concerning a linked page is subject to a de facto veto by changes in the linked page itself. The life span of Web pages can be measured in days or weeks. The term "link rot" is evocative of the speed and likelihood of a link becoming unusable. Although many of these pages might be considered ephemeral in the sense of referring to occasions that have come and gone, the occasion may be worth remembering as part of our shared cultural experience. Some of what we know about William Shakespeare is from the preserved playbills and other ephemera. If a new play by a novice playwright is produced by a small theater company, but the only record of this is on the Web, what will the future know of it?

BOX 6.8
PRESERVATION AND THE WEB

Clifford Lynch observes that there is a set of questions "about stewardship more broadly in the digital age; these are related to preservation but go far beyond preservation, and move into cultural, public policy, and ethical questions about how and what we remember and forget, about when and how it is appropriate to invest in ensuring the survival of memory."[19] What does this mean for reference librarians?

During this period of transition from mostly paper to mostly digital publication, some issues of identity are emerging. In the recent past, it has been possible to refer to a journal or a reference book and have an expectation that all users of the journal or reference book will have the same experience with items of identical content. The title *Statistical Abstract of the United States*, for example, has existed in paper for more than one hundred years. A user of the 1978 volume in Namibia will see the same pages as a user in Virginia. The same is true for such standard reference titles as *Contemporary Authors*. However, as these titles migrate to the Web, the constancy of their content and the ability to reliably predict the information that will be found at the Web site is no longer a certainty. Some journals have a print version and an e-version that differ substantially from one another. The e-version has no page limits, perhaps, or allows for a fuller presentation of the statistical analysis of the data. The e-version may contain links to the full text of the cited articles. It is reasonable to ask, which is the *real* journal? It is also reasonable to ask about the preservation of the full content of both versions. It is likely that major research libraries will maintain a copy of the print version for as long as it is published, and it is likely that the major publishers of journals will keep copies of the e-versions as well.

Mechanisms for maintaining permanent access to the preserved copies are still being developed. OCLC Electronic Collections Online has committed the considerable resources of OCLC to permanently preserving content and access to the e-journals in its collection. Other organizations such as *JSTOR* are committed to developing a permanent collection of digitized journals. In addition, there are projects such as Portico, which began as the Electronic-Archiving Initiative, a collaborative effort of publishers, librarians, and foundations designed and supported to provide a permanent electronic archive of the journals published by the member publishers (http://www.portico.org/digital-preservation/).

All of these efforts are commendable and will result in the preservation of a significant number of the published e-journals and e-versions of journals. There are still concerns about the material that is less mainstream. Which organizations have sufficient resources to spend on developing and maintaining permanent access to the smaller, experimental, and short-lived journals and other publications on the Web? Having recognized that this preservation effort is beyond the resources of any one institution or library, organizations have come together to share in discovering and implementing solutions. Some of the major players include the Digital Preservation Coalition (DPC, http://www.dpconline.org/) from the United Kingdom and the International Internet Preservation Consortium (http://netpreserve.org/about/index.php), composed of national libraries of a number of countries in Asia, Australia/Oceania, Europe, and North America, as well as related organizations such as the Internet Archive (U.S.).

In addition to the commercial, personal, and nonprofit material on the Web, every university and research organization creates digital content. Scholars and researchers conduct experiments, do statistical analyses, create and analyze cultural texts and objects, and present the results in a variety of forums and arenas. Texts of articles and books are created, revised, edited, and printed in electronic formats. Institutions are collaborating in a variety of ways to explore the possibilities for permanently gathering and maintaining these work products and providing access to the contents in perpetuity, typically called an institutional repository. Legal, technical, and resource challenges abound in this effort.

PUBLIC INFORMATION RESOURCES AND THE REFERENCE LIBRARIAN

Many of the developments on the Web that have been touched on in this and other chapters have resulted in an incredible expansion of information resources available to everyone who has access to an Internet connection. The growth in high-speed Web access in homes, hotel rooms, offices, and even trains and cars has greatly lowered the threshold to accessing information. The consequences for reference librarians of the growth of the personal delivery of information services are hard to determine.

People have always had alternative sources of information on any topic. Typically, the primary source is the circle of family and friends. Local and national news sources are likely the second most important information source. Perhaps now many people depend on the news preferences they have configured for their Web portal. Where libraries and reference departments fit into the strategy depends on the education and experience of the person seeking the information. Will the wiring of the world's living rooms change the fundamental nature of reference work, or will it change it only on the margins? As reference librarians expand the scope of their resources and services, will they also expand their audience? Will there be a 24-hour TV librarian on channel 411? Will the person at home punch in a question and the answer appear as an e-mail message on the person's own channel 1? Or will the inquirer turn on the interactive camera on the television set and ask the librarian a question live and get a personal video reply? These are some possible roles for reference librarians.

One can envision other roles for reference librarians in the digital information industry. Some are relatively easy to identify, if hard to solve, such as the need to reach and teach the remote user of the library's resources. Others are more elusive, such as imagining and creating the new role of the library in the planning and implementation of these technologies, nationally and locally.

THE FUTURE OF REFERENCE TECHNOLOGY

One aspect of technological innovation is the fact that the people who interact with the new technology have a mental framework shaped by their previous experience. The ways in which we think about the new are shaped by the old. It takes some maturing of technology before we can start to think about it in entirely new ways. The initial implementation of NCSA's Mosaic Web browser was shaped at least in part by the developers' experiences with Gopher, Archie, and Veronica, to name but a few of the precursors of the World Wide Web. An experienced reference librarian initially approached the Web from the perspective of a skilled command-line searcher. The two technologies share a common base of electronic information with associated retrieval software. However, the Boolean approach is not an ideal match for searching millions of pages of full-text resources, and orderly sets are not the likely outcome of a Web search. With an examination of the Web on its own terms as a reference resource, reference librarians have adopted new strategies and new skills.

The growing body of electronic texts and multimedia resources available over the Internet and the Web requires a fresh look at how information is organized and retrieved. An examination of how users find and utilize information may lead to the conclusion that the traditional lines that have been drawn between different types of materials are not understood by users. For example, do the boundaries drawn between journal articles and books reflect useful distinctions about intellectual activities, or do they reflect the traditional methods of material production and distribution? If a growing understanding of users' needs reveals it to be a distinction that hinders access and use, it is likely that an integrated system of access to all forms of library resources will be developed. Z39.50 is just one mechanism that can be implemented to provide a single, unified interface to a wide variety of information resources. Corporate models, such as Google Scholar, are also shaping the information space of the library's users.

This example can serve as a model for the reexamination and reimagining of other reference tools and systems and how they serve their users. Reference librarians have a vital role to play in designing and conducting the research that will inform the new system designs and in interacting with system developers to ensure that the needed functionalities are built-in from the start. These redesigned information systems will provide reference librarians with the real tools needed to answer the question "May I help you?"

NOTES

1.   Michael M. Roberts, "Lessons for the Future Internet: Learning from the Past," *Educause Review* 41(July/August 2006): 20–24.

2.   Balachander Krishnamurthy, Jeffrey C. Mogul, and David M. Kristol, "Key Differences between HTTP/1.0 and HTTP/1.1," *Computer Networks* 31 (1999): 1737–51.

3.   Jon Bosak, "XML, Java, and the Future of the Web." http://metalab.unc.edu/pub/sun-info/standards/xml/why/xmlapps.htm.

4.   Bob Doyle, "X Marks the Spot: Let's Take Today's XML Content-Creation Tools for a Spin," *EContent* 29 (June 2006): 22–30.

5.   *Wikipedia.* http://www.wikipedia.org/.

6.   "Internet Resources," *College & Research Libraries News.* http://crln.acrl.org.

7.   Greg R. Notess, "Search Engine Showdown: The Users' Guide to Web Searching." http://www.searchengineshowdown.com/.

8.   Randolph Hock, "The Latest Field Trip: An Update on Field Searching in Web Search Engines," *Online* 28 (September/October 2004): 15–21.

9.   Yanbo Ru and Ellis Horowitz, "Indexing the Invisible Web: A Survey," *Online Information Review* 29 (2005): 249–65.

10.   Chris Sherman and Gary Price, "The Invisible Web: Uncovering Sources Search Engines Can't See," *Library Trends* 52 (2003): 282–98.

11.   "About Google Scholar." http://scholar.google.com/intl/en/scholar/about.html.

12.   Dublin Core Metadata Initiative. http://dublincore.org/index.shtml.

13.   "How to Use HTML Meta Tags." http://searchenginewatch.com/2167931.

14.   Xiaotian Chen, "MetaLib, WebFeat, and Google: The Strengths and Weaknesses of Federated Search Engines Compared with Google," *Online Information Review* 30 (2006): 413–27.

15.   Cynthia Hodgson, Andrew Pace, and Jenny Walker, "NISO Metasearch Initiative Targets Next Generation of Standards and Best Practices," *Against the Grain* 18 (February 2006): 79–82; Cynthia Hodgson, Andrew Pace, and Jenny Walker, "NISO Metasearch Initiative Issues First Set of Recommendations," *Against the Grain* 18 (June 2006): 74–76.

16.   Jason Vaughan, "Web Scale Discovery Services," *Library Technology Reports* 47, no. 1 (January 2011), 61 pp.

17.   John Bartlett, *Familiar Quotations*, 14th ed. (Boston: Little, Brown, 1968), 762.

18.   Peter Lyman and Brewster Kahle, "Archiving Digital Cultural Artifacts: Organizing an Agenda for Action," *D-Lib Magazine* 4 (July/August 1998). http://www.dlib.org/dlib/july98/07lyman.html.

19.   Clifford Lynch, "Where Do We Go From Here? The Next Decade for Digital Libraries," *D-Lib Magazine* 11 (July/August 2005). http://www.dlib.org/dlib/july05/lynch/07lynch.html.

ADDITIONAL READINGS

Current Cites: *An Annotated Bibliography of Selected Articles, Books, and Digital Documents on Information Technology.* Ed. Roy Tennant. http://lists.webjunction.org/currentcites/.

This is a current awareness service offered by a team of librarians and library staff. The editors select articles, reports, and some monographs, print and digital, on a wide range of topics under the broad umbrella of electronic information technology. They add clear, evaluative, and helpful annotations and distribute the list monthly to subscribers. There is an accessible archive of the database from August 1990 to the present.

Digital Preservation: The National Digital Information Infrastructure and Preservation Program. http://www.digitalpreservation.gov/.

This site presents information about the National Digital Information Infrastructure and Preservation Program, sponsored by the Library of Congress. Created in December 2000 under Public Law 106-554, the program will provide, through a collaborative effort with federal agencies and other institutions, a national focus on important policy, standards, and technical components necessary to preserve digital content. The program's mission is to "develop a national strategy to collect, preserve and make available significant digital content, especially information that is created in digital form only, for current and future generations."

Hayes, David, and Alan Hopkinson. "Librarians Need Standards." *Library + Information Update* 5 (November 2006): 31–33.

In this brief article, the authors identify and clarify the standards and protocols that are central to the library in the realm of electronic information services.

Hock, Randolph. *The Extreme Searcher's Internet Handbook: A Guide for the Serious Searcher.* 3rd ed. Medford, NJ: CyberAge Books, 2010. 339 pp.

This book includes a discussion of the basics of search engines as well as profiles of several of the most widely used ones. Other chapters cover such topics as directories and portals and finding images, audio, and video.

McDermott, Irene E., and Barbara Quint, eds. *The Librarian's Internet Survival Guide Strategies for the High-Tech Reference Desk*. 2nd ed. Medford, NJ: Information Today, 2006. 298 pp.

This is an updated edition of the popular 2002 title. The first nine chapters cover "Ready Reference on the Web: Resources for Patrons," and the six chapters in Part 2 offer advice for reference librarians on managing e-mail, teaching the Internet, making and maintaining Web pages, making the Web accessible to disabled users, computer troubleshooting, and keeping up with changes on the Web.

Miller, Paul. "Z39.50 for All." *Ariadne* 21 (September 1999). http://www.ariadne.ac.uk/issue21/z3950/intro.html.

This article is an excellent introduction to Z39.50. It draws together the concepts and implementation of Z39.50 in libraries and in other environments. The examples are well selected and clear. A comprehensive list of references to the active players in the development of Z39.50 is included.

Notess, Greg R. *Teaching Web Search Skills: Techniques and Strategies of Top Trainers*. Medford, NJ: Information Today, 2006. 344 pp.

This book is written by the foremost library expert on Web search engines. It will be most useful to the information professional who is training Internet users to search the Web.

Woodyard-Robinson, Deborah, ed. "Digital Preservation: Finding Balance." Special issue. *Library Trends* 54 (Summer 2005). 172 pp.

This special issue of *Library Trends* addresses many of the challenges and issues in digital preservation: technical issues, identification of materials, metadata, and access. It also includes articles from libraries that have started some of the solutions.

Chapter

7

Access-Related Reference Services

Lynn Wiley

INTRODUCTION

How did you obtain this textbook you are reading now? Chances are that you bought it because you needed it for your coursework. But you may have chosen to look for it at a library, your college or university, or even a public library and then borrowed it rather than make the purchase. Maybe you found that your library owned a copy, but it was not available for you to take out because someone else already had borrowed it, or it was on reserve for in-house use only. If it was loaned out, you may have known to place a hold to get an alert on its return, or you may have asked that your local library find it for you elsewhere. And it could be that your book is available online as an e-book or offered by the publisher online for a fee. But the point here is, did you know you had library options for access to a title?

Reference personnel help library users find facts or information sources and are teachers as well, instructing users on effective research and retrieval skills. Accurate and focused bibliographic searching assistance for users seeking materials in any format is an important reference service, especially because an untutored Internet search can retrieve too much that is not useful or that is unreliable. With reference help, users can narrow their search strategies to identify titles covering their topic, but what about that next step, actually getting the materials on that final list? Reference librarians can open doors to the world of information for a library user, but what the user really wants is the actual item and often right away. Usually, what users really want is to do it all in one easy interface that links to one comprehensive database. That service is not yet available, but reference librarians will help build the next new development toward that goal.

Librarians are responsible for building services and tools to best guide users to titles held locally and, if needed, anywhere in the world. Those services include circulation policies that control local use, loan periods, and recalls as well as interlibrary loan and document delivery processes. Librarians do the behind-the-scene negotiations for the best online resource licensing terms and develop the tutorials to advise on searching tools. Those tools include many different databases, indexes, and abstracts used to locate information at the article and chapter levels and guides to online catalogs, including the relatively new Web-based layered interfaces referred to as next-generation catalogs. Librarians know how to interpret serial holdings to find who owns a serial for the date associated with a specific needed article. They understand that the format of a media material will define its usability depending on the equipment available. They are aware of the license agreements that control access to online resources and advise the user on their access rights to those titles. They provide guidance on the copyright issues that may restrict access. They are at the forefront in developing the standards and technology used in information systems and in usability testing to adapt tools for users. Reference personnel are pushing more services to where users live and work. These staff members develop, maintain, and enhance access service options, designed within their local library environment, to provide for the easy discovery and delivery of content, including that which is not directly available, owned, or leased. These staff must also navigate the many options users have for obtaining a title depending on time, cost, or format and make sure that users get the most out of their local library collections and services. Librarians juggle many roles and continually adapt to new environments and technology. One active participant in this process notes, "After looking back over the past 30 years, I can't begin to imagine where we will end up in another 30 years. But the point isn't to be able to predict the future but to help create it. And that we can do."[1]

This chapter describes what access to information can entail and provides an overview of library cooperative networks; those policies and processes, from local to global, that enhance access; the technology and standards available to streamline access; and the legal or contractual and even environmental factors that define and impact access to material that library users want and need.

Access Expectations

How much information is available? (See Box 7.1.) How many secondary sources such as books and journals? How many articles in journals or in newspapers? What about conference proceedings or technical reports and media material from music to movies? Types of primary research materials are countless, including letters, manuscripts, pamphlets, diaries, meeting minutes, data files of all types, medical studies, legal cases, and legislative documents. Users may want access to any or all of these, but the problems in obtaining them are large and complex.

Researchers, students, and other information seekers all want access to all kinds of information more than ever. Not only is there more information out there; it is easier than ever to find out about its existence on the Internet. Libraries simply do not own it all; even the very largest library could not buy all that its users need. This is even truer today as costs have increased and as libraries spend more resources on online content:

Not only have electronic materials expenditures grown sharply in the past decade, they have grown at a rate far exceeding that of library materials

---

BOX 7.1
HOW MUCH INFORMATION IS THERE ANYWAY?

The School of Information Management and Systems at the University of California at Berkeley completed a research project to answer this question. Their reports are available at http://www2.sims.berkeley.edu/research/projects/how-much-info-2003/. The project addresses counts such as how many books have been printed and distributed. Based on their research, they guesstimate that there are anywhere from 74 to 175 million unique books held throughout the world. The researchers also suggest that, counting multiple copies of all those unique titles, more than 4 billion books exist worldwide.

Of those books, others estimate that more than 70 percent are no longer in print.[2] If not in print, they will not be available in bookstores; they are in libraries, with some portion in the hands of private collectors.

Serials and the unique articles they contain are also a vast number. *Ulrich's*, the authoritative source for serial information, currently provides information for more than 300,000 serial titles.[3] This translates into millions of articles published annually and does not include older serials now ceased, which cover even more articles that are still requested by researchers; such articles may be long gone from publisher warehouses but are collectively held by libraries.

---

expenditures overall.... In every year of the last decade electronic materials expenditures have grown sharply, anywhere between two and ten times faster than other materials expenditures have. The average ARL university library now spends 51% of its materials budget on electronic resources and 68 ARL libraries report that they spent more than 50% of their materials budget on electronic resources.[4]

Even as individual library budgets buy less, user demand increases exponentially. This is a library and Internet success story resulting from the added research and discovery tools that better expose content. Those tools include a huge array of online indexes that are easy to use; tables of contents that have been added to monograph records for online chapter-level details; the implementation of software services that allow users to link from an online index directly to a full-text source or online order service; and services to search many online indexes and abstracts simultaneously, retrieving citations from many sources with one easy search input.

A major contribution that will forever change how users obtain books is the Google Books project (see Box 7.2), through which millions of books will be scanned and findable on the Internet. The scanning will make the titles searchable, though not all the content is freely available. The Google settlement with authors and publishers is still not complete, so it is not clear how many publishers are participating or how many authors may choose to opt out and thereby withdraw content. The settlement also does not include nonbooks, such as journals, newspapers, and music scores. Because few international libraries' collections were scanned, titles published overseas

---

BOX 7.2
GOOGLE BOOKS PROJECT

The impact of Google's digitizing millions of books has every potential to revolutionize access, but many questions remain regarding just what anyone may use.

The Google Print Library Project formally began in 2004 with the announcement that it would be digitizing the collections of five major libraries (Harvard, New York Public, Oxford, Stanford, and University of Michigan) and would cover more than 15 million volumes. Since that time, many other libraries, including a few international ones, have joined in this project, which was renamed to Google Books in 2005. Google provides a history at http://books.google.com/intl/en/googlebooks/history.html.

---

may not be as comprehensively covered as those in the United States. But if the settlement does go through, users will be able to purchase many out-of-print titles previously unavailable. With public libraries able to provide full access to the Google content via at least one public station, users should still be able to rely on libraries as a primary source for free access.

Only books in the public domain may be viewed in their entirety or downloaded; the full text of the rest of the titles is searchable, but only very small portions called snippets can be seen by the public. A significant controversy remains over the project with regard to the scanning techniques used, the nature of the agreements reached with the libraries owning the books, and the fear that Google, a commercial enterprise, will have too much control over this content and may not uphold the equitable access desired. The most significant disagreements over the scanning of the materials are due to alleged copyright infringement. A settlement of several lawsuits brought against Google by authors and publishers has been proposed (http://books.google.com/googlebooks/agreement/). That agreement and its implications were still being debated as of 2011. It has the potential to provide for unprecedented access to book content, though Google would most certainly make revenue under the terms of the settlement, which include selling the subscriptions they will be able to offer to the Google Books database, selling individual books as print-on-demand copies, and selling more advertising on the Web pages where the book content resides.

LIBRARY RESPONSES

Library Collections

Librarians do not all buy the same thing. This is a good thing for the public as a whole because the aggregated "collective collection" of libraries then has more breadth and depth. Regarding those 74 to 175 million unique titles and the as many as 4 billion copies, who owns them? In the United States and Canada alone, there are nearly 34,000 libraries.[5] The question then becomes, what do they own collectively? A number of studies have been done on who owns what, on the collection overlap or the lack of that overlap, and on the collection gap that exists across libraries' monograph collections.

Greg Byerly's 1996 report on the OhioLINK libraries' shared titles reveals how little overlap there is for monographs in Ohio academic libraries' collections.[6] In 2005, another group of researchers looked at the holdings of the original group of five libraries participating in the Google Books project to reexamine the overlap question. Looking at a 2005 copy of the biggest bibliographic database in the world, OCLC *WorldCat*, which then covered 32 million book records, they found that the group of five collections together did not cover even two-thirds of the material represented in this database. Further analysis of the aggregated collection of those five revealed that 60 percent of the titles were owned by only one of them.[7] Google has since cast a wider net to cover a greater number of unique titles, expanding its program to include other libraries in addition to that initial group of five.

Having access to deep collections is needed, as is indicated by studies of the large percentage of unique materials that users ask for that must be obtained from another library. These may be single articles from an older journal title, out-of-print books, or older editions of works. The 1997 study by Chandra Prabha and Elizabeth Marsh on interlibrary loan requests illustrated how many requests can be for one article from one single journal title.[8] This was reinforced in another statewide study done in 2001 that again confirmed a long "comet tail" of article requests.[9] Popular literature confirms this as well, in highlighting a new market for more esoteric material that is now better exposed on the Web to potential customers who then want to obtain this material. Chris Anderson made this concept well known in his article and subsequent book about the long tail of products consumers wish to find and obtain (see Box 7.3). Librarians certainly understand the principles he outlines, including one in particular: making it easy to find and then obtain materials that do not always get the attention they deserve. Users seek to cast a wide net for the long tail via the interlibrary loan services or network-based requesting systems offered by their home library.

BOX 7.3
PRINCIPLES OF THE LONG TAIL

Unlimited selection is revealing truths about what consumers want and how they want to get it in service after service, from DVDs at Netflix to music videos on Yahoo! Launch to songs in the iTunes Music Store and Rhapsody. People are going deep into the catalog, down the long, long list of available titles, far past what is available at Blockbuster Video, Tower Records, and Barnes & Noble.[10]

Following are Chris Anderson's principles in brief:

Rule 1: Make everything available.
Rule 2: Cut the price in half. Now lower it.
Rule 3: Help me [the user] find it.

Interlibrary Loan (ILL)

Interlibrary loan, or ILL, also known as *library resource sharing*, covers the process of obtaining the loan of a book or other circulating media, or receiving a copy of a book chapter, a document, or a journal article, from any library willing to share their collections. Copy services are often referred to as document delivery, but ILL in the library vernacular covers both *returnables* (a loan of an item) and *nonreturnables* (a copy). Librarians have been loaning to each other for many years. ILL is a library-to-library loan, with the lending library never knowing much about the ultimate borrower. A researcher may not be able to enter a particular library because of lack of affiliation, but that library user may still obtain a loan from that collection via ILL, whether that library is nearby or thousands of miles away.

Direct Consortial Borrowing (DCB) is different. Here a group of libraries share access to their holdings via one central catalog or system and allow their users to request any available circulating item, such that each library loans directly to borrowers, who are all affiliated with the group of libraries. Typically the borrowers all have similar privileges across the libraries, including onsite access.

Interlibrary loan was once a poor cousin in the suite of library services; it was slow, cumbersome to initiate, and not always successful. Times have changed. The growth and acceptance of ILL as a core service is due to a combination of factors, including a high demand for research material coupled with focused support on the part of many librarians and organizations in developing better systems to make the service more reliable. Revisions to the national Interlibrary Loan Code document the evolution of the service. The changes to this code, a governing protocol for library sharing in the United States, illustrate how perceptions of the service have changed in the library community. Once seen as a privilege for the elite few as evidenced by earlier versions,[11] ILL is now a core part of any routine access program. Librarians are expected to provide excellent lending service to those requesting to borrow, as clearly outlined in the latest version of the *Interlibrary Loan Code for the United States*, approved in 2008 and available at http://www.ala.org/ala/mgrps/divs/rusa/resources/guidelines/interlibrary.cfm. ILL practitioners have also called for libraries to commit to better services in issuing a manifesto for interlibrary loan units everywhere.[12] This manifesto asks for signatures from all engaged in borrowing or lending activity as testimony to their commitment to a series of best practices that together guarantee a more consistent level of service.

The Association of Research Libraries (ARL) sponsored several programs beginning in 1993 to provide for more assessment and support of ILL. Two well-known programs were the North American Interlibrary Loan and Document Delivery Project (NAILDD) and the ILL/Document Delivery Performance Measure Studies. These programs included studies of the process and costs, shared statistics, and cooperative work with vendors and networks to help streamline the service and to adopt standards for new systems for better interoperability. Cost and performance studies of the service conducted by ARL revealed how labor-intensive the process was and also revealed some best practices to emulate. Libraries with better automated processes had lower costs. The studies helped to spotlight changes that could be made and reminded all that the service was expensive. This helped librarians to put the service in context with purchases made for their collections. The ARL ILL cost study was performed three times, with the latest results published in 2004. The most recent study validated previous ones and showed some improvements, with a decrease in cost and decrease in turnaround time. The study collected data on the 2001–02 performance of mediated and user-initiated ILL operations in 72 research, academic, and special libraries. This study showed that the full cost of an ILL transaction from initiation to receipt by the requester, from the borrowing cycle through the lending, is still close to $30, except where direct borrowing systems involving less labor were used.[13] One unexpected consequence was that taking into account the total cost of an ILL transaction, more libraries started experimenting with outright purchases of those titles requested rather then requesting a loan. Purchase-on-demand programs are now part of many ILL or access programs. One of the first published studies documents the success of such a program in two academic libraries.[14] Because not all material requested can be easily purchased, requests filled in this manner typically represent just a small percentage of the total requests any one library may fill for their users. A look at the statistics generated by some of the larger associations or organizations that monitor or facilitate ILL activity reveals how large the volume is (see Box 7.4).

What are the labor-intensive parts of interlibrary loan? For returnables, the borrower locates a source for a title and ideally a copy that is available. The lender must obtain a local call number and then physically retrieve it, which may require additional searching if it is not on the shelf. The title, when located, must be physically delivered to the requesting library, which may require special packaging. Once received at the borrowing site, the loan is tracked for delivery and then circulated to the borrower, which requires notification, pickup, and then return tracking. Article or document requests require a complete citation and, for best fulfillment, not only a source for the title but also information on the holdings to be sure the required year is held. Once the lender locates the item locally, it must be copied and then delivered to the requester. Here at least the item need not be returned, and new systems allow

---

BOX 7.4
ILL STATISTICS: A SAMPLING

- According to the Association of Research Libraries, FY 2008, ILL borrowing totaled 3,511,075, and lending was 4,497,888 (http://www.arl.org/stats/annualsurveys/arlstats/statxls.shtml).
- OCLC ILL borrowing and lending totaled 10.3 million in FY 2009 (http://www.oclc.org/us/en/news/publications/annualreports/2000/2009.pdf).
- The National Library of Medicine DOCLINE reported 1.9 million transactions in FY 2008 (http://www.nlm.nih.gov/docline/doclinepresentations.html).
- The ILL activity for the National Center for Education Statistics Academic Libraries in 2006 included 10,801,531 provided and 10,265,385 received ILL requests (http://nces.ed.gov/pubs2008/2008337.pdf).

for desktop delivery, bypassing labor-intensive manual delivery. Anywhere along the way, a request may stall because of lack of an available copy or a noncirculation policy or because a citation was scrambled, an article was ripped out of a journal, or a license restricted the use of an online copy. Invoicing (for lender sending and borrowing payment), the need for statistics management for both the borrowing and the lending side, and analysis of impact on collections all add to the work level.

Systems have been developed to take more of the labor out of the fulfillment equation. These allow users to initiate requests by capturing the citation of the item sought and then passing this on to a potential lender without mediation. The system may help lenders by automatically matching requests to local call numbers and canceling requests for titles not available or that do not meet parameters defined by the lender. A robust system will facilitate local inventory control of temporarily held loans and will also provide for easy user tracking of their material. Some of these systems are installed locally to help manage ILL, whereas others are network-based and used by groups of libraries. A few of the best-known systems are detailed in Box 7.5. Later sections of this chapter provide more detail on how libraries maximize use of their local collections and work together to build cooperative services to manage the collective inventories.

BOX 7.5
ILL MANAGEMENT SYSTEMS

- OCLC's *WorldCat* Resource Sharing is an easy-to-use Web-based interface that facilitates the ordering of books and articles from a network of thousands of libraries. OCLC has added many features to this service to reduce the labor and decrease the time needed to obtain a book or article from another collection.
- ILLiad is a comprehensive ILL management tool that allows for local control and customization of ILL workflow, including user tracking of requests and options for a local database of ILL transactions. ILLiad works with a variety of systems to provide for paperless and efficient handling of any transaction. It can be purchased directly from the developers at Atlas or through OCLC, which partners with Atlas to optimize ILL options for libraries.
- Relais International is a company that offers software to connect libraries not sharing a system to facilitate loan requesting and also offers document delivery solutions for optimal nonreturnable fulfillment.
- Auto-Graphics AGent Resource Sharing software enables libraries with different automation systems to share resources with one another.
- VDX is a system made available by OCLC to allow groups of libraries to optimize how they work together to share collections when their local systems cannot do that for them.
- SirsiDynix offers URSA (Universal Resource Sharing Application), which resembles VDX in providing for better controls between partner libraries of their OCLC activity.

Library Networks: Local to Shared

Librarians require an accurate inventory of the collection as well as ways to authenticate and link affiliated users to online resources and services so that the material can be used. The term *inventory* invokes images of a retail operation, and the analogy is actually not a bad one. Finding and obtaining what one needs at a library requires some rules. Think about how one orders from an online retail catalog: First one must "search" and then "select" from the list of items or inventory available. The catalog may provide options on colors and sizes, for example, and may indicate whether an item is in stock and therefore available or requestable or backordered.

Librarians need to be able to describe what is owned down to such details as volume holdings, edition statements, and formats as well as item status indicators such as whether a title is on the shelf, what can be charged out, and what cannot. The catalog should also guide users to information about requesting the materials for use, including delivery or pickup options. Good inventory rules can optimize access for users.

Librarians manage their print inventory with the use of automated systems. Librarians in smaller libraries may use off-the-shelf software to handle that, but most large libraries are using the extensive, expensive, complex, and inflexible integrated library systems (ILS). Some of the larger companies offering these systems include Ex Libris, SirsiDynix, Innovative Interfaces, and The Library Corporation (TLC).

Online catalogs are hard to use and slow to change to match the promise of the technology now available. Open source, where programmers collaborate to build their own programs, is drawing a lot of attention. A 2008 issue of *Library Technology Reports* was devoted to an excellent overview of this alternative to purchasing an ILS system.[15] ILS vendors are also looking at offering a more modular approach, calling it the ILS hybrid or disintegrated or even reintegrated approach. Most librarians still use ILS systems because the inventory control that they provide is absolutely critical to the services offered. Librarians may opt to enhance their online catalogs with new solutions to make finding titles easier. These are the next-generation systems, such as Endeca, Aquabrowser, or Primo, that can provide added features on top of the ILS to mitigate the problems so well identified by Andrew Pace, who has written and presented on these services. Box 7.6 describes his summary of what the online catalog cannot do, to underscore the importance of the new systems. The interfaces also allow for the addition of other features users want, such as book covers, tables of contents,

---

BOX 7.6
THINGS THE ONLINE CATALOG DOES NOT DO WELL

- Any search other than known item
- Most anything other than books
- Logical groupings of results
- Faceted browsing
- Relevance ranking
- Sideways searching (suggestions, expansion of searches and search targets)[16]

reviews, and tools to help users both keep their own lists of books and update them with citation formatting tools.

To see a catalog that employs next-generation features, go to http://vufind.carli.illinois.edu/all/vf/ and do a search. For example, search the title *Freakonomics* and see how easy it is to locate other material using the faceted browsing by subject, author, or format. Then look at the record itself to see the citation features. Locate links to Google, tagging opportunities, and listing and citation capabilities and find book reviews all from one easy search.

The ILS systems have separate but integrated modules: an acquisitions system to facilitate ordering material, a cataloging interface for bibliographic record work and item record creation, and serial check-in systems to record issue receipt. The circulation system handles item statuses and the affiliated users database and is the foundation for inventory control. It is the circulation system that controls access to a physical piece, matching the loanability of any item to a patron record. The circulation system also covers short-term loans and reserve readings, as well as enhanced services such as the ability to place a hold or request a title. The circulation systems are integrated with other modules; for example, the library user can view the availability of the item when in the online catalog, and staff working in other modules may have access to change an item status when needed, to perhaps bind a volume or to order a new copy and withdraw a missing one. If items travel from one department to another, then the system also tracks that delivery, allowing users to see where an item is. Items are not always on a shelf; they are updated often and will be used more frequently if users can get access to them at their convenience. Librarians work hard to optimize these systems to allow timely access to material on site. Some libraries implement local request options and pull items for the user to have them available for pickup. Others actually deliver these titles to office or home.

Librarians would like to exert more control over ILS systems and are favoring the layered approaches to catalog design for greater flexibility, though local programming and maintenance help are required. The next few years will likely see more open source development and vendors' developments of hybrid or layered systems, which will impact the local and the shared systems. E-books are also growing in volume, and although they require records with links for access, they do not require the same inventory controls. OCLC is also offering a new approach that may compete with established ILS systems, as described in the later section on OCLC.

Library networks have played a critical role in enhancing access to collections. The growth and development of these networks, local, national, and even international, have made possible large-scale borrowing of material held in libraries worldwide. Once online bibliographic records were available through the creation and adoption of machine-readable records, library networks grew at a rapid rate. Librarians immediately realized the benefits of sharing access to bibliographic records and then the ability to share the actual items through interlibrary loan. The interlibrary loan process is automated in many ways now across disparate systems. One early and cost-efficient method was to share inventory and bibliographic systems. In this case libraries join together to develop or buy programming to create one central access to all their holdings. This may be one database or may be one created from many or may be clusters of shared catalogs within the whole network. Many versions are possible.

With the addition of circulation capabilities, loan transactions between members are greatly facilitated. Shared information on item availability optimizes access. No time is wasted requesting those titles that are charged out or noncirculating. Volume and/or year or summary holdings for serial titles are also available. This helps staff and users to determine who owns a particular volume or issue. Networks have developed many local variants to the structure and details of the programs. Some networks are restrictive in membership requirements; some have more stringent controls over record contribution than others do. Some offer free book loans, with item delivery backed up by courier services, for their member organizations. Others also allow for their own separately maintained union lists and expedited article copy arrangements. It makes sense to use one system to link libraries together. Not all systems are created equally, however, and not all groups of libraries will agree to work together in one consistent way. Some of the successful library networks operating today are the result of long history, some are economically based, some are visionary, some are evolutionary, some are small, and others are now global leaders.

Three examples illustrate the range of possibilities for library network organization:

1.   The OhioLINK group in Ohio and the CARLI group of libraries that participate in I-Share in Illinois are examples of shared systems with a highly structured organization. Each features a central office that maintains the system and offers a suite of services for the membership. These systems typically support an easy borrowing system that is user-driven, with each affiliated user able to initiate an online request for any system-wide available item and have it delivered to a chosen pickup location. Use of the request feature is high. Member institutions must agree on how to load records, on who gets privileges, and to offer equitable access across the membership of users as well as commit to shared governance and all policies.

2.   Hybrid systems may share most of a system but retain more local control. The MOBIUS system in Missouri and the Orbis Cascade group in Oregon and Washington share a system but then utilize additional software or processes to share material effectively.

3.   Other library consortia or partner groups may share software to federate searches across their different systems and to authenticate users to allow for reciprocal borrowing across the libraries that bypasses laborious manual processes. Brown, Columbia, Cornell, Dartmouth, University of Pennsylvania, and Yale developed Borrow Direct and together purchased a software program to allow users access to each other's collections.[17]

Many other local systems are running or developing similar projects. These networks require good governance, with formal agreements and shared policies and procedures to build the shared catalog or agreements to purchase and implement other stand-alone software programs. The benefits are many, beginning with the economic ones, because the members share system costs. Book-request fill rates are high, and resource sharing with cooperative collection development programs can be extended easily. The drawbacks include the investment of time necessary to coordinate such organizations, especially in the governance and issues surrounding fully shared networks. All members must agree on many issues, which may delay action on new services, and local issues may be subordinated to larger consortium needs. Libraries can belong to several networks given that no one partner group does it all. Such networks have provided models illustrating how easily and economically materials may be shared. The very largest network is described in the next section.

OCLC: A Network Leader

OCLC began as a small local network but has grown exponentially, becoming a global cooperative that serves more libraries than any other organization. It represents 72,000 libraries in more than 100 countries. With 220 million records and 1.7 billion holdings, it has the largest bibliographic database (*WorldCat*) in the world and offers services that form the backbone of libraries' local workflow, including cataloging and resource sharing. More than any other network, OCLC has helped to shape how libraries can share their collections in the United States and now worldwide and has provided the tools that allow the large volume of lending and borrowing that occurs today. Statistics reveal that more than 200 million ILL requests have been generated on the OCLC ILL systems since 1979, with 10.3 million in 2009 alone.[18]

OCLC began in 1967 as a small nonprofit corporation, the Ohio College Library Center, a group of 54 libraries interested in sharing resources. An online shared cataloging system was in place in 1971. OCLC quickly expanded to nonacademic libraries, with the offer of attractive membership options. By 1973, it was no longer regional in scope, and in 1981 the name was changed to Online Computer Library Center. Today, it is simply OCLC. A subsystem to facilitate interlibrary loan was implemented in 1979, forever changing the laborious, time-consuming mechanisms previously necessary to transact a remote loan. Begun as a way to share cataloging records, OCLC has grown in so many directions that the use of that system is just a small part of its suite of services now. The organization has seen incredible international growth, both in acquiring several global companies that serve libraries, such as Fretwell Downing and PICA, and in loading a considerable number of national bibliographic databases into *WorldCat*. OCLC merged with several bibliographic utilities that served smaller groups of libraries, taking over WLN, a network serving more than 500 libraries in the Pacific Northwest in 1999, and more recently the Research Libraries Group, or RLG network, in 2007. The national library record loads and the RLG merger both brought many unique records into *WorldCat*, resulting in much more comprehensive access to the world's library holdings. Librarians can share material much more effectively because of the more centralized access that OCLC provides. Since the last edition of this textbook, OCLC has increased the database from 43 million records to 220 million. Librarians and the staff and leadership at the OCLC network have worked steadily to introduce new services and enhancements to enable more cost savings through cooperative work. Their innovation has led to many improvements in the labor-intensive process of resource sharing (see Box 7.7).

One of OCLC's most recent and intriguing projects has been the *WorldCat* Local initiative launched in 2007 to bridge the gap between the discovery of an item and direct access to it. This project capitalizes on the *WorldCat* search interface backed by that extensive database with access to millions of holdings. It provides for many features of next-generation systems combined with Web 2.0 user options, such as adding

---

BOX 7.7
OCLC INNOVATIONS

Since 1979, a number of time-saving enhancements have been added to the OCLC resource-sharing services, including the following:

- Direct borrowing from FirstSearch databases, where users can search for articles or books and then initiate a request from the source used, eliminating the need to retype the citation for the request
- Unmediated borrowing options with requests sent automatically to lending partners as profiled by a borrowing site
- ILL Fee Management (IFM) is a system that simplifies ILL invoicing
- *WorldCat* Resource Sharing: an easy-to-use Web-based service to facilitate borrowing requests and lending fulfillment
- Atlas ILLiad partnership integrating OCLC services with an effective ILL management system
- International Organization for Standardization (ISO) and National Information Standards Organization (NISO) Circulation Interchange Protocol (NCIP) standards compliance for cross-platform interoperability
- RLG merger
- Google Books "find in a library" links to easily link to a nearby library to find a book
- *WorldCat* Database growth with national library database loads
- Serial holdings batch load service
- Fretwell Downing VDX partnership, now Navigator VDX, which is being developed to emulate direct consortial borrowing systems
- *WorldCat* Local

---

tags or reviews, customized lists, and citation aids, and then marries that to local inventory control systems. OCLC is familiar with how the major ILS systems work and has been successful in replicating searches and then transferring availability and holdings information to allow for easy patron-initiated requesting partners. The work takes advantage of the detailed inventory control offered by the ILS systems and then allows users to extend beyond local partner groups to the larger world of holdings on *WorldCat* for seamless and "one-stop shopping" for all their information needs. The University of Washington was one of the first to implement this new service, which can be viewed at http://www.lib.washington.edu/. OCLC is now venturing directly into the ILS arena with this project. The potential cost savings for libraries could well be significant because the service obviates the need to purchase a separate next-generation system and potentially even parts of an integrated library system. The system does require some complex setup, and certainly, any participant must carefully maintain all its holdings on OCLC's *WorldCat*. The e-resources discovery links also need careful vetting because it can be difficult to emulate the local authentication and seamless links to sources on a network. This development nonetheless has the potential to totally change how libraries extend access to users and what options they may have in looking at ILS systems.

Document Delivery: Nonreturnables

Network systems make book requesting easier, so much of the material covered so far in this chapter has focused on interlibrary loans, particularly the newest trends to expedite sharing of returnables. Article copies (and other copies as well, such as book chapters), also known as document delivery, require another set of processes. The nature of serials sets article requesting apart from book loans. In brief, it is imperative that the article citation be complete and accurate, that information exist about exactly what year and volumes a supplying library may have or that a commercial supplier may make available, and that the supplying source employ best practices in fulfilling the order. Open URL and link resolvers have made the citation part easier (see standards section later in the chapter). Users need not retype a citation, no matter what index or database they use, as they are guided along the request submittal process.

Confirming holdings prior to requesting a copy is more challenging because that depends on librarians providing that information consistently to a network such as OCLC, which can be a labor-intensive maintenance issue. Librarians have to maintain their local holdings as well as the network ones, which can be double input. Best practices for fulfillment will vary because every supplier is different. The fee associated with obtaining a copy is another factor and is predicated on the suppliers' policies (libraries or commercial), the options for speedier delivery, and any copyright fees that either may be applied as part of the total fee or may be due to the publisher if the title is heavily requested. The copyright section later in this chapter touches on this.

Delivery options are important because they decide how well a library may rely on the service to meet the quick turnaround expectations of the requester and whether a copy can be downloaded or must be picked up. Document delivery is of growing importance because librarians can no longer afford to subscribe to as many serial titles. The just-in-time document delivery approach can work if library users are well served by the access service model rather than ownership. Innovations in document delivery have meant better guarantees of the service in the fulfillment process. Copyright and licensing restrictions are still barriers, and new budget pressures are resulting in fewer library holdings. One solution for libraries has been consortial purchases of serial content databases. Serial content is offered online in aggregated databases. Here a vendor works with publishers to offer their content online to institutions for annual fees. The EBSCO databases are one example. These databases help libraries offer research support to their users. Access to particular journal articles is not guaranteed because publishers can choose to pull content from these aggregators and may embargo the most current articles, which requires libraries to buy copies of recent articles from the publisher or to acquire them via a document delivery process.

Approaches to Document Delivery

Some networks and services are dedicated to efficient document delivery services. Examples include DOCLINE and RAPID. DOCLINE is a unique library-to-library document delivery service developed by the National Library of Medicine. DO-CLINE requires members, generally medical libraries, to supply and maintain their serial holdings information. Records for orders are easily identified from the *MED-LINE PubMed* index, which is central to all biomedical journal literature and utilizes unique record identifiers. Participating librarians first enter their own biomedical serial holdings into the SERHOLD database and then build a profile of their preferred lenders. When requests are input using the unique record identifier that is automatically captured from *PubMed*, the system matches the serial title and volume needed from that identifier and routes it to the lender based on the holdings available and on the specified hierarchy of lenders. The lender then receives the request and acts on it. This service has eliminated the need to re-verify or reenter citations or search for bibliographic records and holdings. The system is also superb in tracking rerouting and order history, detailing why particular articles could not be sent. New enhancements facilitating the maintenance of serial holdings updating and order management make this an excellent system. Its one major drawback is that it includes only biomedical literature. The use of the record identifiers has prompted more attention to how such a standard number for any article could enhance access if included in an index.

Another system, RAPID, was developed after the Colorado State University Library lost a majority of its journal collection as a result of a devastating flood in 1997. The technology developed at this library to facilitate access to journal literature via ILL and document delivery services resulted in the system named RAPID. This is now a commercially available service and uses some of the basic principles of the DOCLINE system to offer efficient and better-guaranteed access to articles from thousands of serials regardless of the discipline. RAPID requires accurate serial holdings from participants. It also mandates strict adherence to a service commitment for article fulfillment. The software developed offers automated processing and routing of requests and keeps track of lenders, to route requests evenly across partners. Librarians decide how much of their serial collection to offer and work with the RAPID staff to provide holdings information.

Librarians may work with RAPID to support their traditional partner groups and can join other groups as needed. Groups can be private or public, and RAPID offers several options, referring to groups as pods. The system works with the major ILL software systems, and the holdings database it maintains includes open access journals, relieving the requesting library from having to search those independently. Libraries utilizing RAPID or DOCLINE report fast and accurate service with reduced labor costs.[19]

Delivery and Access

Documents obtained through any service can be accessed online or delivered electronically. With the inception of the portable document format (PDF) and widespread availability of Adobe software, anyone can share files across the network, but large-scale sharing requires systems to automate the process in the context of the service and to provide for user file management and protection. Several systems optimize this process to work with libraries' ILL services. These services result in better turnaround time and more convenience for users who like to receive their material on their desktop.

Ariel was developed at RLG (now part of OCLC) to streamline the scanning and sending of large files from library to library to offer faster service and to reduce labor and postage costs. Ariel is proprietary software and requires that the sender and receiver use the same software and, in later versions, sometimes the same version. The service has seen a high volume of use and was enhanced several times by RLG before being sold to the for-profit firm Infotrieve. The software allows the receiving end to convert the file to a PDF for the end user. Many librarians have developed Web sites to track and maintain the files and a Web interface for users to receive and view their documents, while setting restrictions on how long and by whom a file can be accessed. For the service to be most effective to the library community, however, interoperability is a must because there are thousands of libraries sharing. Odyssey was developed by ILLiad to do similar things but optimized the electronic delivery process within ILLiad, thereby reducing keystrokes and integrating it with that management system to provide central controls for such things as address management.

Some innovations in delivery of returnables have been implemented with home delivery for books. Montana sponsored one pilot for libraries statewide in part because of its rural environment, where many residents have no easy access to a public library.[20] Books were delivered directly to the requester's home with a prepaid-postage return envelope. Academic libraries offer such services to campus offices with the support of local campus mail services. More public libraries are experimenting with home delivery, a sort of Netflix for books, but the postage costs can be prohibitive. With the requesting features available from many catalogs, notably OCLC *WorldCat* Local, it may be only a matter of time before such delivery becomes a standard offering, perhaps with a small fee to recoup some of the costs.

STANDARDS AND PROTOCOLS

People rely on standards every day as they go about their daily business. Standards allow one to perform such tasks as use electronic appliances, drive a car, pay for goods, and communicate by phone or e-mail. The International Organization for Standardization (ISO) and the National Information Standards Organization (NISO) are two agencies that develop the standards libraries need (see Box 7.8).

Librarians rely on standards daily. Several underlie computer-based access-related services. They are briefly described in this section, with links to additional information.

Record retrieval, local and across systems

MARC (http://www.loc.gov/marc/) provides a way to represent and communicate bibliographic and related information in machine-readable form, allowing for consistency in searching for items in online catalogs.

Dublin Core is another standard widely used in the description of digital materials.

Z39.50 (http://www.niso.org/standards/resources/Z39.50_Resources) is a protocol for handling the search and retrieval of information across different platforms and allows for federated searches for a one-stop shopping approach to searching different databases and networks and bringing back consistent search

BOX 7.8
ORGANIZATIONS FOR STANDARDS DEVELOPMENT

NISO, the National Information Standards Organization, is a nonprofit association accredited by the American National Standards Institute (ANSI). It identifies, develops, maintains, and publishes technical standards to manage information in our changing and ever-more-digital environment. NISO standards apply to both traditional and new technologies and to the full range of information-related needs, including retrieval, repurposing records, storage, metadata, and preservation.

ISO, the International Organization for Standardization, is a nongovernmental agency and is the largest developer of standards used worldwide. ISO works with more than 160 countries to help make sure that society can work with materials and services developed by businesses. ISO defines a standard as a "documented agreement containing technical specifications or other precise criteria to be used consistently as rules, guidelines, or definitions of characteristics to ensure that materials, products, processes and services are fit for their purpose. It is a living agreement that can have a profound influence on things that deserve to be taken seriously—such as the safety, reliability and efficiency of machinery and tools, means of transport, toys, medical devices, and so on."[21]

Both of these organizations help to promulgate standards used in information science.

results. Of course, this requires that those databases be compliant and on similar versions of the standard to achieve predictable results.

Request management

In ISO ILL, the ISO-10161 protocol is an international communications standard that permits the exchange of ILL messages among ILL systems even if they use different hardware and software. It also controls ILL transactions for both lending and borrowing activities. More information about this protocol is available from the Interlibrary Loan Application Standards Maintenance Agency (http://www.lac-bac.gc.ca/iso/ill/standard.htm).

Circulation Interchange

The Z39.83 NISO Circulation Interchange Protocol (NCIP, http://www.ncip.info/) helps to maximize item availability/location information and is a way to integrate user database and item processes no matter what local system is used. If it is implemented correctly, and the libraries in the group use systems that have NCIP, a union catalog approach to borrowing may be emulated.

Seamless discovery to delivery

The Open URL framework (entry for Z39.88 at http://www.niso.org/kst/reports/standards/) is built on the principle that the full text of an article can be defined by a set of metadata elements (ISSN, volume, issue, page numbers, and so on), rather than by a specific URL. This is quite important given that many URLs are not persistent. The protocol standardizes the way any metadata element that describes the piece is pulled from its source (such as an index or abstract) and is then transmitted to link to a target such as an online journal. The standard also allows for links to redirect a user to local print holdings to see local availability and to capture the citation for an ILL request once the user determines no local availability.

Digital Object Identifier (DOI, http://www.doi.org/) is a suite of protocols that refer to the potential for "naming" a digital object. One wants to be directed not only to the online platform but more specifically to the actual article to avoid researching within that database of content. DOI naming provides a way to persistently find the piece needed. Any document's digital form may change, but the DOI name will remain stable. Publishers of indexes and abstracts use DOI along with publishers of the articles to allow for seamless access. The use of DOI identifiers is one piece of a framework that is making access to smaller content packages such as articles, proceedings, essays, and chapters much easier in a networked environment and is allowing for automated access across services.

Identifiers to help locate a title

The International Standard Serial Number (ISSN, http://www.issn.org) is a unique identifier for serials. Challenges in using ISSNs include frequent title or publisher or format changes and the fact that many older serials do not have them. Best practice requires the publisher to maintain the ISSNs, but many lack the staff to adequately do this. Frequent changes require frequent updates to ISSNs, and often there is a time lag in this work.

The International Standard Book Number (ISBN, http://www.isbn.org/standards/home/index.asp) is a unique identifier for books. Book formats complicate this because one title can have three formats for the same content: paperback, hard cover, and an online e-book.

Data

Extensible Markup Language (XML) is a type of markup language that allows for the sharing of data across different platforms (http://www.w3.org/XML/, http://www.xml.com).

User authentication/access

Lightweight Directory Access Protocol (LDAP) users are authenticated using protocols that can be set up to allow access when a login matches to an existing directory or database of uniquely identified affiliates.

With IP recognition, users are recognized as having access from the IP ranges that libraries provide to those they pay for online content and that users link from on the Internet.

EZproxy is a Web proxy server program used to give access to restricted-access Web sites that authenticate users by IP address. This allows library users to log in through their library's EZproxy server and gain access to the electronic resources to which the library subscribes.

Shibboleth (http://shibboleth.internet2.edu/) is an open source cross-domain sign-on system for easy "federated" user access. Users attempting to access a source that their affiliated institution has licensed can be identified through a shibboleth link presented to them by that source.

Standards offer an ideal that often is very difficult in practice. They take time to develop. Often before a standard has been agreed on, an industry-based standard may emerge when one vendor or firm adopts a workable framework that is adopted by others simply to continue to be players in that marketplace. And it is hard to get a large community to move to them, libraries included!

The only thing librarians don't do with standards is follow them. When it comes to standards, librarians are hypocrites. We want others to follow standards very carefully and predictably, but we're somewhat sloppy ourselves. Need proof? Who uses the MARC standard? Almost everyone. But who follows it without any exceptions? Librarians think of standards the same way we think of traffic laws—when the other guy breaks them he should be punished. When we break them, we have a good reason.[22]

LEGAL ISSUES FOR ILL/DOCUMENT DELIVERY

Interlibrary loan and document delivery are library services directly impacted by copyright legislation and by the license agreements libraries sign that could trump the exceptions that copyright law provides libraries. Digitization projects, the increased availability of online formats, and scholarly communication efforts are changing perceptions of access rights and behaviors on copy procurement. Consumer markets are also widening thanks to all kinds of new sales potential afforded by the Internet, which is both encouraging and challenging to the commercial sector. Librarians are active in helping to update legislation and in developing new guidelines to retain rights to materials for their users.

Copyright

The U.S. Copyright Law protects the holders of copyright from loss of revenue and from unauthorized uses of their material, including adaptations of it. Society protects the investment the copyright holders have made in creating the work. However, U.S. law has also balanced that protection by providing for some exceptions, which allow the citizens of the United States to have access to materials needed to learn and add to our collective knowledge. When, in 1790, George Washington asked Congress to enact copyright legislation, he argued that it would increase the national stock of knowledge. And knowledge, he said, is "the surest basis of public happiness."[23]

Access to copyrighted material is much easier in our networked environment, where copies are enabled with a simple click of the mouse. All librarians must be familiar with the provisions of copyright law and recent updates to that law as well as any published guidelines. Libraries must abide by the law and must also understand and protect the rights allowed them in obtaining copies for users and in maintaining collections. Librarians have been active in speaking for their users' access needs as well as for the preservation needs of their collections whenever copyright has been reviewed or when court cases may seem to tip the balance away from public use. Reference librarians help users gain access to copyrighted material based on their knowledge of the law and the fees that might have to be paid directly to a copyright holder as a result of a copy being made. They also negotiate for the best license to allow for the widest access to digital material and educate users not to pay fees when their library can provide access or proxy access on their behalf.

The Copyright Law of 1976 (Title 17 U.S. Code) was groundbreaking in the exceptions allowed for copying in sections 107 and 108. Since that time, the law has been updated several times to extend protection, to provide for provisions related to new technology such as digitization, and also to provide harsher measures against infringement. The Digital Millennium Copyright Act (DMCA) and the Sonny Bono Copyright Term Extension Act of 1998 are recent updates to the law and have indirectly affected ILL. Details of sections 107 and 108 of the Copyright Law are provided here as they relate to resource sharing activities.

Section 106 of Title 17 describes the copyright owner's rights. The fair use clause is in section 107. Library exceptions are detailed in section 108. Section 107 allows for copying of copyrighted material for purposes of criticism, comment, news reporting, teaching, scholarship, or research. These uses are qualified by a number of factors:

1. the purpose and character of the use, including whether such use is of a commercial nature or is for nonprofit educational purposes;
2. the nature of the copyrighted work;
3. the amount and substantiality of the portion used in relation to the copyrighted work as a whole; and
4. the effect of the use upon the potential market for, or value of, the copyrighted work.

The fact that a work is unpublished shall not itself bar a finding of fair use if such finding is made upon consideration of all the above factors.[24]

Fair use interpretation can be extreme, from those who say the law allows any copying done for any educational use, to the reverse stance taken by copyright holders, who would like to see this clause removed. For that reason, it is perhaps not surprising that attempts to provide guidelines have not been successful. A commission had been set up by Congress to develop guidelines for fair use (Commission on Fair Use, or CONFU), but it was disbanded after several years' work. The panel of educators, scholars, publishers, and librarians could not agree. One of the guidelines was to have covered interlibrary loan. ILL processes are concerned with fair use, but also with very specific sections of the law dealing with systematic reproduction, public domain, and the education of library users.

Libraries were given certain rights to make copies under section 108 of Title 17 (d, g, and e). These rights are spelled out in great detail. The part most concerned with interlibrary loan is 108(g)(2), which covers systematic reproduction of materials:

(g) The rights of reproduction and distribution under this section extend to the isolated and unrelated reproduction or distribution of a single copy or phonorecord of the same material on separate occasions, but do not extend to cases where the library or archives, or its employee—(1) is aware or has substantial reason to believe that it is engaging in the related or concerted reproduction or distribution of multiple copies or phonorecords of the same material, whether made on one occasion or over a period of time, and whether intended for aggregate use by one or more individuals or for separate use by the individual members of a group; or (2) engages in the systematic reproduction or distribution of single or multiple copies or phonorecords of material described in subsection (d): Provided, That nothing in this clause prevents a library or archives from participating in interlibrary arrangements that do not have, as their purpose or effect, that the library or archives receiving such copies or phonorecords for distribution does so in such aggregate quantities as to substitute for a subscription to or purchase of such work.[25]

Systematic reproduction was deliberately not defined here. Congress appointed the U.S. National Commission on New Technological Uses of Copyrighted Works (CONTU) to wrestle with this issue. This group made recommendations to Congress that are not law (although appended to the law), but are guidelines to follow. These guidelines have not been tested in court. The full text can be read in CONTU's *Final Report*.[26] The guidelines offer help in limiting or allowing copying under certain conditions. Periodical copying in any one year is limited to five articles from one title from the last five years' worth of issues, counting back from the date of the request ("five in five"). In ILL, librarians must indicate when they follow the Commission guidelines (CCG) on the request and also must retain their records for three calendar years. Libraries that do not follow through on the guidelines when making requests will see requests delayed or not filled and may be asked later about their CONTU observance.

Once the limit of "five in five" is reached, the requesting library usually seeks other options for obtaining a copy. Some of those options include seeking permission from the copyright holder (the publisher in the case of most periodicals), which often means paying for permission with a *royalty fee*. These fees may also be paid indirectly through a clearinghouse center or commercial supplier. Many ILL offices use the Copyright Clearance Center (CCC) to pay the fees due to publishers by keeping track of the requests and submitting a record of use for the sixth and later copy. CCC is a reproduction rights organization, one of many worldwide, and provides collective copyright licensing services for users of copyrighted materials, including libraries. As a member of the International Federation of Reproduction Rights Organizations (IFRRO), CCC works with many other countries to repatriate fees for overseas use of U.S. works. Another option for librarians if they have exceeded copies allowed is to use a commercial supplier to obtain the article. The supplier will collect the fee on behalf of the publisher. The fees vary widely from publisher to publisher, with the more expensive journals requiring the highest fees. Reference librarians, in seeking the best source for a needed copy, should be aware of these fees because they can be prohibitive.[27]

The DMCA and Bono Copyright Term Extension Act updated the law of 1976 and indirectly ILL. The DMCA mandated a new notice requirement for copies made by libraries (including for ILL) that required them to reproduce any copyright notice that appears on the work or, if there is none, to include a notice similar to those libraries used before the law changed. The Copyright Term Extension Act provided for a limited library exemption to the 20 years added as long as the work was for research and not for commercial use.

Section 108 was subject to extensive review from 2005 to 2008 when the final report of the Section 108 Study Group was issued (http://www.section108.gov). The review was set up to recommend changes; an update was recognized as necessary because the digital revolution has changed assumptions for copying needs, especially when it comes to preserving cultural heritage materials in libraries and museums. Although the report did not cover ILL per se, its recommendations on educational and preservation goals of libraries and museums help to reinforce the need for balance between the commercial and nonprofit sectors in considering the need to reproduce material. The report will serve as the basis for any future legislation.

Recent court cases that may limit copying seem to favor the commercial sector over the nonprofit. It is well known that the Copyright Term Extension Act that extended copyright 20 years was the outcome of the need to be sure the Disney Mickey Mouse character remained under copyright and did not pass into the public domain. Lawrence Lessig's book *The Future of Ideas*[28] is compelling reading on how copyright may stifle creativity as more companies file lawsuits claiming infringement. The Google Books project has initiated many new court cases. Publishers were unhappy that Google scanned copies without permission, even though the full text is not made available online if under copyright. They brought suit alleging that the act of scanning is an infringement of the law. If the purpose of that copy is to better expose the content to citizens, is that an infringement? Is it best to be sure no exposure is allowed to protect copyright holders? The old rules do not apply logically in the digital world. Google will expose more content and could provide for much more business as print-on-demand services emerge for the out-of-print material and links to purchase options are provided for books still in print.

New York Times columnist Paul Krugman offered some hopeful musings on the subject. He was intrigued with how the Kindle reader may impact sales of e-books and reminded readers of how the Grateful Dead made their money: not from music sales, but from all the other things they sold at concerts. He speculates on how consumers may provide for more open access to copyrighted material:

> How will this [Kindles and e-book downloads] affect the publishing business? Right now, publishers make as much from a Kindle download as they do from the sale of a physical book. But the experience of the music industry suggests that this won't last: once digital downloads of books become standard, it will be hard for publishers to keep charging traditional prices. Indeed, if e-books become the norm, the publishing industry as we know it may wither away. Books may end up serving mainly as promotional material for authors' other activities, such as live readings with paid admission. Well, if it was good enough for Charles Dickens, I guess it's good enough for me.... Bit by bit, everything that can be digitized will be

digitized, making intellectual property ever easier to copy and ever harder to sell for more than a nominal price. And we'll have to find business and economic models that take this reality into account.[29]

Licensing Agreements

Acquiring online resources usually requires libraries to sign a license in order to gain access. These licenses are legal documents, contracts that stipulate who, how, how many, and how long a library patron can use a title. Some may have certain ILL restrictions, including limiting copying or stipulating to whom the library may send an article or in some cases even prohibiting it.[30] Librarians are aware of the implications of licensing terms, however, and have been successfully working with publishers to adjust the language to be sure cooperative sharing can continue when a resource is full-text online rather than in print and on a shelf. Restrictions on lending to commercial firms with libraries or internationally and some limitations on electronic delivery are still common. Efforts on the part of many librarians are relaxing these restrictions or at least making them consistent for better workflow practices. The Yale Web site on licensing digital information (http://www.library.yale.edu/~llicense/index.shtml) has model language to encourage publishers and librarians to use standardized language to provide for equitable access to information for all users.

Digital Rights Management (DRM)

Publishers and copyright holders are also using technology to restrict access to their materials. These are devices or software code that limit online usage and are collectively referred to as Digital Rights Management (DRM or DRMs with the "s" for systems). One sees these most often applied to media material, but e-books are often wrapped such that users can view or print only bits at a time. This can mean that local libraries that provide for e-book access that comes with DRMs may see frustrated users who are locked out if a copy is "on loan" or cannot be easily printed. In this case, users may turn to ILL for a print copy. This is an unexpected consequence of providing online access! Other publishers freely allow ILL of e-books, but the mechanics are not quite worked out yet because it is not pragmatic to download and copy the whole book or provide a direct link to the remote and unaffiliated user. A chapter may be sufficient for a user's needs, but which one? Direct Consortial Borrowing systems find that this is impacting their users. If partners in the group buy e-content locally and not for the whole consortium, then the e-books are not available for all to request. ILL practitioners see barriers with efficient delivery of documents that come with a DRM because they may not be able to easily send it on to the requestor, or they may do so only to find the requester locked out from access inadvertently. DRMs are like those large security tags a retail salesperson may forget to remove from a garment as it is bought. They can make the product unusable.

Open Access

The open access movement is helping to protect users' rights to materials created for the greater good. In the academic and research sphere, much of the content that is published is part of a serial title and often an expensive one, where the publisher requires that authors sign over their copyright. The research can often be funded by federal support with additional support from the university for faculty completing the research and writing it up for publication. Federal agencies and academic institutions are becoming more involved in the movement to encourage or even require authors funded by or affiliated with them to retain access to their publications in some form. Faculty members are expected to publish in prestigious peer-reviewed journals and may feel compelled to sign away their rights. Librarians have worked to develop digital repositories and work with publishers to allow their faculty, students, and other researchers to place prepublication versions of their articles in these archives. The National Institutes of Health (NIH) requires scientists supported by NIH to deposit a copy in its digital archive. Authors are required to be sure that they retain the right to deposit before they transfer their copyright. The final manuscript as accepted by reviewers must be made available to the public within 12 months of its official publication date.[31] Harvard University has adopted a similar policy, with its faculty of Arts and Sciences voting to approve the measure in 2008. This policy requires faculty to be sure the publisher accepting their work allows an addendum to the copyright transfer agreement whereby they can post a copy to the university archive. Here the university has first access to the research. The policy also allows faculty to obtain a waiver in the event their publisher will not accept the addendum[32] Many speculate that more universities will follow Harvard's example, leading to more comprehensive access to research that

---

BOX 7.9
FINAL PRODUCT—SATISFIED USERS

Of the many compelling reasons to develop enhanced access programs, the best are library user success stories:

A hospital librarian needed rush access to an article on rare fungi, which a local doctor suspected as a culprit in a patient's strange disorder. The serial title, an obscure agricultural publication, was held at only a few research libraries. One was able to retrieve it and send it over the Internet in less than four hours.

The natural history curator was ecstatic to receive a loan of an older museum bulletin that contained beautiful color plates needed for research. The journal generally did not circulate, but an exception was made for this researcher.

The doctoral candidate was able to obtain copies of theses on one particular subject area, allowing for better focus on that user's own thesis.

A music teacher was looking for that perfect score that would bring out a student's potential in an important competition and located it in a library 300 miles away. ILL services provided for a loan, and the student received the piece in ample time to practice, with much appreciation from the teacher.

is done to contribute to the greater good. Librarians continue to be activists to promote education and a better understanding of scholarly communication issues such as the open access movement, with the goal of better access to information.

SUMMARY: ACCESS ANYWHERE, ANYTIME

The ILL process is a complicated one, but new tools and approaches to resource sharing are available to provide increasingly seamless access to remotely located materials. Access to the world's library collections is important to all. Reference librarians have critical roles to play in setting up new services and in ensuring that users can make effective use of them. With change now a constant in libraries, it is important that librarians keep up with evolving technology and the resulting products because they will help to select and implement new systems that allow for the best options in access. They will also provide for the training and documentation that the users need to be aware of and best realize the benefits of the services. With better delivery options, reference librarians will be called on to help ensure that the user has the needed material in hand in ways not possible before (see Box 7.9).

NOTES

1.   Roy Tennant, "Looking Back to Go Forward," *Library Journal* 132 (August 2007): 28.

2.   Pamela Samuelson, "Legally Speaking: The Dead Souls of the Google Booksearch Settlement," *O'Reilly Radar* (April 17, 2009). http://radar.oreilly.com/2009/04/legally-speaking-the-dead-soul.html.

3.   *Ulrichsweb*. http://www.ulrichsweb.com/ulrichsweb/.

4.   Martha Kyrillidou and Les Bland, eds., *ARL Statistics 2007–2008* (Washington, D.C.: Association of Research Libraries, 2009), 18.

5.   *Library and Book Trade Almanac,* 53rd ed. (Medford, NJ: Information Today, 2008), 462–64.

6.   Greg Byerly, "Ohio: Library and Information Networks," *Library Hi Tech* 14, no. 2–3 (1996): 245–54.

7.   Brian Lavoie, Lynn Silipigni Connaway, and Lorcan Dempsey, "Anatomy of Aggregate Collections: The Example of Google Print for Libraries," *D-Lib Magazine* 11 (September 2005). http://www.dlib.org/dlib/september05/lavoie/09lavoie.html.

8.   Chandra Prabha and Elizabeth G. Marsh, "Commercial Document Suppliers: How Many of the ILL/DD Periodical Article Requests Can They Fulfill?," *Library Trends* 45 (Winter 1997): 551–68.

9.   Lynn Wiley and Tina Chrzastowski, "The State of ILL in the State of IL: The Illinois Interlibrary Loan Assessment Project," *Library Collections, Acquisitions & Technical Services* 25 (Spring 2001): 5–20.

10.   Chris Anderson, "The Long Tail," *Wired* 12, no. 10 (October 2004): 1–5. http://www.wired.com/wired/archive/12.10/tail.html.

11.   The National Interlibrary Loan Code has been revised multiple times. The 1940 version clearly describes the service as one for scholars and researchers only, going so far as to say

that graduate students must be careful to pick only those fields of study supported by their institution's library. A progression of revisions is available from "Revised Code," *Library Journal* 65 (October 1, 1940): 802–3; "National Interlibrary Loan Code," *RQ* 20 (Fall 1980): 29–31; "National Interlibrary Loan Code," *RQ* 33 (Summer 1994): 477–79. This version was revised in 2001 and again in 2008 as the *Interlibrary Loan Code for the United States.* http://www.ala.org/ala/mgrps/divs/rusa/resources/guidelines/interlibrary.cfm.

12.   Rethinking Resource Sharing Initiative, *A Manifesto for Rethinking Resource Sharing*, affirmed by the ALA/RUSA/STARS Executive Committee and the STARS Rethinking Resource Sharing Policies Committee, January 2007. http://rethinkingresourcesharing.org/manifesto.html.

13.   Mary E. Jackson, "Assessing ILL/DD Services Study: Initial Observations," *ARL Bimonthly Report* 230/231 (October/December 2003): 21–22. http://www.arl.org/bm~doc/illdd.pdf.

14.   Suzanne M. Ward, Tanner Wray, and Karl E. Debus-López, "Collection Development Based on Patron Requests: Collaboration between Interlibrary Loan and Acquisitions," *Library Collections, Acquisitions & Technical Services* 27 (Summer 2003): 203–13.

15.   Marshall Breeding, "Open Source Integrated Library Systems," *Library Technology Reports* 44 (November/December 2008): 1–33. http://www.alatechsource.org/ltr/open-source-integrated-library-systems.

16.   Andrew Pace, *Library's Automation: Yesterday's Technology, Tomorrow*, Triangle Research Libraries Network presentation, July 28, 2006. www.trln.org/events/annual2006/future_catalog.ppt.

17.   Robert Krall, "Get It Fast and Get It Cheap—What's an ILL Librarian To Do?," *American Libraries* 31 (November 2000): 41–42.

18.   OCLC publishes annual statistics on their services, which may be found within their annual reports. http://www.oclc.org/news/publications/annualreports/default.htm.

19.   Jane Smith, "The RAPIDly Changing World of Interlibrary Loan," *Technical Services Quarterly* 23, no. 4 (2006): 17–25; Maria Elizabeth Collins, "An Overview of the DOCLINE System, Its Functions, Purposes and Descriptions of Participating Libraries," *Journal of Interlibrary Loan, Document Delivery & Information Supply* 17, no. 3 (2007): 15–28.

20.   *Montana NCIP Home Delivery Report* (Dublin, OH: OCLC, 2009). http://www.oclc.org/services/brochures/213652usf_montana_ncip_home_delivery_report.pdf.

21.   International Organization for Standardization (ISO), *Standards FAQ*. http://www.iso.org/iso/iso_catalogue/faq_standards_2.htm.

22.   Joan Frye Williams, "Unicode: What the Vendors Aren't Telling You," *Information Standards Quarterly* 9 (October 1997): 4.

23.   Charles C. Mann, "Who Will Own Your Next Good Idea?," *Atlantic Monthly* 282 (September 1998): 58.

24.   U.S. Copyright Law of the United States of America, *Circular 92* (Washington, D.C.: Government Printing Office, 1995), 9 pp.

25.   Ibid.

26.   U.S. National Commission on New Technological Uses of Copyrighted Works, *Final Report*, July 31, 1978 (Washington, D.C.: Library of Congress, 1979), 154 pp. http://digital-law-online.info/CONTU/PDF/index.html.

27.   Nancy J. Chaffin, "Examining Copyright Fees for Article Delivery," *Serials Librarian* 31, no. 3 (1997): 67–78.

28.   Lawrence Lessig, *The Future of Ideas: The Fate of the Commons in a Connected World* (New York: Random House, 2001), 352 pp.

29.   Paul Krugman, "Bits, Bands and Books," *New York Times*, late edition—final, June 6, 2008, 21. http://www.nytimes.com/2008/06/06/opinion/06krugman.html.

30.   Lynn Wiley, "License to Deny? Publisher Restrictions on Document Delivery from E-Licensed Journals," *Interlending & Document Supply* 32, no. 2 (2004): 94–102

31.   *The NIH Public Access Policy*, Division G, Title II, Section 218 of PL 110–161 (Consolidated Appropriations Act, 2008). http://publicaccess.nih.gov/policy.htm.

32.   Lila Guterman, "Celebrations and Tough Questions Follow Harvard's Move to Open Access," *Chronicle of Higher Education* 54 (February 29, 2008): A14. http://chronicle.com/article/CelebrationsTough/524.

ADDITIONAL READINGS

Brown, Laura, Rebecca Griffiths, and Matthew Rascoff. *University Publishing in a Digital Age*. New York: Ithaka, 2007. 67 pp. http://www.ithaka.org/ithaka-s-r/strategyold/Ithaka%20University%20Publishing%20Report.pdf.

The authors provide a good review of scholarly communication and the academic community and how universities may redefine their role.

Crews, Kenneth. *Copyright Law for Librarians and Educators: Creative Strategies and Practical Solutions*. 2nd ed. Chicago: American Library Association, 2006. 141 pp.

Kenneth Crews, director of the Copyright Advisory Office at Columbia University, provides guidance to librarians on copyright in this book divided into five sections: the reach of copyright, rights of ownership, fair use, focus on education and libraries, and special features (including music and copyright, the Digital Millennium Copyright Act, archives and copyright, and permission from copyright owners).

Croft, Janet Brennan. "Copyright Basics." *Journal of Interlibrary Loan, Document Delivery & Information Supply* 14, no. 3 (2004): 5–15.

This brief tutorial article provides a helpful overview of concepts and provisions of the law relevant to library handling of copyrighted materials.

Davidson, Ed. "How Close Are We to Having a Global 'Get It for Me' Service?," *Interlending & Document Supply* 37, no. 2 (2009): 64–67.

This article identifies the key features in the process by which an end user finds, requests, and obtains a needed document and the issues that need to be addressed for this process to be successful. The author concludes that most technical issues have been resolved, but additional attention needs to be paid to policy barriers that inhibit seamless access.

Delaney, Tom. "Rapid and the New Interlending: A Cooperative Document Supply System in the USA." *Interlending & Document Supply* 35, no.2 (2007): 56–59.

Details on the RAPID system and its growth and mechanics are covered in this article by the individual who helped develop it in Colorado.

Hazen, Dan. "The Cooperative Conundrum in the Digital Age." *Journal of Library Administration* 46, no. 2 (2007): 101–18.

Dan Hazen reflects on what it means to build library collections with others in the new world of virtual access but physically distributed material. He offers a review of the past and presents possible new models and a framework for how libraries may work together in the future to share and preserve material.

Hilyer, Lee Andrew. *Interlibrary Loan and Document Delivery: Best Practices for Operating and Managing Interlibrary Loan Services in All Libraries*. Binghamton, NY: Haworth Press, 2006. 150 pp. Also published as *Journal of Interlibrary Loan, Document Delivery & Electronic Reserve* 16, no. 1–2 (2006).

This book has two parts: an introduction to interlibrary loan department operations and management and a listing of resources relevant to interlibrary loan operations, including publications, Web sites, associations, and software packages.

Hodgson, Cynthia. *The RFP Writer's Guide to Standards for Library Systems*. Bethesda, MD: NISO Press, 2002. 70 pp.

Though written to assist those engaged in looking at new library systems, this guide offers a thorough review of the major standards that librarians must know today.

Hollerich, Mary A. "STARS Portends a Bright Future for Resource Sharing." *Journal of Access Services* 2, no. 4 (April 2005): 23–33.

The Sharing and Transforming Access to Resources Section (STARS) of the Reference and User Services Association (RUSA) brings together librarians and library staff involved with interlibrary loan, document delivery, access services, and other shared library services as well as vendors of products and services that support them. This article provides an overview of this section and its activities.

Jackson, Mary E. *Assessing ILL/DD Services: New Cost-Effective Alternatives*. Washington, D.C.: Association of Research Libraries, 2004. 154 pp.

This book reports the findings of a study examining the performance of user-initiated services and mediated ILL/DD services using three performance measures—direct costs, fill rate, and turnaround time—for borrowing and lending operations.

Kern, M. Kathleen, and Cherié L. Weible. "Reference as an Access Service: Collaboration between Reference and Interlibrary Loan Departments." *Journal of Access Services* 3, no. 1 (July 2006): 17–35.

The authors, a reference librarian and an interlibrary loan librarian from the University of Illinois at Urbana-Champaign, advocate closer collaboration between reference and interlibrary loan, recognizing that reference librarians can contribute searching expertise to assist interlibrary loan staff in locating otherwise difficult-to-find materials.

Knox, Emily. *Document Delivery and Interlibrary Loan on a Shoestring*. New York: Neal-Schuman, 2010. 225 pp.

Drawing on her own experience in a small academic library, Emily Knox provides guidance on cost-effective strategies for managing document delivery and interlibrary loan operations. Coverage includes copyright considerations, interlibrary loan codes, lending and borrowing policies and procedures, and available technology to support these operations.

Laughlin, Sara, ed. *Library Networks in the New Millennium: Top Ten Trends*. Chicago: ASCLA, 2000. 115 pp.

The editor has assembled chapters that describe the issues for multitype library networks as they adapt to changes in the environment. The result is a good overview of the challenges library networks face and includes coverage of electronic information, restructuring, distance education, buying clubs and cooperatives, skilled workers, diversifying funding, collaboration, users' expectations of one-stop shopping, accountability, and customer service.

Morrison, Heather G. "The Dramatic Growth of Open Access: Implications and Opportunities for Resource Sharing." *Journal of Interlibrary Loan, Document Delivery & Electronic Reserve* 16, no. 3 (August 2006): 95–107.

This article explains open access and highlights major collections, resources, and tools. In addition, the author explores issues and implications from the perspective of resource sharing specialists.

Wanner, Gail, Anne Beaubien, and Michelle Jeske. "The Rethinking Resource-Sharing Initiative: A New Development in the USA." *Interlending & Document Supply* 35, no. 2 (2007): 92–98.

The authors provide an overview of the Rethinking Resource Sharing Initiative in the United States, with the goal of gaining participation by librarians and vendors from other countries. "Rethinking" in this context means finding ways to facilitate users' access to resources.

Chapter

Instruction

Lisa Janicke Hinchliffe

INTRODUCTION

From the Institute of Museum and Library Services initiative "Museums, Libraries and 21st Century Skills" to the information literacy standards and training programs developed by the American Association of School Librarians and the Association of College and Research Libraries, to the thousands of workshops, sessions, and classes offered annually by libraries around the world, the educational role of the librarian is no longer in question. Instruction is a fundamental function of librarianship. Rare is the reference librarian, bibliographer, or even cataloger who does not have responsibility for staff or user education. Particularly because library users no longer need to be physically within a library to locate and use information, librarians are increasingly involved in education so that users can find information efficiently and effectively in independent and self-directed information-seeking environments. At one time, users were required to visit the library building to use the card catalog, leaf through periodical indexes, and browse the bookshelves. With the increasing availability and sophistication of information networks and wireless connectivity, the ever-expanding availability of laptops and mobile devices, and the continued proliferation of information resources outside the domain of the library, greater and greater capacity for information retrieval is put in the hands of the independent information user. Librarians are uniquely prepared by their familiarity with information resources and information seeking to provide instruction to information users in search strategies, critical thinking about information, and resource availability. Becoming skilled with teaching strategies and methods and familiar with different approaches to instruction is the foundation for success with one's educational role.

WHAT IS INSTRUCTION?

In defining *instruction*, a statement on librarians and the teaching role of librarians made in 1876 by Otis Hall Robinson is as applicable today as it was so many years ago. During the Conference of Librarians (the forerunner of the American Library Association's conferences) held in Philadelphia in 1876, a group of distinguished librarians were asked to respond to the paper "Personal Intercourse and Relations between Librarians and Readers in Popular Libraries," authored by Samuel Green, the librarian of the Worcester Free Public Library. In his paper, Green put forth a philosophy of personalized reference service for library users, including the admonition to "give them as much assistance as they need, but try at the same time to teach them to rely upon themselves and become independent."[1] Robinson, then head of the University of Rochester Library, responded in what was a visionary statement on librarians as teachers:

> I wish his paper could be read by every librarian and every library director in the country. A librarian should be so much more than a keeper of books; he should be an educator. It is this that I had in mind yesterday when I spoke of the personal influence of a librarian to restrain young persons from too much novel-reading. The relation which Mr. Green has presented ought especially to be established between a college librarian and the student readers. No such librarian is fit for his place unless he holds himself to some degree responsible for the library education of the students. They are generally willing to take advice from him; he is responsible for giving them the best advice. It is his province to direct very much of their general reading; and especially in their investigation of subjects, he should be their guide and friend. I sometimes think students get the most from me when they inquire about subjects that I know least about. They learn how to chase down a subject in a library. They get some facts, but especially *a method*. Somehow I reproach myself if a student gets to the end of his course without learning how to use a library. All that is taught in college amounts to very little; but if we can send students out self-reliant in their investigations, we have accomplished very much.[2]

Many years after the 1876 Conference of Librarians, the American Library Association echoed the emphasis on instruction in affirming the importance of instruction services in all libraries. The *ALA Policy Manual* states the following:

52.6 Instruction in the Use of Libraries

In order to assist individuals in the independent information retrieval process basic to daily living in a democratic society, the American Library Association encourages all libraries to include instruction in the use of libraries as one of the primary goals of service. Libraries of all types share the responsibility to educate users in successful information location, beginning with their childhood years and continuing the education process throughout their years of professional and personal growth.[3]

Instruction is, then, the teaching of individuals to become "successful bibliographic problem-solvers who learn through information use,"[4] but who also know when they need help. As the amount of information available continues to expand, and as radical changes continue to affect the ways that information is stored, organized, accessed, and used, it has become increasingly apparent that individuals need instruction, not only in the use of libraries, but also in the general handling and use of information throughout their lives. Whereas prior generations may have struggled with a scarcity of information, the challenge for today's user is finding what is needed in an environment of information abundance. In today's world, the information that is needed may be obscured by the sheer volume of resources available or the distraction users face as related but not quite "on topic" information draws attention from one's intended search task.

Theoretical Approaches to Instruction

Numerous terms have been used over time for instruction in the use of libraries and information, most notably *library orientation*, *library instruction*, *bibliographic instruction*, and *information literacy instruction*. At first glance, the various terms may appear to be semantic hairsplitting, and in practice, the terms are often used interchangeably without mention of the distinctions among them.

To claim that each term is completely distinct from the others and that no overlap exists would be misleading. As the terms came into use, the programs that were described by the newer term often included everything indicated by the previous term, in addition to newer developments and initiatives. What the various terms do point to is the evolution of the theory of educational services in libraries and the different approaches that different libraries may use in providing instructional services. As such, each instruction term is worth some attention.

Library Orientation

Library orientation comprises activities designed to welcome and introduce users to services, resources, collections, building layouts, and the organization of materials. Although users may develop some research skills through these activities, the primary purposes are to increase user comfort and to welcome them. Goals for library orientation might include introducing users to the physical facilities of the building (service desks, staff members, and library policies), motivating users to come back and make use of resources, and communicating an atmosphere of service and friendliness.[5]

Library Instruction

Library instruction refers to instruction in the use of libraries, with an emphasis on institution-specific procedures, collections, and policies. The term emphasizes the library as defined by its physical parameters. The focus of library instruction is on in-depth explanation of library materials; it concentrates on tools and mechanics, including techniques in using indexes, reference sources, card and online catalogs, and bibliographies. Sample objectives of a library instruction program include learning to use the *Readers' Guide Abstracts*, finding books on a subject through the library catalog, using microforms and networked information resources, and using specific reference tools such as the *Columbia Gazetteer*.[6]

Bibliographic Instruction

Bibliographic instruction began to be used in the mid-1970s to refer to any educational activities designed to teach learners how to locate and use information.[7] In contrast to library instruction, bibliographic instruction goes beyond the physical boundaries of the library and beyond institution-specific confines.

Proponents of bibliographic instruction suggested that the term better reflects the teaching that was undertaken. Librarians were moving toward critical thinking and problem solving rather than tool-based or institution-specific approaches to instruction. In particular, the 1980s saw the emergence of an emphasis on a conceptual approach to instruction based on learning theory.[8] The more conceptual approach to bibliographic instruction focuses on teaching principles rather than specific tools, for example, the concept of the scholarly publishing cycle rather than the mechanics of a particular database.[9] The intent of teaching principles of information organization and retrieval is to provide learners with the knowledge to function in a broad range of information situations and environments. Such instruction emphasizes developing and using a *search strategy*, a systematic approach to identify, locate, and evaluate information.

Information Literacy Instruction

The most recent development in the theory of instruction is the theory of *information literacy instruction*. Paralleling the developing emphasis on information literacy has been an increasing focus on the process of learning rather than the process of teaching.

In 1989, the American Library Association Presidential Committee on Information Literacy called for individuals to develop information literacy to fully participate in the information society. Key to this document is its definition of information literacy (see Box 8.1).

This definition sparked a sometimes vigorous and confused debate in librarianship about the implications of embracing the notion of information literacy.[10] Loanne Snavely and Natasha Cooper summarized the main points of the debate in their article "The *Information Literacy* Debate." After considering various pro and con arguments, Snavely and Cooper concluded with a recommendation for "embracing the term *information literacy*, using it carefully and with clarity."[11] Indeed, the profession seems to have followed that recommendation, for in 1997 the Association of College and Research Libraries established the Institute for Information Literacy,[12] and the term is now in wide use throughout the professional literature.

Not surprisingly, although the debate about the term *information literacy* continued, librarians accepted the definition as stated in the *Final Report* of the Presidential Committee and set to work establishing information literacy programs. Christine Bruce points out that "in the late 1980s and 1990s, interest in information literacy mushroomed on all continents."[13] Because information literacy instruction includes instruction in the use of information broadly defined, it is necessarily broader than library or bibliographic instruction activities. In addition, information literacy

BOX 8.1
DEFINITION OF INFORMATION LITERACY

To be information literate, a person must be able to recognize when information is needed and have the ability to locate, evaluate, and use effectively the needed information. Producing such a citizenry will require that schools and colleges appreciate and integrate the concept of information literacy into their learning programs and that they play a leadership role in equipping individuals and institutions to take advantage of the opportunities inherent within the information society. Ultimately, information literate people are those who have learned how to learn. They know how to learn because they know how information is organized, how to find information, and how to use information in such a way that others can learn from them. They are people prepared for life-long learning, because they can always find the information needed for any task or decision at hand.

American Library Association Presidential Committee on Information Literacy, *Final Report* (Chicago: American Library Association, 1989), 1.

instruction focuses on what and how students are learning rather than what and how librarians are teaching. The teaching role is defined by the learner's needs and abilities. Librarians engaged in information literacy instruction become involved with a wide variety of educational activities both in the traditional library setting and in nontraditional settings. In many cases, this has led to increased collaboration with other educators, and at some institutions of higher education, librarians have become campus leaders in information literacy efforts across the curriculum.

School and academic librarians have been particularly active in developing instruction programs that replace the traditional library instruction goals of merely teaching physical access to information with information literacy goals. Michael Eisenberg and Robert E. Berkowitz provided an early detailed curriculum for teaching library and information skills in *Information Problem-Solving: The Big Six Skills® Approach to Library and Information Skills Instruction.*[14] In 1998, the American Association of School Librarians (AASL) and the Association for Educational Communications and Technology articulated "The Nine Information Literacy Standards for Student Learning" in *Information Power: Building Partnerships for Learning* (see Box 8.2). These are still important to know about because they served as the basis for many state-level learning standards, but AASL also established a set of learning standards reflecting multiple literacies in 2007 titled *Standards for the 21st-Century Learner*, which articulates skills, dispositions in action, responsibilities, and self-assessment strategies for four learning standards:

1. Inquire, think critically, and gain knowledge.
2. Draw conclusions, make informed decisions, apply knowledge to new situations, and create new knowledge.

3. Share knowledge and participate ethically and productively as members of our democratic society.
4. Pursue personal and aesthetic growth.[15]

In early 2000, the Association of College and Research Libraries approved the *Information Literacy Competency Standards for Higher Education* (see Box 8.3). These standards have been adopted and adapted by many higher education institutions as

---

BOX 8.2
THE NINE INFORMATION LITERACY
STANDARDS FOR STUDENT LEARNING

Information Literacy

Standard 1: The student who is information literate accesses information efficiently and effectively.
Standard 2: The student who is information literate evaluates information critically and competently.
Standard 3: The student who is information literate uses information accurately and creatively.

Independent Learning

Standard 4: The student who is an independent learner is information literate and pursues information related to personal interests.
Standard 5: The student who is an independent learner is information literate and appreciates literature and other creative expressions of information.
Standard 6: The student who is an independent learner is information literate and strives for excellence in information seeking and knowledge generation.

Social Responsibility

Standard 7: The student who contributes positively to the learning community and to society is information literate and recognizes the importance of information to a democratic society.
Standard 8: The student who contributes positively to the learning community and to society is information literate and practices ethical behavior in regard to information and information technology.
Standard 9: The student who contributes positively to the learning community and to society is information literate and participates effectively in groups to pursue and generate information.

From *Information Power: Building Partnerships for Learning*, pp. 8–9, by American Association of School Librarians and Association for Educational Communications and Technology. Copyright © 1998 American Library Association and Association for Educational Communications and Technology. Reprinted by permission of the American Library Association.

BOX 8.3
INFORMATION LITERACY COMPETENCY
STANDARDS FOR HIGHER EDUCATION

Standard 1: The information literate student determines the nature and extent of the information needed.

Standard 2: The information literate student accesses needed information effectively and efficiently.

Standard 3: The information literate student evaluates information and its sources critically and incorporates selected information into his or her knowledge base and value system.

Standard 4: The information literate student, individually or as a member of a group, uses information effectively to accomplish a specific purpose.

Standard 5: The information literate student understands many of the economic, legal, and social issues surrounding the use of information and accesses and uses information ethically and legally.

From *Information Literacy Competency Standards for Higher Education.* Copyright © 2000 Association of College and Research Libraries. Reprinted by permission.

well as in position statements from higher education organizations, such as the *AACC Position Statement on Information Literacy*.[16] Work is underway to evaluate revising these standards and to better align the learning outcomes for secondary and postsecondary education. These documents and many others provide excellent direction for librarians developing information literacy instruction.

The shift to focusing on the literacy of the learner parallels a shift in education more generally from an emphasis on teaching to an emphasis on learning. Many colleges and universities have refocused missions to be institutions of learning rather than teaching. Likewise, developments in corporate training are emphasizing the process of learning rather than the production of training events. The continued development of computer networking technologies points to the continued development of learning on demand in the context of lifelong development of knowledge and skills, including information literacy. Giving evidence to the importance of information literacy for lifelong learning is *Beacons of the Information Society: The Alexandria Proclamation on Information Literacy and Lifelong Learning*,[17] promulgated in 2005 through a colloquium organized by the United Nations Educational, Scientific and Cultural Organization (UNESCO), the International Federation of Library Associations and Institutions (IFLA), and the National Forum on Information Literacy (NFIL). This document, among others,[18] points to the global importance of information literacy.

The theory of information literacy and information literacy instruction is increasingly impacted by research studies that employ ethnographic and phenomenographical approaches to investigating individuals' experiences of information literacy and successes with information literacy. Christine Bruce's *The Seven Faces of Information Literacy*[19] was the first widely considered work in this area, but other studies have followed as well.[20] In keeping with these new understandings of information literacy, librarians are increasingly designing instruction within a broad framework of learner engagement in the development of information literacy as an attribute[21] or "way of life."[22]

Relationship to Reference Services

Although many assume that instruction is a recent outgrowth of reference services, instruction and reference philosophies developed simultaneously as responses to individuals who were unable to use libraries organized for the specialist or scholar. It is certainly true that the last 40 years have seen accelerated advances in the theory and practice of instruction as distinct from one-on-one assistance at the reference desk or through a virtual reference service. The resulting separation of instruction programs from reference services has caused some to wonder about the relationship between reference services and instruction. In considering the relationship, it is best to return to the roots of instruction and reference and remember that reference and instruction are intrinsically linked, complementary, and intertwined services. One study of academic library positions noted that "every announcement for a reference librarian position also mentioned instruction."[23] To separate instruction from reference or reference from instruction is to do a disservice to users.

Reference as a Form of Instruction

Some suggest that reference service is the most intimate form of instruction. Indeed, Samuel Green's approach was one of instruction through individualized and personalized reference service. In some instances, the one-to-one assistance a user receives may be the most effective form of instruction. Increasingly, individualized and personalized reference service is becoming available to everyone, whenever and wherever it is needed; librarians are continuously adding to their reference repertoire through services such as chat and instant messaging. Virtual reality environments and social networks may eventually offer new possibilities for ways of teaching through individual and small group conversation.

Instruction at the reference desk presupposes that a user will approach the desk and ask a question and that the librarian on duty will have the time to provide instruction. What happens if 1 librarian is on duty and 10 individuals are in line? Instruction might be abandoned in favor of the expedient answer. In-depth reference service is typically tied to a place or online communication mechanism and set hours. If dependent on reference services for assistance, how will users get help when they remotely access the online system and do not get the desired results, or when the library is open but the reference desk is closed? The limitations of the reference desk can create barriers to educating users. Cooperative online reference services with partnerships across time zones may offer a partial solution to this challenge, though it can be difficult for a librarian at one institution to provide detailed instruction to students at another.

An Instructional Philosophy of Reference Service

One philosophical approach to reference work is that instruction is a part of reference. When reference librarians approach reference questions with an instructional philosophy, not only do they provide the information that users need; they also capitalize on the opportunity to utilize the experience as a "teaching moment." The old Chinese proverb "Give a man a fish, feed him for a day; Teach a man to fish, feed him for a lifetime" certainly captures the spirit of this approach. James Elmborg's work on the pedagogy of the reference desk has done much to reconnect the reference desk and the philosophy of library instruction by articulating a pedagogy of reference service that aligns reference service with the educational mission of the library.[24]

Every reference encounter requires a decision along a spectrum, with providing the complete answer on one end and only teaching a search strategy on the other end. Most encounters fall somewhere in the middle. Even individuals who feel very strongly about their teaching role may provide "information" without elaboration when it is appropriate for that situation.

Creating handouts, bibliographies, online tutorials, and Web pages; providing better signage; and improving library layout are all reference services within an instructional framework. Providing the information and strategy to the user at the point of need allows users to access library materials and information resources independently, if they so desire. One-on-one instruction at the reference desk provides personalized strategies for research as well as advice on how to use specific tools.

Instruction as a Separate Service

Separate instruction services provide solutions for overcoming the limitations of the reference desk while meeting the needs of users. Moving away from a focus on the librarian as a continuous provider of information, instruction emphasizes information independence for users. This emphasis is important for several reasons:

- An information society requires a citizenry capable of accessing, evaluating, and using information independently.[25]
- "Being able to effectively deal with information and knowledge is required in today's workplace."[26]
- Not all user needs can be addressed through traditional reference services because those services cannot effectively handle the ever-increasing demands for assistance given current and expected staffing levels.[27]
- Institutions of higher education, corporate training, and continuing education programs are emphasizing learning as an outcome rather than teaching, which is a method.[28]
- Users may prefer to work in independent and self-directed ways.

As professionals, librarians must continuously reexamine and question library services, including instruction. Many questions exist and will continue to exist for librarians providing instructional services. How do libraries provide services to "invisible" users remotely accessing information systems? How can technology be integrated into education programs? What impacts do networks, resource sharing, and e-mail have on instruction and how people learn? How can librarians provide instruction for retrieving "better" information if users are satisfied with "good enough" information? Both traditional reference desk service and instruction will continue to undergo changes as technology influences the relationships among librarians, users, and information resources.

DEVELOPING AND IMPLEMENTING INSTRUCTION

As explained earlier in this chapter, *library orientation*, *library instruction*, *bibliographic instruction*, and *information literacy instruction* are terms used to describe various theoretical approaches to instruction in libraries. Like most educational theories, these theories do not necessarily translate directly into practice but rather serve as the underlying philosophical foundations of instructional practices. Regardless of the underlying theoretical approaches, however, developing and implementing instruction is a complex and multifaceted process. The process of developing instruction is called *instructional design*.[29]

One caveat is in order. The instructional design process is often presented as a series of sequential stages distinct from one another, and this is how it is presented here. In reality, the process is much less sequential and the issues far less distinct from one another. Instruction librarians must use their knowledge of the theory of instructional design to guide them through the reality of their work life and organizational circumstances. Scenarios posing circumstances requiring the application of instructional design principles are interspersed throughout the text in this section.

Needs Assessment

Conducting a *needs assessment* prior to developing and implementing a specific instructional program is crucial to ensuring a responsive and appropriate educational program.[30] A need is a discrepancy "between an actual condition or state and a desired standard"[31] and should not be confused with a want or a demand, neither of which is necessarily indicative of a discrepancy between *what is* and *what should be*. A needs assessment is the process of identifying existing discrepancies, prioritizing discrepancies, and then selecting discrepancies to be addressed.[32] Needs assessment must be ongoing to respond to changes in user groups, information structures, and resources. Both external and internal factors need to be assessed to ascertain the educational needs of users and the library's ability to meet them.

Strategies for needs assessment are numerous, including literature reviews, surveys, observations, and testing. Literature reviews include research into local and institutional sources, such as archives, college catalogs, annual reports, and statistical summaries, as well as use of national and international sources, such as clearinghouses, discussion groups, and publications in library science and related fields. Surveys can be conducted that ask users about their needs and preferences or that ascertain staff attitudes toward instruction. Astute observation at the reference desk, in the stacks, or near computer terminals can also provide strong anecdotal evidence of user needs. Reviews of Web site traffic patterns, search strings in the library catalog, and comments from users are also helpful. Some libraries are beginning to make more systematic use of work-practice studies to understand user needs.[33] Finally, users can be tested on their knowledge and skills. User surveys and observation are probably the most commonly used approaches in conducting needs assessment for library instruction.

After gathering and analyzing information about existing needs, the instruction librarian must determine which needs are highest in priority, which can be addressed through formal instructional interventions (not all needs are appropriate for educational

---

BOX 8.4
SCENARIO: THE NEEDS OF GENEALOGISTS

You are one of 10 reference librarians at a large urban public library. Each weekend shift at the reference desk, you notice that you are asked many questions about genealogy research. Raising this observation with your reference colleagues, you learn that they too have noticed this pattern in reference questions on the weekends. The head of the reference department suggests that the library consider offering a genealogy research workshop. You are assigned to conduct a needs assessment to determine whether such a workshop would be useful, who would attend, and what should be taught. Outline your approach.

---

solutions; some are better addressed through signage, policy changes, or one-on-one assistance), which are politically acceptable to address, and so forth. After selecting the needs to be addressed, a general statement of the broad aim of the instruction to be developed should be formulated. This broad aim will serve as a touch point and focus throughout the remaining stages in developing and implementing instruction.[34]

Goals and Objectives

After a needs assessment has been conducted, the instruction librarian is ready to identify the desired learning outcomes: the goals and objectives of the instruction. Goals and objectives do not guarantee successful instruction, but the lack of them could mean failure. Writing goals and objectives is a skill that may be frustrating and time-consuming to acquire at first, but it is essential for good teaching.[35]

Written objectives for instruction are expressions of the intended outcomes or results of learning. Instructional objectives serve both the instructor and the learner. For the instructor, objectives focus and guide instruction, provide consistency in structuring content, facilitate choices of media and methods, assist in determining supplemental learning aids and/or approaches for student activities, and provide a mechanism for evaluation. For the learner, objectives give direction, set clear expectations, increase motivation, focus time, and allow for self-monitoring. For both the learner and the instructor, objectives create a mutual understanding of content, expectations, and outcomes. Objectives help make learning more effective and efficient.

Instruction has three levels of objectives: general, terminal, and enabling.[36] *General objectives* describe the overall goals of a program and what the entire program is designed to achieve in broad terms. Often these objectives are expressed in fuzzy terms such as "understands," "appreciates," or "believes." *Terminal objectives* break the general objectives into more specific, meaningful units that are the intended outcomes of instruction. *Enabling objectives* define the specific knowledge or skills necessary to achieve the terminal objective; they describe the behavior of a person who has mastered the material. Enabling objectives have three characteristics: the performance (observable behavior), conditions (situation statement), and criterion (acceptable behavior and who judges the performance of that behavior).[37] See Box 8.5 for examples.

BOX 8.5
EXAMPLES OF GENERAL, TERMINAL, AND ENABLING OBJECTIVES

General: "The user understands how information is defined by experts, and recognizes how that knowledge can help determine the direction of his/her search for specific information."[38]

Terminal: "The user understands the processes through which information sources are accepted and disseminated in the research community."[39]

Enabling: Given a stack of general magazines and a stack of scholarly journals, clearly labeled (conditions), the student (the learner) can identify (the performance) at least five differences between articles in general magazines and those in scholarly journals (criterion).

Although an understanding of these three levels of objectives is conceptually useful, they are presented here as a framework for consideration, not a prescribed method. In practice, librarians will do well to follow the advice of Norman E. Gronlund to write objectives that are "specific enough to provide focus for both teaching and the assessment of learning, without limiting the teacher's flexibility in selecting instructional methods and materials."[40] This is particularly important given that critics of writing objectives in behavioral terms rightly argue that student performance may not reflect what the student has learned as well as might be supposed.[41]

Gronlund also suggests "using an overall classification of possible learning outcomes to serve as a frame of reference" to help broaden the possible areas considered, to aid in stating and organizing objectives, and to check for possible omissions.[42] Benjamin Bloom's *Taxonomy*[43] gives a hierarchical organization of learning in the cognitive domain (thinking skills) in six levels: knowledge, comprehension, application, analysis, synthesis, and evaluation, with the last three identified as higher-level thinking skills. David R. Krathwohl and colleagues[44] have done the same for the affective domain, which is concerned with motivation and prioritization, and Elizabeth J. Simpson[45] has detailed the psychomotor domain. A. Dean Hauenstein[46] takes a holistic approach to the three domains in rewriting the taxonomies as a unified whole. In applying objectives to libraries, instruction librarians will find assistance in the *Model Statement of Objectives for Academic Bibliographic Instruction*,[47] developed by the Bibliographic Instruction Section of the Association of College and Research Libraries. The *Model Statement* can be customized to a particular library regardless of type and to individual learners regardless of experience, age, or background. As a unique blend of several theoretical traditions, this document presents an excellent framework for thinking about instruction in libraries.[48] The aforementioned *Information Literacy Competency Standards for Higher Education* and *The Nine Information Literacy Standards for Student Learning* will also be helpful in this regard.

Instructional Content

Goals and objectives provide a framework for instructional design by detailing the intended outcomes for an instruction session or program. This framework is not prescriptive of the instructional content, however, because decisions about what content to include in an instruction session are affected as well by the needs assessment and understandings of learners' existing knowledge and skill levels. The framework is instead a guide for making decisions about instruction content.

Though the specific content for any particular instruction program cannot be detailed here, the instruction librarian should keep in mind the kinds of content that might be selected. A useful way of considering the content is to distinguish among declarative, procedural, and conditional content. Declarative content is information that describes and tells what something is. Procedural content is information about how something is done. Conditional content is information about the circumstances under which particular declarative and procedural content is relevant. Conditional content tells learners when to use the "what" and "how" knowledge conveyed in declarative and procedural content. In other words, conditional content ensures that learners can apply other content in appropriate contexts. All three types of content are likely to be needed by learners in every instruction session. *Understanding by Design* is highly recommended for librarians wanting to follow a systematic instructional design process.[49]

Learning Theory and Styles

The most effective instruction efforts take into account learning theory and consider individual styles of learning. Therefore, it is essential that instruction librarians be familiar with learning theory and learning styles.

Views of Learning and Knowledge

What is learning? What is knowledge? Although these may seem like easy questions, the answers are very complex and depend on how one considers the world and

---

BOX 8.6
SCENARIO: THE ONLINE CATALOG WORKSHOP

You have been hired as the instruction librarian at a small liberal arts college that has not previously had an instruction librarian. Your first task is to develop a series of one-hour open workshops for faculty and staff of the college, to be held in the library's hands-on electronic classroom. Because the library is bringing up a new online catalog interface, which has caused numerous faculty members to express frustration with not knowing how to use the new system when they were familiar with the previous system, you decide that the first workshop you will develop will be an introduction to the online catalog. Write objectives that express the intended learning outcomes of the workshop.

the nature of knowledge. Robert M. Gagné defines learning as "a change in human disposition or capability that persists over a period of time and is not simply as-cribable to processes of growth."[50] Theories on how individuals learn continue to be developed and modified. As theories are proposed and become accepted, older ones are not necessarily discarded. Divergent theories exist simultaneously and are often considered equally valid in different situations. Although there is not one definitive, exclusive learning theory, the major schools of behaviorism, cognitivism, and con-structivism have had particular impact on the field of library instruction.[51]

Behaviorists view knowledge as passive, largely automatic responses to external factors in the environment. Ideas are fixed and immutable. The learner adapts or re-sponds to changes in the environment. Learning is largely seen as a passive process that focuses on new behavioral patterns being repeated until they become automatic. B. F. Skinner studied behavioral conditioning, in which reinforcement—positive, negative, or lack of—shapes behavior. Positive reinforcers help one to make connec-tions, negative reinforcers cause learners to avoid undesirable responses, continuous reinforcement increases the rate of learning, and intermittent reinforcement contrib-utes to longer retention. Edward Thorndike theorized that learning is the formation of connections or bonds between stimuli and responses.

Cognitivists view knowledge as symbolic, mental representations in the minds of individuals. The emphasis is on active mental processing or information process-ing. Changes in behavior are observed but only as an indicator of what is going on in the learner's mind. Knowledge is still viewed as given and absolute but is formed and reformed through experience. For cognitivists, the emphasis is on the process of learning. Gagné's information processing theory argues that people can reason with higher-level concepts if they have learned all of the prerequisite lower-level information.

Constructivists view knowledge as a constructed entity made by each learner individually through the learning process, based on individual experiences and sche-mata. Schemata are mental models of how information is organized in an individual's thinking in order to make sense of what is known and to incorporate new knowledge. By having experiences and reflecting on those experiences, individuals construct their own understandings of the world; learning is the process of adjusting and re-structuring mental models to accommodate new experiences. Constructivists argue that teaching should focus on preparing the learner to solve problems in ambiguous situations. Constructivist thought has two branches: cognitive constructivism, which focuses on the individual, and social constructivism, which focuses on social interac-tion. Piaget discussed situated (or shared) cognition, in which learning is viewed as the process of entry into a community of practice.

Though less influential in the development of instruction in libraries, many librarians also find the humanist theories of learning useful. *Humanists* view knowl-edge as the acquisition of information and the personalization of that information. Learning occurs primarily by reflecting on personal experience and as a result of intrinsic motivation; it is defined as an increasing capacity to be self-directing. The role of instruction is to help learners extract the knowledge from their own insights and experience and personalize it. Humanist teachers focus on problem solving, development of human potential, and greater self-direction, making use of self-discovery, goal-setting, esteem-building, and relationship-building activities.

These views of learning affect instruction in libraries. The influence of behaviorists can be seen in the writing of behavioral objectives, workbooks, linear computer-assisted instruction, and institution-specific instruction. The cognitivist theory is reflected in the use of conceptual frameworks and guided design and in an increased awareness of learning styles.[52] Constructivist theory is reflected in the use of collaborative learning, synchronous and asynchronous online learning environments, and problem analysis. As instruction in libraries focuses on information literacy rather than bibliographic problem solving, constructivism is increasingly the learning theory with the greatest explanatory power and instructional design utility. Each instruction librarian, however, will have a personal philosophy of teaching unique to his or her own experiences, beliefs, and goals. Articulating this personal philosophy and exploring how it fits with the philosophy of the instruction program and the library organization's culture reflect maturity of development as an instruction librarian.

Styles of Learning

Individuals also have their own personal preferences for learning. Each individual develops a learning style or a habitual manner of problem solving. Researchers have analyzed these learning styles using a variety of measurements.[53]

One way that educators divide learning styles is into *field-dependent* and *field-independent*.[54] A field-dependent learner prefers learning by observing, is distracted by surroundings, seeks guidance, and likes learning in groups. A field-independent learner tends to learn through question and answer, likes to work alone, and is analytical in problem solving. Cerise Oberman has used "Petals around a Rose," a dice game predicated on this distinction, to illustrate the importance of teaching problem solving.[55]

David Kolb found that individuals have tendencies to both perceive and process information differently. Learners can be concrete or abstract perceivers and active or reflective processors. Concrete perceivers absorb information through direct experience, by doing, acting, sensing, and feeling. Abstract perceivers, on the other hand, take in information through analysis, observation, and thinking. Active processors make sense of an experience by immediately using the new information. Reflective processors make sense of an experience by reflecting and thinking about it. Traditional education practices tend to favor abstract perceiving and reflective processing.[56]

Another theory suggests that the two different sides of the brain control two different modes of thinking and that each individual prefers one mode over the other. Left-brain thinkers are logical, sequential, rational, analytical, and objective and look at parts. Right-brain thinkers are random, intuitive, holistic, synthesizing, and subjective and look at wholes. In general, traditional school settings tend to favor left-brain modes of thinking and downplay right-brain ones.[57]

With so many views of how people learn and prefer to learn, it should not be surprising that there are also many debates about the validity and usefulness of learning styles. Instead of trying to identify a single learning style instrument, instruction librarians will benefit from assuming a multiplicity and complexity of styles and following this advice: "Using only one measure assumes that one inventory is more correct than others. At this time that assumption cannot be made. It may be assumed that, with human individuality, multiple descriptions of learning style are necessary."[58] In addition, it is rare for instruction librarians to be able to test learners before instruction, so they often must use aggregate data and research studies to make reasonable assumptions about user populations. As such, instruction librarians should be prepared to address a variety of learning styles in any learning experience.

Instructional Methods

After a needs assessment is completed, learning goals are articulated, and learning theory and styles are examined, the instruction librarian begins the process of deciding what *instructional methods* to employ. No one instructional method serves all situations, and the effectiveness of an instructional method is contingent on the learning objectives to be achieved, the learning styles of the participants,[59] and the instructor's facility with the method. Commonly, more than one method is used during a single session; for example, a class might begin with a short lecture that incorporates multimedia, go on to student brainstorming in small groups, and end with the entire class discussing solutions. A variety of teaching methods keeps learners involved and responsive, and every instructional strategy has certain advantages and disadvantages. It is essential that careful consideration be given to these advantages and limitations to ensure that the strategy selected for a specific instructional setting is one that will be effective.

Strategy decisions must be based on careful analysis of instructional objectives, subject matter, learner populations, instructors, instructional space, facilities, equipment and materials, time, and costs. Finding the right method may also require some experimentation: "In reality, no one method or combination of methods can be applied with equal success in all circumstances. The instructor will often have to experiment with several different approaches to find the right one for a particular course and class."[60] The overriding consideration in the selection of strategy is the objectives of instruction: what the student will be required to do. Beginning librarians should explore their teaching strengths as well as methods that are most effective for their learners. Instructors should also consider the "Seven Principles for Good Practice in Undergraduate Education" (see Box 8.7), which are easily adaptable to other instructional settings.

Lecture/Discussion

A *lecture* is a semiformal discourse in which the instructor presents a series of events, facts, or principles; explores a problem; or explains relationships.[61] It is a means of "telling" and is used to inform. Lectures are presented by experts and are one-directional; that is, there is little interaction between the instructor and the students, with little or no interchange of ideas. It may be difficult to perceive student reactions, misconceptions, inattention, or difficulties during a lecture. On the other hand, lectures have the benefit of transmitting large amounts of information at one time to a large number of students in a proportionately short period of time. The length and content are also easily modified.

Discussion includes questions, answers, and comments from instructors and students. Discussion can be *instructor-centered* to "clarify content, define terms, identify assumptions, motivate participation, recognize contributions"; *group-centered* to "build on experience, explore hypotheses, strengthen relationships, raise questions,

---

BOX 8.7
SEVEN PRINCIPLES FOR GOOD PRACTICE
IN UNDERGRADUATE EDUCATION

1. Encourages student–faculty contact
2. Encourages cooperation among students
3. Encourages active learning
4. Gives prompt feedback
5. Emphasizes time on task
6. Communicates high expectations
7. Respects diverse talents and ways of learning

Arthur W. Chickering and Zelda F. Gamson, "Seven Principles for Good Practice in Undergraduate Education," *AAHE Bulletin* 39 (1987): 3–7.

---

formulate ideas, examine assumptions"; or *collaborative* to "solve problems, share responsibilities, compare alternatives, test hypotheses, modify assumptions."[62] Leading discussion requires more instructor resourcefulness, initiative, and ability than lecturing and also requires advance preparation of the participants in the form of reading, thinking, and study. Although small group discussion can be used effectively in large classrooms with advanced preparation on the part of the instructor, there are size and time limits. Relatively large blocks of time are needed for discussion to be effective. A high degree of student participation and active involvement promotes better and more permanent learning.

Demonstration

In *demonstration*, the instructor performs a skill or process, showing the students what to do and how to do it, usually accompanied by explanations to point out why, where, and when it is done. Demonstrations give concreteness to oral explanations, helping students learn faster and more permanently and preventing misunderstandings. The student is usually expected to be able to repeat the task or activity after the demonstration. Students must clearly see every part of the demonstration, so environmental factors such as lighting, size of group, and the ability to project screens or pages are important. Equipment must function adequately; instructors need to consider backup approaches if equipment malfunctions.[63] Because sequencing is usually important in demonstration, situation, timing, and pacing are also critical. Students must be given time to see the action, think about it, and then perform the task themselves.

Active Learning

The literature suggests that students should do more than just listen and observe for effective learning to take place.[64] According to Charles C. Bonwell and James A. Eison,

They must read, write, discuss, or be engaged in solving problems. Most important, to be actively involved, students must engage in such higher-order thinking tasks as analysis, synthesis, and evaluation. Within this context, it is proposed that strategies promoting active learning be defined as instructional activities involving students in doing things and thinking about what they are doing.[65]

Active learning provides time for learners to process information and transfer learning to long-term memory and thus promotes greater retention of information and skills and higher cognitive learning. It is a meta-method: active learning incorporates many other instructional methods in a context of considering the whole of the students' instructional experience rather than only considering the component parts. For example, students can be given a short lecture on Boolean operators followed by a practice exercise in which they group themselves using individual characteristics such as hair or eye color to demonstrate their understanding of Boolean concepts, followed by the opportunity to discuss the principles of Boolean operators and how they apply to searching for information on a topic.[66] With such an active learning approach, learners have more opportunities to integrate new information with existing knowledge, so they are better able to translate what they have learned into their own schema. This practice also helps address issues of library anxiety.[67]

Collaborative Learning

Collaborative learning is an umbrella term for a broad array of teaching methods that are learner-centered and based on the premises that learning is an active, constructive process; learning depends on rich contexts; learners are diverse; and learning is inherently social. It is this last factor that distinguishes active learning theories from collaborative learning. The most structured form of collaborative learning is cooperative learning—a systematic instructional strategy in which "small groups work together toward a common goal."[68] Cooperative learning has been used successfully in library instruction.[69]

Five attributes must be present for collaborative learning to be successful: positive interdependence, face-to-face communication, individual responsibility, social skills, and time for reflection.[70] Obviously, establishing this kind of environment in a "one-shot lecture" setting can be extremely difficult, unless the learners are already comfortable in collaborative learning environments. Instruction librarians must learn to feel comfortable with giving up control of the learning process, sharing that control with the students, and taking risks. When collaborative environments are established appropriately, they help students personalize knowledge and apply learning, improving student attitudes, retention, performance, and levels of success. In addition, students develop problem-solving skills and more effective communication skills.[71] Box 8.8 provides a framework for analyzing how time is allocated among different activities in an instructional session.

Instructional Materials

Instructional materials include any and all resources that are created to assist with teaching and learning, including guides, worksheets, videotapes, tutorials, Web

BOX 8.8
STUDENT ACTIVITIES DURING INSTRUCTION

What percentage of instructional time in a typical classroom period is focused on the following activities?

Percent

Students reading	_____
Students watching	_____
Students listening	_____
Students talking	_____
Students writing	_____
Students reflecting	_____
Students acting	_____
Other	_____
Total =	100%

Include all time spent on instructional activities but excluding activities such as passing out handouts, taking roll, etc. Do not total above 100 percent. Even though students are probably thinking and writing while the instructor is speaking, count only the times when students are thinking or writing with no other activity going on.

What percentage of time in a typical classroom period do students spend doing the following?

Working independently	_____
Working in groups	_____
Total =	100%

Adapted with permission from a workshop by Trish Ridgeway, "Integrating Active Learning into Library Instruction: Practical Information for Immediate Use," a pre-conference sponsored by the Bibliographic Instruction Section of the Association of College and Research Libraries, Miami, FL, June 24, 1994.

sites, textbooks, online tutorials, and modules in networked courseware systems such as Moodle and Blackboard. Some instructional materials are designed to be used by the learner without formal instruction, whereas others are designed to be used within the context of an instructional session.

Handouts

Perhaps the most common type of instructional material is the handout. Handouts are used as stand-alone instructional opportunities as well as supplements to point-of-use instruction at the reference desk and during instruction sessions. Plain or fancy, simple or complex, handouts provide information and instructions that are needed by the learner but not easily committed to memory without practice. In some cases, the information might be needed only on rare occasions. In others, the handout supports the learner until a given procedure or informational detail is committed to memory. The handout is very flexible.

Regardless of their intended purpose, handouts must be well designed if they are to be useful to the learner. A poorly developed handout may actually make a given task more difficult than if no handout were available at all. When developing handouts, consider the following:

- Content: Systematic and careful decisions about the information that is included in a handout must be made; equally important to consider is what information will not be included. The type of information to be presented should also be considered in light of instructional objectives—is the content declarative (knowledge that or knowledge about), procedural (knowledge how), or conditional (knowledge when or knowledge why)?[72]—as well as the structure of the content.[73] These factors will help determine how the information should be presented.
- Relationships: The relationship between the handout in development and other handouts and instructional content should be considered.
- Permanence: Decide whether the handout is for one-time use or will be used in multiple situations.
- Design: Size, orientation, white space, line width, typography, justification, fonts, and institutional standards are among the many design issues an instruction librarian should consider.[74] Because handouts may not be provided in print form but rather presented electronically through Web sites or courseware systems, design considerations for print may need to be superseded by design considerations for online display. For online display, however, the design should also accommodate printing because many learners prefer to print online handouts for easy consultation during information searching.

Exercises and Assignments

Unlike handouts, which are often distributed to learners during instruction as well as at various public service points within the library, exercises and assignments are unique to formal instruction sessions. The purpose of an exercise is to provide learners with an opportunity to practice with new resources or skills. Assignments are

---

BOX 8.9
SCENARIO: CALL NUMBERS

You are the school library media specialist in a suburban elementary school that uses the Dewey Decimal system. The teachers have requested a handout explaining what call numbers are and how to use them in locating books in the library. Create this handout, taking into consideration the following factors: content, relationships, permanence, and design.

similar in purpose but with the additional requirement that the learner is in some way responsible for demonstrating skill or knowledge through completion of the assignment, often to receive a grade or credit for the instruction. Although worksheets and research term papers are common assignments, there are many alternative projects such as mock trials and editorials that should be considered as well.[75]

Like handouts, exercises and assignments must be well developed to be effective. When developing exercises and assignments, consider the following:

- Content: Instructional goals and objectives should direct the development of every exercise or assignment.[76] This will ensure that the activities required of the learners are directly related to the learning outcomes expected from the instruction and that the exercise or assignment is not "busy work."
- Realistic expectations: Overly complex activities that fail to provide for the developmental processes of learning will frustrate students. If an exercise or assignment is complex, break the activity into parts and provide students with opportunities to check their work before completing, perhaps incorrectly, an entire activity.
- Grading and feedback: Up-front consideration of how exercises and assignments will be graded or how other feedback will be provided to students will prevent situations in which learner performance cannot be assessed.

Both exercises and assignments can indicate the extent to which learners have accomplished the goals and objectives of the instruction session. Such assessment of learning is vital to evaluating the effectiveness of instruction and identifying areas where student achievement is less than expected or hoped.

BOX 8.10
SCENARIO: THE PERSUASIVE SPEECH

You are one of two reference librarians at a community college. At the beginning of each semester, all 200 students in Speech Communication 109: Principles of Communication are required to do library research in preparation for a persuasive speech. Each student selects a topic from a list of broad social issue topics (e.g., capital punishment, abortion, euthanasia, gun control, and pornography). Each student is required to choose a specific position within the broad topic area and to find three scholarly journal articles about the topic. Presently, the students receive no library use instruction and often fail to narrow their topics and/or locate appropriate articles. More often than not, the result is frustrated students, edgy librarians, and disappointed instructors. As part of the institution's recently articulated commitment to information literacy, the department chair offers to schedule one hour of class time for a librarian to instruct the students in the use of library resources, provided that the students complete a graded exercise as part of the session. Develop objectives for this instruction session and, using those objectives as a guide, create an assignment for the students, which the librarians will grade after the session.

Instructional Technology

New educational technologies have given instruction librarians incredible promises: increased work speed through instantaneous transmissions, increased work efficiency, removal of possibilities of human error, provision of access to those outside the library's walls,[77] accommodation of different learning styles,[78] and improved interactions with others,[79] sometimes at less cost than the traditional methods, though startup costs can be significant. Instruction librarians should use technology in combination with other modes of delivery and teaching methods to make learning more active and interactive, but they must be careful that the glitz of the technology is not the primary reason for the changes. Often the old technology or method is equally, or even more, effective. For example, online tutorials may require less staff time for instruction, but by removing learners from the library environment, the learners are divorced from viewing the librarian as mentor and guide for their research. Making careful and reflective decisions about using technology requires consideration of learning objectives, learner needs, and technological capacity.

Many librarians start by replicating existing materials within a new technological context, such as making paper handouts available on the library's Web site. However, instructional designers warn that "just making content available is not education. Learning requires action, interaction, and application."[80] The next phase of adopting new technology is to more fully utilize the technology's capacity for new and better ways of teaching by creating cooperative and independent learning systems. The ultimate phase of incorporating technology into instruction involves a redesign of programs characterized by unmediated user access to source materials and tools, opportunities for apprenticeships and cooperative learning, and opportunities for self-paced learning where appropriate.[81] Social networking technologies such as Facebook and virtual reality environments such as Second Life hold the potential for deep reconsideration and redesign of current instructional approaches.

Utilizing the full potential of instructional technology takes a great deal of time and requires that instructors learn new skills, develop support systems, and work collaboratively with colleagues to avoid redundancies and costly mistakes. Online tutorials have emerged as a very common approach to supplementing or supplanting classroom-based information literacy instruction. *Developing Web-Based Instruction: Planning, Designing, Managing, and Evaluating for Results*[82] provides a comprehensive resource guide for librarians needing detail in this area. The ALA/ACRL Instruction Section's PRIMO project[83] also highlights exemplary work in this area.

Evaluation and Assessment

Evaluation is "a process involving the collection and presentation of information in a manner intended to increase the credibility and usefulness of that information."[84] Librarians regularly make observations and judgments about the effectiveness and value of instruction initiatives; however, evaluation is set apart from the everyday activity of making decisions by the purposive nature of the collection and analysis of data in evaluation. Although the same conclusions might be reached through everyday observation, conclusions reached through systematic data collection and analysis are likely to be perceived as more reliable and trustworthy.

The primary purpose of instructional evaluation is the improvement of instruction for the benefit of learners. By investigating the success of past instruction efforts, an instruction librarian will be prepared to make sound decisions about future initiatives. Without the information that an evaluation provides, it may be difficult to ensure that instruction efforts are responsive to needs and continue to improve. Evaluation results can also be used to answer queries from library administrators, legislators, or accrediting bodies about the impact of libraries on the information literacy of users.

In conducting a program evaluation, the instruction librarian must return to the goals of the program. Put most simply, a program evaluation will investigate whether the program has met its goals.[85] Specific questions for investigation might include whether teaching methods are effective, program resources are used efficiently, learners develop intended skills, faculty perceive the instruction as valuable, students can transfer skills to another research tool, learners feel more comfortable,[86] and appropriate goals and objectives were selected for the program. Appropriate methods, instruments, data, and conclusions are dependent on which particular question or set of questions is under investigation.[87]

Librarians who are not responsible for overall program evaluation may be interested in using learner feedback to improve their teaching. *Assessment* techniques such as the Minute Paper (see Box 8.11), the Muddiest Point, and the One-Sentence Summary can provide a wealth of information through relatively low-risk and simple procedures;[88] handbooks and examples of information literacy assessment tools are also available.[89] The results of such assessments can inform and strengthen program evaluation conclusions. Recently, librarians have also turned to standardized testing instruments to measure students' information literacy abilities. Two high-profile standardized testing initiatives are SAILS (Standardized Assessment of Information Literacy Skills)[90] and the *iSkills* Information and Communication Technology (ICT) Literacy Assessment from the Educational Testing Service.[91] Critics of these tests are concerned that standardized testing does not provide an authentic assessment of learner abilities and places inappropriate emphasis on information seeking and management rather than information use.

BOX 8.11
THE MINUTE PAPER

Directions to learners: Please take one minute and respond to the following questions:

1. What was the most important thing you learned during this session?
2. What important question remains unanswered?

Direction to instructor: Tabulate responses and reflect on any patterns. Use responses to guide subsequent instructional sessions. In particular, use learner questions to clarify content before moving on to new learning objectives.

ADMINISTRATION AND MANAGEMENT OF INSTRUCTION

Administering instructional services involves many issues, including organizational structures; personnel; budgets and funding; facilities; and promotion, marketing, and public relations. The beginning librarian may not be responsible for the management of a program; however, how and how well the program is managed will greatly affect the ability of all participating librarians to implement effective instruction.

Organizational Structures

The instruction librarian works within at least two organizational structures: that of the library and that of the larger institution.[92] Both organizational structures have the potential to facilitate or hinder instructional efforts. The successful instruction librarian learns how to maneuver within the structures, determine how and where decisions are made, and influence those decisions.

The greater institution may be a college, school system, public library board, community, or company. Within that structure, decisions about policies, budgets, and personnel are made that affect the instruction program either directly or indirectly. The instruction librarian must determine where various decisions are made, who makes them, and what information and processes are used. Some answers may be easily determined from the institution's organizational chart; others may be mired in institutional lore or affected by personalities. To effectively manage an instruction program, the librarian responsible must work within both the official structure of an organization and the informal networks of influence.

Within the library, organization of the instruction program may take a variety of forms, depending on the type and size of the institution. Instruction may be the responsibility of a separate instruction department, the reference department, subject specialists, or any combination of these.[93] Each approach has advantages and disadvantages.

A separate department allows concentration on instructional design and delivery without the distraction of conflicting priorities and responsibilities. Although a separate department establishes visibility for educational services, it can also isolate instruction librarians from related service areas such as reference and collection development.

More typical is for instruction to be the responsibility of reference librarians or subject bibliographers led by a single coordinator of instruction, rather than an entire instruction department.[94] Responsibility for instruction is a reasonable extension of the role of reference librarians and subject bibliographers; however, overwork and confusion of priorities can result when reference librarians or subject bibliographers take responsibility for instruction.[95] In such settings, an instruction coordinator is usually responsible for monitoring the instruction load and providing some type of leadership for the instruction program. In smaller libraries, the instruction coordinator may be a reference librarian with particular instruction coordination duties. In larger libraries, the instruction coordinator is likely to be a separate position filled by an individual specializing in library instruction.

BOX 8.12
SCENARIO: LIBRARY INSTRUCTION
AND THE FIRST-YEAR EXPERIENCE

You are a reference librarian at a research university that is developing a new program to support undergraduate students. This first-year experience program divides students into learning communities. All 20 students in a given learning community will meet in a weekly success seminar and take at least two classes together in the fall and one in the spring. The success seminar will include instruction in library and research skills. The head of public services has asked you to investigate different organizational approaches for providing this instruction. Specifically, you are to recommend whether the library should (1) hire librarians who will be solely responsible for providing the instruction to the 100 learning communities, (2) create a team of librarians who focus on this instruction but have other responsibilities as well, or (3) hire a coordinator and require that current reference librarians each provide instruction for some of the learning communities. Write a report that compares the advantages and disadvantages of each approach and then recommends a course of action.

In a one-person library, it goes without saying that the same person who selects and catalogs materials and provides reference services is also responsible for instruction. In many school and corporate libraries, the organizational structure of the solo librarian is the norm.

Personnel

Instruction services, like most reference services, are personnel-intensive. Regardless of the organizational structure, staff members with appropriate education, experience, and expertise are needed for an instruction program to be successful.[96] Without appropriate personnel, designing and implementing instruction is impossible.

The skills needed by a librarian with instruction responsibilities differ from those needed by the coordinator of an instruction program. In 2007, the ALA/ACRL Instruction Section produced the *Standards for Proficiencies for Instruction Librarians and Coordinators*,[97] which articulated core proficiencies for all instruction librarians and additional proficiencies for coordinators in 12 categories. The 12 categories are as follows:

1. Administrative ability
2. Assessment and evaluation skills
3. Communication skills
4. Curriculum knowledge
5. Information literacy integration skills
6. Instructional design skills

    7. Leadership skills
    8. Planning ability
    9. Presentation skills
  10. Promotion skills
  11. Subject expertise
  12. Teaching skills

Instruction responsibilities, however, are not the sole domain of public service librarians. Technical services librarians may participate in the instruction program. Library support staff is also involved in the implementation of instruction programs, in activities such as handout compilation, scheduling, and marketing and, in some cases, delivery of the instruction. Staff outside of the library in the larger institution may also do work that supports the library instruction program. For example, a university's multimedia unit might assist with the creation of a Web-based tutorial, or a company's marketing department might provide guidance in developing handouts.

Recruitment of qualified professionals and continuing education are major issues for instruction administrators. Because relatively little emphasis is placed on learning to teach in library schools, librarians may feel ill-prepared for instruction responsibilities.[98] School librarians with teacher preparation may fare better, but they often still lack specific background in library instruction and its development. Because of this lack of expertise, some libraries have established in-service training programs.[99] Mentoring, performance appraisal, and coping with stress and burnout are important professional development issues for instruction librarians.[100] Reflective peer coaching is another approach.[101] Many individuals, even those with extensive instruction experience, seek out continuing education opportunities such as the LOEX and WILU[102] conferences and the programs offered by the Institute for Information Literacy, such as the Immersion and Intentional Teacher programs.[103]

Program Structures

The particulars of program structures are somewhat dependent on the type of library—that is, whether a library is academic, school, special, or public; however, all program structures can be thought of as being on a continuum of collaboration.

BOX 8.13
SCENARIO: A POSITION ANNOUNCEMENT

You are one of four reference librarians at a private college. The most senior reference librarian has announced retirement. The reference coordinator has asked you to write a draft position advertisement focusing on instruction coordination for discussion at the staff meeting next week. Review the job advertisements listed on the ALA JobList (http://joblist.ala.org/), create the advertisement, and then draft a cover memo to explain why you crafted the advertisement as you did.

At one end of the continuum is formal instruction that is developed and offered by the librarian alone. At the other end of the continuum is instruction that is developed and offered by the librarians in full collaboration with another organization, group, or institution. Between the two ends exists a variety of collaborative structures involving a variety of collaborative partners.[104]

After identifying the existing instructional needs through an informal or formal needs assessment process, an instruction librarian should consider the available opportunities for collaboration and the desirability of those opportunities. In pursuing a particular structure for an instruction program, librarians must consider the political environment, administrative support, and the degree of inter-departmental and inter-institutional cooperation that exists. In some circumstances, a solo venture by the librarian may be more effective or more desirable than a joint effort. Neither end of the continuum of collaboration is inherently better than the other; what is important is that the structure implemented in a particular setting be the most appropriate and effective for the circumstances and instructional needs. The structure of the program should be decided on before instructional design decisions are made, in order to involve any collaborative partners early in the development process.

The particular mix of instruction offerings and collaborations that exist in a particular library will be unique to that library's situation and mission. In "Structures of Bibliographic Instruction Programs: A Continuum for Planning," Lori Arp and Lizabeth A. Wilson detail a continuum of cooperation for academic libraries.[105] Defining the continuum is the level of cooperation required among librarians, departmental faculty, and university administrators. *Orientation* activities require little to no cooperation, whereas course-related instruction, course-integrated instruction, and team teaching require increasing levels of departmental faculty cooperation, and separate courses require the cooperation of university administrators as well. *Course-related instruction* occurs during class time with the support and cooperation of the course instructor and provides learners in a given course with the information skills needed to carry out one or more activities of that course.[106] *Course-integrated instruction* is developed at the time that the course is designed, is part of the objectives of the course, and is essential to knowledge of the subject.[107] At its most developed stage, course-integrated instruction takes the form of *team teaching*, where the instruction is designed, delivered, and evaluated by the librarian and classroom teacher together. According to Arp and Wilson, as an academic library instruction program develops and cooperation increases, librarians can move toward structures more fully integrated into the institution's educational mission and goals. *Integrating Information Literacy into the Higher Education Curriculum* provides detailed examples of how information literacy can affect and transform campus curricula.[108]

The program structures that develop in school libraries will be similar to those in academic libraries; however, curriculum guidelines, state education regulations, and staff certification requirements will also likely affect the types of collaboration that develop. In schools that embrace resource-based teaching, which uses a variety of primary resources rather than textbooks, high levels of collaboration are likely to develop, and librarians will work closely with teachers and administrators to integrate library instruction into the curriculum. School library media specialists' efforts in learning and teaching, information access, and program administration support partnerships for student learning.[109]

In public libraries, potential collaborative partners are quite varied. In addition to schools and other educational institutions, public librarians might partner with businesses, nonprofit organizations, local governments, church groups, civic groups, or similar groups in developing instructional programs to meet the needs of different user groups. Likewise, special librarians have many opportunities to collaborate with other professionals within their larger institutions.

Even when extensive collaboration is in place, many librarians offer at least some instruction that is developed and sponsored by the library alone. For example, most librarians offer some form of library orientation designed to introduce and orient users to services, facilities, and resources, often in the form of guided building tours. Another type of library-sponsored instruction uses workshops to introduce users to methods and strategies for using particular resources; however, the workshops are developed for a walk-in clientele rather than for a particular group.

Funding

All aspects of designing, implementing, and managing a library instruction program will require financial support. A library instruction program must have ongoing funding to accomplish the program's goals and objectives.[110] Funding is needed for staff, equipment, supplies, facilities, instructional materials, promotion and marketing, and training. Without money, not much happens.

The library's budget for instructional activities should be integrated in the operating budget. In some cases, this will mean funds specifically allocated to the instruction program and managed by the instruction coordinator. In other cases, funding for instruction will be included as appropriate throughout the library's budget, such as funding for instructional equipment in the equipment budget or funding for training in the continuing education and travel budgets.

Funding may also be available for special projects through sources external to the library. An institution may provide funds through internal competitions. For example, a college may sponsor curriculum innovation grants or provide technology-enhancement funds. Instruction librarians might also apply for grants from state and federal government agencies and charitable foundations.

Facilities

Instruction programs have a variety of space needs, including space for instruction, preparation, storage, and staff offices.[111] With respect to the goals of an instruction program, the most important space is the space for instruction, the classroom. In *Designing Places for People*, C. M. Deasy explains that because teaching is fundamentally about communication, "classroom design must therefore focus on providing the proper setting for effective and accurate communications."[112] In other words, the classroom environment itself affects the ability of students to learn.[113] Whether in a computer classroom or a traditional lecture or seminar room, layout, seating configuration, furnishings, heating, ventilation, air conditioning, lighting, and acoustics are some of the many elements to consider in designing classrooms.[114] Spaces in the reference room, microforms area, and other locations in the library may also serve as instruction spaces as demanded by the instructional needs of a particular group of learners. In academic libraries, the development of information commons, or learning commons, is a facilities development initiative that parallels and supports the information literacy agenda of higher education.[115]

Space for preparation is needed for the development of instructional materials, for testing new technologies, and for duplicating materials. Space for storage is necessary for equipment and supplies as well as instructional materials already duplicated and awaiting distribution. Finally, staff of the library instruction program must have office space and equipment to complete their tasks effectively and efficiently.

Publicity and Public Relations

The promotion and marketing of instruction involves educating potential users regarding the availability of instructional services[116] and convincing those users to take part in instructional offerings. Publicity can take place through a variety of mechanisms, including formal liaison relationships, brochures, signage, the library Web page, personal letters, newspaper advertisements, an eye-catching logo, and word of mouth.[117] Naomi Lederer provides librarians with a number of practical ideas for marketing instruction programs.[118]

As has been emphasized with respect to designing and implementing instruction, designing and implementing a program of publicity for instruction should be guided by the development of goals and objectives.[119] Developing marketing and promotional materials demands considerations similar to those that guide the development of instructional materials. Because library instruction programs primarily comprise services and not products, the instruction librarian should consult the general literature on nonprofit services marketing.[120] In addition to promoting instructional services, publicity should also portray librarians as educators and libraries as educational institutions.

FUTURE TRENDS AND CHALLENGES

The fundamental and ongoing challenge of instruction is teaching the content, tools, skills, competencies, attitudes, and processes that users need or need to know to be independent, information-literate individuals in the current information environment and to be able to adapt to the environments that develop in the future. As libraries and information resources change and develop, so too must library instruction.

Technology is changing fundamental information structures and organizational principles. Librarians cannot teach a "one size fits all" strategy to all users because the information environment is constantly transformed into one of greater variety, complexity, opportunity, and confusion. Because users must apply knowledge in so many different environments, librarians must also emphasize concepts rather than teaching individuals to use specific tools.

Instructional technologies are altering the very nature of the learning environment. Distance-learning environments are becoming increasingly commonplace, and even on-campus students and local public library users are accessing materials remotely and are demanding that instructional programs be delivered in the same venue. As fewer individuals come in person to request assistance or to attend workshops held in the library, librarians must find ways to instruct users where they need help. Not only does this mean creating tutorials and online instructional materials, but it also means investigating ways to embed instruction into the information tools that users encounter. Immersive virtual environments and handheld devices are likely to be the technologies of greatest impact in the coming years.

Instruction librarians continue to be challenged to change the focus from teaching to learning. Although it is important for the teacher to plan instruction, the instructional activities themselves are not as important as what happens to the learners through the activities. This shift to emphasize learning requires that one assess the impact that instruction has on the ability of the student to accomplish a task or produce a product. Especially for beginning instruction librarians who are developing their instructional skills, it can be a challenge to focus on student learning rather than teacher performance.

In addition, it is not enough to make instructional materials "available." These materials must also engage users and provide mechanisms to actually involve the users with the materials and increase student time on task. Learning is often a collaborative activity, and librarians need to help students learn problem solving and interactive decision making, in the classroom or asynchronously. The instructor must use a variety of instructional approaches, methods, and materials and be attentive to learning styles, motivation, and outcomes.

Librarians involved in instruction are also challenged to take on a wider variety of roles. Not only do librarians model search strategies, coach users, and facilitate group interaction; they also need to develop skills as advocates for users, developers of collaborative communities, and trainers for other instruction librarians and for volunteers or students involved in peer tutoring. Librarians must seek out institutional partners in recognition that users cannot become information literate in an isolated environment. Preparation of librarians for these roles continues to be a challenge as professional library education engages in reexamination of the foundations of library and information science education and the relationship to professional practice.

Probably the biggest challenge to instruction librarians is to embrace these changes. Quite likely, librarians will always be faced with a changing information environment and changing educational approaches. Working within these changes rather than against them will ensure responsive and successful instruction programs. The challenges of today are the opportunities for tomorrow. Instruction librarians must be ready to take on these challenges in educating users for today and for their lifetimes.

NOTES

1.   Samuel S. Green, "Personal Relations between Librarians and Readers," *American Library Journal* 1 (1876): 80.

2.   Otis H. Robinson, "Proceedings: First Session," *American Library Journal* 1 (1876): 123–24.

3.   "ALA Policy Manual," section 52.6. http://www.ala.org/ala/aboutala/governance/poli cymanual/updatedpolicymanual/section2/52libsvcsandrespon.cfm#52.6.

4.   Harold W. Tuckett and Carla J. Stoffle, "Learning Theory and the Self-Reliant Library User," *RQ* 24 (Fall 1984): 58.

5. James Rice Jr., *Teaching Library Use* (Westport, CT: Greenwood Press, 1981), 5.

6. Ibid., 6.

7. Association of College and Research Libraries, Bibliographic Instruction Section, Policy and Planning Committee, *Bibliographic Instruction Handbook* (Chicago: American Library Association, 1979), 69 pp. Interestingly, the term *bibliographic instruction* was unknown in the field or the literature when the Association of College and Research Libraries Ad Hoc Committee on Bibliographic Instruction was formed in 1971. The term appears to have been coined by the original organizers. Cerise Oberman, in "What's in a Name? The Search for *Bibliographic Instruction*," *Bibliographic Instruction Section Newsletter* (Fall 1993): 2, states, "Where did the term *bibliographic instruction* come from? It is difficult to say. I have offered the honor to Tom Kirk, but he refuses this distinction. Perhaps it emerged from the intense need of a group of librarians fervently seeking an expression to capture the new spirit that was emerging and at the same time distance themselves from old terms. Whatever the origin, it was apparently right. *Bibliographic instruction* not only became the label used to describe the library instruction programs, but it was soon used to characterize a new specialist—a bibliographic instruction librarian."

8. Constance Mellon, ed., *Bibliographic Instruction: The Second Generation* (Littleton, CO: Libraries Unlimited, 1987), xiii. See also Cerise Oberman and Katina Strauch, eds., *Theories of Bibliographic Education: Designs for Teaching* (New York: R. R. Bowker, 1982), 233 pp.

9. Pamela Kobelski and Mary Reichel, "Conceptual Frameworks for Bibliographic Education," *Journal of Academic Librarianship* 7 (May 1981): 73–77. Also reprinted as Pamela Kobelski and Mary Reichel, "Conceptual Frameworks for Bibliographic Instruction," in *Conceptual Frameworks for Bibliographic Education*, ed. Mary Reichel and Mary Ann Ramey (Littleton, CO: Libraries Unlimited, 1987), 3–12.

10. Lori Arp, "Information Literacy or Bibliographic Instruction: Semantics or Philosophy," *RQ* 30 (Fall 1990): 46–49; Christine Bruce, *The Seven Faces of Information Literacy* (Adelaide, Australia: Auslib Press, 1997), 10–13; Edward K. Owusu-Ansah, "Information Literacy and the Academic Library: A Critical Look at a Concept and the Controversies Surrounding It," *Journal of Academic Librarianship* 29 (July 2003): 219–30.

11. Loanne Snavely and Natasha Cooper, "The *Information Literacy* Debate," *Journal of Academic Librarianship* 23 (January 1997): 9–14. For additional readings and discussion, see Trish Ridgeway, "Information Literacy: An Introductory Reading List," *College & Research Libraries News* 51 (July/August 1990): 645–48; Esther Grassian and Susan E. Clark, "Information Literacy Sites: Background and Ideas for Program Planning and Development," *College & Research Libraries News* 60 (February 1999): 78–81, 92; and Michael B. Eisenberg, Carrie A. Lowe, and Kathleen L. Spitzer, *Information Literacy: Essential Skills for the Information Age*, 2nd ed. (Westport, CT: Libraries Unlimited, 2004), 408 pp.

12. Information about the Institute for Information Literacy is available at http://www.ala.org/ala/mgrps/divs/acrl/issues/infolit/professactivity/iil/welcome.cfm. See also Cerise Oberman, "The Institute for Information Literacy: Formal Training Is a Critical Need," *College & Research Libraries News* 59 (October 1998): 703–5.

13. Bruce, *Seven Faces of Information Literacy*, 5.

14. Michael Eisenberg and Robert E. Berkowitz, *Information Problem Solving: The Big Six Skills Approach to Library and Information Skills Instruction* (Norwood, NJ: Ablex, 1990), 156 pp. An extensive complementary Web site is at http://www.big6.com/.

15. A portal Web site for the *Standards for the 21st-Century Learner* is at http://www.ala.org/ala/mgrps/divs/aasl/guidelinesandstandards/learningstandards/standards.cfm.

16.   Available at http://sites.scc.spokane.edu/nclr/InfoLit_statement.htm.

17.   Available at http://archive.ifla.org/III/wsis/BeaconInfSoc.html.

18.   Christine Bruce and Philip Candy, eds., *Information Literacy around the World: Advances in Programs and Research* (Wagga Wagga, New South Wales: Centre for Information Studies, Charles Sturt University, 2000), 304 pp; Allan Martin and Hannelore Rader, eds., *Information and IT Literacy: Enabling Learning in the 21st Century* (London: Facet, 2003), 284 pp.

19.   Christine Bruce, *The Seven Faces of Information Literacy* (Adelaide, Australia: Auslib Press, 1997), 203 pp.

20.   Mandy Lupton, *The Learning Connection: Information Literacy and the Student Experience* (Adelaide, Australia: Auslib Press, 2004), 105 pp.; Sheila Webber, Stuart Boon, and Bill Johnston, "A Comparison of UK Academics' Conceptions of Information Literacy in Two Disciplines: English and Marketing," *Library and Information Research* 29 (2005): 4–15; Clarence Maybee, "Undergraduate Perceptions of Information Use: The Basis for Creating User-Centered Student Information Literacy Instruction," *Journal of Academic Librarianship* 32 (January 2006): 79–85.

21.   Craig Gibson, ed., *Student Engagement and Information Literacy* (Chicago: Association of College and Research Libraries, 2006), 197 pp.

22.   Lisa Janicke Hinchliffe, "Information Literacy as a Way of Life," *Research Strategies* 18 (2002): 95–6.

23.   Chris Avery and Kevin Ketchner, "Do Instruction Skills Impress Employers?," *College & Research Libraries* 57 (May 1996): 258. The same finding was reported in Beverly P. Lynch and Kimberley Robles Smith, "The Changing Nature of Work in Academic Libraries," *College & Research Libraries* 62 (September 2001): 407–20.

24.   James K. Elmborg, "Teaching at the Desk: Toward a Reference Pedagogy," *portal: Libraries and the Academy* 2 (July 2002): 455–64; James K. Elmborg, "Libraries in the Contact Zone: On the Creation of Educational Space," *Reference & Users Services Quarterly* 46 (Fall 2006): 56–64.

25.   American Library Association, Presidential Committee on Information Literacy, *Final Report*. http://www.ala.org/ala/mgrps/divs/acrl/publications/whitepapers/presidential.cfm.

26.   Tom W. Goad, *Information Literacy and Workplace Performance* (Westport, CT: Quorum Books, 2002), 1.

27.   Cheryl LaGuardia, Stella Bentley, and Janet Martorana, eds., *The Upside of Down-Sizing: Using Library Instruction to Cope* (New York: Neal-Schuman, 1995), 249 pp.

28.   Barabara Wittkopf, "Learning Paradigm," *Research Strategies* 14 (Spring 1996): 66–67; Robert B. Barr and John Tagg, "From Teaching to Learning," *Change* 27 (November/December 1995): 13–25; John Tagg, *The Learning Paradigm College* (Bolton, MA: Anker, 2003), 379 pp.

29.   Mary Ellen Litzinger, "Instructional Design," in *Sourcebook for Bibliographic Instruction* (Chicago: Association of College and Research Libraries, 1993), 17–27. For a detailed guide through an instructional design process, see Jerilyn Veldof, *Creating the One-Shot Library Workshop: A Step-by-Step Guide* (Chicago: American Library Association, 2006), 170 pp.

30.   Needs assessment is similar to "auditing" learner needs and expectations. See Jo Webb and Chris Powis, *Teaching Information Skills: Theory and Practice* (London: Facet, 2004), 223 pp., for details on the auditing approach.

31.   Donna S. Queeney, *Assessing Needs in Continuing Education: An Essential Tool for Quality Improvement* (San Francisco: Jossey-Bass, 1995), 3.

32.   Roger A. Kaufman and Fenwick A. English, *Needs Assessment: A Guide to Improve School District Management* (Arlington, VA: American Association of School Administrators, 1976), 20.

33.   Nancy Fried Foster and Susan Gibbons, eds., *Studying Students: The Undergraduate Research Project at the University of Rochester* (Chicago: Association of College and Research Libraries, 2007), 90 pp.

34.   Charles K. West, James A. Farmer, and Phillip M. Wolff, *Instructional Design: Implications from Cognitive Science* (Englewood Cliffs, NJ: Prentice Hall, 1991), 238–41.

35.   Librarians new to writing objectives should consult Robert F. Mager, *Preparing Instructional Objectives* (Belmont, CA: Fearon, 1975), for a useful self-paced lesson.

36.   Jerrold E. Kemp, *The Instructional Design Process* (New York: Harper & Row, 1985), 88.

37.   Mager, *Preparing Instructional Objectives*, 21.

38.   Association of College and Research Libraries Bibliographic Instruction Section, *Read This First: An Owner's Guide to the New Model Statement of Objectives for Academic Bibliographic Instruction* (Chicago: American Library Association, 1991), 8.

39.   Ibid., 8.

40.   Norman E. Gronlund, *How to Write and Use Instructional Objectives* (Englewood Cliffs, NJ: Merrill, 1995), 4.

41.   William D. Rohwer Jr., and Kathryn Sloane, "Psychological Perspectives," in *Bloom's Taxonomy: A Forty Year Retrospective*, ed. Lorin W. Anderson and Lauren A. Sosniak (Chicago: National Society for the Study of Education, 1994), 44.

42.   Gronlund, *How to Write and Use Instructional Objectives*, 31.

43.   Benjamin S. Bloom et al., eds., *The Taxonomy of Educational Objectives. The Classification of Educational Goals, Handbook I: Cognitive Domain* (New York: Longmans, Green, 1956), 207 pp.

44.   David R. Krathwohl, Benjamin S. Bloom, and Bertram B. Masia, *The Taxonomy of Educational Objectives. The Classification of Educational Goals, Handbook II: Affective Domain* (New York: David McKay, 1964), 196 pp.

45.   Elizabeth J. Simpson, "The Classification of Educational Objectives, Psychomotor Domain," *Illinois Teacher of Home Economics* 10 (1966): 111–44. (Also available as ERIC Reproduction Service Document No. 010368.) Others have written taxonomies for the psychomotor domain, for example, Anita J. Harrow, *Taxonomy of the Psychomotor Domain: A Guide for Developing Behavioral Objectives* (New York: David McKay, 1972), 190 pp.

46.   A. Dean Hauenstein, *A Conceptual Framework for Educational Objectives: A Holistic Approach to Traditional Taxonomies* (New York: University Press of America, 1998), 151 pp.

47.   Association of College and Research Libraries, Bibliographic Instruction Section, "Model Statement of Objectives for Academic Bibliographic Instruction: Draft Revision," *College & Research Libraries News* 48 (May 1987): 256–61.

48.   Lori Arp, "An Introduction to Learning Theory," in *Sourcebook for Bibliographic Instruction* (Chicago: Association of College and Research Libraries, 1993), 10.

49.   Grant Wiggins and Jay McTighe, *Understanding by Design* (Alexandra, VA: Association for Supervision and Curriculum Development, 2005), 371 pp.

50.   Robert M. Gagné, *The Conditions of Learning and Theory of Instruction* (New York: Holt, Rinehart & Winston, 1985), 2.

51.   Discussions of contributions by Robert M. Gagné, B. F. Skinner, Edward Thorndike, Jean Piaget, and others can be found in Greg Kearsley, *Explorations in Learning and Instruction: The Theory into Practice Database* (http://www.gwu.edu/~tip/), and Funderstanding's *About Learning* (http://www.funderstanding.com/about_learning.cfm).

52.   See Kobelski and Reichel, "Conceptual Frameworks," and Oberman and Strauch, *Theories of Bibliographic Education.*

53.   See Joan Kaplowitz, "Contributions from the Psychology of Learning: Practical Implications for Teaching," in *Learning to Teach: Workshops on Instruction* (Chicago: American Library Association, 1993), 57–70; Blue Wooldridge, "Increasing the Effectiveness of University/College Instruction: Integrating the Results of Learning Style Research into Course Design and Delivery," in *The Importance of Learning Styles: Understanding the Implications for Learning, Course Design, and Education*, ed. Ronald R. Sims and Serbrenia J. Sims (Westport, CT: Greenwood Press, 1995), 50. Extensive discussion can also be found in Esther S. Grassian and Joan R. Kaplowitz, *Information Literacy Instruction: Theory and Practice* (New York: Neal-Schuman, 2001), 468 pp.

54.   Herman A. Witkin, Carol Ann Moore, Donald R. Goodenough, and Patricia W. Cox, "Field Dependent and Field Independent Cognitive Styles and Their Educational Implications," *Review of Educational Research* 47 (1977): 1–64.

55.   Cerise Oberman, *Petals around a Rose: Abstract Reasoning and Bibliographic Instruction* (Chicago: Association of College and Research Libraries, 1980), 23 pp.

56.   See David A. Kolb, *Experiential Learning: Experience as the Source of Learning and Development* (Englewood Cliffs, NJ: Prentice-Hall, 1984), 256 pp.; Carl Jung, *Psychological Types: Or, The Psychology of Individuation* (New York: Harcourt Brace, 1923), 654 pp.; Gordon Lawrence, *People Types and Tiger Stripes: A Practical Guide to Learning Styles* (Gainesville, FL: Center for Applications of Psychological Type, 1982), 101 pp. See *Learning-Style Inventory: Self-Scoring Inventory and Interpretation Booklet* (Boston: McBer & Company, 1985), 14 pp. for one example of an instrument measuring individual learning style.

57.   Bernice McCarthy, *The 4-MAT System: Teaching to Learning Styles with Right/Left Mode Techniques*, rev. ed. (Barrington, IL: EXCEL, 1987), 220 pp.

58.   Leslie K. Hickcox, "Learning Styles: A Survey of Adult Learning Style Inventory Models," in *The Importance of Learning Styles: Understanding the Implications for Learning, Course Design, and Education*, ed. Ronald R. Sims and Serbrenia J. Sims (Westport, CT: Greenwood Press, 1995), 44.

59.   Wooldridge, "Increasing the Effectiveness," 64.

60.   Ronald R. Sims and Serbrenia J. Sims, "Learning Enhancement in Higher Education," in *The Importance of Learning Styles*, 22.

61.   William R. Tracey, *Designing Training and Development Systems* (New York: AMACOM, 1994), 253–55.

62.   See Jodi Reed, "Engage Students with Variety and Interaction," *Videoconferencing Instructional Strategies* (2006). http://www.kn.pacbell.com/wired/vidconf/instruct.html#Engage.

63.   Tracey, *Designing Training*, 253–55.

64.   A bibliography of active learning articles is available at http://www.cte.usf.edu/bibs/active_learn/intro2.html.

65.   Charles C. Bonwell and James A. Eison, *Active Learning: Creating Excitement in the Classroom* (Washington, D.C.: The George Washington University School of Education and Human Development, 1991), iii.

66.   Paula Dempsey and Beth Mark, "Human Boolean Exercise," in *Designs for Active Learning: A Sourcebook of Classroom Strategies for Information Education*, ed. Gail Gradowski, Loanne Snavely, and Paula Dempsey (Chicago: Association of College and Research Libraries, 1998), 117–18. For more active learning activities, see Jeanetta Drueke, "Active Learning in the University Library Instruction Classroom," *Research Strategies* 10 (Spring 1992): 77–83.

67.   Anthony J. Onwuegbuzie, Qun G. Jiao, and Sharon L. Bostick, *Library Anxiety: Theory, Research, and Applications* (Lanham, MD: Scarecrow Press, 2004), 378 pp.

68.   Robert E. Slavin, "Cooperative Learning," in *Encyclopedia of Educational Research*, ed. Marvin C. Alkin (New York: Macmillan, 1992), 1:235.

69.   Marjorie Markoff Warmkessel and Frances M. Carothers, "Collaborative Learning and Bibliographic Instruction," *Journal of Academic Librarianship* 19 (March 1993): 4–7, found that pairing students allowed them to share ideas and helped alleviate computer anxiety. See also Kim N. Cook, Lilith R. Kunkel, and Susan M. Weaver, "Cooperative Learning in Bibliographic Instruction," *Research Strategies* 13 (Winter 1995): 17–25. Four levels of cooperative skills—forming, functioning, formulating, and fermenting—are described in David W. Johnson, Roger T. Johnson, and Edythe Johnson Holubec, *The New Circles of Learning: Cooperation in the Classroom and School* (Alexandria, VA: Association for Supervision and Curriculum Development, 1994), 111 pp.

70.   Lizabeth Wilson, Sharon Mader, Lori Arp, and Mary Jane Petrowski, "Cooperative Learning: A Guided Discovery Workshop," in *The Impact of Technology on Library Instruction*, ed. Linda Shirato (Ann Arbor, MI: Pierian Press, 1995), 24.

71.   Slavin, "Cooperative Learning," 236–37.

72.   West et al., *Instructional Design*, 15–16.

73.   Ibid., 36–57.

74.   Mary Jane Walsh, "Graphic Design for Library Publications," in *The Impact of Technology on Library Instruction*, ed. Linda Shirato (Ann Arbor, MI: Pierian Press, 1995), 141–58.

75.   See Kris Huber and Patricia Lewis, "Tired of Term Papers? Options for Librarians and Professors," *Research Strategies* 2 (Fall 1984): 192–99; Marilyn Lutzker, *Research Projects for College Students: What to Write across the Curriculum* (New York: Greenwood Press, 1988), 141 pp.

76.   Christina J. Woo, "Developing Effective Library Assignments," in *Learning to Teach: Workshops on Instruction* (Chicago: American Library Association, 1993), 30.

77.   Cheryl LaGuardia et al., *Teaching the New Library* (New York: Neal-Schuman, 1996), 139–54, discuss instruction for remote users.

78.   See Arthur W. Chickering and Stephen C. Ehrmann, *Implementing the Seven Principles: Technology as Lever*, for a discussion of how technology can assist with best practices in undergraduate education (see Box 8.7). http://www.tltgroup.org/programs/seven.html.

79.   Morten Flate Paulsen describes possible technology-based teaching methods based on the number and type of interactions in *The Online Report of Pedagogical Techniques for Computer-Mediated Communication* (1995), http://nettskolen.nki.no/forskning/19/cmcped.html. He describes several communication approaches—(1) One-Alone (online resources paradigm): online databases, online journals, online interest groups; (2) One-to-One (the e-mail paradigm): learning contracts, apprenticeships, correspondence studies; (3) One-to-Many (the bulletin board paradigm): lectures, symposia, skits; and (4) Many-to-Many (conferencing paradigm): discussion groups, debates, simulations, case studies, role plays, brainstorming, group projects.

80.   Rick Ells, "Basic Premises of This Workshop," in *Effective Use of the Web for Education: Design Principles and Pedagogy* (1998). http://staff.washington.edu/rells/effective/premises.html.

81.   Barbara O'Keefe, "Learning Communities, a Paper Presented at the 1997 UIUC Faculty Retreat on College Teaching," in *Tradition, Innovation, and Technology: Teaching for Active Learning*, Urbana, IL, February 6, 1997.

82.   Elizabeth A. Dupuis, ed., *Developing Web-Based Instruction: Planning, Designing, Managing, and Evaluating for Results* (New York: Neal-Schuman, 2003), 279 pp.

83.   Available at http://www.ala.org/ala/mgrps/divs/acrl/about/sections/is/projpubs/primo/accepted.cfm.

84.   David N. King, "Evaluation and Its Uses," in *Evaluating Bibliographic Instruction: A Handbook* (Chicago: American Library Association, 1983), 5.

85.   Litzinger, "Instructional Design," 24.

86.   Carol Collier Kuhlthau, *Seeking Meaning: A Process Approach to Library and Information Services* (Norwood, NJ: Ablex, 1993), 199 pp.

87.   For more information on evaluation, as well as information about specific evaluation methods and instruments, see American Library Association, Library Instruction Round Table, Research Committee, *Evaluating Library Instruction: Sample Questions, Forms and Strategies for Practical Use*, ed. Diana D. Shonrock (Chicago: American Library Association, 1996), 174 pp.; F. Wilfrid Lancaster, *If You Want to Evaluate Your Library* (Champaign: University of Illinois, Graduate School of Library and Information Science, 1988), 193 pp.; and Mignon Adams, "Evaluation," in *Sourcebook for Bibliographic Instruction*, ed. Katherine Branch (Chicago: Association of College and Research Libraries, 1993), 45–57. More experienced evaluators may wish to evaluate the effectiveness of the evaluations that are in place using the Joint Committee on Standards for Educational Evaluation, *The Program Evaluation Standards: How to Assess Evaluations of Educational Programs*, 2nd ed. (Thousand Oaks, CA: Sage, 1994), 222 pp.

88.   Thomas A. Angelo and K. Patricia Cross, *Classroom Assessment Techniques: A Handbook for College Teachers* (San Francisco: Jossey-Bass, 1993), 427 pp.; see also Maryellen Weimer, Joan L. Parrett, and Mary-Margaret Kerns, *How Am I Teaching? Forms and Activities for Acquiring Instructional Input* (Madison, WI: Magna, 1988), 100 pp.

89.   See, for example, Teresa Y. Neely, *Information Literacy Assessment: Standards-Based Tools and Assignments* (Chicago: American Library Association, 2006), 216 pp.; Elizabeth Fuseler Avery, ed., *Assessing Student Learning Outcomes for Information Literacy Instruction in Academic Institutions* (Chicago: Association of College and Research Library, 2003), 299 pp.

90.   Available at https://www.projectsails.org/.

91.   Available at http://www.ets.org/icriticalthinking/about.

92.   Scott Walter, "Using Cultural Perspectives to Foster Information Literacy across the Curriculum," in *Proven Strategies for Building a Successful Information Literacy Program*, ed. Susan C. Curzon and Lynn Lampert (New York: Neal-Schuman, 2007), 55–76.

93.   Anne K. Beaubien, Sharon A. Hogan, and Mary W. George, *Learning the Library: Concepts and Methods for Effective Bibliographic Instruction* (New York: R. R. Bowker, 1982), 230.

94.   For example, Kristin Johnson and Kathleen Carlisle Fountain, "Laying a Foundation for Comparing Departmental Structures between Reference and Instructional Services: Analysis of a Nationwide Survey," *College & Research Libraries* 63 (May 2002): 275–87.

95.   William Miller, "What's Wrong with Reference: Coping with Success and Failure at the Reference Desk," *American Libraries* 15 (May 1984): 303–6, 321–22.

96.   Association of College and Research Libraries, Instruction Section, "Guidelines for Instruction Programs in Academic Libraries," 2003. http://www.ala.org/ala/mgrps/divs/acrl/standards/guidelinesinstruction.cfm.

97.   Available at http://www.ala.org/ala/mgrps/divs/acrl/standards/profstandards.cfm.

98.   Diana Shonrock and Craig Mulder, "Instruction Librarians: Acquiring the Proficiencies Critical to Their Work," *College & Research Libraries* 54 (March 1993): 137–49; Bridgit Shea Sullivan, "Education for Library Instruction, A 1996 Survey," *Research Strategies* 15 (1997): 271–77, reports evidence that an increased number of library schools are offering separate courses in library instruction. Most library schools now offer an elective course, but because it is an elective, many students do not prepare themselves in this area.

99.   Scott Walter and Lisa Janicke Hinchliffe, *Instructional Improvement Programs*, SPEC Kit No. 287 (Washington, D.C.: Office of Leadership & Management Services, Association of Research Libraries, 2005), 135 pp. For information on implementing in-house staff development programs, see Association of College and Research Libraries, Bibliographic Instruction Section, *Learning to Teach: Workshops on Instruction* (Chicago: American Library Association, 1993), 76 pp.; Alice S. Clark and Kay F. Jones, eds., *Teaching Librarians to Teach: On-the-Job Training for Bibliographic Instruction Librarians* (Metuchen, NJ: Scarecrow Press, 1986), 232 pp.; Sheril J. Hook, Marianne Stowell Bracke, Louise Greenfield, and Victoria A. Mills, "In-House Training for Instruction Librarians," *Research Strategies* 19 (2003): 99–127.

100.   Esther S. Grassian and Joan R. Kaplowitz, *Learning to Lead and Manage Information Literacy Instruction* (New York: Neal-Schuman, 2005), 322 pp.

101.   Dale J. Vidmar, "Reflective Peer Coaching: Crafting Collaborative Self-Assessment in Teaching," *Research Strategies* 20 (2006): 135–48.

102.   WILU (the annual Workshop on Instruction in Library Use) alternates in location. Information about the 2011 conference is available at http://www2.uregina.ca/wilu2011/. Information about LOEX conferences is available at http://www.emich.edu/public/loex/conferences.html.

103.   The Institute for Information Literacy offers an Immersion Program with two tracks, one for new librarians and librarians new to teaching and the other for experienced instruction librarians who seek to further develop, integrate, or advance an information literacy program within their institution. The Intentional Teacher program is for experienced instructors to further develop as reflective practitioners. An assessment program is also offered. Additional information is available at http://www.ala.org/ala/mgrps/divs/acrl/issues/infolit/professactivity/iil/immersion/programs.cfm.

104.   For specific examples, see Jean Sheridan, ed., *Writing-across-the-Curriculum and the Academic Library: A Guide for Librarians, Instructors, and Writing Program Directors* (Westport, CT: Greenwood Press, 1995), 240 pp.; Dick Raspa and Dane Ward, *Collaborative Imperative: Librarians and Faculty Working Together in the Information Universe* (Chicago: Association of College and Research Libraries, 2000), 158 pp.; James K. Elmborg and Sheril Hook, eds., *Centers for Learning: Writing Centers and Libraries in Collaboration* (Chicago: Association of College and Research Libraries, 2005), 231 pp.

105.   Lori Arp and Lizabeth A. Wilson, "Structures of Bibliographic Instruction Programs: A Continuum for Planning," in *Integrating Library Use Skills into the General Education Curriculum*, ed. Maureen Pastine and Bill Katz (New York: Haworth Press, 1989), 25–39.

106.   ACRL, *Bibliographic Instruction Handbook*, 58.

107.   Ibid.

108.   Ilene Rockman and Associates, *Integrating Information Literacy into the Higher Education Curriculum: Practical Models for Transformation* (San Francisco: Jossey-Bass, 2004), 260 pp.

109.   American Association of School Librarians and Association for Educational Communications and Technology, *Information Power: Building Partnerships for Learning* (Chicago: American Library Association, 1998), 205 pp. For information on integrating the school library and instruction programs, see also Jean Donham, *Enhancing Teaching and Learning: A Leadership Guide for School Library Media Specialists*, 2nd ed. (New York: Neal-Schuman, 2005), 337 pp.

110.   ACRL, "Guidelines for Instruction Programs in Academic Libraries." http://www.ala.org/ala/mgrps/divs/acrl/standards/guidelinesinstruction.cfm.

111.   Ibid.

112.   C. M. Deasy, *Designing Places for People: A Handbook on Human Behavior for Architects, Designers, and Facility Managers* (New York: Whitney Library of Design, 1985), 105.

113.   Lisa Janicke Hinchliffe, *Neal-Schuman Electronic Classroom Handbook* (New York: Neal-Schuman, 2001), 257 pp.

114.   For a detailed discussion of these elements and much more, see Robert L. Allen et al., *Classroom Design Manual* (College Park, MD: University of Maryland Academic Information Technology Services, 1996), 90 pp.; or Daniel Niemeyer, *Hard Facts on Smart Classroom Design: Ideas, Guidelines, and Layouts* (Lanham, MD: Scarecrow, 2003), 154 pp. A useful "Sample Facilities Assessment Form" is included in May Brottman and Mary Loe, *The LIRT Library Instruction Handbook* (Chicago: American Library Association, Library Instruction Round Table, 1990), 39. Lennie Scott-Webber, *In Sync: Environmental Behavior Research and the Design of Learning Spaces* (Ann Arbor, MI: Society for College & University Planning, 2004), 145 pp.connects research on human interaction with the built environment with decisions about learning spaces.

115.   Donald Robert Beagle, *The Information Commons Handbook* (New York: Neal-Schuman, 2006), 247 pp.

116.   Patricia Breivik, *Planning the Library Instruction Program* (Chicago: American Library Association, 1982), 119.

117.   LaGuardia et al., *Teaching the New Library*, 73–74.

118.   Naomi Lederer, *Ideas for Librarians Who Teach: With Suggestions for Teachers and Business Presenters* (Lanham, MD: Scarecrow Press, 2005), 225 pp.

119.   Breivik, *Planning the Library Instruction Program*, 121.

120.   See, for example, Alan R. Andreasen and Philip Kotler, *Strategic Marketing for Nonprofit Organizations*, 6th ed. (Upper Saddle River, NJ: Prentice Hall, 2003), 536 pp.

ADDITIONAL READINGS

American Association of School Librarians and Association for Educational Communications and Technology. *Information Power: Building Partnerships for Learning*. Chicago: American Library Association, 1998. 205 pp.

Information Power is a valuable handbook for librarians engaged in the development of school library media programs. Reflective of the leadership school librarians have taken in instruction, the book addresses missions and challenges of school libraries, the roles and responsibilities of school library media specialists, leadership, planning, management, personnel, resources, and association support.

American Library Association. Presidential Committee on Information Literacy. *Final Report.* Chicago: American Library Association, 1989. 17 pp. http://www.ala.org/ala/mgrps/divs/acrl/publications/whitepapers/presidential.cfm.

This report convincingly presented the case for librarians taking a leading role in information education. Well-written and engaging, the report explored information literacy in personal life, business, and citizenship. The committee's recommendations had far-reaching implications for all librarians, not just those explicitly involved with education. This is the touchstone document for information literacy programs.

Bransford, John D., Ann L. Brown, and Rodney R. Cocking, eds. *How People Learn: Brain, Mind, Experience, and School.* Washington, D.C.: National Academy Press, 1999. 319 pp.

This report provides a comprehensive review of current research on the science of learning and its application across the lifespan in a variety of educational settings. Chapter 2, "How Experts Differ from Novices," has particular relevance for instruction librarians.

Cox, Christopher N., and Elizabeth Blakesley Lindsay, eds. *Information Literacy Instruction Handbook.* Chicago: Association of College and Research Libraries, 2008. 236 pp.

This handbook presents a comprehensive overview of theories and practical ideas for librarians new to instructional roles in academic libraries, including particularly contemporary topics of diversity, academic integrity, and assessment bracketed by chapters on the history and future of information literacy in higher education.

Grassian, Esther S., and Joan R. Kaplowitz. *Information Literacy Instruction: Theory and Practice.* 2nd ed. New York: Neal-Schuman, 2009. 412 pp.; *Learning to Lead and Manage Information Literacy Instruction.* New York: Neal-Schuman, 2005. 322 pp.

These two complementary handbooks address issues related to information literacy and instruction in academic libraries and are good starting texts for academic librarians new to instruction.

Leckie, Gloria J. "Desperately Seeking Citations: Uncovering Faculty Assumptions about the Undergraduate Research Process." *Journal of Academic Librarianship* 22 (May 1996): 201–8.

Leckie describes information-seeking problems created by the typical research paper assignment. The large "disjuncture" between the expectations of faculty members as expert researchers and undergraduates as novice researchers is revealed in the research paper assignment. Undergraduates are more likely to use whatever sources are familiar, even if those sources are not relevant. She advocates a stratified approach with a six-part structure for the research paper process and urges faculty to take responsibility for teaching library-based research skills, with librarians taking supportive roles as mentors.

Lederer, Naomi. *Ideas for Librarians Who Teach: With Suggestions for Teachers and Business Presenters.* Lanham, MD: Scarecrow Press, 2005. 225 pp.

This text provides practical hints and ideas on a wide range of topics in 17 chapters of bulleted ideas and quick tips complemented by sample syllabi with the ideas in action.

GUIDELINES

American Association of School Librarians. "Information Literacy Standards for Student Learning: Standards and Indicators." 1998. http://www.ala.org/ala/mgrps/divs/aasl/aaslarchive/pubsarchive/informationpower/InformationLiteracyStandards_final.pdf.

American Association of School Librarians. "Standards for the 21st-Century Learner." 2007. http://www.ala.org/ala/mgrps/divs/aasl/guidelinesandstandards/learningstandards/standards.cfm.

Association of College and Research Libraries. "Characteristics of Programs of Information Literacy that Illustrate Best Practices: A Guideline." 2003. http://www.ala.org/ala/mgrps/divs/acrl/standards/characteristics.cfm.

Association of College and Research Libraries. "Information Literacy Competency Standards for Higher Education." 2000. http://www.ala.org/ala/mgrps/divs/acrl/standards/informationliteracycompetency.cfm.

Association of College and Research Libraries. "Guidelines for Instruction Programs in Academic Libraries." 2003. http://www.ala.org/ala/mgrps/divs/acrl/standards/guidelinesinstruction.cfm.

Association of College and Research Libraries. "Standards for Proficiencies for Instruction Librarians and Coordinators." 2007. http://www.ala.org/ala/mgrps/divs/acrl/standards/profstandards.cfm.

Chapter

9

Training and Continual Learning for Reference Staff

Beth S. Woodard

INTRODUCTION

In "The Making of a Reference Librarian,"[1] Samuel Rothstein argues that whether one believes that reference librarians are "made" or "born," for more than a hundred years, a small industry has been devoted to improving their performance at the reference desk. Most librarians agree that merely working with library users and reference sources on a daily basis does not ensure that reference librarians will acquire a thorough knowledge of a wide variety of sources, that they will understand users' requests accurately, or that they will translate the users' requests appropriately. Although some people have natural abilities in working with others and good instincts regarding how to approach reference questions, both asking appropriate questions and listening for what is not expressed, all reference librarians need nurturing and training to expand and complement these innate abilities.

New reference librarians often begin their careers with only the required library and information science courses to support them, occasionally reinforced with paraprofessional or pre-professional work. Beginning reference courses generally cover specific reference sources, types of print and electronic sources, reference query negotiation, selection and evaluation of reference sources, and searching strategies.[2] Only one of these five topics is directly related to the service aspect of reference work. To use this basic knowledge effectively, reference librarians must be trained to apply their professional education to a particular library setting.[3]

Although there are examples in the literature of how students can get a glimpse of what it is like to work with reference queries,[4] the reality is that relatively few students have actual reference experience when they leave library school. It is unreasonable to expect new graduates to perform today's sophisticated reference services successfully, or even adequately, without an investment of time and effort on the part of the employing library. These graduates need careful orientation, training, retraining, development, and continuing education to maximize their potential for providing effective reference service.

In a pilot study conducted in Ohio, almost all librarians surveyed felt that the skills needed in order to conduct a reference interview successfully can be taught. Most indicated that their formal training in conducting interviews had been given by their employer.[5]

Reference librarians rarely see themselves as educators or administrators, even though they often perform traditional educational and administrative functions, such as teaching individuals how to use the library catalog or an index and supervising clerks, students, paraprofessionals, volunteers, or other librarians. These supervisory responsibilities usually include training in some capacity. The average reference librarian is generally only vaguely aware of this role in training, either as a recipient or as a facilitator for others. This chapter describes the role of training in preparing reference staff to provide effective service and in maintaining skill levels.

As reference departments continue the process of "rethinking reference," recognizing limitations on the roles that professionals can play in providing reference service, there has been more of an emphasis on the use of paraprofessionals in reference services. Subsequently, there has been greater interest in designing training programs and in sharing information about the training process.[6] In addition, there has been enormous interest in training generated as a result of studies indicating that reference service is not always accurate (see chapter 10).

When reference department personnel rely only on informal apprenticeships, serious gaps in reference staff training occur. Commonly, trainees, whether new reference librarians, reference assistants, students who shelve books, or volunteers, learn a few specific tasks and never understand the rationale for what they are doing or how these tasks fit into the overall mission of the library. Employees not only need to be trained in specific skill areas related to their direct responsibilities; they also must have a knowledge base broad enough to understand the larger context. A broad knowledge base also allows them to learn new skills that they need to respond to the rapidly changing environment of reference and information services.

Today's reference staff members are expected to handle changes that occur with increasing frequency. Reference personnel must live with uncertainty and must adapt to new management styles, changing user demands, advances in technology, and their own expanding roles in creating and maintaining Web pages or participating in networked campuses or organizations, community outreach, and distance education. Unless training ensures that librarians are committed to the value of reference service, are able to provide instruction to users regarding available services, and are flexible in responding to changes, reference librarians will be limited to using traditional tools, and they will not be able to approach reference service in the context of changed user needs or new technologies.[7]

The terms *training*, *education*, and *development* are often used interchangeably. Leonard Nadler introduced the term *human resource development* in 1969 and defined it as "organized learning experiences in a definite time period to increase the possibility of improving job performance growth."[8] He went on to make fine distinctions between training, education, and development, which Suellyn Hunt further clarified for librarians: "Training = job-related learning experiences; Education = individual-related learning experiences; Development = organizational-related learning experiences."[9] The various aspects of these three activities are explored in this chapter.

ORIENTATION

All staff members, whether part-time employees, temporary workers, or experienced individuals who plan to stay for a while, need *orientation*, or an introduction to the job environment. *Staff orientation* is "an initial training process designed to acquaint new employees with various aspects of the organization, including established goals, policies, and procedures; the physical environment; other personnel and working relationships, job duties and responsibilities; and fringe benefits."[10] Typically, this type of training is not transferable to another setting and provides little that employees could use if they took jobs in other libraries. Box 9.1 provides an example of an orientation program.

BOX 9.1
SAMPLE ORIENTATION CHECKLIST

General Orientation Checklist

Employee's Name: _____

Weeks 1–2

Orientation to Reference Department

1. Meet with library personnel office representative
2. Meet with trainer to cover such things as training plan schedule, employee's work area, position's duties based on job description, and job conditions and benefits; hours, vacations, sick leave, and other matters.
3. Organization and Goals of Reference Department Reading material, such as New Employee Orientation Packet: IV. Reference. Reference Department Policies and Procedures Manual, and last year's departmental annual report. Explanation of the Reference Department's mission, goals, and expectations
4. Tour of Reference, introduction to each staff member below: (list departmental staff, with job titles or areas of responsibility) Location of important files or reading materials such as meeting minutes and staff newsletter

Orientation to Public Services

1. Read New Employee Orientation Packet: III. Public Services
2. Meet with assistant to head of public services. Introduction to Public Services mission, goals, and policies
3. Tour of Public Services. Introduction to key staff, including heads of documents, circulation, and interlibrary loan
4. Location of facilities, files, etc.; including Copying and Digitization Services, Microforms

Weeks 3–4

Orientation to General Library System

1. Read New Employee Orientation Packet: II. The General Library and Library Brochure
2. Tour of the Main Library, Branch Library I, and Branch Library II
3. New Employee Coffee

Orientation to the Campus/Community

1. Read New Employee Orientation Packet: I. The Campus/Community
2. Attend the Campus Personnel Office's new employee orientation session

Donnagene Britt, Patricia Davison, and Judith Levy, eds., *Painlessly Preparing Personalized Training Plans* (Berkeley: University of California Library, April 1982), 7–9.

Enculturation

Orientation provides a sense of support, defines the employee's singular role in the library, and establishes the individual as a part of the team. Dorothy Jones stresses that the training of new librarians should address the political setting, the work organization of the department, the details of each task, and the path to promotion and job retention.[11] The orientation program's ultimate goal is to promote a feeling of self-worth, a sense of belonging, an attitude of pride and confidence in both self and the library, and a desire to succeed. H. Scott Davis stresses that research has indicated that the first few weeks in a new job are important to establishing future job satisfaction and productivity in new employees and in capitalizing on the excitement and anticipation felt in the first few days.[12] One objective should be to address typical issues and answer typical questions before they cause frustration or inhibit productivity. *Enculturation* should be a part of orientation programs, communicating the culture, the expectations for dress and behavior (both the formal and the informal rules of behavior), and the importance of each individual in the organization.

To give the new staff member a sense of the organizational culture, including areas of authority and expertise, individuals should meet with key personnel throughout the organization. This allows them to discover how each unit functions and the interrelationships between units.[13] The personal connection also allows individuals to feel comfortable in returning to the expert to ask questions when needed.

Socialization

Socialization is also an important aspect of the reference orientation session.[14] Employees need time to get acquainted with their coworkers in an informal setting, to discuss their activities in an unstructured environment, and to reflect on and absorb what they have already been told. In any training program, reference staff, as well as staff in other departments with which the trainee comes in daily contact, should be formally introduced, but they should also have some opportunity to meet on a less formal basis, such as a coffee hour or other informal gathering. This is particularly important for reference staff members, who must work together as a team and make referrals to other service points in the library.

Expectations

The first day of orientation is the appropriate time to discuss both the employee's expectations and the employer's. "Time spent here can prevent many misunderstandings and counterproductive situations later."[15] Anne May Berwind stresses the need for staff to discuss the local philosophy of reference service. This discussion should include the nature of the population of users served and the primary purpose of the reference service, whether it is to find answers as rapidly as possible or to teach users how to find information independently. Priorities for service should be agreed on, and reference librarians need to know whether they are expected to work independently or together to provide service.[16] This is particularly important for new librarians, whose preexisting expectations can differ radically from the job reality.[17]

Linda A. Jerris suggests that orientation is "a process, not just a program,"[18] and goes on to state that orientation should communicate the values and priorities of the organization. It should focus on alignment with the organization's mission statement, have a quality and customer focus, and emphasize accountability and teamwork. In order to accomplish this, she urges the participation of supervisors and senior management in orientation programs, fostering two-way communication between new employees and decision makers. She also discusses the importance of conducting follow-up and review.[19]

Environments Conducive for Ongoing Learning

Orientation is only the first step in a continuing process. A positive, upbeat orientation program extending over a period of several weeks or even months can be very effective in helping the new employee to become an efficient, productive member of the library staff.[20] An effective period of induction will help the new staff member become more receptive to continuing training, absorb the details of the job, become a better team player, and feel comfortable in the new position.

A planned orientation also helps to establish an atmosphere that facilitates learning. Orientation reduces stress when opportunities are given for individuals to share

BOX 9.2
LIBRARY ORIENTATION OUTLINE

Organizational Values

First Week	First Month	Fourth Month
Institution's mission Library's mission Individual's role in mission Relationships between mission and evaluations and budget priorities	Library's approaches to rules Departmental rules that may frustrate patrons Goals behind key policies	How and when to bend rules Problem solvers in other units How and when to gather patron concerns and suggestions and what to do with them

General Orientation

First Week	First Month	Fourth Month
Location of primary resources and services Basic desk procedures Library hours Emergency procedures	How to operate equipment How to complete necessary forms Phone system tricks Locations of smaller library units	The sequence of processing orders Directions to popular locations on campus or in the city The importance of continuing education and the types of programs that are available

Reference

First Week	First Month	Fourth Month
How to do simple searches in the catalog Types of reference sources Analyzing reference questions Location of the most frequently requested sources	How to do complicated keyword searches Desk reference collection How to use primary indexes How to use the sources in one popular academic subject area, such as education, that has "user friendly" reference sources	How to use the more complex sources in various academic disciplines and special collections, such as government documents, business, and law How to tap informational resources that extend beyond the local collection by using sources such as OCLC, the Internet, or online table of contents services

Interpersonal skills

First Week	First Month	Fourth Month
Greeting patrons Encouraging patron follow-up	Listening skills Making referrals Receiving referrals	Dealing with irate patrons Saying "no"

Phone techniques Treating staff as patrons	Coping with stressful individuals and situations	Dealing with patrons with special needs Intervening when another staff member is misinforming a patron

Joanne M. Bessler, *Putting Service into Library Staff Training*, LAMA Occasional Papers Series (Chicago: American Library Association, 1994), 15.

work-related problems and questions. When similarly situated individuals share feelings of frustration and isolation, those feelings are reduced, and work relationships can also improve. Orientation can also be a motivator. When individuals see the library as an organization that is willing to put time and effort into orientation and training, they are likely to feel more a part of the organization and make a commitment to it.

When planning orientation and training activities, trainers should attempt to create learning environments that facilitate learning. Trainers need to remember that research about how adults learn suggests that the following elements need to be incorporated into the design of a training program:

- involve participants in mutual planning
- provide for active involvement
- recognize the personal and subjective nature of learning
- accept differences
- recognize people's right to make mistakes
- tolerate ambiguity
- allow cooperation and self-evaluation
- permit confrontation[21]

BASIC TRAINING: LEARNING THE ESSENTIALS

Basic training in job requirements is mainly concerned with helping staff members learn fundamental job skills, but it also covers some skills that employees may be able to take to other jobs. The *ALA Glossary* defines training as "the process of developing the knowledge, skills, and attitudes needed by employees to perform their duties effectively and to meet the expectations and goals of the organization. This diverse process, which may be performed by supervisors, fellow employees, and personnel officers, involves planning, preparation, execution, and evaluation."[22]

Defining Competencies

If supervisors fail to define performance expectations, employees will establish their own acceptable performance levels, either individually or as a group.[23] Staff members will observe colleagues and draw their own conclusions regarding the kind of behavior that is expected if expectations are not clearly articulated.

The mutual development of performance expectations and objectives will avoid hidden expectations of standards. If clear standards and specific models of performance are described, individuals will know what is expected of them and how they are to be evaluated. If librarians, or any group of library workers, are asked to participate in establishing these objectives, the objectives are more likely to be accepted by the group.

After a consensus of what constitutes adequate performance has been established, the next important step is to write a competency description, which describes the correct performance of a job and delineates behaviors that signal when it is done right. *Competencies* are knowledge, skills, or attitudes that enable a person to function satisfactorily in a work situation, either alone or with others. The profession has made great strides in the past few years to come to consensus about competencies for reference service.[24] RUSA's *Professional Competencies for Reference and User*

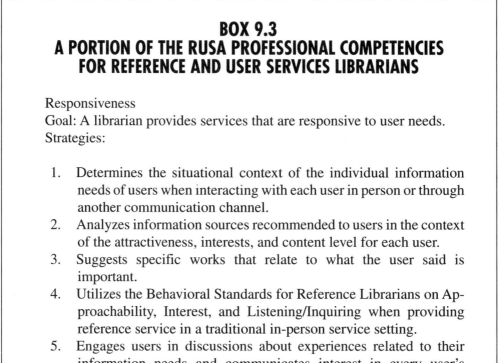

BOX 9.3
A PORTION OF THE RUSA PROFESSIONAL COMPETENCIES FOR REFERENCE AND USER SERVICES LIBRARIANS

Responsiveness
Goal: A librarian provides services that are responsive to user needs.
Strategies:

1. Determines the situational context of the individual information needs of users when interacting with each user in person or through another communication channel.
2. Analyzes information sources recommended to users in the context of the attractiveness, interests, and content level for each user.
3. Suggests specific works that relate to what the user said is important.
4. Utilizes the Behavioral Standards for Reference Librarians on Approachability, Interest, and Listening/Inquiring when providing reference service in a traditional in-person service setting.
5. Engages users in discussions about experiences related to their information needs and communicates interest in every user's experiences.
6. Respects the right of users to determine the direction of their research by empowering them to pursue their own preferences.

Reference and User Services Association, Task Force on Professional Competencies, "Professional Competencies for Reference and User Services Librarians," *Reference & User Services Quarterly* 42 (Summer 2004): 290–95. http://www.ala.org/ala/mgrps/divs/rusa/resources/guide lines/professional.cfm.

Services Librarians include competencies in access; knowledge base; marketing, awareness, and informing; collaboration; and evaluation and assessment of resources and services. When answering questions, librarians must know about available reference sources, be able to find proper sources to answer the questions, be familiar with the library's collection, and use appropriate technology. Although these are only a few of the functions that reference librarians perform, they definitely need to be competent in these areas.[25] See Box 9.3 for an example.

Some other reference competencies can be derived from the various functions performed by reference librarians. In the reference interview, reference staff need to have excellent communication skills, including listening, instructing others, and giving clear directions. Virginia Massey-Burzio emphasized that reference librarians need communication skills: "In addition to verbal skills, writing skills are also needed since a considerable part of a reference librarian's life is spent preparing brochures, pathfinders, flyers, point-of-use instruction guides, grant proposals, articles in the campus newspaper and in library newsletters, and other written communication."[26] Reference staff members need to be able to work well in teams and foster ways of sharing knowledge. They must deal with angry and frustrated users as well as diversity issues. They must prioritize when confronted with multiple demands and long lines of users. They must know when to give information, how far to go in providing information, when to stop, when to refer, and when to teach. Reference staff increasingly must develop presentation skills for dealing with groups.

When answering questions, librarians must know about available reference sources (both electronic and print), be able to find proper sources to answer the questions, be familiar with the library's collection and local resources, and use appropriate technology. They also have to maintain awareness of community resources and optional delivery services through interlibrary loan, consortial agreements, fax, and full-text services. They have to maintain at least minimal skill levels in searching online systems and the Web.

Mary Nofsinger identifies six major categories of competencies: reference skills and subject knowledge, communication and interpersonal skills, technological skills, analytical and critical thinking skills, management and supervisory skills, and commitment to user services.[27] Although these are only a few of the functions that reference librarians perform, they illustrate the diversity of competencies required.[28]

Competencies can be identified for specific staff levels or for particular services. For example, certain groups of staff may provide all levels of reference service, from providing directional assistance to performing complex bibliographic verification and research consultation. Other staff members may only provide directional and ready-reference assistance, referring all other queries to a more experienced staff member, to a different level of staff, or to another service point. These levels can be by service point or may all be located at the same desk. Box 9.4 provides an example of core competencies needed in an academic library.

Assessing Training Needs

Reference departments frequently hire new staff members. Because no department has unlimited time or funds to train, it needs to determine how to get the most

BOX 9.4
CORE COMPETENCIES, UNIVERSITY LIBRARIES, UNIVERSITY OF NEBRASKA-LINCOLN

Analytical Skills/Problem Solving/ Decision Making
Recognizes patterns, draws logical conclusions, and makes recommendations for action. Uses a well-ordered approach to solving problems and sound judgment in making decisions despite obstacles or resistance.

Communications Skills
Listens effectively, transmits information accurately and understandably, and actively seeks constructive feedback.

Creativity/Innovation
Looks for opportunities to apply new and evolving ideas, methods, designs, and technologies.

Expertise and Technical Knowledge
Demonstrates broad, in-depth, and up-to-date knowledge of pertinent fields and awareness of current technology.

Flexibility/Adaptability
Performs a wide range of tasks, responds to changes in direction and priorities, and accepts new challenges, responsibilities, and assignments.

Interpersonal/Group Skills
Builds strong work relationships with a sensitivity to how individuals, organizational units, and cultures function and react. Establishes partnerships at all levels and across department and functional lines to achieve optimum results.

Leadership
Sets and models high performance standards characterized by integrity. Earns trust and respect of others by coaching, inspiring, and empowering teams of people to achieve strategic objectives.

Organizational Understanding and Global Thinking
Demonstrates an understanding of the institution in its entirety and works to achieve results across disciplines, departments, and functions. Develops and maintains supportive relationships across the organization.

Ownership/Accountability/ Dependability
Accepts responsibility for actions, results, and risks. Gets the job done.

Planning and Organizational Skills
Anticipates and predicts internal and external changes, trends, and influences in order to effectively allocate resources and implement appropriate library initiatives.

Resource Management
Demonstrates a consistent focus on minimizing expenses while maximizing results.

Service Attitude/User Satisfaction
Understands and meets the needs of users and addresses their interests and concerns of those affected.

Joan Giesecke and Beth McNeil, "Core Competencies and the Learning Organization," *Library Administration and Management* 13 (Summer 1999): 160.

from training. Therefore, it is essential to conduct a *needs assessment*. A needs assessment is important in order to plan, manage, and allocate scarce training dollars, as well as to evaluate training results. Training needs are competencies that are required or desired but have not yet been developed. Training should never be conducted without identifying its purpose or need.

A great deal of discussion continues about what reference librarians need to know from a general liberal arts and sciences background that gives a basis of knowledge to comprehensive knowledge of reference sources. A public service attitude, communication skills, teaching ability, an ability to evaluate information, knowledge of the structure of literature, and the ability to formulate search strategies effectively are all aspects of reference service that most reference librarians would include as requirements.

Analyzing Tasks

Analyzing what goes on at the reference or information desk can be a good beginning for identifying needs of reference librarians or paraprofessionals. Reference interview techniques; knowledge of reference sources; ability to manipulate online and card catalogs, local files, community information, online databases, or networked resources; and working as a team with colleagues, sharing knowledge in a constructive way, are all areas in which any staff member who works at a reference or information desk should be competent. Although analysis of reference desk activities is a good method to identify basic training needs for new reference desk workers, many other techniques are available.[29]

Interviews

Interviews, either with individuals or in groups, are particularly useful in determining the needs of experienced librarians.[30] From interviews, it may be determined that librarians have specific ongoing training needs, such as further practice in asking open-ended questions and achieving closure in the reference interview. Other areas in which experienced personnel generally identify training needs are in using new equipment or systems, learning new sources and tools, and reviewing little-used reference sources. Box 9.5 provides a sample list of the training needs of a reference assistant.

BOX 9.5
SAMPLE LIST OF TRAINING NEEDS OF A REFERENCE ASSISTANT

Task: "Responds to patron information needs through the use of reference sources"
Needs to know:

Where things are in the building, emphasizing reference area
Library policies regarding amount of help given to each category of patrons

How to conduct a reference interview
What is in the reference collection
What are the types of reference sources (almanacs, dictionaries, etc.)
How to use the local "hard to answer" file
Understand to whom and how to refer difficult questions
How to use the telephone system

Adapted from Julie Ann McDaniel and Judith K. Ohles, *Training Paraprofessionals for Reference Service*, How-to-Do-It Manual for Libraries, no. 30 (New York: Neal-Schuman, 1993), 18.

When Needs Do Not Point to Training

When skill deficiencies exist, certain questions must be answered to determine the best course of action. If the job is one the employee used to do, have procedures changed? If not, then feedback and practice may be the answer. If procedures have changed or it is a new job, then procedures may be simplified, training may be done on the job, or formal training may have to be arranged. If there is no skill deficiency, then the obstacles to adequate performance must be examined and corrected. One obstacle may be that procedures are unrealistic or have not been clearly communicated. Creating practice sessions, a job aid, or a finding guide, or combining them, can be a more practical approach to helping people to perform infrequent complex tasks. Not all deficiencies in performance can be addressed with training; some performance problems are associated with environmental or attitudinal factors that prevent or discourage optimum performance. Other techniques, such as providing feedback on observed behaviors or planning practice sessions, can also be used to improve performance at the reference desk. Some reference departments have found success with having individuals become "the resident expert" in certain areas, resources, or databases and then have the responsibility of teaching others.

BOX 9.6
SCENARIO: IS THIS A TRAINING PROBLEM?

A large university reference department provides occasional reference assistance in using the library's collection of British parliamentary papers. The staff has received training, which consists of reviewing the types of access tools, discussing formats, and examining a bibliography prepared by an experienced librarian. One particular staff member has trouble dealing with these questions. She ordinarily panics and turns to the person who prepared the bibliography. When that person is not available, she can generally muddle through to answer the question.

Is this a training problem? What are the obstacles to adequate performance?

Training Needs of Specific Groups

Every reference department has a variety of individuals who make up the staff and provide varying levels of service. From the students shelving books and the clerical persons who check in the books to the paraprofessionals who work the reference desk a few hours a week, to the senior reference librarian or head of the department, everyone has training needs that need to be addressed.

Volunteers

Although the use of volunteers to provide reference service is a managerial decision that may or may not come under the purview of the individual entrusted with training, the training of volunteers requires flexibility and individuation. Volunteers can range from unemployed librarians to staff members in other departments to well-meaning community members with little or no skills or background in libraries. Consequently, this makes it extremely difficult to lump them into a single category. The kind of responsibilities they have in the department will determine the kind of training they need. Museums and other nonprofit organizations use volunteers very successfully in their educational programs, and there is certainly no reason that libraries cannot do the same.

Students and Clerical Workers

Students and clerical workers have needs similar to volunteers in that they often come to their jobs without library backgrounds or familiarity, so they often need more than basic orientation to know where they fit into the system. They need to understand the terminology and the service mission of the department, with the understanding that they represent the library to many users.

Paraprofessionals

Paraprofessionals often come with a wide variety of backgrounds and skills. Some may have little or no library experience and little formal education; others may have extensive library experience; yet others may have advanced degrees in other subject areas. With such inconsistency, trainers must either test for each person's knowledge or assume no knowledge and begin from scratch.

Reference interview behaviors, as well as general information on how materials are physically and intellectually accessed in the library, need to be included, along with specific tools and sources paraprofessionals are expected to know. Generally, training needs to include an introduction to and practice sessions on the library's catalog and specific tools, such as indexes in all formats that are appropriate. In addition, types of information frequently in demand, such as biographical information, statistics, government information, newspapers or current events, or special types of materials such as government publications, should be covered in a manner determined by the individual library. The chapters of this book on sources can provide suggestions for these sessions or modules of training. Paraprofessionals also need guidance regarding how to examine a new reference source and how to identify strengths and weaknesses of specific sources. In addition, paraprofessionals will need written policies and procedures indicating when it is appropriate to refer users to professional librarians in the department or in other departments, other libraries, or outside agencies.

Because most paraprofessionals do not have the benefit of a library school education, they will need guidance in the process of approaching a reference question. For example, they need to learn how to analyze a question so that when they do not find the answer in the first source they try, they can devise an alternate strategy.

Writing Objectives for Training

If training objectives are to be useful, they must describe the kind of performance that will be accepted as evidence that the learner has mastered that particular task. This definition by behavior is used to measure whether the trainees have achieved the goal of the training and whether the training is successful.

Three kinds of objectives, *acquiring knowledge*, *learning skills*, and *reinforcing attitudes*, are described. Examples of knowledge in the reference setting include information and understanding about the reference collection, the general collection, library services, and policies. Skills of reference librarians include the ability to translate that knowledge into performing tasks, such as conducting reference interviews, instructing users, and communicating in a clear and concise way. Attitudes such as commitment and motivation are observable in the behavior of the reference librarian.[31]

With training as with other educational sessions (see chapter 8), if objectives are to be useful, three elements are necessary: *performance*, *conditions*, and *criteria*.[32] Performance describes what is to be done, what the trainee should be able to do. Conditions describe the situation and the kinds of tools that can be used. Criteria describe the quality and quantity of work expected and the time allowed to complete the job. In reference work, this means the quality of service, including accuracy and completeness.

Selecting Methods

Selection of the most suitable instructional strategy is based on several considerations. One of the most important is congruency with the stated training objective. The strategy should recognize the need for trainees to respond and to receive feedback, should adapt to individuals' different learning styles, and should approximate what happens on the job. Factors that restrict the choice of strategy include the instructor's level of skill, the size of the group, costs, time, and equipment available.

Knowledge

Some methods are more suitable than others in helping trainees attain the objective. Objectives that stress knowledge acquisition, such as "describe the structure of biological literature," are appropriately reached through lecture, discussion, and assigned readings. Lectures and films require only that people listen and watch, whereas programmed texts and computer-aided instruction are specifically designed to require that a choice be made before the trainee can move to the next question, page, or screen. Research has shown that programmed texts are the first choice of trainers for knowledge retention[33] because of the activity involved. A number of good online training resources are available through clearinghouses such as WebJunction.[34]

Skills

The use of videos has been increasingly popular in training, but it is often difficult to find quality clips. For communication and management skills, videos can model appropriate behavior. For technical procedures that apply step-by-step processes, videos not only demonstrate appropriate techniques but also allow slow motion and replay functions that will deepen comprehension. Used to record trainees' behaviors, video can provide opportunities for self-observation and evaluation.[35] *Trigger videos*, or short episodes, can raise a large number of issues, including sexual harassment, the handling of aggression or other problems, or behaviors that affect the image of the library,[36] and can stimulate or trigger discussions.

Skills generally cannot be learned and applied without some sort of practice. Although the general concepts behind the application of skills, such as the steps involved in the reference interview, can be learned through lectures, demonstrations, or other passive forms of teaching, reference staff must *use* a skill if they are to apply it consistently.

Role playing, in which situations are outlined and individuals assume roles to try out behaviors in a realistic manner, is one technique that simulates the job environment. Other methods that simulate job behavior include case studies, management games, practice sessions, and workshops. Often, reference departments compile questions that have really been asked at their desks and ask trainees to identify sources to answer these questions.[37] If the training objective is to select an appropriate search strategy to find a known item in the online catalog, effective methods might include programmed instruction or a combination of reading, lecture, and discussion, as well as practice sessions. Because this objective requires that a choice be made, a method requiring a response will be more effective.

When introducing new staff to database searching, general searching techniques can be explained through lecture and demonstration. This can be followed by a set of practice searches for specific databases. Other databases, search software, and more specific search techniques can again be demonstrated with lectures and demonstration and followed by hands-on practice. As training proceeds over the course of several days with several different databases, trainees should start to ask when they would go to a particular source. Training people *how* to use a particular resource does not guarantee that they will know *when* to use it appropriately. After a discussion of the advantages and disadvantages of each system, the trainees can be divided into small groups and given a series of questions. They can be asked to try them in the different systems and report back to the group what worked and what did not. Providing an environment in which it is acceptable to make mistakes, but simulating the kinds of questions they will be asked at the information or reference desk, helps trainees learn for themselves when it is appropriate to examine a particular tool.

The best training promotes self-discovery, recognizing that "the most important things cannot be taught but must be discovered and appropriated for oneself."[38] As an ancient proverb puts it, "Tell me, I forget. Show me, I remember. Involve me, I understand." Adults learn best with active involvement, by solving realistic problems.

BOX 9.7
SCENARIO: WRITE GUIDELINES FOR PREPARING TRAINING

The information staff consists of 12 library assistants, and introducing them to and updating them on the online databases has gotten out of hand. There are just too many databases and too many software vendors for one person to keep track of. The reference training coordinator has decided to ask each of the 12 library assistants to be responsible for training the others on the use and searching of a particular database. A small committee of reference librarians has been assigned to help the training coordinator come up with guidelines for the training. What should be included in the documentation that each assistant develops? Should they also be asked to develop handouts for users? How much autonomy will each assistant have in creating these training materials?

If adults work things out for themselves, they are more likely to be able to work out a similar problem on the job. Active learning promotes the use of ingenuity and imagination rather than performance of a task in a set manner. Problem-solving skills can be learned effectively in this way, using case studies or in-basket exercises to simulate decisions that must be made on the job. Asking staff to take on training another person can have similar benefits.

Attitudes

Attitudes can be influenced in a variety of ways, and experts differ in the approaches they suggest. With adults, interaction again is important, so sensitivity training, role playing, and discussion groups are useful means of changing attitudes. Trigger videos, or dramatic vignettes illustrating a dilemma, a problem, or a situation with which the audience is familiar without providing the answer as to what should be done to resolve the situation, are useful in stimulating discussions. They are particularly useful for handling issues that are hard to describe or replicate, such as sexual harassment, the handling of aggression or other problems, or behaviors that affect the image of the library.[39]

Factors in Strategy Selection

The availability or lack of experienced trainers, instructional space, facilities, equipment, and materials can do much to facilitate or hinder the training process, and all factors influence the choice of instructional strategy. The time and costs of development, the size of the group, and the learning styles of the trainee population also restrict the choices the trainer can make. A number of training experts have written excellent guides to facilitate selection of training methods for the new trainer.[40] Instruction experts have also identified approaches to teaching library skills to patrons; these approaches transfer well to training situations.

In planning training events, trainers should consider known educational principles. Although individual study and reflection are excellent ways that people learn,

---

BOX 9.8
SCENARIO: IDENTIFY TRAINING ACTIVITIES

The reference librarian and the circulation librarian at a small college library have been asked to improve the staff's dealings with angry patrons. In doing research, they identified three steps: (1) calming the patron, (2) identifying the problem, and (3) providing relief. Staff members have more difficulty with steps 1 and 3. Brainstorm about possible training activities. What are the strengths and weaknesses of each?

BOX 9.9
DEVELOP A CASE STUDY

In small groups, identify a problem area in reference services training and develop a case study. Share the case study with another group, asking them to actually work through the problem. Have them consider the perspectives of both staff and users in considering approaches. Ask the group to identify the strengths of this case study and offer suggestions for improvement.

Sample case study:

You are working alone at a very busy information desk at Green County Public Library. The mayor's secretary calls and says that the mayor needs the names and addresses of the publishers of about twenty periodicals and that she needs it now. Although the source of this information is at your service desk, the information will require multiple look-ups. Furthermore, you see three restless users circling your desk area. Identify three ways to handle this call that could satisfy the mayor and also tend to your on-site users.

Joanne M. Bessler, *Putting Service into Library Staff Training: A Patron-Centered Guide*, LAMA Occasional Papers Series (Chicago: American Library Association, 1994), 30.

---

one should also take into consideration that cooperative learning is a good practice. One study on training library technicians to take on reference responsibilities found that relying too heavily on self-paced study proved difficult with hectic schedules. The program was revised to include more formal courses.[41]

Facilitating Retention of Skills

In learning almost any skill, people go through an awkward phase when the newly acquired skill does not feel natural and does not achieve results. This period, called the "results dip" or "incorporation lag," is particularly difficult.[42] Initially, when reference librarians attempt to substitute a new behavior for an old one, it feels uncomfortable, and results suffer. Some studies have found that up to 87 percent of the skills actually acquired by a training program may be lost if attention is not paid to making sure that these skills are retained.[43] Combating the problem of transferring learned skills to the job environment can take several forms, both during the training itself and back on the job.

Practice

Techniques that simulate the behavior used on the job are more likely to teach skills that will actually be used in that setting. The training program itself should include a sufficient amount of time to practice, which may be as much as a third of the instruction time.[44] Practice away from the job provides an opportunity to fail in a controlled environment without the normal consequences, a frame of reference for tasks to be performed, and an ability to apply new skills learned more easily and readily.

Role-playing, although not a particular favorite with trainees, continues to be one of the best approaches to allow the learner to take part in a realistic, but simulated and therefore nonthreatening, situation. Role-playing is an excellent way to demonstrate appropriate techniques to use with problem patrons and in question negotiation. Role-playing exercises in isolation do not produce skilled performers. They do, however, help ensure that trainees learn the steps appropriate for skilled performance. This technique has been used successfully at Baylor University, where Janet Sheets has developed a role-playing exercise she calls "The Reference Game."[45] In this game, the emphasis is on the interaction with users rather than on the selection of a particular reference tool. For virtual reference, practice is particularly important, given that unfamiliarity with the software may make the interaction more difficult (see Box 9.10).

Drills, or short, repetitive exercises, can be used to master skills in small steps. As skills are practiced under a variety of circumstances, the trainee's ability to perform consistently improves. During these drills, trainees function as coaches for each other, helping to critique as each element or move is practiced and then combined into a series of moves. Drilling then provides confidence, and "confidence builds 'ownership' of the skill. And ownership must occur *during* the training course in order for the skill to transfer to the real job."[46]

Several other techniques can be used during the training session to facilitate retention of skills learned. *Action plans*, in which the participants reflect on program content and write goals of intended implementation, are useful techniques for maintaining behavior. These can take the form of a letter to oneself or an ideas and applications notebook. Other activities that can be incorporated into training sessions include *guided practicing* (as opposed to turning trainees loose for independent practice) and *question-and-answer sessions* that involve some sort of systematic pattern to include everyone.

Other ways to improve the transfer of skills to the on-the-job setting include highlighting similarity of the new information to something that the participants already know, as in illuminating a framework or pattern. Sometimes this can be a completed matrix or a grid that is handed out, or it can be an empty frame where the participants can complete the form for themselves.[47] The other advantage to this kind of activity

BOX 9.10
PRACTICE EXERCISE: ANSWERING QUESTIONS USING CHAT

Instructions

During this exercise, you will be chatting with _____
(screen name)

Sign on to the chat program and send a chat invitation to your partner.
Decide who will ask a question (patron) and who will answer (librarian).

If you are the patron with a question:

• Select one of the questions below or make up your own.
• You may decide to play the role of a student with a homework assignment, a person with a trivia question, etc.
• Word your question and responses accordingly.
• When the librarian sends a URL to you, open a second browser window.
• Let the librarian know if this Web site answers your question.

If you are the librarian answering the question:

• Clarify the patron's question through a reference interview.
• Open a browser window and search for Web sites that will answer the question.
• Once you have found a good source for the answer, use CTRL C and CTRL V to copy and paste the URL in the chat window.
• Keep the patron informed of what you are doing.
• Check to see if the patron is satisfied with what you found.

Then trade roles.

Practice Questions

1. I would like to know the specific death dates of Jessie and Frank James. Where did they die?
2. When did Mount St. Helens erupt?
3. What is the date for Ramadan in 2004?
4. I am writing an essay on teenage suicide. I am looking for sources of teenagers giving personal testimonies who have decided not to commit suicide or have tried suicide and lived.
5. When is Juneteenth celebrated?
6. Who was the first person to walk on the moon?
7. Why do potatoes turn green beneath the skin?
8. I am looking for a playdough recipe.
9. What is the history behind Nobel prizes? When was the first one awarded?
10. When and where was the first World's Fair?
11. I need to know which states were the original thirteen colonies.
12. Who are the Chicago Seven defendants and what did they do?

13. What are the names of the nine muses?
14. Where do I find APA or MLA formats for bibliographies or works cited online?
15. What are the dates of the Black Monday and Black Thursday Stock Market Crashes?
16. When is Deaf Awareness Week?

Buff Hirko and Mary Bucher Ross, *Virtual Reference Training: The Complete Guide to Providing Anytime, Anywhere Answers* (Chicago: American Library Association, 2004), 134–35.

is that it provides specific items to look for. Box 9.11 illustrates this in the context of comparing the contents of two databases.

Feedback

One of the most important methods of facilitating retention of skills on the job is *feedback*. There are two basic types of feedback. The first recognizes good work, general competence, or exemplary performance and encourages employees to keep up the good work. This kind of feedback is important in maintaining skill levels because

BOX 9.11
ONLINE DATABASE COMPARISON

CONTENT EVALUATION		
	Name of Database 1	**Name of Database 2**
Publisher/provider?		
How many periodicals are indexed?		
Are periodicals indexed cover to cover?		
Approx. % English language material?		
What type of information is included? (bibliographic, full text, other)		
What time period is covered? (year range)		
Are there any particular **subject strengths** applicable to your library? (list)		
Are there any particular **gaps in coverage**? (list)		

behaviors can lapse through lack of reinforcement. Addressing the upkeep of these strengths is as important as fixing problems. The other kind of feedback is *improvement feedback*, which sends the message that change is needed. This feedback calls attention to poor work, areas of incompetence, or problem behavior.

Effective feedback is immediate, clear, accurate, specific, and positive. Behaviors should be reinforced as quickly as possible. Trainees need to be informed of the trainer's awareness of their behavior as soon as it happens, through attention, recognition, or praise. Negative feedback is better than no feedback at all, but positive feedback produces the best results. Employees tend to remember longest what they hear first and last in a message and are more likely to apply suggestions if the feedback is personal and private. Approval of or agreement with ideas and behavior is communicated by the absence of feedback, so it is very important for people to be informed when their behaviors are not appropriate.

Feedback on the job can be provided in several ways. Performance can be examined through personal diaries and self-reporting by individuals; through observations and interviews with supervisors, either informally or in a performance appraisal; or through buddy systems, support groups, coaching, or job aids. Very few of these

---

BOX 9.12
SCENARIO: GIVING EFFECTIVE FEEDBACK

Mary, a new reference assistant, is handling the reference desk while the reference librarians are in an extended meeting. An abusive caller telephones the reference desk and demands to speak to a reference librarian. Mary tells the caller that none are available and asks if she can help in any way. He curtly says no and continues to be abusive without actually swearing. Mary hangs up.

When the reference librarians return from their meeting, the abusive individual immediately calls the reference head. After taking the call, John, the reference head, calls Mary into his office and says, "I hear you hung up on one of our users; tell me about it." Mary relates the story in detail. John says, "I think you did the right thing. No one should have to put up with that kind of abuse. However, based on what you told me, I think there may have been a better way to handle the situation. What do you think it might be?"

Was this feedback effective?

---

methods have been reported as having been applied in reference settings. *Coaching*, which is basically one-on-one counseling, is one technique that has been used to provide feedback on reference staff performance in reference interviews, notably in public libraries. Coaching is one of the best ways to make sure that newly learned skills are transferred and maintained on the job, but it is a feedback technique that has only recently been applied in reference situations. Informal coaching situations can be established, however, merely by providing an environment in which an experienced person works with an inexperienced one. At one academic library, during the month of September, reference librarians work alongside newly hired graduate assistants at the information desk to ease them into their new environment, reassure them, and give them additional opportunities for feedback.

Other Interventions

Alternatives to giving feedback include *review sessions*, which give trainees opportunities to refine and polish skills learned and which encourage continued use of the skill; *further practice time*, such as that provided by database vendors who give free time or reduced rates on selected databases; or the use of *job aids*. The use of informational job aids or performance aids helps to transfer skills learned in training. The idea behind job aids is to eliminate the need for people to remember details by providing assistance in the form of checklists, reference manuals, flowcharts, computer databases, templates for keyboards or telephones, and so forth.[48] These performance aids give trainees a better chance to use new skills by providing the minimal guidance so badly needed in the early stages of attempting to apply a newly learned skill on the job. See Figure 9.1 for more intervention techniques.

Evaluating Training

Without evaluation, it is impossible to know whether the training program has done what it was designed to do. Has the performance of the reference staff member improved? If so, is it because of the training program? It is important to build evaluation into the program from the very beginning.

Who Evaluates?

Experts suggest that evaluation be done by as many people as possible to eliminate biases. This means that the supervisor, the trainer (if not also the supervisor), the

IMPROVE PERFORMANCE	ESTABLISH PERFORMANCE
Action research	Employee selection
Business planning	Job aids
Coaching	Mentoring
Feedback	Modeling
Training	Training
MAINTAIN PERFORMANCE	**EXTINGUISH PERFORMANCE**
Compensation	Outplacement
Feedback	Upward evaluation
Performance standards	Withholding information
Work schedules	Withholding rewards

From Danny G. Langdon, Kathleen S. Whiteside, and Monica M. McKenna, eds., *Intervention Resource Guide: 50 Performance Improvement Tools* (San Francisco: Jossey-Bass, 1999), 20.

Figure 9.1 Sample interventions for performance problems.

employee who received the training, coworkers, and outsiders (who could be library users) may be involved in evaluation.

Trainee evaluation. Otherwise excellent staff development programs often fail to provide built-in opportunities for participants' self-assessment. Thomas Shaughnessy argues that "staff development programs which include a self-assessment component should focus on providing each participant with the tools and materials necessary for the individual to test himself or herself and to score the test."[49] Programs that provide for self-assessment ease staff anxiety concerning test results and increase accuracy of results. Videotaping has been suggested as "a useful, and surprisingly comfortable, self-evaluation technique, because it captures actions in context otherwise lost to the person acting."[50] The results of self-evaluation are difficult to validate, however, and should be used in conjunction with other approaches.

Peer evaluation. William Young believes that peers working together at a reference desk are those in the best position to judge reference behaviors and that this is the most promising and realistic approach to evaluating reference desk performance.[51] *Behaviorally anchored rating scales* (BARS) are frequently used to assist in defining degrees of performance on the job. Several libraries have used these satisfactorily. Most have extracted behaviors, skills, and knowledge from a service standard to create a checklist of desirable behaviors, such as a reference librarian asking for assistance in certain situations or suggesting alternative sources of information to the user.[52] Figure 9.2 shows behaviorally anchored rating scales that are a portion of an instrument used in peer evaluations of an information desk staff of an academic library.

Supervisor evaluation. The supervisor's evaluation is the most subjective and can be difficult to rely on in training situations, unless testing, observation, or interviews accompany it. Also, because supervisors have a number of other areas of job performance to attend to, the particular performance related to training may be difficult to determine.

Library user evaluation. Although library users' consistently high ranking of satisfaction with reference services calls into doubt their ability to evaluate reference performance,[53] it has been suggested that library users can evaluate librarians' attitudes, degree of self-confidence, and ability to instruct individuals in the use of reference sources.[54]

Instruments such as the Wisconsin-Ohio Reference Evaluation Program (WOREP)[55] collect data from both users and staff members. Although completing the form does require a significant commitment from the staff and the users, a more complete picture is formed because more than one viewpoint is solicited.

What Is Evaluated and How?

Evaluating training can be very difficult. Decisions have to be made not only concerning how to evaluate but also on what can and should be evaluated. Four different levels can be evaluated in a training program: *reactions*, *learning*, *job behaviors*, and *results*.[56]

Reactions. Although attendees do not necessarily have to enjoy a session, it is important that a positive reaction to the training sessions occur if learning is to take place. A positive reaction to training is a precondition to learning, but it is not a guarantee that learning will transpire. Participants must feel a commitment to training—must

II. Interactions with Users	Seldom	Not Frequently Enough	Sometimes	Frequently	Almost all the time	Cannot Respond
Maintains a Professional Posture						
1. Looks alert, confident, and interested.						
2. Works to minimize the initial barrier between patron and staff member.						
3. Establishes good eye contact (e.g., looks up as patron approaches desk).						
Desk Service Priorities						
1. Handles multiple patrons well.						
2. Maintains awareness of work flow at the desk and utilizes time away from the desk appropriately.						
3. Acknowledges the presence of users not yet served.						
Effective Communication						
1. Avoids unexplained or unnecessary jargon.						
2. Speaks in positive, relaxed, appropriately loud tone of voice.						
3. Listens well.						
4. Seeks definitions.						
One-on-One Teaching						
1. Explains steps taken.						
2. Involves user in the search process when appropriate.						
3. Is sensitive to user's level of skills and knowledge.						
4. Proactively assists patrons through roving and working with patrons away from the desk.						

Figure 9.2 A portion of an instrument used in peer evaluations by staff at an information desk.

feel it is valuable—in order to learn. Most often, reactions are assessed by asking trainees to complete rating scales for individual sessions. Verbal comments or nonverbal cues can also be observed. To supplement the attendees' comments, the supervisor or an observer should also record comments.

Learning. Learning, the acquisition of knowledge, skills, or attitudes, within the training context can be tested through programmed instruction, objective tests, essays, and pen and pencil tests. Testing may also be built into the training, such as judgment of performance in practice sessions or in-class exercises. To determine whether skill improvement can indeed be attributed to the training program or results from outside influences, training experts recommend the use of *pre-tests*, *post-tests*, and *control groups*.[57] All those attending a training session, as well as those in a control group that does not receive training, are given a pre-test, to see what skills and knowledge they already possess. After a period of time has elapsed since training was administered, both groups are again tested to see whether skills improved through training or merely from working on the job. Most librarians, unfortunately, have difficulty finding the time to administer tests in this way.

Job behaviors. Although trainees may learn the skills and be able to perform them in the training session, they may not be able to perform them on the job. If the trainee did achieve the criteria during training sessions, the application exercises may not have been similar to the on-the-job environment. For example, when given citations with the author and title identified, reference assistants may be able to search the online catalog correctly. However, they may not be able to do so effectively on the job because they are unable to identify those key items from a citation that does not have the elements labeled. The evaluation itself can affect the result of training, so if trainers or supervisors wish to reinforce that training, they should use *obtrusive methods*, or testing that is known to the trainee. If it is important that outside factors be limited, *unobtrusive methods*, in which the trainees do not know they are being tested, should be used. Terry Weech and Herbert Goldhor have shown that reference librarians correctly answer a larger proportion of reference questions when they know they are being evaluated.[58] Chapter 10 discusses the advantages and disadvantages of unobtrusive and obtrusive methods in more detail.

When on-the-job benefits of training programs are hard to measure or are unclear, or when outcomes cannot be adequately measured with simple quantitative methods, as is the case in reference librarianship, interviews can be useful. Interviews and group discussions are more informal ways of assessing the effectiveness of a training program.[59]

Results. The final results, or benefit to the organization, should be the last stage of evaluation. Benefits such as users' satisfaction with library service or their ability to access needed information are difficult to measure. If the goal is to determine the effect that training has had on these outcomes, it becomes even more complicated; for this reason, libraries rarely evaluate at this level.[60]

BEYOND THE BASICS: CONTINUAL LEARNING

Training for reference staff should be a continuous process that is never really finished. Although the library can complete its induction phase to orient new staff members and finish on-the-job training for basic job skills, the basic level of skills constantly changes as resources, technology, customer needs, and services evolve. Donna Cromer and Andrea Testi assert that "cultivating an atmosphere of life-long learning, continuing education, and self-evaluation for reference personnel is essential in responding to and anticipating change."[61] Reference staff members have an additional need to go beyond basic-level competencies to mastery of their field, or expertise in a particular area. "Today's dynamic environment of reference work demands that reference staff, whether newly-hired or seasoned, professional or paraprofessional, engage in ongoing professional development opportunities."[62]

Two different approaches to continual or lifelong learning can be identified. Although the two approaches use similar methods and have similar purposes of improving the competence of individuals, each has a different focus. *Staff development* is organizationally centered and directed, whereas *continuing education* is individually centered and directed. They are, however, not mutually exclusive and are in fact complementary approaches. Both approaches are actually beneficial in helping staff members avoid technological obsolescence, develop expertise and knowledge in specialized areas, and widen experiences and practical knowledge.

Mastery or Expertise

A common practice in new employee orientation and training efforts is to have the new employees spend a lot of individual time with other staff members at the beginning of the employment period. Once the overview is given and a foundation is laid, they are often left to jump in and "sink or swim." Because they do not know yet how to choose the most important information out of all they are hearing, they often reach information overload, and "later portions of the orientation process may not even be heard."[63] Alternating tasks with early orientation sessions and providing continuing training and review sessions can help new staff members build full knowledge or mastery of the content more gradually and more interactively.

Expertise in specific areas should also be encouraged. In developing expertise in reference, staff members deepen their understanding of resources and technology and learn how to transfer existing skills to a new environment,[64] a crucial skill in a constantly changing environment.

Change Management

Multiple paradigm shifts in the world economic, political, and cultural order, and simultaneous shifts in organizations, businesses, and information technology, are having a significant impact on library and information services. Joan Giesecke and Beth McNeil suggest that "to succeed, libraries must now be agile, flexible, and able to adjust to a world that resembles an amusement park roller-coaster ride or whitewater rafting."[65]

The sources that record information and the tools that provide access to these sources are revised and updated or appear in different forms. In such a time of profound change, the knowledge that individuals bring initially to their work can become obsolete rapidly. The effort required to maintain current knowledge and understanding is immense.

"In the print era the reference librarian could turn to the Mudge/Winchell/Sheehy *Guide to Reference Books*, or locate an index for a given journal through the listings in *Ulrich's* or other specialized guides. In the online era, new tools will have to be built that can deal comprehensively with a dynamic environment."[66] Reference librarians will always have to keep up with new information, new reference sources and access tools, and the changing needs of their users.[67]

Reference librarians have traditionally been conservators or caretakers of the library's collections. These roles are evolving as reference librarians become mediators between users and materials, information counselors, and educators and guides in teaching how to find and evaluate information. Mary Nofsinger notes that, "The reference librarian must not only be able to find relevant information or documents, but must be able to evaluate them on the criteria of availability, ease of access, authority, presence of biases, scope, and timeliness, regardless of electronic or print format or location. In addition, a critical thinking librarian must estimate the quantity and intellectual level of information required by the user."[68]

Julie Parry is concerned with how staff will deal with a constantly changing environment. She states, "Clearly, ongoing training is necessary to enable staff to keep up-to-date with changes. In responsive service, processes and procedures will be constantly monitored and modified to meet changing needs. Managers and supervisors need to ensure that staff understand new procedures and are able to put them into practice."[69]

Job Stress

Continual learning should help reference librarians deal with the stress that accompanies any kind of front-line position (see Box 9.13). Tina Roose points out that "reference librarians are among the few researchers of this world who are expected to perform with an audience in the midst of many other demands and distractions."[70] Four factors contribute to stress at the reference desk: technology, users, environment, and staffing.

BOX 9.13
REFERENCE SERVICE AS COMBAT: FIGHTING JOB STRESS

Some experts suggest that jobs with a high emotional labor content, jobs where the performer's persona goes on the line time and time again at the customer interface, should be treated as combat, and like combat soldiers, people in high-stress service jobs need to be rotated off the front line frequently, and sometimes permanently. As one expert puts it, "In Vietnam we *knew* come hell or high water, that after so many months, we were out of there. You need to do that for service people. They have to know there is a light at the end of that tunnel—and it isn't from an oncoming train."

Ron Zemke, "Contact! Training Employees to Meet the Public," *Training* 23 (August 1986): 44.

Technology

Computers have assumed a central role in librarianship. Librarians need to maintain basic knowledge of operating systems, learn basic hardware and communications troubleshooting techniques, and develop deep understanding of software used every day.[71]

> When libraries dealt with only one or two database vendors, it was comparatively simple for an individual to remember what databases were available. For unfamiliar subject areas, a quick reference to the paper directories supplied by the online vendor yielded the needed information. As the sources of online information have multiplied, one person can no longer keep a mental catalog of the likely places where individual pieces of information may be found.[72]

In addition to the variety of sources available, in an online environment, available resources can change overnight. Technological obsolescence can occur when individual competence holds constant while professional standards advance.[73]

Users

The technological age has brought further complications in raising users' expectations of libraries and of the ability of library staff to provide information immediately. Users often expect reference staff to provide data that may not be collected or that by nature is confidential. When advised by reference staff on a course of action, the user may not be willing to follow that advice if it seems like too much work. For example, individuals wanting information on a topic from the 1960s are incredulous when told they will have to use print indexes to find information. They may go to the next person on duty in the hope of getting a different answer to their question.

Reference staff are increasingly dealing more directly with diverse populations, including individuals with physical, emotional, and health limitations who may have been served by special agencies before or individuals with different cultural expectations (see chapter 12). Although this recognition of the needs of a diverse population is important, it brings further stresses to a service desk in the amount of knowledge required to handle a particular question and the amount of patience or tact needed.

Environment

Local collections necessarily have limitations, and with today's information explosion, no one institution can be expected to acquire everything its users could reasonably ask about. Additionally, the arrangement of the reference collection, physical desks, and equipment can negatively affect the reference transaction.[74] If desks are cumbersome to use or inhibit the use of a particular kind of source, service is affected. Aging or constantly breaking equipment can also be a stress factor. Service philosophies can vary tremendously from one service desk to another even within the same institution. This, too, can contribute to users' expectations or frustrations and thus the librarian's stress.

Staffing

Individuals have a limit on how much they can work with the public, and this factor is different for each person. Some individuals work better in small stretches of time, whereas others do well working on the desk for longer periods of time. Departments should have limits on the number of hours that staff members are expected to work. Inappropriate staffing can also create stress. Boredom from staffing professionals during slow periods and anxiety from single staffing during busy times are equally problematic. Lack of technological backup, especially on nights and weekends, can be another problem.

Burnout

Burnout is an overwhelming feeling of frustration, apathy, and exhaustion regarding one's work.[75] It is not a problem unique to reference service providers, but it

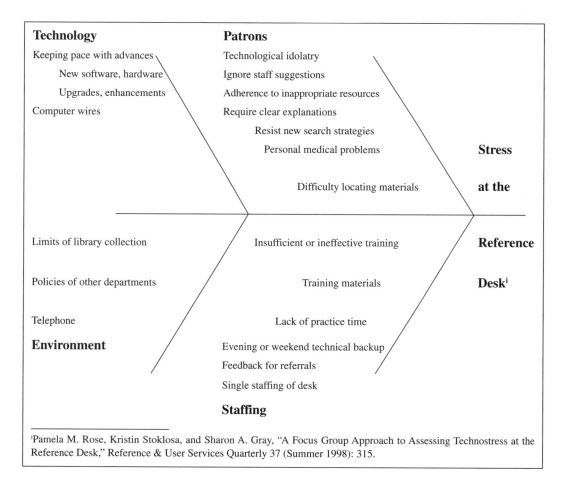

i Pamela M. Rose, Kristin Stoklosa, and Sharon A. Gray, "A Focus Group Approach to Assessing Technostress at the Reference Desk," Reference & User Services Quarterly 37 (Summer 1998): 315.

Figure 9.3 Fishbone diagram: Factors Producing Stress at the Reference Desk.

is very intense and pervasive.[76] "Reference librarians seem most particularly at risk for burnout because of their assignment of general direct availability for an unpredictable stream of requests and demands and their high visibility in most libraries."[77] Various individuals have attributed the problem to

- too many new services and activities added to traditional reference desk service with no increase in staff to handle the new activities,[78]
- "a gap between the ideals of reference librarianship that [librarians] believe and espouse and the realities of reference service that can be practiced,"[79] or
- *technostress*, or the anxiety and psychological pressure created by the continually expanding range of electronic tools that reference librarians must master.[80]

It is important to note that the four stages of burnout—*enthusiasm, stagnation, frustration*, and *apathy*—start with enthusiasm. The challenge to librarians is to rekindle the fire of enthusiasm and not let it burn out—to feed it with challenges, new environments, new information, and new techniques, without letting it engulf reference staff members. Staff development and continuing education can provide the kindling for the fire by presenting new information and techniques for approaching the reference process. When someone is removed from the desk, even temporarily, to attend a development activity, it gives that person breathing room and a chance to reflect on what has happened. The sessions are intended to provide new insights into desk service and new ways of coping with stress by improving knowledge, skills, or attitudes.

Organizational Responses

"The organizational costs of burnout are high. Lost motivation, increased staff turnover, poor delivery of services, increased employee theft, increased tardiness, and greater absenteeism all result in significant indirect costs to organizations."[81] Luckily, the organization has a variety of ways to prevent burnout and to help combat it once it has developed.

Managerial Decisions

The library reference manager can take control of some of the issues that contribute to stress and burnout. By establishing an atmosphere of support and trust, by balancing the kinds of service activities in which reference librarians are engaged, and by establishing service standards and policies and communicating them effectively, the reference department head can help keep burnout from developing. Once burnout has occurred, the department head can change job assignments or institute cross-training to change the environment in which the burnout was initiated.

Developing trust. Janette Caputo identifies "a high level of mutual trust"[82] as the single most important facet to the effective supervisory relationship in terms of burnout prevention. "Supervisors who see themselves as trainers or coaches have the best success in counteracting burnout, as they encourage individual growth and development and open the door for group applications of theoretical knowledge to practical situations."[83] Individuals with good support systems with colleagues develop better coping mechanisms.

Balancing activities. Supervisors can keep reference desk hours at a reasonable level, minimizing excessive contact with the public. Reference managers need to respond when demands are high. Joanne Bessler suggests using a "floater" position to assist in areas with higher workloads, identifying low-priority work that can be deferred or eliminated, and creating a team that can work across units when needed.[84]

Service statements. Department heads can develop reference service policy statements that recognize reasonable limits to service that librarians are expected to provide. "When training staff to apply policies, you should also prepare staff for likely challenges and exceptions. Discussing exceptions at staff meetings is helpful. A staff member who knows why a policy was written and how it has been interpreted is well-prepared to make a reasonable judgement."[85] Explicitly stating to staff at all levels when rules can be modified in providing help to users is important in defining levels of empowerment. For example, volunteers or student staff members who work very limited schedules may not have the comprehensive understanding of overall library operations to be able to judge special user requests, but nonsupervisory staff may be able to bend policies within certain guidelines.

Redesigning a job. Managers can redesign the content of a job through job rotation or exchange or can provide assignments that allow individuals to gain authority, personal achievement, recognition, growth, responsibility, and advancement. They can encourage employees to undertake new and different assignments periodically to ensure that their jobs do not become too routine or lacking in challenge.[86] Staff development programs that help service providers see their job as playing a role for the organization can also provide concrete assistance with job burnout and stress.

Cross-training. "Cross-training is valuable because it helps employees become familiar with co-workers' contributions and get a better idea of how the institution works as a whole. In addition, cross-trained staff members can pinch-hit for each other when the need arises."[87] Lothar Spang states that "librarian participants have agreed that the cross-training opportunities have substantially improved their ability to provide accurate and convenient service to an increasingly cross-discipline user population."[88]

Staff Development

The goal of staff development is to improve the organization's effectiveness, or service to its users, by increasing the competence of its staff. Much of the training that has been discussed up to this point is encompassed by the term *staff development*; orientation and on-the-job training are certainly included. The library administration has a responsibility to improve staff performance, and it is to the library's benefit to produce employees who are committed to the library.

Merely providing the training for basic job skills is not enough. The library administration should provide continual training for reference librarians that develops and maintains competence, updates basic professional foundations, and introduces new concepts. Staff development should emphasize attitude shaping, people-handling skills, dealing with users' feelings, listening skills, and thinking on one's feet. "Given the scope and pace of present and prospective change, training, by itself, will not provide librarians with a satisfactory framework for new understandings, or the basis for responding to the changed environment."[89] An ongoing development program is necessary.

Libraries as Learning Organizations

Although individual learning is important, it needs to impact the overall organizational performance in order to have a long-range benefit. Although a particular individual may become an expert in a specific area, if that information and expertise are not shared with the organization, the organization will lose that expertise when the individual leaves. On the other hand, if individuals share this expertise in such a way that they train others, and the information learned is incorporated into organizational documentation, then the expertise remains in the organization after the individuals leave. Librarians who promote this kind of transfer of knowledge and expertise can call their libraries *learning organizations.*

A learning organization is one that has an enhanced capacity to learn, adapt, and change and is "skilled at creating, acquiring, and transferring knowledge and insights."[90] It is characterized by

- using information technology to inform and empower the many rather than the few;
- collaborating rather than competing, making comparisons of the organization's best practices with the practices of others;
- encouraging self-development opportunities for everyone in the organization and encouraging individuals to take responsibility for their own learning and development;
- exchanging information—getting closer to customers and suppliers; and
- using the people in contact with customers to bring back useful information about needs and opportunities.[91]

Personal Responses: Continuing Education

Individuals must also accept some of the responsibility for refueling the fire by planning their own continuing education activities. Continuing education activities center on the individual's personal interests and include those that promote personal development and growth as an individual, whether to increase personal job satisfaction or to prepare for a promotion. Continuing education includes learning experiences that will introduce new concepts and skills, update basic professional foundations, refresh or reemphasize aspects of professional training, provide additional competencies to make career advancement or change possible, and furnish individuals with an overview of their profession as a changing and evolving discipline.[92]

Charles Bunge discussed methods that reference librarians use to update their reference knowledge and skills. The most frequently mentioned strategy is reading professional literature, followed by reference staff meetings and staff sharing. He also mentioned attendance at conferences, workshops, and other meetings outside the individual's library as much-used methods for reference librarians.[93] One librarian has started a "journal club" in which individuals share what they have learned through professional reading. Another relies heavily on electronic bulletin boards, claiming that it is like "a professional conference online without the airfare."

Opportunities for continuing education originate from many different sources. Courses offered at local community colleges, colleges, or universities range from those in computer and software management to courses in supervisory and teaching skills to courses in subject-related topics that may or may not lead to an advanced degree. Outside groups, such as online database vendors, often offer basic and advanced training in the use of their software, with refresher courses and updates on specific databases. Library professional organizations make many contributions to continuing education for reference librarians. Local interest groups often provide forums for discussing mutual problems, challenges, and potential solutions with peers. State associations sponsor conferences, workshops, and programs in more convenient locations than many nationally sponsored programs. The American Library Association and associations of special groups provide numerous activities that can promote the individual reference librarian's development. As outlined in *Continuous Learning*,[94] a report to the ALA Executive Board, these opportunities include programs and exhibits at conferences, pre-conferences, regional and national institutes, chapters, traveling exhibits, teleconferences, publications, electronic discussion lists, Web sites, online courses, fax-on-demand, speakers' bureaus, and networking and mentoring. The report goes on to recommend that ALA become involved in post-master's certification programs, explore the development of a distance education service, establish a continuing education clearinghouse, enhance public programming, and build library roles in public education. See the *ALA Handbook of Organization* for the names of groups emphasizing staff development and continuing education.[95]

CONCLUSION

The results of a thorough and responsive training program that involves the staff in decision making and uses participatory educational methods will be a highly motivated staff who have high morale and good self-esteem, identify with their peers, cope with changes and stress, make fewer mistakes, and solve problems. On the other hand, unplanned on-the-job training may result in ill-trained, unmotivated employees, with the added danger that necessary skills may not be learned or that undesirable methods and approaches will be reinforced and low standards set. "Employees (new or old) learn, whether we wish it or not. If we are disorganized, indifferent, or sloppy in our approach, the employee will absorb the standards. No amount of future lecturing will erase these standards."[96]

The act of training itself motivates and builds employee confidence and self-esteem, regardless of the actual content of training. Training reduces stress and turnover, improves work relationships, and increases adaptability. Without training, reference librarians cannot keep up with change, develop expertise, or learn how to transfer what they already know to new environments.

Reference librarians are truly in the knowledge business, both on behalf of their users and for themselves. Librarians cannot help the users fulfill their information needs if they themselves are ignorant of the sources, lack the ability to access the information they know exists, or are unwilling to go that extra step to gain that knowledge and skills. A well-planned program of training, development, and continuing education will give the reference staff the tools they need to tackle the tasks at hand and strategies for approaching new problems as they arise.

NOTES

1.   Samuel Rothstein, "The Making of a Reference Librarian," *Library Trends* 31 (Winter 1983): 375–99.

2.   Marsha D. Broadway and Nathan M. Smith, "Basic Reference Courses in ALA-Accredited Library Schools," *The Reference Librarian* 25–26 (1989): 431–48.

3.   Ronald R. Powell and Douglas Raber, "Education for Reference/Information Service: A Quantitative and Qualitative Analysis of Basic Reference Courses," simultaneously co-published in *The Reference Librarian* 43 (1994): 145–72, and *Reference Services Planning in the 90s*, ed. Gail A. Eckwright and Lori M. Keenan (Binghamton, NY: Haworth Press, 1993), 145–72.

4.   Loriene Roy, "Engaging LIS Students in Reference Work Through Online Answer Boards," *The Reference Librarian* 51, no. 2 (April/June 2010): 97–107.

5.   Michele M. Deputy, "A Study of Librarians' Attitudes towards the Reference Interview," ERIC Document 401919, December 1995, 42 pp.

6.   Julie Ann McDaniel and Judith K. Ohles, *Training Paraprofessionals for Reference Service*, How-to-Do-It Manual for Libraries, no. 30 (New York: Neal-Schuman, 1993), 1–5.

7.   Sheila D. Creth, *Effective On-the-Job Training: Developing Library Human Resources* (Chicago: American Library Association, 1986), 6.

8.   Leonard Nadler and Zeace Nadler, *Handbook of Human Resource Development*, 2nd ed. (New York: Wiley, 1990), 1.3.

9.   Suellyn Hunt, "A Structure and Seven-Step Process for Developing In-House Human Resources Programs," *Bookmark* 41 (Summer 1983): 227.

10.   Heartsill Young, ed., *The ALA Glossary of Library and Information Science* (Chicago: American Library Association, 1983), 214.

11.   Dorothy E. Jones, "I'd Like You to Meet Our New Librarian: The Initiation and Integration of the Newly Appointed Librarian," *Journal of Academic Librarianship* 14 (September 1988): 222.

12.   H. Scott Davis, *New Employee Orientation*, How-to-Do-It Manual for Libraries, no. 38 (New York: Neal-Schuman, 1994), v.

13.   Sandra Weingart, Carol A. Kochan, and Anne Hedrich, "Safeguarding Your Investment: Effective Orientation for New Employees," *Library Administration and Management* 12 (Summer 1998): 157.

14.   Angela Ballard and Laura Blessing, "Organizational Socialization through Employee Orientations at North Carolina State University Libraries," *College & Research Libraries* 67 (May 2006): 240.

15.   Weingart, Kochan, and Hedrich, "Safeguarding Your Investment," 157.

16.   Anne May Berwind, "Orientation for the Reference Desk," *Reference Services Review* 19 (Fall 1991): 51–54, 70.

17.   Joanne Oud, "Adjusting to the Workplace: Transitions Faced by New Academic Librarians," *College & Research Libraries* 69 (May 2008): 254.

18.   Linda A. Jerris, *Effective Employee Orientation* (New York: AMACOM, 1993), 3.

19.   Ibid., 6.

20.   Mary W. Oliver, "Orientation of New Personnel in the Law Library," *Law Library Journal* 65 (May 1972): 140.

21.   Susan Imel, "Guidelines for Working with Adult Learners," *ERIC Digest* 77 (1988), ERIC Document 2994546, http://www.ericdigests.org/pre-929/working.htm; and Malcolm Knowles, "Adult Learning," in *ASTD Training and Development Handbook: A Guide to Human Resource Management*, 4th ed., ed. Robert L. Craig (New York: McGraw-Hill, 1996), 253–56.

22.   Young, *ALA Glossary*, 231.

23.   F. J. Roethlisberger and W. J. Dick, *Management and the Worker* (Cambridge, MA: Harvard University Press, 1939), 522.

24.   Reference and User Services Association, Task Force on Professional Competencies, "Professional Competencies for Reference and User Services Librarians," *Reference & User Services Quarterly* 42 (Summer 2004): 290–95. http://www.ala.org/ala/mgrps/divs/rusa/re sources/guidelines/professional.cfm.

25.   Ibid.

26.   Virginia Massey-Burzio, "Education and Experience: Or, the MLS Is Not Enough," *Reference Services Review* 19 (Spring 1991): 73.

27.   Mary M. Nofsinger, "Training and Retraining Reference Professionals: Core Competencies for the 21st Century," co-published simultaneously in *The Reference Librarian* 61 (1999): 9–19, and *Coming of Age in Reference Services: A Case History of the Washington State University Libraries*, ed. Christy Zlatos (Binghamton, NY: Haworth Press, 1999), 9–19.

28.   For further discussion of areas of competency, see Anne F. Roberts, "Myth: Reference Librarians Can Perform at the Reference Desk Immediately upon Receipt of MLS. Reality: They Need Training Like Other Professionals," in *Academic Libraries: Myths and Realities. Proceedings of the Third National Conference of the Association of College and Research Libraries* (Chicago: ACRL, 1984), 402.

29.   See Geary A. Rummler, "Determining Needs," in *Training and Development Handbook*, 3rd ed., ed. Robert L. Craig (New York: McGraw-Hill, 1987), 217–47, for a discussion of alternative needs assessment techniques; and Mel Silberman, *Active Training: A Handbook of Techniques, Designs, Case Examples, and Tips* (Lexington, MA: Lexington Books, 1990), 16–19, for a list of advantages and disadvantages of nine basic needs assessment techniques.

30.   Barbara Conroy, "The Structured Group Interview: A Useful Tool for Needs Assessment and Evaluation," *Mountain Plains Journal of Adult Education* 4 (March 1976): 19.

31.   Creth, *Effective On-the-Job Training*, 31.

32.   Robert F. Mager, *Preparing Instructional Objectives*, 2nd ed. (Belmont, CA: Fearon Publishers, 1975), 21.

33.   John W. Newstrom, "Evaluating the Effectiveness of Training Methods," *Personnel Administrator* 25 (January 1980): 58.

34.   *WebJunction*. http://www.webjunction.org.

35.   Gwen Arthur, "Using Video for Reference Staff Training and Development: A Selective Bibliography," *Reference Services Review* 20 (Winter 1992): 63–68.

36.   Phillipa Dolphin, "Interpersonal Skill Training for Library Staff," *Library Association Record* 88 (March 1986): 134.

37.   Julian M. Isaacs, "In-Service Training for Reference Work," *Library Association Record* 71 (October 1969): 301.

38.   Donald A. Schön, *Educating the Reflective Practitioner: Toward a New Design for Teaching and Learning in the Professions* (San Francisco: Jossey-Bass Publishers, 1987), 92.

39.   Dolphin, "Interpersonal Skill Training for Library Staff," 134.

40.   The following sources are extremely useful: Chip R. Bell, "Criteria for Selecting Instructional Strategies," *Training and Development Journal* 31 (October 1977): 3–7; Vernon S. Gerlach and Donald P. Ely, *Teaching and Media: A Systematic Approach*, 2nd ed. (Englewood Cliffs, NJ: Prentice Hall, 1980), 420 pp.; John W. Newstrom, "Selecting Training Methodologies: A Contingency Approach," *Training and Development Journal* 29 (October 1975): 12–16; William R. Tracey, *Designing Training and Development Systems*, 3rd rev. ed. (New York: AMACOM, 1992), 532 pp.; and Marilla D. Svinicki and Barbara A. Schwartz, *Designing Instruction for Library Users: A Practical Guide* (New York: Marcel Dekker, 1988), 249 pp.

41.   Barbara Bandys, Joan Daghita, and Susan Whitmore, "Raising the Bar or Training Technicians to Assume Reference Responsibilities," paper presented at the Special Libraries Association Conference, Los Angeles, CA, June 9–12, 2002. http://www.sla.org/content/Events/conference/2002annual/confpap2002/papers2002conf.cfm.

42.   Neil Rackham, "The Coaching Controversy," *Training and Development Journal* 33 (November 1979): 14.

43.   Ibid.

44.   Susan N. Chellino and Richard J. Walker, "Merging Instructional Technology with Management Practices," in *Strengthening Connections between Education and Performance*, ed. Stanley M. Grabowski (San Francisco: Jossey-Bass Publishers, 1983), 12.

45.   Janet Sheets, "Role Playing as Training Tool for Reference Student Assistants," *Reference Services Review* 26 (Spring 1998): 37–41.

46.   James C. Georges, "Why Soft-Skills Training Doesn't Take," *Training* 25 (April 1988): 46.

47.   Charles K. West, James A. Farmer, and Phillip M. Wolff, *Instructional Design: Implications from Cognitive Science* (Englewood Cliffs, NJ: Prentice Hall, 1991), 58–92.

48.   Ron Zemke and John Gunkler, "28 Techniques for Transforming Training into Performance," *Training* 22 (April 1985): 62.

49.   Thomas W. Shaughnessy, "Staff Development in Libraries: Why It Frequently Doesn't Take," *Journal of Library Administration* 9 (1988): 7.

50.   Judith Mucci, "Videotape Self-Evaluation in Public Libraries: Experiments in Evaluating Public Service," *RQ* 16 (Fall 1976): 33.

51.   William F. Young, "Methods for Evaluating Reference Desk Performance," *RQ* 25 (Fall 1985): 73.

52.   Diane G. Schwartz and Dottie Eakin, "Reference Service Standards, Performance Criteria, and Evaluation," *Journal of Academic Librarianship* 12 (March 1986): 6; Mignon S. Adams and Blanche Judd, "Evaluating Reference Librarians Using Goal Analysis as a First Step," *The Reference Librarian* 11 (Fall/Winter 1984): 141.

53.   William F. Young, "Evaluating the Reference Librarian," *The Reference Librarian* 11 (Fall/Winter 1984): 123–24.

54.   Schwartz and Eakin, "Reference Services Standards," 4–8.

55.   Wisconsin Ohio Reference Evaluation Program. http://worep.library.kent.edu/.

56.   Donald L. Kirkpatrick, "Techniques for Evaluating Training Programs," *Training and Development Journal* 33 (June 1979): 78–92.

57.   A. C. Hamblin, *Evaluation and Control of Training* (London: McGraw-Hill, 1974), 8.

58.   Terry L. Weech and Herbert Goldhor, "Obtrusive Versus Unobtrusive Evaluation of Reference Service in Five Illinois Public Libraries: A Pilot Study," *The Library Quarterly* 51 (1982): 305–24.

59.   See Robert O. Brinkerhoff, "The Success Case: A Low-Cost, High Yield Evaluation," *Training and Development Journal* 37 (August 1983): 58–59, 61; and Sumru Erkut and Jacqueline P. Fields, "Focus Groups to the Rescue," *Training and Development Journal* 41 (October 1987): 74.

60.   Kirkpatrick, "Techniques for Evaluating Training Programs," 89.

61.   Donna E. Cromer and Andrea R. Testi, "Integrated Continuing Education for Reference Librarians," *Reference Services Review* 22 (Winter 1994): 51.

62.   Karla J. Block and Julia A. Kelly, "Integrating Informal Professional Development into the Work of Reference," *The Reference Librarian* 72 (2001): 207–17.

63.   Janette S. Caputo, *Stress and Burnout in Library Service* (Phoenix, AZ: Oryx Press, 1991), 134.

64.   Nina Stephensen and Deborah J. Willis, "Internet In-Service Training at the University of New Mexico General Library," simultaneously co-published in *The Reference Librarian* 41/42 (1994): 211–14 and *Librarians on the Internet: Impact of Reference Services*, ed. Robin Kinder (Binghamton, NY: Haworth Press, 1994), 211–14.

65.   Giesecke and McNeil, "Core Competencies," 158.

66.   Ron Force, "Planning Online Services for the 90s," simultaneously co-published in *The Reference Librarian* 43 (1994): 113 and *Reference Services Planning in the 90s*, ed. Gail A. Eckwright and Lori M. Keenan (Binghamton, NY: Haworth Press, 1994), 113.

67.   Charles A. Bunge, "Strategies for Updating Knowledge of Reference Resources and Techniques," *RQ* 21 (Spring 1982): 228.

68.   Nofsinger, "Training and Retraining," 15.

69.   Julie Parry, "Continuing Professional Development," in *Staff Development in Academic Libraries: Present Practice and Future Challenge*, ed. Margaret Oldroyd (London: Library Association Publishing, 1996), 23.

70.   Tina Roose, "Stress at the Reference Desk," *Library Journal* 114 (September 1, 1989): 166.

71.   Dan Marmion, "Facing the Challenge: Technology Training in Libraries," *Information Technology & Libraries* 17 (December 1998): 216–18.

72.   Force, "Planning Online Services," 112–13.

73.   Elizabeth W. Stone, "Towards a Learning Community," in *Continuing Education for the Library Information Professions*, ed. William G. Asp et al. (Hamden, CT: Library Professional Publications, 1985), 65.

74.   See Anna M. Donnelly, "Reference Environment," *The Reference Assessment Manual* (Ann Arbor, MI: Pierian Press, 1995), 47–50.

75.   Tina Roose, "Stress at the Reference Desk," 167.

76.   See the following articles for discussions of burnout in librarians: Mary Haack, John W. Jones, and Tina Roose, "Occupational Burnout among Librarians," *Drexel Library Quarterly* 20 (Spring 1984): 46–72; William Miller, "What's Wrong with Reference: Coping with Success and Failure at the Reference Desk," *American Libraries* 15 (May 1984): 303–6, 321–22;

Sandra H. Neville, "Job Stress and Burnout: Occupational Hazards for Service Staff," *College & Research Libraries* 42 (May 1981): 242–47; David S. Ferriero and Kathleen A. Powers, "Burnout at the Reference Desk," *RQ* 21 (Spring 1982): 274–79; Nathan M. Smith and Veneese C. Nelson, "Burnout: A Survey of Academic Reference Librarians," *College & Research Libraries* 44 (May 1983): 245–50; Nathan M. Smith, Nancy E. Birch, and Maurice Marchant, "Stress, Distress, and Burnout: A Survey of Public Reference Librarians," *Public Libraries* 23 (Fall 1984): 83–85; and Pamela A. Rose, Kristin Stoklosa, and Sharon A. Gray, "A Focus Group Approach to Assessing Technostress at the Reference Desk," 311–17.

77.   Caputo, *Stress and Burnout*, 59.

78.   Miller, "What's Wrong with Reference," 303.

79.   Charles Bunge, "Potential and Reality at the Reference Desk: Reflections on a 'Return to the Field,'" *Journal of Academic Librarianship* 10 (July 1984): 131.

80.   John Kupersmith, "Technostress and the Reference Librarian," *Reference Services Review* 20 (Summer 1992): 7–14; Connie Van Fleet and Danny P. Wallace, "Virtual Libraries—Real Threats: Technostress and Virtual Reference," *Reference & User Services Quarterly* 42 (2003): 188–91; Lisa A. Ennis, "The Evolution of Technostress," *Computers in Libraries* 25 (2005): 10–12; Terence K. Huwe, "Running to Stand Still?," *Computers in Libraries* 25 (2005): 34–36; and Henry DuBois and Lesley Farmer, "Technology Impact on Reference and Information Services Staffing," in *The Human Side of Reference and Information Services in Academic Libraries: Adding Value in the Digital World*, ed. Lesley S. J. Farmer (Oxford: Chandos Publishing, 2007), 19–32.

81.   Caputo, *Stress and Burnout*, 32.

82.   Ibid., 136.

83.   Ibid.

84.   Bessler, *Putting Service into Library Staff Training*, 33.

85.   Ibid., 38.

86.   Samuel T. Huang, "The Impact of New Library Technology on Reference Services," *Illinois Libraries* 72 (November 1990): 601–2.

87.   Weingart, Kochan, and Hedrich, "Safeguarding Your Investment," 157.

88.   Lothar Spang, "A Staff-Generated Cross-Training Plan for Academic Reference Librarians: The TQM Approach at Wayne State University Libraries," *Reference Services Review* 24 (Summer 1996): 84.

89.   Howard Harris, "Retraining Librarians to Meet the Needs of the Virtual Library Patron," *Information Technology & Libraries* 15 (March 1996): 48.

90.   David Garvin, "Building a Learning Organization," *Harvard Business Review* 70 (July/August 1993): 80.

91.   Harris, "Retraining Librarians," 51.

92.   Stone, "Towards a Learning Community," 62.

93.   Bunge, "Strategies for Updating Knowledge," 229–31.

94.   *Continuous Learning: A Report to the ALA Executive Board* (photocopy), Summer 1998, 7 pp.

95.   *ALA Handbook of Organization* (Chicago: American Library Association, annual). http://www.ala.org/ala/aboutala/governance/handbook/index.cfm.

96.   Gordon F. Shea, *The New Employee: Developing a Productive Human Resource* (Reading, MA: Addison-Wesley, 1981), 61.

ADDITIONAL READINGS

Allan, Ann, and Kathy J. Reynolds. "Performance Problems: A Model for Analysis and Resolution." *Journal of Academic Librarianship* 9 (May 1983): 83–88. Reprinted in *Performance Evaluation: A Management Basic for Librarians*, ed. Jonathan A. Lindsey,
198–208. Phoenix, AZ: Oryx Press, 1986.

Often, problems with performance are wrongly attributed to training. Allan and Reynolds
describe a flowchart for identifying appropriate solutions to performance problems in libraries. A series of questions helps identify major issues such as environmental issues
that might impact performance.

Allan, Barbara. *Developing Information and Library Staff through Work-Based Learning: 101
Activities.* London: Library Association Publishing, 1999. 191 pp.

"Work-based learning may involve *learning at work* as well as *learning through work*"
(p. 5). Techniques used on the job—such as structured learning in the workplace and
on-the-job training/learning opportunities—complement short courses and gaining academic and/or vocational qualifications. Activities identified as work-based include information discussions with colleagues, taking an active part in staff meetings, giving talks
to groups outside the library profession, visiting other libraries, writing guides/aids for
users, reading library literature, attending conferences and meetings, receiving in-service
training, coaching, mentoring, job rotation, guided reading, and group work.

Auster, Ethel, and Donna C. Chan. "Reference Librarians and Keeping Up-to-Date: A Question of Priorities." *Reference & User Services Quarterly* 44 (Fall 2004): 57–66.

The authors studied the professional development activities of reference librarians in
large urban public libraries in Ontario, finding that most were consciously developing
and updating their technological skills, about half were updating communication and interpersonal skills, and smaller portions were improving instructional and management
skills. No respondents mentioned problem-solving and analytical skills as topics of professional development activities. The authors found that librarians typically spent 3 days
a year in formal professional development activities and about 31 days a year in informal activities. Deterrents to participation were studied, and the most significant ones
were inconvenient scheduling or lack of information, as well as the perceptions of the
library environment as not encouraging of information sharing and innovation. The authors suggest that librarians need to take more responsibility for their own professional
development.

Avery, Elizabeth Fuseler, Terry Dahlin, and Deborah A. Carver. *Staff Development: A Practical Guide.* 3rd ed. Chicago: Library Administration and Management Association, 2001.
194 pp.

This is a step-by-step guide for customizing a staff development program that is both proactive and goal-oriented. Drawing on the advice of 37 top experts with a variety of skill
sets, this work provides assistance in assessing the library's needs and setting training
goals, budgeting appropriately, developing a set of core competencies, and mapping out
a program specifically for a particular setting.

Ballard, Angela, and Laura Blessing. "Organizational Socialization through Employee Orientations in North Carolina State University Libraries." *College & Research Libraries* 67
(May 2006): 240–48.

Ballard and Blessing discuss the importance to the organization of including socialization in the employee orientation program. This particular program has three components:

(1) orientation sessions that encourage participation in sharing knowledge about work in other departments, overview of computing environment, tours of the building and units, a safety presentation, and exploration of the mission and vision statement of the organization; (2) orientation checklists; and (3) one-on-one meetings with appropriate personnel.

Bessler, Joanne M. *Putting Service into Library Staff Training*. LAMA Occasional Papers Series. Chicago: American Library Association, 1994. 72 pp.

This guide aims to help library managers teach staff in all areas of library work—public, technical, and administrative services—the attitudes and skills to make their library a service-oriented organization. Developing a mission statement, recruiting employees with service attitudes, preparing staff to give quality service through orientation and continuous training, and empowering staff are areas addressed.

Davis, H. Scott. *New Employee Orientation*. How-to-Do-It Manuals for Libraries, no. 38. New York: Neal-Schuman, 1994. 144 pp.

The author, a practicing librarian, wrote this book to fill a gap in the professional literature by providing a practical guide to the process of effectively orienting new library employees. A menu of program options and activities is presented. Included are good examples of gathering staff suggestions through surveys, brainstorming, and focus groups for determining the content of and need for orientation. Davis includes an excellent section on anticipating and handling problems such as ineffective participants, short notice, dropouts, resistance, and mismatching of mentors. Some examples from the Indiana State University mentor orientation program are included as a model. Some noteworthy suggestions include creating a glossary of common library terms and abbreviations and maintaining a staff photo album. Participant input is suggested as of primary importance in the evaluation phase.

Ennis, Lisa A. "The Evolution of Technostress." *Computers in Libraries* 25 (September 2005): 10–12.

Ennis updates the literature review she conducted in 1996, which pointed to six primary causes of technostress: pace of change, lack of training, increased workload, lack of standardization, reliability of technology, and the changing role of librarians. In her subsequent study she measured those six aspects using a Likert scale. Of those six causes, the pace of change and lack of standardization appeared the most stressful. She additionally found that stress also came from the level of technological expertise expected of librarians and the gap between what users expected and what librarians could deliver. The coping strategies identified from 1996 are still valid, and she also includes observations of the past 10 years in the field.

Hirko, Buff, and Mary Bucher Ross. *Virtual Reference Training : The Complete Guide to Providing Anytime, Anywhere Answers*. Chicago: American Library Association, 2004. 168 pp.

This practical and hands-on approach to creating training for virtual reference includes guidance in developing curricula, assessment tools, and enjoyable learning activities.

Katz, Bill, ed. "Continuing Education of Reference Librarians." *The Reference Librarian* 30 (1990): 1–273.

This issue of *The Reference Librarian* covers a range of topics concerning training and continuing education of librarians. Several articles stress the need for adaptability and critical thinking skills.

LearningExchange. Quarterly newsletter of the American Library Association Learning Round Table. http://alalearning.org/about/learning-exchange-newletter/.

This newsletter provides reviews of training books, summaries of training workshops, and helpful training tips.

Massis, Bruce E. *The Practical Library Trainer*. Binghamton, NY: Haworth Press, 2004. 122 pp.

This text examines types of staff training, strategies for recruiting and retaining staff, online training, in-house training, how to use professional conferences as continuing education opportunities, and evaluation of training programs.

Messas, Kostas. *Staff Training and Development*. SPEC Kit 224. Washington, D.C.: Association for Research Libraries, 1997. 199 pp.

This survey examines the state of formal staff training and development programs in Association of Research Libraries (ARL) institutions, finding that only 56 percent of the 50 respondents had such a program in place. The most frequently used formats are small group discussions and on-site workshops, followed by off-site workshops, videotapes and films, and lectures. This SPEC Kit includes the best representative supporting documents and materials from the survey, including mission statements, guidelines, needs assessments, training activities, training course catalogs, and evaluations. Another valuable feature is a good bibliography of library staff training materials written since 1990.

Morgan, Pamela J. *Training Paraprofessionals for the Reference Desk*. 2nd ed. New York: Neal-Schuman, 2009. 201 pp.

Revised to reflect the changes in reference service in the past 15 years, this new edition offers guidance in training paraprofessional staff to use both print and electronic resources to handle questions as frontline staff. Training modules include some more specialized areas such as government information, corporate information, statistics, and medical and health information.

Nofsinger, Mary M., and Angela S. W. Lee. "Beyond Orientation: The Roles of Senior Librarians in Training Entry-Level Reference Colleagues." *College & Research Libraries* 55 (March 1994): 161–70.

The authors suggest that more experienced staff members can play four vital roles in training entry-level reference librarians: as teachers or coaches, as interpreters or advisors for the institution's culture, as role models for interpersonal skills and cooperation among professional colleagues, and as mentors in professional development.

Todaro, Julie, and Mark L. Smith. *Training Library Staff and Volunteers to Provide Extraordinary Customer Service*. New York: Neal-Schuman, 2006. 160 pp.

Todaro and Smith focus on the specific concerns that libraries have about customer service that are different than those of for-profit organizations. They emphasize the need to create a framework for gathering customer feedback and building a system of continuous learning.

Tracey, William R. *Designing Training and Development Systems*. 3rd ed. New York: AMACOM, 1992. 532 pp.

This lengthy and detailed overview of every conceivable aspect of training is particularly useful for writing objectives, selecting appropriate media, and constructing evaluative instruments.

Evaluation of Reference Services

Chapter

10

Jo Bell Whitlatch

INTRODUCTION

To evaluate means to establish the value or worth of the service. Concepts often used in discussions of evaluation of reference services are reference service quality, reference service effectiveness, and assessment of reference services. Evaluating reference services is a complex art because there is no simple or single answer to the question of how to best assess the value of reference services. Assessments of reference service depend on values, and values are subjective. Effective evaluation requires understanding the importance of defining and establishing which values are going to drive the assessment project.

The appropriate role of evaluation of reference is often misunderstood by reference practitioners. Reference librarians often believe that their job is just to answer reference questions to the best of their ability. Evaluation can often be perceived as threatening because it may be linked to individual performance, with the results affecting promotion or compensation. Thus, front-line reference librarians often come to believe that evaluation is something that managers should do, not reference librarians. Or reference librarians sometimes feel that only library school faculty with a PhD have the skill set to do evaluation of services.

However, evaluation in today's rapidly evolving information society is the job of all librarians who wish to call themselves professionals. "Most professionals routinely ask themselves, 'Am I giving quality service?' The concern for quality is generally considered a mark of professionalism."[1] For professionals, evaluation must be an integral part of daily practice and may be as simple as reflecting on the process of answering a reference question. How could I have given an answer that provided more value to the user? Did I take the time to conduct an interview to be certain that I understood exactly what information the person needed? Did I ask a follow-up question to ensure that the person was satisfied with the information received? Or, if the reference service was too busy at the time to do more than get the user started, did I encourage that user to return? Should I have consulted with a colleague with more expertise in the subject area and followed up with a phone call or e-mail to the user?

At its most basic level, evaluation can be continual self-assessment and reflection of quality of answers and service process as part of ongoing professional practice. Self-assessment practices are important in building a culture of assessment in an organization. Formal evaluation programs of services in a library by reference practitioners are more easily undertaken when all reference librarians view evaluation as an integral part of being a professional.

This chapter discusses the fundamentals of designing and implementing evaluation plans for reference services in an individual library setting and provides a general overview of evaluation principles, methods, and techniques. Other chapters in this text that cover instruction (chapter 8) and selection and evaluation of resources (chapter 13) discuss evaluation in the context of those topics.

WHY EVALUATE REFERENCE?

In the private sector, a major impetus for evaluation is survival and growth. For example, for-profit service organizations, such as bookstores, attract customers through providing more value than their competition. Historically, in the public sector, the notion of competition is more difficult to appreciate because government utilities have most frequently been the sole provider of unique services, which are viewed as a "public good." However, changes in technology have made it possible for private information vendors to compete in significant ways with publicly funded libraries, by providing easily accessible information sources and services.[2] Public institutions must therefore evaluate their effectiveness to remain competitive and retain public support.

Rapid changes in technology have also been accompanied by an environment of very limited public funding for many competing public services, such as police, fire, welfare, medical care, and education. Organizations in the public sector can no longer rely on stable funding for services. Services now need to demonstrate added value to the community and to potential donors if they are to retain a reasonable share of available funds.

Taxpayers, library users, and potential donors must be able to see the evidence of the value of reference services to the community. If the value of reference services cannot be established through the collection and presentation of evaluations that demonstrate added value, the personal reference service provided by librarians could cease to exist. The methods of evaluation discussed in this chapter can provide the type of evidence that will convince funders to make adequate resources available.

THE ROLE OF STANDARDS IN REFERENCE EVALUATION

Evaluating reference service requires assessing performance against a standard. One of the fundamental questions that reference evaluators must ask at the beginning of the planning process is, "What standard or standards should be used to measure the effectiveness of reference service?" Good examples of standards that address all aspects of digital reference service are *Facets of Quality for Digital Reference Services* (http://www.webjunction.org/quality-standards/) by the Virtual Reference Desk, the Reference and User Services Association (RUSA) *Guidelines for Implementing and Maintaining Virtual Reference Services* (http://www.ala.org/ala/mgrps/divs/rusa/resources/guidelines/virtrefguidelines.cfm), and the *IFLA Digital Reference Guidelines* (http://www.ifla.org/en/publications/ifla-digital-reference-guidelines).

Four different categories of standards can be used to assess reference service effectiveness. Each of the categories represents a different set of values. One category consists of economic assessments, which use productivity or efficiency as the main value to determine reference effectiveness. A performance standard related to productivity might be the following: Reference librarians should answer a minimum of 10 reference questions per hour.

Another category of standards is related to the ability to acquire valued resources. Following is an example of a performance standard for resources: Reference librarians should be able to identify and locate adequate resources for immediate use for 80 percent of user queries.

A third category of standards concerns quality of outcomes. A classic performance standard in this area would be the following: Reference librarians should provide accurate and complete information for 80 percent of all user queries.

The fourth category of standards involves assessments of the reference process. This is the area for which most standards have been developed. Process measures have received the most attention partly because the practicing librarian has some control over behavioral process measures, and users are often more able to judge the process than the outcomes, such as the accuracy of the information provided. Good examples of standards that focus largely on process include the following:

- QuestionPoint *Global Reference Network Member Guidelines*, http://www.questionpoint.org/policies/memberguidelines.html. The policies Web page also has some additional information useful in formulating standards: http://www.questionpoint.org/policies/index.html.
- *RUSA Guidelines for Behavioral Performance of Reference and Information Service Providers*, http://www.ala.org/ala/mgrps/divs/rusa/resources/guidelines/guidelinesbehavioral.cfm.
- *RUSA Professional Competencies for Reference and User Services Librarians*, http://www.ala.org/ala/mgrps/divs/rusa/resources/guidelines/profesional.cfm.
- Washington Statewide Virtual Reference Project's *Core Competencies for Virtual Reference*, http://66.212.65.207/textdocs/vrscompetencies.pdf.

Standards must be very specific statements so that they can serve as yardsticks to measure success. If the standards are vague, general goals, a librarian will have no way to measure the degree to which a standard has been achieved. Thus, "providing high-quality reference services to users," belongs in the reference mission statement because it does not meet the criteria for a standard. On the other hand, "providing correct and complete answers to 80 percent of all factual queries" is an excellent example

---

BOX 10.1
SELECTING APPROPRIATE STANDARDS FOR REFERENCE EVALUATION

The university library has been asked to work with instructors, who have been developing online courses, to provide an integrated model of library services as part of each course. The team of librarians who will develop the proposal have agreed that personal reference assistance should be part of the service and that the success of reference assistance should be evaluated. What standards will be best for evaluating reference assistance to online courses, which will be offered through chat and e-mail? The RUSA *Guidelines for Implementing and Maintaining Virtual Reference Services* (http://www.ala.org/ala/mgrps/divs/ rusa/resources/guidelines/virtrefguidelines.cfm) state that "evaluation of the virtual reference service should be equivalent to and part of a library's regular evaluation of all its reference services" (4.6.3), yet the *Guidelines* also note that "the absence of a physically present patron and the different modes of communication may call for additional skills, effort, or training to provide quality service on par with face-to-face reference services" (3.3.1). What standards should the team recommend in order to measure the success of reference services provided to the online courses?

---

of a standard that is specific and useful for measuring the degree of success achieved in meeting the standard.

WHAT TO EVALUATE

Reference services are defined as personal assistance given by library staff to users seeking information. Reference services can be delivered in person or virtually from a remote location, using telephone, e-mail, or live chat. Thus, evaluating reference is fundamentally about assessing the effectiveness of the process of providing reference service to users. Many elements influence the success of reference service. Figure 10.1 illustrates the major factors that influence the nature of the reference service. All of these factors should be studied in order to obtain a complete understanding of reference service effectiveness.

Because reference service is so complex, evaluators can become overwhelmed with choices, fail to focus, and fall into the common trap of designing a study with data collection requirements that are too labor intensive. The RUSA *Guidelines for Information Services* (http://www.ala.org/ala/mgrps/divs/rusa/resources/guidelines/ guidelinesinformation.cfm) includes a section on evaluation, which recommends emphasizing the factors that are most important to the local community, including response time, accessibility of services, value and effectiveness of services for various groups, and effectiveness in anticipating the community's needs.

Inputs <·····················>	Process <·····················>	Outputs/Outcomes
Quality of Information Resources	User/ Staff Interaction	Quality of Answers
Communication	Quality of Process Librarian and Staff	As Perceived by
Competencies		Users and/or Staff
– knowledge	In Person	
– skills	Telephone	Value Added to
– abilities	Email	User Knowledge
	Live Chat	Base
Quality of Technology		Quality of End
Support		User Project
Building Orientation		Enhancement in
– signage		User Information
– arrangement of		Competencies
– services		
– ease of use		
User Competencies		
– knowledge		
– skills		
– abilities		

Figure 10.1. Factors influencing reference service quality.

The primary focus of this chapter is evaluating reference services that librarians provide to users. Thus, the perspective these studies take is that of the user within the context of existing library reference services. However, in discussing what to evaluate, it is important to look beyond present library services and to consider conducting evaluation studies that focus on the information-seeking patterns and behaviors of people in the library community. Evaluation of existing library services tends to address the question of how good the existing reference services are, whereas studies with an information-seeking perspective are better at addressing questions relating to whether libraries are offering the right type of reference services to the most important community constituencies. The information-seeking perspective is particularly important in attracting special populations of users that the library wishes to serve, such as children, youth, the elderly, people with disabilities, and ethnic populations in the community (see chapter 12 for a discussion of developing services to meet the needs of these specific populations).

Evaluation does require staff time. The time and money invested in evaluation should have definite benefits. All evaluation should be designed to improve services.

If evaluation results do not have the potential to enhance services, the resources may be better used to meet other library needs. However, failure to evaluate reference services means that services are unlikely to realize their potential for success. Continuing improvement of services requires not only planning and implementing services but also obtaining systematic information on successes and failures through evaluation. Without systematic and ongoing evaluation, library staff will never have the opportunity to obtain systematic information so essential for continuing growth and development of the reference service.

Evaluation can focus primarily on inputs to the reference process, such as the quality of the reference collections; the quality of building signage, layout, and organization of the reference desk; or ease of use of the Web site to locate reference assistance. Or evaluation can emphasize the process of the interaction between the librarian and the user. For example, this could include the librarian and/or user behaviors associated with success in locating information. Finally, evaluation may focus primarily on the outputs or outcomes of the transaction. Was the user satisfied with the process and/or the information received? What value did the information add in the context of the life of the user?

Over time, the inputs, process, and outputs should be assessed. One very good diagnostic instrument for getting started is the Wisconsin Ohio Reference Evaluation Program (WOREP, https://worep.library.kent.edu). For traditional reference desk services and phone queries, this instrument collects information from both the user and the librarian on sources used; process elements, such as librarian courtesy; and outputs, such as user satisfaction with the information provided. Results can be compared with those of similar institutions and used to set desirable performance standards. Staff with little experience in evaluation can gain good experience in planning and administering this reliable and valid instrument. Results can also suggest the most profitable areas for additional in-depth study.

EVALUATION METHODS

Four methods of collecting data are useful in evaluating reference services: surveys and questionnaires, observation, focus groups and interviews, and case studies. Each of these methods has strengths and weaknesses. When time and budget permit, combining more than one method produces more reliable results.

Although the delivery of reference services is shifting from heavy reliance on traditional in-person assistance at the reference desk to delivery through a greater range of methods, especially e-mail and live chat, the standard research methods can be utilized very effectively in an electronic environment.[3] Although the manner of applying the methods often changes in the electronic environment, surveys and questionnaires, observation, focus groups and interviews, and case studies remain the standard tools for evaluating the effectiveness of the service.

Surveys or Questionnaires

Surveys or questionnaires are best when an evaluator wants to study people's attitudes and opinions on fairly well-defined topics. Surveys are not the best method

BOX 10.2
EVALUATING REFERENCE TRANSACTIONS

The university reference department has received a number of comments from faculty in history, English, biology, and chemistry that students have not been receiving the help that they needed with their assignments at the reference desk. The reference department head has many responsibilities for collection management and instructional programs in addition to reference services, so she does not work at the reference desk and has had little opportunity to observe the reference librarians interacting with students. Because of the complaints, the dean of the library has told her that she must design an evaluation of reference desk service effectiveness. What methods will provide her with the best evaluative information to help diagnose reasons for the faculty dissatisfaction with the service and to find possible solutions—unobtrusive evaluation, direct evaluation, user surveys, surveys of reference librarians, interviews of students and/or librarians, or focus groups? How should she deal with issues related to the fact that the reference librarians might feel threatened and defensive when told that they must conduct an evaluation of their service because of the faculty complaints?

for studying behavior. People's responses to a survey may not match their actual behavior. For example, on a survey users may respond that they can seldom find materials in the library, but when actually observed, they may find about 60 percent of all materials that they originally sought.

Surveys can collect information from a large number of people and are the most efficient method of obtaining information from a large and representative sample of users. However, surveys appear deceptively simple to design. In reality, difficult questions must be addressed, such as organizing the responses by mutually exclusive categories and minimizing errors resulting from the inaccuracy of people's responses because of ignorance, illiteracy, social bias, time pressures, inaccurate recall, and errors in recording of information. Marjorie Murfin and Gary Gugelchuk's article[4] on designing the WOREP contains an excellent discussion of the problems associated with designing questions, especially the use of overly broad general-satisfaction questions and using single questions to measure complex concepts such as satisfaction. Because surveys and questionnaires are very difficult to design, libraries should use a questionnaire already tested for validity and reliability or work with an expert who has experience in designing and administering surveys.

Follow-up surveys of user perceptions of the success of reference service have some advantages over surveys administered at the reference desk immediately after the user has received the information. E-mailing the questionnaire can be timed to give individuals some time to incorporate the information into their projects and better judge the actual value of the information provided. However, Internet surveys may yield a lower response rate than an immediate request for feedback from the user.

BOX 10.3
EVALUATING REFERENCE COLLECTIONS

The head of a public library reference department has observed that fewer users are consulting books in the reference collection. A survey of reference collection use in the past year shows that only 1 out of every 10 books in the reference collection was used. Reference librarians in the department have various theories on why use is declining. The most popular explanations are that business people have quit coming to the library because they think everything is available through Google; no one in the community is interested in using print materials anymore; users of the library have changed, and the reference department is collecting the wrong types of print materials; and the reference collection needs weeding and would be used more heavily if people could find the most current materials more easily. Identify some methods that could be used to study why use of the reference collection is declining. Discuss the strengths and weaknesses of user surveys, observation methods, and interviews in collecting data to discover why reference collection use is falling and what the public library should do to enhance use of the reference collection.

Observation

Observation is most useful in studying behavior. Common types of observation that have been used in studying the reference process are direct observation (when users and librarians know that someone is observing them), observers disguised as library users (unobtrusive observation), self-observation (e.g., keeping diaries or journals of activities), reference interview recordings and/or videos, and physical traces in books (i.e., use is recorded if the paper is moved).

Observation can provide biased results if the observer is not objective. Observers also need to be certain not to interrupt the regular activities of librarians and users. However, observation can still be a very valuable complement to a well-designed survey. Studies of use of the reference collection generally involve observation.[5] Reference cost studies also have included collection of observational data.[6]

The most extensive use of observation in evaluating reference services has been unobtrusive studies. Unobtrusive testing eliminates possible bias because the effect of being tested cannot influence the normal behavior of the librarian. Unobtrusive studies take time to design and administer. Test questions must be representative of the level of difficulty and range of questions typically received at the libraries under study. In addition, test questions take substantial time to formulate and test. Peter Hernon and Charles McClure[7] provide detailed guidance on unobtrusive testing.

The electronic environment offers new and exciting opportunities for using observational techniques in evaluating reference services.[8] E-mail and chat interactions provide a written transcript of the user and staff interaction, unlike in-person queries. These transcripts can be sampled and the content analyzed to determine the quality of services in relation to predetermined performance standards. The ease of collecting such information has raised concerns about protecting the privacy of both users and librarians.

BOX 10.4
USING REFERENCE STATISTICS IN EVALUATION

The public library reference department has kept statistics on the reference and directional/information questions asked by all users for the past year. The reference staff has used the statistics to study the busy and slow times at the reference desk and to attempt to match reference desk staffing with the patterns that have emerged. However, reference staff would like to use the statistics to evaluate the quality of the services provided. How could the reference librarians collect statistics that could be used to assess the quality of the services and go beyond just simply using the statistics to adjust staffing levels at the reference desk?

BOX 10.5
REFERENCE SERVICES IN A JOINT-USE LIBRARY

The president of the university and the mayor of the city have agreed to offer library services in a combined public and academic library building. At present, both the university and the city have different libraries, but it is clear that both library organizations are going to be in the same library building within a couple of years. The library directors need to determine how services will be organized and delivered to the various user groups in the new library. One of the most controversial areas is offering combined reference services. City reference librarians believe that an important part of the service is to actually provide the information that the user wants, not just tell the user how to find it. On the other hand, university reference librarians are very focused on information literacy and believe that it is important that students learn how to find information on their own once the reference librarian has provided some general instruction. What types of studies could these two libraries conduct to determine whether they ought to offer combined reference services for both the university and the city communities? What evaluation methods might be most helpful in determining whether combined reference services will provide the most effective services to both community members and students in the new city/university library?

When transcripts are archived and sampled, identities of the individuals participating in the transaction should be removed in order to ensure that privacy is respected.

Interviews and Focus Groups

Interviews and focus groups provide a very rich source of data to those who want to understand how library users view libraries through their experiences, perspectives,

---

BOX 10.6
EVALUATING SERVICES FOR SPECIFIC POPULATIONS

A proud public library tradition in this eastern U.S. community has been the role of the library in assisting immigrant populations in achieving success in their new country. Waves of immigrants from Germany, Norway, England, Ireland, Scotland, and Italy have valued the library as a place of independent learning that supplements their formal educational opportunities. In the past decade, new groups of immigrants have started to settle in the area, including many Hmong from Southeast Asia and Latinos from several Central and South American countries. The reference staff has noted that few of the new immigrant populations are using the library. The few people from these new immigrant populations who are using the library are definitely not using reference services. A major focus of the library is devoted to serving immigrant populations, and the new public library director wants to increase the use of the library by this group and has turned to the reference staff to develop an action plan for outreach to this population. What should the reference staff recommend in order to develop an effective plan of action that is likely to be successful in getting more of the new immigrants into the library and using the full range of library services?

---

thoughts, and feelings. Interviews can assist in interpreting both observational and survey data. They are also useful in the early stages of designing questionnaires, particularly in sharpening issues that evaluators wish to address in a questionnaire. Interviews can be either structured or unstructured. A structured interview is led by the interviewer, and questions are predetermined. Unstructured interviews are more exploratory in nature and often take the form of a free-flowing conversation between interviewer and interviewee around a broad general topic or theme.

Focus groups are a form of group interviewing that emphasizes the interaction between participants. The time and costs of organizing and conducting interviews limit interviewers to collecting information from relatively small numbers of people. Findings from focus groups may not apply to larger populations.

Focus groups and interviews are a particularly valuable method of identifying the information-seeking patterns and behaviors of special populations, such as children, youth, the elderly, people with disabilities, and ethnic populations. These populations are often difficult to understand using other research methods, partly because there may be a difference in language skills. Often these special populations are not well represented in the library profession, and therefore their perspectives on the value and need for library services may not be well understood unless evaluation of their needs and information-seeking preferences is conducted through a well-designed study.

Interviews have been used to study why library users do not ask questions,[9] interpersonal dynamics between librarian and user,[10] and how users deal with the rapidly changing technological environment.[11] Interviews and focus groups can also be conducted using chat technology. Although online focus groups do not allow focus group facilitators to observe the nonverbal interactions of participants, benefits include no geographic barriers, lower costs, more rapid turnaround time, and the possibility that people will be more open because of the greater anonymity provided by chat rooms.[12]

Interviews are a worthwhile, but expensive, method of collecting information. Considerable time is required to recruit and schedule interviews and to carefully train staff who will be conducting the interviews. SAGE Publications publishes both survey and focus group kits, which provide excellent detailed practical advice on using these methods.[13]

Case Studies

Case studies generally use several methods to study a single organization and provide an in-depth understanding and evaluation of an organization through the rich data collected. Findings from a case study generally cannot be applied to other situations. For reference librarians interested in improving some aspect of reference service in a single library, a well-designed case study has much promise. Effective case studies require several steps:

1. Defining the purpose of the evaluation and obtaining agreement from the reference staff. A very important consideration is the value of the evaluation project for the improvement of reference services. Does the proposed evaluation project have the potential to provide information that will enhance the value of services for users?
2. Providing the evaluation goals and objectives and defining the information that must be collected to determine whether the objectives are met.
3. Selecting the best methods to collect the needed information. This requires a careful analysis of the strengths and weaknesses of each method and how two or more methods might be combined to collect the most reliable and valid information.
4. Collecting and analyzing the data to reach conclusions about changes in reference service practices that will enhance the quality of services to users.

Good examples of case studies include the following:

*   Wichita State University's case study,[14] which employs problem logs, a suggestion box, the reference transaction instrument from the Wisconsin Ohio Reference Evaluation Program (WOREP), and a quality circle.
*   A Brandeis University study[15] of the effectiveness of the research consultation model, which used direct and unobtrusive observation and focus groups.
*   A Toledo-Lucas County Public Library study,[16] which used the WOREP study instrument, circulation and usage statistics, and ongoing evaluation of staff training.

BOX 10.7
EVALUATING THE EFFECTIVENESS OF REFERENCE TRAINING

The city has just completed a major study of all public services to citizens in the community using "secret shoppers." Results of the study indicate that on the whole, library services are good, but that the secret shoppers who asked for government information (city, county, state, or federal) received inaccurate or incomplete information. On the basis of these results the public library commits to a major training program for locating government information in response to typical user queries. Each reference staff member is required to attend more than two days of training workshops on government information. Staff members evaluate the workshops very positively. Another secret shopper study is conducted a couple of months after all staff have completed the training workshops. Results of the second secret shopper survey indicate that there has been no improvement in government information services provided by the library. Reference staff members are not certain that the results of the secret shopper survey are reliable. What might the staff do to determine whether the secret shopper results are really representative of the service provided? What methods might be most productive in determining why government-information reference services still do not rank highly on the secret shopper survey?

PLANNING AND ORGANIZING DATA COLLECTION AND ANALYSIS

Evaluation must be an ongoing part of regular reference operations. Isolated projects can provide some interesting results, but the value of these single projects is soon lost. Ongoing evaluation is essential for the continual enhancement of reference services.

Ongoing evaluation programs cannot be left to chance, but must be defined as a professional responsibility for each librarian. Evaluation should be part of each librarian's job description, and an assessment committee or assessment coordinator must provide the leadership for ongoing evaluation efforts. New initiatives must include an evaluation component. For example, if a new branch library is to be opened, a plan for an initial community analysis should be an essential part of the planning process. As part of the planning process, performance standards should be established and an evaluation program established to measure how well the branch has met the performance standards after the branch has been open for a year or two.

The assessment committee or coordinator provides the leadership through setting and regularly reviewing the goals and objectives of reference services and by determining the service aspects most in need of assessment. Reference units that do not provide these types of organizational structure will fall into the trap of thinking that evaluation is a good idea, but that someone else should deal with it.

Planning and organizing data collection and analysis requires considering the following factors: participants, data collection instruments, personnel, and equipment and supplies (see Figure 10.2 for a more detailed outline of requirements). Planning and organizing the data collection and analyzing the data collected require expertise, which can be acquired through experience and judicious use of appropriate consultants. For a first study, one of two strategies is highly recommended: (1) replicating another study done elsewhere or (2) working in partnership with someone who has already completed a successful evaluation project, such as a faculty member or a county or city official; these individuals will know much about effective design of surveys, observational studies, sampling, good data analysis software, organizing focus groups, effective interviewing techniques, and so forth.

Data analysis and budget resources should be planned at the beginning of the evaluation project. Data analysis methods and budget resources definitely must be in place after the pilot testing of the data collection instrument.

Participants

- What population will be studied?
- How are study participants selected?
- Will the study results be representative of the entire population?
- What incentives (small gifts, prizes, a raffle) can be offered to encourage people to participate in the study?

Data Collection Methods

- What are the strengths and weaknesses of each method (surveys, observation, focus groups, interviews) relative to the goals and objectives of the evaluation project?
- What data collection instruments are available in the research literature that can be used or adapted for the study?
- How can the instrument be pilot tested?

Environment

- What location(s) will be used to collect the data?
- How will study participants at the location be informed about the goals of the evaluation project?
- Are there other evaluation projects being conducted at that location within the same time frame that need to be coordinated?

Personnel

- How will personnel be trained to collect the data?
- What elements need to be included in the training program for data collection?

Equipment and Supplies

- What specialized equipment and supplies are needed to collect, analyze, and disseminate project evaluation findings?
- How will funding be obtained?

Figure 10.2. Planning and organizing data collection.

THE EVALUATION REPORT

Communication and dissemination of the results of the evaluation project is the final and absolutely essential step in the project. Typically, an evaluation report should include an executive summary, the purpose of the project, the results, the limitations, the recommended changes in reference policies and practices, and appendices (see Figure 10.3).

In communicating the results and implications of the project evaluation findings, considering the audience is important. Is library jargon that would not be understood or appreciated by those outside of the library avoided in the planned presentation? Would the project results be more interesting to the audience if accompanied by an oral presentation? What is the best format to persuade library managers and colleagues that changes in the policies and practices, which are recommended in the report, should indeed be implemented?

CONCLUSION

Every reference librarian is responsible for ensuring that adequate resources and time are allocated to evaluate reference services, so that reference services do indeed provide information that is of value to users. One of the attributes of a professional is to evaluate the effectiveness of the services that a professional provides. Only through ongoing evaluation will librarians be able to ensure that reference services are continually responsive to the needs of users in a rapidly changing economic and technological environment.

None of the evaluation methods will provide a complete picture of the quality of reference services. An ongoing integrated evaluation program is essential to build and

---

Executive Summary

A brief one page summary of purpose, major findings, and implications for reference practice. Keep in mind that the summary may be all that busy librarians and administrators will read.

Purpose

Evaluation project goals and objectives, methods of collecting and analyzing the data.

Results

Major findings of the evaluation project organized around project objectives.

Recommended Changes in Reference Policies and Practices

Describe plans for implementing changes in reference policies and practices based on study findings. Indicate how these changes will improve the value of services to users.

Appendices

Include detailed tables here for the really curious readers.

Figure 10.3. Contents of an evaluation report.

continually update a reliable and valid picture of the effectiveness, quality, and value of reference services to users. Continual dissemination of results is also essential. Funders, the general public, and library administrators need to be regularly reminded of the value of reference services and the importance of adequately supporting and staffing such services.

All librarians engaged in professional practice must acquire in-depth understanding and experience in designing and implementing assessment projects. Evaluation skills should be an essential part of every reference librarian's toolkit so that reference services and reference librarians can change, survive, and prosper in the information world of the 21st century.

NOTES

1. James Shedlock, "Defining the Quality of Medical Reference Service," *Medical Reference Services Quarterly* 7 (Spring 1988): 49.

2. Tim Loney and Arnie Bellefontaine, "TQM Training: The Library Service Challenge," *Journal of Library Administration* 18 (1993): 85–95.

3. Jo Bell Whitlatch, "Evaluating Reference Services in the Electronic Age," *Library Trends* 50 (Fall 2001): 207–17.

4. Marjorie E. Murfin and Gary M. Gugelchuk, "Development and Testing of a Reference Transaction Assessment Instrument," *College & Research Libraries* 48 (July 1987): 314–38. For current administration of the reference transaction instrument, see the Wisconsin Ohio Reference Evaluation Program (WOREP): https://worep.library.kent.edu/.

5. Daniel R. Arrigona and Eleanor Mathews, "A Use Study of an Academic Library Reference Collection," *RQ* 38 (Fall 1988): 71–81.

6. Carol C. Spencer, "Random Time Sampling with Self-Observation for Library Cost Studies: Unit Costs of Reference Questions," *Bulletin of the Medical Library Association* 68 (January 1980): 53–57.

7. Peter Hernon and Charles R. McClure, *Unobtrusive Testing and Library Reference Services* (Norwood, NJ: Ablex, 1987), 240 pp.

8. Jeffrey Pomerantz, "Evaluation of Online Reference Services," *Bulletin of the American Society for Information Science and Technology* 34 (December 2007/January 2008): 15–19.

9. Mary Jane Swope and Jeffrey Katzer, "Silent Majority: Why Don't They Ask Questions?," *RQ* 12 (1972): 161–66.

10. Virginia Massey-Burzio, "From the Other Side of the Reference Desk: A Focus Group Study," *Journal of Academic Librarianship* 24 (1998): 208–15.

11. Marie Louise Radford, "Communication Theory Applied to the Reference Encounter: An Analysis of Critical Incidents," *Library Quarterly* 66 (1996): 123–37.

12. Kate Maddox, "Virtual Panels Add Real Insight for Marketers: Online Focus-Group Use Expanding," *Advertising Age* 69 (June 1998): 34–35.

13. Latest editions of *The Focus Group Kit* and *The Survey Kit* can be located at the Web site of SAGE Publications: http://www.sagepub.com. SAGE is also an excellent source for less expensive one-volume paperbacks on a wide variety of research methods.

14. Janet Dagenais Brown, "Using Quality Concepts to Improve Reference Services," *College & Research Libraries* 55 (1994): 211–19.

15.   Douglas Herman, "But Does it Work? Evaluating the Brandeis Reference Model," *Reference Services Review* 22 (1994): 17–28.

16.   Jane Pinkston, "Assessment and Accountability at Toledo-Lucas County Public Library," *The Reference Librarian* 38 (1992): 41–52.

ADDITIONAL READINGS

ACRL Instruction Section, Research and Scholarship Committee, American Library Association. *A Bibliography of Research Methods Texts*. Chicago: American Library Association, 2006. Updated January 2009. http://www.ala.org/ala/mgrps/divs/acrl/about/sections/is/projpubs/bibliographyresearch.cfm.

This selective, evaluative, annotated bibliography is revised and updated biennially. The bibliography covers texts related to general research methods, qualitative research, quantitative research, library and information science research, research design, data analysis, case studies, interviews, surveys, and questionnaires. Though intended to complement the research agenda for instruction and information literacy, the bibliography is also useful for exploring methods helpful in evaluating reference services.

Carter, David S., and Joseph Janes. "Unobtrusive Data Analysis of Digital Reference Questions and Service at the Internet Public Library: An Exploratory Study." *Library Trends* 49 (Fall 2000): 251–65.

Logs of more than 3,000 questions were analyzed in early 1999 to determine, among other things, how questions were handled, answered, and rejected. This study is an excellent example of how librarians can use question sets to learn about the quality and effectiveness of digital reference service.

Coffman, Steve, and Linda Arret. "To Chat or Not to Chat." Part 1: *Searcher* 12 (July/August 2004); Part 2: *Searcher* 12 (September 2004). http://www.infotoday.com/searcher/jul04/arret_coffman.shtml (part 1), http://www.infotoday.com/searcher/sep04/arret_coffman.shtml (part 2).

In response to the widespread adoption of virtual reference, Coffman and Arret question the costs and encourage librarians to explore alternatives, such as answering the phone. The purpose of this very thoughtful article is to look carefully at reference service as a whole and the methods that provide the best service. The costs and benefits of any new approach need to be carefully considered.

Hirko, Buff, and Mary Bucher Ross. *Virtual Reference Training: The Complete Guide to Providing Anytime, Anywhere Answers*. Chicago: American Library Association, 2004. 160 pp.

This book describes the training program for Washington's Statewide Virtual Reference Project. This model training program emphasizes active learning through a curriculum that creates a learning environment allowing library staff to actively explore, discover, and reflect on the skills needed for reference services in an online environment. The book and the online Virtual Reference Training Program (http://66.212.65.207) provide a section (chapter 9 in the book) and an online module (http://66.212.65.207/fourth.htm) on evaluating and improving reference services. Although the Web site is no longer being updated, very practical and useful information is provided for evaluating virtual reference services.

Janes, Joseph. "Survey Construction." *Library Hi Tech* 17 (1999): 321–25.

One of a series of pieces on research methods that has appeared in *Library Hi Tech*, this concise article covers the basics on writing good questions and designing good questionnaires.

Kawakami, Alice, and Pauline Swartz. "Digital Reference: Training and Assessment for Service Improvement." *Reference Services Review* 31 (2003): 227–36.

This study assesses digital reference competencies in order to determine gaps in training. Observation was used both as the primary assessment method and to improve the training program.

Kuhlthau, Carol Collier. "Learning in Digital Libraries: An Information Search Process Approach." *Library Trends* 45 (Spring 1997): 708–25.

Kuhlthau briefly summarizes her model of the information search process (ISP) and the challenges for librarians to create environments for learning within libraries. She notes that the goal of the learner, which is to move from uncertainty to understanding, cannot be met by merely locating relevant, or even useful, information. For the learner to achieve success, librarians must adopt strategies that are appropriate to the user's stage in the information search process.

Kuruppu, Pali U. "Evaluation of Reference Services—A Review." *Journal of Academic Librarianship* 33 (May 2007): 368–81.

Kuruppu provides an extensive review of the literature on reference service evaluation, with emphasis on evaluation methodologies. Sections include quantitative evaluation methods (reference statistics, surveys, and questionnaires) and qualitative evaluation methods (observations, interviews, focus groups, and case studies). Validity and reliability of quantitative and qualitative research results are also discussed.

LibQUAL+®: Charting Library Service Quality. http://www.libqual.org/.

LibQUAL+® is very useful in assessing user perspectives of library service quality by focusing on the gap between customer expectations and perceptions across various service constructs. One of the constructs of service quality is "affect of service," which includes empathy, accessibility, and personal competence (such as willingness to help users). This instrument is based on SERVQUAL, widely used for assessing service quality in private business service organizations. LibQUAL+® is offered by the Association of Research Libraries (ARL), but it also can be used by public and less intensive research academic libraries. This tool is useful as a general survey to identify priority areas for more in-depth study for reference service evaluation.

McClure, Charles R., R. David Lankes, Melissa Gross, and Beverly Choltco-Devlin. *Statistics, Measures and Quality Standards for Assessing Digital Reference Library Services: Guidelines and Procedures*. Syracuse, NY: Information Institute of Syracuse, School of Information Studies, Syracuse University; Tallahassee: School of Information Studies, Information Use Management and Policy Institute, Florida State University, 2002. 104 pp. http://www.webjunction.org/quality-standards/.

In this report the authors begin to identify, describe, and develop procedures for assessing digital reference service in order to improve the quality of service. The manual covers a wide variety of measures for digital reference: descriptive statistics, log analysis, user satisfaction measures, cost, staff time expended, and other options. The manual also includes useful sample forms and survey instruments.

Murphy, Sarah Anne, Sherry Engle Moeller, Jessica R. Page, Judith Cerqua, and Mark Boarman. "Leveraging Measurement System Analysis (MSA) to Improve Library Assessment: The Attribute Gage R&R." *College & Research Libraries* 70 (November 2009): 568–77.

This paper addresses the development of local standards to interpret and apply the *RUSA Guidelines for Behavioral Performance of Reference and Information Service Providers* for evaluating e-mail reference. Because of the subjective interpretation and application of guidelines in reference evaluation, an ongoing challenge for librarians remains the development of reliable measures. The process utilized in this study improved the reliability of the local quality standards and provided unexpected opportunities for staff to see how others answered questions and reflect on how to improve their own performance.

Novotny, Eric, ed. "Assessing Reference and User Services in a Digital Age." *The Reference Librarian* 95/96 (2006): 1–230.

This collection of articles explores the evaluation of reference services from a variety of perspectives. Approaches vary from case studies of individual libraries to discussions of the best methods and approaches.

The Outcomes Toolkit. http://ibec.ischool.washington.edu/toolkit.php.

This resource is very useful for conducting evaluations based on outcomes (rather than inputs or process measures). The Outcomes Toolkit provides a four-step process: getting started, collecting data, analyzing data, and using what you find. The Toolkit was developed by the Information Behavior in Everyday Contexts (IBEC) team, which is composed of researchers and graduate students from the University of Washington and the University of Michigan. Project leaders are Joan Durrance and Karen Fisher.

Pomerantz, Jeffrey, Lorri M. Mon, and Charles R. McClure. "Evaluating Remote Reference Service: A Practical Guide to Problems and Solutions." *Portal: Libraries and the Academy* 8 (January 2008): 15–30.

This paper identifies key methodological issues affecting the quality of data in the evaluation of virtual reference services. The authors propose strategies for practical ways in which libraries can improve the overall quality and usefulness of data gathered in such studies.

Reference and User Services Association (RUSA). Research and Statistics Committee. http://www.ala.org/ala/mgrps/divs/rusa/sections/rss/rsssection/rsscomm/rssresstat/researchstatistics.cfm

This RUSA committee provides annual bibliographies of recently published research on reference and annual programs on assessing reference services, as well as identifying information on useful Web sites for reference research. RUSA also publishes a quarterly journal, the *Reference & User Services Quarterly*, which frequently features articles on reference research.

The Reference Assessment Manual. Ann Arbor, MI: Pierian Press, 1995. 372 pp.

This manual provides a historical overview of the theory and practice of reference evaluation in libraries. A valuable section contains the reviews of a large number of instruments used in evaluating reference services. The volume was compiled and edited by the Evaluation of Reference and Adult Services Committee, Management and Operation of Public Services Section, Reference and Adult Services Division (RASD), American Library Association.

Rimland, Emily L. "Do We Do It ~~Good~~ Well? A Bibliographic Essay on the Evaluation of Reference Effectiveness." *The Reference Librarian* 98 (2007): 41–55.

Rimland examines recent (1994–2006) research into the evaluation of reference effectiveness. Topics covered include unobtrusive studies, obtrusive studies, emerging trends, and research needs.

Ross, Catherine Sheldrick, and Patricia Dewdney. "Negative Closure." *Reference & User Services Quarterly* 38 (1998): 151–63.

This study uses observational techniques to explore librarian behaviors related to terminating the reference transaction without providing a helpful answer, including unmonitored referral, implying that the user should have done something before asking for reference help, trying to get the user to accept easily found information, claiming the information does not exist, and going off, never to return.

RUSA/RSS Evaluation of Reference and User Services Committee. *Measuring and Assessing Reference Services and Resources: A Guide*. Chicago: American Library Association, December 11, 2007. http://www.ala.org/ala/mgrps/divs/rusa/sections/rss/rsssection/rss comm/evaluationofref/measrefguide.cfm

This guide provides assessment planning advice and measurement tools for volume, costs, benefits and quality, program effectiveness, cost-benefit analysis, patron needs and satisfaction, use, usability, and collection assessment. Each section includes bibliographic references useful for in-depth exploration of a topic.

Von Seggern, Marilyn, and Nancy J. Young. "The Focus Group Method in Libraries: Issues Related to Process and Data Analysis." *Reference Services Review* 31 (2003): 272–84.

This article covers the basics of planning for collecting data using focus groups. Ethnograph software for coding and analyzing focus group data is discussed, and a useful example of the coding is provided. An annotated bibliography includes focus group studies in a library setting.

Wallace, Danny P., and Connie Van Fleet, eds. *Library Evaluation: A Casebook and Can-Do Guide*. Englewood, CO: Libraries Unlimited, 2001. 237 pp.

Chapter 3 (pp. 79–115), written by Kathryn Dana Watson, covers evaluating reference and information services. The chapter includes case studies using the Wisconsin Ohio Reference Evaluation Program (WOREP) and assessing reference behaviors with unobtrusive testing.

Watson-Boone, Rebecca. "Academic Librarians as Practitioner-Researchers." *Journal of Academic Librarianship* 26 (March 2000): 85–93.

Watson-Boone identifies seven steps common to both research- and practice-based problem solving: identify the true problem that needs attention; define the various ways to solve the problem; select the process that appears to have the greatest chance of working; set out criteria against which to measure the success of specific problem-solving efforts; carry out the effort; evaluate what occurs; and reflect on whether the results have solved the problem to a significant degree.

Whitlatch, Jo Bell. *Evaluating Reference Services: A Practical Guide*. Chicago: American Library Association, 2000. 226 pp.

This guide provides information on the basic techniques that are commonly used to collect data for evaluating reference services and also contains an extensive annotated bibliography (pp. 113–213) of reference research studies. Readers wishing to use a method or study a certain type of reference issue can use the research studies as guides to get started on their own research project.

WebJunction. *Virtual Reference*. http://www.webjunction.org/virtual-reference.

This compilation includes resources such as conference proceedings, white papers, quality standards, research agenda, and other materials focusing on assessment and its importance to virtual reference practices and procedures.

Chapter

Organizing and Delivering Reference and Information Services

Jim Hahn and Josephine Z. Kibbee

INTRODUCTION

The commercial bookstore's amiable atmosphere, customer focus, and ease of use is an instructive model for the design of the reference service experience.[1] Bookstores are seen by many as a more desirable place to gather or study, with comfortable chairs, a relaxed atmosphere, and the added perk of an endless supply of caffeine. This competition served as a wake-up call to many librarians, who have refashioned their libraries as welcoming institutions with comfortable ambience and renewed interest in the total library experience. For users who need information more than they need caffeine and conversation, however, libraries are distinctively different from bookstores and cafés.

Libraries not only provide access to books and Internet connections (and maybe even coffee and comfortable chairs) but also offer a critical additional service: reference assistance. From a one-room library to the Library of Congress, an enduring value of the profession since the 19th century has been providing assistance to readers, not just collections, computers, and space.

Contemporary reference service takes place anywhere the library exists, from the library's Web presence to the in-person experience. Reference service has traditionally been available in a reference room, or an otherwise designated area in the library, at a desk staffed by librarians. Now, networked databases and e-resources, not to mention Google, Bing, and other free search services such as *Wikipedia*, have reduced dependence on the reference room as the place where library research begins.

Mobile software applications deliver information directly to the user's smart phone; there are a number of freely available iPhone apps that have reengineered what would have been considered traditional reference tools: dictionaries and encyclopedias, among a few examples. Many users begin (and often end) their research by using the Internet. Today's challenge is to ensure that reference services remain relevant in a wired world and to provide this service not only within the library, but wherever, whenever, and however users prefer to work.

A useful frame for understanding the role of the reference department's online presence is to see the reference Web site as an additional branch of the library. Emerging reference tools such as federated search placed on the reference department's home page offer new services to users at their point of need. Additionally, help tools such as instructional Web sites pointed to from the reference department's online presence serve to help users understand and make use of the array of reference tools available electronically.

This chapter highlights key issues in the organization and delivery of reference and information services as they retool for the future. The first sections discuss the place, figuratively and literally, of the reference department within the library. The next section moves beyond the library to explore ways reference services can be delivered, regardless of physical arrangement. The chapter concludes with a discussion of ways to keep current and stay relevant as we meet the challenges of the digital future.

THE ROLES OF REFERENCE LIBRARIANS

Though the reference department is traditionally associated with a central information desk, reference librarians play many roles. As discussed in chapter 8, instruction is intrinsic to reference, and instructional programs are often administered by reference departments. In many instances, reference librarians serve as subject specialists and hold responsibility for collection development and faculty or community outreach. Reference departments may hold responsibility for managing collections and services such as government documents, periodicals and microforms, and interlibrary loan. In public libraries, reference librarians often manage community information and referral services, offer readers' advisory services, and organize programming. Behind the scenes, reference librarians build Web sites, work on teams that implement new systems, engage in public relations, and otherwise contribute to a wide variety of library initiatives.

The primary responsibility of the reference department, however, still derives from Samuel Green's exhortation to assist readers, even though the reference work environment has changed in ways Green never could have imagined. In recent years, libraries have stressed their role in helping users *access* information, no matter where it resides. In this paradigm, reference librarians function as intermediaries, instructors, and troubleshooters, providing a human connection between the user and sources of information, regardless of format and location.

The availability of online databases and the Internet has irrevocably altered traditional reference tools and strategies. Christen Cardina and Donald Wicks surveyed academic reference librarians to determine how their jobs have changed with the advent of the Web. They found that the "core jobs" of providing reference service to users, collection development, user education, and involvement in library initiatives have remained, but the nature of these jobs has changed. Librarians are serving users they no longer see face to face and are utilizing a far greater number of resources than were available in a print collection. The study concludes that librarians who work

---

BOX 11.1
POSITION OPEN

Information Access Librarian: Digitopia Public Library invites applications for the position of Information Access Librarian. As part of the Information and Research Services Team, the successful applicant will provide reference service in person and virtually, select and organize electronic resources, assist users in accessing information sources and developing information literacy, involve the library in social networking initiatives, and represent the perspective of the user in the design and implementation of access systems.

---

in academic libraries saw vast changes in their work environments and in what is expected of them professionally. Web publishing, virtual reference, online databases, and Google searches are all part of the reference librarian's repertoire. It is encouraging to note that despite these rapid changes, librarians responded enthusiastically and report increased job satisfaction.[2]

REFERENCE AS A PLACE IN THE LIBRARY

Reading Rooms, Mixing Chambers, and Information Commons

Until the advent of the Internet, reference librarians depended solely on a print collection of reference titles. Because reference books are typically consulted for specific information and do not circulate, most library buildings have traditionally designated a reference area or reading room to house these titles and provide reference service. Though digital reference sources are proliferating, an encouraging trend in the past few years has been the restoration and refitting of classic reference or reading rooms. The Library of Congress, Harvard University, the New York Public Library, and other institutions have invested considerable sums in restoring and updating these physically impressive areas. These magnificent reading rooms represent the library as a seat of learning and scholarship and as a repository of recorded knowledge. Often incorporating a time-honored print collection (e.g., many of the titles described in this book), archetypal furnishings, and wireless technology, they combine past and present with oak tables and wireless networks, with classic print titles and computer screens, to provide a space that supports individual productivity and contemplation.

The concept of a reference area is also alive and well in new library buildings, though the area may no longer be called a "reference room." The Seattle Public Library, for example, inaugurated an award-winning building that boasts a "Mixing Chamber." In this 21st-century library space, glossy metal workstations have replaced stately oak tables, but at its essence, the Mixing Chamber sounds remarkably like a reference room (see Box 11.2)

BOX 11.2
THE MIXING CHAMBER

At the Seattle Public Library,

The 19,500-square-foot Mixing Chamber is where patrons go for help with general questions or in-depth research—a "trading floor for information."

In the Mixing Chamber, librarians are able to serve patrons as a team. Staff members are equipped with wireless communication devices, which allow them to contact librarians in the Books Spiral for additional help. Librarians have nearby access to large reference collections and online resources, as well as a dumbwaiter to quickly deliver items from the Books Spiral.

The character of the space is silvery and high tech—the ceiling is black and the floor aluminum. This floor also has the largest configuration of technology in one spot—145 computers—and is the entry to the Books Spiral. The Quick Information Center provides telephone reference service on this floor. Ask a Librarian—virtual reference service via online chat also takes place here.

Description of the Seattle Public Library's Mixing Chamber, http://www.spl.org/default.asp?page ID=branch_central_visit_floor&branchID=1.

Though computer workstations and wireless networks are a common feature, reference rooms were originally built around a print collection and remain generally conducive to solitary research. A different vision of library space, however, is embodied in the evolving notion of the *information commons*, particularly in academic libraries. Although definitions and terminology vary—for example, permutations include "learning commons" or "scholarly commons"—the concept generally refers to a designated area that provides a variety of digital resources, productivity tools, and other technologies to facilitate both research and production. The goal is to provide a place where users can find information, utilize computing and communications technologies, and obtain a variety of services, either individually or in groups.

The information commons includes a large number of computer workstations and a team of staff, including librarians, information technology specialists, and assistants, generally in partnership with the campus computing unit. Here, reference service is provided within the context of a holistic research experience. Users can explore, learn, and create using a variety of library resources and productivity software and other IT tools.[3] Ideally, writing labs, advising centers, and other student services are also collocated into an area that expands the traditional notion of information or learning—or the library.

Will the information commons replace the reference room? Librarians ignore technology at their own peril and risk becoming curators of book museums if they do not acknowledge evolving user preferences for accessing information and modes of working. A library is conceptually and substantively different from a computer lab, but partnerships between libraries and computing centers can capitalize on the respective strengths of each. The challenge for librarians is to create spaces and services that are flexible, responsive to user needs and preferences, and faithful to the principles on which libraries have been built.

Location of Reference Services

Although the place of reference within an information commons is a relatively new concern, the question of optimally configuring reference services within the library has long been debated. Large public and academic libraries frequently provide subject-based departments, such as business, genealogy and local history, music, and science and technology. Medium-sized libraries occasionally follow this model as well. Proponents of decentralized services cite advantages to library users, arguing that the quality of reference assistance is improved because subject specialists are better equipped to provide in-depth, subject-based service. With a smaller and more homogeneous unit, librarians enjoy greater autonomy and control, and user studies have indicated a preference for more focused units of library service and small, client-centered work groups. Proponents of centralizing reference also claim advantages to library users. By providing greater efficiency and fewer referrals elsewhere, libraries are able to extend service hours; offer more consistent availability of professional staff, particularly on nights and weekends; and reduce duplication of resources. As a matter of practicality, however, budgetary constraints often serve as the primary catalyst for reducing service points.

It is interesting to note that the debate over physical service points has cooled considerably in recent years as networking has shifted emphasis from the *location* of services to the *delivery* of services. Increasing demands on library budgets, coupled with increasing demand for networked collections and services, is causing librarians to rethink their library's physical organization. The user-centered library is the ultimate goal of library design. If librarians hope to attract and retain users, they must learn how users prefer to work and organize collections and services accordingly.

The Reference Desk: Critical Mass or Trivial Pursuit?

Historically, the focal point of the reference area is a desk, staffed by one or more librarians, in proximity to a reference collection that holds many of the titles described in this book. Long a cornerstone of reference service, to many the reference desk reflects the values that Charles Bunge and Chris Ferguson identify as being core to reference librarianship: convenient and equitable service to users, individually tailored personal assistance, and high professional standards.[4] Patricia Swanson described the reference desk as representing a "critical mass of resources—human, printed, and now electronic, so configured for a convenient and predictable location so that library patrons can find the service and can find someone to help them."[5]

Not all agree. Writing more than 25 years ago, Thelma Freides asserted that "by establishing the desk as the focal point of reader assistance, librarians not only expend professional time on trivial tasks, but also encourage the assumption that the

---

BOX 11.3
A GOOD USE OF PROFESSIONAL SKILLS?

"Every library that I have worked in over the last twenty-plus years has had at least one staff member grumbling about how often they have to give directions to the restroom . . . My question is this: Why grumble? This is our chance to shine, to invite people in. While it's true that any trained monkey could point in the correct direction, I would like to believe that human beings aspire to be a bit more helpful than this. In the current economy, with declining numbers of reference transactions and dwindling budgets, every patron encounter is important."

Lorraine J. Pellack, "First Impressions and Rethinking Restroom Questions." *Reference & User Services Quarterly* 49 (Fall 2009): 4.

---

low-level, undemanding type of question handled most easily and naturally at the desk is the service norm."[6] Her studies of user behavior indicate that users do, in fact, perceive the reference desk as intended for quick replies. When the opportunity arises for providing detailed bibliographic assistance or research consultation, both user and librarian experience frustration when ringing phones and queues of users with short-answer questions compete for the librarian's attention.

A review of library literature during the past two decades indicates that the desk has been the focus of much reflection. To many, it epitomizes problems with reference service: questionable use of staff expertise, dependence on a physical location, undifferentiated service, and unawareness of user needs. These critics charge that the ideal of the reference desk, staffed by competent professionals whose expertise is consistently challenged by informed library users, is elusive at best. Repetitive and routine questions, such as how to use the library catalog or, worse, how to fix a printer jam, ignore librarians' expertise and contribute to job dissatisfaction. Some have questioned whether the reference desk makes users less self-sufficient and more dependent on library staff.

Although the necessity of a central desk staffed by librarians is best addressed within the context of individual libraries, as the next section illustrates, librarians are moving beyond discussions of furniture to meet the challenge of designing effective service models in a rapidly changing environment.

SERVICE MODELS

In designing the excellent service experience, librarians are rapidly adapting to changing practices of information access and use. A recent approach to service models in libraries of all types is the empathetic concern of designing the user experience.[7] User experience pushes librarians to look at all elements (signage, desk configuration, available resources) of in-person library service and all its components as well as virtual service and its components. Essentially, user experience design critiques the library's service anywhere the user interacts with any attribute of the library. The totality of in-person and virtual services produces a complete "experience" of service for the library. This next section looks at past and emerging models and the issues driving them.

In-Person Service

The holy grail of staffing a reference service is to maximize use of the librarian's expertise. One staffing model that attempts to achieve this, particularly in large public or research libraries, uses *tiered* service. Considerations underlying the notion of tiered service include optimizing the use of the librarian's time and expertise, reduction of stress and burnout, presentation of an appropriate professional image, and more efficient use of human resources. A separate service point, which may be called a help desk or information desk, staffed by paraprofessionals or students, is set up to address directional and quick-answer questions. Complex or in-depth questions are then referred to librarians at the reference desk. Ideally staffed by well-trained individuals who make informed referrals, a separate information desk, preferably near the entrance, can free librarians to focus on questions that require professional expertise.

Tiered service is not a panacea, however. Smaller libraries cannot always afford to designate separate staff and facilities for reference, let alone establish two or more service points. Experience shows that a separately staffed information desk requires a clearly defined mission and a considerable investment in training to operate successfully.[8] Because the entire array of library resources is now available at each library desktop, it is difficult to define the limits of the assistance provided by staff at an information desk. The "simple/complex" dichotomy that once drove tiered service is increasingly blurred, and the public is rarely aware of the difference between the service points.[9]

The idea of eliminating a professionally staffed reference desk and replacing it with a *research consultation* service has received some traction, particularly in light of decreasing reference statistics. This model involves scheduling office hours or setting appointments when librarians can spend uninterrupted time working with a user to offer research assistance and targeted instruction. Although staff-intensive, research consultation takes optimal advantage of professional expertise, eliminates

---

BOX 11.4
ONE SIZE DOES NOT FIT ALL!

Discuss the comparative advantages and disadvantages of tiered service. Is it of primary benefit to users? To librarians? To both? Or to neither? Should librarians be divorced from routine library functions?

the competing demands that often accompany "on the fly" reference encounters, and offers librarians and users a more satisfying and productive encounter. In a much-discussed reorganization at Brandeis University Library several years ago, the reference desk was eliminated in favor of an information desk staffed by paraprofessionals and a research consultation service drawing exclusively on librarians with a combination of office hours and appointments. In an article evaluating this model, Douglas Herman concludes that the project is a "mildly qualified" success.

Though faculty and students enthusiastically endorse the consultation service, informed referrals are not always made from the information desk, and users might not have ready access to the librarians' expertise.[10] However, a more recent study, analyzing Dickinson College's replacement of the reference desk with a consultation service, found the new service model to be beneficial to librarians as well as to users.[11] Other service configurations for desks include a "one desk" model whereby reference librarians answer research questions from the circulation desk; this introduces a seamless experience for the user in which one desk is a "one stop shop" for all the user's information needs.[12] Models will depend on typology of user population as well as library size and mission. What works for a smaller public library may not find similar uptake in an academic setting of any size.

With the convergence of decreasing staff, a reduction in the number of reference questions, and virtual service (see later section), librarians will increasingly experiment with configuring their reference services in upcoming years. However it is configured, in-person reference service offers the personal assistance that most people value and provides a rich opportunity for instruction as well as research assistance as long as people are in the library. In a world of massive networked access to information and data, librarians must meet these users where they are (i.e., on campus, in the community, in cyberspace). To this end, reference librarians have ventured into "embedded librarianship" as well as cyberspace and accompanying social networking platforms as complements to traditional service.

Mobile Librarians and Embedded Service

Entrepreneurial and intrepid, reference and outreach librarians have moved outside the library building literally and virtually. Academic librarians in particular have moved beyond the desk by taking reference service to where users work. These "mobile" librarians move not only beyond the desk but also beyond the library, setting up outposts in student unions, academic departments, campus computing centers, undergraduate dormitories, and wherever their users gather or work. Reports of pilot projects by librarians from Rutgers University, University at Buffalo, and other university libraries describe these various outreach initiatives. Experiences vary, with some services in such sites as student centers and computing labs providing primarily quick-answer service, whereas others report that users indeed take advantage of the opportunity for research consultation.[13] The common denominator of these efforts, however, is positive public relations for the library and the promotion of library research assistance to those who might otherwise be unaware of this service.

At a deeper level, Martin Kesselman and Sarah Watstein discuss the notion of the embedded librarian, who "brings the library and the librarian to the user, wherever they are . . . embedding themselves into research and learning environs."[14] These roles

---

BOX 11.5
EMBEDDED PUBLIC LIBRARIANS?

The literature on embedded librarians has mostly focused on academic libraries. Can public librarians be embedded as well?

---

include involvement in course-integrated instruction, participation in research teams, and collaboration with faculty in scholarly communication activities, and they offer exciting and professionally satisfying opportunities for librarians to share their expertise. If reference services could be plotted along a continuum, the embedded librarian represents the apex of successful outreach and user service.

Digital Reference Service

While librarians struggle to optimize service they provide to their respective communities, they are also keenly aware that large segments of their population never come through the library's doors. Digital reference service encompasses service that can be delivered at the user's point of need. This entails instant messaging (IM) reference services and SMS reference service (also referred to as a Text-a-Librarian service), as well as proprietary online chat platforms, known simply as chat. Twenty-first-century digital culture is such that most people now work and communicate primarily in front of a computer screen and spend a majority of their day connected to the online world. Digital reference service occurs online as a means to meet the needs of users where they are.

Variously referred to as *electronic*, *digital*, or *virtual* reference service, the salient feature is that communication between user and librarian takes place online. Virtual reference services developed in response to a number of interrelated factors: the ubiquitous popularity of the Internet as an avenue of communication, increasing availability of networked digital resources and the corresponding need for service, reports of decreasing numbers of in-person reference transactions, and librarians' continuing efforts to respond to user preferences. As illustrated by the number of articles and programs it has generated, virtual reference has sparked a lively discussion within the profession.[15] Proponents wax enthusiastic about increased responsiveness and outreach capabilities, and opponents decry the decline of the reference interview and increased reliance on online sources. Nonetheless, librarians are increasingly embracing virtual reference, not as a substitute for traditional service, but simply as another means of reaching users. As with in-person service, however, different models of virtual service have developed in response to varying user needs, philosophies of service, and staff resources.

Asynchronous versus Synchronous

The two basic modes of digital service, asynchronous and synchronous, differ substantially in their immediacy, interactivity, and cost. Asynchronous service—that is, service via e-mail—offers many immediate advantages. Software costs are negligible, and the medium is familiar to nearly all users of the Internet. It offers advantages to users who are less technically savvy or who use slow Internet connections. Likewise, users with limited English skills or typing skills might prefer composing at their own pace. This service works particularly well for short-answer or known-item questions: How can I reach the local Internal Revenue Service office? Does the library have any travel books on Belize? A short answer, however, does not necessarily translate to a short amount of time spent finding the answer. As librarians know, a considerable amount of time might be spent in tracking down an address, determining a death date, finding a specific poem, and so forth. Thus, from the librarian's perspective, communicating via e-mail provides an opportunity to work on a question with less time pressure, eliminates telephone tag, and lends itself well to collaborating with colleagues.

On the downside, e-mail does not lend itself well to instructing users in finding or using resources on their own, and questions received via e-mail can be maddeningly vague or open-ended. Though it is possible to engage in a reference interview through a series of e-mail exchanges and clarifications, efficiency and effectiveness can be compromised.

Synchronous reference service offers a partial solution. Though "chat" service implies a casual conversation, in its more sophisticated incarnations, it has the potential to provide a more effective communication and learning tool than e-mail. Useful as a means of humanizing and enhancing online communication, chat can facilitate collaboration between the user and the librarian, particularly through the co-browse feature. In this scenario, the librarian can share screens with users, guiding them to appropriate databases and teaching effective search strategies.

The ideal and the reality, however, are often at odds. Librarians frequently experience frustration with software performance: connections are inexplicably dropped, co-browsing or other features do not work, and users have a difficult time following what is happening. Taking a "less is more" approach, some librarians have adopted instant messaging as a medium for providing real-time reference.[16] Here, librarians are taking advantage of a popular method of communicating via computer. At its most basic level, IM is considerably less sophisticated than chat software, but it offers the advantage of ease of use, speed, reliability, and negligible cost. Though this medium is not optimal for every type of question or every type of user, it offers a good opportunity for librarians to investigate real-time reference service without a significant investment in software.

In further lowering the barriers of online direct engagement with librarians, widgets can be used to create near instant communication. Chat widgets are made up of snippets of HTML code that can be dropped into a library's reference department Web page in order to connect the user directly with that reference staff's IM window. This immediacy of reference service is a new way to engage with users as they experience a service at their point of need.

Librarians are justifiably concerned with the video quality of the user's virtual experience when compared with face-to-face transactions. To that end, some librarians experiment with video chat reference service, and one pilot use is Skype reference services. Skype is a type of video conferencing service whereby librarians and users can converse over video chat, with librarians setting up video kiosks to answer reference queries from users at a distance. Skype applications exist for the iPhone and other mobile devices such that users may be able to get nearly the same type of video service virtually as is available in person. The same network issues may arise with this service as well; that is, depending on the stability of the connection, users may get dropped, or quality may become poor if the user is on a low-bandwidth connection for video chat.

Delivering virtual reference service poses unique opportunities and challenges. Although reference librarians have long grappled with issues such as the level of service that will be offered, the clientele who will be served, the length of time spent on a specific question, how and where to staff, and user privacy and confidentiality, virtual reference brings these questions into sharper relief. When users are physically present, question negotiation and user–librarian collaboration tend to be more straightforward. In the virtual environment, however, responsibilities are more ambiguous, questions can consume significantly more time, users may have unrealistic expectations, staff levels may be too thin to consistently staff virtual reference, and transcripts potentially pose risks to user privacy. On the other hand, users appear to be enthusiastic about the service, and it is gratifying to be considered "awesome."[17] As with in-person transactions, there is no "best" way to run a virtual service, and each institution ultimately needs to establish a model and policies that work for its users.

DELIVERING VIRTUAL REFERENCE SERVICES

Staffing Models

Most reference departments take on virtual reference without a corresponding addition of staff. The challenge then becomes how to integrate virtual reference into existing services. The most common model is staffing the service from an office or other location away from the desk. Underlying this model is a view of virtual reference as a research consultation service. This configuration offers the advantages of better focus and fewer distractions and interruptions and facilitates in-depth transactions and instruction. Because the service is not place-bound, it offers the possibility for flexible staffing from a distance. The primary disadvantage is that libraries cannot always afford enough personnel to staff a separate virtual service point during all the hours that the library is open, and real-time service may thus be available only for limited hours. Although limited service hours have relatively low impact on asynchronous (e-mail) service, given that the user is not expecting an immediate answer, a schedule of limited hours can deter use of real-time service. (Some libraries have addressed this by participating in a cooperative service, which is discussed in the next section). This model can also be an inefficient use of the librarian's time, foster greater dependence on online sources to the exclusion of the print collection, and diminish collaboration with colleagues.

A less frequently used model is staffing from the reference desk. In this model, virtual transactions are seen as just another mode of access to reference service, not unlike the telephone. An early study indicated that the majority of virtual questions are brief or known items and do not require lengthy communication.[18] Thus users are offered a service convenient to their schedule and work preference. The relatively high volume of virtual users at the University of Illinois at Urbana-Champaign is very likely due to the fact that virtual reference is available nearly all the hours the library is open.

This model works well with a team of staff at the desk, with someone on the team theoretically available to take a virtual question. It lends itself well to collaboration with colleagues and can facilitate a tiered system when paraprofessionals are used because difficult questions can be referred to the librarian on duty. Proximity to the print reference collection provides a richer pool of resources to draw upon. This is not an optimal environment for lengthy or involved transactions, however, and frequently requires multitasking on the part of the librarian. In-person users may not understand why they need to wait while a librarian types on the computer, and transactions often cannot be conducted at leisure.

Which is the right model? Just as with in-person service, the best model is the one that fits an institution's philosophy of service, user needs, and staff resources. A singular advantage to virtual reference service is that it offers an excellent opportunity for service analysis and assessment. By reviewing transcripts, reference departments can analyze who uses the service and when, what users are asking, and how well their needs are met.

Cooperative and Collaborative Reference

As librarians struggle to embrace new technologies and services, they rarely receive a corresponding increase in budget and human resources. Small libraries in particular are hard-pressed to keep up, but even large libraries cannot easily meet the challenge of 24/7 service. Consequently, librarians are finding strength in numbers and extending their participation in resource sharing to include sharing reference expertise. These cooperative ventures are further facilitated by the collaborative capabilities of most virtual reference software.

BOX 11.6
QUESTIONPOINT

The QuestionPoint service, available at www.QuestionPoint.org, provides libraries with access to a growing collaborative network of reference librarians in the United States and around the world. Library patrons can submit questions at any time of the day or night through their library's Web site. The questions will be answered online by qualified library staff from the patron's own library or may be forwarded to a participating library around the world. The service, which is available to libraries by subscription, will enable reference librarians to share their resources and expertise with each other and with their patrons free of charge in unprecedented ways.

From "Global Reference Network," http://www.loc.gov/rr/digiref/.

Though informal collaboration was never farther away than the telephone, the idea of institutionalizing collaborative or cooperative reference was born in the late 1990s, when the Library of Congress undertook development of the Collaborative Digital Reference Service. The purpose of the service was to build a system (including software) that capitalizes on the specific strengths of individual libraries in answering virtual questions from users from any of the participating libraries. The service has evolved and expanded and is now part of the Online Computer Library Center (OCLC) and known as QuestionPoint (see Box 11.6). This initiative is an example of one of several whereby librarians create customized consortia in which participating libraries take turns providing virtual reference to all members.

Many libraries are now involved in a cooperative reference service, particularly at a regional or state level. Examples of successful collaborative services include the Maryland AskUsNow! (http://www.askusnow.info) and AskColorado (http://www.askcolorado.org/) networks, among others. Cooperative services often afford librarians their only opportunity to venture into virtual service or enable them to extend service hours. Not all librarians, however, regard cooperative service as the course to follow. Librarians are concerned that local questions may not be effectively answered and are equally reluctant to take on questions relating to another collection or institution. Research indicates that the majority of virtual questions are "local" in that they relate to the holdings, policies, or other specific aspects of the host library.[19] Supporters, however, report positive experiences and argue that with appropriate training, good communication, clear policies and procedures, and a healthy dose of trust, cooperative reference provides a win-win situation for librarians and users.[20]

In some cases, virtual reference service is so popular that multiple chat questions occur simultaneously, and there exists a real need for a virtual reference queuing service. One such platform is the Library H3lp (http://libraryh3lp.blogspot.com) platform that allows a staff of reference librarians to share expertise in answering reference queries that come in virtually. This queuing service can also act as a tool to integrate disparate query sources; for example, you may want to set up your library's Text-a-Librarian service to be answered from this interface. The ideal would be to have all virtual services configured from one shared interface to which librarians in all parts of the library would have access, not only in order to share expertise in answering queries but also as a means to share the responsibilities for staffing the virtual reference service.

Handheld Computing and Reference Service

Cell phones have widespread uptake and use, particularly among the library's younger user population, and can be considered a ubiquitous tool for information access. Higher-end phones are essentially a type of handheld computer, offering their users profound new ways to engage with information in the world. Context-aware services offer users the ability to gain information about their surrounding environment as they experience it, delivering information to their handheld device based on where they are and what filters of information are requested. Mobile applications that deliver this level of interactivity are emerging as an important part of the reference librarian's toolkit. Other types of handheld computing services that augment the in-person library experience are SMS tools that allow users to text the call number of their book to their phone. This service helps the user navigate the library space as they seek to obtain their identified item.

The development of SMS reference service allows librarians to answer reference questions that users ask from their cell phones. Many higher-end phones have "always on" Internet connections, and a user could be asking the library an IM question from a chat interface on his or her handheld device. Other librarians have experimented with catalog notification services delivered to the patron's cell phone by way of SMS: services that allow users to be notified at the exact moment requested books have arrived or to be notified when books they have checked out are about to be overdue. Such "just-in-time" service is the virtue of SMS services.

A useful frame for understanding handheld computing is the matrix of mediated versus unmediated service. In mediated service, the library and library staff serve as a gateway to library information by way of library resources or tools. A librarian may design a library iPhone app that acts as a chat widget or perhaps a video tour of the library. These resources are mediated by the librarian. Alternatively, the library may also have no such gateway when it comes to other types of software components for access to information. Search for information by way of mobile apps cuts out the librarian as intermediary to information and represents unmediated access to information. Every day, more and more reference sources will become available by way of these discrete software components that quickly and seamlessly deliver information to a user's personal computing device. Librarians will come to view informational apps as a new type of reference source for their user and will recommend them accordingly.

KEEPING CURRENT, STAYING RELEVANT

With rapidly evolving technologies and increasing user expectations, how can librarians hope to keep pace and remain relevant? Fortunately, an ever-increasing number of professional outlets help keep librarians current. Through the work of committees and discussion groups of the Reference and User Services Association of the American Library Association (http://www.ala.org/ala/mgrps/divs/rusa/), librarians can keep current on hot topics. Professional literature abounds with articles relevant to reference services, particularly the journals *Reference & User Services Quarterly*, *Reference Services Review*, and *Internet Reference Services Quarterly*. Various Web resources provide an excellent means of learning the latest applications and keeping current (see Box 11.7).

Although the challenges of the future may appear daunting, to paraphrase Mark Twain, reports of the death of reference are greatly exaggerated. As reference librarianship enters its second century, reference librarians are providing "personal assistance to readers" both within the library and far beyond library walls and are embracing new technologies as they retain traditional values. If extinction results from an inability to adapt to a changing environment, reference librarians have no cause to worry.

BOX 11.7
WEB SITES, BLOGS, WIKIS, AND APP STORES

Web Sites

Virtual Reference Desk: Resources related to virtual reference and conference proceedings from the Virtual Reference Desk conferences (http://www.webjunction.org/52).

Current Cites: An annotated bibliography of selected articles, books, and documents on information technology (http://lists.webjunction.org/currentcites/).

Blogs

Digital Reference: A forum for discussion of all aspects of digital reference service. (http://www.stephenfrancoeur.com/digitalreference/).

Wikis

Library Success Wiki—Reference Services and Information Literacy: An openly edited source on staying current with reference service delivery (http://www.libsuccess.org/index.php?title=Main_Page#Reference_Services_and_Information_Literacy).

App Stores

iPhone app store—Periodically browse the reference apps to learn how traditional reference tools combined with user location help to meet users information needs as they experience their surrounding environment (http://www.apple.com/iphone/apps-for-iphone/).

Android Marketplace—Another online app store that can offer free access to information that traditionally has been the domain of the reference librarian (http://market.android.com/).

NOTES

1.   Jeannette Woodward, *Creating the Customer-Driven Library: Building on the Bookstore Model* (Chicago: American Library Association, 2005), 234 pp.

2.   Christen Cardina and Donald Wicks, "The Changing Roles of Academic Reference Librarians Over a Ten-Year Period," *Reference & User Services Quarterly* 44 (Winter 2004): 133–42.

3.   For additional discussion, see "Information Commons" in *The Encyclopedia of Library and Information Science*, 3rd ed., ed. Marcia J. Bates and Mary Niles Maack (Boca Raton: CRC Press, 2009), 2401–8.

4.   Charles Bunge and Chris Ferguson, "The Shape of Services to Come: Values-Based Reference Service for the Largely Digital Library," *College & Research Libraries* 58 (May 1997): 258.

5.   Patricia K. Swanson, "Traditional Models: Myths and Realities," in *Academic Libraries: Myths and Realities: Proceedings of the Third National Conference of the Association of College and Research Libraries* (Chicago: American Library Association, 1984), 89.

6.   Thelma Freides, "Current Trends in Academic Libraries," *Library Trends* 31 (Winter 1983): 466–67.

7.   Aaron Schmidt, "The User Experience," *Library Journal* 135, no. 1 (2010): 28–29.

8.   Beth S. Woodard, "The Effectiveness of an Information Desk Staffed by Graduate Assistants and Non-Professionals," *College & Research Libraries* 50 (July 1989): 455–67.

9.   Pixie Ann Mosley, "Assessing User Interactions at the Desk Nearest the Front Door," *Reference & User Services Quarterly* 47 (Summer 2007): 159–67.

10.   Douglas Herman, "But Does It Work? Evaluating the Brandeis Reference Model," *Reference Services Review* 22 (Winter 1994): 17–28.

11.   Theresa Arndt, "Reference Service without the Desk," *Reference Services Review* 38, no. 1 (2010): 71–80.

12.   Janet Crane and Jeanne A. Pavy, "One-Stop Shopping: Merging Service Points in a University Library," *Public Services Quarterly* 4, no. 1 (2008): 29–45; Pat Flanagan and Lisa R. Horowitz, "Exploring New Service Models: Can Consolidating Public Service Points Improve Response to Customer Needs?," *Journal of Academic Librarianship* 26, no. 5 (2000): 329–38.

13.   See, for example, Triveni Kuchi, Laura Bowering Mullen, and Stephanie Tama-Bartels, "Librarians without Borders: Reaching out to Students at a Campus Center," *Reference & User Services Quarterly* 43 (Summer 2004): 310–17; A. Ben Wagner and Cynthia Tysick, "Onsite Reference and Instruction Services: Setting Up Shop Where Our Patrons Live," *Reference & User Services Quarterly* 46 (Winter 2007): 60–65.

14.   Martin Kesselman and Sarah Watstein, "Creating Opportunities: Embedded Librarians," *Journal of Library Administration* 49 (2009): 383.

15.   The literature on digital reference service, particularly real-time services, is extensive. See the Virtual Reference site for links to many resources: http://www.webjunction.org/52.

16.   See, for example, Marshall Breeding, "Instant Messaging: It's Not Just for Kids Anymore," *Computers in Libraries* 23 (November/December 2003): 38–40.

17.   Jo Kibbee, David Ward, and Wei Ma, "Virtual Service, Real Data: Results of a Pilot Study," *Reference Services Review* 30 (February 2002): 25–36.

18.   Ibid., 35.

19.   Theresa Berry, Margaret Casado, and Lana Dixon, "The Local Nature of Digital Reference," *Southeastern Librarian* 51 (Fall 2003): 8–15.

20.   Thomas A. Peters, "E-Reference: How Consortia Add Value," *Journal of Academic Librarianship* 28 (July 2002): 248–50.

ADDITIONAL READINGS

Bailey, Russell, and Barbara Tierney. "Information Commons Redux: Concept, Evolution, and Transcending the Tragedy of the Commons." *Journal of Academic Librarianship* 28 (September 2002): 277–86.

Bailey and Tierney review the concept of the information commons and describe its administrative and functional integration into an academic library, highlighting the role of the "enhanced" information desk.

Cardina, Christen, and Donald Wicks. "The Changing Roles of Academic Reference Librarians over a Ten-Year Period." *Reference & User Services Quarterly* 44 (Winter 2004): 133–42.

This study assesses the changes that occurred in academic reference librarians' job responsibilities from 1991 to 2001. The authors describe how various reference responsibilities changed over a 10-year period, as did the relative amount of time spent on various activities. The article concludes with a list of traditional as well as newly developed duties of reference librarians.

Ferguson, Chris. "Reshaping Academic Library Reference Service: A Review of Issues, Trends, and Possibilities." *Advances in Librarianship* 18 (1994): 73–109.

Though written in the mid-1990s, this article by Ferguson provides an excellent overview of the issues fueling the debate on the theory and practice of reference services in academic libraries. Beginning with an anatomy of the "crisis" in reference, Ferguson examines factors such as funding, the impact of technology, organizational structures, quality of service, and burnout—all of which call into question the efficacy of the traditional model. He concludes with a prediction that future libraries will see a more fully integrated and user-centered service.

Gray, Suzanne M. "Virtual Reference Services: Directions and Agendas." *Reference & User Services Quarterly* 39 (Summer 2000): 365–75.

Gray discusses issues librarians grapple with in providing virtual reference service, including traffic from nonaffiliated users, response time, optimal service hours, and service evaluation.

Hahn, Jim. "Mobile Learning for the Twenty-First Century Librarian." *Reference Services Review* 36 (2008): 272–88.

A literature review of mobile computing initiatives in public, academic, and special libraries offers a picture of library services for the 21st century by drawing on human–computer interaction papers and approaches from medical libraries.

Janes, Joseph. *Introduction to Reference Work in the Digital Age.* New York: Neal-Schuman, 2003. 213 pp.

Engagingly written, this introductory text provides an excellent overview of the current state of reference services, with a clear articulation of the advantages, as well as the challenges and limitations, of serving users remotely.

"Reference in the (post)Google Age." *Reference Services Review* 38, no. 1 (2010).

This important theme issue includes a variety of articles focused on creating an optimal reference environment, including issues such as research consultations, reference without a desk, and social networking.

Rieh, Soo Young. "Changing Reference Service Environment: A Review of Perspectives from Managers, Librarians, and Users." *Journal of Academic Librarianship* 25 (May 1999): 178–86.

This article examines changes in the traditional reference desk model, with a focus on integrating and maximizing users' information-search processes and librarians' intervention.

"Symposium on Reference Service." *Journal of Academic Librarianship* 21 (January 1995): 3–16.

Leading off with the provocative article "Is Traditional Reference Service Obsolete?," followed by four responses, this series of essays calls into question the notion of "reference librarians answering questions at a reference desk." Evolving responsibilities include the design of user-friendly retrieval systems, negotiation of complex automated reference environments, and continued human mediation.

Tyckoson, David A. "What Is the Best Model of Reference Service?" *Library Trends* 50 (Fall 2001): 183–96.

Tyckoson reviews models of reference service in the context of the professional values they reflect. He compares and contrasts the traditional desk model with the teaching-library model, tiered service, and virtual service and concludes that there is no "right" model.

Chapter

Reference Services for Specific Populations

Frances Jacobson Harris

INTRODUCTION

An underlying philosophy of this book, articulated most explicitly in chapter 2, is a commitment to quality reference service for *all*. Because "all" encompasses individuals with a variety of needs, successful reference service must accommodate those needs. No standard blueprint for reference services exists that is appropriate in all situations. Developing specialized reference services for specific populations within our society is an essential corollary to developing service for the majority. Beyond the provision of basic reference services to an obvious, primary group of users, librarians need to identify significant secondary or special groups of users with common needs and adjust reference service to these groups.

The basis of concern for reference service to specific populations is ethical as well as legal. Reference librarians often must be advocates for members of these groups to ensure they have equitable access to information and materials. In addition, libraries supported by public funds have a legal obligation to provide service without discrimination based on class, race, gender, or other defining social or physical characteristics. As noted in chapter 2, the profession has created the *Library Bill of Rights* to emphasize its commitment to fair use of resources and openness to all users (see Box 12.1).

This chapter examines models of reference service delivery to a selection of groups whose needs are especially well defined, although not always met. The chapter does not address the reference needs of those in the business or technical sector, who would typically be served by special libraries. Instead, the focus is on groups who are defined in terms of socioeconomic, ethnic, or physical characteristics. The specific groups discussed are differentiated on the basis of *age* (children, young adults, and the elderly); *disabling conditions* (physical and developmental disabilities); and *cultural identity*, which may include language facility (non-English-speaking and the adult illiterate). For each of these groups, defining characteristics

BOX 12.1
LIBRARY BILL OF RIGHTS

Article V of the Library Bill of Rights states,

A person's right to use a library should not be denied or abridged because of origin, age, background, or views.[1]

(Adopted June 19, 1939, by the ALA Council; amended October 14, 1944; June 18, 1948; February 2, 1961; June 27, 1967; January 23, 1980; inclusion of "age" reaffirmed January 23, 1996)

Broadly interpreted, this article includes all persons, regardless of characteristics or circumstance. In the interpretation of Article V, *Free Access to Libraries for Minors*, the right of minors is explicitly defended:

Librarians and library governing bodies cannot assume the role of parents or the functions of parental authority in the private relationship between parent and child. Librarians and governing bodies should maintain that only parents and guardians have the right and the responsibility to determine their children's—and only their children's—access to library resources. Parents and guardians who do not want their children to have access to certain library services, materials, or facilities should so advise their children. .

Lack of access to information can be harmful to minors. Librarians and library governing bodies have a public and professional obligation to ensure that all members of the community they serve have free, equal, and equitable access to the entire range of library resources regardless of content, approach, format, or amount of detail. This principle of library service applies equally to all users, minors as well as adults.[2]

(Adopted June 30, 1972 by the ALA Council; amended July 1, 1981; July 3, 1991; June 30, 2004; July 2, 2008)

Reprinted by permission of ALA.

are described, and reference techniques and policy issues associated with the group are discussed.

Within any library service community, there are certainly other groups to consider (such as institutionalized populations, specific ethnic or religious groups, members of the gay and lesbian communities, and others), and not every group discussed here may be part of a given library's service population. The intent of this chapter is to give an overview of issues associated with reference service to individual groups. The assumption is that service to any one group is a microcosm of general reference service—that the basics of reference service are present, and the task is to adapt good reference skills and collections to serve each group. Satia Orange and Robin Osborne argue that librarians need to shift their focus from developing special services for specific user groups (with funds that may disappear) to sustaining quality services for all user groups.[3] They suggest that we reframe what we know as outreach so that it is based on equity rather than on underserved populations per se. If the focus is on underserved or "special" populations, these services tend to be marginalized and are the first to be cut in times of budget crisis. But if the focus is on equitable service delivery, then service to specific populations is part of the whole, part of a systemic approach that serves all. It is in this spirit that this chapter is written.

An equitable reference service model includes these components:

1. Assessing the problems a member of a specific group experiences when trying to access information and services provided by the library
2. Conducting research that includes contact with associations and service providers about how to improve services for specific categories of users (and how to attract nonusers)
3. Planning how to adapt the reference interview, collection development, and delivery of service
4. Training staff to work with users with special needs or cultural differences
5. Implementing periodic evaluation of reference services to members of specific groups

Although school, public, academic, and special libraries may vary in the degree to which certain reference services are provided, elements to be considered in an adequate configuration of reference services to specific groups include the following:

1. Information services commensurate with the group's needs and abilities, such as ready reference, virtual reference service, homework assignment help, personal research assistance, and information and referral services (see chapter 1)
2. Readers' advisory service (see chapter 1)
3. Instructional services that include assistance both in finding materials and in understanding the information found (see chapter 8)
4. Collection development to support the information and developmental needs of each group, including a good reference and circulating collection of materials at appropriate reading and cognitive levels in book and nonbook formats
5. Interlibrary referral and loan services to supplement local sources when necessary
6. Solutions to problems of access caused by physical, cognitive, or emotional barriers[4]

REFERENCE SERVICE IN A PLURALISTIC SOCIETY

Ethnic Diversity

A demographic profile of the United States and Canada reveals a highly diverse, culturally rich picture. Population projections from the U.S. Census Bureau indicate that by 2020, Hispanics will make up 17.8 percent of the U.S. population, African Americans 13.5 percent, and Asians 5.4 percent.[5] Hispanics have already replaced African Americans as the country's largest minority group. The percentage of non-Hispanic whites in the population will continue to decrease, and by 2050, non-Hispanic whites will be at 50.1 percent of the total population.[6] In 2008, 13.2 percent of the total population lived below the poverty level; only 11.2 percent of the white population shouldered this burden, whereas 24.7 percent of African Americans and 23.2 percent of Hispanics lived below the poverty line.[7] The post-September 11 world has also made North Americans much more aware of the religious and ethnic diversity in their midst.

In 1990, 527,000 Americans identified themselves as Muslim. By 2008, that number had risen to 1,349,000, a 156 percent increase.[8] During the same period, the number of self-identified Hindus rose from 227,000 to 582,000, also a 156 percent increase, whereas the total Christian population rose from 151,225,000 to 173,402,000.[9] Although Christians are still the overwhelming majority, these latter figures represent only a 15 percent increase in that population.

Such overwhelming data compel librarians to consider providing reference service that is responsive to different needs and, as stated earlier, does not have a formulaic, one-size-fits-all approach. Marcia Nauratil observes that "the [relatively small] size and composition of the library's traditional clientele might be due more to a library's own middle-class orientation than to various inadequacies on the part of nonusers."[10] Mengxiong Liu notes that nontraditional clientele may not have a conceptual awareness of library services or may come from a culture that embraces an entirely different philosophy of education.[11] As individuals, their information-seeking behavior is affected by "different cultural experiences, language, level of literacy, socioeconomic status, education, level of acculturation and value system."[12]

Phoebe Janes and Ellen Meltzer advocate training that specifically addresses the need to individualize and adapt reference service.[13] They state that training is necessitated by invisible barriers and implicit assumptions of which many librarians are not consciously aware. For example, library staff are often guilty of assuming that users share common experiences in libraries and similar communication styles. Yolanda Cuesta advises that staff training cover three types of techniques: techniques for engaging the community, techniques for effective communication with a diverse customer base, and techniques for analyzing the library from the community's perspective.[14] In terms of communication, she includes cultural awareness and sensitivity training, cultural knowledge, and linguistic competence to help staff convey information in a manner that is easily understood by diverse audiences. She notes that "everything and anything the library does communicates a message to the community."[15] Patrick Andrew Hall argues that the role of *affectivity*, "the more intangible qualities of personal rapport and empathy," is just as important as familiarity with specific cultural experiences and sensitivity to diversity.[16] Thus, although it is useful to know that people of color may regard professional distance as "a sign of rudeness or contempt,"[17] it is the specific *relationship* between librarian and user that builds an effective interaction, more so than the generic, "culturally correct" approach.

Non-English Speakers

Non-English (or new-English) speakers represent every age group, every race, and every level of the socioeconomic spectrum and make use of all types of libraries. In 1990, almost 20 million persons living in the United States (7.9% of the U.S. population) were foreign-born; that number had risen to more than 38 million (12.5%) by 2008.[18] In 2009 there were more than 48 million Hispanics in this country (Hispanics made up more than 15% of the population),[19] and there were 672,000 international students enrolled in institutions of higher education.[20] Clearly, ethnic diversity continues to be a major factor in the composition of the U.S. population. Furthermore, immigrant populations are now settling in a wide variety of communities in the United States and Canada, no longer just in big cities or traditional immigrant enclaves.[21]

New- or non-speakers of English fall into three general categories: long-term residents or citizens; immigrants and newly arrived persons, both permanent and transient; and international students attending institutions of higher education. At issue is not only mastery of the English language but also individual background and experience with the U.S. system of libraries.

Although types of libraries vary in the exact nature of reference services provided, all libraries should adapt their standard reference services to their non-English-speaking users. Particular attention should be paid to collection of materials in different languages, as appropriate, and to materials that describe or reflect the cultures of the library's users. Public libraries, in particular, should provide access to materials for teaching and learning English and to continuing education opportunities, such as literacy programs, study programs for citizenship, and high school equivalency courses. In her library's English as a second language (ESL) classes, Lena Gonzalez made an ally of technology.[22] In addition to ESL software, she had students use word processors to write or dictate stories that became part of the class curriculum. She noted that Internet access to information about her students' home countries was very meaningful to those who were homesick or wished to share their experiences with others. In libraries where this kind of comprehensive programming is not feasible, access to such services should be provided by means of referral or liaison work. When possible, libraries should also provide bilingual or bicultural reference staff or solicit the aid of volunteer groups for translation purposes or peer support. One such example is the Denver Public Library, where Spanish-speaking staff have *Hablo Español* printed at the bottom of their nametags for easy identification.[23] Even assistance in the form of bilingual phone messages and signage will make a big difference to non-English speakers.

School library media centers increasingly serve multiple groups of bilingual children, and librarians need to develop communication skills based on cultural awareness and provide materials in the native languages of their students. School libraries can also form effective partnerships with ESL teachers, which will strengthen students' experiences and expand their understanding of library services.[24] Academic libraries need to include in their reference program information literacy instruction that is accessible to students for whom English is a second language. For example, international students have been recruited to conduct orientation tours in target languages and to act as peer tutors.[25] In order to accommodate larger numbers of students and allow them to proceed at their own pace, Baruch College created multilingual virtual tours in nine languages.[26]

Reference services to non-English-speaking groups are more expensive in terms of required staffing and materials than are services to the general U.S. public. But such services facilitate retention of native languages and traditions while easing integration into the new culture. Such citizens move more quickly to a position to contribute to the economy and the culture of their surroundings and to "pay back" the society that supported their transition.[27]

Cultural Differences and Reference Service

Libraries, as Americans know them, are rather unusual in their approach to library service. In many countries, academic libraries are nothing but vast study halls, or their limited collections are locked in closed stacks. Access to these warehouses is obtained through the beneficence of retrieval clerks who are not trained librarians. Collections are often noncirculating, or users may have to pay fees to check out books. A comparable public library system for the general population may not exist. Reference service is neither provided nor understood in the way that it is practiced in the United States. In support of this type of library service are educational traditions that are often based on rote learning, where the teacher is regarded as the repository of all knowledge; no independent investigation is required, and it may in fact be strongly discouraged.[28]

The characteristics of the U.S. library system are simultaneously wonderful and daunting to many non-English speakers. In these libraries one is permitted direct access to a seemingly unlimited supply of materials, and most exciting of all, one is allowed to take materials home. On the other hand, open access implies independent negotiation of a confusing and unfamiliar environment. Using the catalog can be challenging because of its highly formalized structure. Although some catalog systems now include a Spanish-language interface with title, author, and other data elements labeled in Spanish, users will eventually have to face English-language information.[29] Asking for help does not always seem to be a viable option. From some cultural perspectives, library staff members may be suspect as representatives of the institution, as figures of authority (see Box 12.2). Librarians may exhibit what appears to be confusing body language, or by their gender or perceived social status, they may be deemed unapproachable. From this vantage point, the users must ask questions not about something they know, but about something they do *not* know, a task that is difficult enough to accomplish when English is one's first language.

The Reference Interview

Fundamentally, the librarian's conduct during the reference interview is no different with non-English speakers than it is with other users. As stressed in chapter 3, the librarian should treat all people and queries with respect and seriousness. However, with non-English speakers it is especially important to anticipate some timidity and

---

BOX 12.2
IN THE WORDS OF A FOREIGNER

In some foreign countries, the librarian at the reference desk still possesses the image of the person with the power to claim monopoly of all knowledge, and thus is not to be disturbed. Further, societal demands in some countries require that people of a certain social status, or age, or gender ask nothing but intelligent questions. Thus, with this same perception of the librarian, and the concomitant potential for ridicule, some foreign students will not approach the librarian. And if they have a first (bachelor's) degree, and are large males, they will certainly shy away from the reference desk, abiding by the norm that intelligent people (as shown by possession of a first degree), and mature beings (as shown by size and/or age) do not ask silly questions, even if this is the only way to get much-needed answers. Sometimes it is not easy for foreign students to realize that certain types of ignorance are acceptable, and that librarians are there to help.

Kwasi Sarkodie-Mensah, "In the Words of a Foreigner," *Research Strategies* 4 (Winter 1986): 31.

---

a possible reticence toward public institutions. It is crucial to be aware of and to understand both cultural and individual differences. For example, the terms "Latino" (a reference to Latin America) and "Hispanic" (derived from Hispania, the Latin name for the Iberian Peninsula) hardly describe the huge variety of cultural traditions represented. Although most Hispanics come from Mexico, many are from Puerto Rico, the Dominican Republic, Cuba, and countries in Central and South America. Each cultural grouping has its own traditions, value systems, and social classes. Hispanics may be of any race and also include the indigenous peoples whose native language is something other than Spanish. Within this array of cultural identities, it is *individuals* with unique needs and questions who come to reference desks for help.

It is important to make no assumptions regarding what non-English-speaking users know about libraries.[30] Depending on circumstances, they may not understand the concept of call numbers, be able to decipher commonly used library terms, or know how to distinguish between printed U.S. first names and surnames. In answering reference questions, slang should be avoided and the use of materials explained and demonstrated, giving users the opportunity to observe and then to imitate. Whenever possible, the librarian should escort a new library user through to the end of the process, such as locating a book or a magazine on the shelf. It is easy to mistake nods and smiles as signifying comprehension. This pitfall can be avoided by asking questions that allow users to communicate more precisely what they do or do not understand. Even apparent English-language fluency may not produce an outcome of successful communication and cultural understanding. Between the user and the librarian, it is also possible to misunderstand body language, eye contact (or lack of it), attempts at humor, and other common communication habits.[31] The librarian must abandon assumptions and concentrate on the intent of the user's question. After a question is answered, follow-up is especially important and is vital to proper closure of the interview.

Sharon Moller suggests several behaviors that can help communication. Try to avoid situations that will embarrass the user. "If a staff person cannot understand the patron's request, the staff should apologize and make it his or her fault, and not that of the patron. It would therefore be my fault that I don't understand Spanish or fractured English as well as I should, not the patron's fault that the patron does not speak better English. Sometimes humor at one's own expense will help ease the situation."[32] She also notes that in deciding what to call anyone, it is best to follow that person's lead. "Many may prefer to be known by their country of origin—Chileans or Mexicans or Peruvians. Or, even better, refer to them by name (but try to get the pronunciation reasonably correct). Isn't that the best way to refer to any of us rather than trying to lump many unique individuals into one impersonal category?"[33]

Illiterate/Low-Literate Adults

Current adult literacy statistics are surprisingly hard to come by. Although it is possible to count how many students go to school and subsequently graduate, it is very difficult to determine how many adults can actually read at a competent level. The National Center for Education Statistics (NCES) completed a National Assessment of Adult Literacy in 2003.[34] The first international survey of illiteracy was published in 1995 by Statistics Canada and the Organisation for Economic Co-operation and Development (OECD) and has not been re-administered.[35] Results showed that 46.6 percent of the adult population of the United States was unable to perform Level 3 prose literacy tasks, such as reading a set of four movie reviews to determine which review was least favorable.[36] Of those who were only at the first level of prose proficiency (20.7 percent), 44.2 percent had no income, and 25.9 percent were in the lowest income quintile[37] (see Box 12.3). These statistics suggest that delivery of reference service may need to be adapted for significant numbers of adults, in any community, who do not read well.

Literacy programming is a natural service for libraries, particularly public libraries. However, teaching adults to read has traditionally been the responsibility

---

BOX 12.3
A THIRD OF THE NATION CANNOT READ THESE WORDS

Twenty-five million American adults cannot read the poison warnings on a can of pesticide, a letter from their child's teacher, or the front page of a daily paper. An additional 35 million read only at a level that is less than equal to the full survival needs of our society.

Together, these 60 million people represent more than one-third of the entire adult population.

Jonathan Kozol, *Illiterate America* (New York: New American Library, 1985), 4.

of school systems or social service agencies, so libraries have not always seen it as part of their mandate. At the same time, libraries embrace the role with children, through core services such as story times, summer reading programs, and other reading promotion activities.[38] Adult nonreaders deserve similar consideration. Some libraries host literacy services in the library or provide space for tutoring that other agencies deliver. Other libraries simply provide appropriate referral to community agencies or literacy councils that administer testing and tutoring. Many community colleges or public and school libraries support programs such as GED (General Educational Development—high school equivalency) or formal adult basic education programs, or offer special tutoring services to nonreading adults. Materials explaining tutoring and other services should be written at no higher than a fourth-grade level, using a conversational high-interest/low-vocabulary format, and such services should be promoted through other media, such as television and radio, as well.

For library-based literacy programs to be successful, Dinah O'Brien offers a number of specific suggestions.[39] She stresses the importance of staff training, including preemptive training given during graduate school. "It is in training sessions that we will learn what tutors and learners need to know about the library, how they feel about our services, and what we can do to make the literacy experience beneficial to all."[40] She notes that the public library is a representative of a government structure that may seem exclusionary, indicating that libraries have to work hard to overcome that perspective and establish comfort levels with nontraditional users. Collaboration with other community agencies is essential, as is the participation of non-librarian staff members who may have close ties to the local community.

O'Brien's observations reflect the experiences reported by the 13 libraries that participated in the Literacy in Libraries Across America (LILAA) initiative funded by the Lila Wallace–Reader's Digest Fund and the American Library Association.[41] The Oakland Public Library developed learner-centered participatory literacy education by establishing learner advisory groups and crafting curriculum based on their interests and suggestions.[42] At the Waukegan (Illinois) Public Library, literacy training is folded into computer and Internet training.[43] Participants use e-mail and a variety of software programs. At the Wakefield branch of the New York Public Library, which serves an Afro-Caribbean community, the Center for Reading and Writing staff is Afro-Caribbean and uses materials and curricula that reflect students' cultures and interests such as employment, taxation, and health.[44] Unconventional approaches such as these are more likely to attract those in need.

In its analysis of the OECD survey, the Educational Testing Service noted that "adults with low literacy levels do not usually acknowledge or recognize they have a problem."[45] The reference interview must take this perspective into account. It is important to listen carefully and to observe not just the literal spoken words but also other available cues. In answering specific queries, reference librarians should, without fanfare, be prepared to offer materials on a low reading level, when available, and to read or paraphrase the information contained in them to the user. A variety of associations and publishers provide materials and information for the new adult reader, including ProLiteracy (http://www.proliteracy.org), formed by the 2002 merger of Laubach Literacy International and the Literacy Volunteers of America, and now the oldest and largest nongovernmental literacy organization in the world. Smaller libraries might choose to integrate adult and children's nonfiction collections "to reduce the stigmatization of the adult new learner when selecting materials."[46]

Library reference collections should contain the types of information needed by adolescents or adults who do not read well, in formats or reading levels accessible to them when possible. Because poor reading skills are frequently associated with poor earning power, this information should include coping or basic life skills information, such as health, consumer, employment, and money management data. The general library collection should include materials for developing basic reading skills (materials on beginning to fourth- or fifth-grade reading levels), GED materials (fifth- to seventh-grade reading level), and leisure reading.[47]

REFERENCE SERVICE TO DISABLED INDIVIDUALS

Among the specific populations for whom librarians need to develop a full range of reference services are individuals with disabilities. In 1990, the Americans with Disabilities Act (ADA) was signed into law, representing "a milestone in America's commitment to full and equal opportunity for all its citizens."[48] Title II of the ADA governs public services for disabled individuals. It states that "library services must be provided in a manner that allows *each* eligible user with a disability to equally benefit from the local library....Every decision about ADA compliance must be made on a case-by-case basis, taking into consideration the elements involved in the service or program and the needs of the library patron with a disability."[49] A particular service for persons with disabilities can be denied only if a library can prove that it would incur an undue burden were it required to offer the service. However, thinking in terms of "requirements" masks a simple reality. As Katy Lenn observes, it "is important to remember that the purpose of legislation for the disabled is not to create special rights but equal rights."[50]

Developments in adaptive technology have transformed many dreams into realities, such as speech recognition systems, screen enlargement software, and computerized Braille embossers. But lack of funding for high technology should not inhibit service to disabled users. Many aspects of ADA compliance are not technology-intensive and serve the able-bodied population as well. A magnifying glass and an adjustable piece of furniture are two such examples. Other solutions involve forethought more than cost. If a workstation is set up on a push-button adjustable-height table with an adjustable keyboard tray, with a keyboard that has large-type black-on-white keys, and with two pointing devices such as a conventional mouse and a trackball, the workstation will meet the needs of wheelchair users and people who have computer-related repetitive strain injuries or carpal tunnel syndrome, as well as other dexterity disabilities.[51] Rob Imrie advocates principles of universal design, in which products, environments, and communication systems are designed for the broadest spectrum of users.[52] He stresses that social, attitudinal, and political shifts must first take place so that design principles and technical adaptations take place within an ethos of inclusiveness.[53] By following this advice, libraries simultaneously meet the needs of able-bodied users as well as disabled clientele.

Some services and technologies that are new to mainstream audiences have engendered unexpected benefits for disabled persons. For example, live online chat reference service is an improvement on traditional TTY reference service at Gallaudet

University, whose Internet-adept students are already veteran users of chat and instant messaging technology.[54] Other unanticipated consequences have not been so welcome. Marti Goddard notes that because most computer-based assistive technology is designed for installation on single-user workstations, a networked library environment with secured workstations presents serious challenges for those who need to reconfigure computer settings.[55] Voice recognition software requires users to build a voice file that the computer learns to "recognize," another challenge in a shared-use environment. Some technologies create noise, such as Braille embossers and voice output systems (although headphones can mitigate problems with the latter). Conversely, a workstation that is intended for users with learning disabilities should be installed in a quiet location with a minimum of distractions.[56]

Each library needs to formulate its own service policies, using the ADA as a guideline along with publications that have been written specifically to help libraries through this process.[57] A library, for example, may adopt the policy that when its employees are unable to provide equal, immediate delivery of service, such as photocopying the information in answer to a reference question, they will provide the material within 24 hours. The goal to work toward is equal treatment of all persons, the key ingredient being a positive attitude on the part of the staff. In any library, the reference department will certainly play a central role in developing and implementing services for disabled persons.

Both legally and ethically, librarians should evaluate the reference services they offer from the perspective of the user with a disability. This is a challenging task, given that there are numerous disabling conditions, and in any community served, the incidence of any one disabling condition may be relatively low. The general groups considered here are individuals with physical disabilities and those with developmental or learning disabilities.

Persons with Physical Disabilities

The physically disabled population includes persons who are blind and visually impaired, individuals who are deaf and hearing-impaired, and persons with mobility impairments. Each of these groups requires somewhat different adaptations of reference service. The uniting theme, however, is realistic access to resources and services so that these items are usable by the individual with a physical disability.

Visually Impaired Persons

People who are blind or visually impaired have had the longest tradition of special services from libraries. The Library of Congress developed a special reading room for blind persons in 1897.[58] In the 1930s, the Library of Congress developed a national network of libraries to serve blind persons, and in the mid-1960s, other disabled individuals became eligible for this service. The services of the Library's National Library Service for the Blind and Physically Handicapped are available through a system of regional and subregional centers, with local libraries often acting in a liaison role. For eligible individuals, the service includes the loan of Braille books and audiobooks, magazines, and specialized equipment for playback of the library's custom cassette tapes.[59] The Library of Congress is currently in the process of converting to digital audio technology, a service it had hoped to launch in 2008.[60] It has begun limited online delivery of Braille texts and audio magazines.

In addition to the Library of Congress programs, there are many other programs and agencies whose products and services are useful in helping the person with visual impairment gain access to information. A variety of vendors distribute large-print books and magazines. General audiobook publishing has exploded in recent years, with many audio titles being published simultaneously with book releases. The 2007 Audio Publishers Association Sales Survey, analyzing data for 2006, showed a 6 percent increase over 2005 audiobook sales. Direct-to-library sales continued to increase, reaching 32 percent of the audiobook market in 2006, compared to 28 percent in 2005.[61] *Library Journal*'s 2004 audiobook survey showed an increase in circulation of 13.5 percent in just two years.[62] For those who can use conventional playback equipment, it is now relatively easy to find most mainstream popular reading material in recorded format. Many larger communities have radio stations for blind and other disabled individuals, as well as organizations that arrange for recording text and other materials.

A number of innovative adaptations of computer workstations have reduced the need for human readers for the blind. Libraries should provide visually impaired users with an Optical Character Recognition (OCR) system, which scans printed text, converts the images into recognized words, speaks the text, and then stores the information in electronic form. Current-generation OCR systems are fairly accurate and have become quite affordable.[63] Other devices are also available to help users who are blind or low-vision.[64] Refreshable Braille display units interface with a personal computer to translate text to Braille and vice versa, giving the library user access to information from online databases and the online catalog. Braille and electronic note-takers provide output in print form, speech, or Braille.

As reference services become more Web-driven, librarians must consider whether their Web pages are accessible to visually impaired users and the technical reading devices they employ.[65] Software is available that interacts directly with appropriately designed Web page coding and translates it into speech, making it useful to the learning disabled and learners of new languages as well as the visually impaired. An added bonus is that accessible Web design is closely connected to principles of good Web design and usability, so all users benefit.[66] A number of prescriptions will ensure Web-compliant design:

- Provide native text for images and Java applets, especially the "hot-spots" in image maps.
- Use contrasting colors for text, image, and background, but do not rely on color alone.
- Use standard style sheets and encoding.
- Provide summaries for tables of data.
- Use relative sizing and positioning rather than absolute.
- Avoid blinking and scrolling text, and make pages function without frames.
- Provide context and orientation information.

Standards for Web-compliant design have been developed by the Web Accessibility Initiative of the World Wide Web Consortium (http://www.w3.org/WAI) and

Section 508 of the U.S. Rehabilitation Act (http://www.section508.gov). The former provides guidelines with checkpoint definitions but does not carry the force of law. Section 508 standards do carry the force of law for federal Web sites. The Web Accessibility Initiative maintains a list of Web accessibility evaluation tools (http://www.w3.org/WAI/ER/tools/complete).

Reference librarians, particularly those in public libraries, should know how to connect users with the Library of Congress program and how to make the various services and devices known to persons in the community who would benefit from their use. The ADA will prompt more libraries to supply readers and reading devices for people with visual impairments. In reference service it is important to provide requested information in a readable form as quickly as possible. This may mean reading lengthy passages to the user or requesting documents in a format readable by the user.

Hearing-Impaired Persons

Individuals with hearing impairments have traditionally been less well served by libraries. The language impairment of deaf persons requires both sensitivity and skill on the part of reference staff to provide effective service. It is important to note that needs and communication techniques will vary depending on whether a person is prelingually deaf, profoundly deaf, deafened late in life, or hard of hearing. Those who are prelingually deaf may need literacy training in English, which is a second language for them.[67] Some libraries sponsor American Sign Language instruction, which also serves parents, children of deaf parents, and other family members.[68] Librarians need to be aware that there is continuing debate in the field of deafness surrounding the status of deafness as a disability or a condition of linguistic minority status.[69] Many deaf persons consider themselves culturally deaf and distance themselves from the disability movement.

Several steps can be taken to provide access for users with hearing impairments. First, in the area of collection development, information about hearing impairment; products for hearing-impaired individuals; community resources; and captioned films, videos, and DVDs are important (including the availability of closed caption decoders where there are also viewing facilities). Additionally, clear signage to lead users to these materials is essential. The second step is to provide ways by which the person who is hearing-impaired can communicate with the reference staff. This can include employing librarians who know American Sign Language (or having an interpreter available by appointment); providing TTY (Text Telephone) machines, which can be attached to a regular telephone; acquiring appropriate amplification devices; and, as mentioned previously, taking advantage of instant messaging technology, e-mail, Web boards, blogs, and other online means of communication for reference service. The third step is publicizing references services, through brochures and other means, to the hearing-impaired community, as well as to families and service providers.

Mobility-Impaired Persons

Reference librarians serving mobility-impaired persons should employ appropriate means of communication and document delivery. For example, answering reference questions might entail note-taking, retrieval of books from higher shelves, or

---

BOX 12.4
IT'S NOT JUST THE BOOKS!

"You have to be impressed when you see librarians getting to know you and your physical limitations so quickly," says Carl. "After my accident, the social worker sent me to a support group for people who were recently handicapped and who relied on wheelchairs. What struck me right away was that wheelchair people have different limitations and challenges. There are paraplegics and quadriplegics. Some of us are incontinent, or asthmatic, or depressed, or heavily medicated. Elderly wheelchair users can get drowsy and fall asleep in the reference area. Younger users might require constant supervision. But you don't hear librarians complain about us. We seem to be as welcome as anyone else, no matter how severely challenged we are. And that's why so many of us become regular library users. It's not just the books, it's the quality of the staff and the way they treat us like ordinary people."

Guy Robertson, "'It's Not Just the Books!' Wheelchair Patrons Speak Out," *Feliciter* 50, no. 6 (2004): 258–60.

---

photocopying for the user. The reference area itself should be evaluated to ensure that it is barrier-free. Appendix B of the *Americans with Disabilities Act (ADA) Handbook* contains the "ADA Accessibility Guidelines for Buildings and Facilities."[70] Further information can also be found online, on the United States Access Board Web site (http://www.access-board.gov) and the ADA home page (http://www.ada.gov). Additionally, specific information on adaptations to the environment are part of municipal or state building codes or accessibility standards. Librarians need to start by looking at Appendix B of the *ADA Handbook* and at state and local codes to determine what needs to be done to come into compliance. In addition, state and national advocacy groups may be able to supply information on adapting environments, or local individuals with physical disabilities may be able to help by personally assessing the library's space.[71] Telephone and online reference assistance may help homebound individuals gain access to reference service.

It is also important to publicize to the physically disabled community that the library is accessible. People who are mobility-impaired need information about disabling conditions, available community services and resources, and current legal and medical information. Such guides as the *Complete Directory for People with Disabilities*[72] or the *Complete Product Guide for People with Disabilities*[73] will direct users to sources of information, advocacy, and services.

Persons with Developmental and Cognitive Disabilities

Persons who have *developmental disabilities* fall into a wider variety of categories than is generally assumed. Developmental disabilities include broad categories such as learning disabilities, mental retardation, and attention deficit disorder with hyperactivity. Characteristics that are often common to these disabilities are difficulties with language, communication, perception, and cognition. Some individuals may also experience problems with emotional and social development. In their book on information services for people with developmental disabilities, Linda Lucas Walling and Marilyn M. Irwin include in their definition such specific labels as autism, Down syndrome, epilepsy, deaf-blind, multiply disabled, spina bifida, medically fragile, Tourette syndrome, fetal alcohol syndrome, and cerebral palsy.[74] They note that "the term *developmental disabilities* encompasses individuals who are intellectually gifted and individuals who are mentally retarded; individuals who cannot use arms and legs and individuals who are physically adept; and individuals who communicate with great difficulty and individuals who communicate easily."[75] Because of the potential for confusion and misunderstanding, they recommend that the term "developmentally disabled" be defined whenever it is used. Obviously, with such a variety of characteristics, reference needs will vary, and librarians need to plan accordingly.

Despite a limited ability to manipulate information, individuals with cognitive disabilities have a right to information, and reference librarians can adapt services to meet their needs. Reference interview sessions will need to be short and focused. Rephrasing or repetition may be necessary, and listening creatively will facilitate communication. The most successful materials are those that have large print, brief texts, and uncluttered pictures. Although children's materials often prove to be good reference tools, mentally disabled adults have the full range of adult concerns, such as vocation, social relationships, sexuality, money management, and parenting; thus, they frequently need to go beyond the resources of a children's reference collection. The adult reference collection can include titles from among the increasing number of materials available for the adult new reader. Because the mentally impaired user may be slow in processing information, it is important to have useful reference materials that circulate or to have space so that the materials may be used for extended periods of time in the library.

It is important for librarians to recognize that they may serve developmentally disabled users through intermediaries, such as parents or attendants. Guides such as *Including Families of Children with Special Needs*[76] communicate to caregivers that the library recognizes their role and is ready to assist. Libraries should provide information about developmental disabilities, including the identification of relevant local and national organizations and agencies, so that family and caregivers can understand the conditions as well as make appropriate decisions about care. Reference librarians may offer to create bibliographies and special informational brochures about library services to be used by care providers, special schools, and organizations for individuals with developmental disabilities.

Another category of mental disability is mental illness, which is included in the ADA's definition of disability. With the deinstitutionalization of large numbers of seriously mentally ill individuals without the provision of sufficient community resources to accommodate them, many have become marginalized in our society and even homeless. Libraries have seen an influx of these displaced people in their reference and reading rooms. Thomas Hecker suggests that libraries' "problem patron" response be replaced by casting the situation in terms of disability, where services and protections are provided as appropriate.[77] But he does not intend for libraries to serve as social service agencies in the face of extreme situations:

> Rather, I suggest that librarians apply the disability model to patrons with
> mental illness who have retained, or who have regained, a level of functioning

which is still within the pale of society. Such people may exhibit symptoms which "stretch the envelope" of our tolerance, but if tolerance will allow them to live an acceptable life within society, tolerance is the accommodation which must be accorded them.[78]

In her book on handling problem situations in libraries, Anne Turner proposes that it is possible to deal with the unanticipated consequences of social policy such as the presence in the library of mentally ill homeless, odiferous individuals, unattended children, migrant laborers, substance abusers, patrons who use library restrooms to smoke or to cook and clean, and so on without compromising professional ethics and principles, and also without creating draconian policies and procedures that attempt to address every conceivable situation.[79] She suggests four themes in an approach to library services:

- No one has the right to interfere with anyone else's right to use the library.
- Library staffs, and especially library managers, must be flexible in their approach to delivering information services in a rapidly changing world and in devising the procedures and policies that organize how they do that.
- Good procedures for handling bad situations are a lot more useful than good rules that do not prevent them.
- Our task is to learn how to handle problem situations, not problem people or problem patrons.[80]

REFERENCE SERVICES FOR SPECIFIC AGE GROUPS

Three age groups are discussed in this chapter. In this introduction to thinking about differences in reference services called for because of age, the focus is on children, young adults, and the elderly. Service to adults is not addressed because the basic reference services described elsewhere in this book focus on services to the general adult audience. For this discussion, *children* are defined as persons from birth to age 14, or infancy through junior high school, and *young adults* are defined as persons from age 12 through 18, or middle school and high school students. There is an intentional overlap in the definitions of children and young adults to account for the variety of ways in which public libraries and schools choose to serve persons of junior high or middle school age. The *elderly* include persons who are 65 years of age or older. Although there is little literature on special needs of the elderly for library service, this is one of the fastest-growing segments of our population, constituting 12.9 percent of the population in 2009.[81] To put this figure into context, the median age of the population in 1980 was 30.0 years; by 2009, it was 36.8 years[82] The percentage of people over 65 is projected to rise to 13 percent by 2010 and to 20.2 percent by 2050.[83] Undoubtedly, the library profession should be adapting reference services to meet the needs of this growing population.

Children and Young Adults

Reference service to children and young adults constitutes a significant portion of reference work in general. In their study of reference queries at the *adult* reference desks of 13 public libraries, Melissa Gross and Matthew Saxton found that fully 19 percent of the questions came from persons under the age of 18.[84] Adding these to the questions received directly in children's departments, we begin to develop a true picture of the impact of this user group on reference services.

Reference service to youth in both school and public libraries has been profoundly affected by recent educational reform movements. There has been a trend away from textbook-based teaching and toward inquiry-based learning, which relies on constructivist ideals of active learning and resource-based teaching (based on the belief that individuals construct knowledge rather than receiving it from others).[85] In these models, students take more responsibility for their own learning. Information literacy becomes an integral part of the curriculum, resulting in an increased use of the library and a greater need for reference services. At the same time, members of the "Google generation" are highly likely to turn to the Internet to solve information problems before they even think of the library. An astonishing 87 percent of people between the ages of 12 and 17 are now online.[86]

Reference Services for Children

Some underlying assumptions provide a useful framework for understanding reference service for children. First and most fundamental is that children progress through a series of developmental stages as they mature. These stages define what type of reference service is appropriate to match a child's cognitive capabilities. For example, most third-graders can categorize and use basic classification systems. Carol Kuhlthau found that this ability means that third-graders are capable of understanding the difference between fiction and nonfiction and that the purpose of call numbers is to bring together books on the same topic.[87] However, their use of a library catalog must be guided, as well as their journey from the catalog to the books on the shelf. Children labor under a real handicap in having to use a library system designed for adult users. Vicky Crosson notes that "most subject terms used in library catalogs are on a sixth-grade-or-above reading level and often use words not commonly used by children."[88] Depending on their age, children tend to have difficulty using online catalogs, reference tools, and databases, even when those systems are designed for young users.[89] Children also have mixed success finding and evaluating information on the Web.[90] Clearly, all reference service to children must be conducted within the context of developmental parameters and the design of our information retrieval systems.

Christine Behrmann and Dolores Vogliano assert that a good children's librarian demonstrates two types of skills: cognitive and affective.[91] *Cognitive skills* provide for competence and qualification in fulfilling children's information needs. *Affective skills* are those that enable the librarian to respect and understand the needs of young people. The librarian providing reference service to children has a special responsibility for mastering these affective skills because there is more at stake in these transactions than simply answering questions correctly. It is at this stage in their lives that children often form lifelong attitudes about libraries. Young people can feel either empowered by the library and its resources or intimidated and excluded by those same riches.

Of critical importance in reference service to children is an understanding that a large proportion of reference queries are *imposed*.[92] In other words, children's questions often arise from what others (usually teachers) ask them to find out and do not reflect what children themselves find intrinsically interesting. Further complicating matters, adults often act as agents for children. This situation creates a *double-imposed query* because the agent (the child) receives a question from the imposer (the teacher) and then passes it to another agent (the parent) to process.[93] Not all adults are clear or skilled translators of children's needs, so the reference librarian must develop a range of interviewing skills to determine what the child really wants to know or read. No wonder reference service to children can be difficult! In any case, children's reference service includes users of all ages—children, parents, teachers, and care providers. As intermediaries for children's questions, adults also need guidance in the use of materials housed in the youth services area of the public library or the school library media center.

Information Services. Information service to children is a central part of library services to children and is not secondary in importance to programming for children. Children have limited choices for gathering information and may logically turn to the librarian at the public library or at school for help. Young children's information needs are especially likely to be overlooked because of an emphasis on programming and fiction collection development in service to preschoolers. It is important to supply to young children information that is stated simply. Librarians need to have commercially or locally produced bibliographies of picture book and easy-to-read titles available for both reference staff and users to consult, given that subject cataloging of these materials is often inadequate.

As noted previously, children's reference questions are predominantly school-related (imposed) or stimulated by aspects of popular culture such as television, movies, and sports. Thus, there is a certain predictability in much reference work with children, although it is important not to become complacent. Elizabeth Overmyer observes that children's librarians do not tend to consciously develop their reference skills in the same way that they prepare for the other activities they are responsible for, such as story hours and booktalks. As a result, they are more likely to have limited access to and knowledge of some of the newer tools and techniques of reference work.[94]

It is not easy to get teachers to warn librarians about the assignment needs of children, but often librarians can set up a system of communication whereby assignment sheets are copied and kept on file. Public and school librarians can telephone teachers or approach them informally with questions and can keep notations from year to year about major assignments that are likely to recur perennially. Strong communication links between school library media specialists and public library reference staff can help both institutions provide better reference service to school children (see Box 12.5 for an example of a form that school librarians can use to alert public library reference staff of classroom assignments).

Local or state-mandated curriculum requirements can also be used to identify courses that may involve library use. Also, some time spent reading local newspapers and school newsletters and keeping up with movies, music, and youth culture will help librarians predict and relate to reference questions on personal interest topics. A community resource file that contains a section on children's activities will be extremely useful in answering questions about local events and issues.

Electronic reference tools and databases are increasingly important in children's reference service. Until just a few years ago, most available online catalogs, as well as commercially produced electronic reference tools such as electronic encyclopedias, were not developed with the needs of children in mind. Typing a string of correctly spelled words, often preceded by an arcane code defining a search type, is difficult enough for an adult to accomplish, let alone a child with elementary reading skills. Successful electronic systems share important characteristics, such as multiple search modes, which provide the flexibility to meet the needs of varying levels of cognitive development, and interface designs that capitalize on recognition skills and natural browsing search strategies. For example, KCWeb, formerly the Kid's Catalog, features a graphical user interface that provides age-appropriate searching software that links to the bibliographic data on a public access catalog.[95] Children can identify and select topics by browsing colorful icons that represent the Dewey hierarchy as well as popular topics that cross strict Dewey categories. Children who are adept typists and spellers can use a mode that allows them to type in their search strategies. From each book record, a library map is available that flashes the location of the book on the screen. The product allows customization so that libraries can add curriculum pathfinders, book lists, and selected Web sites in addition to the preselected sites that come with the software.

In this era of shared catalog systems and consortial agreements, interlibrary loan is more accessible to children than it ever has been before. Children can often initiate transactions themselves, with "their" de facto library being the extensive network of libraries on a shared database. However, some local interlibrary loan services may have special limitations with regard to persons below a designated age. Sometimes schools are excluded from interlibrary loan policies and agreements.

The Internet has, without doubt, made a bigger impact on reference service to children than any other advance in recent technological history. Not only do vendors use it as a standard method of delivering information products, but nonprofit and public sector information providers have found it to be an inexpensive and effective means of dissemination as well, usually without having to charge fees. But finding information on the Internet can be extremely problematic for a child. Search engines and Internet directories all use different protocols and retrieve from different parts of Internet space. Commercial sites are mixed in with educational sites, and personal Web pages pop up alongside government agencies. Yet search engines do not connect children to the "invisible Web," the valuable services that are hidden behind proprietary access mechanisms or database search query walls. In other words, a Google search will not yield results from the library's subscription to *World Book Encyclopedia* online or to the online primary sources provided by the American Memory collections from the Library of Congress, which are searchable only from the American Memory query page.

Reference librarians are important advisors in the Web-searching process. They should assist the young user by creating supportive library home pages that provide links to "jumping off" sites specifically designed for children. An example of this type of service is Yahoo! Kids (http://kids.yahoo.com), a hierarchical category search tool that links to sites created for children. Another example is KidsClick!, a highly selective subject directory that is designed and maintained by librarians (http:/www.kidsclick.org). The *ipl2*, with its "For Kids" section (http://www.ipl.org/div/kidspace/), is maintained by the Drexel University College of Information Science and Technology. Even with age-appropriate guides such as these, librarians may need to

BOX 12.5
SAMPLE ASSIGNMENT ALERT FORM

Mass-Assignment <u>Alert</u>!

TO: _____, Public Librarian

Fax #:

(Date)

Dear Public Library Colleague,

We wanted to alert you to a major research project that has been assigned in our school. You may want to keep some of your material on reserve to meet student demand and more equitably distribute your resources. Here are some details you may find helpful.

Teacher _____ Subject/Class _____

Grade _____ Date Due _____

Project/Assignment _____

Expected Product _____

A copy of the student assignment sheet is attached for your convenience. Please feel free to contact us with any questions.

Librarian _____

School _____

Phone _____

E-mail _____

Fax # _____

_____

Joyce Kasman Valenza, *Power Tools Recharged: 125+ Essential Forms and Presentations for Your School Library Information Program* (Chicago: American Library Association, 2004), 1.21. Reprinted by permission of ALA.

help users evaluate the results of their searches, redefine search strategies, and assess the authority and depth of individual Web sites.

Concerns about children's access to inappropriate materials on the Internet resulted in the passage of the Children's Internet Protection Act (CIPA), which requires that libraries receiving certain types of federal funding implement an Internet safety policy and operate "technology protection measures" (blocking and filtering software). Filtering software has enormous implications for students' ability to access information. For example, filters are known to prevent successful searches for information on topics such as breast cancer, which fail because the word "breast" is blocked. The American Library Association has taken the position that the use of filtering software by libraries to block protected speech violates the *Library Bill of Rights*.[96]

Ethics and Confidentiality. Children may request information on sensitive topics, such as sex, drugs, or even child abuse. Reference librarians need to consult and interpret, and in some cases formulate, local policy related to the provision of information to minors on controversial topics. Librarians should not presume to know what kinds of information parents want their children to have access to. Such issues are worked out between parent and child; especially concerned parents should accompany their children to the library.[97] Some institutions are required to act *in loco parentis* (in the place of the parent) unless released from this status by particular parents with respect to their own children. The political or religious affiliation of some libraries may dictate local policy with regard to minors and require library personnel to provide less than the *Library Bill of Rights'* intended level of access to information. For example, in a parochial school library, librarians may be restricted from providing information about abortion.

The ability to maintain confidentiality in a user–librarian relationship is inextricably tied to legal issues. In a school library setting, the librarian is typically governed by the same regulations that govern all personnel, designating them as mandated reporters of certain kinds of information. For example, the Abused and Neglected Child Reporting Act of Illinois specifically states that the privileged quality of communication between designated employees and children does not apply in situations involving abuse and neglect.[98]

The Reference Interview. The reference interview is important for all users, but it is "particularly problematic when dealing with children who form their questions through limited vocabulary and sphere of experience."[99] A friendly, open demeanor and careful listening to children will help them express their needs. Virginia Walter advises librarians "to listen for the silent, 'unasked' questions that children sometimes pose. Children don't formulate questions well, and they usually aren't aware of their own deepest and most important information needs."[100] When it comes to the imposed query, however, some careful prompting may be necessary. When asking a self-generated question, even a poorly articulated one, a child will know many things about the context of the question and will be able to negotiate knowledgably through the process. But when the child is trying to translate someone else's question, the librarian cannot take the question back to its origins because the child does not have intellectual access to its full context.[101] Interviews with children may need to be more directive, with more explanations and fewer open-ended questions than interviews with adults. It may be appropriate to ask to see a copy of the child's assignment and, in some cases, to even contact a teacher.

Children's questions may contain inaccurate information. Verification of spelling, proper names, and facts presented in a child's questions may be a good first step in an interview to ensure that both the librarian and the child are on the right track. Children also have difficulty following directions in sequence. A seemingly reasonable suggestion to a middle-grade child that includes three or four steps (e.g., go to the catalog, find the call number of this book, go to the proper place in the stacks, find the book, look in the index for your topic) may be too difficult for the child to remember at this stage of development. The reference interview may have to be done gradually as the child works through the search step by step. Reference librarians frequently follow a child all the way to the source.

In addition to the problems of getting information from the child and helping the child absorb information from the librarian, time is a factor. Children have a short attention span and are easily discouraged if the search is not successful in the first few attempts. Again, a series of short exchanges may be more successful than one longer, more complete interview. The reference librarian needs to be good at juggling several simultaneous searches, keeping track of each child's progress. Children react to a positive attitude and praise. Although efficiency may sometimes seem to be sacrificed for friendliness, reference service ultimately will be more effective if presented in this manner.

Readers' Advisory. Although libraries vary in the provision of readers' advisory services to the general adult population (see chapter 1), readers' advisory is an essential reference service for children. Virginia Walter notes, "Nearly all public services librarians working in public libraries today practice the craft of reference, but children's librarians have elevated readers' advisory, or reading guidance, almost to an art form."[102] Whether asking for school-related information or a good book to read, children usually need some guidance in choosing materials. Readers' advisory service to children is enhanced when the librarian knows the local collection well, has specialized training in library materials for children, and is an active reader of the literature. As Walter observes, a good children's librarian knows the books, sees the relationships between books, knows the children, and knows how to connect the specific child to the specific book.[103]

When helping children with book selection, the librarian should determine the child's interests or needs, age or grade level, and approximate reading level. Often the child can articulate an interest and age or grade level, but it may be a little more difficult to assess actual reading level. School library media specialists may be able to check school records, but public librarians may have to ask what books the child has been reading recently to get some idea of where to start. It is always wise to give children several choices of titles and encourage personal selection. This gives the child practice in independent book selection but also answers the child's need for some guidance from a knowledgeable adult.

Readers' advisory support is available in the many reading lists provided by professional associations and through professional literature. The Association for Library Service to Children provides book lists on a range of topics and for a variety of audiences (http://www.ala.org/ala/mgrps/divs/alsc/compubs/booklists/index.cfm). Other helpful organizations include the International Reading Association (http://www.reading.org), the Children's Book Council (http://www.cbcbooks.org), and the Center for Children's Books (http://ccb.lis.illinois.edu/), among others. Another way to stay current is to subscribe to an electronic discussion list such as Child_Lit.[104]

BOX 12.6
GUIDELINES FOR SUCCESSFUL REFERENCE SERVICE TO CHILDREN

Developmental Levels

It is important to offer resources appropriate to the child's age and experience. Looks are deceiving. Children may be tall for their age. Don't assume you know they have outgrown the children's section.

Sophistication

Even the brightest child needs the assistance of an adult. A child may lack the life experience to identify the most important facts about a topic.

Vocabulary

The words we use can educate or confuse children. Avoid using library jargon.

Children are still learning English vocabulary words. Give them many words with which to tell others exactly how they feel and precisely what they need.

Powerlessness

Sometimes we forget that many children depend on adults for transportation to and from the library. Determine whether children can stay in the library while you work with them or whether a busy parent has instructed them to run in and run out.

A library policy of charging a fee for printouts and copies may seem reasonable. However, many children depend upon their families for spending money. In a conscientious effort to avoid fines, some parents instruct their children not to check out materials.

Likewise, when a child describes a homework assignment that is difficult to match with library resources, don't kill the messenger! Meet with the teacher to discuss the issue instead.

Knowledge of Library Ways

Do you remember how overwhelming it can be to shop in a new, unfamiliar grocery store? Walk students through the first search. Demonstrate databases when time allows. Pointing out all the options gives children tips for success.

Energetic Body Language

Children need to move. Put them on their best behavior by leaving the desk. Join them where they have the space to move and talk freely. It also allows you to show them materials rather than citations. They can therefore better judge whether the reading level is what they need.

Excerpts from Sunny Strong, "Sights, Sounds, and Silence in Library Reference Service to Children," *Public Libraries* 43 (November/December 2004): 313–14.

Instruction for Children in the Use of Libraries and Materials. Both formal group instruction and individual instruction are generally considered part of reference service to children. Traditionally, formal library instruction has been the responsibility of the school librarian. Integrating library skills in all areas of the curriculum, cooperation between librarian and teacher, and creative learning activities will provide children with the skills they need to succeed in school and become lifelong learners. Unfortunately, library time in many elementary schools is still scheduled in a fixed manner apart from any consideration of what is going on in the classroom. Fixed scheduling is an administrative convenience that allows teachers to use library time as planning time and ensures that students come to the library on a regular basis. *Information Power* notes,

> In a student-centered school library media program, learning needs take precedence over class schedules, school hours, student categorizations, and other logistical concerns. To meet learning needs, the program's resources and services must be available so that information problems can be resolved when they arise.[105]

Fixed schedules inhibit the integration of library instruction into the curriculum. Students may learn library skills in this environment but do not generally have the opportunity to *apply* what they have learned in the context of real educational problems. Even if students are allowed access to the library outside of designated library time, the librarian is generally busy with another scheduled class. These limitations, as well as the natural boundaries of different stages of cognitive development, may explain why students have difficulty transferring skills from school to public libraries.[106]

Library skills that are abstracted from situations where they can be meaningfully applied are difficult for children (or anyone) to generalize to other situations. Instead, learning how to use the library is more meaningful if it is viewed as a *process that occurs in context* rather than as a set of specific discrete skills. Therefore, it is optimal when school libraries are able to employ a system of flexible scheduling. Instruction in this type of environment includes a combination of generic information and library-specific information, taught in the context of a particular application rather than as ends in themselves. Children receive multiple exposures of this process through many trips to the library for different school projects, developing a rich view of how to access information. Again, this approach reflects the values expressed in the *Information Literacy Standards for Student Learning* [107] (see Box 8.2); its successor, the AASL *Standards for the 21st-Century Learner* (http://www.ala.org/ala/ mgrps/divs/aasl/guidelinesandstandards/learningstandards/standards.cfm); and the general educational trend toward project- and resource-based learning that integrates and situates knowledge. Children who have a flexible scheduling experience in their schools also score higher on the reading and writing portions of standardized tests than do students who attend schools with less flexibly scheduled libraries.[108]

Individual instruction also takes place during the reference interview in both school and public libraries. By discussing a question during the reference interview and explaining why and how particular reference tools are used to answer the question, the librarian provides models of search strategies that the young person can emulate. Drawing the user into active involvement in answering the question (e.g., encouraging the child to find an index entry during the reference interview, letting the child lead the way to the book on the shelf) means that the child is immediately applying the new knowledge with the support and encouragement of the librarian/instructor. Children may also need help in interpreting information once it is found.

It is often a creative process to determine at what point library instruction related to homework assignments becomes doing the homework itself. Some public libraries have instituted deliberate policies that limit reference assistance for homework-related questions, reasoning either that children will not get appropriate educational value from their assignments if they do not finish them on their own or that homework help is not the public library's responsibility.[109] Other libraries have found that it makes sense to turn homework assistance into a full-fledged program.[110] Another factor having an impact on reference service in public libraries is the growth of home schooling. Although still constituting only 2.2 percent of school-age children, the home schooling population increased from 850,000 in 1999 to 1.1 million in 2003.[111] In homeschooling, the public library serves as a child's school library, and public librarians are professionally bound to take on the role.[112] Paul Kaplan suggests such strategies as maintaining a homeschooling notebook at the reference desk, devoting a portion of the library newsletter to homeschoolers, and offering programs and orientation sessions to the homeschooling community.[113] The Web site of the Johnsburg (Illinois) Public Library District (http://www.johnsburglibrary.org/content/homeschool-resource-center) connects users to a wide variety of homeschooling resources and to information about grant-funded curriculum materials that can be checked out.

Reference Services for Young Adults

Young adult (YA) reference services are composed of essentially the same components as children's reference services, with some salient age-related differences. For example, young adults require access to adult-level materials as well as to children's collections. They are also less dependent on parents or other adults to act as intermediaries or to assist with the use of materials. Young adults are served by public libraries, school libraries, and in many cases, college and university libraries. Although they constitute a prominent service group, many public libraries are unable to fund young adult specialist positions. Worse, some library staffers actively dislike teenagers, a condition Patrick Jones refers to as "ephebiphobia" in his discussion of setting the stage for public library service to young adults.[114] Although the ephebiphobic staff member may need some heavy-handed remediation, helpful guides are available for those whose attitudes are in the right place. Two such examples are Jones's *New Directions for Library Service to Young Adults*[115] and Virginia Walter and Elaine Meyers's *Teens & Libraries: Getting It Right*.[116]

Adolescence is a time of transition. Public libraries typically purchase unique as well as duplicate copies of selected titles for their young adult users but manage these materials in different ways. Many libraries provide a section or special collection of materials specifically designated for young adults. A smaller number collect young adult materials but shelve them with the adult collection, and a few shelve these materials in the children's section. The concept of giving young adults a separate library space of their own came into favor during the 1940s and 1950s[117] but has often proven to be expensive in terms of staffing and has not decreased the need for duplication of materials among departments.

Mary K. Chelton provides a useful overview of current common models of service to young adults in public libraries, delineating the strengths and weaknesses of each.[118] She points out that specialized services are often marginalized (or their staff is) in the overall library hierarchy. At the same time, generalists tend to be more ignorant of YA interests and materials and sometimes are even dismissive of them. The *Voice of Youth Advocates* publishes a useful column called "YA Spaces of Your Dreams," which features a different public library teen space in each issue. Libraries are also targeting their Web presence to teens, who appreciate such online alternatives as chat groups and special teen Web spaces. For example, the Public Library of Charlotte & Mecklenburg County has a well-developed teen Web site with links and activities designed to engage teens (http://blogs.plcmc.org/libraryloft/).

Information Services. School-related queries account for the majority of the informational activities of young adult reference work. The trend toward inquiry-based education is also thriving at the secondary level. Students progressing to junior high or middle school and then senior high school are faced with assignments of increasing number and complexity. However, the typical strategy students use to solve information problems is to type keywords into the search box of their favorite search engine and hope for the best. Reference intervention is a critical component at this juncture, or students may never find the high-quality information that is available to them. From a teen's perspective, there is often no difference between the sources retrieved from a respected information vendor and those found on the results screen of a Web search. To put it another way, teens do not often recognize a distinction between the "free" Web and the "invisible" or deep Web. It is also important that students have thorough grounding in Web site evaluation. Timely reference service is the key to helping students determine the reliability and authority of online sources. Finally, it must be noted that if Internet filtering software is installed, it can prove to be a real liability, given that students conduct research on topics ranging from drug legalization to assisted suicide.

In the school library, the librarian's best ally in providing assignment-related assistance is a good instruction program that is integrated into the school curriculum. In this way, the intent of such assignments—to teach students how to locate and evaluate information independently—is directly reinforced by the person most qualified to see that this actually happens. In sum, reference service for young adults is inextricably linked to the teaching role for school library media specialists, as supported by *Information Power, Information Literacy Standards for Student Learning*, and the AASL *Standards for the 21st-Century Learner.*[119]

In the public library, librarians have much less control over library-related assignments, although these generate a great deal of their reference activity. For frequently requested topics, many libraries prepare *reference pathfinders* (suggested search strategies that include standard reference tools and their appropriate subject headings). For recurring and popular topics, pathfinders provide a kind of one-on-one instruction in high-use environments where a librarian may not always be readily available. They are especially effective for young adults who are too shy to ask for help or who appreciate the opportunity to work independently. As in children's reference service, it is important to establish a library policy for young adult reference service that delineates what the library can and cannot do in terms of homework assistance. Telephone or online support of assignments, for example, is an amorphous issue; it is difficult enough to define limits of these services among professionals and even more difficult to explain them to an adolescent.

Modern pathfinders, though often also available as print handouts, are generally delivered as Web sites ("Webliographies"), accessible by teens from within the library or from home. Librarians are wise to put their efforts into creating pathfinders that reflect local curricula and interests. They can also supply links to the more comprehensive sites that are known for keeping their links current and up-to-date. The *ipl2* (http://www.ipl2.org/div/teen/) is one such example, as is the Homework Center created by the Multnomah County Library (http://www.multcolib.org/homework).[120] Both sites link to a host of other useful homework help sites.

Teens, who cherish their growing independence and tend to be comfortable with technology, are particularly good candidates for chat and e-mail reference services. Both types of media offer opportunities for point-of-use instruction. The Baltimore County Public Library began marketing virtual reference service to youth in early 2001.[121] Its AskUsNow! service (http://bcpl.info) has now become a consortium of 39 Maryland libraries, which, in turn, is a member of a nationwide consortium called QuestionPoint 24/7, a service of the Online Computer Library Center, or OCLC. A different kind of personalized service is available from the Public Library of Charlotte and Mecklenburg County in the form of "brarydog.net," a library Web site the user customizes with his or her own selection of databases, search tools, and lists of links. The template includes links to the library's virtual reference service and to professional online tutors.[122]

Interlibrary loan service presents special challenges for young adults as well as for children. In practical terms, tight deadlines and the human tendency to procrastinate, coupled with increased mobility on the part of teenagers, usually suggest that direct reciprocal borrowing from nearby libraries is a more viable option than interlibrary loan for young adults. The reference librarian can assist by providing location information to the user. Fortunately, the growing availability of electronic full-text sources has decreased dependence on interlibrary loan services. Even small libraries can take advantage of these subscriptions if they belong to a consortium or district that negotiates group rates.

Ethics and Confidentiality. As a part of growing up, young adults are naturally interested in information of a personal or sensitive nature. In the library, they face the prospect of going through an intermediary to find information on topics such as sexuality or troubled family relationships. The librarian must be seen as a neutral resource yet appear sympathetic and understanding. A school librarian may be in the privileged position of knowing the individuals better, of being the trusted counselor. On the other hand, a student in search of sensitive information may prefer to ask for it where anonymity is more likely. Helma Hawkins suggests that teens searching for information about homosexuality may be afraid to be seen buying a book on the topic, especially in a gay bookstore, "but they might sit in a quiet part of the public library and read."[123] Amy Levine suggests five tips for providing sexuality information: (1) create a supportive environment; (2) provide a wide range of appealing, age-appropriate materials with positive messages about sexuality; (3) identify community and national resources and make them accessible; (4) develop library displays and programming around national observances; and (5) be approachable.[124] Anonymous question boards might give some teens the courage to ask tough questions. The exchanges can be posted electronically or in a publicly accessible area of the library, as fits the situation.

The ability to maintain confidentiality in the user–librarian relationship, however, is dependent on legal issues, as outlined in the previous section regarding confidentiality and children. In a public library, the written reference policy can provide the opportunity to make an explicit statement regarding open access and the library's commitment to confidentiality. By doing so, the library is released from the *in loco parentis* role and can grant young adults independent and adult status in their pursuit of information. In any case, it is incumbent upon the librarian to find out what local laws or policies govern this issue before stumbling into a compromising situation (see Box 12.7).

Readers' Advisory. Young adult reference service began largely as an out-of-school, extracurricular effort to emphasize reading guidance in an era when school courses were taught solely from textbooks.[125] This orientation continued even after teachers began expecting students to use outside sources. In libraries without a young adult specialist, the readers' advisory role is often subsumed by the school-related informational role, one with which reference generalists may be more comfortable and where the techniques and tools more readily translate across age levels.

Readers' advisory service is an aspect of reference work that is of critical importance in the young adult arena. Books present young adults with options, allowing them to glimpse models of conflict resolution and decision making and, in the process, to develop their own critical thinking skills. Librarians who serve young adults need to know the literature, to be able to suggest titles that are similar to other titles a young library user has enjoyed, and to discuss the issues raised therein. Dorothy M. Broderick admonishes today's librarians with the example of Margaret Edwards of the Enoch Pratt Free Library, who required a librarian to read and orally report on 300 titles from the New York Public Library's *Books for the Teen Age* before being granted the title of Young Adult Librarian.[126]

BOX 12.7
WHAT WOULD YOU DO?

David, a quiet 15-year-old, is a regular library user. The staff notices that lately he has been visiting the Web sites of white supremacy organizations and gun owners' interest groups. When he asks for help finding information that denies the existence of the Nazi Holocaust, the librarian, who happens to be Jewish, hesitates at his request. She also wonders whether she should inform David's parents.

What should the librarian do in this situation?

Are there legitimate limits or larger responsibilities when it comes to certain types of reference requests?

As in children's readers' advisory service, professional associations and the professional literature offer much in the way of book lists and annotated bibliographies. Sources of note include the many lists available from the Young Adult Library Services Association (http://www.ala.org/ala/mgrps/divs/yalsa/booklistsawards/booklistsbook. cfm), the Assembly on Literature for Adolescents (http://www.alan-ya.org), and issues of the *Voice of Youth Advocates* and *School Library Journal*. Another way to stay current is to subscribe to an electronic discussion list such as YALSA_BK.[127] Because teens sometimes are reluctant to talk to adults, electronic subscription products are now available that may help bridge the gap. *NoveList* (http://www.ebscohost.com/ novelist/default.php?id=3) allows the user to search for titles at the adult and/or the young adult level. Gale's (http://www.gale.cengage.com) series *What Do Children and Young Adults Read Next?* is a comprehensive guide to readers' advisory for both children and young adults.[128]

The Reference Interview. As young adults begin to move away from the children's department and to ask questions at the adult reference desk, they encounter many librarians who are helpful and friendly, who take their needs at face value, and who treat them as individuals. They also encounter librarians who are uncomfortable with them, who see them as potential problems, and who judge their needs to be less serious than those of adults and therefore less important. Chelton found that in many libraries, teens have been, for all practical purposes, relegated to a "problem patron" category of their own.[129] Complicating the situation, developmental differences often make it extremely difficult to determine a young person's age. Some young adults still look juvenile yet consider themselves beyond that stage. Savvy teens recognize that the visual opacity of online reference service has the potential to mitigate such problems. Regardless, it is incumbent on the librarian to treat all requests with equal weight and respect. Idiosyncratic library organization can also cause awkwardness for young adults. For example, because publishers package most curricular material for the juvenile market, a lot of information very appropriate for adolescents is housed in the children's department. Clearly, navigating between the adult and juvenile departments during the reference process calls for tact and discretion.

During any reference interview, the librarian must determine a user's actual need, as opposed to the need as it is initially expressed. In the case of young adults, vocabulary and self-concept are still developing. Young adults may not yet possess the analytical skills to identify the components of their information need or to approach a problem systematically and sequentially. They tend to be literal-minded, focusing on the end product rather than the process, asking questions or making statements such as "I need a book that compares revenge in *Hamlet* with revenge in Stephen King's books."[130] They have to articulate their needs to a figure of authority in a strange environment. The librarian must therefore take special pains to be approachable, friendly, nonjudgmental, and above all, not condescending. A user's reluctance to come forward must also be respected. Patrick Jones recommends a proactive reference approach, in which the librarian is out on the floor asking whether users are finding what they need, thus sparing teens the mortification of asking for help.

On the most basic level, a teen that must approach a reference desk to pose a reference question is almost assuming the position of a supplicant (I need help, ergo I am helpless; you can help me, ergo you have a power and are more powerful than I.) Is that something a teen wants to do? Of course not, thus many a YA never get to a moment of truth encounter because they won't ask for help.[131]

And when a question is obviously school-related, it is often possible to ask more pointed, direct questions than one normally would: "Can I ask you what your assignment is? Do you have a copy of it with you?" It is always helpful to rephrase the question to make sure both parties are working under the same assumptions.

A Final Thought on Reference Services for Youth

The "future of libraries" is a perennial topic, one that seems to arise every time a new technological advancement is announced.[132] The ubiquity of the Internet seems to have spawned a fresh outburst of concern about the survivability of libraries. Indeed, reports from the Pew Internet and American Life Project (http://www.pewinternet.org) are filled with statistics documenting how all Americans, young and old, are flocking to the Internet before seeking information at their libraries. Initiatives such as Google Books (http://books.google.com), with its wholesale digitization of books, threaten to make even our print collections obsolete. But libraries are not dead yet. Their future depends on how well the library users of tomorrow are treated today. Excellence in service to young people *now* will ensure that they come back to libraries as adults, bringing their own children with them.

Older Adults

Although the other special age groups (children and young adults) have both a body of professional literature and an established separate place in libraries, the elderly often lack recognition as a group with special needs (see Box 12.8). Because the elderly are a fast-growing population, it is likely that their special needs and services will come to the forefront in the next 25 years. In 2009, 12.9 percent of the American population was age 65 or over.[133] By 2025, it is estimated that those 65 or older will have become 17.9 percent of the nation's population.[134] It is also anticipated that because of improved health care, older adults will be more active. At the same time, a longer life means that more people live with physical and mental ailments. In 2005, 25.2 percent of those age 65 to 74 were considered persons with limitation of activity caused by chronic conditions.[135] That percentage rose to 43.5 for those age 75 and over.[136]

In working with older adults, it is important to approach each person as an individual who may not share the characteristics or interests commonly associated with the elderly. One should avoid assuming that older adults experience a decline in cognitive ability because many do not. Indeed, unless disease attacks the brain, intellectual capacities can improve with age.[137] Other assumptions must also be avoided. For example, reading interests may or may not change as individuals grow older. Older persons are not necessarily retired; in 2009, 21.9 percent of men 65 or older were employed in the labor force, and 13.6 percent of women 65 or older were employed.[138] Finally, many grandparents are now raising their own grandchildren; 2.4 million children lived with their grandparents in 2000, without any parents in the household.[139] These older adults have reference needs that do not fit the mold of the "typical" senior citizen.

BOX 12.8
INVISIBLE, NUMEROUS, AND UNDERSERVED

When talking professionally about service to "underserved" populations, what population do we immediately think about? Perhaps persons with disabilities, the homeless, minority populations, or those who are living in poverty. But one of the largest of the underserved library populations is seniors, or older adults.

Older adults can have disabilities; older adults can be living in poverty or can be homeless, wealthy, middle class, African American, Caucasian, Asian, Latino, American Indian, Alaska Native, Native Hawaiian, biracial, lesbian, gay, bisexual, or transgender. Simply put, service to older adults is indeed a cross-cultural concern, as they are a part of almost every library community.

Barbara T. Mates, *5-Star Programming and Services for Your 55+ Library Customers* (Chicago: American Library Association, 2003), 1.

Good reference service for elderly individuals includes all the basic components of good reference service for the general adult population, with particular attention to the individual needs of elderly users. In its guidelines for library service to older adults, the Reference and User Services Association of the American Library Association exhorts libraries to provide a full slate of integrated library services to the elderly.[140] The ALA Office for Literacy and Outreach Services (OLOS) provides a list of quick tips for serving older adults, summarized here:

- Location, location, location! The new books section should be close to the main entrance. Provide plenty of lighting and unblocked windows. Reserve space for video magnifying equipment near or in the large-print section.
- Marketing essentials: Include potted plants, magazine tables, larger font for signage, reference signs for related services, flyers and brochures in at least 14- to 16-point type, high-contrast printing, and signage.
- Seating: Supply "comfy" chairs near bookshelves, several chairs with arms, straight-back wooden or winged-back chairs, and high rather than low seat heights.
- Shelving: Set up shelving at the end of stacks for new large-print books, place books on middle shelves (not lower or upper), create wide aisles, place books facing forward, and locate large-print books near audio books.
- Collection tips: Establish an information center for seniors with collections of brochures from the agencies that serve them in the area, provide magazines such as *Mature Living*, and provide large-type instructions for use of the closed caption television.
- Other support: Provide steel support bars throughout (especially in non-handicapped bathroom stalls, in elevators, and at check-out stations),

basket trolleys, magnifying glasses, ADA computer workstations close by, and cordless mouse devices for those who suffer from arthritis.[141]

Reference librarians need to avoid stereotyping or patronizing older users and should develop effective communication skills so as to encourage them to ask questions and to ensure that each answer is fully understood by the user. Many older adults, for example, have had limited exposure to computers and may experience more computer anxiety than younger library users. Whereas the library was once a friendly, welcoming place, it now feels intimidating and impersonal. Special online catalog instruction sessions tailored for older individuals will create a comfortable atmosphere where users can ask questions and experience self-paced practice and one-on-one coaching.

Because computer use in libraries has become so important, Mates devotes two full chapters of her book to the subject as it relates to seniors.[142] She discusses hardware considerations, the problems seniors tend to have with navigation (mouse coordination being a particularly problematic area), training and marketing approaches, and Web site design recommendations (with special attention to color and font choices). She emphasizes the importance of teaching online safety and evaluation skills, given that many seniors may not be prepared for the preponderance of online misinformation and scam artists. As baby boomers begin reaching retirement age, they are changing the picture of how senior citizens relate to computers. Already, the number of older Americans who go online jumped by 47 percent between 2000 and 2004.[143] Though their relative numbers are still low, librarians need to stay tuned to the computer literacy levels of the senior populations they serve.

Collections should be developed that deal with common concerns such as income, social security, transportation, housing, and health, all from the point of view of older adults as well as from the point of view of their children or other caregivers. It is important to have current directories (local, state, and federal) of services for the elderly, as well as materials that discuss the aging process and how to obtain adequate medical, legal, financial, and psychological help. Libraries can use directories to provide information and referral to appropriate government and private agencies serving the elderly. Online, searchable databases, such as *AgeLine* (http://www.ebscohost.com/public/ageline), are frequently updated. Book sources such as the *Aging Sourcebook*[144] provide an overview of current issues and list sources of services for older adults. Regional and, less frequently, local directories of this type are available also. A community resource file should include information about rights, organizations, local transportation, housing, educational and recreational opportunities, tax changes, social security, and Medicare. A centralized reference collection of this type of information will prove invaluable to older library users and service providers.

To provide reference service to older adults, it may be necessary to offer remote delivery of materials and service. Certainly the most common form of remote delivery of reference service to seniors is by telephone. In libraries where in-person reference service is busy and takes precedence over answering questions over the telephone, special provisions must be made to serve the homebound and the institutionalized elderly. The general rule of serving walk-in users before answering the telephone is logical but may make it difficult for the older adult to access the library. It may be necessary to set up a special telephone service for elderly (or disabled) persons who cannot easily get to the library. Also, it may be possible to take reference service to elderly individuals by including reference materials in the bookmobile collection when making stops at retirement homes, assisted living facilities, nursing homes, or senior citizen centers or by providing chat and e-mail reference service to these agencies. Training bookmobile staff in basic reference service and teaching care-facility staff to assist with online reference services would ensure that questions could be answered in a timely and predictable fashion.

It is important to communicate to older adults the reference services that are available to them and to make them feel welcome. The library can effectively market services of particular interest to older persons through library brochures, specific informational programs held in the library, and outside agencies. Reference librarians should cultivate communications with other service agencies in the community; often, specialists in services to the elderly can provide training for library staff in working with the elderly and make appropriate referrals to the library if interagency cooperation is practiced. Careful assessment of what use older citizens make of a library may reveal a need to publicize existing reference services or a way to adapt services to meet the needs and capacities of older adults.

CONCLUSION

Reference services should be offered to all persons in a library's service community regardless of their circumstances or identifying characteristics. There are several issues to be addressed by librarians responsible for ensuring that specific groups in their service community have equal access to reference service. First, librarians need to acknowledge that reference services *do* need to be adapted, or at least assessed, with respect to the needs and abilities of particular groups. Librarians need to identify groups within their community that might face obstacles to free and full access to information. It should be stressed that this assessment needs to go beyond polling or observing current users of library reference materials or services. If impediments such as physical or communication barriers exist, members of a group affected by the barriers often are nonusers of the library and thus are invisible to the librarian who only observes the behavior of the user group.

Once groups are identified, librarians need to create a plan of service for meeting the special needs of individuals in each. This plan would include determining the adaptations needed by each group, assessing the library's ability to meet identified needs, and establishing priorities for actions to be taken by the library. It is important to work with other agencies, including local ones and regional or national organizations, both to identify needs of special users and to design collections and services that meet the groups' reference needs. The library should have policies and procedures, including staff training, that enhance access to full reference services. Special adaptations to library procedures to accommodate the needs of identified groups should be incorporated in library handbooks or manuals. Finally, librarians should plan regular evaluation of services and facilities for targeted groups, so that they can keep up with—or even anticipate—changes in the population of those groups, as well as relevant changes in library technology.

Librarians need to plan reference services, assemble reference collections, and develop reference skills appropriate to the various groups in their community of users. This planning process must begin with an understanding of the diverse groups that constitute that community.

NOTES

1.   American Library Association, *Library Bill of Rights*. http://www.ala.org/ala/issuesad vocacy/intfreedom/librarybill/index.cfm.

2.   American Library Association, *Free Access to Libraries for Minors: An Interpretation of the Library Bill of Rights*. http://www.ala.org/ala/issuesadvocacy/intfreedom/librarybill/in terpretations/freeaccesslibraries.cfm.

3.   Satia Marshall Orange and Robin Osborne, "Introduction," in *From Outreach to Equity: Innovative Models of Library Policy and Practice*, ed. Robin Osborne (Chicago: American Library Association, 2004), xi–xvii.

4.   Based in part on a list from Shirley Fitzgibbons, "Reference and Information Services for Children and Young Adults: Definition, Services, and Issues," *The Reference Librarian* 7/8 (Spring/Summer 1983): 5–6.

5.   *U.S. Interim Projections by Age, Sex, Race, and Hispanic Origin: 2000–2050* (Washington, D.C.: U.S. Bureau of the Census). http://www.census.gov/population/www/projections/ usinterimproj.

6.   Ibid.

7.   *Statistical Abstract of the United States 2011* (Washington, D.C.: U.S. Bureau of the Census, 2011), table 709.

8.   Ibid., table 75.

9.   Ibid.

10.   Marcia J. Nauratil, *Public Libraries and Nontraditional Clienteles: The Politics of Special Services* (Westport, CT: Greenwood Press, 1985), 12.

11.   Mengxiong Liu, "Ethnicity and Information Seeking," *The Reference Librarian* 49/50 (1995): 123–34.

12.   Ibid., 124.

13.   Phoebe Janes and Ellen Meltzer, "Origins and Attitudes: Training Reference Librarians for a Pluralistic World," *The Reference Librarian* 30 (1990): 145–55.

14.   Yolanda J. Cuesta, "Developing Outreach Skills in Library Staff," in *From Outreach to Equity: Innovative Models of Library Policy and Practice*, 112–15.

15.   Ibid., 113.

16.   Patrick Andrew Hall, "The Role of Affectivity in Instructing People of Color: Some Implications for Bibliographic Instruction," *Library Trends* 39 (Winter 1991): 316–26.

17.   Ibid., 322.

18.   *Statistical Abstract of the United States 2011*, table 38.

19.   Ibid., table 6.

20.   Ibid., table 278.

21.   Roberto Suro and Sonya Tafoya, *Dispersal and Concentration: Patterns of Latino Residential Settlement* (Washington, D.C.: Pew Hispanic Center, December 27, 2004). http://pewhispanic.org/reports/report.php?ReportID=36.

22.   Steve Sumerford, "Creating a Community of Readers to Fight Functional Illiteracy," *American Libraries* 28 (May 1997): 44–48.

23.   Sharon Chickering Moller, *Library Service to Spanish Speaking Patrons: A Practical Guide* (Englewood, CO: Libraries Unlimited, 2001), 19.

24.   "An ESL Orientation," *School Librarian's Workshop* 24 (November 2003): 12–13; Anne H. Filson, "Librarian–Teacher Partnerships: Serving the English-as-a-Second-Language Students," *Journal of Youth Services in Libraries* 5 (Summer 1992): 399–406.

25.   Manuel D. Lopez, "Chinese Spoken Here: Foreign Language Library Orientation Tours," *College & Research Libraries News* 44 (September 1983): 265–69.

26.   Arthur Downing and Leo Robert Klein, "A Multilingual Virtual Tour for International Students: The Web-Based Library at Baruch College Opens Doors," *College & Research Libraries News* 62 (May 2001): 500–502.

27.   Leonard Wertheimer, "Library Service to Ethnocultural Minorities: Philosophical and Social Bases and Professional Implications," *Public Libraries* 26 (Fall 1987): 98–102.

28.   Miriam Conteh-Morgan, "Connecting the Dots: Limited English Proficiency, Second Language Learning Theories, and Information Literacy Instruction," *Journal of Academic Librarianship* 28 (July 2002): 191–96; Ziming Liu, "Difficulties and Characteristics of Students from Developing Countries in Using American Libraries," *College & Research Libraries* 54 (January 1993): 25–31; Kwasi Sarkodie-Mensah, "The International Student on Campus: History, Trends, Visa Classification, and Adjustment Issues," in *Teaching the New Library to Today's Users: Reaching International, Minority, Senior Citizens, Gay/Lesbian, First Generation, At-Risk, Graduate and Returning Students, and Distance Learners*, ed. Trudi E. Jacobson and Helene C. Williams (New York: Neal-Schuman, 2000), 3–16; Dorothy Tao, "Bibliographic Instruction for a Diverse Population: Understanding, Planning, and Teaching in the Twenty-First Century," *Art Documentation* 24 (Spring 2005): 29–37.

29.   Moller, *Library Service to Spanish Speaking Patrons*, 105–6.

30.   Sarkodie-Mensah, "The International Student on Campus," 3–16; Diane DiMartino and Lucinda R. Zoe, "International Students and the Library: New Tools, New Users, and New Instruction," in *Teaching the New Library to Today's Users*, 17–43.

31.   Gary E. Strong, "Teaching Adult Literacy in a Multicultural Environment," in *Literacy & Libraries: Learning from Case Studies*, ed. GraceAnne A. DeCandido (Chicago: Office for Literacy and Outreach Services, American Library Association, 2001), 110–15.

32.   Moller, *Library Service to Spanish Speaking Patrons*, 20.

33.   Ibid., 5.

34.   *National Assessment of Adult Literacy.* http://nces.ed.gov/naal/.

35.   *Literacy, Economy and Society: Results of the First International Adult Literacy Survey* (Ottawa, Ontario: Statistics Canada and the Organisation for Economic Co-operation and Development, 1995), 199 pp.

36.   Ibid., 57.

37.   Ibid., 61.

38.   Dinah L. O'Brien, "Whole Literacy in Plymouth: Literacy as a Library Service," in *Literacy & Libraries: Learning from Case Studies*, 52–59.

39.   Ibid., 58–59.

40.   Ibid., 58.

41.   *Literacy & Libraries: Learning from Case Studies*, ed. GraceAnne A. DeCandido (Chicago: Office for Literacy and Outreach Services, American Library Association, 2001), 181 pp.; Donna D. Grant, "Leading the Way to Adult Literacy: What 13 Public Libraries Are Doing," *American Libraries* 28 (May 1997): 45–47; Kristin E. Porter, Sondra Cuban, and John P. Comings, *"One Day I Will Make It": A Study of Adult Student Persistence in Library Literacy Programs* (New York: MDRC, 2005), 77 pp.

42.   Leslie McGinnis, "A Place in the World: Building a Learner-Centered Participatory Literacy Program," in *Literacy & Libraries: Learning from Case Studies*, 16–29.

43.   Carol Morris, "Computer Skills and Literacy," in *Literacy & Libraries: Learning from Case Studies*, 135–40.

44.   John Comings, Sondra Cuban, Hans Bos, and Cate Taylor, "'I Know This Is the Place for Me': Stories of Library Literacy Learners and Programs," in *Literacy & Libraries: Learning from Case Studies*, 6–15.

45.   "International Adult Literacy," *ETS Policy Notes* (Princeton, NJ: Educational Testing Service, 1996). http://www.ets.org/Media/Research/pdf/PICPNV7N1.pdf.

46.   Nauratil, *Public Libraries and Nontraditional Clienteles*, 90.

47.   Debra Wilcox Johnson with Jennifer A. Soule, *Libraries and Literacy: A Planning Manual* (Chicago: American Library Association, 1987), 31.

48.   U.S. Equal Employment Opportunity Commission and the U.S. Department of Justice, *Americans with Disabilities Act Handbook* (Washington, D.C.: Government Printing Office, 1992), 1.

49.   Michael G. Gunde, "Working with the Americans with Disabilities Act," *Library Journal* 116 (December 1991): 99.

50.   Katy Lenn, "Library Services to Disabled Students: Outreach and Education," *The Reference Librarian* 53 (1996): 14.

51.   Marti Goddard, "Access through Technology," *Library Journal Net Connect* 129 (Spring 2004): 2–6.

52.   Rob Imrie, "From Universal to Inclusive Design in the Built Environment," in *Disabling Barriers—Enabling Environments*, 2nd ed., ed. John Swain, Sally French, Colin Barnes, and Carol Thomas (London: Sage, 2004), 279–84.

53.   Ibid, 282–83.

54.   Laura Jacobi, "Chatting at Gallaudet," *Library Journal Net Connect* 129 (Spring 2004): 3.

55.   Goddard, "Access through Technology," 4.

56.   Ibid., 4.

57.   See, for example, Rhea Joyce Rubin, *Planning for Library Services to People with Disabilities* (Chicago: Association of Specialized and Cooperative Library Agencies, American Library Association, 2001), 80 pp, and Courtney Deines-Jones, ed., *Improving Library Services to People with Disabilities* (Oxford: Chandos Publishing, 2007), 175 pp. Note that some older guides (e.g., Donald D. Foos and Nancy C. Pack, *How Libraries Must Comply with the Americans with Disabilities Act* [Phoenix, AZ: Oryx Press, 1992]) are still useful for information on staff training and building accommodation, but they do not address newer concerns such as Web site compliance.

58.	Steven J. Herman, "Information Center Profile: Library of Congress Division for the Blind and Physically Handicapped," in *Library Services to the Blind and Physically Handicapped*, ed. Maryalls G. Strom (Metuchen, NJ: Scarecrow Press, 1977), 5.

59.	For more information, see the National Library Service Web site at http://www.loc.gov/nls.

60.	John M. Taylor, "Serving Blind Readers in a Digital Age," *American Libraries* 35 (December 2004): 49–51.

61.	Audio Publishers Association, *Americans Are Tuning in to Audio: Audiobook Sales on the Rise Nationally* (August 24, 2007). http://www.audiopub.org/PDFs/2007SalesSurveyrelease.pdf.

62.	Norman Oder, "Feeling a Squeeze," *Library Journal* 129 (November 15, 2004): 34–36.

63.	American Foundation for the Blind, *Optical Character Recognition Systems* (New York: AFB, 2008). http://www.afb.org/Section.asp?SectionID=4&TopicID=31&DocumentID=1283.

64.	See, for example, ABLEDATA at http://www.abledata.com, a project of the National Institute on Disability and Rehabilitation Research of the U.S. Department of Education, which provides information about products for users with disabilities and links to the vendor sites.

65.	Cheryl H. Kirkpatrick, "Getting Two for the Price of One: Accessibility and Usability," *Computers in Libraries* 23 (January 2003): 26–29.

66.	Ibid., 27.

67.	Abigail Noland, "How Cleveland Serves the Deaf Community," *Public Libraries* 42 (January/February 2003): 20–21.

68.	Rosa Rodriguez and Monica Reed, "Our Deaf Family Needs to Read, Too," *Public Libraries* 42 (January/February 2003): 38–41.

69.	Susan Foster, "Examining the Fit between Deafness and Disability," in *Rethinking Disability: The Emergence of New Definitions, Concepts and Communities*, ed. Patrick Devlieger, Frank Rusch, and David Pfeiffer (Antwerp, Belgium: Garant, 2003), 111–29.

70.	*American with Disabilities Act Handbook*, n.p.

71.	Ibid., 123–24.

72.	*The Complete Directory for People with Disabilities 2011* (Millerton, NY: Grey House Publishing, 2010), 1,200 pp.

73.	Laura Thill, ed., *The Complete Product Guide for People with Disabilities*, 2nd ed. (Horsham, PA: No Limits, 2002), 256 pp.

74.	Linda Lucas Walling and Marilyn M. Irwin, eds., *Information Services for People with Developmental Disabilities: The Library Manager's Handbook* (Westport, CT: Greenwood Press, 1995), 4.

75.	Ibid., xvi.

76.	Sandra Feinberg, Barbara Jordan, Kathleen Deerr, and Michelle Langa, *Including Families of Children with Special Needs* (New York: Neal-Schuman, 1999), 208 pp.

77.	Thomas E. Hecker, "Patrons with Disabilities or Problem Patrons: Which Model Should Librarians Apply to People with Mental Illness?," *The Reference Librarian* 53 (1996): 5–12.

78.	Ibid., 10.

79.	Anne M. Turner, *It Comes with the Territory: Handling Problem Situations in Libraries*, rev. ed. (Jefferson, NC: McFarland & Company, 2004), 194 pp.

80. Ibid., 12.

81. *Statistical Abstract of the United States 2011*, table 7.

82. Ibid.

83. Ibid., table 8.

84. Melissa Gross and Matthew L. Saxton, "Who Wants to Know? Imposed Queries in the Public Library," *Public Libraries* 40 (May/June 2001): 170–76.

85. See, for example, Barbara K. Stripling, "Inquiry-Based Learning," in *Curriculum Connections through the Library*, ed. Barbara K. Stripling and Sandra Hughes-Hassell (Westport, CT: Libraries Unlimited, 2003), 3–39; Jean Donham, Kay Bishop, Carol Collier Kuhlthau, and Dianne Oberg, *Inquiry-Based Learning: Lessons from Library Power* (Worthington, OH: Linworth Publishing, 2001), 88 pp.

86. Amanda Lenhart, Mary Madden, and Paul Hitlin, *Teens and Technology: Youth Are Leading the Transition to a Fully Wired and Mobile Nation* (Washington, D.C.: Pew Internet & American Life Project, July 27, 2005). http://www.pewinternet.org/Reports/2005/Teens-and-Technology.aspx.

87. Carol Collier Kuhlthau, "Meeting the Informational Needs of Children and Young Adults: Basing Library Media Programs on Developmental States," *Journal of Youth Services in Libraries* 2 (Fall 1988): 51–57.

88. Vicky L. Crosson, "Hey! Kids Are Patrons, Too!" *Texas Libraries* 52 (Summer 1991): 50.

89. Colleen Cool, "Information-Seeking Behaviors of Children Using Electronic Information Services during the Early Years: 1980–1990," in *Youth Information-Seeking Behavior: Theories, Models, and Issues*, ed. Mary K. Chelton and Colleen Cool (Lanham, MD: Scarecrow, 2004), 1–35; Delia Neuman, "Learning and the Digital Library," *Library Trends* 45 (1997): 687–707.

90. Dania Bilal, "Research on Children's Information Seeking on the Web," in *Youth Information-Seeking Behavior*, 271–91; Andrew Large, "Information Seeking on the Web by Elementary School Students," in *Youth Information-Seeking Behavior*, 293–319.

91. Christine Behrmann and Dolores Vogliano, "On Training the Children's Reference Librarian," *Illinois Libraries* 73 (February 1991): 152–57.

92. Melissa Gross, "The Imposed Query and Information Services for Children," *Journal of Youth Services in Libraries* 13 (Winter 2000): 10–17.

93. Melissa Gross, "Pilot Study on the Prevalence of Imposed Queries in a School Library Media Center," *School Library Media Quarterly* 25 (Spring 1997): 157–66.

94. Elizabeth Overmyer, "Serving the Reference Needs of Children," *Wilson Library Bulletin* 69 (June 1995): 141.

95. Paula Busey and Tom Doerr, "Kid's Catalog: An Information Retrieval System for Children," *Journal of Youth Services in Libraries* 7 (Fall 1993): 77–84.

96. American Library Association Intellectual Freedom Committee, *Statement on Library Use of Filtering Software* (July 1, 1997; rev. November 17, 2000). http://www.ala.org/ala/aboutala/offices/oif/statementspols/ifresolutions/statementlibrary.cfm.

97. Anitra T. Steele, *Bare Bones Children's Services: Tips for Public Library Generalists* (Chicago: Association for Library Service to Children, American Library Association, 2001), 80.

98. "Abused and Neglected Child Reporting Act," *Illinois Revised Statutes*, 325 ILCS 5, from Chapter 23, par. 2051. http://www.ilga.gov/legislation/ilcs/ilcs3.asp?ActID=1460&Ch

apAct=325%AOILCS%A05/&ChapterID=32&ChapterName=CHILDREN&ActName=Abu
sed%20and%20Neglected%20Child%20Reporting%20Act.

99.   Linda Ward Callaghan, "Children's Questions: Reference Interviews with the Young," *The Reference Librarian* 7/8 (Spring/Summer 1983): 55.

100.   Virginia A. Walter, *Children & Libraries: Getting It Right* (Chicago: American Library Association, 2001), 31.

101.   Melissa Gross, "The Imposed Query," 10–17.

102.   Walter, *Children & Libraries*, 29.

103.   Ibid., 29–32.

104.   For more information about Child_Lit and instructions for subscribing, see http://www.rci.rutgers.edu/~mjoseph/childlit/about.html.

105.   American Association of School Librarians and the Association for Educational Communications and Technology, *Information Power: Building Partnerships for Learning* (Chicago: American Library Association, 1998), 89.

106.   Leslie Edmonds, Paula Moore, and Kathleen Mahaffey Balcom, "The Effectiveness of an Online Catalog," *School Library Journal* 36 (October 1990): 28–32.

107.   American Association of School Librarians and the Association for Educational Communications and Technology, *Information Literacy Standards for Student Learning* (Chicago: American Library Association, 1998), 64 pp.

108.   Keith Curry Lance, Marcia J. Rodney, and Christine Hamilton-Pennell, *Powerful Libraries Make Powerful Learners: The Illinois Study Executive Summary Report* (Canton, IL: Illinois School Library Media Association, 2005), ii; see also other studies by the Lance group at http://www.lrs.org/impact.php.

109.   Walter, *Children & Libraries*, 32.

110.   Ibid., 82–84; Cindy Mediavilla, *Creating the Full-Service Homework Center in Your Library* (Chicago: American Library Association, 2001), 141 pp.

111.   *1.1 Million Homeschooled Students in the United States in 2003* (Washington, D.C.: National Center for Education Statistics). http://nces.ed.gov/nhes/homeschool.

112.   Ann Slattery, "In a Class of Their Own," *School Library Journal* 51 (August 2005): 44–46.

113.   Paul Kaplan, "Reaching Out to Homeschooling Families: Services and Programs," *Illinois Libraries* 83 (Winter 2001): 44–46.

114.   Patrick Jones and Joel Shoemaker, *Do It Right! Best Practices for Serving Young Adults in School and Public Libraries* (New York: Neal-Schuman, 2001), 96.

115.   Patrick Jones, *New Directions for Library Service to Young Adults* (Chicago: Young Adult Library Services Association, American Library Association, 2002), 146 pp.

116.   Virginia A. Walter and Elaine Meyers, *Teens & Libraries: Getting It Right* (Chicago: American Library Association, 2003), 154 pp.

117.   Mary K. Chelton, "Young Adult Reference Service in the Public Library," *The Reference Librarian* 7/8 (Spring/Summer 1983): 35; Anthony Bernier, Mary K. Chelton, Christine A. Jenkins, and Jennifer Burek Pierce, "Two Hundred Years of Young Adult Library Services History: The Chronology," *Voice of Youth Advocates* 28 (June 2005): 106–11.

118.   Mary K. Chelton, "Common YA Models of Service in Public Libraries: Advantages and Disadvantages," *Young Adult Library Services* 3 (Summer 2005): 4–6.

119.   AASL and AECT, *Information Power*, 1998; *Information Literacy Standards for Student Learning*, 1998; and American Association of School Librarians, *Standards for the 21st-Century Learner* (Chicago: American Library Association, 2007). http://www.ala.org/ala/mgrps/divs/aasl/guidelinesandstandards/learningstandards/standards.cfm.

120.   See Walter Minkel and Roxanne Hsu Feldman, *Delivering Web Reference Services to Young People* (Chicago: American Library Association, 1999), 121 pp., for an in-depth description of designing a homework reference site.

121.   Joseph Thompson, "After School and Online," *Library Journal Net Connect* 128 (Winter 2003): 35–37.

122.   Robin Bryan, "Brarydog.net: A Homework Assistance Portal for Students," *Public Libraries* 41 (March/April 2002): 101–3.

123.   Helma Hawkins, "Opening the Closet Door: Public Library Services for Gay, Lesbian, & Bisexual Teens," *Colorado Libraries* 20 (Spring 1994): 28.

124.   Amy Levine, "Providing Information on Sexuality: Librarians Can Help Youth Become Sexually Healthy Adults," *Journal of Youth Services in Libraries* 15 (Winter 2002): 45–48.

125.   Chelton, "Young Adult Reference Service," 32.

126.   Dorothy M. Broderick, "On My Mind," *Voice of Youth Advocates* 11 (August 1988): 116.

127.   For more information about YALSA_BK and instructions for subscribing, see http://www.ala.org/ala/yalsa/electronicresourcesb/websitesmailing.htm.

128.   *What Do Children and Young Adults Read Next? A Reader's Guide to Fiction for Children and Young Adults*, 3 vols. (Farmington Hills, MI: Thomson Gale, 2001–2004).

129.   Mary K. Chelton, "Young Adults As Problems: How the Social Construction of a Marginalized User Category Occurs," *Journal of Education for Library and Information Science* 42 (Winter 2001): 4–11; Mary K. Chelton, "The 'Problem Patron' Public Libraries Created," *The Reference Librarian* 75/76 (2002): 23–32.

130.   Mary K. Chelton and James M. Rosignia, *Bare Bones: Young Adult Services Tips for Public Library Generalists* (Chicago: American Library Association, 1993), 30.

131.   Jones and Shoemaker, *Do It Right!*, 119.

132.   Gregg Sapp, *A Brief History of the Future of Libraries: An Annotated Bibliography* (Lanham, MD: Scarecrow Press, 2002), 295 pp.

133.   *Statistical Abstract of the United States 2011*, table 7.

134.   Ibid., table 8.

135.   *Statistical Abstract of the United States 2008* (Washington, D.C.: U.S. Bureau of the Census, 2008), table 181.

136.   Ibid.

137.   Barbara T. Mates, *5-Star Programming and Services for Your 55+ Library Customers* (Chicago: American Library Association, 2003), 17.

138.   *Statistical Abstract of the United States 2011*, table 585.

139.   Tavia Simmons and Jane Lawler Dye, *Grandparents Living with Grandchildren: 2000* (Washington, D.C.: U.S. Census Bureau, 2003). http://www.census.gov/population/www/cen2000/briefs.html.

140.   *Library Services to Older Adults Guidelines* (Chicago: Reference and User Services Association, American Library Association, revised 1999, approved 2008). http://www.ala.org/ala/mgrps/divs/rusa/resources/guidelines/libraryservices.cfm.

141. *Quick Tips for Serving Older Adults* (Chicago: Office for Literacy and Outreach Services, American Library Association, 2004). http://www.ala.org/ala/aboutala/offices/olos/out reachresource/quicktipsolderadults.cfm.

142. Mates, *5-Star Programming and Services*, 63–82.

143. Susannah Fox, *Older Americans and the Internet* (Washington, D.C.: Pew Internet & American Life Project, March 28, 2004). http://www.pewinternet.org/PPF/r/117/report_dis play.asp.

144. Dan R. Harris and Laurie L. Harris, eds., *Aging Sourcebook: Basic Information on Issues Affecting Older Americans, Including Demographic Trends, Social Security, Medicare, Estate Planning, Legal Rights, Health and Safety, Elder Care Options, Retirement Lifestyle Options, and End of Life Issues* (Detroit: Omnigraphics, 1998), 889 pp.

ADDITIONAL READINGS

Alter, Rachel, Linda Walling, Susan Beck, Kathleen Garland, Ardis Hanson, and Walter Metz. *Guidelines for Library Services for People with Mental Illnesses.* Chicago: Association of Specialized and Cooperative Library Agencies, American Library Association, 2007. 48 pp.

These guidelines provide recommendations on providing successful library experiences for people with mental illnesses.

American Association of School Librarians and Association for Educational Communications and Technology. *Information Power: Building Partnerships for Learning.* Chicago: American Library Association, 1998. 205 pp.

Information Power includes the nine "Information Standards for Student Learning," which guide the development of school library media services, including reference service.

Brazier, Helen, and David Owen, eds. "Library and Information Services for Visually Impaired People." *Library Trends* 55 (Spring 2007): 757–993.

This collection of articles offers an international perspective on library services for the visually impaired. The scope includes national models for service delivery and the use of specific technologies to enhance resource discovery and Web accessibility.

Cuban, Sondra. *Serving New Immigrant Communities in the Library.* Westport, CT: Libraries Unlimited, 2007. 255 pp.

Cuban discusses strategies for enhancing services to new immigrant communities, including assessment of needs, addressing these needs through library services, and connecting new immigrants to learning opportunities.

DeCandido, GraceAnne A., ed. *Literacy & Libraries: Learning from Case Studies.* Chicago: Office for Literacy and Outreach Services, American Library Association, 2001. 181 pp.

This volume features stories from the 13 library literacy programs that made up the first phase of the Literacy in Libraries Across America Initiative funded by the Lila Wallace–Reader's Digest Fund and the American Library Association. Together, these contributions make a clear case for the role of literacy programming as an essential reference service in libraries.

Deines-Jones, Courtney, ed. *Improving Library Services to People with Disabilities.* Oxford, England: Chandos Publishing, 2007. 175 pp.

This compilation includes chapters on improving library services to individuals with visual impairments, hearing impairments, and physical disabilities. A chapter by Deines-Jones discusses low-cost/no-cost ways to improve services through strategies such as addressing staff attitudes. The book concludes with a guide to resources, including publications, Web sites, and organizations.

Goddard, Marti. "Access through Technology." *Library Journal Net Connect* 129 (Spring 2004): 2–6.

Goddard's holistic approach to technology planning will keep this guide fresh, even as specific technologies come and go.

Jacobson, Trudi E., and Helene C. Williams, eds. *Teaching the New Library to Today's Users: Reaching International, Minority, Senior Citizens, Gay-Lesbian, First-Generation, At-Risk, Graduate and Returning Students, and Distance Learners.* New York: Neal-Schuman, 2000. 256 pp.

Though focused on instruction in the academic library, this book models how library services should be adapted to meet the needs of diverse users.

Kirkpatrick, Cheryl H. ""Two for the Price of One: Accessibility and Usability." *Computers in Libraries* 23 (January 2003): 27–29.

Kirkpatrick makes a compelling case for why the accessible design of Web sites is also good design for all library users.

Mates, Barbara T. *5-Star Programming and Services for Your 55+ Library Customers.* Chicago: American Library Association, 2003. 154 pp.

This useful guide discusses special needs of older citizens and the approaches libraries must take to meet those needs. The two chapters on computers and seniors are particularly helpful.

Moller, Sharon Chickering. *Library Service to Spanish Speaking Patrons: A Practical Guide.* Englewood, CO: Libraries Unlimited, 2001. 207 pp.

Moller first provides a historical background for the need for service to Spanish-speaking populations and then addresses her topic by age level. The appendix of this useful guide contains glossaries of library and computer terms translated into Spanish and Spanish-language forms that are commonly used in libraries.

Moyer, Jessica E. *Research-Based Readers' Advisory.* Chicago: American Library Association, 2008. 279 pp.

Moyer partners with practitioners to explore many facets of readers' advisory work, such as service to children and young adult readers. The format of each chapter includes two parts: a "research review" analyzing the existing research related to an area of readers' advisory services and a "librarian's view" written by a practicing librarian and readers' advisor. The chapter on work with children and young adult readers (pp. 77–110) includes views from both a youth services librarian and a young adult librarian.

Osborne, Robin, ed. *From Outreach to Equity: Innovative Models of Library Policy and Practice.* Chicago: Office for Literacy and Outreach Services, American Library Association, 2004. 145 pp.

The contributors to this volume present models for differentiated approaches to service. Their innovative programs encompass diverse populations and institutions: immigrants and refugees, the homeless, prisoners, people with disabilities, minority women, teenagers, tribal libraries, and academic libraries.

Rubin, Rhea Joyce. *Planning for Library Services to People with Disabilities*. Chicago: Association of Specialized and Cooperative Library Agencies, American Library Association, 2001. 80 pp.

This title in the ASCLA Changing Horizons Series is essentially a template for a planning process, from assessing the needs of the library and community to drafting and finalizing the plan. Pre-tested user surveys are provided along with other helpful resources.

Turner, Anne M. *It Comes with the Territory: Handling Problem Situations in Libraries*. Rev. ed. Jefferson, NC: McFarland, 2004. 194 pp.

Turner keeps the focus on the user as she discusses ways to deliver quality service to all, even under trying circumstances. She takes a humorous and practical approach to the many unexpected situations that can arise during reference work.

Walter, Virginia A. *Children & Libraries: Getting It Right*. Chicago: American Library Association, 2001. 155 pp.

Walter, a respected children's library specialist and advocate, presents a call to action for libraries serving children. Now a classic in the field, this book places children's services—including reference services—in the context of their changing lives and experiences.

Walter, Virginia A., and Elaine Meyers. *Teens & Libraries: Getting It Right*. Chicago: American Library Association, 2003. 154 pp.

As Walter did in *Children & Libraries*, Walter and her colleague Meyers make the case for the importance of equitable and professional library service to teenagers. They describe the importance of working *with*, not *for*, young adult users and enumerate the many ways in which that can happen.

Part II

Information Sources and Their Use

Chapter

13

Selection and Evaluation of Reference Sources

Linda C. Smith

REFERENCE SOURCES

Part 1 of this text introduced the variety of services provided by reference librarians in all types of libraries and information centers. Essential to the provision of services is a carefully selected collection of sources. This chapter introduces the types of sources used most frequently in reference work and discusses reference collection development and maintenance. This includes consideration of the criteria used to evaluate sources as well as reviewing media and guides to reference materials useful in collection development. Discussion encompasses well-established reference sources and approaches to collection development, as well as responses to the challenges and opportunities posed by the increasing volume of licensed electronic full-text and freely available Web resources. The remaining chapters in Part 2 discuss the characteristics and uses of particular types of reference sources.

What Is a Reference Source?

In considering selection and evaluation of materials for the reference collection, it is helpful first to attempt to characterize the types of materials most commonly included in reference collections. The *ALA Glossary of Library and Information Science* offers the following definitions of a reference book: "1. A book designed by the arrangement and treatment of its subject matter to be consulted for definite items of information rather than to be read consecutively. 2. A book whose use is restricted to the library building."[1] Marcia Bates labels these definitions "functional" and "administrative."[2] She further clarifies the concept of a reference book by describing in greater detail the arrangement and indexing that typically characterize the presentation of information in reference books. Bill Katz provides a history of the development of each of the standard categories of reference books, from encyclopedias to bibliographies, showing the relationship to intellectual and technological developments.[3]

As described in chapter 1, reference librarians must be able to respond to a wide variety of questions, such as ready-reference or research, depending on the needs expressed by library users. Increasingly, the concept of a reference collection made up of reference books is an inadequate characterization of the resources most frequently used by reference librarians. *Harrod's Librarians' Glossary and Reference Book* defines the broader concept of reference source: "any material, published work, database, web site, etc. which is used to obtain authoritative information."[4] Thus, although print materials continue to be important, they are supplemented by materials in microform, CD-ROM, and DVD format and electronic resources accessed via computers and network connections. With the availability of a growing number of freely available resources on the Web, it is limiting to think of the reference collection as only those materials that are purchased or licensed by the library. Nevertheless, reference librarians still have a responsibility to identify resources of value for reference work, developing a "virtual reference collection" to supplement the material housed in the reference section of the library. Where the same title is available in alternative formats, a choice must be made as to which one(s) will be most useful. Reference librarians must also monitor the growing availability of all types of materials in electronic form, given that their enhanced searching, retrieval, and display capabilities may make them useful in answering reference questions even though they are not reference sources per se. As Margaret Landesman observes, "the ability to search full text...turns every collection of online texts into a reference collection and provides an automatic concordance for every title. Titles can no longer be tidily separated into 'reference works' and 'general collection.'"[5]

Types of Sources

As noted, one way to categorize reference sources is by format: print, microform, distributed electronic format such as CD-ROM, or electronically accessible over the Web. Alternatively, it is possible to divide reference sources into two main classes: compilations that furnish information directly and compilations that refer to other sources containing information, merely indicating places where information may be found. In practice, this distinction becomes blurred because sources of the first type often refer to others for fuller information, and those of the second type are adequate for answering some questions. Sources of the first type include encyclopedias, dictionaries, almanacs, handbooks, yearbooks, biographical sources, directories, atlases, and gazetteers; sources of the second type include catalogs, bibliographies, and indexes. Each of these is the subject of one of the remaining chapters in this book. In addition, government publications, which frequently constitute unique sources of information, are treated in a separate chapter. Although not the subject of a separate chapter in this book, pamphlets and clippings files are often part of the reference collection, organized by subject in a vertical file. Such collections tend to feature items of local interest, selected for their potential reference value.[6] Increasingly, reference librarians are building Web sites to link to this type of information in electronic form.

Trends in Reference Publishing

Although some indexes and abstracts have been available in electronic form for as long as 40 years, the electronic availability of other categories of references sources, such as specialized subject encyclopedias and handbooks, is much more recent. The last decade has seen a rapid increase in the availability of reference titles in electronic form, the aggregation of multiple titles into virtual reference collections, and the emergence of new forms of collection that go beyond a simple aggregation of the contents of individual print titles.

Examination of the Web sites of major publishers of reference sources, such as Gale, H. W. Wilson, Oxford University Press, Routledge, ABC-CLIO, and SAGE Publications, demonstrates the proliferation of titles available in electronic form. Many publishers are also becoming distributors of electronic content, creating Web-based virtual reference collections. Other publishers license their electronic content to companies that aggregate access to titles from multiple publishers. Still others do both, making their content available through their own sites as well as other venues. An example of a resource aggregating content from other publishers is *Credo Reference* (formerly *Xrefer*). As of 2011, this included the contents of 531 titles from more than 70 publishers in a variety of subject areas. Adam Hodgkin, developer of Xrefer, argues that to realize the full benefit of such collections, aggregation with searching across a range of titles needs to be supplemented with cross-references implemented as hyperlinks, both within and across the titles included in the collection. Such a feature supplements searching with support for browsing to explore interconnections.[7] Although most such aggregations are accessible only through license or purchase, Péter Jacsó identifies some available as open access resources without charge.[8] Also, although some such freely available resources are quite current, others include older material now out of copyright. For example, *Bartleby.com* (http://www.bartleby.com) has the 10th edition (1919) of *Bartlett's Familiar Quotations* and the 1922 edition of Emily Post's *Etiquette*.

New forms of virtual collections are also emerging, combining electronic versions of both primary source materials and related reference source materials. A comparison of two such collections devoted to African American life illustrates the richness and complexity of this emerging genre. Greenwood Publishing Group has produced *The African American Experience* as an electronic research tool for African American history and culture. It encompasses more than 450 volumes, all cross-searchable and indexed, including material from multivolume print reference sets, such as *Encyclopedia of African American Literature* and *The Greenwood Encyclopedia of African American Civil Rights*; other reference books and monographs; primary documents such as manuscripts, speeches, and court cases; interviews with former slaves; and classics in black scholarship from the Negro Universities Press. Other features include a time line, audio clips, links to vetted Web sites, lesson plans, and photographs, maps, and other images. It is regularly updated with new content, documents, and multimedia. The Oxford University Press *Oxford African American Studies Center* focuses on the lives and events that have shaped African American and African history and culture. Core content includes scholarly encyclopedias and biographical sources such as the *Encyclopedia of African American History, 1619–1895* and *African American National Biography*, as well as articles from other major reference titles. Images, primary sources with specially written commentaries, maps, charts, tables, and time lines have been included to enhance this reference content. The site continues to grow with the addition of new material, such as the latest biographies from the *African American National Biography* project. The interface supports both searching and browsing the various categories of materials included.

This proliferation of Web products has allowed librarians to access content they may not have been able to collect in print. However, it has left librarians with the difficult task of figuring out how best to select and organize the sources they purchase.[9] Rather than having the flexibility to select individual reference volumes from many different publishers, librarians increasingly have to select one aggregated package over another. This can have the effect of increasing the range and depth of a reference collection while also decreasing the flexibility to customize the collection to reflect the interests of the library's specific user community.[10] Following are some of the questions that must be addressed: Which product will best suit one's library? Which product has the best access and search features? What are the options for ownership versus licensing?[11]

REFERENCE COLLECTION DEVELOPMENT AND MAINTENANCE

The work of reference librarians includes selection of an adequate and suitable collection of reference sources and arrangement and maintenance of the collection so that it can be used easily and conveniently. Unplanned collection development and neglect of weeding can impair the efficiency of reference services. Records of unanswered questions are one means of identifying deficiencies in the existing collection.

Components of the Collection

Because reference collections now include materials in a variety of formats, the reference librarian must decide whether to acquire particular titles in more than one format. At present, many titles exist in only one format, be it print, microform, or electronic. Others are available in several different formats. For example, to aid in locating residential telephone numbers, one can purchase print telephone directories, consult a compilation of directories on CD-ROM, or use one of the many freely available telephone directory services on the Web. Although the different formats may be identical or at least overlapping in content, they may differ in search capabilities.

The greater flexibility of searching electronic resources has led to increasing migration from print to electronic sources, with libraries canceling subscriptions to print indexes, for example, in favor of online access.[12] Librarians must weigh such factors as relative costs, amount of use, and likely users and uses in deciding which formats to acquire. These decisions must be continuously reviewed as new titles become available in electronic formats.

Reference Collection Development

Increased costs of reference sources and proliferation of formats and titles have focused attention on the importance of a systematic approach to reference collection development. Librarians have more options than ever before in creating a reference collection that is responsive to the needs of the community served. Many of the sources described in this text commonly form the core of a library's reference collection, but other titles in a specific collection will vary depending on local needs.

Decisions in collection development include whether to buy newly published titles, buy new editions of titles already in the collection, cancel a title that is now freely accessible on the Web, continue serials such as indexes, contract with vendors for online access or load databases locally, and coordinate collection development with other libraries to ensure the availability of at least one copy of an expensive set in a particular geographic area or take advantage of consortial pricing arrangements. A written collection development policy can provide guidance in making these decisions and will help in establishing and maintaining an effective reference collection. Sydney Pierce suggests that developing a reference collection development policy requires the reference staff to identify the objectives to be met by the collection and to define the content of the collection: the nature and organization of its different parts, criteria for placing materials in each part, and formats and degree of duplication desired for reference materials.[13]

Surveys indicate that many libraries do not have written collection development policies.[14] Chapter 2 of Christopher Nolan's text on managing the reference collection outlines possible elements of a reference collection development policy,[15] including (1) an introduction, relating reference collection development to the library's overall collection development plan; (2) scope of the collection; (3) staff responsibilities; (4) selection criteria; (5) any special policies; (6) sources of funds for the purchase of reference sources; and (7) a section on external relationships—that is, on the library's position on working with other libraries for reference collection support. Examples of policies are available in the literature to provide some guidance.[16]

Maintaining the collection is an ongoing process. For example, to provide accurate information in response to questions regarding current addresses, telephone numbers, and statistical data, it is important to have the latest available edition of a tool in the collection and to be aware of the Web resources that may have even more current information. Publishers' announcements and reviews can alert the librarian to the availability of new titles and new editions; publishers' Web sites can also be perused.[17] Regular inventory of the reference collection is needed to identify areas that require updating or strengthening. Chapter 10 provides more discussion of the evaluation of reference collections.

Arrangement of the Collection

Just as different libraries have somewhat different sets of titles making up their reference collections, there are different possible arrangements of titles. One possibility is to maintain a classified arrangement regardless of type. An alternative is to group types of sources together, creating sections for encyclopedias, biographical sources, directories, indexes, and so forth. Most collections designate a portion of the titles as ready-reference because of the frequency with which they are consulted and the need for rapid access to their contents. These titles are often kept at or near the reference or information desk.

It is difficult to integrate sources requiring special equipment, such as microform readers or computer workstations and CD-ROM drives, with other titles of the same type or in the same subject area. Whatever arrangement is chosen, consideration must be given to ease of access by the library user as well as the reference librarian. Special signage or handouts may be required to orient the library user to the location of particular sections of the collection.

With the increasing availability of resources in electronic form, reference librarians are often involved in library projects to design the interface or gateway to orient library users to available electronic resources and aid in their selection. As discussed in chapter 5, the familiar orienting devices of physical collections now need to be supplemented with approaches to guiding navigation and selection via the interface to these electronic resources.

Weeding the Collection

There must be a systematic basis for weeding (i.e., deselection, pruning, deacquisition[18]) as well as for adding new titles to the collection. A reference librarian should discard materials in the same way that they are chosen: by taking into account what is already in the collection and what is actually needed for reference work. Weeding keeps the collection from becoming a depository of out-of-date materials and reduces the danger of giving incorrect information from dated sources. Factors affecting weeding include frequency of use, age of material, physical condition, arrival of a new edition or electronic version that supersedes a volume already on the shelf, and the need for space. Weeded materials may be placed in the circulating collection or discarded, depending on their possible continuing value to users. For example, old directories might be used for historical research. Different types of materials will require different guidelines for retention. Lynn Westbrook provides guidelines for weeding reference serials,[19] and William Katz lists general guidelines for various types of reference sources.[20] For example, Katz notes that almanacs, yearbooks, and manuals are usually superseded by the next edition. However, because the information in each is rarely duplicated exactly, he suggests keeping old editions for at least 5 years and preferably 10. With the growing emphasis on electronic resources in reference collections, librarians must devote increasing attention to policies for retaining access to materials in this form.[21] A growing number of libraries are weeding and reducing the size of their print reference collections, sometimes dramatically, reflecting decreasing use of print resources as more materials become accessible in electronic form.[22]

EVALUATION OF SOURCES

In building the reference collection, the librarian must evaluate the quality of individual sources and their suitability for inclusion in the library's reference collection. Although evaluation criteria were originally developed for print sources, they are also applicable to nonprint sources, such as microforms and databases. It may be more difficult to apply some of the criteria to electronic and other nonprint sources, however, because such media cannot be examined directly in the same way that one handles print sources. The criteria covered in this chapter and listed in Box 13.1 apply

---

BOX 13.1
EVALUATION CRITERIA

Format

print/microform/electronic, physical makeup, illustrations

Scope

purpose, coverage, currency

Relation to similar works

uniqueness, spin-offs, new editions

Authority

authorship, publisher/sponsor, sources of information

Treatment

accuracy, objectivity, style/audience

Arrangement

sequence, indexing

Special features

Cost

price, licensing conditions

---

to all types of reference sources; chapters 14 through 22 include sections on evaluation of particular types of sources and highlight the criteria of special importance for those types. By considering these evaluation criteria, the librarian will be better able to judge whether a particular source meets the needs of the library and its users and is worthy of purchase or licensing using the limited funds available for reference collection development.

The focus in this chapter is on evaluation of individual titles. Although databases are not yet reviewed as extensively as print sources, a number of authors have proposed criteria for evaluating CD-ROM and online databases, as well as Web resources, and these are incorporated in the following discussion.[23] Lynne Martin provides an interesting evaluation of online catalogs as reference tools using similar criteria.[24]

Format

When reviewing print sources, one is concerned with the physical makeup and features of the book, such as binding, paper, typeface, and layout. If a print source includes illustrations, one must judge their quality and relationship to the text. Recent reference publishing has placed increasing emphasis on visual material.[25] Print sources have the advantages of being straightforward to use, predictable in cost, and usable by more than one person simultaneously if produced as a multivolume set. Disadvantages include the space required to house print sources, the problem in maintaining their currency, and the limitations on search strategies.

Microform formats may prove satisfactory for sources with short entries and alphabetical arrangements, such as bibliographies and directories. Microforms can save space and are a recognized medium for preserving content that has continuing value. Disadvantages include equipment costs and maintenance, the need for user orientation, the limit to one user at a time per microform viewer, and the limitations on search strategies.

CD-ROMs allow complex searching and store large amounts of information. The introduction of multimedia CD-ROMs and DVD technology means that they now can store images and sound in addition to text and numerical data.[26] (As with illustrations in print sources, the quality and reference value of such images and sound should be assessed.) On the other hand, CD-ROMs may be expensive, somewhat slow to search, and variable in ease of use because interfaces are not standard. They may lack currency, and they require work space for equipment.

Like CD-ROMs, online databases and Web resources support flexibility and complexity in searching and may contain large amounts of information. In addition, they can be updated more frequently than CD-ROMs. Limitations of online access to commercial databases include unpredictable costs (unless databases are locally loaded or licensed to allow unlimited use), the need for equipment, and the frequent need for special training to use search systems effectively. Web resources may vary in usability and stability. These advantages and disadvantages must be weighed when evaluating a reference source in one or more formats.

Scope

One indication of scope is the statement of purpose, generally found in the preface of print reference sources. In evaluating a source, it is necessary to judge to what extent the statement of purpose is fulfilled in the text. Has the author or editor accomplished what was intended? Aspects of scope include subject and geographical coverage. Time period coverage is also important for many reference works. How current are the contents? For a serial publication, how frequently is it updated? What is the language of publication? Print sources can be examined to assess the various parameters that define the work's scope, but evaluations of electronic sources may have to rely more on documentation—written descriptions that attempt to characterize the coverage of the source. Sample searches can be done to probe various aspects of the scope, but it may be difficult to develop as thorough an understanding of the source's scope as is possible with a print tool, where this "metainformation" about scope is contained in a clearly identifiable preface. Péter Jacsó provides a thorough review of approaches to assessing database scope.[27] Factors to consider include size of the database, the number of sources and time period covered, unique content when compared to other databases, and geographic and language coverage.

When the same source exists in different formats, currency may vary. Online sources are often more current than print and CD-ROM sources. There are many exceptions, however, so the librarian should investigate relative currency for each source being evaluated. Resources providing links to Web sites can suffer from "link rot" (when URLs given are no longer correct) unless an effort is made to update them on a regular basis.[28]

Relation to Similar Works

A newly published title may have different types of relationships to sources already in the collection. These need to be taken into account when assessing the potential value of a new title to the collection. One obvious category is a new edition of a title already held. In this case, it is necessary to assess the extent of revision in the new edition. Is it sufficient to warrant purchase? Another category is works of similar scope. To what extent is there overlap in content, and to what extent is there unique information? If there is overlap in content, is information more easily found in the new source? Is it written for a different audience? Reference book publishers may issue spin-offs from large sets, such as a one-volume physics encyclopedia with articles selected from a multivolume encyclopedia of science and technology. Although the one-volume encyclopedia might be useful in a branch library that does not own the parent set, it would duplicate information already found in a collection that contains the original set.

With the availability of electronic counterparts for many print tools, it is important to assess the extent to which the content corresponds. For example, there are often differences in time period covered. At times, there is more information in electronic formats because it is easy to store additional information in them. In some cases, the same database is available from different vendors; thus, it is necessary to consider differences in search capabilities and coverage.

Authority

Indicators of authority include the education and experience of the editors and contributors, as indicated by degrees earned and organizational affiliations. The reputation of the publisher or sponsoring agency is also an indicator. Certain publishers are well established as sources of quality reference materials. Many reference sources include lists of material used in compiling the source. Beyond leading to additional sources of information, these lists also can be used as an indicator of the authority of the work. It may be easier to evaluate the authority of print reference sources because statements of authorship and lists of references can be easily identified. If a CD-ROM or online database has a print counterpart, authority can likewise be judged. When there is no print counterpart, it may be necessary to judge authority from statements presented in the documentation describing the electronic source.

Treatment

Accuracy is important in reference works. How reliable are the facts presented?[29] How "dirty" is a database? Are there misspelled words,[30] missing data elements, or inconsistent formatting of parts of the record such as author names? Objectivity can be assessed by examining the coverage of controversial issues and the balance in coverage given to various subjects. Because reference works can be addressed to particular audiences, it is important to determine who can best use the work: layperson or scholar, adult or child.[31] Reviewing topics on which one has personal knowledge allows one to assess the accuracy and quality of writing.[32] Again, this type of review may be easier to accomplish with print sources than with works in electronic form.

Arrangement

Print and microform sources arrange entries in a particular sequence, such as alphabetical, chronological, or classified. If the sequence is a familiar one, such as alphabetical, the user of the source may be able to directly find the information sought rather than first having to look up the location in an index. The flexibility of a reference source is typically enhanced by the availability of indexes offering different types of access to the information. In addition, the text itself may offer leads to additional information in the form of cross-references to related entries. In general, electronic sources offer many different indexes to the contents of a database. These may allow the reference librarian to answer questions that cannot be answered in a print source because neither the primary arrangement of entries nor the indexes offer the needed point of access. For example, although a print bibliography may allow one to search by author, title, and subject, a publisher index is not likely to be provided. In an electronic version of the bibliography, however, "publisher" could be a searchable data element, allowing one to locate easily the list of items in the bibliography issued by a particular publisher.

Special Features

One will always be interested in identifying any special features that distinguish a given reference source from others. Any new developments that make database searching easier and more accessible to users will affect the choice among products. In addition, in the case of electronic sources, one must consider the quality of available documentation, training, and customer support. For Web resources, effective use of hyperlinks may add to a source's value.

Cost

The costs of print sources and sources in distributed electronic formats (e.g., CD-ROM) are similar in that a copy is acquired for in-house use in the library, and the purchase or subscription price buys unlimited access to the contents of the source. Pricing of online databases follows a variety of models, from a charge per use to subscription with unlimited access for authorized users. Pricing may depend on the size of potential user populations, ownership of print equivalents, number of simultaneous users of the resource, and whether the library is licensing the database as part of a consortium or individually. In assessing cost, the reference librarian must try to determine whether the price is appropriate in relation to the need and the anticipated frequency and length of use. In the case of nonprint sources, costs include purchase and maintenance of equipment to make the contents accessible. One may also want to consider the costs in terms of the staff support needed to allow users to make use of a nonprint source.

Access to electronic resources often takes place within the confines of a license that defines appropriate use over a specific period of time. Selection of such resources and negotiation of licensing agreements should consider whether the rights assigned by the license are adequate for the library's purposes.[33] Although reference librarians may not be involved directly in negotiating licenses, they should provide input reflecting the needs of library users. Once resources have been licensed for use, reference librarians need to understand how the content may be used (i.e., what is considered fair use), how the content may be accessed (only within the library or also remotely), and who is defined as an authorized "user." As electronic resource publishers try to earn revenue based on levels of use of their products, librarians have to make decisions about how many simultaneous users they can afford to support as they negotiate licensing agreements for database access. Usage data can help fine-tune these decisions as licenses come up for renewal.[34]

VIRTUAL REFERENCE COLLECTION DEVELOPMENT

Discussion to this point has emphasized the key role of the reference librarian in building collections of purchased or licensed materials. As explained in chapter 5, with the advent of the open environment of the Web, where many different organizations and individuals create sites that are freely accessible, it is necessary to expand the well-established notions of reference sources and reference collections to encompass these new resources. When connecting to the Web via a browser and Internet connection, one has access to everything that has been made freely available on the Web.

Two examples can be used to illustrate this change. *Books in Print*, long a standard tool for verifying basic bibliographic information about books in print, now competes with the descriptive and review information about books found on the Web at the sites of Internet booksellers such as Amazon.com (http://www.amazon.com) and Barnes & Noble (http://www.barnesandnoble.com).[35] Many associations of all types now have their own Web sites with much more detailed information than that found in widely used directories of associations such as *Encyclopedia of Associations*. Elizabeth Thomsen suggests that librarians need to examine all areas of their collections to make sure that they are still worth the time and money invested to maintain them.[36] Reference librarians must determine whether such special collections as vertical files, college catalogs, company annual reports, and telephone books can now be replaced with access to resources available on the Web.

Rather than relying solely on search engines, which do not automatically differentiate the authoritative sites from the rest, reference librarians can exercise the same type of selectivity that they do in building physical reference collections by building virtual collections. Librarians can develop special guides for users of their own libraries. Once published on the Web, such guides are available to a much wider audience as well. There is a growing body of literature providing guidance on developing and revising such virtual reference collections.[37] The *ipl2* Reference collection (listed as one of the categories under "Resources by Subject" at http://www.ipl2.org) and the *Library of Congress Virtual Reference Shelf* (http://www.loc.gov/rr/askalib/virtualref. html) are two examples of virtual reference collections.

SELECTION AIDS

A number of tools are available to assist the reference librarian in evaluating sources for possible inclusion in the library's reference collection. Review sources, varying in update frequency from semimonthly to annual, offer critical reviews of newly published titles. Although most titles covered are in print format, reviews are including increasing numbers of electronic titles as well. To identify gaps in existing collections, guides to reference sources can be used. These guides are also valuable as aids in identifying likely sources for answering particular reference questions (as described in chapter 4). Both current reviewing media and guides to reference sources are helpful to librarians in developing collections on which effective service is based, but they are no substitute for informed judgment in selection of titles best suited to the library's users. This requires a thorough knowledge of the library's existing reference collection and user needs.

Reviewing Sources

Because it is impossible to examine all books before purchase, several reviewing sources are useful to the librarian in identifying and evaluating new titles. Analyses of these sources demonstrate that they differ in number of titles covered and that each covers some unique titles.[38] Thus, it is worthwhile to monitor several of these sources for reviews of reference materials. One difficulty with reviews is the time lag in appearance of reviews following publication of the reference work. Generally, the more thorough the review, the longer the time lag. The frequency of publication of the reviewing sources also influences time lag.

Reference Books Bulletin appears in the semimonthly issues of *Booklist*. It provides long, comprehensive, and evaluative reviews prepared by members of the American Library Association's Reference Books Bulletin Editorial Board or by guest reviewers and revised by the board as a whole.[39] Major new reference sources in English are analyzed at length, and many additional titles, as well as selected revisions of standard works, are also evaluated. In recent years, an annual review of general encyclopedias has been included, and reviews of selected electronic sources have been introduced. Reviews are available as part of *Booklist Online*, where they can be searched by author, title, keyword, or ISBN. Titles reviewed are of interest to public libraries and school media centers. *Booklist Online* also hosts a blog, *Points of Reference* (http://pointsofreference.booklistonline.com/), that includes posts about reference sources and trends in reference publishing and services.

In contrast to the lengthy reviews found in *Reference Books Bulletin*, *Library Journal* includes a section of brief, signed reference book reviews in each issue. Books reviewed are generally suitable for public and college libraries. Reviews are also available online at the *Library Journal* Web site (http://www.libraryjournal.com). An annual supplement to the November 15 issue highlights new and forthcoming reference sources in both print and electronic formats. The Web site also includes an "E-Reference" ratings section, assessing some of the most well-known subscription-based electronic resources in various subject categories. *School Library Journal* includes reviews of both reference books and digital resources suitable for K–12 students. These reviews appear in print issues and as part of the companion Web site (http://www.schoollibraryjournal.com). *Choice*, focusing on books suitable for undergraduate collections and published 11 times per year, often reviews more specialized titles than does *Library Journal*. Each *Choice* issue has a section of signed reviews of reference books and electronic resources, and reviewers are encouraged to compare the title being reviewed with related titles. *Choice* is also available on the Web as a licensed database, *Choice Reviews Online* (http;//www.cro2.org). Quick search options in the Web version include keyword (in title), keyword (in review), author/editor, publisher, ISBN, *Choice* issue, and *Choice* review number. Additional options in Advanced Search include keyword in LC subject, LC#, reviewer name, and reviewer affiliation. Reviews published since 1997 in *Reference & User Services Quarterly* are accessible by searching the Sources database on the companion Web site (http://cs.ala.org/ra/rusqsources/index.cfm).

The most comprehensive source of reviews is *American Reference Books Annual* (*ARBA*). The annual volumes aim to review all reference resources published and distributed in the United States and Canada in a given year. Reference resources that are revised on a regular or continuing basis are periodically reassessed. Both print and electronic resources are within scope. Arrangement is classified in 37 chapters in 4 broad categories: general reference works, social sciences, humanities, and science and technology. General reference works are further subdivided by form, such as dictionaries and encyclopedias. Subject areas are subdivided by topic, such as history and law within social sciences. The reviews, written by a pool of more than 500 subject specialists, critically evaluate each work. Each entry includes a full bibliographic citation with price, a description of the reference work, and an evaluation of content. Each volume is indexed by author/title and subject. Indexes cumulate every five years, beginning with 1970–1974 up to 2005–2009. The 2011 edition includes more than 1,500 reviews. *ARBAonline* provides a searchable database of reviews published in the annual volumes since 1997 and is updated monthly. The database can be searched by title, author/editor, subject, publisher, keyword, ISBN/ISSN, or combinations of those fields.

Since 1981, a selection of reviews from *ARBA* has been published as *Recommended Reference Books for Small and Medium-Sized Libraries and Media Centers*, which reprints about one-third of the year's *ARBA* reviews and tags them for type of library (college, public, or school media center).

More selective lists of recommended reference sources appear annually in *American Libraries* and *Library Journal*. The list in *American Libraries* is selected by the Outstanding Reference Sources Committee of the Reference and User Services Association (RUSA) of the American Library Association and appears in the May issue. The list in *Library Journal* is selected by experienced reference librarians and appears in the April 15 issue. These lists are helpful in identifying outstanding reference sources of potential value in many libraries. Both lists now include electronic resources in addition to print titles. Additional reviews can be found at the *Reference Reviews* site, hosted by Gale. The four parts currently include "Péter's Digital

Reference Shelf" for reviews of online products, "Lawrence Looks at Books" for reviews of reference sources for public and academic library reference collections, and "Reference Unbound" and "Doug's Student Reference Room" for reviews of K–12 online and print reference resources (http://www.gale.cengage.com/reference/). The Machine-Assisted Reference Section (MARS) of RUSA annually compiles a list of the "Best Free Reference Web Sites," available both in the fall issue of *Reference & User Services Quarterly* and on the MARS portion of the RUSA Web site (http://www.ala.org/ala/mgrps/divs/rusa/sections/mars/marspubs/marsbestindex.cfm), where a combined index of sites selected since 1999 is also maintained.

Ideally, reviews describe, evaluate, and compare new reference sources so that librarians can make informed decisions about whether to purchase the titles for their reference collections. Some researchers who have completed systematic evaluations of the various reviewing tools have expressed dissatisfaction with the contents of many reviews. James Sweetland found a general lack of comparison within reviews.[40] Most reviews were generally favorable, with few mixed reviews and fewer wholly negative ones. Some reviews were descriptive rather than evaluative, and others made recommendations that did not follow from the text of the evaluation. Overall consensus among the reviewing sources covering the same title was low. Donald Dickinson has noted the lack of reviews of foreign-language reference sources in English-language reviewing media.[41] Nevertheless, although reviews could be improved in content and coverage, they still offer the librarian some basis for assessing new reference sources. At present, coverage of print reference books is more comprehensive than coverage of electronic sources, but the reviewing sources described in this section are trying to be more responsive to the need for reviews of reference sources in all formats. Other journals can be monitored to supplement the reviews found in the primary review journals. For example, periodic articles describing new reference sources appear in *College & Research Libraries*.[42] *College & Research Libraries News* has both a regular column of "Internet Reviews" and topical bibliographies of "Internet Resources" (both also available in issues linked on the Web from http://crln.acrl.org/). Online bookseller sites such as Amazon.com reprint reviews from other sources in addition to featuring reviews contributed by users of their sites.

Guides to Reference Sources

The best-known guide to reference sources in the United States is that published by the American Library Association. *Guide to Reference Books* has served librarians since 1902, with the 11th edition published in print in 1996 and a new updated Web-based 12th edition (titled simply *Guide to Reference*) in 2008. This compilation is frequently referred to by the name of its editor: Alice Bertha Kroeger, Isadore Gilbert Mudge, Constance M. Winchell, Eugene P. Sheehy, Robert Balay, and most recently, Robert H. Kieft have served in that capacity.[43] The 11th edition of the *Guide* provides bibliographic information and descriptions for 15,875 English- and foreign-language reference works in all fields through 1993. Arrangement is in five major parts: part A—general reference works; part B—humanities; part C—social and behavioral sciences; part D—history and area studies; and part E—science, technology, and medicine. Within each part, entries are classified first by subject and then by form. The table of contents displays the subjects in a classified arrangement, and there is an alphabetically arranged author/title/subject index. A bullet next to a title entry indicates that at least a portion of the source is available in electronic form. Entries include complete bibliographic information, publication history (where appropriate), notes or annotations, and often a Library of Congress call number. The new Web-based edition covers more than 16,000 print and Web reference resources, selected and annotated by subject specialist librarians. Annotations are intended to help readers to understand the utility of listed resources and quickly choose among similar works. In addition to the broad subject categories covered in the 11th edition, there is a new section for interdisciplinary fields (cognitive science, communication and media studies, cultural studies, environmental studies, and gender studies). In addition to browsing, options for searching include Quick Search by keyword and Advanced Search by title, author/editor, publisher, or annotation.

The British counterpart to *Guide to Reference Books* was edited for a number of years by A. J. Walford, but now each volume has more than one individual responsible for its compilation. *The New Walford Guide to Reference Resources* appears in three volumes. Because they are not published simultaneously, the three books of the set differ in currency. Volume 1 covers science, technology, and medicine; volume 2 covers the social sciences; and volume 3 covers the visual arts, music, language, and literature. Each volume has its own author/title and topic indexes. Both print and new digital resources (image and text collections, blogs, RSS feeds, Web sites) are covered. Like the ALA *Guide*, *Walford* is international in scope, but it has better coverage of British and European titles. Each entry provides a bibliographic citation and/or URL and a brief annotation describing the content and any notable features.

Although both the ALA *Guide* and *Walford* seek to encompass works from all subject areas, they cannot cover in depth the works in any particular subject area. For this purpose, the librarian must consult guides to the literature of particular subjects, such as Fred Jenkins's *Classical Studies: A Guide to the Reference Literature*. Such works generally serve as introductions both to the subject area and to specialized reference works within each area.

The ALA *Guide* and *Walford* identify many sources likely to be found only in large academic libraries. There are more selective guides to reference sources for smaller libraries. One example is *Reference Sources for Small and Medium-Sized Libraries*, published by ALA. This compilation, last updated in 2008, covers 1,695 print sources, Web sites, CD-ROMs, and electronic databases. In the 20 topical chapters, the contributors, each a subject matter expert, provide an introductory overview of their topics, followed by their recommended selections. Entries include Dewey and Library of Congress call numbers as well as complete bibliographic information and brief annotations. Two texts designed for school media specialists include coverage of selection, evaluation, and maintenance of reference collections in those settings: Barbara Ripp Safford's *Guide to Reference Materials for School Library Media Centers* and Scott Lanning and John Bryner's *Essential Reference Services for Today's School Media Specialists*.

James H. Sweetland has compiled the third edition (2000) of *Fundamental Reference Sources*, reflecting the major changes in reference sources since the second edition was published 20 years earlier. Chapters cover selected sources grouped by type, such as directories, biographical sources, encyclopedias, and indexing and abstracting services. Titles in electronic format are included.

Of particular interest to those in Canadian libraries is *Canadian Reference Sources: An Annotated Bibliography*. Its scope includes sources about Canadian people, institutions, organizations, publications, art, literature, languages, history, and religion; it is indexed by name, title, French subject, and English subject. Annotations are in English and French. The availability of nonprint formats is noted.

Because the widely used guides to reference sources already described in this section provide only limited coverage of electronic sources, there is a need for directories of databases and Internet resources. These directories are useful sources of descriptions of databases, but they typically do not provide evaluative or comparative annotations. The *Gale Directory of Databases*, formed from the merger of three titles (*Computer-Readable Databases*, *Directory of Online Databases*, and *Directory of Portable Databases*), provides extensive coverage of databases in all formats. Volume 1 is devoted to online databases; volume 2 divides the databases into six other media for distribution (CD-ROM, DVD, diskette, magnetic tape, handheld, and batch access). Such a directory is useful in identifying databases covering a particular subject area or containing a particular type of information. The information on producers and online services and vendors indicates how a library can acquire or gain access to these databases.

These guides to reference sources and directories of databases serve dual purposes: as collection evaluation checklists and selection tools for reference and collection development librarians and as aids in reference work to identify appropriate reference sources to use in answering reference questions. In reference work, if the question is unlike one that a reference librarian has answered before, the librarian may not be able to easily identify a likely source without referring to a guide to reference sources or directory of databases. These lead-in tools can direct the librarian to one or more sources likely to provide an answer. The remaining chapters in Part 2 consider each type of source in turn, describing their characteristics and appropriate search strategies.

SOURCES, COLLECTIONS, AND SERVICES IN TRANSITION

As the discussion in this chapter has made clear, one impact of technology on reference is the need to think in new ways about reference sources, collections, and the services they support. The familiar categories of reference sources (such as encyclopedias, dictionaries, and directories) are still useful. Nevertheless, what Vannevar Bush termed "wholly new forms of encyclopedias . . . with a mesh of associative trails running through them"[44] are emerging both in the form of freely available Web resources and in newly aggregated offerings from publishers. As Ken Winter observes, emerging reference sources are "intricate text-and-image databases that harness the power of the Internet to deliver information in profoundly new ways."[45] The Internet has also facilitated new forms of collaborative authorship that make it more difficult to judge the authority and accuracy of the resulting product. For example, *Wikipedia* (http://www.wikipedia.org) is written and edited by numerous volunteers, who can continuously change and add articles. Started on January 10, 2001, by early 2011 this self-described "free encyclopedia that anyone can edit" had grown to nearly 3.6 million articles in English. Articles are of variable quality, but many do have a great deal of accuracy as well as currency. Cass Sunstein explains how this is accomplished:

"Large numbers of knowledgeable people are willing to participate in creating Wikipedia, and whatever errors they make usually receive rapid correction, simply because so many minds are involved. The involvement of many people ensures that Wikipedians are able to produce a much more comprehensive resource than a small group could, even a small group of experts."[46] On *Wikipedia*, because articles can continue to be revised, no person is considered "the" author of an entry. A history page for each article shows the text of every change and the identifier (user name or IP address) of the person who made the change. Berinstein provides a comparison of *Wikipedia* and *Encyclopaedia Britannica*, noting that neither is error-free; each has strengths and limitations. She concludes that "people are becoming more aware of the perils of accepting information at face value. They have learned not to consult just one source. They know that authors and editors may be biased and/or harbor hidden agendas. And, because of Wikipedia's known methodology and vulnerabilities, it provides opportunities to teach (and learn) critical thinking."[47] A recently published detailed evaluation of 106 randomly generated Wikipedia articles from a broad range of subject areas demonstrated that overall the articles were "objective, clearly presented, reasonably accurate, and complete, although some are poorly written, contain unsubstantiated information, and/or provide shallow coverage of a topic."[48] (See chapter 18 for further discussion of *Wikipedia*.)

The proliferation of reference sources in electronic form has led to a shift in which kind of sources are used to answer questions, with the use of print sources diminishing in favor of electronic.[49] At the same time, certain categories of reference sources, such as one-volume dictionaries, thesauri, and almanacs, still function well as print products.[50] Ann Ritchie and Paul Genoni note that "there is great difficulty in assessing what constitutes a 'correct' balance between print and electronic sources for responding to reference questions, and the current practice is likely to differ significantly between libraries."[51] Sara Sluss and Lesley Farmer suggest that the term "access development" is coming to replace, or at least complement, "collection development" as reference librarians have to determine whether to purchase resources, license access, or rely on freely available Web resources.[52]

The increasing reliance on electronic resources also means that physical access to print collections now needs to be supplemented with new forms of intellectual access to digital collections. Michael Buckland observes,

> In a digital environment, one cannot see the collection. One cannot see beyond the screen, although an interface may provide some guidance. We no longer have the familiar pleasure of seeing a well-stocked collection, of being able to grasp the layout and to assess the relative size of each section, and recognize, at a glance, familiar tools that can provide answers. The valuable structured guidance of the arrangement of the reference collection and of each reference work is mostly absent.[53]

Through building online directories to guide library users to available reference sources, both print and electronic, reference librarians are devising intellectual access systems that their user communities can find and use.

As the popular perception that "everything is on the Web" grows, reference librarians must find ways to show "which types of information resources answer which questions best."[54] As Jane Subramanian notes, many users have preconceived attitudes regarding the use of particular formats of indexes and other materials. These attitudes may interfere with the user's retrieval of needed resources as a result of the use of a preferred format rather than the best means of access for the information need.[55] Librarians must maintain knowledge of what is available in print, so as to be in a position to assist users in locating answers to questions in whatever format the information is found.

As reference librarians develop and work with hybrid collections of purchased, licensed, and freely available Web resources, a better understanding of the questions most easily answered by each will emerge. The volume and diversity of information available on the Web opens new possibilities to both reference librarians and users, but both must continue to keep in mind that at present it can be hard to find good content; once found, such information may later disappear (or at least move); and some information found may be completely incorrect. Recalling *Harrod's* definition of a reference source as one used to obtain authoritative information, reference librarians and users alike must be vigilant in their search for answers to questions.

NOTES

1.   Heartsill Young, ed., *The ALA Glossary of Library and Information Science* (Chicago: American Library Association, 1983), 188.

2.   Marcia J. Bates, "What Is a Reference Book? A Theoretical and Empirical Analysis," in *For Information Specialists: Interpretations of Reference and Bibliographic Work*, ed. Howard D. White, Marcia J. Bates, and Patrick Wilson (Norwood, NJ: Ablex, 1992), 9–26.

3.   Bill Katz, *Cuneiform to Computer: A History of Reference Sources* (Lanham, MD: Scarecrow Press, 1998), 415 pp.

4.   Ray Prytherch, comp., *Harrod's Librarians' Glossary and Reference Book*, 9th ed. (Aldershot, England: Gower, 2000), 618.

5.   Margaret Landesman, "Getting It Right—The Evolution of Reference Collections," *The Reference Librarian* 91/92 (2005): 19.

6.   Michael D. G. Spencer, "Pamphlet Collection Development," in *Readings on the Vertical File*, ed. Michael D. G. Spencer (Englewood, CO: Libraries Unlimited, 1993), 21–28.

7.   Adam Hodgkin, "Reference Books on the Web," *Ariadne* 30 (December 2001). http://www.ariadne.ac.uk/issue30/ref-books/

8.   Péter Jacsó, "Open Access Ready Reference Suites," *Online Information Review* 30 (2006): 737–43; for a comparison of five reference e-book collections available for license, see Sarah Witte and Mary Cargill, "Selected Reference Works, 2007–08," *College & Research Libraries* 69 (September 2008): 459–67.

9.   Mirela Roncevic, "E-Reference on a Mission," *Library Journal* 131, supplement (November 15, 2006): 8–11.

10.   Peter Webster, "Implications of Expanded Library Electronic Reference Collections," *Online* 27 (September/October 2003): 24–27.

11.   Sue Polanka, "Options for the E-Reference Collection," *Booklist* 103 (November 1, 2006): 93–95.

12.   Sarah Robbins, Cheryl McCain, and Laurie Scrivener, "The Changing Format of Reference Collections: Are Research Libraries Favoring Electronic Access Over Print?," *The Acquisitions Librarian* 35/36 (2006): 75–95.

13.   Sydney J. Pierce, "Introduction," *The Reference Librarian* 29 (1990): 1–8.

14.   Mary Biggs and Victor Biggs, "Reference Collection Development in Academic Libraries: Report of a Survey," *RQ* 27 (Fall 1987): 67–79.

15.   Christopher W. Nolan, *Managing the Reference Collection* (Chicago: American Library Association, 1999), 32–44.

16.   Links to several reference collection development policies available on the Web can be found in Alice J. Perez, ed., *Reference Collection Development: A Manual* (Chicago: Reference and User Services Association, American Library Association, 2004), 75–78.

17.   Melissa Holmberg, "Using Publishers' Web Sites for Reference Collection Development," *Issues in Science & Technology Librarianship* 25 (Winter 2000). http://www.library.ucsb.edu/istl/00-winter/article3.html.

18.   Eleanor Mathews and David A. Tyckoson, "A Program for the Systematic Weeding of the Reference Collection," *The Reference Librarian* 29 (1990): 129–43.

19.   Lynn Westbrook, "Weeding Reference Serials," *Serials Librarian* 10 (Summer 1986): 81–100.

20.   William A. Katz, *Introduction to Reference Work*, 8th ed. (New York: McGraw-Hill, 2002), 2:196–97.

21.   Jean C. McManus, "Archiving the Content of Print and Electronic Reference Works in the Digital Age: An Analysis and a Proposal," in *Finding Common Ground: Creating the Library of the Future without Diminishing the Library of the Past* (New York: Neal-Schuman, 1998), 375–80.

22.   Frances A. Delwiche and Nancy A. Bianchi, "Transformation of a Print Reference Collection," *Medical Reference Services Quarterly* 25 (Summer 2006): 21–29; Rose M. Frase and Barbara Salit-Mischel, "Right-Sizing the Reference Collection," *Public Libraries* 46 (January/February 2007): 40–44; and Carol A. Singer, "Weeding Gone Wild: Planning and Implementing a Review of the Reference Collection," *Reference & User Services Quarterly* 47 (Spring 2008): 256–64.

23.   For criteria for evaluating online databases and Web resources, see the following: Nolan, "Criteria for Selecting Electronic Products," in *Managing the Reference Collection*, 111–45; James Rettig and Cheryl LaGuardia, "Beyond Cool: Reviewing Web Resources," *Online* 23 (July/August 1999): 51–55; Richard Bleiler and Terry Plum, comps., "Selection Criteria," in *Networked Information Resources* (Washington, D.C.: Association of Research Libraries, 1999), 53–70; and "Best Free Reference Websites: Twelfth Annual List," *Reference & User Services Quarterly* 50 (Fall 2010):19–24.

24.   Lynne M. Martin, "Evaluating OPACs, or, OPACs are Reference Tools, Too!" *The Reference Librarian* 38 (1992): 201–20.

25.   Peggy Langstaff, "Getting the Picture—Along with the Words," *Publishers Weekly* 243 (April 29, 1996): 36–40.

26.   Kayvan Kousha, "DVD: The Next Evolutionary Step for Publishing Multimedia Reference Sources," *Online & CD-ROM Review* 23 (June 1999): 203–5.

27.   Péter Jacsó, "Content Evaluation of Databases," *Annual Review of Information Science and Technology* 32 (1997): 231–67.

28.   Mary K. Taylor and Diane Hudson, "'Linkrot' and the Usefulness of Web Site Bibliographies," *Reference & User Services Quarterly* 39 (Spring 2000): 273–77.

29.   Mark Schumacher, "Accuracy of Reference Sources: The Example of Balzac," *RQ* 32 (Fall 1992): 26–29.

30.   Pamela Cahn, "Testing Database Quality," *Database* 17 (February 1994): 23–30.

31.   Marilyn Domas White, "The Readability of Children's Reference Materials," *Library Quarterly* 60 (October 1990): 300–19.

32.   David Isaacson, "Literary Style in Reference Books," *RQ* 28 (Summer 1989): 485–95.

33.   Trisha L. Davis, "Licensing of Electronic Resources: Resources for Dealing with the Challenge," *Bowker Annual Library and Book Trade Almanac* 50 (2005): 221–31.

34.   Charles T. Townley and Leigh Murray, "Use-Based Criteria for Selecting and Retaining Electronic Information: A Case Study," *Information Technology & Libraries* 18 (March 1999): 32–39. See the Project COUNTER Web site for a discussion of efforts to develop standards to facilitate the recording and reporting of online usage statistics in a consistent way: http://www.projectcounter.org.

35.   Péter Jacsó, "Be Savvy! Sometimes the Free Resources Are Better," *Computers in Libraries* 20 (May 2000): 56–58.

36.   Elizabeth Thomsen, *Rethinking Reference: The Reference Librarian's Practical Guide for Surviving Constant Change* (New York: Neal-Schuman, 1999), 110.

37.   See, for example: Steven W. Sowards, "Structures and Choices for Ready Reference Web Sites," *The Reference Librarian* 91/92 (2005): 117–38; Theresa Mudrock, "Revising Ready Reference Sites: Listening to Users through Server Statistics and Query Logs," *Reference & User Services Quarterly* 42 (Winter 2002): 155–63.

38.   James Rettig, "Reference Book Reviewing Media: A Critical Analysis," *Library Science Annual* 2 (1986): 13–29.

39.   Helen K. Wright, "Reference Books Bulletin Editorial Review Board—ALA," in *Encyclopedia of Library and Information Science*, ed. Allen Kent (New York: Marcel Dekker, 1984), 37:346–52.

40.   James H. Sweetland, "Reference Book Reviewing Tools: How Well Do They Do the Job?," *The Reference Librarian* 15 (Fall 1986): 65–74.

41.   Donald C. Dickinson, "The Reviewing of Foreign Language Reference Books: A Woeful Inadequacy," *RQ* 32 (Spring 1993): 373–80.

42.   For example, see Sarah Witte and Mary Cargill, "Selected Reference Works, 2007–08," *College & Research Libraries* 70 (March 2009): 178–93.

43.   Stuart W. Miller, "Monument: *Guide to Reference Books*," in *Distinguished Classics of Reference Publishing*, ed. James Rettig (Phoenix, AZ: Oryx Press, 1992), 129–37.

44.   Vannevar Bush, "As We May Think," *Atlantic Monthly* 176 (July 1945): 108.

45.   Ken Winter, "From Wood Pulp to the Web: The Online Evolution," *American Libraries* 31 (May 2000): 70.

46.   Cass R. Sunstein, *Infotopia: How Many Minds Produce Knowledge* (Oxford: Oxford University Press, 2006), 151–52.

47.   Paula Berinstein, "Wikipedia and Britannica: The Kid's All Right (And So's the Old Man)," *Searcher* 14 (March 2006): 26.

48.   Kathy West and Janet Williamson, "Wikipedia: Friend or Foe?," *Reference Services Review* 37 (2009): 260–71.

49.   Jane T. Bradford, Barbara Costello, and Robert Lenholt, "Reference Service in the Digital Age: An Analysis of Sources Used to Answer Reference Questions," *Journal of Academic Librarianship* 31 (May 2005): 263–72; and Jane T. Bradford, "What's Coming Off the Shelves? A Reference Use Study Analyzing Print Reference Sources Used in a University Library," *Journal of Academic Librarianship* 31 (November 2005): 546–58.

50.   John M. Morse, "Reference Publishing in the Age of Also," *The Reference Librarian* 91/92 (2005): 69–81.

51.   Ann Ritchie and Paul Genoni, "Print v. Electronic Reference Sources: Implications of an Australian Study," *The Electronic Library* 25 (2007): 440.

52.   Sara Sluss and Lesley Farmer, "Technology Impact on Reference Resources," in *The Human Side of Reference and Information Services in Academic Libraries: Adding Value in the Digital World*, ed. Lesley S. J. Farmer (Oxford: Chandos Publishing, 2007), 37.

53.   Michael K. Buckland, "The Digital Difference in Reference Collections," *Journal of Library Administration* 46, no. 2 (2007): 89.

54.   Judith Metcalf, "Full Circle, Back to Selecting and Organizing," *American Libraries* 30 (May 1999): 42.

55.   Jane M. Subramanian, "Patron Attitudes toward Computerized and Print Resources: Discussion and Considerations for Reference Service," *The Reference Librarian* 60 (1998): 127–38.

LIST OF SOURCES

The African American Experience. Santa Barbara, CA: ABC-CLIO/Greenwood. http://african-american.abc-clio.com.

American Libraries. Chicago: American Library Association, 1970–. 11 issues per year.

American Reference Books Annual. Ed. Shannon Graff Hysell. Santa Barbara, CA: Libraries Unlimited, 1970–. Annual.

ARBAonline. Santa Barbara, CA: Libraries Unlimited. http://www.arbaonline.com.

Booklist. Chicago: American Library Association, 1905–. Twice monthly, September–June; monthly, July–August. Includes Reference Books Bulletin.

Booklist Online. Chicago: American Library Association. http://www.booklistonline.com.

Canadian Reference Sources: An Annotated Bibliography/Ouvrages de Reference Canadiens: Une Bibliographie Annotée. Compiled by Mary E. Bond and Martine M. Caron. Vancouver, BC: UBC Press in association with the National Library of Canada, 1996. 1076 pp.

Choice. Middletown, CT: Association of College and Research Libraries, 1964–. 11 issues per year.

Choice Reviews Online. Middletown, CT: Association of College and Research Libraries. http://www.cro2.org.

Credo Reference. Boston: Credo Reference. http://corp.credoreference.com.

Gale Directory of Databases. Volume 1: *Online Databases*. Volume 2: *CD-ROM, DVD, Diskette, Magnetic Tape, Handheld, and Batch Access Database Products*. Farmington

Hills, MI: Gale, 1993–. Semiannual. Also available online as part of the *Gale Directory Library*.

Guide to Reference. 12th ed. Ed. Robert H. Kieft. Chicago: American Library Association, 2008. http://www.guidetoreference.org.

Guide to Reference Books. 11th ed. Ed. Robert Balay. Chicago: American Library Association, 1996. 2020 pp.

Jenkins, Fred W. *Classical Studies: A Guide to the Reference Literature*. 2nd ed. Westport, CT: Libraries Unlimited, 2006. 401 pp.

Lanning, Scott, and John Bryner. *Essential Reference Services for Today's School Media Specialists*. 2nd ed. Santa Barbara, CA: Libraries Unlimited, 2010. 141 pp.

Library Journal. New York: Media Source, 1876–. 22 issues per year.

The New Walford Guide to Reference Resources. 3 vols. London: Facet, 2005–2011.

Oxford African American Studies Center. Oxford: Oxford University Press. http://www.oxfordaasc.com/.

Recommended Reference Books for Small and Medium-Sized Libraries and Media Centers. Ed. Shannon Graff Hysell. Santa Barbara, CA: Libraries Unlimited, 1981–. Annual.

Reference & User Services Quarterly. Chicago: American Library Association, 1997–. (Formerly *RQ*, 1960–1997.)

Reference Reviews. Farmington Hills, MI: Gale. Monthly. http://www.gale.cengage.com/reference.

Reference Sources for Small and Medium-Sized Libraries. 7th ed. Ed. Jack O'Gorman. Chicago: American Library Association, 2008. 329 pp.

Safford, Barbara Ripp. *Guide to Reference Materials for School Library Media Centers*. 6th ed. Santa Barbara, CA: Libraries Unlimited, 2010. 236 pp.

School Library Journal. New York: Media Source, 1954–. Monthly.

Sweetland, James H. *Fundamental Reference Sources*. 3rd ed. Chicago: American Library Association, 2000. 384 pp.

ADDITIONAL READINGS

Bates, Marcia J. "What Is a Reference Book? A Theoretical and Empirical Analysis." In *For Information Specialists: Interpretations of Reference and Bibliographic Work*, ed. Howard D. White, Marcia J. Bates, and Patrick Wilson, 9–26. Norwood, NJ: Ablex, 1992.

Bates notes that reference books have traditionally been defined administratively (e.g., as books that are noncirculating) or functionally (e.g., as books used for reference) rather than descriptively (i.e., in terms of the essential characteristics that distinguish reference books from other books). This article develops and tests a descriptive definition.

Buckland, Michael K. "The Digital Difference in Reference Collections." *Journal of Library Administration* 46, no. 2 (2007): 87–100.

Buckland argues for the need to design reference works to fit in the digital, networked environment of library users. He provides examples of how genres of reference works might be enhanced. Examples include gazetteers coupled with maps and bibliographies, which could allow new ways to search by place, and biographical directories that could link persons with their contexts in new ways.

Farmer, Lesley S. J. "The Life Cycle of Digital Reference Sources." *The Reference Librarian* 50 (2009): 117–36.

This article examines what Farmer terms "the life cycle" of digital reference sources, with particular attention to assessment of resources, selection processes and policies, acquisitions issues, Web presentation and maintenance, archiving and preservation, and deselection.

Frost, William J., ed. *The Reference Collection: From the Shelf to the Web*. Binghamton, NY: Haworth Information Press, 2005. 310 pp. Also published as *The Reference Librarian*, no. 91/92, 2005.

This collection of articles explores the migration of reference materials in print to an electronic format accessible on the Web. Articles of particular interest include Margaret Landesman's "Getting It Right—The Evolution of Reference Collections," John Morse's "Reference Publishing in the Age of Also," Steven Sowards's "Structures and Choices for Ready Reference Web Sites," and Lori Morse's "100 Best Free Reference Web Sites: A Selected List."

Kieft, Robert H. "The Return of the *Guide to Reference* (Books)." *Reference & User Services Quarterly* 48 (Fall 2008): 4–10.

Kieft, editor of the latest edition of this classic, discusses decisions made in adapting the *Guide* to a Web-based product. He explains the organization, the choice of entries, the inclusion of editor's guides to the disciplinary categories, and the content of annotations. He also highlights the potential role of the *Guide* in teaching future reference librarians.

Nolan, Christopher W. *Managing the Reference Collection*. Chicago: American Library Association, 1999. 231 pp.

Nolan shows how to create "a lean, efficient reference collection that is based on actual user needs." He discusses developing reference collection development policies, selecting and managing electronic reference sources, and evaluating and weeding reference collections. The book concludes with a very helpful annotated bibliography, leading to key literature on reference collection management.

Pearlmutter, Jane. "Policy Components for Online Electronic Resources." In *Library Collection Development Policies: Academic, Public, and Special Libraries*, ed. Frank W. Hoffmann and Richard J. Wood, 218–29. Lanham, MD: Scarecrow Press, 2005.

Pearlmutter outlines collection development policy components encompassing two types of online electronic resources: (1) electronic resources acquired through license, purchase, or subscription; and (2) free Internet resources. She also discusses provision of access to these resources and deselection criteria.

Perez, Alice J., ed. *Reference Collection Development: A Manual*. RUSA Occasional Papers, no. 27. Chicago: Reference and User Services Association, American Library Association, 2004. 80 pp.

Developed by the Reference Collection Development and Evaluation Committee of the Collection Development and Evaluation Section of RUSA, this manual offers guidance in producing collection development policies for reference collections serving adults in academic and public libraries. The manual begins with a checklist for writing a reference collection development policy and then provides a model policy in outline, with illustrative examples. An appendix provides URLs for reference collection development policies available on the Web, as well as a bibliography of useful books and articles.

Rettig, James. "Every Reference Librarian a Reviewer." *RQ* 26 (Spring 1987): 467–76.

   Rettig argues that all reference librarians are obligated to get to know the works in their collections as thoroughly as a reviewer must. This article describes this process with respect to reference tools in all formats, relating strengths and weaknesses to the situations that arise in dealing with the information needs posed by the library's users.

Singer, Carol A. "Ready Reference Collections: A History." *Reference & User Services Quarterly* 49 (Spring 2010): 253–64.

   Singer explores the evolution of ready reference collections from the late 19th century to their transformation by developments in electronic resources beginning in the 1960s. She concludes that such collections of print materials will exist "only as long as they provide the answers to frequently asked questions at the reference desk and do so more efficiently and effectively than online information sources."

Slote, Stanley J. "Weeding Reference Collections." In *Weeding Library Collections: Library Weeding Methods*, 4th ed., 219–26. Englewood, CO: Libraries Unlimited, 1997.

   Slote notes that the problems involved in weeding reference collections are made more complex by the diversity of types of materials they encompass. This chapter reviews methods of weeding the various categories of reference materials.

Directories

Joseph E. Straw

USES AND CHARACTERISTICS

A directory is defined in the *Dictionary for Library and Information Science* as "a list of people, companies, institutions, organizations, etc., in alphabetical or classified order, providing contact information (names, addresses, phone/fax numbers, etc.) and other pertinent details (affiliations, conferences, publications, membership, etc.) in brief format, often published serially."[1] Telephone books and titles such as *The Foundation Directory* and the *Million Dollar Directory* are examples of directory publications that are found in libraries of all types. Directories can cover a wide variety of topics and are available to libraries in print, microform, and electronic formats.

Directories have a long history of serving the human need to know about people and places. Early directory precursors were census-like compilations of property and persons that were used by ancient and feudal governments to account for wealth and taxes. Narrative ancestors of the directory were the travel and topographical histories of the early modern period.

Topographical histories provided geographical descriptions of places that often contained detailed notes about their history and lists of inns, establishments, townships, or other things that travelers would likely encounter on the road. Although these works had literary and historical value, they also served a practical purpose for educated travelers to find out what to expect when moving about the landscape. From 16th-century England, John Leland's *Itinerary*, William Harrison's *The Description of England*, and John Stow's *A Survey of London* are some of the more famous topographical histories. This type of guide served a few highly educated users who needed to know about a broader world. The topographical history was free of the pressure of having to constantly change because it served a slowly changing rural society that was not tied together by efficient communications.[2]

More utilitarian classified listings of people and places began to emerge in the mid-19th century. The growth of cities and population spurred by the Industrial Revolution generated a need for more people to know about things beyond their immediate experience. The linkage of communications by telegraph, railroads, and later the telephone made knowledge of addresses, timetables, and telephone numbers essential for transacting daily life. As economies of scale began to take shape, persons in businesses found it crucial to have a medium that would provide their contact information and serve as a place to advertise their goods and services. Publishers responded to these needs and produced the city directory.

The city directory of the 19th century is the direct precursor of the alphabetical and classified directories of today. These publications sought to be a means for promoting the advantages of doing business in a particular community. City directories also linked businesses, advertisers, and customers, in an effort to market commercial activities in a given area. Typically, a city directory would have a local gazetteer and a classified listing of businesses. The classified listing would often be an alphabetical listing of businesses that could be arranged by street or district within the city or by the service offered by the business: brokerage house, insurance firm, blacksmiths, accountants, and so on. Many companies would be profiled with full-page spreads, and others might have drawings or photographs of their products.[3]

To account for more frequent change, city directories were published annually. Some directories were supplemented at different times during the year to keep up with an even faster pace of change. Many city or local publishers produced these directories, but a few larger publishers tackled larger cities. Perhaps the best known are the *Polk City Directories*, which continue to be published to this day.

The emergence of city directories followed closely the early development of libraries. The information contained in early directories was in high demand, and a marriage between the directory and the library was a logical development. Libraries became important consumers of city directories and significant users of newer directory products that emerged in the later 19th century and first part of the 20th century. Telephone books, listings of professionals, guides to associations, and increasingly more specialized directories made their way into libraries. Directories rapidly became essential components of reference collections, often among the most consulted sources in libraries of all types.

For more than a century, library directory collections were almost exclusively made up of print publications. Many libraries kept long runs of serial directory publications in their reference areas. Crowded shelves of multicolored directories were a common site in reference collections throughout most of the 20th century. Many of these collections became unwieldy to use and difficult to update and maintain. Some directory collections were put on microfilm or microfiche, allowing libraries to keep more extensive back runs of historical directory collections. However, the difficulties of reading this format and the expense of microform readers prevented microform from becoming a widespread option for libraries seeking to maintain large directory collections.

Since the 1980s, computer technology has made serious inroads into the primacy of print directory collections. The speed, storage, and computational advantages of computers were obvious to both librarians and users. In the past few decades, many directories have appeared as online databases, on CD-ROMs, and most recently, on the Web. Directories available commercially or for free on the Web are causing many librarians to look closely at their investment in print directories.

The shape of directory collections in libraries is changing rapidly, with many libraries opting to cancel print directories in favor of comparable electronic versions. Even subscription-based Web directories are feeling the pressure of resources that are freely available on the Web. For many questions, answers from freely available Web resources can suffice, leading to less reliance on subscription-based print and electronic resources.

EVALUATION

Librarians have always placed a high priority on evaluating directory sources. In helping users find people, places, and organizations, having suitable directory resources has always been critical. Criteria for judging directories are often similar to standards that are used for other types of reference sources. Some important criteria to consider in evaluating a directory include scope, currency, accuracy, and arrangement.

Scope

Does this source include addresses and telephone numbers? Can we get Web sites and sales figures from this list of businesses? Will this directory of colleges include schools in Canada? These are all questions that deal with the scope of a directory.

What is covered or included should be one of the first things considered in deciding to use a specific directory to answer a user's question. The scope of directories can be looked at in terms of their *who*, *what*, or *where*. *Who* are the people covered by this directory? Does it even list or cover people? Is it covering lists of people who reside in a given area? The *what* of the directory refers to the things listed in the directory. *What* organizations, schools, agencies, businesses, or funding opportunities are listed in the directory? The *where* of the directory deals with the geographic coverage. Is it local, national, or international? Prefatory material in a print directory can be used to determine the scope and likely usefulness in a particular library setting. Scope can be more difficult to determine for electronic directories, and often librarians have to rely on vendor documentation or promotional material to get an idea of what a given resource may cover.

Currency

How often is this directory published and updated? Does it come out annually, biannually, quarterly, weekly, or daily? These questions of currency are of critical importance. Users of directories are often trying to make connections with people and organizations outside their immediate community. Success in doing so often depends on having the most current available information.

Determining the currency of a directory can be less complicated for a print source. Print directories often follow an established publishing schedule, usually appearing annually with supplements at regular intervals. The print directory will have a lag in reporting changes in addresses or phone numbers, for example, until a supplement or new edition is published. This lag will limit the currency, and this caution should always be taken into account when using a print directory in a reference situation.

The currency of electronic directories can sometimes be problematic. They often have much more frequent updates than their print counterparts, with additions and changes being made several times a year or even more frequently. However, despite frequent updates, the currency claims of electronic directories need to be viewed critically and with caution. Updating for many electronic directories consists of adding new material but not updating the entire database content. Some database vendors will keep separate schedules for adding new entries and for updating the remainder of the database. Librarians should be alert to these possible discrepancies and look for electronic directories that regularly update all entries.

Accuracy

The accuracy of information in directories should also be examined carefully. Is the information about people and organizations correct? Reading the preface or the introduction in a directory can sometimes give clues about its potential accuracy. Introductory material can often reveal how the data compiled in the directory was collected, alerting librarians to potential inaccuracies. For example, did a representative of the organization provide the information compiled in its directory entry, or were other sources used? Clearly, inaccurate information will limit the usefulness of a directory in a reference setting, and users should be made aware that sometimes information obtained from directories will have to be used with caution.

Arrangement

Does this directory have an index? Are the entries alphabetical or classified? Do subject categories appear at the top of the page? Does the electronic version of this directory allow one to sort results by city? These are some of the questions that address the arrangement of a directory. The arrangement determines whether access to the information in the directory will be simple or difficult. If a directory is poorly organized, users are not likely to find the information they need.

Electronic directories often have an advantage over their print counterparts in providing access options. Searching directories electronically allows users to take advantage of multiple access points, search multiple editions of a print counterpart, and create customized lists for entries with common characteristics. Regardless of whether the source is print or electronic, knowledge of indexing schemes and access options will help get information to the user faster and more efficiently.

SELECTION

The selection of directory sources may vary greatly from library to library, depending on size, mission, and users served. Some important criteria to consider in selecting a directory include the user community, cost, and uniqueness. Librarians will also need to carefully consider the advantages of providing access to commercially published directories as opposed to relying on resources that might be available freely on the Web.

User Community

Librarians need to carefully consider their user community when building their directory collections. Directories dealing with the geographic area in which the library is located have long been staples of public library collections. Academic and school libraries serving users involved in specific areas of research or study may need to look at international directories or directories that focus on a specialized subject. A special library serving a corporate clientele can make business directories the mainstay of its reference collection. Clearly, all types of libraries can benefit from having directory collections, but their selection should reflect the needs of their users.

Cost

In all libraries the cost of directory sources is a major consideration. Library size, budget, and availability of alternative funding will often decide the shape of a directory collection. Large libraries may have the funds required to build comprehensive directory collections. Smaller libraries may have to purchase selected parts of larger print directories or purchase more limited access to electronic versions. The availability of free directories and organizational Web sites can offer alternatives to purchase when funds are limited. Such free Web resources can be linked from public terminals or the library Web site, providing easy access for users and librarians.

Uniqueness

The uniqueness of a directory must also be considered when selecting it for a reference collection. Is the information unique, or does it overlap with what can be found in other directories or freely on the Web? Having multiple directories that largely cover the same content may not be cost-effective and may be counterproductive from a service perspective. Specialized directories also need to be examined for uniqueness and measured against what is available in existing directories. By carefully looking at uniqueness, libraries can avoid duplication, excessive costs, and unnecessarily large collections.

Directories as Databases

Given the increasing ability to answer directory-related questions using freely available Web resources, it is important to recognize the potential benefits of commercially published directories, whether in print or in electronic form. Features of these directories can make it easier to answer certain types of questions. These features include the structured format of directory entries and the ease in identifying all entries having certain characteristics. In the *American Library Directory*, for example, each entry has a structured format that includes such elements as size of staff, size of collection, and automation activity and vendor information (see Figure 14.1). Although this information may be discernible from the library's Web site, it will not be in a

SAMPLE ENTRY

[1]P [2]McNeil & Foster, [3]Prescott Memorial Library, [4]500 Terra Cotta Dr, 85005-3126. [5]SAN 360-9070. [6]Tel: 602-839-9108. Toll Free Tel: 800-625-3848. FAX: 602-839-2020. TDD: 602-839-9202. E-mail: mcneilfoster@prescott.org. Web Site: www.fosterpress.com. [7]*Dir* Troy Alan; Tel: 602-839-5522; *Asst Dir* Tasha Brunnell; *Tech Serv* Beverly Greene; *Pub Servs* Tanya Peeley. Subject Specialists: *Bus* Cecil Brown; *Folklore* Peggy Shoree.
[8]Staff 20 (MLS 15, Non-MLS 5)
[9]Founded 1903. Pop served 92,540; Circ 210,000
[10]July 2006-Jun 2007 Income (Main Library and Branch(es)) $439,158, State $300,000, City $139,518. Mats Exp $142,460, Books $53,000, Per/Ser (Incl. Access Fees) $72,900, Micro $1,160, AV Equip $5,100. Sal $97,100 (Prof $32,000)
[11]**Library Holdings:** Bk Vols 110,000; Bk Titles 72,000; Per subs 245
[12]**Special Collections:** Local History (Lehi College)
[13]**Subject Interests:** Child psychology, genetics
[14]**Automation Activity & Vendor Info:** (Acquisitions) Innovative Interfaces Inc.; (Cataloging) Innovative Interfaces Inc.; (Circulation) Gaylord
[15]**Database Vendor:** DRA, Ebsco-EbscoHost
[16]Wireless access
[17]Mem of Southwestern Library System
[18]Partic in Amigos; BRS
[19]Special Services for the Deaf-TDD. Staff member who knows sign language; projector & captioned films
[20]Friends of Library Group
[21]**Bookmobiles:** 1
[22]**Branches:** 1
EASTSIDE, 9807 Post St, 85007-3184. SAN 360-9083. Tel 602-839-9178; *Librn* Linda Rhodes
Library Holdings: Bk Vols 23,000

1. Classification key (see "Arrangement & Coverage" in the Preface for explanation).
2. Official library name.
3. Other name by which library may be known.
4. Address.
5. SAN (Standard Address Number).
6. Communication information.
7. Personnel.
8. Number and professional status of staff.
9. Library background—Data on enrollment and the highest degree offered are included for academic libraries.
10. Income figures—Library income is broken down by source when reported.
    Expenditure figures—Material expenditure figures are requested for AV equipment, books, electronic reference materials (including access fees), manuscripts and archives, microforms, other print materials, periodicals/serials (including access fees), and preservation. In addition, salary figures are broken down by professional status when given.
11. Library holdings.
12. Special collections.
13. Subject interests.
14. Automation activity and vendor.
15. Database vendor.
16. Library with wireless access.
17. Library system to which the library belongs.
18. Networks in which the library participates.
19. Special services.
20. Friends of Library Group.
21. Bookmobiles.
22. Branches (or departmental libraries for academic libraries)—Entries include library name, address, name of librarian, and number of book volumes. Branch libraries are listed under the library of which they are a part.

Figure 14.1. "Sample Entry" page from the *American Library Directory*.

standard location on the site and may require extended exploration of various sections of the site. Likewise, if one wants to identify all the libraries in a particular city, the geographic arrangement of entries in the print directory, by city within state, groups together the relevant entries on consecutive pages. Alternatively, the online version can be searched by location to yield a list of libraries in a particular city. Although it may be possible to generate a list of libraries in a particular city through use of a Web search engine, one would have less confidence in the completeness of the results.

Even more sophisticated use of directory content is possible when multiple electronic titles are aggregated, as in the *Gale Directory Library*. This resource currently provides online access to 43 different directories, such as *Ward's Business Directory of U.S. Private and Public Companies* and the three parts of the *Encyclopedia of Associations*. A single title can be searched by its own unique data fields, or the entire directory collection can be searched at once. Results can be sorted and exported to programs such as Excel for further analysis. Availability of older editions of some of the directory titles as part of the *Gale Directory Library* enables trend analysis.

As these examples suggest, inclusion of commercially published directories in a library's collection can expand the range of questions that can be answered and the efficiency with which answers can be found. Whether investment in such directories is warranted for a particular library will depend on user needs and funds available for collection development. If the investment is made, then librarians should work to ensure that library users are aware of the ways in which use of the library's directory collection can extend beyond what can easily be accomplished using resources freely available on the Web.

IMPORTANT GENERAL SOURCES

The directories profiled in this section include a selected sampling of core directories that could be of use in libraries of all types. In addition to information on identifying directories, the section includes discussions of telephone directories and directory sources that focus on libraries, associations, publishers, education, grants, business, government, and specialized subjects. Standard print sources are highlighted together with information about electronic equivalents where they exist. For commercial electronic sources, emphasis is given to Web-based products because that is now the dominant format in use in libraries. Useful freely available Web-based directory resources are also discussed. One general title that does not fit into any one of these areas that lists Canadian organizations in all fields is the *Canadian Almanac & Directory*, a very useful annual publication discussed more fully in chapter 15.

Identifying Directories

Determining whether a directory exists is a common challenge at the reference desk. Directories of directories can help identify whether a directory exists for a given topic, answering questions such as the following:

- Can I find a listing of addresses and phone numbers for sports agents?
- Is there a directory of law enforcement officials?

Directories in Print is a comprehensive listing of available directories published in the United States and around the world. Directories of all types, including international, national, regional, and local, are listed. Print and nonprint directories covering business, education, trade, professions, and numerous other areas are profiled. Inclusion of a title depends on the source containing at least addresses for its subjects. Two volumes make up the print version of *Directories in Print*. The first volume consists of descriptive entries that are arranged in general subject categories. Under these subject categories, the entries appear alphabetically by title and contain information

---

BOX 14.1
SEARCH STRATEGY: DIRECTORY OF DIRECTORIES

A user in a college library came to the information desk asking for a list of Army/Navy surplus stores. The user had been surfing all over the Web and had found only individual store sites. The user wanted a more systematic list that would list them by state. After failing with the online catalog, the librarian decided to try the *Directories in Print* source in the reference collection. The librarian could not get a sense of where this might be in the *Descriptive Listing* volume of the source. The librarian decided to try the *Indexes* volume and, after striking out under "Army" and "Surplus," finally found an entry for the *Army & Navy Goods Retail Directory* under a heading for "Retail Stores." The directory arranged the stores by geographic location and included contact information, name of owners, and number of employees. A search of the online catalog found that the library did not have the directory, but a *WorldCat* search found that the local public library had the latest version of the directory, and the user was successfully referred to the public library.

---

about coverage, language, frequency, and electronic availability of the directory. The second volume is made up of title, keyword, subject, and alternate-formats indexes. A supplemental volume is issued between annual editions to cover newly published directories. *Directories in Print* is also available online in combination with other Gale directory databases through the *Gale Directory Library*.

Directories in Print is an important source in assisting users to identify the in-print availability of directories and to track down directories that might be available for a certain subject. This source is extremely helpful in finding directories for obscure or specialized subjects such as violinists, magicians, or occupational therapists. *Directories in Print* should be consulted in helping users get to the directory that they need.

Telephone Directories

For most of the 20th century, print telephone directories were standard components of library reference collections. A successor to the 19th-century city directory, telephone books provide important information about local communities. They can be used to answer such questions as the following:

- What's the phone number for Joe's Body Shop?
- I need to find my friend's telephone number and address in Macon, Georgia.
- Where can I go in town to get my bicycle repaired?

Along with the standard residential listings with addresses and phone numbers, telephone directories have maps, building guides, local calendars, and advertisements for businesses. During the era of the AT&T monopoly, libraries could build large collections of telephone directories because the phone company offered them for free. The breakup of AT&T in the early 1980s saw the emergence of local successor companies that no longer offered free print telephone directories. This led libraries to re-evaluate their print telephone directory collections, with many keeping only the print directory for their city or local area.[4]

Librarians with a need for more comprehensive telephone directory coverage have turned to the Web in recent years, relying on Web-based subscription services to get comprehensive contact information about people and businesses. A good example of a resource of this type is *ReferenceUSA* offered by Infogroup. This database contains, in module format, contact information for more than 14 million U.S. businesses; 89 million U.S. residents; 855,000 U.S. health care providers; 1.5 million Canadian businesses; and 12 million Canadian households. Librarians may customize the product by purchasing one or more modules.

The modules have quick and custom search modes that allow access across a number of different parameters. The resident and business information comes from nearly 5,200 white and yellow page telephone directories and is updated on a monthly basis. The business entries are further supplemented by annual reports, SEC filings, and government agencies. *ReferenceUSA* and other subscription services can provide accurate information for libraries looking for wider, more extensive telephone directory coverage.

Librarians are also able to answer many telephone directory questions by using freely available sources on the Web. Sources of this type have been evolving very rapidly in the last few years. An example of a free portal for Web telephone books is *Infobel*, that offers links to phone directories in the United States and internationally. *Switchboard* and *AnyWho* are good examples of free Web-based white and yellow page services used to answer phone directory questions. Both of these services allow searching by a person's name, by business name or category, by ZIP code, and by reverse lookup; a user may also conduct a Web search from the site. Both of these resources have additional features such as maps, advertising services, and personal listing opportunities.

Although accuracy and currency of such free sites cannot be guaranteed, for ready-reference questions, they are often sufficient. Freely available telephone directory sites need to be linked prominently from library Web pages or reference portals so that they can be easily accessed by library staff, in-house users, and remote users. For smaller libraries with more basic telephone directory needs, links to these types of resources may be able to answer the bulk of telephone questions without a major investment in subscription-based resources.

Library Directories

Of special interest to librarians are directories of libraries. They can answer questions such as the following:

- How many people are employed at the Library of Congress?
- Does Uganda have a national library?
- What kind of automation system is used at the Seattle Public Library?

The best-known resource of this kind is the *American Library Directory*, a standard source in reference collections for many years. This directory is the most comprehensive listing of libraries in North America, covering libraries of all types, consortia arrangements, and key library personnel. Still popular in its print form, the *American Library Directory* is often kept at the reference desk or handy in a ready-reference collection.

In print, the *American Library Directory* consists of an annual two-volume set. The first volume consists of a geographical listing of libraries in the United States by state, Alabama through Rhode Island, and further subdivided by city, with the library entries arranged alphabetically under the city. The entries themselves consist of such elements as library name, address, telephone number, fax number, e-mail address, Web site URL, collection size, subject strengths, automation information, director name, and rare or special collections (see Figure 14.1). The second volume covers the remainder of the states, South Carolina through Wyoming, followed by sections for libraries in Puerto Rico and regions administered by the United States, Canadian libraries, consortia, and other institutions that are related to libraries such as library schools and state library agencies. This volume includes organization and personnel indexes. Information Today also makes available an online version of *American Library Directory* that allows searching by library type, location, and all relevant entry fields. Customized lists can be created for libraries based on expenditures, staff, and holdings. The entries in this electronic version contain the same information as those in the print version.

The *American Library Directory* is good for finding out about particular libraries. For those seeking more specific information about specialized collections, the *Directory of Special Libraries and Information Centers* can be helpful. This resource is a comprehensive directory of special libraries that includes collections in corporations, museums, foundations, professional organizations, hospitals, and learned societies. It is arranged alphabetically by the name of the collection or library. The entries contain elements such as name, address, telephone number, fax number, e-mail address, Web site URL, parent organization, director name, and founding date. This directory has access points through geographical, subject, and personnel indexes. Electronic access is provided through the *Gale Directory Library*.

Questions about libraries around the world are not uncommon at the reference desk. An example of a directory with worldwide coverage of libraries is the *World Guide to Libraries*. This annual directory is arranged by country and lists entries under type of library, including national libraries, public libraries, special libraries, government libraries, and academic libraries. The entries include basic contact information, collection size, notable collections, and director name. A single alphabetical index provides access to the directory entries.

With more libraries maintaining their own Web sites, the ability to get library information directly from the Web has been greatly enhanced. Users who know the library's name can just type it into a search engine such as Google and connect directly to the Web site. Library Web sites have basic contact information and often more detailed information about the library and the services it offers. For many public libraries, the Web site can be an important community bulletin board for the city or region that the library serves, providing information that users might not find using a traditional library directory. *Libweb: Library Servers via WWW* (http://lists.web junction.org/libweb/) is a Web-based directory providing links to Web pages from libraries in 146 countries. The site has a keyword search capability in addition to the possibility of browsing the lists of libraries arranged by country and, for the United States, further subdivided by type of library and state. In assisting colleagues and users find information about libraries, librarians need to be knowledgeable about the opportunities that exist at no cost on the Web and be prepared to take advantage of the value-added features of their commercially available resources where appropriate.

Association Directories

Directories of associations can answer contact and basic informational questions about this type of organization, such as the following:

- When was the American Medical Association founded?
- How many members does the American Library Association currently have?
- Does the American Historical Association sponsor a journal?

A core set of resources that provide comprehensive directory coverage for associations are the three *Encyclopedia of Associations* titles. The *Encyclopedia of Associations: National Organizations of the U.S.*, the *Encyclopedia of Associations: Regional, State and Local Organizations*, and the *Encyclopedia of Associations: International Organizations* provide basic profiles of nonprofit associations in the United States and worldwide. *National Organizations of the U.S.* and *International Organizations* are arranged by subject, and the *Regional, State and Local Organizations* volumes are organized by geography. In general, the entries for all of these directories consist of association name, address, phone number, fax number, e-mail address, Web site URL, number of members, budget, founding date, publications, conferences or meetings, and contact person for the organization. Narrative information about the organization's function and mission is also provided as part of the entry for each association. Indexes include a geographic index, an index of names of executive officers, and a keyword index to organization names. These three titles are all available as a component of the *Gale Directory Library*. Available search modes include association name or acronym, location, and subject/any word. Custom and expert search options allow for searching in multiple fields and for customizing lists of associations by different criteria. An additional feature allows users to search for IRS data on organizations that have applied for and been granted nonprofit status. Cross-searching can be conducted simultaneously across all three files (national; international; regional, state, and local) or limited to only one of the directory titles.

Associations Canada: The Directory of Associations in Canada/Le Répertoire des Associations du Canada covers more than 17,000 Canadian organizations and international groups including industry, trade, and professional associations; registered charities; and special interest organizations. Entries include complete contact information and descriptive information such as scope of activity, sources of funding, and founding date. Indexes facilitate access by subject, acronym, geographic location, and executive name. This title is also available online from *Canada's Information Resource Centre*, an electronic suite of general reference resources made available from Grey House Publishing Canada.

A great deal of information about associations can be obtained freely on the Web. The *ipl2* offers a free directory called *Associations on the Net* that provides descriptions and access to the Web sites of more than 2,000 associations of all types (http://www.ipl.org/div/aon). This site can be searched by keyword, but the principal access is by linked subject categories. The University of Waterloo maintains the *Scholarly Societies Project,* facilitating access to Web sites for scholarly societies from around the world (http://www.scholarly-societies.org). Users can also locate association Web sites directly through standard Web search engines. Association Web sites provide basic contact information and in many cases more details about the organization's history, mission, publications, conferences, and member services. Librarians need to be aware of access options that exist, and key resources need to be prominently listed on the library's Web page. Librarians who serve specialized users can also provide direct Web links to the associations of greatest interest to their users.

Publishing Directories

As repositories of books and other materials, libraries are closely connected to the publishing industry. Both librarians and library users are interested in information about publishing and publishers. It is not surprising that questions about contacting and locating publishers would be common in the reference setting. Questions such as the following can be answered by having directories of publishers in the reference collection:

- What is the address of Yale University Press?
- Who publishes science books for children?

A good example of a comprehensive directory of publishers in the United States and Canada is the *Literary Market Place.* In its print form, in two volumes, *Literary Market Place* is an annual publication with more than 12,000 entries for various entities in the publishing industry. Volume 1 is the basic industry directory with information on publishers, literary agents, editorial providers, industry associations, and trade publications. Volume 2 is a directory of supporting services that includes entries for marketers, advertisers, promoters, and suppliers. The entries contain name, address, telephone number, fax number, e-mail address, and Web site URL; key personnel; affiliated offices; and a brief descriptive annotation. Yellow page indexing coverage is provided for companies, personnel, sections, and advertisers at the end of both volumes.

A companion directory to *Literary Market Place* is the *International Literary Market Place.* This annual directory covers the international publishing industry, with nearly 15,500 entries for entities in 180 countries. A single volume in print, *International Literary Market Place* is organized in broad sections: publishing, manufacturing, book trade information, literary associations and prizes, book trade calendar, and library resources. Entries are arranged alphabetically by country and contain basic contact information, key people, and a brief narrative description. An industry yellow pages section covering publishers and supporting companies is available at the end of the directory.

Both *Literary Market Place* and *International Literary Market Place* can be found as a Web-based product called *LiteraryMarketPlace.com* from Information

Today. Subscribers can get complete entries and enhanced searching for publishers by different subject or type of publication. Lists of publishers based on size, sales, city, zip code, and other variables can be generated from this database.

Publishers Directory provides comprehensive coverage of approximately 20,000 U.S. and Canadian publishers, distributors, and wholesalers. A wide range of presses is represented, including major commercial publishers, literary and alternative small presses, scholarly publishers, museums, associations and societies, religious organizations, government agencies, and corporations. Also included are producers of databases and curriculum materials. Entries are arranged alphabetically by name of publisher and provide full contact information, including toll-free telephone and fax numbers, as well as e-mail addresses and Web site URLs. Indexes provide access by subject or area of specialization and geographical area; there is also a publishers, imprints, and distributors index. The directory is available online as part of the *Gale Directory Library*.

The retail end of the book trade industry is also the subject of questions such as these:

- Is there an antiquarian bookseller in this city?
- Can addresses for used bookstores in New Orleans be obtained?

The *American Book Trade Directory* is a comprehensive directory of book retailers and wholesalers in the United States and Canada. It lists more than 20,000 retailers, wholesalers, antiquarians, and dealers in foreign language books, arranged geographically by state or province and then by city. The entries provide store or business name, address, telephone number, fax number, e-mail address, Web site URL, owner/manager, stocked volumes, and subject strengths. A standard alphabetical index and a store-type index provide access to the directory content.

Many publishers have extensive Web sites that can be accessed for free to locate contact and profile information. Many publishers also allow access to product catalogs and often permit direct ordering and buying from their Web sites. Librarians in all types of settings need to know the variety of publisher information that is freely available and how commercial print or electronic resources complement or exceed that information in scope and functionality.

Education Directories

Questions about educational institutions and programs are common in most reference settings, especially in academic and school libraries. Educational directories are often used to answer basic informational questions dealing with schools and other educational entities, such as the following:

- What's the address of Echo Hills Elementary School in Stow, Ohio?
- What are the major universities in Belgium?
- Can I get a list of schools that offer graduate programs in medieval studies?

For users looking for information on elementary and secondary schools in the United States, the Patterson directories are core resources. *Patterson's Elementary*

Education and *Patterson's American Education* provide basic information for K–12 educational institutions. *Patterson's Elementary Education* is an annual one-volume directory that profiles more than 66,000 public, private, and Catholic elementary schools as well as 15,600 middle schools. *Patterson's American Education* is also an annual one-volume publication that provides basic information for more than 40,000 secondary and postsecondary schools. Both of these directories are organized alphabetically by state and then by community, school district, and individual school. The school entries include the name of the school, address, telephone number, fax number, grades taught, enrollment, and the principal's name. Both of these directories are popular in print but are also available in a CD-ROM product that allows for searching across multiple fields and for creating lists of schools that meet certain criteria.

Directory information about higher education can be found in a number of places. A commonly used concise guide to colleges and universities is *Peterson's Four-Year Colleges*. This directory is a single-volume annual publication profiling accredited four-year colleges in the United States and Canada. The college descriptions are arranged alphabetically by state or province, and the college entries contain information such as name, address, phone number, fax number, Web site URL, acceptance rates, majors, current tuition, student life, and campus safety. A detailed section of inserts provides additional in-depth narrative profiles for more than 400 selected colleges and universities. *Peterson's* includes indexes that are based on entrance difficulty, cost, majors, and a standard alphabetical index. Peterson's also provides basic descriptive information about colleges, as well as graduate schools, online degrees, and K–12 private schools, at the company's Web site (http://www.petersons.com) at no charge for users.

A more comprehensive treatment of higher education can be found in *The College Blue Book*. *The College Blue Book* profiles more than 11,300 universities and postsecondary institutions in the United States and Canada. In its popular print form, this resource is organized in six thematic volumes that can largely stand by themselves. Volume 1 contains the narrative descriptions of more than 4,100 colleges and universities. The entries are arranged alphabetically by state and Canadian province and include contact and brief descriptive information. Volume 2 includes tabular data for colleges, with information about tuition, accreditation, enrollment, faculty, and administration. Descriptions of degrees offered by colleges in various subject areas make up Volume 3. Volume 4 profiles more than 6,300 postsecondary occupational and vocational schools. A directory of grant, scholarship, fellowship, and loan opportunities is provided in Volume 5. Volume 6 gives detailed profiles of more than 900 institutions that offer distance education programs in the United States and Canada.

Graduate education is covered comprehensively in *Peterson's Graduate & Professional Programs*. Contact and informational profiles are provided for more than 44,000 graduate programs at more than 2,300 institutions in the United States and Canada. Like *The College Blue Book*, this resource is organized around six thematic volumes that can be used as a set or individually. Across all the volumes in this set, three kinds of entries appear: basic profiles, short announcements, and in-depth descriptions. The basic profiles are the heart of each volume, and every program listed has a profile that includes information such as name, address, graduate director, acceptance figures, and a very brief narrative description. Some profiles have a short announcement at the end of their listing containing information that the school or program wants to emphasize to potential applicants. Many profiles also have a cross-reference to an in-depth description of their program, submitted by the schools themselves. These descriptions are found at the end of subject sections in the individual volumes and appear in a standard format that includes information on programs of study, research facilities, costs, available financial help, and how to apply.

Finding contact information for professors, teachers, and administrators is also a common directory question in the area of higher education. An example of a core resource in this area is the *National Faculty Directory*. This directory is a simple alphabetical listing of almost 768,000 currently active faculty members at universities, colleges, and community colleges in the United States and Canada. The entries are very brief, containing only the name of the faculty member, academic department affiliation, name of his or her college or university, address, and phone number. Addresses and phone numbers for all the institutions that have faculty listed in the directory are also provided. The *National Faculty Directory* is also available online as part of the *Gale Directory Library*.

Many library users are interested in finding contact information for education-related institutions around the world. A core resource for such questions is *The Europa World of Learning*. This widely held annual publication provides basic information for educational and cultural entities in countries around the world. In its print form, the directory is arranged alphabetically by country, with subsections dealing with universities, specialized schools, learned societies, research centers or institutes, libraries and archives, and museums and galleries. Entries include name, address, telephone number, Web site URL, directors or key people, and details about library or museum collections. A standard alphabetical index of institutions is provided at the end of the set.

A subscription Web-based version of *The Europa World of Learning* from Routledge is becoming more popular in libraries. Like many other online directories, this resource allows for a variety of search functions, including browsing by country, institutions, and subjects. The content is basically the same as what can be found in the print version of *The Europa World of Learning*.

Increasingly, schools and other educational institutions are maintaining their own free Web sites. Colleges and universities in particular have made a vast amount of information available on the Web. A comprehensive freely available directory to Web sites in higher education is *General Education Online*. This resource provides links to college and university sites in the United States and internationally. *General Education Online* is arranged by country with the college links appearing in an alphabetical list.

Locating college sites can be important for users because many of them offer both contact information and access to basic services. Users can go to a university or college site and get full contact information, fill out paperwork, and in many cases actually apply to the school. In libraries of all types, librarians need to know the extent to which educational information of interest is freely available on the Web and when it is appropriate to turn to the commercial print and online resources in their collections.

Foundations and Grants Directories

Individuals seeking funds to advance their education and organizations seeking funds to support development of new initiatives may need assistance in identifying potential funding sources. Directories of foundations and grants can assist in answering such questions as the following:

- What organizations fund programs for libraries?
- Does the Monroe Fund give to individuals?
- What is the address of the Astra Foundation?

Questions of this type are common in all types of libraries.

The most comprehensive resource covering private grant-giving to nonprofit organizations is *The Foundation Directory*. In its print form, this annual publication comes in two parts: *The Foundation Directory* and *The Foundation Directory Part 2*. *The Foundation Directory* profiles the top 10,000 foundations in terms of annual giving, and *The Foundation Directory Part 2* profiles the next 10,000 in terms of giving. Entries are organized alphabetically by state, and the foundations are listed alphabetically by name. Entries can be quite detailed, including elements such as foundation name, address, telephone number, contact person, establishment date, fields of interest, principal donors, foundation assets, and expenditures. Indexes by geography; international giving; types of support; subject; names of donors, officers, and trustees; and foundations new to the edition provide wide access to *The Foundation Directory*.

Foundation Grants to Individuals is the most extensive resource covering private grant-giving to individuals. In its print form, this annual single-volume publication profiles nearly 9,000 U.S. granting institutions that have ongoing programs geared to individuals. The entries are listed geographically by state and alphabetically by the name of the grant maker. Elements of the entries include full contact information, assets, expenditures, total giving, grants to individuals, loans to individuals, fields of interest, types of support, program information, and application details. Access is facilitated by indexes arranged by geography, international giving, company name, specific school, type of support, subject, and grant-maker name.

Online access to these resources is available through *The Foundation Directory Online* and *Foundation Grants to Individuals Online*, provided by the Foundation Center. Access to *The Foundation Directory Online* can be customized through a number of different subscription packages, with the top-level option profiling more than 100,000 grant makers, including entries for smaller foundations not found in the print *Foundation Directory*. The content of the *Foundation Grants to Individuals Online* follows more closely the arrangement of its print counterpart. For users seeking less comprehensive information, the "Foundation Finder" section of the Foundation Center Web site offers free basic information on grant makers in the United States and can be searched by grant-maker name as well as geography to identify grant makers in a given city, state, or ZIP code (http://foundationcenter.org/findfunders/foundfinder/).

Information about grant-giving organizations can also be found in the *Annual Register of Grant Support*. This one-volume directory profiles public and private foundations, government agencies, corporations, community trusts, unions, educational organizations, professional associations, and interest groups that are involved in grant- giving. The directory is divided into a number of funding areas that are further divided into more specialized categories. Entries include contact information for the funding entity, Web site URL, duration of grants, amount of funding for awards, areas of interest, eligibility requirements, and application process. Subject, organization, program, geographic, and personnel indexes give users access options to identify the best funding opportunity.

A great deal of information about grant-giving organizations is freely available on the Web. Perhaps the largest source of grants is the U.S. government, and the essential resource for finding federal funding is freely available online. The Web-based *Catalog of Federal Domestic Assistance* (www.cfda.gov) provides access to all federal funding programs that are available to individuals, state and local governments, private organizations, and nonprofit groups. This directory can be searched by functional area, agency, program title, applicant eligibility, deadlines, program number, grant, and keyword. Of course, foundations, government agencies, and other grant makers can be identified directly using a search engine, and many of their Web sites provide detailed information about available funding opportunities. Many potential funding sources have key application documents linked directly from their Web sites. Libraries should be cognizant of the kind of grant opportunities their users might pursue and be ready to highlight available directory resources from their own collections and the open Web.

Business Directories

Business directories have long been staples of reference collections in libraries of all types. They can be used to answer questions such as the following:

- Who is the current CEO for General Motors?
- Where is the corporate headquarters for Kraft Foods?
- What company makes regulators for HVAC units?

One of the most comprehensive business directories is *Ward's Business Directory of U.S. Private and Public Companies*. *Ward's* lists 112,000 public and private companies in the United States. The entries include company name, address, sales figures, number of employees, SIC codes, NAICS codes, public or private status, ticker symbol, stock exchange, founding year, principal company officers, and main product or service. A unique feature of the *Ward's* product is the arrangement of its eight volumes. The first three volumes list companies alphabetically by name. Volume 4 offers a geographic approach to the companies by state. Volume 5 lists the companies by the Standard Industrial Classification (SIC) code that most closely fits their industry and further ranks them by sales within the industrial codes. Volumes 6 and 7 organize the companies by state and then rank by sales within SIC code. Volume 8 ranks the companies by sales under the six-digit North American Industry Classification System (NAICS) codes that best describe their industry. This directory allows users to go beyond brief descriptive information to look at customized lists of companies that are strong in a particular industry, or those companies that are prominent in certain geographic markets. The *Ward's* product is also available on CD-ROM and online as part of the *Gale Directory Library*. Online users can search by almost any field of information included in the directory, such as industry, state, ZIP code, type of company, and sales ranges.

Another well-recognized business directory is *Standard & Poor's Register of Corporations, Directors and Executives*. This annual directory profiles more than 85,000 corporations and also provides names and biographical sketches for their executives and top-level managers. The *Standard & Poor's* directory is published in two volumes, with the first volume being an alphabetical listing by the name of the company. The entries contain the name of the company, street address, telephone number, Web site URL, company officers, ticker symbol, number of employees, products or services, yearly sales figure, subsidiaries, parent company, and the NAICS codes. Volume 2 features the biographical dictionary of people currently serving as officers, partners, executives, and directors of these companies. The biographical entries include company affiliation, business address, home address, year of birth, place of birth, college graduation, e-mail address, and association memberships. This volume also includes indexes by geography, NAICS codes, corporate family, and an obituary section that reports deaths of executives during the past year.

The *Standard & Poor's Register* is available electronically through *NetAdvantage*, an electronic set of Standard & Poor's reference products. This Web version can be used to retrieve the standard company profiles and executive biographies. Customized searching can also be used to generate lists by NAICS codes, geography, sales, size, and other variables.

Dun & Bradstreet's *Million Dollar Directory* is one of the best-known business directories in use in libraries today. The annual print directory profiles 160,000 top public and private companies in the United States. To qualify for the directory, a company must have more than $9,000,000 in sales and 180 employees at a headquarters or single location. The directory has five volumes, with the first three listing companies alphabetically by name and the last two providing profiles by SIC code and geography. Entries include business description, name, address, telephone number, fax number, Web site URL, e-mail address, number of employees, SIC codes, date of founding, annual sales, and key officers. The *Million Dollar Directory* is available online as part of the Dun & Bradstreet *Million Dollar Database*. The enhanced version of this product includes listings for 8 million American, Canadian, and international companies. This database enables searching for specific companies or by industries designated by NAICS or SIC codes, and the opportunity for selecting multiple criteria permits customized lists to be developed using a variety of variables.

Many users seek to identify affiliates and parents for given companies. A specialized directory that identifies these relationships is the *LexisNexis Corporate Affiliations*. The current annual print version appears in eight volumes, with the first two being the master indexes and volumes 3 through 8 containing the A–Z company listings (U.S. public companies in volumes 3 and 4; U.S. private companies in volumes 5 and 6; and international public and private companies in volumes 7 and 8). The affiliate entries contain elements such as company name, phone number, address, fax number, Web site URL, e-mail address, net worth, earnings, year founded, products, number of employees, and principal officers. An electronic version of this directory is available as a CD-ROM or online through various subscription options from *LexisNexis*.

Library users are often interested to know what companies provide certain products or services. For years the *Thomas Register of American Manufacturers* was used to answer such questions. Its 100th and final edition was published in print in 2006. Now *ThomasNet.com* provides this information through the Web. The site can be browsed by product category or searched by product/service, company name, or brand name. These searches can cover all states and provinces or be limited to a particular state or province. Company profiles include name, address, phone number, fax number, Web site URL, principal products, sales, number of employees, and export markets.

In recent years, searching for company information has become easier with the advent of the Web. The company Web site has become an important sales and marketing tool for many businesses. Users can now access company Web sites for free and get basic contact information or locate more detailed information such as annual reports, job listings, financials, stock reports, and detailed product descriptions. For users who want information about a specific company, the Web can often be the choice of first resort. For those who are seeking information about multiple companies or who wish to create lists using varied criteria, librarians should be prepared to promote the scope and functionality of their subscription-based business directories that can often provide more enhanced service for users.

Government Directories

Contact and basic informational questions about government at all levels are common for reference librarians to handle in all settings. The following are examples of questions that can be answered using a government directory:

- How do I contact my congressman?
- What is the address for the Department of Defense?
- What does the Small Business Administration do?

This section highlights examples of directories covering each level of government, from international to local. More detailed treatment of government information sources can be found in chapter 22.

One of the more comprehensive government directories with an international perspective is the *Worldwide Government Directory with International Organizations*. In print, this directory is a one-volume source that identifies elected and appointed officials in 201 countries and the European Union as well as the leadership of more than 100 international organizations. For each country, entries provide the official name of the country, names of key government offices, and names of important executive and legislative officials. The profiles for the government offices include addresses, telephone numbers, fax numbers, e-mail addresses, and Web site URLs. The international organizations section lists the organizations alphabetically, and the entries include name, address, telephone number, e-mail address, Web site URL, and key officers. The content of the print *Worldwide Government Directory* is included in the online searchable *World PowerBase* from CQ Press.

An extensive directory covering governmental and nongovernmental organizations in the U.S. capital region is *Washington Information Directory*. This directory is organized by broad subjects, such as energy, health, and education. Entries include name, address, telephone number, fax number, contact person, Web site URL, and a narrative description of the organization. The narrative descriptions are a unique feature of this directory, allowing the user to get a sense of an organization's basic charge and mission. Name, organization, and subject indexes are provided. An online edition is also available on the Web from CQ Press, updated annually in conjunction with the print edition.

Directory information for state and local governments is provided by a family of directories published by the Council of State Governments (CSG). The *CSG State Directory I: Elective Officials* covers contact information for elective officials for all the states and territories. *CSG State Directory II: Legislative Leadership, Committees & Staff* provides profiles of officers, staff, and standing committees for legislative bodies in all the states. *CSG State Directory III: Administrative Officials* lists names, addresses, telephone numbers, fax numbers, and e-mail addresses for elected and appointed officials for state executive agencies.

Information on local municipalities and counties is covered by a series of directories put out by Carroll Publishing. *Carroll's Municipal Directory* provides contact information for officials at the city, township, and village level of government. *Carroll's County Directory* profiles officials of county governments across all the states. These directories are updated several times a year and are available online through Carroll's *GovSearch*.

During the past few years, there has been a proliferation of freely available government information on the Web. State and federal government Web sites have contact and directory information that librarians and users can browse and search for free. The Internet also has many portals and freely available directories of government information at all levels. A good example of such a site is *State and Local Government on the Net*, a free directory of official state, county, and city government Web sites. As with other types of directories, libraries should be aware of the kind of government information their users are seeking and be prepared to mix the best features from subscription-based resources and those that can be found freely on the Web.

Specialized Directories

Specialized directories cover a certain segment of the population or profile very specific organizations. Directories of this type come in all kinds of formats and vary greatly in the information they provide. Some examples of the many available specialized directories include *A Directory of the Parochial Libraries of the Church of England and the Church of Wales*, the *Directory of Native American Museums and Cultural Centers*, the *Directory of American Philosophers*, and *The Official Museum Directory*. The extent to which specialized directories will be represented in a particular collection depends on the needs of the individual library. In considering acquisitions of specialized titles, librarians should look at their existing directory collections to see whether the content of a specialized resource is duplicated by directories that are wider in scope. Librarians in all types of libraries need to look closely at their user population, available budget, and basic mission in deciding which specialized directories will best suit their needs.

SEARCH STRATEGIES

Directory questions are at the same time both the easiest and the most difficult questions that come into the reference setting. The nature of many directory questions puts them into the realm of ready-reference questions that often may be answered by simply opening a print resource or typing a name into an electronic database. Others may require careful deliberation and involve consulting a number of different resources. The process of working through a directory question will take a good reference interview and careful consideration of the advantages, disadvantages, and features of the available print and electronic directory resources.

Reference Interview

The starting point in working through any directory question is finding out what the user actually needs, and clearly, this is best done through the reference interview. Questions can be asked to clarify exactly what information is needed:

- Are you looking for an address or telephone number for this person?
- Would you like to find this association's Web site?
- Would you like financial information with the company's phone number and e-mail address?
- Would you like the database to sort these manufacturing companies by city?

Good follow-up questions can be used to ascertain whether the initial question is ready-reference or is a hidden research question that may require consulting multiple reference resources.

Print Directories

Once the need of the user has been determined, the librarian will have to choose a directory that best meets the information need. In a general sense, the librarian will be faced with a large array of print and electronic resources that can answer potential questions in different ways. Certainly, a librarian can consider using a print directory to locate the specific information sought by the user. Libraries still have substantial collections of print directories. In some cases, they may be the only available directory for certain kinds of information. Other print directories have commercial electronic equivalents, or their content may be freely found on the Web. Deciding to use a print directory brings with it advantages and disadvantages for searching and overall use.

Print directories have the advantage of coming from reputable publishers with information that is filtered and largely accurate. Publication schedules are regular, so the availability of the next installment can be predicted. For certain users, information from a print directory may have more authority than comparable electronic sources. Print directories are also easy to browse, allowing users to thumb through information that may be of interest.

The print directory also has very real limitations. Print directories may not be as current as electronic resources. Getting information from a print directory may be slow and sometimes cumbersome. Limited access points restrict what can be retrieved from a print resource. The organization of the entries and the types of indexes determine the possible approaches to the print directory's contents.

Although weighing the advantages and disadvantages of using a print directory is important, ultimately the success of using the resource will depend on using it correctly to get the desired information. Knowing the basic arrangement of the directory is critical to locating the right answer. Librarians need to be aware of the intuitive alphabetical and geographic organizations of many print directories that allow for easy browsing. A good sense of the indexes included can also provide flexibility in helping the user to search for information without knowing the name of a person or organization.

Electronic Directories

Electronic directory options are becoming more and more prominent in libraries. Many users are finding answers to directory questions quickly by using electronic resources. Some electronic directory products are unique and have no equivalents in any other format. Other commercial electronic directories are direct equivalents of well-known print products. In recent years, many users have also been turning to directories and Web sites that are freely available. Like using comparable print products, using an electronic directory brings with it advantages and disadvantages that need to be considered.

Generally, electronic directories have the advantage of being more current than comparable print resources. Information is easier to update in electronic form, and users are more likely to get the most current information in this format. The speed of processing is a real advantage of using a commercial electronic directory or conducting free searches on the Web. For both commercial Web sources and freely available Web sources, users can often access them remotely without having to come into the library. Perhaps the most powerful advantage is the ability to search multiple access points. Being able to search several indexes at a time or combining fields to create customized lists greatly adds to the retrieval power of electronic resources.

Despite the real advantages of electronic directories, they also have disadvantages that can limit their effectiveness. Electronic directories, like other online resources, depend on working equipment and network connections. Although outages are usually temporary, librarians may be forced to have alternatives on hand to meet such contingencies. Subscription-based electronic resources have protocols that might limit where or how many users can access a product at a given time. Users who are searching for directory information for free on the Web may face the disadvantage of getting information that may not have gone through a filtering or editorial process and may be unreliable. Browsing may also be limited in many electronic resources, and users may need to formally search a database before they can retrieve any information.

The success of using an electronic option, like its print counterpart, will depend on the librarian's knowledge of the source. Knowing the basic rules of database searching and applying techniques such as Boolean logic, field searching, truncation, and other general principles are key in opening up the contents of most electronic resources. Familiarity with the search features and protocols of individual databases

---

BOX 14.2
SEARCH STRATEGY: DIRECTORY INFORMATION ON THE WEB

A user in a public library came to the reference desk wanting to find information on a small local company. Through a reference interview, the reference librarian determined that the user needed the e-mail address of the president and some information about the products made by the company. The librarian could not find anything using either the *Standard & Poor's Register* or the state manufacturing directory. Because the library collection was small, the availability of additional print or electronic business resources was limited. The librarian turned to her computer and searched for the company name in Google, finding the company Web site. The Web site included the president's e-mail address as well as that of all the principal officers. Pictures and descriptions of the products made by the company were also provided. Because the user did not have his own computer, the librarian printed out the contact information and product descriptions sought by the user.

---

is also a key element in using them effectively. Knowledge of how information is displayed and how it might be manipulated is often critical to taking full advantage of an electronic resource's capabilities.

CONCLUSION

Libraries today are populated with a vast array of directories that cover a wide variety of topics and meet a diversity of user needs. The shape of the directory resources in the contemporary library is a hybrid mix of print and electronic resources that is increasingly evolving toward a more electronic future. The move toward an electronic future has not changed the need for librarians to apply high standards in selecting quality directory resources and getting this information into the hands of library users quickly and effectively.

NOTES

1. Joan M. Reitz, *Dictionary for Library and Information Science* (Westport, CT: Libraries Unlimited, 2004), 221.

2. Fred J. Levy, *Tudor Historical Thought* (San Marino, CA: Huntington Library, 1967), 133.

3. Ivan Basar, "Directory Publishing in Canada: The Last Hundred Years," *Serials Librarian* 37 (1999): 61.

4. Douglas J. Ernest, Joan Beam, and Jennifer Monath, "Telephone Directory Use in an Academic Library," *Reference Services Review* 20 (Spring 1992): 50.

LIST OF SOURCES

American Book Trade Directory, 2010-2011. 56th ed. Medford, NJ: Information Today, 2010. 1700 pp.

American Library Directory, 2010-2011. 63rd ed. 2 vols. Medford, NJ: Information Today, 2010.

American Library Directory Online. Medford, NJ: Information Today. http://www.american librarydirectory.com/.

Annual Register of Grant Support, 2011. 44th ed. Medford, NJ: Information Today, 2010. 1306 pp.

AnyWho. http://www.anywho.com/.

Associations Canada: The Directory of Associations in Canada/Le Répertoire des Associations du Canada. 32nd ed. Toronto: Grey House Publishing Canada, 2010. 1886 pp. Also available online from *Canada's Information Resource Centre*.

Associations on the Net. http://www.ipl.org/div/aon.

Canada's Information Resource Centre. Toronto: Grey House Publishing Canada. http://circ. greyhouse.ca/.

Canadian Almanac & Directory. 164th ed. Toronto: Grey House Publishing, 2010. 1936 pp. Also available online from *Canada's Information Resource Centre*.

Carroll's County Directory. Bethesda, MD: Carroll Publishing, 1984–. Semiannual.

Carroll's Municipal Directory. Bethesda, MD: Carroll Publishing, 1984–. Semiannual.

Catalog of Federal Domestic Assistance. http://www.cfda.gov.

The College Blue Book. 38th ed. 6 vols. New York: Gale-Macmillan Reference USA, 2010.

CSG State Directories. I. Elective Officials; II. Legislative Leadership, Committees & Staff; III. Administrative Officials. 3 vols. Lexington, KY: Council of State Governments, 2011.

Directories in Print. 32nd ed. 2 vols. Farmington Hills, MI: Gale, 2010. Also available online as part of *Gale Directory Library*.

Directory of American Philosophers. 25th ed. Ed. Elizabeth Stombock. Charlottesville, VA: Philosophy Documentation Center, 2010. 674 pp.

Directory of Native American Museums and Cultural Centers. Nashville, TN: American Association of State and Local History, 1998. 50 pp.

Directory of Special Libraries and Information Centers. 38th ed. 3 vols. Farmington Hills, MI: Gale, 2010. Also available online as part of *Gale Directory Library*.

A Directory of the Parochial Libraries of the Church of England and the Church of Wales. Rev. ed. Ed. Michael Perkin. London: Bibliographical Society, 2004. 496 pp.

Encyclopedia of Associations: International Organizations. 49th ed. 3 vols. Farmington Hills, MI: Gale, 2010. Also available online as part of *Gale Directory Library*.

Encyclopedia of Associations: National Organizations of the U.S. 49th ed. 3 vols. Farmington Hills, MI: Gale, 2010. Also available online as part of *Gale Directory Library*.

Encyclopedia of Associations: Regional, State and Local Organizations. 22nd ed. 5 vols. Farmington Hills, MI: Gale, 2010. Also available online as part of *Gale Directory Library*.

The Europa World of Learning 2011. 61st ed. 2 vols. London: Routledge, 2011.

The Europa World of Learning Online. London: Routledge. http://www.worldoflearning.com.

The Foundation Directory. New York: Foundation Center, 2010. 2730 pp.

The Foundation Directory Online. New York: Foundation Center. http://fconline.fdncenter.org.

The Foundation Directory Part 2. New York: Foundation Center, 2010. 2148 pp.

"Foundation Finder." New York: Foundation Center. http://foundationcenter.org/findfunders/foundfinder.

Foundation Grants to Individuals. New York: Foundation Center, 2010. 1427 pp.

Foundation Grants to Individuals Online. New York: Foundation Center. http://gtionline.foundationcenter.org/

Gale Directory Library. Farmington Hills, MI: Gale. http://www.gale.cengage.com/DirectoryLibrary.

General Education Online. http://www.findaschool.org.

GovSearch. Bethesda, MD: Carroll Publishing. http://www.carrollpub.com/govsearch.asp.

Infobel. http://www.infobel.com/en/world.

International Literary Market Place, 2011. Medford, NJ: Information Today, 2010. 1800 pp.

LexisNexis Corporate Affiliations. 8 vols. New Providence, NJ: LexisNexis Business Data Group, 2010.

LexisNexis Corporate Affiliations Online. New Providence, NJ: LexisNexis Business Data Group. http://www.corporateaffiliations.com.

Libweb: Library Servers via WWW. http://lists.webjunction.org/libweb.

Literary Market Place, 2011. 2 vols. Medford, NJ: Information Today, 2010.

LiteraryMarketPlace.com. Medford, NJ: Information Today. http://www.literarymarketplace.com.

Million Dollar Database. Bethlehem, PA: Dun & Bradstreet. http://www.dnbmdd.com/mddi.

Million Dollar Directory. 5 vols. Bethlehem, PA: Dun & Bradstreet, 2010.

National Faculty Directory. 42nd ed. 2 vols. Farmington Hills, MI: Gale, 2010. Also available online as part of *Gale Directory Library*.

NetAdvantage. New York: Standard & Poor's Corporation. http://www.netadvantage.standardandpoors.com.

Official Museum Directory. 2 vols. New Providence, NJ: National Register Publishing, 2011.

Patterson's American Education 2011. Schaumburg, IL: Educational Directories, 2011. 934 pp.

Patterson's American Education/CD. Schaumburg, IL: Educational Directories. CD-ROM.

Patterson's Elementary Education 2011. Schaumberg, IL: Educational Directories, 2011. 1103 pp.

Peterson's Four-Year Colleges 2011. Lawrenceville, NJ: Peterson's, 2010. 1516 pp.

Peterson's Graduate & Professional Programs 2011. 45th ed. 6 vols. Lawrenceville, NJ: Peterson's, 2011.

Publishers Directory. 35th ed. Farmington Hills, MI: Gale, 2010. 1426 pp. Also available online as part of *Gale Directory Library*.

ReferenceUSA. Omaha, NE: Infogroup. http://www.referenceusa.com/.

Scholarly Societies Project. Waterloo, Ontario: University of Waterloo Library. http://www.scholarly-societies.org.

Standard & Poor's Register of Corporations, Directors and Executives. 2 vols. New York: Standard & Poor's Corporation, 2011. Also available online as part of *NetAdvantage.*

State and Local Government on the Net. http://www.statelocalgov.net/index.cfm.

Switchboard. http://www.switchboard.com.

ThomasNet.com. New York: Thomas Publishing. http://www.thomasnet.com.

Ward's Business Directory of U.S. Private and Public Companies. 53rd ed. 8 vols. Farmington Hills, MI: Gale, 2010. Also available online as part of *Gale Directory Library.*

Washington Information Directory 2010–2011. Washington, D.C.: CQ Press, 2010. 976 pp.

Washington Information Directory. Washington, D.C.: CQ Press. http://library.cqpress.com/wid.

World Guide to Libraries 2011. 25th ed. 2 vols. München: K.G. Saur, 2010.

Worldwide Government Directory with International Organizations. Washington, D.C.: CQ Press, 2011. 2016 pp.

World PowerBase. Washington, D.C.: CQ Press. http://library.cqpress.com/world-powerbase/.

ADDITIONAL READINGS

Basar, Ivan. "Directory Publishing in Canada: The Last Hundred Years." *Serials Librarian* 37 (1999): 59–82.

Basar discusses the history of directory publishing in Canada, tracing the growth of the city directory and its relationship to emerging industrial and advertising interests in the 19th and early 20th centuries.

Boettcher, Jennifer, and Bruce R. Kingma. "Telephone Directories: Alternatives to Print." *Reference Services Review* 22 (Summer 1994): 53–61.

This article provides a literature review and comparative cost analysis of different phone directory formats.

Gooden, Susan. "College Guides." *Booklist* 104 (May 15, 2008): 84–85.

Gooden describes both print and electronic guides suitable for library collections, including guides from the College Board, Peterson's, Princeton Review, Macmillan, and *U.S. News & World Report.* Selected more specialized guides, such as *Treasure Schools: America's College Gems,* are also profiled.

Harrison, William. *The Description of England.* Ed. Georges Edelen. Ithaca, NY: Cornell University Press, 1968. 512 pp.

Harrison's *Description* is a well-known antiquarian and topographical classic that provides a comprehensive portrait of late 16th-century England. He profiles many features of the English landscape of the time, including inns, roads, and townships. The descriptions and presentation influenced later reference resources such as gazetteers, almanacs, and directories.

Hartman, Donald K., and Charles A. D'Aniello. "Subscribe to an Online Directory Today, Frustrate a Researcher Tomorrow: Are Print Directories Dead?" *College & Research Libraries News* 67 (April 2006): 222–26.

Hartman and D'Aniello argue that "superseded directories have a value and utility that transcend their immediate purpose," providing details of use to historical researchers. They give examples of reference questions that can be answered through consultation of superseded volumes. The article concludes with guidelines for building and retaining a core directory collection.

Leland, John. *John Leland's Itinerary: Travels in Tudor England*. Ed. John Chandler. Stroud, Gloucestershire, UK: Sutton Publishing, 1998. 601 pp.

This book presents descriptions of parts of Leland's 1535–1543 journeys across England, Wales, Scotland, and Ireland. Of particular interest are the directory-like profiles of church and monastic library collections in the British Isles at the time.

Stow, John. *A Survey of London, Written in the Year 1598*. Ed. William J. Thoms. London: Chatto & Windus, 1876. 222 pp.

Stow's work is a classic view of late Tudor London and includes descriptions of churches, businesses, and other establishments for travelers of that period.

Tobin, Carol M. "The Book That Built Gale Research: The *Encyclopedia of Associations*." In *Distinguished Classics of Reference Publishing*, ed. James Rettig, 89–97. Phoenix, AZ: Oryx Press, 1992.

This chapter provides a description of the evolution of the *Encyclopedia of Associations*, including such topics as the method of compilation and computerized production of this directory.

Almanacs, Yearbooks, and Handbooks

Lori S. Mestre

USES AND CHARACTERISTICS

Almanacs, yearbooks, and handbooks frequently provide quick answers and summaries for factual questions. Even though much of this information may be available from other sources (such as atlases, directories, encyclopedias, journals, newspapers, and Web sites), almanacs, yearbooks, and handbooks provide a type of "one-stop shopping" as they consolidate, summarize, and synthesize information on various topics. Some of those topics include facts about people and organizations, current and historical events, countries, geographical data, political and historical data, statistics, and popular culture items such as sports and entertainment.

These sources are works that are designed to be consulted for specific information and can be enormously helpful for a wide range of uses. Some examples include:

- finding statistics, dates, addresses, formulas, and other sorts of factual information;
- getting a broad overview and background information on a topic;
- gaining a clear understanding of a topic, or a definition of an unfamiliar term;
- locating additional resources on a topic;
- learning more detailed information about a specific person, place, or topic;
- obtaining a summary of events and developments surrounding a topic; and
- discovering how to complete a task, solve a problem, or answer a question.

Many times, these tools can satisfy an initial query of a user, as they typically cover a broad spectrum of topics. However, because they do not include in-depth information, librarians need to evaluate the information needs of users, given that their initial query may have clues embedded in it that lead the librarian to consult other sources that would yield more detailed or analytical information.

Almanacs

Almanacs are collections of facts, statistics, and lists gathered together in a convenient format for easy reference. They are filled with up-to-date answers to all kinds of questions. The print version is generally updated annually and may contain a "year in review" summary. Two print examples of standard almanacs are *The World Almanac and Books of Facts* and the *Time Almanac*. The online version of the latter is the *Information Please Almanac*, part of the *Infoplease* Web site. General almanacs provide a snapshot of what the world or country was like in a given year, including summaries of major events, names of people in power, things that were prominent in the arts, and statistical information.

Some almanacs are focused on a given field and will provide a glimpse of the state of the world in regard to that particular topic, as well as show trends in that area. They are a significant source for statistical information and often contain citations for their sources of information. Additionally, they can be utilized for biographical or directory information.

Whether one is looking for specific dates, facts, statistics, measures, or information on topics such as state funding of welfare programs or recent winners of the Davis Cup, one can likely find the information in an almanac, along with charts, figures, and tables. Many times, the almanac can be the first source to consult, and then, after further reassessment of the query, one may need to consult other sources.

Almanacs are available in print and online. Many excellent online almanacs require no subscription fees, such as the *Information Please Almanac*. Although online almanacs can be more up-to-date than the print versions, the disadvantages may include a confusing interface, poor search options, and annoying advertisements. Additionally, when finding quick factual information, many times, it is faster to grab the print almanac behind the reference desk and flip to the chart or page (assuming there is a good index) than it is to go online, find the resource, and navigate through it to find that piece of information.

Brief History of Almanacs

Almanacs first appeared in the 16th and 17th centuries as calendars, containing days, weeks, and months and astronomical data such as the phases of the sun and moon, home remedies, and folk wisdom. They were among the most widely owned books in 18th- and early 19th-century America. The main role of almanacs was to show the progress of time. The first annual almanacs were published at the turn of the 15th and 16th centuries, recording events of the previous year, and soon afterward, additional parts were appended to the original content. By the end of the 16th century, they included practical advice for many topics of everyday life, such as the weather forecast, the expected harvest, advice about nourishment, health regulations, and economic guidelines.

It was noted that Christopher Columbus used the *Perpetual Almanac* of Abraham Zacuto, an astronomer from Spain. Columbus used the astronomical data in this almanac to help him navigate as he attempted a new passage to the Indies, which instead led him to the New World.[1] Using information he got from his almanac, he even impressed the natives on his fourth visit (to Jamaica) with his forecast of a solar eclipse on February 29, 1504. They believed he had control over celestial matters and consequently supplied him with food.[2]

By the 17th and 18th centuries, almanacs had developed into a form of folk literature, with notations of anniversaries and interesting facts, home medical advice, statistics of all sorts, jokes, and even fiction and poetry. The most famous American almanac was Benjamin Franklin's *Poor Richard's Almanack* (published by him 1732–1757), which, in its title, recalled one of the most popular and long-lasting of English almanacs, that of "Poor Robin" (founded ca. 1662). *The Old Farmer's Almanack* was first published in 1792 by Robert Bailey Thomas, continuing from Franklin's almanac, and is still published today. Other important almanacs that are still key resources are *The World Almanac and Book of Facts* (first published as a booklet in 1868, discontinued in 1876, and revived in 1886) and the *Information Please Almanac* (first published in 1947, now the *Time Almanac*).

In the 19th century, American newspapers began to publish almanacs. These almanacs developed from the newspapers' need for easy access to accurate, factual information about political, historical, and current events[3] and were more like the contemporary almanacs discussed in this chapter. These latter-day almanacs include some astronomical and calendar data, but more importantly, they are compendia of current and retrospective statistics and facts.

Contemporary Usage of Almanacs

Although most almanacs are broad in geographical and subject coverage, many of the best-known general almanacs emphasize a particular country, such as the *Canadian Almanac and Directory*, or state, such as the *Texas Almanac*. Although the contemporary almanac consists of fact rather than folklore, the most famous general almanacs are still rooted in popular culture, which explains many aspects of their content. Sports, entertainment, practical information such as ZIP codes, first aid treatment, and business addresses are typically part of the content.

Because of the broad range of factual material in almanacs, they are often used for trivia contests. In fact, rare is the librarian who has not been consulted by someone trying to "win a bet" with a friend by recalling a certain fact or needing to answer a question. The librarian reaches instinctively for the almanac at hand and in a matter of seconds can solve the dispute. If, by chance, the user wants to delve further into a topic, the librarian can provide the citation of the originating source and then consult that as well. Following are other examples of questions whose answers can be found in an almanac:

- What is a Category 5 hurricane?
- How many calories are in a tablespoon of butter?
- How many centimeters are in an inch?
- Who was the youngest president of the United States?
- What is the address of the Special Libraries Association?
- What percentage of adult Americans smoke?

- What is the suicide rate among teenagers?
- Where can one find a map showing international time zones?
- What is the population of Australia?
- For how many seasons was Michael Jordan a scoring leader in the National Basketball Association?

Yearbooks

Yearbooks are useful for giving an overview of trends that occurred in a particular year. Most yearbooks are released annually and are sometimes referred to as *annuals*. Although yearbooks do not contain information from previous years, they do contain quite a bit of information dealing with that one particular year, often organized by characteristics such as subject area or geographic boundary. They can serve as a factual and historical account of the year and may be documentary in nature. Although many yearbooks are general in scope, there are also many that deal with particular topics and include statistical information. Sometimes yearbooks are subject-specific—for instance, *Yearbook of the United Nations* or *Africa South of the Sahara*—and will provide a snapshot of the state of the world that year in regard to a particular topic. They can also be used to find factual information about the events, organizations, people, places, and trends that had an effect on the lives of people living during the time period.

Because nomenclature for reference books is not consistent, almanacs may be called yearbooks and vice versa. Encyclopedias often issue yearbooks that supplement the main set and chiefly review a specific year, such as *Britannica Book of the Year*. These yearbooks contain a chronology of the year, biographies of newsmakers, obituaries, sports news, current statistical data, and articles about events of the year.

A general yearbook is the place to find information such as the following:

- An obituary for a person who died during the year
- A description of a disaster that occurred during the year
- The winner of a major athletic event that happened during the year
- Discussion of a current controversial social problem
- Chronology of important political happenings

Comparison of Almanacs and Yearbooks

Although a general almanac also provides some of the same information as a yearbook, the yearbook's presentation of the information is different. Almanacs are full of bits of data on a wide spectrum of topics, whereas a yearbook can provide more in-depth information on a specific topic. They fill different information needs. If a library user wants to know whether someone died in a given year, he or she can consult an almanac, looking under "obituaries." However, for more in-depth information and perhaps a picture, a library user could consult an encyclopedia yearbook under personal name and find a longer entry. A general almanac will satisfy a sports fan wanting box scores from the most recent World Series, but a yearbook will be a more suitable tool for a fan wanting a game-by-game description of the series.

Yearbooks regularly index personal names, whereas almanacs, in print format, index personal names sparingly. Yearbooks usually contain longer descriptions of events and more analysis and evaluation, and articles are almost always signed (meaning the name of the author of that article is included, rather than no attribution). Yearbooks customarily have larger and more readable type than almanacs in book format. With the abundance of online sources, the distinction between almanacs and yearbooks blurs, given that online almanacs now tend to include more in-depth information or link out to additional information.

Handbooks and Manuals

The terms *handbook* and *manual* are used almost interchangeably. In fact, some of these resources are called *guides*. Although some reference works of this type actually do explain how to do something (for example, how to format a citation to a journal article or how to repair your car), these books are more than just "how to" books.

Handbooks

A handbook generally covers a limited area of knowledge and can be used by people interested in gaining in-depth knowledge about a specific topic. Handbooks generally pertain to a specific subject, such as chemistry or physics, and contain quick facts, charts, formulas, tables, statistical information, historical background, and perhaps lists of organizations connected to the subject. A handbook can serve as a handy guide to a particular subject, with all of the critical information that one might need for a particular field in one book. Often, large amounts of information about a subject are compressed into a single volume.

Some handbooks are geared to those who have a basic knowledge of the subject area and may contain information and language that may be difficult for casual readers to comprehend. Because they are updated frequently, handbooks may include information about new developments. References to additional information are usually included.

Handbooks organize bits of important data that will enable the reader to do something. For instance, the *CRC Handbooks* (the most important in the physical sciences) provide the data needed for the equations necessary for doing scientific experiments. The *DSM-IV* (*Diagnostic and Statistical Manual of Mental Disorders*) is the diagnostic manual for psychiatry and provides all of the necessary diagnostic criteria for diagnosing a patient. The *Physicians' Desk Reference* (*PDR*) provides physicians with the necessary information to prescribe medications.

In addition to the multitude of specialized handbooks available, there are many subject handbooks that are guides to various scientific fields and to religion, history, literature, and social sciences. Many of these are available in *Oxford Reference Online*, including *The Oxford Companion to Medicine*, *The Oxford Companion to Philosophy*, *The Oxford Companion to American Theatre*, and so on. *Credo Reference* is another online subscription service that contains more than 475 full-text reference sources (from more than 70 publishers). There are freely available handbooks as well, such as the online government handbook *Statistical Abstract of the United States*, which is a standard statistical resource. This handbook is almost always within reach of reference librarians for the quick statistical information it provides.

Manuals

Manuals, much like handbooks, deal with very specific subject matter and are narrow in scope. They are often used when one needs information dealing with a topic or procedure on a much more focused, detail-oriented level.

Manuals provide step-by-step instructions on how to do specific tasks. They can show one how to rebuild a carburetor, conduct a scientific experiment, apply for financial aid, correctly format papers or cite information in a bibliography, and so on. One example of a manual frequently found in public libraries or linked from their web pages is Chilton's automotive repair guides. There are more than 40,000 from 1910 onward of these types of manuals on how to repair automobiles.

Handbooks and manuals provide answers to questions such as the following:

- Are there any adverse side effects to this drug?
- What happened in history on November 23, my birthday?
- Is the Willis Tower the world's tallest building?
- How do I format a bibliography?
- What do I wear to a formal evening wedding?

EVALUATION

In evaluating almanacs, yearbooks, and handbooks, accuracy, comprehensiveness, currency of information, and ease of use are all important to both user and librarian.

Accuracy

Accuracy is the single most important characteristic of works that present factual information. When assessing resources for accuracy, reference librarians can read reviews, compare data in different sources, and rely on personal expertise. The long-time reputation of a work is also a guide, subject to continual reevaluation. In online sources and even in the most prestigious works, however, errors can occur. Librarians can take a proactive role in reporting these errors to the publisher so that they can be corrected in subsequent editions or by addenda.

Indexing

The index in a fact book should be helpful, accurate, and internally consistent in style and terminology, and it should complement the overall arrangement of the work. Some yearbooks include a cumulative index that covers more than the current volume. This is an extremely useful feature if, for example, the exact date of an event is unknown.

Indexes are critical tools, especially in almanacs because they contain lots of bits of information. To help guide the reader, the first page may list the types of topics covered. Both a very specific index and a "Quick Reference Index" (very general) may also be available.

Documentation

Many almanacs, yearbooks, and handbooks are composed, at least in part, of secondhand information. The statistics should be recent and from identified sources. Identification should be complete enough to lead to the original source where additional information might be located. Reference works without documentation are of questionable reliability.

Comprehensiveness

Almanacs, yearbooks, and handbooks are a source of information on a single subject or on many subjects. They should be comprehensive within their stated scope, or they have little value.

Uniqueness

A certain amount of overlap in reference collections is desirable because users' needs vary in terms of the amount and presentation of information. Nonetheless, the reference work should provide either some unique information or a unique approach to information. One should assess the existing collection to ascertain whether the purchase or subscription will fill a gap in the collection.

Format

Almanacs, yearbooks, and handbooks should be organized in a logical manner, one that the user can understand. Because many of these publications are inexpensive, they are sometimes less physically attractive than other types of reference books, but readability is still an important consideration. With many of the resources now available online, there is a great possibility of enhanced access through the use of keyword and Boolean searching, as well as multiple access points. The design of the interface needs to be user-friendly and intuitive to the user. If the indexing and search engine of the resource are incomprehensible, the resource will be of little value. Good search features should include a well-designed main page with multiple search possibilities, browsing capabilities, and organization by categories. Some government online sources suffer from their interface design and lack of good search features. Finding information online through some of these resources can be frustrating and time-consuming and can end with incomplete answers. Even though the government online sources may be free, it is important for librarians to select Web pages and resource lists that will assist users rather than frustrate them. Part of the role of librarians, in cases where they see a need for improvement in the pages, should be to contact the organizations (or Web managers) with suggestions. Oftentimes, this gesture results in improved navigation and features.

Currency

Almanacs and yearbooks are published yearly with the most up-to-date information. However, one should keep in mind that a 2011 almanac will contain statistics and events from 2010. For example, the 2008 *World Almanac and Book of Facts* includes obituaries and a chronology of events through October 11, 2007. When looking for the current Secretary of State, the librarian must be sure to use the most recent edition of the almanac and possibly do a second check on the Web site for the Secretary of State's office. For historical information (e.g., who *was* the Secretary of State during the Clinton administration?), older books are acceptable sources. Online editions of these tools can be updated more frequently, but this varies, so it is always important to check the date of the information and verify the information. For example, a user recently asked for the salary that members of Congress receive. The answer varied in two reputable online almanacs. In one of the almanacs, that piece of information had not been updated in five years.

SELECTION

All libraries need reference works that answer the information demands of their users. Even libraries with minimal budgets should have a few standard sources in their ready-reference collection, and one is a good almanac, even if it is a paperbound edition. Not all almanacs contain identical information, so purchasing a couple could be useful in ferreting out those little nuggets of information. However, if the library has Internet access, it can bookmark some freely available (good-quality) almanacs, such as the *Information Please Almanac*.

Almanacs, yearbooks, and handbooks tend to offer very good value at a low cost. However, cost may be a determinant. Some general reference departments in public and academic libraries and many school libraries can afford to purchase a moderately priced yearbook such as *The Statesman's Yearbook* but not the more expensive *Europa World Year Book*.

Characteristics of users, such as age, education, and occupation, influence decisions about which works to purchase. Various types of libraries have some of the same almanacs, yearbooks, and handbooks, but there are significant differences in emphasis between these types. Public libraries often get requests for information about how to make or repair household items and machinery. Some of the standards in this area are now available online, such as *HowStuffWorks*. Automobile repair manuals are also in demand, and all but the smallest public library will have at least one such manual. However, if a library can afford it, it can subscribe online to a large number of manuals through *ChiltonLibrary.com*, rather than having to purchase and shelve individual manuals. Reference works relating to hobbies and games—for example, bird watching, various kinds of collecting, craft work, card games, and the like—are standard tools in public library reference departments, even still in print, because users want to have the book in hand to consult. Other common specialized almanacs, yearbooks, and handbooks in public libraries relate to questions of health, investments, consumer affairs, legal matters, and popular entertainment. Again, there are many excellent online options, many freely available that librarians could bookmark or add to their virtual reference collection. Some selected titles are described in this chapter.

Academic libraries may have a representative set of almanacs, yearbooks, and handbooks such as those found in public libraries, but because they generally serve a different clientele, they concentrate on scholarly and educational sources and acquire the resources that support teaching and research. School libraries generally have smaller collections, and the intellectual level of the student body affects the books selected. Some almanacs, yearbooks, and handbooks are available in youth editions. Special libraries have as many specialized handbooks in their field as budgets will allow.

Almanacs and encyclopedia yearbooks consist of information that may be more extensively treated in other sources. The decision of whether to rely on the almanac and yearbook to supply information or to purchase specialized sources depends on budget, similar sources available, and the frequency of demand for the type of in-depth information. For example, *The World Almanac* has a list of "Associations and Societies." This list provides the founding date, address, and number of members of approximately a thousand organizations. The *Encyclopedia of Associations* (discussed in chapter 14) provides additional information about more organizations. Most general reference collections own the *Encyclopedia of Associations*, but small or specialized libraries may find that *The World Almanac* meets most of their needs, especially if they have Internet access and can search for information online.

For many librarians, regardless of the size and budget of their library, referral is another way of responding to a request that cannot be answered using the library's collection, the Internet, or expertise. The availability of other reference collections, colleagues in other libraries, and services in a community can be tapped, thus allowing the library to forgo an unnecessary purchase of a little-used reference tool. The Web can also expand the resources of libraries. The *ipl2* is an example of a freely available resource that librarians can bookmark, add to Web pages, and perhaps even catalog. It includes a searchable, subject-categorized directory of authoritative Web sites and links to online texts, newspapers, magazines, and special collections. *Ipl2* merged the collections of resources from the Internet Public Library (IPL) and the Librarians' Internet Index (LII), creating an indispensable resource for answering reference queries. There are also numerous electronic discussion groups that librarians can join to post questions for hard-to-find answers. Many electronic discussion groups are archived, and users can check the archive to see if a question has already been answered.[4]

Online Options

With so many resources available online now, librarians need to consider whether they are viable options and whether they should be acquired as an alternative to the print version, along with the print, or not at all. Two categories of online options are available to librarians: *open source* (freely available sources) that do not require subscription and *subscription sources*. Generally, one would think that the subscription sources would be more reliable, be easier to search, and have better formatting and access. That is not always the case, and it may be that a subscription source is not any better than a freely available source. Careful evaluation of the resources is required.

The acquisition of an electronic edition of an almanac, yearbook, or handbook depends on several factors. Does the electronic edition facilitate the retrieval of information better than a print version? Is it more current? Is it frequently used? Can it be easily integrated into the existing workspace? Is it part of a larger electronic product? For example, yearbooks are frequently part of the electronic edition of their parent encyclopedia. Because many of these tools are available from different vendors offering different interfaces, a secondary decision may be necessary to determine which version to acquire. Compatibility with other electronic products may determine vendor selection.

Many other factors influence the acquisition of electronic tools. The reliability and completeness of information is important, but enhanced search capabilities, including reliable links and full text, are also important. Online searching using vendors such as FirstSearch or Dialog, which allow a charge-per-search arrangement, may serve as an alternative to subscribing to a service, if occasional use of a tool is all that is required.

Other considerations for acquiring an online version of an almanac, yearbook, or handbook include selection process, system support, licensing agreements, cost, cataloging, and training. Regardless of whether the resource is free or part of a subscription, it should be treated as any other resource as far as the selection criteria are concerned. Librarians should get a trial to the product in all of the available interfaces. Some interfaces provide excellent search functions, formatting, categorization, and help. Others are not very intuitive and can be frustrating. If the resource does not provide better access than a print version or, in fact, makes finding the information difficult, one needs to determine whether the online version is a good choice. Additionally, though, one needs to consider whether the current library system or technology department is set up to support the resource. Are there additional plug-ins or features that the site uses that the librarian needs to add to public workstations? Will the resource be networked and, if so, for how many simultaneous users? Cost factors increase with more users.

Licensing agreements also need to be considered. Some of these negotiations can be quite lengthy. Many libraries belong to consortia that acquire electronic products at discounted rates. A representative from each reference department should be on the committee deciding which resources to select, so that the decisions of which tools to purchase are representative of the needs of each library. If it is decided to acquire an electronic resource, it should be cataloged (regardless of whether or not it was free). Tools should have multiple ways to be accessed, such as through the catalog, the library Web pages, and the library's electronic resource list. Training in use of these online tools also needs to occur, so that the highlights, pitfalls, and tips can be shared. For example, if the interface for the almanac (such as *The World Almanac* in *Lexis-Nexis*) is not very intuitive, training should be offered.

With the abundance of resources available on the Web, librarians are expected to use the Web and online databases as routine sources for information and need to continually upgrade their knowledge of what is available, as well as be informed about the credibility, currency, and reliability of the information. It may be, though, that librarians still prefer to consult the print version of a handbook because of the ease of referring quickly to the handbook's index and locating the information in a matter of seconds.

IMPORTANT GENERAL SOURCES

The reference collections in most libraries will contain almanacs, yearbooks, and handbooks. In this section, some examples of these genres are discussed. The examples were chosen either because they are widely used classics or because they are illustrative of subject-specific almanacs, yearbooks, and handbooks.

Almanacs

According to *Merriam-Webster's Online Dictionary*,[5] there are two kinds of almanacs. The traditional type is defined as "a publication containing astronomical and meteorological data for a given year and often including a miscellany of other information." The other is "a usually annual publication containing statistical, tabular, and general information."

Astronomical and Meteorological Data Almanacs

The Old Farmer's Almanac, published in print since 1792, is an example of the first type of almanac. It provides traditional almanac content, including astronomical information, weather forecasts, and gardening tips. It offers a freely available companion site that has been online since 1996. The weather pages in the almanac offer detailed seven-day forecasts for thousands of cities and towns across the United States and Canada. A searchable weather history database contains weather conditions for 2,000 locations in the United States and Canada for any date from 1946 to the present. Weather Features pages explain such phenomena as tornadoes and droughts. Gardening pages include frost charts, planting tables, and source lists for seeds and flowers. Astronomy pages offer charts and tables for various celestial events, including moon phases, comet and meteor appearances, and rise/set times for the sun, moon, and planets. Cooking pages, household pages, forums, and a Country Store are also available.

Some of the same features can be found at a similarly named site: the *Farmers' Almanac*. The editors of this site update the Weather, Gardening, and Best Days pages a few days before the beginning of each month. Also available are household tips; astronomy information; a message board; and fishing, gardening, and other calendars.

Statistical, Tabular, and General Information Almanacs

Examples of the second type of almanac are the *Information Please Almanac*, *The World Almanac and Book of Facts,* and *The New York Times Almanac*. Although these almanacs serve as general almanacs, they contain easily accessible statistical information.

The World Almanac and Book of Facts began in 1868 as a publication of the *New York World* newspaper. Although it prominently bears the date of the following year, the almanac is usually published annually at the end of November. In the print version, the center of the almanac contains a series of colored plates of countries' flags, a map of world time zones, and maps of various parts of the world. Millions of copies of *The World Almanac* are sold each year, and it annually makes the *New York Times*

"Paperback Best Sellers" list, not just because of library purchases, but also for home purchases.

Earlier in this chapter there was a comment about the importance of good indexes for almanacs. In the print version of *The World Almanac*, there are three indexes: a general index, a quick reference index on the last page, and a quick thumb index that uses black marks on the fore-edge of the volume to indicate the location of some sections of the almanac. The back cover of the paperback and the book jacket of the hardcover edition feature the list of headings for the quick thumb index. Although these sections have varied somewhat from year to year, they often include Year in Review, Astronomy and Calendar, Noted Personalities, Nations of the World, and Sports. A user can find the population of Botswana, for example, by using the quick thumb index to turn to Nations of the World, an alphabetically arranged summary of information about countries of the world, including the United States. The general index consists of topical subject headings and includes only a few personal names. The quick reference index is composed of keywords for some of the most sought-after information in the almanac. Those who understand the organization of the almanac will find this quick reference index easier to use, but less complete, than the general one.

The World Almanac is also available online from vendors such as OCLC First-Search and *LexisNexis*. Generally, the online search capabilities are enhanced because of different types of searching, including keyword searching. However, in some cases, the print edition is faster and easier to use. The general index of the print edition includes many subentries that do not appear in the electronic editions. The definition of a "Category 5 hurricane," the population of Australia, and the percentage of adult Americans who smoke can be easily ascertained through the use of the general index because "hurricanes," "Australia," and "smoking" are appropriately subdivided by "classifications," "area, population," and "adults," respectively. The electronic edition relies on keyword searching, and thus, results may not be as precise, depending on the terms used.

The *Information Please Almanac* has been published annually since 1947 by a series of publishers with variant titles. Its most recent title is the *Time Almanac*. "Information Please" was the name of a famous radio quiz program. The *Information Please Almanac* is very similar to *The World Almanac* both in content and in style. The print in the *Time Almanac* is more readable than that of *The World Almanac*, and the *Time Almanac* indexes more personal and place names. Each almanac has some information the other almanac does not. *Time Almanac*, for instance, has a TIME 100 list of influential individuals for the year but does not have a glossary for scientific concepts frequently in the news.

The *Information Please Almanac* online (http://www.infoplease.com) includes information from the *Time Almanac* and the *ESPN Sports Almanac*. The almanac information is integrated with the *Random House Unabridged Dictionary* and *The Columbia Encyclopedia* (6th ed.) into a single reference source with a wealth of facts. The search page offers several ways to find information, including a keyword box, an index of topics, and a directory of information divided into the following categories: World and News, United States, History and Government, Biography, Sports, Arts and Entertainment, Business, Calendars and Holidays, Health and Science, Homework Center, and Fact Monster. One can click the Daily Almanac link near the top of the search page to access such features as "This Day in History," "Today's Word

Quiz," "Today's Weather Fact," and "Today's Birthdays." The site is continuously updated, offering more recent information than can be found in the paper edition. However, there are annoying pop-up ads from time to time.

The New York Times Almanac began publication in 1997. Coverage includes profiles of U.S. states and nations of the world, politics, education, health and medicine, the economy, the environment, science and technology, awards and prizes, sports, and obituaries. It features an extensive index.

The question "What percentage of Americans smoke?" illustrates the way in which two almanacs can differ. Figure 15.1 shows how this question is answered in *The World Almanac* and the *Time Almanac*, both with the publication year of 2009. Although the information came from the same source, the characteristics used in the charts differ (see Figure 15.1).

Almanacs for Children

The World Almanac for Kids appears annually in print and has a corresponding Web site. It offers a plethora of "kid-friendly" information on such topics as animals, the environment, nations, population, religion, birthdays and holidays, and mythology, and it has sections on sports, books, and states as well as a U.S. history time line. The site also offers a games area with puzzles, educational games, and quizzes.

Another online almanac for children is *Factmonster.com*. Drawing on the contents of the print *Time for Kids Almanac*, the freely available Web site offers information in various categories: World, United States, People, Science, Math and Money, Word Wise, and Sports. The Cool Stuff area includes information on art, architecture, business, entertainment, fashion, holidays, music, and worldwide dating and marriage customs. *Factmonster.com* also offers a Games and Quizzes area and a Homework Center. The Word Wise section includes information on children's literature, language facts, and a handy grammar and spelling resource. This reference also has a Reference Desk area. One can search all the information on the site through a simple keyword search box on the home page.

Country and Regional Almanacs

Many almanacs focus on countries or regions. *Whitaker's Almanack* was founded in London in 1868 by the publisher Joseph Whitaker. It emphasizes the United Kingdom in the way that *The World Almanac* and *Information Please Almanac* emphasize the United States. For this reason, it is a useful source for current information about the United Kingdom. For example, it lists historic landmarks, museums, and monuments, giving where appropriate a brief history, hours open, and admission charge. Other features include sections on British taxation, laws, and passport regulations. The almanac has extensive coverage of the British nobility, including a list of the English kings and queens, a list of peers and their heirs, orders of chivalry, and a list of baronetage and knightage. *Whitaker's* has a very extensive index, although personal names are generally not included. The *Cambridge Factfinder* has some of the same information as *Whitaker's*, from politics to sports to the arts, but includes more illustrations and features a thorough 100-plus page index.

Time Almanac 2009 with Information Please

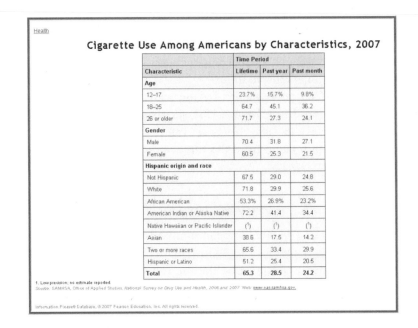

Cigarette Use Among Americans by Characteristics, 2007

Characteristic	Lifetime	Past year	Past month
Age			
12–17	23.7%	15.7%	9.8%
18–25	64.7	45.1	36.2
26 or older	71.7	27.3	24.1
Gender			
Male	70.4	31.8	27.1
Female	60.5	25.3	21.5
Hispanic origin and race			
Not Hispanic	67.5	29.0	24.8
White	71.8	29.9	25.6
African American	53.3%	26.9%	23.2%
American Indian or Alaska Native	72.2	41.4	34.4
Native Hawaiian or Pacific Islander	(¹)	(¹)	(¹)
Asian	38.6	17.5	14.2
Two or more races	65.6	33.4	29.9
Hispanic or Latino	51.2	25.4	20.5
Total	65.3	28.5	24.2

1. Low precision; no estimate reported.
Source: SAMHSA, Office of Applied Studies, *National Survey on Drug Use and Health, 2006 and 2007.* Web: www.nas.samhsa.gov.

Information Please® Database. © 2007 Pearson Education, Inc. All rights reserved.

The World Almanac and Book of Facts 2009

Cigarette Use in the U.S., 1985-2007

Source: Substance Abuse and Mental Health Services Administration (SAMHSA), U.S. Dept. of Health and Human Services
(percentage reporting use in the month prior to the survey; figures exclude persons under age 12)

	1985	2000	2004	2005	2006	2007
TOTAL	38.7	24.9	24.9	24.9	25.0	24.2
Sex						
Male	43.4	26.9	27.7	27.4	27.8	27.1
Female	34.5	23.1	22.3	22.5	22.4	21.5
Age group						
12-17	29.4	13.4	11.9	10.8	10.4	9.8
18 and older	47.4	38.3	39.5	39.0	38.4	36.2
26 and older	45.7¹	24.2	24.1	24.3	24.7	24.1

	1985	2000	2004	2005	2006	2007
Race/Ethnicity						
White	38.9	25.9	26.4	26.0	26.1	25.6
Black	38.0	23.3	23.5	24.5	24.4	23.2
Hispanic	40.0	20.7	21.3	22.1	22.4	20.5
Education²						
Non-high school graduate	37.3	32.4	34.8	34.8	35.6	32.9
High school graduate	37.0	31.1	30.4	31.8	31.9	31.9
Some college	32.6	27.7	29.0	28.1	27.7	26.8
College graduate	23.0	13.9	13.6	13.8	14.3	14.0

(1) Figures are for all persons aged 26 to 34 only. (2) Estimates for education are for persons aged 18 and older.

Figure 15.1. Comparison of statistics on smokers from the *Time Almanac* and *The World Almanac*.

Another almanac, the bilingual (English/French) *Canadian Almanac & Directory*, is introduced by a contents page that outlines its sections. In addition to statistical and other factual information specific to Canada, coverage includes directory information for organizations, federal and provincial governments, municipal governments, communications and information management, arts and culture, business and finance, health, education, and the legal system. A keyword index appears at the end of the volume, which is sent to press in November of the year prior to the date of publication. It is also available online from Grey House Publishing Canada. Many U.S. states have almanacs or yearbooks that describe their government, environment, population, and other facts and statistics about the state. The *Texas Almanac* is one example of this kind of almanac.

Specialized Almanacs

Numerous specialized almanacs are published, although some of these could easily be called either handbooks or yearbooks. In fact, one can now find an almanac or handbook for nearly every subject, from cults to politics to pseudonyms. A few examples give an indication of the wide variety available. The *International Motion*

BOX 15.1
ALMANAC SEARCH STRATEGY

An undergraduate student approached the librarian on duty at the reference desk. "I have just spent two hours on the Web searching for a list of counties that make up South Texas. Can you tell me how to find a list?" The librarian asked the student to show him her Web search strategy. The student had searched for "counties, South Texas" and "South Texas counties" on Google. The result was pages of results to scan through. A likely possibility had the heading of *DFPS—Counties in Region 8—San Antonio*. Indeed, this did include some charts with counties by region, and this link was for Region 8 and did mention South Texas. Had the student not been vigilant, she might have accepted this. In fact, there was another table with other counties from South Texas listed. Because the student had already searched through numerous links from Google, the librarian felt it prudent not to reproduce the search on other online sources, although he did see a link for *The Handbook of Texas Online* and various sites by government organizations. Knowing that the search capabilities within the sites might not be very intuitive, robust, or quick, he instead walked over to the reference shelf and looked in the *Texas Almanac* under "Counties" in the table of contents. He quickly located a table near the end of the chapter that classified counties by geographical region, as used by the Secretary of State in reporting election results. Later, the librarian double-checked those entries found on Google (at least on the first few pages) and realized that none of the Web lists corresponded to this official list, which the student used for her assignment.

Picture Almanac is a compilation of biographical, organizational, and statistical information concerning the motion picture industry, primarily in the United States. British, Irish, and Canadian film industries are reviewed, and basic information on the world market is provided. A table of contents and subject index are included. *The Almanac of American Politics* provides biographical information and political records of state governors and members of Congress. Published every two years, it is organized by state and, within each state, by congressional district.

Cities Ranked & Rated ranks more than 400 U.S. and Canadian cities according to climate, housing, health care, crime, transportation, education, the arts, recreation, and economics. *Library and Book Trade Almanac* (formerly *The Bowker Annual*) consists of reports written by library and information industry professionals about events of the previous year, topics of current importance, and activities of national associations and government agencies. In addition, it includes statistics, directories, awards, and other information of interest to librarians. The *NEA Almanac of Higher Education* highlights current information on employment conditions in higher education, including national salary data, trends in bargaining, and faculty workload. Two media giants publish sports almanacs: The *Sports Illustrated Sports Almanac* and the *ESPN Sports Almanac* include extensive statistics and coverage of sporting events for the preceding year. Commentaries are written by staff of the respective organizations.

Gale publishes a series of almanacs that describe the history and culture of American ethnic and racial minorities: *The African American Almanac*, *The Hispanic American Almanac*, *The Native North American Almanac*, and *The Asian American Almanac*. These reference works contain a vast amount of information about the present condition and past history of their respective groups, including heavily illustrated biographical information as well as photographs of famous places and events. The works also have some information related to the roots of the groups covered. For example, *The African American Almanac* has a section profiling the various countries in Africa. Each has a comprehensive index.

Yearbooks

As previously mentioned, yearbooks can cover general or specific areas of knowledge. One general yearbook that many libraries own is the *Britannica Book of the Year*. It updates articles in the *Encyclopaedia Britannica* (discussed in chapter 18) and is a chronicle of the events of a given year. It bridges the gap between editions of the *Encyclopaedia Britannica*. The majority of each yearbook is a review of happenings of the previous year. In addition, about a third of each volume provides a largely statistical description of the nations of the world, called "Britannica World Data." Sections cover images of the year and people of significance in the previous year, as well as obituaries for prominent people who died during the previous year. Special reports appear throughout "The Year in Review" and provide several-page discussions of topics of current interest. A cumulative, decennial index is an important feature of *Encyclopaedia Britannica Book of the Year* because it allows the user to locate information when the exact year is not known. Unlike many almanac indexes, yearbook indexes also contain personal names. In the decennial index, the date of the yearbook is indicated by boldface type followed by a page number; for example, **89:**14 refers to page 14 of the 1989 yearbook. The *Britannica Book of the Year* is included in *Britannica Online* (discussed in chapter 18). Articles from the yearbook are identified in the "search results" list after performing a search. The on-line edition offers the advantage of single-stop searching but is not necessarily more current than the print version.

Other encyclopedia annuals are similar in content and format to *Britannica Book of the Year* and have much in common with the almanacs previously discussed in this chapter. Both almanacs and this type of yearbook list such things as winners of sporting events, disasters, election results, and awards. Biographies in the yearbooks are more detailed and often include a photograph. Encyclopedia yearbooks help stretch the reference collection and are valuable in helping students, especially those in junior and senior high school.

Facts on File World News Digest, a yearbook in the making, is a weekly digest of information published in newspapers. Information about political, social, cultural, and athletic events is summarized in the weekly classified digest. Classifications such as "World Affairs," "Finance," "Science," "Arts," and "Sports" are used as headings. Lists of best-selling records, movies, and books are included, as are obituaries of notable people. The digests have references to related stories. Each weekly issue of *Facts on File* is placed in a yearly loose-leaf volume that includes a quick reference world atlas. A color-coded index is issued twice a month, with each index superseding the previous one; this index is replaced by a quarterly cumulative index that is in turn replaced by an annual index.

The text of *Facts on File* is divided into three columns and further subdivided by letters that appear on the margins. The index refers first to the date of the event (not the publication date of *Facts on File*) and then to one of the pages numbered continuously throughout the year, the margin letter, and column number. The index entry "8-26, 735G3" refers to page 735, margin letter G, column 3. The date (8-26) in the citation is helpful in identifying the time of an event but is not necessary to locate a specific item. Items are indexed under personal names, place names, subjects, and, where appropriate, title. The same news item is usually indexed in several ways. For example, an obituary of a business leader is indexed under personal name; under the heading "Deaths," which is subdivided by an alphabetical list of personal names; and under "Business and Industry," subdivided by obituaries.

Five-year cumulative indexes are issued for *Facts on File*, which has been published since 1940. An annual bound volume called *Facts on File World News Digest Yearbook* has been published since 1941. *Facts on File* in paper is an excellent resource. However, its index is daunting, and it may be necessary to consult more than one year to find certain kinds of information.

The online version of *Facts on File World News Digest* offered by Facts on File and LexisNexis helps to eliminate the aforementioned problems. It offers easy access to all of *Facts on File* with a complete archive of this publication of record back to 1940, which is updated every week. It also provides important indexing features not available in paper. The main menu offers a keyword search with the option of specifying date ranges to find news stories from a particular period. The online version offered by Facts on File also has a section titled "Need a Research Topic?" that offers short summaries of suggested research topics with a fully linked list of articles for each.

Facts that appear in *Facts on File* also appear in encyclopedia yearbooks and almanacs, but because *Facts on File* is updated every week, it is much more up-to-date. Another advantage to the digest is that it can serve as an index to other newspapers and newsmagazines. Because *Facts on File* gives specific dates for events, it aids users in locating newspaper articles. Although news magazines are indexed in periodical indexes, these indexes are not as detailed as the *Facts on File* index. However, *Facts on File* does not have the information organized in the concise way that almanacs do.

The print volumes of *Facts on File* occupy a large amount of space on the shelves and thus are not typically within reach at the reference desk. Some librarians have even had to take them out of Reference because of space needs. Therefore, having an online version of this indispensable resource is a great asset.

Two excellent yearbooks with international foci, commonly kept behind a reference desk, are *The Europa World Year Book* and *The Statesman's Yearbook*. Both consist of an initial section on international organizations, followed by alphabetically arranged countries of the world. They both aim to give a concise but complete description of organizations and countries and to emphasize the political and economic aspects of the world. However, each has unique characteristics.

Europa is published annually in two thick volumes. Volume 1 contains international organizations and the first part of the alphabetically arranged survey of countries; volume 2 contains the second part of the alphabet. International organizations are described in terms of structure, function, and activities. Names of important officials, budget information, and addresses are given. Information about individual countries is divided into three parts: introductory survey, statistical survey, and directories. The introductory survey has short essays on location, climate, language, religion, recent history, government, defense, economic affairs, and education. The statistical survey provides summary data about the country and is followed by separate directories for government, the press, religion, finance, and other areas. Entries for some of the industrialized countries include directories for periodicals, banks, and trade unions. The directory also has either a summary of or the complete constitution for each country.

The inclusion of this varied information makes *The Europa World Year Book* a one-stop reference work. The yearbook contains a short index to territories of the world. Statistical tables compare life expectancy, population, gross national product, and other topics among countries of the world. *The Europa World Year Book* obtains information from the institutions listed, as well as from many other sources, such as national statistics offices, government departments, diplomatic missions, and United Nations publications. The publisher of *The Europa World Year Book* also publishes nine regional surveys: *The Far East and Australasia*; *South Asia*; *The Middle East and North Africa*; *South America, Central America and the Caribbean*; *The USA and Canada*; *Central and South-Eastern Europe*; *Eastern Europe, Russia and Central Asia*; *Western Europe*; and *Africa South of the Sahara*. These surveys are similar in content to *Europa World Year Book* but include more information and a bibliography. The publication schedules range in frequency from annual to triennial. *Europa World Plus* enables online searching of *The Europa World Year Book* together with the nine regional surveys. In addition to search and browse options, the interface supports retrieval of comparative statistics from data included in the country profiles.

The Statesman's Yearbook, published annually since 1864, is a one-volume book. It includes country profiles covering key historical events, territory and population, social statistics, climate, constitution and government, government chronology, recent elections, current administration, current leaders, defense, international relations, economy, energy and natural resources, environment, industry, international trade, communications, social institutions, religion, culture, diplomatic representatives, and a list for further reading. The volume also has a chronology of world events from the previous year. *The Statesman's Yearbook* does have some special features, including lists of books about each country. The place and international organizations index is helpful in finding specific information. *The Statesman's Yearbook Online* supports searching and browsing the contents of the volume and is updated throughout the year.

A freely available Web-based resource that offers a bit of what *Europa* and *Stateman's* offer is *The World Factbook*. Made available by the U.S. Central Intelligence Agency, it provides only brief data and small maps for each country and does not compare in coverage to *Europa* or *Statesman's*. This site provides a reliable resource for information on independent states, dependencies, areas of special sovereignty, uninhabitable regions, and oceans. Each entry typically includes concise physical and demographic statistics, an outline of government, and an economic overview, as well as communications, transportation, and military information.

Yearbooks featuring only one country, such as the *Canada Year Book*, are also available. Profusely illustrated, in 31 chapters, it combines statistical data and short descriptions about every aspect of Canadian life, from aboriginal peoples and agriculture to transportation and travel and tourism. The volume also includes a list of maps, charts, and tables; a glossary; and an index.

As is true for almanacs, there are many yearbooks on special topics. Sometimes topical yearbooks update either a special or a general encyclopedia. The *McGraw-Hill Yearbook of Science and Technology*, for example, is an annual review and supplement to the *McGraw-Hill Encyclopedia of Science and Technology* (discussed in chapter 18). The yearbook updates the most recent edition of the encyclopedia and is arranged alphabetically by topic. Practitioners and researchers write entries. Bibliographies, cross-references, and an index are also included.

BOX 15.2
YEARBOOK SEARCH STRATEGY

An author writing a science fiction story about space flight wanted information about recent space expeditions. The librarian showed the writer entries under "space exploration" in the recent *Britannica Book of the Year* volumes. Although she found these articles helpful, the author wanted more technical information. When the librarian showed her the *McGraw-Hill Yearbook of Science and Technology*, the author found exactly the information she wanted. She did, however, have to look through several years, sometimes under "space flight" and sometimes under more specific topics, because coverage and indexing varied from year to year.

Other yearbooks review the activities of organizations or groups. The *Yearbook of American and Canadian Churches* and the *Yearbook of the United Nations* are examples. These annuals furnish statistics, directories, facts, and trends about a specific group and are often published as a handbook for the group's members. For example, the *Yearbook of American and Canadian Churches*, prepared and edited at the National Council of the Churches of Christ in the U.S.A., has directories and statistics of religious denominations and affiliated organizations in North America. The *Yearbook of the United Nations* summarizes events of a designated year, provides texts of important United Nations documents, and lists member nations and important officeholders.

Handbooks

That famous trivia book, *Guinness World Records* (formerly *The Guinness Book of Records*), is also a useful reference work. The first American edition of *Guinness* was published in 1956, and it has appeared annually since that time. With sales of more than 100 million copies in 100 different countries and 37 languages, *Guinness World Records* is the world's best-selling copyrighted book ever. A hurdle to using *Guinness* as a reference tool is in understanding what a record means. The records in the book are for every type of extreme: largest and smallest, worst and best, widest and narrowest, oldest and newest, and the like.

The reference librarian will find the subject index essential when using *Guinness*. The subject index, which does not include personal names, lists many specific terms in boldface type, in some cases also subdividing the term using normal typeface. In addition there is a superlatives index, with entries such as *first, heaviest, deepest,* and *youngest.* The Web-based version features only a selection of the records in the Guinness World Records database. Visitors can browse world records by category (such as "Natural World" or "Travel & Transport") or search by keyword.

Another record book, Joseph Nathan Kane's *Famous First Facts*, is an alphabetical subject list of "first happenings, discoveries, and inventions in American history."[6] Firsts included are quite diverse, from the invention of the tape measure to the first appearance of billiards in the United States. Five indexes, by subject, years, days of the month, personal names, and geographical areas, expand the usefulness of the work. *Famous First Facts*, now in its sixth edition, can be used to establish historical fact, to identify anniversaries, and to gather information about a specific place or time. The index to days of the month serves as a "book of days" for the United States. It is available online through WilsonWeb. *Notable Last Facts* includes an eclectic selection of the last of something (event, person, place, or thing), such as the last game played by Red Sox legend Ted Williams or the last works of some major author. The volume has broad topic areas and includes both individual lasts as well as those that can be grouped together.

Other "books of days" are common in reference collections. *American Decades* is a set of 11 volumes spanning the period 1900–2009. Each volume begins with a chronology of the decade, and the subject chapters concentrate on the important aspects of the period under consideration by providing biographies of prominent individuals; statistics; and information on arts, music, literature, government and politics, business, science and technology, and more. The set includes bibliographies and indexes. *Chase's Calendar of Events* lists birthdays of famous people (living and dead), festivals, historical anniversaries, presidential proclamations, special events, and the like for every day of the year. It contains more than 12,500 entries and is 752 pages long. Brief biographical information is included with each name, and the name and telephone numbers of event organizers are given where applicable. *Chase's* also lists the winners of many popular awards, such as television's Emmy Awards. Aside from the detailed index, the accompanying CD-ROM offers enhanced searching capabilities, as well as scheduling and grouping features. *The Folklore of World Holidays*, also arranged by the Gregorian calendar, describes customs and folklore surrounding 340 holidays in more than 150 countries, excluding the United States. *Today in History*, a Web site from the Library of Congress, highlights an event from American history with digitized items from the American Memory historical collections.

Another useful resource that serves as a type of handbook is *The New York Public Library Desk Reference*. It is a compilation of information frequently requested at library reference desks. "Religions," "Etiquette," "Personal Finances," and "Libraries and Museums" are a few of the chapter headings in this single-volume work. An important feature of *The New York Public Library Desk Reference* is a listing of additional sources of information at the end of each chapter. The source list consists of a directory of related organizations and a bibliography of reference works.

A standard handbook in almost all reference collections is the style manual. A style manual is consulted by writers, students, and librarians to help determine the format of papers, bibliographies, footnotes, and endnotes. Such a manual may also include helpful information of interest to authors and others concerned with publishing, such as information on the bookmaking process and copyright law and the rules of spelling and grammar.

Many publishers, organizations, and faculty prescribe a particular bibliographic style. One of the most common is that described in *The Chicago Manual of Style*. The manual is subdivided into numbered paragraphs. The paragraph numbers appear on the left-hand margin of a page. References in the index, except for tables and figures, are to paragraph numbers rather than page numbers. The volume has a glossary of technical terms, a bibliography, and an index. Since 2006, users have been able to subscribe online to *The Chicago Manual of Style Online,* which provides a searchable interface to the popular Chicago Style Q&A, updated advice on style issues from the editorial staff, and the content of *The Chicago Manual of Style.* Although the full online version requires a subscription, nonsubscribers can use the search function to identify a specific paragraph number and then refer to a hard copy of the manual. *A Manual for Writers of Research Papers, Theses and Dissertations*, by Kate L. Turabian, is adapted from *The Chicago Manual of Style* and is aimed primarily at students. Although there is generally a style guide for each discipline, the other commonly required style manuals are the *MLA Handbook for Writers of Research Papers* and the *Publication Manual of the American Psychological Association*.

Citation style guides also include information on how to cite electronic publications and resources found on the Web. The bibliographic conventions for these sources are continuously under development as new types of formats emerge. Some publications have developed bibliographic styles exclusively for electronic publications. One useful source that focuses on electronic style and the Internet is Janice R. Walker and Todd Taylor's *Columbia Guide to Online Style*. It is divided into two sections, "Locating and Citing Source Materials" and "Preparing Manuscripts for Print and Electronic

Publication." Librarians can also subscribe to bibliographic management systems, such as RefWorks, NoodleBib, Reference Manager, and EndNote.[7] These systems are like personal databases of citations that allow one to insert citations in papers and create bibliographies in a matter of seconds based on almost any citation style. Some of them, such as RefWorks, are Web-based and allow for exporting of citations from databases.

Because many library users ask for assistance in solving practical problems of day-to-day living, etiquette books, another type of handbook, are a part of most public and academic library reference collections. Long considered the standard, *Emily Post's Etiquette*, currently edited by Peggy Post, has a subject arrangement covering such topics as "Greetings and Introductions," "Table and Party Manners," and "The Finer Points of Tipping." It has an excellent index. *Miss Manners' Guide to Excruciatingly Correct Behavior* is one of several additional or alternative guides. *Miss Manners*, written by Judith Martin, is also organized by subject and well indexed but differs from *Emily Post's Etiquette* in that it consists of letters written to "Miss Manners" and her responses to the letters.

When Henry M. Robert discovered that associations, societies, and other organized groups needed rules of etiquette to govern their conduct at meetings, he wrote his classic reference work on parliamentary procedure, *Robert's Rules of Order*. It was originally published in 1876, and many editions have appeared since then.[8] *Robert's Rules of Order Newly Revised* has been updated to incorporate new rules, interpretations, and procedures made necessary by the evolution of parliamentary procedure. A companion volume, *Robert's Rules of Order Newly Revised in Brief*, offers guidance in applying the rules.

Questions about sickness, health, and medicine are commonplace in many reference departments. Fortunately, the quality and amount of consumer health information has increased over the past few years.[9] Although reference librarians should not attempt to provide medical advice, a number of handbooks assist the user in understanding health-related issues. Merck Research Laboratories publishes *The Merck Manual of Diagnosis and Therapy*, a widely used medical handbook that provides essential information on diagnosing and treating medical disorders, with 22 major sections by body system and medical specialty. *The Merck Manual of Medical Information* is a comprehensive consumer health version of the previous title, offering straightforward discussions of diseases and other health problems. It describes symptoms and suggests possible treatments. Both titles are also available online. Another excellent handbook, *Mayo Clinic Family Health Book*, describes various parts of the body and their diseases or ailments. Written in easy-to-understand language, it is abundantly illustrated and has a comprehensive index. The Web site *MayoClinic.com*, sponsored by the Mayo Foundation for Medical Education and Research, provides extensive consumer health information under the categories "Diseases and Conditions," "Symptoms," "Drugs and Supplements," "Tests and Procedures," and "Healthy Living."

Physicians' Desk Reference (PDR), a handbook intended for physicians, is also at home in a general reference department. It is a compilation of product information on package inserts found in all available prescription drugs. The *PDR* includes Food and Drug Administration (FDA)–approved information on more than 4,000 prescription drugs and important data on more than 250 drug manufacturers. Data comply with FDA regulations and are fairly uniform and concise. *PDR* is alphabetically arranged by manufacturer and then by trade name of drugs, and access is provided by several indexes at the beginning of the book. *PDR* indexes manufacturers, brand and generic names, and product categories. The product identification section of the work shows pictures of the different drugs and aids in verifying the name of a particular drug. An online resource, *PDRHealth*, is written in lay terms and is based on the FDA-approved drug information found in the *PDR*. Coverage includes prescription drugs, over-the-counter drugs, and herbals and supplements, all organized alphabetically. A search option looks for keywords within the entries for each drug. In October 1998 the National Library of Medicine launched the *MedlinePlus* Web site, an extensive portal that links users to high-quality sources of consumer health information. The site has a "Drugs & Supplements" section with profiles of prescription and over-the-counter medications as well as herbs and supplements.

Legal and business questions occur frequently at the reference desk. Though they cannot offer legal or business advice, reference librarians can guide users to appropriate sources. Many guides are available, such as *The Legal Researcher's Desk Reference*, *Legal Research: How to Find and Understand the Law*, and *Legal Research in a Nutshell*, that help librarians locate information. These tools, however, usually require a bit of effort on the user's behalf to interpret and proceed. The *American Bar Association Family Legal Guide* is a book designed for the average user.

Handbooks such as *Hoover's Handbook of American Business* are useful guides to business. *Hoover's Handbook* profiles more than 750 companies. The profiles contain descriptions of each enterprise, its management, its key competitors, and its history of sales and growth. Hoover's also publishes the *Hoover's Handbook of World Business*, covering 300 of the most influential firms from Canada, Europe, and Japan as well as companies from the fast-growing economies of such countries as China, India, and Brazil. *Hoover's Online* combines its series of handbooks and offers free but limited access to company information, with full profiles and additional features available to subscribers. Many librarians subscribe to the full version. For questions about occupations, the biennial *Occupational Outlook Handbook* is a valuable source. Entries cover the nature of the job, working conditions, employment statistics, job outlook, training, earnings, and sources of further information. The contents of the

---

BOX 15.3
HANDBOOK SEARCH STRATEGY

A user is headed to the public library after being advised by his doctor to consider drug therapy in addition to diet to help lower his elevated cholesterol level. The librarian found a reference in the *Physicians' Desk Reference* "product category" index from cholesterol reducers to cardiovascular agents known as antilipemic agents. Several types of cholesterol-reducing drugs were listed under antilipemic agents. The user was able to consult the listed references to learn more about the drugs, including warnings about possible negative effects. If the user had known the specific name of a drug, he could have also consulted *PDRHealth* or the "Drugs & Supplements" listings on the *MedlinePlus* Web site.

free Web-based version can be searched by keyword or browsed by category or in alphabetical order by occupation name.

Hobbies and special interests bring many users to the reference desk. Handbooks on topics such as genealogy, sports, and films are invaluable aids in helping them. *The Researcher's Guide to American Genealogy*, by Val D. Greenwood, is considered by many to be the best single guide to genealogical research. It explains both the principles of genealogical research and the use and value of specific records. David Wallechinsky's *The Complete Book of the Olympics* answers many questions about the Olympic Games. This handbook not only summarizes Olympic records in every competitive sport; it also provides descriptions and stories of human interest for each event. Because *The Complete Book of the Olympics* is updated every four years, it does not include records of the latest Olympic games and is valuable for retrospective, rather than current, information.

Students of film, as well as movie buffs, will find answers to many of their questions in *Halliwell's Who's Who in the Movies*. The alphabetically arranged guide includes short biographies of actors, directors, writers, and other film-related persons; definitions of terms; plots of selected movies; descriptions and examples of movie genres and themes; and more. Information ranges from a country-by-country breakdown of national film industries to lists of prize-winning films. The *Internet Movie Database* is a comprehensive Web source, with similar information and extensive links to other related Web sites. It offers free access to some information, but to get additional content, there is a subscription fee. Librarians may also want to refer users to *Leonard Maltin's Movie Guide* for quick plot summaries, basic movie credits, and video/DVD availability. Published annually and arranged alphabetically by title, the *Guide* includes a star index and a director index.

Handbooks also solve educational, professional, or research problems. In the sciences, the *CRC Handbook of Chemistry and Physics*, published since 1913, is a basic reference work for chemistry and physics. Composed primarily of tables, it describes or defines the structure, formulas, and phenomena of chemistry and physics. Physicists, chemists, and students of physics and chemistry use the handbook for research and study, and reference librarians consult it to answer questions for them. The handbook is available online as part of *CHEMnetBASE*.

The Science and Technology Desk Reference is a different sort of science reference book. Compiled by the Science and Technology Department at the Carnegie Library of Pittsburgh, *Desk Reference* provides answers to frequently asked or hard-to-answer questions. The questions answered are the kind that an average citizen or amateur scientist might ask. With questions arranged by subject, such as "Animal World," "Cars, Boats, Planes, Trains," "Health and Medicine," and "Weather," each answer has a citation to its source of information.

Literary handbooks are commonplace in most reference departments. *Benét's Reader's Encyclopedia* is a useful one-stop guide to authors, titles, plots, characters, literary terms, movements, and other information sought by book enthusiasts. Oxford University Press produces a series of respected "Oxford Companion" handbooks. Some of these companions, such as *The Oxford Companion to American Literature* and *The Oxford Companion to Canadian Literature*, serve as comprehensive guides to the literature of a particular country. These guides include historical themes and trends; biographies of writers; summaries of plots; and descriptions of literary awards, journals, societies, and so forth. *The Oxford Companion to the English Language* is a fascinating compendium of information about English, including histories of the countries where English is spoken. All the companions are arranged alphabetically by topic, with cross-references where necessary. They can be searched online as part of *Oxford Reference Online: Premium Collection.*

Masterplots is a series that has caused debate among librarians. This famous reference work summarizes the plots of major literary works, but it also offers critical assessments of the same works. The full text of the 70 volumes of all *Masterplots* series is available online through EBSCOhost as part of *MagillOnLiterature Plus.* Whether it is a prop for lazy students or an aid to research, it remains a staple in many reference collections. Another similar tool is *CliffsNotes* for summaries, character analyses, critical essays, and study help. The Web site allows one to read literature notes online free as well as purchase them.

SEARCH STRATEGIES

The first step in developing a search strategy is to determine the nature of the question. The sources described in this chapter provide simple, factual answers and in some cases lead users to more complex or detailed sources. If an almanac, yearbook, or handbook is an appropriate choice to answer a user's question, the librarian draws on a thorough personal knowledge of the collection to choose a source. Wise decisions depend on knowledge gained from previous use and continual reexamination of these reference works. The scope of the work and its strengths and weaknesses, publishing schedule, special features, and indexes are all factors to be considered. As more and more "fact books" appear in electronic formats, choice of format must also be considered. If the librarian keeps in mind that current, accurate information is the goal of every reference transaction, some of the decisions will be easy to make. C. Alan Joyce argues for the continuing value of titles such as *The World Almanac* "in a world where terabytes of information are a mouse-click away": they serve users and librarians "by filtering through massive quantities of data to bring its readers only the most essential statistics, in readable format; by delivering authoritative, reliable facts and practical information; and by avoiding, as much as is humanly possible, the modern urge to editorialize and manipulate data to support a particular point of view."[10]

Other factors influence the choice of source. If current information is required, frequently updated databases or Web sites are preferable. For difficult or hard-to-find information, the search capabilities of electronic resources make them better choices. On the other hand, for quick facts or simple information, books are often faster. Reference works with a national or regional slant usually have more information about these geographic areas than other sources and may be better sources for questions about those areas. It is important to remember, especially when relying on fact books, that more than one source can answer the same question. Often, comparing information in two or more sources may be the best way to serve the user.

The effective use of almanacs, yearbooks, and handbooks requires both patience and imagination. Successful search strategies can be written down and shared with colleagues. New technology can enhance the use of older sources, and an effort should be made to keep abreast of developments. There is no single magic formula

---

BOX 15.4
SEARCH STRATEGY: LOCATING INFORMATION ABOUT A COUNTRY

A high school student in a social studies course is engaged in a semester study of Liberia, requiring at least 25 different sources. He needs to discover information about the culture and language, geography, history, and political climate of the country. He begins by looking for Liberia on the Web using Google and finds the entry in *The World Factbook* ranked near the top of the list. Because he is overwhelmed by the number of listings, he consults his high school librarian for additional help. The librarian refers him to the *Infoplease* Web site and the high school's access to *Britannica Online*. Although he cannot rely on general encyclopedia articles, he finds that both of these sites give him additional resources to consult, including books and Web sites.

He goes to the public library to search for the books and to seek help from a reference librarian. One of the Web sites he located was about the colonization of Africa, and he wants more information on this topic. The librarian feels that *The African American Almanac* will be a good starting point. For more information about English as it is spoken in Liberia, she recommends *The Oxford Companion to the English Language*. Further, she suggests that the student consult *Facts on File World News Digest* online, where the student finds useful information about current political, social, and economic events of the country. Because he is also interested in locating primary sources, he asks the librarian for the name, address, and Web site (if applicable) of Liberian newspapers. She recommends that he look in *The Europa World Year Book*. She also suggests that he write to the Liberian Embassy in Washington, D.C., and that the address for the embassy can be located in *The Statesman's Yearbook*, but he tells her that he has already located the embassy's Web site. This background reading and research enable him to prepare to search the periodical indexes described in chapter 21.

---

to apply to the use of these reference works. This makes using them a challenge, but a rewarding one.

NOTES

1.   Abraham Zacuto, Joseph Vizinus, and Luciano Pereira da Silva. *Almanach Perpetuum Celestium Motuum: Radix 1473: Tabulae Astronomicae Abraham Zacuti*. Munich: Obernetter, 1915 facsimile. The almanac was found among Christopher Columbus's papers by his son, Ferdinand Columbus. There are no annotations in it, but the astronomical data correspond exactly with the calculations of Columbus, who was an expert in the science of navigation.

2.   William H. Calvin, *How the Shaman Stole the Moon: In Search of Ancient Prophet-Scientists: From Stonehenge to the Grand Canyon* (New York: Bantam Books, 1991), 223 pp.

3.   Margaret Morrison, "All Things to All People: The World Almanac," in *Distinguished Classics of Reference Publishing*, ed. James Rettig (Phoenix, AZ: Oryx Press, 1992), 313–21.

4.   Electronic discussion lists or Web pages that are useful for finding answers to difficult reference questions include LIBREF-L with archives and information for joining at http://listserv. kent.edu/cgi-bin/wa.exe?A0=LIBREF-L and the ipl2, with frequently asked reference questions at http://www.ipl.org/div/farq/.

5.   *Merriam Webster Online Dictionary*, "Almanac." http://www.merriam-webster.com/dictionary/almanac.

6.   Joseph Nathan Kane, Steven Anzovin, and Janet Podell, *Famous First Facts*, 6th ed. (New York: H. W. Wilson, 2006), title page.

7.   Jane Kessler and Mary K. Van Ullen, "Citation Generations: Generating Citations for the Next Generation," *Journal of Academic Librarianship* 31 (July 2005): 310–16.

8.   Sarah B. Watstein, "Demystifying Parliamentary Procedure: *Robert's Rules of Order*," in *Distinguished Classics of Reference Publishing*, ed. James Rettig (Phoenix, AZ: Oryx Press, 1992), 211–19.

9.   Mary L. Gillaspy, "Factors Affecting the Provision of Consumer Health Information in Public Libraries: The Last Five Years," *Library Trends* 53 (Winter 2005): 480–95.

10.   C. Alan Joyce and the Editors of *The World Almanac 2008*, "The Almanac in the Internet Age," *The World Almanac and Book of Facts* (New York: World Almanac Books, 2008), 7.

LIST OF SOURCES

Africa South of the Sahara 2009. 39th ed. London: Routledge, 2010. 1536 pp.

The African American Almanac. 10th ed. Farmington Hills, MI: Gale, 2008. 1468 pp. (The 11th edition is scheduled for publication in 2011.)

The Almanac of American Politics. Washington, D.C.: National Journal, 1972–. Biennial.

American Bar Association Family Legal Guide. 3rd ed. New York: Random House, 2004. 794 pp.

American Decades. 11 vols. Farmington Hills, MI: Gale, 1994–2011.

The Asian American Almanac. 2nd ed. Ed. Irene Natividad and Susan B. Gall. Detroit: U.X.L., 2004. 268 pp.

Benét's Reader's Encyclopedia. 5th ed. New York: Collins, 2008. 1168 pp.

Britannica Book of the Year. Chicago: Encyclopaedia Britannica, 1938–. Annual. Also available online as part of *Britannica Online*.

Cambridge Factfinder. 4th ed. Ed. David Crystal. New York: Cambridge University Press, 2000. 938 pp.

Canada Year Book. Ottawa: Statistics Canada, 1906–. Annual.

Canadian Almanac & Directory. Toronto: Grey House Publishing Canada, 1847–. Annual. http://circ.greyhouse.ca/.

Central and South-Eastern Europe 2010. 10th ed. London: Routledge, 2009. 852 pp.

Central Intelligence Agency. *The World Factbook*. https://www.cia.gov/library/publications/the-world-factbook/index.html.

Chase's Calendar of Events. Chicago: McGraw-Hill, 1995–. Annual. (Formerly *Chase's Annual Events*, 1954–1994.) Also available on CD-ROM.

The *Chicago Manual of Style*. 16th ed. Chicago: University of Chicago Press, 2010. 1026 pp. Also available online by subscription: http://www.chicagomanualofstyle.org/home.html.

ChiltonLibrary.com. Farmington Hills, MI: Gale. http://www.gale.cengage.com/ChiltonLibrary/.

Cities Ranked & Rated: Your Guide to the Best Places to Live in the U.S. & Canada. 2nd ed. By Bert Sperling and Peter Sander. Hoboken, NJ: John Wiley & Sons, 2007. 850 pp.

CliffsNotes. Hoboken, NJ: Wiley Publishing. http://www.cliffsnotes.com/WileyCDA/.

The *Columbia Guide to Online Style*. 2nd ed. By Janice R. Walker and Todd Taylor. New York: Columbia University Press, 2006. 288 pp.

The *Complete Book of the Olympics*. Ed. David Wallechinsky. London: Aurum Press, 2008. 1181 pp.

CRC Handbook of Chemistry and Physics. Boca Raton, FL: CRC Press, 1913–. Annual. Also available online as part of *CHEMnetBASE*.

Credo Reference. Boston, MA: Credo Reference. http://corp.credoreference.com/.

Diagnostic and Statistical Manual of Mental Disorders: DSM-IV-TR. 4th ed. Washington, D.C.: American Psychiatric Association, 2000. 943 pp. Also available online as part of STAT!REF: http://www.statref.com.

Eastern Europe, Russia and Central Asia. 10th ed. London: Routledge, 2009. 780 pp.

Emily Post's Etiquette. 17th ed. By Peggy Post. New York: HarperCollins, 2004. 876 pp.

ESPN Sports Almanac. New York: Hyperion ESPN Books, 1998–.

The *Europa World Year Book*. 2 vols. London: Routledge, Annual. Also available online as *Europa World Plus* at http://www.europaworld.com/pub/.

Factmonster.com. Boston, MA: Information Please, Pearson Education. http://www.fact monster.com.

Facts on File World News Digest with Index. New York: Facts on File, 1940–. Weekly. http://www.facts.com.

Famous First Facts. 6th ed. By Joseph Nathan Kane, Steven Anzovin, and Janet Podell. New York: H.W. Wilson, 2006. 1307 pp.

The *Far East and Australasia 2010*. 41st ed. London: Routledge, 2009. 1536 pp.

Farmers' Almanac. Lewiston, ME: Farmer's Almanac. http://www.farmersalmanac.com.

The *Folklore of World Holidays*. 2nd ed. Ed. Robert H. Griffin and Ann H. Shurgin. Detroit: Gale, 1999. 841 pp.

Guinness World Records. New York: Guinness World Records, 1956–. Annual. (British edition began publication in 1955. Previously titled *Guinness Book of Records*.) http://www.guinnessworldrecords.com.

Halliwell's Who's Who in the Movies. 4th rev. ed. By John Walker. New York: HarperCollins Entertainment, 2006. 639 pp.

The *Hispanic American Almanac: A Reference Work on Hispanics in the United States*. 3rd ed. Detroit: Gale, 2003. 886 pp.

Hoover's Handbook of American Business. Austin, TX: Hoover's, 1992–. Annual.

Hoover's Handbook of World Business. Austin, TX: Hoover's, 1992–. Annual.

Hoover's Online. Austin, TX: Hoover's. http://www.hoovers.com.

HowStuffWorks. Atlanta, GA: HowStuffWorks.com. http://www.howstuffworks.com/.

Information Please Almanac. Boston, MA: Information Please, Pearson Education. (Now titled *Time Almanac* in print.) http://www.infoplease.com/almanacs.html.

International Motion Picture Almanac. New York: Quigley, 1929–. Annual.

Internet Movie Database. http://www.imdb.com.

ipl2. http://www.ipl2.org.

Legal Research: How to Find and Understand the Law. 15th ed. By Stephen Elias, Susan Levinkind, and Richard Stim. Berkeley, CA: Nolo Press, 2009. 386 pp.

Legal Research in a Nutshell. 9th ed. By Morris L. Cohen and Kent C. Olson. St. Paul, MN: Thomson/West, 2007. 507 pp.

The Legal Researcher's Desk Reference. Teaneck, NJ: Infosources, 1990–. Biennial.

Leonard Maltin's Movie Guide. New York: Plume, 1993–. Annual.

Library and Book Trade Almanac. 55th ed. Medford, NJ: Information Today, 2010. 830 pp. (Formerly titled *The Bowker Annual*.)

A Manual for Writers of Research Papers, Theses and Dissertations. 7th ed. By Kate L. Turabian. Revised by John Grossman and Alice Bennett. Chicago: University of Chicago Press, 2007. 466 pp.

Masterplots. 4th ed. Ed. Laurence W. Mazzeno. 12 vols. Pasadena, CA: Salem Press, 2010. Also available online from the publisher and as part of *MagillOnLiterature Plus*.

Mayo Clinic Family Health Book. 3rd ed. Ed. Scott Litin. New York: Collins, 2009. 1448 pp.

MayoClinic.com. Rochester, MN: Mayo Foundation for Medical Education and Research. http://www.mayoclinic.com.

McGraw-Hill Yearbook of Science and Technology. New York: McGraw-Hill, 1962–. Annual.

MedlinePlus. Bethesda, MD: National Library of Medicine. http://www.medlineplus.gov.

The Merck Manual of Diagnosis and Therapy. 18th ed. Whitehouse Station, NJ: Merck Research Laboratories, 2006. 2991 pp. http://www.merck.com/mmpe/index.html.

The Merck Manual of Medical Information. 2nd ed. By Mark H. Beers. Whitehouse Station, NJ: Merck Research Laboratories, 2003. 1907 pp. http://www.merck.com/mmhe/index.html.

The Middle East and North Africa 2010. 56th ed. London: Routledge, 2009. 1440 pp.

Miss Manners' Guide to Excruciatingly Correct Behavior. By Judith Martin. New York: Norton, 2005. 858 pp.

MLA Handbook for Writers of Research Papers. 7th ed. New York: Modern Language Association of America, 2009. 292 pp.

The Native North American Almanac. 2nd ed. Ed. Duane Champagne. Detroit: Gale Research, 2001. 1472 pp.

NEA Almanac of Higher Education. Washington, D.C.: NEA Communications Services, 1984–. Annual.

The New York Public Library Desk Reference. 4th ed. New York: Hyperion, 2002. 999 pp.

The New York Times Almanac. New York: Penguin Group, 1997–. Annual.

Notable Last Facts: A Compendium of Endings, Conclusions, Terminations, and Final Events through History Organized in a Single, Easy-to-Use Reference. Ed. William Brahms. Haddonfield, NJ: Reference Desk Press, 2005. 834 pp.

Occupational Outlook Handbook. Washington, D.C. : Bureau of Labor Statistics. 1949–. Biennial. http://www.bls.gov/OCO/.

The Old Farmer's Almanac. Dublin, NH: Yankee Publishing, 1792–. Annual. http://www.almanac.com.

The Oxford Companion to American Literature. 6th ed. Ed. James David Hart and Philip Leininger. New York: Oxford University Press, 1995. 779 pp. Also available online from *Oxford Reference Online: Premium Collection*.

The Oxford Companion to Canadian Literature. 2nd ed. Ed. William Toye and Eugene Benson. Oxford: Oxford University Press, 1997. 1199 pp. Also available online from *Oxford Reference Online: Premium Collection*.

The Oxford Companion to the English Language. Ed. Tom McArthur. Oxford: Oxford University Press, 1992. 1184 pp. Also available online from *Oxford Reference Online: Premium Collection*.

Oxford Reference Online. Oxford: Oxford University Press. http://www.oxfordreference.com/views/GLOBAL.html.

PDRHealth. Montvale, NJ: Thomson PDR. http://www.pdrhealth.com.

Physicians' Desk Reference. Montvale, NJ: Thomson PDR, 1946–. Annual. http://www.pdr.net/.

Publication Manual of the American Psychological Association. 6th ed. Washington, D.C.: American Psychological Association, 2009. 480 pp.

The Researcher's Guide to American Genealogy. 3rd ed. By Val D. Greenwood. Baltimore, MD: Genealogical Publishing, 2000. 662 pp.

Robert's Rules of Order Newly Revised. 10th ed. Cambridge, MA: Da Capo Press, 2000. 802 pp.

Robert's Rules of Order Newly Revised, in Brief. Cambridge, MA: Da Capo Press, 2004. 208 pp.

The Science and Technology Desk Reference. 2nd ed. Edited by the Carnegie Library of Pittsburgh Science and Technology Department. Detroit: Gale Research, 1996. 795 pp.

South America, Central America and the Caribbean 2010. 18th ed. London: Routledge, 2009. 1128 pp.

South Asia 2010. 7th ed. London: Routledge, 2008. 768 pp.

Sports Illustrated Sports Almanac. New York: Sports Illustrated, 1992–. Annual.

The Statesman's Yearbook. Ed. Barry Turner. Basingstroke, Hampshire: Palgrave Macmillan. Annual. http://www.statesmansyearbook.com/public/.

Statistical Abstract of the United States. Washington, D.C.: U.S. Census Bureau, 1878–. Annual. http://www.census.gov/compendia/statab/.

Texas Almanac 2010–2011. 65th ed. Denton, TX: Texas State Historical Society, 2009. 736 pp. Biennial. http://www.texasalmanac.com/.

Time Almanac. Boston: Information Please, 1998–. Annual. (Formerly titled *Information Please Almanac*.)

Time for Kids Almanac. New York: Time for Kids Books, 2008–. Annual.

Today in History. Washington, D.C.: Library of Congress. http://memory.loc.gov/ammem/today/today.html.

The USA and Canada 2010. 12th ed. London: Routledge, 2009. 624 pp.

Western Europe 2010. 12th ed. London: Routledge, 2009. 888 pp.

Whitaker's Almanack. London: A&C Black, 1868–. Annual.

The World Almanac and Book of Facts. Mahwah, NJ: World Almanac Books, 1868–1876, 1886–. Annual. Also available online via FirstSearch and LexisNexis.

The World Almanac for Kids. Mahwah, NJ: World Almanac Books, 1996–. Annual. http://www.worldalmanacforkids.com.

Yearbook of American and Canadian Churches. Nashville, TN: Abingdon, 1915–. Annual.

Yearbook of the United Nations. New York: United Nations, 1946/47–. Annual.

ADDITIONAL READINGS

Frost, William J., ed. *The Reference Collection: From the Shelf to the Web*. Binghamton, NY: Haworth, 2005. 310 pp. (Copublished as *The Reference Librarian* 91/92.)

This source combines 16 articles on all aspects of electronic reference sources, including "a survey of the most important Web-accessible reference tools." Two of the relevant chapters for almanacs, handbooks, and yearbooks are "Structures and Choices for Ready Reference Web Sites" by Steven W. Sowards and "Electronic vs. Print Reference Sources in Public Library Collections" by Jeanne Holba Puacz.

Grogan, Denis. *Encyclopedias, Yearbooks, Directories and Statistical Sources*. Grogan's Case Studies in Reference Work, vol. 2. London: Clive Bingley, 1987. 170 pp.

Grogan uses the case study method to illustrate both search strategy and the content of ready-reference works. Although the sample questions are oriented to the United Kingdom, the discussion of the search process is informative.

Harrell, Merrilee. "Self-Help Legal Materials in the Law Library: Going a Step Further for the Public Patron." *Legal Reference Services Quarterly* 27, no. 4 (2008): 283–304.

This article explores the history of self-help legal materials, with an emphasis on recommendations for collection development. The author encourages development of a legal self-help collection and provides guidelines for evaluating and producing such materials.

Huber, Jeffrey T., Jo Anne Boorkman, and Jean Blackwell. *Introduction to Reference Sources in the Health Sciences*. 5th ed. New York: Neal-Schuman, 2008. 381 pp.

Chapter authors have selected and described the features and use of the most important resources for answering various categories of health sciences reference questions. Relevant chapters include "Handbooks and Manuals," "Drug Information Sources," and "Consumer Health Sources."

Katz, Bill. *Cuneiform to Computer: A History of Reference Sources*. Lanham, MD: Scarecrow Press, 1998. 417 pp.

This book emphasizes the use of reference sources throughout history. Almanacs, for example, date back to the mid-1100s B.C.E. and handbooks to 200 B.C.E. The book contains a chapter titled "The Reference of Time: Almanacs, Calendars, Chronologies, and Chronicles." Another relevant chapter is "Ready Reference Books: Handbooks and Manuals." This chapter discusses yearbooks as well.

Moss, Rita W. *Strauss's Handbook of Business Information: A Guide for Librarians, Students and Researchers*. 2nd ed. Westport, CT: Libraries Unlimited, 2003. 480 pp.

This book covers business information sources in two parts, with the first seven chapters divided by format (e.g., statistics and consolidated electronic business information) and the second part by topic (e.g., marketing, accounting and taxation, and the many aspects of investment). Both print and electronic resources are profiled.

Perkins, Maureen. *Visions of the Future: Almanacs, Time, and Cultural Change 1775–1870*. Oxford: Clarendon Press, 1996. 270 pp.

Perkins has written a thought-provoking book about the history and use of almanacs. It is a detailed work covering Australian and English almanacs, with such chapter titles as "Almanacs, Astrology, and the Stationers' Company," "Comic Almanacs," and "Australian Almanacs and Popular Culture." This source would be useful for anyone who wanted to explore the boundaries of the use and history of almanacs outside the United States.

Rettig, James. *Distinguished Classics of Reference Publishing*. Phoenix, AZ: Oryx Press, 1992. 356 pp.

This wonderful history of famous reference books includes the following works discussed in this chapter: *The Chicago Manual of Style*, *Emily Post's Etiquette*, *Guinness Book of Records*, *Robert's Rules of Order*, *The Statesman's Yearbook*, and *The World Almanac*.

Chapter

16

Biographical Sources

Jeanne Holba Puacz

USES AND CHARACTERISTICS

From investigating potential corporate board members to learning about presidents for school reports, from exploring personal genealogical relationships to researching figures for dissertations, biographical questions abound at the reference desk. At all types of libraries and for all types of reasons, users ask questions about the lives of others. Although the questions may focus on the lives of local personages or family members, they will more commonly focus on the lives of the famous and the infamous.

In order to best determine what sources are most appropriate and most helpful for the users of a particular library, it is necessary to evaluate both the sources available and the needs of the users. Source evaluation and selection should encompass such considerations as scope, accuracy, currency, format, and cost, among others. The types of questions commonly received, the depth of response generally required, and the age and educational level of the average user are often included in an evaluation of user needs.

In addition to classic biographical sources such as *Current Biography*, the *Who's Who* titles, and *Encyclopedia of World Biography*, a number of excellent electronic sources have recently evolved that greatly reduce the time required for many biographical searches. Sources such as *Biography in Context* and *Biography Reference Bank* allow simultaneous searching of numerous biographical sources, and many of the results are available in full text. These sources allow cumulative access to and searching of multiple editions, titles, and series; many included resources were previously available only in print.

When pursuing biographical information, search strategy will be affected by a number of factors. How much information is needed, how quickly it is needed, and by whom it is needed must all be considered. The number and type of sources consulted

---

BOX 16.1
SOURCES OF INTEREST IN BIOGRAPHY

"Man's sociality of nature evinces itself . . . [in] the unspeakable delight he takes in Biography."

—Thomas Carlyle, *The Carlyle Anthology,* 1876

"For one who reads, there is no limit to the number of lives that may be lived, for fiction, biography, and history offer an inexhaustible number of lives in many parts of the world, in all periods of time."

—Louis L'Amour, *Education of a Wandering Man,* 1989

---

for an elementary student will, obviously, be more limited than the number and type consulted for a graduate student. The subject of the biographical search and what is already known about the subject will also impact the search process. Information concerning a well-known historic figure is often readily available, even if the user is unsure about the spelling of the name, the time period, or the subject area in which the biographee was most influential. Unfortunately, searches for information pertaining to lesser-known individuals can be significantly hampered by such a lack of knowledge.

Although it is true that, as William Katz has said, "answering reference questions may involve the resources of the whole library, and, for that matter, libraries and collections elsewhere,"[1] there are a number of standard sources with which any student of reference should become familiar. In addition to the classic biographical sources, standard encyclopedia and indexing sources can also be extremely useful when pursuing information about people. Many specialized biographical sources exist, so many that it is impossible to know all of them. Therefore, numerous excellent guides to biographical sources have been produced to assist librarians in locating specialized sources to meet the needs of their users. Primary sources, such as vital records, city directories, census data, and the like, may be necessary for some types of questions. However, because this goes beyond reference to research, it is important for the reference librarian to know when to direct users to this type of source and where to direct them so that they can obtain the documents they need.

Although a number of biographical sources may be considered universal, in that they include persons regardless of their nationality, their subject of interest, or whether they are living or dead, many sources consulted in biographical research are subdivided into a variety of categories. These subdivisions can be determined by the type of information the source provides, the type of persons included in the source, or the format of the source itself. The strengths and limitations of each category of source, as well as the goal of the user's research, must be considered when choosing the sources to be consulted.

Direct versus Indirect

Biographical sources are typically designated as either direct or indirect. This designation refers to the type of information that the sources provide. Direct sources provide information within the source itself, whereas indirect sources indicate which titles should be consulted in order to locate the needed information. Direct sources are often further classified as being either directory sources or dictionary sources. In general, directory sources provide basic and brief information about the biographee. Titles of the *Who's Who* variety are classic examples of the biographical directories. More detailed, essay-length descriptions of the person of interest are provided by those sources commonly referred to as biographical dictionaries. *Current Biography* and *American National Biography* exemplify the category of biographical dictionary. Indirect sources provide very little biographical information within the body of the source; rather, they indicate which works the searcher should consult to obtain additional information. Indexes, such as *Biography and Genealogy Master Index* and *Biography Index*, are commonly used indirect biographical sources. These titles provide just enough information about the person of interest for identification purposes and then point the user to supplementary data.

Although the categorizations of direct and indirect are very common when describing biographical sources, there are many works that can be classified as both direct and indirect. Sources that provide any type of bibliography, list of works consulted, or recommended sources for further reading at the end of a biographical entry easily qualify for both categories. The *Encyclopedia of World Biography* and *Contemporary Authors* provide both direct and indirect access to information. *Biography in Context* and *Biography Reference Bank*, which are electronic sources that provide aggregated and cumulative coverage of numerous and varied biographical sources, also provide both types of information.

Current versus Retrospective

Biographical sources are also often categorized by the type of persons included in the work and are commonly designated as being either current or retrospective. Persons included in the current sources are generally assumed to be living at the time of publication. The *Who's Who* variety of source serves as a representative example of current sources. Retrospective sources are understood to provide information about persons from the past and to include only those who are deceased. The *Dictionary of American Biography* and *American National Biography* are two such sources. A number of sources provide information on both current and retrospective figures. *Current Biography* profiles only current individuals but provides access to obituaries for deceased individuals who were previously profiled by the publication and a citation for the issue of *Current Biography* in which that profile appeared. *Biography in Context* and *Biography Reference Bank* regularly include both living and deceased individuals.

International versus National

Biographical sources are often classified as either international or national in scope. International sources, such as *Who's Who in the World* and *Encyclopedia of*

World Biography, are international in coverage and include persons regardless of their ethnicity or country of birth. National sources restrict their coverage to individuals born in the nation in question and, as is becoming more common in today's shrinking world, to those persons of prominence in, or importance to, the nation being covered. *Who's Who in America* and *American National Biography* are two examples of sources that are limited nationally in their scope. Sources may be further restricted to cover only a particular region of a country, such as with *Who's Who in the Midwest*, or to cover only a particular field of interest, such as *American Men and Women of Science*.

Alternative Sources

Although persons included in major biographical works have, obviously, obtained some level of fame, the area in which they have achieved their status may dictate into which sources they are placed. Those of longstanding fame, such as classical Greek poets, or of outstanding achievement, such as past presidents of the United States, are likely to be included in the selective and well-respected dictionary sources, whereas those of sport or entertainment fame may be restricted to sources with good coverage of individuals of broad popular interest, such as *Current Biography* and *Biography.com*.

Newspapers and magazines can serve as excellent sources of biographical information, particularly for those figures who are newly famous, fleetingly famous, or famous for notorious or criminal reasons. Although perpetually of interest, the notorious are often excluded from many of the standard biographical sources. However, this does nothing to lessen the interest of the general public, and periodicals can often fill the gap. In the past, limited indexing made locating periodical articles challenging and time-consuming, with *Biography Index* often being the best resource for locating articles about people. Periodical indexes have made great strides both in content and in format, and periodical articles are now much more readily available (see chapter 21). In addition, these indexes act as an excellent supplement to the traditional sources by providing access to very current information before the standard sources have been updated. However, it should be noted that these indexes are limited in their retrospective coverage; therefore, if older articles are required, a lack of indexing may still hamper the search process.

Encyclopedias can also act as supplementary biographical sources and should not be overlooked (see chapter 18). Encyclopedia articles can provide concise and helpful overviews concerning the person sought and are quite useful for historical figures. Encyclopedias, particularly those created for young people, are often an excellent source for pictures. Valuable information may also be included in topical encyclopedia articles for subjects related to the individual in question; therefore, it is important that the index to the encyclopedia be consulted. Important references to the life, work, and influence of a person may be missed if the index is ignored.

The Web can serve as another outstanding alternative for very current information or for difficult-to-locate persons. In addition to some of the well-known biographical Web sites, such as *Biography.com* and *Infoplease Biography*, a wealth of additional biographical information may be gleaned from the Web. Personal Web sites of the famous (and infamous), company Web sites that provide profiles of corporate officials, and the Web sites of smaller, local newspapers are a few examples of potential Web resources that may be tapped. Although general Web searching is likely to produce some kind of results for most searches, they may or may not be results of quality. Although numerous sites containing quality information are available, many Web sources lack editorial control. Thus, it is important to view each site critically and evaluate it for such qualities as accuracy, reliability, and currency. Although users may contend otherwise, searching accepted electronic biographical sources of known quality is often far more efficient than general Web searching. The *ipl2* can provide recommendations to quality Web sites with biographical information.

EVALUATION

A staggering amount of biographical information is available, and myriad new works are published yearly. It is imperative for librarians to carefully evaluate the sources available and to work diligently to direct users to those sources deemed to be of the highest quality. Whether adding a print source to the traditional reference collection or an electronic source to the Web-based collection, librarians should strive to ensure that users are consulting sources that are current, accurate, comprehensive, and easy to use.

Currency

When evaluating the currency of a work, it is important to consider how quickly, how often, and how thoroughly the work is updated. The entries in retrospective sources generally do not need regular updating and will be updated only if significant new information about a historical figure is discovered. However, because lives and fortunes can change very quickly, it is extremely important for current sources to be regularly and thoroughly updated. Dated entries have the serious potential consequence of providing incorrect information to the researcher. Although many directory sources have regularly scheduled updates, other dictionary sources are updated infrequently, offering updates and revisions only when a new edition is published. Some dictionary sources that are published serially, such as *Contemporary Authors* and *Current Biography*, periodically include revised entries to keep the information provided more accurate. Print sources, by their nature, cannot be updated as often or as quickly as electronic sources. However, it must be noted that the potential for electronic sources to be updated more quickly and more often does not guarantee that the sources are updated or indicate how thorough those updates may be. During the evaluation process, careful attention should be paid to the editorial policy regarding updates.

Accuracy and Authority

Issues of accuracy and authority can be considered on several levels. When evaluating any reference work, it is important to investigate what kinds of reviews the source received upon publication and whether the work has been included in the standard guides to reference works. The reputation of the publisher of the work can also serve as a good indicator of the overall quality. Gale, H. W. Wilson, and Marquis Who's Who are some of the best-known and most trusted names in biographical reference publishing.

A consideration that is somewhat unique to biographical works encompasses the source of the biographical data. Often, the biographees themselves are asked to provide the information included in the entry. Theoretically, self-compiled information will be superior because it will be most accurate. However, the accuracy and legitimacy of the information provided is dependent on the honesty and thoroughness of the individual entrant. Although the entrant may not actually provide factually incorrect information, the information may be, effectively, edited to provide a more flattering, if not more complete picture. If the information located in a source seems at all questionable or incomplete, it is highly advisable to consult additional sources in an effort to provide the user with the most complete answer possible.

Scope and Comprehensiveness

The scope statement of the source will indicate which individuals are eligible for inclusion. A clearly worded and well-defined statement of scope will help to lend legitimacy to the source and its entries. Common ways to limit scope include whether the entrants are living or deceased, whether the entrants are residents of a particular country or region, and whether the entrants are employed in a particular field or profession. Inclusion of as many individuals as possible that meet the stated scope results in a more comprehensive source. If prominent individuals who meet the stated scope are overlooked, the overall legitimacy of the source will suffer. Likewise, if individuals who do not meet the qualifications set down by the scope statement are included, the quality of the source could and should be questioned.

Format

The usefulness of information, even information of the highest quality, can be greatly diminished if the source of that information is difficult to access. Information can be rendered useless if it is inaccessible as a result of poor organization or lack of access points. The number and type of available indexes in a print source will greatly impact the overall effectiveness of the work. Electronic sources have great potential in terms of searching and accessibility. Many sources allow for searching essentially all of the fields of the record, searching a number of factors in combination to refine the search, or even searching the entire contents of the database by keyword. This search power of electronic sources should be exploited to the fullest so that searchers can locate the information of interest quickly and effectively. The ability of electronic sources to allow for cumulative searching of multiple editions of a title, such as with the *Biography and Genealogy Master Index*, is an excellent and time-saving advantage for any searcher. Likewise, the ability to search a large number of biographical sources at one time, as allowed for by the large aggregate sources such as the *Biography Reference Bank* and *Biography in Context*, can make the process of biographical searching fast, easy, and effective. Some librarians find the variety of works included in the aggregate sources somewhat detrimental. There are many different source types, of varying breadth and depth, so there is no guarantee of consistency

---

BOX 16.2
BIOGRAPHICAL DETAILS

"Discretion is not the better part of biography."

—Lytton Strachey

---

in information located for included individuals. However, for most, the increased efficiency and convenience of such sources outweigh these concerns.

Careful attention should be paid to the spelling of names when using electronic sources. Unlike print sources, where the traditional alphabetical arrangement of the source and/or its index may help the searcher to stumble upon the correct entry even if the spelling is inaccurate, electronic sources are far less likely to return a result if the name is spelled incorrectly. Increasingly, sources are beginning to offer close matches, suggest alternative spellings, or offer an alphabetical browse feature in order to assist the searcher in locating the correct individual.

Cautions

A number of cautions should be taken into account when discussing biographical sources. Many early biographical works, particularly those from 19th- and early 20th-century America, were essentially vanity publications. Prominent citizens would be offered inclusion in the source for a fee, and the publishers would profit. Although these works are now useful to scholars as historical snapshots of the era and the locale, they are not legitimate and unbiased biographical sources. A large number of vanity publications continue to exist in the biographical realm; any publication that requires an individual to purchase a copy of the title before he or she is included or that offers to include an individual for a fee should be viewed as suspect. Librarians may be questioned about such sources by users who have received an invitation for inclusion; tact should be employed when discussing these invitations and sources.

Quality and completeness of information included in biographical entries has varied greatly over time. Whether deliberately or subconsciously, biographers can be selective in their coverage. The Victorian era was notorious for including only acceptable and complimentary information about biographical subjects. Obituaries, which can serve as another important source of biographical information, are also often considered to be more complimentary than complete. For this reason among others, knowing what sources have been consulted during the creation of a biographical work and knowing where to look to locate additional information can be quite helpful to the biographical researcher. Because it is often necessary to consult multiple works in order to obtain a clear picture of an individual, particularly an individual from the past, references and recommendations for sources of further information are an important component of many, and especially retrospective, works.

SELECTION

Although the type and depth of information needed can vary greatly by library, it is interesting to note that a number of classic biographical sources are useful in all libraries. Sources such as *Who's Who in America*, *Current Biography*, and the *Biography and Genealogy Master Index* can be just as useful to a corporate librarian as to a school media specialist. The succinct information provided in a directory such as *Who's Who in America* may provide the answer to a simple ready-reference question. The essay format and excellent coverage of popular figures from *Current Biography* may provide the supplemental information needed for a more in-depth query. The *Biography and Genealogy Master Index* provides efficient and effective direction to those pursuing biographical research.

Needs of Users

Although some sources are useful at multiple levels, the needs of the users of specific types of libraries will impact each library's selection of biographical tools. Dictionaries that are written at an appropriate level for the students being served and that provide illustrations are likely to be more useful than directories in a school media center. Such dictionary sources will be far more useful to students as they work to complete reports and projects on prominent individuals. Dictionaries are also likely to be more useful than directories to the student users of academic libraries. However, the directory sources may be extremely useful to the staff and faculty users of the library. Identifying researchers specializing in a particular field, locating colleagues at different educational institutions, and obtaining contact information for potential donors are just a few of the possible uses for biographical directories at academic libraries. Directories that provide very current contact information and brief biographical data are often the most useful biographical sources for users of special libraries. The narrative entries provided by dictionary sources are likely to provide substantial retrospective information and thus be less useful in these settings. Because it is difficult to anticipate the broad range of questions that may be faced in a public library, it is important to provide a cross-section of sources. Both dictionary and directory sources, in a progression of difficulty and detail, should be made available for use.

Cost

Unfortunately, librarians are not financially able to afford all of the sources that might be helpful to their users. Therefore, in addition to evaluating sources for quality and usefulness, the prices of the sources must also be considered. Some classic biographical sources offer abridged versions that may be sufficient for smaller libraries with limited budgets. For example, the *Almanac of Famous People* acts as a significantly abridged version of *Biography and Genealogy Master Index*, covering more than 39,000 of the larger work's 19 million-plus entries. The uniqueness of works considered for a collection should be taken into account, and titles with similar scope statements should be studied closely; it is unlikely that smaller libraries truly need or can easily afford titles that duplicate coverage. For example, does the library actually need both *Who's Who in the World* and *The International Who's Who*? Or would one of the titles suffice?

Electronic versions of some sources may be available at reduced prices for those libraries that hold the print version of the source, thus providing additional access without significant extra cost. Though still costly, electronic aggregate sources that provide full-text access to numerous classic biographical sources may enable libraries to provide access to more sources than they would otherwise be able to afford in print. Consortial pricing, which may result in a substantial discount in price, should be investigated for those sources that may be useful to multiple libraries in an area. A number of quality biographical sources are available free of charge on the Web. For example, *Biography.com* and *Infoplease Biography* are free resources that can be used by libraries of any budget to supplement their collections.

IMPORTANT GENERAL SOURCES

Although it is not possible to provide a detailed description of every biographical source, a number of regularly used sources of widely accepted worth are discussed in this chapter. Several of the texts listed under "Additional Readings" at the end of this chapter can be used to identify more specialized biographical sources suitable for particular collections.

Directories of the Who's Who Form

Who's Who directories, in one variation or another, are commonly used biographical sources. They provide succinct, noncritical access to biographical facts for currently prominent individuals, including name, age, education, family, contact information, and so on. The original *Who's Who* was first published in England in the 19th century and limited entry to those of British citizenship. The source retains its British focus to this day, although it now also includes foreigners influential in Britain. It should be noted that this is the original work of this type and is the only *Who's Who* title that is not qualified by some additional designation, such as *Who's Who in America* or *Who's Who in the Midwest*. *Who's Who* includes more than 33,000 influential people in British public life today.

Who's Who in America, which began approximately 50 years after the original *Who's Who*, is a premier source for basic information about more than 96,000 eminent Americans. "Americans," for this source, includes those from the United States, Canada, and Mexico. Inclusion in *Who's Who in America* is restricted to those deemed to be of "reference interest" and is dictated by an individual's achievements. Achievement may be measured by positions of leadership or responsibility held, significant creative or educational works, public speaking, publishing, or noteworthy contributions to the community. These are the same criteria used to measure all entrants into the Marquis Who's Who sources; however, achievements for those being considered for *Who's Who in America* are generally at the national level. Government officials at the national or state level, upper-level administrators from academic institutions, and key personnel from major businesses are generally ensured inclusion. Those selected for inclusion are sent a questionnaire and are asked to provide information about their life, family, career, and achievements, which is compiled in a standardized format. Figure 16.1 shows a sample entry. It should be noted that although the *Who's Who* sources have generally been found to be reliable, the answers provided by the biographees may not undergo any editorial review or revision.

The *Who's Who* directories have expanded to include numerous additional titles. Four regional titles based on the *Who's Who in America* format cover the East, Midwest, South and Southwest, and West. Multiple topical *Who's Who* titles are in publication, including those limited by profession or vocation, such as *Who's Who in Science and Engineering*; by gender in *Who's Who of American Women*; or by ethnic identity, such as *Who's Who among African Americans*. Because these works are more limited in scope, focusing only on the prominent individuals in a particular region or field instead of the whole country, more members of the subgroups are included in these limited titles than in the original, national source. Many countries of the world produce some type of *Who's Who* directory, providing information about their prominent citizens. For example, *Canadian Who's Who* includes more than 13,000 biographies of persons of current national interest. *Who's Who in the World* and *The International Who's Who* provide access to individuals who are prominent in a broader scope.

Who's Who in America - Sample Listing

---

1 **FIELD, MARSHALL,** 2 retail executive; 3 b. Charlottesville, Va., May 13, 1941; 4 s. Marshall IV and Joanne (Bass) F.; m. Joan Best Connelly, Sept. 5, 1964 (div. 1969); 1 child, Marshall; m. Jamee Beckwith Jacobs, Aug. 19, 1972; children: Jamee Christine, Stephanie Caroline, Abigail Beckwith. 5 BA, Harvard Coll., 1963. 6 With N.Y. Herald Tribune, 1964-65; pub. Chgo. Sun-Times, 1969-80, Chgo. Daily News, 1969-78; dir. Field Enterprises, Inc., Chgo., 1965-84, dir., mem. exec. com., 1965-84, chmn. bd., 1972-84, The Field Corp., 1984–, Cabot, Cabot & Forbes, 1984–, chmn. exec. com., 1985-89, sr. dir., chief exec. officer, 1989–; 7 pub. World Book-Childcraft Internat. Inc., 1973-78, 8 dir., 1965-80. Bd. trustees Art Inst. Chgo., Chgo. Pub. Libr. Found., Rush-Presbyn.-St. Lukes Med. Ctr., Chgo. Cmty. Trust; chmn. bd. trustees Field Mus. Natural History; chmn. bd. Terra Mus. Am. Art; adv. bd. Brookfield Zoo; mem. charitable adv. coun. Office of Atty. Gen. of State of Ill.; active Chgo. Orchestral Assn.; mem. bd. visitors, vice chair Nicholas Sch. of the Environment, Duke U.; bd. dirs. First Nat. Bank Chgo., 1970–85, Field Found. Ill., Lincoln Park Zool. Soc.; chmn. Nat. Coun. of the World Wildlife Fund; bd. dirs. Atlantic Salmon Fedn., Openlands Project. Mem. Nature Conservancy, River Club, Chgo. Club, Comml. Club, Harvard Club, Racquet Club, Onwentsia Club, Jupiter Island Club, Shore Acres Club. 9 Office: 225 W Wacker Dr Ste 1500 Chicago IL 60606-1235 Office Phone: 312-917-1810.

Key:

1 **Full Name** ensures the proper spelling of the biographee name for correspondence and other written work.
2 **Occupation** describes the subject's current profession and identifies areas of expertise.
3 **Date/Place of Birth** indicate age and national origin.
4 **Family Background** provides the names of parents, spouse and children.
5 **Education Summary** reveals the level of education and areas of expertise, including professional certifications.

6 **Career Summary** details full career history to indicate areas of expertise and facilitate contact.
7 **Writings and Creative Works** list books published, contributions to professional journals, exhibits, and commissioned works.
8 **Civic and Political Activities, Military Service, Awards, Memberships, Political Affiliation, Religion and Avocations,** where available, complete your knowledge of an individual's accomplishments and highlight vital interests.
9 **Address** provides vital contact information.

Figure 16.1. Sample entry from *Marquis Who's Who on the Web*, including the key to interpret the entry.

The *Who's Who* directories are current sources and aim only to include those who are among the living. As individuals pass away, they are removed from the print work and added, for the next edition, to a list of those who have died. *Who Was Who* and *Who Was Who in America* provide reprints of entries for those individuals who are the subject of continued reference interest even after they have died. A cumulative index lists the names and years of birth and death of all those whose entries appear in *Who Was Who* from 1897 to 2000, indicating the volume in which they are to be found. Volumes of *Who Was Who in America* span 1607–2010. A cumulative index enables quick identification of the volume covering each of more than 158,000 biographies.

The *Marquis Who's Who on the Web* database provides aggregate, searchable access to 23 Marquis Who's Who titles. More than 1.4 million individuals are included in the database, which may be searched by 15 fields, including name, occupation, gender, degrees, colleges or universities, year of graduation, hobbies, religion, and more. These fields may be searched individually or in combination to create specific search statements. Such access points, and particularly the ability to combine criteria, far surpass the access points available in the print format. Another advantage of the electronic format is the daily updating, both of biographical facts and of included figures.

The International Who's Who includes more than 22,000 of the most distinguished men and women from around the world. Entries typically provide nationality, date and place of birth, current position and career to date, honors and awards, publications and artistic achievements, and contact details. The online version is updated quarterly and includes recently deceased entrants as well as the living individuals covered in the print version. *Who's Who in the World* contains approximately 60,000 entries for persons of note from around the world, including heads of state, politicians, writers, artists, businesspeople, and religious leaders. Each entry includes an individual's date and place of birth, nationality, marital/family information, education, career background, awards and honors, artistic achievements, publications, leisure interests, and contact information.

Two specialized directories useful for finding biographical information on contemporary scholars are *American Men and Women of Science* (*AMWS*) and the *Directory of American Scholars* (*DAS*). *AMWS* includes biographical entries on nearly 135,000 living scientists from the United States and Canada. Entries include birth date and place, field of specialty, education, career history, awards, memberships, research/publication information, and contact information. Volume 8 lists scientists by field and then by state within field. *AMWS* is also available online as part of the *Gale Virtual Reference Library*. The six-volume *DAS* is arranged by discipline from the humanities and social sciences, with a geographic index. Entries for more than 24,000 scholars from the United States and Canada include the same type of information as *AMWS*.

Indexes

The *Biography and Genealogy Master Index* includes citations from more than 2,100 print sources that provide biographical information. Currently, the index provides access to more than 19 million citations relating to more than 5 million individuals. The number of citations is continually rising, as an estimated half-million or more new entries are added every year and existing citations are retained, not removed. Although the source provides little biographical data within its entries— just name and birth and death dates—it effectively points the researcher to where biographical information is published. The print source is updated with supplement volumes twice a year and exists in multiple volumes, and the cumulative searching offered by the electronic version is quite beneficial, saving both time and effort. A note of caution regarding *Biography and Genealogy Master Index* relates to the method of including names. Names and dates are included as they appear in the title that has been indexed; no attempt is made at authority control. Therefore, a single individual may have multiple entries under various forms of the same name (see Figure 16.2).

Biography Index provides access to biographical information published in more than 3,000 magazines and journals and 2,000 books each year. Citations are not limited to biographies and autobiographies but also include interviews, obituaries, letters, diaries, memoirs, juvenile literature, reviews, and bibliographies. Coverage includes persons from the past and the present, of all nationalities, and from all fields of interest. Unlike *Biography and Genealogy Master Index*, authority control is employed to ensure easy access to individuals regardless of possible name variations. The source,

Figure 16.2. Sample results screen from the online *Biography and Genealogy Master Index* showing multiple forms of entry for the same individual.

which has been available in print since the 1940s, is also available online. As with *Biography and Genealogy Master Index*, the online source may be searched cumulatively and is updated daily instead of quarterly, as is the case with the print format. Retrospective coverage of the online version now goes back to 1946, covering the full span of the corresponding print index.

Biographical Dictionaries
Current

Current Biography, which began publication in 1940, is a useful biographical source, enduringly popular with users and librarians. Complete with photographs, family life, and physical descriptions of the biographees, *Current Biography* provides accurate and quite readable essay-length biographies of international personalities. Subjects often tend to have had some impact on American life and are often important figures in popular culture. The print source is published monthly, with about 20 profiles in each issue as well as brief obituaries for past entrants who are recently deceased. The monthly issues are gathered into an annual yearbook that also contains additional current and cumulative indexing. A cumulated index volume covering the period 1940–2005 has been published to facilitate retrospective searching. The title is also available electronically via WilsonWeb, and the database contains the entire contents of all print issues, more than 20,000 articles and obituaries in total. The source is also included in *Biography Reference Bank*.

Containing profiles of almost any published American writer, including novelists, poets, columnists, cartoonists, screen and television writers, and more, *Contemporary Authors* is an extremely comprehensive choice for biographical information about authors. Begun in 1962, it references more than 130,000 authors. Described as a bio-bibliographical guide, the work contains biographical details, references to recent news about the author, biographical and critical references, and more. Modern writers and significant writers from the early 20th century from around the world are included, and when possible, biographical information is provided directly from the entrant. It should be noted that several different series of *Contemporary Authors* are published, and the print volumes and their indexes may be cumbersome for novice users. The online version is significantly easier to use and may provide more current entries than the print format. The source is available online individually or as a part of *Biography in Context*. *Contemporary Authors* is also offered online as part of Gale's *Literature Resource Center*.

Newsmakers is designed to complement and supplement *Contemporary Authors* by providing biographical information about prominent individuals who are not writers. Like *Current Biography*, *Newsmakers* covers all fields, from government and business to entertainment and sports. Issues appear quarterly, covering about 200 newsmakers each year. Indexes enable location of entries by name, nationality, occupation, and subject. A separate obituaries section provides concise profiles of recently deceased newsmakers. Also published by Gale, *Contemporary Black Biography* focuses on important persons of African heritage. Each volume contains 55 biographies. Name, occupation, nationality, and subject indexes are included in each volume. Both *Newsmakers* and *Contemporary Black Biography* are available online as part of *Biography in Context*.

Current and Retrospective

The *Encyclopedia of World Biography* contains more than 7,000 biographical sketches of current and historical figures. In addition to the expected historical entrants, movie, television, and music stars are included. The text is eminently readable and, thus, quite accessible to students as well as the general public. Illustrations and bibliographical references are provided for many of the entries, and extensive indexing is available. The source is well organized and easily usable in print, but it is also available online as part of *Biography in Context*. Annual supplements update the set with additional biographical sketches.

African American National Biography contains more than 4,000 entries written and signed by distinguished scholars under the direction of editors in chief Henry Louis Gates Jr. and Evelyn Brooks Higginbotham. The time span is almost 500 years, from 1528 to the present day. The scope includes slaves and abolitionists; writers, artists, and performers; politicians and business people; athletes; and lawyers, journalists, and civil rights leaders. Each entry is followed by a section of suggestions for further reading. Indexes allow access by category or area of renown and by birthplace. There are also lists of African American prizewinners, medalists, members of Congress, and judges. The entries are available online as part of the *Oxford African American Studies Center*, with updates on a regular basis.

Retrospective

The *Dictionary of American Biography*, or *DAB*, is a massive work containing narrative biographical accounts for more than 19,000 prominent deceased Americans. All entries are evaluative, are written by scholars, and focus on the public life of the featured individual. Some personal information is also included, as are bibliographical references for further reading. The first volumes of this source were published in the late 1920s, with the index following in the late 1930s; updates and supplements provide coverage through 1980. A comprehensive index, published in 1990, has six sections, including subject of the biography, birthplace, schools and colleges attended, occupations, topics discussed in the biography, and contributors' names. Although long accepted as an excellent reference source, it should be noted that this source has been criticized for its lack of diversity; entries for women and minorities are quite limited. Because it is now quite dated, researchers should consult additional sources, when possible, to guarantee accuracy and thoroughness. Continuing biographical coverage of prominent individuals in the tradition of the *DAB*, *The Scribner Encyclopedia of American Lives* includes eight volumes to date, with the first volume covering 1981–1985 and the most recent covering those who died between 2006 and 2008.

Compared to *DAB*, *American National Biography* is an equally massive, but far more recent biographical work focusing on significant deceased Americans. Foreigners who have had a significant impact on the country are included. Providing new entries for approximately 10,000 of the figures covered in *Dictionary of American Biography*, *American National Biography* also includes entries for more than 7,000 figures not included in that source. Given that *DAB* stopped updating its coverage in 1980, many of the 7,000 are persons who died after that date. However, *American*

National Biography has also worked to include those persons overlooked by *DAB*, especially women, minorities, and precolonial figures. Entries are signed and quite lengthy, include bibliographical references, and may also include illustrations. Four indexes are provided in the print edition: subject, contributors, birthplace, and "occupations and realms of renown." Originally published in 1999, the title is available in print and online. The online version is revised, updated, and expanded semiannually to ensure accuracy. Access points that may be searched singly or in combination go beyond the print indexes to also include fields such as gender, birth and death dates, and limits to special collections (e.g., Black History, Women's History, Asian Pacific American Heritage, Hispanic Heritage, American Indian Heritage). Serious scholars who are researching figures included in both *ANB* and *DAB* should consult both entries; these sources, although written from different perspectives and in different eras, are both works of significant scholarship and are viewed by many as complementary.

The *Dictionary of National Biography*, the inspiration for the *Dictionary of American Biography*, was originally published in the late 1800s in an attempt to profile deceased persons of distinction from Great Britain and Ireland. During the 20th century, supplements were published approximately every 10 years. A new edition of the *Dictionary of National Biography*, titled *Oxford Dictionary of National Biography*, was released in 2004. This edition continues to focus on deceased Britons, but foreign-born persons who have achieved significance in Britain are also included. The revised source contains in excess of 54,000 biographies, more than 16,000 of which are new to this edition. The popular and the scholarly, the ancient and the modern, are all included in this revision. The new edition has received excellent reviews for its content, coverage, and quality of writing. Although the original title was somewhat lacking in available indexes—an extensive index to the basic set and its supplements not being published until 1985—the revised edition has rectified this problem. In the online format, search options include searches by person, full text, bibliographic references, contributors, and images. Selected biographies are also grouped by theme, such as "Astronomers royal," "Climbers of Mount Everest," and "Poets laureate." Online updates are done three times per year, including new biographies, themes for reference, illustrations, and corrections and additions to articles already published. The complete text of the original *DNB* with all supplements is also available online.

The major source for historically important Canadians is the *Dictionary of Canadian Biography* (*DCB*). The 15 volumes of this work published to date cover Canadian history from 1000 to 1930. The *DCB* is arranged chronologically rather than alphabetically. Each volume contains essays about individuals who contributed to a specific period of Canadian history. Entries in the *DCB* average several hundred words in length, and all conclude with citations for further reading and research. Library and Archives Canada has provided free online access to the contents of the set, with the possibility of searching by name or keyword and limiting by date range, gender, or occupation.

Developed by the Australian National University, the *Australian Dictionary of Biography*, which is available online, contains more than 10,000 articles on 11,237 persons who were important in Australian history, or who represent the diverse nature of the Australian experience. Coverage currently extends to 1980, with plans to extend coverage to prominent individuals who died in subsequent decades. Browsing may be done by name or occupation, and the advanced search feature enables searches based on dates and places of birth and death, religious influence, cultural heritage, occupation, and gender. Entries include physical description, family details, distinctions gained, career, occupation, and religious affiliation.

Retrospective sources may also focus on particular ethnic or gender groups or professions. Examples include the *Dictionary of Scientific Biography* (*DSB*) and its supplement *New Dictionary of Scientific Biography*. The two publications exist in an online version called the *Complete Dictionary of Scientific Biography* as part of the *Gale Virtual Reference Library*. The *New Dictionary of Scientific Biography* includes 575 new biographies, treating scientists deceased since 1950 or overlooked in the original *DSB*. In addition, 225 of the original articles have been updated to reflect more recent scholarship. More women and African Americans have been included as well as more scientists from Arabic and Asian countries. Articles describe work and career and conclude with a bibliography of works by and about the scientist. In addition to a general index, volume 8 contains a list of scientists organized by field, a list of Nobel Prize winners, and an alphabetical list of articles. *Notable American Women* provides scholarly essays on historically significant American women. The first three volumes, published in 1971, cover the period 1607–1950, and the fourth volume, published in 1980, focuses on women who died between 1951 and 1975. Modeled on the *DAB*, each entry contains a fairly lengthy life history covering personal and career events. Each entry concludes with a list of primary and secondary sources for further research, and indexes by occupation are provided.

Aggregate Sources

Although general aggregators of online reference sources, such as *Credo Reference*, include a growing number of biographical titles (including both *Who's Who in America* and *Who's Who in the World*), two aggregate sources devoted to biographical information provide even richer coverage. *Biography in Context* (based on *Biography Resource Center*), an easy-to-use online source, provides access to biographical information on more than 500,000 individuals. It is universal in scope, including current and historical figures from around the world and from all areas of interest. Biographical information from more than 170 Gale titles, such as *Newsmakers*, *Contemporary Authors*, and *Contemporary Black Biography*, to name just a few, are indexed and made available full-text. Full-text articles from magazines and multimedia content are also included in this comprehensive database. For example, the entry for "Maya Angelou" includes five biographical profiles from titles such as *Contemporary Black Biography* and *Newsmakers*, as well as images, audio files, and a concise fact box. The database is regularly updated, to include new content and to update existing entries. There are several different search options: name, occupation, nationality, birth place, death place. A search for a person can be limited by occupation, nationality, ethnicity, gender, birth year, and/or death year. Advanced search allows additional limiting options including content type (such as reference or audio) and content level (basic, intermediate, advanced). The convenience and time savings of searching so many standard and accepted reference works at one time is quite significant, as are the collection development implications; libraries that might be unable to afford a fraction of these biographical sources in print may be able to access all of them full-text online via this database.

Similar in function to *Biography in Context*, the *Biography Reference Bank* is an aggregate source from H. W. Wilson. This source provides biographical entries for more than 600,000 individuals, with up to 1,500 new profiles added annually. *Biography Index*, *Current Biography*, the Wilson World Authors Series, the Junior Authors & Illustrators Series, and more are combined with biographical content from other Wilson databases and selected biographical material from other reference publishers (such as Greenwood Publishing and Oxford University Press) to provide the substance for this resource. In addition to narrative biographies, more than 36,000 images and links to more than 380,000 full-text magazine articles are provided, as are interviews, reviews, speeches, and obituaries. This extensive database allows searching by name, profession, place of origin, gender, ethnicity, birth and/or death date, titles of works, and keywords. As with *Biography in Context*, the overall convenience and time that may be saved by accessing these numerous valuable titles via one interface and one search is quite substantial.

Free Web Resources

Biography.com is an outgrowth of the Arts & Entertainment channel's popular *Biography* television program. Providing more than 25,000 entries, the database is not limited to those who have been featured on the program; however, the coverage and content for those who have been featured is much more complete. Although it emphasizes coverage of figures in popular culture, historical figures and scholars are also included. The search feature, though easy to use, is somewhat inexact, providing links to all entries that contain any part of the name searched. Regardless, this user-friendly and familiar site is a useful free source of legitimate biographical content with which many users will already be comfortable. Another free Web resource, *Infoplease Biography*, has more than 30,000 brief biographical entries. These can be searched by name or browsed by occupational category or by race and ethnicity.

SEARCH STRATEGIES

When developing a search strategy to be used to locate biographical information, a number of factors should be considered, such as what the user knows about the individual being sought, what the user is hoping to learn about the individual, and at what level the information is needed. Whether the person is well known or obscure, whether the coverage should be scholarly or popular, whether the user is sure of the spelling or unsure of even the name, there are sources and strategies that can be employed to attempt to locate the required information.

When the subject of the search is well known, it is possible, even likely, that the problem will not lie in being able to find something about the individual; rather, it will lie in finding too much. When there is an abundance of information available, the librarian may find it wise to assist the user in evaluating the search results to determine which sources are most appropriate. When the individual sought is not well known, finding anything may become an issue, and it may be necessary to employ sources with a regional or local focus. If the user knows very little about the individual being sought, it can be very difficult to narrow the search or even to be sure that the located results are actually for the correct person. It is extremely important for the librarian to obtain any and all information possible from the user. Information that the user may feel is insignificant or information that the user is hesitant to share because he or she is unsure of its accuracy may well be the information that the librarian will need in order to conduct a successful search. It also may happen that a user claiming to need biographical information on an individual in fact needs information related to that person's work instead. Thus, a thorough reference interview, investigating everything from where the user heard of the individual to any variations on the name or spelling of the name, to what the user is actually hoping to find, is essential, and no detail obtained should be discounted as unimportant.

Biographical information exists in a range of depth and completeness, from thorough, scholarly articles to popular, gossipy coverage. In order to perform a successful reference transaction, it is necessary for the librarian to ascertain the level of coverage desired by the user. It is unlikely that an elementary school student would find an article from the *Dictionary of American Biography* useful and readable or that a graduate student would find a single profile from *Current Biography* sufficient for term paper research; however, it is equally unlikely that a librarian can assume what level of coverage is most appropriate for a specific user. Therefore, in order to avoid misunderstandings and assumptions that could leave the user feeling uncomfortable, the librarian should try to investigate the level and depth of coverage desired during the interview process. If the user is hesitant to clarify the level needed, the librarian may wish to consider offering a number of sources at varying levels of complexity. The user can then choose the desired source, thus indicating to the librarian the type of coverage preferred if additional information is necessary.

Factual Data

If the user is looking for brief, factual data, such as birth or death dates, full name, education, or contact information, biographical directories are excellent sources. If the individual is famous, basic information such as nationality and whether the individual is still alive may be known to the user and the librarian. If so, it may be possible to go without hesitation to the appropriate directory, such as *Who's Who* for those of British nationality, *Who's Who in America* for those from North America, and so on. *Marquis Who's Who on the Web* is another noteworthy possibility for locating living North American figures. Because this source includes the regional and many of the subject-specific *Who's Who* titles, multiple sources can be consulted quickly and easily. In addition to biographical directories, encyclopedia articles may well prove an effective resource for general, factual data about well-known individuals.

Single-volume universal biographies, which do not restrict by time, place, or subject and which include both the living and the dead, have long served as effective starting points when little is known about the individual sought. Titles of this type include *Merriam-Webster's Biographical Dictionary*, providing very brief biographical information for about 30,000 world figures, and *Chambers Biographical*

Dictionary, with entries for 17,500 individuals. Because these volumes are not updated on a regular basis, they are most useful for historical figures. *Biography in Context* and the *Biography Reference Bank*, regularly updated electronic aggregate sources, may now be the best options to serve in their stead for individuals from all periods.

When the subject in question is not known to the librarian, and the user can provide little detail, the librarian may find it efficient to consult an indirect source, such as the *Biography and Genealogy Master Index*, in order to determine in which directories the individual will be found. If available, an electronic source such as *Biography in Context* can act as both an indirect and direct source for this type of question. A single search in this type of source can provide the searcher not only with results for directory information but also with dictionary-type information, as well as references in the event that the user decides to pursue the subject further.

Narrative Biographies

If the user is looking for essay-length coverage, biographical dictionaries should be consulted. Again, if the figure is well known, it may be possible to progress directly to an appropriate source. Important historical figures of British descent may be available in the *Oxford Dictionary of National Biography*; historical figures of American heritage may be found in either the *Dictionary of American Biography* or *American National Biography*. If the person sought is fairly well known, but the nationality of the person is in question, a source such as *Encyclopedia of World Biography*, which is international in scope, may provide an entry. If the figure sought is well known but currently famous or popular, sources such as *Current Biography* or even *Biography.com* may be most appropriate. As noted previously, if very little is known about the figure being sought, an indirect source such as the *Biography and Genealogy Master Index* or an aggregate source that provides both direct and indirect access to information, such as *Biography in Context* or *Biography Reference Bank*, should be consulted early in the search in order to locate information with a minimum of lost time and fruitless searching.

If the user is hoping to locate detailed or exhaustive coverage of an individual, a number of steps will be required. Indirect biographical sources should be consulted to obtain references to the articles on the biographee that are available in the standard biographical reference sources. Then the articles located should be consulted for any bibliographic references or recommendations that may be included. Information about the individual of interest may also be available in nonbiographical periodical articles. Sources such as *Biography Index*, *Biography in Context*, the *Biography Reference Bank*, or even a general periodical index can provide access to such articles. If the user is hoping to obtain as much information about the person in question as possible, the existence of a full-length biography or autobiography of the individual should be investigated. The library catalog, available union catalogs such as *WorldCat*, and biographical bibliographies (such as Daniel Burt's *The Biography Book* and related titles listed in this chapter's "Additional Readings" section) may be consulted to determine whether such a work is available.

Subject Inquiries

A number of sources are designed to help searchers locate information on individuals prominent in a particular subject area or vocation. Sources such as *Contemporary Authors*, *American Men and Women of Science*, and *Who's Who in American Politics* are just a few of the numerous subject-specific sources available. These specialized sources, because of their more limited scope, are often able to include a larger number of entrants from the field and information at a greater level of detail. If the profession or field of the individual sought is known to the user, these subject-specific sources may be a good starting point for the search. If it is not known whether a subject-specific source is available, a guide to biographical sources (see "Additional Readings") should be consulted for further information. A number of excellent subject-specific free Web sites also may be consulted for biographical information. The *Union List of Artist Names* (*ULAN*), the *Internet Movie Database* (*IMDb*), the *All Music Guide*, *POTUS: Presidents of the United States*, and the *First Ladies Gallery* are just a few of the subject-specific free Web sites that can provide reliable biographical information. The *ipl2* provides useful Web guides and recommendations for available subject-specific Web resources. Professional directories, although limited in the biographical information they provide, may also serve a purpose in biographical searching. These directories often provide an opportunity to verify the name, licenses, and educational credentials of individuals who are not included in more standard biographical sources.

Authors and writers are particularly well covered in many general biographical sources. Additionally, there are a number of excellent sources that focus on this vocation. If the subject of the search can be considered a writer by any definition, *Contemporary Authors* should be checked for coverage. The *Dictionary of Literary Biography*, a related work to the *Contemporary Authors* series, is also an excellent source of biographical information for literary figures. These sources offer thorough cross-referencing and can be quite valuable when dealing with questions of pseudonyms. *Contemporary Authors*, the *Contemporary Authors New Revisions Series*, the *Dictionary of Literary Biography*, and more are available electronically via Gale's *Literature Resource Center*. Because this aggregate source also includes works focusing on literary criticism, it is a particularly effective resource for those searching not only for biographical information about an author but also for critical information about the author's works. *Contemporary Authors* and *Contemporary Authors New Revisions* are also included in *Biography in Context*, which may be more widely available than the *Literature Resource Center*, especially in smaller libraries.

It is not uncommon for a librarian to be asked to help a user identify an individual who fits a particular set of biographical criteria. Often in relation to school assignments, librarians may be faced with the challenge of finding an individual of a certain race or ethnicity who is prominent in a particular field or profession. Searches of this type have been, historically, difficult and labor-intensive. However, with the additional search capabilities and excellent access points of the electronic biographical sources, such searches have become much simpler. *American National Biography*, the *Oxford Dictionary of National Biography*, *Biography in Context*, and the *Biography Reference Bank*, among others, allow searching by a variety of criteria

---

BOX 16.3
COMBINING CRITERIA IN BIOGRAPHICAL SEARCHING

An elementary student was assigned to write a report on a male ballet dancer of African American descent. Such a task seemed hopeless to the student and his father when they approached the reference desk; however, with the assistance of the *Biography in Context*'s Person Search, an appropriate individual was identified in a matter of minutes. The librarian used the various options in the search interface to specify Occupation = ballet dancer, Ethnicity = African American, and Gender = male. The search resulted in several matches, including Arthur Mitchell, one of the first African Americans to become successful and internationally known as a classical ballet dancer. The search yielded links to articles on Mitchell in *Contemporary Black Biography*, *Notable Black American Men*, *Newsmakers*, *Encyclopedia of African American Culture and History*, and *International Dictionary of Ballet*. In addition there was a link to an image and two related Web sites.

---

such as gender, vocation, ethnicity, religion, place of birth, date of birth, date of death, and more.

Images

If a picture of the subject is required, there are a number of sources that may be useful. Although some may feel that images are sought only by schoolchildren writing reports, a vast amount of information that may not be readily available elsewhere can be gleaned from the image of an individual. Details of a person's appearance are not regularly included in many of the traditional sources; however, that information may be observed firsthand by the searcher if an image is available. Standard biographical sources, such as the *Encyclopedia of World Biography* and *Current Biography*, generally provide images of their entrants. The *Encyclopedia of World Biography* and *Current Biography* may be searched electronically: the *Encyclopedia* via *Biography in Context* and *Current Biography* either individually or via the *Biography Reference Bank*. With many electronic sources, such as *Biography in Context*, the *Biography Reference Bank*, *American National Biography*, and the *Oxford Dictionary of National Biography*, it is possible to limit the search to entries with illustrations. Encyclopedias, especially those designed for young people, can serve as an excellent source for images. Web search tools, such as Google Images, may provide quick electronic access to hard-to-find pictures. Images relating to the work of the individual in question, such as campaign posters and political cartoons, may provide additional insight and perspective. When dealing with requests for images, the librarian may be faced with the dilemma of having to explain to users why no photographs exist for certain figures of historical significance. It is important for the librarian to remain patient and tactful when explaining the time limitations of photographic technology and to offer artists' renderings as a possible alternative.

BOX 16.4
IMAGES AS A FORM OF BIOGRAPHICAL INFORMATION

"A good portrait is a kind of biography."

—Alexander Smith, *On Vagabonds*

Recently Deceased

Individuals who are recently deceased may, for a brief period, still be listed in the current sources; however, after they are removed from the current sources, it may take some time before they are included in the retrospective. During this gap, it may be necessary to consult alternative sources. Electronic resources that are regularly updated, particularly sources that include newspaper, magazine, or journal articles, may fill this need. Biographical sources that index periodicals, such as *Biography Index*, *Biography in Context*, and the *Biography Reference Bank*, as well as general periodical indexes, may be extremely useful.

Obituaries

Obituaries can provide a wealth of biographical information on the famous as well as on the lesser known. Obituaries for famous individuals may be accessed in a number of ways. The *New York Times Obituaries Index* is a standard source to use when searching for obituaries of the well known. The index is available in print, or obituaries can be searched online from the *New York Times* Web archive. The online *New York Times* archive may be searched for citations free of charge; however, full-text coverage must be purchased. *Current Biography* provides short obituary notices with references to the *New York Times* obituaries for past biographees. The content of *Current Biography* and, thus, the obituaries, is available electronically. The *Biography and Genealogy Master Index* may also be used to find some obituary references. Often, obituaries will be published even for lesser-known figures, particularly in the person's local newspaper. Historically, the obituaries published in these small-town newspapers became quite inaccessible over time. Although the newspaper itself may have been preserved in microform, access to the contents of said paper was often quite limited because of a lack of indexing. Currently, a number of retrospective indexing and digitization projects are helping to save these valuable records from obscurity. Librarians should be sure to investigate this possible avenue of access for obituaries published in local papers. Because newspaper Web sites may make their obituary sections freely available, searches using a Web search engine such as Google may also yield a needed obituary.

Local and Lesser-Known Personalities

If the user is attempting to locate information on local or lesser-known personalities, it will be necessary to alter the search strategy and sources employed. Because users can pose queries about anyone, and comparatively few persons are ever included in biographical reference sources, biographical requests for the local and lesser-known can be quite daunting. However, it is important to remember that virtually all persons are listed somewhere, even if only in local sources. Locally compiled and created resources, particularly local newspapers, are excellent potential sources. Vital records, city directories, or yearbooks from local institutions may also provide biographical insights. Until recently, using such sources necessitated research visits and interlibrary loan requests. Now, because many libraries and institutions have begun creating databases of local history information and records, much information is available via the Web. Visiting the Web sites of the libraries in the area where the individual lived or achieved prominence should give some indication as to what information is available electronically or, if not yet available online, what is available in print. If sources are available for use remotely, the librarian should explain their use and worth to the user to ensure the user's ability to utilize them. If the sources are not available for use remotely, the librarian should again explain what sources are held, what they may contain, and what options exist for consulting those sources, including interlibrary loan, photocopy requests, or site visits.

Genealogical Information

Genealogical queries are a subset of biographical questions and are quite popular, especially in public libraries and in libraries that house a special collection focusing on family or local history. Because of their popularity, it is necessary for all reference librarians, even those not choosing to specialize in this field, to be familiar with some of the basic genealogical sources. A number of excellent electronic options exist when searching for genealogical information. *FamilySearch*, a free resource from the Church of Jesus Christ of Latter-Day Saints, provides information on how to conduct genealogical research as well as a searchable database of information. Subscription databases, such as *Ancestry Library Edition* and *HeritageQuest Online*, provide extensive coverage and access to works of genealogical research. *Cyndi's List of Genealogy Sites on the Internet* provides a categorized index to genealogical resources on the Internet, serving as a free starting point for online research. Self-published family history Web sites, which may be inconsistent, incomplete, or inaccurate, should be approached with caution and carefully evaluated.

As when searching for information on local personalities, genealogical requests may necessitate consultation of primary source materials, and the reference request may quickly move into the realm of research. Primary source materials such as birth, death, and marriage certificates, census records, and tombstones provide a wealth of genealogical and biographical information but can be very time-consuming and labor-intensive to locate and consult. The responsibility of the librarian in this realm usually does not lie in conducting the research for the user; rather, it lies in conveying to the user the types of sources that may be available, the information that they may contain, and suggestions on how to locate and obtain the records.

Fictional Personalities

Reference questions may arise that are presumed to be biographical in nature but that, in fact, focus on a fictional personality instead of an actual person. Although the librarian may determine that the name in question is that of a fictional personality, conveying this information to a user who believes the person to be real may require some tact. Literary characters, gods, or epic heroes may be the focus of such inquiries. General and subject encyclopedias, such as those focusing on literature, folklore, mythology, and religion, may be helpful when searching for references to fictional figures. *The New Century Cyclopedia of Names* has entries for places, events, literary works, and fictional and mythological characters, as well as for important people from the past. Individuals who were alive at some point but who have since attained legendary status, such as saints, folk heroes, and outlaws, may also pose unique challenges. It should be noted that biographical studies of saints are often quite glorified, frequently to the point that they are considered hagiography. Legends surrounding folk heroes and outlaws (and especially outlaws who have evolved into folk heroes) are often quite exaggerated as well, and careful checking will be required to verify occurrences as fact.

Book-Length Biographies

Biographical queries are perennially popular at the reference desk, and some users do not wish to stop their investigation with a few mere articles. Recommendations for book-length biographical works may also be requested. This type of request may be considered both a biographical query and a readers' advisory request. Both factual and fictionalized book-length biographies exist, and the librarian should take care to ascertain which type of coverage interests the user. Standard readers' advisory sources may be useful, and readers' advisory tools with a biographical or historical focus should also be consulted. *The Biography Book* provides recommendations for factual biographies, biographical novels, fictional portraits, and even juvenile biographies, and *What Historical Novel Do I Read Next?* and *Historical Figures in Fiction* will, obviously, focus on fictionalized accounts. Theatrical and cinematic adaptations of biographies may also be of interest to users. *The Biography Book* provides references to both, and free Web sources, such as the *Internet Movie Database*, may also be helpful.

BOX 16.5
SEARCH STRATEGY: SEEKING MR. ROGERS

A media studies student had an assignment to write a paper on an individual who was influential in television programming for children. She chose Mr. Rogers, recalling her own experience as a child watching the *Mister Rogers' Neighborhood* program. Searching for "Mr. Rogers" in *Wikipedia*, she found an article on Fred Rogers that included his full name ("Fred McFeely Rogers") and his birth and death dates (March 20, 1928–February 27, 2003). Not satisfied with this article and its associated references and external links, she e-mailed the reference librarian at her college library for assistance in locating more complete and authoritative sources. The librarian began by consulting the online version of *Biography and Genealogy Master Index* and discovered several variant forms of his name: Rogers, Fred; Rogers, Fred (1928–); Rogers, Fred (1928–2003); Rogers, Fred (McFeely) (1928–); Rogers, Fred (McFeely) (1928–2003); Rogers, Fred M. (1928–); Rogers, Fred M. (1928–2003); Rogers, Fred McFeely (1928–); Rogers, Fred McFeely (1928–2003). Scanning the entries associated with each of these variant forms, the librarian identified the sources likely to provide the most substantive information (in contrast to briefer *Who's Who* type entries). These included *Contemporary Authors*, *The Scribner Encyclopedia of American Lives*, the *Encyclopedia of World Biography*, and the *Current Biography Yearbook*. Because Mr. Rogers had died a few years earlier, the librarian also checked *American National Biography* online and found a detailed biographical sketch together with a photograph. This entry concluded with a very helpful bibliography including various published sources and a three-hour documentary by PBS, *Fred Rogers: America's Favorite Neighbor*. The librarian sent the student an e-mail summarizing her search strategy and recommended sources. The student replied with a "thank you" e-mail and a further request for help in locating the documentary. The librarian did a title search in *WorldCat* and found more than 500 holding libraries. Although the college library did not have a copy, the librarian was able to direct the student to a copy in the video collection at the local public library.

NOTE

1.   William A. Katz, *Introduction to Reference Work*, 8th ed. (Boston: McGraw-Hill, 2002), 2:191.

LIST OF SOURCES

African American National Biography. 8 vols. New York: Oxford University Press, 2008. Also available online as part of the *Oxford African American Studies Center*.

All Music Guide. http://www.allmusic.com/.

Almanac of Famous People. 9th ed. 2 vols. Farmington Hills, MI: Gale, 2007. Also available online as part of *Biography in Context*.

American Men and Women of Science. 28th ed. 8 vols. Farmington Hills, MI: Gale, 2010. Also available online as part of the *Gale Virtual Reference Library*.

American National Biography. 24 vols. New York: Oxford University Press, 1999. Supplements, 2000–. http://www.anb.org.

Ancestry Library Edition. Ann Arbor, MI: ProQuest. Available online via ProQuest.

Australian Dictionary of Biography. http://www.adb.online.anu.edu.au/adbonline.htm.

Biography and Genealogy Master Index. 2nd ed. Farmington Hills, MI: Gale, 1980–. Annual. Also available online from Gale.

Biography in Context. Farmington Hills, MI: Gale. Available online from Gale.

Biography Index. New York: H. W. Wilson, 1946–. Quarterly, with annual cumulations. Also available online via WilsonWeb.

Biography Reference Bank. New York: H. W. Wilson. Available online via WilsonWeb.

Biography.com. http://www.biography.com.

Canadian Who's Who, 2010. 45th ed. Toronto: University of Toronto Press, 2010. 1449 pp.

Chambers Biographical Dictionary. 7th ed. Edinburgh: Chambers, 2002. 1650 pp.

Contemporary Authors Series. Farmington Hills, MI: Gale, 1962–. Also available online as part of *Biography in Context* and *Literature Resource Center*.

Contemporary Black Biography. Farmington Hills, MI: Gale, 1992–. Also available online as part of *Biography in Context*.

Credo Reference. Boston: Credo Reference. http://corp.credoreference.com.

Current Biography. New York: H. W. Wilson, 1940–. Monthly, with an annual cumulative yearbook. Also available online via WilsonWeb and as part of the *Biography Reference Bank*.

Cyndi's List of Genealogy Sites on the Internet. http://www.CyndisList.com.

Dictionary of American Biography. 20 vols. and index. New York: Scribner, 1928–1937. Supplements, 1944–1980. Index, 1996. Also available online as part of *Biography in Context*.

Dictionary of Canadian Biography. 15 vols. Toronto: University of Toronto Press, 1966–2006. http://www.biographi.ca/index-e.html.

Dictionary of Literary Biography Series. Farmington Hills, MI: Gale, 1978–. Also available online and as part of the *Literature Resource Center*.

Dictionary of Scientific Biography. 18 vols. New York: Scribner, 1970–1980, 1990. Also available online as part of the *Gale Virtual Reference Library*.

Directory of American Scholars. 10th ed. 6 vols. Farmington Hills, MI: Gale, 2002. Also available online as part of *Biography in Context*.

Encyclopedia of World Biography. 2nd ed. 18 vols. Farmington Hills, MI: Gale, 1998. Supplements, 1999–. Also available online as part of *Biography in Context*.

FamilySearch. The Church of Jesus Christ of Latter-Day Saints. https://www.familysearch.org/.

First Ladies Gallery. http://www.whitehouse.gov/history/firstladies/.

HeritageQuest Online. Ann Arbor, MI: ProQuest. Available online via ProQuest.

Infoplease Biography. http://www.infoplease.com/people.html.

The International Who's Who 2010. 73rd ed. London: Routledge, 2009. 2482 pp. http://www.worldwhoswho.com.

Internet Movie Database (IMDb). http://www.imdb.com/.

ipl2. http://www.ipl2.org/.

Literature Resource Center. Farmington Hills, MI: Gale. Available online from Gale.

Marquis Who's Who on the Web. New Providence, NJ: Marquis Who's Who. Available online from Marquis Who's Who.

Merriam-Webster's Biographical Dictionary. Rev. ed. Springfield, MA: Merriam-Webster, 1995. 1170 pp.

The New Century Cyclopedia of Names. 3 vols. Englewood Cliffs, NJ: Prentice Hall, 1954.

New Dictionary of Scientific Biography. 8 vols. Detroit: Scribner's, 2007. Also available on-line as part of the *Gale Virtual Reference Library*.

New York Times Obituaries Index, 1858–1968. New York: New York Times, 1970. Additional coverage from 1969–1978, http://www.nytimes.com/pages/obituaries/index.html.

Newsmakers. Farmington Hills, MI: Gale, 1988–. Quarterly, with an annual yearbook. Also available as part of *Biography in Context*.

Notable American Women: 1607–1950. 3 vols. Cambridge, MA: Belknap Press of Harvard University Press, 1971.

Notable American Women: The Modern Period. Cambridge, MA: Belknap Press of Harvard University Press, 1971. 773 pp.

Oxford African American Studies Center. Oxford: Oxford University Press. http://www.oxfordaasc.com/.

Oxford Dictionary of National Biography. Rev. ed. 61 vols. Oxford: Oxford University Press, 2004. http://www.oxforddnb.com.

POTUS: Presidents of the United States. http://www.ipl.org/div/potus/.

The Scribner Encyclopedia of American Lives. 1981–. New York: Scribner, 1998–. Irregular.

Union List of Artist Names (ULAN). http://www.getty.edu/research/tools/vocabularies/ulan/index.html.

Who Was Who, 1897–2010. 12 vols. London: A & C Black, 1929–2010. Irregular.

Who Was Who: A Cumulated Index, 1897–2000. London: A & C Black, 2002. http://www.ukwhoswho.com.

Who Was Who in America, 1897–2010. 21 vols. and index. New Providence, NJ: Marquis Who's Who, 1942–2010. Irregular. Also available online as part of *Marquis Who's Who on the Web*.

Who Was Who in America: Historical Volume, 1607–1896. Rev. ed. Chicago: Marquis Who's Who, 1967. 689 pp.

Who's Who, 2011. 163rd ed. London: A & C Black, 2010. 2650 pp. http://www.ukwhoswho.com.

Who's Who among African Americans. 25th ed. Farmington Hills, MI: Gale, 2010. 1502 pp. Also available online as part of *Biography in Context*.

Who's Who in America, 2011. 65th ed. 2 vols. New Providence, NJ: Marquis Who's Who, 2010. Also available online as part of *Marquis Who's Who on the Web*.

Who's Who in American Politics, 2011. 24th ed. New Providence, NJ: Marquis Who's Who, 2011. 1046 pp. Also available online as part of *Marquis Who's Who on the Web*.

Who's Who in Science and Engineering, 2011–2012. 11th ed. New Providence, NJ: Marquis Who's Who, 2010. 2508 pp. Also available online as part of *Marquis Who's Who on the Web*.

Who's Who in the East, 2011. 38th ed. New Providence, NJ: Marquis Who's Who, 2010. 1664 pp. Also available online as part of *Marquis Who's Who on the Web*.

Who's Who in the Midwest, 2011. 37th ed. New Providence, NJ: Marquis Who's Who, 2010. 886 pp. Also available online as part of Marquis Who's Who on the Web.

Who's Who in the South and Southwest, 2011. 37th ed. New Providence, NJ: Marquis Who's Who, 2010. 990 pp. Also available online as part of *Marquis Who's Who on the Web*.

Who's Who in the West, 2011. 38th ed. New Providence, NJ: Marquis Who's Who, 2010. 954 pp. Also available online as part of *Marquis Who's Who on the Web.*

Who's Who in the World, 2011. 28th ed. New Providence, NJ: Marquis Who's Who, 2010. 3108 pp. Also available online as part of *Marquis Who's Who on the Web.*

Who's Who of American Women, 2010–2011. 28th ed. New Providence, NJ: Marquis Who's Who, 2010. 2004 pp. Also available online as part of *Marquis Who's Who on the Web.*

ADDITIONAL READINGS

American Library Association, Reference and User Services Association, History Section, Genealogy Committee. *Guidelines for a Unit or Course of Instruction in Genealogical Research at Schools of Library and Information Science.* 1995, revised 2004. http://www.ala.org/ala/mgrps/divs/rusa/resources/guidelines/guidelinesunit.cfm.

These guidelines provide an outline of the expertise needed to support library users undertaking genealogical research, including basic genealogical research methodology and major genealogy research resources. Notes accompanying the guidelines identify several sources useful in developing this expertise.

Burt, Daniel S. *The Biography Book: A Reader's Guide to Nonfiction, Fictional, and Film Biographies of More than 500 of the Most Fascinating Individuals of All Time.* Westport, CT: Oryx Press, 2001. 629 pp.

More than 500 historical figures are included in this biographical reader's advisory tool. In addition to recommended biographies, citations to autobiographical or primary source material, biographical fiction, juvenile biographies, and biographical films and theatrical adaptations are noted.

Cimbala, Diana J., Jennifer Cargill, and Brian Alley. *Biographical Sources: A Guide to Dictionaries and Reference Works.* Phoenix, AZ: Oryx Press, 1986. 146 pp.

This guide, in an effort to help researchers locate relevant sources, provides annotated bibliographic access to almost 700 English-language biographical sources.

Clarke, Jack. "Biographical Dictionaries, the Fine Line between Vanity and Pride." *RQ* 22 (Fall 1983): 76–78.

Designed to help librarians deal with questions surrounding vanity publications, this concise article offers information about a large number of questionable biographical sources.

Grogan, Denis. *Biographical Sources.* Grogan's Case Studies in Reference Work, vol. 6. London: Clive Bingley, 1987. 154 pp.

Grogan describes and explains search strategies and sources that are relevant and useful when pursuing biographical inquiries.

Mann, Rupert. "Searching the *Oxford Dictionary of National Biography.*" *The Indexer* 25 (April 2006): 16–18.

Mann, electronic publication manager for the *Oxford Dictionary of National Biography,* explains how the option to "search for biography of person" can exploit the metadata associated with each name to enable retrieval on alternative forms, such as maiden and married surnames. Although the index stores variants in spelling of names that appear in the historical record (e.g., searching "shakspere" will lead to "Shakespeare"), misspellings will not yield a match.

Schellinger, Paul E., ed. *St. James Guide to Biography*. Chicago: St. James Press, 1991. 870 pp.

This guide provides citations to and critical analysis of book-length biographies of 700 historic individuals. Living and deceased persons of either general or scholarly interest are included.

Schreiner, Susan A., and Michael A. Somers. "Biography Resources: Finding Information on the Famous, Infamous and Obscure." *College & Research Libraries News* 63 (January 2002): 32–35, 39.

Though somewhat dated, this article serves as a brief guide to free Web sites that provide general and subject-specific access to biographical information.

Searing, Susan E. "Biographical Reference Works for and about Women, from the Advent of the Women's Liberation Movement to the Present: An Exploratory Analysis." *Library Trends* 56 (Fall 2007): 469–93.

Searing compiled a database of more than 400 English-language biographical dictionaries and collective biographies devoted to women and published in the period 1966–2006. This database was analyzed to identify trends in subject content over this period. She also highlights problems with some sources, including duplicative content, subjectivity, and factual errors and omissions. A bibliography of sources used in this study, grouped by decade, is available at http://www.library.uiuc.edu/lsx/BiogRefWorksAboutWomen.htm.

Slocum, Robert B. *Biographical Dictionaries and Related Works*. 2nd ed. 2 vols. Detroit: Gale Research, 1986.

Arranged in three sections, "Universal Biography," "National or Area Biography," and "Biography by Vocation," this classic guide details citations and annotations of more than 16,000 biographical works.

Wick, Robert L., and Terry Ann Mood, eds. *ARBA Guide to Bibliographical Resources, 1986–1997*. Englewood, CO: Libraries Unlimited, 1998. 604 pp.

Full bibliographic citations and critical annotations are provided for more than 1,100 biographical sources. The work is divided into two parts, "International and National Biographies" and "Biographies in Professional Fields."

Dictionaries

Stephanie R. Davis-Kahl

USES AND CHARACTERISTICS

Purpose: Past and Present

Dictionaries have long been the tool by which people from all walks of life find the definitions, pronunciations, usage, and etymology of words. According to the *Encyclopaedia Britannica*, "a dictionary lists a set of words with information about them."[1] They are fascinating glimpses into how words and their meanings are shaped by aspects of our culture and society such as commerce, technology, entertainment, trends, politics, and globalization. In the last century, dictionaries have expanded their reach from words to images and visual information, an excellent development for a wide range of users, including children, teachers, librarians, and English as a second language learners. By far the most exciting development in the dictionary's long history is the convergence of Web technology with the dictionary and the plethora of information contained within, making dictionaries more accessible and versatile.

Although a short word list from the 7th century B.C.E was found in central Mesopotamia, the dictionary as we know it today in the 21st century has its roots in Greece and later in Italy, from the 1st century C.E. into the Middle Ages. In the early Middle Ages, manuscripts often included *glosses*, marginal or interlinear notes, to define or translate words. Oftentimes, glosses from different works were collected and printed as a stand-alone publication. Clerics, spelling reformers, and teachers heavily influenced the development and creation of dictionaries. These could be divided into two schools of thought: the first stressed standardizing the language (that is, dictionary as authority, a *prescriptive* approach), whereas the second emphasized recording language as it is used by the people (that is, dictionary as reflection of reality, a *descriptive* approach). An excellent example of the divergence between the two perspectives is illustrated by the reaction to one of the first dictionaries compiled in America, *The Columbian Dictionary of the English Language*, published in 1800. According to the *Encyclopaedia Britannica*, "it received abuse from critics who were not yet ready for the inclusion of American words."[2]

Although Britain's contribution to the evolution of the dictionary is exemplified best in the massive and incomparable *Oxford English Dictionary*, it is worth noting that dictionaries created up until the 18th century were authored by amateur lexicographers. John Kersey the Younger published *A New English Dictionary* in 1702, the first work to be compiled by a professional lexicographer. Another major name in the history of dictionaries is Samuel Johnson, a poet and critic, whose *Dictionary* included quotations showing the usage of the word as well as a definition. Johnson's *Dictionary* went through multiple editions and was even imported to America for schoolchildren.

Kinds of Information Found in Dictionaries

The kinds of information found in a dictionary depend on the goal of the dictionary itself. A standard, general dictionary will contain pronunciation (including syllabication and emphasis), definitions, function, variant spellings, and an example of usage. Dictionary entries may also include deeper information, such as etymological history, dates of use, and—depending on the objective, scope, and size of the publication—an illustration or photograph. A specialized subject- or discipline-focused dictionary will go into more detail in its definition, examples, and usage but may omit elements found in a general dictionary such as pronunciation. Dictionaries are generally organized alphabetically, but visual dictionaries, in which the focus is on associating terms with their corresponding objects, are often organized by subject. Dictionaries in electronic form can include enhancements such as hyperlinks for cross-references or audio samples of correct pronunciation.

Types of Dictionaries

General dictionaries are one of two types: abridged and unabridged. An *abridged* dictionary is usually based on a larger work, such as the two-volume *Shorter Oxford English Dictionary*, which has fewer than 3,900 pages, whereas the full 20-volume *Oxford English Dictionary* has 22,000 pages. The goals of an abridged dictionary are convenience, conciseness, and selectivity. An *unabridged* dictionary strives to be comprehensive in its goal to record and reflect the usage and definition of words in use at the time of the dictionary's creation. Also, an unabridged dictionary provides more information about its contents than an abridged dictionary. Whereas an abridged dictionary may include only a word's definition, part of speech, pronunciation, and usage, an unabridged dictionary may include variant spellings, word etymology and dates of use, lengthy notes about usage (including examples), synonyms or word history, and color pictures. Specialized types of dictionaries focus in depth on particular aspects of words, such as etymology or synonyms (see Box 17.1). Examples of these specialized types are discussed later in this chapter.

BOX 17.1
SPECIALIZED DICTIONARIES

Etymological dictionary. An etymological dictionary gives the history of individual words with linguistic derivation and examples from writings of the past.

Slang dictionary. A slang dictionary defines terms used in ordinary, informal speech. These terms may include jargon, obscenities, or ephemeral words that go in and out of use quickly.

Thesaurus. A thesaurus contains synonyms and antonyms, usually without definitions. Its purpose is to provide writers with alternate or more specific words.

Dual-language dictionary. A dual-language dictionary has two sections, the first being a dictionary of terms in one language with definitions in a second language. The second section is the reverse, with terms in the second language and definitions in the first language.

Dialect dictionary. A dialect dictionary gives regional variants and usage for words within a language. It may include some slang.

Usage dictionary. A usage dictionary prescribes how a word should be used, based on the way it has been used in the past.

EVALUATION

When evaluating dictionaries, an assessment of their authority and accuracy is essential. Scope considerations include both the number and the content of entries. Because a growing number of titles are available in electronic form, a comparison of the features of print and electronic formats becomes important.

Authority

Authority can be difficult to ascertain in the case of large, unabridged, comprehensive dictionaries because they are usually the product of editorial staffs of publishers. As a consequence, investigating the authority of the publisher is usually a more productive endeavor. In the United States and Canada, several publishers are well known for the quality of their previously published work: Houghton Mifflin (*American Heritage Dictionary*), Merriam-Webster, NTC/Contemporary, Oxford University Press, Random House, Macmillan USA, and World Book. Internationally, Dorling Kindersley (DK) is noted for its visual dictionaries, and Cambridge University Press is noted for its overall reputation and quality of content. In addition, attention should be paid to university presses, which often publish dictionaries of regional interest, with a focus such as slang or regionalisms. In general, judging the authority of a dictionary can be informed by print, online publisher or user reviews, reviews in the library literature, posting queries to mailing lists or blogs, and browsing catalogs or bookstores. Publishers are seeking to make dictionaries "more accessible, more inviting, more popular with individual users" but without "sacrificing the imprimatur of authority."[3]

Accuracy and Currency

The three key factors in judging a dictionary's accuracy and currency are spelling, definition, and usage. Spelling should be up-to-date, keeping pace with how a word's spelling might have changed in common use. The inclusion of variant spellings is also important for loanwords that have been subsumed into a language from other languages or dialects, such as the word *airplane*, which is an alteration of the French word *aéroplane*. Typically, dictionaries also demonstrate where hyphens should go if necessary. This is a helpful feature especially with terms that sometimes appear as a single word, for example, e-mail, home page, and Web site. Definitions of words should be succinct and clear, without using the word itself. It is important to note here that some dictionaries organize definitions chronologically, whereas others order definitions by the most to the least commonly used. In addition, a comprehensive unabridged dictionary will include several, if not many, definitions, but a general desk dictionary will usually limit itself to commonly used definitions. The same holds true for usage, which is fundamental to understanding how the word is used in context, not only grammatically but also in modern connotations. For example, the word "cookie" has three definitions listed in *The American Heritage Dictionary of the English Language*:

1. A small, usually flat and crisp cake made from sweetened dough.
2. *Slang* A person, usually of a specified kind: *a lawyer who was a tough cookie*.
3. *Computer Science* A collection of information, usually including a username and the current date and time, stored on the local computer of a person using the World Wide Web, used chiefly to identify users who have previously registered or visited the site.[4]

Some dictionaries create their own usage examples, and others use phrases or sentences from literature, poetry, science, or news to demonstrate usage.

Format

The Internet has brought along another wave of evolution in dictionaries. In contrast to dictionaries that were once static representations of language and word use, publishers are now taking advantage of the fluid nature of technology and putting it to excellent use. An article published in *Booklist* in 2003 reported that pre-Internet, Merriam-Webster would receive about 1,000 letters every year from dictionary users with new definitions, corrections, and questions. At the time of the article, the company received 1,000 emails per month. In addition, "the company can observe which words are most frequently looked up online at any given time."[5]

A plethora of free and subscription-based dictionary Web sites are active on the Internet. Some are from publishers, such as *Merriam-Webster Online*, which is divided into free and fee resources, but which also includes extras such as word games, word of the day, and free downloads such as dictionary toolbars. In evaluating and selecting which online dictionaries to link from a library Web site, criteria to consider are similar to criteria used to evaluate print dictionaries with the additional factors of ease of navigation, ease of printing, and quick response time.

In both print and online dictionaries, aesthetics make a difference. Because dictionaries are traditionally text with some pictures (if any), layout is a key factor in assessing usability. Good use of white space, color choices, use of boldface or italics for emphasis, use of different fonts, and size of typeface all have an impact on the ease of locating a definition and readability. In some cases, how a page looks may seem frivolous; however, for users who are visually impaired or who just prefer not to squint over a page of small words, user-friendly aesthetics will improve the accessibility of the information.

Scope

A dictionary's scope is often communicated in its introduction, usually written by the primary author or lead editor. In addition to explaining the purpose and content of the dictionary, the introduction often contains information such as abbreviations and acronyms, pronunciation guides, names of contributors, and how the dictionary came to be compiled and published. This information will help gauge whether the dictionary will supplement or replace other items in the current reference collection, and its content will help decide if the dictionary is age-appropriate (i.e., children, college students) and contains a useful amount of information. For instance, language derivation is less important for children than visual representations and a clear pronunciation guide. Last, some dictionaries may include charts, tables, and time lines that make up a sort miniature ready-reference collection. Such information is definitely helpful but, for many libraries, not a requirement for selection, given that libraries will have other materials such as almanacs and encyclopedias that include such information.

Comparing Similar Dictionaries

In evaluating dictionaries that cover similar topics, regions, or time periods, an excellent rule of thumb is to choose a few words, look them up in each dictionary, and compare the elements of the dictionary entry discussed earlier in this chapter. The words selected should represent commonly used terms, slang, technical jargon, and rarely used words. Other considerations include the presence of a chart or legend explaining the abbreviations used to represent word derivation, part of speech, stress marks, and regionalisms.

SELECTION

With the many varieties of dictionaries available, assessing the value of a particular dictionary is vitally important. Ideally, this process should begin with an exploration of user needs. No matter the type of library, there are often several choices for purchasing dictionaries. Therefore, in the public library setting, the librarian must consider the needs of children, adolescents, adults, and senior citizens. Also important is the demographics of the community; as the ethnic makeup of the community changes, so do the reading and reference needs of library users. In a school library, dictionaries (as all reference works in general) should be useful for a range of ages, learning styles, reading levels, curricula, and topics. In addition, teachers' and administrators' needs should be addressed, so a more comprehensive dictionary or a dictionary specific to education may be a good purchase (depending on other factors such as cost). In academic libraries, considerations include type of institution. For example, a research university's students, faculty, and staff will differ from those of a school of art and design. In any academic library, the balance between curriculum and research needs is key to creating a responsive reference collection. There is no one-size-fits-all solution to selecting dictionaries, especially when considering more specialized, subject-focused dictionaries. Fortunately, publishers provide a wide range of options for dictionaries, so libraries have many choices.

Sources for Reviews

Selecting dictionaries for purchase takes time to compare and contrast individual titles and to decide whether an online resource will best fit the needs at hand. Luckily, there are several sources that aid librarians by providing objective opinions. *Kister's Best Dictionaries for Adults and Young People: A Comparative Guide* is an excellent starting point. Though this book is more than 15 years old, it provides useful insight into how dictionaries are produced and published and also provides criteria for purchasing. More than 300 sources for both adults and children are evaluated and annotated, making it a comprehensive, if somewhat dated, source for reviews. Appendices include a listing of dictionary publishers and associations. A slightly more updated book is the second edition of Thomas Kabdebo's *Dictionary of Dictionaries*, published in 1997. Kabdebo's work covers nearly 9,000 sources, primarily language- and subject-oriented dictionaries, glossaries, and wordbooks. Each evaluative annotation includes the dictionary's organization and topic coverage, and the book itself has three indexes (title, author, and keyword) to aid users in finding a dictionary. Other monograph sources include the *ARBA Guide to Subject Encyclopedias and Dictionaries* and Andrew Dalby's *A Guide to World Language Dictionaries*. Other review sources are discussed in chapter 13. In addition, general sources such as Amazon.com can be helpful in understanding what consumers look for in a dictionary.

Electronic Options

Electronic options for dictionaries include both freely available and subscription-based titles. Features of some specific titles are discussed in the following section. Electronic dictionaries may be single titles or aggregations of titles that can be searched simultaneously. The best-known title available by subscription is the *OED Online*, the electronic version of the *Oxford English Dictionary*. An example of a single, freely available title is Joan M. Reitz's *ODLIS: Online Dictionary for Library and Information Science*, based on the print *Dictionary for Library and Information Science*. The online version supports browsing by initial letter in a word or phrase and searching either headwords or headwords and definitions. Like many subject-specific titles, entries include only definitions. Extensive hyperlinks connect terms within a definition to entries elsewhere in the dictionary. In addition, several entries include links to other Web sites for additional explanations of terms.

Increasingly, multiple dictionaries are available as part of collections in electronic form. As noted in chapter 13, *Credo Reference* aggregates access to 531 titles from more than 70 publishers. Among the titles aggregated include English-language dictionaries, bilingual dictionaries, and subject dictionaries in areas such as art, business, medicine, and law. Several sources of quotations are also included. Oxford University Press is making increasing numbers of titles from its rich collection of reference material available in electronic form. *Oxford Dictionaries Online* gives users access to the publisher's modern English dictionaries, thesauri, and usage guides. Coverage includes more than 350,000 definitions covering U.S., British, and worldwide English; more than 600,000 thesaurus entries; and more than 1.9 million usage examples. Users of such subscription-based collections can have confidence in their accuracy and authority. Tools are also available to facilitate simultaneous searching of freely available dictionaries on the Web. For example, *OneLook Dictionary Search* indexes words in more than 1,000 online dictionaries and provides a range of search options in addition to exact match, such as **bird* to find words and phrases that end with *bird*. When a word is searched, the resulting list of matches identifies the titles of sources that provide a definition, allowing the user to select the one(s) likely to be most authoritative.

IMPORTANT GENERAL SOURCES

This section focuses on several kinds of dictionaries and related tools that are found in typical school, public, or academic library reference collections. Under each category, a few representative titles are described. For information on titles not discussed here, the reader can consult the sources for reviews listed earlier and relevant articles in the "Additional Readings" section.

Unabridged Dictionaries

Though unabridged dictionaries are expensive to develop and maintain, the quality ones continue to keep high standards in comprehensiveness, description, and usage. First, a note on the prodigious use of the name "Webster" in the dictionary world is required. Though Merriam-Webster purchased the copyright from Noah Webster in 1843, the name "Webster" is still seen in dictionary titles. The name "Webster" has become a sort of colloquialism for the word "dictionary," and this is reflected in the publishing world.

Noah Webster's first unabridged dictionary, *An American Dictionary of the English Language*, appeared in 1828, and the first Webster's dictionary published by Merriam was released in 1847. The latest in the modern series of the Webster's unabridged dictionary, *Webster's Third* (first published in 1961), is infamous for the decision of its editors to be descriptive in its style and content, rather than prescriptive. Traditionalists were unsupportive of the inclusion of colloquial and slang words, but others welcomed the change as a true reflection of how new words and phrases contribute to the English language.

Its most current edition, titled *Webster's Third New International Dictionary, Unabridged,* was published in 2002. Two versions of this edition are available, one with a CD-ROM and the other with a complimentary one-year subscription to *Merriam-Webster Unabridged* online. Both editions contain nearly a half-million entries with 14,000 new words. Entries include pronunciation, part of speech, definition, example of usage, etymology, labels (obsolete, slang, dialect, regional), cross-references, and more. In the matter of pronunciation, description over prescription also holds true; entries reflect "general cultivated conversational usage, both formal and informal, throughout the English-speaking world."[6] The 2002 edition of *Webster's* included a new label especially for scientific and technical terms: ISV, or International Scientific Vocabulary. ISV labels denote current, in-use words with uncertain language of origin, such as "endoscope" and "cholesterolemia."[7]

In addition to Merriam-Webster, the other authoritative publisher of unabridged dictionaries is Random House. A revised, single-volume edition of the *Random House Webster's Unabridged Dictionary* was published in 2005 with an updated word list, definitions, and etymologies. In addition, the dictionary includes illustrations, maps, and supplements in the form of lists, tables, time lines, style guides, and more. A CD-ROM version is also available. Like other dictionary publishers, Random House also boasts an ever-growing database of new words, new uses for words, and updated definitions.

Etymological Dictionaries

The *Oxford English Dictionary* (*OED*) is by far the most comprehensive etymological dictionary available. The story of the *OED* is a fascinating history of an incredible human achievement that began in 1857 and continues to the present day (see "Additional Readings" at the end of this chapter). The publication has had countless contributors throughout its development and reflects the technology of its time; it was made available in microfilm in 1971, on CD-ROM in 1992, and on the Web in 2000. The most recent edition in print was published in 1989, combining the text of the first edition (published between 1884 and 1928) with four supplements published between 1972 and 1986. Three volumes of supplements, the *Oxford English Dictionary: Additions Series*, were subsequently published in 1993 and 1997. At this time, the master copy of the *OED* was digitized (previous editions had been typeset in hot metal), paving the way for both CD-ROM and online editions. Last, the second edition contains nearly 300,000 main entries, a 15 percent increase over the first edition, but more importantly, the second edition also contains 34 percent more text, with expanded citations, usage examples, and notes. The *Additions Series* not only contained new words such as "acid house," but also added new meanings to older words; for example, to the entry for the word "read," editors added the following definition: "To interpret or translate (genetic information); *spec.* to extract genetic information from (a particular sequence of nucleic acids), or to extract from a given sequence the genetic information necessary to synthesize (a particular substance)."[8] The *OED Online* is now the home for the second edition and the *Additions Series*, and on its Web site, the Help section lists the new words added to the database on a quarterly basis. The *OED Online* can be thought of as a database with extensive searching options, from simple word and proximity searching to Boolean searching across one or more fields (such as headword, definition, and etymology) in the dictionary entries. The quotations illustrating word usage are also searchable.

Though the full 20-volume second edition is usually out of the price range of most public and school libraries, Oxford University Press has several smaller options for these libraries. The *Shorter Oxford English Dictionary* is a two-volume set that is currently in its sixth edition, published in 2007. The purpose of the *Shorter OED* is to provide a "historical dictionary of modern English."[9] It is also available on CD-ROM. The *Oxford Dictionary of Word Histories* was published in 2002 and provides narrative descriptions of words, tracing their development through other languages and time periods to present-day English, including regionalisms and older spellings. The *Shorter OED* and the *Oxford Dictionary of Word Histories* are excellent options for those libraries that choose not to purchase the full *OED*. Another choice is the *Barnhart Concise Dictionary of Etymology*. Though not as comprehensive as the *OED*, it is equally informative and useful as a single-volume etymological dictionary. The most attractive aspect of the *Barnhart* is its focus on current and modern language, with more than 20,000 words and their language derivations.

Desk

Desk dictionaries are usually single-volume, more concise than an unabridged dictionary. Content is more focused and more up-to-date, with rare, technical, and obsolete words and definitions omitted. Etymologies are usually abbreviated or do not appear in a desk dictionary, and appendices usually contain supplemental lists of things such as weights and measures, abbreviations, names, and dates. The biggest difference between the dictionaries discussed in this section is layout; any of the works listed would be excellent choices for home, school, or office.

The American Heritage Dictionary of the English Language is published by Houghton Mifflin and is well known for its readable and aesthetically pleasing layout. Words are in boldface, printed with a dark green ink, and appear in syllabicated form, distinguishing them from accompanying pronunciation, part of speech, definitions, brief etymological note (when included), usage example, and variant forms (also when included). Illustrations are in color, and nearly every page has a mini-guide to pronunciation. The updated fourth edition, published in 2006, includes terms such as "blog" and "9/11."

The *Merriam-Webster's Collegiate Dictionary* is part of the Merriam-Webster family of publications. The strength of the *Collegiate Dictionary* lies in its content, taken from the Merriam-Webster word database. The 11th edition, published in 2003, contains about 10,000 new words, more examples of usage, idioms, and updated definitions. Illustrations are black-and-white drawings, and entries include the usual pronunciation, brief etymology, and usage examples. Considering that the 10th edition of the *Collegiate Dictionary* was published in 1993, the new additions and changes to the 11th edition are significant. The 11th edition comes with the dictionary on CD-ROM and a free year's subscription for consumers (not libraries or schools) to the *Collegiate Dictionary* online, which includes the *Collegiate Thesaurus*, *Collegiate Encyclopedia*, and *Merriam-Webster's Spanish-English Dictionary*. With Merriam-Webster's stellar reputation, libraries may want to investigate a subscription to the Merriam-Webster online products in addition to or instead of purchasing print, depending on factors such as user needs and budgets. An extensive subset of the *Collegiate Dictionary* is freely available at *Merriam-Webster Online.*

Funk & Wagnalls New International Dictionary of the English Language was published in early 2005 and is a two-volume set, setting it apart from other desk dictionaries. In the introduction, editors share their three major objectives: "To present the fundamental facts and characteristics of the language accurately, fully and interestingly.... To present adequately the significant contributions to English made in the United States, [and] To secure the widest possible coverage of both established word stock of English and of the rapidly expanding vocabularies of the arts, sciences, trades, and professions."[10] To this end, definitions are succinct and easy to understand; entries include pronunciation, usage, brief etymology note, and variant spellings when necessary. A mini-guide to pronunciation appears on each odd-numbered page of the book, and black-and-white line drawings serve as illustrations. Although the readability and layout are not as contemporary as *Merriam-Webster's Collegiate,* *Funk & Wagnalls* organizes its definitions with the most currently used appearing first, followed by other less-used definitions. This not only allows editors the flexibility to shape the dictionary's content to the language but also allows the user to learn the word in chronological context.

Two well-regarded titles from Oxford University Press, the *New Oxford American Dictionary* and the *Canadian Oxford Dictionary*, emphasize coverage of current American and Canadian English, respectively. The *New Oxford American Dictionary* has entries organized around core meanings, supplemented by illustrative, in-context usage examples. The *Canadian Oxford Dictionary* entries provide the meaning most familiar to Canadians first. Among the words defined are 2,200 uniquely Canadian words. Coverage also includes 5,500 biographical entries and 5,600 place names.

School

Dictionaries for children and young adults are published by nearly every reputable dictionary publisher, including Oxford University Press, Houghton Mifflin, Macmillan, Merriam-Webster, and World Book, leaving readers to decide between a visual or textual focus. Visual dictionaries can be exciting ways to introduce new words to children, with bright colors, images, and simple definitions. Textual dictionaries may be more appropriate for older children, depending on reading ability and grade level. In each case, important criteria for selection include clear layout, easy-to-understand definitions, and enough words to interest and educate a child using the dictionary. Large print and the highlighting of main words are both helpful at this level, as are simple examples of usage. Dictionaries are available for specific age groups, organized alphabetically and by subject, both with their advantages and drawbacks. For settings serving children and young adults, having a few of both types of dictionaries is a wise choice. Because use of the word "children's" or "student" in the title does not always correspond to a specific age range or grade level, evaluation of such a dictionary should include determining the target audience. For example, Merriam-Webster has a series of four titles: *Merriam-Webster's Primary Dictionary* (grades K–2), *Merriam-Webster's Elementary Dictionary* (grades 3–5), *Merriam-Webster's Intermediate Dictionary* (grades 6–8), and *Merriam-Webster's School Dictionary* (grades 9–11).

A few examples of the many titles available are given here; the article by Terri Tomchyshyn in the "Additional Readings" section includes many more. *DK Merriam-Webster Children's Dictionary* combines the design strengths of Dorling Kindersley with the lexicographic strengths and reputation of Merriam-Webster. The collaboration between the two publishers results in an easy-to-read and informative reference work, with design and images from DK and text based on *Merriam-Webster's Elementary Dictionary*. For older readers, *The American Heritage Student Dictionary* is focused on providing more detailed information such as etymology and usage notes. The *World Book Dictionary* is a two-volume set with more than 225,000 entries and 3,000 illustrations. Words likely to be used by students are clearly defined, and usage examples are included.

Foreign-Language/English-Language Dictionaries

In the case of foreign-language/English-language (dual) dictionaries, the options available include everything from mini-abridged dictionaries for travelers to comprehensive dictionaries for scholars and academics. In between the two are dictionaries for those traveling on business, dictionaries for students studying abroad, and dictionaries devoted to single subjects, such as food. In the case of foreign languages, the authority of the publisher is key. Cassell's, HarperCollins, Cambridge University Press, and Larousse have excellent reputations in the world of dual-language dictionaries, and Oxford University Press also publishes dual-language dictionaries suitable for a range of readers. In addition to print titles available from Oxford, *Oxford Language Dictionaries Online* includes bilingual dictionaries in French, German, Spanish, Italian, Russian, and Chinese with up-to-date translations of words and phrases, illustrative examples, and native speaker audio pronunciation of words. An increasing number of free Web sites can serve as aids to translating from one language into another as well.[11]

An exciting development for foreign-language dictionaries is the visual dictionary. As previously noted, Dorling Kindersley (DK) is a well-known publisher in this area. DK's *5 Language Visual Dictionary* includes English, French, German, Spanish, and Italian. The book is organized by broad categories, including people, appearance, health, home, services, shopping, food, leisure, and other. Each image is accompanied by the word printed in a different font according to its language. Images are all in color and are pleasing to the eye. The book also includes helpful short phrases, such as "Do you have any vegetarian dishes?" and "Where can I park?" An index of all the words in the dictionary, arranged alphabetically by language, is also included. This type of book would be an excellent addition to any type of library with either foreign-language or English-language learners.

For scholars and researchers of languages, Andrew Dalby's *A Guide to World Language Dictionaries* is a highly selective annotated bibliography of dictionaries for 275 languages. The dictionaries included in the book define vocabulary as well as establish and sustain the language's history and evolution. As a result, the book includes historical, modern, classical, etymological, and slang dictionaries, and each language category contains a very brief overview of the language. Alphabetical order and script are also shown to give readers information as to how an alphabet is arranged. The index contains a list of dictionary titles and personal names cited in entries. A large number of dual-language dictionaries in many languages can be accessed on the Web. A good source for these is the list of links provided by *YourDictionary.com* for about 300 languages, from Afrikaans to Zulu.

Dialect and Regionalisms

One of the most fascinating types of dictionaries is that which chronicles the evolution and use of language from a specific geographic area. Three such works are the *Dictionary of American Regional English* (*DARE*), the *Dictionary of the American West*, and the *Dictionary of Smoky Mountain English*. The first is legendary in its scope: 10 years, 1,000 communities, nearly 3,000 informants, and 80 fieldworkers, ultimately totaling more than 2 million responses to the survey created by the American Dialect Society (ADS). The ADS had planned *DARE* since the beginning of the society in the late 1800s and held on to this goal through the Depression and two World Wars, finally appointing an editor in the 1960s. Thanks to federal funding, the editors and staff developed a survey (included in an appendix) to record the use of English throughout the country. Responses from informants, a listing of whom is included, complemented other primary and secondary sources of usage, such as oral histories, diaries, letters, regional fiction, and newspapers, to name a few. *DARE* contains entries for single words, phrases, and compounds, with each entry including parts of speech, etymology, geographical and usage labels, definitions, and cross-references for variant spellings. At five volumes, it lives up to its goal of "testify[ing] to the wondrous variety and creativeness of human language, and specifically of the English language as it is used regionally in the United States."[12]

Michael Montgomery and Joseph Hall's *Dictionary of Smoky Mountain English*, published in 2004, achieves a similar level of comprehensiveness for the "traditional and contemporary folk language of Appalachia."[13] Based on the life work of Joseph Hall, a trained phonetician who studied Appalachian English over his entire career, the book chronicles and identifies two centuries' worth of words, phrases, and definitions from three generations of members of the Appalachian community. In fact, Hall's work was consulted by the editors of *DARE*. Like *DARE*, other primary and secondary sources, such as documents, recordings, and transcripts from archives; historical societies; and libraries were also used to create the word and definition list. Entries include definitions, usage examples and their supporting citations, variant spellings, labels, and cross-references. The book also includes fascinating historical material, such as informative chapters about the grammar and syntax of the Great Smoky Mountain areas.

Win Blevins's *Dictionary of the American West* began as a pamphlet for book editors unfamiliar with the vernacular of the American West. As the author researched and wrote, his goal expanded to "restore some of the full richness of the history of the West."[14] The book is fascinating, given that the American West was home to a wide diversity of people: Native Americans, Mormons, Hispanics, French-Canadians, Mexicans, slaves, and immigrants from Europe, to name a few. The book's entries include definitions, some black-and-white illustrations and photos, history of how the word came to be used, and occasionally, examples of use. The book's introduction is a fascinating overview of the history of the area and also lists books on the topic of the American West.

For readers more interested in modern English, two sources from Houghton Mifflin cater to the contemporary English-language learner. *The American Heritage Dictionary for Learners of English* is for learners of all ages, and *The American Heritage Thesaurus for Learners of English* is directed at learners at the high school level and above. Both focus on building vocabulary, and the textual layout of both supports this goal. The text is easy to read, and examples are easy to understand while imparting a word's meaning at the same time. The *Thesaurus* includes an appendix of irregular verbs and idiomatic uses of prepositions, and the *Dictionary* includes several appendices useful for quick reference, such as lists of state capitals, units of measure, and the periodic table of elements. Both would be suitable for public, school, and university libraries serving multi-language communities.

Slang and Euphemisms

The most entertaining types of dictionaries are those that keep a record of the various words in our language that do not appear, as a rule, in general dictionaries. The word "slang" has several synonyms, including *vernacular, colloquialism, mumbo jumbo, vulgarity, lingo*, and *jargon*. In general, slang is either language used by a specific group, such as teenagers, or language that is informal and conversational, used for added effect. Euphemisms are closely related to slang at first glance, given that both are colloquialisms, but the difference is that they seek to restate or deflect a harsh, perhaps too-realistic term or phrase. For example, the term "person of interest," when used by police, usually equates with the word "suspect" or "witness." Both slang and euphemisms can be geographic- and occupation-based as well.

Words, at least the ones we use in conversation, seem to be a fascination for people. Publications recording the rise and fall of slang and euphemisms exist for libraries as well as for consumers' personal libraries. One such book is Paul McFedries's *Word Spy: The Word Lover's Guide to Modern Culture*. *Word Spy* is a combination of dictionary and sociocultural commentary. Each chapter delves into a different part of society, such as food, advertising, the workplace, politics, or relationships. A typical entry usually includes the main word or phrase, the year it first appeared, a short definition, and a citation of the word's first or most demonstrative use. The chapter titled "Words for Activists" chronicles the rise of blending words with the suffix "-vist/-vism." Examples include hacktivist ("a computer hacker who breaks into computer systems to further an activist agenda")[15] and lactivist ("an activist who promotes breast-feeding over the use of infant formula").[16] As a reference source, it provides context for words often used in the news, on talk shows, or in newspapers coined by journalists, politicians, or pundits. It provides a look into language from a popular-culture vantage point.

Another source that provides a different, geographic perspective is R. W. Holder's *How Not to Say What You Mean: A Dictionary of Euphemisms*. Published by Oxford University Press, the fourth edition of this resource covers American and British euphemisms, both contemporary and traditional. The most interesting aspect of this dictionary is the number of words shared by both countries. Each entry contains the main word, definitions, usage examples or citations, and notes, such as "obsolete" or "American." Ewart James's *NTC's Dictionary of British Slang and Colloquial Expressions* also covers modern English in Britain, including terms from

America. Terms in *NTC's Dictionary* were culled not only from individuals but also from television, movies, and radio. Verification of terms came from reference sources (including the *OED*), newspaper stories, and old movies. Besides the standard entry information (word, definition, usage, and citation), entries also include notes to further contextualize the word, such as "cant," to denote crime jargon, and "taboo," to denote unacceptable speech. Jonathan Bernstein's *Knickers in a Twist: A Dictionary of British Slang*, while less scholarly, is a more portable guide to usage of British colloquialisms. The book is organized by broad categories of slang, including "Vintage Vocabulary," "Catchphrases," and "Posh."

Americans are not without their own dictionaries of slang. *McGraw-Hill's Dictionary of American Idioms and Phrasal Verbs* by Richard Spears stands out from the rest with its focus on two-word verbs, such as "check out" or "work out." Native, near native, or speakers of other varieties of English are the audience of this book. As the introduction states, the goal of the dictionary is to "provide learners with enough information to recognize and use phrasal verbs in speech, writing and other contexts, and to make details of idioms accessible."[17] Phrases and idioms from the last 50 years are the focus, and among the most helpful elements of the entry are the notes, including designations such as *informal, literal, figurative, jocular, rural,* or *euphemism.* Spears has also compiled *McGraw-Hill's Dictionary of American Slang and Colloquial Expressions*, which provides definitions of more than 12,000 slang and informal expressions.

A standard source for American slang is the *Random House Historical Dictionary of American Slang*, to be completed in four volumes. For libraries that seek to show the development of the English language in America from colonial times to the present day, this would be an excellent source. *The Routledge Dictionary of Modern American Slang and Unconventional English* provides an authoritative source for contemporary American slang with 25,000 entries accompanied by citations and examples of usage. *The New Partridge Dictionary of Slang and Unconventional English* encompasses the entire English-speaking world and focuses on slang and unconventional English used or created since 1945. Entries list the term, identify its part of speech, explain its meaning, identify the country of origin, and cite sources or provide quotations showing how the term is used. The old *Partridge* remains the best record of British slang antedating 1945.

Thesauri and Usage Guides

A thesaurus is an invaluable tool to anyone who writes for work or pleasure. Essentially a dictionary of synonyms and antonyms, a thesaurus helps novice and expert writers alike add variety and clarity to their work.

First published in England in 1852 by physician Peter Mark Roget, *Roget's International Thesaurus* is the standard thesaurus of choice. Currently in its seventh edition, *Roget's* is organized not alphabetically but instead by category. Fifteen classes of words contain more than 1,000 categories, and 325,000 synonyms, antonyms, and phrases serve to guide readers, writers, and speakers to the best word or phrase for their purpose. Classes are broad, including "Place," "Natural Phenomena," "Measure and Shape," "Behavior," and "Language." Categories are more detailed; for example, under the class "Mind and Ideas," categories include "Comparison," "Discrimination,"

"Judgment," and "Theory and Philosophy," among others. Cross-references and quotations help to add meaning and context to each category and each entry, and an alphabetical index helps users to locate specific words when necessary. Lists of words without synonyms appear in sidebars throughout the book with their related class; for instance, names of muscles and bones appear in the "Body" class. The layout of the book is clear and helpful to the reader, with main words in bold and numbered for easy location. Editor Barbara Ann Kipfer holds an MPhil and PhD in linguistics from the University of Exeter and is lexicographer for several Roget's publications, including the *Roget's 21st Century Thesaurus* and *The Concise Roget's International Thesaurus*, both desk versions of the original.

In addition to *Roget's*, Oxford University Press has entered the thesaurus market with its usual quality and authority. The *Oxford American Writer's Thesaurus*, published in 2004, is suitable for middle school and high school students, as is the *American Heritage Thesaurus*. *Merriam-Webster Online* includes a thesaurus search option in addition to the dictionary. Academic libraries invest heavily in general thesauri but also invest in discipline-specific works that will aid students and scholars in their research. Examples include the *Thesaurus of Psychological Index Terms*, published by the American Psychological Association; the *Thesaurus of Aging Terminology*, published by AARP; and *The Art and Architecture Thesaurus*, published by the Getty Research Institute of the J. Paul Getty Trust. Writers and speakers of any age will enjoy popular thesauri, written as much to inform as to entertain, such as *The Dimwit's Dictionary: 5,000 Overused Words and Phrases and Alternatives to Them* by Robert Hartwell Fiske and *Words That Sell* by Richard Bayan.

Usage guides are another important resource for writers. These go one step further than a general desk dictionary by providing quotations and citations illustrating grammar and word use. Two examples published in the last decade are given here. The third edition of *Garner's Modern American Usage*, published by Oxford University Press in 2009, not only includes nouns, verbs, adjectives, idioms, and exclamations, but also explains distinct jargon such as "commercialese" and "computerese" and figures of speech such as the "zeugma." In addition to examples of word and phrase use, Garner includes a lengthy bibliographic time line of usage guides and a bibliography of sources used to gather examples. The *Cambridge Guide to English Usage*, published in 2004, is a descriptive reference work that answers questions of grammar and word use. Written and spoken examples of the English language originate from the British National Corpus and the Cambridge International Corpus. The book is intended for speakers and readers of English and is international in its coverage of American, British, Canadian, Australian, and New Zealand English.

Abbreviations and Acronyms

Dictionaries of abbreviations and acronyms are key sources for any type of library, especially those that serve writers, researchers, journalists, or students. The sheer number of abbreviations and acronyms in the United States alone is mindboggling, so a quality dictionary is an essential reference tool. The two largest and perhaps most comprehensive publications are Gale's *Acronyms, Initialisms and Abbreviations Dictionary* and its counterpart, *Reverse Acronyms, Initialisms and Abbreviations Dictionary*. Each is a multivolume set covering abbreviations and acronyms from specific subjects and disciplines, associations, organizations, companies, and periodical titles. The latter is organized alphabetically by organization name, and the former is organized alphabetically by abbreviation. Published annually, the two sets could easily stand alone as core sources. *Abbreviations Dictionary*, now in its 10th edition with more than 300,000 entries, is a more compact one-volume work. There are also numerous publications for special subjects, such as medicine, politics, business, and law, among others. Because abbreviations dictionaries are usually compiled and published by publishing houses within specific disciplines or industries, the information is usually authoritative and credible.

Quotations

Another core source for any reference collection is a dictionary of quotations. Questions from users often focus on the source of a particular quotation or on how a quotation appeared originally; reasons for researching quotations can vary from a planned toast at a wedding to a speech for a class or event or even to the settling of a bet. The challenge with answering a quotation question is the frequent misinformation provided by the user. However, if a quotation book has a decent index, quotations can be easy to locate and verify. In addition to the two sources noted in this section, libraries may also like to supplement their collections with more focused quotation books, such as dictionaries of song lyrics, movie quotations, political speeches, or Shakespeare or of quotations specific to weddings, graduations, birthdays, retirements, and other special occasions.

The core quotations source is *Bartlett's Familiar Quotations*, now in its 17th edition, published since 1855. With 25,000 quotations from more than 2,000 authors, *Bartlett's* covers a wide variety of subjects, time periods, and people, from the Bible and Shakespeare to such contemporary authors as Maya Angelou and Frank McCourt. It is arranged chronologically and includes an author index and a keyword index to provide and enhance access. Its moderate price puts it within the reach of many libraries' budgets, and for the content and history contained in *Bartlett's*, it should be part of every library's collection.

Other publishers have emulated *Bartlett's* and developed their own quotation books. Oxford University Press has an impressive array of choices, from the general and comprehensive to the specialized. *The Oxford Dictionary of Quotations*, now in its seventh edition, is another core source for libraries of any type. Like *Bartlett's*, sources of quotations come from traditional works and from elements of modern culture. An excellent keyword index helps the reader locate authors and verify quotations, and informative sidebars contribute to the comprehensive nature of the work. Citations provide context for quotations, and cross-references help readers find quotations on related topics. Oxford also publishes many other quotation dictionaries focusing on literature, science, politics, law, business, humor, and other specific topics, industries, or occupations.

SEARCH STRATEGIES

Definitions of words or phrases can be among the most important reference answers a librarian provides. Sometimes just giving an example of how to correctly use a word or illustrating a word's definition with a sentence can help a user understand a topic in a whole new way. Librarians need to be cognizant of both the tools and the many ways users can approach them. The key to understanding how to use a specific dictionary is to actually use it. Make a list of words and look them up in different dictionaries, and read the introduction and any "how to use this book" section that the title offers so that the information in the book can be used to its fullest extent. For some of the more subject-specific dictionaries and word books, this is crucial to understanding the organization and access methods of the information within the book.

Just as one must work to become familiar with the scope and organization of print titles, the features and search capabilities of electronic sources, both freely available and subscription-based, need to be explored so that an informed choice can be made as to when turning to the Web is likely to be more efficient and effective than consulting print sources. Depending on the source, electronic format dictionaries may allow users to differentiate between exact and "near" spellings and to search other elements of an entry (definition, quotations, word usage, word history) in addition to the entry word. The capability to simultaneously search multiple sources increases the chances of locating the information sought. Enhancements such as audio pronunciation go beyond the capabilities of print resources.

Readers of all ages, from children to adults to senior citizens, have a need for dictionaries, which can explain the wide variety of print and online dictionaries available today. Reference librarians have the enviable task of getting to know the character and strengths of the dictionaries, quotation books, and thesauri in their collections for the benefit of the users in their community. As the example in Box 17.2 illustrates, it is important to develop an appreciation for the range of answers that different sources can provide for even a seemingly simple definitional question. Understanding why the information is being sought and how it will be used can be helpful in developing a search strategy to guide the user to the sources most likely to be helpful in responding to a particular word-related question.

BOX 17.2
SEARCH STRATEGY: DEFINING "SUFFRAGETTE"

In seeking a definition, it would be natural to begin with a desk dictionary such as *Merriam-Webster's Collegiate Dictionary*, where one finds the following definition:

"*n* (1906): a woman who advocates suffrage for women."

This is not particularly informative. *The American Heritage Dictionary of the English Language* adds a bit more detail but still requires the user to look further if unfamiliar with the meaning of "suffrage":

"An advocate of women's suffrage, especially in the United Kingdom."

The *Oxford English Dictionary* provides a more detailed definition, accompanied by numerous examples of the word's use in context, beginning with a quotation from the 1906 *Daily Mail*:

"A female supporter of the cause of women's political enfranchisement, *esp.* one of a violent or 'militant' type."

Thus far, only general dictionaries have been consulted. A search on *Credo Reference* yields definitions from subject-specific dictionaries, reflecting the particular perspective of each. Some examples include the following:

"A woman who campaigned for women to be given the right to vote in the early part of the 20th century." In *Dictionary of Politics and Government* (2004). Retrieved from http://www.credoreference.com/ entry/acbgovtpol/suffragette.

"A member of the militant female movement which, in the early part of the 20th-century, advocated the extension of the right to vote to women" In *Collins Dictionary of Sociology* (2006). Retrieved from http://www.credoreference.com/entry/collinssoc/suffragette.

"A suffragist. Today, the term *suffragette* is often considered demeaning." In *The New Dictionary of Cultural Literacy, Houghton Mifflin* (2002). Retrieved from http://www.credoreference.com/entry/ hmndcl/suffragette.

Finally, one can turn to a usage guide to differentiate between "suffragist" and "suffragette":

"The word *suffragist*, meaning an advocate of the extension of political voting rights, especially to women, is used of both men and women. The word *suffragette*, which refers only to female suffragists, became popular in the early 20th century and was favored by many female British suffragists as well as some groups and individuals who mocked women's attempts to gain suffrage. In the United States, however, the word *suffragist* was preferred by advocates of women's suffrage, who regarded *suffragette* as a sexist diminutive." In *The American Heritage Guide to Contemporary Usage and Style* (2005). Retrieved from http://www.credoreference.com/entry/hmcontempusage/ suffragist_suffragette.

NOTES

1.   Allen Walker Read, "Encyclopaedias and Dictionaries," *Encyclopaedia Britannica*, 15th ed. (Chicago: Encyclopaedia Britannica, 2005), 18:257.

2.   Ibid., 280.

3.   Robert Dahlin, "You're as Good as Your Word," *Publishers Weekly* 246 (November 15, 1999): 34.

4.   *The American Heritage Dictionary of the English Language*, 4th ed. (Boston: Houghton Mifflin, 2000), 403.

5.   Molly McQuade, "Defining a Dictionary," *Booklist* 99 (May 15, 2003): 1688.

6.   *Webster's Third New International Dictionary of the English Language, Unabridged* (Springfield, MA: Merriam-Webster, 2002), 4a.

7.   Ibid., 16a.

8.   John Simpson and Edmund Weiner, eds., *Oxford English Dictionary: Additions Series* (New York: Oxford University Press, 1993), 1:220.

9.   William R. Trumble and Angus Stevenson, *Shorter Oxford English Dictionary on Historical Principles*, 5th ed. (New York: Oxford University Press, 2002), vii.

10.   *Funk & Wagnalls New International Dictionary of the English Language: Comprehensive Millennium Edition* (Naples, FL: World Publishers, 2005), iv.

11.   Rebecca A. Martin and Sarah McHone-Chase, "Translation Resources on the Web: A Guide to Accurate, Free Sites," *College & Research Libraries News* 70 (June 2009): 356–59.

12.   Frederic G. Cassidy, ed., *Dictionary of American Regional English* (Cambridge, MA: Belknap Press of Harvard University Press, 1985), xxii.

13.   Michael B. Montgomery and Joseph S. Hall, eds., *Dictionary of Smoky Mountain English* (Knoxville: University of Tennessee Press, 2004), vii.

14.   Win Blevins, *Dictionary of the American West: Over 5,000 Terms and Expressions from Aarigaa! to Zopilote*, 2nd ed. (Seattle: Sasquatch Books, 2001), vii.

15.   Paul McFedries, *Word Spy: The Word Lover's Guide to Modern Culture* (New York: Broadway Books, 2004), 187.

16.   Ibid.

17.   Richard A. Spears, ed., *McGraw-Hill's Dictionary of American Idioms and Phrasal Verbs* (Chicago: McGraw-Hill, 2005), v.

LIST OF SOURCES

5 Language Visual Dictionary. New York: DK Publishing, 2003. 400 pp.

Abbreviations Dictionary. 10th ed. Ed. Dean A. Stahl and Karen Kerchelich. Boca Raton, FL: CRC Press, 2001. 1529 pp.

Acronyms, Initialisms, and Abbreviations Dictionary. 43rd ed. 4 vols. Detroit: Gale, 2010. Also available online as part of the *Gale Virtual Reference Library*.

The American Heritage Dictionary of the English Language. 4th ed. updated. Boston: Houghton Mifflin, 2006. 2074 pp.

The American Heritage Dictionary for Learners of English. Boston: Houghton Mifflin, 2002. 999 pp.

The American Heritage Student Dictionary. Updated ed. Boston: Houghton Mifflin, 2010. 1068 pp.

The American Heritage Thesaurus. New York: Bantam Dell, 2005. 713 pp.

The American Heritage Thesaurus for Learners of English. Ed. Joyce LeBaron and Susannah LeBaron. Boston: Houghton Mifflin, 2002. 326 pp.

ARBA Guide to Subject Encyclopedias and Dictionaries. 2nd ed. Englewood, CO: Libraries Unlimited, 1997. 482 pp.

The Art and Architecture Thesaurus. http://www.getty.edu/research/tools/vocabularies/aat/index.html.

Barnhart Concise Dictionary of Etymology. New York: HarperCollins Publishers, 1995. 916 pp.

Bartlett's Familiar Quotations. 17th ed. Boston: Little, Brown, 2002. 1431 pp.

Bayan, Richard. *More Words That Sell: More Than 6000 Entries to Help You Promote Your Products, Services, and Ideas*. Rev. and expanded ed. New York: McGraw-Hill, 2006. 134 pp.

Bernstein, Jonathan. *Knickers in a Twist: A Dictionary of British Slang*. New York: Canongate, 2006. 194 pp.

Blevins, Win. *Dictionary of the American West*. 2nd ed. rev. and expanded. Fort Worth, TX: TCU Press, 2008. 429 pp.

Cambridge Guide to English Usage. New York: Cambridge University Press, 2004. 608 pp.

Canadian Oxford Dictionary. 2nd ed. Ed. Katherine Barber. Don Mills, Ontario: Oxford University Press, 2004. 1830 pp.

The Concise Roget's International Thesaurus. 6th ed. rev. and updated. Ed. Barbara Ann Kipfer. New York: HarperCollins, 2003. 929 pp. (7th ed. forthcoming in 2011.)

Credo Reference. Boston, MA: Credo Reference. http://corp.credoreference.com.

Dalby, Andrew. *A Guide to World Language Dictionaries*. Chicago: Fitzroy Dearborn, 1998. 470 pp.

Dictionary of American Regional English. 5 vols. Cambridge, MA: Belknap Press of Harvard University Press, 1985–. (Vol. 4 published 2002.)

DK Merriam-Webster Children's Dictionary. Rev. ed. New York: Dorling Kindersley, 2008. 960 pp.

Fiske, Robert Hartwell. *The Dimwit's Dictionary: More Than 5,000 Overused Words and Phrases and Alternatives to Them*. Oak Park, IL: Marion Street Press, 2006. 383 pp.

Funk & Wagnalls New International Dictionary of the English Language: Comprehensive Millennium Edition. 2 vols. Naples, FL: Literary Guild World Publishers, 2005.

Garner, Bryan A. *Garner's Modern American Usage*. 3rd ed. New York: Oxford University Press, 2009. 942 pp.

Holder, R. W. *How Not to Say What You Mean: A Dictionary of Euphemisms*. 4th ed. New York: Oxford University Press, 2007. 410 pp.

James, Ewart. *NTC's Dictionary of British Slang and Colloquial Expressions*. Lincolnwood, IL: NTC Publishing Group, 1997. 573 pp.

Kabdebo, Thomas, and Neil Armstrong. *Dictionary of Dictionaries and Eminent Encyclopedias: Comprising Dictionaries, Encyclopedias, and Other Selected Wordbooks in English*. 2nd ed. New Providence, NJ: Bowker-Saur, 1997. 418 pp.

Kister, Kenneth F. *Kister's Best Dictionaries for Adults and Young People: A Comparative Guide*. Phoenix, AZ: Oryx Press, 1992. 438 pp.

McFedries, Paul. *Word Spy: The Word Lover's Guide to Modern Culture*. New York: Broadway Books, 2004. 419 pp.

Merriam-Webster Online. http://www.merriam-webster.com.

Merriam-Webster Unabridged. http://unabridged.merriam-webster.com.

Merriam-Webster's Collegiate Dictionary. 11th ed. Springfield, MA: Merriam-Webster, 2003. 1623 pp.

Merriam-Webster's Collegiate Thesaurus. 2nd ed. Springfield, MA: Merriam-Webster, 2010. 1162 pp.

Merriam-Webster's Elementary Dictionary. New and expanded ed. Springfield, MA: Merriam-Webster, 2009. 824 pp.

Merriam-Webster's Intermediate Dictionary. Springfield, MA: Merriam-Webster, 2004. 1005 pp.

Merriam-Webster's Primary Dictionary. Springfield, MA: Merriam-Webster, 2005. 436 pp.

Merriam-Webster's School Dictionary. Springfield, MA: Merriam-Webster, 2004. 1251 pp.

Montgomery, Michael B., and Joseph S. Hall, eds. *Dictionary of Smoky Mountain English*. Knoxville: University of Tennessee Press, 2004. 710 pp.

New Oxford American Dictionary. 3rd ed. New York: Oxford University Press, 2010. 2096 pp.

The New Partridge Dictionary of Slang and Unconventional English. Ed. Tom Dalzell and Terry Victor. 2 vols. New York: Routledge, 2005.

OED Online. Oxford: Oxford University Press. http://www.oed.com.

OneLook Dictionary Search. http://www.onelook.com.

Oxford American Writer's Thesaurus. 2nd ed. Compiled by Christine A. Lindberg. New York: Oxford University Press, 2008. 1052 pp.

Oxford Dictionaries Online. Oxford: Oxford University Press. http://english.oxforddictionaries.com.

The Oxford Dictionary of Quotations. 7th ed. Ed. Elizabeth Knowles. New York: Oxford University Press, 2009. 1155 pp.

Oxford Dictionary of Word Histories. Ed. Glynnis Chantrell. New York: Oxford University Press, 2002. 559 pp.

Oxford English Dictionary. 2nd ed. 20 vols. New York: Oxford University Press, 1989.

Oxford English Dictionary: Additions Series. Ed. John Simpson, Edmund Weiner, and Michael Proffitt. 3 vols. New York: Oxford University Press, 1993–1997.

Oxford Language Dictionaries Online. Oxford: Oxford University Press. http://www.oxford-languagedictionaries.com.

Random House Historical Dictionary of American Slang. Ed. J. E. Lighter. 4 vols. New York: Random House, 1994–. (3rd vol. published in 2007.)

Random House Webster's Unabridged Dictionary. 2nd ed. rev. and updated. New York: Random House Reference, 2005. 2230 pp.

Reitz, Joan M. *Dictionary for Library and Information Science*. Westport, CT: Libraries Unlimited, 2004. 788 pp.

Reitz, Joan M. *ODLIS: Online Dictionary for Library and Information Science*. http://lu.com/odlis.

Reverse Acronyms, Initialisms and Abbreviations Dictionary. 43rd ed. 3 vols. Detroit: Gale, 2010.

Roget's International Thesaurus. 7th ed. Barbara Ann Kipfer. New York: Collins, 2010. 1312 pp.

Roget's 21st Century Thesaurus in Dictionary Form: The Essential Reference for Home, School, or Office. 3rd ed. Ed. Barbara Ann Kipfer. New York: Bantom Dell, 2005. 962 pp.

The Routledge Dictionary of Modern American Slang and Unconventional English. Ed. Tom Dalzell. New York: Routledge, 2009. 1104 pp.

Shorter Oxford English Dictionary. 6th ed. Ed. Angus Stevenson and Lesley Brown. 2 vols. New York: Oxford University Press, 2007.

Spears, Richard A. *McGraw-Hill's Dictionary of American Idioms and Phrasal Verbs.* Chicago: McGraw-Hill, 2005. 1080 pp.

Spears, Richard A. *McGraw-Hill's Dictionary of American Slang and Colloquial Expressions.* 4th ed. New York: McGraw-Hill, 2006. 546 pp.

Thesaurus of Aging Terminology. 8th ed. Ed. Ann Rimkus, Michael D. Melinchok, Kathleen McEvoy, and Amy K. Yeager. Washington, D.C.: Ageline Database, Research Information Center, AARP, 2005. 236 pp.

Thesaurus of Psychological Index Terms. 11th ed. Ed. Lisa Gallagher Tuleya. Washington, D.C.: American Psychological Association, 2007. 463 pp.

Webster's Third New International Dictionary, Unabridged. Rev. ed. Springfield, MA: Merriam-Webster, 2002. 2662 pp.

World Book Dictionary. 2 vols. Chicago: World Book, 2009.

YourDictionary.com. http://www.yourdictionary.com/languages.html.

ADDITIONAL READINGS

Battistella, Edwin L. "Groping for Words: A Guide to Slang and Usage Resources." *Choice* 46 (December 2008): 619–31.

This bibliographic essay offers a wide-ranging discussion of some of the many books on grammar, pronunciation, spelling, diction, and punctuation. The scope includes guides to both American and British English, as well as slang and dialect. Concluding sections of the article discuss "grammar as entertainment" and "language and the Web."

Brewer, Charlotte. *Treasure-House of the Language: The Living OED.* New Haven, CT: Yale University Press, 2007. 336 pp.

This book brings the history of the *Oxford English Dictionary* forward from the completion of the first edition in 1928 to its current electronic form in the 21st century.

Grogan, Denis. *Dictionaries and Phrase Books.* Grogan's Case Studies in Reference Work, vol. 5. London: Clive Bingley, 1987. 153 pp.

Grogan gives students examples of reference questions involving the use of dictionaries and phrase books.

Kendall, Joshua C. *The Man Who Made Lists: Love, Death, Madness, and the Creation of Roget's Thesaurus.* New York: Berkley Books, 2008. 307 pp.

This recent biography of Peter Mark Roget (1779–1869) traces Roget's life and the thesaurus project that occupied his retirement years, with the first edition published in 1852.

Landau, Sidney I. *Dictionaries: The Art and Craft of Lexicography.* 2nd ed. London: Cambridge University Press, 2001. 477 pp.

Landau offers a description of how dictionaries are researched and written, with particular attention to how computers have changed modern lexicography. The final chapter addresses legal and ethical issues.

Martin, Rebecca A., and Sarah McHone-Chase. "Translation Resources on the Web: A Guide to Accurate, Free Sites." *College & Research Libraries News* 70 (June 2009): 356–59.

This article provides a selected, annotated list of sites useful as aids in translating from one language into another. Resources are grouped under headings for online dictionaries, online translator services and directories, gateways to glossaries, and blogs.

Mulac, Carolyn. "Other People's Words: Recent Quotation Books." *Booklist* 98 (July 2002): 1870–72.

In order to highlight the range of specialized quotation books that are available for purchase, this article looks at 20 titles, ranging from *African American Quotations* to *The Ultimate Dictionary of Sports Quotations*. Annotated entries are grouped by broad topic.

Tomchyshyn, Terri. "Children's Dictionaries." *Booklist* 97 (October 15, 2000): 475–77.

Although somewhat dated, this article still provides a helpful introduction to the range of dictionary titles published for children. The author reviews 22 titles designed for children in elementary grades, junior high, or high school. The annotations, which are detailed and evaluative, are arranged under four headings; Kindergarten to Grade 3; Grades 3–6; Grades 6–9; and High School.

Winchester, Simon. *The Meaning of Everything: The Story of the Oxford English Dictionary.* New York: Oxford University Press, 2003. 260 pp.

Winchester provides an interesting history of the first edition of the *Oxford English Dictionary*, including prior efforts to document the English language beginning in the 17th century. He describes the people and processes involved in the project over a 70-year period concluding with completion of the first edition in 1928.

Encyclopedias

Melissa A. Wong

USES AND CHARACTERISTICS

The encyclopedia is the quintessential reference tool, a source that seems to cover any topic imaginable and the one many people remember learning to use at an early age. More than any other book, the encyclopedia has long been associated with an educated mind. In the 20th century, traveling salesmen sold encyclopedias door-to-door, and many families bought an encyclopedia for their school-age children. The home encyclopedia set provided ready access to information for school reports and symbolized the family's commitment to education and knowledge. Thus, it seems only fitting that A. J. Jacobs's memoir about reading the entire *Encyclopaedia Britannica* is titled *The Know-It-All: One Man's Humble Quest to Become the Smartest Person in the World.*[1]

Whether the encyclopedia is a single volume on one specific subject, a multi-volume work such as the *Encyclopaedia Britannica*, or an online multimedia resource, the goal remains implicit: to provide a summarized compendium of multidisciplinary knowledge in a verifiable, organized, and readily accessible manner that allows its users to meet their information needs first on a general level and then on a specific level by pointing them to more detailed sources of information. Kenneth Kister reinforces this: "Encyclopedias, in short, aim to encompass and codify that knowledge and information educated people deem essential or universally worth knowing."[2]

Given the varied role of encyclopedias and because they provide summary information, it is valuable to categorize the types of questions best answered through their use:

1. Ready-Reference Information

   - What is the size of Jupiter?
   - Where can I find a picture of a koala bear?
   - Where can I see the periodic table of elements?

The preceding are types of questions suited to the encyclopedia.

2.   General Background Information

- How does photosynthesis work?
- What construction techniques were used to build the Golden Gate Bridge?

As in the case of locating answers to ready-reference questions, one can also consult encyclopedias to garner background information. They are unique in that they give definitions, explain phenomena, and provide illustrations. Children's encyclopedias are particularly helpful in this regard, given that they typically provide simplified explanations accompanied by illustrations. Encyclopedias are also helpful in that they often list cross-references to related information located in other parts of the encyclopedia or include bibliographic citations to similar, yet more in-depth information found in outside sources.

3.   "Pre-research" Information
Encyclopedias provide a useful launch point for learning basic research skills and for embarking on research itself. For a novice researcher, the encyclopedia provides an introduction to the organization and procurement of information, as well as succinct overviews of topics of interest. This allows the novice to make connections between topics and to see that all information lies in a broader context. Through this understanding, novices can readily seek out more substantive and focused sources of information, thus embarking on a path that could make them better researchers.

Jacques Barzun notes that "encyclopedias should be 'learned' and not blindly used: The childhood faith in *the* encyclopedia that happened to be the one large book of knowledge in the house should be replaced by a discriminating acquaintance with others."[3] Barzun's comments aptly describe the mixed perceptions many people have of encyclopedias. Although few would dispute their convenience, others, particularly those in academe, may not view them as scholarly works and may encourage students not to overuse them when engaging in research. Barzun's advice seems particularly appropriate today, when traditional multivolume print sets with recognizable names are giving way to robust online products that combine multiple encyclopedia titles in two or more languages with multimedia and a choice of user interfaces. In addition, the Internet offers users free online titles such as *Wikipedia*, with content created by volunteer authors and editors. The responsibility of the librarian is to have the "discriminating acquaintance" with encyclopedias that allows him or her to direct the user to the right encyclopedia for the information need.

Kinds of Information Contained in Encyclopedias

Encyclopedias provide a well-organized overview of *selected* topics of major importance. They deliver a survey presentation, a snapshot of how topics are and were. Encyclopedias are written in an objective rather than an analytical style, imitating the textbook rather than the scholarly monograph. Although most people are familiar with the traditional, multivolume encyclopedia (such as the *Encyclopaedia Britannica*), other equally important types exist.

Single-Volume Encyclopedias

Single-volume encyclopedias such as the *Encyclopedia of Animal Science* deliver condensed, factual information, often with accompanying illustrations. Typically arranged in dictionary format without an index, single-volume encyclopedias are inexpensive alternatives to multivolume sets. They can be readily purchased by individuals for home use or by libraries seeking cost-effective ways of augmenting their core or ready-reference collections. Desktop versions, when available, are even more compact and inexpensive.

Encyclopedias for Children and Young Adults

Children's encyclopedias tend to place more emphasis on format, illustrations, and pedagogical tools, as a way of making it easier for children to learn how to use them. Typically, the arrangement of these encyclopedias mirrors those targeted to adults. The principal difference between the two lies in content. Children's encyclopedias are written for young readers, a domain that contains a variety of abilities and audiences. Consequently, one finds a variety of titles to choose from in both print and electronic formats. For example, World Book's *Childcraft* targets elementary school students, whereas *Compton's by Britannica* targets middle school and high school students. *School Library Journal* regularly reviews reference books written for children and young adults and occasionally highlights specific genres such as encyclopedias, devoting pages to comprehensive and candid reviews of the latest versions. Although children's encyclopedias are generally less expensive than those written for adults, they are by no means inexpensive.

Subject Encyclopedias

Subject encyclopedias, unlike their single- or multivolume counterparts that have a broader scope, give more in-depth coverage to a specific field of knowledge. Varying in price and size, subject encyclopedias can deliver depth and breadth of information not covered in general encyclopedias and can easily be used to augment the reference collection of a library. Inexpensive single-volume titles such as *The Pacific Islands: An Encyclopedia* or the *Encyclopedia of Forensic Science*, although highly specialized, can function as cost-effective alternatives that facilitate ready-reference access to subjects underrepresented in the overall library collection. Some mid-sized sets, such as the *Worldmark Encyclopedia of the Nations* or *Women in World History*, can also add immediate depth to a library's circulating collection, which may not represent these subjects adequately. And unlike single-volume titles, multivolume sets can address their subjects in greater detail. Such titles can exceed general multivolume encyclopedias in price. The *McGraw-Hill Encyclopedia of Science and Technology* is a case in point. The 20-volume 10th edition was listed at $3,495 in 2010.

Encyclopedia Yearbooks and Supplements

Yearbooks have always functioned as "year-in-review" reference tools, providing users with either chronological or topical reports of the events and/or people that shaped the world in a given year. Yearbooks, such as the 2010 *Britannica Book of the Year*, also include a plethora of statistical data rivaling the information contained in *The World Almanac and Book of Facts*. It is important to note that yearbooks do not act as encyclopedia updates (although some, such as *Britannica*, include articles that update those contained in the parent set); instead, they are tools that complement the information contained within the encyclopedia, whether it be in print or online.

Supplements, on the other hand, are designed to update print encyclopedias, which are "current" only on the day they go to press. Britannica's *New Views of the Solar System* is a supplement to *Compton's by Britannica* that was published to provide updated information on the solar system when Pluto was stripped of its planetary status. Web-based encyclopedias have no need for supplements because information can be updated on an ongoing basis.

Foreign-Language and Non-English-Language Encyclopedias

Traditionally, large public and academic libraries purchased "foreign-language" encyclopedias, titles published in another country that might or might not be translated into English, in order to augment their holdings on other countries or cultures. *Japan: An Illustrated Encyclopedia*, the successor to the *Kodansha Encyclopedia of Japan*, is a national encyclopedia available in an English-language version that can be considered a subject encyclopedia on that country. Like their American counterparts, foreign encyclopedias can appear as single- or multivolume entities.

Increasingly, American publishers are offering Spanish, French, and even Chinese versions of their major titles (see Table 18.1). Non-English-language encyclopedias may or may not be based on an English-language title and typically include general content with additional articles appropriate to the language of publication. For instance, World Book publishes the Spanish-language *Gran Enciclopedia Hispanica*, aimed at ages 13 and up, which offers global coverage with increased emphasis on the Hispanic world, as well as the *Enciclopedia Estudiantil Hallazgos*, an online, Spanish version of its *Discovery Encyclopedia*, aimed at younger readers. Non-English-language encyclopedias are valuable additions to libraries supporting bilingual communities, English-language learners, and students studying other languages.

EVALUATION

Like dictionaries, encyclopedias are published to meet the general information needs of a particular group, such as schoolchildren or scholars. Unlike dictionaries, encyclopedias typically contain lengthy essays, compact factual discussions, and a variety of tools that teach research skills. Consequently, the writing style and syndetic structure of encyclopedias assume great importance when one attempts to assess their usefulness. Format, accuracy and objectivity, and currency are other factors to keep in mind when evaluating specific titles.

TABLE 18.1   NON-ENGLISH-LANGUAGE ENCYCLOPEDIA COMPARISON CHART

Encyclopedia	Language & age range	Print contents	Online availability
Britannica Enciclopedia Universal Ilustrada (Britannica, 2006)	Spanish 13–adult	• 20 volumes • 24,000 articles • 4,800 illustrations	*Spanish Reference Center / Global Reference Center*
Gran Enciclopedia Planeta (Britannica, 2004)	Spanish 13–adult	• 20 volumes • 135,000 articles • 21,000 illustrations	*Spanish Reference Center / Global Reference Center*
La Nueva Enciclopedia Cumbre (Grolier)	Spanish 11–adult	• Online only • 19,000 articles • 8,000 illustrations	*Grolier Online*
Enciclopedia Estudiantil Hallazgos (World Book, 2001)	Spanish 7–11	• 13 volumes • *World Book Discovery Encyclopedia* in Spanish	*World Book Online*
Gran Enciclopedia Hispanica (World Book, 2006)	Spanish 13–adult	• 18 volumes and DVD • 105,000 articles • 13,000 illustrations • Global coverage with increased emphasis on Hispanic world	*Gran Enciclopedia Online*
Universalis Junior (Britannica, 2008)	French 7–12	• 10 volumes • 3,000 illustrations • Based on *Britannica Student Encyclopedia*	*Universalis Junior Online*
Encyclopaedia Universalis (Britannica, 2004)	French 13–adult	• 28 volumes • 50,000 articles • 32,000 illustrations • Index	*Encyclopaedia Universalis Online / Global Reference Center*
L'encyclopédie Découverte (World Book, 2009)	French All ages	• 15 volumes • *World Book Discovery Encyclopedia* in French	*L'encyclopédie Découverte Online*
World Book Encyclopedia Chinese Version (World Book, 2007)	Chinese All ages	• 20 volumes • 17,000 articles • Chinese, English, and bilingual indices • Based on *World Book Encyclopedia* with 300 additional articles on Chinese culture and history	Not available

Reviewing Tools

When evaluating any reference work for acquisition, librarians use a variety of reputable reviewing sources, including reviews written in scholarly journals or trade magazines, books, and even colleagues. Standard reviewing titles such as *Choice* and *Library Journal* routinely review encyclopedias. In addition to regular reviews of new titles, *Booklist* publishes an annual encyclopedia update that facilitates comparisons across titles. *American Reference Books Annual*, available as an annual print publication or electronically as *ARBAonline*, is an excellent source of reviews for both general and subject encyclopedias. Discipline-specific journals often include reviews of encyclopedias and can provide more in-depth or subject-specific insights. Finally, one can also speak to colleagues in similar institutions to ascertain their opinions before purchasing a new encyclopedia.

Scope

Focus or Purpose

The focus or purpose of an encyclopedia is generally found in its prefatory remarks. There, its editors should clearly delineate its intended audience, its scope, and its format. For example, with regard to content, the editors of the first edition of the *Encyclopedia of African-American Culture and History* wrote, "It was the Board's opinion that it was far more important to reserve space for information about a wide range of African Americans and to preserve a record of achievement not covered elsewhere."[4] Reviews often describe the focus or purpose of encyclopedias and even point out where emphasis is placed. Some encyclopedias, such as *World Book*, place great emphasis on visual appeal, carefully balancing illustrations and text. *Encyclopaedia Britannica*, on the other hand, values textual content above all.

Subject Coverage

With regard to multivolume general encyclopedias, coverage should be even across all subjects; however, it is important to note that some subjects, by their very nature, demand greater emphasis. It would also be naïve to assume that general encyclopedias do not have inherent biases. General encyclopedias published in the United States contain far more information about the United States than they do about any other country. When assessing whether an encyclopedia is balanced with respect to subject coverage, one merely has to examine the length and depth of articles written on a variety of subjects. One also must take into account the extent to which current affairs are covered and how.

Audience

Subject matter, writing style, and presentation determine an encyclopedia's audience. Clearly, *The Blackwell Encyclopedia of Management* sees its audience as adults who have a scholarly or professional interest in business. *Encyclopaedia Britannica* is appropriate for readers at the ninth grade level and above. The *Scholastic Children's Encyclopedia*, with its short entries, numerous illustrations, and larger print, is clearly aimed at young readers. Some titles aim to serve a wide audience and can be used by children, young adults, and adults. Although targeted at primary and secondary school students, *World Book Encyclopedia* prides itself on being suitable as a "family reference tool" that is also used by "librarians, teachers, and the general public to satisfy their everyday reference needs."[5] Many librarians find *World Book* useful for adult users seeking an illustration or a simple explanation of a topic.

Format

The physical format of an encyclopedia is inextricably intertwined with its accessibility and overall usefulness. An encyclopedia whose physical format looks daunting or appears confusing in spite of its content may dissuade potential users from choosing it. On the other hand, looks can be deceiving, and librarians should not confuse slick packaging or cutting-edge multimedia clips with usability or reliable content.

The key to evaluating an encyclopedia in terms of its physical format lies in understanding one's target audience. With regard to adult general encyclopedias, a plethora of photographs and illustrations and a dearth of content might indicate a lack of substance; however, in the case of encyclopedias for children, this scenario would be welcome, particularly if the photographs and illustrations are current and targeted to a child's viewpoint. Page layout also figures prominently. Minimal or excessive "white space," poor placement of illustrations, and incorrect choice of fonts for headers and text would again detract from content, no matter how scholarly or substantive that content may be.

The arrangement of volumes also impacts the usability of an encyclopedia. Children's encyclopedias are often arranged so that one volume encompasses an entire letter of the alphabet, ensuring for example, that entries beginning with M are not split between two volumes, which can be confusing for younger users. In *Discover America*, an encyclopedia of the states, each state is given its own volume, which simplifies access and allows an entire classroom of children to conduct simultaneous research. Additionally, librarians should consider the presence and design of indexes, user guides, and supplemental materials, such as study guides.

Online versions of encyclopedias have become increasingly more common and cost-effective. Their presence has also begun to change the nature of encyclopedia publication. Some publishers, such as Britannica, continue to publish and sell their multivolume print encyclopedias while simultaneously producing CD-ROM and DVD versions for the home market and offering both free and fee-based online versions. Other publishers, such as Grolier, have ceased publication of selected print titles in favor of a robust online product.

Online encyclopedias typically contain the full text of their print counterparts with embedded links between articles and a variety of multimedia enhancements. These media enhancements can include animations, video clips, sound files, and even three-dimensional "virtual tours." When evaluating media, it is important to ask what contribution their inclusion makes to the overall efficacy of the encyclopedia. Do video clips or sounds enhance the reference value of the encyclopedia, or are they merely intrusive? Do images, sounds, and text work together to provide a rich and substantive learning experience, or do they act disharmoniously, distracting the user from finding information or understanding better how the product works? Online encyclopedias offer the ability to both search and browse content. Features such as

"Today in History," prominent links to timely topics, and trivia or puzzle-type games all add visual appeal and encourage users, particularly children, to explore the resource. Online encyclopedias may also offer additional research resources such as primary documents and periodical articles, making them a cost-effective way to support student research.

In selecting an online encyclopedia, another variable comes into play: the computer screen and one's interaction with it. The interface design of an electronic encyclopedia plays the greatest role in terms of usability and accessibility. Interfaces for online encyclopedias must be age-appropriate and as intuitive as the usage guides and indexes included in their print counterparts. They must readily and effortlessly guide their users to desired information. With extensive online help features and a sparing use of graphics and search buttons, these interfaces should not intimidate even novice or computer-phobic users.

A growing trend in children's encyclopedias is for publishers to offer multiple online versions aimed at different types of libraries. In addition to age-appropriate interfaces, these online products combine content from a variety of print titles, allowing libraries to purchase content tailored for their user group. For example, libraries interested in the online World Book can select from *World Book Kids* (an online version of the *World Book Discovery Encyclopedia*), *World Book Student* (an online version of the *World Book Encyclopedia*), *World Book Advanced* (the encyclopedia with additional primary source material and research tools), and *World Book Online Reference Center* (combining multiple products). In addition, libraries can add on access to *Enciclopedia Estudiantil Hallazgos*, a Spanish-language version of the *World Book Discovery Encyclopedia*, for younger readers; *Gran Enciclopedia Hispanica* for older Spanish-language readers; and/or *L'encyclopédie Découverte* for French-language readers.

All of the major multivolume, general encyclopedias now have online equivalents, and publishers have started to publish online versions of subject and single-volume encyclopedias. Although some of these are available as stand-alone products, most are made available through large reference packages, such as *Oxford Reference Online*, *Credo Reference*, and the *Gale Virtual Reference Library*.

Uniqueness

An encyclopedia is unique if it contains features that set it apart from other encyclopedias. The inclusion of a variety of reading guides and study aids makes *World Book* unique. *Encyclopaedia Britannica* has a *Propaedia*, a single volume that acts as an outline of knowledge. An encyclopedia can also be unique within the context of a library's reference collection. The presence of certain subject encyclopedias may bolster areas underrepresented in the circulating collection or may augment the broad, general information contained in a traditional, multivolume set such as *Encyclopedia Americana*. Online encyclopedias might add further depth to a collection by providing users with sound and video images that supplement the text.

Authority

As with any reference source, authority, or the staff responsible for the content, has immense value when one chooses to use or purchase the source. An examination of a source's prefatory remarks can reveal much about its authority and thus its worthiness. With regard to encyclopedias, the editorial board and contributors are deemed to be specialists in their respective fields. In the case of general, multivolume, adult-level encyclopedias, the editorial staff serves to review and revise authors' contributions so that they conform to the editorial guidelines typically set forth by the publishers. For example, there must be conformity in style and length. Author credit appears either at the beginning or at the end of each article, and a separate list of authors and their credentials generally follows the prefatory remarks. Some articles may not provide an author credit; therefore, one might conclude that the editorial staff, in concert with a subject expert, wrote those pieces.

Accuracy

Although one would like to believe otherwise, reference works such as encyclopedias contain errors and misinformation. Copy editors may miss typographical errors, and even the most diligent editors and authors can get their facts wrong. As with any source, librarians should not assume complete accuracy and reliability. Instead, they should choose an encyclopedia wisely and be mindful that they should look at other sources to verify information located in that encyclopedia.

Objectivity

Because encyclopedias have numerous contributors and because, in the case of general encyclopedias, they cover a broad range of subjects, users may initially assume that encyclopedias maintain an objective viewpoint. However, without examining an encyclopedia's prefatory material as well as its text and images, a librarian would be naïve to make such an assumption. Although the publishing industry has made great strides in the past decade to eliminate gender-biased and racially biased language or stereotyped images from their publications, bias has not been eliminated entirely.

When reviewing an encyclopedia, a librarian should pay careful attention to what an article includes or omits. A librarian should also be concerned with balanced coverage and language. With respect to controversial issues such as the death penalty or abortion, does the article present both sides? Is inflammatory language used, or is the article entirely neutral in its treatment? A librarian must also consider photographs, illustrations, sounds, and digital images when evaluating an encyclopedia for objectivity. Do images portray women solely in traditional settings? Do multimedia encyclopedias developed in the United States devote equal media space to all ethnic groups?

Currency

Encyclopedias lose value soon after they are purchased. Given the lengthy lead times for publication of print works, one could even posit that print encyclopedias lose value while in press. This poses a greater problem for publishers of multivolume sets than it does for those who produce single-volume encyclopedias. It is a Herculean and economically infeasible task to revise a multivolume general encyclopedia yearly. Consequently, publishers tend to update only a portion of the encyclopedia with each new edition.

Online encyclopedias have no limitations, other than those imposed by their producers, on the level and frequency of updates, and most publishers update their online versions more frequently than their print counterparts. For example, in *Britannica Online*, just two months after the Haitian earthquake of January 2010, entries such as "Haiti" and "Port-au-Prince" mentioned the impact of the disaster, and an entry "Haiti earthquake of 2010" had been added.

Arrangement and Indexing

Print encyclopedias typically follow a common format: alphabetical arrangement with associative cross-references and indexes. Bibliographies often follow articles or sections within long articles. Alphabetization can vary between the word-by-word method, where *San Salvador* comes before *sandman*, and the letter-by-letter method, where *sandman* comes before *San Salvador*. Most encyclopedias provide *see* references to direct users to preferred entries (e.g., from a variant spelling of a name to the correct spelling), and *see also* references at the end of articles direct users to related entries.

Although many users instinctively look up topics alphabetically to find a main entry, use of the index generally reveals additional information that would not be found by relying on *see* and *see also* references alone. For example, in *Encyclopaedia Britannica*'s index, an index entry for "Woodville, Elizabeth" directs the user to a main entry under her name, as well as additional information under "Edward IV," "Edward V," and "Richard III." The index entry for "work" refers the user to main entries in both the *Micropaedia* and *Macropaedia*, as well as the *Propaedia*. It also references entries about work in eight other *Micropaedia* and *Macropaedia* articles and provides *see also* references to four other index entries. Some children's sets enhance accessibility with the inclusion of an index at the end of each volume. These indexes, which may be set off by the use of colored paper, refer to pages within the volume as well as to related information in other volumes.

In addition, although alphabetical arrangement is the most common, it is not the only possible arrangement. Some encyclopedias aimed at young children, such as *My First Britannica*, organize each volume around a broad topic, such as plants or the human body. The *Encyclopedia of American History* is arranged chronologically, with individual volumes devoted to a specific time period and the entries within organized alphabetically.

Ease of access to information in electronic encyclopedias is theoretically superior to the ease of locating information in print versions. With the presence of robust, Boolean-based search engines, the inclusion of controlled vocabulary, and the presence of good authority control and indexing, one can, in effect, access any word contained in an electronic encyclopedia through keyword searching. Using Boolean operators such as *and*, *or*, *not*, and phrase searching can make a search more precise and productive; however, because many users do not have experience using Boolean logic, several current versions of electronic encyclopedias allow for natural language searching, through which the users type in a question such as "What was England's role in the American Civil War?" and the search engine returns articles containing any of the question's key words (England, American, Civil, and War). Although this latter method lacks precision and yields a number of false hits, the users will presumably retrieve some relevant articles that could lead them to other related information. Some products automatically spell-check searches and offer alternate spellings of words, and some provide a "fuzzy search" feature that allows users to indicate they are unsure of a spelling. Both options can greatly ease a user's search for information. In addition, most electronic encyclopedias rank retrieved articles for relevance, thus allowing users to quickly discard irrelevant information.

In online encyclopedias, internal hyperlinking between articles has replaced the *see also*; however, most products have separate indexes similar to those seen in their print counterparts. Again, the difference lies in the user's ability to click on an index term and go directly to the article or illustration and back to the index again with ease. With multivolume print sets, the user must constantly go back and forth between the index and the content volumes themselves, a method that often proves tiresome and inefficient.

SELECTION

Purchasing an encyclopedia, whether a print or online version, is a major investment in terms of cost. Cost alone, however, is not a sufficient reason for a librarian to select between versions of an encyclopedia. Other factors such as available shelf space, preservation goals, and type and number of users are equally important. It is incumbent upon the librarian to choose an encyclopedia that best addresses all of these issues. Table 18.2 is a chart of several common encyclopedia titles available today, showing both print and online availability.

Determining Need in Different Library Settings

The needs of a library's users determine which encyclopedias a librarian should select for purchase. A business information center would probably not need *Childcraft*, just as a small public library probably would not purchase the *Encyclopedia of Mathematics*. Librarians at large academic or public libraries face a different problem: how best to serve the varied needs of a large and diverse population.

Regardless of where they are located, people who seek information fall into one of three information-seeking categories: learners, users with general needs, and users with scholarly or specialized needs. These categories are not mutually exclusive, and it is not uncommon to find a modicum of overlap. A doctor who consults a drug encyclopedia while at work might visit the local public library to obtain information about organic gardening.

Learners

Anyone can be a learner, and publishers of encyclopedias generally target their products to this individual. Encyclopedias play a didactic role regardless of the age of the learner. They provide a range of tools that can help a wide variety of people learn how to access, synthesize, and in some cases, analyze information. Encyclopedias also tend to present information clearly and briefly so that the learner will not feel overwhelmed or intimidated. Children's encyclopedias are probably the best

TABLE 18.2   ENCYCLOPEDIA COMPARISON CHART

Encyclopedia	Age range	Print contents	Online availability
My First Britannica (Britannica, 2008)	7–11	• 13 volumes • 500 articles • 800 illustrations • Topical arrangement, index	Not available
Britannica Student Encyclopedia (Britannica, 2010)	8–12	• 16 volumes • 2,300 articles • 3,800 illustrations • Index	*Britannica Online* (various editions available)
Compton's by Britannica (Britannica, 2008)	10–17	• 26 volumes • 37,000 articles • 23,000 illustrations • Fact-Index: ready-reference guide and index	*Britannica Online* (various editions available)
Encyclopaedia Britannica (Britannica, 2010)	13–adult	• 32 volumes (*Micropaedia, Macropaedia, Propaedia*) • 65,000 articles • 24,000 illustrations • 2-volume index	*Britannica Online* (various editions available)
The New Book of Knowledge (Grolier, 2008)	8–13	• 21 volumes • 9,000 articles • 25,000 illustrations • Index in every volume; cumulative index	*Grolier Online* (various editions available)
Encyclopedia Americana (Grolier, 2006)	13–adult	• 30 volumes • 45,000 articles • 23,000 illustrations • Index	*Grolier Online* (various editions available)
World Book Discovery Encyclopedia (World Book, 2009)	7–11	• 13 volumes • 2,300 articles • 3,300 illustrations • Index and atlas	*World Book Online* (various editions available)
World Book Encyclopedia (World Book, 2010)	All	• 22 volumes • 17,000 articles • 27,500 illustrations • Index	*World Book Online* (various editions available)

examples of encyclopedias geared to learners. They provide only the most basic information, include a multitude of illustrations, and use vocabulary that allows children not only to expand their own vocabulary but also to locate information in other sources. Adult encyclopedias can also aid learners. Research and study skills guides can act as mini-refresher courses for an older adult who is returning to college after graduating from high school 30 years earlier or can help a high school senior choose a topic for a term paper.

Users with General Needs

People who need brief factual information or leads to sources about a particular topic qualify as users with general needs. Unlike learners, general users will not consult an encyclopedia's research guides but rather will focus on locating information quickly and easily. To meet those needs, librarians should acquire encyclopedias whose emphasis is on breadth of subject coverage as opposed to those that emphasize scholarly depth and treatment of subject matter.

Users with Scholarly or Specialized Needs

Although users with scholarly or specialized needs might find some information of value in a general, multivolume encyclopedia, it is more likely that subject encyclopedias would be a better choice. A graduate student in library science would obviously benefit from access to the *Encyclopedia of Library and Information Science*, and the library and information science librarian would undoubtedly choose that for inclusion in the reference collection in print and/or online. Because the University of California at Davis has a prominent viticulture and enology program, it would necessarily follow that its university library would acquire encyclopedias about wine and winemaking.

Which subject encyclopedias a librarian chooses to acquire depends entirely on the needs of the library's users. However, it would be foolish for most public and academic libraries not to include a variety of subject encyclopedias in their collections. New titles can always be added when user needs change.

Cost

Cost plays a major role in the acquisition of any library material. Encyclopedias, by their very nature, can be viewed as investment pieces, and their acquisition should not be a cavalier matter. In addition to the often substantial cost of purchasing a print encyclopedia set, annual updates and supplements are often purchased as separate items. Subscription rates for electronic encyclopedias vary according to the number of users a library serves, although institutions often can get a discount by purchasing as part of a consortium or by subscribing to multiple products from the same vendor.

Some publishers of multivolume sets such as the *McGraw-Hill Encyclopedia of Science and Technology* may offer compact, one-volume versions containing material extracted from the larger set. As of 2010, McGraw-Hill offered several compact volumes, including the *McGraw-Hill Concise Encyclopedia of Engineering* and the *McGraw-Hill Concise Encyclopedia of Physics*. These one-volume titles allow a smaller library to grow or vary its collection cost-effectively.

Choosing between Print and Online Options

For years, librarians could purchase only print encyclopedias. Multivolume general sets cost the most and had limited shelf lives. However, once a library made the purchase, it owned the set outright and could provide unlimited access to it. The downside lay in having to make this investment over and over because encyclopedias lose their currency rather quickly. Before the current trend of moving to electronic encyclopedias, libraries typically followed a pattern whereby they would purchase a new multivolume set on a fairly regular schedule determined by user needs and the amount of revision work undertaken by encyclopedia publishers from year to year.

With recent advances in technology and the desire to make information widely accessible, many libraries have begun to purchase electronic encyclopedias. One of the greatest advantages of online encyclopedias lies in their ability to be accessed by several people simultaneously, as well as by people located in a variety of places, both inside and outside the physical library. However, in the case of online encyclopedias, subscriptions are negotiated annually; the library must pay the subscription fee each year or lose access to the information. In addition, given the current obsolescence rate of personal computers, librarians have to consider the cost of upgrading or replacing this equipment every two to four years to keep up with the system requirements that new and improved software always requires.

Selection decisions are further complicated by the growing number of free encyclopedias available on the Web. Some, such as the Encyclopedia section of *Infoplease.com* and the *Stanford Encyclopedia of Philosophy*, are free in their entirety. In other cases, commercial publishers offer free access to a limited amount of information via their Web sites; users who desire access to the complete encyclopedia are encouraged to start an individual or library subscription. An example in this latter category is *Britannica Online*.

As with any other Web site, librarians must carefully evaluate the content of free encyclopedias for authority, accuracy, objectivity, and currency before recommending them to users. The encyclopedia content on *Infoplease.com* is from *The Columbia Encyclopedia*, a preeminent single-volume encyclopedia. Thus, this site reflects the authority of its print predecessor. The *Stanford Encyclopedia of Philosophy*, on the other hand, has been developed solely as a Web-based resource. Its authority stems from its reliance on expert scholars as authors of individual articles and its use of a scholarly publishing model, in which articles are reviewed by an editorial board before publication. At the same time, the *Stanford Encyclopedia of Philosophy* is a work in progress; some articles have yet to be written. Thus, although libraries could point users to this site for reliable information on philosophy, they would not want to discard their more complete print reference tools just yet.

Ultimately, librarians need to examine a variety of issues before deciding whether to abandon print encyclopedias in favor of their online counterparts. Although some libraries point users to free Web sites, it seems preferable for libraries to purchase access to a complete and authoritative encyclopedia through a library-based subscription. In addition to cost and access issues, librarians need to consider shelf space, preservation goals, and user needs. A large academic or public library may subscribe to online encyclopedias in order to provide their users access to information from homes and offices. A small school library with limited computer workstations, however, might find a print encyclopedia provides the best access, given that each volume can be used by a different student simultaneously. In the end, libraries will want to achieve the balance of print and online encyclopedias that best serves their particular users.

IMPORTANT GENERAL SOURCES

This section focuses on general encyclopedias typically purchased by school, public, or academic libraries. Although there are many subject encyclopedias, only a few important titles are discussed. For information about titles not described in this section, the reader is referred to sources listed in the "Additional Readings" section.

Encyclopedias for Children and Young Adults

The strength of the *World Book Encyclopedia* is its ability to help a wide variety of users find information quickly and effectively. The 2010 revision has 22 volumes containing more than 17,000 signed articles and 27,500 illustrations, the vast majority in color, including approximately 2,200 maps. All subjects are arranged alphabetically using the word-by-word method. Cross-references also play a significant role in this alphabetical arrangement. As the preface notes, articles vary in length and treatment depending on the subject matter and intended audience. The "mouse" article targets young readers and includes age-specific vocabulary, whereas the "cell" article targets advanced readers. Many of the lengthier articles, like the "leaf" article, use a graduated approach; that is, its authors use simple concepts and vocabulary at the beginning of the article and build toward incorporating more advanced ideas and vocabulary at its conclusion.[6] Technical terms such as those found in the "moon" article are italicized and their meanings given within the context of the sentence or within parentheses.

World Book is heavily illustrated and conveys much of its information in tables and charts, which are set apart from the text on a given page. This method makes the layout more visually appealing and acts as a vehicle for helping its readers digest what they have read thus far. For example, the "tree" article has 28 illustrations covering, among other things, the parts, growth cycle, and uses of trees; instructions on correctly planting and growing a tree; and a guide to more than 75 tree species that includes an illustration of each tree with and without leaves and detailed views of the leaf, seed, and bark.

Another great strength of *World Book* is its ability to be used as a learning and instructional tool. Lengthy articles are often followed by an outline of the article for quick review purposes, references to related entries, and a list of study questions. Related reading lists often appear at the end of articles and are often split into two levels, easy and advanced. Volume 22 contains an index with more than 175,000 entries and the "Research Guide," an instructional section with guides to writing, speaking, and researching.

World Book is also available electronically as *World Book Online*. Depending on the version selected, it contains the complete contents of the print set plus thousands more articles, as well as links to multimedia content, periodical articles, primary sources, and Web sites. Multimedia features include 100-plus 360-degree photographs and more than 10,000 audio files. Students can explore history through a series of imaginary Web sites called "Surf the Ages," as well as historical articles from previous editions of *World Book*. *World Book Online* is suitable for even novice users. Users can browse or search content. A simple search option is prominent, and an advanced search link takes users to a page that provides Boolean search options, the ability to limit to particular types of media, and numerous browse options.

Another perennial favorite with librarians is Grolier's 21-volume *New Book of Knowledge* (*NBK*), aimed at elementary and middle-school students, as well as their parents. The 2008 edition has 21 volumes with more than 9,000 articles. Articles are heavily illustrated with photos, maps, tables, and time lines (more than 25,000 color illustrations total, including 1,300 maps). The editors work with educators and librarians to determine content that supports the public school curriculum, as well as student interests. Articles are written at different levels of reading comprehension, depending on the perceived audience, with topics that appeal to younger readers written for lower levels of comprehension and with articles aimed at older readers containing more technical vocabulary.

To make *NBK* even more child-friendly, its editors use bold subheadings to break up longer articles, provide word guides at the bottom of each page to facilitate searching, and have made each volume a stand-alone (letters of the alphabet are not split between volumes). Every volume of *NBK* contains an index, printed on blue paper to separate it from the volume's contents, which is cross-referenced to the contents of the entire encyclopedia. In addition, all of the indexes are brought together in a cumulative index.

The New Book of Knowledge aims to be more than just a reference tool for factual knowledge. Entries include a variety of activity projects as well as stories and poems that users can read aloud. An additional volume written for parents and teachers contains a "Home and School Reading" guide, which recommends nearly 6,000 fiction and nonfiction children's and young adult titles covering more than 1,300 topics. In the same volume, the "Study Guide" contains information on child development and the school curriculum for various grade levels, along with recommended activities for parents and children to do together.

The *NBK*'s online counterpart is *Grolier Online*, a suite of databases that includes the *NBK*; *Grolier Multimedia*, a ready-reference encyclopedia aimed at middle and high school students; an online version of *Encyclopedia Americana*, which is discussed in more detail later in this chapter; *La Nueva Enciclopedia Cumbre*, a Spanish-language encyclopedia; and three subject encyclopedias: *The New Book of Popular Science*, *Lands and Peoples*, and *America the Beautiful*. Libraries can combine a subscription to two or more of these titles to create an online encyclopedia package that best suits their needs. The *Grolier Online* interface allows users to search all the titles in a library's package or go to the interface for an individual encyclopedia. Current events are highlighted through a daily news feature (taken from the Associated Press) and weekly "Feature Stories" that combine news articles, links to photos and "fast facts," and suggested lesson plans for teachers.

The online version of the *NBK* mimics the best features of the print version and adds many multimedia tools to enhance a child's learning experience. It includes the content of the print set with the addition of an interactive time line, "Wonder Questions" to encourage further research and exploration, games, and selections from literary works. *NBK*'s online interface is well organized and provides alphabetical browse, subject browse, and search functions.

Aimed at upper-elementary through high-school-age users, *Compton's by Britannica* can be used in school or at home. The 2008 edition has 26 volumes containing more than 37,000 articles and approximately 23,000 illustrations. Longer articles have their own table of contents. Volume 26, called the Fact-Index, contains the index, as well as nearly 30,000 brief articles suitable for ready reference. Other notable features include "Exploring," a list of questions that introduces each volume; "Here and There," a topical guide to each volume; and time lines. *Compton's* is also available online through the *Britannica Online School Edition* and the *Britannica Online Public Library Edition* (*Britannica Online* is discussed in more detail in the following section).

Britannica offers *My First Britannica*, a 13-volume set aimed at elementary school children. Instead of an alphabetical organization, each of the volumes is devoted to a topic such as mammals, plants, or Africa. Volume 13 includes an index and reference guide. The set contains 525 articles and more than 800 color photos and illustrations. Each volume also includes a glossary. Features such as "Did You Know?" (interesting facts) and "Search Light" (questions encouraging reading comprehension) break up the text and help engage young readers.

Another thoughtful print encyclopedia for children is the *World Book Discovery Encyclopedia*. Designed for early elementary children, its 13 volumes have 2,300 articles in an alphabetical arrangement and more than 3,300 illustrations. Most articles are brief, but special feature articles on high-interest topics contain more detailed treatments, as well as colored backgrounds and additional illustrations. Volume 13 contains both an index and a collection of maps. The *World Book Discovery Encyclopedia* is available online as *World Book Kids*, which features the content of the print version along with activities and teacher guides.

There are several single-volume encyclopedias available for children and young adults as well. The 2004 edition of *The Kingfisher Children's Encyclopedia* contains more than 400 brief, alphabetically arranged entries on a broad range of subjects. The volume is heavily illustrated, has an index, and includes a section of time lines and data tables. Kingfisher also makes a number of single-volume subject encyclopedias for children, such as *The Kingfisher History Encyclopedia*. Dorling Kindersley's *DK Children's Illustrated Encyclopedia* contains hundreds of well-crafted illustrations and sharp photographs, as well as 500 main entries. The *Scholastic Children's Encyclopedia* contains approximately 600 short entries and 2,000 illustrations. Designed to appeal to young readers, each entry starts with a two-sentence summary, followed by more detailed information. Sidebars labeled "Amazing Facts," "Key Facts," and "Did You Know" contribute to the visual appeal of the book. A reference section at the end contains maps of countries, time zones, and Native American tribes; quick facts on nations, states, and U.S. presidents; tables of plant and animal classifications; and a guide to measurements.

Encyclopedias for Adults

The largest of the multivolume English-language general encyclopedias, *Encyclopaedia Britannica* is considered by many to be the most scholarly. The 2010 revision contains approximately 65,000 articles in 32 volumes and comes in three parts: the *Micropaedia*, the *Macropaedia*, and the *Propaedia*. The 12-volume *Micropaedia* contains thousands of shorter entries, whereas the 17-volume *Macropaedia* contains lengthy, detailed articles. Together they contain more than 24,000 illustrations, primarily in black and white. The single-volume *Propaedia* acts as an "outline of knowledge." The extensive index comes in two volumes. Purchasers can also buy *Britannica Book of the Year* separately.

Britannica's Micropaedia is designed primarily for ready reference. Entries are arranged alphabetically using the word-by-word method. The *Micropaedia* can be used as a resource on its own or in combination with the *Macropaedia*. Several entries conclude with bibliographies of scholarly research material. The structure of the *Micropaedia* facilitates easy access to the information contained within. Entries for individuals follow certain conventions. For example, individuals of Eastern origin will have their entries listed with the surname preceding the personal name (for example, Deng Xiaoping, Nguyen Cao Ky). Certain titles, such as those for institutions or structures, also receive special treatment with regard to entry arrangement (for example, the Tower of London is listed as London, Tower of). Cross-references have several functions within the *Micropaedia*. They can act as referents to alternate names or spellings or operate as *see also*, *see under*, *q.v.* (quod vide—"which see," singular), or *qq.v.* (quae vide—"which see," plural) within or following the conclusions of articles. Page format tends toward the crowded, with little white space, use of smallish fonts, and small illustrations.

The *Macropaedia* has detailed survey articles that range from a few pages to more than 100 pages in length. A bibliography follows every article. Unlike the *Micropaedia*, use of the *Macropaedia* almost always requires consulting the index given that individual topics are typically addressed within larger articles. For example, the *Micropaedia* has a one-column entry under "Kalahari"; the *Macropaedia* contains more than two pages of information on the same desert, as well as a map, but it is found in the "Africa" entry. As in the *Micropaedia*, page layout in the *Macropaedia* tends to be dense. The *Macropaedia* incorporates larger illustrations and several color-insert plates; however, *Britannica*, in spite of adding more graphics in recent editions, will never rival *World Book* in terms of number of photographs, images, and illustrations used.

The *Propaedia* serves as "a topical guide to the contents of *Encyclopaedia Britannica*, enabling the reader to carry out an orderly plan of reading in any field of knowledge or learning chosen for study in some depth."[7] Although this is indeed correct, the *Propaedia*, or "outline of knowledge," can seem daunting to the uninitiated. It has a unique structure that allows the user to find relationships and connections within and across disciplines and thus to relevant information in the *Micropaedia* and *Macropaedia*. In comparison, the index includes more than 700,000 references and cross-references and provides ready access to the information contained in the *Micropaedia* and the *Macropaedia*. Whereas the index tells the user where to find information, the *Propaedia* tells the user what information can be found.

Another tool connected to *Britannica* is its *Book of the Year*. Purchased separately, this single volume includes vast statistical information in the "World Data" section, a collection of current facts and figures for the countries and dependencies of the world. Because *Britannica* does not cover statistical information in depth in its *Propaedia*, *Micropaedia*, and *Macropaedia*, it is imperative for libraries to order *Book of the Year*. In addition, a "World Affairs" section provides narrative updates for individual countries, and additional articles provide updates on cultural topics such as fashion and literature. The *Book of the Year* also includes brief biographies of notable figures, obituaries, and a time line of noteworthy events. It is important to note that the date given on the spine reflects the publication year; the data comes from the preceding year (i.e., the 2010 *Book of the Year* actually reflects data and events from 2009).

Although locating information in the *Encyclopaedia Britannica* can be difficult or intimidating for some, the depth and breadth of scholarship contained within outweigh these difficulties. Nevertheless, because the online version eliminates the need to move through multiple print volumes, libraries may want to consider switching from the print set to an online version to give users easier access to information housed in what many deem the premier English-language encyclopedia produced today.

Britannica Online maintains the high standards that are the hallmark of the print version and augments what is available in the print edition. *Britannica Online* is available in a variety of packages, including the School Edition, the Academic Edition, and the Public Library Edition, which offers two interfaces, one for children and one for adults. Depending on the edition, articles come from *Encyclopaedia Britannica*, *Britannica Concise Encyclopedia*, *Compton's by Britannica*, and other Britannica titles, as well as the *Book of the Year*. Textual information is supplemented by a wealth of images, multimedia, tables, and figures. Searches can be conducted across multiple titles or limited to any combination thereof. Browsing is available by time period, index, and subject (in an easy-to-use arrangement similar to the *Propaedia*). Special features include interactive time lines, statistical profiles of countries worldwide, the *Merriam-Webster's Collegiate Dictionary*, a biography of the day, a "This Day in History" link, headline news from the *New York Times* and BBC News, and a list of recently updated articles.

The first encyclopedia published in the United States, in 1829, *Encyclopedia Americana* prides itself on its focus on U.S. history, geography, and biography, as well as on science and technology. This is not to say that it sacrifices coverage of other countries or topics to make room for these emphases; *Encyclopedia Americana* is second only to *Britannica* in terms of depth and breadth. The 30-volume 2006 version includes 45,000 articles and 23,000 illustrations, including 1,200 maps. Entries are arranged alphabetically using the word-by-word method, and cross-references are numerous. Longer articles are given their own table of contents and contain bibliographies. Although *Americana*'s structure is more straightforward than that of *Britannica*, librarians will still want to consult the index, located in volume 30, to be sure of finding all the relevant information on a topic. Like *Britannica*, *Encyclopedia Americana* uses illustrations sparingly, and the majority are black and white.

An online version of *Encyclopedia Americana* is available through *Grolier Online* (discussed previously). The online version provides the contents of the print *Americana*, as well as news items from the *Americana Journal* and links to thousands of periodical articles, as well as external Web sites. The interface is spare compared to other online encyclopedias. However, two special features invite readers to browse. "Editor's Picks" highlights selected content of the encyclopedia, and "Profiles" provides topical access to biographies. A search function is prominent and allows users to search only *Americana* or all the Grolier encyclopedias in a library's subscription.

With regard to encyclopedias written for a Canadian audience, *The Canadian Encyclopedia* does an admirable job of including information on a wide variety of

Canadian personalities, places, events, and achievements. Previously published in print and as a CD-ROM, the encyclopedia is now produced as a free Web site available in both English and French. The site also offers the *Encyclopedia of Music in Canada* and selected content from *Maclean's* magazine. A simple search interface allows keyword searching, and features such as picture galleries, time lines, and "On This Day in Canadian History" invite the user to explore the site.

Wikipedia is a free online encyclopedia that anyone can author and anyone can edit. Authors are asked to maintain a neutral point of view and include only verifiable information (and are encouraged, but not required, to provide references). Unlike more traditional encyclopedias, there is not an editorial system that verifies or certifies articles or their authors prior to "publication." Instead, *Wikipedia* assumes other user-authors will check for and correct erroneous information. Each article includes a "discussion" page where authors can explain a change they have made or otherwise discuss the article's content. Lengthy guidelines and policies set expectations for appropriate content, writing style, and what constitutes a reliable source.

Because of the open authorship, reviews of *Wikipedia* have been mixed, although the site has steadily been gaining a reputation for quality. A study published in *Nature* found that science articles in *Wikipedia* were nearly as accurate as those in *Britannica* (three errors per article on average for *Britannica* and four for *Wikipedia*). Studies also have found that errors and vandalism are quickly fixed. However, *Wikipedia*'s reputation came under attack after an incident in 2005 when a *Wikipedia* biography of a well-known journalist and political figure was altered to implicate him in the Kennedy assassinations. Also, studies have noted that *Wikipedia*'s articles can provide uneven treatment of topics—thus, although the information given in an article is generally accurate thanks to eager fact-checkers and editors, the same article can be missing important aspects of a topic that a more conventional source would include.[8] Recognizing the need to provide high-quality, reliable content, *Wikipedia* has created "protected" articles that are restricted to established members in order to prevent vandalism and a ranking system of "featured" and "good" articles to highlight higher-quality work.

One of the advantages of *Wikipedia* is its sheer size—in early 2011 the site had almost 3.6 million articles in its English-language version. *Wikipedia* covers topics from the scholarly (phenomenology) to the mundane (San Pedro, California) to the trivial (a comparison chart of characters from six different versions of the television show *The Office*). Thus, the encyclopedia can be a source of information on even the most unusual of topics. In addition, *Wikipedia*'s open editing structure means articles can be updated almost simultaneously with world events. In June 2008, an article on Phar Lap was updated the same day researchers announced tests that revealed the noted racehorse, who died in 1932, had been poisoned with arsenic. Although librarians should be wary of consulting *Wikipedia* for ready-reference factual information, the encyclopedia can be a valuable resource for general background information and pre-research information. Bibliographies and cited references, when present, can direct researchers to additional sources of information, and careful reading of the "discussion" page associated with a topic can reveal diverse points of view worthy of further study.

Citizendium, an online encyclopedia started by one of the cofounders of *Wikipedia*, follows a similar format to its open predecessor by allowing anyone to author a page but uses experts to provide editorial oversight. Unlike *Wikipedia*, the site requires that all authors and editors use their real names. Although growth has been slow, and it is still in the early stages as of this writing, the site bears watching.

Single-Volume Encyclopedias

Although the number of single-volume subject encyclopedias continues to grow, there are not many recent single-volume general encyclopedias from which to choose. *The Columbia Encyclopedia* was most recently published in 2000 as a sixth edition. It includes more than 50,000 brief entries with limited black-and-white illustrations. This sixth edition of *Columbia* is available on the Web for free. In addition, a version of *Columbia*, updated in 2004, is available through *Credo Reference*. The fourth edition of *The Cambridge Encyclopedia* was published in 2000. It includes more than 36,000 brief entries, of which 26,000 are main entries presented in alphabetical order and 10,000 are ready-reference entries located at the back of the encyclopedia. A slightly more recent publication is the *Britannica Concise Encyclopedia*, published in 2006. This title contains more than 28,000 brief entries.

Subject Encyclopedias

Although there are numerous high-quality subject encyclopedias, the limits of a single chapter allow for discussion of only a few important titles: *McGraw-Hill Encyclopedia of Science and Technology*, *Encyclopedia of Religion*, *Grzimek's Animal Life Encyclopedia*, and *Worldmark Encyclopedia of the Nations*. In addition to their availability in print, the last two titles are available in electronic form as part of the *Gale Virtual Reference Library*.

Perhaps the most important subject encyclopedia is the 20-volume *McGraw-Hill Encyclopedia of Science and Technology*. Unsurpassed in scope and coverage, the 10th edition, published in 2007, contains more than 7,000 articles and 12,000 illustrations, more than 1,900 of which are new or revised. Articles are authored by experts from universities, industry, and government organizations, including a number of Nobel Prize winners. In spite of having so many world-renowned experts, the *McGraw-Hill Encyclopedia of Science and Technology* is written to accommodate a wide variety of readers, from the layperson to the specialist. Specific disciplines, such as meteorology and physics, are covered in broad survey articles. Each entry begins with a definition and a general overview of the topic. The entry then progresses from the general to the specific in an effort to provide comprehensive coverage of the topic. Bibliographies typically come at the end of an article. Pure science remains the focus; there are no articles devoted to sociological, historical, or biographical aspects of science or technology. More than 60,000 cross-references are included. Perhaps the best feature of this subject encyclopedia is its organization. One can locate information using four methods: find an article alphabetically in its appropriate volume; consult the 500-page "Analytical Index" (a traditional index of terms, concepts, and names); browse the "Topical Index" (which groups all article titles under general subjects, such as Organic Chemistry); or use the "Study Guides." The last three features are found in volume 20. The "Study Guides" outline major disciplines and provide a guide for reading and self-study. The final volume also contains a guide to scientific notation. Supplementing the

McGraw-Hill Encyclopedia of Science and Technology is the single-volume *McGraw-Hill Yearbook of Science and Technology*. Since 1962, these yearbooks have reviewed the previous year's scientific accomplishments and advancements.

The *McGraw-Hill Encyclopedia of Science and Technology* is available online under the name *AccessScience*. From the initial screen, users can search or browse, and an advanced search screen allows users to limit by content type or subject area. The online version includes more than 2,000 biographies from the *Hutchinson Dictionary of Scientific Biography*. A Nobel Prize section provides a list of all prize winners (including those for literature, peace, and economics), with links to relevant articles. *AccessScience* enhances the textual content of the print set with a number of multimedia features designed for the non-expert. The "Image Galleries" has slide-shows, some of which can be downloaded as PowerPoint files for use in the classroom, and animated tutorials on selected topics. For students, an "Essay Topics" page suggests research topics for beginner, intermediate, and advanced students, and a section of study guides for Advanced Placement (AP) tests combines topical outlines, links to encyclopedia content, specially developed animations and tutorials, and practice quizzes to help high schoolers study for the AP exams in physics, biology, chemistry, and environmental science. Podcasts and an RSS feed, which allows users to receive automatic updates about encyclopedia content and scientific news, are available.

Another important title is the *Encyclopedia of Religion*, most recently revised in 2004. The 15-volume set contains approximately 3,300 articles on religion and spiritual practice. The *Encyclopedia of Religion* takes a valuable cross-cultural approach, highlighting practices and beliefs in different faiths and countries. Because of this cross-cultural approach and because one of the goals of the *Encyclopedia of Religion* is to place religion in the context of daily life, the content is relevant to users interested in art, history, sociology, and other fields. Articles are arranged alphabetically, and longer articles include a table of contents. Cross-references and bibliographies, many with annotations, are located at the end of articles. Composite articles start with an overview of a topic (e.g., Afterlife) followed by articles that explore the topic in the context of a particular faith or place (e.g., Afterlife: Oceanic Concepts, Afterlife: Jewish Concepts). Interestingly, this second edition retains approximately 50 prominent articles in their original form, providing updates in a second article subtitled "Further Considerations." All articles are signed and dated. Volume 15 contains an index.

A second important science encyclopedia is *Grzimek's Animal Life Encyclopedia*. The 17-volume set contains more than 700 articles and 12,000 color illustrations. *Grzimek's* is arranged taxonomically by class, order, and family, which can be confusing for the novice user. However, finding aids abound. Each volume includes a table of contents and index for the volumes in that class (so the five volumes on mammals have the same table of contents and index reprinted in each volume). Volume 17 contains a cumulative index. Each article provides an overview of a family (e.g., slit-faced bats), including biology, habitat, behavior, and conservation status, followed by more detailed information on individual species. Information is presented in both narrative and tabular form, and each article is accompanied by at least one distribution map. Articles end with a list of resources for further study. The complete content of the print encyclopedia is available in the *Gale Virtual Reference Library*, and in fall 2009, the publisher released the online *Grzimek's Animal Life* with additional multimedia content.

The five-volume *Worldmark Encyclopedia of the Nations* is another essential title for most libraries. Country information is contained in four volumes that are organized by continent, with country entries organized alphabetically within each volume. Each entry starts with basic country facts, followed by detailed information organized under 50 subheadings. These subheadings are numbered and are consistent across all entries to aid users in finding the desired information. Information is presented primarily in narrative form, although some tabular data is given. Illustrations are black and white and consist of the coat of arms and flag, as well as a map of each country. A full-color regional map is printed at the front of each volume. Volume 1 provides detailed information about the United Nations, as well as information on polar regions, tables of statistical data, and an index (unfortunately, its location in the first volume is counterintuitive to most users, and it is easily overlooked). Although librarians would want to verify some information in a more up-to-date source, the *Worldmark Encyclopedia of the Nations* continues to be an excellent source for succinct background information about a nation's history, politics, economy and culture.

SEARCH STRATEGIES

As is the case with any reference source, knowledge of how and when to use that source plays a key role with respect to locating required information quickly and efficiently. Given the unique role of encyclopedias, having an understanding of how to use them properly has greater significance. Because no two encyclopedias are alike in terms of format and scope, librarians need to become familiar with as many as possible to best guide users in their selection. No one encyclopedia can meet every information need. Therefore, a librarian must conduct a reference interview with the user to determine what information is specifically needed. If the librarian determines that encyclopedias would be the best source, the information need can then be categorized into one of the three areas discussed earlier in this chapter: ready reference, general background information, or pre-research information. Once categorization has been determined, a librarian can then choose an encyclopedia or encyclopedias that would best allow the user to locate the needed information. With the advent of online encyclopedias, search strategies with regard, first, to selection of an encyclopedia and, second, to locating information contained within the encyclopedia have become more complex. Although online encyclopedias generally have some sort of help tool, a novice computer user would benefit from librarian instruction.

Which Encyclopedia Should I Use?

When determining which encyclopedia to use, librarians must consider the user's age, knowledge level, and information need. In addition, because many encyclopedias are now available both in print and online, librarians must consider not only which encyclopedia to choose but also which format.

A ninth grader asks, "I am writing a report about Martin Luther King. My teacher said that he wrote a speech about a dream. Where can I find it?" Not only does *Britannica Online* provide an article about Dr. King as well as links to the text of his "I Have a Dream Speech"; it also includes a video clip of Dr. King delivering that speech. The

BOX 18.1
WHAT DID YOU NEED TO KNOW ABOUT GIRAFFES?

A library user has approached the desk and asked for some information on giraffes. *Britannica* and *Americana* both provide short articles accompanied by a photo of a giraffe. In *Britannica*, the article is a few paragraphs long. In *Americana*, the article is one page and focuses on physical appearance, diet, behavior, and reproduction. A final paragraph addresses the environmental status of the animal. The article is signed and includes a short bibliography. After reviewing both sources, the user indicates she would like more information. Which source would you pick?

Both *World Book* and *The New Book of Knowledge* contain more in-depth information. In *World Book*, the article is almost two pages long and is accompanied by multiple illustrations. The article addresses physical appearance and reproduction, as well as the family life of giraffes, how they move, and their interaction with people. In addition to two photos of giraffes, one of which shows how giraffes bend to the ground to lick salt or drink, there is an illustration of the giraffe's skeleton, an illustration of its footprints, and a world map showing distribution. Although there is no bibliography, the article is signed. *The New Book of Knowledge* also has a two-page, signed article. This article addresses physical appearance, life cycle, and how giraffes interact with people but also includes detailed information on the activities of giraffes—how they eat, drink water, and lie down. There are three photos, including one of a giraffe bending down to drink.

Grzimek's Animal Life Encyclopedia has a 12-page entry on the family Giraffidae, which includes giraffes and okapis. The article includes in-depth information and numerous photos. One section provides scientific names and descriptions for nine subspecies of giraffes, as well as photos illustrating the markings of all nine subspecies and a short discussion of current scientific debates about whether all nine are truly distinct subspecies.

Britannica Online provides a moderate-length article with two photos and a video. This article has more detail than its print counterpart and lists the nine subspecies of giraffes. *AccessScience* provides a short article, as well as a research update with detailed information on the neck vertebrae of giraffes. *World Book Online Reference Center* provides a moderate-length article with a map, two photos, and a video of giraffes running, as well as a link to an article from *Ranger Rick*, a children's magazine.

Wikipedia provides an extensive article with a table of contents, an illustration with the complete scientific classification and conservation status, numerous photos (including one of the tongue and one of giraffes bending down to drink), a map of the distribution of all nine subspecies, and an illustration of the skeleton. The article provides information on evolution, anatomy and morphology, behavior, and conservation, as well as giraffes in art and culture. The entry ends with a list of references and links to further information on other sites.

student would benefit from reading and listening to this speech and might gain a better understanding of the impact Dr. King had on U.S. history.

Nearly all university freshmen take a rhetoric and composition class during their first semester. Typically, their teachers have them write a position piece about a controversial topic such as gun control or the death penalty. A common question might be "I have to write a paper about the history of gun control in the United States; where would I find some good introductory material?" Because these students will be conducting pre-research, two encyclopedias, *Encyclopaedia Britannica* and *Encyclopedia Americana*, would be good places to start. *Encyclopedia Americana* takes pride in its focus on American history. Because the possession of guns has figured in U.S. history since its founding, this encyclopedia would provide the student with a good historical overview. The index and *Micropaedia* of the *Encyclopaedia Britannica* would provide, respectively, locations of information about gun control in the *Macropaedia* as well as ready reference or broad topical information.

Another question might be "Where can I read about the structure of DNA?" Because of the specificity of this question, a subject encyclopedia would be the first place to look. In particular, the *McGraw-Hill Encyclopedia of Science and Technology* lends itself to this question because it is the standard for in-depth information on science and technology. For younger users, *World Book* or *The New Book of Knowledge* would provide comparable information written at a level they would better understand.

NOTES

1.   A. J. Jacobs, *The Know-It-All: One Man's Humble Quest to Become the Smartest Person in the World* (New York: Simon & Schuster, 2004), 386 pp.

2.   Kenneth F. Kister, "Questions and Answers about Encyclopedias," in *Kister's Best Encyclopedias: A Comparative Guide to General and Specialized Encyclopedias*, 2nd ed. (Phoenix, AZ: Oryx Press, 1994), 3.

3.   Jacques Barzun, *The Modern Researcher*, 5th ed. (New York: Houghton Mifflin, 1992), 73.

4.   *Encyclopedia of African-American Culture and History* (New York: Simon & Schuster Macmillan, 1996), vii.

5.   *World Book Encyclopedia* (Chicago: World Book, 2010), iii.

6.   Ibid., iv.

7.   *New Encyclopaedia Britannica Propaedia* (Chicago: Encyclopaedia Britannica, 2005), 4.

8.   "Wiki's Wild World," *Nature* 438 (December 15, 2005): 890; Jim Giles, "Internet Encyclopaedias Go Head to Head," *Nature* 438 (December 15, 2005): 900–901; Gregory M. Lamb, "Online Wikipedia Is Not Britannica—But It's Close," *Christian Science Monitor* (January 5, 2006): 13; Jon Udell, "Wikipedia's Future," *InfoWorld* 28 (January 9, 2006): 30; Brock Read, "Can Wikipedia Ever Make the Grade?," *The Chronicle of Higher Education* 53 (October 27, 2006): A31–A36.

LIST OF SOURCES

AccessScience. New York: McGraw-Hill. http://www.accessscience.com (subscription required).

American Reference Books Annual. Ed. Shannon Graff Hysell. Santa Barbara, CA: Libraries Unlimited, 1970–.

ARBAonline. Santa Barbara, CA: Libraries Unlimited. http://www.arbaonline.com (subscription required).

The Blackwell Encyclopedia of Management. 2nd ed. 12 vols. Hoboken, NJ: Wiley, 2005.

Britannica Book of the Year. Chicago: Encyclopaedia Britannica, 1938–. Annual.

Britannica Concise Encyclopedia. Chicago: Encyclopaedia Britannica, 2006. 2115 pp.

Britannica Enciclopedia Universal Ilustrada. 20 vols. Chicago: Encyclopaedia Britannica, 2006. http://www.info.eb.com/ (subscription required).

Britannica Macropaedia, Britannica Micropaedia, and *Britannica Propaedia.* See *Encyclopaedia Britannica.*

Britannica Online. Chicago: Encyclopaedia Britannica. http://search.eb.com (subscription required); http://www.britannica.com (free).

Britannica Student Encyclopedia. 16 vols. Chicago: Encyclopaedia Britannica, 2010.

The Cambridge Encyclopedia. 4th ed. Ed. David Crystal. New York: Cambridge University Press, 2000. 1336 pp.

The Canadian Encyclopedia. Toronto: Historica Dominion Institute. http://www.thecanadian encyclopedia.com.

Childcraft: The How and Why Library. 15 vols. Chicago: World Book, 2006.

Citizendium. http://www.citizendium.org.

The Columbia Encyclopedia. 6th ed. Ed. Paul Lagassé. New York: Columbia University Press, 2000. 3156 pp. http://www.infoplease.com/encyclopedia. Also available in an updated form: http://www.credoreference.com (subscription required).

Compton's by Britannica. 26 vols. Chicago: Encyclopaedia Britannica, 2008. http://www.info.eb.com/ (subscription required).

Credo Reference. Boston, MA: Credo Reference. http://www.credoreference.com/ (subscription required).

Discover America. 51 vols. Chicago: Encyclopaedia Britannica, 2005.

DK Children's Illustrated Encyclopedia. 7th ed. New York: Dorling Kindersley, 2010. 600 pp.

Enciclopedia Estudiantil Hallazgos. 13 vols. Chicago: World Book, 2001.

Encyclopaedia Britannica. 32 vols. Chicago: Encyclopaedia Britannica, 2010. http://www.info.eb.com/ (subscription required).

Encyclopaedia Universalis. 28 vols. Chicago: Encyclopaedia Britannica, 2004. http://www.info.eb.com/ (subscription required).

Encyclopedia Americana. 30 vols. Danbury, CT: Grolier, 2006.

Encyclopedia of African-American Culture and History. Ed. Jack Salzman, David Lionel Smith, and Cornel West. 5 vols. New York: Simon & Schuster Macmillan, 1996.

Encyclopedia of African-American Culture and History. 2nd ed. Ed. Colin A. Palmer. 6 vols. Detroit: Macmillan Reference, 2006. Also available online as part of the *Gale Virtual Reference Library.*

Encyclopedia of American History. 2nd ed. Ed. Gary B. Nash. 11 vols. New York: Facts on File, 2009.

Encyclopedia of Animal Science. Ed. Wilson G. Pond and Alan W. Bell. New York: Marcel Dekker, 2005. 926 pp.

Encyclopedia of Forensic Science. Rev. ed. Ed. Suzanne Bell. New York: Facts on File, 2008. 432 pp.

Encyclopedia of Library and Information Science. 3rd ed. Ed. Marcia J. Bates and Mary Niles Maack. 7 vols. Boca Raton, FL: CRC Press, 2010. http://www.informaworld.com (subscription required).

Encyclopedia of Mathematics. Ed. James Stuart Tanton. New York: Facts on File, 2005. 568 pp.

Encyclopedia of Religion. 2nd ed. Ed. Lindsay Jones. 15 vols. Detroit: Macmillan Reference, 2005.

Gale Virtual Reference Library. http://www.gale.cengage.com (subscription required).

Gran Enciclopedia Hispanica. 18 vols. Chicago: World Book, 2006. http://www.worldbookonline.com (subscription required).

Gran Enciclopedia Planeta. 20 vols. Chicago: Encyclopaedia Britannica, 2004. http://www.info.eb.com/ (subscription required).

Grolier Online. http://go.grolier.com (subscription required).

Grzimek's Animal Life Encyclopedia. 2nd ed. 17 vols. Detroit: Gale, 2003–2004. Also available online as part of the *Gale Virtual Reference Library* and at http://www.gale.cengage.com (subscription required).

Japan: An Illustrated Encyclopedia. 2 vols. Tokyo: Kodansha, 1993.

The Kingfisher Children's Encyclopedia. Boston: Kingfisher, 2004. 468 pp.

The Kingfisher History Encyclopedia. Boston: Kingfisher, 2004. 491 pp.

L'encyclopedie Découverte. 15 vols. Chicago: World Book, 2009. http://www.worldbookonline.com (subscription required).

La Nueva Enciclopedia Cumbre. http://go.grolier.com (subscription required).

McGraw-Hill Concise Encyclopedia of Engineering. New York: McGraw-Hill, 2005. 912 pp.

McGraw-Hill Concise Encyclopedia of Physics. New York: McGraw-Hill, 2005. 832 pp.

McGraw-Hill Encyclopedia of Science and Technology. 10th ed. 20 vols. New York: McGraw-Hill, 2007.

McGraw-Hill Yearbook of Science and Technology. New York: McGraw-Hill, 1962–. Annual.

My First Britannica. 13 vols. Chicago: Encyclopaedia Britannica, 2008.

The New Book of Knowledge. 21 vols. Danbury, CT: Grolier, 2008.

The New Book of Knowledge Online. http://go.grolier.com (subscription required).

New Views of the Solar System. Chicago: Encyclopaedia Britannica, 2007. 106 pp.

Oxford Reference Online. New York: Oxford University Press. http://www.oxfordreference.com (subscription required).

The Pacific Islands: An Encyclopedia. Ed. Brij V. Lal and Kate Fortune. Honolulu: University of Hawaii Press, 2000. 664 pp.

Scholastic Children's Encyclopedia. New York: Scholastic Reference, 2004. 710 pp.

Stanford Encyclopedia of Philosophy. Stanford, CA: Stanford University. http://plato.stanford.edu.

Universalis Junior. 10 vols. Chicago: Encyclopaedia Britannica, 2008. http://www.info.eb.com/ (subscription required).

Wikipedia. http://www.wikipedia.org.

Women in World History: A Biographical Encyclopedia. Ed. Anne Commire and Deborah Klezmer. 17 vols. Farmington Hills, MI: Gale, 1999–2002.

World Book Discovery Encyclopedia. 13 vols. Chicago: World Book, 2009. http://www.worldbookonline.com (subscription required).

World Book Encyclopedia. 22 vols. Chicago: World Book, 2010. http://www.worldbookonline.com (subscription required).

World Book Encyclopedia Chinese Version. 20 vols. Chicago: World Book, 2007.

World Book Online. Chicago: World Book. http://www.worldbookonline.com (subscription required).

Worldmark Encyclopedia of the Nations. 12th ed. 5 vols. Farmington Hills, MI: Gale, 2007. Also available online as part of the *Gale Virtual Reference Library*.

ADDITIONAL READINGS

American Reference Books Annual. Ed. Shannon Graff Hysell. Santa Barbara, CA: Libraries Unlimited, 1970–. Annual.

This work examines all categories of reference works, covering general encyclopedias in three-, four-, and five-year cycles. Initial reviews give detailed background about an encyclopedia, whereas subsequent reviews focus solely on updates and revisions undertaken. A Web-based version, *ARBAonline*, allows searching current and past issues, as well as the ability to browse recent reviews and browse by subject.

Badke, William. "What to Do with Wikipedia." *Online* 32 (March/April 2008): 48–50.

Written by a librarian, this article provides a good overview of *Wikipedia*, as well as ideas for how librarians should respond to the ubiquitous encyclopedia by helping students to understand both its strengths and its limitations.

Berinstein, Paula. "Wikipedia and Britannica: The Kid's All Right (And So's the Old Man)." *Searcher* 14 (March 2006): 16–26.

For those interested in an in-depth evaluation of *Wikipedia*, Berinstein's article is well researched and features extensive quotes from an interview with *Wikipedia* founder Jimmy Wales. She contrasts the *Wikipedia* process of production with that of *Britannica*.

Cohen, Noam. "Start Writing the Eulogies for Print Encyclopedias." *New York Times*, March 16, 2008. http://www.nytimes.com/2008/03/16/weekinreview/16ncohen.html.

This article looks at the decline in demand for print titles, as well as the emergence of online-only encyclopedias.

Jacobs, A. J. *The Know-It-All: One Man's Humble Quest to Become the Smartest Person in the World*. New York: Simon & Schuster, 2004. 386 pp.

Entertaining and informative, this book describes the author's attempt to read the entire *Encyclopaedia Britannica* and what he learned in the process.

Katz, Bill. *Cuneiform to Computer: A History of Reference Sources*. Lanham, MD: Scarecrow Press, 1998. 417 pp.

For those interested in the origins and evolution of encyclopedias (as well as other reference sources), this book provides an in-depth overview.

Miller, Nora. "Wikipedia Revisited." *et Cetera* 64 (April 2007): 147–50.

This article provides a good summary of concerns regarding *Wikipedia*. Miller concludes, "In some ways, we can see Wikipedia as a metaphor for the evidence of our own senses: we have little control over what we receive, and we do well to remember to take a cautious view of what we think it tells us."

Recommended Reference Books for Small and Medium-Sized Libraries and Media Centers. Ed. Shannon Graff Hysell. Santa Barbara, CA: Libraries Unlimited, 1981–. Annual.

This title is a wonderful resource for librarians and school media specialists who work in small institutions. Although it covers all types of reference sources, the encyclopedias section thoughtfully discusses which encyclopedias would be most appropriate, and why, for the small or medium-size library or media center.

Reference Books Bulletin. Chicago: American Library Association, 1983–. 22 issues per year.

RBB appears as a separate section in every issue of *Booklist*. It devotes one issue annually to the review of encyclopedias; see, for example, *Booklist* 106 (September 15, 2009): 74–75, 78–79. Other issues often include lengthier reviews of newly released titles.

Geographical Sources

David A. Cobb

USES AND CHARACTERISTICS

Geographical sources are materials that are especially conducive to electronic formats, and such transformations continue at a rapid rate. Many atlases and maps, being graphical in nature, are transferable to many Web applications. And yet, although this is an age in which many believe everything can be found on the Internet, there is still value in collecting print materials that users may study and review. This chapter introduces a diversity of resources in both formats and, in some cases, even offers the same title in both formats.

Geographical sources are most often used to answer location questions: "Where is Frankfurt, Germany, where my grandmother was born?" or "Where is the location of yesterday's environmental catastrophe?" or "How do I find an Italian restaurant in Boston?" Although these are the types of questions asked most often, readers should not have the false impression that geography refers only to specific places or that those answers will be found only in traditional print reference volumes. Geographers study spatial problems involving environmental issues, regional planning, medical geography, political geography, mapping, and the general relationship between humans and their physical world. It is beyond the scope of this chapter to discuss specialized works of geography in great detail, but readers are encouraged to pursue further studies if they should find themselves in charge of administering even a small geography collection or acquiring materials in geography.

The publications discussed in this chapter represent the basic sources used in an average academic or large public library. For larger academic libraries that have greater financial resources, reference is made to additional sources. Similarly, it is impossible to discuss more than a few of the many resources that are now available via the Web. The most dramatic change for geographical sources is the amount of digital data widely available and the number of electronic map products available via the Web and on commercial CD-ROM.

Because many librarians will not be able to answer all geographical questions using the sources in their own collections, they should identify the closest large collection of geographical and cartographic materials in their state or region. The third edition of *Guide to U.S. Map Resources* is the most comprehensive listing of such collections in the United States, providing information on almost 600 individual map collections. The geographical and cartographic collections in this guide are the locations to which one may direct questions requiring more detail or expertise.

Librarians must always justify the cost of their materials, and some geographical sources have suffered in the library environment because of their cost, size, and storage requirements. Good-quality atlases, which often cost more than $100, create an added burden on budgets that are usually already unable to meet demands. The recent increase in the number of such atlases, along with political changes in an ever-changing world, makes it even more difficult for the reference librarian to make choices among geographical materials. Although it may be impossible to purchase all the different atlases, an alternative solution would be to purchase one or two titles annually and thus develop a well-rounded collection over several years.

Oversized materials and particularly geographical atlases and maps present obvious storage problems for the average reference department. All too often, oversized atlases are filed on bottom shelves, only to be forgotten. The acquisition of oversized atlases is more cost-effective if they are stored on atlas stands where they can be seen and used more frequently.

Almost all maps, especially larger ones that are not easily folded, present a unique problem for the library because they require specialized storage equipment. Ideally, large atlases should be stored on oversized atlas shelves, and maps should be placed in either vertical or horizontal cases designed specifically for map storage. Unfortunately, these may be luxury items for some libraries. For smaller libraries, maps can also be placed in large flat boxes and stored on top of filing cabinets to provide protection from light and dust. If a library's collection of maps grows to several hundred, metal map cases are the alternative of choice.

The primary purpose for the majority of geographical sources is to help one locate places. All of the sources described in this chapter locate something, tell something about a location, or show how to get there. Another general characteristic of geographical sources is that they usually deal with a time period, either current or historical. Although currency is very often important, historical information is also often critical to a reference question. In addition, some geographical sources deal with thematic or subject information. Examples of thematic information are a population atlas, a geological map, and an electronic road atlas.

Location questions can be grouped into three general categories: current events, recreation, and business. Current events are one of the strongest reasons for maintaining up-to-date geographical sources. Just as last night's talk-show novel will be requested in the library the next day, so too will information on yesterday's volcanic eruption, earthquake, revolution, or other human or physical disaster. Human society has become more global than ever, and the media bring the world's crises and disasters into the living room. It is the library's role to provide additional information on this global society. Current detailed geographical sources are one important means to accomplish this.

Recreation has become an important part of many lives, and travel is now more common than it was in the past. As a result, a larger segment of the population is interested in information, not only on local, state, or national parks but also on cities and regions all over the world. The amount of travel literature available today is more than any library could possibly accumulate, but an attempt should be made to provide a modest collection of travel literature for general user needs.

Finally, business travel is also more common, and the information required to answer these questions is related to travel literature. This particular type of travel requires more information on cities and detailed information regarding subjects such as hotels and restaurants.

Another category of questions concerns historical geography. This category can generally be divided into genealogy, military history, and place name changes. All three of these areas are covered in many specialized sources that are merely introduced in this chapter. Many genealogy questions are specific. For example, the user may want a map of the town where an ancestor lived in southern Germany in 1860. Few libraries can provide this information, and referral to a more specialized map collection may be required. However, often a quality atlas with large-scale maps or an older atlas in the collection may show the location of the town. The most valuable asset in answering these questions may be a late 19th- or early 20th-century atlas. Age should not be a primary criterion when weeding geographical sources because historical sources are especially valuable for these questions. Most historical atlases provide some treatment of military history, and if more specialized information is needed, large atlases are available that restrict themselves to a particular war or country (such as the American Civil War).

Similarly, place name changes can present a special problem for the general reference librarian. Because of its many place name changes, Eastern Europe presents particularly difficult challenges no matter how many sources the library has. Again, older atlases are excellent sources for early place names. Gazetteers, which list place name locations, are also discussed later in this chapter.

The types of geographical sources considered in this chapter include maps, atlases, gazetteers, travel literature, and general sources. Maps are purposely listed first because many librarians find them problematic, for reasons already mentioned. Nevertheless, maps generally provide more detailed information on a specific area, and provide more comprehensive thematic coverage, than do atlases. The advantage of atlases, however, is that they can provide the whole world, or a single country or state, in one volume at a nominal cost. Individual atlases may cover many types of subjects and offer basic reference information on geological features, the oceans, space, or the historical geography of a particular country. Gazetteers are also important reference tools because they provide information on geographical place names. Some gazetteers simply give precise information about a location, such as latitude and longitude; others describe the locations and give information on population, climate, economy, and notable tourist attractions. The titles making up travel literature have grown considerably in the last few years because of the travel patterns of society. Fortunately, there are many good options available from which libraries and individuals can choose. The section covering other geographical sources briefly describes the genre of titles that relate to geography, such as climatic information, political and geographical information on individual countries, mileage guides, geographical dictionaries, and online sources.

EVALUATION

Although atlases may be evaluated using criteria applicable to other reference books, there are criteria unique to atlases. Maps also must be evaluated differently than other reference sources. The criteria to be considered in evaluation of atlases and maps include scale and projection, color and symbols, publisher/authority, indexing, and currency. These criteria are equally important when evaluating digital cartographic formats.

Scale and Projection

Scale and projection are the two most common characteristics that make cartographic materials different from all other library materials. These two concepts are difficult for many persons to understand and are also difficult to explain. Essentially, *scale* is the ratio of the distance on the map to the actual distance on the face of the Earth. Maps must be drawn to scale so that accurate comparisons may be made between the map and the corresponding distance on the Earth. This scale may be given as a verbal scale (e.g., 1 inch equals 4 miles), as a representative fraction (e.g., 1:253,440), or as a graphic scale or bar scale normally found below the map. The verbal and representative fraction examples here are the same because there are 253,440 inches in 4 miles. Scale is the most important element of a map because it defines the amount of information that can be shown as well as the size of the geographical area (see Figure 19.1). Maps are generally classed by scale: large-scale maps are normally 1:100,000 or larger; medium-scale maps are between 1:100,000 and 1:1,000,000; and smaller-scale maps are 1:1,000,000 or smaller. Note the cartographic aberration that, as the number increases, the scale is considered smaller rather than larger, and vice versa.

A good map or atlas, even in electronic form, will always identify the scale, and the librarian must decide the appropriate scale for the user or library. Topographic maps, with large scales of 1:50,000, are excellent sources for geographical place names but would be the wrong choice for someone looking for a country's administrative boundaries. A smaller geographical area is shown on a 1:50,000-scale map; therefore, such a map is very detailed in the amount of data it shows. A more appropriate scale for administrative divisions would be 1:250,000 or even 1:500,000. It is important that maps in an atlas not vary their scales greatly. Quality atlases make an attempt to map nations and states at similar scales. An inferior atlas may show each U.S. state on its own page, which leads the user to believe that all states are "page-size." Similar examples should be carefully reviewed when looking at world atlases.

Map projection is one of the most complicated aspects of cartography, and scholars continue to discuss the value of one projection over another. Suffice it to say that when a spherical globe is drawn on a flat piece of paper (*projected*), there will be some distortion and unavoidable error. Certain projections are better suited to large-scale maps and others to small-scale maps. Furthermore, some projections are preferred for their

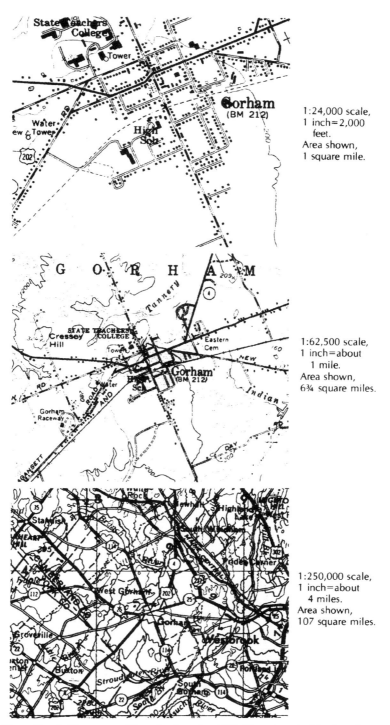

1:24,000 scale,
1 inch≈2,000
feet.
Area shown,
1 square mile.

1:62,500 scale,
1 inch=about
1 mile.
Area shown,
6¾ square miles.

1:250,000 scale,
1 inch=about
4 miles.
Area shown,
107 square miles.

From Morris Thompson, *Maps for America*, U.S. Department of the Interior, 1987.

Figure 19.1. Comparison of various map scales.

mapping characteristics (e.g., equal area, navigation, least distortion). The map user should be aware of these distortions and differences. A current globe will decrease the degree of distortion found in many maps and atlases. One of the well-known examples of distortion is the "large" Greenland on the Mercator projection world map. Find such a map and compare it to a globe to see how projections can slant one's understanding of the Earth. It is difficult for the average user, or librarian, to be aware of the many characteristics of the various projections used. *Map Appreciation*, by Mark Monmonier and George Schnell, provides an expert and clear explanation of this mapping concept.[1]

Color and Symbols

Color is used on maps in many different ways and for different purposes. The simplest of maps use color to show political boundaries: for example, France, green; Germany, yellow; and Italy, red. Color is also used on many government maps to show standard types of information. The U.S. Geological Survey, for example, uses five basic colors on its topographic maps: Brown is used to show contours (altitude lines), their elevations, and certain unverified altitude heights. Blue shows lakes, rivers, canals, and other waterways. Black indicates roads, buildings, railroads, and other human impact on the land. Red is another "culture color," showing road classifications for major highways, some administrative boundaries, and built-up areas in the center of many cities. Green displays vegetation, such as woodlands, vineyards, and orchards.

Color also may be used to show land heights, ocean depths, or gradients on a thematic map. An example of the latter might be the use of color shading to indicate population distribution from an inner city to its suburbs. Many atlas maps use color to portray the varying land heights in a country or across Europe, for example. Usually, deeper colors are used to show the highest land, with pastel shades used for lowlands and coastal plains. Another subtle use of color is the shading that creates shadows along the eastern side of mountains, assuming a light source from the northwest. The results create an easy-to-read relief map. Figure 19.2 shows the relationship between shaded relief and contour elevations. Excellent examples of this map type are the many country maps produced by the Central Intelligence Agency and distributed by the U.S. Government Printing Office.

Symbols and color on a map allow it to communicate its information to the reader. Users must not expect too much from a map, which can communicate effectively only when it is not cluttered. The scale of the map controls the number of symbols. To state the obvious, a map of Denver will show far more detail and symbols for that city than will a map of Colorado. A successful map differentiates between geographical features. For example, there should be a clear indication of the difference between the symbols for roads and railroads, external and internal boundaries, and rivers and canals. Each map or atlas should provide a key or index to its symbols. The first question that should be asked of a map is "Is it too cluttered?" A map that attempts to provide too much information can be as misleading as a map that shows very little.

Publisher/Authority

As with any area of publishing, there are reputable map and atlas publishers and those that are less so. On the whole, few publishers produce inferior products because

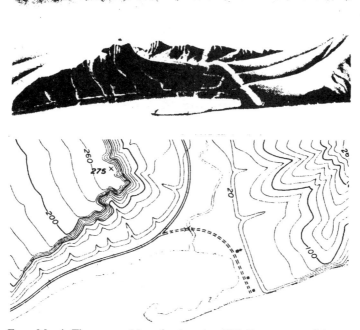

From Morris Thompson, *Maps for America,* U.S. Department of the Interior, 1987.

Figure 19.2. Shaded relief and contours.

they face a marketplace that has become far more qualified to evaluate their products. Nevertheless, librarians need to be familiar with the literature and study reviews of maps and atlases, as they would for other reference materials.

With very few exceptions, national mapping agencies (see *World Mapping Today* and *Inventory of World Topographic Mapping*) produce high-quality, current, authoritative maps for their nations. These agencies, such as the U.S. Geological Survey, the Ordnance Survey in Great Britain, and Canada's Centre for Topographic Information, are sources of quality mapping products at reasonable costs for their countries. Today, however, several national mapping agencies have decided to cease publication of printed maps and plan to offer them only on demand through commercial dealers (e.g., Canada) or via the Web (e.g., Finland).

Commercial map products are more difficult to evaluate if the librarian is not familiar with the firm or its products. Well-known U.S. firms that produce both maps and atlases are Rand McNally, the National Geographic Society, and Universal Map. The number of smaller firms producing high-quality products is growing rapidly and includes such companies as DeLorme, Raven, Northern Cartographic, and ADC. The international market is equally prolific, although several large firms again stand out: Collins Bartholomew (formerly John Bartholomew and Son) of Scotland, Kümmerly & Frey of Switzerland, and Michelin of France. Numerous smaller firms also produce maps, especially city maps of individual foreign countries, such as ITMB of British Columbia in Canada. Finally, although good maps are available from many sources, it is prudent to purchase materials from established, reputable dealers. Now several Web map sites offer maps from several publishers, ranging from the more general offerings of Omni Resources (http://www.omnimap.com) to the large-scale topographic map series offered by East View (http://www.eastview.com), which specializes in Russian materials.

Indexing and Place Names

The heart of an atlas or a map is the map itself. By analogy, then, the brain is the index or guide to that atlas or map. An atlas without an index to the maps, their locations, and the place names they contain is of questionable value as a reference tool. Similarly, a map of a city without an index to its streets or geographical features is equally suspect. How is the index to be used? Does the index locate the feature on the map with grid references or exact coordinates, as well as references to page numbers? Does the index include all of the place names on the map? Does the index include not only cities and towns, but also national parks, administrative divisions, and mountains? It is important to find an atlas or map that indexes as many of these features as possible. A publisher's higher-priced atlas or map is usually the best buy because it offers more information, more maps, and a larger index.

Currency

After scale, currency is probably the most important criterion for geographical source material. Because the world is changing so rapidly, it is imperative that libraries be able to provide current information. A world atlas that is five years old portrays enough obsolete information that it should be used only for historical purposes. So many changes occur annually: place name changes, new roads, railroad abandonment, and boundary changes (consider Israel and Yugoslavia). Also many subtle changes occur within cities that can be shown only on the most detailed of maps, including growth of the city's boundaries, its suburbs, and redevelopment projects, including the replacement of old buildings with new ones.

SELECTION

Geographical sources vary extensively. Each library must determine the needs of its users and the community that it is trying to serve. A large academic library will require a greater complexity of geographical sources for its users than will a smaller, rural public library. The academic library may require several world atlases as well as selected national atlases to supplement its map collection, whereas a small public library may be satisfied with a new world atlas every few years. No library can satisfy all of its users all of the time, and it is imperative that librarians communicate among themselves to become aware of expertise that is available to them. This may be especially important with geographical sources, given that very few libraries have large, comprehensive collections.

The library must also decide, within its collection development guidelines, whether it will collect primarily ready-reference materials or develop a more comprehensive collection for in-depth research purposes. A ready-reference collection may consist of only 100 titles,[2] whereas research collections may include tens of thousands of maps and hundreds of atlases. The basic collection is the focus in this chapter; one can refer to many sources for the development of larger collections.

Finding appropriate selection tools for geographical sources is perhaps the most difficult task in this area of collection development. Although *Publishers Weekly*, *Choice*, and other reviewing sources include atlas reviews, it is not possible to use only the standard tools for current awareness of geographical sources. As in other fields, there is a specialized literature of unique publications. A current and regular listing of current cartographic publications appears in *base line*, the newsletter of the American Library Association's Map & Geography Round Table.[3] Published six times annually, this small newsletter contains information in each issue on new publications. Other publications useful for selection purposes are included in the "List of Sources" near the end of this chapter. Several Web sources, such as Omni Resources (www.omnimap.com), also announce new cartographic publications.

Format

The choice of format is quickly becoming a dilemma for those using geographical sources. Maps and atlases are now being offered as print publications and as CD-ROMs or DVDs. In addition, numerous Web sites are available that offer maps. With these formats come the demands for additional library equipment, such as personal computers, CD-ROM or DVD drives, scanners, and color printers.

Digital products range from the simplest CD-ROMs to complex combinations of geographical data and boundaries using compression technology. An example of the first is *Centennia*, which allows the user to view the boundaries of Europe and the Middle East from the year 1000 C.E. to the mid-1990s. A user can select boundaries for a particular year, compare boundaries, or allow the boundaries to move forward in time with a "movie" option. The major limitation of such products is their inability to interact with other data that a user may have or wish to map. Nevertheless, they are reasonably priced (under $100) and provide color graphic maps that can be reproduced for applications such as term papers. Essentially, such products provide a variety of international and domestic document information in map form that is easy to use. Slightly more complex is DeLorme's *Street Atlas USA*, a DVD product that is suitable for almost every library. Using a complicated Census mapping database (the TIGER street file boundaries), DeLorme has created a seamless street and road map for the entire United States that is very easy to use. Similarly, the online offerings are increasing almost exponentially, and anyone with a home computer and Internet access now has access to road and travel information via *MapQuest*, *Google Maps*, *Bing Maps*, and *Yahoo! Maps*. The next step is to consider the use of geographical information systems (GIS), discussed later in this chapter.

IMPORTANT GENERAL SOURCES

As mentioned earlier in this chapter, categories of geographical sources that librarians find useful in reference work include atlases, travel guides, gazetteers, and maps. In this section, major publishers and their geographical products are discussed, as well as a selection of the most useful gazetteers and geographical dictionaries. Three distinct types of atlases are identified, and a few of the best of each type are described. Finally, additional important geographical sources that do not fit into any of these categories are described.

Maps

Even though individual maps may present storage problems, librarians should not forgo them entirely in favor of atlases. The major disadvantage of the atlas map is its small scale and inability to depict many geographical regions with sufficient detail. Local detail is usually provided only through individual maps, unless one is fortunate enough to live in a large metropolitan area that has its own street atlas. Some of the sources for maps that should be collected and included in all library collections are described here.

The U.S. Geological Survey (USGS) is the national agency officially responsible for domestic mapping. It creates maps at many scales, prints maps for other agencies of the federal government, and produces maps both on printed paper and in electronic formats. Librarians should focus on providing coverage of the local area at various scales to show varying amounts of detail. Librarians may request the free state indexes and other information for their states by calling 1-888-ASK-USGS or contacting them via their Web site (http://www.usgs.gov). This number may also be used to ask any questions regarding maps or map products. Libraries, including public and school, should purchase maps covering their cities or towns at the following scales: 1:250,000 (one sheet); 1:100,000 (one to two sheets); and 1:24,000 (one to six sheets). These maps provide valuable information on the town and surrounding area: topography, drainage systems, transportation, woodland coverage, and other physical and cultural features.

An electronic option worth considering is DeLorme's *Topo North America*, which provides complete topographic coverage of the United States as well as road details for Canada and Mexico on one DVD for under $100. For those libraries unable to store nearly 60,000+ paper maps or acquire the map cases to store them in, this is an alternative that should receive serious consideration. Libraries located in coastal cities or near the Great Lakes are encouraged to contact the National Ocean Service in Silver Spring, Maryland (http://oceanservice.noaa.gov/), for information on nautical charts of their local areas. These charts are valuable for boaters, fishermen, environmentalists, and others interested in the coastline environment.

A variety of commercial sources also produce local maps that are useful when answering reference questions on local streets, public buildings, schools, and so forth. Companies such as Rand McNally, American Map, and Universal Map produce numerous maps for local government agencies and chambers of commerce. Once again, online sources such as *MapQuest*, *Google Maps*, *Bing Maps*, and *Yahoo! Maps* provide viable options for librarians wishing to offer street-level access for cities and towns in the United States. Realistically, these products provide the average librarian with more street detail than the librarian could ever hope to collect in paper form. The online sources are also now offering aerial photography and bird's-eye views for selected regions, and such services are only going to improve and increase. And yet librarians should remember that paper maps for their local area are still important primary sources. All librarians should maintain contacts with local tourism offices for new publications, including maps. Regular visits to local bookstores also may provide information on new maps.

Some of the most important, and often overlooked, sources for local information are local governments and regional agencies. Most municipal governments and regional agencies produce maps for planning purposes and now digital data and digital maps for geographic analysis. Sadly, many of these items are simply discarded once they are out-of-date (including the old digital data information). It is important to maintain contacts with these agencies because their discards can be a valuable source of information for libraries. Although maps and aerial photographs are seldom free, these items are usually available for reasonable reproduction costs. Besides the usual chamber of commerce maps, librarians are encouraged to seek out aerial photographs and maps showing neighborhoods, school districts, and parks, as well as examples of out-of-date maps to show the changing landscapes and human impacts thereon within their geographical area.

Online and Digital Map Sources

Additional products are appearing that provide greater detail and allow some interaction with the map display and printed output. It is important to maintain currency with online titles. DeLorme's *Street Atlas USA* remains a popular DVD program but is being severely challenged by the online programs. For example, *Google Maps* provides accurate and up-to-date road maps for the United States and a satellite image option. Full functionality is available for the United States and selected other countries. *Google Earth*, which can be installed on one's local computer, is an image-based system using satellite imagery and aerial photography from around the world. *Bing Maps* allows users to browse and search topographically shaded street maps for many cities worldwide and also includes satellite and aerial imagery for many locations. For several cities, a bird's-eye view provides aerial photos using images from multiple angles that are much more detailed than the aerial views from directly above buildings.

General online sources are represented by the National Geographic Society's *MapMachine*. A place name can be entered in the search box and the resulting map is displayed, with options for a road map, satellite view, bird's eye view, and 3D view. Librarians interested in census materials should review the Census Bureau Web site (http://www.census.gov), which has many maps as well as census data. Many publications previously available in print form have been digitized and are now available as online subscriptions. Two map examples are the *Digital Sanborn Maps, 1867–1990*, for more than 12,000 American towns and cities, and the *LexisNexis* online access to maps in the *U.S. Serial Set*, including historical geological, soil, and population maps.

The next level of data and software begins to bring libraries near or into the development and use of geographical information systems (GIS). Although this often requires sophisticated equipment and additional training and staff expertise, GIS has the potential to offer sophisticated enhancements to existing numeric data and geographical datasets to create unique and specialized reference services. Librarians are

---

BOX 19.1
MAP SEARCH STRATEGY

A traveling businesswoman asked a reference librarian in a public library for city maps. She had client addresses and wanted to make her hotel reservations nearby. The librarian's first response was to refer to the current general atlases, but none of them provided maps detailed enough for such a query. A quick check of the current Rand McNally *Road Atlas* was more useful for major cities, but the businesswoman requested more detail. The librarian then turned to an online resource, *Bing Maps*. She was able to quickly search the city maps for Boston, Massachusetts, and Washington, D.C. Not only was she able to identify the location of each address, but she could also show an aerial photograph and provided the woman with an oblique bird's-eye view so that she could almost walk around the building.

---

encouraged to pursue this path if they have an interested staff and financially supportive administration. A review of the literature and various Web sites (e.g., http://www.gis.harvard.edu) can provide additional information and sources for learning, software, and data.

Atlases

Atlases, like maps, can be divided into three groups: current, historical, and thematic. Current atlases are needed for up-to-date information on geographical and political changes in the world. Historical atlases are necessary for the study of boundary changes, military campaigns, early exploration, and similar topics. Thematic, or subject, atlases emphasize a specific subject or region. Examples include national atlases, population atlases, and geological atlases.

General World Atlases

The finest general world atlas available is *The Times Comprehensive Atlas of the World*. The *Times* is regarded as the highest-quality English-language world atlas, providing balanced geographical coverage. The scales of many maps are generally larger and show greater detail than the *Hammond* or Oxford atlases, also discussed in this section. Its map pages, produced by the highly respected firm of Collins Bartholomew, provide excellent regional maps to answer all but the most specialized reference questions. This atlas is divided into three general sections: an introductory section including general physical information and thematic world maps, a series of regional maps showing political and physical features, and a final section that is a large index-gazetteer with more than 200,000 names. Locations are indexed by map page, a map-page grid system, and latitude and longitude.

Three additional atlases that deserve attention are the *Hammond World Atlas*, the *National Geographic Atlas of the World*, and the *Oxford Atlas of the World*. Each of these atlases has advantages and should be seriously considered for inclusion in reference collections. The *Hammond* atlas, now in its fifth edition, contains 64 pages of thematic maps and was one of the earliest computer-generated atlases. Its satellite photo section contains 48 pages of images revealing environmental problems and settlement patterns. Its reasonable pricing makes it a good choice for smaller and medium-size libraries. The physical and political maps of the *Hammond* atlas indicate relief using shading. Included in its appendices are a large gazetteer (more than 111,000 entries), statistical tables, and the population of major cities. The results are crisp, easy-to-read maps, uncluttered place names, good choice of color throughout, and an affordable price for public and school libraries.

The *Oxford Atlas of the World*, in contrast, represents a more traditional atlas like the *Times*. Its use of color tints to show relief results in large patches of purples and browns to show mountains. To its credit, it provides an encyclopedia of geographical information in its introductory pages, with color maps illustrating climate, the greenhouse effect, health, population and migration, global conflicts, and more, and also provides a glossary of geographical terms and a gazetteer of nations. This atlas has a large collection of world metropolitan maps and a separate index with more than 83,000 place names.

The *National Geographic Atlas of the World* has a long tradition of publication. This latest edition, the ninth, brings the world up-to-date, including new regional maps for several areas such as Afghanistan and Pakistan, the Korean Peninsula, and Iraq and Iran. Maps include a large number of place names. Arrangement is by continent, including satellite, political, and physical maps and a section with country summaries, with official flags and demographic and economic data for all independent nations, arranged alphabetically. Political maps for regions and specific countries follow. New thematic maps treating environmental issues, natural resources, and human culture have been added as well as maps of space, the ocean floor, and Earth's poles. The index includes more than 150,000 entries for cities and natural features.

Historical Atlases

The *Atlas of World History* is an atlas divided into five parts: "The Ancient World," "The Medieval World," "The Early Modern World," "The Age of Revolutions," and "The Twentieth Century." The atlas includes 450 maps showing topics such as the golden age of Athens, the breakup of the Soviet Union, and the development of Australia and New Zealand. It also includes thematic topics such as migration patterns and environmental changes across the globe. Other features include an index with 8,000 entries and alternate name forms and a classified bibliography.

The *National Geographic Historical Atlas of the United States* provides a unique and current perspective on America's history. In addition to hundreds of maps, this atlas incorporates more than 450 photographs, 80 graphs, and 140,000 words of text. It is an interesting volume that interweaves the historical time line of American history throughout its chapters: "Land," "People," "Boundaries," "Economy," "Networks," and "Communities." The atlas also includes a useful bibliography and index.

Kenneth Martis's *Historical Atlas of Political Parties* offers a wealth of information in a political atlas. Its multicolored maps, combined with judicious text and tables, provide an authoritative record and geographical understanding of American political history.

The significant three-volume *Historical Atlas of Canada* also must be mentioned here. Too often, such projects are restricted to a single volume, and their reference and scholarly value are somewhat diminished; not so with this exquisite Canadian effort. Bringing together scholars from many disciplines, this collaborative effort has resulted in a publication recommended for all libraries whose users are interested in Canada and Canadian history. Volume 1 includes topics on Canada's early prehistory and settlement to 1800; volume 2 focuses on the 19th century, 1800–1891; and volume 3 reviews the changes in the 20th century, 1891–1961.

Many other historical atlases concentrate on either particular periods in history or particular regions. Examples of the former are Martin Gilbert's *Atlas of the Holocaust* and *The Times Atlas of the Second World War*. Regional atlases are appearing with greater frequency today. Gerald Hanson's *Historical Atlas of Arkansas* and the *Historical Atlas of Massachusetts* are significant examples of the proliferation of this atlas type.

Thematic Atlases

The National Atlas of the United States of America is included in this category because it focuses on a specific nation. Even though this atlas has long been out of print, it provides a cornucopia of knowledge about the United States through its many statistical and graphical maps. Although much of the economic and social information is now out-of-date, many of the sections, such as general reference maps, landforms, climate, and history, are still valuable for reference purposes. An updated version is now being compiled digitally, and the information is provided on the Web. The site includes a variety of products and services, including printable maps, dynamic maps, and the capability of customizing maps to display certain types of data.

In spite of the ever-increasing popularity of the Web and its various geographic travel sites, librarians still consult the venerable road atlas. *The Road Atlas* by Rand McNally, updated annually, is in its 87th edition and features more than 400 maps, including city and national park maps. Each year, it shows thousands of changes, including new roads, construction hot lines, and new travel Web sites.

The *Atlas of North America* includes three parts: satellite images; a thematic section covering physical, historical, economic, urban, social, and cultural topics; and detailed cartographic, statistical, and narrative coverage of Canada, the United States, and Mexico. Both maps of states and provinces and maps of urban areas are included. An extensive index provides latitude and longitude notations, grid references, place names, and geographic features.

The *Atlas of Canada* has taken a unique path in deciding to issue the maps separately and was a good example for many countries to follow. Today, Canada is one country that has decided to cease printing national maps; its atlas updates and new maps are now available only online. Like similar national atlases, this series of maps reveals the country's social, economic, and physical characteristics. Existing maps show election results, population density, native populations, farm types, and climatic regions, to name a few topics covered. The *Atlas of Canada's* many maps may be accessed via its Web site.

Numerous titles are available in thematic atlas publishing, and a library's budget and collection development goals will define the depth of its coverage in this area. Examples of titles focused on specific subjects include Joni Seager's *Penguin Atlas of Women in the World*, Dan Smith's *Penguin Atlas of War and Peace*, and Smith's *Penguin State of the World Atlas,* to name but a few.

Gazetteers

Gazetteers may be the most often used geographical reference source. A gazetteer is usually a list of geographical names or physical features, or both, either appended to an atlas or published as a separate volume. There are two types of gazetteers: locational and descriptive. *Locational* gazetteers usually provide information precisely locating the feature, either by atlas page and grid index or by even more precise latitude and longitude on the Earth's surface. *Descriptive* gazetteers may provide some or all of the preceding information and then describe the place. Such a description may include such features as a brief history, commodity production, population, and altitude.

Almost every atlas includes a gazetteer as an appendix, used to locate the place names in that volume. Therein lies its limitations. Atlas gazetteers are useful for locating major towns, cities, administrative divisions, and physical features. Answering questions requiring information on those cities beyond the scope of the normal world atlas requires a more detailed volume, such as a gazetteer.

A standard library gazetteer in the past has been *The Columbia-Lippincott Gazetteer of the World.* Although its 130,000 entries made it one of the most comprehensive descriptive gazetteers, it has become too outdated (1961) to be used for current reference. Fortunately, *The Columbia Gazetteer of the World*, a three-volume work containing more than 170,000 entries, has taken its place as the standard general library reference gazetteer. As a descriptive gazetteer, no other single resource resembles *The Columbia Gazetteer of the World* in scope, coverage, and amount of detail about so many places. Its scope encompasses the political world (from neighborhoods to major geographic regions), the physical world (from continents and oceans to deserts and streams), and special places (national parks, historic sites, and so forth). The gazetteer is also available as an online resource for libraries preferring this format for quick searches on place names. Nevertheless, librarians should not discard the 1961 volume because its value for historical information (including its earlier historical editions) will continue to be significant for many reference questions.

Similar in format, in that it provides descriptive information for locations, is the third edition of *Merriam-Webster's Geographical Dictionary.* This has become a "best buy" for U.S. libraries, although it is restricted by having about 54,000 entries. Its inclusion of more than 250 maps showing national and international boundaries, cities, physical features, and national parks is very useful. Its lists of administrative divisions for major countries and U.S. states also make it a useful world gazetteer for smaller libraries.

The most valuable gazetteer for U.S. libraries is the U.S. Geological Survey's *Geographic Names Information System* (*GNIS*). The original plan was for publication of the individual state data as individual volumes, but it was decided to deliver the data via an online service instead. In cooperation with the U.S. Board on Geographic

Names (BGN), this database contains information about more than 2 million physical and cultural geographic features in the United States. It includes the following information: federally recognized feature name, feature type, elevation, estimated population, state and county in which the feature is located, latitude and longitude, on which 7.5-minute topographic map the feature is located, and links to sites offering map viewers. This database includes names found on various maps and public documents but excludes railroads, streets, and roads. The database also includes information on U.S. territories and Antarctica. Lists of features for individual states can be downloaded. The amount of detail can be illustrated by comparing the Indiana volume, with 23,000 entries, to *Merriam-Webster's Geographical Dictionary*, which has about 54,000 entries to cover the entire world. The entire *GNIS* database is currently available on the Web.

An important set of gazetteers is the series of foreign-country volumes produced by the U.S. Board on Geographic Names and published by the then-named Army Map Service and the Defense Mapping Agency. Similar to the USGS volumes, these are locational gazetteers providing latitude and longitude for geographical places. These are the best volumes for locating any place-name information for foreign countries. Most of these titles have been distributed to libraries through the GPO depository library program. This dataset is also now available on the National Geospatial-Intelligence Agency's *GEOnet Names Server* Web site.

The *Rand McNally Commercial Atlas and Marketing Guide* contains a wealth of economic information in addition to large maps for each state. It is noted in this context because it has long been considered an unofficial gazetteer for the United States. The annual editions include more than 125,000 principal cities, towns, and inhabited places. Furthermore, each entry includes information on population, elevation, zip code, airlines, railroads, and so forth.

Travel Guides

Travel literature continues to proliferate at an unprecedented rate as publishers attempt to provide sources for a large number of travelers, both domestic and international. It is difficult for libraries to decide among the multiplicity of choices for travel guides to various regions of the United States or to other countries. As publishers try to take advantage of a growing market, there is also considerable duplication. The traditional areas of Europe, the Caribbean, and the United States are the mainstays of the U.S. travel industry, but many firms are now producing guides for Eastern Europe, the former Soviet Union, and adventure travel locations, expecting increased travel in these areas.

Librarians are encouraged to refer to the *Publishers Weekly* annual issues on travel literature. These articles provide descriptions of sources for both foreign and domestic travel and list the major publishers and their specialties. The accompanying advertisements are useful for reviewing the most current titles for selection.

An article by Carolyn Anthony provides an interesting division of travel literature into four general categories.[4] First are the popular annuals, Fodor, Frommer, and Birnbaum, that cover all topics, including passports, restaurants and hotels, and car rentals. Most of these guides are revised annually by local authorities and provide reliable, up-to-date information on restaurants, accommodations, and sightseeing. They usually provide current pricing for a variety of budgets. A second group, "Let's Go" from Let's Go Publications, "Shoestring Guides" from Lonely Planet Publications, and business traveler guides, is aimed at particular groups or types of traveler. These guides may target adventurous travelers looking for out-of-the-way locations, special groups such as students and budget travelers, business travelers who intend to extend their stays for short vacations, or upscale travelers looking for premier accommodations and sightseeing. Third, there is a growing literature for the specialized traveler: guides to museums, cathedrals, pubs, and similar tourist attractions. Guides in this category include "maverick" guides, trail guides, diving and snorkeling guides, and so forth. Finally, there is a resurgence in the literary travel book for the armchair tourists who enjoy taking an imaginary trip or satisfying their curiosity.

As one might suspect, the increasing use of personal computers has resulted in the introduction of electronic travel guides. Some incorporate navigation technology, whereas others simply pinpoint locations. Several alternatives are available from a variety of Web sites, including *MapQuest* and *Yahoo! Maps*. These sites are usually quite user-friendly and offer a variety of options for trip planning: identification of the quickest, shortest, or most scenic route; production of a map and directions for a specific trip; and/or the provision of detailed plans of individual cities.

Other Geographical Sources

Geography's supplementary reference sources, like those of so many disciplines, are turning to the digital world and the Web. Several sources for travel have already been mentioned, such as *MapQuest*, *Street Atlas USA*, and *Yahoo! Maps*. These sources have literally replaced several print publications of the past, such as Rand McNally's *Standard Highway Mileage Guide*. A variety of more specialized Web sites can be useful in reference work. For example, ZIP code information is available from the U.S. Postal Service (http://zip4.usps.com/zip4/citytown_zip.jsp). It is now possible to check on local environmental hazards using the U.S. Environmental Protection Agency's Enviro Mapper Web site (http://www.epa.gov/emefdata/em4ef. home). The *geodata.gov* geographic information system portal provides access to federal, state, and local geographic data. Datasets can also be found at ESRI's Web site (http://www.esri.com/products/index.html#data). The Perry-Castañeda Map Library at the University of Texas offers a spectacular collection of online maps from government sources on its Web site (http://www.lib.utexas.edu/maps/index.html). This site is especially cognizant of world affairs and provides maps for current world crises. One of the most comprehensive Web sites is Matt Rosenberg's Geography Guide (http://geography.about.com/). This Web site provides hundreds of links to other sites and is updated and revised continually. It also features geography in the news that focuses on world crisis areas and provides links to maps and geographical information.

A useful publication on foreign countries is *Background Notes*, compiled by the U.S. Department of State. It is a series of brief, authoritative pamphlets on selected countries and geographical entities. Each pamphlet contains relevant information on history, geography, culture, government, politics, and economics. These pamphlets also include base maps (easily photocopied) for each country, showing cities, rivers, railroads, roads, and airports. The series now includes approximately 230 titles, which are updated every few years. These *Notes* are now available on the Department of State Web site.

A geographical dictionary is useful for any reference collection. Many specialized terms developed for the lexicon of this field are not included in standard dictionaries. Audrey Clark's *Longman Dictionary of Geography* is a compact volume incorporating terms from both physical and human geography, including definitions for terms such as *bathymetric*, *gobolala*, *portulano*, and *zymogenous*. *The Weather Almanac* provides information on U.S. weather and weather fundamentals. This volume summarizes many U.S. government documents and provides weather information using maps and statistical tables. The *Almanac* includes topics such as storms and severe weather phenomena, retirement and health weather, air pollution, weather fundamentals, record-setting weather, round-the-world weather, and detailed weather data for 109 selected U.S. cities. Additional weather information is available on various Web sites, including *The Weather Channel*.

An additional, and increasingly useful, source for geographic information is the MAPS-L electronic mailing list. MAPS-L is like many discussion lists, providing access to reference expertise in a specific area, in this case the area of geography, maps, and map librarianship. Its significance lies in its members in many countries, working in a variety of libraries, large and small, who can provide valuable reference expertise through electronic communication. One may subscribe to MAPS-L by sending the following message to Listserv@listserv.uga.edu: "SUBSCRIBE MAPS-L."

SEARCH STRATEGIES

Geographical sources should be used when the question asked involves location. Such inquiries could be as simple as "I need to know where Vilnius is" or "Could I have a map showing Beethoven's birthplace?" They also may be more complicated, such as a request for information on the distribution of radioactive waste from a specific nuclear arsenal or power plant. Both cases require maps and other reference sources as well, which may be more easily accessible in a smaller library where all of these sources are grouped together. Reference librarians must become thoroughly familiar with basic mapping concepts, such as scale and projection, and must understand how these concepts are represented in general and historical maps. This knowledge will allow the librarian to focus on finding the needed information without having to struggle to interpret mapping symbols.

Map reference work also requires a reference interview. Most users are unfamiliar with the resources of the map collection and, therefore, generally ask for maps of a much larger area rather than for one of a specific area that they would really prefer. For example, a map librarian may encounter a genealogist requesting a map of Germany, when the user really needs a detailed map of the outskirts of Hanover, Germany. Too often, users ask for general maps because they do not know the resources of the library and are not sufficiently questioned by the librarian so that they can be helped to use those resources correctly. Conversing with the user better defines the query so that the appropriate map will be retrieved. Similarly, users will often consult an atlas in an attempt to locate a particular place name; if they fail to find it, they may leave, believing that the library does not have the answer. Again, a discussion with the user would probably lead the librarian to examine a gazetteer, which has considerably more place names for an area, to provide the answer to such a question.

One of the more difficult concepts for many map users to accept is that it may be possible to use a map of a larger area to answer a question for a smaller one. This is especially important for libraries that do not have large, detailed collections of maps for foreign countries. An example would be a question on the location of Angel Falls, Venezuela. Although the collection may not contain maps of Venezuela, a map of northern South America or of the whole continent may provide the correct location. Similarly, users may ask for a small map of a particular country but be shown only a wall-size map that is too large. Again, using the previous example, a map of South America would be able to provide a Venezuelan map for the user at a smaller size.

A "sliding scale" concept should be used when answering geographic reference questions. The reference interview allows the librarian to ask specific questions to define the appropriate type of map to be used to answer the question. For example, suppose a user asks for a railroad map of Europe. Although the library has such a map, further questioning reveals that the user is really looking for railroads in Germany, and additional questions reveal that the user really wants to know whether there is a subway system in Berlin. This question is probably going to require a different map than a railroad map of Europe. Librarians should let their minds "slide" through the various kinds of maps in the collection as the discussion with the user progresses. Users often do not define their questions before they approach the librarian; thus, the librarian must help clarify questions so that appropriate reference sources can be used to answer them.

BOX 19.2
SEARCH STRATEGY: A MAP OF OBERWEIS

A user entered the map library one afternoon to inquire into whether the library had any maps of Germany because she was tracing her family history. A brief reference interview revealed that she was really looking for a detailed map that would show the town of Oberweis. The librarian first checked the gazetteer in *The Times Comprehensive Atlas of the World*, only to discover that this town was not listed. Two additional world gazetteers, the *Columbia Gazetteer of the World* and *Merriam-Webster's Geographical Dictionary*, were also consulted with no success. It became apparent that this was a small village that would require a specialized place-name gazetteer, usually available only in research collections. Fortunately, the librarian had access to such tools in the collection, and the town was located in *Müllers Grosses Deutsches Ortsbuch*, which included a brief description of the village. An additional source, *Gazetteer to AMS 1:25,000 Maps of West Germany*, volume 2, also listed Oberweis and provided location information: latitude/longitude and an individual map number for libraries having this map series. The user not only found the location of the small village but also was able to view a detailed map (1:25,000) revealing the plan of the town. This map provided the user with the necessary information to locate her family's birthplace.

Today's cartographic reference services must also include knowledge of Internet sources and an ability to search and find the increasing amount of cartographic information available via the Web. This may include the use of historical maps, such as the Library of Congress Panoramic Maps 1847–1929 Web site, to view historical landscapes (http://lcweb2.loc.gov/ammem/pmhtml/panhome.html). Such maps could be used to identify landmarks in the 19th and early 20th centuries.

NOTES

1.   Mark Monmonier and George A. Schnell, *Map Appreciation* (Englewood Cliffs, NJ: Prentice-Hall, 1988), 15–25.

2.   David A. Cobb, "Developing a Small Geographical Library with Special Emphasis on Indiana," *Focus on Indiana Libraries* 26 (Fall 1972): 114–20.

3.   American Library Association, Map & Geography Round Table, *base line,* 1980–. Six times per year.

4.   Carolyn Anthony, "The World in the '90s," *Publishers Weekly* 237 (January 19, 1990): 20–30.

LIST OF SOURCES

Atlas of Canada. 6th ed. Ottawa, Ontario: Natural Resources Canada, 2002–. http://atlas. nrcan.gc.ca/site/english/index.html.

Atlas of North America. Ed. Harm J. de Blij. Oxford: Oxford University Press, 2005. 320 pp.

Atlas of World History. 2nd ed., rev. Oxford: Oxford University Press, 2010. 312 pp.

Background Notes. Washington, D.C.: U.S. Government Printing Office, 1954–. Irregular. http://www.state.gov/r/pa/ei/bgn/.

Bing Maps. http://www.bing.com/maps.

Centennia. Chicago: Centennia, 2003. CD-ROM.

Clark, Audrey N. *Longman Dictionary of Geography, Human and Physical.* Essex, England: Longman, 1985. 724 pp.

The Columbia Gazetteer of the World. 2nd ed. 3 vols. New York: Columbia University Press, 2008. http://www.columbiagazetteer.org/

Digital Sanborn Maps, 1867–1970. Ann Arbor, MI: ProQuest. http://sanborn.umi.com/.

Gazetteer to AMS 1:25,000 Maps of West Germany. 3 vols. Washington, D.C.: U.S. Army Map Service, 1954.

Geodata.gov. http://gos2.geodata.gov/wps/portal/gos.

Geographic Names Information System. http://geonames.usgs.gov.

Gilbert, Martin. *Atlas of the Holocaust.* New York: Pergamon Press, 1993. 282 pp.

Google Earth. http://earth.google.com.

Google Maps. http://maps.google.com.

Guide to U.S. Map Resources. 3rd ed. Compiled by Christopher J. J. Thiry. Lanham, MD: Scarecrow, 2006. 511 pp.

Hammond World Atlas. 5th ed. Maplewood, NJ: Hammond, 2008. 464 pp.

Hanson, Gerald T. *Historical Atlas of Arkansas*. Norman: University of Oklahoma Press, 1989. 142 pp.

Historical Atlas of Canada. 3 vols. Toronto, Ontario: University of Toronto Press, 1987–1993.

Historical Atlas of Massachusetts. Ed. Richard Wilkie and Jack Tager. Amherst: University of Massachusetts Press, 1991. 152 pp.

Inventory of World Topographic Mapping. Ed. Rolf Böhme. 3 vols. London: Elsevier, 1989–1993.

MapMachine. Washington, D.C.: National Geographic Society. http://ngm.nationalgeographic.com/map-machine.

MapQuest. http://www.mapquest.com.

Martis, Kenneth C. *The Historical Atlas of Political Parties in the United States Congress, 1789–1989*. New York: Macmillan, 1989. 518 pp.

Merriam-Webster's Geographical Dictionary. 3rd ed. rev. Springfield, MA: Merriam-Webster, 2007. 1392 pp.

Müller, Friedrich. *Müllers Grosses Deutsches Ortsbuch . . .* Wuppertal, Germany: Post- und Ortsbuchverlag, 1996/97. 1266 pp.

The National Atlas of the United States of America. Washington, D.C.: U.S. Geological Survey, 1970. 417 pp. http://www.nationalatlas.gov.

National Geographic Atlas of the World. 9th ed. Washington, D.C.: The Society, 2010. 424 pp.

National Geographic Historical Atlas of the United States. Rev. ed. Washington, D.C.: National Geographic Society, 2004. 240 pp.

National Geospatial-Intelligence Agency. *GEOnet Names Server*. http://earth-info.nga.mil/gns/html/index.html.

Oxford Atlas of the World. 17th ed. New York: Oxford University Press, 2010. 448 pp.

Rand McNally Commercial Atlas and Marketing Guide. Chicago: Rand McNally, 1876–. Annual.

The Road Atlas 2011: United States, Canada, Mexico. 87th ed. Chicago: Rand McNally, 2010. 140 pp.

Seager, Joni. *The Penguin Atlas of Women in the World*. 4th ed. New York: Penguin, 2008. 128 pp.

Smith, Dan. *The Penguin Atlas of War and Peace*. 4th ed. New York: Penguin, 2003. 128 pp.

Smith, Dan. *The Penguin State of the World Atlas*. 8th ed. New York: Penguin, 2008. 144 pp.

Street Atlas USA. Yarmouth, ME: DeLorme, 2009. DVD.

The Times Atlas of the Second World War. Ed. John Keegan. New York: Harper & Row, 1989. 254 pp.

The Times Comprehensive Atlas of the World. 12th ed. London: Times Books, 2007. 544 pp.

Topo North America. Version 9.0. Yarmouth, ME: DeLorme, 2010. DVD.

U.S. Serial Set Maps Digital Collection. Bethesda, MD: LexisNexis, 1789–.

The Weather Almanac. 11th ed. Ed. Richard A. Wood. Farmington Hills, MI: Gale, 2004. 820 pp.

The Weather Channel. http://www.weather.com.

World Mapping Today. Ed. R. B. Parry and C. R. Perkins. 2nd ed. London: Bowker-Saur, 2000. 1064 pp.

Yahoo! Maps. http://maps.yahoo.com.

ADDITIONAL READINGS

American Library Association, Map & Geography Round Table. *base line.* 1980–. Six times per year. http://www.ala.org/ala/magert/publicationsab/publicationsa.cfm.

This newsletter provides current information on cartographic materials, other publications of interest to map and geography librarians, meetings, related government activities, and map librarianship.

Berinstein, Paula. "Location, Location, Location: Online Maps for the Masses." *Searcher* 14 (January 2006): 16–25.

Although features of online mapmaking sites continue to evolve, this article is useful as an introduction to the capabilities of *Google Maps, Google Earth, Yahoo! Maps,* and *Microsoft Live Search Maps* (now *Bing Maps*). Berinstein includes a thoughtful discussion of issues for information professionals presented by these new mapping resources, including the possible need to assist users in developing geographical literacy.

Hock, Randolph. *The Traveler's Web: An Extreme Searcher Guide to Travel Resources on the Internet.* Medford, NJ: CyberAge Books, 2007. 400 pp.

Covering travel by air, train, car, ferry, ship, boat, and barge, this book presents a range of useful online travel resources and advice on travel research and planning. There is also a chapter on exploring countries and cultures online.

Johnson, Jenny Marie. *Geographic Information: How to Find It, How to Use It.* Westport, CT: Greenwood Press, 2003. 216 pp.

This book offers guidance on how to use a wide range of geographic information sources efficiently and effectively. Topics encompass maps, atlases, aerial photography, remotely sensed images, general geography works, and geographic information systems. Full bibliographic citations are given for all books and Web sites.

Larsgaard, Mary Lynette. *Map Librarianship: An Introduction.* 3rd ed. Englewood, CO: Libraries Unlimited, 1998. 487 pp.

This text constitutes the most comprehensive description of map librarianship, including information on collection development, cataloging, reference, and care of maps. The appendices provide useful information for those just beginning to work with maps.

Mathenia, Brenda G. "A Guide to Online Map and Mapping Resources." *Journal of Library Administration* 44 (2006): 325–48.

This article highlights the best online resources for both map image collections and interactive mapping sites found on the Web. The section on virtual map collections identifies sources of world maps, historic maps, and physical maps. Interactive mapping sites include both street mapping sites and data mapping sites. Online atlases, gazetteers, and other online sources of geographical information are also covered.

Monmonier, Mark, and George A. Schnell. *Map Appreciation*. Englewood Cliffs, NJ: Prentice-Hall, 1988. 431 pp.

Written by two geographers, this book provides an excellent explanation of the different types of maps (e.g., photomaps, population maps, political maps, computer maps).

Stoltenberg, Jaime, and Abraham Parrish, eds. "Geographic Information Systems and Libraries." Special issue. *Library Trends* 55 (2006): 217–360.

This special issue includes 10 articles exploring current issues and trends in geographic information systems (GIS) in libraries. Topics covered include geospatial data acquisition, distribution, and preservation; analysis of GIS reference statistics; GIS services models; and geoarchiving.

Weessies, Kathleen. "Electronic Maps: Sources and Techniques." *Reference Services Review* 31 (2003): 248–56.

The author reviews strategies for finding, using, saving, and printing electronic maps. She includes discussion of selected Web sites useful for finding general maps.

Western Association of Map Libraries. *Information Bulletin*. 1969–. Three times per year.

This lively journal includes articles, announcements, and news regarding new maps, atlases, and related publications.

Western Association of Map Libraries. *Map Librarians' Toolbox*. http://www.waml.org/map tools.html.

This resource page organizes information on frequently asked questions related to map librarianship, providing access by subject (cartobibliographies and indexes; cataloging and processing; equipment and supplies; federal depository library program; geographic information systems; map vendors; reference resources) and an alphabetical keyword index.

Wood, Denis. *The Power of Maps*. New York: Guilford Press, 1992. 248 pp.

The author challenges traditional cartographic ideas and lays a framework for the map as an influential communication medium.

Bibliographic Sources
Carol Bates Penka

USES AND CHARACTERISTICS

Knowledge of bibliographic sources is essential for both librarians and scholars. Bibliographies are used to answer a wide variety of questions and to further research by identifying resources on various topics. A historian studying the American Civil War may seek a better understanding of plantation life by locating and reading novels written by women in the South during that time period. A school librarian may wish to select books on dinosaurs for the library's collection to satisfy the scientific interests of the students in the school. A rare-book librarian may need to study books published in a particular place during a particular period to identify a fragment of a work. A library user wants to read the best translation of a literary work originally published in German. In each case, a bibliographic source would be consulted to achieve the desired result.

In addition, many of the most challenging questions that a reference librarian faces deal with bibliographic puzzles involving the verification of incomplete or inaccurate information. A user wants to find a particular book in the library. The librarian must then determine the following:

1. Do the library's catalog records show that the library owns the book?
2. If not, is the user looking for a book that really exists? That is, has it actually been published? Or is the user looking for a type of item not indexed in the catalog? Depending on the scope of the individual catalog, the item might be a journal article or a conference presentation.
3. Is the user's information correct, or only partially correct? For example, could the author's name be misspelled, thus rendering the search of the library's catalog fruitless?

4.   If the information is not completely correct, did the user get the information about the book title from a reliable source, or has it perhaps been garbled in an oral communication?

The librarian must decide what path to take to recreate the information in correct form or to verify that the information is correct. A seemingly simple question—"Does the library own this book?"—may turn into a puzzle requiring the skills of a legendary detective and the use of multiple bibliographic sources.

In this chapter, we look at bibliographic sources from the perspective of both the print environment and the electronic universe. Many of the techniques we use to create new electronic bibliographic products and the criteria we use to evaluate them are derived from the way we have interacted with bibliographic information in print for more than 400 years. An additional reason for looking at both environments is that bibliographic products may be produced as hybrids. Reference sources published in print format may be updated electronically, or they may be published simultaneously in multiple formats. A full-text electronic version of the print bibliographic source (an e-book) may be accessed from within the library's online public access catalog alongside the bibliographic record for the print source.

"The term *bibliography* can have two definitions: there is bibliography itself, an activity, and there is a bibliography, the product of this activity."[1] Bibliographies generally belong to two groups. *Enumerative* or *systematic* bibliographies are concerned with the listing of books and other documents. The second group of bibliographies, which are composed of several subtypes, are concerned primarily with the study of books as physical objects. Some define the cultural impact of texts as yet a third type of bibliographical study. In this chapter the focus is on bibliographic products that meet the first definition.

In the print environment, the usual definition of enumerative bibliography refers to a list of works compiled on some common organizing principle, such as authorship, subject, place of publication, chronology, or printer/publisher. The primary arrangement of the list is usually alphabetical, although a subject classification scheme, such as the Dewey Decimal Classification System, may be used. Secondary arrangement schemes may also be employed. To illustrate, a bibliography of writings by Ernest Hemingway (author approach, with primary arrangement by title) may be secondarily arranged by the dates the works were published. Indexes to the main listings are usually included to provide access points not covered by the primary and secondary arrangements. For example, the Ernest Hemingway bibliography would probably include an index of the publishers of the works listed and an index to the type of literature, such as short stories, novels, and so forth. Most print bibliographic sources are derived or printed from an electronic database and may be sold in either or both formats. The two formats may or may not be identical in content.

Electronic resources differ from print sources and usually provide a superior bibliographic product. The internal file structure of the electronic database, which is invisible to the user, is usually based on the date and time the item was entered into the database. Each record is identified by a unique accession number assigned to the record at the time of its entry into the database. Most fields or elements of the bibliographic record are searchable by keyword or phrase, although fields can be made "display only" (not searchable). Using the Boolean operators *and*, *or*, and *not*, the searcher is able to perform extremely precise queries based on the information needs of the moment. Other commands may limit the search to particular publication years, publishers, formats, languages, or other factors. Depending on the capabilities of the database, a search for all books published in Canada in the 1980s on the subject of immigration could be conducted quickly and easily. Because of the limited number of access points, the same search in a print source would be difficult and time-consuming, if not impossible. The printout from the computer search could be produced as an author list, as a title list, as a list in chronological or reverse chronological order, or in any number of other ways. In cases where license agreements permit, search results downloaded from a computer search can become a freestanding database searchable in a similar fashion to the larger database from which it was derived.

Electronic databases have proven their superiority for both users and compilers. For users the electronic product is superior because of the ease and speed of producing precise, customized search results. "Perhaps the greatest advantage of an electronic catalog from the compiler's perspective is the fact that future additions and corrections can be made, location symbols added, and re-sequencing accomplished with relative ease and low cost."[2]

The theory of bibliographic control is discussed more fully in chapter 4. This chapter discusses the concepts of bibliographic control necessary for the study of bibliographies. The process of providing bibliographic control generally means providing two different kinds of access to information: bibliographic access (that is, letting the user know of the existence of the work), and physical access (that is, letting the user know where the work can be found). In the current library environment, both types of access can be provided by a wide variety of methods.

To achieve the aims of bibliographic control, providing bibliographic and physical access, three major types of reference sources have evolved: bibliographies, library catalogs, and bibliographic utilities. The firm distinctions between types of sources are rapidly disappearing in the electronic environment.

Distinctions between types of bibliographic sources are often made based on the bibliographic level of material that is listed and whether the physical location of the work is indicated. Does the bibliography or catalog include journal articles and book chapters, or are only whole books listed? In general, bibliographies list works or parts of works regardless of their physical location; library catalogs aim to list the works located in or accessible online from one or more libraries. Bibliographic utilities serve both functions, providing complete machine-readable cataloging copy and a list of libraries that own the item reflected in the catalog record.

The desire to achieve universal bibliographic control (UBC) is shared by librarians and scholars alike. "Simply put, the ideal of UBC is that each document should be cataloged once in its country of origin and that cataloging should be made available to libraries around the world."[3]

On a more theoretical level, Patrick Wilson, in *Two Kinds of Power*, defines universal bibliographic control as the creation of an "exhaustive inventory" of all the works that have ever been published.[4] Although extremely noble, these aspirations toward UBC are unattainable. However, we are now able to go a long way toward achieving this aim through the cooperative efforts of national libraries, national standards organizations, and the efforts of the bibliographic utilities in various countries.

Types of Bibliographies and Catalogs

Bibliographies and catalogs fall into several basic types. One should study these basic distinctions before reading about specific tools. The first are national bibliographies.

National bibliographies list the materials published in a particular country. In addition, the scope of the work may be enlarged to include works written about the country or in the language of the country, regardless of the place of publication. Because the intent is that the publication be as comprehensive as possible, material written by the citizens of the country, wherever published, may also be included.

Most national bibliographies are published under the auspices of the national library or other governmental agency charged with the responsibility for the production of the national bibliography. Usually, this entity is the recipient of copies received to satisfy the provisions of legal deposit. Under legal deposit, certain libraries or agencies are entitled by law to receive one or more copies of certain types of publications printed or published in the country. Often, legal deposit is required for copyright protection under copyright law, but the two do not always go together. For example, in Canada copyright protection is administered by the Canadian Intellectual Property Office. Publishers send copies of publications under legal deposit requirements to Library and Archives Canada. In the United States, all works under copyright protection and published in the United States are subject to mandatory deposit requirements that are similar to legal deposit in other countries. These copies are sent to the Register of Copyrights in the Library of Congress.

Print versions of current national bibliographies usually appear weekly or monthly, with both annual and multiyear cumulations. Electronic versions may be updated as often as daily. In many cases, retrospective national bibliographies, which give a record of the country's publishing history over a long period of time, have also been published.

The terms *current* and *retrospective*, as applied to bibliographies, refer to the time period covered by the items selected for inclusion in the bibliography. Current bibliographic sources list books or other items close to the time at which they are published. A retrospective bibliography covers materials published during an earlier time period. Compilations of current bibliographic sources turn into retrospective sources when the time period covered recedes into the past.

Trade bibliographies are produced by commercial publishers and serve to provide the information necessary to select and acquire recently published materials. Usually, the materials included in trade bibliographies are trade books, those intended for sale to the general public and generally available for sale in bookstores, as opposed to mass market books, which are sold in grocery stores or on newsstands. Nontrade publications, such as textbooks, government documents, encyclopedias, and dissertations, are not listed in trade bibliographies. As a consequence, lists of these must be acquired directly from the publisher or specialized dealers. They may, however, be listed in the national bibliography of the country in which they are produced.

The predominant form of trade bibliography is the in-print list, such as R. R. Bowker's *Books in Print* (*BIP*). In-print lists show which titles are currently available from publishers. In another form, trade bibliographies such as *American Book Publishing Record*® provide lists of books as they are published. The various electronic products discussed later in the chapter are blurring the distinctions between types of bibliographic publications, but these distinctions should still be understood.

Library catalogs exist to serve the users of a particular library by listing the holdings and location of materials accessible to users in that library. The term *online public access catalog*, or OPAC, refers to an electronic catalog designed for end users, as opposed to a version of the catalog that may be used by reference librarians or staff in other units. OPACs generally have user-friendly interfaces. Union catalogs (or union lists) identify the material held in the collections of more than one library. Shared cataloging networks such as OCLC (Online Computer Library Center) create union catalogs for their member libraries. The geographic area covered by union lists may vary from local to multinational. In the case of serials, it is quite common to find not only the lists of libraries holding a particular title but also a record of which volumes each library holds.

Bibliographies of bibliographies are lists of bibliographies that have been created as a means of bibliographic control. They are usually general in scope and offer a good starting place when trying to locate a list of works on a particular subject.

Subject bibliographies, as the name implies, are lists of materials that relate to a particular topic. Some authorities consider national bibliographies that include material written about a country as being subject bibliographies rather than true national bibliographies.

Kinds of Information Contained in Bibliographies and Library Catalogs

The data elements in a bibliography entry depend largely on the intent of the publication. Current national bibliographies exist in part to facilitate the international exchange of cataloging data in a standardized format. Therefore, the entries reflect the information available in machine-readable cataloging records. In addition to author, title, and publication data, each entry usually includes subject headings, contents notes, and suggested classification numbers. Name entries, both personal and corporate, are standardized with appropriate *see* references from alternate forms of the name. Ordering information such as price is often included.

Because trade bibliographies are produced for the use of book dealers, they contain information that is essential for book purchases. Examples include price, availability, publishers' addresses, and International Standard Book Number (ISBN). The ISBN is a code number assigned by the publisher to provide unique identification of a particular work. There will be, for example, different ISBNs for the hardback and paperback versions of the same title. The ISBN consists of a country code, a publisher identifier, a title identifier, and a check digit. For example, the ISBN for the third edition of this textbook is 1-56308-624-7 for the paperback edition and 1-56308-621-2 for the hardback edition. The ISBN was expanded from a 10-digit to a 13-digit number effective January 1, 2007. The International Standard Serial Number serves a similar role, uniquely identifying each serial title with an 8-digit number.

Use of bibliographies depends on the type of information needed. If one needs simply to verify the existence of an item, a source giving short entries may be sufficient. If one needs both to identify and to locate copies, a union list is necessary. If the intent is to purchase materials, information such as price, ISBN, and availability is definitely required.

EVALUATION

Evaluation of general bibliographies and library catalogs is primarily concerned with the following criteria: authority, scope of the bibliography, arrangement of contents, frequency of publication, and currency of the included material. These criteria are used to evaluate the bibliography itself. Additional criteria should be considered when choosing a bibliography for inclusion in a collection, and these are discussed in the section on selection.

Authority

Authority concerns the qualifications of the compiler or sponsor of the bibliography. Compiling a national or trade bibliography is a massive undertaking. It usually involves the resources of a major publisher, national library, or governmental agency. Therefore, the issue of authority usually concerns the compilers of subject bibliographies or resources found on the Web. Do the compilers have the educational background or academic stature to justify their roles in compiling these bibliographies? Does the organization sponsoring the bibliography have a particular political agenda or viewpoint?

Scope

The scope of any reference tool is of primary importance when evaluating its usefulness. "The domain or set of items in the bibliographic universe from which a bibliography's content is selected and drawn defines the outer limits of the scope of a bibliography. Ordinarily, the domain will be larger than the number of items actually listed, as some principle of selection is applied to define and restrict the bibliography's scope."[5] The scope of the bibliography, meaning the domain of items selected for inclusion, should be stated by the compilers in the preface or introduction. Furthermore, any exclusion of materials, for reasons such as place of publication, language, time, type of materials, level of bibliographic unit, format, or subject, should also be noted. The librarian will need to make frequent use of the introductory material because this type of information is not always immediately apparent simply from reading the entries in the body of the work. For example, the *Union List of Serials* does not contain entries for newspapers, a fact not readily discernible simply from scanning the listings.

Reading the introductory material is essential, but it may not be enough. Commercial publishers may not be too eager to point out the limitations of their publication, and the introductions to national bibliographies are often in a language unfamiliar to the librarian. Therefore, it is also essential to consult guides to the tools of reference work that give clear and concise descriptions of the coverage, accuracy, intent, and scope of the bibliographic sources. *Guide to Reference* and its predecessor *Guide to Reference Books*, *New Walford Guide to Reference Resources* (the British counterpart to *Guide to Reference Books*), and *Canadian Reference Sources* serve this purpose. (These sources are discussed more fully in chapter 13.) Other, more specialized tools exist for specific types of bibliographies, and a selection of these tools is listed in the "Additional Readings" section at the end of this chapter.

When a bibliography or catalog includes coverage dates in its title, the librarian must learn what those dates mean. In some cases, the dates may indicate the years in which the items included were published. In the case of the *National Union Catalog*, the dates mean the years in which the cataloging copy was reported to the Library of Congress. On the other hand, the title of the printed catalog of the New York Public Library includes the dates 1911–1971. Here 1911 refers to the date of the founding of the library and has no relation to the dates of the publications listed in the catalog.

Similarly, the word "international" may be included in a title merely as a selling point. The true geographical coverage of an international or regional work must be determined by reading introductory material and examining the contents for depth of inclusion from the countries or areas intended to be covered. The coverage may be uneven, or spotty entries from a few countries may be included to justify the use of the word "international."

Arrangement

The titles discussed in this chapter vary widely in the primary form of arrangement. Some catalogs have author, title, and subject entries in separate alphabetical sequences. Dictionary catalogs interfile all three types of entries in a single alphabetical listing. A classified subject catalog arranges the contents by subject according to a classification scheme. The index/register arrangement consists of a register that contains the complete bibliographic descriptions of all entries arranged in accession number order. Alphabetical indexes contain a brief bibliographic description and the register (or accession) number that locates the complete entry in the register. The register is never superseded. Cumulated indexes are published at regular intervals.

Practically any combination of arrangement and subarrangement is possible. In each case, indexes, which complement the primary arrangement, are essential to enhance the effectiveness of access. Any of these arrangements may be helpful at a given time, depending on the user's need. In reference work, the librarian needs to be aware of the possible arrangements and to make the appropriate choice of tools depending on the information at hand and the information to be located.

Currency

Currency refers to the delay, or lack thereof, between the date of publication and the time at which the publication is entered in the bibliography. Obviously, publications designed for the book trade should offer the most recent information to fulfill the intent of their publication: providing current information on currently available materials. Book trade publications may also list publications announced for publication but not yet published.

Countries that maintain no formal system of legal deposit are at a disadvantage in trying to keep up with publishing output in the areas of their coverage. In addition, bibliographies produced in developing countries, where the production of a national bibliography is a major undertaking, have perhaps the greatest problem with currency. In regions such as Latin America or Africa, where a prompt book order is necessary to obtain one of the few copies produced before the title goes out of print, national bibliographies are rarely produced fast enough to be of help in acquisitions.

Librarians must rely on the services of book jobbers in the region and other means to supplement information obtained in national and trade bibliographies.

SELECTION

The selection of a particular bibliographic source for inclusion in a library's collection depends on the mission of the library and on its collection development policies. Library units using bibliographic tools may well stretch across administrative or budgetary divisions in the library. Therefore, the reference department may be called on to purchase and house a title that is more frequently used by catalogers or subject bibliographers than by reference librarians. Yet all concerned may feel that the title should be in the reference department because of the use of the material by so many different personnel in the library: acquisitions, cataloging, interlibrary loan, reference, and subject bibliographers. Reference librarians can be encouraged by the knowledge that all sources are eventually used for reference purposes. Often, reference library budgets are increased in anticipation of this demand on their monetary resources by other departments.

Many of the sources discussed in this chapter would be found in most libraries. Current sources, such as *Books in Print*, are essential tools for selection and acquisitions in both public and academic libraries of all sizes. National and trade bibliographies of foreign countries, however, are most often found in large research libraries. Nevertheless, large public libraries maintaining foreign-language collections would frequently need at least some of these foreign sources, particularly in-print lists.

Most often, the choice is fairly clear-cut; only one source will fill a particular need. Therefore, the most frequent decisions to be made involve choice of format (print or microfilm versus electronic access), number of copies, and the retention of those copies.

The selection of format involves weighing several factors concerned with use of the item. In general, providing electronic access offers the greatest advantage to users. The first and most obvious advantage is the enhanced searching capability provided by electronic access. The ability to search a database by phrase or keyword and to combine the resultant sets using Boolean searching techniques simply cannot be matched by the indexes in a print product. Search sets may also be limited by other criteria, such as date, language, or year. Electronic products are accessible through the Web or local area networks to multiple users at the same time. These users may be located anywhere in the world.

Cost must also be considered when selecting which form of a bibliography or catalog to purchase. So many factors come into the equation that it is hard to generalize; each library's situation is unique. The use of electronic access involves the purchase and upkeep of supporting equipment in addition to the cost of the bibliographic product itself. The exact cost of electronic access may vary depending on the number of simultaneous users allowed and whether the product will be networked or run on a stand-alone computer. Moreover, the cost of some products varies depending on the size of the library's overall budget. In much the same way, bibliographic sources (both print and electronic) produced by the H. W. Wilson Company are sold on a service basis, under which the price depends on the size of the library's book budget.

In some cases, the cost of an electronic product is discounted if the library also sub-scribes to the print version or vice versa.

Small libraries of all types generally keep only the latest edition of a biblio-graphic source. They would simply be overrun if they retained superseded issues or volumes. Large academic or research libraries retain all copies of bibliographic tools to provide a historical perspective on publishing. In other cases, if libraries require that payment of lost book fees reflect the actual price of the book at the time of its publication, historical publishing information is needed for accounting purposes. However, the choice of format complicates this issue. Libraries that provide access to bibliographic information via the Web are actually leasing access to that data, but they do not own the material. Indeed, the data do not even reside on computers owned by the library itself.

The provision of online access thus does not guarantee the archival coverage that will form the basis of future historical research. To ensure a retrospective collection, a library must often acquire either a microform or a print copy of the same title acquired electronically. To do so is an expensive proposition. Among the current issues facing librarians today are the following: How many times and in how many formats should a library buy the same data? And how many libraries should do so? Should libraries cooperatively provide for historical access rather than having each library do so indi-vidually? And how will this cooperation be coordinated and under whose auspices?

IMPORTANT GENERAL SOURCES

The following discussion covers those bibliographic compilations that provide the most comprehensive coverage of books or serials or both. For the United States, both current and retrospective sources are described; for Canada, Great Britain, and France, only current bibliographies are included. Works providing information about materials currently available from commercial publishers (in-print lists) are discussed, as are a few of those that offer lists of recommended works in a particular area or for a specific group of users. The printed catalogs of a few of the world's largest libraries, as well as a selection of bibliographies of bibliographic materials, are also included.

Shared Cataloging Networks

The most important bibliographic sources in today's library have neither a long history nor a traditional format. Shared cataloging networks, often called bib-liographic utilities, such as OCLC, were established about 40 years ago to provide machine-readable cataloging records and holdings information for their member li-braries. Their services have expanded to support access to article databases and re-source sharing through interlibrary loan and document delivery. Cooperative research projects enhance the effectiveness of member organizations.

OCLC provides services not just to libraries for the use of librarians, as in cata-loging, interlibrary loan, and document delivery; it also provides services for library users. Thus, such bibliographic utilities are not only revolutionizing access to the bib-liographic universe; they are also rapidly changing the interactions between libraries and their users. As of early 2011, OCLC *WorldCat* provided bibliographic records and holdings information for more than 72,000 member institutions in 170 countries. A new bibliographic record is added every 10 seconds. The database contained more than 220 million unique bibliographic records for books, serials, audiovisual materials, maps, archives/manuscripts, sound recordings, music scores, Web sites, and computer files. Retrospective conversion projects, whereby some of the world's leading libraries enter into the system newly created machine-readable records for older materials, make the shared cataloging networks the first bibliographic source of choice for materials from all time periods, not just from the period since 1971, when computerized cataloging began. Following the merger of the Research Libraries Group (RLG) with OCLC, *WorldCat* was enriched with records for many specialized materials held by RLG member libraries.

Access to *WorldCat* and other OCLC services is provided by several different systems, each to be used for specific purposes. The Connexion, CatExpress, and ILLiad services provide access for cataloging and resource sharing (interlibrary loan and the production of union catalogs). The FirstSearch service is aimed at end users, who may access not only *WorldCat* but also article databases that may include both abstracts and full-text materials. FirstSearch, which is menu-driven, also allows users to search their own catalog for holdings and then to input an interlibrary loan request if their library does not own the item. *WorldCat.org* opens up *WorldCat* so that any Web user can search the database and link to online catalog records. Libraries holding an item are also displayed as part of the search results.

As projects to digitize large numbers of books proceed, one can supplement searches of the document surrogates found in catalog records with a search of the full text of a growing number of books. Libraries are licensing full-text content from vendors such as ebrary (http://www.ebrary.com) and NetLibrary (http://www.netlibrary.com). *Google Books* is currently the most ambitious digitization project, allowing a simple Web search of book contents or an advanced search on combinations of fields such as keyword or phrase, language, title, author, publisher, subject, and publication date. It is also possible to browse through the digital collection under broad subjects such as "fairy tales," "photography," and "mathematical recreations." What can be viewed online depends on the copyright status of the book. Full view is possible if the book is out of copyright or if the publisher or author has asked to make the book fully viewable. Limited preview of selected pages is possible if the author or publisher has given permission. Otherwise, a "snippet view" is provided: information about the book plus a few sentences to display the search term or terms in context. If no text is available online, then basic bibliographic information about the book is provided. Entries for each book include a "find this book in a library" link that automatically provides a holdings list from *WorldCat.org*.

U.S. Bibliography

The study of bibliography in the United States is complicated by several factors. First, there is no official list of books published in the United States. Second, the mandatory deposit requirements for works copyrighted and published were enacted as part of the 1978 Copyright Act and were broadened in 1989. Prior to these laws, no provision for mandatory deposit existed. The retrospective coverage of publishing in the United States must be pieced together by using many sources. The earliest sources were produced by individual bibliographers, and they reflect their compilers' biases and idiosyncrasies. More recently, commercial publishers have dominated the field. Currently, the products and services of the Library of Congress and the shared cataloging network OCLC are the dominant elements in the provision of bibliographic control in the United States.

For most bibliographic quests, a search of *WorldCat* is the first order of business. The speed, ease of searching, and depth and breadth of coverage make this the first choice in almost all cases. However, a study by Beall and Kafadar and a follow-up study be DeZelar-Tiedman demonstrate that there are still a significant number of bibliographic records, especially for old and rare materials, found in the *National Union Catalog, Pre-1956 Imprints* that are not found in a search of *WorldCat*.[6] A reference librarian, therefore, still needs a thorough knowledge of these early bibliographic sources (see Figure 20.1). Additionally, to answer a question, the librarian may need to look at several tools and may well find pieces of the bibliographic puzzle in each of them. Knowledge of these sources will assist the librarian in deciding which tools to examine and, in some cases, may narrow the search to only one tool that will give a particular type of information. For example, a bibliographic description of a book published in 1857 might be found in the *National Union Catalog* or in *WorldCat*, but the price is likely to be found only in Roorbach's *Bibliotheca Americana*.

U.S. Retrospective Bibliography (to 1876)

Charles Evans's *American Bibliography* lists books, pamphlets, and periodicals published in the United States from 1639 through 1800. It is the most important of the

Figure 20.1. Time line of major sources for American bibliography.

bibliographies covering this period. The titles included are arranged in chronological order by date of publication. Evans made every effort to include all publications and to give a complete bibliographic description of each item. Each volume includes an index of authors and anonymous titles and a list of printers and publishers. The 14th volume, published in 1959, provides a cumulative author-title index to the whole set. The references in the index are to the item numbers assigned to each entry, not to pages. Library locations are given, by code, for each item listed.

Early American Imprints: Series I, Evans (1639–1800) is a microform set of the full texts of the nonserial titles listed in Evans's work. It is published by Readex in cooperation with the American Antiquarian Society. The microforms are filed in order by the item numbers in the Evans bibliography. The cataloging records for these microform copies have now been entered in the OCLC database as part of the Major Microforms Project, and the American Antiquarian Society has fully cataloged *Series I*.

Ralph R. Shaw and Richard H. Shoemaker continued the Evans bibliography with *American Bibliography: A Preliminary Checklist for 1801–1819*. This 23-volume set includes 19 annual volumes and 4 additional volumes containing addenda, as well as author, title, publisher, and geographic indexes. Library locations for copies are given whenever possible. A microform reprint set of the full texts of the contents, *Early American Imprints Series II, Shaw-Shoemaker (1801–1819)* is also available from Readex. The set is arranged by the Shaw-Shoemaker numbers. The series continues with Shoemaker's *A Checklist of American Imprints for 1820–1829*. Next, *A Checklist of American Imprints for 1830–* extends coverage through 1846.

The major project of digitizing the full text of items, plus images, in the Evans and Shaw-Shoemaker bibliographies has been completed by Readex. The digital collections, part of the Readex *Archive of Americana*, feature fully text-searchable facsimile images. Library users can link directly to the full text from their library's own online catalog, provided enhanced catalog records produced by the American Antiquarian Society have been loaded in the online catalog.

Orville Roorbach's *Bibliotheca Americana...1820–1861* and James Kelly's *The American Catalogue of Books...Jan. 1861 to Jan. 1871* are trade bibliographies listing books published during the periods covered. They are alphabetical lists by author and title and give publisher and price information. Neither title is as complete or as accurate as one would like, but they are the only general bibliographies that cover the period.

Joseph Sabin's *Bibliotheca Americana* is an extremely valuable bibliography of books relating to the United States from its European discovery to 1868. It lists books, pamphlets, and periodicals published in the Western Hemisphere as well as elsewhere. Sabin differs from the titles discussed previously in that the emphasis is on complete bibliographic description. Therefore, contents notes and varying editions are frequently included. The entries also often give locations of copies and references to reviews. Primary Source Media is currently filming items listed in Sabin to produce *The Sabin Collection: Selected Americana from Sabin's Dictionary of Books Relating to America*. Also, *The Sabin Collection Catalog* on CD-ROM provides indexing for the collection by title, author, year of publication, and subject. Cataloging records for individual items in the collection are available from OCLC or Primary Source Media. Gale is currently producing *Sabin Americana, 1500–1926* as a digital collection.

U.S. Retrospective Bibliography (since 1876)

To counter the weakness in U.S. national bibliography, R. R. Bowker produced *American Book Publishing Record Cumulative, 1876–1949*, published in 1980, and *American Book Publishing Record Cumulative, 1950–1977*, published in 1978. Both sources have the same type of arrangement and scope. The main arrangement is by Dewey Decimal Classification System, with separate volumes for fiction and juvenile fiction. These volumes are followed by author and title indexes. They do not include periodicals, government publications, theses, or a few other types of publications. The information in these bibliographies is taken from many sources, and the great value of the cumulation is the unique subject access combined with multiyear coverage.

The *American Catalogue of Books*, published by Publishers Weekly, covers the period 1876 to 1910 in volumes spanning varying numbers of years. Each volume provides author, title, and subject access to all books that were in print at the time the volume was published. *United States Catalog* was an in-print list published by H. W. Wilson in four editions from 1899 to 1928. Supplements to the *United States Catalog*, titled *Cumulative Book Index*, were published in the years between editions. *Cumulative Book Index* is also the title of H. W. Wilson's bibliography of works in English published from 1928 to 1999.

Current U.S. Bibliography

Current bibliographic sources are heavily used by librarians because they provide a timely list of books and other media at the time of publication and often in advance of publication. Librarians use these listings to perform the core functions of libraries: selection, reference, and cataloging. Subject access to newly published books allows both librarians and users to determine those books that have been published on the topic of interest. In addition, reference librarians use them to answer reference questions, including the verification and identification of bibliographic citations. National bibliographic agencies have a broader societal ambition when producing current bibliographic sources: to capture the record of the national publishing output for posterity.

In the United States, the only title being published that meets the definition of a current bibliography is the *American Book Publishing Record* (*ABPR*), a monthly publication from R. R. Bowker. *ABPR* provides full cataloging information for approximately 10,000 new titles as they are published. It does not include government publications, subscription books, dissertations, or pamphlets under 49 pages in length. It is arranged by the Dewey Decimal Classification System, with author and title indexes complementing the primary arrangement. Separate sections for adult fiction and juvenile fiction are arranged alphabetically by main entry author or title. In addition, the subject guide, arranged alphabetically, directs the user from the traced subject headings to the corresponding Dewey Decimal Classification System numbers. The annual *ABPR*, published in March, is compiled from the 12 monthly issues. Five-year cumulations are available for 1970–1974, 1975–1979, and 1980–1984, with only annual cumulations available from 1985. For smaller libraries without access to a bibliographic utility, *ABPR* supplies information for cataloging at the cost of only $335 (in 2011) per year.

Current Bibliographies from Britain, France, and Canada

British National Bibliography (*BNB*) is the national record of publishing in the United Kingdom and the Republic of Ireland. Although the *BNB* is the single most comprehensive listing of UK titles, the coverage of the *BNB* has always been selective, with an emphasis on monographs available through normal book-buying channels. New books and serials have been recorded in *BNB* since publication of the bibliography began in 1950. Since February 2003, records for UK online electronic resources have also begun to appear. *BNB* content is based on the books and e-resources received by the Legal Deposit Office of the British Library under the Legal Deposit Libraries Act 2003 and the Irish Copyright Act 1963. *BNB* also contains advance notification of forthcoming titles that is supplied by publishers under the Cataloging in Publication (CIP) program. CIP is a program through which participating publishers provide galley proofs or the front matter of their books to the national library or other centralized catalog agency. A cataloging record is then prepared and returned to the publisher. The cataloging record becomes a part of the book and is published on the verso of the title page. CIP originated in the Library of Congress in 1971, and the program now operates internationally. The British Library catalogs *BNB* entries in the MARC21 format according to the second edition of the *Anglo-American Cataloguing Rules*. Full subject access is provided by Library of Congress Subject Headings and Dewey Decimal Classification System numbers. In addition, such essential ordering information as ISBN and price is included as part of the entry. The *BNB* is now freely available to search online from the British Library's Web site.

The current national bibliography of France is the *Bibliographie Nationale Française* (*BNF*; until 1990, *Bibliographie de la France*), which records titles received by the Bibliothèque Nationale de France through legal deposit. It has been continuously published since 1811, although the frequency, arrangement, supplements, and format have varied through the years. *BNF* has five sections listing books ("Livres"), publications in series ("Publications en série"), audiovisual materials ("Audiovisuel"), printed music ("Musique"), and cartographic materials ("Cartographie"). Its primary arrangement is by Universal Decimal Classification (UDC), which began as a French translation of the Dewey Decimal Classification System. It contains the same basic arrangement but is much more detailed than Dewey. Author and title indexes in each issue complement the classified arrangement. Frequency varies among the sections, but cumulations of all sections are produced annually. Since 2001, it has been published only as an online file accessible from the Bibliothèque Nationale de France Web site.

Canadiana is the current national bibliography of Canada. Its listings are composed of cataloging records for a wide variety of publications produced in Canada, including books, periodicals, sound recordings, microforms, music scores, pamphlets, government documents, theses, educational kits, video recordings, and electronic documents. Canadian publishers are required to send two copies of these items to the Library and Archives Canada (LAC) as they are published. In Canada, legal deposit of Canadian publications is not related to copyright, but it is required by law. In addition, *Canadiana* lists titles published outside Canada that are of special interest because they are about Canadian topics or because they are written by Canadian authors. *Canadiana* is produced by Library and Archives Canada/Bibliothèque et Archives Canada and is currently available as an online service and via FTP. *Canadiana* can be searched free of charge through the *AMICUS* database, but it is not available as a separate subset of records.

Sources of Purchasing Information

In-print lists identify titles that are currently available from publishers. Because books may remain in print for a number of years, the current list can also be useful in identifying material published much earlier. In reference work, in-print lists are often used to determine whether an announced book has been published, whether a later edition of a work has been published, or what volumes of a series are still in print. Subject specialists use in-print lists as a way of determining what is being published in the subject area they cover. Virtually every in-print list is available in electronic format, with the enhanced access that Boolean logic and keyword searching allow.

The primary advantage of the in-print list is that it consolidates book purchasing information from thousands of publishers into one integrated list. Additional value is added when book reviews, awards, ratings, reading level, and best-seller status are linked to the listings. Other resources, however, are rivaling the in-print list in usefulness. Almost all publishers worldwide now produce catalogs available through the Web. Frequently, these electronic catalogs provide more accurate, up-to-date information than that available from in-print lists. In addition, materials vendors such as Baker and Taylor and even independent booksellers have Web-accessible databases for their customers to use in purchasing books and serials. Materials vendors such as Casalini Libri and Otto Harrassowitz have become OCLC WorldCat Cataloging Partners. Cataloging partners load cataloging records for the books they sell into *WorldCat*. These records include purchase price, status (such as backordered), and a vendor control number to link the vendor to the bibliographic record.

Currently a business unit of ProQuest, R. R. Bowker has been producing reference materials for the U.S. market since 1872 and has totally dominated the in-print list field for more than 50 years. Through the use of BowkerLink.com, Bowker maintains electronic contact with publishers regarding the status of books: date of publication, availability, price, and so on. From the database thus developed, an extensive family of in-print products, both print and electronic, is produced. The electronic products are available from Bowker via the Web, or as licensed data feeds.

Books in Print (*BIP*) is an annual listing of books available from U.S. publishers. It is a seven-volume set with separate author and title sections. Each entry includes price, ISBN, publisher, binding, and other ordering information. Volume 7 also includes contact and ordering information for more than 75,000 publishers. The lists are compiled from information provided by publishers. *BIP* is a list of what publishers report is in print at a given moment. Because data are collected from thousands of sources, errors of omission and commission are not uncommon. No attempt is made to standardize the form of an author's name. It is, therefore, possible to have a single author listed in more than one form, so one must be careful when searching the author volume. The works of an author whose name is listed as both W. Kenneth Smith and as Kenneth Smith would be entered far apart in the alphabetical listings. The annual volumes of *BIP* are updated by *Books in Print Supplement*, which appears in March six months after the main volumes are published in September. *Forthcoming Books*, published four times a year, lists books projected to be published within the next several months as well as postponements and changes in price, edition, title, or ISBN. Each issue of *Forthcoming Books* expands on the previous issue, updating entries and adding new ones.

Subject Guide to Books in Print arranges the contents of *BIP* according to the Library of Congress Subject Headings assigned to the books. Although *BIP* and the *Subject Guide* are separate publications, most libraries subscribe to both titles because both are useful for acquisitions and reference work.

Children's Books in Print and the *Subject Guide to Children's Books in Print* list material selected by age level. Other titles cover specific formats—*Books Out Loud: Bowker's Guide to Audiobooks* and *Bowker's Complete Video Directory* are examples.

The *BooksInPrint.com* Web-based product offers information on book, audio book, and video titles, including in print, forthcoming, and out-of-print items. It offers multiple search options. A quick search can be conducted by keyword, author, title, or ISBN/UPC and limited by status (in print, out of print, and/or forthcoming) and format (book, audio, and/or video). It is also possible to browse by general subject (such as juvenile, history, computers, self-help, sports) or by index (author/contributor, award name, award year, publisher name, review source, series title, subject, title language). Advanced search allows even more precise searching through combinations of various fields. *GlobalBooksinPrint.com*, also from Bowker, provides comparable search capabilities for books, audio books, and video titles from other countries, with the added option of limiting search to publications from specific countries.

Canadian Books in Print (*CBIP*), produced by the University of Toronto Press and long a standard work in the field, ceased publication with the 2006 edition. However, *New Books Service* (*NBS*) of the Library and Archives Canada (LAC) is a source for information on current and forthcoming Canadian books. The *NBS* database contains bibliographic information for English- and French-language books that have been announced by Canadian publishers over the past six months. The database is derived from information received directly from publishers through the Library and Archives Canada's Cataloguing in Publication program.

Library Catalogs

In reference work, library catalogs are used most often for verification purposes, but those that include a subject approach can also be used as subject bibliographies. The catalogs of some special libraries also include indexing at the article level for periodicals in the fields covered. This is particularly important because there may not have been a journal index for the subject involved during the time period covered by the catalog.

Although hundreds of library catalogs have been published, few are still being printed today. Production costs have made printed library catalogs prohibitively expensive. The storage space required to house them is excessive even in the largest of libraries. These catalogs are now much more likely to appear in electronic format, where they can be accessed via the Internet, on CD-ROM, or as part of the larger database in a bibliographic utility.

It is important to note here that libraries gradually began to use machine-readable cataloging in the late 1960s. The cataloging of materials in non-Roman alphabets did not begin until the late 1970s. Large libraries did not go back and create machine-readable cataloging copy for materials acquired earlier. It was simply too expensive to do so. Only in the late 1990s did large research and national libraries conduct widespread massive retrospective conversion projects, allowing libraries such as Princeton and Yale to convert earlier holdings to machine-readable cataloging. The reference librarian, when looking at the librarian's own catalog as well as remote electronic catalogs, must determine what materials have been converted. In other words, what precisely is being searched? Without this information, it is impossible to evaluate the results of a search that had negative results.

Most individual library catalogs may be searched free of charge by using Web access. The application of common standards allows users to search remote catalogs without knowing the exact search syntax required by the remote catalog. Z39.50 is a national standard defining a protocol for computer-to-computer information retrieval. The MARC communications format is an international standard for representing and exchanging bibliographic data in machine-readable form. The Library of Congress (LC) maintains a Z39.50 gateway to individual library catalogs on the LC Web page (http://lcweb.loc.gov/z3950/). In addition, library consortia produce gateways or portals that allow searchers to search multiple libraries' catalogs simultaneously. The European Library, which offers access to the combined resources of the 48 national libraries of Europe, is an example of such unified data access (http://www.theeurope anlibrary.org/portal/index.html).

Most often, it is preferable to search the bibliographic utilities rather than individual library catalogs. Either successful or negative search results cost the librarian very little time. However, the presence of locally produced cataloging copy that might not be present in the utilities occasionally merits searching catalogs individually. Subject bibliographers may wish to search a local collection to determine its holdings in a particular area of strength. An example of such a collection might be that of a local historical society library. In addition to the online catalog, conditions of use, hours of operation, and other worthwhile information may be found on a library's Web site.

United States

Whether one is the sole librarian in a small public library or one of many reference librarians in a large academic library, one needs to be familiar with the *National Union Catalog* (*NUC*) and its publishing history. In a nation that has no official national bibliography and had no system of mandatory deposit for most of its history, the products and services of the Library of Congress are, next to the bibliographic utilities, the most important resource for bibliographic methods of research.

NUC began as the actual card catalog of the Library of Congress. Later, when increased access to the card catalog was deemed desirable, more than 1,000 depository (duplicate) sets of cards were distributed to and maintained by large research libraries throughout the United States. The first printed book catalog version of the card set, *The Library of Congress Catalog: A Cumulative Catalog of Books Represented by Library of Congress Printed Cards*, was published in 1942 under the sponsorship of the Association of Research Libraries. This set represented cataloging done at the Library of Congress, at some libraries of government departments, and at 1,500 research libraries. Cards printed from 1898 to July 31, 1942, were reproduced. Its supplement included cards produced from August 1, 1942, to December 31, 1947; the next cumulation was *Library of Congress Author Catalog...1948–1952*. In 1953 the scope was enlarged to include cataloging entries and holdings information of additional contributing North American libraries, and consequently, the title of the catalog was changed to *National Union Catalog* (*NUC*).

The publication of the Library of Congress catalog has continued to the present, with additional title changes reflecting its variations in scope, frequency, and format. For an extended description of the publishing history of *NUC*, see the entry for it in Balay's *Guide to Reference Books*.[7]

The large retrospective set now in use is *National Union Catalog, Pre-1956 Imprints*. For this set the entries are photocopies of catalog cards. Location symbols for research libraries in the United States and Canada that own a particular title are added to the bottom of the card. *NUC, Pre-1956 Imprints* is an author, or main entry, catalog. Necessary cross-references are included, but subject headings are not. Furthermore, only selected added entries are included. Thus, knowledge of the cataloging code that governs the choice and form of the main entry is necessary to use *NUC* effectively. For almost all entries in *NUC, Pre-1956*, this means using the *ALA Cataloging Rules for Author and Title Entries*, 1949 edition. For example, general rule 92 stated, "Enter an institution (using the latest name) under the place in which it is located."[8] Therefore, Southern Methodist University in Dallas, Texas, was entered under Dallas. Similarly, many subdivisions of governments were entered first under the largest unit of a government agency, with subdivisions for the successive layers of government structure. Subsequent cataloging codes have allowed for entry under the smallest subdivision of a government agency that can logically stand alone, and for entry directly under the name of an institution (e.g., Southern Methodist University).

Because the set was published over a period of 12 years, supplementary volumes were necessary almost immediately. These volumes (686 to 754) add titles identified after publication began and add locations to titles published earlier. *NUC, Pre-1956* was continued as *National Union Catalog* through 1982. Five-year cumulations, except for 1978 to 1982, have been published.

From 1983 until December 2002, *National Union Catalog* editions were published in microfiche, with no print version available. The microfiche edition used the register/index form of arrangement. Full bibliographic records appeared only once in the register, numbered sequentially. Separate alphabetically arranged indexes for names, titles, subjects, and series provided access points to the register. The indexes supplied a brief cataloging record and the item number under which the full record could be found in the register. Although briefer than the register records, index entries frequently provided sufficient bibliographic information to complete a search. The full record in the register provided complete cataloging information as well as information such as ISBN, price, and suggested Dewey Decimal Classification System number. With this arrangement, the indexes could be cumulated without having to reprint the full record. *National Union Catalog: Books* provided bibliographic records for books, pamphlets, manuscripts, map atlases, monographic microform publications, and monographic government publications. Records for all non-Roman-language materials were in Romanized form only, however. With the publication of the 1990 edition, *National Union Catalog: Books* no longer included records for books from OCLC and the Research Libraries Group. The national union catalogs of the

Library of Congress also included the following titles in microfiche: *National Union Catalog: Audiovisual Materials*, *National Union Catalog: Cartographic Materials*, and *The Music Catalog*.

Since production of the microfiche catalog series ceased in December 2002, LC cataloging records have been available only electronically from the MARC (MAchine Readable Cataloging) Distribution Service (MDS), which is part of the Cataloging Distribution Service (CDS) of the Library of Congress. Records are available via Internet ftp (file transfer protocol). Most libraries will, however, simply access OCLC for LC's cataloging output. The Library of Congress Online Catalog (http://catalog.loc.gov/) is a database of approximately 14 million records representing books, serials, computer files, manuscripts, cartographic materials, music, sound recordings, and visual materials in the library's collections. The online catalog also provides references, notes, circulation status, and information about materials still in the acquisitions stage. The catalog is available for searching 7 days a week, 24 hours a day. Research tools, specialized databases, legislative information, and full-text digital resources are also available through the LC Web site (http://www.loc.gov).

Great Britain and France

The library catalogs of Great Britain and France follow similar publishing patterns to those in the United States. The British Library's *General Catalogue of Printed Books to 1975* (*BLC*), the last edition of this printed catalog, was completed in 1985. Editions published before the establishment of the British Library in 1973 were known as the *British Museum Catalogue*. As of 2003, published supplements (published by K. G. Saur) brought the coverage to the end of 2002. This catalog is an invaluable source of bibliographic data because it lists the holdings of one of the world's largest libraries. Because the British Library is a depository for all materials copyrighted in the United Kingdom, its catalog is the most complete record of such publications.

The catalog is arranged by main entry in one alphabetical sequence. Most entries are personal authors, but corporate author and title entries are included where necessary. Serials are included, but they are listed under "periodical publications." Newspapers are not included, but the British Library has published a catalog of its newspaper library.[9] The completeness of the bibliographic description provided varies a good deal depending on when the book was cataloged. In the supplements, complete MARC records are the rule. Newer entries give complete cataloging information.

A subject approach to the BLC was provided under the title *Subject Index of the Modern Works Added to the Library*, which appeared in multivolume sets published from 1906 to 1985. These indexes excluded "pure" literature and personal names, which were included in the *General Catalogue*. The early catalogs are rather difficult to use because the material is arranged in very broad subjects that are then subdivided. The subjects are in alphabetical rather than classified order.

A massive retrospective conversion project was undertaken at the British Library between 1987 and 1991 to convert the entire British Library *General Catalogue of Printed Books to 1975* to machine-readable form. Such conversion does not merely change the format of the catalog; it also enhances use of the catalog by making almost all elements of the entries searchable.

The resulting British Library Integrated Catalogue (http://www.bl.uk) provides free access via the Web to bibliographic records in the library's main catalogs for 14 million books, 920,000 journal and newspaper titles, 58 million patents, and 3 million sound recordings. The catalog also includes records for printed music and maps. Additional resources that can be searched simultaneously include 9 million articles from 20,000 journals; 30,000 historical pictures and sounds; and 10,000 pages on the British Library Web site. Despite the vast coverage of the online catalogs, some categories of materials in the British Library are described only in printed catalogs and are not yet available on the Web.

Catalogue Général des Livres Imprimés from the Bibliothèque Nationale in Paris is the most important source for French publications. It is an alphabetical list of books by personal author only. It does not include entries for anonymous works, serials, or works of corporate authorship. The catalog was published alphabetically in sequential volumes from 1897 to 1981, so there is a great difference in the dates of coverage in different parts of the alphabet. Even in the volumes published after 1960, nothing is included that was published after 1959. A supplement covering 1960 to 1969 has been published that includes entries for corporate authors and anonymous works, as well as for personal authors. Because of the unevenness in coverage over time, the Bibliothèque Nationale has published a microfiche supplement that brings all parts of the original up to 1959. *Le Catalogue Général de la Bibliothèque Nationale de France*, an electronic catalog on six CD-ROMs, lists almost every book published in France up to 1970. The catalog is produced by the Bibliothèque Nationale de France, and the vendor is ProQuest.

Three electronic catalogs of the Bibliothèque Nationale de France (http://www.bnf.fr) are available on the Internet. BnF Catalogue Général combines into one catalog the bibliographic records for the library's print, sound, audiovisual, and multimedia materials from its beginnings to the present day, as well as special materials such as maps, drawings, and engravings. Mandragore is the database of iconographic collections held in the library's Department of Manuscripts. Gallica is the library's online digital library, which includes digitized texts, images, and sound recordings.

Canada

Library and Archives Canada (LAC, http://www.collectionscanada.gc.ca/index-e.html) was established in 2004 by a merger of the services, collections, and staff of the former National Library of Canada and the National Archives of Canada. *AMICUS*, Canada's national catalog, includes the holdings of published materials held at LAC and at more than 1,300 libraries across Canada. It contains more than 30 million records for books, magazines, newspapers, government documents, theses, sound recordings, maps, and electronic texts, as well as items in Braille and large print. Access to *AMICUS* is free and is available from LAC's Web site.

Serial and Newspaper Sources

The term *serial* can be extremely confusing to the neophyte. It simply means "a publication that is issued in successive parts, usually at regular intervals, and, as a rule, intended to be continued indefinitely."[10] Types of serials include periodicals, annuals (e.g., reports, yearbooks), proceedings, and transactions of societies. Irregular serials are issued irregularly at unspecified intervals. The term *periodical* refers to a type of serial that has a distinctive title intended to appear in successive (usually unbound) numbers or parts at stated or regular intervals and, as a rule, for an indefinite time. Each part generally contains articles by several contributors. Each serial title is assigned an ISSN that is unique to that title. If the serial title changes, a new ISSN must be assigned to the new title.

Two types of sources are discussed in this section. One is lists of serial titles that are currently being published. The other is union lists that include the location and holdings of each title listed. In these examples, *location* means a library in the United States or Canada; *holdings* means a record of which volumes or years each library holds.

Retrospective and Union Lists

Union List of Serials in Libraries of the United States and Canada (*ULS*) lists serials that began publication before 1950. It is arranged in alphabetical order by main entry. Although the holdings information is limited to libraries located in the United States and Canada, the serials may be published in any country, making this work international in its coverage. Each entry includes a detailed publication history of the title and notes any variation that has occurred in the title. *ULS* contains no newspapers and very few government publications. Entries include library locations and specific holdings; location symbols used are the same as those used in the *National Union Catalog*.

New Serial Titles (*NST*) continued *ULS*. Its first cumulation covers serials that began publication between 1950 and 1970. Since that time, there have been several multiyear cumulations. In 1981, *NST* expanded its entries to include complete cataloging information; the entries were produced from OCLC tapes and are the reproduction of the OCLC record. *NST* ceased publication with the 1999 cumulation.

American Newspapers, 1821–1936 is similar in format to *ULS* in that it lists locations in the United States and Canada and gives a complete bibliographic description of each title. However, entries are arranged by place of publication. Detailed holdings for each location are included. Because there has been no supplement, other titles must be used to identify more current holdings and to locate descriptions of titles that began publication after 1936.

Newspapers in Microform: United States and *Newspapers in Microform: Foreign Countries* are union lists for Canadian and U.S. libraries. In addition to listing libraries where the newspaper can be consulted or borrowed, sources for purchasing microform copies are indicated. Both of these titles, like *American Newspapers*, are arranged by the place of publication of the newspaper. A title index is provided.

At some point, weakness in a particular bibliographic area is usually addressed by a new product. As can be seen from the preceding descriptions, bibliographic coverage of newspaper holdings in the United States is one such weak area. The United States Newspaper Program (USNP) is a cooperative national effort among the states and the federal government to locate, catalog, and preserve on microfilm newspapers published in the United States. Participants in the program use the OCLC Cataloging and Union List services to create an online database of newspaper bibliographic, location, and holdings information. *United States Newspaper Program National Union List* (*USNP NUL*) is computer output microfiche of the online (*USNP*

NUL) cataloging records database available from OCLC. It first became available in 1985, and the fifth edition was published in January 1999. The arrangement of the list is alphabetical by title; indexes by date, intended audience, language, and place of publication are included. The most current information is, of course, available online through OCLC.

Current Lists

Ulrich's Periodicals Directory is an annual guide to more than 201,000 currently available periodicals and, since 1993, newspapers. The arrangement is by broad subject area, with separate indexes providing access to title, ISSN, and publications of international organizations. Providers of online periodicals and serials on CD-ROM are listed alphabetically in separate sections. Entries include the information needed to order the title: publisher, address, price, and ISSN. In addition, frequency, beginning date, circulation figures, advertising rates, refereed status, and telephone and fax numbers are usually included. *Ulrich's* has several other features that greatly increase its usefulness in the reference collection. Each entry lists the indexes and online databases that cover the contents of the periodical. This feature allows the librarian or other user to locate the complete citation for an article in a periodical by identifying the index or database where the citation can be found. Another valuable feature is the list of cessations, which lists periodicals that have ceased publication during the previous three years. Since 1988, *Ulrich's* has incorporated *Irregular Serials and Annuals* in its coverage and title, thus providing publication and ordering information for most directories, almanacs, and yearbooks.

Web-based access to *Ulrich's* is now provided by Serials Solutions as *Ulrichsweb*. Quick search options include ISSN, keyword, subject, exact title, and keyword from title. Entries can be browsed by general subject or by a variety of indexes, including country of publication, language, Dewey Decimal number, and LC classification number. The advanced search option allows more complex combinations of fields. The database is updated weekly.

Newspapers currently published in the United States and Canada are listed in the *Gale Directory of Publications and Broadcast Media*. This directory has been published annually since 1880 (until 1982, as *Ayer Directory of Publications*). Because it has been published for such a long time, back volumes are an excellent source for historical information on U.S. newspapers. In addition to newspapers, the *Gale Directory* includes information about magazines, journals, college publications, radio and television stations, and cable stations and systems. *Ulrich's* lists more periodicals than does the *Gale Directory*, but *Ulrich's* does not include broadcast media.

The *Gale Directory of Publications and Broadcast Media* is published annually in five volumes. The first two volumes (U.S. and Canada) and volume 5 (international) are arranged geographically, with the print and broadcast entries listed alphabetically under the place of publication. In addition to information that can be used for ordering, such as address and price, the entries include information specific to individual media, such as circulation figures, number of columns, size, and advertising rates for print sources. The third volume includes statistical tables and indexes. In addition to the index of publishers and master name and keyword index, there are several different subject or type listings, such as for Jewish publications, free newspapers, and radio format. The fourth volume has a regional market index and maps. Tables are provided showing statistics by type of publication and geographical region. The maps section includes maps for individual states and provinces and shows the cities and towns in which the titles listed in the directory are published. Newsletters and directories are specifically excluded. This directory is also available on the Web as part of the *Gale Directory Library*.

A series of publications from Oxbridge Communications replicates the coverage offered by other periodical directories and expands coverage into other areas such as newsletters. *The Standard Periodical Directory* includes more than 63,000 U.S. and Canadian periodicals; *The National Directory of Magazines* provides production specifications and rates for more than 20,000 U.S. and Canadian publications; and the *Oxbridge Directory of Newsletters* covers more than 15,000 newsletters, loose-leafs, bulletins, and fax letters. All these titles are produced in print and are accessible on the Web through the MediaFinder subscription service. The strength of these sources lies in the provision of narrower, more numerous subject categories (more than 250) and in the listing of some unique titles not found in other sources.

In recent years, there has been growth in open access journals, publications that make the full text of their articles freely available via the Internet. The *Directory of Open Access Journals* has been developed to simplify identification of and access to these scientific and scholarly journals. As of early 2011, the directory included 6,297 journals, with 2,740 of those searchable at the article level. Journals included in the directory can be browsed by title and subject or searched by keyword.

Bibliographies of Bibliographies

Bibliographies of bibliographies are usually general in scope and are used to identify bibliographies on a specific subject. The major titles of the genre are Theodore Besterman's *A World Bibliography of Bibliographies* (often referred to as Besterman) and *Bibliographic Index*. Besterman includes more substantial bibliographies, but it is not current. *Bibliographic Index* is current and provides information appropriate to any level of inquiry.

Besterman lists in five volumes separately published bibliographies only. It is international in scope and arranged by subject. The last volume is an index that includes authors, titles, and subjects. The last edition covers material through 1963. It has been supplemented by Alice F. Toomey's *A World Bibliography of Bibliographies, 1964–1974*. The supplement, compiled from Library of Congress printed cards, is arranged by subject, based on Library of Congress Subject Headings. In 1998, K. G. Saur began publishing the massive 11-volume *International Bibliography of Bibliographies 1959–1988*, which is intended to serve as yet another supplement to Besterman.

Bibliographic Index is a subject index to bibliographies that have been published in books, pamphlets, and more than 2,800 periodicals. H. W. Wilson began publishing the index in 1937. It currently appears in two paperbound issues per year and an annual permanent clothbound cumulation, which includes four additional months of coverage. This is an excellent source for beginning a search for scholarly and popular works in all subject areas. *Bibliographic Index* includes material published in English and other Western European languages. Each entry gives complete information on the bibliography and indicates whether it is annotated. The arrangement is by Library of Congress Subject Headings. *Bibliographic Index Plus* offers expanded coverage online via WilsonWeb. The database is updated daily. It provides indexing to more than 600,000 bibliographies, and more than 245,000 of the bibliographies, dating from 1994, are full text.

Recommended Lists

Recommended lists are highly selective, evaluative bibliographies. They list only the best titles published in a particular area. The evaluative nature of recommended lists saves the librarian time by eliminating from consideration lesser titles that have been found lacking in some way. The compiler of the bibliography, however, should always carefully define the criteria used to evaluate materials. Quality is a very subjective measure. Therefore, selection of materials by a group of qualified experts is perhaps the most frequently used method of compiling such lists. However, the number of copies sold can also be a valid criterion for lists of popular reading material.

Recommended lists are used by librarians in three integral ways: building a collection to meet the needs of users, measuring (evaluating) the library collection against these standard lists, and advising readers. In carrying out these activities, one must keep in mind that recommended lists are created for an average collection, whereas the librarian is collecting for a particular library with a unique user population.

The term *readers' advisory service* is usually used in the public library context. In reality, all reference interviews essentially provide a bridge between the reader and the sources required to meet the reader's information needs. The difference may be that the true readers' advisory service offered in public libraries is an expanded reference service that includes advice on the selection of recreational reading titles. To assist in this type of service, some recommended lists offer indexing by criteria not often used in other types of bibliographies. Primary examples are lists of fiction and nonfiction by age or reading level and lists of fiction by genre, geographic area, or historical period. Finding books on astronomy written for the layperson in a collection that contains both technical and nontechnical works would be extremely time-consuming without the use of these special indexes.

The titles discussed here are general sources covering broad subject areas. Readers' advisory service is a current hot topic in librarianship, and publishers' output in this field reflects this high interest. Publishers such as Libraries Unlimited, the American Library Association, Gale, Scarecrow Press, and Neal-Schuman produce multiple titles covering narrower subjects, particularly genre fiction.

H. W. Wilson has published *The Wilson Core Collections* (formerly the *Wilson Standard Catalogs*), which are lists of recommended books for particular audiences, for many years. These titles are used for collection development, book selection and acquisition, and readers' advisory services. A subscription to the core collections brings an initial hardcover volume followed by three annual paperbound supplements. Two of the titles are used by public libraries: *Public Library Core Collection: Nonfiction* and *Fiction Core Collection*. *Public Library Core Collection: Nonfiction* lists adult nonfiction in-print titles arranged by Dewey Decimal Classification System; it includes annotations. *Fiction Core Collection* is an annotated bibliography arranged by author with title and subject indexes. With this catalog, it is possible to identify novels about specific places or historical periods, for example. Another popular use is to locate genre fiction, such as spy novels or murder mysteries. The other three titles in this series are aimed at school libraries: *Children's Core Collection*, *Middle and Junior High Core Collection*, and *Senior High Core Collection*. Electronic editions of *The Wilson Core Collections* became available online through WilsonWeb in 2000. In addition to files corresponding to the five print titles, Wilson has added a *Graphic Novels Core Collection* and a *Nonbook Materials Core Collection* online. The latter includes more than 5,300 electronic resources, video recordings, sound recordings, audio books, games, and simulations recommended for various types of libraries. Search options online include subject, author, title, genre, grade level, classification number, publication date, or any combination.

Magazines for Libraries is an annotated listing by subject of more than 6,000 periodicals, both print and electronic journals. Selection is limited to those titles considered to be the most useful for the average elementary or secondary school, public, academic, or special library. The title also serves as a readers' advisory tool for the user who wants to select a magazine in a subject area of particular interest. Annotations from *Magazines for Libraries* are included in *Ulrichsweb*.

A proliferation of online readers' advisory tools have appeared over the past few years. Libraries Unlimited has introduced *The Reader's Advisor Online*, bringing together the volumes in their *Genreflecting* series as well as other material, covering both fiction and nonfiction. There are multiple ways to browse and access titles, including by subgenre, subjects/themes/character, location, title, genre, reading interests, appeal features, author, and series title. Bowker makes available *Fiction Connection*, which allows users to search for similar titles by entering the title of a book or by browsing by characteristics such as location, topic, character, genre, time frame, or setting. Based on these criteria, the user is then provided with a comprehensive list of suggested reading that has characteristics matching their original search criteria. Bowker's *Non-Fiction Connection* was launched in 2007, featuring narrative nonfiction (titles with characters, storylines, and drama that read much like a traditional novel). EBSCO's *NoveList Plus* covers both fiction and nonfiction titles, with sections for teens, older children, and younger children. Recommended reading lists, book discussion guides, and awards lists are also included. The newest addition is Gale's *Books and Authors*, based on the company's print products, including *What Do I Read Next?* Its scope includes fiction, nonfiction, and young adult and children's materials. Multiple browsing and searching options provide a number of ways to discover titles of interest. In addition to these subscription databases, there are a number of free Web-based tools, such as Amazon.com (http://www.amazon.com), which can also be useful for readers' advisory.[11]

SEARCH STRATEGIES

Verification is necessary when trying to identify, and eventually locate, a given item. Often the bibliographic information presented by a library user to the reference librarian is so incomplete that a good deal of ingenuity must be used to locate a copy. The sources of incomplete citations can vary from partial information gathered from a chance reference on a television or radio talk show to a poorly

---

BOX 20.1
SEARCH STRATEGY: A BOOK ON HOMESCHOOLING

An out-of-town researcher appeared at a university library's reference desk. A colleague at her home institution had recommended a book by Eva Boyd. The book was about a single mother who homeschooled her son, who then completed college by age 17. She remembered neither the date of publication nor the title of the book. The first step was searching the university library's own catalog. Because the university had a strong collection in the field of education, it was assumed that the book would turn up immediately as the result of an author search. No author with the name of Eva Boyd appeared in the list of authors. A widening of the OPAC search to include the holdings of all libraries in the state resulted in one book by Eva Jolene Boyd on the subject of stagecoach travel in the American West, *That Old Overland Stagecoaching*. A search of *WorldCat* and *Books in Print* on the Web turned up more books by the same Eva Jolene Boyd. A perusal of the print *Subject Guide to Books in Print* under the subject Home Schooling was unsuccessful. Finally, the librarian revised her strategy on *WorldCat*. A subject search on "Home Schooling" and keyword author search on "Eva" produced two matches, including *About Face* by Eva Seibert. The alternative title is "How both sons of a single mother were homeschooled and admitted to college by the time they were twelve." The record indicated that the book was self-published, and only four holding libraries were listed, none close by. The librarian turned to Amazon.com to determine whether a copy was available inexpensively. Eight sources for purchase were identified with several copies priced at $5.00 or less.

---

constructed bibliography in a scholarly book. Practice and experience make the process easier, but there are a number of factors to keep in mind when deciding where to start.

If the incomplete citation lacks a date, it is best to start looking in a cumulated list that will allow searching a number of years simultaneously. Shared cataloging networks such as OCLC are especially useful in cases such as this because of the wide range of dates covered. Unfortunately, a citation lacking a date frequently also lacks some other important element.

When selecting the bibliography or catalog to use for verification, the librarian needs to keep in mind the stated purpose of the tools. National bibliographies usually list materials published during the time period covered. Most library catalogs list material cataloged during the stated time. Thus, a title published in 1850, but not cataloged and reported to *NUC* until 1965, would not have appeared in *NUC* until the 1963–1967 cumulation.

Using *New Serial Titles* presents some of the same concerns. That is, a serial that began publication in 1975 may very well not appear until the 1981–1985 cumulation. In addition, the librarian needs to keep in mind the changes in rules of entry that have occurred over time.

The search in Box 20.1 illustrates several points. First, one should note that current English usage indicates that the word *homeschooling* should be spelled as one word, yet the Library of Congress Subject Headings (LCSH) uses two words. The listings in *WorldCat* and *Books in Print* use LCSH. When one goes back and checks the electronic *Books in Print* entry for the book, the entry shows only one subject heading: Education—Aims and Objectives. At no place in the *Books in Print* entry does the concept "home schooling" appear. Had the librarian relied on only one source, this query would never have been answered.

Further questioning of the library user indicated that Eva Boyd married again after rearing her boys and before publishing the book. Thus, Eva Seibert is a later form of her name. She has written only under the name Eva Seibert; therefore, there is no *see* reference from the earlier form of name to the later form. Most users would not be aware of the earlier form of her name. This case shows how resourceful and creative reference librarians must be when tackling complex bibliographic questions. Name and title variations, or uncertainties regarding specific editions of works or which libraries might own these editions, are just a few of the difficulties that may arise from a seemingly simple request for a book or journal article. Often, the librarian must carefully question the user and consider all available resources to successfully answer bibliographic reference questions.

The rapid changes in the information marketplace are perhaps more evident in the field of bibliographic tools than in any other area of librarianship. Large numbers of titles considered to be the standard works in the field have ceased publication in the last 10 years. The mergers of what used to be competing publishers have eliminated the economic viability of producing tools with overlapping coverage. Joint ventures between publishers result in efforts such as *Bowker's Book Analysis System*, which enables a qualitative analysis of a library's holdings by comparing a collection to H. W. Wilson's *Core Collections* series and Bowker's *Resources for College Libraries*. The emergence of the bibliographic utilities as sources of book-buying information, including publishing status, have weakened the demand for in-print lists and other traditional sources of information.

The aforementioned changes make it difficult for the student to understand the conceptual framework of bibliography. However, those working in a research library environment will still have to learn "the way it used to be"—because despite all the retrospective conversion and new electronic sources, there will always be the elusive citation that requires research in an old print catalog or serial union list.

NOTES

1.   D. W. Krummel, *Bibliographies: Their Aims and Methods*. (London: Mansell Publishing, 1984), 4.

2.   Robert W. Melton, "'The Baby Figure of the Giant Mass': Pollard & Redgrave's and Wing's Short-Title Catalogues," in *Distinguished Classics of Reference Publishing*, ed. James Rettig (Phoenix, AZ: Oryx Press, 1992), 254.

3.   Glen Holt, "Catalog Outsourcing: No Clear-Cut Choice," *Library Journal* 120 (September 15, 1995): 34.

4. Patrick Wilson, *Two Kinds of Power: An Essay on Bibliographic Control* (Berkeley: University of California Press, 1968), 13.

5. Mary Ellen Soper, "B. Procedures or Processes," in *The Librarian's Thesaurus: A Concise Guide to Library and Information Terms* (Chicago: American Library Association, 1990), 44.

6. Jeffrey Beall and Karen Kafadar, "The Proportion of NUC Pre-56 Titles Represented in OCLC WorldCat," *College & Research Libraries* 66 (2005): 433; Christine DeZelar-Tiedman, "The Proportion of NUC Pre-56 Titles Represented in the RLIN and OCLC Databases Compared: A Follow-Up to the Beall/Kafadar Study," *College & Research Libraries* 69 (2008): 401–6.

7. Robert Balay, ed., *Guide to Reference Books*, 11th ed. (Chicago: American Library Association, 1996), AA106–AA114.

8. *ALA Cataloging Rules for Author and Title Entries*, 2nd ed. (Chicago: American Library Association, 1949), 151.

9. British Library, Colindale, *Catalogue of the Newspaper Library, Colindale*, 8 vols. (London: British Museum Publications, 1975).

10. Heartsill Young, ed., *The ALA Glossary of Library and Information Science* (Chicago: American Library Association, 1983), 203.

11. Jessica Moyer, "Electronic Readers'-Advisory Tools," *Booklist* 104 (July 2008): 10–11.

LIST OF SOURCES

American Book Publishing Record. New Providence, NJ: R. R. Bowker, 1960–. Monthly with annual cumulative volumes.

American Book Publishing Record Cumulative, 1876–1949. 15 vols. New York: R. R. Bowker, 1980.

American Book Publishing Record Cumulative, 1950–1977. 15 vols. New York: R. R. Bowker, 1978.

American Catalogue…1876–1910. 8 vols. in 13 pts. New York: Publishers Weekly, 1880–1911.

American Newspapers, 1821–1936. New York: H. W. Wilson, 1937. 791 pp.

AMICUS. Ottawa: Library and Archives Canada. http://www.collectionscanada.gc.ca/amicus/index-e.html.

Archive of Americana. Chester, VT: Readex. http://www.readex.com/readex/?content=93.

Ayer Directory of Publications. Philadelphia: Ayer, 1880–1982. Annual.

Besterman, Theodore, comp. *A World Bibliography of Bibliographies and of Bibliographical Catalogues, Calendars, Abstracts, Digests, Indexes, and the Like.* 4th ed. 5 vols. Lausanne, Switzerland: Societas Bibliographica, 1965–1966.

Bibliographic Index: A Cumulative Bibliography of Bibliographies. New York: H. W. Wilson, 1937–. 3 issues per year.

Bibliographic Index Plus. New York: H. W. Wilson. Available online via WilsonWeb.

Bibliographie Nationale Française. Paris: Bibliothèque Nationale, 1990–2000. Biweekly with annual indexes. (Title varies: 1811–1989, *Bibliographie de la France.*) Paris: Bibliothèque Nationale, 2001–. http://www.bnf.fr.

Books and Authors. Farmington Hills, MI: Gale. http://www.gale.cengage.com/booksand authors/.

Books in Print. New Providence, NJ: R. R. Bowker, 1948–. Annual with semiannual supplements.

BooksInPrint.com. New Providence, NJ: R. R. Bowker. http://www.booksinprint.com.

Bowker's Book Analysis System. New Providence, NJ: R. R. Bowker. http://www.bowkers bookanalysis.com/bbas/.

British Library. *General Catalogue of Printed Books to 1975.* 360 vols. London: K. G. Saur, 1979–1987. Also available on CD-ROM.

British Library. *General Catalogue of Printed Books 1976–1982.* 50 vols. London: K. G. Saur, 1983.

British Library. *General Catalogue of Printed Books 1982–1985.* 26 vols. London: K. G. Saur, 1986.

British Library. *General Catalogue of Printed Books 1986–1987.* 22 vols. London: K. G. Saur, 1988.

British Library. *General Catalogue of Printed Books 1988–1989.* 28 vols. London: K. G. Saur, 1990.

British Library. *General Catalogue of Printed Books 1990–1992.* 27 vols. London: K. G. Saur, 1993.

British Library. *General Catalogue of Printed Books 1993–1994.* 27 vols. London: K. G. Saur, 1995.

British Library. *General Catalogue of Printed Books 1995–1996.* 27 vols. London: K. G. Saur, 1997.

British Library. *General Catalogue of Printed Books 1997–1998.* 27 vols. London: K. G. Saur, 1999.

British Library. *General Catalogue of Printed Books 1999–2000.* 27 vols. London: K. G. Saur, 2001.

British Library. *General Catalogue of Printed Books 2001–2002.* 27 vols. London: K. G. Saur, 2003.

British Library. *Subject Index of the Modern Works Added to the Library.* London: British Library, 1906–1985.

British National Bibliography. London: British Library, 1950–. http://catalogue.bl.uk/F/?func=file&file_name=find-b&local_base=BNB.

Canadian Books in Print: Author and Title Index. Toronto: University of Toronto Press, 1975–2006. Annual.

Canadian Books in Print: Subject Index. Toronto: University of Toronto Press, 1975–2006. Annual.

Canadian Catalogue of Books: Published in Canada, about Canada, as well as Those Written by Canadians, with Imprint 1921–1949. 2 vols. Toronto: Toronto Public Libraries, 1959.

Canadian Reference Sources: An Annotated Bibliography/Ouvrages de Reference Canadiens: Une Bibliographie Annotée. Compiled by Mary E. Bond and Martine M. Caron. Vancouver, BC: UBC Press in association with the National Library of Canada, 1996. 1076 pp.

Canadiana: Canada's National Bibliography/La bibliographie nationale du Canada, 1950–1991. Ottawa: National Library of Canada, 1951–1991.

Canadiana. Ottawa: National Library of Canada, 1973–2000. Microfiche.

Canadiana. Ottawa: National Library of Canada, 1998–. CD-ROM. Also available online as part of *AMICUS.*

Children's Core Collection. 20th ed. New York: H.W. Wilson, 2010. 2318 pp. Annual supplements. Also available online via WilsonWeb.

Cumulative Book Index. A World List of Books in the English Language. New York: H. W. Wilson, 1933–1999. (Coverage from 1928.)

Directory of Open Access Journals. Lund, Sweden: Lund University Libraries. http://www.doaj.org.

Early American Imprints: Series I, Evans (1639–1800). New Canaan, CT: Readex. Also available online from Readex.

Early American Imprints: Series II, Shaw-Shoemaker (1801–1819). New Canaan, CT: Readex. Also available online from Readex.

Evans, Charles, comp. *American Bibliography; A Chronological Dictionary of All Books, Pamphlets, and Periodical Publications Printed in the United States of America from the Genesis of Printing in 1639 Down to and Including the Year 1800.* 14 vols. Chicago: printed for the author, 1903–1959. Also available on CD-ROM.

Fiction Core Collection. 16th ed. New York: H. W. Wilson, 2010. 1317 pp. Annual supplements. Also available online via WilsonWeb.

Fiction Connection. New Providence, NJ: R. R. Bowker. http://www.fictionconnection.com.

Forthcoming Books. New Providence, NJ: R. R. Bowker, 1966–. Quarterly. Also available online as part of *BooksInPrint.com.*

France. Bibliothèque Nationale. *Catalogue Général des Livres Imprimés: Auteurs.* 231 vols. Paris: Impr. Nationale, 1897–1981.

France. Bibliothèque Nationale. *Catalogue Général des Livres Imprimés: Auteurs, Collectivités-Auteurs, Anonymes, 1960–1969.* 27 vols. Paris: Impr. Nationale, 1972–1978.

France. Bibliothèque Nationale. *Catalogue Général des Livres Imprimés, 1897–1959, supplement sur fiches.* Paris: Chadwyck-Healey France, 1986. 2,890 microfiche.

France. Bibliothèque Nationale. *Le Catalogue Général de la Bibliothèque Nationale de France.* Paris: Bibliothèque Nationale de France. CD-ROM

Gale Directory Library. Farmington Hills, MI: Gale. http://www.gale.cengage.com/DirectoryLibrary.

Gale Directory of Publications and Broadcast Media. Farmington Hills, MI: Gale, 1990–. Annual. (Continues *Gale Directory of Publications* and *Ayer Directory of Publications.*) Also available online as part of the *Gale Directory Library.*

GlobalBooksinPrint.com. New Providence, NJ: R. R. Bowker. http://www.globalbooksinprint.com/.

Google Books. Mountain View, CA: Google Inc. http://books.google.com/.

Graphic Novels Core Collection. New York: H. W. Wilson. Available online via WilsonWeb.

Guide to Reference. Chicago: American Library Association. http://www.guidetoreference.org.

Guide to Reference Books. 11th ed. Ed. Robert Balay. Chicago: American Library Association, 1996. 2020 pp.

International Bibliography of Bibliographies 1959–1988. 11 vols. München: K. G. Saur, 1998–2007.

Kelly, James, comp. *The American Catalogue of Books (Original and Reprints), Published in the United States from Jan. 1861 to Jan. 1871.* 2 vols. New York: John Wiley, 1866–1871.

Magazines for Libraries. 18th ed. New Providence, NJ: ProQuest, 2009. 1045 pp. Also available online as part of *Ulrichsweb.*

Middle and Junior High School Core Collection. 10th ed. New York: H. W. Wilson, 2009. 1600 pp. Annual supplements. Also available online via WilsonWeb.

The National Directory of Magazines. New York: Oxbridge, 1987–. Annual. Also available on CD-ROM and online: http://www.mediafinder.com.

National Union Catalog, Pre-1956 Imprints. A Cumulative Author List Representing Library of Congress Printed Cards and Titles Reported by Other American Libraries. 754 vols. London: Mansell, 1968–1981.

National Union Catalogs in Microfiche. Washington, D.C.: Library of Congress, 1983–2002. Irregular. (Includes *National Union Catalog: Audiovisual Materials*, *National Union Catalog: Books*, *National Union Catalog: Cartographic Materials*, *The Music Catalog*, and *National Union Catalog Register of Additional Locations.*)

New Books Service. Ottawa: Library and Archives Canada. http://www.collectionscanada.gc.ca/newbooks/index-e.html.

New Serial Titles: A Union List of Serials Commencing Publication After Dec. 31, 1949. Washington, D.C.: Library of Congress, 1953–1999.

New Walford Guide to Reference Resources. 3 vols. London: Facet, 2005–2011.

Newspapers in Microform: Foreign Countries, 1948–1983. Washington, D.C.: Library of Congress, 1984. 504 pp.

Newspapers in Microform: United States, 1948–1983. 2 vols. Washington, D.C.: Library of Congress, 1984.

Non-Fiction Connection. New Providence, NJ: R. R. Bowker. http://www.nonfictionconnection.com/

Nonbook Materials Core Collection. New York: H. W. Wilson. Available online via WilsonWeb.

NoveList Plus. Ipswich, MA: EBSCO. http://www.ebscohost.com/novelist.

Oxbridge Directory of Newsletters. New York: Oxbridge Communications, 1979–. Annual. (Continues *Standard Directory of Newsletters.*) Also available on CD-ROM and online: http://www.mediafinder.com.

Public Library Core Collection: Nonfiction. 13th ed. New York: H. W. Wilson, 2008. 1445 pp. Annual supplements. Also available online via WilsonWeb.

The Reader's Advisor Online. Westport, CT: Libraries Unlimited. http://www.readersadviso
ronline.com.

Resources for College Libraries (RCL). 7 vols. New Providence, NJ: R. R. Bowker, 2006.
http://www.RCLweb.net.

Roorbach, Orville Augustus, comp. *Bibliotheca Americana... 1820–1861*. 4 vols. New York:
Roorbach, 1852–1861.

Sabin, Joseph, comp. *Bibliotheca Americana. A Dictionary of Books Relating to America,
from Its Discovery to the Present Time*. 29 vols. New York: Sabin, 1868–1892.

Sabin Americana, 1500–1926. Farmington Hills, MI: Gale. Available online from Gale.

The Sabin Collection Catalog. Woodbridge, CT: Primary Source Media, 1997. CD-ROM.

*The Sabin Collection: Selected Americana from Sabin's Dictionary of Books Relating to
America*. Woodbridge, CT: Primary Source Media.

Senior High Core Collection. 17th ed. New York: H. W. Wilson, 2007. 1514 pp. Annual supplements. Also available online via WilsonWeb.

Shaw, Ralph R., and Richard H. Shoemaker, comps. *American Bibliography: A Preliminary
Checklist for 1801–1819*. 23 vols. New York: Scarecrow Press, 1958–1983.

Shoemaker, Richard, comp. *A Checklist of American Imprints for 1820–1829*. 10 vols. New
York: Scarecrow Press, 1964–1971. (Continued by *A Checklist of American Imprints for
1830–*. Metuchen, NJ: Scarecrow Press, 1972–.)

The Standard Periodical Directory. New York: Oxbridge Communications, 1965–. Annual.
Also available on CD-ROM and online: http://www.mediafinder.com.

Subject Guide to Books in Print. New Providence, NJ: R. R. Bowker, 1957–. Annual.

Toomey, Alice F., comp. *A World Bibliography of Bibliographies, 1964–1974: A List of Works
Represented by Library of Congress Printed Cards. A Decennial Supplement to Theo-
dore Besterman, a World Bibliography of Bibliographies*. 2 vols. Totowa, NJ: Rowman &
Littlefield, 1977.

Ulrich's Periodicals Directory, Including Irregular Serials and Annuals. 48th ed. 4 vols. Ann
Arbor, MI: ProQuest, 2010. Annual.

Ulrichsweb. Seattle, WA: Serials Solutions. http://www.ulrichsweb.com/ulrichsweb/.

Union List of Serials in Libraries of the United States and Canada. 3rd ed. 5 vols. New York:
H. W. Wilson, 1965.

United States Catalog: Books in Print. 4 vols. New York: H. W. Wilson, 1899–1928.

United States Newspaper Program National Union List. 5th ed. Dublin, OH: OCLC, 1999.
102 microfiche.

WorldCat. Dublin, OH: OCLC. Available online via FirstSearch.

WorldCat.org. Dublin, OH: OCLC. http://www.worldcat.org.

ADDITIONAL READINGS

Bell, Barbara L. *An Annotated Guide to Current National Bibliographies*. 2nd rev. ed.
München: K. G. Saur, 1998. 487 pp.

Bell's bibliography lists national bibliographies for 181 countries. The introduction includes a valuable discussion of bibliographic control, and a selective but extensive bibliography lists books, articles, and conference papers dealing with various aspects of current national bibliography.

De Beer, Joan F. "National Libraries Around the World, 2002–2004: A Review of the Literature." *Alexandria* 18 (2006): 1–39.

This literature review article is a recurring feature of *Alexandria, The Journal of National & International Library and Information Issues.*

Embleton, Kimberly, and Helen Heinrich. "Searching to Find: Opening up the World with Open WorldCat." *Searcher* 16 (February 2008): 22–25, 42–46.

The authors describe the various ways in which *WorldCat*, formerly accessible to library users only through FirstSearch, is now woven into the Web through partnerships with Google and Yahoo! Features of *WorldCat.org* and possible future developments are described.

Hall, Danielle. "Mansell Revisited." *American Libraries* 35 (April 2004): 78–80.

Hall highlights the decrease in usage of the *National Union Catalog* by U.S. libraries, coinciding with the growth of bibliographic utilities. She provides a brief history of this ambitious publication project, commenting that "even as the project progressed, the profession recognized that this 'greatest single instrument' would be the last great bibliographic effort in a paper format."

Krummel, D. W. *Bibliographies: Their Aims and Methods.* London: Mansell Publishing, 1984. 192 pp.

This basic text discusses the various types of bibliographic study and the evaluation of bibliographies.

Lawrence, John R. M. "The Bibliographic Wonder of the World: The National Union Catalog." In *Distinguished Classics of Reference Publishing*, ed. James Rettig, 161–73. Phoenix, AZ: Oryx Press, 1992.

Lawrence provides a readable account of the publishing history of the *National Union Catalog.*

Saricks, Joyce G. "Reference Sources." In *Readers' Advisory Service in the Public Library*, 3rd ed., 14–39. Chicago: American Library Association, 2005.

In this chapter Saricks offers guidelines for evaluating readers' advisory reference sources, followed by detailed descriptions of both electronic and print resources for readers' advisors. In addition to titles that must be purchased or licensed, she highlights some freely available Web-based resources such as Fiction-L. She also explains how online bookselling sites such as Amazon.com and Barnesandnoble.com may be helpful to readers' advisors.

Soper, Mary Ellen, Larry N. Osborne, and Douglas L. Zweizig. *The Librarian's Thesaurus.* Chicago: American Library Association, 1990. 164 pp.

Section B, by Soper, presents an excellent overview of the concepts of bibliography and bibliographic control.

Wyatt, Neal, ed. "A Selection of Core Resources for Readers' Advisory Service." *Reference & User Services Quarterly* 50 (Fall 2010): 6, 8–12.

This annotated bibliography of recommended readers' advisory tools is divided into multiple sections: books, key articles, blogs, Web sites, and databases.

Chapter

Indexes and Abstracts

Linda C. Smith

USES AND CHARACTERISTICS

A library's catalog, whether in card format or online, generally does not provide access to the entire contents of a library's collection. The catalog may confirm the holdings of a periodical title but not its contents, a poetry collection but not individual poems, the title of an author's collected works but not an individual essay, and newspaper titles but not individual news stories. Indexes and abstracts can more fully reveal resources not covered in the general catalog, in addition to listing additional resources not held in a given library's collection. With the availability of online catalogs and indexes and abstracts in electronic form, more efforts are being made to provide direct links between them. For example, when the user of an index locates the record of a journal article likely to be of interest, information about the library's holdings of that journal title should be directly accessible. As more material becomes available in electronic form, mechanisms for index entries to link directly to the full texts of the publications indexed are likewise being developed.

Indexes such as periodical indexes usually list the authors, titles, or subjects of publications without comment. Abstracts, on the other hand, present a brief summary of content. Most abstracts are descriptive, but a few abstracting services contain evaluative abstracts, including the abstractor's critical comments, in the summary. Many abstracting services at present rely on author abstracts (or translations thereof) rather than having staff read each article and abstract it (a very costly practice). Abstracts serve as an aid in assessing the content of a document and its potential relevance, and they continue to be valued.[1] Although indexes and abstracts existed before 1900, there was a dramatic growth in their number during the 20th century, as the scholarly community demanded improved access to a growing number of publications. The advent of the Web made it possible for libraries to subscribe to indexing and abstracting databases that the user could view over the Web.

In the first decade of the 21st century, increasing questions are being raised about the future of indexes and abstracts, especially those covering specialized subject areas.[2] A growing number of publications are available in full text online, with the entire text searchable for occurrences of the keywords sought, potentially reducing the need for document surrogates such as indexes and abstracts. Nevertheless, Dennis Auld argues that the skills of classifying, indexing, aggregating, and structuring content still are needed in the Web environment.[3] Traditional databases remain superior in their ability to describe, organize, and connect information in a consistent, structured way. Indexes and abstracts are often thought of as value-added services because a human indexer or abstractor has analyzed the document content and developed a document surrogate, including indexing terms and (often) an abstract. It is assumed that this effort benefits the user by improving retrieval performance, enabling the identification of the best set of items for the user's purposes. More research is needed to determine how searching full text compares with established indexes and abstracts (and their electronic counterparts) in their usefulness for reference work.

Publishers of indexes and abstracts are introducing a number of enhancements to better meet user needs: (1) addition of newspaper, newswire, and radio and television transcript indexing to indexes formerly limited to coverage of periodicals; (2) inclusion of abstracts in what were formerly only indexing services; (3) inclusion of at least some full-text articles in what were formerly only abstracting services; (4) marketing of different subsets of a service to meet the needs of different sizes and types of libraries; (5) creation of rich networks of links between indexes and multiple full-text resources; and (6) enhanced retrospective coverage available in electronic form. As noted in chapter 7, library users increasingly demand rapid access to full texts, and indexes and abstracts are evolving to support that. This has led to what can seem to be a bewildering array of choices for librarians seeking to make selections among competing indexes and abstracts, increasing the need for careful evaluation.

EVALUATION

As reference librarians use the tools in reference work, they evaluate indexes and abstracts and choose those that will best reveal the contents of their own collections or that will refer users to needed information beyond library walls. Important characteristics to consider are format, scope, authority, accuracy, arrangement, and any special features that enhance effectiveness or ease of use.

Many of the indexes and abstracts discussed in this chapter are devoted to a particular type of publication: periodicals, newspapers, or dissertations. More specialized services devoted to indexing and abstracting the literature of a discipline often try to encompass many different types of publications to provide more comprehensive coverage in one source. Other differences arise if there are restrictions on place and language of publication of the source materials. Some indexes and abstracts cover only English-language material; others try to identify material relevant to a particular subject area in any language and from any part of the world. There may also be differences in the level of material covered. Some indexes of science materials may focus on the popular science literature, whereas others cover the scholarly research literature. In print indexes and abstracts, introductory matter may provide a clear statement of materials covered. For electronic databases, it is necessary to rely on database descriptions found in directories or in documentation provided by the database producer or vendor/aggregator. Many publishers of periodical indexes are now posting lists of journals covered on their Web sites, making comparison among competing services easier.[4] The JISC Academic Database Assessment Tool (ADAT, http://www.jisc-adat.com/adat/home.pl) facilitates automatic comparison of lists of journals covered by different databases.

Format

As explained in chapter 5, many indexes and abstracts now exist in electronic form accessible via the Web. Some still have a print counterpart; others exist only in electronic form. The print format may still lend itself best to browsing, especially for abstracts, but the electronic forms usually have much more powerful search capabilities, with more access points and the possibility of refining searches by using Boolean logic to combine terms. Because many databases do not cover the literature before the mid-1960s, searches of indexes and abstracts for older literature must rely on the print versions for the period of interest. Although most databases contain the same records as their print counterparts, some databases include more or combine the records from several print counterparts in a single database. Thus, when comparing alternative formats for a particular index or abstract, the librarian should study available documentation to determine the extent of correspondence between the content of each format and to understand the search capabilities of each. Over the past decade, the debate in libraries over retention of print subscriptions seems to have been settled largely in favor of cancellation of print and a move toward online access instead.

The readability of entries is important, whether the index is in print or in electronic form. Indexes vary in type size, use of boldface, and other aspects of presenting entries. Extensive use of abbreviations may make the entries hard to interpret without frequent reference to lists of abbreviations and symbols elsewhere in the set.

Scope

Several characteristics define the scope of indexes and abstracts. The time covered does not necessarily coincide with the period of publication because the publisher may go back and index some older material valuable to the users of the index. For example, *Science Citation Index* has now extended its coverage back to 1900, although it originally began publication in the 1960s. Related factors are the frequency of publication and cumulation. Frequency of publication also affects currency; a monthly publication is likely to be more current than a quarterly one. Frequency of cumulation affects the ease with which retrospective searching can be done. If a print index is semimonthly but cumulates only annually, for example, then many individual issues must be searched until the annual cumulation is issued. An advantage of searching indexes and abstracts online is that the contents are automatically cumulated.

Types of materials covered are another aspect of scope. Indexes and abstracts differ in the number of publications covered and the depth or specificity of the indexing. General periodical indexes tend to index all substantive articles from the periodicals selected for indexing, whereas subject-specific indexes and abstracts are more likely to index selectively from a much larger list of periodicals, with indexers identifying those articles of most relevance to the subject scope of the service. Some indexes and abstracts are more inclusive in the types of articles indexed, indexing such things as letters to the editor and editorials, whereas other services restrict their coverage to research articles. As the number of electronic-only journals has grown, publishers of indexes and abstracts have had to develop criteria for covering such titles. As Brian Quinn notes, electronic journals may have difficulty gaining acceptance in the mainstream of academic research and scholarship unless they are covered in major indexes.[5]

Authority

Considerations in assessing the authority of indexes and abstracts are the reputation of the publisher or sponsoring organization and the qualifications of the editorial staff. Publishers of indexes include commercial firms, professional associations, and government agencies. The H. W. Wilson Company is one of the longest-established commercial firms and has a well-deserved reputation for the quality of its indexes.[6] As reference librarians use various indexes, the authority of the indexers will usually reveal itself over time.

Accuracy

The quality of indexing and accuracy of bibliographic citations affect the usefulness of indexes. Questions to consider include the following: Are all authors associated with an indexed item included in the author index? Are all major facets of the content of the article represented by entries in the subject index? Accuracy can also apply to both author and subject indexing. Author names should be spelled in the index as they are spelled in the work. Unfortunately, indexing guidelines for some indexes and abstracts dictate that only initials of given names be retained, even when a fuller form of the name appears on the original publication. This can make it difficult, when searching authors, to distinguish between different authors who share a common surname and initials. Accuracy of subject indexing depends on the indexer's ability to represent the content of a publication using terminology drawn from the controlled vocabulary to be used in indexing. Cross-references should be included where needed to lead from a form not used to the proper form or to link related terms. Some indexes include augmented titles, where the indexer supplements the original title with additional terms to characterize the article's content more completely. Abstracts should provide an accurate summary of the original article's content.

Arrangement

Arrangement of entries in print indexes or abstracts determines one possible approach to the items indexed. Although indexes generally employ an alphabetical arrangement, abstracts often appear in a classified arrangement that makes it easier to browse entries for related material. If additional indexes are present, they offer other access points to the publications indexed. Access points in print sources are generally limited to subject, author, and occasionally, title. Indexes and abstracts in electronic form generally offer many additional options for searching, such as keywords from title and abstract, journal title, and author affiliation. When accessing indexes and abstracts online, the search engine will instantly reveal the location of a term no matter where it is in an entry.

Special Features

When indexes and abstracts are evaluated, any special features that enhance their usefulness should be noted. Examples include a list of periodicals or other sources indexed and a published list of subject headings. The list of sources indexed is helpful in providing a clear indication of the materials covered as well as complete bibliographic information for those materials not available locally. This can be helpful in acquiring documents, whether ordering copies for inclusion in the library's collection or making requests through interlibrary loan or a document delivery service. A published list of subject headings can help in formulating effective search strategies in print and electronic indexes and abstracts because the user can see a comprehensive list of terms available to the indexer and thus have a better chance of locating the appropriate terms to search. This is especially the case for those lists of subject headings that include scope notes or instructions for indexers, explaining how particular terms are to be used in indexing (and hence in searching). A growing number of indexing and abstracting services are developing approaches to ease the task of locating the full text of documents covered by their services. In some cases the full text of documents is available as page images or searchable full text. Copies of other documents can be ordered directly from the indexing and abstracting service, with various alternatives for rapid delivery.

When a library subscribes to multiple indexing and abstracting databases and full-text resources, it can be a challenge to determine whether the full text of an article cited in one database is available in another resource. Link resolving software makes this task easier by creating a bridge between databases. Users easily go from a journal citation in one database to the full text of the journal article in another database.[7]

SELECTION

Indexes and abstracts are often expensive reference tools, no matter what format is selected. Selection of titles for a particular collection must take into account the characteristics of that collection as well as the needs of users for access beyond what is already provided by the library's catalog. Directories of periodicals can be used to identify available indexes and abstracts. *Ulrichsweb*, described in chapter 20, has a section on abstracting and indexing services. In addition, for each periodical covered, *Ulrichsweb* provides an indication of the indexes and abstracts that include the periodical in their coverage, meaning inclusion of at least some of the periodical's articles as entries in the index or abstract. The *Gale Directory of Databases* provides good coverage of indexes and abstracts in electronic form.

Needs of Users

Indexes and abstracts selected for a particular library collection should reflect the types of information and publications that library users wish to access. They should allow more complete use of the local collection as well as identification of publications of possible value available elsewhere. General periodical indexes and newspaper indexes could be useful in libraries of all types. Selection of periodical indexes devoted to particular subject areas will reflect the subject interests of the library's users. Citation indexes, with their emphasis on scholarly literature, will be of most use in academic and special libraries. Indexes to special types of materials are also likely to be found most often in academic and special libraries. Selection of indexes to reviews should reflect user demand for this information. Indexes to literary forms can prove useful wherever collected works and anthologies make up part of the collection. Fortunately, the availability of so many indexes and abstracts in electronic form has meant that access to at least a portion of most indexes is possible online even if the library does not have a subscription to the print version. Usage of indexes and abstracts in electronic form can be measured, providing a tool to guide the choice of which resources to retain and which to cancel when licenses come up for renewal.[8]

Cost

The discussion of alternative formats in chapter 13 identifies a number of factors affecting the cost of using indexes and abstracts in different formats. Some publishers of indexes and abstracts offer discounted pricing on a second format if one format is already part of the library's collection. A complete analysis of cost factors for each format has to take into account subscription prices, binding, and shelving costs for print copies; equipment costs for using online databases; and per-search charges or licensing costs for online access. The tradeoffs may be different for different indexes given that each publisher develops its own pricing policy. Increasingly, libraries are gaining access to electronic versions through participation in consortial licensing arrangements, which may reduce the price paid by each participating library.

In a discussion of cost of indexes, it is important to describe the service basis of charging for some of the print indexes published by the H. W. Wilson Company. To make the indexes available to the widest possible audience, such indexes are priced so that each subscriber is charged according to the amount of service provided. For periodical indexes such as *Business Periodicals Index*, *General Science Index*, *Humanities Index*, and *Social Sciences Index*, subscribers pay an amount determined by the number of indexed periodicals they hold. A library holding only a few of the indexed periodicals would pay less than a library holding most of the titles. For some book indexes, such as *Book Review Digest*, the price of the index paid by a particular library reflects that library's expenditure for books. The idea underlying this approach is that the users of a library with a large collection derive more benefit from the index than the users of a library with a small collection. This principle is also reflected in instances where online licensing rates are determined in part by the number of users served by the library, with those serving more users paying a higher rate.

Most of the major index publishers have several products, usually for different types of libraries and often different size packages, so libraries can choose which package they need and can afford. For example, the H. W. Wilson Company's *Readers'*

Guide to Periodical Literature indexes nearly 350 periodicals, whereas the same company's *Wilson OmniFile Full Text, Mega Edition* indexes nearly 3,600 periodicals.

Uniqueness

Uniqueness relates to both the coverage and the arrangement of the indexes and abstracts being considered for selection. Although overlap in sources indexed is one indicator of the degree of uniqueness of indexes, the access points and search capabilities provided by the indexes must also be considered. Two indexes could cover many of the same periodicals, but the subject indexing provided may give the user different ways of approaching the content in each. Thus, examination of overlap in materials covered must be supplemented by an assessment of the approaches provided to those materials by the different indexes.

Full-Text Coverage

Given the growing demand for the full text of periodicals, newspapers, and other publications in electronic form, criteria for selecting these resources deserve special consideration. Unfortunately, "full text" does not have a standard definition when applied to electronic publications with print counterparts. At the article level, "full text" may include the main text but not any sidebars or illustrations.[9] At the issue level, "full text" may include major articles but omit such things as letters to the editor, short columns, book reviews, and advertisements. At the journal level, one expects "full text" to cover all the issues of the publication, including any supplements. As Walt Crawford notes, these differences may result in a loss of important context for the content.[10]

Factors to consider in comparing full-text databases include which titles are covered in various subject areas (and whether any are unique, not covered elsewhere), coverage dates, currency, policy on inclusion of article types and illustrations, whether text is searchable or only displayable, indexing, output formats, and pricing. Delivery of full text in a Web environment also opens up the possibility of creating links among articles, reflecting the relationships among them.

As journal publishers experiment with the electronic medium, the situation becomes even more complex. Electronic journals now range "from simplistic (and quite old-fashioned looking) ASCII texts to complex multimedia and interactive electronic journals."[11] Because of possible differences between the electronic and print versions of the same title, indexing and abstracting services may have difficulty deciding which is the authoritative version to index. Reference librarians also need to be aware of the different models of supplying full text that have emerged in the Web environment: publisher-supplied full text; third-party or aggregator-supplied full text (e.g., *Wilson OmniFile*); and distributed, "linked" full text, in which an indexing or abstracting service links to publisher-supplied full text.[12]

IMPORTANT GENERAL SOURCES

This chapter describes some of the most widely held general periodical indexes, newspaper indexes, broad-subject periodical indexes, citation indexes, indexes for special types of materials, indexes of reviews, and indexes for different literary forms. Many other indexing and abstracting services are devoted to coverage of the literature of a specific subject area and lie outside the scope of this chapter. Selection among competing products should include evaluation of the quality of the abstracts as well as the indexing.[13]

General Periodical Indexes

General periodical indexes are held by all types of libraries. They index periodicals covering current events, hobbies, popular culture, and school curriculum–related areas. The *Readers' Guide to Periodical Literature* has filled this need since 1900.[14] In print the main body of the index consists of subject and author entries to articles from nearly 350 English-language periodicals arranged in one alphabet. Since 1976, each issue has included a listing of citations to book reviews, arranged by author of the book reviewed, following the main body of the index. An *Abridged Readers' Guide* covering 71 periodicals selected from those in the unabridged edition is available for use in school and small public libraries.

Extensive cross-references lead the user from a term not used to the proper term (for example, "Freedom of religion, *See* Religious liberty") and from a term to related terms (for example, "Freedom of speech, *See also* Freedom of the press, Libel and slander"). Specific aspects of a subject are indicated by subdivisions under the main heading. Under authors and subjects, titles are arranged in alphabetical order by the first word, disregarding initial articles. Under personal names, titles *by* an author precede those *about* an author. When titles are not sufficiently descriptive of an article's content, supplementary notes are added in brackets following the original title (as in "Free speech on the Net? Not quite [companies suing over statements made anonymously online]"). Subdivisions of a subject are arranged alphabetically under the subject, with geographical subheads following the other subdivisions in a separate alphabet. The instructions for use explain how to locate reviews of books, dance performances, motion pictures, musicals, opera, radio programs, sound recordings, television programs, and theater, together with how to locate the index entries for fiction, poems, and short stories. The subject headings try to make use of common language, so that users can easily find the topics sought.

Readers' Guide is published monthly, with quarterly cumulations and an annual bound cumulation. Since 1952, the Committee on Wilson Indexes of the American Library Association's Reference and User Services Association has advised the publisher on indexing and editorial policy for *Readers' Guide* and other Wilson indexes.[15] Complementing the coverage of *Readers' Guide*, the *Alternative Press Index*, which began publication in 1969, seeks to provide subject indexing for more than 300 journals and newspapers covering alternative or radical points of view. It is available online through EBSCO.

During the 1980s, the H. W. Wilson Company introduced a number of additions to the *Readers' Guide* family, and competitors emerged with new products taking advantage first of CD-ROM technology and now the Web. Wilson's *Readers' Guide Abstracts* provides summaries of the articles indexed in *Readers' Guide* and can be accessed online with coverage from 1983. More recently, the full text of many of the periodicals indexed has been part of online versions. For example, *Readers' Guide Full*

Text, Mega Edition has full-text coverage of more than 220 periodicals from January 1994. *Readers' Guide Retrospective: 1890–1982* enables a search of articles from 375 periodicals. *Readers' Guide* and other Wilson indexes are characterized by quality subject indexing and author-name authority control. Linda Mark and Hope Tarullo discuss the challenges in creating the *Readers' Guide Retrospective* with regard to quality and consistency of indexing.[16] The print index volumes had to be digitized, and indexing standards that had evolved over decades had to be rationalized so that the final product appears uniform and can be searched effectively and efficiently.

The other major publishers of general periodical indexes include Gale Cengage Learning (InfoTrac), EBSCO Publishing, and ProQuest. Each now markets a family of databases via the Web, with products ranging from those for school libraries to those intended for large academic and public libraries. Many of these products now provide the full text of articles from selected journals as well as citations and abstracts for articles from a larger number of journals. These competing products continue to change their coverage (both of titles indexed and of titles available in full text) and search capabilities. Therefore, librarians need to follow these developments to determine which approaches to providing access to periodicals best meet the needs of the library's users and which are affordable. Publisher Web sites are very helpful for current listings of product offerings. H. W. Wilson Company (http://www.hwwilson.com), EBSCO Publishing (http://www.ebscohost.com/), Gale Cengage Learning (http://www.gale.cengage.com), and ProQuest (http://www.proquest.com) should all be investigated. Increasingly, these databases encompass material in addition to periodicals, such as newspapers and transcripts of television and radio programs. As of early 2011, the most comprehensive multidisciplinary database offered by each of these vendors had the following coverage:

EBSCO Publishing, *Academic Search Complete*

> More than 12,500 publications indexed; more than 8,500 in full text

Gale, *Academic OneFile*

> More than 14,000 publications indexed; more than 6,000 in full text

H.W. Wilson, *Wilson OmniFile Full Text, Mega Edition*

> Nearly 3,600 publications indexed; approximately 2,200 in full text

ProQuest, *ProQuest Central*

> More than 17,000 publications indexed; more than 11,400 in full text

Comparison among these offerings should consider not only how many of their titles are full text but also how far their backfiles go, how many of their titles are unique, and how many of their titles are peer reviewed. In addition, librarians need to be aware that the most recent issues of a journal may be *embargoed*: to protect subscriptions, journal publishers may not immediately release the full text of their most recent issues for inclusion in these aggregated collections. Barbara Fister and colleagues also caution that undergraduate students in particular may be overwhelmed with retrievals from these large databases.[17]

OCLC's *ArticleFirst* also indexes a large number of periodicals (more than 16,000 with coverage beginning in 1990 and updated daily). Records are brief, including only the bibliographic information provided in the tables of contents of the journals indexed, so the database may be more useful for bibliographic verification tasks than for in-depth searching of the literature.

Google released *Google Scholar* in a beta version in 2004 to enable Web-based search of the scholarly literature. Because it is simple to use, free, and available to anyone with access to the Web, *Google Scholar* has rapidly gained in popularity. Nevertheless, a number of questions have been raised: "[*Google Scholar*] is not like the carefully structured, library-based databases we treasure."[18] Concerns include that its selection criteria for "scholarly" materials are unknown, its scope and currency are unknown, and its formatting of citations for items retrieved is very nontraditional. Recognizing that many of their users are turning to *Google Scholar* despite its potential shortcomings, librarians are partnering with Google to include links to their resources as part of *Google Scholar* search results (http://scholar.google.com/scholar/libraries.html). Research studies such as that by Chris Neuhaus and colleagues seek to compare library database coverage with *Google Scholar* to better understand its strengths and weaknesses.[19] Their comparison with 47 databases showed *Google Scholar*'s strengths at the time of their study to be coverage of scientific and medical databases, open access databases, and single publisher databases. Weaknesses included lack of coverage of social science and humanities databases and an English-language bias.

Major retrospective indexing projects are becoming available in electronic form, overcoming a longstanding weakness of most online indexes. *19th Century Masterfile* from Paratext merges entries from 19th-century indexes to periodicals, newspapers, government documents, and books into a searchable database. Where applicable, links are provided to full text available online in the HathiTrust archive (http://www.hathitrust.org/). *Periodicals Index Online* from ProQuest provides access to citations for more than 18 million periodical articles from as early as 1665 in the arts, humanities, and social sciences, including titles in several Western European languages in addition to English. Libraries can gain access to the digitized full text of hundreds of these periodicals through *Periodicals Archive Online* from ProQuest.

Although indexes like *Readers' Guide* include some magazines of interest to children, other products are targeted specifically at children. Examples include EBSCO's *Primary Search*, a full-text database covering more than 80 popular, elementary school magazines; EBSCO's *Middle Search Plus*, with the full text of more than 140 popular, middle school magazines; *InfoTrac Junior Edition*, with 300 indexed journals, of which 230 are full text; and *InfoTrac Student Edition*, with 1,200 indexed journals, of which 1,100 are full text. In addition to the journal content, these resources include supplementary reference material useful to students such as encyclopedias, dictionaries, almanacs, and biographical sources.

Two indexes provide good coverage of Canadian periodicals. *CPI.Q*, or *Canadian Periodicals Index Quarterly*, available from Gale, indexes nearly 1,200 Canadian periodicals (both English and French), with full text from more than 550 periodicals. This resource also covers more than 130 newspapers, including the *Toronto Star* and *The Globe and Mail*, as well as reference material related to Canada. *Canadian Business & Current Affairs (CBCA) Complete* combines full text and indexed content from four *CBCA* database subsets (Business, Current Events, Education, and Reference). Coverage includes full text of nearly 600 periodicals and daily news sources (over 480 of which are Canadian), plus indexing to an additional 1,100 other titles (over 95% Canadian).

As library users become more diverse, libraries need to consider databases in languages other than English. Gail Golderman and Bruce Connolly review several Spanish-language and Latin American studies sources,[20] including *¡Informe!* from Gale, which covers more than 420 Spanish-language and bilingual periodicals and newspapers.

Newspaper Indexes

General periodical indexes include coverage of the major news magazines and selected newspapers, thus offering some access to information on current events at the national and international level. Many library users also want access to more extensive newspaper coverage of national and international topics, as well as regional and local news. The effect of technology on newspaper indexing has been considerable. Well-established newspaper indexes are now supplemented with indexes and abstracts online and an increasing number of full-text newspapers in electronic form. More recently, the Web has developed into a rich and diverse source of current news. These changes have made it possible to make much fuller use of news sources in answering reference questions, especially those on current events.

Gale (*InfoTrac Newsstand*), ProQuest (*ProQuest Newsstand*, *ProQuest Historical Newspapers*), and EBSCO Publishing (*Newspaper Source*) all offer coverage of newspaper resources. *InfoTrac Newsstand* provides access to more than 1,700 major U.S. regional, national, and local newspapers as well as leading titles from around the world. *ProQuest Newsstand* has indexing and abstracting for more than 900 newspapers, with more than 850 in full text. Both U.S. newspapers and titles from around the world are included, and libraries can select which titles to subscribe to. *ProQuest Historical Newspapers* offers digital archives of the full run of major national (e.g., *New York Times*), international, and black newspapers. *Newspaper Source* contains the full text of more than 40 national and international newspapers as well as selective full text for more than 370 regional (U.S.) newspapers. In addition, full-text television and radio news transcripts are included for several major broadcast networks. *Newspaper Source Plus* expands coverage to include more than 860 full-text newspapers as well as a large number of radio and television news transcripts. Other vendors providing access to news databases via the Web include *NewsBank* (http://www.newsbank.com), *LexisNexis* (http://www.lexisnexis.com), *Dialog* (http://www.dialog.com), and *Factiva* (http://www.factiva.com).

Publishers are creating other specialized online products to complement coverage of indexes for general newspapers. For example, *Ethnic NewsWatch* from ProQuest is a full-text database with articles from more than 330 ethnic newspapers and magazines published in the United States, including African American, Caribbean, Hispanic, Native American, Asian American, Jewish, Arab American, Eastern European, and multiethnic publications. Nearly one-fourth of the articles are in Spanish. Coverage begins with 1990; *Ethnic NewsWatch: A History* provides coverage for the period 1959–1989.

At present, news sources freely available on the Web are most valuable for the access they provide to very current news from around the world.[21] Newspapers, newsmagazines, wire services, and broadcast networks are among the sources of news on the Web. Useful directory sites for locating news sources include Newslink (http://newslink.org), NewsVoyager (http://www.newspaperlinks.com/voyager.cfm), and *ipl2*'s newspaper collection (http://www.ipl.org/div/news/).

Google has also entered the arena of providing access to news with its *Google News* service. As with *Google Scholar*, the range of sources indexed is not known. When a user searches for a topic, the News Archives section of the site creates a time line showing the distribution of the articles found for that topic over time.

Broad-Subject Periodical Indexes

When the scope of a library's periodical collection exceeds that of the coverage of a general periodical index, the library should acquire one or more additional indexes. One index commonly found in public and academic libraries is *PAIS International*. It contains citations to journal articles, books, government documents, statistical directories, research reports, conference reports, publications of international agencies, and more. *PAIS International* includes publications from more than 120 countries throughout the world, with coverage back to 1977. Entries include English-language abstract-like notes and indications of special features, such as maps, charts, tables, and bibliographies. The scope of *PAIS* includes public policy, business, legal, economic, social science, and related literature. In introducing a library user to this index, it is helpful to point out the types of publications indexed, given that different strategies may be needed to locate periodicals, books, and documents in the library's collection. For users seeking to go back further in time, *PAIS Archive* covers the period from 1915–1976.

The H. W. Wilson Company publishes indexes to periodicals in a variety of subject areas, such as *Social Sciences Index*, *Humanities Index*, and *General Science Index*, supplementing the coverage of general periodicals provided by *Readers' Guide*. One or more of these indexes are likely to be found in academic, public, and special libraries, with the choice depending on the subject strengths of the collection and interests of the library's users. They are all limited to English-language periodicals but include some titles published outside the United States. Selection of periodicals for indexing is accomplished by subscriber vote, with an emphasis on the reference value of the periodicals under consideration. An effort is made to give consideration to subject balance. Details of subject scope and lists of journals covered can be found at the H. W. Wilson Company Web site. As with *Readers' Guide*, the electronic versions of the subject indexes are now being augmented with abstracts and full text. For example, *Wilson Business Abstracts* began publication in 1991, the first of the Wilson subject titles to offer abstracts as an enhancement of the electronic version. *Wilson Business Full Text* now offers the full text of more than 500 periodicals back to January 1995 and indexing and abstracting of more than 900 publications as far back as 1982. Although ProQuest, Gale, and EBSCO Publishing have emphasized multidisciplinary indexing and full-text products, they also have databases covering more specific subject areas. For example, Gale's *Business and Company ASAP*, ProQuest's *ABI/INFORM*, and EBSCO Publishing's *Business Source Complete* are rich sources of business journal literature as well as related reference material.

The relative value of general periodical indexes, periodical indexes with a more specific subject focus, and Web resources will vary by discipline. As Erik Nemeth suggests, different types of tools are likely to be complementary in value for discovery of scholarly literature.[22] Specialized subject databases emphasize metadata in the form of abstracts and indexing, full-text databases support keyword searching and document access, and Web search engines enable discovery of material on Web pages.

Citation Indexes

The periodical indexes described thus far allow the user to find articles written by the same author or indexed under the same subject heading. Citation indexes allow the user to locate items based on a different type of relationship: the links created when authors cite earlier works by other authors (or even some of their own previously published works). The primary use of a citation index is to find, for a particular publication known to the searcher, later items that have cited it. Thomson Reuters publishes three indexes that allow the user to carry out such searches in broad subject areas: *Science Citation Index*, *Social Sciences Citation Index*, and *Arts & Humanities Citation Index*, searchable singly or in combination online as *Web of Science*. Coverage includes journals and chapters in some multiauthored books.

All three citation indexes are international in scope, covering many journals published outside the United States as well as the major U.S. titles in each subject area. *Science Citation Index* now covers the period back to 1900; *Social Sciences Citation Index* goes back to 1956; *Arts & Humanities Citation Index* goes back to 1975. Citation networks are an inherently hypertext approach to navigating the literature. *Web of Science* has three types of internal links among records in the database: "cited references" lead to the items cited by a publication (going backward in time), "times cited" links lead to the items citing a publication (going forward in time), and "related records" identify other publications that have overlapping items cited with the publication of interest. *Web of Science* also provides external links to the full text of journal articles indexed in the database.[23] If the library subscribes to a given journal, then the user can link from the record in *Web of Science* to the full text of the journal article.

The dominance of *Web of Science* in the citation searching arena has now been challenged by both fee-based and freely available resources. Elsevier's *Scopus* has particular strengths in coverage of the scientific and medical literature but also covers journals in the social sciences. Some discipline-specific indexes as well as full-text journal databases have introduced citation-searching capabilities. Finally, *Google Scholar* includes a "cited by" link as part of the bibliographic information for items retrieved through a search. Péter Jacsó cautions that citation counts displayed in *Google Scholar* are often in error because they are generated automatically and not through the careful editorial process exercised in compiling *Web of Science* and *Scopus*.[24] Yet *Google Scholar* has merit in retrieving citations made by documents not readily found elsewhere, such as online theses, technical reports, and course syllabi. There is a growing body of literature comparing the features and retrieval effectiveness of these various tools for citation searching.[25] An exhaustive search for cited references requires searching more than one resource.

BOX 21.1
SEARCH STRATEGY: IS GOOGLE MAKING US STUPID?

An education student recalled having heard part of an interview on National Public Radio a couple of years ago with the author of an article titled "Is Google Making Us Stupid?" He could not recall the name of the author or where the article had appeared, but he was curious to find out whether others felt the author's arguments were sound. He was having difficulty thinking of search terms that would locate what he wanted. He e-mailed the question to his college library's e-mail reference service. The librarian who handled the question recognized *Web of Science* as a likely tool for such a search, but she first needed to verify the bibliographic information for the original article. Doing a title word search in *ArticleFirst*, she found the original article by Nicholas Carr in *Atlantic Monthly*, July 2008, beginning on page 56. Completing a cited reference search in *Web of Science* using "Carr N" as the cited author and 2008 as the cited year and looking for entries for *Atlantic Monthly* as the cited work, she found that the article had been cited 28 times by subsequently published articles with titles such as "Digital natives and ubiquitous information systems" and "Exploring relationships between traditional and new media literacies: British preteen texters at school." She e-mailed the student instructions on how to repeat the cited reference search and navigate the links in *Web of Science* and encouraged him to contact the reference desk again if he had further questions.

Indexes for Special Types of Materials

The indexes discussed thus far in this chapter provide good coverage of periodicals and newspapers but are not helpful for gaining access to some other special types of materials that may be important in certain library collections. Academic library users frequently want access to dissertations. Indexes devoted to these and other special types of materials, such as conference proceedings and research reports, can be useful for both collection development and reference work. This section describes the indexes for dissertations. Other indexes to special materials are described in more specialized guides to reference sources, such as books on patent searching.[26]

Students have been earning doctoral degrees in U.S. universities for almost 140 years. Research for the doctorate is reported in dissertations, many of which are deposited with ProQuest UMI Dissertation Publishing in Ann Arbor, Michigan, to enable their use outside the institution in which the research was originally completed. The *ProQuest Dissertations and Theses Database* provides bibliographic information for theses from around the world since 1861 and full text for most dissertations since 1997. The record for each dissertation published since July 1980 includes an abstract written by the author. Increasingly, universities are encouraging students completing a dissertation to deposit it in electronic form, as described at the Networked Digital Library of Theses and Dissertations Web site (http://www.ndltd.org). Nancy

Herther presents a helpful overview of trends in production of and access to theses and dissertations.[27]

Indexes of Reviews

Reference librarians may be asked to assist the user in locating reviews of books. Although periodical indexes such as *Readers' Guide* can sometimes help with such requests, it may be more efficient and effective to use indexes specifically designed for this purpose. Three tools available to libraries include H. W. Wilson's *Book Review Digest*, Gale's *Book Review Index Online*, and EBSCO's *Book Index with Reviews*. *Book Review Digest*, with coverage since 1905, provides excerpts of and citations to reviews of current juvenile and adult fiction and nonfiction in the English language. It continues to be published in print but is more easily consulted online, where it exists in two parts: *Book Review Digest Retrospective: 1905–1982*, covering 300,000 books, and *Book Review Digest Plus*, with coverage from 1983 forward. For the current database, contents include at least a citation to every book review that appears in one of the more than 5000 journals indexed by H. W. Wilson. Excerpts from reviews or full reviews are included for many books. *Book Review Index Online* contains entries for reviews of books, periodicals, books on tape, and electronic media from 1965 to the present. Citations are drawn from thousands of periodicals and newspapers. *Book Review Index Online Plus* supplements more than 800,000 of the citations with full-text reviews. *Book Index with Reviews* includes citations for reviews of thousands of books, music, and DVD and video titles, with more than 800,000 reviews in full text. Of course, there are several freely available sources of book reviews on the Web, including online bookseller sites such as Amazon (http://www/amazon.com) and Barnes and Noble (http://www.barnesandnoble.com) and a range of sites identified by AcqWeb (http://www.acqweb.org/book_review). The book review index databases identified in this section remain valuable for the wide range of sources of book reviews that they index and for their retrospective coverage of books both in and out of print.

Indexes for Different Literary Forms

Library collections in school, public, and academic libraries generally include many collected works: poetry anthologies, collections of plays or short stories, and collections of essays. Unless the contents of these volumes are analyzed during the cataloging process and the analytical entries made searchable directly in the library's catalog, the user of the catalog cannot easily determine whether the library holds an anthology that includes a particular play, short story, poem, or essay. The H. W. Wilson Company publishes three indexes that provide access to the contents of collections by author and subject: *Essay and General Literature Index*, *Play Index*, and *Short Story Index*. *Essay and General Literature Index* is an author and subject index to essays published in collections, with particular emphasis on materials in the humanities and social sciences. It is published semiannually, with an annual cumulation. *Essay and General Literature Index* is now online in two parts: a retrospective index covering the period 1900–1984 and a regularly updated index for the period from 1985 forward.

Play Index is published at several-year intervals. The most recent volume, *Play Index 2003–2007*, indexes nearly 3,000 plays that were published during the period 2003–2007. The index covers both individual plays and plays in collections, written in or translated into English. Plays are tagged with *c* for children (through grade 6) or *y* for young people (grades 7 through 12), when those designations apply. The index can be searched by authors, titles, subjects, or dramatic styles. A cast analysis index helps one locate plays by number of characters and their gender. For separately published plays, bibliographic information is given; for plays in collections, the name of the collection is identified. This tool can be used to identify plays meeting certain requirements, such as subject and cast composition, as well as to identify one or more collections containing a play when the title or author is known. Past volumes of the index have been compiled as an online database with coverage back to 1949.

Short Story Index appears annually, with five-year cumulations (the most recent covering 2005–2009). The indexed stories appear in collections and periodicals. The short stories are indexed by title, author, and subject in a single alphabetical listing. *Short Story Index* is now online in two parts: a retrospective index covering the period 1915–1983 and a regularly updated index for the period from 1984 forward. All three of these indexes to literary forms may be helpful in collection development as well as in reference, given that order information is provided for the indexed collections.

In their online format, all three of these indexes have linking capability, so that essays, plays, and short stories available in digital form in a library's collection can be linked to the corresponding entry in one of the indexes. H. W. Wilson has also provided links from these indexes to full-text public domain material available on the Web.

Indexes to poetry anthologies are comparable to the indexes to collections in providing author, title, and subject indexing. In addition, indexes such as *The Columbia Granger's Index to Poetry in Anthologies* also index poems by first line and last line because that may be the information the user remembers rather than the poem's title.[28] The most recent edition of *The Columbia Granger's* indexes anthologies published through May 31, 2006. Coverage includes 85,000 poems by 12,000 poets. Several of the anthologies are collections of poetry translated from other languages, and for the first time, the index covers poems published in Spanish, Vietnamese, and French. Because the most recent edition does not cover all anthologies indexed in the previous editions, the latter should be retained to allow access to poems found only in older anthologies.

Online, *The Columbia Granger's World of Poetry* includes 250,000 poems in full text in English and other languages and 450,000 citations. Search options include title, first line, last line, full text, subject, and author. Other reference material includes biographies and bibliographies on poets and commentaries on poems. Gale's *LitFinder* provides a repository of full-text literature including 150,000 full-text poems; 880,000 additional poem citations and excerpts; 6,400 full-text stories; 3,800 full-text essays; 1,250 full-text plays; and 2,400 full-text speeches, as well as related reference material. Basic search includes keyword, title, author, or subject options, and advanced search provides additional options such as character name and literary movement.

SEARCH STRATEGIES

In performing searches of indexes and abstracts and in guiding library users in search strategy development, today's reference librarian must be able to locate the appropriate databases and take full advantage of the search capabilities. This requires a sophisticated understanding of specifics regarding content, organization, and interface. Almost anyone can find something from an electronic index without any knowledge of searching. It requires skilled searching to find precisely what is needed rather than everything with the same general descriptor.

The reference interview is an important part of assisting library users in accessing indexes and abstracts. Many users may be familiar only with Google or other Web search engines. As a starting point for database selection, it is important to determine the subject of interest and direct the user to the most appropriate indexes for the subject and type of material desired. Because online databases are often limited in the time period covered, library users must be aware that using only these tools for literature searching may lead to inadequate coverage of the published literature.

If a library user is in search of an article that is known to have appeared in a certain periodical, but for which no other information is available, the librarian can consult an index or abstract that covers the periodical in order to identify the complete bibliographic information and possibly a link to the full text. The entry for the periodical in *Ulrichsweb* provides notations to indicate coverage by indexes and abstracts. Because many indexes and abstracts cover periodical titles only selectively, it may be necessary to look in more than one index to find the particular article sought. Indexes may also differ in time lag for indexing the same article. For topical searches, it is likewise necessary to identify the index or indexes most likely to provide the best coverage of the topic. As noted in chapter 5, individual libraries are developing gateways and portals to offer some guidance in database selection.

For the first-time user of an index in print or electronic form, some instruction may be necessary. This is also an opportunity to advise on search strategy. It may also be necessary to explain how to interpret the various components of a bibliographic citation as well as how to locate materials in the library's collection. Chapters 4 and 5 provide additional discussion of search strategies for indexes and abstracts in both print and electronic form. Knowing the scope of the various indexes and abstracts is essential in selecting the most appropriate sources when verifying a citation or searching for information on a subject. Awareness of the conventions used by a particular database for author indexing is essential to doing a thorough search for works by an author. Familiarity with the approaches to subject indexing used in each index or abstract is necessary to select the sources most likely to have the terminology required in searching a particular subject. If the librarian is unfamiliar with the topic sought, it may be necessary first to check reference books such as encyclopedias and dictionaries to develop a list of related terms under which to search. As noted in chapter 4, indexing vocabularies are not standardized, so it may be necessary to reformulate a subject search when checking multiple indexes and abstracts. Access to online sources allows the use of terms appearing in titles and/or abstracts in addition to terms selected from controlled vocabularies.

Recognizing that library users may be accessing library resources, both in the library and remotely, without the assistance of reference librarians, many libraries are implementing some type of *federated searching* (also known as metasearch, parallel search, broadcast search, or cross-database search).[29] This approach provides the ability for search and retrieval to span multiple databases, search systems, and vendors at one time, merging the results of these simultaneous searches. Because federated searching cannot take advantage of unique features in particular databases, most expert searchers prefer to exploit the specific access points and search features provided by individual databases in order to produce thorough, comprehensive searches. As Miriam Drake observes, "effective information finding...requires users to know the type and quality of required information, to have extensive knowledge of sources, to understand how to build effective search strategies, and to have the experience to evaluate results."[30] Knowing that user needs vary, the librarian should seek to understand the kind and quality of information desired by the user before starting an index search. If the user just wants general, nonscholarly articles on a subject, then multidisciplinary periodical and newspaper indexes are places to begin. Should the user's interest be more specialized, however, the librarian can assist the user in finding appropriate subject-based indexes and developing strategies to exploit their capabilities.

BOX 21.2
SEARCH STRATEGY: EARTH DAY

A college student in an environmental policy class came to the reference desk looking frustrated. She explained that she was trying to locate sources that would be useful in writing a paper comparing the first Earth Day celebration with Earth Day 2010. She had tried some Web searching using Google but was overwhelmed with the amount of material that was retrieved when she searched on "Earth Day." She had also tried the "easy search" option (a federated search capability) on the library's home page but still was getting far too many matches to wade through. The librarian checked the Infoplease.com Web site and confirmed that the first Earth Day celebration took place on April 22, 1970; April 22, 2010, was the 40th anniversary. He explained that most databases had limited retrospective coverage, so she might need to use print indexes to locate material contemporary with the first Earth Day.

Together they reviewed the categorized lists of databases available through the library's online gateway. Under General Interest, the librarian pointed out that the student might be interested in exploring the discussion of Earth Day 2010 events in a range of databases with varying perspectives. He suggested that *Ethnic Newswatch* and EBSCO's *Academic Search Complete* would be good starting points for Earth Day 2010. He showed her how to limit the search to 2010 and search for "Earth Day" as subject. *Ethnic Newswatch* included articles from African American, Spanish-language, and Native

American publications; *Academic Search Complete* included both newspapers and periodical articles and President Barack Obama's statement on the 40th anniversary of Earth Day from the *Daily Compilation of Presidential Documents*. For material on the original Earth Day, he turned to *Readers' Guide Retrospective: 1890–1982*, this time limiting the search to 1970 and searching on the subject "Earth Day." This yielded several relevant articles in general magazines. Checking the library's online gateway for the list of journals and newspapers in full text showed that the library had full retrospective coverage of the *New York Times*. A search for articles published on "Earth Day" in 1970 turned up images of relevant article texts and even display ads. The librarian also did a subject search on the online catalog for "Earth Day," finding a biography, *The Man from Clear Lake: Earth Day Founder Senator Gaylord Nelson* (2004), including a chapter on the history of Earth Day. As an active member of the American Library Association, the librarian was aware that ALA's Social Responsibilities Round Table (SRRT) included a Task Force on the Environment. He entered the URL for the ALA Web site (http://www.ala.org) and quickly found the home page for SRRT (http://www.ala.org/ala/mgrps/rts/srrt/srrt.cfm), which had a link for the Task Force on the Environment. That page included an entry for "Earth Day" under Key Issues. This led to a "CyberExhibit" commemorating the 40th anniversary of Earth Day, which included a number of helpful links to other Web resources. Satisfied that she had several promising leads to resources for her paper, the student went to one of the public terminals to spend time exploring the electronic sources in more depth.

NOTES

1.   David Nicholas, Paul Huntington, and Hamid R. Jamali, "The Use, Users, and Role of Abstracts in the Digital Scholarly Environment," *Journal of Academic Librarianship* 33 (July 2007): 446–53.

2.   Xiaotian Chen, "The Declining Value of Subscription-Based Abstracting and Indexing Services in the New Knowledge Dissemination Era," *Serials Review* 36 (June 2010): 79–85; Valerie Tucci, "Are A&I Services in a Death Spiral?," *Issues in Science and Technology Librarianship* 61 (Spring 2010). http://www.istl.org/10-spring/viewpoint.html.

3.   Dennis Auld, "The Future of Secondary Publishing," *Online & CD-ROM Review* 23 (June 1999): 173–78.

4.   Xiaotian Chen, "Overlap between Traditional Periodical Indexes and Newer Mega Indexes," *Serials Review* 32 (December 2006): 233–37.

5.   Brian Quinn, "Mainstreaming Electronic Journals through Improved Indexing: Prospects for the Social Sciences," *Serials Review* 25 (June 1999): 23–34.

6.   *The H. W. Wilson Company: A Centennial Celebration 1898–1998* (Bronx, NY: H. W. Wilson, 1998), 25 pp.

7.   Doris M. Munson, "Link Resolvers: An Overview for Reference Librarians," *Internet Reference Services Quarterly* 11, no. 1 (2006): 17–28.

8.   International Coalition of Library Consortia, "Guidelines for Statistical Measures of Usage of Web-Based Indexed, Abstracted, and Full-Text Resources," *Information Technology & Libraries* 18 (September 1999): 161–63; Oliver Pesch, "Ensuring Consistent Usage Statistics, Part 1: Project COUNTER," *Serials Librarian* 50, nos. 1–2 (2006): 147–61.

9.   Xiaotian Chen, "Figures and Tables Omitted from Online Periodical Articles: A Comparison of Vendors and Information Missing from Full-Text Databases," *Internet Reference Services Quarterly* 10, no. 2 (2005): 75–88.

10.   Walt Crawford, "Here's the Content—Where's the Context?," *American Libraries* 31 (March 2000): 50–52.

11.   Carol Tenopir, "Should We Cancel Print?," *Library Journal* 124 (September 1, 1999): 138.

12.   Bette Brunelle, "Quieting the Crowd: The Clamour for Full Text," *Online & CD-ROM Review* 23 (1999): 297–302; Larry Krumenaker, "'A Dillar, a Dollar . . .' Where's That Article, Scholar?," *Searcher* 7 (September 1999): 36–40; Carol Tenopir, "Linking to Full Texts," *Library Journal* 123 (April 1, 1998): 34–36.

13.   Carol Tenopir and Péter Jacsó, "Quality of Abstracts," *Online* 17 (May 1993): 44–55.

14.   Mary Biggs, "'Mom in the Library': *The Readers' Guide to Periodical Literature*," in *Distinguished Classics of Reference Publishing*, ed. James Rettig (Phoenix, AZ: Oryx Press, 1992), 198–210.

15.   Charles R. Andrews, "Cooperation at Its Best: The Committee on Wilson Indexes at Work," *RQ* 24 (Winter 1984): 155–61.

16.   Linda Mark and Hope Tarullo, "Technology and the Transformation of Abstracting and Indexing Services," *Serials Review* 29, no. 3 (2003): 213–20.

17.   Barbara Fister, Julie Gilbert, and Amy Ray Fry, "Aggregated Interdisciplinary Databases and the Needs of Undergraduate Researchers," *portal: Libraries and the Academy* 8 (July 2008): 273–92.

18.   William Badke, "Google Scholar and the Researcher," *Online* 33 (May/June 2009): 47–49.

19.   Chris Neuhaus, Ellen Neuhaus, Allen Asher, and Clint Wrede, "The Depth and Breadth of Google Scholar: An Empirical Study," *portal: Libraries and the Academy* 6 (April 2006): 127–41.

20.   Gail Golderman and Bruce Connolly, "Spanish Online," *Library Journal, netConnect Supplement* 131 (October 15, 2006): 18–26.

21.   Greg R. Notess, "Searching for Current News," *Database* 22 (June/July 1999): 57–60; Peter Williams and David Nicholas, "The Migration of News to the Web," *Aslib Proceedings* 51 (April 1999): 122–34.

22.   Erik Nemeth, "Complementary Value of Databases for Discovery of Scholarly Literature: A User Survey of Online Searching for Publications in Art History," *College & Research Libraries* 71 (May 2010): 223–35.

23.   Helen Atkins, "The ISI Web of Science—Links and Electronic Journals," *D-Lib Magazine* 5 (September 1999). http://www.dlib.org/dlib/september99/atkins/09atkins.html.

24.   Péter Jacsó, "Metadata Mega Mess in Google Scholar," *Online Information Review* 34, no. 1 (2010): 175–91.

25.   Stephanie Ballard and Marcia Henry, "Citation Searching: New Players, New Tools," *Searcher* 14 (October 2006): 24–33; Nancy K. Herther, "Web-Based Tools for Citation Data

Management," *Searcher* 16 (May 2008): 18–21, 50–54; Christoph Neuhaus and Hans-Dieter Daniel, "Data Sources for Performing Citation Analysis: An Overview," *Journal of Documentation* 64, no. 2 (2008): 193–210.

26.   David Hunt, Long Nguyen, and Matthew Rodgers, eds. *Patent Searching: Tools & Techniques* (Hoboken, NJ: Wiley, 2007), 188 pp.

27.   Nancy K. Herther, "Dissertations and Research in an Era of Change," *Searcher* 18 (March 2010): 22–35.

28.   Milton H. Crouch, "'Of Permanent Use and Usefulness': *Granger's Index to Poetry*," in *Distinguished Classics of Reference Publishing*, ed. James Rettig (Phoenix, AZ: Oryx Press, 1992), 113–16.

29.   Alexis Linoski and Tine Walczyk. "Federated Search 101," *Library Journal, netConnect Supplement* 133 (Summer 2008): 2–5

30.   Miriam A. Drake, "Federated Search: One Simple Query or Simply Wishful Thinking?," *Searcher* 16 (July/August 2008): 22–25, 61–62.

LIST OF SOURCES

ABI/INFORM. Ann Arbor, MI: ProQuest. Available online via ProQuest.

Abridged Readers' Guide to Periodical Literature, 1935–. New York: H. W. Wilson, 1936–. Monthly except June–August, with quarterly and annual cumulations. Available online as part of *Readers' Guide to Periodical Literature*.

Academic OneFile. Farmington Hills, MI: Gale. Available online via InfoTrac.

Academic Search Complete. Ipswich, MA: EBSCO Publishing. Available online via EBSCOhost.

Alternative Press Index. Chicago, IL: Alternative Press Center, 1969–. Semiannual. Available online via EBSCOhost.

ArticleFirst. Dublin, OH: OCLC. Available online via OCLC FirstSearch.

Arts & Humanities Citation Index. Philadelphia: Thomson Reuters. Available online as part of *Web of Science*.

Book Index with Reviews. Ipswich, MA: EBSCO Publishing. Available online via EBSCOhost.

Book Review Digest. New York: H. W. Wilson, 1905–. Monthly except February and July, with quarterly and annual cumulations.

Book Review Digest Plus. New York: H. W. Wilson. Available online via WilsonWeb.

Book Review Digest Retrospective: 1905–1982. New York: H. W. Wilson. Available online via WilsonWeb.

Book Review Index Online. Farmington Hills, MI: Gale. Available online via InfoTrac.

Book Review Index Online Plus. Farmington Hills, MI: Gale. Available online via InfoTrac.

Business and Company ASAP. Farmington Hills, MI: Gale. Available online via InfoTrac.

Business Periodicals Index. New York: H. W. Wilson, 1958–. Monthly except August, with quarterly and annual cumulations. Available online via WilsonWeb.

Business Source Complete. Ipswich, MA: EBSCO Publishing. Available online via EBSCOhost.

Canadian Business and Current Affairs (CBCA). Ann Arbor, MI: ProQuest. Available online via ProQuest.

The Columbia Granger's Index to Poetry in Anthologies. 13th ed. Ed. Tessa Kale. New York: Columbia University Press, 2007. 2416 pp.

The Columbia Granger's World of Poetry. New York: Columbia University Press. http://www.columbiagrangers.org/.

CPI.Q, Canadian Periodical Index Quarterly. Farmington Hills, MI: Gale. Available online via InfoTrac.

Essay and General Literature Index, 1900–. New York: H. W. Wilson, 1934–. Semiannual with bound annual and five-year cumulations. Available online via WilsonWeb.

Essay and General Literature Index Retrospective: 1900–1984. New York: H. W. Wilson. Available online via WilsonWeb.

Ethnic NewsWatch. Ann Arbor, MI: ProQuest. Available online via ProQuest.

Ethnic NewsWatch: A History. Ann Arbor, MI: ProQuest. Available online via ProQuest.

Gale Directory of Databases. Volume 1: *Online Databases*. Volume 2: *CD-ROM, DVD, Diskette, Magnetic Tape, Handheld, and Batch Access Database Products*. Farmington Hills, MI: Gale, 1993–. Semiannual. Available online as part of the *Gale Directory Library*.

General Science Index. New York: H. W. Wilson, 1978–. Monthly except June and December, with quarterly and annual cumulations. Available online via WilsonWeb.

Google News. http://news.google.com.

Google Scholar. http://scholar.google.com.

Humanities Index. New York: H. W. Wilson, 1974–. Quarterly with annual cumulations. (Formerly *International Index*, 1907–1965; *Social Sciences and Humanities Index*, 1965–1974.) Available online via WilsonWeb.

¡Informe! Farmington Hills, MI: Gale. Available online via InfoTrac.

InfoTrac Junior Edition. Farmington Hills, MI: Gale. Available online via InfoTrac.

InfoTrac Newsstand. Farmington Hills, MI: Gale. Available online via InfoTrac.

InfoTrac Student Edition. Farmington Hills, MI: Gale. Available online via InfoTrac.

LitFinder. Farmington Hills, MI: Gale. Available online via Gale.

Middle Search Plus. Ipswich, MA: EBSCO Publishing. Available online via EBSCOhost.

Newspaper Source. Ipswich, MA: EBSCO Publishing. Available online via EBSCOhost.

Newspaper Source Plus. Ipswich, MA: EBSCO Publishing. Available online via EBSCOhost.

19th Century Masterfile. Austin, TX: Paratext. Available online via Paratext.

PAIS Archive. Ann Arbor, MI: ProQuest. Available online via ProQuest.

PAIS International. Ann Arbor, MI: ProQuest. Available online via ProQuest.

Periodicals Archive Online. Ann Arbor, MI: ProQuest. Available online via ProQuest.

Periodicals Index Online. Ann Arbor, MI: ProQuest. Available online via ProQuest.

Play Index, 1949–. New York: H. W. Wilson, 1953–. Irregular with multiyear volumes. Available online via WilsonWeb.

Primary Search. Ipswich, MA: EBSCO Publishing. Available online via EBSCOhost.

ProQuest Central. Ann Arbor, MI: ProQuest. Available online via ProQuest.

ProQuest Dissertations and Theses Database. Ann Arbor, MI: ProQuest. Available online via ProQuest.

ProQuest Historical Newspapers. Ann Arbor, MI: ProQuest. Available online via ProQuest.

ProQuest Newsstand. Ann Arbor, MI: ProQuest. Available online via ProQuest.

Readers' Guide Abstracts. New York: H. W. Wilson. Available online via WilsonWeb.

Readers' Guide Full Text, Mega Edition. New York: H. W. Wilson. Available online via WilsonWeb.

Readers' Guide to Periodical Literature, 1900–. New York: H. W. Wilson, 1905–. Monthly with quarterly and annual cumulations. Available online via WilsonWeb.

Readers' Guide Retrospective: 1890–1982. New York: H. W. Wilson. Available online via WilsonWeb.

Science Citation Index. Philadelphia: Thomson Reuters. Available online as part of *Web of Science*.

Scopus. Amsterdam, The Netherlands: Elsevier. http://info.scopus.com.

Short Story Index, 1900–. New York: H. W. Wilson, 1953–. Semiannual with annual and five-year cumulations. Available online via WilsonWeb.

Short Story Index Retrospective: 1915–1983. New York: H. W. Wilson. Available online via WilsonWeb.

Social Sciences Citation Index. Philadelphia: Thomson Reuters. Available online as part of *Web of Science*.

Social Sciences Index. New York: H. W. Wilson, 1974–. Quarterly with annual cumulations. (Formerly *International Index*, 1907–1965; *Social Sciences and Humanities Index*, 1965–1974.) Available online via WilsonWeb.

Ulrichsweb. Seattle, WA: Serials Solutions. http://www.ulrichsweb.com/ulrichsweb/.

Web of Science. Philadelphia: Thomson Reuters. Available online via Thomson Reuters Web of Knowledge.

Wilson Business Abstracts. New York: H. W. Wilson. Available online via WilsonWeb.

Wilson Business Full Text. New York: H. W. Wilson. Monthly. Available online via WilsonWeb.

Wilson OmniFile Full Text, Mega Edition. New York: H. W. Wilson. Available online via WilsonWeb.

ADDITIONAL READINGS

Andrés, Ana. *Measuring Academic Research: How to Undertake a Bibliometric Study.* Oxford: Chandos Publishing, 2009. 169 pp.

This books offers a guide to the many analyses that could be included in bibliometric studies, including author and journal citation analysis. Such studies rely on citation indexes as their data sources.

Broderick, James F., and Darren W. Miller. *Consider the Source: A Critical Guide to 100 Prominent News and Information Sites on the Web.* Medford, NJ: Information Today, 2007. 457 pp.

Reflecting the proliferation of news sites available via the Web, this book provides in-depth critical reviews of sites that have achieved prominence and that provide content that is largely freely available. Coverage includes sites from different parts of the world, such as Al Jazeera and BBC.

Cleveland, Donald B., and Ana D. Cleveland. *Introduction to Indexing and Abstracting*. 3rd ed. Englewood, CO: Libraries Unlimited, 2001. 283 pp.

The authors describe the types of indexes and abstracts, indexing and abstracting methods and procedures, and index evaluation. New chapters in this edition cover indexing and the Internet as well as Web resources for indexers and abstractors.

Lancaster, F. W. *Indexing and Abstracting in Theory and Practice*. 3rd ed. Champaign: University of Illinois, 2003. 451 pp.

Intended as a text for students in library and information science, this book reviews indexing and abstracting theory together with a discussion of practice and sample exercises. Evaluation of indexes and abstracts is also emphasized. Chapters new to this edition cover multimedia and Internet sources.

Mann, Thomas. *The Oxford Guide to Library Research*. 3rd ed. New York: Oxford University Press, 2005. 293 pp.

Several chapters in this guide provide helpful discussions on search strategy for effective use of indexes and abstracts in both print and electronic form. See in particular the chapters on "Subject Headings and Indexes to Journal Articles," "Keyword Searches," "Citation Searches," and "Related Record Searches."

Tenopir, Carol, Gayle Baker, and Jill Grogg. "Feast and Famine: More and Better Choices, but Belt-Tightening Forces Libraries to Cut Subscriptions." *Library Journal* 135 (May 15, 2010): 32–38.

The latest in an annual survey of fee-based information companies highlights trends and provides comparative data about their offerings.

Wellisch, Hans H. *Glossary of Terminology in Abstracting, Classification, Indexing, and Thesaurus Construction*. 2nd ed. Reston, VA: American Society of Indexers, 2000. 77 pp.

The *Glossary* defines terms used in texts on abstracting, indexing, classification, and thesaurus construction, as well as terms for the most common types of documents and their parts. The definitions are derived from several authoritative sources.

Chapter

22

Government Information and Statistics Sources

Eric Forte and Mary Mallory

INTRODUCTION

Government information is often considered a unique and separate area of reference service. Government documents have their own classification schemes, their own Internet domains, and sometimes their own departments and librarians. Most importantly, they have their own mission. Although other publishers and information providers aim to educate, enlighten, entertain, and make a profit, governments publish to inform and serve their citizens and to publicly document their activities.

Governments operate in nearly every discipline that is of importance or interest to their citizenry, and government documents and information cover nearly every imaginable topic. These sources are used by the general public, statisticians, social workers, scientists, students, retirees, teachers, politicians, parents—in short, by anyone who has a need for information. Nearly every library, regardless of its type, size, or location, uses government information.

For several reasons, government information is an increasingly important aspect of general reference work, rather than a specialty. Although government information specialists remain part of the librarianship landscape, changing government information distribution patterns (government information free on the Web) and evolving service attitudes have increasingly brought government information sources and service to the general reference desk. The reference skills discussed thus far in this text, combined with familiarity with several specialized government information tools and superior knowledge of civics, lay the foundation for providing excellent reference service using government information.

GOVERNMENT INFORMATION: A BRIEF HISTORY

Government information can be said to have existed forever. Governments used to record and communicate their actions on animal hides, on stone tablets, through the oral tradition, and so forth. But the United States, with its unique representative democracy (by the people, for the people...), took the idea of government information further: because the people were governing themselves, they had a right and a need to be informed about their government's activities.[1]

The U.S. Constitution contains the first mention of U.S. government information, calling on Congress to keep and publish a journal of its proceedings.[2] By 1795, Congress was distributing copies of laws to the states, and in 1813, it passed the first law authorizing systematic printing of government materials. At this time, just about all federal government information went through Congress, given that executive agencies, when reporting on their activity, would submit their reports to Congress. This material was published in a large set called the *United States Serial Set*.[3] The *Serial Set* was a shifting composition of congressional publications, messages and communications from the president and other executive agencies, or anything else chartered or commissioned by Congress and was the primary vehicle for publishing and distributing *all* federal government information. Soon, documents and the *Serial Set* began to be distributed more widely to states, historical societies, and universities, in an early version of the system of distributing government information to locations throughout the country via depository libraries, ideally never located too far from any particular citizen.

In 1895, the General Printing Act advanced this idea much further: it streamlined and expanded the arrangement into a system called the Federal Depository Library Program (FDLP), through which documents were distributed, free of charge, to designated libraries throughout the nation.[4] This act also mandated the creation of a catalog of all such documents, the first effort at systematic, ongoing bibliographic control of government documents, because by this time, more and more executive branch documents were being printed separately from the *Serial Set*.

Over the next century, the federal government itself expanded quickly, and with it the amount of government information. The system of distribution via depository libraries also continued to mature. It is worth noting that although public access to the material may have been considered implicit, it was not until 1962 that Congress passed a law specifically requiring depository libraries to allow all members of the public to have access to these documents.[5]

The third century of government information has seen more profound evolution. The bicentennial era (1976–1977) saw the beginnings of nonprint formats, primarily microfiche, and the evolution of cataloging: all bibliographic records for government documents began to be included in the Online Computer Library Center (OCLC) database, laying the grounds for bibliographic integration of government documents into regular library catalogs. Of course, the most significant evolution of this third century has occurred in the last 15 years, as government agencies distribute most of their information directly to citizens via the Web rather than through printed documents sent to depository libraries.

USES AND CHARACTERISTICS

U.S. government documents are officially defined as "informational matter which is published as an individual document at Government expense, or as required by law."[6] Basic government information sources include the laws and official records of government entities, such as the *Congressional Record*, the *United States Code*, the *Federal Register*, the *Public Papers of the President*, and the *United States Reports*. Government information also includes information of a more administrative nature, such as the *Annual Report of the Department of Energy* or *Foreign Per Diem Rates* for federal employee travel. In the course of carrying out their responsibilities, government agencies often produce demographic and economic data, such as reports from the *United States Census of Population and Housing*, the *Statistical Abstract of the United States*, and *Economy at a Glance*. Government information may be technical or scholarly in nature, as in the case of the myriad research included in U.S. Geological Survey's *Bulletins* and *Professional Papers*, or technical reports about aeronautics and physics from NASA. Many documents are informational matter for general use by citizens, such as *Chances Are You Need a Mammogram: A Guide for Midlife and Older Women* or *How To Apply for Social Security Retirement Benefits*; the suite of databases available via the Environmental Protection Agency's *Where You Live*; or the *Catalog of Federal Domestic Assistance*, which lists federal funding sources and opportunities for municipalities.

On a significantly smaller scale, state governments produce a similar variety of state government information. So do local governments, foreign-country governments, and intergovernmental organizations (IGOs), such as the United Nations (UN) and the European Union, although the output of all of these entities varies greatly and always pales in volume comparison with that of the U.S. federal government.

Historically, federal government documents were published and printed by the U.S. Government Printing Office (GPO), the official printer for the federal government. During the printing process, GPO would print extra copies of each document, which were sent to depository libraries in the FDLP. This arrangement survives to this day, although in a drastically reduced form, because the Internet age has led to the publication of most government information online, often directly by the producing agency. The percentage of current federal government information available online is extremely high, and trending ever-closer toward 100 percent. GPO, meanwhile, continues a rapid transformation away from physical printing. Although "essential" titles[7] are still printed by GPO as before, GPO is increasingly moving its emphasis to discovery and stewardship of government information, regardless of format. GPO is continuing to work hard in the areas of identification of materials, cataloging and metadata, preservation, and ensuring perpetual access to government information in all formats.[8]

This chapter focuses on current strategies for discovering, locating, and using government information. It also discusses the most indispensable government documents and information sources. U.S. federal government information sources are stressed, with further sources and tools from nongovernmental or commercial sources discussed as appropriate. Selected state and intergovernmental sources, such as the UN, are also discussed, and Canadian government information is covered in its own section. Because governments are arguably the most important publishers of statistics, another section of the chapter introduces the reader to strategies and resources for statistical reference service. Strategies for reference service using government information and statistics are discussed throughout.

Organization of Documents

Federal government documents in physical formats use a unique classification system called the Superintendent of Documents system, referred to as SuDoc. Unlike Dewey or Library of Congress, the SuDoc system is based not on subject area, but on issuing agency. Class numbers are based on agency, subagency, and publication type. For example, the SuDoc number for the *County and City Data Book*, C3.134/2:C83/2/2007, is constructed as follows:[9]

C	Department of Commerce
3.	Bureau of the Census
134/:	*Statistical Abstract of the United States*
2:	Supplement
C 83/2	*County and City Data Book*
2007	2007 edition

SuDoc numbers are devised and assigned by GPO. Although some libraries classify and integrate their documents into their regular collections using the Library of Congress or Dewey classification schemes, the SuDoc system is universal and used in many standard bibliographies, such as *Catalog of United States Government Publications*, *ProQuest Statistical Insight*, and *PAIS International*. A library user often can identify a government document and its SuDoc number via one of these bibliographies or indexes and then find that document in libraries across the country without having to check local catalogs. For the print government documents collection, the system also allows the user to browse an agency or subagency's publications and allows the librarian to eliminate one step in the cataloging process. The classification system chosen will, to some extent, determine how the collection is used and the extent to which reference service is provided by documents specialists or by general reference staff. Libraries with a separate documents collection arranged by SuDoc, for example, may be more likely to have a separate service point for the documents collection.

Most states and some intergovernmental entities (notably the UN) and foreign governments use their own classification system. A librarian's decision to use these classification systems or to add these items to regular Library of Congress or Dewey collections may be based on numerous factors, including how many of these items a library collects and their level of use. However, in an era of ever-tightening budgets and ubiquitous online access, printed state government documents are decreasing in number even faster than federal government documents.

Acknowledging that in this Internet age the vast majority of recent government information is now online, how important are SuDoc numbers today? No clear answer has yet been given to this question. Obviously, most government information (200+ years of it) predates the Internet age, is only available in print, and is arranged by call number, often SuDoc. Interestingly, because federal government information is not under copyright, its great potential for mass digitization projects is beginning to be realized.[10] Emerging projects are beginning to digitize large runs of historical government documents. GPO itself has proposed a massive historical digitization project, as yet unfunded. The most significant current project is the nonprofit HathiTrust Digital Library, which is believed to hold more than one million government document items in digital form. *Google Books* also includes copies of these government documents, although questions remain when those that digitize are private companies, rather than the government itself. As of 2010, documents in *Google Books*, despite their status as non-copyrighted, are largely unavailable to the public, and their future remains unclear.[11] Digitization is discussed further in the section on "Web Search Engines."

Although the SuDoc system is used for paper, microfiche, and CD-ROM formats, the rules and policies for classifying online government information continue to evolve. URLs for government Web sites contain no unique style beyond generally using the ".gov" domain.[12] But again, the public domain nature of all federal government information can create situations where non–.gov sites, perhaps a university or even a private company, may host digital versions of government documents. Though not considered to be official, authoritative versions, such digital versions may in reality be more than sufficient.

GPO is aggressive in its cataloging of government documents found on government Web sites. And several specialized search engines, especially that of USA.gov and Google U.S. Government Search, mine the Internet for government-only information. Use of standard catalogs, bibliographies, and Web search tools is discussed later in this chapter.

Uses of Government Information

Librarians rely on a broad range of federal government information, including Web sites, directories, yearbooks, handbooks, bibliographies, indexes and abstracts, geographical sources, and others, both in print and online, to answer factual questions about the government, its personnel, its activities, and the nation. Government information also contains a wealth of historical and current information about the country and its citizens. Many of these government documents are among the most important primary sources in their fields.

Often, users need government information as the primary source material documenting our government's activities. For instance, tracing legislation, finding laws, and researching actions of the president or executive agencies all make use of primary source government information. Many reference questions involve statistics. As discussed later in detail, the U.S. federal government compiles more statistical data than any other entity in the world, and many questions require using government information.

Another major category of reference use of documents is bibliographic verification, or supplying bibliographic information about a particular document. The question may take the form of "What is the *Serial Set* volume number of House Document 91-102?" or "What series includes the title *House Bat Management*?" Similarly, government reports are cited daily in newspapers and news sources, and the government information librarian may be asked to find the original source document. Standard government information catalogs and, increasingly, general tools such as Web search engines can identify current known-item requests.

Some government documents are indexed only in highly specialized tools, such as *ProQuest Congressional* or the Department of Energy's *Energy Citations Database* of energy-related technical reports. The librarian will need to understand when a Web search engine may provide a good chance of success and when specialized tools must be used (given that general Web search engines such as Google are still sometimes incapable of finding certain types of government information).

Government information reference work may require an instructional component. Because certain bibliographic tools are specific to particular genres of government information, users may be unfamiliar with the content, organization, and best approaches to using any given tool. Government information librarians frequently find themselves in the position of teaching library users about unique reference sources and helping them to acquire government information access skills. Time may be spent teaching some basics about the organization and operation of government (a mini-civics class), knowledge of which is often necessary to most clearly explain government information. Instructional guides on numerous topics, prepared by government librarians throughout the United States and Canada, have been compiled and made available via the GODORT Handout Exchange, an ongoing project of the Education Committee of the Government Documents Round Table (GODORT) of the American Library Association (ALA). This is a good place to begin to learn about specific components of documents reference work or about specific resources.

EVALUATION

Government information may be the only authoritative source on a subject. There may be no similar sources with which to compare its currency and accuracy. The *2010 United States Census of Population and Housing*, the 23rd decennial census, is an example. No other census or statistical survey contains the breadth and scope of this massive undertaking done to count the U.S. population. However, because the federal government is the largest collector of statistical data in the world, many trade publishers obtain their data from government sources. They then repackage it, perhaps abridge or enhance the data, offer the data online or in other electronic media, or add special features such as expanded indexing, data manipulation, a better interface, or a variety of added features and "mashups." For instance, the privately produced *SimplyMap* does wonderful things with census data. Evaluation of reference tools from the government or use of government data, therefore, depends mainly on comparing features, format, indexing, ease of use, and price, as well as the inclusion of complete and accurate citations to the original sources. Government-funded research and its report literature and administrative records of government agencies also present unique and original information. Geologists working for the U.S. Geological Survey (USGS), for example, have conducted much of the original research in American geology; as such, the government documents of the USGS are just as important to many geologists as are the standard scholarly journals in geology.[13] Likewise, much of the cutting-edge research in energy and aeronautics is also government information. These considerations must be accounted for in the evaluation process.

Additionally, materials may still be published in paper, microfiche, and electronic formats and are listed in distinct bibliographies, catalogs, and databases or are discovered using search engines. The materials budget, space constraints, and user demand, as well as the quality of the pertinent bibliographic tools, can influence choices to continue to receive, and to retain, certain titles in tangible formats.

Commercially published reference sources that provide background, present additional factual information, and offer analyses on politics, socioeconomic matters, and public officials help to supplement the vast array of government-produced information tools. For instance, a user interested in legislation might prefer the *CQ*

Weekly, a weekly magazine that surveys current public policy, significant legislation, and other activities of Congress and includes major votes and other activities, to the often-more-difficult task of wading through the primary source materials found in *THOMAS*, a legislative research system discussed later in the chapter. As with any reference source, the government information librarian must always take into account the needs of the library's users when making choices regarding government and government-related materials.

Government information should be evaluated as to its nature and purpose. For instance, most government information is by nature designed to be strictly factual and may be taken for accurate. Proceedings, records, and most statistical undertakings are relatively straightforward, and the research involved is done by career staff and scientists. Other government information, but perhaps less than one might think, is potentially subject to disagreement, depending on politics and interpretations of specific issues.

SELECTION

The dramatic reduction of government information in print format has clearly altered the nature of selection and acquisition of government information. The traditional method of acquiring government documents was for a library to be part of the FDLP, through which some 1,300 depository libraries would select "classes" (a designation for a particular series or type of publication from a particular government entity) of items and receive the items from GPO at no cost. The law required libraries to house and retain the materials and make them available to the general public.[14] GPO continues to produce a number of "essential titles" in print, and these titles are indeed sufficiently essential that depository libraries will generally want to receive them.

The number of print-only government documents is fast dwindling, and most federal government information is on the Internet, free, and generally accessible to all with online access. So selection of government information by depositories is becoming a two-part process: first, identify which titles beyond the essential titles need to be received in print versions; and second, identify what online government information requires localized discovery tools.

Because of the preponderance of online government information, one could make the statement that every library is now a depository library or, more, that every Web-connected computer or device is a depository library. Although this increased access is why government information is now more important to all reference librarians, depositories still must make selection decisions. Those decisions now have as much to do with whether the depository library wants records for free electronic documents in their local catalogs, with electronic versions potentially linked to print holdings. The future of library catalogs themselves affects this issue, as emerging Web-scale discovery systems generally include records from items from GPO.[15] Linda Ennis addresses these issues of managing a depository library in this new era in her book *Government Documents Librarianship: A Guide for the Neo-Depository Era*.

In an informal sense, government information selection is still not significantly different from any other selection process: one must be aware of the needs of local users. Although every depository will want to own the essential titles, decisions of what else to acquire are informed by local needs. Librarians in rural libraries located among public lands might make sure they are receiving in print, if available, pertinent publications from the U.S. Forest Service or the Bureau of Land Management. Similarly, librarians in the Delaware suburbs of Philadelphia might want to make sure they receive *Census of Population and Housing* volumes not only about Delaware but about Pennsylvania and Maryland as well. When items are electronic-only, libraries will use similar logic to decide whether they would like local catalog records for particular electronic documents. Although the basic government information sources are easily identified and are discussed later in this chapter, the less common sources needed by users of a particular library have to be identified through librarians' alertness and sensitivity to their users' needs.

USING IMPORTANT GOVERNMENT INFORMATION SOURCES

Government-produced reference sources fall into many categories. The remainder of this chapter addresses the following topics, outlining major sources and strategies for using the information in reference work:

- *General guides*, or descriptive surveys of government information and its use, which are essential tools for the initial and continuing education of the government information librarian
- *General facts and directories*, including many standard, ready-reference resources related to government information
- *Web search engines*, which have an ever-increasing importance and have in many instances all but replaced some of the traditional indexes and bibliographies, especially for known-item searching
- *General catalogs and bibliographies*, the standard indexes to government publications
- *Specialized catalogs, indexes, bibliographies, and directories*, which provide comprehensive coverage to some aspect of government information outside the reach of general government information discovery tools and Web search engines
- *Periodical indexes*, covering the numerous governmental products that index periodical content both within and outside of the government
- *Law and legislative information*, a frequently needed type of government information with unique strategies and resources
- *Statistical sources*, which, because governments compile and publish more numerical data than anyone else, are a key resource for all reference librarians
- *Canadian government information*, including guides, catalogs and indexes, factual/directory information, legislative documents, and statistical sources for Canada

General Guides: Learning Government Information Reference Strategies

Guides to government information are useful both to newcomers to government information and to librarians who need to know when and how to use a particular source. For example, when library users need to know details about an 18th-century report, a legislative document from the current Congress, or 30 years of data on the gross domestic product, and librarians are uncertain about which source to consult for help in answering those questions, they can turn first to a guide.

Guides may provide information about government in general, publication practices of government agencies, and details about coverage of important sources. Even veteran government-documents librarians make frequent use of guides, which often serve as library and information science textbooks as well. Web search engines are nearly always useful, yet the most important knowledge for providing reference service related to government information remains knowledge of civics and awareness of specific information products and patterns of specific government agencies. These guides all provide surveys of key government sources and needs.

As of 2011, there is a delay in the publication of new, up-to-date, comprehensive guides to government information, although that is expected to change very soon with publication of both original guides and updated versions of some of the titles discussed in the following paragraphs.

Jean L. Sears and Marilyn K. Moody's *Using Government Information Sources* (3rd ed.) is arguably the single most comprehensive survey of government information sources. It offers actual search strategies for locating more than 50 different categories of government information. Unique in its encyclopedic coverage, this thorough volume can be used as a map for finding key reference sources for scores of specific needs. Each themed chapter provides comprehensive coverage of the essential resources in that subject area. When reference librarians receive questions that call for use of government sources, they can consult one or two chapters for an overview of the major, classic sources in that particular subject. As with the other sources in this section, this guide does not always have the most up-to-date information about online versions of these sources. However, the titles and strategies referenced are often similar in print or online formats and remain accurate.

Notable textbook treatments of government documents are highlighted by Joe Morehead's *Introduction to United States Government Information Sources*, a long-time standard government documents textbook; Peter Hernon's *United States Government Information: Policies and Sources*; and Judith Schiek Robinson's *Tapping the Government Grapevine: The User-Friendly Guide to U.S. Government Information Sources*, an excellent and very popular short text. Each of these textbooks covers major sources and strategies, as well as discussions of trends and characteristics of government information and its dissemination.

Government publications of other countries are covered in the valuable *Guide to Official Publications of Foreign Countries*, compiled by ALA/GODORT's International Documents Task Force.[16] A long-standing handbook to UN information, the European Union, and other international organizations is *International Information: Documents, Publications, and Electronic Information of International Governmental Organizations*, edited by Peter I. Hajnal. A most welcome addition to the realm of government information guides is Andrea Morrison and Barbara Mann's *International Government Information and Country Information: A Subject Guide*, which offers a subject-based approach, not unlike Sears and Moody, to sources from both international organizations and foreign governments.

All of these publications can be used both for collection development (identifying major publications by country or organization) and for reference. For instance, often a particularly detailed statistic about a foreign country may not be available in any of the expected sources (as noted in the later "Statistical Sources" section); one might then consult the aforementioned books to attempt to identify a more esoteric foreign or international source.

A volume similar to the previously discussed guides for federal and international government information exists for local and regional government information: *Local and Regional Government Information: How to Find It, How to Use It*, edited by Mary Martin. Perhaps most useful is *Tapping State Government Information Sources*, in which a number of expert authors detail the key publications and state government information climate for *each* of the 50 states.

Another useful approach to learning about government information, especially in the era of mass government information online, is to brush up on one's civics. A solid understanding of the missions of various government agencies and the types of information they provide informs wise use of a Web search engine. One great way to review these civics is to use the official handbook of the federal government, the *United States Government Manual*, discussed in detail in the next section. This civics-based strategy to learning potential government information sources can also be aided by a number of the other directories covered in the next section, especially the USA.gov directory and the *Federal Agency Directory*.

General Facts and Directories

The standard way to obtain information about the federal government is to consult its official handbook, the *United States Government Manual*, which has been published annually since 1935 and which is online. Normally, a new edition is released in late summer. The *Manual* describes the federal government (see Figure 22.1) and provides mission statements, descriptive information, organizational charts (see Figure 22.2), and directory information for legislative, judicial, and executive agencies and offices, as well as for independent boards, commissions, committees, and quasi-official agencies. Entries cover dates of establishment, key personnel, major subagencies, and programs and services. It is a convenient source for locating contacts, including those for public information inquiries and regional offices.

Federal government agency Web sites may be just as useful, more up-to-date, and more convenient. Many agency Web sites include similar descriptive information and details, such as a staff directory and agency mission, although coverage is not consistent across agencies and is sometimes nonexistent. An excellent, comprehensive directory to government Web sites, arranged hierarchically and alphabetically, is *Federal Agency Directory*, a joint project of the GPO's FDLP and Louisiana State University Libraries.

The U.S. General Services Administration is responsible for a third federal resource that functions as the primary portal to federal government information online, as a government services directory, and as a reference tool and also points to basic directory information. USA.gov was begun as Firstgov.gov by entrepreneur Eric Brewer in 2000 and, after some uncertainty, became the official single portal to federal government information (the E-Government Act of 2002 further pushed

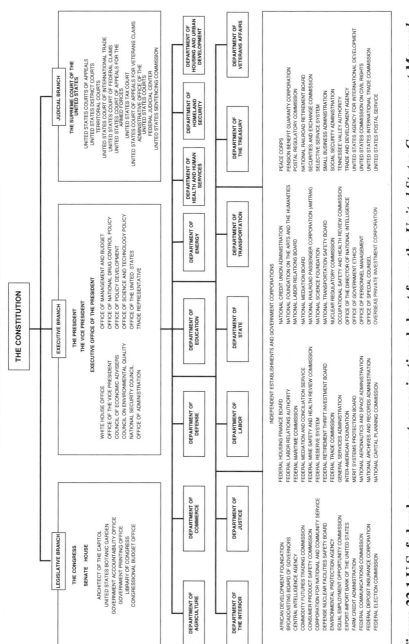

Figure 22.1 U.S. federal government organizational chart from the *United States Government Manual*.

DEPARTMENT OF HOMELAND SECURITY

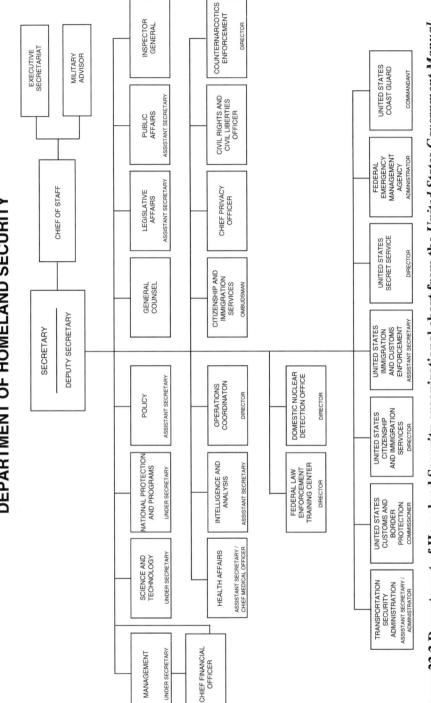

Figure 22.2 Department of Homeland Security organizational chart from the _United States Government Manual_.

development of government Internet sites and services and effectively served to provide funding for, and legitimize, USA.gov). It became known as USA.gov in 2007. USA.gov offers subject-based access to government information, as well as a series of in-depth, user-friendly portals aimed at seniors, students, exporters, workers, small businesspeople, and people with disabilities, to name a few. It also provides access to state, local, and tribal government Web sites. It is organized centrally by broad topics, such as "Consumer Guides," "Jobs and Education," "Science and Technology," and "Travel and Recreation," to name a few. Convenient interactions with government are facilitated. "Shop Government Auctions," "Passport Application," "Flu Clinic Locator—Get Your Flu Shot," and "Loans—GovLoans.gov" are examples illustrative of its service-delivery focus. USA.gov features specialty portals for "Citizens," "Businesses and Nonprofits," "Government Employees," "Seniors," "Military and Veterans," and "Visitors to the U.S." USA.gov also includes a Spanish-language version.

Many federal depository libraries listed in the *Federal Depository Library Directory* (FDLD) create agency or subject Web lists with current links for their institution's primary clientele. These can also be used as directories, and librarians and other users of government information may find the local or nearest depository's Web site to be of particular use for their purposes. A number of model Web sites are in existence that have fairly extensive directory-style links. One is the award-winning site developed by the University of Michigan Documents Center, which offers federal, foreign, international, local, and state links. Another is the ALA/GODORT Federal Documents Task Force's set of Web pages, "Frequently Used Sites Related to U.S. Federal Government Information."

The Web sites of Congress (http://www.house.gov and http://www.senate.gov) are a rich source of directory information as well, although they too can be inconsistent in their coverage, generally relying on individual representative and senator Web sites for directory information. The traditional government handbook that covers Congress is the comprehensive, biennial *Official Congressional Directory*. It can be thought of as a directory *for use by* members of Congress, as well as *about* the Congress. A major portion of this one-volume tool (also available online) provides brief biographies and committee appointments of senators and representatives and directory information for them, their office staff, and congressional committee staff. It includes descriptions and maps of congressional districts and ZIP codes. Although the *United States Government Manual* presents useful descriptions of agencies and their programs, the *Official Congressional Directory* usually provides more personnel information.

Various other directories are published commercially, so unlike nearly all sources discussed in this chapter, they are not free online or available via the FDLP. They provide directory information deeper than is provided free online. Some are descriptive, such as the *Washington Information Directory*, which includes brief information about the programs or purpose of an agency or congressional committee, as well as the address and telephone number and the names of directors or committee members and staff. The *Washington Information Directory* also covers nongovernmental groups interested in federal activities; these include associations, lobbying organizations, and foundations. A Congressional Quarterly (CQ) annual publication, it has been produced since 1975–1976 and is now also available via online subscription. CQ has a number of other useful titles in its directory series, including the *Congressional Staff Directory*, the *Federal Staff Directory*, and the *Judicial Staff Directory*.

Carroll Publishing and Leadership Directories, Inc. are two other excellent publishers of government information directories. The Carroll series constitute phonebooks more than the directory concept. Each publisher has federal, regional, state, and municipal and/or county government directories. In cases where only local government information is required, a Web site may provide a quick, no-fee answer, although coverage may be incomplete. If broader-based information is required on, for example, different geographical locales or political jurisdictions, these subscription services, in print, online, or both, may be preferable.

In addition to these comprehensive directories, individual federal agencies sometimes publish their own directories, phonebooks, guides, or handbooks that give the user more detailed information about the programs, services, and organization of an agency and that also may provide factual material for reference purposes. An example is the *Social Security Handbook*, which tells what the Social Security Administration programs encompass and how to apply for benefits. Other examples are *General Information Concerning Patents* (U.S. Patent and Trademark Office) and the *Occupational Outlook Handbook* (Bureau of Labor Statistics), which is revised every two years. The former describes the process of patenting, in a question-and-answer format. The latter provides detailed descriptions of occupations and careers, informing the user about preparation for that career, salary expectations, job descriptions, job prospects, and where to obtain additional information.

The preceding titles are only a few examples of an enormous variety of sources useful in answering factual, ready-reference questions such as the following: "How can I determine if my invention is already patented?" "Do I need a master's degree to be a medical technologist?" "I'd like to contact my congressional representative at her office in Washington, D.C. Can you give me the phone number?" "What was Frederick Law Olmsted's involvement with the Capitol site?"

Most state governments publish directories to their state government agencies and officials. Like their federal counterparts, state agency Web sites contain directory and other factual information, which is in some cases extensive. Common-sense Web searching should turn these up, although useful, freely accessible lists of links to state government Web sites include *State and Local Government on the Net*. That said, *Book of the States*, published biennially, offers a wealth of factual information about individual states in one place that is unmatched online. *Book of the States* is the standard ready-reference source to check for recent information on state officials, state legislatures, and the state judiciary, as well as on state elections and finances. Whether seeking information on the qualifications of secretaries of state, the methods for the removal of judges and filling of vacancies, or allowable state investments, this source is the place to start. Tables abound: state excise tax rates, motor vehicle laws, and time-series data on state minimum wages are examples. State mottoes, flowers, songs, birds, and so forth are also given.

For international and foreign governments and organizations, an excellent guide is the print and online *Worldwide Government Directory with International Organizations*. This is especially useful because finding equivalent information free online for foreign government entities can be difficult or impossible. This directory provides names, addresses, and telephone numbers for foreign governments and their major agencies, as well as major international intergovernmental organizations, from the UN to the North Atlantic Treaty Organization (NATO). Still, collections of Web links for other national-level governments, such as those at the "International Documents/Foreign Governments" section of the Northwestern University Library Government and Geographic Information and Data Services Department Web site, are certainly useful.[17]

Linking users to the government information they require can occasionally involve making referrals to other government information specialists or to specific collections of government information. The *Federal Depository Library Directory* is useful for this. Of course, the best thing about knowing one's fellow government documents specialists is being able to call on their expertise, which can also be tapped by using electronic mailing lists such as GOVDOC-L. As with all reference transactions, the cardinal rule in government information reference situations is "If you can't answer the question or find the source, ask a colleague."

All of these directories, in addition to providing information, can serve as important instructional tools for the librarians doing government information reference. As mentioned previously, a solid knowledge of civics related to government information publishing—that is, having a basic understanding of which agencies produce what types of information—is key to successful and efficient use of government information discovery tools of all types.

Web Search Engines

Web search engines have become absolutely key sources for identifying and finding government information. As mentioned previously, the civics-and-Web-search approach is increasingly the best method for identifying government information. USA.gov, the earlier-discussed government information directory, indexes millions of government Web pages at all levels of government. Google's U.S. Government Search service also indexes government Web pages (despite its name, it also includes state and local governments). Each one of these is generally excellent for known-item searches and has good potential for subject searching, with some significant exceptions: several major categories of government information remain outside the reach of search engine indexing (for instance, some of the technical reports servers), or their nature usually does not lend itself to discovery via a general search engine (bills and bill status, laws and codes, and specific statistical information). So although typical, recent government monographs that appear on government Web sites are usually somewhat easily found using these search engines (and, increasingly, historical documents through services such as HathiTrust), many types of government information require knowledge of, and skills with, the specialized sources to be discussed later in this chapter.

Armed with a title of a government publication, a librarian can make extremely effective use of Google U.S. Government Search and USA.gov, not to mention a general Web search engine. One might also use them to quickly get to the Web sites of agencies and programs. More difficult is using these sites for subject searching, but with current government information, most of the material is online and free. Google U.S. Government Search benefits from the popularity of the Google search engine. It does an excellent job for known-item searches and known-agency searches. USA.gov's search engine is generally not as successful at returning the desired result to the top of the results list, but real-world testing has shown numerous examples where each of these two services is more successful than the other.

As alluded to earlier in the chapter, digitization projects are revolutionizing discovery strategies for government documents. Right now, a general Web search engine does a great job with current government information, and is fast becoming a viable discovery method for an increasing amount of historical government documents through HathiTrust. Efforts to digitize historical documents continue to change the nature of searching, as almost overnight, thousands upon thousands of historical government documents are being digitized and hopefully made freely available perpetually. Because federal government publications are (with few exceptions) not copyrighted, government information avoids the murky copyright issues surrounding mass book digitization efforts; yet, as in the case of *Google Books*, access is not necessarily open (see note 11). So a mass digitization project could and hopefully will someday enable a Web search engine to quickly discover the full text of federal government documents right back to the beginning of the nation.

GPO itself is working on large-scale digitization projects. The vision is to have hundreds of thousands of legacy documents, eventually approaching everything ever published by the government, in online versions and hosted by the federal government or its partners (under agreements to ensure public access without restriction), all accessible from the traditional catalogs and with the advantages of standard cataloging.[18]

Notably, both USA.gov and Google U.S. Government Search also include state government information. They do not, as of 2011, include foreign or international government information. Although a general search engine may be useful in finding and identifying foreign and international government information, it is also often necessary to consult general catalogs (see next section) or to simply browse the official foreign government's Web pages (see note 17).

General Catalogs and Bibliographies

General catalogs and bibliographies serve an important role in responding to government reference needs. They will continue to have at least some role even in the rosiest of digitization/metadata/harvesting scenarios, especially in their function as a conduit to scores of historical government documents, right from 1790 until today. Because of indexing and cataloging, catalogs are often superior to a Web search engine. Also, understanding these basic tools means understanding much of the nature of government publishing, knowledge necessary for authoritative work with government information, even when a search engine provides the answer itself. Finally, general catalogs often provide the only bibliographic access to the two centuries of government information that predate the Web age.

Catalogs and bibliographies are used to identify what publications a government agency or department has produced, to find out what the government has published on certain subject matter, to determine format of publication, and to understand historical publishing patterns. Catalogs generally include Web addresses for online sources and SuDoc numbers for print format items. They may also indicate the depository status of an individual title or series, which can be consulted to determine the likelihood of locating the item in a particular depository print collection.

The basic bibliographic tool for federal documents is the *Catalog of United States Government Publications*. Although it does not include all unclassified documents, the *Catalog* represents the most complete bibliography available. The free online *Catalog*, part of the suite of tools of the FDsys, the Federal Digital System (the successor to the long-running GPO Access system), contains bibliographic records created since 1976 and is updated on a daily basis. In addition to keyword, title, and SuDoc class number searches, the system supports depository item and GPO stock number searches, among other options. With many electronic records, the *Catalog* links to online documents. A "Locate in a Library" option is included, in which the user can enter a state or area code and can identify which depository libraries should own the item based on their item selection profile.

The traditional print version of the *Catalog* is titled *Monthly Catalog of United States Government Publications*, often referred to as *MOCAT*. Published since 1895, *MOCAT* underwent significant format changes in July 1976 when GPO catalogers began to create machine-readable cataloging records (MARC format), based on the Anglo-American Cataloguing Rules and other national standards, and these records became available electronically through OCLC and other vendors. The *Catalog*'s subject index employs headings derived from the latest *Library of Congress Subject Headings* and is used by those who want to know whether the government has published anything on a particular topic, such as semiconductors, grizzly bears, or U.S. relations with Cuba.

For many known-item searches, *WorldCat.org* is sufficient because enough libraries have cataloged their pre-1976 government documents to make many historical documents included in *WorldCat*. In a library in which documents are not typically cataloged and entered into an online catalog, the *Catalog* may function as the primary access tool to the library's physical U.S. documents collection, especially for the wealth of older material.

One of the trickiest aspects of working with government information is discovering that historical publications, especially items that were quite possibly never cataloged anywhere, have not been scanned and placed online *and* predate the *Catalog*'s creation in 1895. For these items, specialized historical indexes are necessary.

A number of private and government-sponsored ventures attempt to index government publications before 1895 (see Figure 22.3). For most of the nation's first century, government publishing was somewhat haphazard, often sloppy, and neither streamlined nor controlled. Printing was subject to political pressures, and no single system existed whereby citizens could necessarily know about, much less access, information about their government. In 1881, Congress passed a law to create a catalog of all known government publications up to that point and put a man named Benjamin Poore (a clerk in the Senate) in charge. Poore sent a team out scavenging to identify every document it could find. They searched libraries, government offices, agency archives, and the Library of Congress, among other collections. They briefly cataloged all that they found (title, author/agency, date, abstract), and the result was the index called *A Descriptive Catalogue of the Government Publications of the United States, September 5, 1774–March 4, 1881*, popularly referred to as "Poore's." The *Catalogue* is arranged chronologically (the first item is called *Abridgement of Laws in the American Plantations*) and contains 63,000 records. It is estimated to have missed 10,000. A similar project fills in the gap between Poore and the time the *Monthly Catalog* began in 1893 and is called the *Comprehensive Index to the Publications of the United States Government, 1881–1893* (commonly known by its editor's name, Ames).

Timeline Of Government Documents Indexes/Catalogs

	1776	1800	1825	1850	1875	1900	1925	1950	1975	2000s
GENERAL INDEXES	1774------				----------Poore's---------- 1881					
						1881--Ames--1893				
			1824----------Tables of and Annotated Index----------1895							
			1789----------1909 Checklist----------		----1909				
			1789----------Cumulative Title Index ('Checklist 76 plus'----------			----1976			
						1893----Document Catalogue----1940				
							1895----Monthly Catalog + Quinquennial Indexes (print)----2004			
							1895--Cumulative Subject Index to the Monthly Catalog--1971			
								1976- Online Catalog→		
	All dates ----------- WorldCat / other online catalogs and union catalog ----------→									

	1776	1800	1825	1850	1875	1900	1925	1950	1975	2000s
SERIAL SET INDEXES	1789----------*CIS U.S. Serial Set Index (incl. American. State Papers)----------1969									
	1789---Greeley---1817									
								1970--*CIS Annual----→		

	1776	1800	1825	1850	1875	1900	1925	1950	1975	2000s
SERIAL SET	1789---Amer. St. Paps---1823									
	1817----------Serial Set----------→									

* included in LexisNexis Congressional.

- **Poore's:** Poore, Benjamin Perley. *A Descriptive Catalogue of the Government Publications of the United States, September 5, 1774-March 4, 1881.* Washington, D.C.: Government Printing Office, 1885
- **Ames:** Ames, John G. *Comprehensive Index to the Publications of the United States Government, 1881-1893.* Washington, D.C.: Government Printing Office, 1905.
- **Tables Of... :** *Tables of and Annotated Index to the Congressional Series of United States Public Documents.* Washington, D.C.: Government Printing Office, 1902.
- **1909 Checklist:** *Checklist of United States Public Documents 1789-1909.* Washington, D.C.: Government Printing Office, 1911.
- **Cumulative Title Index** to *United States Public Documents, 1789-1976.* Arlington, VA: United States Historical Documents Institute, 1979-1982.
- **Document Catalog:** *Catalog (ue) of the Public Documents of the (53rd -76th) Congress and of All Departments of the Government of the United States for the Period from March 4, 1893 to Dec. 31, 1940.* Washington, D.C.: GPO, 1895-1945.
- **Monthly Catalog:** *Monthly Catalog of United States Government Publications.* Washington, D.C.: GPO, 1895-2004 . Continued by the *Catalog of United States Government Publications.*
- **Cumulative Subject Index** to the Monthly Catalog of United States Government Publications, 1900-1971. Washington, D.C.: Carrollton Press, 1973.
- **Online Catalog:** *Catalog of United States Government Publications.* Washington, D.C.: GPO. Available: http://catalog.gpo.gov/.
- **WorldCat:** *WorldCat.* Dublin, Ohio: Online Computer Library Center (OCLC). Available on subscription via the *FirstSearch* service; see http://www.oclc.org for more information. See also the free worldcat.org.

Figure 22.3 Time line of government documents indexes/catalogs.

When using these older catalogs, it is important to understand that for the first century of the nation, most government publications were published in the single set called the *United States Serial Set*. So historical catalogs are often used in conjunction with the *Tables of and Annotated Index to the Congressional Series of United States Public Documents* or the *Checklist of United States Public Documents 1789–1909*, each of which provides a bridge between the catalogs and the actual place within the *Serial Set* where each item is located. The *Serial Set* has private indexes created by Congressional Information Service; these are available online via the fee-based *Pro-Quest Congressional*, to be discussed later with regard to legislative sources.

Another useful source for tracking historical government publications is the *Guide to U.S. Government Publications*, popularly known as "Andriot" after its founder. The brilliance of this volume is its historical survey of government publishing. It is arranged by SuDoc number and therefore by agency and includes defunct and discontinued agencies and classes alongside the current ones. It is a valuable tool for understanding publication patterns of historical agencies.

Selective depositories choose categories of materials, series, and titles from the *List of Classes of United States Government Publications Available for Selection by Depository Libraries*. Although not in the strict sense a catalog or bibliography, the *List of Classes* is a valuable tool in many reference situations. By enumerating all of the "classes," categories, and series of federal government documents, it provides format, frequency, title, and SuDoc numbers for all classes. Because the *List of Classes* includes electronic classes (classes of publications free online), it remains a useful tool even for the non-depository library.

Bibliographies of state government publications have a venerable heritage as a separate publishing endeavor, beginning with R. R. Bowker's four-volume set, covering the years 1899 through 1908, titled *State Publications; a Provisional List of Official Publications of the Several States of the United States from their Organization*. Adelaide Hasse's *Index of Economic Material in the Documents of the States of the United States*, 1908–1919, continued the tradition. From 1910 to 1994, the most comprehensive bibliography of state government information sources was the *Monthly Checklist of State Publications* from the Library of Congress. It was compiled by Collection Services of the Library of Congress Exchange and Gift Division. Typically, bibliographic information and price were given for monographs, annuals, and monographic series, arranged by state and issuing agency. This massive undertaking ceased in the mid-1990s, as state governments increasingly used Web publishing. *StateList: The Electronic Source for State Publication Lists*, however, aims to bring some organization to these efforts by providing links to those state publication checklists and shipping lists that are currently available on the Web.[19]

The amount and variety of state and local government information in electronic format has increased rapidly. Legislative information, business and economic data, and agency reports are representative of the types of information that are currently available to the public on the Web. Using these electronic sources to answer questions about state and local government issues has become the norm. Librarians should be aware of how their own state catalogs and distributes its documents and what the best sources are for identifying those documents.

Foreign governments and IGOs vary widely in the availability of catalogs of their materials. Sources mentioned in the previous section, *International Government*

656   22—Government Information and Statistics Sources

Information and Country Information: A Subject Guide and *Guide to Official Publications of Foreign Countries*, provide a good starting point for the publishing activities of foreign governments, and the librarian may do well by seeking out a foreign country's national bibliography, should one exist for the country in question.

Both foreign and IGO documents will, hopefully, be cataloged by someone and be discoverable via a library catalog or a union catalog. The UN, the largest IGO, does have several catalogs of its publications and documents. The *Official Document System of the United Nations* is freely available, and it both indexes and has the full text (except for sales publications) of UN materials from 1993 forward, with selected older material. The *UNBISnet* catalog, also free, indexes (with selected full text) UN materials from 1979 forward. The second most prominent IGO for libraries is the European Union, whose *ECLAS* catalog provides bibliographic access to EU documents.

Specialized Catalogs, Indexes, Bibliographies, and Directories

The preceding sources are all broad and relatively comprehensive access points to government information. However, several types of government information needs fall outside the useful realm of Web search engines and general catalogs. The two most obvious examples are tracking legislation and regulatory actions and finding specific statistical data; those are covered in separate subsequent sections. This section focuses on several other types of government information that require specialized tools.

Although most government information that the reference librarian deals with is public and relatively widely accessible (publications and Web sites designed for public consumption on some level), there are also endless amounts of archival material, seemingly mundane government records, and material considered by the government to be of a more private nature, especially information that concerns specific individuals or entities or is considered politically sensitive. Most of these records of the government are held by the National Archives and Records Administration (NARA) and its network of regional archives, more than 20 facilities spread out across the nation. The papers of agencies or government officials may often be found and accessed through a trip to the National Archives.

The *Guide to Federal Records in the National Archives of the United States* is the general index and finding aid to what is held by the National Archives. The *Guide* does not attempt to describe individual items and pieces, but does *outline* NARA's holdings. For instance, a person researching the Tennessee Valley Authority (TVA) could use the guide to see the general types of materials held by NARA from the TVA, where they are located, and what format they are in, as well as get the relevant bibliographic data to begin researching with the collection. Many more popular archival records have been microfilmed, and microfilm copies are available at many of the regional archives.

NARA continues to develop the *Archival Research Catalog* (ARC), which *does* attempt to catalog and describe individual archival items held in the National Archives, any of the regional archives, or the presidential libraries. This monumental undertaking has been going on for many years and currently describes the majority of, but not all, archival holdings. Also, NARA continues to digitize many of its most popular materials, and the ARC increasingly leads one to digitized versions of the archival material.

In addition to the archives, various government agencies may have specific items that could be of interest but are not readily available because they were not printed by the GPO and so did not become part of the depository library program. This information may be requested informally directly from the publishing agency or formally via the Freedom of Information Act. Several resources are available to aid in this effort, including *Your Right to Federal Records: Questions and Answers on the Freedom of Information Act and the Privacy Act* and *A Citizen's Guide on Using the Freedom of Information Act and the Privacy Act of 1974 to Request Government Records* (from the General Services Administration and the U.S. Congress, respectively). Each of these sources outlines the procedures that individuals can use to obtain access to federal records and agency files. The FBI's Freedom of Information Act Electronic Reading Room site is the home to many popular FBI records and features the FBI files on Bertolt Brecht, John Lennon, Martin Luther King, Albert Einstein, Elvis Presley, and Thurgood Marshall, among other prominent individuals, and also on incidents, groups, and institutions, such as the Highlander Folk School, People for the Ethical Treatment of Animals, and the Ruby Ridge shooting incident. The FBI material on famous persons notwithstanding, one should note that nearly all government information about private individuals or entities is barred by law from being released to anyone because of privacy restrictions. In no instance, often not even via law enforcement search warrant or subpoena, can anyone get access to someone else's income tax returns, social security or welfare records, census questionnaires, or any other documents related to their participation in government programs.

The federal government produces specialized indexes to provide access to scientific and technical reports prepared as a result of government-funded or contract research. These reports are generally not cataloged, so are rarely discoverable via regular catalogs. Because many of them are not available online (especially older ones), they also often fall beyond the realm of Web search engines. Identifying such reports, then, requires a specialized database. The most comprehensive such database is the collection accessible via *NTIS Search*, from the National Technical Information Service (NTIS), an agency dedicated to gathering technical reports from across the many scientific agencies of government. The catalog provides free access to citations for its reports and products produced from 1964 to the present; reports themselves must generally be purchased, sometimes online or sometimes via a print-on-demand service. Why, one might wonder, are taxpayer-funded technical reports not available free online, as with the rest of U.S. government information? The answer may not be satisfying, but NTIS's statutory authority (the laws that Congress passed that create and govern its operations) requires NTIS to operate on a cost-recovery basis for its bibliographic control. That said, one should also do a Web search for any known technical report before paying for it via NTIS; reports indexed in the *NTIS* database can often be found elsewhere free on the Web.

Many libraries have large sets of depository technical reports, often on microform. But going from the bibliographic record in *NTIS* to the item can be difficult. Because items are rarely cataloged, one must know which libraries have sets of NTIS or other technical reports and then must rely on the numbering system used by the specific report series to find the item. The traditional, most comprehensive source to NTIS's technical report literature, *Government Reports Announcements and Index* (*GRAI*), ceased publication in 1994, so use of the *NTIS Search* is now required. These sources are crucial in verifying the accuracy of a citation and in obtaining NTIS accession and report numbers.

Although *NTIS* is the largest index to technical report literature, several other agencies maintain their own databases, which often contain additional technical reports. Major databases include the Department of Energy's Information Bridge and *Energy Citations Database*, the Department of Defense's *Defense Technical Information Center* (*DTIC*), and the several access tools via the *NASA Scientific and Technical Information* Web page. Their contents are sometimes redundant with those reports included in the *NTIS* database, but they do often yield unique reports. So a complete technical reports search may include traditional catalogs, Web search engines, *NTIS Search*, and specific databases of likely sponsoring agencies.

Declassified government information represents another substantial, typically uncataloged body of literature that has its own unique catalogs or access tools. Although a handful of declassified documents are among those at the FBI Electronic Reading Room, many declassified documents may be identified and accessed through the *Declassified Documents Reference System*, a privately produced database of full-text declassified documents, documents that generally cannot be identified using traditional government documents catalogs and indexes such as the *Catalog* or Web search engines. The *Digital National Security Archive* is a similar product.

Patents and trademarks also require their own separate tools. In fact, patent and trademark research is sufficiently specialized to merit its own set of Patent and Trademark Depository Libraries. Although these depository libraries remain the best places to conduct patent and trademark research, one can now accomplish quite a bit of patent and trademark research on the Web, provided one knows something about the material. The basics are covered in the companion publications *General Information Concerning Patents* and *Basic Facts, Trademarks*, which describe the nature of patents and trademarks and how the United States Patent and Trademark Office (USPTO) handles them. The USPTO now has searchable databases of all patents and trademarks ever issued, although accurately finding the information requires knowledge of patents and trademarks as well as an understanding of how they are indexed and classified. This information is available either by reading the aforementioned publications and browsing the materials on the USPTO homepage or by consulting a patent and trademark depository library. Google, meanwhile, has uploaded all patents from USPTO into its own patent search database.

Periodical Indexes

Governments publish a number of periodicals. Examples from the federal government include titles such as *Survey of Current Business* (articles and data on the U.S. economy), *Monthly Labor Review* (articles and data on U.S. labor conditions), and *Morbidity and Mortality Weekly Report* (articles and data on infectious diseases). The articles in these periodicals are indexed right along with titles such as *Time* or the *New England Journal of Medicine* in many standard periodical indexes. In addition, government periodicals are picked up by appropriate subject-based indexes as well. For instance, research articles from the National Institute of Environmental Health Sciences' journal *Environmental Health Perspectives* are indexed in *SciFinder* (online access to *Chemical Abstracts*), the premier source that indexes chemical literature, and *PubMed*, the preeminent index to medical literature.

The *Government Periodicals Index* indexes articles from more than 160 government periodicals, with retrospective coverage to 1988. Articles selected for indexing are judged to be of research or general interest value. Although the *Government Periodicals Index* is devoted exclusively to coverage of government periodicals, *PAIS International* includes indexing of government periodicals and other materials with a focus on international public affairs. *PAIS* covers topics in government, public policy, economics, political science, and international relations. Coverage includes periodicals from the U.S. government, some foreign governments, and many IGOs.

The *American Statistics Index* (*ASI*) is an example of a highly specialized indexing and abstracting tool related to government information. This index offers access to the hundreds of statistical reports and other sources of statistical information, including those found in journals produced by the U.S. government that are frequently not covered in other indexing tools. *ASI*, more prominently known now as part of *ProQuest Statistical Insight*, is discussed in greater detail in the "Statistical Sources" portion of this chapter.

The previously described sources are examples of private information providers whose periodical indexes feature government titles. However, the U.S. government also produces several very important periodical indexes itself, which include indexing for government *and* nongovernment titles. Several of these are the primary indexes to the literature in their disciplines.

PubMed (derived from *MEDLINE* and the former print set *Index Medicus*), from the National Library of Medicine, is the premier index to periodical literature in medicine. Anyone searching the medical research literature will need to search *PubMed*. Available free online, the *MEDLINE/PubMed* database is also licensed by several private vendors, who may add special indexing or searching capabilities.

The *Educational Resources Information Center*, or *ERIC* as it is popularly known, is another long-running government-produced database to periodical literature. Produced by the Institute of Education Sciences of the U.S. Department of Education, *ERIC* indexes and abstracts education-related research. It includes both periodical and nonperiodical content. The former makes *ERIC* a premier index to materials in education research journals, and the latter includes hundreds of thousands of documents, which could include monographs, lesson plans, classroom activities, and just about anything else education-related that was not published in a journal. Many recent *ERIC* documents are full text in the database; thousands of others are collected in *ERIC* microfiche, a staple of depository library collections for decades. Armed with their *ERIC* document number, users can find microfiche copies of these generally uncataloged *ERIC* documents.

Finally, there is *AGRICOLA*, created by the National Agricultural Library. The records in this free database describe publications and resources encompassing all aspects of agriculture and allied disciplines, including plant and animal sciences, forestry, entomology, and more. *AGRICOLA* includes both monographs and journal articles.

Law and Legislative Information

Law and its creation are major government information needs. Although legal research can be difficult (which is partly why law libraries and law librarians exist), certain aspects of legal research, especially the materials within the legislative process, including bills, laws, reports, and testimony from Congress, and regulatory documents are frequent government information needs, so understanding of the processes and publications is necessary for almost anyone working with government information.

The major types of law are constitutional, statutory, administrative, and case. *Constitutional law* refers to law regarding the Constitution and its amendments. *Statutory law* is also referred to as legislative law. Statutory law is what results from the constitutional mandate for Congress to make laws, and it is the basis for the other two types of law. Statutory law originates in the legislative branch, which in the case of federal law is Congress. Bills passed by both houses of Congress become law when signed by the president and are referred to as "statutes."

The third type of law is *administrative law*, also referred to as regulatory law. It originates in the executive branch of government and generally refers to the rules and regulations issued by departments or agencies as part of their constitutional mandate to enforce the law. Regulatory law details exactly how the executive branch will enforce the laws of Congress and so is rooted in statutory law. Administrative law also refers to executive orders or proclamations issued by the president.

Finally, there is *case law*, or judicial law. This is the law that originates in the court system, the judicial branch of government, which examines the validity of laws as they relate to the Constitution and existing law, or legal precedent. The rulings that result from this examination are referred to as case law. Historically, case law was the type of law most likely to be handled by law librarians, although the free Web and publishing changes have made case law more accessible to everyone than ever before.

This section discusses the most important government information needs related to law, focusing on the information created during the legislative process and documents of regulatory law, followed by a very brief introduction to working with case law. It should be noted that this section centers heavily on U.S. federal law but that nearly every state has a similar process of statutory, administrative, and case law. Foreign countries, meanwhile, have endless varieties of law far beyond the scope of this section, although Canadian law is introduced in the later section dealing with Canadian government information.

The Legislative Process

First, we present an overview of the legislative process, followed by further discussion on finding the source documents resulting from the process.

Statutory law, promulgated by the U.S. Congress, is one of the major foundations for national policies. It is incumbent on the government information provider to acquire and maintain an in-depth understanding of what is commonly referred to as the legislative process. Comprehension of this process and an awareness of the resultant publications ensure that the most accurate, authoritative information is located.

Statutes begin as legislative proposals, usually in the categories of "bills" or "resolutions." Although the ideas behind legislative proposals and bills do not always originate in Congress, only members of Congress may introduce a measure, and it is at this step that the formal life cycle of a measure begins. For instance, something that the media may refer to as "the president's health care law" may indeed be a bill written by the president's staff, yet the bill itself must be introduced for consideration by a member of Congress. Upon introduction, each House or Senate bill or resolution is printed and numbered sequentially within a specific Congress, and here lies the first publication that a user may need: the text of a bill as introduced. The number and session of the pertinent Congress is printed as part of the header of the bill, and if provided, the bill's "Short Title" appears at the beginning of the bill text. The sponsor and cosponsors are listed. For example, on January 26, 2009, Representative David Obey of Wisconsin introduced a bill "making supplemental appropriations for job preservation and creation, infrastructure investment, energy efficiency and science, assistance to the unemployed, and State and local fiscal stabilization, for the fiscal year ending September 30, 2009, and for other purposes." The line "111th Congress, 1st Session H. R. 1" precedes the text. The bill's short title also appears, in this case "The American Recovery and Reinvestment Act of 2009." The numbering is important, given that the bill will often be referenced by number. For instance, the first bill introduced in the Senate during a session of Congress will be given the number "S.1," and the second bill will be "S.2," and so on. Likewise, the first bill introduced in the House will be numbered "H.R. 1." At this point, it is important to revisit civics: each session of Congress lasts for two years, between the elections that occur during each even-numbered year; so "S.1" for the 111th Congress will either become law or die by the end of the two-year duration of the 111th Congress. If it does not become law, a new version (which could be identical) would need to be introduced again in the next Congress, at which time it would receive a new number and begin the process anew. Further, each two-year session of Congress consists of a "first" and "second" session, usually one for each calendar year to comply with the Constitutional mandate for Congress to meet at least once each year. Action does continue from the first to the second session *within* each Congress.

The preceding example illustrates an important concept: high-profile legislation may be popularly known by unofficial names. "The American Recovery and Reinvestment Act of 2009" was consistently referred to in the popular press and by representatives and the president himself as the "stimulus" bill, law, or package; the government information librarian may have to figure out exactly which bill is being referred to in the popular media.

Once a bill has been introduced, it is usually referred to a congressional committee, the "nerve endings" of Congress. After referral to a congressional committee or subcommittee, the committee may hold hearings on the bill, and usually a transcript of these is published. Such committee hearings are popular congressional publications, containing the oral and/or written testimony of both legislators and experts on the subject at hand. Contentious issues usually have several experts testifying on both sides of an issue, making hearings of particular use to students, the public, and casual and serious researchers alike. Further committee action may occur in the form of a bill "markup," during which the committee may debate and edit the bill. If the committee decides to move the measure to the next stage, consideration by the full chamber, the bill is "reported" out of committee and accompanied by a written Senate or House report. The report, "to accompany H.R. [bill no.]" or "S. [bill no.]," contains the latest version of the proposed legislation and may include more detailed information, such as an overview of the proposal, a cost estimate, and supplemental views. Committee roll-call votes on whether to report the bill are also incorporated into the report. These committee reports are, along with hearings, the other major committee publications. The discussion therein often renders the legislation in something closer to plain language and provides insight into the intent of the legislation (in fact, in reviewing a law, the judicial branch may actually examine the committee report to better understand what the law is trying to accomplish). More in-depth analyses about a policy, subject, or issue may also be authorized, and these studies are published as committee prints.

Note that sometimes a bill can be "held at the desk" or "placed on the calendar" in lieu of assignment to committee. In either case, the bill would then be available for consideration by the full House or Senate chamber, bypassing the committee process.

Once a bill is sent to the entire chamber for consideration, usually after it has come back out of a committee, it may be debated on the floor of the chamber and then voted on. These debates appear in the *Congressional Record*, and the vote activity is recorded there as well. If passed, it is sent to the other chamber to follow a similar path. Upon passage by both chambers, it is sent to the president for consideration. Note that occasionally the same legislation, or extremely similar legislation with a few differences, could make its way through both chambers concurrently. If this is the case and both bills pass their respective chambers, a "conference" of senators and representatives is appointed to iron out the differences between the two bills and make a single piece of legislation to send to the president. The result and details of the conference are published in "conference reports." The results of the conference are then sent back to each chamber to consider for passage by all members. These conference reports can be popular, especially for more contentious legislation where the House and Senate may not agree on some major provision, with the conference effecting a compromise.

Finally, once signed by the president, the legislation is known as a "public law" and is assigned a sequential number based on the Congress. For instance, although the stimulus bill was the first bill introduced in the House for the 111th session of Congress and was therefore numbered H.R. 1, it was only the fifth piece of legislation actually passed by both chambers of Congress and signed by President Obama in that session, becoming "Public Law 111-5." Each public law is eventually compiled sequentially into the bound series the *United States Statutes at Large*. At this point, it is usually cited using its *Statutes at Large* citation (see Box 22.3 for citation examples) rather than its public law citation. This codification process is discussed more later in the chapter.

As indicated previously, there are numerous steps in the process by which a formal bill or resolution becomes a public law. Upon completion, the entire process is often referred to as a law's *legislative history*. Judith Schiek Robinson cites a potential 153 steps in the process, as well as "the undocumented political activities interwoven at every stage."[20] At each stage of this activity, information results, and in most cases the congressional publications noted previously are issued as the primary and official mechanisms for disseminating that information. Bills and resolutions, hearings, reports and committee prints, floor debates, votes, presidential actions, laws, and other congressional publications are the tangible representations and textual records of the legislative process. Detailed explanations of the legislative process are contained in the publications *How Our Laws Are Made* by Charles W. Johnson, from the House of Representatives, and *Enactment of a Law* by Robert B. Dove, from the Senate.

The following example is meant to illustrate the consecutive steps by which a single bill became law and to cite the relevant congressional publications that were produced as part of this process. On January 27, 2003, Representative Bart Gordon, Democrat, Tennessee, introduced the "Sports Agent Responsibility and Trust Act." The bill had 76 cosponsors. This bill was designated H.R. 361, 108th Congress, 1st Session, and was referred initially to the House Committee on Energy and Commerce. The committee held a markup session (markup is when bills are edited) and ordered it to be reported (voted on and recommended to the entire chamber for potential passage) by voice vote. On March 5, 2003, it was reported by the committee, and House Report 108-24, Part I, was produced. It was referred subsequently to the House Committee on the Judiciary to consider provisions that fell within its jurisdiction; Judiciary referred it to its Subcommittee on Commercial and Administration Law on May 1, 2003. The subcommittee held hearings on May 15, 2003 (published as "Sports Agent Responsibility and Trust Act, hearings before the Subcommittee on Commercial and Administrative Law, Committee on the Judiciary. House, May 15, 2003"). These were followed by a markup session, and the subcommittee sent it to the full committee as amended by voice vote that same day. On May 21, 2003, Judiciary held a markup session and also ordered that it be reported as amended by voice vote. On June 2, 2003, it was reported by the committee, and House Report 108-24, Part II, was produced. Once on the floor on the entire chamber, the House passed the bill as amended by voice vote as specified in the *Congressional Record.*

The measure then moved on to the Senate, where it was read twice and referred to the Committee on Commerce, Science, and Transportation on June 5, 2003. Further action on this bill occurred in the 108th Congress, 2nd Session. The Senate committee discharged it back to the floor of the Senate by unanimous consent with neither hearings nor a committee report produced on September 9, 2004, more than a year after it was referred to committee; and the Senate passed it by unanimous consent the same day. A message regarding this action was sent to the House, and the bill was presented to President Bush on September 16, 2004. He signed it on September 24, 2004, at which time it became Public Law (P.L.) 108-304.[21]

Legislative Research: Guides and Indexes

Answering questions about legislation and public laws is standard practice in government information reference service. A user may be looking for a specific fact, such as the date the president signed a bill into law, or may want to review a known discrete source, such as a public law, a House report, or committee hearings on a bill. Frequently, the testimony of a particular individual at the hearing is requested. A user may be interested in the status of proposed legislation or may want either a succinct overview or in-depth coverage of a particular legal or social policy. Usually, current information is needed, but historical queries are common. Standard congressional information tools may provide answers to ready-reference or basic requests, although in some cases congressional publications must be consulted. Locating official versions of these publications, whether in print or in electronic format, can be straightforward, as long as an accurate citation is available or can be fairly easily ascertained. Each legislative measure—that is, bill or resolution—has a legislative history, whether brief or extensive, and the process of ascertaining this information or tracking current legislative proposals has become much less time-consuming and cumbersome as a result of the development of excellent electronic tools and databases, including both free and fee-based resources.

The Library of Congress's *THOMAS* and the congressional section of FDsys (formerly GPO Access) are the permanent, no-fee electronic gateway to bills and resolutions, legislative actions, congressional publications, and related information. *THOMAS* has the full text of most congressional publications, except congressional hearings, and its "Bill Summary and Status" section, which begins coverage with the 93rd Congress, 1973/74–present, includes bill text and comprehensive bill tracking along with coverage of congressional actions. The full text of appropriate congressional actions, including committee reports and links to pages in the *Congressional Record*, begin in earnest with the 104th Congress in 1994. The comprehensive search options of *THOMAS* include searching legislation by bill number or keyword, sponsor, assigned committee, or stage in the legislative process. Once a bill is found, *THOMAS* offers an abundance of information: title, text, and sponsors/co-sponsors; related bills; bill status; cost estimates related to the legislation provided by the Congressional Budget Office; useful summaries of the legislation from the Congressional Research Service; detailed legislative histories with links to publications; and even subject terms. If one understands the legislative process as outlined, *THOMAS* is very easy and complete (see Figure 22.4).

Alternatively, GPO's FDsys also covers legislation, with browseable and searchable collections of congressional bills, congressional reports, the *Congressional Record*, and a "History of Bills" section that provides the bill summary and status information akin to *THOMAS*. FDsys also adds the full text of hearings that are not available via *THOMAS*. Most information in FDsys goes back to the 104th Congress in 1994.

Both *THOMAS* and FDsys provide excellent Web site user guides in the form of Frequently Asked Questions (FAQ) sections and Help screens. *THOMAS* includes revised and updated copies of Charles W. Johnson's basic pamphlet on the legislative process, *How Our Laws Are Made,* and Robert B. Dove's *Enactment of a Law*, and FDsys's detailed Help screens explain both the content and the use of the site. Generally, *THOMAS* has become the tool of choice for quick and easy tracking of legislation.

Tracing older legislation using free depository materials is not as easy. The former print serial *Digest of Public General Bills and Resolutions*, which the Library of Congress's Legislative Reference Service compiled from the 74th Congress (1936) through the 101st Congress (1990) did much the same as *THOMAS*'s "Bill Summary and Status." The Library of Congress was also responsible for *Major Legislation of the Congress*, which covered the 97th Congress (1982) through the 102nd Congress (1992). The *Calendars of the United States House of Representatives and History of Legislation* and the *Senate Calendar of Business* are also helpful in obtaining historical bill tracking (beginning with the 104th Congress, 1995–1996, these can be found on FDsys). These print format editions are still essential when investigating earlier legislation, unless one has access to the fee-based *ProQuest Congressional*.

ProQuest Congressional and the suite of products available from Congressional Quarterly (CQ) are Web-based subscription services offering near real-time access to congressional activity. Commercial competitors, each of these resources operates as

Figure 22.4 *THOMAS*.

guide and index to the legislative process and to the literature, serves as a centralized locale for electronic versions of primary publications, and functions as an educational tool. The full text of bills, the *Congressional Record*, and other types of congressional materials are available; legislative histories or current status of bills are readily accessible; and voting records of members of Congress can quickly be obtained in both systems. Furthermore, more detailed coverage and indexing of historical legislation and congressional documents is provided. In sum, heavy users of legislative information may strongly consider investing in these value-added products.

ProQuest Congressional includes brief bill synopses, summaries, and digests, and CQ maintains bill digests from the Congressional Research Service. Each features news services and transcripts of hearings, press briefings, and other events. The complexities of the legislative and regulatory process have created a legitimate demand among government documents librarians for some of the value-added coverage that these private products offer. As with *THOMAS*, these services can be used to answer basic questions—"What were the details of the legislation that funded but opposed the 'Iraq surge'?" "What was the vote on overriding the veto?" "What were the details of the revised legislation that funded the surge and was passed?"—and more complex questions: "I'd like to identify the legislation that has been proposed over the past five years related to public libraries and rural library services, examine some of the congressional publications relevant to a selected number of the bills that became public law, and compile a list of the senators and representatives who supported passage of these. I would also like to know whether or not the president signed these into law."

ProQuest Congressional features various subscription options with coverage of congressional activity back to the first Congress in 1789. It has detailed bill tracking and legislative histories back to 1970, and its historical indexing covers committee hearings and committee reports back as far as 1819 and indexing to the *U.S. Serial Set*, which often contains committee reports all the way back to 1789. *ProQuest Congressional*'s bill tracking and legislative history component is based on the print *CIS/Index*, a long-standing, comprehensive indexing and abstracting tool for congressional publications. Begun in 1970 by the Congressional Information Service (CIS), this originally print-only, multivolume series provides access to hearings, committee prints, and other types of congressional publications, including Senate and House reports and documents that form the *Serial Set*, starting with the 91st Congress (1969).

All regional and many selective depository libraries house congressional hearings and maintain these collections over time. The source documents cited in *ProQuest Congressional* or the CIS series are also available for purchase on microfiche. Subscriptions to the monthly index and abstract volumes in paper format are still available.

CQ's congressional products are many and varied and cover much of the same territory. CQ offers bill tracking, committee publications, and various value-added analysis features. Other products from CQ are likely to appeal to those who desire readable background information on political activities, but not necessarily primary documents from Congress. These users can consult *CQ Weekly*, *CQ Researcher*, and *CQ Almanac*. These three major publications cover Congress, the presidency, the Supreme Court, the issues, and politics. *CQ Weekly* discusses major legislation, events, and issues. It also furnishes roll-call votes. At the end of the year, information from *CQ Weekly* is reorganized by subject and summarized in chronological order in the *Almanac*. *CQ Weekly* and *CQ Almanac* provide the user with a well-organized, succinct, and readable account of national politics and congressional, presidential, and judicial consideration of major issues affecting the American public. They are excellent resources to get an overview of the major legislation that one is likely to be researching on *THOMAS* and elsewhere. *CQ Researcher*, on the other hand, offers in-depth, unbiased coverage of political and social issues, including regular coverage of topics as diverse as health, international affairs, education, the environment, technology, and the economy. Each nearly weekly issue focuses on a single theme. Topics covered in 2009 include "Rethinking Retirement," "Legalizing Marijuana," "High-Speed Trains," "The Auto Industry," and the "Obama Presidency." The journals and other CQ electronic products are available as separate Web subscriptions or as part of the *CQ Press Electronic Library*.

Another outstanding subscription title is the *National Journal*. Available as either a print or online journal subscription, it is dedicated to covering American politics, Congress, and public policies in an unbiased fashion and is very popular on Capitol Hill. Although described as a comprehensive resource for the academic community, its easy layout and readability are sufficient to attract even the most complacent political naysayer and lead the expert easily to the correct primary source. Its markup reports provide a brief behind-the-scenes look at congressional activities and dynamics on specific legislation.

Of course, new media are covering Congress as well. *Wikipedia* may have articles about significant pieces of legislation that include legislative histories. Various blogs such as *OpenCongress.org* and Twitter feeds from reporters and even representatives feature congressional news as well, from every conceivable political angle.

Legislative research is often centered on finding information about a specific piece of legislation, and one of the biggest challenges is identifying which, among a number of similar bills, is the one the user is interested in. Often, the librarian will know a topic of legislation and first have to use various keyword searches and then browse results to find the right item, given that users may come with only a general topic such as "health care reform" or "climate change," words that may not even be in the title of the bill. This can be confounded by multiple bills on the same topic and also by some bills folding into other ones. It can get even trickier if short but significant pieces of legislation are tacked onto another seemingly unrelated bill. So the research really requires some detective work. Users are most likely to have heard of, and be interested in, whichever of these bills is furthest along in the process, given that such bills are the most likely to be garnering attention. Take an example of three health care bills, one whose history stops at referral to committee, one that resulted in hearings but nothing more, and one that was reported back to the floor of the chamber; it is the final one that is most likely to be of interest because it is the reported bill that has made it out of committee and back to the floor of the chamber for consideration for passage. This does not preclude interest in either of the other two bills; indeed, the hearings on the other bill are likely relevant to the user. In fact, one of the advantages of *ProQuest Congressional*'s "Legislative Histories" section is that it even includes information on versions of the bill from *previous* Congresses; just because a bill died and had to be reintroduced in the next Congressional session before gaining passage does not mean that previous hearings, reports, and the text of the previous bills themselves are not of interest to the user and important parts of the history of the legislation. Within a single Congress, *THOMAS* also does an excellent job of listing and linking to related bills and measures. Box 22.1 illustrates how the various guides and indexes support tracking legislative history.

Legislation: Primary Sources

After reading about legislation in the CQ sources or having identified documents in *THOMAS*, the next step for many users is to view the actual primary publications. These are usually available within the Web-based services in electronic format. Older items are in print or microfiche in most depository libraries. Key items include the *Congressional Record*, the transcripts of proceedings, debates, and votes from the floor of Congress; congressional bills, the form in which legislation is introduced;

BOX 22.1
BASIC LEGISLATIVE HISTORY WITH KEY PUBLICATIONS

ACTION	OUTPUT	SOURCE
Measure introduced, usually a bill.	Text of bill. Sometimes comments made on floor of entire chamber upon introduction, recorded in *Congressional Record*.	Bill in *THOMAS*, FDsys, *ProQuest Congressional*, and CQ products. *Congressional Record* in THOMAS, FDsys, *ProQuest Congressional*, and CQ products. Also depository in print or microfiche.
Referred to committee. Hearings sometimes held.	Transcript of hearings.	Hearings not in *THOMAS*. Many hearings in FDsys, *ProQuest Congressional*, and CQ's *Congressional Transcripts*. Hearings in print and microfiche through depository program. Some hearing testimony also on committee Web sites.
Committee markup and vote.	Committee reports summarizing bill's intent, scope, purpose, and recommendations for passage. Sometimes also committee prints, which may include further analysis, statistics, other supplemental material.	Reports in *THOMAS*, FDsys, *ProQuest Congressional*, and CQ. Also depository in print or microfiche. Committee prints in FDsys, *ProQuest Congressional*. Also depository in print or microfiche.
Back to floor of entire chamber for debate, amendments, and vote.	Testimony, amendments, votes in *Congressional Record*.	*Congressional Record* in *THOMAS*, FDsys, *ProQuest Congressional*, and CQ products. Also depository in print or microfiche.
Passed measure goes to other chamber, repeats process.		
Both chambers pass a measure—if measures differ, a conference of members from both chambers is appointed to iron out the differences.	Conference report published with text and discussion of changes based on compromises.	Conference reports in *THOMAS*, FDsys, *ProQuest Congressional*, and CQ. Also depository in print or microfiche.

Conference report sent back to floor of both chambers for debate, amendments, and vote.	Testimony, amendments, votes in *Congressional Record*.	*Congressional Record* in THOMAS, FDsys, *Pro-Quest Congressional*, and CQ products. Also depository in print or microfiche.
Bill passes both chambers; sent to president.	President signs, vetoes, or lets become law after 10 days of inaction. Called a *public law*.	*Public Laws* in THOMAS, FDsys, *ProQuest Congressional*, and CQ products.
Public law compiled into statutes.	*U.S. Statutes at Large*	*U.S. Statutes at Large* in FDsys. Also depository in print.
Law codified—inserted into subject arrangement of current statutory law in *United States Code*.	*United States Code*	*United States Code* in FDsys, *ProQuest Congressional*, depository in print, and excellent free law site http://www4.law.cornell. edu/uscode/ from Cornell's Legal Information Institute.

committee hearings, the testimony and discussion that occur during a public hearing, as well as appendices of supplementary material; committee prints, research reports requested by a committee; and congressional reports, a description, often with a detailed analysis, of the legislation that is prepared when the bill is sent to the House or Senate floor. All of these primary sources are most easily identified and found by using one of the indexes.

The House and Senate also may order the printing of standard titles or request specialized materials, analyses, or studies, either monographic or serial in nature. Examples include the president's State of the Union message and the *Economic Report of the President*, an annual publication. Each of these congressional publications is numbered and categorized as a "congressional document," and these and the congressional reports described previously form what is known as the *Serial Set*. This long-standing, ongoing series has been compiled since 1789, with the current set consisting of House reports, Senate reports, House documents, Senate documents, Senate treaty documents, and Senate executive reports.

Compilation and Codification of Statutory Law

In addition to tracing legislation from a bill to a public law, another frequent need is to find an older law or to find the current state, or codification, of statutory law on a particular subject. These two needs are filled by use of two key sources, the *United States Statutes at Large* and the *United States Code*.

Laws enacted by each Congress are compiled into the bound volumes called the *United States Statutes at Large*. The *Statutes at Large* presents a chronological

BOX 22.2
SEARCH STRATEGY: TRACKING CURRENT LEGISLATION

A user read on a blog that Congress passed a law that would ensure that safe drinking water was available throughout the world, and she would like to find out more. A search of "drinking water" in *THOMAS*'s current Congress bill-text section yielded a moderately long list. Browsing this list, the librarian found "H.R.2030 : To provide 100,000,000 people with first-time access to safe drinking water and sanitation on a sustainable basis by 2015 by improving the capacity of the United States Government to fully implement the Senator Paul Simon Water for the Poor Act of 2005." It appeared that this might be the law the user had in mind, but a quick glance showed that it was only in committee and had not become law. However, the result inspired the librarian to check out the "Senator Paul Simon Water for the Poor Act of 2005." By using *THOMAS*'s handy "Search Multiple Congresses" feature and limiting results to "Enrolled Bills sent to the President," the librarian quickly located the right bill, H.R. 1973 of the 109th Congress, originally titled *Water for the Poor Act of 2005*, which became the *Senator Paul Simon Water for the Poor Act of 2005*. Looking at the "Bill Summary and Status" information, specifically "All Congressional Actions," allowed the user to trace the bill's passage through Congress. The user was happy to see that her representative, Susan A. Davis, Democrat from the 53rd District in California, was a cosponsor of the bill, along with 100 other cosponsors. It had initially been referred to the House Committee on International Relations and eventually had been signed by President Bush as Public Law (P.L.) 109-260 on December 1, 2005.

Information provided in the congressional actions and bill summary sections allowed her to readily learn more details about the legislative process and an overview of the purpose of the bill. She was also able to find out cost estimates from 2006 to 2010. Note that legislation can be reported in the press at various stages, and a bill's particular status at any given time is not always made clear. Within *THOMAS*, direct links to *Congressional Record* remarks and activities and the relevant House Report 109-260 were available within the "All Congressional Actions" section, allowing her to see the remarks made on the floor of the House at the time of introduction and also the tally of the final House vote. From *THOMAS*, the user was also able to access the full text of both the bill and the public law in FDsys.

The user could also examine the "All Congressional Actions" section to obtain information on related hearings. However, as indicated previously, the formal titles of hearings are not provided. These could be identified by the bill number or public law number from within FDsys and/or *ProQuest Congressional*. In general, a nearly identical process would be followed to obtain the same information in another legislative resource, such as FDsys, *ProQuest Congressional*, or CQ.

arrangement of the laws in the exact order that they have been enacted, with the text of the law as passed. Each volume contains a subject and title index. A user looking for the text of the Civil Rights Act of 1964 could find the 1964 volumes of statutes and use the indexes to easily locate the text. Once found, the law will include the original bill number and also a brief legislative history of that bill, with major actions only. This strategy of finding laws requires knowing when the law was enacted in order to locate the correct volume. When the user lacks knowledge of the date of passage, there are a few other approaches. First, because it is such a famous piece of legislation, it would likely be simple to nail down the year of passage through a quick Web search. A more traditional method would be to use one of several reference books that cite laws by popular name[22] and then use the citation to find the text of the law (see Box 22.3) in the *Statutes at Large*.

In the example of the stimulus law of 2009, Public Law 111-5 is the same as 123 Stat. 115. What this means is that the law appears in the sequentially numbered volume 123 of the series of public laws known as the *Statutes at Large*, and it begins on page 115 of that volume—generally meaning that Public Laws 1 through 4 of the same congressional session take up the first 114 pages.

FDsys contains all public laws back to 1995. Note that public laws from the current Congress will not be bound as the newest volume of the *Statutes at Large* until after the end of the current session of Congress; still, these newest laws do appear in FDsys exactly as they will look in the *Statutes* volume and also contain the *Statutes* citation. The *United States Statutes at Large* are the official record of laws passed by Congress as they are passed (see Figure 22.5).

Another common need is for the current state of the law on a subject. For instance, if the user who wanted the Civil Rights Act of 1964 were to follow up with a request for *current* federal law on civil rights, a different strategy and source would be necessary. This is because of a key truth to statutory law: a law or pieces of it will frequently be amended or deleted by subsequent legislation. So although seeing the Civil Rights Act of 1964 is instructive and shows the historical document, many sections or even specific words have since been changed by subsequent laws, so the law as it appears in the *Statutes* volume is not the actual current law of the land.

The current law of the land is contained in the *United States Code*. The *Code* is the codification by subject matter of the general and permanent laws of the United States at a given time. It is divided by broad subjects into 50 titles and published by the Office of the Law Revision Counsel of the U.S. House of Representatives. It has been published in print every six years since 1926, with annual supplements published between editions. The *United States Code* is now on FDsys. It is also available via the Cornell Legal Information Institute site at http://www4.law.cornell.edu/uscode/. Cornell adds a valuable feature: when looking up the latest portion of any law in the *U.S. Code*, users will see that Cornell includes a link to "pending updates" and lists more recent public laws that update the last published version of the *U.S. Code*.

Thus, a user who wants to know the current law regarding civil rights in the employment process would need to consult the *United States Code*. Finding the right sections of the *Code* can be a difficult process, and such a request is sometimes best referred to a law librarian. But there are a few strategies for finding the right section. First, if one knows the public law that was a primary source of the law, one can look

U.S. Statutes at Large Citation

Public Law Number

Public Law 109–362
109th Congress

An Act

Date of Passage and Original Bill Number

Oct. 17, 2006
[H.R. 233]

To designate certain National Forest System lands in the Mendocino and Six Rivers National Forests and certain Bureau of Land Management lands in Humboldt, Lake, Mendocino, and Napa Counties in the State of California as wilderness, to designate the Elkhorn Ridge Potential Wilderness Area, to designate certain segments of the Black Butte River in Mendocino County, California as a wild or scenic river, and for other purposes.

Be it enacted by the Senate and House of Representatives of the United States of America in Congress assembled,

Popular Title

Northern California Coastal Wild Heritage Wilderness Act. Conservation. 16 USC 460sss note.

U.S. Code Location

SECTION 1. SHORT TITLE AND TABLE OF CONTENTS.

(a) SHORT TITLE.—This Act may be cited as the "Northern California Coastal Wild Heritage Wilderness Act".

(b) TABLE OF CONTENTS.—The table of contents for this Act is as follows:

Sec. 1. Short title and table of contents.
Sec. 2. Definition of Secretary.
Sec. 3. Designation of wilderness areas.
Sec. 4. Administration of wilderness areas.
Sec. 5. Release of wilderness study areas.
Sec. 6. Elkhorn Ridge Potential Wilderness Area.
Sec. 7. Wild and scenic river designation.
Sec. 8. King Range National Conservation Area boundary adjustment.
Sec. 9. Cow Mountain Recreation Area, Lake and Mendocino Counties, California.
Sec. 10. Continuation of traditional commercial surf fishing, Redwood National and State Parks.

SEC. 2. DEFINITION OF SECRETARY.

In this Act, the term "Secretary" means—
(1) with respect to land under the jurisdiction of the Secretary of Agriculture, the Secretary of Agriculture; and
(2) with respect to land under the jurisdiction of the Secretary of the Interior, the Secretary of the Interior.

U.S. Code Location for this Section

16 USC 1132 note.

SEC. 3. DESIGNATION OF WILDERNESS AREAS.

In accordance with the Wilderness Act (16 U.S.C. 1131 et seq.), the following areas in the State of California are designated as wilderness areas and as components of the National Wilderness Preservation System:

(1) SNOW MOUNTAIN WILDERNESS ADDITION.—
(A) IN GENERAL.—Certain land in the Mendocino National Forest, comprising approximately 23,706 acres, as generally depicted on the maps described in subparagraph (B), is incorporated in and shall considered to be a part of the "Snow Mountain Wilderness", as designated by section 101(a)(31) of the California Wilderness Act of 1984 (16 U.S.C. 1132 note; Public Law 98–425).

Figure 22.5 Example of page from *United States Statutes at Large*.

BOX 22.3 BASIC LEGAL CITATIONS

- *United States Statutes at Large*: 118 Stat. 1125 (volume-publication-page)
- *United States Code*: 15 U.S.C. 7801 (title-publication-section, sometimes edition in parentheses)
- *Federal Register*: 70 FR 51984 (2005) (volume-publication-page-date in parentheses)
- *Code of Federal Regulations*: 8 CFR 204.3 (2003) (title-publication-section, sometimes date in parentheses)
- *United States Reports*: 537 U.S. 86 (volume-publication-page)

---

at that law, the sections of which will contain notations specifying exactly where in the *United States Code* they will go (see Figure 22.5). Note that a single public law, especially a large law incorporating multiple distinct measures, could have its pieces incorporated into several different places in the subject arrangement of the *Code*. The *United States Code Classification Tables* also list each section of a public law with its corresponding text in the *United States Code*. Or, one can simply use the subject index to the *United States Code* itself.

One can also work backward and see where exactly each piece of the current law in force came from. Each section of the *United States Code* cites its source in statutory law. In other words, one can trace each word in the *Code* to the laws as passed and compiled in the *United States Statutes at Large*. For instance, 42 U.S.C. 2000e, the *United States Code* section on "Unlawful Employment Practices," is several pages long. At the end of the section, notes reveal that it originated in Public Law 88-352 (which is the original Civil Rights Act of 1964). The *United States Code* section goes on to note other laws that amended that section of the *Code*. By using these notes, one could examine each of the laws and trace every word that is in force in the current *United States Code*.

For reference, Box 22.3 provides examples of basic legal citations for statutory law and for key regulatory and case law sources discussed in the next two sections.

Regulatory Documents

Rules and regulations constitute another principal type of legal document. The U.S. Constitution states that the legislative branch makes the laws and that the executive branch enforces the laws. A key method of enforcing laws is via rules and regulations, by which executive agencies and departments issue detailed requirements pertaining to statutory law and its actual implementation. Considered "quasi-legislation or bureaucratic law,"[23] these administrative rulings, notices, and presidential executive orders and proclamations appear in the daily *Federal Register*. Central to the regulatory process is the publishing of *proposed* rules and regulations, followed by a public comment period and completed with publication of *final* rules, all appearing in the *Federal Register*. The publishing and distribution of the proposed regulations give citizens, officials, and experts the opportunity to comment on and critique them in advance of the final ruling. It is just as common for users to seek proposed rules as final versions.

For instance, in August 2008, Congress passed the "Consumer Product Safety Commission Improvement Act," Public Law 110-314. This law required children's products to be tested for lead to ensure that levels were below acceptable health levels, with products required to meet healthy benchmarks. The law itself did not spell out exactly what was to be tested and how the testing was to occur; those details were to be worked out by the appropriate executive agency charged with enforcing the law, in this case the Consumer Product Safety Commission (CPSC). On January 15, 2009, the CPSC published proposed regulations detailing how it would enforce various aspects of the law. These were published in that day's *Federal Register* (see Figure 22.6). To quote, "In this document, the Commission solicits written comments concerning preliminary determinations on certain natural, untreated and unadulterated materials and metals that have not been found to exceed the lead content limits prescribed under section 101(a) of the CPSIA."[24] The note then instructs the public on how to make comments and gives a due date for comments of February 17, 2009.

Once a proposed rule has been announced, the public, experts, and officials have the opportunity to comment by a certain deadline. The comment period is normally 30, 60, or 90 days. In addition, the agency must list the name and telephone number of a person to contact for further information. Most agencies accept comments electronically or in writing. Whereas the *Federal Register* is the official source for regulatory rulemaking, *Regulations.gov* is the federal rulemaking portal, whereby agencies publish proposed regulations and seek comment.

After comments were collected, the CPSC published a final regulation (on March 11, 2009) "on procedures and requirements on requests for: a Commission determination that a commodity or class of materials or a specific material or product does not exceed the lead content limits specified under section 101(a) of the Consumer Product Safety Improvement Act of 2008...."[25] These procedures, then, become administrative law.

Federal Register notices can also be announcements of meetings, opinions, or other miscellaneous information, such as the availability of an environmental impact statement or a research grant. For example, on January 13, 2006, the Forest Service announced its intention to prepare an environmental impact statement for the Lolo National Forest through a third-party contractor. The major focus of the study was to evaluate the consequences of a proposed expansion of the Montana Snowbowl Ski Area in Missoula County, Montana. Comments on the scope of the analysis were solicited, and in this instance, either written or oral comments were acceptable.[26]

Final rules and regulations, and presidential executive orders and proclamations, are incorporated into the *Code of Federal Regulations* (*CFR*), the codification of the general and permanent rules from executive departments and agencies of the federal government. The *Federal Register* publishes rulemaking as it occurs, much as the *United States Statutes at Large* compiles laws as they are passed. Likewise, the *CFR* compiles and codifies all current, in-force regulations into a subject arrangement, just as the *United States Code* does for statutory law. The latter titles, then, are the source for current, in-force laws and regulations.

and explain that the request may be resubmitted when the deficiency is corrected.

(e) Each complete request for exclusion will be reviewed by the Office of Hazard Identification and Reduction, who will preliminarily recommend granting or denying the request. Where the preliminary determination is to grant, the Commission will publish a notice of proposed rulemaking inviting public comment on whether the proposed exclusion should be issued in final form, and the Office of Hazard Identification and Reduction will review and evaluate the comments and supporting documentation before making its recommendation to the Commission for final agency action.

(f) The filing of a request for exclusion does not have the effect of automatically staying the effect of any provision or limit under the statutes and regulations enforced by the Commission. Even though a request for an exclusion has been filed, unless an exclusion is issued in final form by the Commission after notice and comment, materials or products subject to the lead limits under section 101 of the CPSIA are considered to be banned hazardous substances if they do not meet the lead limits.

Dated: January 9, 2009.

Todd A. Stevenson,

Secretary, Consumer Product Safety Commission.

[FR Doc. E9–715 Filed 1–14–09; 8:45 am]

BILLING CODE 6335–01–P

CONSUMER PRODUCT SAFETY COMMISSION

16 CFR Part 1500

Children's Products Containing Lead; Proposed Determinations Regarding Lead Content Limits on Certain Materials or Products; Notice of Proposed Rulemaking

AGENCY: Consumer Product Safety Commission.

ACTION: Notice of proposed rulemaking.

SUMMARY: On August 14, 2008, Congress enacted the Consumer Product Safety Improvement Act of 2008 (CPSIA), Public Law 110–314, 122 Stat. 3016. This notice of proposed rulemaking (NPR) initiates a proceeding under section 3 of the CPSIA authorizing the Commission to issue regulations, as necessary, to implement the CPSIA. In this document, the Commission solicits written comments concerning preliminary determinations on certain natural, untreated and unadulterated materials and metals that have not been found to exceed the lead content limits prescribed under section 101(a) of the CPSIA.

DATES: Written comments and submissions in response to this notice must be received by February 17, 2009.

ADDRESSES: Comments should be e-mailed to *Sec101Determinations@cpsc.gov.* Comments should be captioned "Section 101 Determinations of Certain Materials or Products NPR." Comments may also be mailed, preferably in five copies, to the Office of the Secretary, Consumer Product Safety Commission, Room 502, 4330 East West Highway, Bethesda, Maryland 20814, or delivered to the same address (telephone (301) 504–7923). Comments also may be filed by facsimile to (301) 504–0127.

FOR FURTHER INFORMATION CONTACT: Kristina Hatlelid, PhD, M.P.H., Directorate for Health Sciences, Consumer Product Safety Commission, 4330 East West Highway, Bethesda, Maryland 20814; telephone (301) 504–7254, e-mail *khatlelid@cpsc.gov.*

SUPPLEMENTARY INFORMATION:

A. Background

Under section 101(a) of CPSIA, consumer products designed or intended primarily for children 12 years old and younger that do not contain more than 600 ppm of lead (as of February 10, 2009), 300 ppm of lead (as of August 14, 2009); 100 ppm after three years (as of August 14, 2011), unless the Commission determines that it is not technologically feasible to have this lower limit, are not considered to be banned hazardous substances under the Federal Hazardous Substances Act (FHSA). However, in the absence of Commission action, these products and materials remain subject to the testing requirements of section 102 of the CPSIA (codified at § 14 of the Consumer Product Safety Act (CPSA)).

Under these provisions, on and after February 10, 2009, general conformity certificates certifying that they comply with the applicable lead content limit are required for children's products. The certification must be based on tests of each product or a reasonable testing program. On and after August 14, 2009, absent Commission action to the contrary, the certificates must be based on testing performed by a laboratory whose accreditation to perform the testing has been accepted by the Commission.

Section 3 of the CPSIA grants the Commission general rulemaking authority to issue regulations, as necessary, to implement the CPSIA. There may be certain products or materials that inherently do not contain lead or contain lead at levels that do not exceed the lead content limits under section 101(a) of the CPSIA. To the extent that such materials or products exist, the Commission, of its own initiative, is proposing to exercise its section 3 authority to make preliminary determinations that certain commodities or classes of materials or products do not exceed the lead limits prescribed in section 101(a) of the CPSIA. The effect of such a Commission finding would be to relieve the material or product from the testing requirement of section 102 of the CPSIA for purposes of supporting the required certification. Of course even where a material or product has been so relieved of the testing requirement, it must still meet the statutory lead level requirements in actual fact. The Commission will obtain and test products in the marketplace to assure that this remains the case and will take appropriate enforcement action in situations where that is not the case.

B. Proposed Determinations on Certain Products and Materials

The Commission staff identified a number of commodities or classes of materials that do not inherently contain lead or contain lead that does not exceed the CPSIA lead limits of 600 ppm or 300 ppm.

Certain Natural Materials

Based on the staff's review, the Commission preliminarily determines that the following natural materials do not exceed the 600 ppm or 300 ppm lead content limits under section 101(a) of the CPSIA. These preliminary determinations are based on materials that are untreated and unadulterated with respect to the addition of materials or chemicals, including pigments, dyes, coatings, finishes or any other substance, and that do not undergo any processing that could result in the addition of lead into the product or material:

1. Precious gemstones: Diamond, ruby, sapphire, emerald

2. Certain semiprecious gemstones provided that the mineral or material is not based on lead or lead compounds and is not associated in nature with any mineral that is based on lead or lead compounds (minerals that contain lead or are associated in nature with minerals that contain lead include, but are not limited to, the following: Aragonite, bayldonite, boleite, cerussite, crocoite, linarite, mimetite, phosgenite, vanadinite, and wulfenite)

3. Natural or cultured pearls

4. Wood

Figure 22.6 Page from the *Federal Register*.

The *CFR* is divided into 50 numbered titles, such as Title 3, The President; Title 17, Commodity and Securities Exchanges; and Title 44, Emergency Management and Assistance. In the example for the CPSC (see Figure 22.6), the rule in question includes a notation, below the title, of its CFR citation, 16 CFR Part 1500, which is with the other regulations pertaining to the Consumer Product Safety Commission.

FDsys has direct links to the daily *Federal Register* and the *CFR* from its central Web page and also allows a variety of searching options, such as by agency and proposed or final rule. There is one other essential title that is regularly used in updating and verifying the latest regulations: the *Code of Federal Regulations: List of CFR Sections Affected (LSA)*. The *LSA* lists proposed, new, and amended federal regulations that have been published in the *Federal Register* since the most recent revision date of a *CFR* title and so allows the user of the *CFR* to ascertain whether any recent, new rules have been published in the *Federal Register* affecting that *CFR* section. The *LSA* on FDsys provides access to the monthly *LSA* series. In the same manner, the "CFR Parts Affected" list in the daily print edition of the *Federal Register* can be used to update the information provided in the *LSA*. The monthly cumulative and annual print-format *Federal Register* indexes can also be consulted.

When a library user needs regulations for an agency and its programs, the research may start with the CFR (see Box 22.4). It is possible to search the *CFR* database by keyword or to browse the subject-based volumes. At FDsys, the complete *CFR* is available (including past years for historical reference). The *CFR* volumes contain only those final regulations in effect at the time of publication. Whether a librarian is responding to a specific query or assisting a user in conducting research, the *LSA* must be consulted to determine whether there are more recent rules and regulations than those in the latest annual edition of the *CFR*. The U.S. Government Printing Office (GPO) and the National Archives and Records Administration (NARA) Office of the Federal Register (OFR) also have an "unofficial," constantly updated version of the *CFR*. This demonstration project is titled the *e-CFR*, although it is not yet considered

BOX 22.4
SEARCH STRATEGY: LOCATING REGULATORY DOCUMENTS

A citizen hears that legislation has been passed affecting bird hunting for both tribal members and nonmembers on tribal lands in the Midwest and on the West Coast. He is particularly interested in Kalispel Reservation in Usk, Washington, where he regularly goes hunting in the fall with relatives who reside near there. He believes that a law has been passed, but searches of congressional bills on FDSys, *THOMAS*, and *ProQuest Congressional* result in no promising matches. But perhaps the "legislation" is really a new regulation: a keyword search of "Kalispel" in the *Federal Register* locates the pertinent final regulation. As it turns out, nontribal hunters are allowed to hunt geese only, specific bag and possession limits have been established, and specified fall hunting days have also been set by the tribe for nonmembers.

BOX 22.5
STATUTORY AND REGULATORY LAW SUMMARY

1. Bills signed by the president are commonly called "slip laws" and have a public law number. For example, Public Law 108-54 is the 54th law passed by the 108th Congress.
2. All the laws passed in a Congress are eventually compiled into bound volumes called the *United States Statutes at Large*. Each volume of the *Statutes* corresponds to a session of Congress. For instance, volume 123 will contain all laws passed in the 1st session of the 111th Congress (2009–2010), and volume 124 will contain all laws passed in the 2nd session of the 111th Congress (2011–2012). The laws appear in the *Statutes* in public law order, which is the order in which they were passed.
3. Many of these laws are simply amendments of existing laws, adding a section here, deleting a section there, or changing some words. Every new public law that is passed is reviewed by the Office of the Law Revision Counsel of the U.S. House of Representatives, which updates (codifies) the *United States Code*, adding sections, deleting sections, changing words, and so on, as specified in the public law. So the federal law currently in force is reflected in the *United States Code*. The *United States Code Classification Tables* do a nice job of listing each public law number and including (1) what the *Statutes* citation will be for each specific part of the law and (2) where it will go in the *United States Code*.
4. Often, the executive branch will then need to write regulations explaining how it will enforce the enacted law. For example, Congress might pass a law that prohibits import of all narcotics, and then the appropriate agency (in this case, perhaps the Food and Drug Administration [FDA] or U.S. Customs and Border Protection) would issue regulations listing the exact items to be banned. As the years go by, FDA or Customs might continue issuing new regulations to reflect new products to be banned under the existing law. The regulations are first issued in draft as proposed regulations (or rules) in the daily publication of the *Federal Register*, and interested parties can comment. (Did FDA catch everything? Did they list something that should not be included?) After that process, the final regulation is also published in the *Federal Register*.
5. Somewhat like the process from the *United States Statutes at Large* to the *United States Code*, all final regulations are then compiled and codified by subject into the *Code of Federal Regulations* (*CFR*). One regulation may add to, replace, or delete what was in a previous regulation, and the *CFR* will then reflect the current administrative law in force.

> States: All 50 states generally follow a similar publication process, both with their state statutory law and with their state administrative (or regulatory) law. The titles, however, do not always mimic federal law. "Statutes" can mean different things at different levels. For instance, the Illinois equivalent to the *U.S. Statutes* is called *Laws of the State of Illinois,* and the Illinois equivalent to the *United States Code* is called the *Illinois Compiled Statutes.*

an official legal edition of the *CFR. ProQuest Congressional* includes regulatory information as well. Its version of the *Federal Register* is updated daily; its *CFR,* weekly.

Finally, when one thinks of the executive branch, one thinks of the president. The president may also make law, although such overt lawmaking is generally limited to executive orders, which detail some function of how the government will operate and do not often have large policy implications, and proclamations, which tend to be more ceremonial. All such presidential actions, along with the text of speeches, press conferences, bill-signing ceremonies, and other activities, are recorded in the *Compilation of Presidential Documents* (a former weekly which, as of the Obama administration, has become a daily), which is eventually compiled into the bound *Public Papers of the President.* Of course, the White House's Web site (http://www.whitehouse.gov/) is also a good source for information about presidential activity and publications.

Case and Judicial Law

Courts may issue decisions on some aspect of law that is unclear or disputed. Such decisions, when considered significant by the courts, are published and make up what is called "case law." Historically, the only foray government documents librarians made into case law was using the *United States Reports,* the decisions of the U.S. Supreme Court. This was largely because the *United States Reports* were the only judicial decisions that were (and still are) printed by the U.S. government as government documents. Other court decisions, when they were published at all, were published by private publishers, and access required subscriptions to large, expensive sets. Also, these publishers did not just print the decisions; they created the numbering and citation system that has become the standard for legal referencing (see Box 22.6), rendering the public ownership of case law even murkier. While these privately produced sets remain the standard sources of case law, recently, decisions were freed from only being published privately, and many decisions can be found on court Web sites and via free services such as the Public Library of Law (http://www.plol.org) and *Google Scholar* (http://scholar.google.com). Access aside, working with case law can be complicated and often is best referred to a law librarian. A basic understanding of the nature of the court system and knowledge of what is available can help the librarian know which queries can be answered and which should or must be referred. It is also important to remember that although the librarian may help patrons locate law materials, interpretation and legal advice are strictly off-limits, to be provided only by attorneys.

In order for a federal court to hear a case, there must be a federal question, usually some dispute about a federal law or a dispute between two states. Such cases go to a federal district court, also known as a trial court. Decisions of the district courts are generally published in the privately published *Federal Supplement* (see Box 22.6),

---

BOX 22.6
FEDERAL JUDICIAL/CASE LAW OVERVIEW

U.S. District Courts

- "Trial courts": 90+ courts, at least 1 in each state.
- Decisions may be published on the particular court's Web site (see http://www.uscourts.gov/courtlinks/ and also at http://www.law.cornell.edu/), the Public Library of Law, and *Google Scholar.*
- Official decisions are published selectively in West's *Federal Supplement.*
- Once published in West's, citations appear as follows: 984 F. Supp. 1288 (decisions on the court's Web sites are cited by party names only).

U.S. Court of Appeals

- "Appellate courts": 1 for each of 12 districts, plus 1 general federal appellate court.
- Decisions may be published on the particular court's Web site (see http://www.uscourts.gov/courtlinks/ and also at http://www.law.cornell.edu/), the Public Library of Law, and *Google Scholar.*
- Official decisions are published selectively in West's *Federal Reporter.*
- Once published in West's, citations appear as follows: 169 F. 3d 646 (decisions on the court's Web sites are cited by party names only).

U.S. Supreme Court

- Decisions from 1937–1975 and 1992–2000 are online in the Supreme Court decisions database via FDsys; decisions from 1992 on are available online at the Supreme Court Web site at http://www.supremecourt.gov/.
- All Supreme Court cases back to 1893 are available online at the Public Library of Law and *Google Scholar.*
- Published in *United States Reports.* Cite: 206 U.S. 285 (KESSLER v. ELDRED from 1907).
- Use the Case Citation Finder at http://www.supremecourt.gov/opinions/casefinder.aspx to find the official citation.

but as noted previously, recent decisions are usually online at the specific court's Web site, accessible from http://www.uscourts.gov/courtlinks/. Also note that such decisions, though public information, are published and easily accessible only for the very small fraction of district court cases that are noteworthy for their interpretation of a law and that may set legal precedent. Most decisions are not published at all.

If a party to a district court case feels a legal error has been made, the case might go to the second level of federal courts, a court of appeals. Like district court opinions, recent decisions of the appeals courts are usually online via the particular court's Web site, and are also in the Public Library of Law and *Google Scholar.* Historically, these decisions were printed in the privately published *Federal Reporter*, yet even at this level, only 20 percent of all decisions are actually considered noteworthy enough to warrant publishing.

Finally, a party to a case at an appeals court may petition to have the case heard by the U.S. Supreme Court, all of whose decisions are published in the *United States Reports* (as well as in several private sets) and are free online. Although asked to hear some 8,000 cases per year, the Supreme Court ultimately takes on only about 1 in every 100 of these requests. So someone can claim that he or she will fight "all the way to the Supreme Court," but that does not mean the Supreme Court will listen. The Supreme Court Web site (http://www.supremecourt.gov/) also has selected transcripts of oral arguments before the court.

More serious users of federal court opinions and documents might also want to register to use *PACER* (Public Access to Court Electronic Records), providing "online access to U.S. Appellate, District, and Bankruptcy court records and documents nationwide." Regrettably, access to these federal documents is not free.

States handle the majority of legal cases. A divorce, a traffic ticket, a small claim—all these will begin in a local court that is part of a state's court system, and the decisions are very unlikely to be original enough to warrant publishing. States have their own system of courts and appeals similar to the federal system, so the local case can be appealed to a state appeals court. Noteworthy decisions of state appellate courts may be published in various state law reporters. A case from a particular state's supreme or highest court may also be referred to the U.S. (federal) Supreme Court, so both state courts and the federal court system all lead to the U.S. Supreme Court. Librarians may want to familiarize themselves with their own state's court system and decision-publishing mechanisms but will definitely want to know the closest place to get help from a law librarian.

Statistical Sources

Requests for statistics are among the most common of reference queries. Governments collect and analyze a tremendous amount of statistical data in the course of satisfying the missions of their various agencies and branches. Indeed, the U.S. federal government is the largest statistics-gathering agency in the world. Data gathered and published include popular items such as population demographics and economic statistics, as well as more esoteric items such as personal computer ownership or the flow rates for various rivers. A librarian can quickly and easily determine how many persons were arrested last year by such variables as race, sex, and place, as well as how many high school graduates went to college. If an event can be counted, it is likely that the government has reported it.

This next section identifies the major statistical reference sources and discusses strategies for their use.[27] It is essential to note that to protect confidentiality, public data from the government never identify individuals by name. Companies or business establishments are identified by name only when the mission of the statistical program specifically calls for it, such as in company reports appearing in the U.S. Securities and Exchange Commission's *EDGAR* database.[28] This confidentiality sometimes results in suppression or deletion of data if it could possibly be used to identify characteristics or information about a specific individual or business. For instance, names from the *United States Census of Population and Housing* are kept secret for 72 years after each census. Likewise, if there are only a handful of auto repair shops in Garfield County, Utah, all information about auto repair shops in Garfield County may be suppressed in *County Business Patterns, Utah*, in order to protect a user from deducing data about a particular auto repair business.[29]

Indexes and Guides to Statistical Resources

Statistics come from numerous sources. In addition to the programs of the federal government, most state governments and foreign nations conduct various statistics-gathering programs. International organizations such as the UN and World Bank also gather statistics in the course of their operations. Private data publishers, industry or nonprofit organizations, and individual scholars may also collect data. With so many resources, an index of some kind is extremely helpful, especially for users doing significant statistical research.

The *Statistical Abstract of the United States* is at once both an index to statistical material and a source of statistics itself. For the librarian who can purchase only one statistical reference volume, or even only one government document, the *Statistical Abstract of the United States* is a likely choice. An annual compendium published by the Census Bureau, the *Statistical Abstract* compiles the most popular statistical data not only from all federal agencies but also from various nongovernmental publishers. A few of the topics included are births and birth rates, high school dropouts, arrests for drug crimes, attendance of performing arts, visitation of national parks, voting patterns, federal aid to states and local governments, unemployment, women-owned businesses, and government spending by topic. The free online version of the *Statistical Abstract* presents the same data, with all tables available as both PDF and spreadsheet files. The *Statistical Abstract* itself has been published annually since 1878.

The *Statistical Abstract* is easily browsed, but even better, it offers excellent subject indexing. To use the online version, browse the contents or use the search option, although results may be incomplete. To use the print or online PDF version, begin by browsing the comprehensive index. Subjects are arranged by broad headings over more specific subheadings. Many data tables are for the United States as a whole. Others provide state and metropolitan area data, and there is a separate chapter that features comparative international statistics.

For instance, if you are looking for data on Americans lacking health insurance, the online and print editions are easy to browse successfully. In the online version, it is simple to see the "Health and Nutrition" section and "Health Insurance" subsection and access relevant data. In print or using the PDF version, the same data is relatively easy to find by browsing the "Health and Nutrition" chapter. In this example, using the print or PDF index adds little. However, a user looking for data on Internet usage is not served as well by this strategy. One can browse either in the online edition or in the print edition to the "Information and Communications" section/chapter and, online, to the "Internet Publishing and Broadcasting and Internet Usage" subsection and find some data, but there are relevant tables outside of these chapters. The online search function likewise discovers several good tables, but a search of the print or PDF index supplies a more comprehensive listing of tables, including several that cannot be found without it. So when looking for data in the *Statistical Abstract*, do not neglect the print or online PDF version of the print index.

Although the *Statistical Abstract* is often sufficient to answer a reference question, much of its real value lies in its role as an index to more detailed or historical statistical data. Each table includes a source note that provides the original source for table data. One may then go to the original source (more often than not another government document) and find more detailed or complete data on the particular topic. For instance, Figure 22.7 shows "Household Internet Usage In and Outside of the Home, by Selected Characteristics: 2007." The data in this particular table, however, presents only highlights of all available data. The source note at the bottom cites

Table 1118. Household Internet Usage In and Outside of the Home, by Selected Characteristics: 2007

[As of October. Based on the Current Population Survey and subject to sampling error. See Appendix III]

Characteristics		In the home			Anywhere		No internet use	
		Percent						
	Total house-holds	All house-holds	Dial-up	Broad-band	Total house-holds	Percent of total	Total house-holds	Percent of total
All households	117,840	61.7	10.7	50.8	83,708	71.0	34,132	29.0
Age of householder								
Under 25 years old	7,028	57.7	5.6	51.9	5,238	74.5	1,791	25.5
25 to 34 years old.	19,718	65.6	7.0	58.3	15,566	78.9	4,152	21.1
35 to 44 years old.	22,854	71.8	10.1	61.4	18,862	82.5	3,992	17.5
45 to 54 years old.	24,773	70.7	12.4	58.0	19,763	79.8	5,010	20.2
55 years and older	43,467	50.2	12.4	37.5	24,280	55.9	19,188	44.1
Sex of householder								
Male.	59,871	65.3	10.6	54.4	43,985	73.5	15,887	26.5
Female	57,969	58.0	10.8	47.0	39,723	68.5	18,245	31.5
Race and ethnicity of householder [1]								
White	83,294	67.0	11.8	54.9	62,593	75.2	20,701	24.9
Black	14,303	44.9	8.4	36.4	8,433	59.0	5,870	41.0
American Indian/Alaskan Native.	643	41.5	11.2	29.8	385	59.9	258	40.1
Asian	4,477	75.5	6.1	69.1	3,672	82.0	805	18.0
Hispanic	13,619	43.4	8.0	35.2	7,463	54.8	6,156	45.2
Educational attainment of householder								
Elementary	5,812	18.5	5.4	13.1	1,490	25.6	4,322	74.4
Some high school	9,264	28.2	7.4	20.5	3,542	38.2	5,721	61.8
High school diploma/GED.	35,295	49.1	12.1	36.8	20,973	59.4	14,322	40.6
Some college.	33,078	68.9	12.1	56.5	26,498	80.1	6,580	19.9
Bachelors degree or more	34,392	84.1	9.7	74.2	31,205	90.7	3,187	9.3
Family Income of householder [1]								
Less than $15,000	13,939	82.7	18.5	63.9	5,433	120.9	8,506	179.1
$15,000 to $24,999.	10,848	76.2	20.2	55.7	5,468	100.3	5,382	99.7
$25,000 to $34,999.	11,650	50.9	11.2	39.7	7,565	64.9	4,085	35.1
$35,000 to $49,999.	13,718	65.7	14.4	51.0	10,723	78.2	2,995	21.8
$50,000 to $74,999.	17,101	80.2	13.8	66.0	15,151	88.6	1,949	11.4
$75,000 to $99,999.	9,872	88.6	11.4	76.8	9,326	94.5	546	5.5
$100,000 to $149,000	8,481	92.1	8.0	83.7	8,118	95.7	363	4.3
$150,000 and over	5,570	95.5	5.0	90.3	5,450	97.9	120	2.2

[1] Includes other groups not shown separately.

Source: U.S. Department of Commerce, National Telecommunications and Information Administration, *Networked Nation: Broadband in America 2007, January 2008.* See also <http://www.ntia.doc.gov/reports/2008/NetworkedNation.html>.

Figure 22.7 Tables from the *Statistical Abstract of the United States*.

"Networked Nation: Broadband in America 2007, January 2008. See also <http://www.ntia.doc.gov/reports/2008/NetworkedNation.html>." This report contains much more detailed information on the topic, which is why each table in the *Statistical Abstract* can be considered an index to further statistical data.

Notes at the beginning of many *Statistical Abstract* tables with available historical data cite related tables in *Historical Statistics of the United States, Colonial Times to 1970.* This two-volume set compiles popular statistical data from the earliest time data were available. It includes an index and presents comprehensive source notes from which the user can often track data to their earliest published sources. One should remember that statistics were gathered on a much smaller scale in the past, so *Historical Statistics* is unable to provide older data for many data items treated in the *Statistical Abstract. Historical Statistics* is among the most important statistical sources, and an updated, five-volume print and fee-based online version is available from Cambridge University Press. The *Statistical Abstract* also features useful appendices: "Appendix I. Guide to Sources of Statistics; Guide to State Statistical Abstracts; and Guide to Foreign Statistical Abstracts." These list major statistical publications of the federal agencies, states, and foreign countries and by themselves are excellent reference guides.

The *Statistical Abstract*, then, serves as an index to most of the popular statistical topics that come to a reference desk and is a great source for the presentation of data itself. It does not, however, lead one to every government statistical table. The most comprehensive statistical index is *ProQuest Statistical Insight*, a subscription product. Largely the Web version of three classic Congressional Information Service (CIS) indexes, *ProQuest Statistical Insight* attempts to comprehensively identify all published statistical data and lead the user to the needed data. The three CIS Indexes included are the *American Statistics Index* (*ASI*), which indexes and abstracts federal government statistical sources from 1973; the *Statistical Reference Index* (*SRI*), which indexes and abstracts state, industry, and about 1,000 other non-federal statistical publications, from 1980 on; and the *Index to International Statistics* (*IIS*), which indexes and abstracts about 2,000 international organizations' statistical sources since 1983.[30]

By combining these three indexes, *ProQuest Statistical Insight* allows users to search all the citations and abstracts of all indexed statistical publications at once, which is nearly equivalent to searching the indexes of thousands of statistical publications simultaneously. Users may search by subject terms, titles, authors, and other keywords and may further filter searches by geography and by data category. These useful data category filters allow one to look only for data available in certain categories, a great feature when seeking comparative statistics. Category searches can be conducted by state, by foreign country, by race, by age, by industry, and many more factors.

The results come from two distinct modules, although they are seamlessly integrated: abstracts and tables. Abstracts are from the three aforementioned sources, *ASI, SRI,* and *IIS,* providing voluminous coverage back decades. The tables are from the online-only effort (beginning in 1999) to index all of the specific data in a particular table. So if a table has been indexed as part of the tables module, indexing down to specific lines in the table exists, allowing discovery by any word in an actual table itself; for abstracts, indexing is broader and at the publication level only. Nearly all of these indexed tables are included full-text as image and/or spreadsheet files.

ProQuest Statistical Insight may be purchased in a slimmed-down version containing just the tables and their indexing, and omitting the abstracts from *ASI, SRI,* and *IIS.* Cheaper access to this indexing may be had by purchasing any or all of the ongoing print editions of *ASI, SRI,* and *IIS.* Each print service consists of two complementary volumes: *Index* and *Abstracts.* Volumes are published annually and kept current with monthly updates. Additionally, multiyear cumulations are put together approximately every four years. In using these print tools, begin with the index and browse by CIS subject terms. Under the appropriate subject term, browse for content notes that describe the specific data needed. The content note in the *Index* volume provides an abstract number, which leads to complete bibliographic information and a detailed abstract in the companion *Abstracts* volume. These abstracts generally list every statistical table in the cited source. Nearly all of the government sources included in *ASI* are free online; the state and private sources in *SRI* and the international sources in *IIS* are mixed. In addition to the subject-based indexing, each *Index* volume contains a "category" index section, just as in the Web version, useful for comparative data. *ProQuest Statistical DataSets* are a possible add-on to *ProQuest Statistical Insight,* providing access to data from licensed and public-domain datasets within an easy-to-use interface.

The breadth of the publications covered by the CIS indexes and *ProQuest Statistical Insight* is beyond what most library collections are likely to own. CIS does, however, publish a microfiche set of nearly every report included in the indexes. Libraries may purchase any of the three sets: the *ASI* Microfiche Library, the *SRI* Microfiche Library, and the *IIS* Microfiche Library. The microfiche reports are numbered by CIS abstract number and are therefore simple to find from the abstracts.

Although there is nothing quite like the breadth of coverage offered by the CIS/ ProQuest statistical products, many librarians may not have the need for such comprehensive indexing or the budget to pay for them. Several other publications aid the librarian in gaining an understanding of the various statistical programs that exist while helping to identify specific statistical publications. In addition to the *Statistical Abstract of the United States,* the four-volume set *Statistics Sources* contains almost 135,000 citations to statistical sources covering the United States and the world, arranged alphabetically by subject.

Just as important as a librarian's bibliographic knowledge of statistical sources, however, is that all-important knowledge of civics. If the librarian is armed with familiarity with the right government agencies and a little sleuthing, agency Web sites are the best and often the only way to find the most timely statistical information. A librarian with a thorough knowledge of statistical programs and sources (based on civics knowledge or use of the *Statistical Abstract* or *Statistical Programs of the U.S. Government*) can often identify standard statistical publications by browsing the appropriate agency's Web site.

The best index to federal government statistical data on the Web is *FedStats,* which aims to provide links to all federal statistical data on the Web. *FedStats* (see Figure 22.8) is an undertaking of the Federal Interagency Council on Statistical Policy. Users may browse *FedStats* by subject or search by keyword. Librarians familiar with statistical programs and agencies may always go directly to the Web site of the various statistical agencies to browse for the needed statistical data, beginning with the key, important statistical sources discussed in the next section.

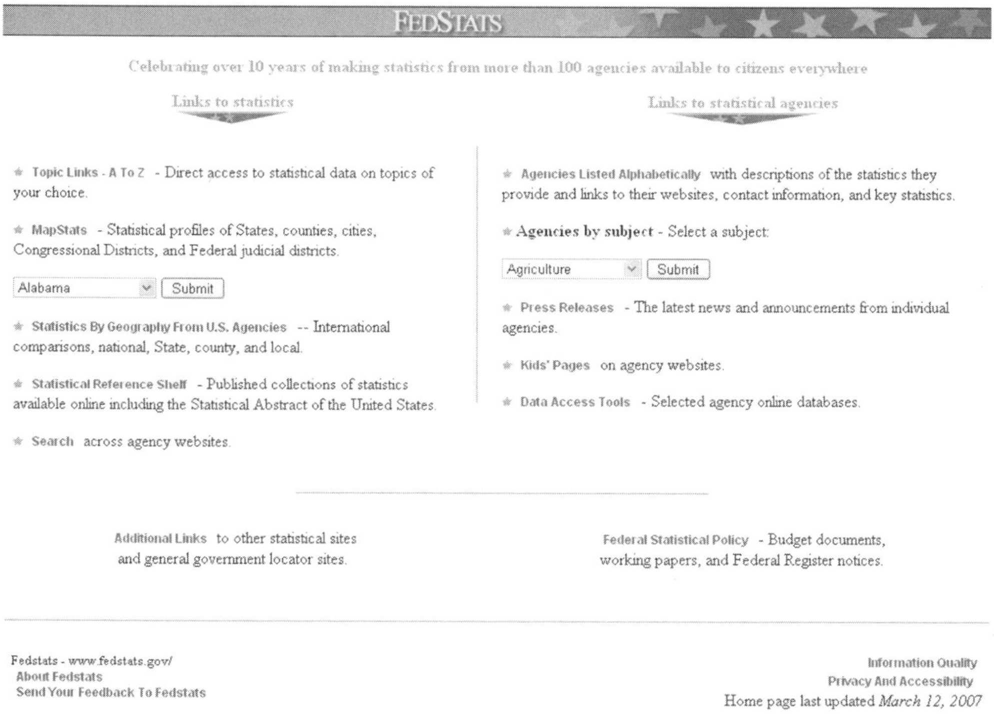

Figure 22.8 *FedStats.*

Important Statistical Sources

Beyond the *Statistical Abstracts of the United States*, for a broad range of statistical data on states, counties, and cities, one can consult the Census Bureau's *Quick-Facts* online or its *County and City Data Book* and the *State and Metropolitan Area Data Book*. Each of these Census Bureau compendiums compiles statistics for smaller geographic areas, from many agencies, on topics such as population, housing, retail trade, crime, agriculture, education, and employment. Generally, there is more data available for counties and metropolitan areas than for smaller cities.

In addition to compiling statistics from many government agencies into these compendiums (and the *Statistical Abstract*), the Census Bureau gathers and publishes a wealth of information based on its own programs. The *United States Census of Population and Housing* is its single largest endeavor. The original and core function of the *United States Census of Population and Housing* remains that of providing the official population counts to calculate each state's congressional apportionment.[31] Although it still serves this purpose, its results are also important in the allocation of federal monies to states and metropolitan areas for various federal programs and as an unparalleled statistical portrait of the country that is of vital use to researchers and general citizens alike.[32]

The *United States Census of Population and Housing* provides a representative picture of the U.S. population. It consists of a small number of questions given to every single household in the United States, in order to gather data on every citizen. Data are then published for the nation as a whole and for states, counties, metropolitan areas, cities, and several smaller geographic representations called Census Tracts, Block Numbering Areas, Block Groups, and Blocks. Because it provides data on the population right down to the equivalent of a city block, the census is a prime source for small businesses, marketers, and researchers of all kinds.

These basic questions cover age, sex, relationship, Hispanic origin, race, and nature of the housing unit (owned, rented, etc.).[33] However, as users of decennial census data know, the census has not stopped at these basic questions. From the early 1800s right up through 2000, each census asked different additional questions of the populace, questions about educational attainment, ancestry, language spoken at home, employment, commuting habits, disability status, military history, and income and many questions about the physical characteristics of the home structure. For most of this time, all citizens answered the same census questions; but beginning in 1940, statistical sampling was put in place, allowing accurate data collection of these additional questions even as the majority of respondents answered only the few basic questions. The percentage of people answering the extended questions (via what became known in 1960 as the "census long form") varies by geography but on the whole comes out to about one in six. Through this long form and its very large sample (one in six Americans is still a massive statistical sample), data on all of the more detailed questions were also available down to the same, small geographic levels as the basic data.

The long form was discontinued for 2010 because the Census Bureau's American Community Survey (ACS) project is up and running. Through this survey, random people are asked questions similar to those from the long form, but not just in census years. The survey is continuously distributed to sampled households and thereby provides information in a timelier manner. Over any 10-year period, it will sample a sufficient number of people as to provide the same detail as was previously provided via the census long form. By surveying approximately 3 million households per year, the ACS will have a large enough sample to provide long-form-equivalent data for every year for places with a population of 65,000 or more; every three years for places with 20,000 or more; and every five years for places with fewer than 20,000 residents. All in all, the ACS promises much more data than the long form could deliver and allowed everyone to answer only the short census questionnaire in 2010.

Many libraries collect the decennial census volumes, from the skinny single 1790 volume to the large set of 1990 volumes.[34] Since 2000, only summary volumes and DVDs have been issued to depositories, given that almost all data were available online via the Census Bureau's *American FactFinder*. A similar distribution was planned for 2010.

American FactFinder and its census and ACS data may be used in several ways. A simple approach is to use its Factsheets, or its handy options of entering a city or even an address and being taken to the available data for that geographic area. In either case, the most recent data are presented, including data from both the decennial census and the American Community Survey. For instance, entering the author's address results in both current data from the ACS and slightly older data (as of this writing) from the latest decennial census. The most robust way to access decennial census and American Community Survey data via *American FactFinder* is by going straight to the "data sets." When 2010 census data are released, users will be able to access a variety of predefined statistics and reports via the *American FactFinder* and its data sets and will also be able to build tables per specifications on the fly. Similarly, ACS data sets may be used to build tables from ACS data. The 2000 decennial census presents a more complicated scenario, as there are four data sets: Summary File 1, Summary File 2, Summary File 3, and Summary File 4. When using these data sets, it is important to remember the two prongs to the 2000 census: (1) that everybody was asked a few basic questions (via the "short form") and (2) that a sample was asked a much longer set of questions (the "long form"). Summary Files 1 and 2 use 100 percent (short form) data, with SF 2 presenting the data by race. SF 3 and 4 use the sample data, with SF 4 focusing on data by race. SF 3 and 4, then, gather statistics that are now compiled using the ACS.

A total population count for an area, for example, may differ depending on whether the data are taken from the short or the long form (or the decennial census versus the American Community Survey). Always use the file most appropriate for the question: if the user does not specifically need something from the long form or ACS, use the short form so that the results are for everybody, and not just the sample. Choosing which ACS data set to use requires knowing the population of the desired geographic entity and then choosing the one-year, three-year, or five-year datasets from *American FactFinder*.

The Census Bureau has recently made available on its Web site electronic versions of a number of historical census reports, right back to 1790. Also deserving special mention is the Historical Census Browser, from the University of Virginia Geospatial and Statistical Data Center, which provides selected data from the U.S. census back to 1790 (the first census).

In addition to the large census conducted every 10 years and the related American Community Survey, the Census Bureau conducts various surveys and makes statistical estimates and projections every year. Many of the results of these other census efforts are published in the topical series *Current Population Reports*. These reports, retrievable online under the census's "People and Households" section as "Data by Subject," cover topics such as poverty, education, income, and various demographics. These reports are based on the broadest ongoing government statistical survey, the *Current Population Survey* (*CPS*). The *CPS* is a monthly survey of some 50,000 people, administered jointly by the Bureau of the Census and the Bureau of Labor Statistics. The CPS asks a number of questions every month and others on a rotating basis (and some just once); the result is the wide range of *Current Population Reports* on many topics.[35]

Although not as large as the *U.S. Census of Population and Housing*, the *Economic Census* is conducted every five years and presents a statistical portrait of U.S. businesses. The latest survey covers the year 2007 (this means that the survey was conducted in 2008 in order to get 2007 data, and reports began to become available in late 2009 and beyond). Businesses are counted and categorized by type, and data such as number of employees and net sales are collected. Data are available by type of business and for states and counties. The results of the *Economic Census* are online, alongside the data from several smaller but related census programs, via the Census Bureau's Business portal, and also from the *American FactFinder* system.

An important concept with economic and business data is that types of businesses and industries are defined and classified using special codes. The 1997 *Economic Census* marked the first time businesses were categorized using the North American Industry Classification System (NAICS) codes; previously, the Standard Industrial

Classification Manual (SIC) codes were used.[36] The NAICS codes include categories for many new types of businesses and industries, such as Internet Service Providers. NAICS and SIC codes are also widely used in numerous private business reference products.

The annual *Economic Report of the President*, from the Council of Economic Advisers, includes a long discussion of current economic policy and trends, followed by a series of time-series tables of U.S. economic data on topics from GDP to employment to interest rates. For popular economic data over the years, the *Economic Report of the President* may be the most useful general volume. Much of the data in the *Economic Report of the President* is collected from historical Bureau of Labor Statistics data and the monthly *Economic Indicators*, a congressional publication featuring official statistics, mostly on macroeconomic topics. Similarly useful is the Department of Commerce's *EconomicIndicators.gov*, which compiles newsworthy economic releases from the U.S. Census Bureau and the Bureau of Economic Analysis. Combined with the data from the Bureau of Labor Statistics (such as employment and price data), the site contains most popularly cited data about the U.S. economy.

Important statistical reports from several other major agencies are used frequently for reference service. These include the Bureau of Labor Statistics, the National Center for Health Statistics, the National Center for Education Statistics, the Bureau of Justice Statistics, and the Bureau of Economic Analysis.

The Bureau of Labor Statistics (BLS) publishes numerous statistical data, nearly all of which is available via its comprehensive and user-friendly site. Chief among BLS statistics are the monthly *Consumer Price Index*, the source for official price and inflation data; *Wages by Area and Occupation*; various data on employment and unemployment; and the *Consumer Expenditure Survey*, an ongoing look at how Americans spend money. BLS also publishes a classic reference tool, the *Occupational Outlook Handbook*, a popular annual overview of the conditions of occupations such as "What is the job market like? What is the current average salary? What are the usual education and training required for the occupation? What is the nature of the work performed?"

The many surveys conducted by the National Center for Health Statistics (NCHS), such as the National Health Interview Survey, form the basis of numerous reports on various topics relating to the health of the American people. NCHS publishes *Health, United States*, an annual volume summarizing the health condition and trends of the nation. NCHS data is also easily accessed via the center's *FastStats*. Note that NCHS is also in charge of gathering vital statistics and is the source for information on births, deaths (including causes of death by various diseases and demographics), marriages, and divorces.

The National Center for Education Statistics (NCES) collects data about American education and its institutions. Popular volumes on education are the annuals *Digest of Education Statistics* and *Condition of Education*, both of which present statistics on current educational trends and exist in print and online. Like other federal statistical agencies, NCES provides quick and easy online access to its popular data via the "Data Tools," "Tables and Figures," and "Fast Facts" options on its Web site.

Crime in the United States (also known as *Uniform Crime Reports*) and the *Sourcebook of Criminal Justice Statistics* are valuable statistical reports on American crime and criminal justice published by the Bureau of Justice Statistics (BJS). The former is the key source for data about the number, type, and location of crime activity and has been published annually for decades. The latter focuses more on the justice system, with data on criminal court cases, sentencing, prisons, and prisoners, among other topics. BJS also publishes a variety of smaller, single-topic statistical reports on crime topics available at the BJS Web site.

The Bureau of Economic Analysis publishes economic data, including statistics on income and national accounts, in its monthly *Survey of Current Business*. Further BEA data include many of the most basic of macroeconomic statistics, including gross domestic product, balance of payments, personal income, and foreign trade.

Many of the raw results of these various surveys have publicly accessible datasets. The researcher using this raw data, or "microdata," has much more flexibility in pulling out exactly the data needed as opposed to relying on packaged statistical tables from the various agencies. Although expertise with raw data and the statistical software packages that use raw data may be outside the scope of most librarians, being able to locate the raw data, whether original decennial census data, Current Population Survey data, or the various health and education survey datasets, is an important skill, made easier by *Data.gov*, a growing compilation of government datasets from various federal agencies.

Federal statistical data are generally in the public domain. This means that private publishers may use federal data to create their own statistical reference works. In fact, many excellent statistical reference sources are published in this way, given that private publishers may repackage statistical data in formats that are easier to use than official government documents. They also may publish data that are difficult to find or may bring together statistics from government and nongovernment sources. Online services that repackage government data in useful ways include *SimplyMap* and *Demographics Now*. Other useful titles include CQ Press's *State Fact Finder Series* (state rankings, health care state rankings, crime state rankings, education state rankings, city crime rankings). Bernan Press produces a number of useful volumes using mostly federal government data, such as *Business Statistics of the United States*, *Handbook of U.S. Labor Statistics*, and *Datapedia of the United States: American History in Numbers*. A number of useful volumes focus on specific demographic groups such as Information Publications' *American Profiles Series*: *Black Americans*, *Asian Americans*, and *Hispanic Americans*.

In addition to the many federal publications that feature statistics for states, state governments themselves collect and publish statistical data. One may identify these publications through an index such as the *Statistical Reference Index (SRI)*. Lacking the *SRI*, librarians should familiarize themselves with the major state government statistical publications available about their particular state. Examine state statistical data by starting with Census Bureau's *Guide to State Statistical Abstracts* (one of the appendices to the *Statistical Abstract of the United States*). One should familiarize oneself with anything that may be a state equivalent to the *Statistical Abstract of the United States* and also with any key publications of major state agencies. Most states, for instance, have important sources for crime and education data.

International Statistics

International and foreign country data are compiled in many excellent sources. The *Statistical Abstract of the United States* contains a section of basic comparative international statistics, with broader data on topics related to the United States (foreign

BOX 22.7
SEARCH STRATEGY: STATISTICS

A user asks for "statistics about computers." The reference interview reveals that the user is looking for data such as how many people use computers at home, how many use the Internet at home, and so forth. You begin with the most current *Statistical Abstract of the United States*. Browsing the online edition reveals no categories about computers. A search of the *Statistical Abstract* online for "computers" yields a few economic tables about shipments of computer products and international computer usage. The PDF index to the 2009 edition has "Personal Computers" cross-referenced to "Computers." Looking under "Computer Use," you see a list of tables. Many of the tables have some relevant information, but Table 1118, "Household Internet Usage Inside and Outside of the Home, by Selected Characteristics: 2007," appears the most on target, with information on home computer use and Internet use by several socioeconomic and demographic factors.

The source of this table is listed as "U.S. Department of Commerce, National Telecommunications and Information Administration, *Networked Nation: Broadband in America 2007, January 2008*. See also <http://www.ntia.doc.gov/reports/2008/NetworkedNation.html>." For more detailed data, one then can look at this report, which has many tables that provide more detailed data than the one in *Statistical Abstract*.

It is always important to the reference librarian working with statistics to consider the source of the data. How might statistics on home computer use be gathered? One might guess that sales of home computers might be tracked; similarly, subscribers to online services might be tracked, and those results published by a business magazine or a trade association. For the report found in this example, the original source of the data is the Current Population Survey, which is a likely source for statistics on many topics.

If the user still wants more data, one could approach the question by using *FedStats*. Browsing the topics section of *FedStats* does lead to a heading titled "Computer and Internet Use," which leads to the same report. Meanwhile, searching *FedStats* turns up some further interesting data, such as the Census Bureau's page on "Computer Use and Ownership," at http://www.census.gov/population/www/socdemo/computer.html, which compiles a number of (older) tables from Current Population Survey data.

An even more interesting approach is to simply try to answer the question by using Google. Searching "personal computer use" or "home computer use" does turn up some interesting reports, and quickly. However, the most comprehensive source, *Networked Nation*, does not come up anywhere near the top of the results, and the data that are returned were from tables also discovered via the *Statistical Abstract*. In this case, Google took us to *some* data much *faster* and more easily, although it missed the best data.

aid, immigration, exports and imports). The *Index to International Statistics* (*IIS*, part of *ProQuest Statistical Insight*) is an excellent way to identify international statistics. Major statistical publications of international organizations and foreign governments are also listed in an appendix to the *Statistical Abstract of the United States.*

Some of the best international statistics are those produced under the broad umbrella of the United Nations. The UN's statistical volumes are highlighted by the *Statistical Yearbook* and *Demographic Yearbook*, each of which compiles a number of useful demographic, social, and economics statistics for countries worldwide. Much data may also be found via the UN Web site, highlighted by the comprehensive, free *UNdata* service.

Also worthy of special mention is the World Bank's *World Development Indicators*, among the most detailed statistical compilations for the world's nations. Social, demographic, and economic statistics are included, as well as data on environmental factors and government finance. *World Development Indicators* is available in print, but also online and on CD-ROM. The electronic versions include time-series for many more indicators, often back to 1960. A free online version exists with less data.

Many other international organizations produce statistics. There are significant statistical publications and products, especially from the International Monetary Fund, the International Labour Organization, the Food and Agricultural Organization, the World Trade Organization, the World Health Organization, the World Tourism Organization, and the United Nations Industrial Development Organization. Librarians working with global data should familiarize themselves with the relevant major international organizations and their available data.

In addition to the various international organizations' statistical volumes, many of the world's nations publish their own statistical compendiums, somewhat akin to the U.S. *Statistical Abstract of the United States.* Such volumes from major countries can be identified using the appropriate appendix to the *Statistical Abstract*, especially if they are consistently produced; it will take more work to identify available data from other countries with more haphazard statistical collection programs and publishing. Although no nation can quite match the U.S. Census Bureau's wealth of information via the Web, statistical agencies of many nations do have Web sites with varying amounts of data.

Finally, many private publications do an excellent job of gathering international and foreign statistics. Sources such as *The Europa World Year Book* and *The World Almanac and Book of Facts* (see chapter 15) contain summary statistics for the world and its nations and also include a variety of other data and information.

Canadian Government Information

Like their U.S. counterparts, Canadian government documents and other officially disseminated information products are up-to-date, authoritative, relatively inexpensive to acquire or access, and indispensable as reference tools. The Canadian government's official Web site, available at http://www.canada.gc.ca, is in both English and French. Resembling USA.gov, the site's organization is user-friendly, even for novices such as tourists or other visitors, and well organized. It achieves the near impossible by providing ready access through this initial page to the most significant and in-demand types of information, including links to government departments and agencies; an A-to-Z index, which covers programs, services, and subjects, as disparate as bullying, climate change, and nanotechnology; government contacts; online forms and services; the prime minister's Web site; publications and reports; and links to the official Web sites of the governments of the provinces and territories. The "About Government" section takes the user to another series of convenient links based on the government's organization and functions.

Links to specific sections oriented toward citizens and residents, non-Canadians, and the business sector are also available. In addition, there is a direct link to an extensive "About Canada" suite of topical Web guides. Also from the home page it is possible to set up a "My Government Account" and develop a personalized set of individualized links to the government's information and services. The Mobile Wireless Portal has an array of services, a sample of which includes border wait times, a currency converter, and contact information for members of Parliament.

Canadian government documents and information sources are also disseminated to the public in tangible formats. They are administered and distributed through the relatively new Publishing and Depository Services (PDS) directorate, in a fashion somewhat analogous to the GPO's Federal Depository Library Program. At present, PDS's three program areas include Publishing Programs, Crown Copyright and Licensing, and the Depository Services Program. Part of the Consulting, Information, and Shared Services Branch of the Public Works and Government Services Canada, the PDS functions as one of the directorates that make up the Government Information Services (GIS) Sector. Overall, the sector exists to ensure integrated and effective communications. The Depository Services Program now has 51 *full* depository libraries in Canada, and 1 in England. These libraries automatically receive all depository publications. Library and Archives Canada and the Library of Parliament receive the complete collection of publications as well. The rest of the depositories in Canada and elsewhere are *selectives*. These libraries purposefully acquire those publications of interest or potential interest to their users, mainly based on the *Weekly Checklist of Canadian Government Publications*. Canadian public libraries and libraries of the country's educational institutions that are open to the public or their clientele 20 or more hours per week and that have one full-time employee are granted selective status. Central libraries of the federal government departments, Parliamentarians, and press libraries represent other types of libraries that are depositories. In total, more than 800 libraries in Canada and libraries and institutions worldwide form the network of collections of Canadian government publications.

The Government of Canada Publications and Reports Web site (http://canada. gc.ca/publications/publication-eng.html) hosts the major Canadian depository and official publications links and access options. Major links appear centrally on the main page under three headings, "Government of Canada Publications," "Libraries," and "Related Resources." Links under the first heading include by Departments and Agencies; Search for Government of Canada Publications; How to Order Government of Canada Publications; Information Guides; *Canada Gazette*; Find a Bookstore; and Browse the *Weekly Checklist*. The "Libraries" section includes a Canadian Library Gateway, Depository Libraries, and Library and Archives Canada. Related resources cover the Depository Services Program, Crown Copyright and Licensing (CCL), and services for booksellers and distributors. The Depository Libraries link (http://publi cations.gc.ca/site/eng/locatingOurPublications/depositoryLibraries/index.html) provides brief descriptions of three types of depositories, including full, selective, and map. The depositories libraries listings provide links to depositories in Canada and international locations. Instructions for locating publications in depository libraries and bookstores are included.

The *Government of Canada Publications* catalogue (http://publications.gc.ca/site/eng/home.html) contains records for more than 180,000 tangible items. These can be ordered through a shopping cart service or, in the case of the e-collection titles for more than 70,000 items, downloaded for free. In addition, through basic and advanced search functions, users are able to readily search publications by date and language and browse serials publications, the *Weekly Checklist*, and the e-collection.

For historical background, a complete discussion of the early history, evolution, problems, and status of the Canadian Depository Library Program through the late 1980s can be found in Elizabeth Dolan's *The Depository Dilemma: A Study of the Free Distribution of Canadian Federal Government Publications to Depository Libraries in Canada*. The author describes the official origins of the program, the role of various agencies, and the pressures that combined to form the system in place until recently. The *Quick Reference Guide for Depository Libraries* offers current relevant policy information and guidelines.

Identification and Selection of Canadian Documents

Following is a brief discussion of the identification and acquisition of some of the basic guides, indexes, and primary sources used for Canadian administrative, parliamentary, and statistical research. The *Weekly Checklist of Canadian Government Publications* is the standard source for acquiring books, serial titles, and other types of publications from federal departments, the Parliament, and Statistics Canada. The *Weekly Checklist* includes both free and priced items. URLs are provided within entries for Web-based electronic sources. In addition to the online edition, a print edition is still mailed. Full depositories receive a single copy in English and French of all publications listed for distribution in the program, and selectives choose publications from the *Weekly Checklist*. Each library is responsible for claiming, processing, maintaining, and providing access to the publications received. Different types of materials are required to be kept for varying lengths of time. The *Weekly Checklist* is a useful acquisitions tool in nondepositories as well, and free publications can usually be obtained from the issuing agencies.

Important General Canadian Sources

Canadian government reference sources fall into many of the same categories already discussed for U.S. federal sources. Like other titles treated in this text, they include directories, fact books, catalogs, and indexes, and like U.S. federal reference materials, they are the authoritative sources for laws, regulations, and statistics. A selection of the most important sources is discussed in the following sections.

Guides: Canada

Canadian government publications are described in various specialized reference sources. One of these is the ALA/Government Documents Round Table's *Guide to*

Official Publications of Foreign Countries, which includes a Canada section compiled by Carol Goodger-Hill and Doug Horne. This core list of essential reference tools focuses on current resources and includes a selection of topical resources, such as publications on the economy, health, human rights, and the status of women. An older work is *Canadian Official Publications*, by Olga B. Bishop, volume 9 of the Pergamon *Guides to Official Publications* series. This source offers very detailed annotations of parliamentary, administrative, and statistical publications. In addition to listing important titles, the author discusses the agencies responsible for the documents, as well as the publication history of long-standing series. The descriptive notes are particularly helpful. Meanwhile, Karen F. Smith's succinct, excellent introduction to Canadian government documents and information in *Tapping the Government Grapevine* (chapter 15, "Foreign and International Documents") can be used to update Bishop's book. The new online *Guide to Reference*, published by the American Library Association in 2008 and continuously updated, contains a "Government Publications" subject category. This section is also helpful in identifying new reference tools produced by and about the Canadian government.

The importance of networking and utilizing local resources cannot be overemphasized on the road to success as a government information specialist. For example, the Maps, Data & Government Information Centre at Queen's University Learning Commons has a well-organized, convenient set of links (http://library.queensu. ca/webdoc/) on Canada that highlight the main government divisions and the major tools, publication series, and other types of information and data resources. The list provides nearly one-stop access to the basics. Another example is the Canadian Government Native/Aboriginal Affairs Websites resource (http://www.lib.purdue.edu/ govdocs/canind.html).

Guides for the documents of multiple foreign countries will also be useful in locating Canadian official publications, including the aforementioned *Guide to Official Publications of Foreign Countries* and, for historical works, Vladimir Palic's *Government Publications: A Guide to Bibliographic Tools*. A related ALA Government Documents Round Table reference book, edited by Marian Shaaban, is the *Guide to Country Information in International Governmental Organization Publications*. This annotated guide is helpful in determining appropriate sources in a reference situation, as well as for building a collection.

Catalogs and Indexes: Canada

The bibliographic control of Canadian documents remained in its nascency until the late 1920s. Publications for sale by the Department of Public Printing and Stationery were listed in the *Price List of Government Publications*, first published in 1895. A more complete catalog, the *Catalogue of Official Publications of the Parliament and Government of Canada*, was issued in 1928 and included all types of official publications, whether copies were available from the King's Printer or the issuing agency. In 1953, a formal system for control and recording of dominion government publications was begun with the issuance of a daily checklist and monthly and annual catalogs titled *Canadian Government Publications*, which existed until 1978. The *Government of Canada Publications: Quarterly Catalogue* and its annual cumulation continued through 1992. The *Weekly Checklist*, mentioned previously, was also a component of this series, and it remains current. A *Weekly Checklist Supplement*, meanwhile, is a series of themed special issues.

As indicated earlier, the site *Government of Canada Publications* catalogue represents the DSP's searchable database of information about Canadian government publications. The "Browse" feature is extensive. Abstracts are included, as is ordering information. Hot links are also provided.

Canadiana, the country's national bibliography, began in 1951. Issued by the National Library of Canada in parts, originally only dominion official publications were included. In 1954, provincial government publications were added to the multipart annual series. *Canadiana* is discussed in more detail in chapter 20. For a detailed list of retrospective bibliographies of Canadian government publications, including titles that record provincial documents, consult Palic's *Government Publications: A Guide to Bibliographic Tools*.

Factual/Directory Information: Canada

Regularly revised directories, handbooks, and manuals are produced by the government as well as by commercial publishers. *Info Source*, in its Web edition (http://www.infosource.gc.ca/index-eng.asp), represents a series of publications that contain information about and/or collected by the government. Its purpose is to enable individuals to exercise rights under the Access to Information Act and the Privacy Act. It is also a source of information about the government itself. The site menu allows access to the major publication in the three-part series, *Sources of Federal Government and Employee Information*. Its essential components include the Index of Standard Personal Information Banks, a Description of Standard Personal Information Banks, and a List of Institutions. A table of contents link and a link to an e-copy of the published version are both useful. Anyone seeking this type of information should be sure to review the foreword, which outlines the two acts and describes the application procedures and fees. The Glossary of Terms found within the publication is key to interpretation of the information in the data banks. The Web site includes a link to the Access to Information Act and Privacy Act annual bulletins from 1997 to the present with summaries of federal court cases and statistics of requests made under the Access to Information Act. A CD-ROM version of *Info Source* is available for purchase.

The *Canada Year Book* is a well-indexed standard reference work that includes statistical tables and graphs, along with descriptive information concerning all aspects of Canada's natural resources, economic and social conditions, government organizations, finance, and industries. It is published biennially in print and online. *Canada: A Portrait* is a collection of essays, including photographs, chronicling the country's "social, economic and intellectual life." It also is published biennially, is indexed, and complements the *Year Book*. Both volumes are available from Statistics Canada. The *Canadian Almanac & Directory*, from Grey House Publishing Canada, is an expansive compendium of directory information for governmental and nongovernmental organizations, and it includes coverage for municipalities. From abbreviations and airline companies to the Yukon government and zoological gardens, it is a convenient source for quick facts, basic statistics, and street and e-mail addresses, as well as URLs, if available. Color plates of flags, arms and emblems, honors, and a map of Canada add to this important tool. Many of the sections have been revised to include the new territory of Nunavut. *Canadian Government Programs and Services*, from CCH Canadian Ltd., is an updated, loose-leaf reporting service that provides information on the latest changes in the organization of the government. Detailed information on the structure, functions, and responsibilities of the government's departments and agencies is presented.

Legislative Documents: Canada

The *Canadian Parliamentary Guide/Guide Parlementaire Canadien* is an annual publication that details the current membership of the legislative and judicial branches of the government. It includes biographical information on the members of the Senate and House of Commons, the Supreme Court and Federal Court of Canada, and the provincial legislatures. Canadian government representatives abroad and foreign representatives in Canada, members of boards and commissions, results of general elections dating back to 1867, members of the Privy Council, and members of the royal family are also listed.

For a detailed discussion of the process through which bills become laws, refer to a general guide such as Bishop's *Canadian Official Publications* or a pertinent Web site. The Parliament of Canada Web site (http://www.parl.gc.ca/) includes "About Parliament," and its "Parliamentary Process" section links to "The Parliament of Canada—Democracy in Action," which provides the basic steps in the legislative process. More detailed reference works, such as the "Standing Orders of the House of Commons," are accessible via the Chamber Business page and its series of links. The more extensive guides, such as Bishop's text or the several guides available within Chamber and Committee business sections, will either take the researcher through the parliamentary process or describe the role of primary sources, including *Bills of the House of Commons*; *Bills of the Senate of Canada*; *Debates of the Senate: Official Report* and *House of Commons Debates: Official Report* (both of which are referred to as Hansard after the first King's Printer); *House of Commons Journals*; *House of Commons Votes and Proceedings*; *Journals of the Senate of Canada*; and *Minutes of the Proceedings of the Senate*. The site's other easy access tools, such as Quick Links, the A to Z index, and the site map, are all equally useful, depending on one's understanding of Parliament.

Bishop also discusses the *Canada Gazette*. As described in the *Guide to Official Publications of Foreign Countries*, the *Canada Gazette, Part I* contains government notices of a general nature, official proclamations, certain orders-in-council, and various other types of statutory notices; *Part II* gives the text of all regulations that must be reported according to the Statutory Instruments Act (1971) and certain other statutory instruments and documents. *Part III* publishes the text of the public acts of Canada, including a list of those acts that have been proclaimed from the date of the last issue of the *Canada Gazette Part III*. The purpose of this publication is to make available those acts that have received royal assent and will be published as the *Statutes of Canada* (also called *Acts of the Parliament of Canada*) at the end of the parliamentary session. Occasionally, *Part III* also includes the "Table of Public Statutes" from 1907 to the date of the current issue, which shows the chapters of the *Revised Statutes* and amendments to statutes and a listing of acts and the ministers responsible for them. Bishop's guide also elaborates on the functions and relationships of the *Consolidated Regulations of Canada, Revised Statutes of Canada*, and the historical set of the *Statutes of Canada*.

LEGISinfo (http://www2.parl.gc.ca/Sites/LOP/LEGISINFO/index.asp?Language=E) is an outstanding tool for finding information about legislation currently before Parliament. The Parliament of Canada site also contains a "Bills" section, which includes government bills from 1994 to the present, whereas the "Senators and Members" section lists both current and historical members of Parliament, 1867 to the present.

Statistical Sources: Canada

Statistics Canada is the central federal government agency responsible for the collection, analysis, and publication of statistical data about Canada. Statistics Canada publishes several excellent catalogs of its own publications. These include *Historical Catalogue of Statistics Canada Publications, 1918–1980*, which provides information on all Statistics Canada titles ever published. Publication histories are included for recurring titles, as are brief abstracts. *Statistics Canada Catalogue* is similar in format but is a comprehensive listing of all currently available Statistics Canada publications. It is arranged by subject categories (e.g., general, manufacturing, commerce, education, health, and welfare). The Statistics Canada Web site contains a plethora of data and detailed information concerning *CANSIM*, a large database of Canadian socioeconomic data.

As mentioned earlier, the major official statistical reference work is the *Canada Year Book*. This is supplemented by *Historical Statistics of Canada*, edited by F. H. Leacy, which presents a broad spectrum of statistical time-series dealing with social and economic data covering the period from 1867 to 1974.

A major census is taken every 10 years in the year ending in "1." In addition, a less detailed census is taken decennially in the year ending in "6." Publications of these censuses are listed in the *Statistics Canada Catalogue* and in the *Historical Catalogue of Statistics Canada Publications, 1918–1980*.

This discussion of Canadian documents has been necessarily brief. The reader is advised to consult the "List of Sources" and "Additional Readings" in this chapter for detailed information on research sources and their uses.

SEARCH STRATEGIES

Current government information is nearly all online and free. Locating a known, recent government publication can usually be accomplished through a general Web search and may even be accomplished more efficiently with a search of a specialty government Web search service such as USA.gov. When an item is known, or characteristics are known but the title is not, a civics-informed strategy often may be successful, namely, navigating to the Web site of the appropriate government agency or branch and browsing for the desired information. The *United States Government Manual* describes agencies and their missions and, along with USA.gov, is an excellent way to familiarize oneself with the necessary civics.

The *Catalog of United States Government Publications* remains and has long been the key bibliographic tool for locating government publications. If a Web search is not appropriate, or if the needed item is older, search the *Catalog*. The *Catalog* benefits from the usual bibliographic advantages, such as subject headings and author information featuring the issuing agency. GPO aggressively catalogs online documents and includes links in the *Catalog*. A number of specialty tools exist to aid the search for historical government information.

Many government information needs require the use of specialty tools. When neither Web searches nor the *Catalog* are successful in locating the item sought, identify and utilize the appropriate tool. When seeking technical reports or archival documents, for instance, use tools such as *NTIS Search* or the *Archival Research Catalog*, respectively.

Legislation, bill history, and congressional documents are frequently needed. When specific legislation or information about a bill is sought, search *THOMAS*, which provides easy access to bills, their text, their status in the legislative process, and documents related to the bill. Some understanding of the basic legislative process is extremely useful; *THOMAS* includes such information. *THOMAS*, along with FDsys, leads to key congressional publications: committee hearings, committee reports, and the *Congressional Record*. *THOMAS* and FDsys are also used to find the text of laws passed, known as public laws and compiled into the *United States Statutes at Large*. To find the text of current law in force, search the *United States Code* via FDsys.

Regulations are a type of law whereby executive agencies explain how they will enforce laws passed by Congress. To locate the documents of the regulatory process—characterized by a draft rule, a comment period, and a final rule—search the *Federal Register*, accessible via FDsys. Regulations are then compiled and codified into the *Code of Federal Regulations*; to find currently in-force regulations, search the *CFR* via FDsys. Case law, the decisions of courts and the third type of law, is generally best found in law libraries by legal specialists, but recent Supreme Court opinions and the opinions of other federal courts can be found via their Web sites. State laws, legislation, court decisions, and regulations are usually found via state-specific sources somewhat akin to federal sources; the reference librarian should learn the appropriate tools for the state or states of interest to the library's clientele.

When searching for statistical data, start with the *Statistical Abstract of the United States*. The *Statistical Abstract* contains much data itself. Use its source notes to locate more in-depth statistical sources on the topic. Also search or browse the online compilation *FedStats*. The search for statistical data may also be approached using knowledge of civics and browsing to data on sites of key statistical agencies, such as the U.S. Census Bureau, the Bureau of Labor Statistics, the National Center for Health Statistics, the National Center for Education Statistics, the Bureau of Justice Statistics, and other statistics-producing agencies. If international statistics are desired, begin with the international chapter of the *Statistical Abstract of the United States*, *UNdata*, or *World Development Indicators*, or browse the Web sites of other appropriate IGOs or foreign governments. Learn the key state-level statistical sources and agencies for the specific state or states of interest.

For Canadian government information, pursue a strategy similar to that for the United States. Start with the official Canadian government Web site, and also search the *Weekly Checklist* for Canadian government documents. Canadian legal information may be widely accessed via Parliament's Web site, and Statistics Canada is the best place to begin the Canadian statistical search.

By developing knowledge of sources of government information and associated search strategies, reference librarians can ensure public access to government information. Given the range of material published by the government, librarians in any setting can enhance service to their users by more fully integrating access to government information into reference services.

NOTES

1. Whether the founding fathers really believed that the masses wanted, or even needed, access to government information is debatable. For a compelling discussion, see Aimee C. Quinn, "Keeping the Citizenry Informed: Early Congressional Printing and 21st Century Information Policy," *Government Information Quarterly* 20 (July 2003): 281–93. John Walters, meanwhile, has published extensively on the history of the ideology surrounding government information. See especially his monograph *U.S. Government Publication: Ideological Development and Institutional Politics from the Founding to 1970* (Lanham MD: Scarecrow, 2005), 296 pp.

2. See Article 1, Section 5, Clause 3.

3. For a nice explanation and discussion of the *Serial Set*, see Virginia Saunders, "U.S. Congressional Serial Set: What It Is and Its History," available at http://www.access.gpo.gov/ su_docs/fdlp/history/sset/index.html. Ms. Saunders was probably the foremost expert on the *Serial Set* until her death in 2009.

4. The original General Printing Act may be found at 28 Stat. 601 (and the current laws about public printing are codified at 44 U.S.C. 1901). For more discussion, see Ridley R. Kessler, "A Brief History of the Federal Depository Library Program: A Personal Perspective," *Journal of Government Information* 23 (July–August 1996): 369–80.

5. 76 Stat. 352.

6. 44 U.S.C. 1901.

7. The list of *Essential Titles for Public Use in Paper or Other Tangible Format* is available at http://www.access.gpo.gov/su_docs/fdlp/pubs/estitles.html. It represents titles with which a librarian working with government information should be familiar.

8. For a view of the future GPO from within, see Ted Priebe, Amy Welch, and Marian MacGilvray, "The U.S. Government Printing Office's Initiatives for the Federal Depository Library Program to Set the Stage for the 21st Century," *Government Information Quarterly* 25 (January 2008): 48–56. A more detailed description, with analysis and discussion, is in the *Federal Depository Library Program Strategic Plan, 2009–2014: Creating an Informed Citizenry and Improving Quality of Life*, available at http://www.fdlp.gov/home/about/237-strategicplan. For an alternative and more critical perspective, see James A. Jacobs, James R. Jacobs, and Shinjoung Yeo, "Government Information in the Digital Age: The Once and Future Federal Depository Library Program," *Journal of Academic Librarianship* 31 (May 2005): 198–208.

9. For more discussion of the Superintendent of Documents Classification system, see U.S. Government Printing Office, *An Explanation of the Superintendent of Documents Classification System* (Washington D.C.: GPO, 1990), available at http://www.access.gpo.gov/su_docs/ fdlp/pubs/explain.html.

10. For instance, see the *Registry of U.S. Government Publication Digitization Projects*, available at http://registry.fdlp.gov/.

11.   The *Google Books* project has digitized thousands upon thousands of historical government documents from such collections as those at the University of Michigan and Stanford University. However, despite these documents' residence in the public domain (like nearly all federal government information, regardless of publication year), *Google Books* still treats post-1924 government publications as if they were privately published (partly because a small percentage of federal documents, notably congressional hearings, do contain some copyrighted material) and therefore still under the limits of copyright law. Although that problem may still see a solution, as of 2011, the future of *Google Books* remained extremely uncertain, remaining in the hands of courts and the U.S. Justice Department as its antitrust and copyright implications continued to be examined. A related Google/Committee on Institutional Cooperation (CIC) project specifically targets federal government publications and should be free of the access problem noted above.

12.   Although the .gov extension is the standard for government Web sites, military organizations use .mil, and some quasi-governmental entities, such as the Smithsonian Institution, may use another domain, such as .org or .edu. Most international government organizations use .org; many state governments use either some variation on their postal abbreviation and *us* or their state name with .gov; and other national governments generally use their assigned country extension. Private digitization projects yield many government documents located under .com extensions.

13.   Important, large series of U.S. Geological Survey research include *Bulletins*, *Professional Papers*, *Monographs*, *Open-File Reports*, and *Water Supply Papers*.

14.   The laws regarding the U.S. depository library program are found at 44 U.S.C. 1901. For more details on the rules regulating depository libraries, see the *Federal Depository Library Handbook* (*FDL Handbook*), available at http://www.fdlp.gov/administration/handbook.

15.   MARCIVE (http://www.marcive.com) is a company that provides cataloging records (among other services) based on a depository library's selection profile.

16.   This chapter makes occasional mention of the work of various committees and task forces of GODORT, the Government Documents Round Table of the American Library Association. For more information, see the GODORT Web site at http://www.ala.org/ala/mgrps/rts/godort/.

17.   Excellent guides to the official Web pages of foreign governments and IGOs have been compiled by Northwestern University and the University of Michigan. Northwestern, for foreign countries: http://www.library.northwestern.edu/libraries-collections/evanston-campus/government-information/international-documents/foreign; and for IGOs: http://www.library.northwestern.edu/libraries-collections/evanston-campus/government-information/international-documents/list-igos. Michigan, with options for searching by topic: http://www.lib.umich.edu/government-documents-center/explore.

18.   For an overview of major government information digitization projects, see GPO's *Federal Publications Digitization and Public Access Files Initiatives*, http://www.fdlp.gov/home/about/453-digitization. Also, refer back to notes 10 and 11.

19.   For background about the *StateList* project and its predecessors, see "About StateList" at http://www.library.illinois.edu/doc/researchtools/guides/state/statelist.html.

20.   Judith Schiek Robinson, *Tapping the Government Grapevine: The User-Friendly Guide to U.S. Government Information Sources*, 3rd ed. (Phoenix, AZ: Oryx Press, 1998), 90.

21.   118 Stat. 1125.

22.   For instance, Cornell's Legal Information Institute makes available "Popular Names of Acts in the US Code" at http://www.law.cornell.edu/uscode/topn/. The *United States Code* itself, in print, has a finding aid for popular laws called the "Acts Cited by Popular Name."

And a classic reference work is *Shepard's Acts and Cases by Popular Names*, published by Shepard's, which aids in finding not only public laws but popular judicial cases too.

23.   Robinson, *Tapping the Government Grapevine*, 118.

24.   74 FR 2433.

25.   74 FR 10475.

26.   71 FR 2178.

27.   An excellent summary of federal government statistical programs is the annual *Statistical Programs of the U.S. Government*, prepared by the Office of Management and Budget, which details spending on statistical programs (5.1 billion dollars in FY2009) and discusses priorities and planning in government statistics collection. For an in-depth discussion of federal statistics programs focusing on the nature and methodology of their collection, see Jean Slemmons Stratford and Juri Stratford, *Major U.S. Statistical Series: Definitions, Publications, Limitations* (Chicago: American Library Association, 1992),147 pp.

28.   The Securities and Exchange Commission (SEC) ensures that securities markets are fair and honest. They require publicly traded companies to file various reports, some of which are made public via the *EDGAR* system. Securities laws are generally found in 15 U.S.C.; the SEC in particular is covered at 15 U.S.C. 78a–78jj.

29.   The laws regarding privacy of census information may be found at 13 U.S.C. 9.

30.   Information about *ProQuest Statistical Insight* is available at http://cisupa.proquest.com/ws_display.asp?filter=Statistical%20Overview.

31.   The U.S. Constitution mandates that an apportionment of representatives among the states, for the House of Representatives, be carried out every 10 years. More information may be found at http://www.census.gov/population/www/censusdata/apportionment/why.html.

32.   For details on the disbursement of various federal funds to states, counties, and municipalities, see the *Consolidated Federal Funds Report*, available at http://www.census.gov/govs/cffr/.

33.   Definitions and reporting of race have changed over the years. The "Census 2000 Brief Overview of Race and Hispanic Origin," at http://www.census.gov/prod/2001pubs/cenbr01-1.pdf, discusses changes to the way race data was asked and tabulated in 2000 (unchanged for 2010).

34.   For a nice discussion of the census through the years, including details on what questions were asked on each census, see *Measuring America: The Decennial Censuses from 1790 to 2000*, available at http://www.census.gov/prod/2002pubs/pol02marv-pt1.pdf.

35.   Information about and some data from the *Current Population Survey* are available at http://www.census.gov/cps/. More complete data from the CPS through the years are available to subscribers at the Inter-university Consortium for Political and Social Research (ICPSR), http://www.icpsr.umich.edu/.

36.   For a discussion of NAICS, see Carole A. Ambler and James E. Kristoff, "Introducing the North American Industry Classification System," *Government Information Quarterly* 15 (1998): 263–73.

LIST OF SOURCES

AGRICOLA (AGRICultural OnLine Access). Beltsville, MD: National Agricultural Library. http://agricola.nal.usda.gov/.

American Community Survey. Washington, D.C.: U.S. Bureau of the Census, 1996–. http://www.census.gov/acs/www/. Also available via *American FactFinder*: http://factfinder.census.gov/.

American FactFinder. Washington, D.C.: U.S. Bureau of the Census. http://factfinder2.cen
sus.gov/.

American Profiles Series. Woodside, CA: Information Publications, 1990–.

American Statistics Index (ASI). Washington, D.C.: Congressional Information Service,
1973–. Monthly; quarterly cumulative index; annual. (Also available as part of *ProQuest
Statistical Insight.*)

Ames, John G. *Comprehensive Index to the Publications of the United States Government,
1881–1893.* Washington, D.C.: GPO, 1905. 1590 pp.

Archival Research Catalog. Washington, D.C.: National Archives and Records Administration. http://www.archives.gov/research/arc/.

Basic Facts, Trademarks. Washington, D.C.: U.S. Patent and Trademark Office. http://www.
uspto.gov/web/offices/tac/doc/basic/.

Bishop, Olga B. *Canadian Official Publications.* Guides to Official Publications, vol. 9. Oxford: Pergamon, 1981. 297 pp.

Book of the States. Lexington, KY: Council of State Governments, 1965–. Annual.

Bowker, R. R. (Richard Rogers). *State Publications; a Provisional List of Official Publications of the Several States of the United States from their Organization.* New York: Publishers Weekly, 1899–1908. Issued in four parts.

Bureau of Justice Statistics. Washington, D.C.: Bureau of Justice Statistics. http://bjs.ojp.
usdoj.gov/.

Bureau of Labor Statistics. Washington, D.C.: Bureau of Labor Statistics. http://www.bls.
gov/.

Business Statistics of the United States. Lanham, MD: Bernan Press, 1996–. Annual. (Continues *Business Statistics.* Washington, D.C.: U.S. Bureau of Economic Analysis, 1951–
1992. Biennial.)

Calendars of the United States House of Representatives and History of Legislation. Washington, D.C.: GPO. http://www.gpo.gov/fdsys/.

Canada. House of Commons. *Bills of the House of Commons.* Ottawa, Ontario: Queen's
Printer, 1867–. http://www.parl.gc.ca.

Canada. House of Commons. *House of Commons Debates: Official Report (Hansard).* Ottawa, Ontario: Queen's Printer, 1875–. Daily. http://www.parl.gc.ca.

Canada. House of Commons. *House of Commons Journals.* Ottawa, Ontario: Queen's Printer,
1867–. Annual. http://www.parl.gc.ca.

Canada. House of Commons. *House of Commons Votes and Proceedings.* Ottawa, Ontario:
Queen's Printer, 1867–. Daily. http://www.parl.gc.ca.

Canada. Senate. *Bills of the Senate of Canada.* Ottawa, Ontario: Queen's Printer, 1867–. http://
www.parl.gc.ca.

Canada. Senate. *Debates of the Senate: Official Report (Hansard).* Ottawa, Ontario: Queen's
Printer, 1867–. Daily. http://www.parl.gc.ca.

Canada. Senate. *Journals of the Senate of Canada.* Ottawa, Ontario: Queen's Printer, 1867–.
Annual. http://www.parl.gc.ca.

Canada. Senate. *Minutes of the Proceedings of the Senate.* Ottawa, Ontario: Queen's Printer,
1867–. Daily. http://www.parl.gc.ca.

Canada: A Portrait. Ottawa, Ontario: Statistics Canada, 1989–.

Canada Gazette: Parts I, II, and III. Ottawa, Ontario: Queen's Printer, 1867– (Part I); 1947– (Part II); 1974– (Part III). http://www.gazette.gc.ca/.

Canada Year Book. Ottawa, Ontario: Statistics Canada, 1867–. Biennial. http://www.statcan. gc.ca/. Also available on CD-ROM.

Canadian Almanac & Directory. Toronto, Ontario: Grey House Publishing Canada, 1947–. Annual. http://circ.greyhouse.ca/.

Canadian Government Programs and Services. Don Mills, Ontario: CCH Canadian Ltd., 1973–.

Canadian Government Publications. 24 vols. Ottawa, Ontario: Supply and Services Canada, 1955–1978.

Canadian Parliamentary Guide/Guide Parlementaire Canadien. Ottawa, Ontario: Queen's Printer, 1912–. Annual. (Continues *Parliamentary Companion*, 1862–1911.)

Canadiana. Ottawa, Ontario: Library and Archives Canada, 1953–. Monthly with annual cumulations. http://www.collectionscanada.gc.ca/canadiana/.

CANSIM. Ottawa, Ontario: Statistics Canada. http://cansim2.statcan.ca/.

Catalog of Federal Domestic Assistance. Washington, D.C.: Office of Management and Budget, 1969–. http://www.cfda.gov/.

Catalog of United States Government Publications. Washington, D.C.: GPO. http://catalog.gpo. gov/. (Continues print *Monthly Catalog of United States Government Publications.*)

Catalogue of Official Publications of the Parliament and Government of Canada. 11 vols. and supps. Ottawa, Ontario: King's Printer, 1928–1948.

Checklist of United States Public Documents 1789–1909. Washington, D.C.: GPO, 1911. 1707 pp.

CIS/Index. Washington, D.C.: Congressional Information Service, Inc., 1970–. Annual. (Includes *CIS Annual, Legislative Histories of U.S. Public Laws*), with monthly supplements. Also available via *ProQuest Congressional.*

A Citizen's Guide on Using the Freedom of Information Act and Privacy Act of 1974 to Request Government Records: First Report. Washington, D.C.: GPO, 1999. 76 pp.

Code of Federal Regulations. Washington, D.C.: National Archives and Records Administration, 1949–. Revised annually. http://www.gpo.gov/fdsys/. Also available from various commercial vendors.

Code of Federal Regulations. LSA, List of CFR Sections Affected. Washington, D.C.: National Archives and Records Administration, 1977–. Monthly. http://www.gpo.gov/fdsys/.

Condition of Education. Washington, D.C.: U.S. National Center for Education Statistics, 1975–. Annual. http://nces.ed.gov/programs/coe/.

Congressional Record. Washington, D.C.: U.S. Congress, 1873–. Daily when Congress is in session. http://www.gpo.gov/fdsys/. Also available via *THOMAS* and from various commercial vendors.

Congressional Staff Directory. Washington, D.C.: Congressional Quarterly, 1959–. Three times a year. http://library.cqpress.com/csd/.

Consolidated List of Serials of the Government of Canada. Ottawa, Ontario: Government of Canada Depository Services Program. http://dsp-psd.pwgsc.gc.ca/Consolidated/con list-e.html.

Consolidated Regulations of Canada. 18 vols. Ottawa, Ontario: Queen's Printer, 1978. (Updated by *Canada Gazette, Part II.*) http://laws.justice.gc.ca/en/index.html.

Consumer Expenditure Survey. Washington, D.C.: U.S. Bureau of Labor Statistics. http://www.bls.gov/cex/.

Consumer Price Index Detailed Report. Washington, D.C.: U.S. Bureau of Labor Statistics, 1953–. Monthly. Data also available at http://www.bls.gov/cpi/home.htm.

County Business Patterns. Washington, D.C.: U.S. Bureau of the Census, 1964–. Annual. http://www.census.gov/econ/cbp/.

County and City Data Book. Washington, D.C.: U.S. Bureau of the Census, 2007. 1026 pp. http://www.census.gov/prod/www/abs/ccdb07.html.

CQ Almanac. Washington, D.C.: Congressional Quarterly, 1945–. Annual. http://www.cq press.com/product/CQ-Almanac-Online.html.

CQ Press Electronic Library. http://library.cqpress.com.

CQ Researcher. Washington, D.C.: Congressional Quarterly, 1991–. Weekly. http://www.cq press.com/product/Researcher-Online.html.

CQ Weekly. Washington, D.C.: Congressional Quarterly, 1946–. Weekly. http://library.cq press.com/cqweekly/.

Crime in the United States. Washington, D.C.: Federal Bureau of Investigation, 1930–. Annual. (Also known as *Uniform Crime Reports*.) http://www.fbi.gov/ucr/ucr.htm.

Cumulative Title Index to United States Public Documents, 1789–1976. Arlington, VA: United States Historical Documents Institute, 1979–1982.

Current Population Reports. Washington, D.C.: U.S. Bureau of the Census, 1946–. Irregular. http://www.census.gov/.

Current Population Survey. Washington, D.C.: U.S. Bureau of Labor Statistics. http://www.census.gov/cps.

Data.gov. http://www.data.gov.

Datapedia of the United States: American History in Numbers. 4th ed. Lanham, MD: Bernan Press, 2007. 736 pp.

Declassified Documents Reference System. Woodbridge, CT: Primary Source Media. http://www.gale.cengage.com/psm/.

Defense Technical Information Center (DTIC). Fort Belvoir, VA: Department of Defense Technical Information Center. http://www.dtic.mil/dtic/.

Demographic Yearbook. New York: United Nations, 1948–. Annual. http://unstats.un.org/unsd/databases.htm.

Department of Energy Information Bridge. Oak Ridge, TN: Department of Energy Office of Scientific & Technical Information. http://www.osti.gov/bridge/.

Depository Libraries. Ottawa, Ontario: Government of Canada. http://dsp-psd.pwgsc.gc.ca/Depo/table-e.html.

Digest of Education Statistics. Washington, D.C.: U.S. National Center for Education Statistics, 1962–. Annual. http://nces.ed.gov/programs/digest/.

Digest of Public General Bills and Resolutions. Washington, D.C.: Library of Congress, Congressional Research Service, 74th Cong., 2nd sess.–101st Congress, 2nd sess., 1936–1990. Two cumulative issues, occasional supplements, and a final edition for each session. Ceased. (Continued by "Bill Summary and Status" section of *THOMAS*.)

Digital National Security Archive. Alexandria, VA: Chadwyck-Healey. http://nsarchive.chad wyck.com/.

Dolan, Elizabeth Macdonald. *The Depository Dilemma: A Study of the Free Distribution of Canadian Federal Government Publications to Depository Libraries in Canada.* Ottawa, Ontario: Canadian Library Association, 1989. 131 pp.

Dove, Robert B. *Enactment of a Law.* Washington, D.C.: Library of Congress, 1997. http://thomas.loc.gov/home/enactment/enactlawtoc.html.

ECLAS: European Commission Libraries Catalogue. Brussels, Belgium: European Commission Libraries. http://ec.europa.eu/eclas/.

Economic Census. Washington, D.C.: U.S. Bureau of the Census, 1954–. Quinquennial. 2007 products available at http://www.census.gov/econ/census07/.

Economic Indicators. Washington, D.C.: U.S. Congress, Joint Economic Committee, 1948–. Monthly. http://www.gpo.gov/fdsys/.

EconomicIndicators.gov. Washington, D.C.: U.S. Department of Commerce. http://www.esa.doc.gov/about-economic-indicators.

Economic Report of the President. Washington, D.C.: Executive Office of the President, Council of Economic Advisors, 1947–. Annual. http://www.gpo.gov/fdsys/.

Economy at a Glance. Washington, D.C.: U.S. Bureau of Labor Statistics. http://www.bls.gov/eag/.

EDGAR Database of Corporate Information. Washington, D.C.: U.S. Securities and Exchange Commission. http://www.sec.gov/edgar.shtml.

Energy Citations Database. Oak Ridge, TN: Department of Energy, Office of Scientific & Technical Information. http://www.osti.gov/energycitations/.

Ennis, Linda. *Government Documents Librarianship: A Guide for the Neo-Depository Era.* Medford, NJ: Information Today, 2007. 174 pp.

Environmental Health Perspectives. Research Triangle Park, NC: National Institute of Environmental Health Sciences, 1972–. Monthly. http://ehp03.niehs.nih.gov/home.action.

ERIC. Washington, D.C.: Department of Education, Institute of Education Sciences. http://www.eric.ed.gov/.

The Europa World Year Book. London: Routledge, 1959–. Annual. http://www.europaworld.com.

FastStats. Atlanta, GA: Centers for Disease Control. http://www.cdc.gov/nchs/FASTATS/.

FDsys (Federal Digital System). Washington, D.C.: GPO. http://www.gpo.gov/fdsys/.

Federal Agency Directory. Washington, D.C.: GPO; Baton Rouge: Louisiana State University Libraries. http://www.lib.lsu.edu/gov/index.html.

Federal Depository Library Directory. Washington, D.C.: GPO. Irregular. http://cata log.gpo.gov/fdlpdir/.

Federal Depository Library Handbook. Washington, D.C.: GPO. http://www.fdlp.gov/administration/handbook.

Federal Register. Washington, D.C.: National Archives and Records Administration, 1936–. Daily. http://www.gpo.gov/fdsys/.

Federal Reporter. St. Paul, MN: West Pub. Co., 1988–.

Federal Staff Directory. Washington, D.C.: Congressional Quarterly, 1959–. Three times a year. http://library.cqpress.com/fsd/.

Federal Supplement. St. Paul, MN: West Pub. Co., 1988–.

FedStats. Washington, D.C.: Federal Interagency Council on Statistical Policy. http://www.fedstats.gov.

Freedom of Information Act Electronic Reading Room. Washington, D.C.: Federal Bureau of Investigation. http://www.fbi.gov/foia/electronic-reading-room/electronic-reading-room/.

"Frequently Used Sites Related to U.S. Federal Government Information." Nashville, TN: American Library Association Government Documents Round Table Federal Documents Task Force, comp. http://www.library.vanderbilt.edu/romans/fdtf/.

General Information Concerning Patents. Washington, D.C.: U.S. Patent and Trademark Office, irregular. http://www.uspto.gov/web/offices/pac/doc/general/.

GODORT Handout Exchange. Ann Arbor, MI: American Library Association, Government Documents Round Table, Education Committee. http://wikis.ala.org/godort/index.php/Exchange.

Google Books. Mountain View, CA: Google Inc. http://books.google.com.

Google U.S. Government Search. Mountain View, CA: Google Inc. http://www.google.com/unclesam.

GOVDOC-L Discussion List LISTSERV. January 16, 1990–. For more about govdoc-l, including subscription instructions and access to the archive, see http://govdoc-l.org/.

Government of Canada Primary Internet Site (Canada Site). Ottawa, Ontario: Government of Canada. http://canada.gc.ca.

Government of Canada Publications: Quarterly Catalogue and Checklist of Canadian Government Publications. Ottawa, Ontario: Canadian Government Publications Centre, 1979–1992. http://publications.gc.ca/site/eng/home.html.

Government Periodicals Index. Bethesda, MD: Congressional Information Service/ProQuest, October–December 1993–. Available online via ProQuest.

Government Reports Announcements and Index (GRAI). Springfield, VA: National Technical Information Service, 1946–1994. Ceased. (Continued by *NTIS Search*.)

Guide to Federal Records in the National Archives of the United States. 2nd ed. 3 vols. Washington, D.C.: GPO, 1998. Updated version available:http://www.archives.gov/research/guide-fed-records/.

Guide to Official Publications of Foreign Countries. Compiled by American Library Association Government Documents Round Table International Documents Task Force. 2nd ed. Bethesda, MD: Congressional Information Service, 1997. 494 pp.

Guide to Reference. Chicago: American Library Association. http://www.guidetoreference.org.

Guide to U.S. Government Publications. Farmington Hills, MI: Gale, 1953–. (Commonly called "Andriot.")

Hajnal, Peter I., ed. *International Information: Documents, Publications, and Electronic Information of International Governmental Organizations*. 2nd ed. Englewood, CO: Libraries Unlimited, vol. 1, 1997, 528 pp.; vol. 2, 2001, 402 pp.

Handbook of U.S. Labor Statistics. Lanham, MD: Bernan Press, 1997–. Irregular. (Continues *Handbook of Labor Statistics*. Washington, D.C.: U.S. Bureau of Labor Statistics, 1924–1989.)

Hasse, Adelaide Rosalia. *Index of Economic Material in the Documents of the States of the United States*. Washington, D.C.: Carnegie Institution of Washington, 1908–1919. Various volumes for individual states.

Health, United States. Washington, D.C.: U.S. National Center for Health Statistics, 1975–. Annual. http://www.cdc.gov/nchs/hus.htm.

Hernon, Peter. *United States Government Information: Policies and Sources*. Westport, CT: Libraries Unlimited, 2002. 430 pp.

Historical Catalogue of Statistics Canada Publications, 1918–1980. Ottawa, Ontario: Statistics Canada, 1982. 337 pp.

Historical Census Data Browser. Charlottesville: University of Virginia, GEOSTAT: Geospatial and Statistical Data Center. http://mapserver.lib.virginia.edu/.

Historical Statistics of the United States: Colonial Times to 1970. 2 vols. Washington, D.C.: U.S. Bureau of the Census, 1975. http://www.census.gov/prod/www/abs/statab.html.

Historical Statistics of the United States Millennial Edition. 5 vols. New York: Cambridge University Press, 2006. http://hsus.cambridge.org/.

History of Bills. Washington, D.C.: GPO. http://www.gpo.gov/fdsys/.

Index to International Statistics. Bethesda, MD: Congressional Information Service, 1983–. Monthly; quarterly cumulative index; annual. (Also available as part of *ProQuest Statistical Insight*.)

Info Source. Ottawa, Ontario: Government of Canada, 1991–. Annual. http://www.infosource. gc.ca/.

Johnson, Charles W. *How Our Laws Are Made*. Washington, D.C.: Library of Congress. http://thomas.loc.gov/home/lawsmade.toc.html.

Judicial Staff Directory. Washington, D.C.: Congressional Quarterly, 1959–. Three times a year. http://library.cqpress.com/jsd/.

Leacy, F. H., ed. *Historical Statistics of Canada*. 2nd ed. Ottawa, Ontario: Statistics Canada, 1983. 900 pp. http://www.statcan.gc.ca/bsolc/olc-cel/olc-cel?catno=11-516-X& lang=eng.

LEGISinfo. Ottawa, Ontario: Library of Parliament. http://www.parl.gc.ca/LEGISinfo/.

List of Classes of United States Government Publications Available for Selection by Depository Libraries. Washington, D.C.: GPO, 1960–. Semiannual. Supplement: *Inactive or Discontinued Items from the 1950 Revision of the Classified List*. http://www.fdlp.gov/ collections/selection/150-list-of-classes.

Major Legislation of the Congress. Washington, D.C.: Congressional Research Service, 97th Cong., 2nd sess.–102nd Congress, 2nd sess., 1982–1992. Monthly. Ceased in print; now available via *THOMAS*.

Martin, Mary, ed. *Local and Regional Government Information: How to Find It, How to Use It*. Westport, CT: Greenwood Press, 2005. 239 pp.

Monthly Catalog of United States Government Publications. Washington, D.C.: GPO, 1895– 2004. Monthly. Supplemented by *Periodicals Supplement and Serial Set Catalog*. (Continued by the *Catalog of United States Government Publications*.)

Monthly Checklist of State Publications. Washington, D.C.: Library of Congress, 1910–1994. Monthly. Ceased.

Monthly Labor Review. Washington, D.C.: U.S. Bureau of Labor Statistics, 1915–. http:// www.bls.gov/opub/mlr/.

Morbidity and Mortality Weekly Report. Atlanta, GA: Centers for Disease Control. http:// www.cdc.gov/mmwr/.

Morehead, Joe. *Introduction to United States Government Information Sources.* 6th ed. Englewood, CO: Libraries Unlimited, 1999. 491 pp.

Morrison, Andrea M., and Barbara J. Mann. *International Government Information and Country Information: A Subject Guide.* Westport, CT: Greenwood Press, 2004. 298 pp.

NASA Scientific and Technical Information. Hanover, MD: NASA Scientific and Technical Information. http://www.sti.nasa.gov/STI-public-homepage.html.

National Center for Education Statistics. Washington, D.C.: U.S. National Center for Education Statistics. http://nces.ed.gov/.

National Center for Health Statistics. Washington, D.C.: U.S. National Center for Health Statistics. http://www.cdc.gov/nchs/.

National Health Interview Survey. Hyattsville, MD: U.S. National Center for Health Statistics, 1987–. Annual. Data available at http://www.cdc.gov/nchs/nhis.htm.

National Journal. Washington, D.C.: National Journal Group. Weekly. http://nationaljournal.com/.

North American Industry Classification System. Washington, D.C.: U.S. Office of Management and Budget, 1998. 1247 pp. http://www.census.gov/eos/www/naics/.

NTIS Search. Springfield, VA: National Technical Information Service. http://www.ntis.gov/search/.

Occupational Outlook Handbook. Washington, D.C.: U.S. Bureau of Labor Statistics, 1949–. Biennial. http://www.bls.gov/OCO/.

Official Congressional Directory. Washington, D.C.: GPO, 1887–. Biennial. http://www.gpo.gov/fdsys/.

Official Document System of the United Nations. New York: United Nations. http://documents.un.org/.

OpenCongress.org. New York: Participatory Politics Foundation; Washington, D.C.: Sunlight Foundation. http://www.opencongress.org/.

PACER, Public Access to Court Electronic Records. Washington, D.C.: Administrative Office of the U.S. Courts. http://pacer.psc.uscourts.gov/.

PAIS International. Ann Arbor, MI: ProQuest. Available online via ProQuest.

Palic, Vladimir. *Government Publications: A Guide to Bibliographic Tools.* Washington, D.C.: Library of Congress, 1975. 441 pp.

Parliamentary Internet Parlementaire. Ottawa, Ontario: Canadian Senate, House of Commons and Library of Parliament. http://www.parl.gc.ca/.

Poore, Benjamin Perley. *A Descriptive Catalogue of the Government Publications of the United States, September 5, 1774–March 4, 1881.* Washington, D.C.: Government Printing Office, 1885. 1392 pp.

Price List of Government Publications. Ottawa, Ontario: Department of Public Printing and Stationery, 1895.

ProQuest Congressional. Bethesda, MD: Congressional Information Service/ProQuest. http://cisupa.proquest.com/ws_display.asp?filter=Congressional%20Overview.

ProQuest Statistical Insight. Bethesda, MD: Congressional Information Service/ProQuest. http://cisupa.proquest.com/ws_display.asp?filter=Statistical.

Public Papers of the President. Washington, D.C.: GPO, 1929–1933, 1945–. (Equivalent volumes for many earlier presidents and FDR published by various private publishers.)

PubMed. Bethesda, MD: National Library of Medicine. http://www.ncbi.nlm.nih.gov/PubMed/.

QuickFacts. Washington, D.C.: U.S. Census Bureau. http://quickfacts.census.gov/qfd/states/00000.html.

Quick Reference Guide for Depository Libraries. Ottawa, Ontario: Public Works and Government Services Canada, 2010. 19 pp. http://dsp-psd.pwgsc.gc.ca/collection_2010/tpsgc-pwgsc/P109-6-2010-eng.pdf.

Regulations.gov. http://www.regulations.gov/.

Revised Statutes of Canada. 8 vols. Ottawa, Ontario: Queen's Printer, 1985. http://lois.justice.gc.ca/en/R-7.7/index.html.

Robinson, Judith Schiek. *Tapping the Government Grapevine: The User-Friendly Guide to U.S. Government Information Sources*. 3rd ed. Phoenix, AZ: Oryx Press, 1998. 286 pp.

Sears, Jean L., and Marilyn K. Moody. *Using Government Information Sources*. 3rd ed. Phoenix, AZ: Oryx Press, 2000. 632 pp.

Senate Calendar of Business. Washington, D.C.: GPO. http://www.gpo.gov/fdsys/.

Shaaban, Marian, ed. *Guide to Country Information in International Governmental Organization Publications*. 11th ed. Chicago: American Library Association, Government Documents Round Table, 1996. 343 pp.

Shepard's Acts and Cases by Popular Names: Federal and State. 3 vols. Colorado Springs, CO: Shepard's, 1999. Cumulative supplements.

Social Security Handbook. Washington, D.C.: U.S. Social Security Administration, 1960–. Irregular. http://www.ssa.gov/OP_Home/handbook/ssa-hbk.htm.

Sourcebook of Criminal Justice Statistics. Washington, D.C.: U.S. Bureau of Justice Statistics, 1973–. Annual. http://www.albany.edu/sourcebook/.

Standard Industrial Classification Manual. Washington, D.C.: U.S. Office of Management and Budget, 1987. 705 pp. http://www.osha.gov/pls/imis/sicsearch.html.

State and Local Government on the Net. Louisville, KY: Clicker LLC. http://www.statelocalgov.net/.

State and Metropolitan Area Data Book. Washington, D.C.: U.S. Bureau of the Census, 2006. 285 pp. http://www.census.gov/prod/www/abs/smadb.htm.

State Fact Finder Series. Washington, D.C.: CQ Press, 1993–. Annual.

StateList: The Electronic Source for State Publication Lists. Urbana-Champaign: Documents and Law Libraries at the University of Illinois. http://www.library.illinois.edu/doc/researchtools/guides/state/statelist.html.

Statistical Abstract of the United States. Washington, D.C.: U.S. Bureau of the Census, 1878–. Annual. http://www.census.gov/compendia/statab/.

Statistical Programs of the U.S. Government. Washington, D.C.: Office of Management of Budget, Annual. http://www.whitehouse.gov/omb/inforeg_statpolicy/.

Statistical Reference Index (SRI). Bethesda, MD: Washington D.C.: Congressional Information Service, 1980–. Monthly; quarterly cumulative index; annual. (Also available as part of *ProQuest Statistical Insight*.)

Statistical Yearbook. New York: United Nations, Statistical Office, 1948–. Annual. http://unstats.un.org/unsd/syb/.

Statistics Canada Catalogue. Ottawa, Ontario: Statistics Canada, 1922–. Title varies. http://www.statcan.ca/english/search/ips.htm.

Statistics Sources. Detroit, MI: Gale, 1962–. Annual.

Statutes of Canada. Ottawa, Ontario: Queen's Printer and Controller of Stationery. Sessional. http://laws.justice.gc.ca/.

Survey of Current Business. Washington, D.C.: U.S. Bureau of Economic Analysis, 1921–. Monthly. http://www.bea.gov/scb/.

Tables of and Annotated Index to the Congressional Series of United States Public Documents. Washington, D.C.: Government Printing Office, 1902. 769 pp.

Tapping State Government Information Sources. Westport, CT: Greenwood Press, 2003. 477 pp.

THOMAS. Washington, D.C.: Library of Congress. http://thomas.loc.gov.

UNBISNET: United Nations Bibliographic Information System. New York: United Nations. http://unbisnet.un.org/.

UNdata. New York: United Nations. http://data.un.org/.

United States Census of Population and Housing. Washington, D.C.: GPO, 1790–. Decennial. Data from the 2000 and 2010 census are available at http://factfinder2.census.gov.

United States Code. 2006 ed. with supplements. Washington, D.C.: GPO, 2006–. http://www.gpo.gov/fdsys/. Also available from various commercial vendors.

United States Code Classification Tables. Washington, D.C.: U.S. Congress, Office of Law Revision Counsel. http://uscode.house.gov/classification/tables.shtml.

United States Government Manual. Washington, D.C. Office of the Federal Register, 1935–. Annual. http://www.gpo.gov/fdsys/.

United States Reports. Washington, D.C.: U.S. Supreme Court, 1790–1991. http://www.supremecourt.gov/opinions/opinions.aspx.

United States Serial Set. Washington, D.C.: U.S. Congress, 1817–.

United States Statutes at Large. Washington, D.C.: GPO, 1789–. Annual. (*Public Laws*, of which the *Statutes at Large* are a compilation, also available at http://www.gpo.gov/fdsys/; via *THOMAS*; and from various commercial vendors.)

University of Michigan Documents Center. http://www.lib.umich.edu/government-documents-center/explore/.

USA.gov. Washington, D.C.: U.S. General Services Administration. http://www.usa.gov.

Wages by Area and Occupation. Washington, D.C.: U.S. Bureau of Labor Statistics. http://www.bls.gov/bls/blswage.htm.

Washington Information Directory. Washington, D.C.: Congressional Quarterly, 1975/76–. Annual. http://www.cqpress.com/product/Washington-Information-Directory-2010.html.

Weekly Checklist of Canadian Government Publications. Ottawa, Ontario: Canadian Government Publishing. http://publications.gc.ca/control/weeklyChecklistMain. (Continues *Weekly Checklist of Canadian Government Publications*. Hull, Ontario: Supply and Services Canada.)

Weekly Compilation of Presidential Documents. Washington, D.C.: Office of the Federal Register, National Archives and Records Administration, General Services Administration. http://www.gpo.gov/fdsys/browse/collection.action?collectionCode=CPD.

Where You Live. Washington, D.C.: Environmental Protection Agency. http://www.epa.gov/epahome/whereyoulive.htm.

Wikipedia. http://www.wikipedia.org.

The World Almanac and Book of Facts. Mahweh, NJ: World Almanac Books. 1868–. Annual. Also available online via FirstSearch and LexisNexis.

World Development Indicators. Washington, D.C.: IBRD, World Bank, 1997–. Annual. Some data available free at http://www.worldbank.org/data/dataquery.html.

WorldCat. Dublin, OH: Online Computer Library Center (OCLC). http://www.worldcat.org.

Worldwide Government Directory with International Organizations. Washington, D.C.: CQ Press, 1981–. Annual.

Your Right to Federal Records: Questions and Answers on the Freedom of Information Act and the Privacy Act. Washington, D.C.: U.S. General Services Administration, 2006. 44 pp. http://www.pueblo.gsa.gov/cic_text/fed_prog/foia/foia.htm.

ADDITIONAL READINGS

Aldrich, Duncan, Gary Cornwell, and Daniel Barkley. "Changing Partnerships? Government Documents Departments at the Turn of the Millennium." *Government Information Quarterly* 17 (2000): 273–90.

The authors discuss the implications for depository library services and operations as material transforms from tangible formats to electronic formats.

American Library Association, Government Documents Round Table, Federal Documents Task Force. "Report of the Federal Documents Task Force on Permanent Public Access to Government Information." *DttP: Documents to the People* 32 (Winter 2004): 32–34.

The rapid move to electronic formats has sometimes seen the need for preservation and permanent public access lag behind the pace of change. This report discusses the current situation.

Arrigo, Paul. "The Reinvention of the FDLP: A Paradigm Shift from Product Provider to Service Provider." *Journal of Government Information* 30 (2004): 684–709.

Arrigo discusses the "identity crisis" facing depository libraries as their materials shift to ever-more exclusively online formats.

Block, Marylaine. "A Day in the Life: Dealing with Digital." *Library Journal* 128 (July 2003): 40–43.

As the title says, this short article discusses the current environment of providing government information in the Web era.

Center for Democracy and Technology. http://www.cdt.org/.

This organization is dedicated to the promotion of open Internet and includes a focus on open government information.

Cheney, Debora. *The Complete Guide to Citing Government Information Resources*. 3rd. ed. Bethesda, MD: LexisNexis Congressional Information Service, 2002. 222 pp.

This comprehensive manual provides complete details on how to cite U.S. federal, state, local, international, intergovernmental, and other representative national level government documents and electronic sources in bibliographies and footnotes. A detailed index gives the user quick access to hundreds of individual examples.

DttP: A Quarterly Journal of Government Information Practice and Perspective. Chicago: American Library Association, Government Documents Round Table, September 1972–. Quarterly.

Formerly *Documents to the People* (*DttP*), this is the official publication of the Government Documents Round Table (GODORT) of the American Library Association (ALA). It is an important source for articles, news items, and other information on government publications, technical reports, and maps; related governmental activities; documents librarianship; and ALA/GODORT matters, as well as other professional organizations, such as the Council of Professional Associations on Federal Statistics.

Farrell, Maggie. "Training for Documents Reference in a Merged Reference Center." *Documents to the People* 28 (Winter 2000): 11–16.

Recent years have seen many libraries combine their government information reference service with a central reference service unit. This article discusses the challenges of such a union, especially for helping the nonspecialist provide service for government information.

Feinberg, Lotte E. "FOIA, Federal Information Policy, and Information Availability in a Post-9/11 World." *Government Information Quarterly* 21 (2004): 439–60.

Part of a themed issue, the article discusses post-9/11 government secrecy and its consequences for the public's right to government information.

Government Technology. Folsom, CA: e.Republic, January 1995–. Monthly; semimonthly, February, May, August, and November. http://www.govtech.com/.

A useful magazine that contains news and publication, conference, and product announcements. The focus is on state and local governments' use of technology. A free print subscription to the regular issues and supplements, such as *Visions*, is available; a complete set of previous issues is accessible and searchable at the Web site.

Herman, Edward. "The American Community Survey: An Introduction to the Basics." *Government Information Quarterly* 25 (2008): 504–19.

This article provides background and overview to the important American Community Survey, the huge census bureau survey that supplements, expands, and updates data from the decennial Census.

Hernon, Peter, and Laura Saunders. "The Federal Depository Library Program in 2023: One Perspective on the Transition to the Future." *College & Research Libraries* 70 (July 2009): 351–70.

The authors present the future of the depository program in the digital age through the eyes of directors of large academic and research libraries.

Jacobs, James A., James R. Jacobs, and Shinjoung Yeo. "The Once and Future Federal Depository Library Program," *Journal of Academic Librarianship* 31 (May 2005): 198–208.

The authors argue that in the digital age, depository libraries are more important than ever.

Journal of Government Information: An International Review of Policy, Issues and Resources. New York: Pergamon Press, January/February 1994–. Bimonthly. (Continues *Government Publications Review* 1–20 [1973–1993].)

Librarians should consider obtaining an individual subscription or make sure their local library has one. Articles cover government policy, current practice, new developments, and history in government information.

Pew Internet and American Life Project. http://www.pewinternet.org/.

These reports from the Pew project are excellent studies on how the public interacts with the Internet and online information. The project is especially enlightening in our era of electronic government information.

Priebe, Ted, Amy Welch, and Marian MacGilvray. "The U.S. Government Printing Office's Initiatives for the Federal Depository Library Program to Set the Stage for the 21st Century." *Government Information Quarterly* 25 (January 2008): 48–56.

This article describes some of the initiatives that the Government Printing Office has undertaken to increase access to electronic U.S. government information.

Public.Resource.Org. http://public.resource.org/.

This is the Web site of a project headed by noted open government advocate Carl Malamud, who began the SEC EDGAR project, among other accomplishments related to government information.

Quinn, Aimee C. "Keeping the Citizenry Informed: Early Congressional Printing and 21st Century Information Policy." *Government Information Quarterly* 20 (July 2003): 281–93.

Quinn provides an interesting review of early government information policy and includes discussion of whether early leaders really were committed to the needs for government information for citizens.

Robbin, Alice. "The Problematic Status of U.S. Statistics on Race and Ethnicity: An 'Imperfect Representation of Reality.'" *Journal of Government Information* 26 (1999): 467–83.

Classification and tabulation of race-based data is a long-standing statistical problem. This article discusses the issues and attempts at solutions.

Seavey, Charles A. "Documents to the People: Musings on the Past and Future of Government Information," *American Libraries* 36, no. 7 (August 2005): 42–44.

Seavey provides a brief, excellent overview of the state of depository libraries and public information, with historical context.

Stratford, Juri. "Responding to Reference Queries for Numeric Data and the Problems Inherent in Interpreting Statistical Sources: A Note." *Journal of Government Information* 25 (1998): 413–17.

Numbers expert Stratford discusses statistical reference service in some depth. Through examples, the author demonstrates how a general knowledge of statistical measures can lead to better-informed reference service.

Sunlight Foundation. http://www.sunlightfoundation.com/

This organization is dedicated to protecting and expanding access to government information.

Walters, John Spencer. "The Ideological Development of U.S. Government Publication, 1820–1920: From Jefferson to Croly," *Journal of Government Information* 29, no. 1 (2002): 1–15.

Walters, John Spencer. "The Presuperhighway Politics of U.S. Government Printing and Publishing, 1917–1960." *Journal of Government Information* 23, no. 2 (1996): 93–121.

Walters, John Spencer. *U.S. Government Publication: Ideological Development and Institutional Politics from the Founding until 1970.* Lanham, MD: Scarecrow Press, 2005. 296 pp.

Walters's contemporary work on the history of government information provides a comprehensive, critical look at the development of the idea and practice of government publications and their distribution.

Author / Title Index

Subject Index

About the Editors

RICHARD E. BOPP earned degrees in history from Northwestern University (bachelor's) and the University of Missouri-Columbia (master's). He received his master's degree in library science from the University of Illinois at Urbana-Champaign in 1974. In 1978, he joined the University of Illinois Library faculty and held positions in the Reference Department, the Government Documents Library, the Health Sciences Library, and the Map and Geography Library. He served as head of the Reference Department from 1986 to 1988 and taught the introductory reference course in the University of Illinois at Urbana-Champaign's Graduate School of Library and Information Science in the summer of 1988. In addition to co-editing and contributing to previous editions of *Reference and Information Services: An Introduction*, he has also written several book chapters and journal articles in the field of library services to persons with disabilities. He retired from the University of Illinois in 2000.

LINDA C. SMITH holds degrees from Allegheny College (BS, physics and mathematics), the University of Illinois at Urbana-Champaign (MS, library science), Georgia Institute of Technology (MS, information and computer science), and Syracuse University (PhD, information transfer). She has served as the associate dean for academic programs at the University of Illinois at Urbana-Champaign's Graduate School of Library and Information Science since 1997 and has been a member of the faculty since 1977. She teaches courses in information organization and access, reference, and science reference both face-to-face and online. She has served as president of both the Association for Library and Information Science Education and the American Society for Information Science and Technology and is a recipient of the Isadore Gilbert Mudge Award from the Reference and User Services Association for distinguished contribution to reference librarianship.